SOUTH AFRICAN

COMPANY LAW

THROUGH THE CASES

SOUTH AFRICAN
COMPANY LAW
THROUGH THE CASES

A COLLECTION OF LEADING SOUTH AFRICAN AND
ENGLISH CASES ON COMPANY LAW, WITH
EXPLANATORY NOTES AND COMMENTS

by

H R HAHLO LLD
Professor Emeritus, University of the Witwatersrand, Johannesburg

THIRD EDITION

1977

JUTA & COMPANY, LIMITED

CAPE TOWN   WYNBERG   JOHANNESBURG

First Published March 1958

Second Edition April 1969

Third Edition February 1977

Hard Cover ISBN 0 7021 0788 3

Soft Cover   ISBN 0 7021 0789 1

❀ SET, PRINTED AND BOUND IN THE REPUBLIC OF SOUTH AFRICA BY
THE RUSTICA PRESS (PTY) LTD, WYNBERG, CAPE

Preface to the Third Edition

As Professor Gower remarked in his Foreword to the first edition of my English company law case book, the 'unity' of 'British' company law is fast becoming a thing of the past. When the second edition of *Company Law through the Cases* was published in 1969, it could still be said with some truth that South African company law was a facsimile of its English progenitor. Since then, there has been a parting of the ways. By joining the European Economic Community in 1972–3, Britain committed itself to a new approach to company law. The European Communities Act 1972 was its first fruit. In South Africa the 1973 Act severed the English connection. It is true that in its overall picture the new Act still exhibits the familiar lineaments of an English company law system, but in important respects it has departed from the orthodox English pattern.

One of the main difficulties the author of a case book has to contend with is to decide which cases he should include and which cases he should leave out or relegate to the notes. If he includes too many cases, the book will become too long and expensive and, more importantly, it may become difficult to see the wood for the trees. If, on the other hand, he errs on the side of parsimony, he may fail in what is after all the main object and justification of a case book: to make the law come alive through the medium of the cases.

These difficulties are compounded if owing to the promulgation of a new Act it becomes impossible in many instances to foretell with any degree of certainty which ones of the earlier cases the courts will continue to regard as relevant. Placing safety first, I have acted on the principle that it is better to have too many cases than too few.

Designed primarily as a teaching tool, a case book is intended to supplement and not to supplant textbooks. This does not, if I have been correctly informed by my friends in the profession, mean that practitioners will find *Company Law through the Cases* useless for their purposes. I have enlarged and strengthened the Notes which contain the fine print: advanced material which is not always readily obtainable elsewhere, and in which even those learned in the theory and practice of company law may occasionally find something to their benefit.

Apart from some minor rearrangement of subjects, there has been no change in style or format. After prolonged thought I decided to include a chapter on winding-up and judicial management. I have felt for some time that the omission of this important subject constituted a serious gap.

I am deeply indebted to Mr J S McLennan of the Law School of the University of the Witwatersrand, who once again undertook the thankless but important task of preparing the General Index, and who made a number of valuable suggestions. My thanks are also due to Miss Joyce Miller, a McGill law graduate, for preparing the Table of Cases, and to Mr Gerard Fick of the Potchefstroom Faculty of Law, who is spending a year at McGill on post-graduate work, for preparing the Table of Statutes. Messrs Juta & Co Ltd and the Rustica Press displayed their customary helpfulness and patience.

In the Preface to the second edition of this work I expressed my gratitude to Messrs Harper and Rowe of New York for granting me permission to include an excerpt from Peter F Drucker's *New Society* (1949), and to the Brookings Institution of Washington DC for permission to include an excerpt from Robert A Gordon's work on *Business Leadership in the Large Corporation* (1966). I reiterate my thanks to authors and publishers.

H R HAHLO

Cape Town
January 1977

Table of Contents

Section		*Page*	*Cases and Materials*

CHAPTER 1

INTRODUCTION

CHAPTER 2

COMPANIES IN GENERAL

Table of Statutes

(A) COMPANIES ACT, 61 OF 1973

(B) COMPANIES ACT, 46 OF 1926

(C) OTHER STATUTES

Table of Cases

Key to Citations of Law Reports

Current

AD	Appellate Division of the Supreme Court
C	Cape Provincial Division
E	Eastern Cape Division (formerly: Eastern Districts Local Division)
NC	Northern Cape Division (formerly: Griqualand West Local Division)
N	Natal Provincial Division
O	Orange Free State Provincial Division
T	Transvaal Provincial Division
SWA	High Court of South-West Africa; South-West Africa Division
SR	High Court of Southern Rhodesia
R	High Court of Rhodesia (General Division)
RAD	High Court of Rhodesia (Appellate Division)
FC	Supreme Court of the Federation of Rhodesia and Nyasaland (no longer in existence)
SA	South African Law Reports (division of Supreme Court indicated by appropriate letters as above)

Pre-Union

SC	Supreme Court of the Cape of Good Hope (cited thus: (1909) 26 SC)
NLR	Supreme Court of Natal
ORC	Orange River Colony High Court
SAR later Off Rep	Official Reports of the High Court of the South African Republic (Transvaal)
Kotzé, Hertzog	Private Compilations of judgments of the High Court of the South African Republic, by Mr Justice Kotzé and Mr Justice Hertzog respectively
TS	Transvaal Supreme Court (highest court in the Transvaal, 1902 to Union)
TH	Transvaal High Court (1902 to Union—present WLD)
EDC	Eastern Districts Court of the Cape of Good Hope
HCG	High Court of Griqualand
Buch AC	Buchanan's Appeal Cases (appeals to the Court of Appeal of the Cape of Good Hope, 1880-6, 1904-9)
CTR	Cape Times Law Reports (Cape Supreme Court, 1891–1910)

First Series (1865–75)

HL	House of Lords (English and Irish Appeals)
CP	Common Pleas
ChApp	Chancery Appeal Cases
Eq	Equity Cases
Ex	Exchequer Cases
QB	Queen's Bench

Second Series (1875–90)

App Cas	Appeal Cases (House of Lords and Privy Council (PC) Appeals)
ChD	Chancery Division
CPD	Common Pleas Division
ExD	Exchequer Division
QBD	Queen's Bench Division

Third Series (1891–   )

AC	Appeal Cases (House of Lords and Privy Council (PC) Appeals)
Ch	Chancery Division
KB or QB	King's Bench or Queen's Bench Division

Weekly Series (1953–   )

WLR   Weekly Law Reports (all-inclusive series)

All the aforementioned law reports are published by the Incorporated Council of Law Reporting for England and Wales.

All England Law Reports

All ER   All England Law Reports (this is a concurrent all-inclusive series of English law reports, published by Messrs Butterworth & Co (Publishers) Ltd, London)

Old Reports

ER   English Reports, reprint of reports of English cases prior to 1865

Scottish Reports

SC	Court of Session (cited thus: 1953 SC)
SC (HL)	House of Lords Appeal Cases from Scotland
SLT	Scottish Law Times

I — *Introduction*

I. OF JURISTIC PERSONS

A TEXT

A juristic person is a body or association other than a natural person, which is endowed by law with the capacity to have rights and duties apart from its members: *1–3*.

According to the 'concession theory', a juristic person is a fictitious body which can only be created by an act of concession of the State, whether by charter, Act of Parliament, or administrative act: *1, 2*. According to the 'realist theory', it is a reality and does not necessarily require State concession: *14* below.

B CASES AND MATERIALS

[1] **Corpus Juris**

D 3.4.1 pr: The right to form a corporation, an association or some similar body, is not conceded to all, but is regulated by laws, decrees of the Senate, and constitutions of the Emperors. Only in a few cases are corporations of this sort permitted; thus, partners in the collection of public taxes or in the working of gold, silver and salt mines have permission to have a corporation. There are also certain gilds in Rome whose corporate existence has been confirmed by decrees of the Senate and constitutions of the Emperors, for example, the gild of bakers and several others, and also that of ship-owners, which also exists in the provinces.

D 3.4.1.1: But those to whom permission has been given to have an association under the name of a corporation, gild or similar body are, in the same way as municipalities, entitled to have common property, a common treasury and an agent or a syndic and whatever is transacted and done by such an agent is, in the same way as in the case of a municipality, deemed to have been transacted and done by all.

D 3.4.7.1: If something is being owed to a *universitas*, it is not being owed to its individual members; and what a *universitas* owes, its members do not owe.

D 3.4.7.2: Nor does it matter whether all the members remain the same or only some of them remain or all are changed.

D 34.5.20(21): As the Senate, in the time of Emperor Marcus, permitted legacies to be left to corporations, there can be no doubt that if a legacy is left to a body which has been permitted to unite, that body will be entitled to it. If, however, a legacy is left to a body which has not obtained this permission, it will not be valid, unless the legacy has been left to its individual members: they will then be admitted to the legacy, not as a corporation, but as individuals.

D 48.18.1.7: The slave [of a corporation] is deemed not to belong to the plurality of members, but to the corporation.

[2] Blackstone *Commentaries on the Laws of England*
17 ed vol 1 (London, 1813)

We have hitherto considered persons in their natural capacities, and have treated of their rights and duties. But, as all personal rights die with the person; and, as the necessary forms of investing a series of individuals, one after another, with the same identical rights, would be very inconvenient, if not impracticable; it has been found necessary, when it is for the advantage of the public to have any particular rights kept on foot and continued, to constitute artificial persons, who may maintain a perpetual succession, and enjoy a kind of legal immortality.

These artificial persons are called bodies politic, bodies corporate, (*corpora corporata*) or corporations: of which there is a great variety subsisting, for the advancement of religion, of learning, and of commerce: in order to preserve entire and for ever those rights and immunities, which, if they were granted only to those individuals of which the body corporate is composed, would upon their death be utterly lost and extinct [at 467].

The honour of originally inventing these political constitutions entirely belongs to the Romans. They were introduced, as Plutarch says, by Numa; who finding, upon his accession, the city torn to pieces by the two rival factions of Sabines and Romans, thought it a prudent and politic measure to subdivide these two into many smaller ones, by instituting separate societies of every manual trade and profession. They were afterwards much considered by the civil law, in which they were called *universitates*, as forming one whole out of many individuals; or *collegia*, from being gathered together: they were adopted also by the canon law, for the maintenance of ecclesiastical discipline; and from them our spiritual corporations are derived [at 468].

Corporations, by the civil law, seem to have been created by the mere act, and voluntary association of their members; provided such convention was not contrary to law, for then it was *illicitum collegium*. It does not appear that the prince's consent was necessary to be actually given to the foundation of them; but merely, that the original founders of these voluntary and friendly societies, for they were little more than such, should not establish any meetings in opposition to the laws of the state.

But, with us in England, the king's consent is absolutely necessary to the erection of any corporation, either impliedly or expressly given [at 471–2].

When a corporation is erected, a name must be given to it; and by that name alone it must sue and be sued, and do all legal acts; though a very minute variation therein is not material. Such name is the very being of its constitution; and, though it is the will of the king that erects the corporation, yet the name is the knot of its combination, without which it could not perform its corporate functions [at 474].

After a corporation is so formed and named, it acquires many powers, rights, capacities, and incapacities, which we are next to consider. Some of these are necessarily and inseparably incident to every corporation; which incidents, as soon as a corporation is duly erected, are tacitly annexed of course. As, 1. To have perpetual succession. This is the very end of its incorporation: for there cannot be a succession for ever without an incorporation; and therefore all aggregate corporations have a power necessarily implied of electing members in the room of such as go off. 2. To sue or be sued, implead or be impleaded, grant or receive, by its corporate name, and do all other acts as natural persons may. 3. To purchase lands, and hold them. . . . 4. To have a common seal. . . . 5. To make bye-laws or private statutes for the better government of the corporation; which are binding upon themselves, unless contrary to the laws of the land, and then they are void . . . [at 474–5].

NOTES

There exists no Roman text in which a *universitas* is called a *persona*. Nearest to it comes D 46.1.22, where it is said that a *hereditas* before adiation functions as if it were a person, like a municipality, a decurion or a partnership.

[3] Webb & Company Ltd v Northern Rifles
1908 TS 462

In an action against a volunteer corps, formed under Transvaal Ordinance 37 of 1904, for the purchase price of goods sold and delivered the court held that the corps was a *universitas* capable of being sued as such.

SMITH J: This question depends entirely upon whether it was the intention of the legislature to create an *universitas*, and we have not in this case to consider the question . . . as to whether an *universitas* can come into being otherwise than through the sanction of the legislature. . . .

. . . An *universitas personarum* in Roman-Dutch law is a legal fiction, an aggregation of individuals forming a *persona* or entity, having the capacity of acquiring rights and incurring obligations to a great extent as a human being. An *universitas* is distinguished from a mere association of individuals by the fact that it is an entity distinct from the individuals forming it, that its capacity to acquire rights or incur obligations is distinct from that of its members, which are acquired or incurred for the body as a whole, and not for the individual members.

Among the most important rights appertaining to an *universitas* is the right to acquire and hold property. It continues to exist though the individual members comprising it change, so long as one member remains in whom the rights of the *universitas* can vest. . . . It has what is sometimes termed perpetual succession. Being formed of an aggregation of individuals, it is, if not a matter of necessity, at all events in the highest degree convenient that it should act through agents, and where created by statute it is frequently the case that these agents are defined by the statute. It does not, however, seem to me to be necessary to the creation of an *universitas* that this should be done, and if no such agent is pointed out or defined at the time of its creation, the *universitas* would have the right to appoint its own agent just as an ordinary individual may do. . . . The main characteristics of an *universitas*, therefore, are the capacity to acquire certain rights as apart from the rights of the individuals forming it, and perpetual succession.

II OF THE HISTORY OF JURISTIC PERSONS IN GENERAL AND COMPANIES IN PARTICULAR

A TEXT

Roman law knew a *universitas personarum* and a *universitas bonorum* (the terms are post-Roman). *Universitates personarum* were associations of persons, and included the State in its financial aspects (*aerarium populi Romani*, fisc); municipalities; various religious bodies; certain trade unions; associations of financiers (*societates publicanorum*), formed for the exploitation of mines or the collection of taxes (in Rome taxgathering was usually 'farmed out' to individuals) (see *1*, above). The *universitas bonorum* was a complex of assets and liabilities. Charitable foundations (*piae causae*), such as hospitals or alms-houses, fell into this category. Another type was a deceased estate before adiation by the heir.

During the early Middle Ages the Roman conception of *universitas* was kept alive by the Church. Every cloister, abbey, chapel or almshouse was regarded as a separate legal entity. At first, the corporation was considered to represent the sum or aggregate of its members. Later, the canonists invested the corporation with a personality of its own. Pope Innocent IV (1243–54), a lawyer by training, was apparently the first to speak of a corporation as a fictitious person: '*cum collegium in causa universitatis fingatur una persona*' ('since a corporation is in a matter concerning the *universitas* deemed by a fiction to be a single person'). As it was thought that only the Prince or State can create a fiction—'*solus princeps fingit quod in rei veritate non est*', said Lucas da Penna, one of the Post-glossators—it followed that incorporation required the sanction of the State. Pope Innocent IV proclaimed that a corporation could commit neither sin nor wrong (Maitland *Preface to Gierke, Political Theories of the Middle Ages* (Cambridge, 1900) xix).

With the reception of Roman law during the latter part of the Middle Ages, the *universitas bonorum* (*afgezonderde vermogen*: mainly the *pia causa* or charitable foundation (*stigting*)) became part of Continental common law. By the time Roman-Dutch law reached its full development, the concept of juristic personality was fully understood: *4*.

The association between trading companies and juristic personality is a relatively recent development. Today, most businesses are in the form of incorporated companies, but until the nineteenth century one-man (or one-family) businesses were the rule. During the Middle Ages, trading associations took the form either of the *commenda*, in which a financier *(commendator)*, in return for a share in the profits of the business, lent money to a trader *(commendatarius)*, without incurring personal liability beyond the amount of his agreed contribution; or of the open partnership *(societas)* in which every partner *(socius)* was an agent of the others, and all the partners were personally liable for the partnership debts. The *commenda* developed later into the partnership *en commandite*, predecessor of the Continental *société en commandite*, and of our partnership *en commandite* as well as of our anonymous partnership. (In England it was not until 1907 that this type of partnership was introduced by the Limited Partnership Act 1907 (7 Edw VII c 24). The Cape Special Partnerships Limited Liability Act 24 of 1861 and the Natal Special Partnerships Limited Liability Act, Law 1 of 1865, make provision for a statutory limited partnership in the Cape and Natal respectively. Neither the partnership *en commandite* or anonymous partnership of the common law, nor the statutory limited partnership is used on any significant scale in modern commercial practice.)

Occasionally there was a trading association on the grand scale, such as the *Grosse Ravensburger Handelsgesellschaft* (1380 to 1530). A society *en commandite*, it had active partners as well as depositors, and was managed by a directorate. Another one was the *Casa* (later *Banca*) *di S Giorgio*, established in the twelfth century. By the fifteenth century, it had a common capital, divided into shares, which were freely transferable and made the holders members of the bank.

As early as the eighth century, merchants travelling to the same markets or fairs formed themselves for mutual protection into convoys or travelling 'companies'. Sometimes they pooled their wares and divided the profits. More usually, each trader conducted his own business with his own stock. At journey's end the 'company' broke up.

The Middle Ages abounded in associations and corporations. The early charters were instruments for the conferment of self-government on towns, gilds, cloisters etc. Merchant and craft gilds also received charters, but they were employers' associations, not trading combines. Each gild had the monopoly of its particular trade. Subject to gild regulations, members conducted their own business.

From the eleventh century groups of merchants trading abroad formed themselves into associations, which were granted by charter the monopoly of specified foreign trades. Such were the German *Hanses*, carrying on trade in France, Holland, England, Scotland, Ireland and the Baltic countries. The 'Mayor, Constables and Fellows of the Merchants of the Staple of England', an association of wool merchants formed to organize their trade on a national basis, had its privileges confirmed in a royal charter of 1353 (27 Edw III st 2 c 1). Another early English trading association was the 'Fellowship of the

Merchant Adventurers of England', consisting of English merchants trading in the Netherlands. Formed early in the fifteenth century, it received its charter from Henry VII in 1505. In 1564, Queen Elizabeth I granted it the corporate privileges of a common seal, perpetual succession, capacity to own and deal with real property, and of making by-laws. Bodies such as the Merchants of the Staple and the Merchant Adventurers were 'regulated companies'. Subject to the regulations of the 'company', each member traded on his own.

The era of the charter companies commenced during the second half of the sixteenth century. The granting of charters to companies carrying on overseas trade, or some other activity which the State wished to encourage in the national interest, became common practice in England and on the Continent. Thus, in England charters were conferred upon the Muscovy Company (1555), the Society of Mines Royal (1568), the Mineral and Battery Works (1568), the Levant Company (1581) and the East India Company (1600). The 'Mines Royal' and the 'Mineral and Battery Works' were the first corporations chartered to exploit patented inventions. Charles II created in 1660 the Company of the Royal Adventurers into Africa: 5.

The Dutch East India Company (*Vereenigde Geoctroyeerde Oost-Indische Compagnie* or *VOC*), which established the first European settlement at the Cape (1652), was founded in 1602 by charter of the Dutch Republic. It was vested with the monopoly of trade with the East Indies: 6.

The later charter companies were 'joint stock' companies. Unlike the older 'regulated company', the 'joint stock' company traded as a single person with a stock jointly contributed by its members. The capital was divided into transferable shares. If the company required additional capital it called upon its members for further contributions. To start with, profits were divided after each single venture, but by stages the organization became permanent. The Dutch East India Company was one of the earliest European associations with the managerial and capital structure of a modern company.

In England whence South Africa derived its early company law, the company charter changed in character after the middle of the seventeenth century. From an instrument for the conferment of a trade monopoly, it became a means for the creation of nationally important domestic companies. In 1688, the grant of monopolistic powers passed from the King to Parliament, which effected it no longer by charter but by statute. The Bank of England was incorporated in 1694, the Bank of Scotland in 1695, the Company of Scotland trading to Africa and the Indies in 1695.

The charter company had general legal capacity analogous to that of a natural person. In accordance with the principle that the debts of a corporation are not the debts of its members, the members of a company were not personally liable for its debts: 7. However, some

companies provided in their charters for unlimited personal liability
of their members. Others, by express provision or usage, were entitled
to claim contributions—'leviations'—from their members. It would
seem that if the corporation could not meet its liabilities, the creditors
could force the company to make calls: *8.*

A charter was expensive and difficult to obtain. Most business
associations were in the form of unincorporated joint-stock companies
—partnerships created by 'deed of settlement' (predecessor of the
modern memorandum and articles of association). Transferable shares
were created, and capital was raised by subscriptions from the public.
The property of the company was usually vested in trustees who could
sue on the company's behalf, while actions against the company had
to be brought against all its members who, as partners, were personally
liable for its debts. By agreement with third parties these unincorporated companies sought to limit liability to the company assets, but
such agreements were of doubtful validity: *9.*

Neither the chartered company nor the unincorporated joint-stock
company was legally entirely satisfactory. As there was no doctrine
of *ultra vires*, a chartered company could undertake anything an
individual could do and was not bound by its original objects. As a
result, there was a flourishing trade in the charters of defunct companies. On the other hand, a person dealing with an unincorporated
joint-stock company was never quite certain with whom to deal or
whom to sue. A bout of company promotion and wild speculation in
stocks and shares, culminating in the bursting of the 'South Sea Bubble',
led to the Bubble Act of 1720 (6 Geo I c 18). It prohibited unincorporated trading associations from acting or purporting to act as
incorporated bodies. It also prohibited the use of charters for purposes
other than those for which they had been granted (see e g *The King* v
Webb (1811) 14 East 406, 104 ER 658).

The first Act to use the term 'public company' was the Public
Companies Act 1767 (7 Geo III c 48). The first modern Companies
Act was the Joint-Stock Companies Act of 1844 (c 110). Its fore-
runners were an Act of 1825 (c 91), which repealed the Bubble Act
and empowered the Crown in future charters to provide that the
members of the corporation should be individually liable for its debts
without limit or to such extent as the Crown should deem fit (prior
to the 1825 Act the Crown could not create a corporation with
unlimited liability: *Elve* v *Boyton* [1891] 1 Ch 501 (CA) at 507); the
Trading Companies Act 1834 (c 94), which empowered the Crown
to confer by letters patent on an incorporated trading association all
or any of the privileges of incorporation, except limited liability; and
the Chartered Companies Act 1837 (c 73). The 1837 Act, which is
still in force but rarely used, re-enacted the provisions of the 1834 Act,
but required the registration of certain particulars regarding the
partnerships in question with an officer of the Court of Chancery,

and laid down that the letters patent might limit the personal liability of its members to a specified amount per share. It also provided for the establishment of companies of limited duration.

The Joint Stock Companies Act 1844 (*supra*) resulted from the labours of a Select Committee, since 1834 under the chairmanship of Gladstone, then President of the Board of Trade. It borrowed many of its ideas from Bellenden Ker's report on the Law of Partnership (1837, BPP *1837* (399) XLIV, reprinted as an appendix to the report of the Select Committee, 1844 (119) VII). As Professor Gower remarked in (1956) 69 *Harvard LR* 1369 at 1371–2,

> '. . . the modern English business corporation has evolved from the unincorporated partnership, based on mutual agreement, rather than from the corporation, based on a grant from the State. . .'.

The Act provided for incorporation by registration, without charter or special Act, and was the first enactment to distinguish clearly between an incorporated company and an unincorporated partnership. The office of a Registrar of Companies was set up. A register of shareholders and certain other information had to be filed with the Registrar on registration and kept up to date by periodical returns. If subscriptions from the public were to be invited, a prospectus was to be registered. A 'full and true' balance sheet, duly audited, had to be submitted to the annual general meeting, and thereafter, together with the auditor's report, filed with the Registrar where it was open for inspection. There was unlimited personal liability of members, but the company had to be excussed first. Personal liability of a member ceased three years after transfer of his shares. All partnerships having more than 25 members or freely transferable shares had to be registered as companies. A separate Act, also of 1844 (c 111), subjected insolvent companies to the bankruptcy laws.

The Companies Clauses Consolidation Act 1845 (8 & 9 Vict c 16; still in force) set out the provisions which at that time used to be normally contained in the statutes of public utility companies, such as railways, waterworks, gasworks, and canal companies. It restricted the liability to creditors of members of these companies, as well as of chartered companies, to the amount unpaid on their shares. Payment of dividends out of capital was expressly prohibited.

The Winding-Up Act 1848 (11 & 12 Vict c 45) entitled shareholders to petition for the winding-up of their company.

The Joint Stock Companies Act 1844 was amended by the Limited Liability Act 1855 (18 & 19 Vict c 133), which adopted the principle of limited liability for all registered companies, provided the word 'limited' was added to the name of the company. The Act fixed the minimum nominal value of shares at £10 each, and required no fewer than 25 shareholders holding shares to the amount in the aggregate of not less than three-fourths of the nominal capital of the company. Each shareholder had to pay up on his shares at least twenty pounds per centum.

Directors were to be personally liable if they paid dividends knowing that the company was insolvent or that the payment of the dividends would render it insolvent. A company which had lost three-quarters of its subscribed capital had to be wound up. Loans by the company to its shareholders were prohibited. Every company had to appoint auditors approved by the Board of Trade.

After having been in force for a few months only, the Limited Liability Act 1855 was repealed, and its main provisions were incorporated in the Joint Stock Companies Act 1856 (19 & 20 Vict c 47). This Act first introduced the requirement of a memorandum of association and articles of association. It took over the principle of limited liability, but dropped the requirement of a minimum capital, the rule that a company which had lost three-fourths of its subscribed capital had to be wound up, and the compulsory auditing requirements.

The 1856 Act and the Winding-Up (Insolvent) Act 1857 (20 & 21 Vict c 78) removed companies from normal bankruptcy jurisdiction and provided, instead, for winding-up proceedings. (This explains why to this day companies do not go insolvent but are wound up.) Winding-up at the instance of creditors was introduced, and the distinction between compulsory and voluntary winding up was established. The 1855–7 legislation laid the foundations of modern English company law.

In 1862, company legislation in England was consolidated and amended in the Companies Act 1862 (c 89), which remained the principal Act until 1908. Among other changes, it introduced the company limited by guarantee. The words, 'Joint Stock', redolent of an earlier dispensation, were dropped.

The Companies Act (1862) Amendment Act 1867 (30 & 31 Vict c 131) provided, inter alia, for reduction of capital, associations not for profit, calls upon shares, and share warrants to bearer. It also prescribed that every prospectus should contain certain particulars, including the date of, and the names of the parties to, any contract entered into by the company or its promoters, directors or trustees before the issue of the prospectus.

The modern rules governing the reduction of capital were first laid down in the Companies Act 1877 (c 26). The Director's Liability Act 1890 (c 64) introduced the principle, now enshrined in s 160 of our Companies Act, that a promoter or director can be held liable in damages for a negligent misrepresentation in a prospectus. It was the legislature's answer to Derry v Peek (1889) 14 App Cas 337 (69), where it was held that at common law a director or promoter cannot be held liable for a negligent, as distinguished from a fraudulent, misrepresentation in a prospectus.

The Companies Act 1907 (c 50) introduced the private company.

The Companies Act of 1862 was replaced, in turn, by the Companies (Consolidation) Act 1908 (8 Edw VII c 69); the Companies Act 1929 (19 & 20 Geo V c 23); and the Companies Act 1948 (11 & 12 Geo VI c 38). The latter was amended by the Companies Act 1967 (c 81), which, among other changes, abolished the 'exempt' private company and tightened up disclosure and accounting requirements.

To prevent fraud in connection with dealings in investments, the Prevention of Fraud (Investments) Act 1939 (c 16) was passed, since replaced by the 1958 Act of the same title (c 45).

In 1972 the United Kingdom joined the European Economic Community. In compliance with the First Directive of the European Economic Community of 9 March 1968 (68/151/EEC), as amended by the Act of Accession of 27 March 1972, Britain passed the European Communities Act 1972 c 18, which, amongst other changes, virtually abolished the *ultra vires* doctrine, except for internal purposes, and reshaped the law relating to pre-incorporation contracts (on the *ultra vires* doctrine in present English law, see pp 80–1 below).

For more than a hundred years South African company legislation trailed faithfully behind English company law. The Joint Stock Companies Limited Liability Act 23 of 1861 (C) of the Cape was based on the English Limited Liability Act 1855 (*supra*), as incorporated in the Joint Stock Companies Act 1856 (*supra*). The Companies Act 25 of 1892 (C), which replaced the 1861 Act, was based on the English Companies Act of 1862 (*supra*).

Law 5 of 1874 of the Transvaal closely followed the 1861 Cape Act. Law 1 of 1891 (T) adopted, in substance, the provisions of the Directors' Liability Act 1890 of the United Kingdom. Act 31 of 1909 (T), which replaced these statutes, leaned heavily on the English Act of 1908. It served as model for the Union Companies Act of 1926.

Early company law legislation in the Orange Free State was on simple lines. Law 2 of 1892 ('to provide for the winding-up of Joint Stock Companies') and Chapter C of the Law Book ('On Limited Liability of Joint Stock Companies') followed English legislation.

In Natal the Joint-Stock Companies' Limited Liability Law 10 of 1864 was substantially based on the Cape legislation. It was supplemented by the Winding-up Law 19 of 1866 (N).

The provincial company statutes, as amended from time to time, continued to apply after Union. They were replaced in 1926 by the Companies Act 46 of 1926, which was repeatedly amended, generally on the lines of the current English legislation.

The appointment of the Van Wyk de Vries Commission of Enquiry into the Companies Act in October 1963 (see 1963 *Annual Survey* 347) initiated a new era in the story of South African company law. The Companies Act 61 of 1973, result of its labours, effectively cut the umbilical cord between English and South African company legislation. (On the work of the Commission see R C Beuthin 1970 *Annual*

Survey 251–69, 1972 *Annual Survey* 220–8.) It is true that the new Act continues to be based on the principles of English company law, but in several respects it strikes out along new lines. (For some of the more important changes, see R C Beuthin 1973 *Annual Survey* 244–9; also Basil Wunsh 1974 *De Rebus Procuratoriis* 461.) While English cases will continue to carry great weight in South Africa, the time when South African company law mirrored the company law of England is past.

Acting under powers vested in him by s 18 of the Companies Act the Minister of Economic Affairs has set up a standing advisory committee on company law (see R C Beuthin 1973 *Annual Survey* 249). The first major piece of amending legislation was the Companies Act 76 of 1974 (on the more important changes made by this Act see R C Beuthin 1974 *Annual Survey* 251–5), followed in 1976 by the Companies Amendment Act 111 of 1976. Further amending legislation can, no doubt, be expected from time to time.

What are the main problems of modern company law? In respect of the small, private company, modern equivalent of the old partnership with the advantages of incorporation and limited liability, there is the time-old problem of how to protect the minority against oppression by a rapacious majority. A variety of remedies has been evolved to this end. (See chapter 14, below).

In the large public company the main problem is a different one: how can the diffuse mass of small shareholders, who may well constitute the majority, be protected from the concentrated power of the controlling shareholders? In theory a company is a democracy, but while this may still hold true of the small company, it has long ceased to be true of the giant corporation which may be effectively controlled by as little as 10 per cent of the voting capital.

The divorce of ownership and control characteristic of the modern company has been accompanied by the 'managerial revolution'. In large companies the tendency has been for management to pass from the full board of directors, comprising part-time, 'outside' directors, as well as full-time, 'inside' directors to the 'inside' directors, assisted and often guided by the 'technostructure', consisting of the professional managers, departmental heads and technical experts of the company: *11–13*.

The strongly felt need to strengthen shareholder democracy and provide more effective protection for the small investor has motivated many of the reforms in the 1973 Act. In common with recent company legislation elsewhere, it provides for more disclosure and stricter accounting. Directors are subjected to a host of restrictions. The rights of minority shareholders are enlarged. Expanded powers of inspection and, if need be, intervention by the Minister of Economic Affairs, nearest South African equivalent of the English Secretary of Trade and Industry (until 1970 the Board of Trade) and the American Federal

Securities and Exchange Commission (SEC), is another device by which it is sought to keep companies on the straight and narrow path of corporate virtue. Further, partly extra-legal, safeguards are found in the stock exchange rules. Indeed, it would probably be true to say that the vigilance of stock exchange committees is the most effective protection of the investing public.

Companies are an essential element in the modern social and economic structure. Shares have replaced land-ownership as the most important form of wealth. The policy decisions of a country's leading companies may make or mar the fortunes of cities, regions, and provinces. The result is a growing public demand that companies should display a 'social conscience' and consider not only the interests of their shareholders, but also those of their workers and customers and, indeed, of the community at large.

In wealth, power and organization, large companies are States within the State, but in the contest for dominance between them and the State, political power has proved itself superior to economic power. 'Like the slave of Aladdin's lamp, it [the corporation] must increasingly follow the mandate of the state': Adolf A Berle (1965) 65 *Columbia LR* at 15.

B CASES AND MATERIALS

[4] *Voet Commentarius ad Pandectas*

1.8.28. As it is clear that individual persons are not bound for the debts of a *universitas*, the directors of the [Dutch] East India Company cannot be sued in their private capacities. It does not follow, however, that there is no personal obligation. As anyone who is not a stranger to law knows, in respect of contracts and last wills *universitates* are in the position of natural persons. They make contracts through their agents and representatives. Like natural persons, they may be left inheritances, legacies and even usufructs, despite the fact that a usufruct is a personal servitude, adhering to the bones of a person. . . .

3.4.1. Whoever has *locus standi in judicio* can issue a summons, be he an individual, the State, or a *universitas*, provided that in the latter case those who preside over the corporation must appoint an agent. . . .

3.4.2. *Universitates* have the rights of private persons and are treated as being in the position of private persons. In the same way as the State, they have estates of their own, treasuries of their own, and their own common property. Hence they can both owe and be owed; sue and be sued. . . .

[5] Charter of the Company of the Royal Adventurers into Africa

18 December 1660

(*Select Charters of Trading Companies AD 1530–1707*, Publications of the Selden Society, vol 28 (1913) 172–7)

CHARLES THE SECOND *by the Grace of God King of England Scotland France and Ireland, Defender of the Faith*, &c., To all to whom these presents shall come, Greeting;

Whereas all and singular the regions countries dominions territories continents coasts and places now or at any time heretofore called or known by the name or names of Guinney and Binney or by either of them . . . and all and singular ports havens rivers creeks islands and places in the parts of Africa to them or any of them belonging, and the sole trade and traffic thereof, are the undoubted right of Us our heirs and successors and are and have been enjoyed by Us and our predecessors for many years past as in right of this our Crown of England,

We, taking into our royal and princely consideration how much the re-settlement of the trade and traffic into the parts aforesaid may and will redound to the good of our service and the honour and enriching of this our Kingdom of England by employing of good store of mariners and shipping and venting of divers of our home manufactures, have for the encouragement of the persons hereafter named, who have undertaken so hopeful an enterprise and must be at great costs and charges likewise to go through with the same, *of our especial grace certain knowledge and mere motion* given and granted, and by these presents for Us our heirs and successors do give and grant, unto our right dear and entirely beloved Brother *James Duke of York and Albany*, our High Admiral of England, and to our most dear and entirely beloved Sisters the most illustrious *Princess Royal, Maria Princess of Aurange*, and most illustrious *Princess Henrietta*, to our right dear and entirely beloved Cousin the most illustrious *Prince Rupert*, etc., etc. . . . , their executors administrators and assigns, All and singular the regions countries dominions territories continents coasts and places lying and being within the limits and bounds hereafter mentioned, that is to say, beginning at Cape Blance lying in twenty degrees of northerly latitude and extending from thence to Cape de Bona Speranza lying in thirty four and a half southerly latitude or thereabouts with all the islands near adjoining to those coasts. . . .

And if otherwise the said grant and demise to them made as aforesaid be not void and determined, then to have and to hold all and singular the said regions . . . for and during the term and unto the full end and term of one thousand years, Yielding and rendering therefore unto Us our heirs and successors two elephants whensoever We our heirs or successors or any of them shall arrive land or come into the dominions regions [&c.] before mentioned or any of them:

And therefore for the setting forward and furthering of the trade intended in the parts aforesaid and the encouragement of the undertakers in discovering the golden mines and settling of plantations there, being an enterprise so laudable and conducing to so worthy an end as the increase of traffic and merchandise wherein this nation hath been famous, *of our further and more ample grace and favour certain knowledge and mere motion* do will ordain constitute appoint give and grant to our said dearest Brother *James Duke of York*, etc., etc. . . . that they and all such other as they shall think fit and convenient to receive into their Company and Society to be traders and adventurers with them to the said countries shall be one body politic and corporate of themselves in deed and in name by the name of The Company of the Royal Adventurers into Africa:

And We do therefore *of our more especial grace certain knowledge and mere motion* for Us our heirs and successors grant unto the said Company and their successors that they the said Company and their successors shall and may have the ordering rule and government of all such Plantations as shall be by them at any time hereafter settled within the parts of Africa aforementioned, And do by these presents for Us our heirs and successors grant unto them full power licence and authority to name and appoint Governors from time to time in the said Plantations, which said Governors shall and by these presents We do for Us our heirs and successors give to them full power and authority to raise arm train and muster such military forces as to them shall seem requisite and necessary and to execute and use within the said Plantations the law called the martial law for the defence of the said Plantations against any foreign invasions or domestic insurrections or rebellions,

And further We will and it is the true intent and meaning of these presents that We our heirs and successors shall have take and receive two third parts of all the gold mines which shall be seized possessed and wrought in the parts and places aforesaid, We our heirs and successors paying and bearing two third parts of all the charges incident to the working and transporting of the said gold, And that the said Company and their successors shall and may have take and enjoy the other third part of all the said gold mines, . . .

In witness &c. witness our self at Westminster the eighteenth day of December

per ipsum Regem.

[6] *Het Oost-Indische Octroy*

(By de Hooch-Mogende Heeren Staten Generael der Vereenichde Nederlanden, inden jare sesthien hondert ende twee verleent ende uyt-ghegeven.) (*GPB* I 30.)

De Staten Generael der Vereenichde Nederlanden, Allen den geenen die dese tegenwoordige sullen worden getoont, Saluyt. DOEN TE WETEN, Aengesien den welstant der Vereenichde Nederlanden principalick is bestaende in de Navigatie, Handelinge ende Commercie die uyt de selve Landen van alle oude tijden gedreven, ende van tijt tot tijt loffelick vermeerdert zijn, niet alleen met de nagebuere Coninckrijcken ende Landtschappen, maer oock met de gene die verder van dese Landen in Europa, Asia ende Africa gelegen zijn, ende dat beneffens de selve inde naeste thien Jaren herwaerts by eenige principale Coopluyden der voorsz Landen, Liefhebbers vande Navigatie, Handelinge eende Commercie op vreemde Landen, in Compagnie binnen der Stadt Amstelredam op gericht met groote kosten, moeyten ende periculen by de hant genomen is, die seer loffelijke Navigatie, Handelinge ende Traffijcque op de Oost-Indien, daer van de apparentie goet ende groot bevonden zijnde, waren onlancks daer naer by verscheyden andere Coopluyden, soo in Zeelandt, op de Mase, als in't Noorder-quartier, ende West-Vrieslandt, mede gelijcke Compagnien op gerecht, ende de voorschreven Navigatie, Handelinge ende Commercie datelick by de hant ghenomen, ende 't welck by ons gheconsidereert ende rijpelick overwogen wesende, hoe vele de Vereenichde Landen, ende de goede Ingesetenen der selver daer aen ghelegen was, dat de selve Navigatie, Handelinge ende Commercie onder een goede generale ordre, Policie, correspondentie ende ghemeenschap, beleyt, onderhouden ende vermeerdert werde, hadden goet ghevonden daer toe Bewinthebbers der voorsz Compagnie voor ons te beschrijven, ende de selve te proponeren, dat eerlick, dienstelick ende profijtich, niet alleen voor de Vereenichde Landen, maer oock voor allen den genen die dese loffelijcke handelinge by de handt ghenomen hadden, ende daer inne waren participerende, soude wesen, dat de selve Compagnie vereenicht, ende de voorsz handelinge onder een vaste ende seeckere eenicheyt, ordre ende Policie soude mogen gemeyn ghehouden, ghedreven ende vermeerdert worden, voor alle de Ingesetenen der Vereenichde Landen, die daer in souden believen te participeren: 't Welck by den Gedeputeerden der selver Compagnie wel verstaen, ende over sulcx na verscheyden communicatien, deliberatien, inductien ende rapporten, tot vereeninge gebracht zijnde, hebben wy nae rijpe beraetslaginge daer op gehouden, tot vervorderinge vanden welstant der Vereenichde Landen, eensamentlijck het profijt van alle de Ingesetenen der selver, de voorsz vereeninge geaggreëert ende bevesticht, aggreëren ende bevestigen mits desen, uyt Souveraine macht ende authoriteyt, oock met vaste wetenschap, onder de Poincten, vryheden ende voordelen hier naer verklaert. Als inden eersten:

I.

Dat in dese equipagie tot dienst ende profijt van dese Compagnie, de Camer van Bewinthebbers binnen Amsterdam sal hebben te bevorderen en te besorgen de helft, de Camer van Zeelant een vierde-part, ende de Cameren op die Mase, Noort-Hollant ende West-Vrieslant elcx een achtste-part.

II.

Dat soo dickwils als het van noode zijn sal, een generale Vergaderinge oft Collegie uyte voorschreven Cameren te houden, die gehouden sal worden van seventien Persoonen, daer inne uyt de Camer van Amsterdam sullen compareren acht, uyt Zeelandt vier, uyt de Mase twee, ende van ghelijcken uyt Noort-Holland twee: Welverstaende dat den seventhienden Persoon by ghebeurte van die Zeelandt, Mase, ende Noort-Hollandt sal werden inde Vergaderinge ghebracht, by de meeste stemmen van welcke Persoonen alle saecken dese vereenichde Compagnie aengaende, sullen verhandelt werden.

III.

't Voorschreven Collegie, als het beschreven sal worden, sal te samen komen, om te resolveren wanneer men sal equiperen, met hoe veel Schepen, waer men die sal seynden, ende andere dingen den Handel betreffende. Ende sullen de Resolutien van 't voorschreve Collegium by de voorschreve Cameren van Amsterdam, Zeelandt, Mase ende Noort-Hollant geeffectueert ende in 't werck gestelt worden.

. . .

VI.

Of 't ghebeurde, dat in 't Collegie eenige swaerwichtige saecken voor vielen, daer inne de Collegianten niet wel en konden verdragen oft accorderen, oft daer sy haer selfs souden in beswaert vinden, om mal-

kanderen to overstemmen, dat het selve sal gelaten worden tot onse ver-
klaringe ende decisie, ende 't geene dien aengaende goet ghevonden sal
worden, sal achtervolcht ende nagekomen worden.

VII.

De vereeninge ende Compagnie sal beginnen ende aenvangh nemen
met desen Jare sesthienhondert ende twee, ende sal gedueren den tijdt van
een en twintich Jaren achtervolgende, midts dat men t'elcke thien Jaren
een generael slot van reeckeninge sal maecken, ende sal elck een t'eynde
die Jaren vry staen, te mogen daer uytscheyden, ende sijn gelt naer hem
nemen. Welverstaende dat vande tegenwoordige equipagie ende uytreedinge van dese Schepen, die binen desen Jare sullen uyt varen, bysonder
reeckeninge gedaen sal worden.

. . .

X.

Alle Ingesetene van dese Landen sullen mogen in dese Compagnie
participeren, met soo weynich ende veele Penningen, als het hun gelieven
sal: dan of het ghebeurde, datter meer penningen waren aen geboden ofte
gepresenteert, dan de Navigatie wel soude vereyschen, sullen die gheene,
die inde Compagnie hebben meer als dertich duysent gulden, moeten nae
rato ende proportie hun Capitael minderen, om anderen plaets te geven.

XI.

Ende sullen de Ingesetenen by openbare affixien van biljetten, ter
plaetse daer men ghewoonlick is biljetten te affigeren, binnen den tijdt van
een Maent naer date deser ghewaerschouwt worden, dat sy binnen den
tijdt van vijf Maenden, ingaende primo Aprilis eerst-komende, in dese
Compagnie sullen worden geadmitteert, ende hare penningen, diese sullen
willen in leggen, mogen op brengen in drie termijnen, te weten ongeveer-
lijck een derde-part tot de toe-rustinge voor den Jaere sestienhondert end
drie, noch een derde-part voor de equipagie vanden Jare sesthien-hondert
ende vier, ende 't resterende derde-part voor de uytreedinge vanden Jare
sesthien-hondert ende vijf, een Maent daer naer dat hy daer van vande
Bewinthebbers sullen zijn vermaent.

. . .

XIIII.

Dat men de reeckeninge vande equipagie ende uyt-rustinge vande
Schepen, met de dependentien van dien sal doen drie Maenden naer het
vertreck vande Schepen, ende een Maent daer naer Copye aende respective Cameren seynden: Ende van de retouren, sullen de Cameren soo
dickwils sy dies versocht worden, Staet aen malkanderen over seynden,
ende de reeckeninge daer van, sal men soo haest sluyten, als doenlijck is,
ende te generale reeckeninge nae de thien Jaren sal geschieden in 't
openbaer, midts datter al vooren Biljetten aen geslagen sullen worden, om
elck een te waerschouwen, die over d'auditie der selver sal begeeren te
komen.

. . .

XVII.

Alsser vande Retouren vijften hondert in Casse sal wesen, sal men aen
de Participanten uytdeelinge doen.

XVIII.

Ende sullen de respective Cameren bedient worden by de tegenwoordige Bewinthebbers, als namelick: De Camer van Amsterdam, by Geraert Bicker, Reynier Paeuw, Pieter Dircxsz Hasselaer, . . .

. . .

XXVII.

De Bewinthebbers sullen op eere, Eedt ende vromicheyt solemnelick beloven, dat sy sich in hare administratie wel ende ghetrouwelick sullen dragen, goede ende deuchdelijcke rekeninge houden ende doen. . . .

. . .

XXXII.

Of 't ghebeurde dat onder d' een oft d' ander Camer, yemandt vande Bewinthebbers in sulcken staet gheraeckte, dat hy niet en konde voldoen 't geene hem sijne administratie aengaende betrouwt ware, ende daer door eenige schade mochte komen, sal sulcx wesen tot last vande penningen, onder de selve Camer resorterende, ende niet tot schade vande generale masse, dies sullen de penningen, welcke de Bewinthebbers in dese Compagnie hebben, specialijck verbonden zijn voor hare administratie.

XXXIII.

De Bewinthebbers vande respective Cameren sullen responderen voor hare Cassiers.

XXXIIII.

Ende op dat het voornemen van dese Compagnie met meerder vrucht uyt ghevoert mach worden, tot welstant der Geunieerde Provincien, conservatie ende augmentatie der Neeringe, midtsgaders tot profijt vande Compagnie, Soo hebben wy de voorsz Compagnie geoctroyeert ende gheaccordeert, octroyeren ende accorderen mits desen, dat niemant van wat qualiteyt ofte conditie die zy anders dan die vande voorsz Compagnie uyt dese Vereenichde Landen sal mogen varen, binnen den tijdt van een-en-twintich Jaren eerstkomende, beginnende met desen Jare sestienhondert ende twee incluys, beoosten de Cape de bonne Esperance, oft door de Straet van Magellanes, op de verbeurte vande Schepen en goederen, . . .

XXXV.

Item, dat die vande voorsz Compagnie sullen vermogen beoosten de Cape van bonne Esperance, mitsgaders in ende door de engte van Magellanes, met de Princen ende Potentaten verbintenissen te maecken, ende contractien op den naem vande Staten Generael vande Vereenichde Nederlanden, oft Hooge Overheden der selver, mitsgaders aldaer eenige Forteressen ende verseeckertheden te bouwen, Gouverneurs, Volck van Oorloge, ende Officiers van Justitie, ende tot andere nootelijcke diensten, tot conservatie vande Plaetsen, onderhoudinge van goede ordeninge, Policie ende Iustitie eensamelijck tot voorderinge ende Neeringe te stellen, behoudelick dat de voorsz Gouverneurs, Officiers, Volck van Justitie, ende Volck van Oorloge, sullen Eedt van ghetrouwicheyt doen aende Staten Generael, ofte de Hooge Overigheyt voorsz, ende aende Compagnie, soo veel de Neeringe ende Trafficque aengaet, ende die sullen de voorschreve Gouverneurs ende Officiers van Justitie af stellen, by soo verre sy bevinden, dat de selve hun qualick ende ontrouwelick dragen, met dien verstande, dat sy-luyden de voorsz Gouverneurs oft Officiers niet en sullen beletten, herwaerts over te komen, om hare doleantien oft klachten, so sy eenige meynen te hebben, ane ons te doen, ende dat die vande Compagnie t' elcker wederkomste vande Schepen gehouden sullen wesen de Heeren Staten Generael te informeren vande Gouverneurs ende Officieren, die sy inde voorsz Plaetsen sullen hebben gestelt, omme hunne Commissie als dan geaggreëert ende geconfirmeert te worden.

. . .

XLII.

Item, dat men geene Bewinthebbers, hare Persoonen ofte goederen sal mogen belasten ofte becommeren, om vande selve te hebben reeckeninge van hare administratie inde voorschreven Compagnie, noch ter cause van gagien van eenige Commisen, Schippers, Stierlieden ende Boots-gesellen, ofte andere persoonen ten dienste der Compagnie aen ghenomen, maer die desen aengaende yet tegen haer sal willen pretenderen, sal ghehouden zijn, de selve te trecken voor hare ordinarise Rechters.

. . .

XLVI.

Alle welcke Poincten, voordelen ende vryheden, hier boven verhaelt, wy gheordonneert hebben ende ordonneren. . . . Gegeven onder onsen Zegel ende Signature van onsen Griffier, in 's Gravenhage den twintichsten Meert sesthienhondert ende twee.

[7] *In Banco Regis* Edmunds against Brown and Tillard
(1668) 1 Lev 237, 83 ER 385

Debt on an obligation of £500. The defendant pleads *non est factum*, and on the evidence it appears that the defendants were two of the principals of the Company of Woodmongers lately dissolved; and that the money was borrowed in the name of the company, and the obligation sealed in the company's name, and with their seal; and the defendants, as was usual, set their names to the obligation. . . . And now the company being dissolved, the plaintiff brought the action against the defendants, intending to charge them in their own right. But it was ruled by the Chief Justice at Nisi Prius at Guild-hall, that he could not so do . . . whereupon the plaintiff was nonsuit.

[See also *The Case of the City of London* (1680) 7 Ventr 351, 86 ER 226.]

[8] De Term Sanct Trin Anno Regis 23 Car II [1671] in Cancellaria
(1671) 1 Ch App Cas 204, 22 ER 763

Doctor SALMON *against the* HAMBOROUGH *Company, by the Name of the Governor, Assistants and Fellowship of Merchant Adventurers of* ENGLAND, *and divers particular Members of that Company by Name, in their natural Capacities.*

The Bill charged, that the Company were incorporated *prout per* Letters Patent, and had Power to make By-Laws, and to assess Rates upon Cloaths (which was the Commodity they dealt in) and by Poll upon every Member to defray the necessary Charge of the Company, and that the Company had imposed Rates accordingly, as namely, 4s. 6d. upon every white Cloath exported, and divers others, and thereby raised £8 000 *per Ann.* towards the Support of the Common Charge of the Company, and that they had thereby got great Credit, and borrowed great Sums of Money by their Common Seal, and particularly the plaintiff lent £2 000 upon that Security many Years since. And the Bill did set forth divers Advantages they had in trade by being Members of this Corporation, which others wanted. And the Bill did charge, That the Company having no Common Stock, the Plaintiff had no Remedy at Law for his Debt, but did charge that their Usage had been to make Taxes, and levy Actions upon the Members and their Goods, to bear the Charge of their Company to pay their Debts, and did complain that they now did refuse to execute that Power, and did particularly complain against divers of the Members by Name, that they did refuse to meet and lay Taxes, and that they did pretend want of Power by their Charter to lay such Taxes, whereas they had formerly exercised Power, and thereby gained Credit; whereupon the Plaintiff lent them £2 000, which was for the Use and Support of the Company's Charge, and so ought to be made good by them, and so prayed to be relieved.

Paschae, 1656, this Bill was filed, and the Company served with Process, but would not appear, they having nothing by which they may be distrained: But divers particular Members being served in their natural Capacities, did appear and demur, for that they were not in that Capacity liable to the Plaintiff's Demands. 10 *May* 1666, On the Argument the Demurrer was allowed, and the Bill dismist as to them . . . and thereupon a Petition of Appeal was preferred to the Lords in Parliament, . . .

The matter upon the Petition of *Salmon*, Dr. of Physick, exhibited to the Lords Spiritual and Temporal in Parliament assembled,

Their Lordships on reading the said Petition, the Answer, Plea and Demurrer thereto, and the said Dismission, and the Charter by which the said Governor and Fellowship are incorporated, and hearing what was alleged on both sides, do order that the Dismission, for so much as concerns the said Company, be, and do stand reversed, and that the Lord Chancellor, or the Lord Keeper of the Great Seal of *England* for the Time being, do retain the said Bill. And that the said Court of Chancery shall issue forth the usual Process of that Court, and if Cause be, Process of *Distringas* thereupon against the said Corporation; . . . And if upon Return of the Process, the said Corporation shall not file an Appearance, or shall appear and not answer, the said Bill shall be taken *pro confesso*, and a Decree shall thereupon pass. But in case the said Corporation shall appear and answer within the Time aforesaid, then the Court of Chancery shall proceed to examine what the Plaintiff's just Debt is, and shall decree the said Company to pay so much money as the same shall appear to amount unto, with reasonable Damages. And in case the Corporation shall not pay the Sum decreed within ninety Days after the Service of the said Decree . . . then the Lords Spiritual and Temporal do farther order . . . that the Lord Chancellor or Lord Keeper for the Time being shall order and decree, that the Governor or Deputy-Governor and the twenty-four

Assistants of the said Company, or so many of them as by the Tenor of their Charter do constitute a *Quorum* for the making of Leviations upon the Trade, or Members of the said Company, for the Use of the' said Company, shall within such Time as by the Lord Chancellor or Keeper shall be thought fit, make such a Leviation upon every Member of the said Company as is to be contributary to the Publick Charge, as shall be sufficient to satisfy the said Sum to be decreed to the Plaintiff in that Cause, and to collect and levy the same, and to pay it over to the Plaintiff as the Court Shall direct. . . .

[On *Edmunds* v *Brown and Tillard*, 7 above, and the *Hamborough Case*, 8, above, see Daffyd Jenkins 'Skinning the Pantomime Horse: Two Early Cases on Limited Liability' (1975) 37 *CLJ* 308.]

[9] *In re* The Sea Fire and Life Assurance Company:

Greenwood's Case

(1854) 3 De G M & G 460, 43 ER 180

The LORD CHANCELLOR (Lord Cranworth): The case arose thus: An order was made for winding up a company, called the Sea Fire and Life Assurance Company. It was evidently a sort of bubble company: there were to have been a hundred thousand shares, but nothing like that number were subscribed for, and still fewer were paid up. . . .

Several attempts having been made to get in assets, costs were necessarily incurred, and it thus became needful to have a sum of money raised for the purpose of providing the official manager with funds. . . .

It was eventually considered by the Master necessary to raise a sum of £1 000 at the least, in order to enable the official manager to proceed safely, and for that purpose a call of £1 per share was made, which together with the money it was reasonable to anticipate might be recovered from those members who had not paid up their shares, would be sufficient to provide the amount required. . . .

The question now raised is, whether it was proper to make the call. . . .

I will now proceed to state the grounds why, upon the main question of the liability of the shareholders, I cannot agree with the Vice-Chancellor. Supposing that the parties had really stipulated that, in no contingency and under no circumstances whatever, whether the affairs of the company prospered or failed, should any one of the shareholders be liable for more than £1 per share, what would be the consequence of such a stipulation. His Honour's judgment proceeds upon the ground, that no creditor could then come upon a shareholder beyond the £1 per share. That is a very strong assumption, for it militates against the principle of partnership as hitherto understood in this country. Whether the principle is a right or wrong one is a matter now under investigation before the Legislature, but that it is the principle cannot, I think, for one moment be disputed, namely, that every person engaged in a partnership is liable solidarily, as they say upon the Continent, for everything. Thus A, B and C carrying on business together, may stipulate among themselves that no one of them shall be liable for more than £1 000, yet, if in the conduct of their business they incur a debt to the extent of £10 000, every one of them would be liable for it, notwithstanding any stipulation they might have made with one another. That doctrine does not depend upon the persons dealing with the partners having notice, and any notice would be quite immaterial. . . . If the deed of partnership, containing such a provision as I have mentioned, were hung up in the shop, it would make no difference; for how could a person dealing with the firm tell whether each partner would be liable to him or not. They might have already incurred debts with other persons to the extent provided, and thus it would not be possible for him to ascertain the limit of their liability. . . .

The law as to common partnerships being such as I have stated, what is the case of a joint stock company? It might be rather a curious and interesting speculation to inquire in what manner exactly, and when, these partnerships became distinguished from ordinary partnerships, and by what steps they advanced to their present position. That long before the Joint Stock Acts they were distinguished, is a proposition that cannot be controverted, although it may be difficult to say precisely in what points they differed. They certainly differed in this, that whereas, according to the ordinary laws of partnership, any one partner acting within the scope of the partnership might bind all the other partners, it was not so with a joint stock company; for, independently of the Joint Stock Companies Act, partnerships consisting of a number of persons too numerous to act in the way that an ordinary partnership does, had been in the habit of exercising many of their functions, accepting bills, giving orders for goods, &c., solely through the means of directors. I have never, however, heard it suggested that, independently of the Act, partners could absolve themselves from the ordinary liabilities or partnership *quoad* third parties because they were very numerous, though Lord Eldon frequently said that it would be extremely difficult to enforce the rights of third parties against bodies so numerous, and he therefore, I believe, doubted whether they were not illegal. But it is idle to speculate upon that point; for these companies, being consonant with the wants of a growing and wealthy community, have forced their way into existence, whether fostered by the law or opposed to it; they have not, however, proceeded to the extent of enabling their members to enter into arrangements absolving themselves from liabilities without the circle of their own deed, that is, from liabilities to third persons.

[10]   Herbert Spencer 'Railway Morals and Railway Policy' *Edinburgh Review*

1854 vol C 420–1 (quoted from Bishop Carleton Hunt *The Development of the Business Corporation in England (1800–1867)* (1936) 136)

As devised by Act of Parliament, the administrations of our public companies are almost purely democratic. The representative system is carried out in them with scarcely a check. Shareholders elect their directors, directors their chairman; there is an annual retirement of a certain proportion of the board giving facilities for superseding them. . . . Yet, not only are the characteristic vices of our political state reproduced in each of these mercantile corporations—some even in intenser degree— but the very form of government which, remaining nominally democratic, is substantially so remodelled as to become a miniature of our national constitution. The direction, ceasing to fulfil its theory as a deliberative body whose members possess like powers, falls under the control of some one member of superior cunning, will or wealth, to whom the majority become so subordinate that the decision on every question depends on the course he takes. Proprietors, instead of constantly exercising their franchise, allow it to become on all ordinary occasions a dead letter; retiring directors are so habitually re-elected without opposition, and have so great a power of insuring their own re-election when opposed, that the board becomes practically a closed body; and it is only when the mis-government grows extreme enough to produce a revolutionary agitation among the shareholders that any change can be effected.

[11] Monograph 11 of the Temporary National Economic Commission

(Bureaucracy and Trusteeship in Large Corporations (1940) 20–1)

Minority control is much more common than majority control among the large companies. It arises where a compact group owns a substantial but minority interest which constitutes a majority of the stock actually represented at stockholders' meetings, or to which the control group can attract a sufficient number of proxies from scattered holders to constitute a majority at such meetings. The latter rather than the former is the usual means of minority control.

Once in power a minority group is difficult to dislodge. It has, of course, picked a management which is congenial and cooperative. Then the proxy machinery, with expenses paid by the company, is commonly at its disposal. The proxy committee is in effect chosen by the control group and is used as a means of perpetuating itself. Naturally, the larger the corporation and the more dispersed the stock, the more difficult it is for a noncontrol faction to amass a sufficient number of proxy certificates to oust the control group and assume command.

As long as management is cooperative with the minority control group, therefore, the minority is relatively secure in its power. When, however, the minority and the management disagree, a major battle may impend in which the management holds a powerful and strategic position. In the ensuing struggle for proxies the management may deny the use of the proxy machinery to the minority, which is then faced with formidable obstacles. The expense of circularizing stockholders with arguments sufficiently convincing to result in their sending in proxy certificates to the minority is a considerable item when stockholders are numbered in thousands. Then there is the natural tendency of the stockholders to let well enough alone and to vote for the existing management, if they vote at all. Thirdly, there are always two sides to the arguments, and to many the side of management may be the more convincing.

[12] Gordon *Business Leadership in the Large Corporation*

Published in co-operation with the Brookings Institution by the U of California Press, 1966

In the broader of the two senses in which the word is used, 'management' includes not merely the executives but also the board of directors. The board stands between the stockholders and the executive group. It is not expected even in theory to direct the affairs of a business in any detail, but it *is* supposed to exercise a broad supervision. This broad supervision presumably includes several types of activities: choice of the major executives (or at least the chief executive), establishment of general objectives, formulation of broad policies, a general appraisal of the operating and financial results of the firm's activities, and distribution of profits. The chief executive reports to the board, and the board reports to the stockholders and — though its responsibilities here are very nebulous — to the community at large [at 116].

It is no secret of course that the board's actual role in most large corporations is far different from the conventionalized picture given in the preceding paragraphs. The extent to which boards of directors have become inactive is indicated in part by the dissatisfaction expressed in many quarters with the role which the typical board now plays in the operations of the large corporation [at 116–17].

The fact that executives make up a large fraction of the total board assumes great significance when management has become separated from ownership. If the executive group holds a majority of the stock, the fact that officers predominate on the board does not of itself prejudice the interests of any group. The officer-directors, whether as officers or as directors, represent the majority stockholders. When the great bulk of stock ownership is divorced from management, however, a board made up primarily of officers creates an entirely different situation. In this case, the officers are given the right to supervise themselves; there is no continuous independent link between management and stockholders; and the interests of the latter can be protected, except as management chooses to protect them, only through the medium of the annual stockholders' meetings and through resort to legal action by particular stockholders. The weakness of the protection provided by these two media needs no elaboration. Thus, in effect, the officer board means that the board as an independent supervisory body has ceased to exist [at 120].

While the officer board, taken in conjunction with the separation of ownership and management, represents a significant development, its importance should not be overstressed. In the first place, officers *may*, despite their lack of ownership, take their responsibilities to stockholders quite seriously. In addition, the executive group is in a better position to recognize and protect the interests of other groups — for example, workers and customers — than are directors elected by and owing allegiance to particular stockholding and other interests [at 120–1].

Those who seek to restore the board as a true decision-making body misread the problem of large-scale management organization. The withering away of the active leadership function of the board is unavoidable. It is merely a reflection of the fact that large-scale business leadership can be performed efficiently only by a single group of working officials willing and able to devote the necessary time to the business. Non-officer directors, however, have other roles to play. Executives need the advice of outside directors, and, what is even more important, we must rely on the board as an independent body to provide the link between executives and those outside groups whose welfare the company exists to serve [at 145–6].

[13] Peter F Drucker *The New Society*
(New York, 1949) 34–5

One symptom of the autonomy of the enterprise is the process known in this country as the 'divorce of control from ownership'. . . . Even in those few big corporations where ownership is still concentrated, the actual control is increasingly being exercised by professional managements. The legal owners are represented on the Board of Directors, but they take less and less part in the running of the business. Management considers them 'outsiders' and resents any 'interference' from them. . . .

In this country the 'divorce of control from ownership' has been regarded widely as both undesirable and unnatural. Undoubtedly, it poses serious problems—though the one that is discussed most generally, that of the 'legitimacy' of management power, has actually nothing to do with the divorce but arises in exactly the same form where the management of a big enterprize is still based on property. But the divorce is not only natural. It is also in the social interest. It expresses clearly the idea that the enterprize cannot and must not be operated in the interest of any one group: stockholders, workers or consumers, but in the interest of society.

NOTES

On the role of the corporation in the modern State, see also A A Berle & G C Means *The Modern Corporation and Private Property* (1932); Paul P Harbrecht 'The Modern Corporation Revisited' (1964) 64 *Columbia LR* 1410; Adolf A Berle 'Property, Production and Revolution' (1965) 65 *Columbia LR* 1; Gerard Nash 'Administrative Law, Criminal Law and Inspection under the Companies Act' (1967) 8 *University of Western Australia LR* 143.

On modern managerial practice, see F J Willett 'Conflict between Modern Managerial Practice and Company Law' (1967) 5 *Melbourne ULR* 48; on publicity in company law, H S Cilliers *Die Leer van Openbaarmaking in Die Maatskappyereg met Besondere Verwysing na die Funksie van Gepubliseerde Finansiële State* (Pretoria, 1964).

Useful starting points for research on the historical development of English company law are: *Select Charters of Trading Companies, A.D. 1530–1707*, Selden Society vol 28 (1913); L C B Gower *Modern Company Law* 3 ed (1969) 22 ff; Bishop Carleton Hunt *The Development of the Business Corporation in England (1800–1867)* (Cambridge, Mass, 1936) (containing an excellent bibliography, at 163–71); C A Cooke *Corporation, Trust and Company* (Manchester UP, 1950); Sir Frederick Pollock *The Law of Partnership in England* (London, 1882); Remarks on Joint Stock Companies by an Old Merchant, London, 1825; W R Scott *The Constitution and Finance of English, Scottish and Irish Joint Stock Companies to 1720* 3 vols (Cambridge, 1910–12); H A Smith *The Law of Associations, Corporate and Unincorporate* (Oxford, 1913); *The South Sea Bubble* 2 ed (London, 1825); Virginia Cowles *The Great Swindle* (1960); H S Cilliers 'A Critical Enquiry into the Design, Development and Meaning of the Concept "Limited Liability" in Company Law', Thesis U of SA 1963; Leonard W Hein 'The British Business Company' (1963) 15 *U of Toronto Law Journal* 134; M L Benade 'The South Sea Bubble' (1965) 6 *Codicillus* 27; S Williston 'History of the Law of Business Corporations before 1800' (1888) 2 *Harv LR* 105, 149; Yves Caron 'Le Droit Corporatif en Evolution: de la "Corporation Sole" à la "Compagnie Simple" ' (1967) 13 *McGill Law Journal* 424 (dealing especially with the 'one-man' company); Clive M Schmitthoff, 'The Origin of the Joint Stock Company' (1939) 3 *U of Toronto LJ* 74; Armand Budington du Bois *The English Business Company after the Bubble Act 1720–1800* (1938).

2   *Companies in General*

I How Juristic Personality is acquired

A TEXT

In South Africa today corporations (*universitates personarum*) of all kinds, public and private, abound: municipalities and universities; trade unions and employers' associations; companies, building societies, co-operative societies and friendly societies; and so on *ad infinitum*.

Leaving aside corporations of the public law, there are three ways in which a juristic person may acquire legal personality:

(*a*) By special Act of Parliament, modern equivalent of the old charter. There are numerous corporations of this kind, usually of a semi-public character. Escom (incorporated by the Electricity Act 42 of 1922, since replaced by Act 40 of 1958) and Iscor (incorporated by the Iron and Steel Industry Act 11 of 1928) may serve as examples.

(*b*) By incorporation under a general enabling Act, such as the Companies Act 61 of 1973, the Co-operative Societies Act 29 of 1939, the Building Societies Act 24 of 1965, the Friendly Societies Act 25 of 1956 (cf s 3 of the Companies Act).

(*c*) By conducting itself as a juristic person. Until 31 December 1939, an association of persons which had all the characteristics of a juristic person could acquire juristic personality without being formally incorporated: *14*. Since 31 December 1939, only an association of persons which does not carry on business for the purpose of gain can acquire legal personality in this manner: s 31. (On the meaning of 'business' and 'gain' see below: *27, 28*.) In effect, therefore, the 'concession' theory applies to associations carrying on business for gain, the 'realist' theory to others. (See above, p 1.)

25

Whether the charitable foundation (*pia causa, stigting*) is a living institution of South African law is an open question. In practice, it plays no significant role. The purposes of the old charitable foundation are achieved by the establishment of trusts or the incorporation of associations not for gain under s 21 of the Companies Act. It cannot be regarded as settled whether it is possible to create a trust with legal personality without registering it as a company.

Deceased estates are, according to the prevailing view, not juristic persons.

B CASES

[14] Morrison v Standard Building Society
1932 AD 229

WESSELS JA: The plaintiff in the court below (respondent in this court) claimed in the Transvaal Provincial Division an order for the ejectment of the appellant from certain premises . . . and for damages. The appellant set up the defence that the Society has no *locus standi in judicio* because it is an unincorporated society and cannot sue in its own name. . . .

The first question to decide is whether the Society was entitled to sue in its own name. [It was contended], on behalf of the appellant, that by the Roman law an association of persons for gain, which has not obtained the permission of the State to act as a corporate body, has no *locus standi in judicio*. Such an association is not a *universitas* or corporation and therefore cannot sue in its own name. . . . There is little or no doubt that the older commentators thought that according to the Roman law an association or combination of individuals could not form a *corpus* or *universitas* unless it had the sanction of the State. Amongst the more modern jurists skilled in Roman law a controversy exists whether in fact all corporations required the sanction of the State. Owing to the sparsity of authority in the texts it is a very difficult matter to determine exactly what associations required the sanction of the State and what did not need a special sanction in order to give them the character of a corporation. Some jurists are of opinion that we must consider the objects and constitution of the association and judge from these whether it possesses the character of a corporation or not. If it has the characteristics of a corporation, and if such a combination is not specially forbidden, then it did not require special permission of the State in order to function as a corporation. . . . Others again hold that the sanction of the State is essential except in the case of religious bodies, institutions *ad pias causas* and combinations for public purposes. . . .

. . . This particular building society has been in existence in the Transvaal since October 1891, under the name of the 'Transvaal Permanent Building and Investment Society'. It has been actively operating as a building society since 1891 and only its name was changed in 1929. Its funds amount to £726 559, and it holds property in all the provinces of the Union. The Society has brought many actions in its own name in the law courts. Even therefore if it has not obtained

State sanction, it certainly has been allowed to carry on business in its corporate name, to hold property and to sue. It therefore falls under the category of associations which have been permitted or suffered to act as corporate bodies without let or hindrance. This review of our law upon the subject has led me to the conclusion that Gregorowski J was right when he held in the case of *Committee of the Johannesburg Public Library* v *Spence* (1898) 5 Off Rep 84 that an association of individuals does not always require the special sanction of the State in order to enable it to hold property and to sue in its corporate name in our courts. In order to determine whether an association of individuals is a corporate body which can sue in its own name, the court has to consider the nature and objects of the association as well as its constitution, and if these show that it possesses the characteristics of a corporation or *universitas* then it can sue in its own name. Nor can I see any valid objection to such a society suing in its own name. It is true that a partnership cannot sue or be sued in its own name, with certain exceptions, but this is because one partner is the agent of the others and the property of its individual members can be executed upon. A building society is not a partnership in any shape or form. One member of a building society is not the agent of the others and his acts cannot bind his fellow members. Nor can a member of such a society be held liable for the debts of the society. The Society exists as such quite apart from the individuals who compose it, for these may change from day to day. It has perpetual succession and it is capable of owning property apart from its members. . . .

. . . But for the fact that it has not obtained the special sanction of the State [the Society] possesses all the characteristics of a *universitas* or corporate body, and therefore in my opinion it can sue in its own name. . . .

NOTES

See further *Nederduitsch Hervormde Congregation of Standerton* v *Nederduitsch Hervormde of Gereformeerde Congregation of Standerton* (1893) Hertzog 69 (common-law corporation can only be dissolved by consent of all members); *Committee of the Johannesburg Public Library* v *Spence* (1898) 5 Off Rep 84; *Cassim* v *Molife* 1908 TS 748; *Tilbrook* v *Higgins* 1932 WLD 147; *Leschin* v *Kovno Sick Benefit and Benevolent Society* 1936 WLD 9; *Van Rensburg* v *Afrikaanse Taal en Kultuurvereniging (SAS en H)* 1941 CPD 179; *Ex parte Doornfontein-Judiths Paarl Ratepayers Association* 1947 (1) SA 476 (W) (association without a constitution held incapable of being a *universitas*); *Klerksdorp and District Muslim Merchants Association* v *Mahomed* 1948 (4) SA 731 (T); *Malebjoe* v *Bantu Methodist Church* 1957 (2) PH M13 (W); *Ex parte Johannesburg Congregation of the Apostolic Church* 1968 (3) SA 377 (W). See also R D Lumb 'Corporate Personality' (1964) 4 *University of Queensland LJ* 418.

There is no presumption that a voluntary association is a corporate body: *SA Cooling Services (Pty) Ltd* v *Church Council of the Full Gospel Tabernacle* 1955 (3) SA 541 (N).

On 'quasi-corporations' which, though unincorporated, are treated for certain purposes as separate entities, see e g *Taff Vale Railway Co* v *Amalgamated Society of Railway Servants* [1901] AC 426; *Knight and Searle* v *Dove* [1964] 2 All ER 307; K W Wedderburn (1965) 28 *MLR* 62.

II THE LEGAL NATURE OF A COMPANY

A TEXT

South African company law is based on the Companies Act 61 of 1973, as amended. The Act is a statute, not a code. Large areas of company law are governed by the common law.

As a juristic person a company is, legally, an entity apart from its members. Its property is not the property of its members, its debts are not the debts of its members, and it has perpetual succession: *1* above; *15–17*. By a legal fiction nationality, a domicile and a place of residence are attributed to a company: *18, 19, 19A*.

In South African, as in English, American and Dutch company law, a company is governed by the law of the country where it is incorporated. In French and German law, on the other hand, it is governed by the law of the country where its central administration or principal place of business (*siége social*) is situated. In most cases, of course, the country of incorporation is also the country where a company's *siége social* is.

On jurisdiction in respect of a company, see s 12 and *Dowson & Dobson Ltd* v *Evans & Kerns (Pty) Ltd* 1973 (4) SA 136 (E).

In exceptional cases the courts will 'lift (or "pierce") the veil of corporate personality' and look at what lies behind it: *20–23*.

B CASES

[15] Salomon *v* Salomon and Company
[1897] AC 22

A trader sold his business as a leather merchant and wholesale boot manufacturer to a limited company with a nominal capital of 40 000 shares of £1 each. The only shareholders in the company were the vendor, his wife, a daughter and four sons, who subscribed for one £1 share each. In part payment of the purchase-money debentures were issued to the vendor. 20 000 shares were also issued to him and paid for out of the purchase-money. The vendor was appointed managing director.

When a year later the company was wound up, it was found that if the amount realized from the assets of the company would be, in the first place, applied in payment of the debentures, there would be no funds left for payment of the ordinary creditors.

The liquidator, alleging that the company was a mere *alias* or agent of the vendor, claimed that the vendor was liable to indemnify the company against the claims of the ordinary creditors, and that no payment should be made on the debentures held by him until the ordinary creditors had been paid in full.

LORD HALSBURY LC: . . . It seems to me impossible to dispute that once the company is legally incorporated it must be treated like any other independent person with its rights and liabilities appropriate to itself, and that the motives of those who took part in the promotion of the company are absolutely irrelevant in discussing what those rights and liabilities are.

I will for the sake of argument assume the proposition that the Court of Appeal lays down—that the formation of the company was a mere scheme to enable Aron Salomon to carry on business in the name of the company. I am wholly unable to follow the proposition that this was contrary to the true intent and meaning of the Companies Act. I can only find the true intent and meaning of the Act from the Act itself;

and the Act appears to me to give a company a legal existence with, as I have said, rights and liabilities of its own, whatever may have been the ideas or schemes of those who brought it into existence.

LORD MACNAGHTEN: My Lords, I cannot help thinking that the appellant, Aron Salomon, has been dealt with somewhat hardly in this case.

Mr Salomon, who is now suing as a pauper, was a wealthy man in July 1892. He was a boot and shoe manufacturer trading on his own sole account under the firm of 'A. Salomon and Co.', in High Street, Whitechapel, where he had extensive warehouses and a large establishment. He had been in the trade over thirty years. . . . Beginning with little or no capital, he had gradually built up a thriving business, and he was undoubtedly in good credit and repute.

It is impossible to say exactly what the value of the business was. But there was a substantial surplus of assets over liabilities. And it seems to me to be pretty clear that if Mr Salomon had been minded to dispose of his business in the market as a going concern he might fairly have counted upon retiring with at least £10 000 in his pocket.

Mr Salomon, however, did not want to part with the business. He had a wife and a family consisting of five sons and a daughter. Four of the sons were working with the father. The eldest, who was about thirty years of age, was practically the manager. But the sons were not partners: they were only servants. Not unnaturally, perhaps, they were dissatisfied with their position. They kept pressing their father to give them a share in the concern. . . . So at length Mr Salomon did what hundreds of others have done under similar circumstances. He turned his business into a limited company. . . .

All the usual formalities were gone through, all the requirements of the Companies Act 1862 were duly observed. There was a contract with a trustee in the usual form for the sale of the business to a company about to be formed. There was a memorandum of association duly signed and registered, stating that the company was formed to carry that contract into effect, and fixing the capital at £40 000 in 40 000 shares of £1 each. There were articles of association providing the usual machinery for conducting the business. The first directors were to be nominated by the majority of the subscribers to the memorandum of association. The directors, when appointed, were authorized to exercise all such powers of the company as were not by statute or by the articles required to be exercised in general meeting; and there was express power to borrow on debentures, with the limitation that the borrowing was not to exceed £10 000 without the sanction of a general meeting.

The company was intended from the first to be a private company; it remained a private company to the end. No prospectus was issued; no invitation to take shares was ever addressed to the public.

The subscribers to the memorandum were Mr Salomon, his wife, and five of his children who were grown up. The subscribers met and appointed Mr Salomon and his two elder sons directors. The directors then proceeded to carry out the proposed transfer. By an agreement dated 2 August 1892, the company adopted the preliminary contract, and in accordance with it the business was taken over by the company as from June 1892. The price fixed by the contract was duly paid. The price on paper was extravagant. It amounted to over £39 000 — a sum which represented the sanguine expectations of a fond owner rather than anything that can be called a businesslike or reasonable estimate of value. That, no doubt, is a circumstance which at first sight calls for observation; but when the facts of the case and the position of the parties are considered, it is difficult to see what bearing it has on the question. . . . The purchase-money was paid in this way: as money came in, sums amounting in all to £30 000 were paid to Mr Salomon, and then immediately returned to the company in exchange for fully paid shares. The sum of £10 000 was paid in debentures for the like amount. The balance, with the exception of about £1 000 which Mr Salomon seems to have received and retained, went in discharge of the debts and liabilities of the business at the time of the transfer, which were thus entirely wiped off. In the result, therefore, Mr Salomon received for his business about £1 000 in cash, £10 000 in debentures, and half the nominal capital of the company in fully paid shares for what they were worth. No other shares were issued except the seven shares taken by the subscribers to the memorandum, who, of course, knew all the circumstances and had therefore no ground for complaint on the score of overvaluation.

The company had a brief career: it fell upon evil days. Shortly after it was started there seems to have come a period of great depression in the boot and shoe trade. There were strikes of workmen too; and in view of that danger contracts with public bodies, which were the principal source of Mr Salomon's profit, were split up and divided between different firms. The attempts made to push the business on behalf of the new company crammed its warehouses with unsaleable stock. Mr Salomon seems to have done what he could: both he and his wife lent the company money; and then he got his debentures cancelled and reissued to a Mr Broderip, who advanced him £5 000, which he immediately handed over to the company on loan. The temporary relief only hastened ruin. Mr Broderip's interest was not paid when it became due. He took proceedings at once and got a receiver appointed. Then, of course, came liquidation and a forced sale of the company's assets. They realized enough to pay Mr Broderip, but not enough to pay the debentures in full, and the unsecured creditors were consequently left out in the cold.

In this state of things the liquidator met Mr Broderip's claim by a counterclaim, to which he made Mr Salomon a defendant. He disputed the validity of the debentures on the ground of fraud. On the same ground he claimed rescission of the agreement for the transfer of the business, cancellation of the debentures, and repayment by Mr Salomon of the balance of the purchase-money. In the alternative, he claimed payment of £20 000 on Mr Salomon's shares, alleging that nothing had been paid on them.

When the trial came on before Vaughan Williams J the validity of Mr Broderip's claim was admitted, and it was not disputed that the 20 000 shares were fully paid up. The case presented by the liquidator broke down completely but the learned judge suggested that the company had a right of indemnity against Mr Salomon. The signatories of the memorandum of association were, he said, mere nominees of Mr Salomon—mere dummies. The company was Mr Salomon in another form. He used the name of the company as an *alias*. He employed the company as his agent; so the company, he thought, was entitled to indemnity against its principal. The counterclaim was accordingly amended to raise this point; and on the amendment being made the learned judge pronounced an order in accordance with the view he had expressed.

The order of the learned judge appears to me to be founded on a misconception of the scope and effect of the Companies Act 1862. In order to form a company limited by shares, the Act requires that a memorandum of association should be signed by seven persons, who are each to take one share at least. If those conditions are complied with, what can it matter whether the signatories are relations or strangers? There is nothing in the Act requiring that the subscribers to the memorandum should be independent or unconnected, or that they or any one of them should take a substantial interest in the under-taking, or that there should be anything like a balance of power in the constitution of the company. In almost every company that is formed the statutory number is eked out by clerks or friends, who sign their names at the request of the promoter or promoters without intending to take any further part or interest in the matter.

When the memorandum is duly signed and registered, though there be only seven shares taken, the subscribers are a body corporate 'capable forthwith', to use the words of the enactment, 'of exercising all the functions of an incorporated company'. Those are strong words. The company attains maturity on its birth. There is no period of minority —no interval of incapacity. I cannot understand how a body corporate thus made 'capable' by statute can lose its individuality by issuing the bulk of its capital to one person, whether he be a subscriber to the memo-randum or not. The company is at law a different person altogether from the subscribers to the memorandum; and, though it may be that after incorporation the business is precisely the same as it was before, and the same persons are managers, and the same hands receive the profits, the company is not in law the agent of the subscribers or trustee for them. Nor are the subscribers as members liable, in any shape or form, except to the extent and in the manner provided by the Act. That is, I think, the declared intention of the enactment. If the view of the learned judge were sound it would follow that no common law partnership could register as a company limited by shares without remaining subject to unlimited liability. . . .

Among the principal reasons which induce persons to form private companies . . . are the desire to avoid the risk of bankruptcy, and the increased facility afforded for borrowing money. By means of a private company a trade can be carried on with limited liability, and without exposing the persons interested in it in the event of failure to the harsh provisions of the bankruptcy law. A company, too, can raise money on debentures, which an ordinary trader cannot do. Any member of a company, acting in good faith, is as much entitled to take and hold the company's debentures as any outside creditor. Every creditor is entitled to get and to hold the best security the law allows him to take. . . .

It has become the fashion to call companies of this class 'one man companies'. That is a taking nickname, but it does not help one much in the way of argument. If it is intended to convey the meaning that a company which is under the absolute control of one person is not a company legally incorporated, although the requirements of the Act may have been complied with, it is inaccurate and misleading: if it merely means that there is a predominant partner possessing an over-whelming influence and entitled practically to the whole of the profits, there is nothing in that that I can see contrary to the true intention of the Act or against public policy, or detrimental to the interests of creditors. If the shares are fully paid up, it cannot matter whether they are in the hands of one or many. If the shares are not fully paid, it is as easy to gauge the solvency of an individual as to estimate the financial ability of a crowd.

[16] Dadoo Ltd v Krugersdorp Municipal Council
1920 AD 530

Under the legislation relating to Non-Whites, as it stood in 1915, Asiatics were prohibited from owning immovable property in the Trans-vaal but nothing was said as to Asiatic companies. In 1915 the company of Dadoo Ltd was registered in the Transvaal, with a share capital of 150 shares, of which one Mahomed Mamojee Dadoo held 149, and one Dindar held the other one. Both Dadoo and Dindar were Asiatics. The court (De Villiers JA dissenting) held that the statutory prohibition did not apply to companies even though their shares were held by Asiatics.

INNES CJ: Taking the intention then [of the legislature] to be the prohibition of ownership of fixed property by Asiatics and the pro-hibition of the acquisition and the occupation of mining rights by coloured people, I come to inquire whether the transaction complained of is a contravention of the statutes. In other words, whether ownership by Dadoo Ltd is in substance ownership by its Asiatic shareholders. Clearly in law it is not. A registered company is a legal *persona* distinct from the members who compose it. . . . Nor is the position affected by the circumstance that a controlling interest in the concern may be held by a single member. This conception of the existence of a company as a separate entity distinct from its shareholders is no merely artificial and technical thing. It is a matter of substance; property vested in the company is not, and cannot be, regarded as vested in all or any of its members.

[17] Macaura v Northern Assurance Company Ltd
[1925] AC 619 (HL(Ir))

The appellant, the owner of a timber estate, assigned the whole of the timber to a company known as the Irish Canadian Saw Mills Ltd the total amount to be paid to him for the timber being £42 000. Payment was effected by the allotment to the appellant or his nominees of 42 000 fully paid £1 shares in the company. No further shares than these were ever issued. The company proceeded with the cutting of the timber. In the course of these operations the appellant became the creditor of the company for £19 000. Beyond this the debts of the company were trifling in amount. The appellant insured the timber against fire by policies effected in his own name. The timber was destroyed by fire. The insurance company refused to pay out on the ground that the plaintiff had no insurable interest in the timber, and was upheld in this contention by the court.

LORD SUMNER: My Lords, this appeal relates to an insurance on goods against loss by fire. It is clear that the appellant had no insurable interest in the timber described. It was not his. It belonged to the Irish Canadian Saw Mills Ltd of Skibbereen, Co Cork. He had no lien or security over it and, though it lay on his land by his permission, he had no responsibility to its owner for its safety, nor was it there under any contract that enabled him to hold it for his debt. He owned almost all the shares in the company, and the company owed him a good deal of money, but, neither as creditor nor as shareholder, could he insure the company's assets. The debt was not exposed to fire nor were the shares, and the fact that he was virtually the company's only creditor, while the timber was its only asset, seems to me to make no difference. He stood in no 'legal or equitable relation to' the timber at all. He had no 'concern in' the subject insured. His relation was to the company, not to its goods, and after the fire he was directly prejudiced by the paucity of the company's assets, not by the fire. . . .

NOTES

Macaura was followed in Canada in *Zimmerman* v *St Paul Fire and Insurance Co* (1967) 63 DLR 2d 282. On the question whether a shareholder has an insurable interest in a corporate venture, see *Wilson* v *Jones* (1867) LR 2 Exq 139.

'. . . a shareholder has a proprietary interest in the company, but not in the business of the company': Hoexter ACJ in *Stellenbosch Farmers' Winery Ltd* v *Distillers' Corporation (SA) Ltd* 1962 (1) SA 458 (AD) at 472.

See, further, *In re George Newman & Co* [1895] 1 Ch 674 at 685 (company's assets are its property and not the shareholders'); *Reynolds* v *Oosthuizen* 1916 WLD 103 (clause in lease prohibiting assignment to Chinese does not operate against a company all the members of which are Chinese); *Madrassa Anjuman Islamia* v *Johannesburg Municipal Council* 1919 AD 439, affirmed on appeal to Privy Council [1922] 1 AC 500 (statute prohibiting a standowner permitting any Asiatic, other than the bona fide servant of a White person residing on the stand, from occupying the stand, contravened where the owner leases the stand to a company all the officers and servants of which are Asiatics: 'a company . . . is incapable of being physically present at any place. It follows . . . that the occupation of the stand was by the . . . employees of the company': per Solomon ACJ at 449); *EBM Co Ltd* v *Dominion Bank* [1937] 3 All ER 555 (PC) at 564; *Goodall* v *Hoogendoorn Ltd* 1926 AD 11 at 16; *R* v *Gillett* 1929 AD 364, 22, below; *Estate Salzmann* v *Van Rooyen* 1944 OPD 1 (a debt owed by a 'one-man company' controlled by A cannot be held to be A's debt so as to justify the sequestration of A's estate); *Roberts* v *Coventry Corporation* [1947] 1 All ER 308 (a shareholder has no direct claim for a loss the company suffers through expropriation); *Ex parte Donaldson* 1947 (3) SA 170 (T), esp at 173 (a company cannot validly be appointed guardian of a minor: 'the relationship is a personal one, necessitating personal contract and a human relationship which cannot be rendered by a corporation'); *Gumede* v *Bandhla Vickani Bakithi Ltd* 1950 (4) SA 560 (N) (a company is not susceptible to a racial test).

Since *Dadoo's* case (*16* above) the legislature, when disqualifying racial groups from owning or occupying land in certain areas, has made special provision for companies 'controlled' by members of the disqualified groups, e g Group Areas Act 36 of 1966 s 1 s v 'controlling interest', 'disqualified company' and 'disqualified person'.

While a company and its shareholders are separate entities, a 'one-man' company and its controlling shareholder-director have been held in England not to constitute two separate minds for the purposes of a criminal conspiracy: *R v McDonnell* [1961] 1 All ER 193. For an example of a statutory remedy available to a natural person but not to a company see *Trafalgar Centre (Pty) Ltd*, 1976 (4) SA 940 (N).

[18] Gasque *v* Commissioners of Inland Revenue
[1940] 2 KB 80

MACNAGHTEN J: It was suggested . . . that by the law of England a body corporate has no domicil in the same sense as an individual any more than it can have a residence in the same sense as an individual. But by analogy with a natural person the attributes of residence, domicil and nationality can be given, and are, I think, given by the law of England to a body corporate. It is not disputed that a company formed under the Companies Acts, has British nationality, though, unlike a natural person, it cannot change its nationality. So, too, I think, such a company has a domicil—an English domicil if registered in England, and a Scottish domicil if registered in Scotland. The domicil of origin or the domicil of birth, using with respect to a company a familiar metaphor, clings to it throughout its existence.

[It follows that a company cannot change its domicile, which is the place of its registration.]

[19] Estate Kootcher *v* Commissioner for Inland Revenue
[1941] AD 256

WATERMEYER JA: The dispute between the parties centres round the question whether the Standard Bank of SA Ltd is in law to be regarded as 'ordinarily resident within the Union'.

The Standard Bank of SA Ltd is a company incorporated with limited liability under the English Companies Acts. Its registered office is in London and its business is controlled by a board of directors which meets in London. It has many branches throughout the Union and South-West Africa which are under the supervision of a general manager in Cape Town, responsible to the directors in London. . . .

Now it has been frequently pointed out that when the words 'reside' or 'resident' are used in connection with a corporation to indicate its presence in a place for some period of its corporate existence, the words are used in a figurative sense and can only be given a meaning analogous to the meaning of the words when used with regard to a human being. A human being has a body and a mind and the mind always accompanies the body; the mind therefore resides (if a mind can be said to reside) where the body resides. A corporation has no body but it has what by analogy can be called a directing mind. In a human being the location of the body with its attendant mind, if such location be periodic or usual or habitual, determines the residence of that human being, and it is therefore to be expected that the residence of a corporation will be determined by the periodic, usual or habitual location of the directing mind. In the case of *De Beers Consolidated Mines v Howe* [1906] AC 455 at 459, Lord Loreburn stated the law as follows:

'In applying the conception of residence to a company, we ought, I think, to proceed as nearly as we can upon the analogy of an individual. A company cannot eat or sleep, but it can keep house and do business. We ought, therefore, to see where it really keeps house and does business. An individual may be of foreign nationality, and yet reside in the United Kingdom. So may a company. Otherwise it might have its chief seat of management and its centre of trading in England under the protection of English law, and yet escape the appropriate taxation by the simple expedient of being registered abroad and distributing its dividends abroad. . . . A company resides for purposes of income tax where its real business is carried on . . . the real business is carried on where the central management and control actually abides. . . .'

[On the facts it was held that the Standard Bank was 'ordinarily resident' in England. Since then, the Standard Bank has become 'naturalized' in South Africa.]

[19A] Dairy Board *v* John T Rennie & Co (Pty) Ltd
1976 (3) SA 768 (W)

ELOFF J: Arising from a special plea in bar filed on behalf of defendant in this action, the question presently falls to be decided whether this court has jurisdiction to entertain the suit. . . .

Section 19(1)(*a*) of the Supreme Court Act 59 of 1959 *inter alia* provides as follows:

'A provincial or local division shall have jurisdiction over all persons residing or being in and in relation to all causes arising . . . within its area of jurisdiction.'

I should at once say that plaintiff's cause of action, which is for the enforcement of an undertaking made by defendant at Durban in terms of s 309(1)(*a*) of the Merchant Shipping Act 1951, plainly did not arise in the Witwatersrand area. Consequently, the initiation of proceedings in this Division can only be justified if it can be shown that the defendant resides or is in the Witwatersrand.

The business of the defendant, which is a company having been incorporated as such on 10 May 1963, was before that date conducted by a partnership. The partnership business was that of a ship's agency and it was conducted at Durban and Cape Town. On incorporation of defendant, its registered office was recorded as being at 10th floor, Rennie House, 13 Melle Street, Braamfontein, Johannesburg. It became a wholly owned subsidiary of a company styled Rennies Consolidated Holdings (Pty) Ltd, which thereafter became a public company with its registered head office also at Rennie House, Melle Street, Braamfontein, Johannesburg. Defendant retained complete autonomy in its affairs, however, and Rennies Consolidated Holdings Ltd merely, from time to time, gave directions from above to defendant and the other companies in its group on such matters as the policy to be adopted regarding staff leave, pension funds and so on. For the rest, defendant's business activities were conducted from Durban. That is where its management was situated; that is where its books of account were kept; that is where its directors met most of the time; that is where most of its directors resided, and that is the point from which its business was controlled.

In the light of these circumstances can it be said that defendant 'resides or is' in the Witwatersrand within the meaning of s 19?

As to the significance of the fact of the situation of the registered office of a company, Pollak *The Law of Jurisdiction* 94–5 states:

'In the normal case the registered office and the principal place of a company are one and the same place. They may however be different, and in such case the situation of the principal place of business and not that of the registered office, is the relevant factor for the purposes of jurisdiction in an action for a judgment sounding in money against the company.'

No authority is quoted for this proposition, however, and there is, as far as I have been able to ascertain, no decided case in which it was laid down that the place given as the registered address of a company incorporated in South Africa is not the place where the company resides or is. On the contrary, there is a dictum which goes the other way. In *Frank Wright (Pty) Ltd* v *Corticas 'BCM' Ltd* 1948 (4) SA 456 (C), Searle J said at 460:

'The residence of a company is however determined by the place where it carries on business or the locality of its registered office.'

I should add that reliance for this is placed on the decision in the cases of *Appleby (Pty) Ltd* v *Dundas Ltd* 1948 (2) SA 905 (E) at 911 and *T W Beckett & Co Ltd* v *H Kroomer Ltd* 1912 AD 324 at 334–5, neither of which laid down that the situation of the registered office *per se* fixes the residence of a company.

For defendant, reliance was placed on certain dicta in *Beckett's* case (*supra*) to the effect that, for jurisdictional purposes, a company has only one residence, and that is where its general administration and business is centred. From that it follows — so it was argued — that the fact that its registered office is centred elsewhere cannot give it a second residence and the situation of the registered office is irrelevant. It is necessary that I should consider *Beckett's* case in some detail.

The defendant in that case had its registered head office and principal place of business in Pretoria. It also maintained a branch at Johannesburg. It was sued in this Division, and the process commencing the action was served on one of its Johannesburg managers. Objection was raised to the jurisdiction of this court. The appropriate legislation stated that the Local Division —

'. . . shall have cognisance of all pleas and jurisdiction in all civil causes and proceedings arising . . . within the said Colony with jurisdiction over His Majesty's subjects and all other persons whomsoever residing or being within the said Colony'.

In regard to the meaning of the phrase 'persons . . . residing or being within the Colony', the following was said at p 334:

'The residence of a legal *persona* like a company artificially created, must be a mere notional conception introduced for purposes of jurisdiction and law. . . . The only home which a corporation can be said to have is the place where the operations for which it was called into existence, are carried on. So far as it can be said to reside anywhere, that is where it resides. And if the analogy of a natural person is to be followed, one would say that it can only reside in one place at a time.'

Later on it was further said:

'The doctrine is firmly established that where a company carries on business at more places than one, its true residence is located where its general administration is centred.'

Now the court did not have to consider the question whether a company might not be said to reside or be where its registered address is; it had merely to deal with the question whether a corporation with a firmly established residence in the sense described in the above-quoted passage could acquire a second residence by reason of having a further place of business elsewhere. The problem with which I am presently concerned is unusual for the reason, as is pointed out by Pollak, *supra*, that it is reasonable to suppose that a company will normally select as its registered head office its principal place of business. And I do not think that is the sort of situation to which the learned judge of appeal addressed his mind when expressing himself as he did.

What is, in my opinion, of importance in the judgment in *Beckett's* case, is that the court considered that there is a close correlation between the duty of a company to accept service at a particular place and its place of residence. On p 339 the concluding paragraph of the judgment reads:

'For the purpose of this case it is not necessary to say more than that a company should not be compelled to accept service anywhere, save at its central office, of process the object of which is to enforce or recover damages in respect of a contract entered into with the officials of its central administration.'

This correlation between the address at which service may be effected and jurisdiction over a corporation is, I think, in accordance with what was said by Cheshire *Private International Law* 7 ed 174 as follows:

'If he is found here he can be served here and at common law the exercise of jurisdiction depends on service. It is the same in the case of a corporation.'

Gower *Modern Company Law* 3 ed 447 is to similar effect where he says *sub voce* 'The company's home':

'By the expression "home" we mean the office at which the registers have to be kept and where service of process is to be effected.'

This factor—that is, the place at which a company can be served with process—assumes importance if it be borne in mind that s 170(1) of the Companies Act 61 of 1973, as also its predecessor in the 1926 Companies Act, mentions the registered office as the one 'at which all process may be served'. And not only does the Companies Act render the registered office the place at which service can be effected; it is also the place where a minute book of the general meetings of the company is to be kept (s 204); as also the register of allotment of shares (s 93); the register of members (s 105); a register of pledges and bonds (s 127); a register of debenture holders (s 128); a register of directors and officers (s 216); a register of material interest of directors and other insiders in the shares and debentures of the company (s 230 and s 231); a register of declaration of interest in contracts by directors and officers (s 240); a register of attendance of directors' and managers' meetings (s 245); and a register of fixed assets (s 284).

The totality of these provisions seem to me to attract the inference that the legislature intended to endow the registered office with the quality of being the place to which the world can look as the legal home and administrative centre of the company.

There is, in my view, the further feature that to view the registered office as the residence of a company for jurisdictional purposes is to create certainty and to bring about commercial convenience. . . . To hold that the registered office is the place of residence for purpose of jurisdiction is to remove all doubt as to the court in which a person intending to sue a company conducting business at various places may do so. In this regard it is not inappropriate to remark that in these days companies sometimes conduct their affairs so that it may be difficult to determine where its 'general administration is centred'. And although it may in fact have been true in 1912 that a company and a person has only one residence, one finds it said in Palmer's *Company Law* 21 ed 66 that:

'Moreover, a company—like an individual—may have several residences at the same time'.

In my view, a company registered in South Africa resides in law where the registered office is. If its principal place of business is situated elsewhere it may *also* reside at the latter place. I accordingly hold that this court has jurisdiction in the present matter.

NOTES

See also 1963 *Annual Survey* 548 and ITC 1054 (1964) 24 SATC 260. In *Unit Construction Co Ltd v Bullock (Inspector of Taxes)* [1960] AC 351, [1959] 3 All ER 831 (HL) three wholly-owned subsidiaries of a company in the United Kingdom were registered in Kenya. The boards of the three subsidiaries were distinct from the board of the parent company, and under their articles of association directors' meetings could not be held in the United Kingdom. Nevertheless, the management of the subsidiaries was in fact in the hands of the board of the parent company in England. The House of Lords, reversing the decision of the Court of Appeal, held that for taxation purposes the three Kenya companies were resident in the United Kingdom. The question was not where, according to the constitutions of the three companies, central management and control ought to have been, but where they in fact were. That for the purposes of Kenyan law the companies might also be resident in Kenya, did not affect the position.

On residence, domicile and nationality of a company, see further *Trustee Insolvent Estate Haydon & Co v Thistle Reef Gold Mining Co Ltd* (1895) 2 Off Rep 175; *Epstein v Manchester Assurance Co* (1903) 24 NLR 41; *Janson v Driefontein Cons Mines Ltd* [1902] AC 484; *Beckett & Co Ltd v Kroomer Ltd* 1912 AD 324; *Grimshaw v Mica Mines Ltd* 1912 TPD 450, esp at 456–7; *Sibisi v Hermansberg Mission Society* (1916) 37 NLR 409; *Rhodesia Railways v Commissioner of Taxes* 1925 AD 438; *Nathan's Estate v Commissioner for Inland Revenue* 1948 (3) SA 866 (N), esp at 879; *Union Corporation Ltd v Inland Revenue Commissioners* [1953] AC 482, [1953] 1 All ER 729. Also A Farnsworth *The Residence and Domicile of Corporations* (1939); R E L Vaughan Williams & M Crussachi 'The Nationality of Corporations' (1933) 49 *LQR* 334; E H Young 'The Nationality of a Juristic Person' (1908) 22 *Harvard LR* 1.

[20] Daimler Company Ltd *v* Continental Tyre and Rubber Company (Great Britain) Ltd

[1916] 2 AC 307

The plaintiff company (the Continental Tyre and Rubber Company) was incorporated in England for the purpose of selling in England tyres made in Germany by a German company which held the bulk of the shares in the English company. The holders (save one) and all the directors were Germans resident in Germany.

After the outbreak of war between England and Germany in 1914, the plaintiff sued the defendant company (the Daimler Company) for payment of a trade debt. The defendant company alleged that the plaintiff company was an alien enemy company and that payment of the debt would be a trading with the enemy.

The plaintiff's action was dismissed on a point of procedure, but in the course of their judgments four of the Lords of Appeal in Ordinary expressed themselves in favour of the view that a company could be an alien enemy.

LORD PARKER OF WADDINGTON: The principle upon which the judgment under appeal proceeds is that trading with an incorporated company cannot be trading with an enemy where the company is registered in England under the Companies Acts and carries on its business here. Such a company it calls an 'English company', and obviously likens to a natural-born Englishman, and accordingly holds that payment to it of a debt which is due to it, and of money which is its own, cannot be trading with the enemy, be its corporators who they may. The view is that an English company's enemy officers vacate their office on becoming enemies and so affect it no longer, and that its enemy shareholders, being neither its agents nor its principals, never in law affect it at all.

My Lords, much of the reasoning by which this principle is supported is quite indisputable. No one can question that a corporation is a legal person distinct from its corporators; that the relation of a shareholder to a company, which is limited by shares, is not in itself the relation of principal and agent or the reverse; that the assets of the company belong to it and the acts of its servants and agents are its acts, while its shareholders, as such, have no property in the assets and no personal responsibility for those acts. . . . I do not think, however, that it is a necessary corollary of this reasoning to say that the character of its corporators must be irrelevant to the character of the company; and this is crucial, for the rule against trading with the enemy depends upon enemy character.

A natural person, though an English-born subject of His Majesty, may bear an enemy character and be under liability and disability as such by adhering to His Majesty's enemies. If he gives them active aid, he is a traitor; but he may fall far short of that and still be invested with enemy character. . . . Voluntary residence among the enemy, however passive or pacific he may be, identifies an English subject with His Majesty's foes. . . . In the case of an artificial person what is the analogue to voluntary residence among the King's enemies? Its impersonality can hardly put it in a better position than a natural person and lead to its being unaffected by anything equivalent to residence. . . .

My Lords, I think that the analogy is to be found in control, an idea which, if not very familiar in law, is of capital importance and is very well understood in commerce and finance. The acts of a company's organs, its directors, manager, secretary, and so forth, functioning within the scope of their authority, are the company's acts and may invest it definitely with enemy character. It seems to me that similarly the character of those who can make and unmake those officers, dictate their conduct mediately or immediately, prescribe their duties and call them to account, may also be material in a question of the enemy character of the company. . . . For certain purposes a court must look behind the artificial *persona* — the corporation — and take account of and be guided by the personalities of the natural persons, the corporators. . . .

My Lords, having regard to the foregoing considerations I think the law on the subject may be summarized in the following propositions:

(1) A company incorporated in the United Kingdom is a legal entity, a creation of law with the status and capacity which the law confers. It is not a natural person with mind and conscience. To use the language of Buckley LJ, 'it can be neither loyal nor disloyal. It can be neither friend nor enemy.'

(2) Such a company can only act through agents properly authorized, and so long as it is carrying on business in this country through agents so authorized and residing in this or a friendly country it is prima facie to be regarded as a friend, and all His Majesty's lieges may deal with it as such.

(3) Such a company may, however, assume an enemy character. This will be the case if its agents or the persons in *de facto* control of its affairs, whether authorized or not, are resident in an enemy country, or wherever resident, are adhering to the enemy or taking instructions from or acting under the control of enemies. A person knowingly dealing with the company in such a case is trading with the enemy.

(4) The character of individual shareholders cannot of itself affect the character of the company. This is admittedly so in times of peace, during which every shareholder is at liberty to exercise and enjoy such rights as are by law incident to his status as shareholder. It would be anomalous if it were not so also in a time of war, during which all such rights and privileges are in abeyance. The enemy character of individual shareholders and their conduct may, however, be very material on the question whether the company's agents, or the persons in *de facto* control of its affairs, are in fact adhering to, taking instructions from, or acting under the control of enemies.

[On the same point see, further, *Sovfracht* (VO) v *Van Udens Scheepvaart en Agentuur Maatschappij* (*NV Gebr*) [1943] AC 203, [1943] 1 All ER 76 (HL); *Kuenigl* v *Donnersmarck* [1955] 1 QB 515; A Farnsworth 'Enemy Character of Corporations' (1944) 7 *MLR* 80.]

[21] *In re* **Yenidje Tobacco Company Ltd**
[1916] 2 Ch 426

W and R, who traded separately as tobacco and cigarette manufacturers, agreed to amalgamate their businesses, and in order to do so
formed a private limited company in which they were the only shareholders and directors. Under the articles, W and R had equal voting
powers.

Differences arose between W and R resulting in a complete deadlock
in the management of the company. The court decided that it was just
and equitable that a winding-up order should be made.

WARRINGTON LJ: In substance it seems to me these two people are
really partners. It is true they are carrying on the business by means of
the machinery of a limited company, but in substance they are partners;
the litigation in substance is an action for dissolution of the partnership,
and I think we should be unduly bound by matters of form if we treated
either the relations between them as other than that of partners or the
litigation as other than an action brought by one for the dissolution of
the partnership against the other; but one result which of course follows
from the fact that there is this entity called a company is that, in order
to obtain what is equivalent to a dissolution of the partnership, the
machinery for winding-up has to be resorted to. Now, if this had been
an ordinary partnership and an action had been brought for dissolution,
it seems to me quite clear that the plaintiff, who is the petitioner in this
case, would have had sufficient ground for a dissolution of partnership
according to the ordinary principle by which the court is guided in such
matters. Then s 129 of the Companies (Consolidation) Act 1908 [s 222(*f*)
of the 1948 Act and s 344(*h*) of the present Act], which defines the
grounds upon which the court in the case of a company can make an
order for winding up, includes the provision that such an order may be
made if the court is of opinion that it is just and equitable that the company should be wound up. . . . I am prepared to say that in a case like
the present, where there are only two persons interested, where there are
no shareholders other than those two, where there are no means of overruling by the action of a general meeting of shareholders the trouble
which is occasioned by the quarrels of the two directors and shareholders
the company ought to be wound up if there exists such a ground as would
be sufficient for the dissolution of a private partnership at the suit of
one of the partners against the other. Such ground exists in the present
case. I think, therefore, that it is just and equitable that the company
should be wound up.

[22] **Rex *v* Gillett**
[1929] AD 365

A moneylender of the name of Gillett conducted his business by means
of two companies, Marais Agencies Ltd and Gillett's Ltd. Marais Agencies
Ltd did the lending. Gillett's Ltd, to which all applications for loans had
to be made, purported to act as adviser to the first company, charging
the borrower a substantial commission and regular renewal fees. Taken
separately, neither the interest charged by the first company nor the
fees charged by the second company were usurious. Taken together,

they were. All the moneys so paid eventually found their way into the pockets of the accused. The magistrate's court found him guilty of usury. His appeal to the Transvaal Provincial Division, and his further appeal to the Appellate Division, failed.

DE VILLIERS ACJ: The difficulty which presents itself in reading the reasons of the magistrate as well as of the members of the Provincial Division is that full effect does not appear to be given to the decision of this court in *Dadoo Ltd* v *Krugersdorp Municipality* [*16*, above]. It may of course loosely be said that Gillett, Marais Agencies Ltd and Gillett's Ltd are all one and the same person; but that is not the correct legal position. In law a registered company is a separate and distinct legal *persona*, and every company is entitled to do whatever is authorized by its memorandum and articles of association. Marais Agencies Ltd is entitled, if so authorized, to make loans of money at legal rates of interest, while Gillett's Ltd may charge a borrower 10 per cent commission for recommending a loan or its renewal. And as long as they do what they are authorized to do, it makes no difference that they are controlled or even dominated by Gillett. Always provided that they stay within the law. For a company or two companies, acting singly or in concert, may not, any more than a physical person, disguise the real nature of the transaction by making a charge of usurious interest appear as other than it is. . . .

It was apparently thought that if Marais Agencies Ltd charged only a legal rate of interest, the commission to Gillett's Ltd would be allowed to pass as a genuine remuneration for services rendered by Gillett in his capacity as sole director and managing director of Gillett's Ltd. But when the transaction comes to be analysed it is seen that no genuine services were rendered to the business by Gillett's Ltd in recommending the loan for which any legitimate remuneration could be exacted. By arrangement between the two companies through Gillett, who, by manipulating the Company Law as he had done would eventually draw all the profits, the transaction was merely cloaked in this form to obtain a larger rate of interest than the law allows. . . . That being the case, it is clear that there has been a conspiracy on the part of the two companies to contravene the Usury Act for which, according to s 384(1) of the Criminal Procedure Act, every director is liable in the absence of proof that he was no party thereto. Gillett, the originator of the scheme, is therefore liable as director of Gillett's Ltd. But as he was the instigator of the offence, he is also liable as *particeps criminis*.

STRATFORD JA: If we regard all the facts of the case, as we are entitled and bound to consider them, it is manifest that throughout there was one purpose, the purpose of Gillett—and one will—that of Gillett. He floated Gillett Ltd and acquired Marais' Agency clearly for the purpose of lending money at an illegal rate, with absolute knowledge and confidence that they were bound inevitably to achieve that purpose. For he made himself practically sole shareholder in one company and sole manager in the other to keep the control he designed. The evidence of the borrowers completes the picture—Gillett was the presiding spirit— the *deus ex machina*.

[It will be noted that the court used the concepts of conspiracy and instigation to deal with the wrongdoer.]

[23] **Wallersteiner v Moir (1)**
[1974] 1 WLR 991, [1974] 3 All ER 217 (CA)

LORD DENNING MR: It is plain that Dr Wallersteiner used many companies, trusts, or other legal entities as if they belonged to him. He was in control of them as much as any 'one-man company' is under the control of the one man who owns all the shares and is the chairman and managing director. He made contracts of enormous magnitude on their behalf on a sheet of notepaper without reference to anyone else. Such as a contract on behalf of the Rothschild Trust to buy shares for £518 786 15s or to vary it; or a contract on behalf of Stawa AG for a commission of £235 000. He used their moneys as if they were his own. When money was paid to him for shares which he himself owned beneficially, he banked it in the name of IFT of Nassau. Such as the £50 000 for the shares in Watford Chemical Co Ltd. When he paid out money on personal loans by himself, he drew the cheques on the account in the name of IFT of Nassau. Such as the £125 000 lent to Camp Bird to pay off the Pearl charge. His concerns always used as their bankers the Anglo-Continental Exchange Ltd. That was a merchant bank in the City of London of which he was chairman and which he effectively controlled.

Counsel as *amicus curiae* suggested that all these various concerns were used by Dr Wallersteiner as a façade, so that each could be treated as his *alter ego*. Each was in reality Dr Wallersteiner wearing another hat. Counsel for Dr Wallersteiner repudiated this suggestion. It was quite wrong, he said, to pierce the corporate veil. The principle enunciated in *Salomon* v *Salomon & Co Ltd* [*15* above] was sacrosanct. If we were to treat each of these concerns as being Dr Wallersteiner himself under another hat, we should not, he said, be lifting a corner of the corporate veil. We should be sending it up in flames.

I am prepared to accept that the English concerns—those governed by English company law or its counterparts in Nassau or Nigeria—were distinct legal entities. I am not so sure about the Liechtenstein concerns—such as the Rothschild Trust, the Cellpa Trust or Stawa AG. There was no evidence before us of Liechtenstein law. I will assume, too, that they were distinct legal entities, similar to an English limited company. Even so, I am quite clear that they were just the puppets of Dr Wallersteiner. He controlled their every movement. Each danced to his bidding. He pulled the strings. No one else got within reach of them. Transformed into legal language, they were his agents to do as he commanded. He was the principal behind them. I am of the opinion that the court should pull aside the corporate veil and treat these concerns as being his creatures —for whose doings he should be, and is, responsible. At any rate, it was up to him to show that any one else had a say in their affairs and he never did so:

[For a full discussion of this case, see J H Farrar & N V Lowe (1975) 38 *MLR* 455.]

NOTES

See also *R P Crees (Pvt) Ltd* v *Woodpecker Industries (Pvt) Ltd* 1975 (2) SA 485 (R), where Goldin J said (at 487):

'The lifting of the corporate veil is possible and may be necessary in order to prove who determines or who is responsible for the activities, decisions and control of a company. Thus, a company can be under complete control of and its activities entirely dictated by another person but that does not deprive it of its distinct legal personality. A person in captivity may be entirely subject to and his conduct completely dictated by his captor. Nevertheless he still retains an existence and is a separate entity from the person who has complete power over and direction of him.'

See further *Forman* v *Barnett* 1941 WLD 54, esp at 60 (restraint of trade agreement by a company with only two members binding upon its members who had agreed to be bound); *Lawrence* v *Lawrich Motors (Pty) Ltd* 1948 (2) SA 1029 (W) ('just and equitable' to wind up a company where one of the two shareholders and directors had committed adultery with the wife of the other). But see also *Re Davis Investments Ltd* [1961] 1 WLR 1396, [1961] 3 All ER 926, where it was held that the mere fact that one of two shareholders in a private company, holding equal amounts of shares, no longer had any confidence in the other, was not sufficient to establish that it was just and equitable for the company to be wound up.

Yenidje was applied in South Africa, *inter alia*, in *Moosa NO* v *Mavjee Bhawan (Pty) Ltd* 1966 (4) SA 462 (T). (See 1966 *Annual Survey* 265–7.) The leading English case on the *Yenidje* principle is now *Ebrahimi* v *Westbourne Galleries Ltd 213* below.

Cases in which the courts' 'lifting the veil', identified a company with the person or company controlling it include, in South Africa, *Cattle Breeders Farm (Pvt) Ltd* v *Veldman* 1974 (1) SA 169 (R), and *Gering* v *Gering* 1974 (3) SA 358 (W); in England, *Smith, Stone & Knight Ltd* v *Birmingham Corporation* [1939] 4 All ER 116, *Jones* v *Lipman* [1962] 1 WLR 832 and *In re Littlewood Mail Order Stores Ltd* v *ICR* [1969] 1 WLR 1241, [1969] 3 All ER 855 (CA). See also *J R McKenzie Ltd* v *Gianoutos & Booleris* [1957] NZLR 309 and *Kaiser Aluminium and Chemical Corporation* v *The Reynolds Metal Co* (1969) 43 *ALJR* 156.

Generally, 'English legal thinking . . . shows no inhibition to piercing the veil where it is intended to use the veil for the protection of interests which are unworthy of such protection': E J Cohn & C Simitis (1963) 12 *ICLQ* 189 at 219. Thus, in *Gilford Motors Company Ltd* v *Horne* [1933] Ch 935 (CA) the court held that a former director of plaintiff company who had bound himself by a 'restraint of trade' clause could not escape its operation by hiding behind a company formed as 'a mere cloak or sham for the purpose of enabling him to commit a breach of his covenant . . .'. An injunction was accordingly granted against both the defendant personally and the company formed by him.

In America the courts are disregarding the corporate façade whenever it is being abused for the purposes of fraud or illegality. As Sanborn J put it in *United States* v *Milwaukee Refrigerator Transit Co* 142 F (1906) 247 at 255: 'when the notion of legal entity is used to defeat public convenience, justify wrong, protect fraud, or defend crime, the law will regard the corporation as an association of persons.' In *Wooddale Inc* v *Fidelity and Deposit Company of Maryland* US Court of Appeals Eighth Circuit 378 F 2d 627 (1967), it was held that equity will not allow the corporate structure to be used to perpetuate a fraud or obvious injustice, but that in the absence of allegations of fraud the corporate veil cannot be removed merely to give the other litigant an advantage at law.

Another instance where American courts have 'pierced the veil' and held shareholders personally liable, is where shareholders have started a company with an obviously inadequate capital, throwing in effect the whole risk of the business on the creditors.

But see also the Canadian case of *Clarkson Co Ltd* v *Zhelka* (1967) 64 DLR (2d) 457, where, in the absence of proof of fraud, the court refused to disregard the separate corporate identity of a family of companies under the control of an insolvent, notwithstanding the facts that although none of the companies was in the legal sense a subsidiary of another, there had been a confusing sequence of transfers of assets and advances between them, and that the only person who had benefited from these operations was the insolvent.

On the whole subject, see (1958) 5 *South African Accountant* 215; Mervyn Woods 'Lifting the Corporate Veil in Canada' (1957) 35 *Canadian BR* 1176; K W Wedderburn (1960) 23 *MLR* at 666–8; E J Cohn & C Simitis ' "Lifting the Veil" in the Company Laws of the European Continent' (1963) 12 *ICLQ* 189, (1964) 15 *Mercer LR* 508–9; George A Pelletier Jnr (1967) 21 *South Western LJ* 141–50; M L Benade (1967) 30 *THR-HR* 224–30; G Seymour Wood (1969) 5 *Speculum Juris* 30; also R C Beuthin 'Dissolving a Quasi-partnership' (1969) 86 *SALJ* 5; E K B Ruthven 'Lifting the Veil in Scotland' (1969) *Jur Rev* 1; 'Lifting the Veil in the EEC' (1974) 2 *Law and Policy in International Business* 375.

III The Distinction Between a Company and a Partnership; Illegal Partnerships

A TEXT

Whereas a company is a corporate body with rights and duties apart from its members, a partnership is an unincorporated association of persons carrying on business together for the purpose of common gain. The assets and liabilities of a partnership are the assets and liabilities of its members. While a company acts through its directors, a partnership acts through its partners, each partner being an agent of the partnership. A company has potentially perpetual existence; a partnership comes to an end with a change in the composition of the firm. One partner cannot transfer his shares in the partnership without the consent of the other partners, while shares in a company are freely transferable unless the articles otherwise provide: *24.* (Though not a corporate body, a partnership may sue and be sued in its own name: Magistrates' Courts Act 32 of 1944 rule 11; Uniform Rules of Court rule 14. On insolvency proceedings against a partnership, Insolvency Act 24 of 1936 s 13.)

It is not lawful to form a partnership or other unincorporated association of more than twenty members for the purpose of carrying on any business that has for its object the acquisition of gain, s 30(1): *25–28.* This does not apply to the members of organized professions designated by the Minister of Economic Affairs, under s 30(2), for the purpose of carrying on such professions. Professions so designated include attorneys, notaries and conveyancers, and public accountants and auditors.

B CASES

[24] **Baird's Case**
(1870) 5 Ch App Cas 725

Sir W M James LJ: Ordinary partnerships are essentially in kind, and not merely in the magnitude of the partnership or the number of the partners, different from joint stock companies.

Ordinary partnerships are by the law assumed and presumed to be based on the mutual trust and confidence of each partner in the skill, knowledge, and integrity of every other partner. As between the partners and the outside world (whatever may be their private arrangements between themselves), each partner is the unlimited agent of every other in every matter connected with the partnership business, or which he represents as partnership business, and not being in its nature beyond the scope of the partnership. A partner who may not have a farthing of capital left may take moneys or assets of this partnership to the value of millions, may bind the partnership by contracts to any amount, may give the partnership acceptances for any amount, and may even—as has been shewn in many painful instances in this court—involve his innocent partners in unlimited amounts for frauds which he has craftily concealed from them.

That being the relation between partners, of course, when the court had to consider whether a partner could substitute or let in some other person for or with him, or whether a partner's executor could claim to succeed to him, there could be no difficulty in saying that this could not be done without the consent of all the partners.

It was because these were the ordinary law and consequences of an ordinary partnership—it was to escape from these, that joint stock companies were invented. That was the very cause and reason of their existence.

At first they existed under the favour of the Crown, which gave them charters of incorporation, and nobody ever supposed that the holders of stock in the Bank of England or the East India Company had anything to do with the law of partnership, or were partners.

But there were large societies on which the sun of royal or legislative favour did not shine, and as to whom the whole desire of the associates, and the whole aim of the ablest legal assistants they could obtain, was to make them as nearly a corporation as possible, with continuous existence, with transmissible and transferable stock, but without any individual right in any associate to bind the other associates, or to deal with the assets of the association.

A joint stock company is not an agreement between a great many persons that they will be co-partners, but is an agreement between the owners of shares, or the owners of stock, that they or their duly recognized assigns, the owners of the shares for the time being, whoever they may be, shall be and continue an association together, sharing profits and bearing losses. No shareholder in a joint stock company is, in the legal sense of the word, any more a partner than the owner of bank stock is; he may not have the same limit of liability, but in every other respect he is the same; he has the same right to take part in public meetings of the body, he has the same right to elect or remove directors, he has the same right to vote for or against the resolutions of the body, he has the same right to such dividends as may be declared, and he has the same right to dispose of his share as a separate and distinct piece of property, and no other rights in or over the association, its assets, or its transactions.

[25] Smith *v* Anderson
(1880) 15 ChD 247

JAMES LJ: The Act was intended, as it appears to me, to prevent the mischief arising from large trading undertakings being carried on by large fluctuating bodies, so that persons dealing with them did not know with whom they were contracting, and so might be put to great difficulty and expense, which was a public mischief to be repressed.

[26] *In re* Arthur Average Association for British, Foreign, and Colonial Ships
(1875) 10 Ch 542

JESSEL MR: . . . Now, if you come to the meaning of the word 'gain', it means acquisition. It has no other meaning that I am aware of. Gain is something obtained or acquired. It is not limited to pecuniary gain. We should have to add the word 'pecuniary' so as to limit it. And still less is it limited to commercial profits. The word used, it must be observed, is not 'gains', but 'gain', in the singular. Commercial profits, no doubt, are gain, but I cannot find anything limiting gain simply to a commercial profit. I take the words as referring to a company which is formed to acquire something, or in which the individual members are to acquire something, as distinguished from a company formed for spending something, and in which the individual members are simply to give something away or to spend something, and not to gain anything. . . .

[27] South African Flour Millers' Mutual Association *v* Rutowitz Flour Mills Ltd
1938 CPD 199

DAVIS J: The applicants are the South African Flour Millers' Mutual Association . . . and the milling firms which purport now to constitute it; the respondent is another milling firm which is alleged by applicants at one time also to have been and still to be a member. The application is brought . . . for [an order] declaring that the South African Flour Millers' Association is a legal association. . . .

The respondent opposes on the ground that on its own showing the Association, which was formed as from 1 January 1936, increased its membership to twenty-one on 1 October 1936, and thus became an illegal association within the meaning of s 4 of the Companies Act of 1926, because it had been formed for the purpose of carrying on a business that had for its object the acquisition of gain. . . .

. . . Was the object of the business the acquisition of gain either by the Association or by its members? In this inquiry the principle must not be lost sight of that we must look at 'the object'; and by this I understand that we must look at the main object, in contra-distinction to objects which are merely subsidiary. . . . Mr Fagan, for the applicant, says that the real object of the Association is to establish and work a quota system. He says that the bulk of the constitution deals either with that or with the internal machinery of the Association. So far he is right, but it does not follow, therefore, that the quota is the true object of the Association. . . . In truth, the quota scheme is a means, and not an end. The main object of the Association is thus described in its constitution: 'To improve the organization of the flour-milling industry in the Union for the purpose of securing economic production and distribution.' What is this for? It surely is with one object, namely the acquisition of gain by the members. That is fully recognized by Mr Mills when he says: 'The Association was formed as from 1 January, 1936, with the object of organizing millers so that they should, by regulating their various enterprises according to a quota system, rationalize the wheat-milling industry in the Union, and thus save it from the chaotic state into which it had drifted, owing to uneconomic production and distribution. But for such organization a large proportion of capital in a number of milling concerns publicly and privately subscribed would have been lost, whereas owing to the existence of the said Association the value of such investments has been secured without directly increasing the cost of wheaten products to the consumer.'

The true object of this Association, if the matter be carefully analysed, is thus seen to be the acquisition of gain by its members, if there were no anticipated gain to be had the members would certainly never have started this Association. . . .

Mr Fagan argued further that even if at one stage the Association became an illegal one, and thus disappeared from the ken of the law, yet that when the membership was again reduced below twenty-one it automatically revived. In my opinion this is not so. When once the Association became, as it has been put, a phantom . . . it could not revive. 'Once dead, always dead' seems to me a terse way of putting the situation. I cannot believe that an association can automatically one day be legally dead and the next day be alive and fully functioning, according as to whether it happens to have more than twenty members or not at any particular time. The very evil of uncertainty aimed at by the section would be increased a thousand-fold if this were so. . . .

[28] Shaw v Benson
(1883) 11 QBD 563

The objects of a society were to form a fund from which money might be lent to shareholders, against interest. The society consisted of more than twenty members and was not incorporated. The society advanced moneys to the defendants who signed promissory notes by way of security for the loan. An action on the notes was dismissed.

BRETT MR: The Thornhill Arms Society is prohibited by the Companies Act 1862 s 4 and is illegal. . . .

[I]s the contract illegal? . . . The mere contract to lend is not illegal, and the question is whether the contract of the borrowers is not merely a contract to repay money advanced: it seems to me that their contract is not a mere contract of repayment, for the liability was undertaken, and the money was to be repaid according to the rules of the society: therefore the rules of the society form part of the contract for repayment, and as the society is illegal, the contract for repayment also must be illegal. The borrowing and the lending were parts of one transaction, which had for its object the carrying out of the illegal purposes of the society.

NOTES

On the meaning of 'carrying on business for gain', see also Jessel MR in *Smith* v *Anderson* (1880) 15 ChD 247 at 258: 'Anything which occupies the time and attention and labour of a man for the purpose of profit is business'; and Simonds J in *Armour* v *Liverpool Corporation* [1939] Ch 422 at 437, [1939] 1 All ER 363 at 371: 'Neither "business" nor "gain" is a word susceptible of precise or scientific definition. The test appears to me to be whether that which is being done is what ordinary persons would describe as the carrying on of a business for gain. . . .' As to the meaning of 'business' and 'gain', see further *In re Padstow Total Loss and Collision Assurance Association* (1882) 20 ChD 137; *Cornish Mutual Assurance Co Ltd* v *Commissioners of Inland Revenue* [1926] AC 281, esp at 286–8; *Maple Leaf Services* v *Townships of Essa and Petawawa* (1962) 37 DLR (2d) 657; and *Nadir (Pty) Ltd* v *Commissioner of Taxation* (1972–3) 129 CLR 595 (HC of Australia). Of 'trade' Lord Reid had this to say in *Ransom* v *Higgs* [1974] 3 All ER 949 (HL) at 955: 'As an ordinary word in the English language "trade" has or has had a variety of meanings or shades of meaning. Leaving aside obsolete or rare usage it is sometimes used to denote any mercantile operation but it is commonly used to denote operations of a commercial character by which the trader provides to customers for reward some kinds of goods or services.'

On associations prohibited by s 30(1), see also *Greenberg v Cooperstein* [1926] ChD 657, where members of an illegal association sued its treasurer and secretary on behalf of all the members for an account of the subscriptions received by the defendants and payment of the account found due. Tomlin J said (at 665–6): '*Wilkinson v Levison* (42 Times LR 97); *Jennings v Hammond* (9 QBD 225); and *Shaw v Benson* (*supra*) were all cases where an illegal association was seeking to recover money lent by it; and it was necessarily held that the association being illegal the contract with it could not be enforced by it. It is a different case where those who have subscribed money for an illegal purpose come requiring the agents in whose hands it is and who were to apply it for that purpose and have not done so, to return it to them. I am happy to think that the law is not so feeble that it cannot protect the subscribers by ordering an account.'

The same view was taken by our courts in *R v Twala* 1952 (2) SA 599 (AD), where the Appellate Division confirmed the conviction of an employee of an illegal loan funds association, who had appropriated moneys to his own use, of theft. His defence that as an illegal body, the association had no right to own or possess property was rejected. Fagan JA said (at 608): 'English decisions . . . have held an association formed in contravention of the corresponding provision in the English Company Law to be incapable of suing or of being sued, and have refused to give legal effect to the agreement purporting to set out the constitution of the association or to contracts purporting to have been entered into by or concluded with the association. I am assuming that our courts will apply s 4 [now s 30(3)] of our Act in the same way, as, indeed, the court seemed to be prepared to do in the *SA Flour Millers' Mutual Association* case [27 above]. But that does not mean that assets purporting to be owned, possessed or controlled by such an association are *res nullius*. The assets must have been derived from people who had a legal title to them, and who, if no legal bond was created by the conditions under which they purported to hand over those assets, must have retained the right to reclaim them in so far as they had not yet been expended in terms of those conditions. And that was the view taken in England by Tomlin J in *Greenberg v Cooperstein* [1926] ChD 657, when he granted an order against the treasurer and the secretary of such an association to account to the subscribers for moneys received by them on behalf of the association . . .'. See also *Wakefield v ASA Seeds (Pvt) Ltd* 1976 (4) SA 806 (R).

As to actions by or against illegal associations, see further *In re Day: Ex parte Day* (1876) 1 ChD 699; *In re Thomas: Ex parte Poppleton* (1884) 14 QBD 379; *Opperman NO v Taylor's All Africa Services* 1958 (4) SA 696 (C). An illegal association of more than twenty members cannot be liquidated in terms of ss 344, 345: *Suid-Westelike Landbou-Koöperasie Bpk v Phambili African Traders Association* 1976 (3) SA 687 (Transkei).

IV TYPES AND FORMS OF COMPANIES

A TEXT

The Act provides for two types of company: a company having a share capital and a company limited by guarantee, s 19(1). A company having a share capital may be a public or a private company. It may have shares of par value or of no par value, s 19(2) p 167 below. All companies limited by guarantee are deemed to be public companies, s 19(3). The 1973 Act does not provide for the formation of unlimited companies but unlimited companies in existence at the commencement of the Act are preserved, s 25(2). (On the conversion of such a company into another type or form of company, s 25(1).)

An association not for gain is incorporated as a company limited by guarantee, s 21.

Under s 20 (see also s 173(4)) the articles of a private company must place restrictions on its right to transfer its shares, limit the number of its members (subject to certain exceptions) to 50, and prohibit any invitation to the public to subscribe for its shares or debentures.

A private company is exempt from several of the more onerous obligations of a public company. Thus, unlike a public company, a private company is not required to lodge copies of its annual financial statements, with the Registrar; to render its members half-yearly interim reports, s 303; or to send to its members provisional annual financial statements if it does not within three months after the end of its financial year issue copies of its annual financial statements in terms of s 304(1) (but see s 304(2)). If a private company fails to comply with the restrictions in its articles, it does not become a public company but becomes subject to ss 302(4), 303 and 304(1) as if it were a public company, unless the court orders otherwise, s 20(4).

Seven or more persons are required to form a public company, a single person can form a private company, ss 32, 54. A public company, but not a private company, may have share warrants to bearer, s 101. Other differences relate to the name of the company (ss 49, 50); proxies (s 189); quorum at meetings (s 190); voting rights (s 195); number of directors (s 208); loans to directors (s 226); and the appointment of auditors (s 275).

A private company may provide in its memorandum that its directors and former directors shall be personally liable, jointly and severally, together with the company, for debts contracted during their periods of office, s 53(b).

Conversion of one type or form of company into another type or form requires a special resolution and compliance with the statutory requirements for the new type or form, ss 22–29: 29.

A shareholder whose shares are paid-up (and a company may not allot or issue shares unless they are fully paid-up, p 212 below) incurs no personal liability for debts of the company. An exception applies if a public company other than a wholly-owned subsidiary carries on business for more than six months with fewer than seven members, s 66.

Chapter 13 of the Companies Act deals with 'external' companies, ie companies incorporated outside the Republic which establish a business in the Republic. An external company must register its memorandum with the Registrar, as provided in s 322. Once registered it can own immovable property in the Republic, s 324, and may offer its shares and debentures to the public, s 142 s v 'company'. Section 334 deals with the transfer of the undertaking of an external company to a company incorporated under the Act, see *Dage Properties (Pty) Ltd* v *General Chemical Corporation Ltd* 1973 (1) SA 163 (AD). If an external company can show that it conducts the whole or the greater part of its business in the Republic, that most of its assets are in the Republic, that the majority of its directors are or will be South African citizens, that the majority of its shareholders are resident in the Republic, and that its registration in the foreign country will be lawfully terminated in that country, it may be transformed by Proclamation of the State President into a South African company, s 335.

See also *Ex parte General Chemical Corporation Ltd* 1971 (2) SA 159 (W) and *Ex parte Reckitt & Coleman (Africa) Ltd* 1971 (2) SA 545 (C), further M L Benade (1968) 1 *CILSA* 128. A foreign company without a place of business in the Republic is not an external company even if it occasionally conducts business in South Africa.

In accordance with the doctrine of sovereign immunity a foreign company which is a branch of a foreign government is immune from suit. Whether this immunity is confined to acts *de jure imperii* or extends to acts *de jure gestionis*, such as ordinary commercial transactions, is not settled, *Lendalease Finance (Pty) Ltd* v *Corporacion de Mercadeo Agricola* 1976 (4) SA 464 (AD).

Extinctive prescription under the Prescription Act 68 of 1969 does not operate in favour of a peregrine company. *Grinaker Mechanicals (Pty) Ltd* v *Société Francaise Industriale et d'Equipment* 1976 (4) SA 98 (C).

B CASES

[29] *Ex parte* **H J Ivens & Company Ltd**
1945 WLD 105

Application by two public companies for confirmation of their conversion into private companies.

MILLIN J: [It was] contended that once a company is seen to have complied with the formal requirements of s 104(2) for its conversion into a private company the court is bound to give its confirmation. . . . I cannot accept this view. I am of opinion that in s 104(2), as in all other sections of the Act requiring the court's confirmation of any proceeding, it is the court's duty to consider the merits of the matter and not to give its confirmation unless the proposed proceeding appears to be fair to all persons affected.

NOTES
Under the new Act confirmation by the court is no longer required, and the court comes into the matter only if a minority shareholder applies under s 252 for relief on the ground of oppression.

V CONTROLLING AND CONTROLLED COMPANIES; HOLDING AND SUBSIDIARY COMPANIES; THE 'GROUP'

A TEXT

The Act speaks of controlling and controlled companies as well as of holding and subsidiary companies.

A controlling company is one which directly or indirectly has power enabling it to control another company. Without prejudice to the generality of the term 'controlling company', a company is deemed to control another if it holds more than 50 per cent of the equity share capital of that other company or is entitled to exercise more than half of the voting rights in respect of the issued shares of that company or is entitled or has the power to determine the composition of the majority of its board of directors, s 1(1) s v 'controlled company' and 'controlling company'.

A company is deemed to be a subsidiary of another company if that other company either is a member of it and controls the composition of its board of directors, or if it holds more than one-half of its equity share capital, or if it is a subsidiary of a company which is a subsidiary of that other company, or if subsidiaries of that other company, or of that other company and one or more of its subsidiaries together, hold more than one-half of its equity share capital, s 1(1), (3) and (4). For the circumstances in which the composition of a company's board of directors is deemed to be controlled by another company, see s 1(3)(b), for shares held and powers exercisable which are disregarded in determining whether one company is a subsidiary of another, s 1(3)(c). An external company may be a subsidiary of a South African company, and so may a foreign company which is not an external company, s 1(3)(d).

A subsidiary is deemed to be a wholly-owned subsidiary of another company if it has no members except that other company and a wholly-owned subsidiary of that other company and its or their nominees, s 1(5).

The following are the main consequences of the 'holding–subsidiary' companies relationship:

(1) The subsidiary company cannot be a member of its holding company, provided that a subsidiary which was lawfully a member of its holding company before it became a subsidiary may continue to be a member but has no right to vote at meetings of the holding company or any class of its members, s 39 (for exceptions see ss (2) and (3)): *30, 31.*

(2) Subject to exceptions, a subsidiary company may not provide financial assistance for the purchase of, or subscription for, any shares of its holding company, s 38, and see below p 212.

(3) The subsidiary company may not make a loan to a director or manager of its holding company, or of any company which is a subsidiary of its holding company, s 226(a)(ii), (iii).

(4) The subsidiary may not make a loan to any company or body corporate controlled by one or more directors or managers of its holding company or of any company which is a subsidiary of its holding company, or provide security to any person in connection with an obligation of such director, manager, company or other body corporate, s 226(1). (See also s 295.)

(5) The accounting periods of the holding company and the subsidiary must be the same, s 293.

(6) Group accounts must (subject to exceptions) be prepared by

the holding company and laid before its annual general meeting, ss 288ff. On accounting requirements for holding and subsidiary companies, see Schedule 4, paras 17, 18, 29, 36, 45 ff, 62–65.

A wholly-owned subsidiary (s 1(5)) is in several respects treated differently from a not wholly-owned subsidiary, e g s 117(4) (a wholly-owned subsidiary has power to mortgage any of its property as collateral security for the issue of debentures of its holding company); s 288(1) (the obligation to lay group accounts before the annual general meeting does not apply to a wholly-owned subsidiary).

The following are the main consequences of the 'controlling–controlled' companies relationship:

(1) No part of the funds of a company may be employed directly or indirectly in loans to its controlling company, unless all its members consent to the loan. The prohibition does not extend to the lending of money in the ordinary course of its business by a company actually carrying on a business which includes the lending of money, s 37.

(2) Included among the persons to whom a company may not, without a special resolution, grant retirement benefits etc (see pp 83ff below) are the directors and past directors of its controlled or controlling company, and of any company controlled by its controlling company s 227(1).

Companies which do not stand in the relationship of controlling and controlled or holding and subsidiary companies may be linked together in a group by the fact that they are controlled by the same persons and, as often as not, have a single secretary. A 'group' has no legal existence apart from the companies comprised in it: *32*. Its characteristic feature is that 'control and management, through subservient boards of directors associated together in that group, become concentrated in the hands of one or two dominant personalities . . .': per Trollip J in *S* v *Heller* 1964 (1) SA 524 (W) at 535.

B CASES

[30] Incorporated Industries Ltd *v* Standard Finance Corporation Ltd
1961 (4) SA 254 (W)

The question was whether under s 24*bis*(3) (now s 39(3)(*a*)) a subsidiary company which was lawfully a member of its holding company at the time when it became a subsidiary, could thereafter acquire further shares in its holding company.

KUPER J: The provisions of the section . . . were designed to prohibit membership by a subsidiary in its holding company in the future or any future trafficking in the shares of the holding company by the subsidiary. The question to be determined is whether the exceptions mentioned in ss (3) and foreshadowed in ss (1) apply both to continued membership and to future acquisition of shares. In seeking a positive answer to the question the applicant contends that every subsidiary which was a

member of a holding company at the time the Act came into force is
not subject to the restriction of the acquisition of shares in the holding
company, nor is any subsidiary which, whenever it becomes a subsidiary,
is at that moment of time a member of the holding company; in other
words, such subsidiaries could freely continue to follow the practice which
was to be stopped in regard to every other subsidiary. This conclusion
would render the provisions largely nugatory, for in any given case it
would be a simple matter for the company which it was proposed should
become a subsidiary to acquire a few shares in the holding company
immediately before its conversion. In my view this conclusion runs counter
to the ordinary meaning of the words employed in the section.

It was common cause that the phrase 'except in the cases hereafter in
this section mentioned' in ss (1) apply both to the membership of the
company and the allotment or transfer of shares. Consequently any
exception mentioned in the later portions of the section could apply to
either or both of the limitations. The exceptions in ss (3) enable the
subsidiary to 'continue to be a member' and there is no warrant for construing these words as lifting the limitation contained in ss (1) in regard
to the acquisition of shares. . . . If the legislature had intended the
subsidiaries mentioned to be free of both limitations the opening words
of the section would not have read 'This section shall not prevent . . .'
but 'nothing in this section shall apply . . .' in the same manner as the
opening section ss (2). The words actually used show that all that was
intended was that the subsidiaries mentioned should not be compelled
to sell the shares they had previously legally acquired, but that even in
such a case the right was to be limited so as to prevent their voting on
such shares. The possible hardship of having to dispose of the already
held shares is averted, and no possible hardship is created by the provision
that once the relationship of subsidiary and holding company has been
established, the former is thereafter debarred from acquiring the shares
of the latter.

[31] Inland Property Development Corporation (Pty) Ltd v Cilliers
1973 (3) SA 245 (AD)

Mr Cilliers (the respondent) had sold to the Inland Property Development Corporation (the appellant) certain shares in the Master Development Corporation, the holding company of the Inland Property Development Corporation. In terms of the deed of sale Mr Cilliers undertook to
deliver the scrip, together with signed share transfer forms in blank, to
the Master Development Corporation. What the Master Development
Corporation was to do with the shares was left open.

The Inland Property Development Corporation claimed that by
reason of the provisions of s 24*bis*(1) of the Companies Act 46 of 1926
(s 39 of the 1973 Act) the transaction was void. The Witwatersrand
Local Division dismissed the claim, and its decision was confirmed by
the Appellate Division.

RUMPFF JA: It will be convenient to deal first with the claim that the
transaction between Inland and Cilliers was void in terms of s 24*bis*(1)

of the Companies Act, on the assumption that Inland was subsidiary to Master. For contextual purposes, I think, it is necessary to quote s 24 of the Act, as well as those subsections of s 24*bis* that have a bearing on this issue. Section 24*bis* was inserted in the Act in 1952. Section 24 reads as follows:

> '(1) The subscribers of the memorandum of a company shall be deemed to have agreed to become members of the company, and upon its registration shall be entered as members in its register of members.
>
> (2) Every other person who agrees to become a member of a company, and whose name is entered in its register of members, shall be a member of the company.'

Subsections (1) and (2) of s 24*bis* contain the following provisions:

> '(1) Except in the cases hereafter in this section mentioned, a body corporate cannot be a member of a company which is its holding company, and any allotment or transfer of shares in a company to its subsidiary shall be void.
>
> (2) Nothing in this section shall apply where the subsidiary is concerned in a representative capacity, or where it is concerned as trustee, unless the holding company or a subsidiary thereof is beneficially interested under the trust and is not so interested only by way of security for the purposes of a transaction entered into by it in the ordinary course of a business which includes the lending of money.'

On behalf of Inland it was submitted that in terms of s 24*bis*(1) the transfer of shares was prohibited and not only the registration thereof, and that the prohibition nullifies a right in the shares which would enable the subsidiary company to deal with the shares. In the result, the shares cannot freely be assigned or otherwise dealt with in the ordinary way in which shares are dealt with. It was also submitted that the prohibition against transfer nullifies any transaction under which the shares are to be transferred because the transaction would become impossible of fulfilment. Both these objects are stultified by the prohibition since the right to hold the shares with its corresponding benefits, *inter alia*, to receive dividends and to vote, cannot, so it was contended, be achieved. The argument advanced on behalf of the appellant is based on the meaning of the word 'transfer'.

In regard to shares, the word 'transfer', in its full and technical sense, is not a single act but consists of a series of steps, namely an agreement to transfer, the execution of a deed of transfer and, finally, the registration of the transfer. As was put by Lord Reid in the House of Lords in *Lyle and Scott Ltd* v *Scott's Trustees and British Investment Trust Ltd* [1959] AC 763 (a case which dealt with the word 'transfer' in the articles of association of a company) at 778:

> 'The word transfer can mean the whole of these steps. Moreover, the ordinary meaning of "transfer" is simply to hand over or part with something and a shareholder who agrees to sell is parting with something. The context must determine in what sense the word is used.'

Because of the view I take of the matter it is, however, unnecessary to determine the true meaning of the word 'transfer' in s 24*bis*(1), and it will be assumed, for the purpose of this judgment, that it ought to be given its 'ordinary' meaning, that is the delivery or transfer of shares in a company to its subsidiary, without the necessity of registration in the company's register. It will also be assumed, in favour of the appellant, that the prohibition in s 24*bis*(1) against the transfer of shares in a company to its subsidiary nullifies not only the actual transfer itself but also any transaction contemplating such a transfer.

The question on this assumption is whether the transaction reflected in the agreement annexure A comes within the assumed ambit of the prohibition. It is clear, according to the provisions of s 24*bis*(2), that not every agreement providing for the transfer or delivery of shares in a holding company to its subsidiary is void. If the subsidiary company is to hold the shares in a representative capacity or as a trustee, the transfer or delivery of the shares for that purpose would not be void, nor the antecedent agreement to effect such transfer or delivery.

Inland's case is . . . essentially and entirely based on the fact that Cilliers agreed . . . to 'sell' to Inland shares in Master. It was not alleged in Inland's particulars of claim, nor was it contended that Cilliers undertook to transfer or deliver the shares to Inland or that Inland was intended to acquire the shares. . . .

. . . In regard to the sale to Inland, Cilliers, by agreeing to deliver the transfer form to Master, undertook to put Master in the position to deal with the shares, and what Master intended to do with the shares seems to me to have been deliberately left undisclosed in annexure A. It cannot be said, therefore, that Cilliers . . . transferred or undertook to transfer the shares to Inland or that Inland was to receive the shares. If it had been the intention of Inland to acquire the shares of Master through some internal arrangement with Master, and if it did acquire the shares from Master after Cilliers had provided Master with the transfer form, such acquisition would, in my opinion, for the purposes of s 24*bis*(1), be the result of a transaction between Master and Inland and not the result of the transaction between Cilliers and Inland as set out in annexure A.

I am of the view, therefore, that, although Cilliers undertook to sell the shares to Inland, he did not in terms of annexure A undertake to deliver the shares to Inland and that the undertaking by Cilliers to sell the shares to Inland in this case is not a transaction providing for the transfer of the shares to Inland within the assumed meaning of s 24*bis*(1) of the Act and is, therefore, not void.

NOTES

Under the old Act it was held that a bond given by a subsidiary company over its assets as a security for the obligations of its hopelessly insolvent parent company is liable to be set aside as a 'disposition without value' under s 26 of the Insolvency Act if the mortgaging subsidiary has not received value: *Langeberg Koöperasie Bpk* v *Inverdoorn Farming and Trading Company Ltd* 1965 (2) SA 597 (AD). The same would, no doubt, apply under the present Act.

For cases in which the courts identified a subsidiary company with its holding company, see p 44 above.

[32] **R v Milne and Erleigh** (7)
1951 (1) SA 791 (AD)

The board of directors in terms of the articles had passed a resolution to the effect that 'authority be and is hereby conferred on E as managing director of the company to buy and sell on behalf of the company shares or options on shares in other companies at his sole discretion'. The court held that any implied powers conferred on a director could not give him the right to do as he pleased with everything belonging to the company, including taking it for himself or using it for his own gain. It also held that E could not have believed that he had this right.

CENTLIVRES CJ: . . . The court addressed itself to the question whether E could have believed that his wide powers included a power to benefit himself at the expense of the company concerned and in the absence of any evidence from E himself it was fully justified in coming to the conclusion that he did not have that belief. Indeed it is difficult to imagine that any person of ordinary intelligence would believe that he had a power to despoil a company in relation to which he stood in a fiduciary capacity. . . .

The appellants relied upon the existence of a group of companies some of which had appointed E their managing director and all of which had allowed him wide powers in carrying on their affairs. It was contended that, apart from the actual existence of wide powers granted to E expressly or by acquiescence in their exercise, allowance must be made, in judging his state of mind, for the reasonable possibility that he believed he had powers more extensive than he actually had. The word 'group' has been used with many shades of meaning. The basic idea seems to be: An association of companies, created not by resolutions to associate but by the acts of individuals, and depending on the facts that they have a single secretary, generally itself a company, and are controlled as to the appointment of their directors, and therefore as to the administration of their affairs, by one or a few people. The persons who wield the controlling power are the only legal *personae* apart from the companies themselves. There is no *persona* which is the group, and there are no interests involved except the interests of the companies and the interests of the controllers. This is no mere legal technicality. No doubt it may be convenient to talk of the interests of the group, but no one could seriously think of the group as having interests distinct from those of the companies and controllers. The fact that in a group bargaining between companies may often be non-existent, because the controllers decide, does not support the idea of a single *persona* with single interests. No business man would be deceived into thinking that in a group there is, in effect, a pooling of assets and a right in the controllers to deal with assets belonging to the companies without regard to their respective interests. Those interests must be adjusted by the controllers as honest boards would agree to do if there were no group, ie on fair and reasonable lines, having regard to the circumstances of each transaction. E owed duties to the companies of which he was a director and not to any concept called the group, and he certainly knew that. . . .

. . . The duty of all agents, including directors of companies, is to conduct the affairs of their principals in the interest of the principals and not for their own benefit. If an act is done which falls within the terms of an express power but is done by the agent for his own benefit and not for the benefit of his principal, it is not an authorized act. . . .

In exceptional circumstances there might conceivably be features that would justify directors in agreeing to the transfer of an obligation to their company, or the transfer of earned profits away from their company, but clearly there could in general be no justification for such a course. . . .

SCHREINER JA: . . . Where . . . a person takes another's money without authority to do so and intending to consume it . . . he commits theft, even if he intends to return other money, if it is proved that he did not, when he took it, believe that he had the right to take it or that the owner, had he been consulted, would have consented to the taking. Where the consent that the taker might have relied on is that of an agent of the owner it must be such as the agent, acting honestly in the interests of his principal and with knowledge of the fact, might have been expected to give. . . .

. . . I shall assume in the appellant's favour that although he has not given evidence to that effect, he expected a resolution to be prepared by a clerk and sent round by a messenger for signature; and if such an expectation would suffice to raise a doubt as to whether the requisite *mens rea* was present, his conviction could not be sustained. On that view the submission to the directors would be no more than a formality, like putting the company's seal upon its contract duly agreed upon. But in deciding whether E intended to steal one must, in my view, ask, not whether he expected the formalities to be put through, but whether he thought that the board, if honest and informed of the facts, would consent. E has not said, nor would it have helped him to say, that he believed that he could without consulting the board take whether by way of loan or otherwise, from the company what he knew that an honest, informed board would not allow him to take. Nor would it help him if he believed no more than that the directors would sign the relative resolution without making an inquiry. Equally, in my view, it would not suffice for him to have believed that he would get the consent of the board because of his personality and dominating position in the group. . . . For a belief so founded would mean no more than that for the reasons stated he thought that he could do any act however dishonest and prejudicial to the company, with safety. . . .

NOTES

'Each company in the group is a separate legal entity and the directors of a particular company are not entitled to sacrifice the interests of that company', per Pennycuick J in *Charterbridge Corporation Ltd* v *Lloyds Bank* [1970] 1 Ch 62 at 74. This does not mean that the courts have to ignore the reality of the group. Thus, in *Meyer* v *Scottish Co-operative Wholesale Society* 1954 SC 381 the Lord President stated (at 391) that 'whenever a subsidiary is formed as in this case with an independent minority of shareholders, the parent company must, if it is engaged in the same class of business, accept as a result of having formed such a subsidiary on obligation so to conduct what are in a sense its own affairs as to deal fairly with its subsidiary' (p 527 below).

The German *Aktiengesetz* of 6 September 1965 is so far the only companies legislation which deals in detail with the relations between all kinds of interconnected enterprises *verbundene Unternehmen*).

VI COMPANIES AND THE STOCK EXCHANGE

Stock exchanges provide organized markets for trading in securities of companies. A company which desires to have its shares or debentures dealt with on a stock exchange must apply for a listing, Stock Exchanges Control Act 7 of 1947, ss 9 and 9A. Before it will be granted a listing it must comply with the listing requirements of the stock exchange concerned.

One of the requirements of the Johannesburg Stock Exchange, whose rules are typical, is that the directors must by resolution of the board undertake, *inter alia*, that the company will comply with the Stock Exchange rules 'now or hereafter in force': *32A*. Other requirements are that all shares in any one class must rank equally; that in the event of the sale of a major portion of the company's assets, or the acquisition of a material asset, the agreement will be submitted to a general meeting of shareholders for approval; that there must be a minimum subscribed capital; and that there must be a 'public interest', normally evidenced by the fact that at least 30 per cent of any issued shares are held by at least 300 shareholders, not associated in any way with the directors or the majority shareholders. The memorandum or articles must provide, *inter alia*, that at least one-third of the directors (unless under contract) must retire annually by rotation. Limitations must be imposed on the borrowing powers of directors.

A company whose securities are listed may be required by the president of the stock exchange to disclose such information as the president considers to be in the public interest, s 9C(1) of the Stock Exchange Control Act 7 of 1947. And if a company discloses any information to registered holders of its securities it must make the information available at the same time for publication to the press and the president of the stock exchange concerned, s 9C(3) of the Act.

The Stock Exchange rules ensure that once a company is listed there will be adequate initial and continuing disclosure of its affairs (see also s 9C(1) of the Stock Exchanges Control Act).

Purchases and sales of listed securities by stock brokers are governed by ss 13, 13A, and 13B of the Stock Exchanges Control Act, and the stock exchange rules relating to 'transactions' (pp 252–3 below). Manipulative practices calculated to create a false market, are prohibited, ss 21A, 21B, supplemented by stock exchange rules. (On 'rigging the market' as a common-law offence, pp 279–83 below.)

In common with other stock exchanges in South Africa and elsewhere, the Johannesburg Stock Exchange has a detailed body of rules, corresponding to the London City Code on Take-overs and Mergers, regarding take-over bids and offers to purchase by or to listed companies (pp 656–7 below).

[32A]   Herbert Porter & Co Ltd *v* Johannesburg Stock Exchange
1974 (4) SA 781 (W)

COETZEE J: The first applicant, Herbert Porter & Co Ltd (to which I shall refer as 'Porter') is the controlling shareholder in the second applicant, Vrede Securities Ltd (to which I shall refer as 'Vrede'). Both are listed companies on the Johannesburg Stock Exchange (to which I shall refer as the 'JSE'), the respondent in this application, against whom they claim a *mandamus* directing it to approve a certain circular to Vrede shareholders dated 14 November 1973. This circular contained a notice of an extraordinary general meeting of shareholders on 7 December 1973, which was being convened for the purpose of considering, *inter alia*, an increase in Vrede's share capital and various acquisitions by Vrede. . . .

Until December 1973 Vrede's name was Vrede Gold Exploration Company Ltd. Before October 1972, when Porter acquired a controlling interest in Vrede, it had suffered substantial losses. During May to September 1973, Vrede acquired various assets in the property, general investment and industrial fields. The immediate effect of these transactions is said to be an increase of about 150 per cent in its net tangible assets and earnings per share. In the course of these negotiations, announcements relating thereto were made, and the listing of Vrede's shares was suspended from time to time at the request of Vrede.

Soon after the last announcement of 12 September 1973 there occurred an event which subsequently figures large in the deliberations of the committees of the JSE. The manager informed Fergussons, who were Vrede's sponsoring brokers, that the transactions referred to in the announcement could be construed by the committee as a 'back door' listing and, therefore, might not be approved. Representations were thereafter made by Fergussons and Hill Samuel (who were Vrede's sponsoring brokers and merchant bankers respectively) to the manager of the JSE and also to the chairman of the listings committee, that no 'back door' listing was involved. . . .

The rules of the JSE . . . provide that where a listed company proposes to acquire assets such as involved in Vrede's acquisitions, shareholders must be given full details by circular and an extraordinary general meeting must be held to obtain shareholders' approval of the proposed transaction. Twelve copies of such circular

'should be submitted for the committee's prior approval at least 21 days before the date of issue to shareholders'.

On 2 October 1973 Fergussons submitted a proposed draft circular to the manager of JSE. During the ensuing weeks both Fergussons and Hill Samuel conveyed additional information to the manager who, in turn, told them of further requirements regarding the amendment and clarification of certain wording in the circular. By 2 November 1973 a new draft circular embodying the required amendments was submitted, and since that date no further point was made by the JSE regarding the adequacy or otherwise of the disclosure by Vrede. It seems clear that it was satisfied with the circular on this score as all its difficulties had been met.

Between 5 and 27 November 1973, however, a series of meetings of the listings and general committees took place at which the transactions and proposals described in the circular were discussed at great length. These committees concerned themselves with questions such as whether the transactions 'constituted a "back door" listing', particularly in the light of the number of shares that had to be issued to make the acquisitions; whether the combined profits of the companies being acquired complied with the JSE's minimum profit requirements for a primary listing; and whether the profit forecast could be achieved. . . .

On 13 November 1973, at a meeting of the general committee, the chairman reviewed the matter and advised the meeting that the reasons for the subcommittee's recommendation 'not to approve the scheme' were the poor past profit records of the companies acquired, the magnitude of the transactions in relation to Vrede's present issued capital, and that the scheme was in conflict with JSE's policy regarding 'back door' listings. After full discussion the committee resolved that the recommendation of the subcommittee be adopted and that Vrede be requested to make an announcement to the effect that 'Stock Exchange approval of the various acquisitions had not been granted'. . . .

The JSE's views on 'back door' listing are contained in para 13 of the president's answering affidavit, which reads as follows:

> 'Words such as "back-door listing" are only labels which are useful both to the committee and the public in conveying sometimes quite complex concepts in a conveniently compressed form. They normally have a core of meaning which is well accepted in everyday usage, but the totality of situations which may be covered by the label can never be circumscribed by any particular definition.
>
> . . . In general, however, the committee applies the concept to attempts to sidestep the requirements for a new listing, considering an application for a new listing as the "front door".'

[After deciding that the JSE's refusal to approve the circular was a reviewable decision, Coetzee J continued:]

In coming to an examination of the content of the contractual relationship between the parties *in casu*, and of a proper construction of various clauses, phrases and words, one bears in mind not only their context but also the setting of this relationship. . . . Crisply, the question is whether this market place in which are traded shares, debentures and other securities, has, in maintaining an orderly market and fair dealing in the public interest, the power to veto certain proposed commercial transactions by listed companies. Is it, in addition to being a market place, also the 'upper guardian' of shareholders whose power to enter into or authorize deals by their companies in their unfettered discretion, is severely curtailed by the overriding veto power of the Exchange?

That Stock Exchanges not only exist in modern developed capitalistic economies but that they are indispensable is a simple fact of life. It is equally true that public interest demands that they should be orderly and fairly conducted, which is ensured by a measure of statutory control. To refer, however, to the Stock Exchange Control Act 7 of 1947 as its 'empowering Act' is inaccurate. . . .

... Neither directly, nor indirectly, does the Stock Exchange Control Act create *statutory* stock exchanges. This Act falls nicely in the general pattern of South African legislation enacted to control a large variety of financial institutions such as banks, building societies, pension funds, benefit funds, insurance companies, etc. It is fundamentally *licensing* legislation. Any stock exchange which functions as such requires to be licensed under the Act. Its rules must conform with certain standards laid down in the Act, and must be approved by the Registrar of Financial Institutions. A board of appeal is established by s 11 of the Act, to which appeals may be made under s 10, but this does not affect the purely contractual nature of the relationship between a licensed exchange and its listed companies. In effect it is a condition of its licence that any company may apply to it for a listing and that it has not an absolute discretion to refuse such an application. . . .

. . . This does not detract from the contractual quality of its subsequent relationship with such company. The JSE is no more a creature of statute than any bank or building society, and I am not going to approach these problems of construction as if they arise in the field of public law.

In the undertaking which was originally signed when application was made for a listing of its shares on behalf of Vrede, the first term thereof read as follows:

'That the applicant company will comply with the committee's requirements as set out in the "General information and requirements for listed companies" booklet, as amended from time to time.'

The latest edition of this publication, to which I shall refer as 'the booklet', was handed to me during the hearing. . . .

Before dealing with the contents of the booklet, I should quote a few paragraphs from the original written undertaking which are indicative of the purposes of certain obligations laid upon the applicant and the JSE's corresponding powers. I quote clause 11(v):

'(v) That the directors report or chairman's statement will contain:

(*a*) The main reason for any significant variation of trading profits and of any fortuitous profit or unforeseen loss by the company and its subsidiary or associated companies.

(*b*) A review of the business conditions and trading results, between the date of the end of the financial year and the date of issue of the annual report and accounts.

(*c*) The failure of the company, or its subsidiary or associated companies, to pay any predetermined

(i) capital repayment, dividend or interest on any fixed dividend or interest bearing security;

(ii) instalment or interest on a loan.

(*d*) The reason for any significant change in the amount of the remuneration or other emoluments paid or accrued to the directors of the company or its subsidiary or associated companies.

(e) A statement of the major trading activities of the company
and its subsidiaries during the year, the towns and areas in
which they operate and the names of the subsidiary companies.'

Clause 14, under the heading of 'Purchase or sale of assets', reads as
follows:

'That the company undertake that, initially, an agreement will be
provisional and it shall be submitted to ordinary shareholders in
general meeting for approval in regard to transactions of the following
nature:'

These transactions are set forth and the clause continues:

'That the full details of the proposed transactions will be included
in a circular to shareholders and that such circular shall be prepared
in accordance with the requirements of the committee that from time
to time be in force. That 225 copies of the circular, carriage paid,
will be lodged with the secretary for distribution to broking members.'

These passages which I have quoted show how concerned the JSE
is that all the persons who trade shares in the market place, as purchasers or sellers, should have full information from the companies
concerned of all those facts which bear upon an assessment of the price
which shares should fetch for all purchasers and sellers are shareholders
or potential shareholders. In addition, it is concerned that the shareholders should have a say specifically in certain transactions of the
company over and above their general right of control of the directors;
moreover, in order to be properly qualified to exercise this right they
should be fully briefed on all the aspects which could conceivably be
considered by them. Nowhere, however, is there the slightest suggestion
of any kind of overriding power residing in the JSE either to influence
the voting on such occasions, or to prevent the very occasion itself from
occurring on the ground that it does not approve of the proposed
transaction.

With but few variations these themes are repeated in the booklet.
At pp 35 et seq the requirements in respect of disclosure of the disposal
or acquisition of assets are stated. Clause 1 provides:

'Where a listed company proposes to acquire an asset involving —
(a) payment in shares of the acquiring company in excess of 15 per
cent in number of its issued share capital; or
(b) payment in cash in excess of 15 per cent of the acquiring company's issued share capital, plus reserves; or
(c) in the case of a combination of shares and cash in excess of 15
per cent of the relative (a) and (b) above:

shareholders must be given full details . . . by circular, and the company must also hold an extraordinary general meeting in order to
obtain shareholders' approval of the proposed transaction. Similarly,
where a listed company disposes of an asset representing more than
15 per cent of its own issued capital plus reserves, shareholders must
be given full details and the company must hold an extraordinary

general meeting in order to obtain shareholders' approval of the proposed transaction.

A statement in the circular to what effect the acquisition or disposal will have on the company's net tangible assets and earnings per share.'

Clauses 3 to 7 lay down the matters to be dealt with in the circular, the reports which must be obtained, and the particulars which must be set forth fully. Read together, these clauses establish clearly the standard of disclosure which must be made by way of the circular. Once the circular has been drafted, rule 2 of s I (at p 8) comes into play:

'Twelve copies of all announcements made, or circulars or notices relating to matters dealt with, or referred to, in this booklet (other than dividend announcements), should be submitted for the committee's prior approval at least 21 days before the date of issue to shareholders.'

This is the only rule in which the approval of circulars is dealt with, and it is in this rule, read contextually, that the power to veto proposed transactions must lurk for the JSE's contentions to have any validity.

Once the circular is approved and the extraordinary general meeting, at which the additional shares of the same class as those already listed have been created, has been held, the rules in s IV A at p 39 et seq apply. It is there provided that the company must now make immediate *application for a listing* (my italics) of such shares. This 'application' is one to which many rules and conditions apply. It must be in writing. A pre-listing statement must be settled, or a circular may be accepted in lieu thereof provided it contains, once again, clearly specified information. This application is then 'considered' by the committee. The information which this circular must contain is a formidable catalogue ... and is yet a further example of the high level of the disclosure of facts to shareholders which is required. This is underlined by the following paragraph at p 39 of the booklet:

'If the circular does not contain all the relevant particulars (set out hereunder) the committee, before considering the application for listing, may require to be issued to shareholders an additional circular embodying the information omitted. Draft circulars to be submitted for approval (original plus 11 copies). Where a rights issue is concerned a proposed time table prepared in accordance with the requirements set out on p 50 to be submitted with the draft circular (original plus 11 copies).'

At this stage, when the application for listing of the new shares is considered, there can be no doubt that JSE functions as an adjudicating body which must weigh up the pros and cons in deciding whether these additional shares ought to be listed. It may be that it is now proper for it to consider such matters as 'back door' listing, the profitability of acquisitions, all the surrounding circumstances of the transactions, and many other matters which may bear on the question of whether such shares merit a listing, but this is not a question on which a decision is called for at present and I say no more about it. That, however, is a very far cry from its function at the stage of the initial circular, where clearly its only concern is to ensure that the required standards of disclosure to shareholders have been adhered to by the company. There is no adjudication in the juristic sense at all. What takes place bears a closer analogy to an auditing function which is essentially one of checking facts for accuracy and to ensure compliance with objectively established standards. . . .

I hold therefore that clause 2 at p 8 of the booklet was no warrant at all for the committee's purported exercise of powers. Properly construed, the clause means no more than that the committee cannot withhold approval if there is substantial compliance with the disclosure requirements in the rules or any additional reasonable *ad hoc* requirement which the committee may make which is calculated to fill in any gaps in the existing picture of information which a shareholder needs in order to hold an informed opinion when he decides how to cast his vote at the extraordinary general meeting of shareholders. To any person reasonably versed in company finance and associated matters, these standards are easily capable of being clearly and objectively established in every case depending upon the facts. Employing their own jargon, one may say that the Johannesburg Stock Exchange have *in casu* perpetrated a 'back door' veto of the proposed transactions by withholding approval of the circular, instead of waiting for the 'front door' occasion when the application for a listing is made to it! Only then would they have performed adjudicating functions. Its failure or refusal to approve was a simple breach of contract, and the remedies of Vrede are those which the innocent party usually has *ex contractu.* . . .

I make the following order:

(1) It is declared that the refusal of the respondent to approve the circular to shareholders issued by the second applicant, dated 14 November 1973, which is annexure A to the founding affidavit, was improper and in breach of the agreement between the parties. . . .

VII The Multinational Company; the Company in the Common Market; the European Company

A TEXT

The multinational company or enterprise is a group or cluster of companies carrying on business in different countries, 'a combination of companies of different nationality, connected by means of shareholdings, managerial control or contract and constituting an economic unit', Clive M Schmitthoff *Nationalism and the Multinational Enterprise* (1973) at 24. It may be 'ethnocentric' (home-country oriented), 'polycentric' (host-country oriented) or 'geo-centric' (world oriented), and must be distinguished from the international company, such as the Bank for International Settlements, which is established under international law. (On the registration of a foreign company in the Republic, pp 50–1 above.)

Special rules apply within the European Economic Community (EEC). The four basic freedoms for which the Community stands—freedom of movement of goods; freedom of movement of persons; freedom of movement of services; and freedom of movement of capital—imply freedom of establishment. A company established in any one of the member states may establish branches, subsidiaries and affiliates in any other member State, and must be treated in every member State in the same way as a domestic company. In pursuance of this objective the member States concluded on 29 February 1968 a Convention on the Mutual Recognition of Companies and Legal Persons.

In order to protect persons dealing in good faith with companies throughout the Community, the EEC has as one of its objectives the approximation of such provisions in the company laws of its member States as directly affect the functioning of the Common Market. The means it employs to this end is the Directive. Unlike a Regulation, which is directly applicable in all the member States, a Directive is binding upon each member State as to the result to be achieved but leaves the choice of form and methods to achieve this result to the member States.

Only one Directive on company law has so far been passed by the EEC Council, the First Directive of 9 March 1968. It deals with compulsory disclosure of certain information regarding companies and, most importantly, with pre-incorporation contracts and the protection of persons dealing with a company in good faith: 33. It was in compliance with this Directive that the United Kingdom passed the European Communities Act 1972 c 18, which, among other changes, virtually abolished the *ultra vires* doctrine (pp 80–1 below). Further Directives dealing, *inter alia*, with capital maintenance, mergers, accounts and balance sheets, management and prospectuses have been prepared by the EEC Commission but have not as yet been approved by the Council. When they are, Britain will have to change its company law accordingly.

For some years now the EEC has been planning a European Company—*Societas Europeae, SE*—which is to have the status of a national company in every EEC member State without being legally attached to any one. The final draft of the proposed statute was submitted by the Commission to the Council of Ministers in May 1975 (Com (75) 150 final, of 30 April 1975. See Clive M Schmitthoff (1975) *JBL* 322). Formation of an SE will be open to two or more public or private companies falling under the laws of at least two different member States, or to an existing SE, and will be effected by merger or by the formation of a holding company or joint subsidiary. The SE will be registered with the Court of the European Communities in Luxembourg, and will be governed, where the statute is silent, by general legal principles—a kind of Western European *jus gentium* of companies.

B MATERIALS

[33] First Directive of the Council of the European Economic Community of 9 March 1968 (68/151 EEC), as amended by the Act of Accession of 27 March 1972

SECTION II: VALIDITY OF OBLIGATIONS ENTERED INTO BY A COMPANY

Article 7

If, before a company being formed has acquired legal personality, action has been carried out in its name and the company does not assume the obligations arising from such action, the persons who acted shall, without limit, be jointly and severally liable therefor, unless otherwise agreed.

Article 8

Completion of the formalities of disclosure of the particulars concerning the persons who, as an organ of the company, are authorised to represent it shall constitute a bar to any irregularity in their appointment being relied upon as against third parties unless the company proves that such third parties had knowledge thereof.

Article 9

1. Acts done by the organs of the company shall be binding upon it even if those acts are not within the objects of the company, unless such acts exceed the powers that the law confers or allows to be conferred on those organs.

However, Member States may provide that the company shall not be bound where such acts are outside the objects of the company, if it proves that the third party knew that the act was outside those objects or could not in view of the circumstances have been unaware of it; disclosure of the statutes shall not of itself be sufficient proof thereof.

2. The limits on the powers of the organs of the company, arising under the statutes or from a decision of the competent organs, may never be relied on as against third parties, even if they have been disclosed.

3. If the national law provides that authority to represent a company may, in derogation from the legal rules governing the subject, be conferred by the statutes on a single person or on several persons acting jointly, that law may provide that such a provision in the statutes may be relied on as against third parties on condition that it relates to the general power of representation; the question whether such a provision in the statutes can be relied on as against third parties shall be governed by Article 3. Art 3 requires member states to keep a central register and to enter in it, *inter alia*, the names of the persons who have authority to represent the company.

VIII Non-Applicability of the Companies Act

The Companies Act does not apply to building societies, trade unions, friendly societies, employers' organizations, or co-operative societies or companies, s 3(1)(*a*). It is of restricted application in the case of banking and insurance companies or societies, s 3(1)(*b*).

3   *The Constitution of a Company*

I THE MEMORANDUM OF ASSOCIATION

(*a*) General

A TEXT

The memorandum of association is the constitution of a company, the articles are its by-laws. The Registrar of Companies grants the certificate of incorporation after the memorandum and the articles have been registered, s 64. Once registered they bind the company and its members, including future members, as if they had been signed by each member, s 65(2).

The form and contents of the memorandum of association must comply with ss 52–54. The purpose for which a company is being formed and the main business which it is to carry on in achieving its purpose must be stated, s 52. More specifically, the memorandum must state,

(i) the name of the company;

(ii) the main object of the company, which must correspond to its purpose and main business;

(iii) the specific ancillary objects (if any) which are to be excluded from the unlimited ancillary objects referred to in s 33(1);

(iv) the specific powers (if any) which are to be excluded from the plenary powers which a company normally has, s 34 and Schedule 2.

If the company is to have a share capital, the memorandum must further state:

(v) the amount of the share capital with which the company is to be registered and the division thereof into shares of a fixed amount or, if the company is to have shares of no par value, the number of shares;

(vi) the number of shares which each subscriber undertakes to take up.

In addition to the aforegoing the memorandum may contain special conditions, and the requirements, if any, additional to those prescribed in the Act, for the alteration of such conditions, s 53(a).

In the case of a private company the memorandum may provide that the directors and past directors are to be personally liable for debts contracted by the company during their periods of office, s 53(b).

The memorandum concludes with the 'association clause'.

Subject to the provisions of s 53(a) as to special conditions, a company may by special resolution make additions to or alter the provisions of its memorandum with respect to objects and powers, s 55(1). Unless prohibited by the condition itself, a special condition contained in the memorandum may be altered by special resolution or in the manner prescribed by such condition, s 56(1). Thus a special condition may be made either unalterable or alterable only by, say, an 80 or 90 per cent majority. A condition which requires a special resolution for its alteration cannot be altered by the unanimous informal consent of all the shareholders: 34 (and below, p 322). The special rights of any class of members enshrined in the memorandum may not be varied or abrogated unless the memorandum itself provides so, s 56(5) and p 196 below. On change of name, see s 44 (p 72 below), on alteration of capital, ss 75, 88ff (p 149 below).

A private company may by special resolution and with the consent of each person being then a director insert a provision providing for personal liability of its directors, s 56(2). Alteration or removal of such a provision, whether contained in the original memorandum or subsequently inserted, requires a special resolution as well as confirmation by the court, s 56(3).

Under s 57, a company may by special resolution substitute for its existing memorandum a translation thereof into the other official language.

Subject to the aforegoing any clause in the memorandum may be altered by special resolution, s 56(4).

(On alteration of the provisions of the memorandum as part of a compromise or arrangement under s 311 or in connection with relief from oppression, under s 252, see respectively, pp 632 and 511 below.)

B CASES

[34] Quadrangle Investments (Pty) Ltd v Witind Holdings Ltd
1975 (1) SA 572 (AD)

A clause in the memorandum of association of the plaintiff company provided that one of the objects of the company was to sell, realize and vary investments made by the company, 'provided always that any surplus or profits resulting therefrom shall be credited to capital reserve or used to write down the book value of the company's assets or for some other capital purposes, and shall not be regarded as profits arising from the business of the company, and therefore, shall not be treated as revenue available for the payment of dividends'. In contravention of this condition the company, with the unanimous assent of its shareholders, declared a dividend out of profits which had accrued to it on the sale of shares.

TROLLIP JA: The crisp question raised by this appeal is whether a dividend declared by a company in contravention of a condition contained in its memorandum, which could lawfully have been contained in its articles of association instead of its memorandum (as predicated in s 11*bis* of the Companies Act 26 of 1946), is valid or validated because all its shareholders unanimously assented to it. . . .

In view of the arguments advanced before us, I think that a few introductory words about the applicability of the doctrine of *ultra vires* relating to companies registered under the Act are warranted. According to s 5 of the Act the requisite number of persons, by subscribing their names to a memorandum of association and otherwise complying with the requirements of the Act in respect of registration, may form an incorporated company. The memorandum must state, *inter alia*, the objects of the company (ss 6 and 7). Section 9 prohibits such a company from altering 'the conditions' contained in its memorandum

'except in the cases, and in the mode, and to the extent for which express provision is made in this Act'.

'Conditions' applies to all conditions in the memorandum, and also includes those that the Act does not require to be inserted in the memorandum. . . .

The articles of association are subordinate to the memorandum. They prescribe the regulations for the internal management of the company (ss 12, 13, and 14) and, subject to the provisions of the Act and the conditions contained in the memorandum, they may be freely altered or added to by special resolution (s 15).

Consequently, according to the Act, the memorandum is the constitution of the registered company; affirmatively it empowers the company to act within the provisions expressed or implied in its memorandum; negatively, it forbids the company to do anything which is beyond or contrary to those provisions; if any such thing is done, whilst it would not be illegal, it would be null and void, as having been, in effect, prohibited by the Act; and it would therefore be incapable of validation by subsequent ratification by the shareholders, even if they unanimously assent thereto. On the other hand any act or activity, contrary to the articles but within the ambit of the memorandum, is at worst merely voidable and can be validated by the shareholders ratifying it the requisite manner.

That is the essence of the *ultra vires* doctrine as applied to registered companies. In English law it was first authoritatively expounded by the House of Lords in *Ashbury Railway Carriage and Iron Co Ltd* v *Riche* (1875) LR 7 HL 653, the *locus classicus* on the subject. . . .

Counsel for Witind relied heavily on s 11*bis* which reads:

'(1) Subject to the provisions of s 111*bis*, any conditions contained in a company's memorandum which could lawfully have been contained in articles of association instead of in the memorandum may, in accordance with the provisions of this section, be altered by the company by special resolution: Provided that if an application is made to the Court for the alteration to be cancelled, it shall not have effect except in so far as it is confirmed by the Court.'

According to ss (3), read with s 11(2), the application to court may be made by the holders of not less than 15 per cent in nominal value of the issued shares or 15 per cent of the company's debentures.

The contention, as I understood it, was that this provision, in particular, had in effect relaxed the *ultra vires* doctrine in relation to the conditions mentioned in ss (1); that, because these conditions, like the articles, can now be altered merely by special resolution, an alteration could also be duly effected, and the otherwise offending act simultaneously authorized, by the unanimous assent thereto of the shareholders, that being an *a fortiori* way of expressing their will; or that, alternatively, the offending act is not *ultra vires* 'in the strict sense of that term', and it can be validated *pro hac vice*, ie without having to alter the conditions, by the shareholders' unanimous assent thereto, according to the decision in this court in *Gohlke and Schneider & another* v *Westies Minerale Bpk & another* 1970 (2) SA 685 [*190* below]. Counsel sought to reinforce that argument by also maintaining that, according to s 11*bis*, only the shareholders and debenture-holders are concerned in the alteration of any such condition in the memorandum.

That argument cannot prevail. When a condition, which could have been contained in the articles, is inserted in the memorandum, it becomes part of the latter and subject to all those sections of the Act, mentioned above, relating to the memorandum (see *Ashbury* v *Watson* (1885) 30 ChD 376, previously referred to). In particular, it becomes one of 'the conditions contained in the memorandum' which, according to s 9, cannot be altered 'except in the cases, and in the mode' for which express provision is made in the Act; that is, in cases under s 11*bis*, by special resolution; secondly, it also becomes one of 'the provisions of the memorandum' which s 16 enjoins the company and its members to observe. It follows:

(i) that such a condition cannot be altered by the unanimous assent of the shareholders; that can only be done by a special resolution; and

(ii) that anything done in contravention of such a condition, without its first being altered, is *ultra vires* and void, and it cannot be validated by the unanimous assent of the shareholders.

As to (i), I would emphasize that s 65 requires that a copy of the special resolution must be recorded by the Registrar before it becomes effective. . . .

As to (ii), it is unnecessary to decide whether, without first duly altering such a condition, a company could by special resolution authorize or subsequently ratify the offending act. For, in the present case, only the unanimous assent of shareholders was relied on, which, for the reasons given, was insufficient for the purpose, since it purported to validate the doing of something which the Act forbids unless its requirements are first complied with. *Gohlke's* case (*supra*) is distinguishable, since it applied the principle of unanimous assent to validate the doing of a particular act of internal management that was *intra vires* the company's memorandum, and which, at worst, was merely contrary to its articles.

NOTES

While there is no equivalent to s 11*bis* of the 1926 Act in the 1973 Act, the judgment in *Quadrangle Investments* remains relevant in as far as it deals with the general question whether a condition which requires a special resolution for its alteration can be altered by the unanimous informal consent of the shareholders.

(b) Name Clause

A TEXT

If the name chosen by a company to be incorporated is, in the opinion of the Registrar, undesirable, he will refuse to register the proposed memorandum, s 41. The old Act provided in s 10, *inter alia*, that the name of a company must not: (1) be identical with the name by which another company is already registered or so nearly resembling it as to be calculated to deceive; (2) be calculated to mislead the public or to cause annoyance or offence to any person; (3) be suggestive of blasphemy or indecency; (4) be calculated to cause damage to any company or other person: *35, 36.*

Presumably, considerations on these lines will guide the Registrar in determining whether or not the chosen name is undesirable in terms of s 41 of the present Act (see the Registrar's Directive on Names of Companies, GN 709 GG 4055 of 19 October 1973).

Certain words, titles and names may not be used without special authorization, e g 'bank' (Banks Act 23 of 1965 s 49), 'funds' (Unit Trusts Control Act 18 of 1947 s 37(1)) and 'insurance' (Insurance Act 27 of 1943 s 5).

The name of a public company must include as its last word the word 'Limited' ('Ltd') or 'Beperk' ('Bpk'). The name of a private company must include as its last two words the words '(Proprietary) Limited' ('(Pty) Ltd') or '(Eiensdom) Beperk' ('(Edms) Bpk'), ss 49, 50. A private company whose memorandum provides for personal liability of its directors must have 'Incorporated' ('Inc') or 'Ingelyf' ('Ing') as the last word in its name, ss 49, 50. The name of an external company must conclude with the words 'Incorporated in . . .' (whatever country it may be), s 49(2).

A company may change its name by special resolution, s 44.

Any director or officer of a company who signs or authorizes to be signed any bill of exchange, promissory note, endorsement, cheque or order for money or goods without describing the company by its proper name can be held personally liable by the other party if the company fails to pay, s 50(3): *37.*

To trade under a name of which 'Limited' or 'Incorporated' is the last word without being incorporated is an offence, s 51.

B CASES

[35] **Aerators Ltd *v* Tollett**
[1902] 2 Ch 319

FARWELL J: The plaintiffs, 'Aerators, Limited', claim an injunction to restrain the defendants from registering a company under the name of 'Automatic Aerators Patents, Limited', on the ground that such name so nearly resembles the plaintiffs' name as to be calculated to deceive. . . . The plaintiffs were incorporated in the year 1900, and took over the business of a similar company of the same name incorporated in 1896. . . . [The plaintiff's business] consists in the sale of 'Sparklets'; this word is their trade mark, and they have largely advertised 'Sparklets'. I understand them to be a small apparatus containing compressed carbonic acid gas, by means of which contents of bottles are aerated. One of the merits claimed for them is their portability and their applicability to a small quantity of liquid. The defendants propose that the new company to be formed by them shall acquire patents for the aeration of liquids contained in tanks or cisterns of large size, and shall either work such patents themselves or shall form subsidiary companies for the development of such patents. The 20th section of the Companies Act 1862 enacts that 'no company shall be registered under a name identical with that by which a subsisting company is already registered, or so nearly resembling the same as to be calculated to deceive', except in certain cases which are not material to the present case. It will be observed that a company has, therefore, a greater right than an individual in respect of names that are identical. For John Smith cannot prevent other persons of the same name from using their own name; but John Smith, Limited, can prevent the registration of any other company as John Smith, Limited. I do not, however, consider that it follows that the legislature has intended to give companies any greater rights than individuals possess in respect of names which are not identical, but only similar, and it has been held that 'calculated to deceive' does not point to intentional fraud; but it is a question of fact in each case whether the name of the new company is so similar to that of the old company as to induce the belief that the two companies are identical. In considering this question it is material to ascertain (1) what business has been or is intended to be carried on by the old company, and what is intended to be carried on by the new one; (2) what sort of name has been adopted by the old company. . . . In the present case the plaintiffs have taken a word which, and which only, aptly and rightly describes a machine for producing a particular result. The word has been in common use in the English language for at least thirty years. It is to be found in dictionaries such as the *Century* (1889), *Oxford English Dictionary* (1888, in a quotation dated 1861), and the *Dictionary of Mechanics* (1876), to which one of the witnesses referred. It would obviously lead to the greatest inconvenience if any company could prevent all other companies from using as part of their title the one word in the English language which aptly describes the articles they manufacture or deal in, or the name of the individual associated for years with a particular firm. For example, suppose a company had registered the name of 'Motors, Limited', and another the name of 'Automobiles, Limited', it appears to me impossible to say that they thereby prevent all other companies from using as part of their title these two words, which, so far as I know, are the only words which represent the fashionable locomotives of the day, although their sole trade was the manufacture and sale of motors and automobiles. . . . In considering whether a name is calculated to deceive, it is, as I have said, material to see what that name is, and if the name is simply a word in ordinary use representing a machine or an article of commerce, the probability of deception is out of all proportion less than it would be in the case of an invented or fancy word, or even of the name of a place. . . .

In my opinion, the plaintiffs' action is an attempt to monopolize for the purpose of nomenclature a word in ordinary use in the English language . . . and must be dismissed with costs.

[36] Pick 'n Pay Discount Stores *v* Registrar of Companies and Pick-'n-Pay Stores Ltd
1972 (1) SA 147 (N)

In 1963 one Goldin started a food store under the name 'Pick-'n-Pay'. By 1964 he owned three stores carrying on business in the Cape Peninsula under that name, and he formed a company called 'Pick-'n-Pay (Pty) Ltd', together with other companies incorporating the name 'Pick-'n-Pay' to conduct these businesses. In February 1967 one Ackerman acquired their businesses, and in July 1968 'Pick-'n-Pay Stores Ltd' was promoted. Half a million shares were placed with the public and the company was granted a listing on the Johannesburg Stock Exchange. In October 1968 one Rawat opened a self-service retail business in partnership with his wife. He gave it the name 'Pick 'n Pay Discount Stores' and it was licensed in that name.

Section 5(1) of the Business Names Act 27 of 1960 reads as follows:

'Upon the application in writing of any aggrieved person the Registrar may in writing order any person who carries on any business under any name, title or description which is in the opinion of the Registrar calculated to deceive or to mislead the public or to cause annoyance or offence to any person or class of persons or is suggestive of blasphemy or indecency, to cease to carry on the business under that name, title or description.'

Acting under this section the Registrar of Companies in October 1970 ordered 'Pick 'n Pay Discount Stores' to change its name. 'Pick 'n Pay Discount Stores' applied to court to set the order aside. The application failed.

SHEARER J: It was common cause between the parties that I must decide the issues raised in this matter, not upon the information which was before the first respondent when he reached his decision, but on all the evidence and information before me. I must therefore refuse the application if I conclude that the use by the applicant of the name under which it trades is 'calculated to deceive or mislead the public' and that the second respondent is 'aggrieved' thereby. In my judgment the second respondent is 'aggrieved', within the meaning to be given to that word in s 5(1), if it suffers or is likely to suffer material prejudice as a result of deception or confusion arising through the use of the name by the applicant.

[Counsel for the applicant] laid stress on a number of factors which, he contended, militated against any deception or confusion. He drew attention to the interposition before and after the ' 'n' of dashes or hyphens, a feature which is absent from the applicant's use of the name. As I have said, I regard this distinction as of no significance. It is one which is likely to escape even the most alert member of the public. Then there is the use of the word 'Discount' in association with the name. In view of the nature of the business carried on by the second respondent and the publicity which its participation in 'price-wars' received, this feature is likely to add to rather than subtract from any confusion. The fact that the second respondent is a public company whereas the applicant is a partnership may impress more sophisticated members of the public as significant, but would undoubtedly make no impression on the great majority.

I turn now to a consideration of whether or not the applicant's use of that name is, in the particular context of the applicant's sphere of business operations and the nature of its business and those of the second respondent, likely to deceive or mislead the public. Here [Counsel for the applicant] drew attention initially to the fact that the applicant carries on business in a small unimposing store with a small turnover and limited stock, whereas the second respondent had no less than fifteen stores in the Cape Province and two in the Transvaal and carries on business in large modern premises. The applicant is owned and controlled by Asiatics, with a predominantly Bantu clientele, whereas the second respondent's business, owned and controlled by Whites, operates in White areas. He also emphasized the fact that the second respondent has, at present, no stores in Natal and its only immediate plans for expansion into Natal are to open stores in Westville and in Durban. Against this background, he contended that it is extremely unlikely that a person doing business with the applicant might be misled into thinking that it was a store operated by the second respondent. This submission is supported by affidavits from customers to the effect that they had never heard of the second respondent. Most of the customers are persons who live in the area. I think that, upon the information before me, I am justified in concluding that, at present, very few of its customers would be misled.

That does not, however, conclude the matter. The second respondent is a large concern which has expanded rapidly in recent years, and which has plans for further expansion which involve extending its trading into Natal. It has received extensive publicity and has acquired a business reputation which extends beyond the bounds of its immediate operations. It is a public company, listed on the Johannesburg Stock

Exchange, and its shares are bought and sold by members of the public. Its reputation is therefore a valuable asset. Anything which detracts from its public image is likely to cause it prejudice sounding in money. That public image is one which it is entitled to exploit in the future, and when it does trade in Natal, the existence of another trading concern with a substantially similar name carries with it the potentiality of considerable embarrassment. The nature of the goods advertised by the applicant and the prices quoted for such goods may cause confusion in the minds of customers, both actual and potential. The small scale of the applicant's business operations and its limited stock suggest that it may not be immune from financial difficulties in the future. If such difficulties become known, they may appear to reflect discredit on the second respondent. . . .

The existence of a store with a substantially identical name may inhibit the second respondent's decision to trade in Pietermaritzburg or its immediate environs. It may be possible for one of the second respondent's trade competitors to acquire both the applicant's business and the name under which it trades, and thus further embarrass the second respondent. Indeed there is implicit in the state of affairs, presently obviated by the first respondent's order, a real prospect of embarrassment in the future. This embarrassment is, in my judgment, sufficient to constitute the second respondent an 'aggrieved person' within the meaning of the section.

I must emphasize that my conclusions in this matter are largely based upon the fact that the second respondent is a concern, carrying on business in a large number of branches, which has already acquired a national reputation and which has aspirations to trade throughout all provinces in the Republic. It is clear that these aspirations took root before the applicant adopted its present name, and I am satisfied that I may have regard to the second respondent's plans for the future. The nature and scope of its operations entitle me to have regard to considerations which are not normally present when a small localized concern seeks to prevent another from using a name similar to its name. . . .

To summarize my conclusions, there is attached to the second respondent's name a substantial and widespread goodwill. It has not a single store but a chain, which will extend into Natal. It has registered trade marks for products marketed under that name. The applicant's use of the name carries with it substantial potentiality of deception and confusion and the second respondent will suffer material prejudice if the applicant continues to use the name which its predecessor contrived.

I conclude therefore that the application must fail.

[Although the principal opponents in this action were a partnership and a company, similar considerations apply where a company assumes a name which so nearly resembles the name of another company as to be calculated to deceive or confuse.]

[37] Abro v Softex Mattress (Pty) Ltd
1973 (2) SA 346 (D)

The defendant signed a note, of which the plaintiff was the holder, for and on behalf of 'Henwoods'. 'Henwoods' was a firm owned by

Libertas (Andries Street) (Proprietary) Limited. The defendant was director and manager of Libertas. The plaintiff sought to hold him liable under s 58 of the old Companies Act, corresponding to s 50(3) of the present one. The defendant excepted to the action as disclosing no cause of action. The exception was dismissed.

HENNING J: A limited or unlimited company registered under the Companies Act 46 of 1926 has only one name, which is readily ascertainable, particularly by those persons mentioned in s 58(3). It is provided in s 58(1)(c) in unmistakable terms that the company's name shall be mentioned in legible characters in all the documents specified, the name obviously being the registered name of the company. So far there is no difficulty in ascertaining what the legislature requires. The use of the imperative 'shall', and the partial relaxation permitted by the proviso and ss (4) lends support to the view that, subject thereto, the legislature had in mind that any misdescription of a company's name or any omission therefrom was intended to render operative the provisions of ss (3), which impose personal liability on the individual or individuals responsible for the defect as well as a criminal sanction. It seems to me that *a fortiori* is this the position where a name is used which bears no resemblance at all to the name of the company. I have not overlooked the principle of interpretation that a statute which creates a criminal offence should be strictly construed. A benign construction is, however, adopted only if the language used is obscure or ambiguous. (See Steyn *Uitleg van Wette* 3 ed 111 et seq.) I have been unable to discover any obscurity or ambiguity in either ss (1)(c) or (3), or the two read together. As to the reason for the enactments it might well be that the legislature considered it in the public interest that a company's name should in all respects properly appear so as to avoid misunderstanding or confusion. As I read it, there is nothing harsh in s 58, nor does accurate observance of its terms present any difficulty.

NOTES

In *Pick-'N-Pay Stores Ltd* v *Pick-'N-Pay Superette (Pvt) Ltd* 1974 (1) SA 597 (RAD) the Rhodesian courts refused an application by a South African company which had never traded in Rhodesia nor acquired a goodwill there for an order restraining a Rhodesian company from trading under a similar name in Rhodesia.

In *Legal & General Assurance Society Ltd* v *Daniel* The Times 10 October 1967, (1967) 117 *New Law Journal* 1113, it was held that the words 'Legal & General', though descriptive, had become specifically associated with the plaintiff company.

See also *Slabbert* v *Airways Booking Office (Pty) Ltd* 1933 WLD 204; further, *Union Steel Corporation Ltd* v *Registrar of Companies* 1920 TPD 266; *Cash Wholesalers Ltd* v *Hogan* 1933 NPD 117; *Ex parte The Club, Benoni Ltd* 1936 WLD 89; *Ex parte SA Farm Products Protective Association Ltd* 1939 CPD 331; *Builma (Cape) (Pty) Ltd* v *Registrar of Companies* 1956 (3) SA 690 (SR); *Charmfit of Hollywood Inc* v *Registrar of Companies* 1964 (2) SA 739 (AD), all cases decided under the old Act; further, *Burnkloof Caterers (Pty) Ltd* v *Horseshoe Caterers (Greenpoint) (Pty) Ltd* 1976 (2) SA 930 (AD) and *William Bartfield & Co (Pty) Ltd* v *Job Hypermarket* 1976 (3) SA 157 (T), both dealing with 'passing-off', and L L Hart 'Company Names considered in the light of Trade Marks' (1970) *De Rebus Procuratoriis* 189.

(c) Objects Clause: 'Failure of Substratum'; Ultra Vires

A TEXT

The capacity of a company is determined by its main object. Included in it are, without limitation, all objects ancillary to its main object, except such specific ancillary objects as are expressly excluded in its memorandum, s 33, and plenary powers (including the common powers stated in Schedule 2), except such specific powers as are expressly excluded or qualified in its memorandum, s 34.

It used to be the law that if a company acted outside its objects, its act was void as being beyond its powers (*ultra vires*): *38*. In view of the provisions of ss 33 and 34 regarding ancillary objects and plenary powers the issue of *ultra vires* can no longer readily arise. Where it does a third party dealing with the company is protected under s 36 which provides that

'No act of a company shall be void by reason only of the fact that the company was without capacity or power so to act or because the directors had no authority to perform that act on behalf of the company by reason only of the said fact and, except as between the company and its members or directors, or as between its members and its directors, neither the company nor any other person may in any legal proceedings rely upon any such lack of capacity or power or authority.'

Under the old dispensation *ultra vires* was relevant in two contexts: (i) externally, in a transaction between the company and an outside party; (ii) internally, as between the company and its members or directors, or as between its members and its directors: *39*. It is clear that for the purposes of (i) the *ultra vires* doctrine no longer exists. An *ultra vires* contract between the company and an outside party is binding both on the company and the other party to the contract even if both knew that the contract fell outside the main object of the company.

The effect of s 36 on contracts between the company and a director is not equally clear, but it is well arguable that as regards contracts the *ultra vires* rule has been abolished in respect of insiders as well, S J Naudé (1974) 91 *SALJ* 315 at 327–9. On the other hand, it follows from the wording of s 36 that *ultra vires* has not been abolished as regards internal company affairs. Shareholders will still be able to apply to court for an interdict if the directors propose to embark on a course of action which is outside the company's main object or otherwise *ultra vires*; the company will still be able to recover damages from directors who have acted *ultra vires* for any loss it may have suffered in consequence; and an *ultra vires* issue of share will still be void. (But note that under s 97 the court is empowered to validate the irregular creation, allotment or issue of shares. This would undoubtedly include an *ultra vires* issue of shares. On repayment of subscriptions where the issue is not validated, see *Linz* v *Electric Wire Company of Palestine Ltd* [1948] AC 371 (PC).)

Section 36 deals with acts which are illegal because they are beyond the company's capacity, not with acts which are beyond the company's capacity because they are illegal. Acts such as providing financial assistance for the purchase of the company's own shares or paying dividends out of capital are not covered by the section.

Unlike its nearest English equivalent (s 9 of the European Communities Act 1972) s 36 does not protect parties contracting with a company in respect of limitations which follow from causes other than lack of the company's capacity, e g restrictions imposed by the articles.

What a company's objects and powers are is important still for another reason. If the main object of a company is or becomes impossible of fulfilment the company may be wound up for 'failure of substratum' on the 'just and equitable ground', s 344(*h*): *39–41*, and p 686 below.

B CASES

[38] Ashbury Railway Carriage and Iron Company v Riche
(1875) LR 7 HL 653

The memorandum gave the company power to make and sell railway carriages. The directors entered into a contract to purchase a concession for constructing a railway in Belgium. The question was whether this contract was valid or, if not, whether it could be ratified by the shareholders.

LORD CAIRNS: . . . A contract of this kind was not within the words of the memorandum of association. In point of fact it was not a contract in which, as the memorandum of association implies, the limited company were to be the employed, they were the employers. They purchased the concessions of a railway—an object not at all within the memorandum of association; and having purchased that they employed, or they contracted to pay, as persons employing, the plaintiffs in the present action, as the persons who were to construct it. That was reversing entirely the whole hypothesis of the memorandum of association, and was the making of a contract not included within, but foreign to, the words of the memorandum of association. . . .

The provisions under which that system of limiting liability was inaugurated, were provisions not merely, perhaps I might say not mainly, for the benefit of the shareholders for the time being in the company, but were enactments intended also to provide for the interests of two other very important bodies; in the first place, those who might become shareholders in succession to the persons who were shareholders for the time being; and, secondly, the outside public, and more particularly those who might be creditors of companies of this kind. . . .

[The] mode of incorporation . . . contains in it both that which is affirmative and that which is negative. It states affirmatively the ambit and extent of vitality and power which by law are given to the corporation, and it states if it is necessary so to state, negatively, that nothing shall be done beyond that ambit, and that no attempt shall be made to use the corporate life for any other purpose than that which is so specified. . . .

The memorandum of association is, as it were, the area beyond which the action of the company cannot go; inside that area the shareholders may make such regulations for their own government as they think fit. . . .

The question is not as to the legality of the contract; the question is as to the competency and power of the company to make the contract. Now, I am clearly of opinion that this contract was entirely, as I have said, beyond the objects in the memorandum of association. If so, it was thereby placed beyond the powers of the company to make the contract. If so, my Lords, it is not a question whether the contract ever was ratified or was not ratified. If it was a contract void at its beginning, it was void because the company could not make the contract. If every shareholder of the company had been in the room, and every shareholder had said, 'That is a contract which we desire to make, which we authorize the directors to make, to which we sanction the placing the seal of the company', the case would not have stood in any different position from that in which it stands now. The shareholders would thereby, by unanimous consent, have been attempting to do the very thing which, by the Act of Parliament, they were prohibited from doing.

But, my Lords, if the shareholders of this company could not *ab ante* have authorized a contract of this kind to be made, how could they subsequently sanction the contract after it had, in point of fact been made ? . . . It appears to me that it would be perfectly fatal to the whole scheme of legislation to which I have referred, if you were to hold that, in the first place, directors might do that which even the whole company could not do, and that then, the shareholders finding out what had been done, could sanction subsequently, what they could not antecedently have authorized. . . .

This contract, in my judgment, could not have been ratified by the unanimous assent of the whole corporation.

NOTES

In England where the strict *ultra vires* doctrine, as laid down in *Ashbury Railway Co v Riche*, 37 above, originated, it was reduced to relative insignificance by s 9 of the European Communities Act 1972 (passed in compliance with the First EEC Directive of 9 March 1968, 33 above). Section 9(1) provides as follows:

'In favour of a person dealing with a company in good faith, any transaction decided on by the directors shall be deemed to be one which it is within the capacity of the company to enter into, and the power of the directors to bind the company shall be deemed to be free of any limitation under the memorandum or articles of association; and a party to a transaction so decided on shall not be bound to enquire as to the capacity of the company to enter into it or as to any such limitation on the powers of the directors, and shall be presumed to have acted in good faith unless the contrary is proved.'

It will be seen that in some respects s 36 of our Act goes further than s 9 of the European Communities Act in protecting third parties, in others not so far. Section 9(1) only protects a party in good faith, while good faith is, apparently, irrelevant for the purposes of s 36. However, since s 9(1) abrogates the doctrine of constructive notice and presumes good faith, this difference does not amount to much in practice. What is important is that s 36 protects the third party only in respect of a limitation on the authority of the directors which follows from their having acted beyond the objects and powers of the company, whereas s 9 provides protection in respect of any limitation on the power of the directors, whatever its cause.

In *Contemporary Refrigeration (Pty) Ltd (in liquidation) v Leites and Sonpoll Investments (Pty) Ltd* 1968 (1) SA 58 (AD) it was held that even where a director with authority to endorse and discount bills on behalf of his company does so with the intention of using the proceeds entirely for his own benefit, the company is bound unless the other party knew or suspected that the director was using his authority for his own, and not for the company's purposes.

Section 36 does not cover friendly societies, *Oranje Benefit Society v Central Merchant Bank Ltd* 1976 (4) SA 659 (AD), where it was held that the rule that a party contracting with a corporate body is deemed to know of the limitations on its powers does not apply where the party is induced to enter into a contract with the corporation by the fraudulent non-disclosure of knowledge that it would be *ultra vires*. See also *Oranje Benefit Society v Volkskas* 1976 (4) SA 656 (T).

[39] Cotman *v* Brougham
[1918] AC 514

LORD PARKER OF WADDINGTON: The question whether or not a company can be wound up for failure of substratum is a question of equity between a company and its shareholders. The question whether or not a transaction is *ultra vires* is a question of law between the company and a third party. The truth is that the statement of a company's objects in its memorandum is intended to serve a double purpose. In the first place, it gives protection to subscribers, who learn from it the purposes to which their money can be applied. In the second place, it gives protection to persons who deal with the company, and who can infer from it the extent of the company's powers. The narrower the objects expressed in the memorandum the less is the subscribers' risk, but the wider such objects the greater is the security of those who transact business with the company.

NOTES

Lord Parker also said (at 521): 'For the purpose of determining whether a company's substratum be gone, it may be necessary to distinguish between power and object and to determine what is the main or paramount object of the company, but I do not think this is necessary where a transaction is impeached as *ultra vires*. A person who deals with a company is entitled to assume that a company can do everything which it is expressly authorized to do by its memorandum of association, and need not investigate the equities between the company and its shareholders.'

Commenting on Lord Parker's statements Trollip JA remarks in *Marrock Plase (Pty) Ltd v Advance Seed Co (Pty) Ltd* 1975 (3) SA 403 (AD) at 414H: 'All that those dicta were intended to convey, I think, was that in the validity cases the question is solely one of law—the proper construction of the memorandum—whereas in the winding-up cases a question of fact is also involved, relating to the activities of the company and the equities of the shareholders, and, for that reason, the two different approaches should not be confused. The dicta cannot mean that the memorandum must be interpreted differently according to the kind of case that the court is dealing with. For, after all, its interpretation, whether for winding-up or validity purposes, is a matter of law in which the same canons of constructions are applied and the same meaning of the relevant objects or powers must therefore be arrived at.'

[40] *In re* Rhenosterkop Copper Company
(1908) 18 CTR 931

MAASDORP J: The circumstances of the present case are these: The company has been formed with the object, among others, of adopting an agreement entered into between F W Warren, of the one part, and W Stern and Ferdinand Gerber of the other part. The agreement which they contemplated adopting is one on which Warren appears as the vendor of certain rights which he had acquired from third parties, and the rights so acquired by him are prospecting and mining rights in respect of all base metals and other kinds of minerals and precious stones on the farm Rhenosterkop. It is stated in this case the substratum of the company has fallen away, because it has been ascertained that there are no metals upon the farm Rhenosterkop which can be worked by the company. If there are no metals, then the prospecting rights and mining rights are worthless. Anyway, it has been ascertained that the property is of such a character that it will not be for the benefit of the company to proceed further with this transaction. The property has been inspected by an expert in these matters, and he has reported that there are no indications of copper on it, which was the metal the parties mainly had in view when they entered into this agreement. The whole of the evidence goes to show that there is very good ground for the shareholders of this company to have arrived at the view that it is not worth while proceeding with the company. Under the circumstances, they ask for relief from the court to wind up this company. As a matter of fact, nothing has been done yet by the company to acquire the rights which they had in view, and no steps have been taken in respect of incurring any debts so far as is known, except the debts which have been incurred, if there be any, to Mr Stern himself. Notwithstanding that, an end can only be put to the company by voluntary winding up or by the interposition of the court. Now the aid of the court is sought in this matter, and I think the company is entitled to it.

[41] *Re* Baku Consolidated Oilfields Ltd
[1944] 1 All ER 24

BENNETT J: This is a petition [for compulsory winding-up] by two gentlemen who are the holders of fully-paid shares in the company, on the ground, *inter alia*, that the company has ceased to carry on its business since 1920; and that the whole substratum of the company is gone. . . .

It appears from art 4 of the memorandum of association that the purpose of the company was to acquire the undertakings of four separate limited companies, carrying on the business of getting and selling oil in or near Baku. Agreements were entered into by the Baku Consolidated Oilfields Ltd with these four companies then carrying on business in or near Baku. . . .

Shortly after the respondent company was formed, the undertakings and businesses of the four companies were confiscated. It seems pretty clear that, in no true sense of the word did the Baku Consolidated Oilfields Ltd carry on any business at all. . . .

In my judgment, it is clear on the facts that the purpose for which this company was originally formed has gone. It can never carry on the business it was formed to carry on, that of consolidating the undertakings of these four oil-producing companies at Baku and selling the oil. . . . It also seems to me to be clear that the majority of the shareholders have no right to compel a minority to embark upon any other undertaking.

[Order granted.]

NOTES

See further *In re German Date Coffee Company* (1882) 20 ChD 169, esp at 187, 188. But see also *Taldua Rubber Co Ltd* [1946] 2 All ER 763.

(*d*) *Donations, Pension Schemes, etc*

A TEXT

The common powers of companies set out in Schedule 2 to the Act include powers to make donations ('o') and to pay gratuities and establish pension schemes, profit sharing plans and other incentive schemes in respect of directors, officers and employees ('r'). For internal purposes the exercise of these powers remains presumably subject to the limitation that the donation, gratuity or pension scheme must be in the interests of the company: *42–45.*

B CASES

[42] Cyclists' Touring Club *v* Hopkinson
[1910] 1 Ch 179

Clause 4 of the memorandum of association of the Cyclists' Touring Club provided as follows:

'The income and property of the club, whencesoever derived, shall be applied solely towards the promotion of the objects of the club as set forth in this memorandum of association, and no portion thereof shall be paid or transferred directly or indirectly by way of dividend, bonus, or otherwise howsoever by way of profit to the members of the club.

'Provided that nothing herein contained shall prevent the payment in good faith of remuneration to any officers or servants of the club, or to any member of the club or other person in return for any services actually rendered to the club.'

The court had to decide whether the grant of a pension by way of gratuity to a retired secretary was *intra vires.*

SWINFEN EADY J: In my opinion, in promoting the objects of a club such as the present one, it is most desirable to encourage faithful service amongst the officers and servants. This is a club with some 20 000 members, and it must obviously rely in great measure upon the services of its employees. It is of as much importance to a club as to a trading company to be able to hold out such inducement to officers and servants as will secure the best assistance. . . .

. . . The payment to a retired servant of the club by way of an annuity, or by way of pension, or by way of gratuity, is within the powers of the club as being a payment in furtherance of the best objects of the club. The fact that the payment is made by way of gratuity and not under any legal liability does not make it a payment outside the objects of the club. . . .

[43] *In re* Lee, Behrens & Company Limited
[1932] 2 Ch 46

EVE J: Lee, Behrens & Co Ltd was incorporated in January 1909 and went into voluntary liquidation on 10 March 1931. The applicant,

Mrs Gertrude Elizabeth Southerden, lodged a proof in the winding-up
for the sum of 8 000*l*, the capitalized value of an annuity of 500*l* per
annum, alleged to be payable to her by virtue of a deed of covenant dated
29 June 1928. . . . The liquidator rejected the claim on the grounds: (1)
That the contract to pay the annuity was *ultra vires* of the company and
void; (2) alternatively, that the contract could only be authorized by a
meeting of the shareholders duly convened for that purpose, and there
was no such meeting ever convened or held; and (3) that the annuity was
a mere gratuity which it was *ultra vires* of the company to pay otherwise
than out of profits, and that since June 1928 there have not been, and
there never will be, any profits out of which to pay it. The company is
insolvent.

It is not contended, nor in the face of a number of authorities to the
contrary effect could it be, that an arrangement of this nature for reward-
ing long and faithful service on the part of persons employed by the
company is not within the power of an ordinary trading company such
as this company was, and indeed in the company's memorandum of
association is contained . . . an express power to provide for the welfare
of persons in the employment of the company or formerly in its employment, and the widows and children of such persons and others dependent
upon them by granting money or pensions, providing schools, reading
rooms or places of recreation, subscribing to sick or benefit clubs or
societies or otherwise as the company may think fit.

But whether they be made under an express or implied power, all such
grants involve an expenditure of the company's money, and that money
can only be spent for purposes reasonably incidental to the carrying on of
the company's business, and the validity of such grants is to be tested, as
is shown in all the authorities, by the answers to three pertinent questions:
(i) Is the transaction reasonably incidental to the carrying on of the
company's business? (ii) Is it a bona fide transaction? and (iii) Is it
done for the benefit and to promote the prosperity of the company?

In the present case the court is left entirely without any material for
determining whether the transaction was characterized by any of these
several attributes. Assuming, as I am quite prepared to do, that there are
no grounds for impugning the bona fides of the Board or the applicant,
no one of them has given evidence to suggest that the course adopted was
taken for the benefit or to promote the prosperity of the company or that
the execution of the deed of covenant and the assumption of so burdensome a liability was reasonably incidental to the carrying on of the company's business. . . .

The conclusion to which in my opinion such evidence as is available
irresistibly points is that the predominant, if not the only, consideration
operating in the minds of the directors, was a desire to provide for the
applicant, and that the question what, if any, benefit would accrue to the
company never presented itself to their minds. . . .

If there were nothing more in the case than what I have just indicated,
I should feel myself bound in the circumstances to support the liquidator's
rejection of this lady's proof.

But there is another and perhaps more insurmountable difficulty with
which she is faced, and it is this, that this annuity is a gift or reward

given out of the company's assets by the directors to one of their own body, and this is something they cannot do unless authorized by the instrument which regulates the company or by the shareholders at a properly convened meeting—that is, a meeting convened by a notice disclosing the intention to make the proposal.

[44] Evans v Brunner, Mond & Company Ltd
[1921] 1 Ch 359

The principal object of the company was carrying on business as a chemical manufacturer. There were various ancillary objects, concluding with one, whereby the company was enabled to do 'all such business and things as may be incidental or conducive to the attainment of the above objects'. A meeting of the company authorized the directors to distribute to such universities or other scientific institutions in the United Kingdom as they might select for the furtherance of scientific education and research, the sum of £100 000. A shareholder asked the court for a declaration that this resolution was *ultra vires*.

EVE J: You cannot pick out one of the objects enumerated under the letters (*a*) to (*r*) of para 3, and having determined the particular act to be incidental or conducive to that object thereupon decide that the act is *intra vires*. The wide and general objects are to be construed as ancillary to the company's main purpose, and I apprehend that the act to be *intra vires* must be one which can fairly be regarded as incidental or conducive to the main or paramount purpose for which the company was formed. It is on these principles I propose to consider the questions raised upon this motion. It is beyond dispute that the paramount object for which this company was incorporated was the carrying on in all its branches of the trade or business of chemical manufacturers, and in order that any particular application of its funds can be justified under clause (*s*) it is essential that it should be established that it is an application incidental or conducive to the business of chemical manufacturers. . . .

It appears from the evidence of the chairman of the company, supported by the evidence of all the other directors, that the company is not aiming by this contribution at securing the education of scientific men as specialists in its business. What it desires is to encourage and assist men who will cultivate the scientific attitude of mind, and be prepared to devote their time and abilities to scientific study and research generally. According to the evidence that is the class of men for whom the company is constantly looking out, a class of men of which the supply is very inadequate but who when obtainable are readily capable of adapting themselves to the investigation, research and scientific work of the company. It is not intended to impose on the universities and other institutions who may benefit under this grant any obligation to train men as specialists in the particular scientific work which the company undertakes. What is desired is to offer attractions to those who are prepared to take up science and to cultivate the scientific mind and scientific habits, and thereby to establish what one of the deponents speaks of as 'a reservoir of trained experts' from which the company will be able to select the right men to instruct in the particular branches of scientific investigation necessary for the purpose of the company. The evidence establishes this much, that the company is in constant need of a reserve of scientifically trained men for the purpose of its business — that the business cannot be maintained if the supply of such men is deficient — that a deficiency is almost inevitable unless substantial inducements are forthcoming to attract men to scientific study and research — that the best agencies for directing these studies are the well-equipped universities and scientific institutions, and that the interest of the company does not require that the education and training should necessarily be confined to scientific work of the nature of that in which the company is solely interested. These considerations dispose, I think, of the objection raised to the wide and general nature of the reference in the resolution to scientific education and research; it is not intended to limit the application of the money to the special branches of science affecting the company's business but to promote the training and education calculated to produce the class of men qualified to assist in maintaining the company's business. . . .

. . . On the evidence I think that the company . . . has proved that the proposed expenditure will not only be to the direct advantage of the company but is also conducive to, and indeed necessary for, its continued progress as chemical manufacturers.

[Order refused.]

[See C W de Kiewiet 'Industry's Obligations to University Education' *Optima* December 1962 p 187:

'It is of capital importance to recognize that many business leaders in America no longer support higher education out of charity, or a spirit of good citizenship. They tend increasingly to support university education because it is sound business practice to do so. . . .

'Today most competent academic and business economists accept the generalization that three forms of investment were the motive forces behind the great expansion of commerce and industry: they were money investment, labour and education. . . . Education is a form of capital which commerce and industry must have to prosper. . . .']

[45] Herald Company *v* Seawell
472 F 2d 1081 (1972)

This was a shareholders' derivative action filed on behalf of a newspaper publishing corporation by a minority shareholder against its officers for misconduct, breach of trust, and misuse of corporate assets, in that they had purchased at an exorbitant price stock of the company for an employee stock trust plan. The plaintiff succeeded in the trial court. On appeal the United States Court of Appeals, Tenth Circuit, reversed and remanded with directions to dismiss the action. Holding that the evidence did not sustain the finding that the purchase price paid by the corporation for its own stock had been exorbitant, Hill J said (at 1091):

'We are fully cognizant of the well established corporate rule of law which places corporate officers and directors in the position of fiduciaries for the stockholders. Basic in that rule of law is the profit motive of the corporate entity. In this case we have a corporation engaged chiefly in the publication of a large metropolitan newspaper, whose obligation and duty is something more than the making · of corporation profits. Its obligation is threefold: to the stockholders, to the employees, and to the public.'

NOTES

Anonymous, commenting on *Herald Company* v *Seawell*, remarks ((1973) 121 *U of Penn LR* 1157 at 1166):

'Despite its broad dicta, much of the language of the opinion supports a narrower reading: that director responsibility in operational decision making is necessary and justified only in the newspaper business. The importance of a vital and responsible "fourth estate" might have been a primary, though unspoken, concern of the court. . . .'

In *Hutton* v *West Cork Railway Co* (1883) 23 ChD 654 Bowen LJ put the principles governing charity by companies thus: 'Most businesses require liberal dealings. The test is not whether it is bona fide, but whether as well as being done bona fide, it is done within the ordinary scope of the company's business, and whether it is reasonably incidental to the carrying on of the company's business for the company's benefit. Take this sort of instance. A railway company, or the directors of the company, might send down all the porters at a railway station to have tea in the country at the expense of the company. Why should they not? It is for the directors to judge, provided it is a matter which is reasonably incidental to the carrying on of the business of the company, and a company which always treated its employees with Draconian severity, and never allowed them a single inch more than the strict letter of the bond, would soon find itself deserted – at all events, unless labour was very much more easy to obtain in the market than it often is. The law does not say that there are to be no cakes and ale, but there are to be no cakes and ale except such as are required for the benefit of the company. . . . Charity has no business to sit at boards of directors *qua* charity. There is, however, a kind of charitable dealing which is for the interest of those who practise it, and to that extent and in that garb (I admit not a very philanthropic garb) charity may sit at the board, but for no other purpose.' (See also *Henderson* v *Bank of Australasia* (1889) 40 ChD 170.)

Similarly, De Vos J in *Amalgamated Society of Woodworkers of SA* v *Die 1963 Ambagsaalvereniging* 1967 (1) SA 586 (T) at 594: '[I]t seems to me that the power of a corporate body . . . to donate a major asset cannot be lightly inferred. In my view, the words "dispose of" in the phrase quoted do not include "donate". But even if I err in this, it seems to me that donations should, in any event, to the extent that the power to donate might be read into the empowering clause, be limited to such donations as are reasonably incidental to the carrying on of the activities of the donor or which are for the benefit of the donor.' (For the sequel, see 1968 (1) SA 283 (T).)

On pension schemes, more especially, see, further, *Ex parte Frasers Ltd* 1937 OPD 34; *Ex parte American Swiss Watch Co Ltd* 1944 CPD 62; *Ex parte Woolworths (Pty) Ltd* 1946 CPD 186.

Re Lee, Behrens & Co Ltd was applied in *Re W & M Roith Ltd* [1967] 1 All ER 427, [1967] 1 WLR 432, where a service agreement with a director providing for a pension to his widow was held to have been *ultra vires* the company because it was on the facts not reasonably incidental to the company's business nor entered into bona fide for the benefit of the company. In *Hall Parke* v *Daily News Ltd* [1961] 1 All ER 695, [1962] Ch 927, [1962] 2 All ER 929 (noted (1962) 25 *MLR* 715, (1962) *Cambridge LJ* 141) a company, which had sold the two newspapers which constituted the major part of its business, proposed to apply most of the purchase price of nearly £2 000 000 in the payment of pensions and other retirement benefits to employees about to become redundant. In holding that the scheme was *ultra vires* and incapable of ratification by the shareholders, Plowman J said ([1962] 1 Ch at 963): 'the defendants were prompted by motives which, however laudable, and however enlightened from the point of view of industrial relations, were such as the law does not recognise as a sufficient justification. Stripped of all its side issues, the essence of the matter is this, that the directors of the defendant company are proposing that a very large part of its funds should be given to its former employees in order to benefit those employees rather than the company, and that is an application of the company's funds which the law, as I understand it, will not allow.'

On the whole subject, see also H R Hahlo 'Benefactions by Companies' (1967) 84 *SALJ* 260; Bert S Prunty 'Love and the Business Corporation' (1960) 46 *Virginia LR* 467; R C Beuthin 1967 *Annual Survey* 216–18; 'The Range of a Company's Interests' (1969) 86 *SALJ* 155.

II The Articles of Association

(a) Registration

A TEXT

The articles of association contain regulations for the internal affairs of the company. A public company may adopt all or any of the articles contained in Table A of Schedule 1; a private company may adopt all or any of the articles contained in Table B of Schedule 1, s 59(2). Every private company must adopt the restrictions in s 20(1). In so far as its provisions are not excluded or modified, Table A in Schedule 1 applies to public, Table B to private companies.

Articles may not contravene the Companies Act or any other statutory or common-law rule, and are subordinate to the memorandum: *46, 47*.

B CASES

[46] *In re* Peveril Gold Mines Ltd
[1898] 1 Ch 122

The Court of Appeal, affirming the decision of the court of first instance, held that the right given by the Companies Act to a contributory to petition for the winding-up of the company cannot be excluded or limited by the articles of association of the company.

CHITTY LJ: . . . We have not now to consider whether an individual shareholder can or cannot bind himself not to petition for the winding-up of the company, nor generally how far the provisions of the Act may be modified by the articles of association. In my opinion, this condition is annexed to the incorporation of a company with limited liability—that the company may be wound up under the circumstances, and at the instance of the persons, prescribed by the Act, and the articles of association cannot validly provide that the shareholders, who are entitled . . . to petition for a winding-up, shall not do so except on certain conditions. . . .

[47] Guinness *v* Land Corporation of Ireland Ltd
(1822) 22 ChD 349

COTTON LJ: . . . Now the articles cannot in my opinion alter or vary that which would be the result of the memorandum standing alone. A special resolution cannot alter the memorandum in any way, and in my opinion (though the case may be different where, as may sometimes happen, the memorandum introduces something which the Act does not require to be stated in it), that which is required by the Act to be provided for, and is provided for in the memorandum can no more be altered by the articles than by a special resolution. . . .

NOTES

See further *Welton v Saffery* [1897] AC 299 (a company cannot, by its memorandum of association, give itself the right to issue shares at a discount); *Payne v Cork Co Ltd* [1900] 1 Ch 308; *Bisgood v Henderson's Transvaal Estate Ltd* [1908] 1 Ch 743, esp at 758–63; *In re Greene* [1949] Ch 333, [1949] 1 All ER 167; *Angostura Bitters Ltd v Kerr* [1933] AC 550 (PC); *R v Alexander* 1935 (2) PH H172 (W) (the appeal of the accused before the Appellate Division succeeded, but on another ground—see 1936 AD 445); *Rosslare (Pty) Ltd v Registrar of Companies* 1972 (2) SA 524 (D); *Quadrangle Investments v Witind, 38* above. The articles may be used to clarify ambiguities in the memorandum, *Re Duncan Gilmour and Co Ltd* [1952] 2 All ER 871.

(b) *Effect of Articles as Between Company and Members*

A TEXT

Like the memorandum, the articles of association, when registered, bind the company and its members to the same extent as if they had been signed by each member, s 65(2): *48*. They constitute a contract between the company and its members, and regulate the rights of members *inter se*; non-members acquire no rights under the articles, and even a member cannot enforce provisions which do not concern him as a member: *49–52*.

Acts done in contravention of the articles are not covered by s 36. It follows that, subject to the operation of the 'unanimous consent' principle, they are not binding on the company. As the articles are registered, persons doing business with a company cannot be heard to say that they were unaware of the provisions of the articles.

An act which has been performed otherwise than in accordance with the articles can be ratified by the shareholders in general meeting or by that organ of the company which, in terms of the articles, has the authority to perform the act in question. In appropriate circumstances the act can also be ratified by the unanimous informal consent of the shareholders. Where the act is forbidden by the articles a special resolution is required, *Quadrangle Investments (Pty) Ltd v Witind Holdings Ltd, 34* above, but it seems possible that even in this situation ratification can be effected informally by unanimous consent: *Gohlke and Schneider v Westies, 190* below.

B CASES

[48] **Malleson *v* National Insurance and Guarantee Corporation**
[1894] 1 Ch 200

NORTH J: . . . Section 16, providing that the articles shall bind the members as if each member had affixed his seal, means the articles as originally framed, or as they may from time to time stand after they have been altered or varied under the provisions of this Act. . . .

[49] Eley v Positive Government Security Life Assurance Company Ltd
(1876) 1 ExD 88

Clause 118 of the articles of association of the defendant company provided that the plaintiff should be solicitor to the company, and that he should transact all the legal business of the company, for the usual fees and charges. The plaintiff acted as solicitor to the company for some time, but ultimately the company ceased to employ him. . . . The plaintiff brought an action against the company for breach of contract.

LORD CAIRNS LC: . . . Articles of association, as is well known, follow the memorandum, which states the objects of the company, while the articles state the arrangement between the members. They are an agreement *inter socios*, and in that view, if the introductory words are applied to article 118, it becomes a covenant between the parties to it that they will employ the plaintiff. Now, so far as that is concerned, it is *res inter alios acta*, the plaintiff is no party to it. No doubt he thought that by inserting it he was making his employment safe as against the company; but his relying on that view of the law does not alter the legal effect of the articles. This article is either a stipulation which would bind the members, or else a mandate to the directors. In either case it is a matter between the directors and shareholders, and not between them and the plaintiff.

[The judgment of the lower court dismissing the action was confirmed.]

[50] Welton v Saffery
[1897] AC 299

LORD HERSCHELL: . . . It is quite true that the articles constitute a contract between each member and the company, and that there is no contract in terms between the individual members of the company; but the articles do not any the less, in my opinion, regulate their rights *inter se*. Such rights can only be enforced by or against a member through the company, or through the liquidators representing the company. . . .

[51] Hickman v Kent or Romney Marsh Sheep-breeders' Association
[1915] 1 Ch 881

ASTBURY J: . . . I think this much is clear, first, that no article can constitute a contract between the company and a third person; secondly, that no right merely purporting to be given by an article to a person, whether a member or not, in a capacity other than that of a member, as, for instance, as solicitor, promoter, director, can be enforced against the company; and, thirdly, that articles regulating the rights and obligations of the members generally as such do create rights and obligations between them and the company respectively. . . .

[52] Rayfield v Hands
[1960] 1 Ch 1, [1958] 2 All ER 194

The plaintiff was the registered holder of 725 fully paid shares of £1 each in the capital of a company named Field-Davis Ltd. The defendants

were also members of the company as well as its sole directors. The articles
of the company provided as follows:

'(6) No shares in the company shall be transferred to a person not
a member of the company so long as any member of the company may
be willing to purchase such shares at a fair value.'

'(9) The directors may at any time in their absolute discretion
refuse to register any transfer of shares.'

'(11) Every member who intends to transfer shares shall inform
the directors who will take the said shares equally between them at a
fair value.'

The plaintiff called upon the directors to take his shares at fair value.
They refused to do so.

VAISEY J: It is art 11 with which I am mainly concerned in the
present case, in the following circumstances. On or about 4 April 1955
the plaintiff, by a notice in writing bearing that date, informed the defendants as the directors of the company of his intention to transfer his
shares to them as provided by art 11. The defendants were and are, however, unwilling and contend that they are not liable to take and pay for the
plaintiff's shares. They say that art 11 imposes no enforceable liability on
them, and they base their contention first on the wording of art 11 itself,
arguing that on its true construction it does not purport to impose any
liability on the company's directors. It is admitted that the words 'every
member . . . shall inform' the directors does create an obligation but it is
argued by the defendants that the words 'the directors . . . will take
the shares' imports in some way the idea of an option or choice or volition
on the part of the directors having regard to the inherent difference (not
always observed) in the English language between the words 'shall' and
'will'.

I appreciate the force of that argument, but I cannot accept it. In this
context, while the word 'shall' clearly imports compulsion and obligation,
the word 'will' indicates as it seems to me a resultant prospective eventuality, in which the member has to sell his shares and the directors have
to buy them, each being under an obligation to bring that eventuality into
effect. There is thus in the language of art 11 a mutual obligation.

The next and most difficult point taken by the defendants, as to which
it would appear that there is no very clear judicial authority, is that art 11,
as part of the company's articles of association, does not do what it looks
like doing, that is to create a contractual relationship between the plaintiff
as shareholder and vendor and the defendants as directors and purchasers.

Now the question arises at the outset whether the terms of art 11
relate to the rights of members *inter se* (that being the expression found in
so many of the cases), or whether the relationship is between a member
as such and directors as such. I may dispose of this point very briefly by
saying that in my judgment the relationship here is between the plaintiff
as a member and the defendants not as directors but as members.

On the whole, if the proper way to construe the articles of association
of a company is as a 'commercial' or 'business' document to which the
maxim 'validate if possible' applies, I think that the plaintiff in this
action ought to succeed. Not one of the judges in *Dean* v *Prince* [[1954]

Ch 409 (CA), [1954] 1 All ER 749] showed any signs of shock or surprise in the assumption there made of a contract between directors being formed by the terms of a company's articles. I am encouraged, not I hope unreasonably, to find in this case a contract similarly formed between a member and member-directors in relation to their holdings of the company's shares in its articles.

[*Rayfield* v *Hands* was noted by L C B Gower in (1958) 21 *MLR* 401 and 657, and by K W Wedderburn in (1958) *CLJ* 148.]

NOTES

See also *Gohlke Schneider* v *Westies Minerale (Edms) Bpk, 190* below, where Trollip JA, with reference to s 16 of the Companies Ordinance 19 of 1928 (SWA), which is in the same terms as s 65(2) of the present South African Act, said (at 692): As to the articles it will be immediately apparent that the section does not render them absolutely binding on the company and its members as though they were statutory enactments. . . . The company and its members are bound only to the same extent *as if* the articles had been signed by each member, that is, as if they had contracted in terms of the articles. The articles, therefore, merely have the same force as a contract between the company and each and every member as such to observe their provisions.' His Lordship then refers to *Hickman's* case, *51* above, and *De Villiers* v *Jacobsdal Saltworks (Michaelis and De Villiers) Pty Ltd* 1959 (3) SA 873 (O), *202* below, where Potgieter J said (at 876, 877): '. . . it is clear . . . that the articles of association of a company do not create a contract between the company and a member except in his capacity as a member. The articles constitute a contract between the members *inter se* and between the company and the members but only in their capacity as members. They do not for instance constitute a contract between the company and a director in his capacity as such.' The statements in these two cases were approved by Milne J in *Rosslare (Pty) Ltd* v *Registrar of Companies* 1972 (2) SA 524 (D) at 528 (*86* below).

Though the articles do not constitute a contract between the company and a third party, including a director, they can (*a*) be embodied in a contract between the company and a third party, e g a director (see below, p 347) or the company's attorney (*Isaacs Geshen & Co (Pty) Ltd* v *Ellis* 1964 (2) PH A59 (N)); or of some other official (*Gründling* v *Beyers* 1967 (2) SA 131 (W) at 139); (*b*) confer a power on a third party, e g to appoint a director of the company: *Woodlands Ltd* v *Logan* [1948] *New Zealand LR* 230; (*c*) serve as evidence of the terms upon which a director, auditor or third party serves the company: *Re City Equitable Fire Insurance Company Ltd* [1925] Ch 407 at 520–1.

In as far as the articles amount to a contract between the members *inter se*, e g by establishing a right of pre-emption in respect of shares, they may (despite the rule in *Foss* v *Harbottle*, p 534 below) be enforced by direct action between the members, Cilliers & Benade p 39, L C B Gower pp 262–3.

See further *Miller* v *Miller* 1963 (2) SA 199 (SR) at 201–2; *Rooibokoord Sitrus (Edms) Bpk* v *Louw's Creek Sitrus Koöperatiewe Maatskappy Bpk* 1964 (3) SA 601 (T) at 605.

A company can be compelled to act in accordance with, or restrained from acting contrary to, its articles: *Salmon* v *Quin & Axtens Limited* [1909] 1 Ch 311.

(c) Alteration

A TEXT

Articles of association may be altered by special resolution, s 62. The altered articles must not contain anything illegal, must not go outside the powers given by the memorandum of association and must not constitute a fraud on the minority, for though a company has almost unlimited power to alter its articles, this power must be exercised bona fide for the benefit of the company: *53*.

A company cannot, either by a statement in the articles or by a contract outside the articles, deprive itself of the power to alter its articles in the manner prescribed by the Act, but where an alteration of the articles is effected in breach of a contract outside the articles, the company will be liable for breach of contract: *53*. Special rules apply to the variation of class rights, pp 196ff below.

It would seem that the court has no jurisdiction to rectify articles of association, even though they do not accord with the intention of the signatories at the time when they were entered into (*Scott* v *Frank F Scott (London) Ltd* [1940] Ch 794, [1940] 3 All ER 508). It may, however, order alterations in the articles in relief of an oppressed minority under s 252.

B CASES

[53] **Allen** *v* **Gold Reefs of West Africa Ltd**
[1900] 1 Ch 656

Z held both fully paid-up shares and not fully paid-up shares in the company. Under its articles the company had a lien for all debts and liabilities of any member to the company 'upon all shares (not being fully paid) held by such member'. By special resolution, the company altered the article by omitting therefrom the words 'not being fully paid', thus creating a lien on Z's fully paid shares. It was held that the company had power to alter its articles by extending its lien to fully paid shares.

LINDLEY MR: The facts . . . raise the following very important questions, namely (1) Whether a limited company, registered with articles conferring no lien on its fully paid-up shares, can by special resolution alter those articles by imposing a lien on such shares? (2) Whether, if it can, the lien so imposed can be made to apply to debts owing by fully paid-up shareholders to the company at the time of the alteration of the articles? (3) Whether, if it can, fully paid-up shares allotted to vendors of property to the company are in any different position from other fully paid-up shares issued by the company? (4) Whether, assuming the altered articles to be valid and to be binding on the general body of the holders of fully paid-up shares in the company, there are any special circumstances in this particular case to exclude the fully paid-up shares held by Zuccani from the operation of the altered articles?

The articles of a company prescribe the regulations binding on its members: . . . They have the effect of a contract . . .; but the exact nature of this contract is even now very difficult to define. Be its nature what it may, the company is empowered by the statute to alter the regulations contained in its articles from time to time by special resolutions; and any regulation or article purporting to deprive the company of this power is invalid on the ground that it is contrary to the statute.

The power thus conferred on companies to alter the regulations contained in their articles is limited only by the provisions contained in the statute and the conditions contained in the company's memorandum of association. Wide, however, as the language of s 50 [now s 10 of the

United Kingdom Companies Act 1948 and s 62 of our Act] is, the power conferred by it must, like all other powers, be exercised subject to those general principles of law and equity which are applicable to all powers conferred on majorities and enabling them to bind minorities. It must be exercised, not only in the manner required by law, but also bona fide for the benefit of the company as a whole, and it must not be exceeded. These conditions are always implied, and are seldom, if ever, expressed. But if they are complied with I can discover no ground for judicially putting any other restrictions on the power conferred by the section than those contained in it. How shares shall be transferred, and whether the company shall have any lien on them, are clearly matters of regulation properly prescribed by a company's articles of association. . . . Speaking, therefore, generally, and without reference to any particular case, the section clearly authorizes a limited company, formed with articles which confer no lien on fully paid-up shares, and which allow them to be transferred without any fetter, to alter those articles by special resolution, and to impose a lien and restrictions on the registry of transfers of those shares by members indebted to the company.

But then comes the question whether this can be done so as to impose a lien or restriction in respect of a debt contracted before and existing at the time when the articles are altered. Again, speaking generally, I am of opinion that the articles can be so altered, and that, if they are altered bona fide for the benefit of the company, they will be valid and binding as altered on the existing holders of paid-up shares, whether such holders are indebted or not indebted to the company when the alteration is made.

The conclusion thus arrived at . . . is in conformity with such authorities as there are on the subject. *Andrews* v *Gas Meter Co* [[1897] 1 Ch 361] is an authority that . . . a company's articles can be altered so as to authorize the issue of preference shares taking priority over existing shares, although no power to issue preference shares was conferred by the memorandum of association or by the original articles. The answer to the argument that the company could not alter existing rights is that, within the limits set by the statute and the memorandum of association, the rights of shareholders in limited companies, so far as they depend only on the regulations of the company, are subject to alteration by s 50 of the Act. . . .

It was urged that a company's articles could not be altered retrospectively, and reliance was placed on Rigby LJ's observations in *James* v *Buena Ventura Nitrate Grounds Syndicate* [[1896] 1 Ch 466]. The word 'retrospective' is, however, somewhat ambiguous, and the concurrence of Rigby LJ in *Andrews* v *Gas Meter Co* shows that his observations in *James* v *Buena Ventura Nitrate Grounds Syndicate* are no authority for saying that existing rights, founded and dependent on alterable articles, cannot be affected by their alteration. Such rights are in truth limited as to their duration by the duration of the articles which confer them.

But, although the regulations contained in a company's articles of association are revocable by special resolution, a special contract may be made with the company in the terms of or embodying one or more of the articles, and the question will then arise whether an alteration of the articles so embodied is consistent or inconsistent with the real bargain between the parties. A company cannot break its contracts by altering its articles, but, when dealing with contracts referring to revocable articles, and especially with contracts between a member of the company and the company respecting his shares, care must be taken not to assume that the contract involves as one of its terms an article which is not to be altered. . . .

This brings me to the last question which has to be considered, namely, whether there is in this case any contract or other circumstance which excludes the application of the altered article to Zuccani's fully paid-up vendor's shares.

First, let us consider the shares. I am unable to discover any difference in principle between one fully paid-up share and another. Whether a share is paid for in cash or is given in payment for property acquired by the company appears to me quite immaterial for the present purpose. In either case the shareholder pays for his share, and in either case he takes it subject to the articles of association and power of altering them, unless this inference is excluded by special circumstances.

Next let us consider whether a vendor who makes no special bargain except that he is to be paid in fully paid-up shares is in any different position from other allottees of fully paid-up shares. I fail to see that he is, unless he stipulates that his shares shall be specially favoured. Zuccani bargained for fully paid-up shares and he got them. The imposition of a lien on them did not render them less fully paid-up than they were before. They remained what they were. Zuccani did not bargain that the regulations relating to paid-up shares should never be altered, or that, if altered, his shares should be treated differently from other fully paid-up shares. I cannot see that the company broke its bargain with him in any way by altering its regulations or by enforcing the altered regulations as it did.

NOTES

In *Southern Foundries (1926) Ltd* v *Shirlaw* [1940] AC 701, [1940] 2 All ER 445 (HL) Lord Porter put the principle thus: 'The general principle . . . may, I think, be thus stated. A company cannot be precluded from altering its articles thereby giving itself power to act upon the provisions of the altered articles—but so to act may nevertheless be a breach of contract if it is contrary to a stipulation in a contract validly made before the alteration.'

'Nor can an injunction be granted to prevent the adoption of the new articles and in that sense they are binding on all and sundry, but for the company to act upon them will none the less render it liable in damages if such action is contrary to the previous engagements of the company. . . .'

In *Andrews* v *Gas Meter Co* [1897] 1 Ch 361, the Court of Appeal held that a company which has no authority under its memorandum or articles to create any preference between different classes of shares may by special resolution alter its articles so as to authorize it to issue preference shares. Lord Lindley LJ stated (at 368–9):

'. . . So far as the constitution depended on the articles, it clearly could be altered by special resolution under the powers conferred by . . . the [Companies] Act. A company cannot deprive itself of this power. . . . If the memorandum of association really prescribed equality amongst all the shareholders . . . the articles of association could not override the memorandum of association in that particular. . . . [But although under the provisions of the Act] the memorandum is to state the amount of the original capital and the number of shares into which it is to be divided, yet in other respects the rights of the shareholders in respect of their shares and the terms on which additional capital may be raised are matters to be regulated by the articles of association rather than by the memorandum, and are, therefore, matters which (unless provided for by the memorandum . . .) may be determined by the company from time to time by special resolution. . . .'

See, further, *Shuttleworth* v *Cox Brothers and Co, 210* below; *De Villiers* v *Jacobsdal Saltworks, 202* below; further, *Walker* v *London Tramways Co* (1879) 12 ChD 705; *Malleson* v *National Insurance and Guarantee Corporation* [1894] 1 ChD 200; *Punt* v *Symons & Co Ltd* [1903] 2 Ch 506; *Bishop* v *Nannuci* (1908) 25 SC 464 (*312* below); *Ex parte Huguenot Carriage Works and Timber Mills Ltd* 1921 CPD 491; *Levin* v *Felt and Tweeds Ltd* 1951 (2) SA 401 (AD). By altering its articles, a company cannot deprive non-consenting shareholders or third parties retrospectively of rights already accrued to them: *Bradford Banking Co Ltd* v *Henry Briggs, Son & Co Ltd* (1886) 12 App Cas 29; *In re North West Argentine Railway Co* [1900] 2 Ch 882.

The question whether and when an alteration of the articles amounts to a breach of contract has proved itself of special importance when the terms of employment of a director are changed or he is dismissed from office (see below, p 354).

That a company cannot preclude itself from altering its articles, is settled law. But can it make the alteration of its articles more difficult than the Act requires by insisting on a ninety per cent majority or unanimity for a special resolution altering its articles or, for that matter, any special resolution? In *Swerdlow* v *Cohen* 1977 (1) SA 178 (W) Botha J seems to have taken it for granted that the articles may require all resolutions to be passed by an increased majority, or unanimously, and this would presumably include special resolutions. See also the Canadian case of *Minister of National Revenue* v *Dworskin* 1967 [RSC] 223, where a clause in the articles providing that all motions put before any meeting of shareholders or directors of the company should require the unanimous consent of all its members was upheld as being neither illegal nor *ultra vires*. On the other hand, an article reducing the majority required by the Act for a special resolution would clearly be invalid.

It will be remembered that if a special resolution is inserted in the memorandum, the memorandum may prescribe in what manner it may be altered, p 69 above.

4   *Promoters and Prospectuses*

I PROMOTERS

A TEXT

A promoter is one who takes it upon himself to bring a company into existence: *54*. (Cf s 142 s v 'Promoter'.)

Failing an undertaking to the contrary, a promoter is not personally liable to prospective shareholders if his efforts to 'float' the company come to naught: *55, 56*. Whether expenses incurred in connection with the attempted promotion have to be borne by him depends upon the facts: *57*.

A promoter stands in a fiduciary relationship to the company which he floats. He may make profits for himself but must fully disclose them to the company: *58–60*. (See also s 423. On disclosure in the prospectus, see Schedule 3, paras 13 and 17; also paras 10, 11, 12, 16 and 26.)

As to the liability of promoters for omissions or untrue statements in a prospectus, see below, p 113.

B CASES

[54] **Twycross *v* Grant**
(1877) 2 CPD 469

COCKBURN CJ: . . . A promoter, I apprehend, is one who undertakes to form a company with reference to a given project and to set it going, and who takes the necessary steps to accomplish that purpose. That the defendants were the promoters of the company from the beginning can admit of no doubt. They framed the scheme; they not only provisionally formed the company, but were, in fact, to the end its creators; they found the directors, and qualified them; they prepared the prospectus; they paid for printing and advertising, and the expenses incidental to bringing the undertaking before the world. In all these respects the directors were passive; without saying that they were in a legal sense the agents of the defendants, they were certainly their instruments. All the things I have just referred to were done with a. view to the formation of the company, and so long as the work of formation continues, those who carry on that work must, I think, retain the character of promoters. Of course, if a governing body, in the shape of directors, has once been formed, and they take, as I need not say they may, what remains to be done in the way of forming the company, into their own hands, the functions of the promoter are at an end. . . .

NOTES

See, also, *The Emma Silver Mining Company Ltd* v *Lewis & Son* (1879) 4 CPD 396, per Lindley J: 'As used in connection with companies the term "promoter" involves the idea of exertion for the purpose of getting up and starting a company (or what is called "floating" it) and also the idea of some duty towards the company imposed by or arising from the position which the so-called promoter assumes towards it.'

[55] Mayhew *v* Maynard
(1890) 3 SAR 193

KOTZÉ CJ: This is an appeal from the judgment of Esselen J, sitting in the Circuit Court at Johannesburg. In the court below a certain John Mayhew sued the defendants Maynard, Wrey, Farrell, Knox, and George Brown 'both in their capacity as directors of the Crocodile Gold Mining and Prospecting Company Ltd, and in their private capacity', for the sum of £858. The summons alleges that the plaintiff Mayhew is entitled, by virtue of three provisional certificates issued to him, to 858 fully paid-up £1 shares in the Crocodile Company; that the provisional certificates were given to the plaintiff on 4 May 1888, but that owing to the negligence of the said directors the company was not floated and established, in consequence of which the plaintiff suffered damage to the extent of £858. The defendants deny that the failure to float the company is attributable to any negligence on the part of the directors, and they plead further that they were under no obligation to float the company if they were of opinion that the prospects did not justify such flotation. They also deny that the plaintiff has suffered any damage. . . . Now the certificates in question merely award 858 shares to the plaintiff provisionally in the Crocodile Company for what they may be worth, but they do not guarantee that the company has been established, or that the whole amount of capital has been subscribed according to the prospectus, or that the company will in any case issue scrip to the plaintiff on these provisional certificates. Everything was in embryo, and if the provisional directors deemed fit to resolve to abandon the formation of the proposed company because the whole capital had not been subscribed and the prospects of the property in their opinion were bad, it does not follow that they were in any way bound to compensate the plaintiff. The plaintiff has not shown that he gave the defendants, either as directors of the Crocodile Company or in their private capacity, any money or other consideration for the provisional certificates, and even if this were so, he does not sue for the return of his money with interest, but for damages suffered owing to the alleged negligence on the part of the defendants because they did not properly float the company. Such an obligation, in the absence of further evidence, does not arise between the parties on the provisional certificates on which the action is based. The contract to float a company, dated 23 September 1887, binds the defendants neither in their capacity as directors of the Crocodile Company nor in their private capacity. . . .

[The action failed.]

[56] Scott v Poupard
1971 (2) SA 373 (AD)

HOLMES JA: On 13 July 1967 Poupard acquired from the Government of Mauritius the right to prospect for minerals 'in or under any land in the Colony of Mauritius and its Dependencies'. The grant was valid for a year, subject to renewal. The grant was subject, *inter alia*, to the condition that within six months he should enter into a contract with a competent person, company, partnership or syndicate for the carrying out of the prospecting. The document emphasized that the right to mine should be the subject of separate negotiations at some appropriate time. Poupard came to Johannesburg to discuss the matter with Lobel. His main concern was to find a mining company which would undertake the prospecting and eventually the mining operations. The two men entered into an agreement of partnership on 10 November 1967, in terms of which they would share equally in the sale of the prospecting rights and ultimately the mining rights.

On 9 April 1968 Poupard entered into a written contract with Scott and Du Preez, who were to form a company. The contract ceded to them Poupard's right to prospect for minerals, and it provided that, upon the grant to the company by the Mauritian Government of the right to mine for minerals (on terms which I shall discuss later), certain shares in the company were to be transferred into the name of Poupard and Lobel, and each of them was to be paid £100 000 sterling.

On the day after the signing of the contract in Johannesburg, most of the party went to Mauritius, that is to say, Scott, and his secretary Colonel Johnstone, and Poupard and Lobel. On the following day Scott called on the Prime Minister of Mauritius and put forward in detail the basis on which he would form a company with an authorized capital of fifteen million rupees (about R2 000 000). The discussion was confirmed in a very full letter by Scott to the Prime Minister on 16 April 1968, which formally requested that the company to be formed be granted the exclusive right to prospect and mine for all minerals in Mauritius and its Dependencies.

On 19 April 1968 (the day on which the party was due to return to Johannesburg) the appropriate Minister replied favourably in a Letter of Intent

'which will in due course be superseded by a formal contract between your company and the Government of Mauritius'.

Paragraph 3 of the letter stated that the Government agreed to grant exclusive rights to prospect and mine for all minerals. The terms and conditions were then set out in considerable detail in the paragraph. . . .

Meantime, Col Johnstone was busy in the matter of the formation of the company. And early in May 1968 Scott went to Europe. Johnstone told Poupard that this was in connection with the Mauritian venture. Johnstone also wrote to Poupard saying that there was no obstruction in the way of reaching final agreement with the Government and forming a company.

Scott returned to Johannesburg on 16 May 1968. Abruptly, on 3 June 1968, Scott and Du Preez sent a cable to Poupard in Mauritius saying that they had decided to withdraw from all arrangements regarding mineral rights in Mauritius. Scott also wrote to the Minister of Industry and Commerce withdrawing his application for prospecting and mining concessions. This letter contained no explanation beyond the cryptic phrase, 'as a result of certain information received by us'.

The company was never formed.

Poupard and Lobel responded by suing Scott and Du Preez, averring a failure to perform their obligations under the contract, and/or a deliberate frustration of the fulfilment of the conditions upon which the payment of money and delivery of shares were to be made under the contract. The particulars averred were that they failed to procure the formation of the company, and/or to complete the negotiations with the Government of Mauritius for the right to mine. In the premises, they claimed that the conditions, upon the happening of which they would be entitled to money and shares under the contract, were deemed to have been fulfilled. Accordingly, relying on clause 2 of the contract, they each claimed, *inter alia*, £100 000. . . .

The trial court awarded [them this amount].

[After analysing the agreement between the parties Holmes JA arrived at the conclusion that, as a matter of interpretation, Scott and Du Preez had bound themselves to procure the formation of a company and to negotiate on behalf of that company with the Mauritian Government for a mining concession. He continued:]

I come now to the issue of fictional fulfilment of the condition upon the occurrence of which the money was to be paid and the shares transferred to Poupard and Lobel, ie to say, the grant of mining rights. The relevant principle had its origin in Roman law, was received into Roman-Dutch law, and was discussed by this court in *Gowan* v *Bowern* 1924 AD 550; *MacDuff & Co Ltd (in liquidation)* v *Johannesburg Consolidated Investment Co Ltd* 1924 AD 573; *Koenig* v *Johnson & Co Ltd* 1935 AD 262. In essence it is an equitable doctrine, based on the rule that a party cannot take advantage of his own default, to the loss or injury of another. The principle may be stated thus: Where a party to a contract, in breach of his duty, prevents the fulfilment of a condition upon the happening of which he would become bound in obligation and does so with the intention of frustrating it, the unfulfilled condition will be deemed to have been fulfilled against him.

. . . In the initial stages the condition in question depended for its fulfilment on the performance by Scott and Du Preez of their obligation to form a company and to conduct bona fide negotiations with the Government of Mauritius for mining rights. But breach of that term would not give rise to the specific claim here in issue, namely the cash sum of £100 000 sterling (ie R170 360). In the ultimate the fulfilment of the conditions depended upon a favourable decision by the Mauritian

Government. It is the fulfilment of that condition which the conduct of
Scott and Du Preez frustrated. In my view there is a preponderance of
probability, on the facts set out earlier herein, that the breaking off of
negotiations with the Mauritian Government by Scott and Du Preez
was intended to frustrate the condition precedent to their liability to
Poupard and Lobel: that it resulted in no mining rights being granted;
and that, but for such discontinuance of negotiation, mining rights, on
terms entirely acceptable to Scott and Du Preez, would have been granted
by the eager Government and sanctioned by the legislature. On the
arguments it was accepted that, if those were found to be the facts, and
if the other defences failed, the plaintiffs were entitled to succeed. It
follows that the award to each of them of the sum of R170 360 cannot be
disturbed.

NOTES

See further *Vogelman* v *Bantjies* (1890) 3 SAR 200. As to the right of a prospective
shareholder to rescind the contract to take shares if the company is not formed within a
reasonable time, see *Geddes* v *Kaiser Wilhelm Gold Mining Co* (1888) 6 SC 263.

[57] **De Drukpers Maatschappy** *v* **Oosthuizen**
1915 CPD 401

Action by the proprietors of *Ons Land* newspaper for the price of an
advertisement against the provisional directors of a projected company
(the 'Agricultural Fertiliser Co, Ltd') which was never formed. The
advertisement was inserted upon the order of one Fitzpatrick who acted
as 'secretary' for the intended company.

GARDINER J: . . . The principles which, in my opinion, should be
applied, were set forth by Pollock CB in *Reynell* v *Lewis* (1846) 15 M
and W 517, and the following conclusions may be drawn from his judgment. The mere fact that a person agrees to become a member of a
provisional committee of a proposed railway company—a provisional
director, as in the present case, would be in the same position as a provisional committeeman—does not render him liable for goods supplied
on the order of the solicitor or the secretary of the company, nor is he
necessarily rendered liable by allowing his name to appear on a prospectus as a provisional committeeman. Whether he is to be held liable
or not will depend upon the terms of the prospectus. If it merely states
that he is a provisional committeeman and nothing more, the fact
that his name is on the published prospectus will not render him liable.
If, however, the prospectus represents that a person named as solicitor
or as secretary of the company is not merely a person who is to act as
such when the company shall have been formed, but is a person already
appointed to act as solicitor or secretary of the persons who style themselves provisional committeemen, then the latter will be liable for such
business as is usually transacted by the solicitor or secretary of persons
who are forming a company. . . .

If the advertisement of the Agricultural Fertiliser Company had
been confined to stating who the directors and officials were to be, and
what would be the capital of the company, and the nature of its operations, the defendants would not have been liable for the actions of

Mr Fitzpatrick. But the advertisement went further. It disclosed that the defendants were not merely persons who would direct the company when formed, but that they were persons who were already actively engaged in operations which would ordinarily fall to the lot of the promoter, for according to the prospectus they had made inquiries and entered into a contract for the supply of offal. It held out Mr Fitzpatrick not as a gentleman who would be appointed as secretary but as one who had already assumed the duties of that office. Samples of fertilizers, it stated, 'manufactured under conditions under which the company's factory would be conducted, have been prepared by Dr Marloth, and these can be seen at the office of the company's secretary'. The prospectus was obtainable 'from the secretary'. There was no mention of anyone as promoter of the company, no statement that the preliminary expenses were being borne by the vendor, and I think that the plaintiff company was justified in assuming that the directors were promoting the company, that they had appointed Mr Fitzpatrick to act as their secretary for the purpose of such promotion, and that he was authorized to incur on their behalf such expenses as a person acting in that capacity would usually incur. . . . The legal position, in my opinion, is that the four defendants have rendered themselves liable because the form of advertisement sanctioned by them held out Fitzpatrick as their agent.

NOTES

Whether co-promoters or a promoting syndicate are partners depends upon the circumstances: *Hollis and Horn* v *Argus Company (Ltd)* (1890) 7 SC 326; *Con-Force Products, Ltd* v *Rosen* (1967) 64 DLR (2d) 63; *Keith Spicer Ltd* v *Mansell* [1970] 1 WLR 333 (CA).

See further *Guardian Insurance and Trust Co* v *Lovemore's Executors* (1887) 5 SC 205; *P J Joubert et alii* v *Voss Bros* (1893) Hertzog 202; *Walker and Jacobsohn* v *Norden* (1904) 14 CTR 995.

On promoters generally, see Joseph H Gross *Company Promoters* (1972), and (1970) 86 *LQR* 493.

[58] Erlanger *v* New Sombrero Phosphate Company
(1878) 3 App Cas 1218

LORD CAIRNS LC: My Lords, the appellants in this case complain of a decree of the Court of Appeal which has set aside a sale made to the Sombrero Company, of the island of Sombrero, and ordered a repayment and re-transfer by the appellants of large sums of money and shares which had passed to them from the company on the occasion of the sale. . . .

In my view which I take of the case, the facts of which it is necessary to remind your Lordships are in a very narrow compass. Sombrero is a small island in the West Indies, about a mile and a quarter long, in which are deposits or beds of phosphate of lime. It belongs to the Crown, and a lease was made of it for twenty-one years from March, 1865, at a rent of £1 000. This lease was assigned, in the first instance, to a company called the Old Sombrero Company, who paid £100 000 for it, taking it besides subject to a mortgage of £12 400. This company was wound up by the Court of Chancery, and in the winding-up the lease of the island came in 1871 to be sold. The appellants along with one Thomas Westall, a solicitor, thought well of the speculation, and wished to buy the lease, and for this purpose they formed what is called a syndicate or partnership, and ultimately, on 30 August 1871, did agree to buy the lease by private contract from the official liquidator for £55 000, the contract being made in the name of Westall on behalf of his principals.

My Lords, I stop at this point for the purpose of saying that I think it to be clear that the syndicate in entering into this contract acted on behalf of themselves alone, and did not at that time act in, or occupy, any fiduciary position whatever. It may well be that the prevailing idea in their mind was not to retain or work the island, but to sell it again at an increase of price, and very possibly, to promote or get up a company to purchase the island from them; but they were, as it seems to me, after their purchase was made, perfectly free to do with the island whatever they liked; to use it as they liked, and to sell it how, and to whom, and for what price they liked. The part of the case of the respondents which, as an alternative, sought to make the appellants account for the profit which they made on the resale of the property to the respondents, on an allegation that the appellants acted in a fiduciary position at the time they made the contract of 30 August 1871 is not, as I think, capable of being supported. . . .

I now proceed to state what happened subsequently to 30 August 1871.

Shortly before 20 September 1871 the syndicate determined to form a joint stock company, and to sell the island to the company for £110 000, and the syndicate took the necessary steps for this purpose; preparing the memorandum of association, and the articles, and also the prospectus which was to be issued.

The memorandum of association stated that the object of the company was the purchasing, leasing, and working of mines or quarries of phosphate of lime in the island of Sombrero. The articles stated that the number of directors should from time to time be determined by a general meeting, and that till any other number was determined there should be not less than four nor more than seven directors. Two directors should be a quorum for the transaction of business; and among the acts which the directors were empowered to do were the adoption and carrying into effect of the contract for the assignment to the company of the island of Sombrero. . . .

This contract was a contract by which John Marsh Evans agreed to sell, and Francis Pavy agreed to purchase, the lease of the island and the property on it for £110 000, £80 000 to be paid down, and £30 000 in fully paid-up shares of the new company. John Marsh Evans was a trustee or agent for Baron Erlanger and the other members of the syndicate, and Pavy was a person whose name was introduced into the contract as a matter of form, to represent the company about to be created, in case it should adopt the contract. The contract was, on the face of it, a provisional one, subject to the formation of the company, and the adoption of the contract by it.

In the whole of this proceeding up to this time the syndicate, or the house of Erlanger as representing the syndicate, were the promoters of the company, and it is now necessary that I should state to your

Lordships in what position I understand the promoters to be placed
with reference to the company which they proposed to form. They
stand, in my opinion, undoubtedly in a fiduciary position. They have
in their hands the creation and moulding of the company; they have
the power of defining how, and when, and in what shape, and under
what supervision, it shall start into existence and begin to act as a
trading corporation. If they are doing all this in order that the company
may, as soon as it starts into life, become, through its managing directors,
the purchaser of the property of themselves, the promoters, it is, in my
opinion, incumbent upon the promoters to take care that in forming the
company they provide it with an executive, that is to say, with a board
of directors, who shall be aware that the property which they are asked
to buy is the property of the promoters, and who shall be competent and
impartial judges as to whether the purchase ought or ought not to be
made. I do not say that the owner of property may not promote and
form a joint stock company, and then sell his property to it, but I do
say that if he does he is bound to take care that he sells it to the company
through the medium of a board of directors who can and do exercise an
independent and intelligent judgment on the transaction, and who are
not left under the belief that the property belongs, not to the promoter,
but to some other person. . . .

LORD SELBORNE: My Lords, the contract in this case was adopted
as the contract of the company (having been previously prepared for that
purpose by the vendors) through the machinery of a board of directors
of the vendors' own creation, who were so constituted as to be practically
incapable of exercising (and who did not, in fact, exercise) any independent judgment on the subject. All the documents were prepared by
the vendors' solicitor, who was also made solicitor to the company, and
who participated, to the extent of £500, in the vendors' profit. Of the
five directors named in the articles of association, two were absent from
this country, and were at that time practically incapable of acting; the
other three were present when the contract was adopted; but of these,
one was the nominal vendor, and the paid agent and trustee of the real
vendors; another was a mere instrument in the hands of the vendors,
qualified (contrary to the articles) by a loan of shares from Baron
Erlanger. The third was the Lord Mayor of London, and it seems only
fair to him to suppose that he was too much occupied with other duties
to be able to give much attention to this. The consideration for the sale
was £110 000 (partly in shares of the company), being twice as much as
the vendors had paid for the property a month before. Whether this was,
or was not, an excessive price to be asked from a company, is a question
into which I do not enter. If there had been an independent purchaser
and a real bargain, the vendors would have been at liberty to ask what
price they pleased; and if that purchaser had agreed to pay more than
the property was worth, he could not complain. But there was, in fact,
no such purchaser and no such bargain. The vendors themselves
managed the whole thing, and they made those who through their means
undertook a trust for others, their passive instruments. . . .

[The court accordingly held that the contract could be rescinded by
the company.]

[59] Gluckstein v Barnes
[1900] AC 240

EARL OF HALSBURY LC: My Lords, in this case the simple question is whether four persons, of whom the appellant is one, can be permitted to retain the sums which they have obtained from the company of which they were directors by the fraudulent pretence that they had paid £20 000 more than in truth they had paid for property which they, as a syndicate, had bought by subscription among themselves, and then sold to themselves as directors of the company. . . .

My Lords I am wholly unable to understand any claim that these directors, vendors, syndicates, associates, have to retain this money. I entirely agree with the Master of the Rolls that the essence of this scheme was to form a company. It was essential that this should be done, and that they should be directors of it, who would purchase. The company should have been informed of what was being done and consulted whether they would have allowed this profit. I think the Master of the Rolls is absolutely right in saying that the duty to disclose is imposed by the plainest dictates of common honesty as well as by well-settled principles of common law. . . .

My Lords, I decline to discuss the question of disclosure to the company. It is too absurd to suggest that a disclosure to the parties to this transaction is a disclosure to the company of which these directors were the proper guardians and trustees. They were there by the terms of the agreement to do the work of the syndicate, that is to say, to cheat the shareholders; and this, forsooth, is to be treated as a disclosure to the company, when they were really there to hoodwink the shareholders, and so far from protecting them, were to obtain from them the money, the produce of their nefarious plans. . . .

[60] *In re* Contributories Rosemount Gold Mining Syndicate
1905 TH 169

BRISTOWE J: . . . It is well established that promoters stand in a fiduciary relation to the company which they promote. They are not merely its parents, but they are its creditors. They fashion and mould it according to their will. They endow it with powers or limit its activities in any manner they think fit. And they cannot complain if the law makes them (as it does) the guardians and protectors of its infant life. The duties and obligations which this position of trust places upon promoters are (to use the words of Lindley MR in *Re Olympia Limited* [1898] 2 Ch 153 at 166), 'imposed by the plainest dictates of common honesty as well as by well-settled principles of company law'. They include the duty of not making a secret profit at the company's expense, and also (if they wish to enter into contracts with or make payments to themselves) to furnish it with a board of directors 'who can and do exercise an independent and intelligent judgment on the transaction' (see *Erlanger* v *New Sombrero Phosphate Company* (1878) 3 App Cas 1218 at 1236, per Lord Cairns). It was held in the *Erlanger* case that a contract for sale between the promoters and the company could not stand where the company's concurrence had been obtained by means of a board of directors who were merely the nominees and creatures of the promoters. It does not seem to me to make any difference whether the company is asked to buy property or to remunerate for services. In either case the promoters seek to obtain a payment for themselves out of the company's assets, and it is plain that they must furnish the company with a body of agents who can fairly and impartially consider whether such payment ought to be made or not. What was the position of the directors in this case? Bernard Scott himself was one of them, and the other five had all accepted promises of shares from the promoters. For nearly two months before the company was formed they had been holding (with two other persons who dropped out, and for one of whom Anderson was substituted). periodical meetings under the name of provisional directors. There was no objection to this (except that persons who call themselves provisional directors are liable to be misled into thinking that they have powers which they have not), if only they had devoted themselves to safeguarding and protecting the interests of the public who were to be asked to subscribe the whole cash capital of the company. But in fact they simply identified themselves with the nominal promoters, becoming, in all but name, promoters themselves. They sanctioned a prospectus which the promoters had prepared, and which was fraudulent because it represented that there were to be 5 000 promotion shares, whereas in fact there were to be 18 000. They took in common with the promoters their quota of paid-up shares; and not at one single meeting of either the provisional or the actual board was the issue of the paid-up shares sanctioned or even discussed. . . . In these circumstances it is idle to say that there was a bona fide issue by the company of fully paid shares in consideration of services rendered. In my opinion the whole proceeding was collusive and fraudulent. The promoters obtained their shares by means of a gross breach of fiduciary obligations, and those which the directors received they issued to themselves in nominal performance of a promise which was nothing but a bribe.

It may be said that the principles which I have enunciated bear hardly on promoters who render great services and undertake great liabilities, for which it is only fair that they should be remunerated. I agree that it is only fair. There is no objection whatever to promoters being remunerated, and the articles in the present case provide a method by which the promoters could have been remunerated had the funds of the company been sufficient for the purpose. The objection is not to the promoters being remunerated, but to their fixing their own remuneration and paying it out of the coffers of the company without giving it an opportunity of saying yea or nay. To take such remuneration as a proper board of directors after due deliberation has thought fit to award is one thing. To take it from the hands of a board whose discretion, through the contrivance of the promoters themselves, is paralysed and their wills held fast by corruption and self-interest, is a proceeding which morality and law alike combine to condemn. . . .

NOTES

See also Rugg J in *Old Dominion Copper Mining Smelting Co* v *Bigelow* Supreme Judicial Court of Massachusetts, 203 Mass 159 (1909), LRA NS 314, 89 NE 193: 'Notwithstanding [the] fiduciary relation the promoter may sell property to the company which he is promoting. But in order that the contract may be absolutely binding he must pursue one of four courses: (*a*) He may provide an independent board of officers in no respect directly or indirectly under his control, and make full disclosure to the corporation through them; (*b*) He may make a full disclosure of all material facts to each original subscriber of shares in the corporation; (*c*) He may procure a ratification of the contract after disclosing its circumstances by vote of the stockholders of the completely established corporation; (*d*) He may be himself the real subscriber of all the shares of the capital stock contemplated as a part of the promotion scheme.

'. . . The fiduciary relation must in reason continue until the promoter has completely established according to his plan the being which he has undertaken to create. His liability must be commensurate with the scheme of promotion on which he has embarked. If the plan contemplates merely the organization of the corporation his duties may end there. But if the scheme is more ambitious and includes beside the incorporation, not only the conveyance to it of property but the procurement of a working capital in cash from the public, then the obligation of faithfulness stretches to the length of the plan. It would be a vain thing for the law to say that the promoter is a trustee subject to all the stringent liabilities which inhere in that character and at the same time say that, at any period during his trusteeship and long before an essential part of it was executed or his general duty as such ended, he could, by changing for a moment the cloak of the promoter for that of director or stockholder, by his own act alone, absolve himself from all past, present or future liability in his capacity as promoter.' See also *In re Olympia Ltd* [1898] 2 Ch 153, where Lindley MR said (at 166): 'A promoter of a company, whose duty it is to disclose what profits he has made, does not perform that duty by making a statement not disclosing the facts, but containing something which, if followed up by further investigation, will enable the inquirer to ascertain that profits have been made and what they amounted to'; further *Atwool* v *Merryweather* (*325* below).

Directors who in league with the promoters allow the latter to make secret profits are jointly and severally liable for these profits: *Balmoral Diamond Syndicate Ltd (in liquidation)* v *Liddle, Smith, Leeb, Harger and Schuller* 1907 TH 89.

The principle laid down in *Erlanger* v *New Sombrero Phosphate Co* (*58*) does not apply where full disclosure has been made to all members (existing or potential) of the company or the company confirms the promoter's action with full knowledge of the facts: *Salomon* v *Salomon & Co* [1897] AC 22 at 33 and 37; *Lagunas Nitrate Co* v *Lagunas Syndicate* 1899] 2 Ch 392.

An agent of the promoter is also bound to exercise good faith towards the company. See Smith J in *Herzfelder* v *McArthur, Atkins & Co Ltd* 1908 TS 332 at 353: 'Just as a sub-agent is bound to exercise good faith towards the principal of the agent who directly employs him, so, as it seems to me, is the agent of a promoter bound to exercise good faith towards the company which his principal is to his knowledge forming. I see no distinction in principle as regards the matter between the agent of an agent and the agent of a promoter.'

In view of the detailed disclosure requirements of Schedule 3, cases such as *Erlanger* v *New Sombrero Phosphate Company, Gluckstein* v *Barnes*, and *In re Contributories Rosemount Gold Mining Syndicate* are unlikely to recur.

II PROSPECTUSES

(*a*) Offering Shares to the Public

A TEXT

A public company may offer its shares to the public, a private company may not (p 50 above). Shares of a foreign company which is not registered as an external company may not be offered to the public.

An offer to the public may take one of two forms: the shares may be offered to the public for subscription; or they may be allotted to a bank or issuing house which offers them to the public for sale. No offer for the subscription or sale of shares to the public may be made unless a prospectus is registered and issued. A prospectus is defined in the Act as 'any prospectus, notice, circular, advertisement or other invitation offering any shares of a company to the public', s 1 s v 'Prospectus'. For the purposes of chapter VI, entitled 'Offering of Shares and Prospectus', an 'offer to the public' means 'any offer to the public and includes an offer of shares to any section of the public, whether selected as members or debenture-holders of the company concerned or as clients of the person issuing the prospectus or in any other manner', s 142 s v 'offer to the public'. This covers an offer of shares through an issuing house or other intermediary. 'Company' for the purposes of chapter VI includes an external company, s 142.

Section 144 lays down that an offer of shares is not to be construed as an offer to the public (a) if it is not calculated to result, directly or indirectly, in the shares becoming available to persons other than those to whom the offer has been made; or (b) if it is an offer for subscription to members or debenture-holders without the right to renounce any right to take up the shares in favour of other persons; or (c) if the offer can properly be regarded as a domestic concern of the person making or receiving it; or (d) if it is a 'rights offer' as defined in s 142.

A prospectus is 'issued' when it is made public: 61, 62. 'Issued generally' means issued to persons who are not existing members or debenture-holders of the company, s 142 s v 'issued generally'. Before a prospectus may be issued, it must be registered as prescribed in s 145. No prospectus will be registered unless the requirements of ss 151–153, 155 (in so far as they are applicable) are satisfied. No prospectus may be issued more than three months after the date of its registration, s 156.

Every prospectus must contain a fair presentation of the affairs of the company and must at least state the matters specified in, and contain the reports referred to in, Schedule 3, s 148. No person may be named as a director unless his consent so to act has been lodged with the Registrar, s 150. Where the prospectus contains a statement by, or reference to a statement by, an expert it may not be registered unless the expert has given his consent, as provided in s 151. Copies of written contracts required to be stated in the prospectus must be attached to it, oral contracts must be set out in detail in a memorandum, s 152. Where the issue is underwritten the requirements of s 153 must be complied with.

A prospectus must be attached to any form of application for shares, failing which the contract of allotment is voidable at the instance of the allottee, ss 147, 166. A clause in a prospectus which requires applicants for shares or debentures to waive compliance with the statutory requirements is invalid, s 158.

Every advertisement offering or calling attention to an offer of shares, even if it states in so many words that it is not a prospectus, is deemed in law to be a prospectus unless it confines itself to the information set out in s 157.

Renounceable rights issues by listed companies do not require a prospectus. Instead, a 'letter of allocation' (ie a document conferring a right to subscribe for shares in terms of a 'rights offer', s 142 sv 'letter of allocation' and 'rights offer') must be lodged with the Registrar, s 146A. It must be accompanied by the documents required and approved by the stock exchange concerned. No letter of allocation may be issued, distributed or delivered unless it is accompanied by these documents, s 145A.

Where a rights offer relates to unlisted shares, it must be accompanied by a prospectus, but this prospectus may confine itself to the matters specified in Part III of Schedule 3, s 148(1)(*b*). (See A Hyman, 'Requirements for Prospectuses', 1976 *De Rebus Procuratoriis* 111.)

An advertisement relating to a renounceable right issue by a listed company is not deemed to be a prospectus if it contains no more information than the issue price, the ratio in which the offer is made, and the last day for registration, s 157(1)(*f*). Subject to exceptions, no person, other than a stock exchange, may, as a regular feature of his business, carry on a scheme in pursuance whereof particulars of securities to be bought or sold are published, s 2B of the Stock Exchanges Control 7 of 1947. As to restrictions on offering of shares for sale, see s 141. If a person is convicted of having made an offer in contravention of the section, the court may order that any contract made as a result of the offer shall be void, s 141(9).

Variation of a contract referred to in the prospectus requires ratification by a general meeting, s 159.

B CASES

[61] **Nash *v* Lynde**
[1929] AC 158

Viscount Sumner: . . . Though the word 'issue' is not defined in the Act, it must be noticed that in dealing with such a subject-matter the legislature invariably uses in many places the idiom of company business. In connection with the issue of a prospectus the word does not mean mere delivery. I am anxious not to say anything that would make the way of the share canvasser less hard than [the Act] makes it already, but to me it is difficult to think of a prospectus being issued without some measure of publicity, however modest, and I think it is also impossible to do so, unless the steps taken are taken with the intention of inducing a subscription by the person invited to subscribe for the securities. I do not think that the term is satisfied by a single private communication between friends, even if they are business friends, or even though preparations have been made for other documents to be used in other communications, if none such take place. In the present case all that constituted the 'issue' was that one of the directors, in the course of a general endeavour to find money, was furnished with some copies of these typewritten documents and gave one of them to a friend who, as requested, passed it on to a friend of his own. I cannot believe that any one in business would call this the issue of a prospectus.

'The public', in the definition section . . . is of course a general word. No particular numbers are prescribed. Anything from two to infinity may serve: perhaps even one, if he is intended to be the first of a series of subscribers, but makes further proceedings needless by himself subscribing the whole. The point is that the offer is such as to be open to any one who brings his money and applies in due form, whether the prospectus was addressed to him on behalf of the company or not. A private communication is not thus open. . . .

[62] S *v* Rossouw
1971 (3) SA 222 (T)

NICHOLAS J: The present respondent was charged before the regional magistrate at Johannesburg with a contravention of s 80*bis*(4) [now s 141(8)] of the Companies Act 46 of 1926. It was alleged in the charge that, on 7 August 1966, and at Johannesburg, the accused wrongly offered for sale to one Herman Radecker, a member of the public, shares in a company known as Parys Diamante (Edms) Bpk, for the sum of R500, without such offer being accompanied by a document such as is referred to in s 80*bis*(1). The accused pleaded not guilty. At the end of the State case, an application was made for his discharge, and he was found not guilty and discharged.

The Attorney-General, acting under s 104(1) of Act 32 of 1944, required the magistrate to state a case for the consideration of the court of appeal. The magistrate duly did so and, in the case as stated, the question of law was set out as follows:

'Question of law: Whether accused made an offer to sell shares in the company to Radecker without showing him a prospectus in contravention of s 80*bis* of Act 46 of 1926.'

The unchallenged facts were as follows. On 7 August 1966, Radecker, who up to that date had been a stranger to the respondent, travelled on the same aircraft as the respondent from Windhoek to Johannesburg. During the flight he and the respondent engaged in conversation, in the course of which the respondent told Radecker that a private company (Parys Diamante (Edms) Bpk), in which the accused was interested, was developing a diamond mine near Parys, and that it would become a public company in February 1967. He offered to sell shares in the public company to Radecker. Radecker was interested and, at the suggestion of the respondent, met him at the respondent's hotel the following morning. After a long discussion Radecker agreed to buy 1 000 50 cent shares in the company for R500, which he paid to the respondent.

The relevant portions of s 80*bis* are as follows:

'(1) No person shall either verbally or in writing (including any newspaper advertisement) —

   (i) make an offer of shares for sale to the public or any member of the public; or

(ii) invite offers from the public or any member of the public to purchase any shares;

and no person shall issue, distribute or publish any material which in its form and context is calculated to be understood as an offer or invitation as aforesaid unless it is accompanied either by a prospectus complying with the provisions of this Act or by a written statement containing the particulars required by this section to be included therein. . . .

(4) If any person acts in contravention of this section he shall be guilty of an offence and liable, on conviction, to a fine not exceeding five hundred pounds or to imprisonment for a period not exceeding two years, or to both such fine and imprisonment. . . .

(6) . . . [For] the purposes of this section a person shall not in relation to a company be regarded as not being a member of the public by reason only that he is a holder of shares in the company or a purchaser of goods from the company. . . .'

There was unchallenged evidence that the offer was not accompanied by a prospectus or by a written statement in terms of ss (1). The only question is, therefore, whether Radecker was a 'member of the public' within the meaning of that provision.

In the case of *S* v *Rossouw* 1968 (4) SA 380 (T) this court considered the meaning of the word 'publiek' as used in the Afrikaans version of s 80*bis*(1). The learned judge who delivered the judgment of the full bench is reported at 385 to have said:

'Die woord „publiek" verwys gewoonlik na die gemeenskap as 'n geheel, eerder as na die gemeenskap as 'n georganiseerde eenheid. Dit verwys dus na die lede van die gemeenskap as sulks. Dit kan ook verwys na 'n besondere deel van die gemeenskap, maar dit sal afhang van die sin waarin dit gebruik word. In so 'n geval is daar gewoonlik 'n aanduiding na watter deel van die gemeenskap verwys word. In art 80*bis* is daar niks wat die woord, soos dit daarin gebruik word enige beperkte betekenis gee nie. Trouens, in sub-art (6) word die betekenis verder uitgebrei deurdat dit bepaal dat by die toepassing van die artikel word 'n persoon nie met betrekking tot 'n maatskappy geag 'n lid van die publiek te wees nie slegs omdat hy 'n houer van aandele is in die maatskappy of 'n koper is van goedere van die maatskappy.'

The learned judge then proceeded to consider the policy of the section, and came to the following conclusion:

'Daar is niks in die artikel wat enigsins aantoon dat aan die woord „publiek" 'n ander betekenis as sy gewone betekenis gegee moet word nie. Daar is ook niks in die artikel wat toon dat die beskerming beperk word tot gevalle van ventery aan aandele nie. Elke lid van die publiek word beskerm insoverre die uitsonderings van sub-art (1)(*a*), (*b*), (*c*), (*d*) en (*e*) nie van toepassing is nie.'

With the view of the learned judge may be compared the statement of Scott LJ in the case of *Tatem Steam Navigation Company* v *Inland Revenue Commissioner* [1941] 2 KB 194 (CA) at 203:

'There is no reason why the word "public" should be given anything but its ordinary meaning. The definition contained in Murray's *Oxford Dictionary* is: "The community" as an aggregate, but not in its organised capacity; hence, "the members of the community", and it is in that sense, as it seems to me, that the words "the public", are used in this section.'

It does not seem to me, however, that the learned judge in *Rossouw's* case would have formed the opinion that the effect of ss (6) was to give an extended meaning of the word 'publiek', if he had been aware that the English text, which is the official text, differed in a small but important respect from the Afrikaans text—in the Afrikaans version the word 'nie' has been omitted after the word 'maatskappy' where it is used for the first time.

The English version of ss (6) [now s 141(10)] which provides that

'a person shall not in relation to a company be regarded as not being a member of the public by reason *only* that he is a holder of shares in the company or a purchaser of goods from the company',

shows clearly that the legislature contemplated cases in which 'a person' would not be 'a member of the public' for the purposes of s 80*bis*(1) [now s 141(1)]. No guide is given in the section as to what those cases are. I should think, however, that one such case would be a member of the immediate family of the offeror. In *IRC* v *Park Investments Ltd* [1966] 2 All ER 785 (CA) at 795, Danckwerts LJ said with reference to a provision in the British Income Tax Act 1952:

'It is unfortunate that no definition or guide is given in ss (5) of what is meant by "the public". I think that I know what a public house is, or what a public meeting is, or what a public procession is. I do not know, however, what exactly is meant by "the public" in ss (5). At any rate, I am sure that it does not mean the family of those in control of the company as defined in ss (3). No one would regard a party to which only relatives of the giver of the party were invited as a "public" party.'

And one can visualize other cases in which the connection between the offeree and the company concerned, or the connection between the offeree and the offeror, is such that in relation to the company or in relation to the offeror, the offeree would not be a member of 'the public' for the purposes of s 80*bis*(1). Where, for example, a private company is administered by two shareholders, each of whom holds half of the issued shares, an offer by one to sell his shareholding to the other would not, in my view, be an offer to a 'member of the public'.

In so far, therefore, as the statement from *Rossouw's* case, which is quoted above, suggests that a 'member of the public' is in s 80*bis*(1) the equivalent of a 'member of the community' I am constrained to come to the conclusion that it is, with respect, clearly wrong, and that Van den Heever J was correct when, in considering the meaning of s 80*bis*(1) in the case of *S* v *Rossouw* 1969 (4) SA 504 (NC), she said at 509 that:

'. . . 'n aanbod van aandele aan „die publiek" of „'n lid van die publiek" nie sinoniem is met 'n aanbod van aandele van „enige persoon" nie.'

It is not necessary for the decision of this case, nor would it be desirable, to attempt to define the limits of what is meant by the 'public' in the section, and I respectfully agree with Van den Heever J, when she stated in that case (at 509H) that the question of whether an offeree is or is not a member of the 'public' can only be answered with reference to the circumstances of a particular case.

In the present matter, there are on the record no circumstances which would justify the conclusion that Radecker was, in relation to the company or to the respondent, anything other than a member of the public. The magistrate was therefore wrong in granting the application for a discharge at the end of the state case and the appeal is upheld.

The magistrate's verdict is set aside and the matter is remitted to the magistrate's court to proceed with the trial of the accused.

NOTES

See also *R v Akoob* 1951 (4) SA 683 (T), where Price J said: 'A prospectus is plainly not issued until it is passed around. The mere handing of a prospectuš to one or two people is not issuing a prospectus; it must be so used as to have become an invitation to the public before it can be said to have been issued.' Further *S v National Board of Executors Ltd* 1971 (3) SA 817 (D), critically discussed by R C Beuthin (1972) 89 *SALJ* 8.

In *In re South of England Natural Gas and Petroleum Co Ltd* [1911] 1 Ch 573 it was held that the distribution of a prospectus, headed 'for private circulation only', to shareholders in certain gas companies, was an offer to the public.

A circular sent to shareholders in connection with an offer to acquire shares under an amalgamation scheme is not a prospectus: *Governments Stock & Other Securities Investment Co Ltd v Christopher* [1956] 1 All ER 490, [1956] 1 WLR 237.

(b) Omissions and Untrue Statements in a Prospectus

A TEXT

Any person who is knowingly a party to the contravention of any of the provisions of s 148 is guilty of an offence, s 148(4). So is every one of the persons referred to in s 160(1) or (2) if the prospectus contains an untrue statement, s 162 (for defences, see ss (3) and (4)). They may also be guilty of criminal fraud: *63*.

A person who has been induced to subscribe for shares or debentures on the faith of a prospectus which contains an untrue statement may rescind his contract to take shares and claim return of the amount paid for them, irrespective of whether the false statement was made fraudulently, negligently or innocently: *64, 65*. A subscriber to the memorandum cannot rescind: *66*.

The remedy is lost if the subscriber delays unduly in repudiating the contract, *67*, and there can be no rescission once the company is being wound up. Where the misrepresentation was fraudulent the subscriber, in addition to rescinding the contract, may claim damages from the company, but he cannot remain a subscriber and claim damages: *68*.

In addition to his remedies against the company a subscriber who has taken shares on the faith of an untrue statement in the prospectus may have an action for damages against the directors, promoters or other persons responsible for the prospectus, either at common law or under s 160 (note the definition of 'promoter' in s 142 for the purposes of chapter VI). In an action for damages at common law fraud used to be required: 69. In an action under s 160, all the plaintiff has to show is that the statement was untrue. The defendants can escape liability only by proving one of the defences stated in s 160(3). In substance they have to show either that they did not act fraudulently or negligently (s 160(3)(a), (b), (c)) or that they dissociated themselves in time from the company or the prospectus, s 160(3)(i), (ii), (iii).

The statutory liability extends to directors who have been appointed after the issue of the prospectus, s 160(1)(b) and (c). As to contributions and rights of recourse, see s 160(4) and (5). On the liability of experts, see s 161.

Both at common law and under the Act an omission may amount to an untrue statement, and a statement which is literally true may become an untrue statement by reason of its form or context, s 142 s v 'untrue statement': 70.

As a general rule only an original allottee of shares may claim relief. A subscriber to the memorandum has no action, nor, as a rule, has a purchaser of the shares: 71–73.

An 'expert' who has made an untrue statement, is liable in damages to allottees, both at common law and under the Act, s 161; see also ss 160 and 162.

B CASES

[63] R v Bishirgian
[1936] 1 All ER 586 (CCA)

Appeal against a conviction of an offence under the English Larceny Act (in South Africa the charge would be one of common-law fraud or an offence under s 162 of the Companies Act) in knowingly making a false statement in a prospectus with intent to induce persons to become shareholders.

LORD HEWART LCJ: The complaint which is made here by these appellants is that the prospectus for preference shares and ordinary shares in James & Shakespeare Ltd was not false in any material particular within the meaning of the statute. The case for the Crown was that the evidence proved conclusively that the prospectus was false as a whole in that it gave an entirely false description of the business in which the public was being invited by the prospectus to invest its money. The public was invited by this prospectus to subscribe £300 000 for preference shares and £112 500 for ordinary shares in James & Shakespeare Ltd, a company which was carrying on, as it said, a business in London as metal

dealers and brokers, a business founded in 1844, and carried on uninter-
ruptedly from that time. . . . Out of the total amount for which subscription was being asked, £162 000 was to be used in acquiring a majority
interest in a company called Williams Henry & Co Ltd, a company with
similar interests having important agencies and connections in the United
States of America, India, and the Colonies. . . . The words of the prospectus are: 'The substantial amount of additional working capital which
will now become available for that purpose—namely, the carrying of
stocks on the London market for account of clients—should assist
materially in extending both the volume and scope of the company's
activities.' It is contended by the prosecution that the prospectus, by that
which it did state with regard to James & Shakespeare Ltd and Williams
Henry & Co Ltd, and especially by contrast with what it omitted to
state, gave, and was intended to give, an utterly false description of the
business into which at that time the public was really, though it did not
know it, being invited to put its money. . . . The case made out was that
the persons behind this prospectus were really at this time engaged
not in ordinary business, but in a gamble described indeed in various
phrases, but always the same thing: a gamble to make a corner in pepper,
or to control the price or to command the market. That gamble had been
conducted by the company William Henry & Co, a private company
belonging wholly in different proportions to Bishirgian and Howeson. . . .

Anyone who is at all acquainted with business and anybody who
reads about these companies with intelligence may be taken to know that
some future commitments there must be. So the learned judge ruled, and
indeed it is obvious, because they are future commitments, although they
ought no doubt to be entered in a properly kept minute book, they may
fail to find a place in accounts duly audited, and for this reason: that
future commitments do not become material for the work of the auditor
inasmuch as the time has not yet arrived when the commitments have
crystallized either into profit earned or into a loss incurred. The future
commitments of a normal business are one thing. The future commitments of a colossal gamble are different not merely in degree, but in kind.
[Counsel for the appellants] in his argument developed the proposition
that inasmuch as it is apparent, not from express words, but from a
reasonable inference, that there must be some future commitments, it is
really not material for the purposes of the present case, at any rate, to
examine the dimensions of those commitments. Given the fact, the quantum, it is said, does not matter. There, it seems to me, lurks the fallacy.
Future commitments of a normal business are one thing. The airy specu-
lations of a colossal gamble are quite a different thing. It is not a difference of degree, but it is a difference of kind. As the learned judge
explained in the course of his summing up . . . there is not merely some
difference, but all the difference between future commitments of normal
trade and future commitments of an attempt to corner. The financing
as it is called is different. The risks are different. And to advertise a
business as an ordinary business seeking development when money is
really being asked to feed and supply an ambitious gamble is simply
deceit.

It is said that no suitable words could have been included into the prospectus to repair the omission. It is not quite clear what that proposition means. If suitable and true words had been there, it might well be that the prospectus would not have been of much use. Suppose there had been a note: 'N.B.—You are apparently being invited to subscribe in a well-known old-established ordinary business carrying on its operations on approved lines. You are really being invited to trust your money to a gambling speculation to make a corner in pepper.' It would have been the truth, but the utility of the prospectus might have been extremely small. There may be some dispute as to the precise moment of time when the gamble began, but it was all antecedent to the prospectus, and the purpose for which this money was wanted, and the purpose to which it was, in fact, applied was the bolstering up of a very ambitious scheme — which failed — to control the pepper supply of the world.

In order to ascertain the question whether this document was false in a material particular or in all material particulars, one may ask oneself this question: 'If the facts had been revealed or even clearly indicated, would any man of sense have put his money into it?' That question is sought in argument and to some extent in the evidence to be answered on the part of the appellants by the statement: 'the appellants themselves put money into it and themselves took large personal risks. They believed, and they said, that they were on a good thing.' No doubt there was a time when they entertained sanguine expectations of the enormous operations upon which by degrees they had entered. That does not alter the nature of the operation. The public was not told what the good thing was. The public was told that the good thing was quite a different good thing and really, when one analyses, after hearing all the argument, the excuse which is offered on behalf of these appellants, it comes to no more than the excuse of the office-boy who takes a half-crown from the till because he has a good thing for the Grand National. Morally and legally the transactions are on the same footing. The dimensions greatly differ.

NOTES

See also *R* v *Lord Kylsant* [1932] 1 KB 442 (CCA). This case was an appeal by Lord Kylsant against a conviction under s 84 of the Larceny Act 1861 of making, circulating or publishing a prospectus relating to an issue of 2 000 000 5 per cent debenture stock, which he knew to be false in a material particular, with intent to induce persons to invest or advance property to the Royal Mail Steamship Packet Company, he being a director of that company.

. The prospectus stated, *inter alia*, that 'Although this company in common with other shipping companies has suffered from the depression in the shipping industry, the audited accounts of the company show that during the past ten years the average annual balance available (including profits of the insurance fund), after providing for depreciation and interest on existing debenture stocks, has been sufficient to pay the interest on the present issue more than five times over.

'After providing for all taxation, depreciation of the fleet, etc, adding to the reserves and payment of dividends on the preference stocks, the dividends on the ordinary stock during the last seventeen years have been as follows:—'

A table was then set out showing that, between 1911 and 1927, the company had paid dividends varying from 5 to 8 per cent, except in 1914, when no dividend was paid, and in 1926, when a dividend of 4 per cent was paid. What it did not say was that, although the company made very large profits in 1918, 1919 and 1920, when, owing to the European war, there was a shipping 'boom', in 1921, 1922, 1923, 1924, 1925, 1926 and 1927 it made substantial trading losses, and was only able to pay the dividends and to produce the 'balances available', by the introduction of items of a non-recurring nature, earned in the abnormal war period, such as repayments by the revenue authorities in connection with excess profits duty and adjustments of income tax reserves, the war contingency reserves, deferred repairs account and so on.

The conviction was upheld. 'The falsehood in this case consisted in putting before intending investors, as material on which they could exercise their judgment as to the position of the company, figures which apparently disclosed the existing position, but in fact hid it. In other words, the prospectus implied that the company was in a sound financial position and that the prudent investor could safely invest his money in its debentures. This inference would be drawn particularly from the statement that dividends had been regularly paid over a term of years, although times had been bad—a statement which was utterly misleading when the fact that those dividends had been paid, not out of current earnings, but out of funds which had been earned during the abnormal period of the war, was omitted': per Avory J at 448–9.

[64] Directors of Central Railway Company of Venezuela *v* Kisch
(1867) LR 2 HL 99

LORD CHELMSFORD LC: . . . The alleged representations are contained in a prospectus, the object of which was to invite the public generally to join the proposed undertaking. In an advertisement of this description some allowance must always be made for the sanguine expectations of the promoters of the adventure, and no prudent man will accept the prospects which are always held out by the originators of every new scheme, without considerable abatement.

But although, in its introduction to the public, some high colouring, and even exaggeration, in the description of the advantages which are likely to be enjoyed by the subscribers to an undertaking, may be expected, yet no misstatement or concealment of any material facts or circumstances ought to be permitted. In my opinion, the public, who are invited by a prospectus to join in any new adventure, ought to have the same opportunity of judging of everything which has a material bearing on its true character, as the promoters themselves possess. It cannot be too frequently or too strongly impressed upon those who, having projected any undertaking, are desirous of obtaining the co-operation of persons who have no other information on the subject than that which they choose to convey, that the utmost candour and honesty ought to characterize their published statements. As was said by Vice-Chancellor Kindersley, in the case of the *New Brunswick and Canada Railway Company* v *Muggeridge* (1860) 1 Drew & Sm 363, 'those who issue a prospectus holding out to the public the great advantages which will accrue to persons who will take shares in a proposed undertaking, and inviting them to take shares on the faith of the representations therein contained, are bound to state everything with strict and scrupulous accuracy, and not only to abstain from stating as fact that which is not so, but to omit no one fact within their knowledge the existence of which might in any degree affect the nature, or extent, or quality of the privileges and advantages which the prospectus holds out as inducement to take shares'.

But the appellants say that even admitting the prospectus to be open to the objections which are made to it, the respondent has no ground of complaint, because he had an opportunity of ascertaining the truth of the representations contained in it, of which he did not choose to avail himself; that he was told by the prospectus that 'the engineer's report, together with maps, plans, and surveys of the line, might be inspected, and any further information obtained, on application at the temporary offices of the company'; and in his letter of application he agreed to be bound by all the conditions and regulations contained in the memorandum and articles of association of the company, which, if he had examined, would have given him all the information necessary to correct the errors and omissions in the prospectus.

But it appears to me that when once it is established that there has been any fraudulent misrepresentation or wilful concealment by which a person has been induced to enter into a contract, it is no answer to his claim to be relieved from it to tell him that he might have known the truth by proper inquiry. He has a right to retort upon his objector, 'You, at least, who have stated what is untrue, or have concealed the truth, for the purpose of drawing me into a contract, cannot accuse me of want of caution because I relied implicitly upon your fairness and honesty'.

[The respondent was held entitled to rescind the contract entered into by him to take up shares in the company.]

[65] Alexander v African Investment and Credit Company
(1917) 38 NLR 133

DOVE WILSON JP: The plaintiff applied for and obtained an allotment of 1 000 shares of the defendant company. The action is for rescission of the contract and repayment of the sum paid on account of the shares, on the ground that the contract to take them was induced by misrepresentations made by two persons, Van Santen and Harrison, as the duly authorized agents of the company appointed to introduce the shares to the public. . . .

As regards Harrison, while he was a shareholder for a large amount, and certainly one of the most active and prominent of the shareholders, I am not satisfied that he ever occupied any position as the authorized agent of the company. He never occupied the position of director or servant of the company in any way. Misrepresentations by a shareholder who has been too zealous in the interests of himself and the other shareholders, which induce a member of the public to take up shares, will not entitle the person so induced to rescission of the contract although it may give a right of action against the particular shareholder; but unless it can be shown that in making the misrepresentations the shareholder was in the position of a duly authorized agent for the company, which merely as a shareholder he is not, no liability attaches to the company to forgo the contract on the ground of the misrepresentations. Had the case therefore depended only on the misrepresentations by Harrison it must have failed. But there remains the question of the relations of Van Santen to the company. . . .

[After discussing the facts, the learned judge continued:]

All these circumstances in my opinion afford only one reasonable inference, and that is that Van Santen was acting as the agent of the company appointed by the secretary, Mr Sinclair: and that leads me to consider whether or not Mr Sinclair had authority to appoint agents for this purpose. . . . It is clear that a secretary's duties are merely ministerial and that his general authority does not entitle him to make representations to induce people to take up shares, and that a contract made on the faith of them will not be rescinded for fraud or misrepresentation. But I know of no authority for the proposition that these directors might not entrust or leave to the secretary, as a detail of the management, the task of finding suitable convassers to secure purchasers for the new shares, a task which, even if it did involve the exercise of some discretion, I cannot think was one which they were expected to undertake personally. The directors were merely instructed in the most general terms to take any steps they thought necessary to insure the new issue being adequately brought before the public; they were not expected to actually make the publication personally. The publication might be by public advertisement, by the issue of circulars or by canvassers; and the only step which the directors thought necessary, so far as they were concerned, to give effect to the wishes of the shareholders, was to leave it to the secretary—to whom so many things were habitually left—to proceed by any or all of these methods as he thought fit; and it must have been in their contemplation that he might adopt the method of canvassers. . . . If in these circumstances he did, as I think he did, appoint Van Santen, it was within the authority committed to him by the directors; he was merely the hand of the directors in appointing Van Santen, who thereby became the agent of the company. . . .

[*Held*, plaintiff was entitled to the relief claimed.]

NOTES

In *Lynde* v *Anglo-Italian Hemp Spinning Company* [1896] 1 Ch 178 Romer J summarized the cases where a company will be liable for misrepresentations inducing a contract to take shares as follows:

(1) Where the misrepresentations were made by the directors or other general agents of the company entitled to act and acting on its behalf as, for example, by a prospectus issued by the authority or sanction of the directors of a company inviting subscriptions for shares; (2) Where the misrepresentations were made by a special agent of the company while acting within the scope of his authority—as, for example, by an agent specially authorized to obtain, on behalf of the company, subscriptions for shares; (3) Where the company can be held affected, before the contract was complete, with the knowledge that it was induced by misrepresentations—as, for example, when the directors, on allotting shares, knew, in fact, that the application for them had been induced by misrepresentations, even though made without any authority; (4) Where the contract was made on the basis of certain representations, whether the particulars of those representations were known to the company or not, and it turns out that some of those representations were material and untrue—as, for example, if the directors of a company knew when allotting that an application for shares was based on the statements contained in a prospectus, even though that prospectus was issued without authority or even before the company was formed and even if its contents was not known to the directors.

[66] *In re* **Metal Constituents Ltd: Lord Lurgan's case**
[1902] 1 Ch 707

Lord L signed the memorandum of association of the M Company for 250 shares. Thereafter it was incorporated, but Lord L refused to pay for his shares on the ground that he was induced to apply for them by misrepresentations of a promoter of the company, and sought rescission of the contract.

BUCKLEY J: I will assume that before the incorporation of the company Sims made to Lord Lurgan a representation which was untrue, and on the faith of which Lord Lurgan signed the memorandum of association of the company for 250 shares. Is Lord Lurgan entitled to rescission of his contract to take shares on the ground of the assumed misrepresentation? I think not. Before the incorporation of the company Sims was not the agent of the company, because the company did not exist, and therefore Lord Lurgan could not have been induced to sign for the shares by the misrepresentation of the company or its agent. The contract of the subscriber of a memorandum of association is of a very peculiar kind. . . . There is no contract at all until the moment when the incorporation and the character of membership in the signatories to the memorandum come simultaneously into existence. I must, therefore, hold that the subscriber to the memorandum cannot have rescission on the ground that he was induced to become a subscriber by the misrepresentations of an agent of the company. . . .

NOTES

As to rescission, see also *Klette* v *South African Cycle Factory Ltd* (1899) 16 SC 240; *Burnard* v *African Mercantile Co* (1903) 20 SC 378; *Ottoshoop Proprietary Mines Ltd* v *Reeves* 1907 TH 76; *Johannesburg Motor Mart Ltd* v *Schonken* 1919 OPD 90; *Agricultural Co-operative Union* v *Chadwick* (1922) 43 NLR 135; *Pathescope (Union) of South Africa Ltd* v *Mallinick* 1927 AD 292; *Pretorius* v *Natal South Sea Investment Trust* 1965 (3) SA 410 (W).

On the proposition that in an action for rescission of the contract to take shares, it is not necessary to prove that the defendant knew that the representation was false, see further *Viljoen* v *Hillier* 1904 TS 312; *Parke* v *Hamman* 1907 TH 47; *Symons and Moses* v *Davies* (1911) 32 NLR 69, esp at 81, per Broome J: 'If the representation is untrue, the contract can be rescinded; if fraudulently untrue, damages can also be recovered'; *Brink* v *Robinson* 1916 CPD 88.

Where a person applies for shares in a company without disclosing that he is acting on behalf of a principal, the only person entitled to rescind the contract on the ground of misrepresentations is the agent, and in order to succeed he must prove that he himself was induced by the misrepresentations to enter into the contract to take shares: *Collins* v *Associated Greyhound Racecourses Ltd* [1930] 1 Ch 1.

[67] Pathescope (Union) of South Africa Ltd *v* Mallinick
1927 AD 292

STRATFORD JA: . . . In considering whether or not it would be equitable to grant the relief prayed, the court will have regard, not only to the likelihood of his position being prejudiced by the delay, but also to the prejudice to third parties which may result if relief is granted. This view is aptly illustrated in cases, like the present, where the plaintiff seeks to have his name removed from the register of shareholders of a company. 'It it obviously of the utmost importance in these cases that a shareholder should come at the earliest possible opportunity, before other persons have entered into engagements with the company upon the faith of his being a member': per Lord Romilly MR in *Heymann* v *Central European Railway Co* (1868) LR 7 Eq 154 at 169. Thus the court is left free in the circumstances of each case to judge of the equity of granting the relief in face of the delay in asking for it. And the doctrine (called in English law '*laches*') can only be stated in somewhat vague and general terms. Where there has been undue delay in seeking relief the court will not grant it when in its opinion it would be inequitable to do so after the lapse of time constituting the delay. And in forming an opinion as to the justice of granting the relief in face of the delay, the court can rest its refusal upon *potential* prejudice, and that prejudice need not be to the defendant in the action but to third parties. These are principles of the doctrine which at once distinguish it from a defence of estoppel and are clearly illustrated in cases, like the present, where a rectification of the share register is prayed for. . . .

NOTES

See also *Atlas Diamond Mining Company Ltd v Poole* (1882) 1 HCG 20: 'I am bound to add that I can feel no special sympathy for a man who, after entering on a speculation and not finding it so good as he had expected, then endeavours to cry back upon his bargain', per Buchanan JP; further *Adamanta Diamond Mining Co Ltd v Wege* (1883) 2 HCG 172; *Pandora Syndicate v Ramsay* (1902) 9 HCG 213; *Johannesburg Motor Mart Ltd v Schonken* 1919 OPD 90; *Pretorius v Natal South Sea Investment Fund* 1965 (3) SA 410 (W).

On the general principle, see Innes CJ in *Bowditch v Peel and Magill* 1921 AD 561: 'A person who has been induced to contract by the material and fraudulent misrepresentation of the other party may either stand by the contract or claim a rescission. . . . It follows that he must make his election between those two inconsistent remedies within a reasonable time after knowledge of the deception. And the choice of one necessarily involves the abandonment of the other.'

[68] Houldsworth *v* City of Glasgow Bank and Liquidators
(1880) 5 App Cas 317

EARL CAIRNS LC: The question . . . upon which the decision of this case must, as I think, depend, was this: Can a man, induced by the fraudulent misrepresentations of agents of a company to take shares in the company, after he discovers the fraud, elect to retain the shares, and to sue the company for damages?

There is no doubt that according to the law of England a person purchasing a chattel or goods, concerning which the vendor makes a fraudulent misrepresentation, may, on finding out the fraud, retain the chattel or the goods and have his action to recover any damages he has sustained by reason of the fraud. . . . But does the same rule apply to the case of shares or stock in a partnership or company? We are accustomed to use language as to such a sale and purchase as if the things bought or sold were goods or chattels, but this it certainly is not. The contract which is made is a contract by which the person called the buyer agrees to enter into a partnership already formed and going, taking his share of past liabilities, and his chance of future profits or losses. He has not bought any chattel or piece of property for himself; he has merged himself in a society, to the property of which he has agreed to contribute, and the property of which, including his own contributions, he has agreed shall be used and applied in a particular way and in no other way. . . .

[In claiming damages from the company] he is making a claim which is inconsistent with the contract into which he has entered, and by which he wishes to abide; in other words, he is in substance, if not in form, taking the course which is described as approbating and reprobating, a course which is not allowed. . . .

NOTES

See further *Cargill v Bower* (1878) 10 ChD 502 and *Pathescope (Union) of South Africa Ltd v Mallinick* 1927 AD 292 (67 above).

[69] Derry v Peek
(1889) 14 App Cas 337

By a special Act which incorporated it, a company was given the right to construct tramways to be moved by animal power and, with the consent of the Board of Trade, by steam or mechanical power. The defendants as directors issued a prospectus stating that the company had the right to use steam or mechanical power. The plaintiff subscribed for shares in reliance on this representation. Subsequently the Board of Trade refused to give its consent to the use of steam or mechanical power, and as a result the company was wound up. The plaintiff brought an action for deceit for alleged fraudulent misrepresentations. It was held, however, that the defendants were not liable as they had made the incorrect statement in the honest belief that it was true.

LORD HERSCHELL: . . . I think the authorities establish the following propositions: First, in order to sustain an action of deceit, there must be proof of fraud, and nothing short of that will suffice. Secondly, fraud is proved when it is shown that a false representation has been made (1) knowingly, or (2) without belief in its truth, or (3) recklessly, careless whether it be true or false. Although I have treated the second and third as distinct cases, I think the third is but an instance of the second, for one who makes a statement under such circumstances can have no real belief in the truth of what he states. To prevent a false statement being fraudulent, there must, I think, always be an honest belief in its truth. And this probably covers the whole ground, for one who knowingly alleges that which is false, has obviously no such honest belief. Thirdly, if fraud be proved, the motive of the person guilty of it is immaterial. It matters not that there was no intention to cheat or injure the person to whom the statement was made. . . .

In my opinion making a false statement through want of care falls far short of, and is a very different thing from, fraud, and the same may be said of a false representation honestly believed though on insufficient grounds. . . . The whole current of authorities, with which I have so long detained your Lordships, shows to my mind conclusively that fraud is essential to found an action of deceit, and that it cannot be maintained where the acts proved cannot properly be so termed. . . .

NOTES

See further *Akerhielm v De Mare* [1959] 3 All ER 485 (PC), where, dealing with a false representation in a letter relating to the formation of a private company, Lord Jenkins said (at 503): 'The question is not whether the defendant in any given case honestly believed the representation to be true in the sense assigned to it by the court on an objective consideration of its truth or falsity, but whether he honestly believed the representation to be true in the sense in which he understood it, albeit erroneously, when it was made.'

He hastened to add that, 'This general proposition is, no doubt, subject to limitations. For instance the meaning placed by the defendant on the representation made may be so far from the sense in which it would be understood by any reasonable person as to make it impossible to hold that the defendant honestly understood the representation to bear the meaning claimed by him and honestly believed it in that sense to be true.'

In *Shepheard v Broome* [1904] AC 342 it was held that where a director is sued under the act for damages for omission of prescribed matter in the prospectus, it is not a good defence for him to say that he did not think the prescribed matter material—the test is whether it was material.

See further *Edgington v Fitzmaurice* (1885) 29 ChD 459; *Tait v Wicht* (1890) 7 SC 158; *Benjamin v Minter* (1896) 8 HCG 37; *In re Leeds and Hanley Theatres of Varieties Ltd* [1902] 2 Ch 809; *Symons and Moses v Davies* (1911) 32 NLR 69; *Adams v Thrift* [1915] 1 Ch 557, [1915] 2 Ch 21 (CA); P C Heerey 'Directors and Public Issues' (1967) 5 *Melbourne University LR* 395.

The measure of damages under the Act is the same as in the common-law action for fraudulent misrepresentation (in England, the action of deceit): *Clark v Urqubart* [1930] AC 28.

The rule in *Derry v Peek* (*supra*) that at common law a director or promoter is not liable in damages for a negligent (as distinguished from a fraudulent) misrepresentation in a prospectus, is no longer true either for English or South African law, see pp 617–31 below.

[70] Brownlie *v* Campbell
(1880) 5 App Cas 925

LORD BLACKBURN: . . . I quite agree in this, that whenever a man in order to induce a contract says that which is in his knowledge untrue with the intentions to mislead the other side, and induce them to enter into the contract, that is downright fraud; in plain English, and Scotch also, it is a downright lie told to induce the other party to act upon it, and it should of course be treated as such. I further agree in this: that when a statement or representation has been made in the bona fide belief that it is true, and the party who has made it afterwards comes to find out that it is untrue, and discovers what he should have said, he can no longer honestly keep up that silence on the subject after that has come to his knowledge, thereby allowing the other party to go on, and still more, inducing him to go on, upon a statement which was honestly made at the time when it was made, but which he has not now retracted when he has become aware that it can be no longer honestly persevered in. That would be fraud, too, I should say, as at present advised. And I go on further still to say, what is perhaps not quite so clear, but certainly it is my opinion, where there is a duty or an obligation to speak, and a man in breach of that duty or obligation holds his tongue and does not speak, and does not say the thing he was bound to say, if that was done with the intention of inducing the other party to act upon the belief that the reason why he did not speak was because he had nothing to say, I should be inclined myself to hold that that was fraud also. . . .

NOTES

See further *Peek v Gurney* (1873) LR 6 HL 377, per Lord Chelmsford: 'It is said that the prospectus is true as far as it goes, but half a truth will sometimes amount to a real falsehood'; and Lord Colonsay: 'I think that this prospectus did suppress important matter, and if it did not contain any direct allegation of what was false, it was at least of a misleading character. It was a *suppressio veri*, which, if it did not amount to an *allegatio falsi*, at least amounted to a *suggestio falsi*. . . .' If the action in *Peek* v *Gurney* nevertheless failed, it was because the plaintiff was not an original allottee of the shares, but a purchaser in the market, see 71 below . . .

See also *In re Leeds and Hanley Theatres of Varieties Ltd* [1902] 2 Ch 809; *Greenwood* v *Leather Shod Wheel Co* [1900] 1 Ch 421; *S* v *De Jager* 1965 (2) SA 616 (AD) at 627.

[71] Peek *v* Gurney

(1873) LR 6 HL 377

The plaintiff sued the directors of the Overend & Gurney Company, and the executors of a deceased director, for the loss which he had sustained by reason of his having become the purchaser of 2 000 shares in the company. He alleged that he had been deceived and misled by a prospectus put forth by the directors, containing several misrepresentations and suppressions of material and important facts. Having lost in the trial court, the plaintiff appealed.

LORD CAIRNS: . . . The object of the prospectus on the face of it is clearly to invite the public to take shares in the new company. The prospectus is, as is usual in such cases, an invitation, and there is appended to it a form of application for shares, which was to be filled up, and upon which form the invitation was to be answered. It is a prospectus in this shape addressed to the whole of the public, no doubt, and any one of the public might take up the prospectus and appropriate it in that way to himself by answering it upon the form upon which it is intended by the prospectus that it should be answered. The appellant, however, did not take up and did not appropriate the prospectus in this way. For reasons which it is unnecessary to inquire into he declined to take, or at all events he did not originally take any shares in the company. The allotment of shares began on 24 July; it appears to have been completed on 28 July; and it is stated that two or three times the number of shares to be had in the company were applied for. The allotment having been completed, the prospectus, as it seems to me, had done its work; it was exhausted. The share list was full; the directors had obtained from the company the money which they desired to obtain. The appellant subsequently, upon 17 October, several months afterwards, bought 1 000 shares at a premium of something over £7, and again, still later, on 6 December, he bought 1 000 other shares at a premium of something over £6. He bought them on the Stock Exchange, and he, of course, did not know in the first instance from whom he bought them. In point of fact, it appears that as to the greater part of them they were shares which had originally been allotted to one of the old partners, Samuel Gurney, by whom they were transferred to a nominee for himself, in whose name they were registered; they were then sold upon the market, and resold apparently several times, because the premium seems to have risen from a much smaller to a much larger sum, and ultimately they were sold, at the premium which I have stated, to the appellant, and were registered in his name.

Now, my Lords, I ask the question: How can the directors of a company be liable, after the full original allotment of shares, for all the subsequent dealings which may take place with regard to those shares upon the Stock Exchange? If the argument of the appellant is right, they must be liable *ad infinitum*, for I know no means of pointing out any time at which the liability would, in point of fact, cease.

[The appeal was dismissed by the House of Lords.]

[72] Tait *v* Wicht
(1890) 7 SC 158

DE VILLIERS CJ: . . . The action is for damages resulting from false and fraudulent statements, alleged to have been made to the plaintiffs. . . . The objection [raised by the defendants] is that there is no averment that the defendants made the alleged misstatements with the view of inducing the shareholders or the public to buy shares or to refrain from selling those which they already had—and the question is whether such an averment was necessary in order to entitle the plaintiffs to succeed. In my opinion, after fully considering the weighty arguments to the contrary, such an averment is not necessary, inasmuch as it is implied in the allegation that the misstatements had been made 'fraudulently'. A mere lie, which is foolishly acted upon by others to whom it is addressed, does not constitute a fraud, in the legal sense of the term, unless the utterer intended or must, from the mode and circumstances in which he uttered it, be presumed to have intended that it should be acted upon. The word 'fraud' as used in this Colony is a very wide one and embraces within its meaning the terms *'dolus malus'*, *'falsum'* and *'stellionatus'* as used by the Roman-Dutch text writers. The first of these terms is only used in civil cases and especially in matters of contract, the two last terms are only applied to criminal offences. The definition of *dolus* given by Labeo (D4.3.1), which has been followed with slight variations by the text writers, is *'omnis calliditas, fallacia, machinatio ad circumveniendum, fallendum decipiendum alterum adhibita'*. Each of the expressions *calliditas* (artifice), *fallacia* (deceit), *machinatio* (contrivance) assumes an intention on the part of the wrongdoer to bring about the result of *circumventing, cheating*, or *deceiving* someone else, but, as has been properly observed by Voet (4.3.2), seeing that such intention is an operation or condition of the mind, it can in no way be better ascertained than from the nature of the acts or words complained of and from the circumstances under which they were done or spoken. The acts or words and the circumstances under which they were done or spoken may be such as to raise a conclusive presumption that the intention to effect the object complained of existed, whatever the doer or speaker may say to the contrary. A jeweller exposes a brass watch chain for sale in his shop. A customer enters and after asking whether it is made of pure gold and being told that it is, buys it. The jeweller could not be heard to say that he did not intend the customer to act upon his statement, for every circumstance shows conclusively that the false statement was made with a view to induce the customer to buy the chain. . . . In the case of *Peek* v *Gurney* (1873) LR 6 HL 377, the House of Lords had held that when the allotment was completed the office of a prospectus inviting applications for shares was exhausted, and that a person who had not become an allottee, but was only a subsequent purchaser of shares in the market, was not so connected with the prospectus as to render those who had issued it liable to indemnify him against the losses which he had suffered in consequence of his purchase. The real ground of this decision could only have been that the issuers of the prospectus were only liable to those persons whom the prospectus was intended to deceive. . . . Proof of very special circumstances would be required to justify any court in conclusively presuming that the purchase of shares from persons not parties to the fraud was the object of a third party in making representations having no direct reference to the purchase of such shares. No doubt by our law a person who has been induced to enter into a contract with one person by the falsehood of a third party has his remedy against such third party for any damages which the entering into the contract has directly entailed, but the instances given by Voet (4.3.5) all refer to cases where the obvious object of the falsehood was to induce the particular contract which entailed the loss. For example, a broker who by deceit circumvents a person into lending money to a man of straw, who is represented as being a man of means, is said by Voet to be liable for damages sustained in consequence by the lender, but the avowed object of the false representation being to induce the loan of the money there was no necessity for introducing any presumption. Where such an avowed object exists difficulty can arise, but where a misrepresentation is made for one purpose and acted upon in a different manner from that which ostensibly at least was intended by the person making the misrepresentation, it would require very special circumstances to raise the presumption that his real intention was different from his avowed object. The fraudulent intention must be associated with the particular contract which resulted in the loss, but when once it is so associated the link in the chain of legal reasoning is complete, and the person defrauded is entitled to recover all losses which he has sustained as a direct consequence of having been induced to enter into the contract. . . .

[73] Andrews v Mockford
[1896] 1 QB 372

A L SMITH LJ: . . . The plaintiff in this action seeks to recover damages from the defendants for having by fraudulent devices induced him to purchase shares in a sham or pretended gold-mining company, for which he has paid the sum of £411 15s 6d; and the jury in answer to specific questions left to them by the Lord Chief Justice, have found that the plaintiff has established his allegation, and have given a verdict for him for the amount claimed, for which judgment has been entered.

Application is now made to this court to enter judgment for the defendants or for a new trial, upon the grounds that there was no evidence to support the plaintiff's case; misreception of evidence; misdirection. The case made by the plaintiff against the defendants is this —that the defendants fraudulently agreed together to publish and to [send] to the plaintiff, and did send to him, a prospectus of a company, the Sutherland Reef Company, which they knew, when brought out, would be a sham or pretended company, in order to induce the plaintiff to purchase shares therein; that the plaintiff did not then do so; that the prospectus so issued having produced but a scanty subscription for shares, the defendants thereupon fraudulently caused to be published in the *Financial News* a telegram, which they knew to be false, in order to stimulate and bring about that which the prospectus had been intended to effect but had failed in doing; that the plaintiff, believing in the truth of the telegram confirming, as he thought it did, the statistics given in the prospectus, was thereby induced to purchase the shares; whereby he was damnified. . . .

. . . The plaintiff gave evidence, and there was none brought forward to contradict him on the part of the defendants, who were both in court, that he received the prospectus sent to him by post (it was not disputed that the prospectus had been issued by the defendants); that having read it he did not then apply for shares, but laid it aside for a time; that he afterwards saw the telegram in the *Financial News*, and, believing that its contents were true, and that it confirmed the statistics in the prospectus, he thereupon purchased the shares — in other words, that he purchased, upon the faith of the statements contained in the prospectus, supplemented by the statements in the telegram, which last statements were that a shaft had been driven, and that a large body of payable ore had then been opened, assaying by Government assay twenty-four ounces to the ton. . . .

It was said that, assuming all this, and that the telegram was proved to have been published at the instance of the defendants with a fraudulent intent, and that the contents were false to their knowledge, and that the plaintiff really did act upon the conjoint representation of the prospectus and the telegram, nevertheless the Lord Chief Justice should have directed judgment for the defendants upon the grounds, firstly, that *Peek* v *Gurney* (1873) LR 6 HL 377, in the House of Lords, has decided that when shares are purchased upon the market, and not taken by allotment from a company, fraudulent misstatements in a prospectus cannot be relied upon by a purchaser, because the prospectus had theretofore performed its function, which was only to obtain purchasers from the company of shares by allotment, and so the plaintiff had no cause of action on the prospectus; and, secondly, that the false statements in the telegram could not be relied upon by the plaintiff, because it had been pointed out in reference to the case of *R* v *De Berenger* (1814) 3 M & S 67, that the propagation of false news of peace, whereby the price of funds was sent up, did not give a cause of action for damage to one of the public who had been deceived and injured thereby, through having purchased stock when unduly inflated by the false news. . . . In my opinion, without discussing the effect of these cases, neither decision governs the present one, which is a case of continued systematic fraud from its commencement to its end. . . .

. . . There was proved against the defendants a continuous fraud on their part, commencing with the sending of the prospectus to the plaintiff, and culminating in the direct lie told in the telegram, which was intended by the defendants to operate upon the plaintiff's mind as well as on the minds of others, and did so operate to his prejudice, and to the advantage of the defendants. It is not taking the correct view of the case to sever it into parts, as the defendants' counsel sought to do, and to argue that the prospectus by itself would not support a cause of action, and that the telegram by itself would not do, and since two nothings make nothing, the combination of the two does not support a cause of action. This case must be taken as a whole. In this case the function of the prospectus was not exhausted, and, indeed, in answer to the third question, the jury so find; and the false telegram was brought into play by the defendants to reflect back upon and countenance the false statements in the prospectus.

For these reasons the plaintiff, in my opinion, is entitled to retain the judgment entered for him.

RIGBY LJ: . . . In my judgment, there is nothing in *Peek* v *Gurney* (1873) LR 6 HL 377, or in any other case, which precisely meets the present one. Undoubtedly, if there be a prospectus issued for the sole purpose of obtaining subscriptions for the original capital of the company, or subscriptions for any issue of shares about to take place, and if that can be treated as a separate transaction, people who did not respond to that invitation, and did not act upon it in the way which it was intended to be acted upon, but who afterwards bought shares in the open market, cannot rely on statements in the prospectus, which they may be able to establish as being fraudulent misrepresentations. It is, however, a totally different matter when the conclusion is arrived at that the prospectus was not intended solely, or even primarily, for the purpose of getting the public to subscribe to the shares. If the object was, in pursuance of a deliberate scheme of fraud, to impress the minds of all persons who read the prospectus with the idea that the sham company which was created was a real and most prosperous company —if that was a part of the scheme, and if, after the issue of the prospectus, that scheme was continued by other devices intended to produce the same results, it is idle to say there is any rule of law or any principle which should oblige us to shut our eyes to that portion of the fraud which was contained in the prospectus. . . .

. . . I agree that the appeal should be dismissed with costs.

5 Incorporation, Pre-incorporation Contracts and Deregistration

I INCORPORATION AND COMMENCEMENT OF BUSINESS

A TEXT

When all the prescribed documents have been lodged with the Registrar of Companies and the prescribed fees have been paid, the Registrar registers the memorandum and articles of association and endorses thereon the date and the certificate of registration, ss 63, 64. If the objects of the company are unlawful the Registrar may not register the company, if lawful he may not refuse to register it: 74; see also 86.

In the absence of fraud in its procurement, the certificate of incorporation is conclusive evidence that all the requirements of the Act relative to the formation of the company have been complied with and that the company has been incorporated on the date stated on the certificate, ss 64, 65. See *In re Yolland, Husson and Birkett Ltd* [1908] 1 Ch 152; *Jubilee Cotton Mills Ltd v Lewis* [1924] AC 958. The certificate is not conclusive evidence as to the legality of the objects of the company (*Society of Incorporated Accountants and Auditors v Powell* 1929 CPD 453). See further *Registrar of Asiatics v Salajee* 1925 TPD 71 at 72, per Stratford J: 'To say that a certificate is to be conclusive proof of the facts to which it speaks is not the same thing as saying that the certificate cannot itself be attacked on the ground of fraud in its procurement.' See also *Bowman v Secular Society Ltd* [1917] AC 406 at 420–1; *In re Hampstead Garden Suburb Trust Ltd* [1962] 1 Ch 806 at 824–5.

The fact that one or other of the subscribers to the memorandum signs it in a fictitious name does not prevent the company from coming into existence: *R v Meer* 1958 (2) SA 175 (N), decided under the old Act when a private company required no fewer than two members for its formation.

No company having a share capital may commence business or exercise any borrowing powers unless and until the Registrar has issued under his hand and seal a certificate entitling it to commence business, s 172(1). Before such a certificate is granted every company, public or private, has to satisfy the requirements of s 172(3). A public company which has issued a prospectus must, in addition, comply with the requirements of s 172(2). A certificate by the Registrar that the company is entitled to commence business is conclusive evidence that the company is so entitled, s 172(4). Whether the Registrar may, or must, refuse to grant the certificate if he is not satisfied that the capital of the company is adequate for its purposes (s 172(3)(a)), is not clear.

A contract made by a company before the date on which it is entitled to commence business is provisional only and does not become binding on the company until it becomes entitled to commence business, s 172(5): 75. Until the certificate is issued the director and subscribers to the memorandum are personally liable for debts and liabilities from any business conducted by the company, s 172(5).

A person who is responsible for or knowingly a party to a contravention of s 172 is guilty of an offence, s 172(7): 76.

A company which commences business before the Registrar has certified that it is entitled to do so, is liable to be wound up by the court in terms of s 344(1)(b).

A trading licence ought not to be granted to a company before its incorporation, but if it is granted and the company is subsequently incorporated, it will not be cancelled in the absence of prejudice (or, quaere, fraud): Rajah & Rajah (Pty) Ltd v Ventersdorp Municipality 1961 (4) SA 402 (AD). See also Ventersdorp Town Council v Rajah 1960 (2) SA 141 (T).

B CASES

[74] The King v Registrar of Joint Stock Companies
[1931] 2 KB 197

The Registrar of Companies refused to register a company formed in England for the sale of tickets in the Irish Lottery. An application for a writ of mandamus ordering the Registrar to register the company was unsuccessful.

SCRUTTON LJ: This is a short point involving the construction of s 41 of the Lotteries Act 1823. Two gentlemen proposed to sell tickets in England in connection with an Irish lottery. For some reason they did not propose to do this themselves; they proposed to form a private company to do it. It is merely conjecture on my part that this may be due to the fact that the provisions in the Act of 1823 making offenders liable to be punished as rogues and vagabonds do not apply to a company, and so the two gentlemen intending to form this company wished in this way to avoid the risk of being prosecuted under the Act. They accordingly lodged the memorandum and articles of association of the proposed company with the Registrar of Companies, who, when he saw that the object of the company was to sell tickets in a lottery known as the Irish Free State Hospitals Sweepstake, refused to register the company. Thereupon an application was made to the court for a writ of *mandamus* directing the Registrar to register the company. To succeed in that application the applicant must show that it is legal to sell in England tickets for the Irish Free State Hospital Sweepstake authorized by an Act of the Irish Free State. The only Act which can be supposed to authorize the selling in England is an Irish Act, but the Irish Parliament has no jurisdiction in England, and that being so, the Irish Parliament cannot authorize lottery tickets to be sold in England. The authority to sell in any place must be given by the Parliament having jurisdiction in that place, and the Imperial Parliament has given no authority to sell lottery tickets in England.

[75]   *In re* **Otto Electrical Manufacturing Company** (1905) **Ltd:** **Jenkins' Claim**
[1906] 2 Ch 390

A company went into liquidation without having become entitled to commence business. Jenkins claimed that the company was indebted to him for, among other things, furnishing offices for the company at the request of the directors. The claim was disallowed.

BUCKLEY J: The question to be determined is whether Mr Jenkins . . . can . . . be heard to say that he is a creditor. . . .

Now this company never did become entitled to commence business; therefore any contract made by the company was provisional and not binding on the company. But [counsel for the claimant] has argued that the Act of Parliament does not mean what it says, that it does not mean any contract, but any contract of a certain kind; and his next difficulty is to define of what kind. He says that it means any contract entered into for the purpose of carrying on its business, and that there are some contracts which are not entered into for the purpose of carrying on the business, but which are what he calls 'preliminary' — as for expenses incurred with a view to the future carrying on of business.

I think that argument is altogether unsound. A company of this kind has no purpose of existence other than the carrying on of its business, and every contract which it enters into must be a contract entered into for the purposes of its business in some form or other; whether it is preliminary or final, or one in the course of carrying on its business, makes no difference. . . .

[76] **R *v* Milne and Erleigh** (7)
1951 (1) SA 791 (AD)

CENTLIVRES CJ: It was common cause that BNU commenced business on 30 August 1946 in contravention of s 84(2) [now s 172(2) and (3)] of the Companies Act. Subsection (5) of s 84 [now s 172(7)] provides that

'if any company commences business or exercises borrowing powers in contravention of this section, every person who is responsible for the contravention shall . . . be guilty of an offence and liable, on conviction, to a fine not exceeding £50 for every day during which the contravention continues'.

... It is clear from [the] facts that Erleigh was responsible for the fact that BNU commenced business and exercised borrowing powers before the Registrar of Companies had certified in terms of s 84(2)(d) of the Companies Act that BNU was entitled to commence business, for it was he who bought the 100 000 Freddies shares from JCI and obtained £600 000 from Rooderand in order to pay JCI for these shares.

There was no evidence to show that Erleigh, who had entrusted the duty of registering the company to Jacobson, knew that a certificate to commence business had not yet been granted, but there can be no doubt that the Crown has proved that Erleigh was responsible for the commencement of business by BNU. Prima facie, therefore, s 84(5) of the Companies Act was satisfied ... and, assuming that the principle that *actus non facit reum nisi mens sit rea* applies to the offence created by the section, it then lay upon Erleigh to prove that the violation of that section which had taken place had been committed accidentally or innocently as far as he was concerned. This onus has not been discharged. . . .

II PRE-INCORPORATION CONTRACTS

A TEXT

A pre-incorporation contract may be made under s 35 of the Companies Act or under the common-law rules relating to contracts for the benefit of a third party. Under s 35 a company may after its incorporation ratify or adopt a contract entered into prior to its incorporation, if—

(a) the contract was made in writing; and

(b) the person who made it professed to act as agent or trustee for the company not yet incorporated; and

(c) the memorandum of association of the company on its registration contained as an object of the company the adoption or ratification of or the acquisition of rights and obligations in respect of such contract; and

(d) two copies of the contract, one certified as correct by a notary public, have been lodged with the Registrar together with the memorandum and articles of association.

At common law a company cannot adopt or ratify a contract entered into prior to its incorporation by a person professing to act as its agent, for an agent cannot act on behalf of a non-existing principal (rule in *Kelner* v *Baxter* (1866) LR 2 CP 174), but it can adopt a contract made for its benefit by a person acting as principal (*stipulatio alteri*). Such a contract need not comply with the requirements of s 35. It is a question of fact in each case whether a person who acts for a company prior to its incorporation does so as an agent or trustee under s 35 or as a principal at common law: 77–80.

A person who enters into a pre-incorporation contract as an agent under s 35 does not normally incur personal liability, and the ratification or adoption of the contract by the company does not normally have retroactive effect. A person who enters into a pre-incorporation contract by a *stipulatio alteri* acts as a principal. Personal entitlement and liability, and retroactivity depend upon intention.

B CASES

[77] McCullogh v Fernwood Estate Ltd
1920 AD 204

Action based on a contract of sale entered into between the plaintiff and one A on behalf of a company to be formed.

INNES CJ: . . . Grotius divides all unauthorized agreements for the benefit of third persons into two classes—those made with principals in favour of third persons, and those made with agents purporting to act on behalf of third persons. Both are valid, and both, if duly accepted or ratified, are enforceable by the third person concerned. The division seems satisfactory; for it is exhaustive and founded on principle. There may be difficulty, however, in ascertaining whether a particular transaction falls under one class or the other, especially where the third person was not in being at the date of the agreement, a position with which Grotius in the passage referred to does not deal. Yet the enquiry is of importance, because the rule that there can be no ratification by a principal not in existence at the date of the transaction is recognized by our law as well as by the law of England. . . . The English doctrine as laid down in *Kelner v Baxter* (1866) LR 2 CP 174 . . . seems clear. A company cannot ratify a contract made for its benefit before it was formed; nor can it adopt such contract by resolution. A new agreement on identical lines is necessary. The result may sometimes be unfortunate, but follows logically from an application of the doctrine that a principal not in being at the date of an agreement, and therefore not in a position to be bound by it then, cannot ratify it thereafter. Now the rule of English law that there must in every contract be consideration moving from the promisee, prohibits any agreement for the benefit of and enforceable by a third person, except one made by an agent on his behalf. And such an agreement cannot be entered into on behalf of a non-existent principal. But by our law, as already explained, it is possible to contract independently for the benefit of a third person; it is not necessary to do so as agent. Such a contract when duly accepted by the person for whose benefit it was made may be enforced by him. I know no reason in principle why this right of acceptance should be confined to cases where the third person was in being at the date of the contract. There is nothing in the authorities which points to such a conclusion. The sole test is whether the offer is open. And I cannot see why by our law a man should not himself stipulate in favour of his unborn child, or of the company which he is engaged in bringing into existence, leaving it to the beneficiary in due time to decide whether or not he will accept the benefit offered. . . .

[78] **Peak Lode Gold Mining Company Ltd *v* Union Government**
1932 TPD 48

GREENBERG J: The question in dispute in this appeal is whether the appellant is liable to the respondent for certain transfer duty. It is common cause that if the appellant is deemed to have entered into a certain agreement, to which I shall refer later, on 7 April 1927, then it is liable for the amount claimed and for which the magistrate has given judgment against it. On the other hand, if the appellant is deemed to have entered into this agreement on 21 July 1927, with no retroactive effect, then there is no liability.

The facts lie within a small compass. On 7 April 1927, an agreement was entered into between William Deans and Claudius Marais de Vries, as vendors, and Edward Rooth 'for and on behalf of Peak Lode Gold Mining Co Ltd, a company about to be registered with limited liability according to the law in the Union of South Africa'. Under this agreement Deans and De Vries purported to sell to the appellant certain base metal and gold-mining claims and also certain movable property. In consideration of this sale the appellant purported to agree to allot to the vendors certain shares in the company. On 12 May 1927, the company was incorporated according to law, and on 21 July 1927, the Registrar of Companies issued to the appellant a certificate under s 84 [now s 172(5)(*a*)] that it was entitled to commence business. On the same day the appellant, by resolution, adopted the agreement of 7 April 1927. It is clear from these facts that until the date of adoption the appellant was not liable under the agreement. Apart from s 84(3) of the Companies Act . . . there was nothing until that date to establish any contractual relationship between the appellant and the vendors. The respondent, however, contends that by the adoption of the agreement on 21 July 1927 effect must be given to the maxim *omnis ratihabitio retrotrahitur et mandato priori aequiparatur*, with the result that the appellant must be deemed to have entered into the agreement on the date on which it was signed, namely, 7 April 1927.

The first question to be decided is whether Rooth subjected himself to any liability by entering into this agreement. Ordinarily when a person enters into an agreement professing to act on behalf of another he subjects himself to certain liabilities to the other party to the agreement if in fact he has no authority and his alleged principal refuses to ratify the agreement. He is not liable on the contract but on a warranty of authority: *Blower* v *Van Noorden* 1909 TS 890. But it is clear from this decision that if the other party knows at the time of the contract that he has no authority, then this liability does not arise. . . . In *Blower* v *Van Noorden*, however, the court (at 897) expressly excluded from its inquiry the case of a person who professes to act on behalf of a principal not in being at the time, while in *Kelner* v *Baxter* (1866) LR 2 CP 174 it was held that where a person professes to contract on behalf of a principal, who is non-existent, then the so-called agent is personally liable on the contract. I think that the decision is based on the ground that under English law a contract made on behalf of a principal who is not in being at the time cannot thereafter be ratified or adopted by the principal, and the agent is therefore deemed to have contracted on his own behalf. This was also the position under our law until the passing of the Companies Act of 1926, but I think the position is altered by s 71 [now s 35]. This section enables a company, after its incorporation, to ratify or adopt a contract made before its incorporation by an agent professing to act on its behalf. It seems to me, therefore, to follow that the position of an unauthorized agent is now the same whether the alleged principal was or was not in existence at the time of the contract and that such an agent is not liable as a party to the contract, nor is he liable under a warranty of authority if the other contracting party knew at the time of the contract that he had no authority. . . .

In the present case there can be no doubt that the vendors knew that Rooth had no authority from the appellant seeing that . . . the appellant was not yet registered. He was, therefore, not liable under the agreement under any warranty of authority, and if I am right in my view as to the effect of s 71, he would not be deemed to have entered into the contract of sale on his own behalf. . . . In my opinion Rooth was under no liability to the vendors between the time the contract was entered into and when it was adopted, and the binding force of the agreement was conditional upon its adoption. The effect of the agreement was that the appellant, within a reasonable time after its incorporation, and after receipt of the certificate under s 84, was entitled to adopt the contract which, until that date, merely had the effect of granting an option to the appellant. Nor do I think that Rooth was under any liability for payment of transfer duty under s 25 of Proclamation No 8 of 1902. I think that this section deals with the case of a person who represents that he has authority and not to the case of a contract such as the present one. If I am right in the view that Rooth would in no case become liable either to the vendors or to the respondent then I do not think that the maxim applies. In my opinion the maxim would only apply to cases where, until the ratification, the liability existed, but it does not operate to create a liability which never existed.

The result is that the contract was conditional until adoption by the appellant, and only became binding at that date with no retroactive effect, and that the appellant became liable for transfer duty on and as from 21 July, 1927 from which date the period of six months referred to in ss 7 and 9 of Proclamation No 8 of 1902, commenced to run. It it were otherwise there would be the anomaly that although neither the appellant nor any person was liable for transfer duty before 21 July, nevertheless the period of six months during which transfer duty must be paid would commence to run on 7 April 1927.

The only other question is whether this conclusion is affected by the words 'as if it had been duly formed, incorporated and registered at the time when the contract was made' in s 71 of the Companies Act. In my opinion it is not. Under the law before this Act was passed, as laid down in *McCullogh* v *Fernwood Estate Ltd* (*supra*), difficulties were likely to arise as to whether a person who purchased property which was to be taken over by a company about to be formed was acting as an agent or a trustee, and I think that the whole object of s 71 was to make it immaterial in which of these capacities he acted and to do away with the difficulty of deciding in which capacity he had acted. It may be that under the contract Rooth warranted not that he had authority from appellant to enter into the contract, but that appellant after its incorporation would bind itself in terms of the contract. Assuming that this is so, it does not assist the respondent because if this is the right view then clearly there was no sale until 21 July, when the company entered into the contract and so enabled Rooth to fulfil his bargain. It is, I think, clear, even if there was this liability on Rooth, that the maxim of retroactivity cannot apply to this view of the contract. . . .

[Since the passing of the Transfer Duty Act 40 of 1949, there is liability for transfer duty in a case such as *Peak Lode Gold Mining Company*. Section 1 defines the 'date of acquisition' as 'the date on which the transaction was entered into, irrespective of whether the transaction was conditional or not *or was entered into on behalf of a company* already registered or *still to be registered*'.]

[79] *Ex parte* **Vickerman**
1935 CPD 429

WATERMEYER J: The contract was made between Vickerman and certain three parties by which the latter persons purchased land for and on behalf of a limited liability company to be formed. They now wish to transfer this land to the company which was formed the day after this contract was entered into but the Registrar of Deeds raised a difficulty, which is caused by s 71 of the Companies Act. The company has agreed to adopt and ratify that contract, but he contends that they cannot get transfer of the land unless the memorandum of association contains a clause which states that one of the objects of the company is to adopt and ratify that particular contract. . . . Now previous to [the] Act there was the case of *McCullogh* v *Fernwood Estate Ltd* 1920 AD 204, where it was held that a company can by adoption or ratification obtain the benefit of a contract made on its behalf before it came into existence where such contract has been made by a person acting individually and not as the agent of the company. I think that s 71 of the Companies Act was not intended to curtail the right of a company to adopt a contract made for its benefit but to extend that right to cover the case where the person acting for the company about to be formed was acting as agent and not individually. . . .

In the present case the contract made between Vickerman and the purchasers seems to me a contract in which those purchasers acted not as agents for the company about to be formed, but in which they acted in their individual capacities, but stipulating for a company about to be formed. The only difficulty is the heading of the contract, in which the purchasers are described as purchasers for and on behalf of a limited liability company about to be formed. That, prima facie, looks as if they were acting as agents for the company about to be formed. But from the terms of the contract it appears that the purchasers agreed personally to pay £500 on the signing of the contract and agreed personally to take possession of the property, and personally to pay transfer duty to the Government and to pay rates and taxes, and personally undertook, should the company not be registered by the time transfer had to be taken, to take transfer in their respective names jointly; and undertook to pay the sum of £2 200 in cash against registration of transfer. . . . All these things show that they were acting as principals and undertaking personal liabilities, and not merely contracting as agents for a company about to be formed. That being the case, it seems to me that the company, independently of s 71 of the Companies Act, could adopt and ratify this contract, and consequently it seems to me that the applicants are entitled to an order directing the Registrar of Deeds to register transfer.

[80] Nordis Construction Co (Pty) Ltd v Theron, Burke and Isaac
1972 (2) SA 535 (N)

A tender by the plaintiff to do certain work for a company was accepted by the defendant who professed to act as agent of the company. Both parties believed the company to be already in existence but in fact it was still in course of formation. The requirements of s 71 were not complied with. The company was subsequently incorporated but did not adopt or ratify the contract. The plaintiff sought to hold the defendant personally liable on the contract. It was clear, on the facts, that the rule in *McCullogh* v *Fernwood Estate, 77* above, did not apply as the defendant had not acted as a principal.

LEON J: In this action the plaintiff, a construction company, is claiming R4 274,63 from the defendant a partnership firm of consulting civil and structural engineers.

During October 1969, the plaintiff tendered to carry out certain work near the Umgeni River Mouth in Durban. That tender was made by the plaintiff in response to a request by the defendant professing to act as agent for a company known as Hi-Slide (Pty) Ltd. Although disputed on the pleadings it became common cause at the trial that the aforementioned tender was made in response to a request by one Burke a partner of the defendant firm.

The tender, which is dated 6 October 1969, was in writing and was signed by E H Karsten on behalf of the plaintiff. . . .

It is alleged by the plaintiff in its particulars of claim that the defendant accepted the plaintiff's tender on 9 October 1969 and that such acceptance was:

(i) in writing, and
(ii) signed by T J Burke on behalf of the defendant.

The plaintiff further alleges that, in accepting the plaintiff's tender, the defendant:

(i) professed to be acting as agent for Hi-Slide (Pty) Ltd; and
(ii) represented that it had authority so to act. . . .

There is no dispute on the pleadings that Hi-Slide was only incorporated on 27 November 1969. It was in issue on the pleadings as to whether or not the provisions of s 71 of the Companies Act 46 of 1926 were complied with 'as regards the apparent contract which resulted from the acceptance of plaintiff's tender'. At the commencement of the trial, however, Mr F, on behalf of the defendant, admitted that neither the company's memorandum nor its articles of association made any reference to any pre-incorporation contract and that the company has no minute reflecting that the directors had ever ratified or adopted any such contract. Finally, counsel for the defendant stated that despite the issue raised in the pleadings it was admitted by the defendant that the provisions of s 71 of the Companies Act had not been complied with. . . .

I will deal with the issues raised *seriatim*. [Mr B, on behalf of the plaintiff] submitted that the evidence established that the defendant acted at all material times as an agent and not as a mere channel of communication. [Mr F], on the other hand, [on behalf of the defendant] urged that Burke was merely a 'boodskapper of *nuntius*' (see De Wet en Yeats *Kontraktereg en Handelsreg* 3 ed 82). I am unable to accede to the submissions made by counsel for the defendant. The defendant has admitted para 3(*b*) of the plaintiff's particulars of claim, ie that the plaintiff's tender was submitted in response to a request by the defendant purporting to act as agent for Hi-Slide (Pty) Ltd. Furthermore the evidence shows that at the time when the telephone call took place between Karsten and Burke:

(1) Burke knew that the defendant's principal was Hi-Slide (Pty) Ltd.
(2) Karsten believed that Burke was acting on behalf of Hi-Slide (Pty) Ltd.
(3) Both parties accepted the position that the defendant was acting as the agent for Hi-Slide (Pty) Ltd. . . .

There remains to be considered the point to which most of the argument was devoted, ie whether, as a matter of law the defendant is liable. Mr B submitted that this case was governed by the principle referred to in the English case of *Kelner* v *Baxter & others* (1867) LR 2 CP 174, which was approved by the Privy Council in *Natal Land and Colonization Company Limited* v *Pauline Colliery Syndicate Ltd* [1904] AC 120 (PC). In *Kelner* v *Baxter* the plaintiff sent a written proposal to the defendants for the sale of certain stock and the defendants sent the plaintiff a written acceptance thereof. The proposal was directed to and accepted by the defendants on behalf of 'the proposed Gravesend Royal Alexandra Hotel Co Ltd'. The company was not then in existence. The plaintiff sued the defendants on the agreement. It was held that as the company was non-existent at the time of the agreement, the defendants were personally liable. . . .

It was submitted by Mr F that *Kelner* v *Baxter* is distinguishable from the present case in the following important respects:

(i) In *Kelner's* case both parties were aware of the non-existence of the company. In this case they were ignorant of its non-existence.
(ii) In *Kelner's* case the parties intended that there should be a liability on the part of the agent. In this case the facts show that the parties intended only the company to be bound. . . .

In *Wolhuter* v *Smith & another* 8 HCG 109 the defendant, acting on behalf of a syndicate about to be formed, purchased certain farms from the plaintiffs. The syndicate was never formed and the defendant refused to pay for the farms. The plaintiff claimed damages for breach of contract. The defendant excepted to the plaintiff's declaration. The exceptions were dismissed. The very brief report (at 110) states that the court held that the case clearly fell within the principle that, when a person contracts on behalf of a principal not in existence at the time, such person binds himself and must be held liable as an individual.

Kelner v *Baxter* was also applied and followed in *L and SA Exploration Co* v *Murphy* 4 HCG 322 at 335, which was a similar case. Laurence J expressed himself as follows at 335:

'I think that there can be no doubt on the authority of the cases cited by *Pollock on Contracts* 4 ed 107, 108; *Kelner* v *Baxter* LR 2 CP 174; *Scott* v *Lord Ebury* ibid 225; *Re Empress Engineering Company* 16 ChD 125, that the defendant by this agreement made himself personally liable and that, as stated in the headnote of *Kelner* v *Baxter*, which is quite opposed to the contention of his counsel upon this point, "parol evidence was not admissible to show that personal liability was not intended".' ...

The full bench of the Transvaal Provincial Division in *Gompels* v *Skodawerke of Prague* 1942 TPD 167 also approved the decision, although the case was held not to be applicable to the facts with which the court was there concerned. However, Greenberg JP, who gave the judgment of the court, referred to *Kelner* v *Baxter* in these terms at 170:

'The decision in that case was that where a person enters into a contract with another, the first person professing to act as agent for a company which is not yet in existence, then the law regards it as a contract between the first person in his individual capacity and the other person. In intendment of law he is taken to contract on his own behalf.'

It should be pointed out that the phrase 'professing to act for a company which is not yet in existence' is capable of meaning that it was expressly stated that the company was not yet in existence.

Some years earlier the same learned judge in *Peak Lode Gold Mining Co Ltd* v *Union Government* [*78* above] explained the basis of the decision in *Kelner* v *Baxter* thus at 50–1:

'I think that the decision is based on the ground that under English law a contract made on behalf of a principal who is not in being at the time cannot thereafter be ratified or adopted by the principal and the agent is therefore deemed to have contracted on his own behalf. This was also the position under our law until the passing of the Companies Act of 1926, but I think that the position is altered by s 71 of the Act. This section enables a company, after its incorporation, to ratify or adopt a contract made before its incorporation by an agent professing to act on its behalf. It seems to me, therefore, to follow that the position of an unauthorized agent is now the same whether the alleged principal was or was not in existence at the time of the contract and that such an agent is not liable as a party to the contract, nor is he liable under a warranty of authority if the other contracting party knew at the time of the contract that he had no authority.' ...

Section 71 of the Companies Act has no application to this case nor does the principle referred to in *McCullogh* v *Fernwood Estate* [*77* above] apply as the defendant contracted as agent and not as principal. If follows that the company could not ratify. There is therefore some force in Mr B's contention that, in order to render the contract operative it should be construed in such a way as to render the defendant personally liable. In answer to this argument counsel for the defendant relied, *inter alia*, on *Blower* v *Van Noorden* 1909 TS 890. That case was not concerned with a similar situation to the present case. Indeed Innes CJ (at 897) specifically excluded from consideration the case of an agent acting in good faith on behalf and in the name of a principal not in being at the time. It was there held that an agent who has exceeded his authority in contracting for a named principal is liable in damages to the other contracting party on the ground that, from his representations of authority, a personal undertaking on his part is to be implied that his principal will be bound, and that, if not, the other party will be placed in as good a position as if he were.

Although that case did not deal with the position with which I am concerned, counsel for the defendant urged that an agent without authority is in a similar position to a so-called agent for a non-existent principal. An agent acting without authority is not liable *ex contractu* because he is not a party to the contract. Similarly, it was contended, a so-called agent for a non-existent principal could only be liable *ex contractu* if it could be shown as a matter of construction that the agent was in fact a party to the contract. It was at this level that reliance was placed on the following remarks of Innes CJ at 899:

> 'During the two hundred years which have passed since Voet wrote, the doctrine of commercial agency has been developed along lines then already recognized, though not fully explored, with the result that an agent is now regarded as one to whom no contractual liability in respect of agreements entered into in the name of his principal, can possibly attach. He is simply and solely the representative of another. This view of the position of a modern agent is now so firmly established and so generally recognized, that no person dealing with an agent, as such, can be held to have intended to contract with him personally unless the terms of the contract itself make it clear that he did. To hold under these circumstances that an agent, acting in the name of an existing principal, but in excess of his authority, is liable on the contract itself, or takes the place of the named principal as a party thereto, would be to make a new contract which neither of the parties contemplated. And it is impossible to fall back upon the doctrine of the general liability of an agent upon all contracts made by him, because that doctrine cannot coexist with the modern idea of his position and responsibilities.' . . .

A similar approach is to be found in the case of *Newborne* v *Sensolid (Great Britain) Ltd* [1953] 1 All ER 708. There the plaintiff was the promoter and prospective director of a limited company, Leopold Newborne (London) Ltd, which, at the time when the contract (to which I shall presently refer) was entered into, had not yet been registered. A contract for the supply of goods to the defendants was signed: 'Leopold Newborne (London) Ltd' and the plaintiff's name was written underneath. In an action for breach of contract brought by the plaintiff against the defendants it was held that the contract was made, not with the plaintiff, whether as agent or as principal, but with a limited company which at the date of the making of the contract was non-existent, and, therefore, it was a nullity and the plaintiff could not adopt it or sue on the contract.

Unlike the situation in *Kelner* v *Baxter* the contract in *Newborne's* case was *ex facie* one with an existing company whereas in *Kelner* v *Baxter* the contract was *ex facie* a contract with a non-existent company.

Lord Goddard CJ, in giving the judgment of the Court of Appeal, and after having set out the facts in *Kelner* v *Baxter*, went on to say at 710:

> 'It seems to me a very long way from saying that every time a prospective company, not yet in existence, purports to contract everybody who signs for the company makes himself personally liable.'

Although that case is not on all fours with the present case I have found the reasoning therein both persuasive and helpful.

It would therefore seem that this case has one important feature in common with *Kelner* v *Baxter*, namely that the company could not ratify. On the other hand there is a crucial point of distinction between this case and that of *Kelner* v *Baxter*. There, *ex facie* the contract, the parties intended that the 'agent' was contracting on behalf of a non-existent person. Even if, therefore, some straining of language was involved in holding the 'agent' personally liable it was not a matter of great difficulty to do so *as a matter of construction* in view of the fact that *ex facie* the contract there was a non-existent principal—a 'nonentity'. In such circumstances the contract proclaimed that the 'agent' was not, strictly speaking, an 'agent' at all. . . . In the present case the common intention of the parties which appears from the contract was to contract with a company in existence; the parties intended that the defendant was acting *as an agent for such a company*. . . .

. . . That principal was intended and believed to be a company. To hold the defendant personally liable upon such a contract would be to make a new contract for the parties which neither of them ever intended. There can be no justification for construing the agreement in such a way. Whatever the precise limits of the *Kelner* v *Baxter* principle may be, I am of the opinion that that principle has no application to the present case.

I express no opinion on the question as to whether the defendant is liable for damages for breach of warranty of authority and, if so, whether such damages can be proved.

NOTES

Nordis Construction Co (Pty) Ltd v *Theron, Burke and Isaac* was followed in *Terblanche* v *Nothnagel* 1975 (4) SA 405 (C). In *Black* v *Smallwood* (1966) 39 *ALJR* 405, the High Court of Australia, following *Newborne* v *Sensolid (Great Britain) Ltd* [1954] 1 QB 45, had arrived at the same result.

Barwick CJ, with whom Kitto, Taylor and Owen JJ concurred, said (at 408): '. . . in the present case the respondents did not contract, or purport to contract, on behalf of the non-existing company. They simply subscribed the name of the non-existent company and added their own signatures as directors in the belief that the company had been formed and that they were directors. The fact that their signatures appeared as part of the company's signature did not make them parties to the contract nor could, as was possible in *Kelner* v *Baxter*, an intention to be bound personally be imputed to them. . . .'

Where, however, the person contracting does not make it clear that he is merely acting in a representative capacity, he may be personally liable: *Con-Force Products Ltd* v *Rosen* (1967) 64 DLR 63. Again, he may be personally liable on breach of warranty of authority if he represents the company as already existing.

In *Sentrale Kunsmis Korporasie (Edms) Bpk* v *NKP Kunsmisverspreiders (Edms) Bpk* 1970 (3) SA 367 (AD) three legal questions were in issue: (1) whether a company which does not have the adoption of a pre-incorporation contract as one of its objects at the time of its incorporation can subsequently remedy the defect by altering its objects clause. The majority of the court answered the question in the affirmative. Since s 35 of the 1973 Act, unlike s 71 of the 1926 Act, requires that the adoption or ratification of the pre-incorporation contract must be contained as an object of the company in its memorandum *on its registration*, the question can no longer arise.

(2) Whether failure to lodge two copies of the contract, one certified, invalidates it. The majority of the court held that this requirement was merely directory. Trollip JA dissented, holding that the failure to lodge two copies was fatal to the contract.

(3) Whether the contract in the case before the court could be construed as a *stipulatio alteri*, which did not have to comply with s 71. On this point, Holmes JA said (at 394):

'Maar die hof *a quo*, dws die Voltallige Regbank, het verder beslis dat die respondent op die beginsel van 'n beding ten behoewe van 'n derde kan staatmaak, wat niks te make het met arts 71 en 11 van die Maatskappyewet nie. In die hof van eerste instansie is namens die huidige respondent melding daarvan gemaak, maar beswaar daarteen is deur die advokaat van die appellant gemaak. Na my mening kan die respondent nie op hierdie grond steun nie. Die hele uiteensetting van die eerste aansoek, en ook dié in die huidige saak, is op die veronderstelling van agentskap gefundeer. Dit was presies om hierdie rede dat die respondent gebruik van arts 71 en 11 wou maak. Die beëdigde verklaring namens die respondent bevat geen feite-bewering, òf uitdruklik, òf stilswyend, dat die betrokke vier persone nie verteenwoordigers was nie maar wel prinsipale was, wat met die appellant ten behoewe van 'n derde ooreengekom het. Inteendeel word in die beëdigde verklaring gesê dat die ooreenkoms ,,namens" die respondent aangegaan is; en in 'n brief aan die appellant gedateer 4 Augustus 1966 word gesê dat, na inkorporasie, die ooreenkoms ,,geratifiseer is". Sulke woorde kan slegs in verband met agentskap gebruik word. As die respondent hom op 'n beding ten behoewe van 'n derde wou verlaat, sou die appellant geregtig gewees het om feite te beweer ten opsigte van die uitleg van die woorde ,,in hulle respektiewelike persoonlike hoedanighede en in hulle hoedanighede as trustees van 'n maatskappy wat geregistreer staan te word". Na my mening het die hof *a quo* verkeerdelik beslis dat, op die oorkonde soos dit staan, die huidige respondent op 'n *stipulatio alteri* kan staatmaak.'

On the meaning of the words 'professing to act as agent or trustee . . .' in s 71 (now s 35), Trollip JA had this to say (at 397):

'Now the use of the words "professing to act as an agent" in s 71 is understandable, for prior to the company's incorporation no person can act in law as its agent; he can only profess to act as such. On the other hand, according to our common law a person can act as a trustee for a company to be formed (see *McCullogh* v *Fernwood Estate Ltd (supra)* at 208–9); the section does not however refer to a contract made by a person acting as a trustee, but to one "professing to act as a trustee"; that connotes that, whilst the person declares that he is acting as a trustee, he is in fact or in law not one; and, as he is actually not a trustee, the only other relevant capacity in which he can be acting for the company is that of an agent. That shows, I think, that s 71 was only meant to apply to a pre-incorporation contract made by a person acting as an agent for the company, whether he calls himself an agent or a trustee. The reference later in the section to the binding effect of the company's ratifying the contract supports that conclusion: it is to be as binding as if the company had existed at the time the contract was made "and such contract had been made without its authority". That provision points clearly to the postulated contract being one by an agent.'

[*Sentrale Kunsmis* was noted by Lila E Isakow (1971) 88 *SALJ* 165 and by N C (1971) 11 *Rh LJ* 7.]

In *Olifants Trust Co* v *Pattison* 1971 (3) SA 888 (W) it was held that the mere fact that the person who enters into the pre-incorporation contract binds himself personally in the event of the company's not being formed, does not necessarily mean that he is acting as a principal.

A pre-incorporation contract may validly specify a date by which the proposed company has to ratify the agreement, *Malcolm* v *Cooper* 1974 (4) SA 52 (C).

'In my opinion . . . there is no rule of law entitling a person who contracts as trustee for a company to be formed, to claim transfer of property into his own name, merely by reason of the fact that the company has not been formed', *Gardiner* v *Richardt* 1974 (3) SA 768 (C) at 773, per Friedman AJ. But see also *Bagradi* v *Cavendish Transport Company (Pty) Ltd* 1957 (1) SA 663 (N).

In *Swart* v *Mbutzi Development (Edms) Bpk* 1975 (1) SA 544 (T) the pre-incorporation contract took the form of an option agreement. The memorandum of the company did not have its adoption or ratification as one of its objects. The court held that on the alleged exercise of the option by the company no legally valid agreement of sale came into being.

In *Pledge Investment (Pty) Ltd* v *Kramer NO* 1975 (3) SA 696 (AD) the Appellate Division, overruling *Nicolau* v *Navarone Investments (Pty) Ltd* 1971 (3) SA 883 (W), held that a sale by public auction, once it has been confirmed by the signing of the conditions of sale, is a 'contract made in writing' within the meaning of s 71 (now s 35).

A person acting for the future company as a principal at common law will be held more readily personally liable than one who acted as an agent under s 71 (now s 35): *Peak Lode Gold Mining Co Ltd* v *Union Government* (78, above); *Semer* v *Retief and Berman* 1948 (1) SA 182 (C); and *Maree* v *Du Preez* 1956 (2) PH F127 (T). See also I B Murray in (1958) 75 *SALJ* at 196, and W E D Davies 'Personal Liability of "Directors" of Non-Existent Companies' (1964) 6 *Univ of Western Australia LR* 400.

See further *Gompels* v *Skodawerke* 1942 TPD 167; *Ackermann NO* v *Burland and Milinsky* 1944 WLD 172; also *Kynochs Ltd* v *Transvaal Silver and Base Metals Ltd* 1922 WLD 71 (cf *Rand Trading Co Ltd* v *Lewkewitsch* 1908 TS 108); *Naik* v *Westville Estates (Pty) Ltd* 1934 NPD 152; *Ex parte Elands Properties (Pty) Ltd* 1945 TPD 37; *African Organic Fertilizers and Associated Industries Ltd* v *Premier Fertilizers Ltd* 1948 (3) SA 233 (N); *Martian Entertainments* v *Berger* 1949 (4) SA 583 (E). In *Gaybelle Investments (Pty) Ltd* v *Hermer* 1951 (1) SA 486 (W) it was held that as long as a contract for the purchase of fixed property entered into by a person acting as agent for a company not yet formed in terms of s 71 complies with the requirements of that section, it is valid and binding even though the requirements of ss 28 and 30 of the Transfer Duty Proclamation 8 of 1902 (Transvaal) (now the Formalities of Contracts of Sale of Land Act 71 of 1969 s 1) are not satisfied in that the name of the future company as the purchaser is not inserted in the deed of sale. Per Millin J at 488: 'As ss 28 and 30 of the proclamation cannot be applied in contracts for sale of fixed property falling under s 71 of the Companies Act, the legislature, in my opinion, intended that their operation should be excluded. Section 71 is self-contained and nothing more is required to validate a contract, including a contract for the purchase of fixed property, than compliance in every respect with the section. See also B R Bamford (1963) 80 *SALJ* at 82; M Laubscher (1971) 2 *Responsa Meridiana* 119; J D M Swart (1974) 7 *De Jure* 19; and p 470 below.

III DEREGISTRATION

In the circumstances set out in s 73 a company's memorandum and articles of association may be cancelled by the Registrar. This process is known as deregistration, s 1 s v 'deregistration'. The effect is that the company ceases to exist as a corporation, see *Silver Sands Transport (Pty) Ltd* v *SA Linde* 1973 (3) SA 548 (W). On re-registration, see *Ex parte Smith: In re Parkside Trading Co (Pty) Ltd (now dissolved)* 1974 (2) PH E9 (C).

6 *Capital*

I CAPITAL AND THE CAPITAL MAINTENANCE RULE

A TEXT

Share capital may be divided into shares having a par value, or it may consist of shares having no par value, provided that all the ordinary shares and all the preference shares must consist of either the one or the other, s 74. The capital of a company and its division into shares, or the number of shares if the company is to have shares of no par value, must be stated in its memorandum, ss 52(2)(*a*), 74. That part of the stated or nominal capital of a company which has been issued constitutes its issued share capital: *81*. It is no longer permissible to issue or allot any shares unless the full issue price or other consideration has been paid to and received by the company, s 92(1). In the case of shares having no par value the whole of the proceeds of the issue is paid-up capital and must be transferred to a 'stated capital account', s 77.

In contradistinction to most continental company laws but in common with English company law, our law does not prescribe a minimum capital for either a public or a private company. However, before a company is issued with a certificate to commence business it must lodge, *inter alia*, a statement of the opinion of each director to the effect that the capital of the company is adequate for its purposes or, if he is of the opinion that it is inadequate, the reasons therefor and the manner in which and the sources from which the company is to be financed, s 172(3)(*a*) (see also Schedule 3 para 22), and a company issuing a prospectus may not proceed to the allotment of shares until it has received the minimum subscription in cash, ss 165, 167, and Schedule 3 para 21.

Moreover, while no minimum capital is prescribed, the capital maintenance rule applies: *82–84*. Save by a reduction of capital in terms of ss 83ff or in terms of a compromise or arrangement under s 311, a company may not (subject to minor exceptions) diminish its capital otherwise than by expenditure upon its business, see eg *338, 346* below. More specifically, a company may not

(1) purchase its own shares (p 211 below); or
(2) finance the purchase of its own shares by others (pp 214ff below); or

(3)   issue shares at a discount (p 237 below); or
(4)   pay dividends out of capital: *84* (and p 558 below).

B CASES

[81] Benoni, Brakpan and Springs Board of Executors, Building Society and Trust Company Ltd *v* Commissioner of Inland Revenue
1921 TPD 170

WESSELS JP: [It is contended that] 'the uncalled capital cannot be considered capital employed in the business of the company, inasmuch as it is capital which is still in the hands of the shareholders of the company and does not become a debt due until it has been called up by resolution of the company'. Mr Lucas has argued that the uncalled capital of the company should be considered as part of its capital, either because it is an asset of the company, or because it is a debt due to the company. It is not necessary to go through all the argument again; it is quite sufficient to say that we abide by the decision in *Whittaker* v *Kershaw* (1890) 45 ChD 320, where it is clearly laid down that the uncalled capital of a company is not a debt due to the company.

Then the next question is whether the uncalled capital of a company can be regarded as part of the assets of the company. Now the word 'assets' is used in so many different ways and has such a large and varying meaning that before you can determine the meaning of the word in any particular statute, you have to take the whole scope of the statute into consideration. In *Page* v *International Agency and Industrial Trust Ltd* (1893) 62 LJ Ch 610 Kekewich J deals with the meaning of 'assets'. He says (p 613): 'The primary meaning of "assets" is that which is available for payment of debts on taking proper accounts into liquidation. It means what can be got, and is enough, or generally less than enough to satisfy the liabilities.' That is the ordinary meaning, and when we are dealing with the assets of a company it is a relative term which refers to the liquidation of the company; it refers to a comparison between what it has got and what is due by it. In that respect if a company is actually in liquidation, then the uncalled up capital of the company may be regarded as part of its assets, but when we are regarding the company from the point of view of a trading concern, something for making profits out of its capital, then the uncalled capital of a company cannot be regarded as part of its assets. Until the amount of uncalled capital is called up, until it has been liquidated, and until the company is entitled to claim from its shareholders it cannot be said to be part of its assets. It may one day become an asset of the company, something tangible that can be transferred away, but in the ordinary sense it is not part of the assets of the company. . . .

NOTES

In a number of cases decided before the 1973 Act it was held that a company can mortgage its uncalled capital, *In re Pyle Works* (1890) 44 ChD 534; *Ex parte Gunn NO: In re Contributories of Krag Engineering (Pty) Ltd (in liquidation)* 1965 (3) SA 231 (O). As a company may no longer issue or allot shares unless they are paid in full (see p 144), the question can no longer arise.

[82] Trevor v Whitworth
(1887) 12 App Cas 409

A company having gone into liquidation, a former shareholder claimed from the company the balance of the price of his shares which he had sold to the company before the liquidation and which were not wholly paid for. The claim was dismissed.

LORD WATSON: ... One of the main objects contemplated by the legislature, in restricting the power of limited companies to reduce the amount of their capital as set forth in the memorandum, is to protect the interests of the outside public who may become their creditors. In my opinion the effect of these statutory restrictions is to prohibit every transaction between a company and a shareholder, by means of which the money already paid to the company in respect of his shares is returned to him, unless the court has sanctioned the transaction. Paid-up capital may be diminished or lost in the course of the company's trading; that is a result which no legislation can prevent; but persons who deal with, and give credit to a limited company, naturally rely upon the fact that the company is trading with a certain amount of capital already paid, as well as upon the responsibility of its members for the capital remaining at call; and they are entitled to assume that no part of the capital which has been paid into the coffers of the company has been subsequently paid out except in the legitimate course of its business.

When a share is forfeited or surrendered, the amount which has been paid upon it remains with the company, the shareholder being relieved of liability for future calls, whilst the share itself reverts to the company, bears no dividend, and may be reissued. When shares are purchased at par, and transferred to the company, the result is very different. The amount paid up on the shares is returned to the shareholder; and in the event of the company continuing to hold the shares (as in the present case) is permanently withdrawn from its trading capital. It appears to me that, as the late Master of the Rolls pointed out in *In re Dronfield Silkstone Coal Company* (1880) 17 ChD 76 at 83, it is inconsistent with the essential nature of a company that it should become a member of itself. It cannot be registered as a shareholder to the effect of becoming debtor to itself for calls, or of being placed on the list of contributories in its own liquidation. ...

When a company, in order to get rid of a troublesome shareholder, buys his shares and continues to hold them, as in *In re Dronfield Silkstone Coal Company*, the object may be different, but the result, so far as regards the capital of the company, is precisely the same as if it had purchased the shares as an investment. If the shares are purchased with a view to being resold, that is simply a speculation with the funds of the company. If they are purchased with the view of their being retained by the company, that is a permanent withdrawal of the money invested in them from the trading capital of the company. I do not agree with Cotton LJ [in the court below], in thinking that if such a transaction is invalid no forfeiture or surrender could be supported. When shares are forfeited or surrendered and not reissued, that affects only the nominal amount of the shares so far as unpaid; when they are bought and not reissued that diminishes the paid-up as well as the nominal capital. ...

[83] Guiness *v* The Land Corporation of Ireland

(1882) 22 ChD 349

The articles of a company which had A and B shares provided, *inter alia*, that the capital produced by the issue of B shares should be invested and that the income, and so far as necessary, the capital, should be applied so as to make good to the holders of A shares a preferential dividend of £5 per cent on the amounts paid up. The court held that the capital provided by the B shares could not be used to pay a dividend to the holders of the A shares.

COTTON LJ: The Act requires the memorandum to state the objects of the company and the amount of capital with which the company proposes to be registered. What is the meaning of the word 'capital', and what is the effect of the statement of the amount of capital in the memorandum, having regard to the other sections of the Act? We have first to ascertain what is meant by 'capital', and to my mind s 38 as to the liability of members is of the utmost importance as a guide to answering that question. That section provides that in the case of a company limited by shares being wound up, no contribution shall be required from any member exceeding the amount if any unpaid on the shares in respect of which he is liable as a present or past member; that the capital of the company as mentioned in the memorandum is to be the fund which is to pay the creditors in the event of the company being wound up. From that it follows that whatever has been paid by a member cannot be returned to him. In my opinion it also follows that what is described in the memorandum as the capital cannot be diverted from the objects of the society. It is, of course, liable to be spent or lost in carrying on the business of the company, but no part of it can be returned to a member so as to take away from the fund to which the creditors have a right to look as that out of which they are to be paid. In former days proceedings could be taken against members of a company, but under the present law a creditor has no remedy except execution against the goods of the company, or winding-up proceedings. If a winding-up order is made each shareholder is liable to contribute the amount not paid up on his shares, including what if anything he has had returned. It follows, as I have said, that no part of the capital mentioned in the memorandum can be taken out of the fund to which the creditors have to look except for the purpose of employing it for the objects of the company.

[84] Cohen NO *v* Segal

1970 (3) SA 702 (W)

BOSHOFF J: In this action the liquidator of the Johannesburg Timber Co (Pty) Ltd in liquidation is in effect claiming from the defendant a refund of money which it is alleged was constructively paid out of the company to the defendant and one Harber by the operation of set-off as the result of the wrongful declaration of a dividend, which declaration was *ultra vires* the company inasmuch as there were no profits at all from which a dividend could be declared. The claim is being brought against the defendant because at the time of the declaration of the dividend he was a director and shareholder of the company. . . .

The question which immediately arises for consideration is the legal effect of the declaration of the dividend in the circumstances of this case. A shareholder is not entitled to claim his *aliquot* share of the profits made by the company unless a dividend is declared. Upon a declaration of a dividend the sums due for dividend become debts due from the company to the shareholders and the shareholders can sue the company for the dividend; *Boyd* v *Commissioner for Inland Revenue* 1951 (3) SA 525 (AD) at 534. As was pointed out in the case of *Estate McGregor* v *De Beer's Consolidated Mines* 20 SC 284 at 291, there may, however, be special circumstances in which a company might resist the payment of a dividend which had been declared, and by way of illustration a reference is made to the case where it is subsequently discovered that there was no profit to warrant the declaration of the dividend.

Section 6 of the Companies Act 46 of 1926 [s 52 of the 1973 Act] . . . requires that the object of a limited company must be stated in the memorandum of association. These objects cannot be enlarged by anything to be found in the articles of association or by anything outside the memorandum. Everything beyond that is prohibited. The amount of the share capital and the division thereof into shares of fixed amount must also be stated in the memorandum. Such capital is to be devoted to the objects of the company. Whatever has been paid by a member cannot be returned to him and no part of the *corpus* of the company can be returned to a member so as to take away from the fund to which the creditors have a right to look as that out of which they are to be paid. The capital may be spent or lost in carrying on the business of the company, but it cannot be reduced except in the manner and with the safeguards provided by the statute. As will appear from ss 44 to 50 [now ss 83ff] of the Companies Act it is against the policy of the Act that any portion of the capital should be returned to the shareholders without the statutory conditions being complied with. . . .

It follows from all this that a dividend cannot be declared which has the effect of diverting a portion of the *corpus* of the company to the shareholders. A dividend may thus, generally speaking, only be declared out of profits, and a resolution which declares a dividend to be paid out of the capital of the company is *ultra vires* the company.

The directors of a limited company are the creatures of statute and occupy a position peculiar to themselves. It has often been said that they are really commercial men managing a trading concern for themselves and all other shareholders in it. They occupy a fiduciary position towards the company and must exercise their powers bona fide solely for the benefit of the company as a whole and not for an ulterior motive. . . .

Directors are from time to time spoken of as agents, trustees or managing partners of a company, but such expressions are not used as exhaustive of the powers and responsibilities of those persons, but only as indicating useful points of view from which they may for the moment and for the particular purpose be considered, points of view at which, for the moment, they seem to be falling within the category of the suggested kind. It is not meant that they belong to the category, but that it is useful for the purpose of the moment to observe that they fall, *pro tanto*, within the principles which govern that particular class. . . .

An application of a company's money *ultra vires* the company is in fact a breach of trust on the part of the directors. In the case of such misapplication the directors are not only liable for what they put into their own pockets but also for what they, in breach of trust, pay to others. They have to account to the company for such moneys and their liability need not necessarily be based on fraud or delict. If it is sought to base their liability on fraud or delict it is necessary to prove the fault or blameworthiness which is essential for actions of that kind. In our law the action based on breach of trust is *sui generis*; . . .

[The plaintiff's action for damages nevertheless failed because no money was paid out by the company pursuant to the declaration of the dividend and the plaintiff failed to show that he had suffered any pecuniary loss.]

NOTES

On the liability of directors for payment of dividends out of capital, see also *Flitcroft's case 235* below. On their liability for authorizing, in contravention of s 38, the use of the company's funds in providing financial assistance for the purchase of its own shares, see *Selangor United Rubber Co v Cradock (No 3)*, p 235 below, and *Wallerstein v Moir (1), 128* below.

In *Ex parte Rietfontein Estates Ltd* 1976 (1) SA 175 (W), where a company had illegally purchased its own shares, the court confirmed a reduction of capital which had the effect of curing the illegal use of the company's funds.

Though a company cannot purchase its own shares or be a member of itself, there is no reason why shares acquired otherwise than by purchase (e g under a will) should not be held by a trustee for the benefit of the company: *In re Castiglione's Will Trusts* [1958] 1 All ER 480, [1958] Ch 549. See also *Kirby v Wilkins* [1929] 2 Ch 444.

II ALTERATION OF CAPITAL OTHER THAN A REDUCTION

A TEXT

Under s 75 a company, if so authorized by its articles, may by special resolution increase its share capital; increase the number of its issued no par value shares without an increase of its stated capital; consolidate or subdivide its shares; convert share capital consisting of shares having a par value into capital constituted by shares of no par value or vice versa (see also s 78); cancel shares which have not been taken or agreed to be taken and diminish the amount of its authorized share capital accordingly, such cancellation not to be deemed to be a reduction of capital; convert any of its shares, whether issued or not, into shares of another class: *84A*.

A company which is not authorized by its articles to alter its capital must alter its articles by special resolution so as to give itself this power. The special resolution altering the articles and the special resolution altering the capital may be passed at the same meeting, s 201.

The issue of hitherto unissued shares which form part of the nominal capital of the company is not an increase of capital in terms of s 75. In issuing new shares, shareholders' special rights must be observed.

B CASES

[84A] M Dalley & Co v Sims
(1968) 120 CLR 603 (HC of Australia)

A company was run by the managing director 'as if it were her own business', with 'no more than perfunctory attention to the requirements of the articles or of the Companies Acts'. An issue of bonus shares was proposed, for the implementation of which a resolution in general meeting to increase capital was required. No notice of a general meeting was given, and no meeting was held, but proceeding as though the capital had been increased, the company on the managing director's instructions issued the bonus shares and allotted them as a gift to one of its employees. The court held that the issue was invalid.

BARWICK CJ: . . . without valid increase in the amount of the company's nominal capital, there could not have been a valid bonus issue. I am unable to agree with the learned judge that the purported increase in capital was validated by the acquiescence or approbation of all the shareholders. My reasons for not agreeing with the conclusion that there was effective increase of the capital of the company are, first, that though undoubtedly all the active shareholders both agreed in advance to the steps which ought to have been taken to increase the capital of the company and subsequently acquiesced in the company being treated as if the capital had been duly increased, I do not think that the evidence linked all the shareholders with that agreement or that acquiescence: and, secondly, that in any case I entertain some doubt as presently advised as to whether the lack of a resolution duly passed to increase the capital can be overcome by acquiescence on the part of all the shareholders.

III REDUCTION OF CAPITAL

A TEXT

A company having a share capital may, if so authorized by its articles, reduce its capital by special resolution. If it has no creditors or all its creditors have consented to the reduction and the reduction will affect all its shares or any class of shares proportionally, and the reduction will be effected in some way other than by paying off capital in instalments or in future payments, no confirmation by the court is required, s 83. The remedy of a shareholder who considers that the reduction is unfairly prejudicial to him is to apply to court for relief under s 252. Where a reduction cannot be effected under s 83, a special resolution as well as confirmation by the court is required, s 84. In this case the reduction may be effected in any way the court deems fit to confirm, including the cancellation of paid-up share capital which is lost or not represented by available assets or repayment of any paid-up share capital which is in excess of the wants of the company, s 84(1). Payment in instalments or by future payments may be authorized, subject to the safeguards of s 84(4) and (5).

Where the proposed reduction under s 84 involves the payment to any shareholder of any paid-up capital, and in any other case if the court so directs, creditors who would be entitled to claim if the company were being wound up may object to the reduction, s 85. The court may not confirm the reduction unless it is satisfied that every creditor who is entitled to object under s 85 has either consented to the reduction or his claim has been discharged, secured, or determined, s 86(2). As to the provisions which apply to special resolutions for the reduction of capital, see s 87. The special resolution may not be acted upon before it is registered by the Registrar but may be given retrospective effect to a date not earlier than the date at which the special resolution was passed, s 88.

Any scheme or transaction which reduces the stated capital of a company amounts to a reduction within the meaning of the Act, but a reduction does not necessarily involve a reduction of the nominal or stated capital: 85, 86.

The following do not constitute a reduction within the meaning of the Act:

(a) the cancellation of unissued shares, s 75(2);
(b) the redemption of redeemable preference shares, s 98(3);
(c) the surrender of fully paid-up shares in exchange for new fully paid-up shares of equal value: 87;
(d) the forfeiture of partly paid-up shares for non-payment of calls, and the surrender of shares as a short-cut to forfeiture (since the 1973 Act does not permit the issue of partly paid-up shares (s 92(1)) this can now happen only with shares that were issued under the 1926 Act).

The provisions relating to the reduction of share capital apply, subject to certain exceptions, to the capital redemption reserve fund, s 98(1)(b), and the share premium account, s 76(1). (Note that s 76(1) covers premiums which came into existence prior to the commencement of the Act, s 76(5). Thus, *Ex parte Slater, Walker Securities (SA) Ltd* 1974 (4) SA 657 (W) is no longer law. On the question whether s 76 applies to no par value shares, see S W L Villiers *CILSA* 348.)

In those cases where confirmation by the court is required the court will not confirm the reduction unless it is satisfied that it will not work injustice on the shareholders or any class of shareholders and that the interests of creditors and the public are safeguarded: *88–91, 384* below.

B CASES

[85] *Ex Parte* **Associated Lead Manufacturers (Pty) Ltd**
1960 (2) SA 36 (D)

JANSEN J: The petitioner is a duly registered company with limited liability. Its nominal capital is £175 000, divided into 175 000 shares of £1 each, of which 150 000 have been issued and fully paid for. The remaining 25 000 shares have not been issued. Of the issued shares 149 997 are held by Goodlass Wall and Lead Industries Ltd of London, and the remaining 3 by 3 nominees of that company, who each hold 1 share on behalf of that company. The directors of petitioner have come to the conclusion that the issued share capital of the company is 'in excess of the needs of the company to the extent of £50 000 and that such surplus cannot profitably be employed in the company's business.'

The articles of association of petitioner provide *inter alia*:

'44. The Company may by special resolution:

(a) Alter the provisions of its memorandum of association in such manner and to such extent as may be permitted by s 11 or s 11*bis* of the Companies Act 1926, but subject always to the provisions of these sections.

(b) consolidate and divide all or any of its share capital into shares of larger amount than its existing shares.

(c) subdivide its existing shares or any of them, into shares of smaller amount than is fixed by the memorandum of association, subject nevertheless to the provisions of para (d) of ss (1) of s 39 of the Companies Act 1926.

(d) cancel any shares which, at the date of the passing of the resolution, have not been taken or agreed to be taken by any person.

(e) reduce its share capital and any capital redemption fund in any manner authorized and with, and subject to, any consent and incident required by law.

Pursuant to these powers all the shareholders, at a duly constituted special meeting, unanimously passed *inter alia* the following special resolution:

'1. That subject to the confirmation of the court in terms of s 44 of the Companies Act 1926 —

 (i) the issued share capital of the Company be reduced to £100 000, divided into 100 000 shares of a nominal value of £1 each.

 (ii) the aforesaid reduction be effected by paying off and returning to Goodlass Wall and Lead Industries Ltd the sum of £50 000 paid up in respect of 50 000 of the shares held by it in the Company.

 (iii) that the said 50 000 shares so paid off be treated as unissued.'

The present application is for a rule nisi with the object of obtaining the necessary confirmation. . . .

The only difficulty in the way of granting a rule is that the scheme of 'reduction of capital' leaves the nominal capital of the company (as it appears in the memorandum of association) unaltered. There is weighty authority for the proposition that the jurisdiction conferred on the court by s 44 to confirm a special resolution of a company 'to reduce its share capital' relates to 'nominal share capital', and that unless the scheme of reduction embraces a reduction of the nominal capital, it cannot be confirmed (see *Ex parte Witwatersrand Board of Executors Building Society & Trust Co Ltd (and reduced)* 1926 WLD 205; *Ex parte Seafoods Successors Ltd* 1957 (3) SA 73 (D)). It is clear that without such confirmation a company cannot simply pay off paid up capital and take back the relative shares because, it seems, it would amount to an *ultra vires* trafficking in shares and also because a company cannot be a shareholder itself.

The High Court of Southern Rhodesia, however, has recently considered this difficulty in *Ex parte Rattham and Son (Pvt) Ltd* 1959 (2) SA 741 (SR). This decision deals with s 67(1) of the Companies Act (SR) 47 of 1951, the wording of which is identical with that of s 44(1) of the Union Act. After considering the authorities (including the cases referred to above) Young J came to the conclusion that the term 'share capital' in s 67(1) is not restricted to nominal share capital but also includes issued share capital, and that it follows that a 'reduction of share capital' does not necessarily embrace a reduction of nominal share capital. He refused to follow the two cases referred to above and preferred the decision in *Ex parte Power Industries Co Ltd* 1944 CPD 404. He decided that he had jurisdiction to confirm a resolution to pay off capital against surrender of issued shares, the company maintaining 'its nominal capital intact by the device of deeming shares which have been issued and subsequently surrendered for value to be unissued'.

I am in respectful agreement with the conclusion and reasoning of Young J. It is unnecessary to repeat the reasoning in detail. But a few remarks may not be inapposite. The learned judge says *inter alia*:

'The fact that capital is sometimes increased contingently on a reduction . . . suggests that the rule' (viz every reduction of capital must reduce the nominal capital), 'if valid, would be artificial. . . .'

A recent example of such a contingent increase is to be found in *Ex parte Rhodesian Pulp and Paper Industries Ltd* 1959 (2) SA 735 (SR). It would certainly be the height of artificiality in the present case to hold that the court has no jurisdiction because it is proposed to allow the nominal capital to remain at £175 000 by making use of the device of treating the £50 000 shares to be paid off 'as unissued' and yet recognize a jurisdiction if it be proposed 'to reduce the nominal capital' to £125 000 and, conditional upon and simultaneously with the aforementioned reduction of the nominal share capital becoming effective, to increase the nominal capital from £125 000 to the former amount of £175 000. Moreover, it is plain that the jurisdiction to allow and control a reduction of capital, under s 44 as elaborated in the sections following upon it, is actually concerned with the danger that the reduction of paid up or issued capital may affect adversely creditors of the company. If it is merely a question of the decrease or increase of the nominal capital alone, the intervention of the court is unnecessary (s 39 of Act 46 of 1926). Hinging the jurisdiction of the court on a change in nominal capital and not in the real matter of importance, is but another facet of the artificiality inherent in attaching a restricted meaning to the term 'share capital' in s 44.

In determining the meaning of the term 'share capital' in s 44 it would be legitimate to trace the history of the section back to s 9 of the Companies Act, 1867 (30 & 31 Vict c 131):

'Any company limited by shares may, by special resolution so far modify the conditions contained in its memorandum of association, if authorized so to do by its regulations as originally framed or as altered by special resolution, as to reduce its capital: but no such resolution for reducing the capital of any company shall come into operation until an order of the court is registered by the Registrar of Joint Stock Companies, as is hereinafter mentioned.'

In *Re Ebbw Vale Co* (1877) 4 ChD 827, and *In re Kirkstall Brewery Co Ltd and Reduced* (1877) 5 Ch 535, a limited meaning was placed upon the term 'capital' (as a result of reasoning largely based on the context). In this regard the following remarks by Lord Macnaghten in *British and American Trustee Finance Corp* v *Couper* [1894] AC 399 at 412 are instructive.

'The Companies Act 1877 was passed mainly in order to remove certain doubts created by the decision of Sir George Jessel in the *Ebbw Vale* case 4 ChD 827, which was a surprise to the profession at the time, and which is, I believe, generally thought to have been incorrect.'

Section 3 of the Companies Act 1877 (40 & 41 Vict c 26) is as follows:

'The word "capital" as used in the Companies Act, 1867, shall include paid-up capital; and the power to reduce capital conferred by that Act shall include a power to cancel any lost capital unrepresented by available assets, or to pay off any capital which may be in excess of the wants of the company; and paid-up capital may be reduced either with or without extinguishing or reducing the liability (if any) remaining on the shares of the company, and to the extent to which such liability is not extinguished or reduced it shall be deemed to be preserved, notwithstanding anything contained in the Companies Act, 1867.'

It is difficult to understand how the word 'capital' could thereafter in subsequent statutes (including our own) have acquired a limited meaning of 'nominal capital' in sections obviously based on these sections of the statutes of 1867 and 1877.

Acceptance of the views expressed by Young J brings one in conflict with a decision of this court (viz *Ex parte Seafoods Successors Ltd* (*supra*)). But in this decision all the matters mentioned by Young J were not considered, nor the historical background of s 44; the case of *Ex parte Power Industries Co Ltd* 1944 CPD 404 was, as pointed out by Young J, distinguished on insufficient grounds; an additional ground for refusing the application for reduction of capital was a contravention of s 86*bis* of the Act.

With the greatest of respect I feel constrained in these circumstances to depart from this decision and follow the judgment of Young J. . . .

[86]   **Rosslare (Pty) Ltd & another** *v* **Registrar of Companies**
1972 (2) SA 524 (D)

MILNE J: These proceedings commenced as a review, in terms of s 215(2) [now s 12(2)] . . . of the refusal by the respondent to register amended articles of association of the first applicant which, in terms of a special resolution of 27 April 1971, were substituted for its original articles of association. . . .

It is clear from the provisions of s 15 and s 17 [now s 62 and s 63(1)] of the Companies Act that a company may, provided it complies with the procedural requirements laid down, validly amend its articles of association, and that the Registrar of Companies is obliged to register them if they are 'in accordance with' the Act. . . .

Articles which are not in conflict with the general law, nor with any express or implied provision of or underlying assumption in the Companies Act, are registrable and the Registrar of Companies is obliged to register them.

The original articles of association of the first applicant were in a fairly standard form, whereas the amended articles of association now sought to be registered are in the form commonly encountered where the company owns a block of flats, and individual flats in the building are 'sold' on the basis that ownership of a particular number or block of shares entitles the owner of those shares to occupation of a particular flat. This device has been resorted to because our law does not recognize the separate ownership of sections of a building [though provision has since been made therefor in the Sectional Titles Act 66 of 1971]. The amended articles also provide for the directors to make levies upon the shareholders for the purposes of meeting expenses of the company, and for shareholders to make loans to the company for the purposes of discharging the company's loan obligations. . . .

[Counsel for the Registrar submitted that] while the division of the shares into blocks might well be a competent division and while it might be possible for the company to enter into arrangements of the nature contemplated . . . with third parties or even with persons who are in fact members of the company, it was not permissible for the company to enter into such arrangements with members *in their capacity as members,* since the permanent right to occupy a particular portion of the company's property, without any obligation to pay rental or anything equivalent to a valid profit or gain for the company, amounted to a return of capital to the shareholders constituting an unauthorized reduction of capital of the company. The proposition is a somewhat startling one and, if correct, will have far reaching consequences, as it is common knowledge that there are a large number of companies in existence which have registered articles substantially in this form. The fact that it will have such consequences cannot, of course, affect the validity, or otherwise, of the proposition, which is directly supported by the decision of the New Zealand Court of Appeal in *Jenkins* v *Harbour View Courts Ltd* [reported in 1966 NZLR at 1]. . . . [T]he headnote which is in the following terms, correctly reflects the decision of the Court of Appeal:

'Where a company which has erected a building of flats, contracts to grant to each holder of certain of its shares a lease for 99 years of one of such flats at a rental to be fixed each year by the directors of the company at an amount sufficient only to meet out-goings with some provision for a reserve fund but not including any amount as landlord's reward, a grant of such lease amounts to a return of capital to shareholders and is *ultra vires* the company, even though such an arrangement may be expressly authorized by the company's memorandum of association.'

I deal firstly with the submission that it is the fact that the amended articles give the shareholders rights to the company's property *in their capacity as members* which renders the article objectionable. It was submitted that the amended articles were endeavouring to promote a purely personal arrangement into an arrangement with persons as members. There is a well recognized distinction between contracts made by a company with a member in his private capacity and those made with him in his capacity as a member. In *De Villiers* v *Jacobsdal Salt Works (Michaelis and De Villiers) (Pty) Ltd* 1959 (3) SA 873 (O) at 876–7 Potgieter J said

'the articles constitute a contract between the members *inter se*, and between the company and the members, but only in their capacity as members. They do not, for instance, constitute a contract between the company and a director in his capacity as such'.

This passage was approved by the Appellate Division in *Gohlke and Schneider & another* v *Westies Minerale (Edms) Bpk & another* 1970 (2) SA 685 (AD) at 692F–G, where Trollip JA said

'the articles therefore merely have the same force as a contract between the company and each and every member as such to observe their provisions'.

A member of a company has, of course, no separate legal personality 'in his capacity as a member' which is distinct from him 'in his private capacity'. It seems clear, however, that what is meant by a contract with a member 'in his capacity as such', is a contract between him and the company which is connected with the holding of shares *and* which confers rights which are 'part of the general regulations of the company applicable alike to all shareholders'. See the judgment of Astbury J in *Hickman* v *Kent or Romney Marsh Sheepbreeders' Association* [1915] 1 Ch 881 at 897 and at 896, citing the judgment of Lindley LJ in *Browne* v *La Trinidad* 37 ChD 1 at 14. The rights which are given to shareholders in terms of the amended articles are 'part of the general regulations of the company applicable alike to all shareholders' and they are, therefore, contracting in their capacity as members. Accordingly, if, as [Counsel for the Registrar] submitted, it would be permissible for persons who are members of the company to contract outside the articles for such rights, I have some difficulty in seeing why it is not equally permissible for them to do so in the articles. In other words, if the grant of rights to occupy the company's property for no rental does constitute a return of capital to the shareholders, it seems to me to make no difference in law whether the contract embodying such provisions is contained in an agreement outside the articles of association or whether it arises from the terms of the articles themselves. Furthermore, if the granting of the rights does constitute a reduction of capital then, in each case, the share capital, that is to say, the fund to which creditors have a right to look as that out of which they are to be paid, would be diminished by precisely the same amount. On the other hand, as pointed out ... in *Jenkins's* case [[1966] NZLR 1], the situation would be different if the agreement between the company and a shareholder had been, say, for the purchase and allotment of one share followed (on different articles of association) by a purchase of a lease. Neither the Companies Act nor the policy of the law requires a company to operate at a profit, nor (subject to the provisions of s 70*dec* [now s 228]) do they prevent the disposition by a company of the whole or the greater part of its assets. What is the position where the company grants perpetual rights of occupation of various portions of its property to strangers, ie persons who are not members of the company, on the basis that no rental is to be paid? This would include a situation where the share capital has been raised and has been converted into a building say, for example, a block of flats. In my view, there is nothing, subject to the provisions of s 70*dec* being complied with, which would, in such circumstances, prevent the company from thereafter selling perpetual rights of occupation of the flat in that building to persons who were not members of the company, provided that such sale was within the objects of the company, because the company would, in return for the rights granted to such strangers, receive moneys or assets of equal value which would, in the words of Boshoff J in *Cohen NO* v *Segal* 1970 (3) SA 702 (W) [*84* above], constitute 'the fund to which creditors have a right to look as that out of which they are to be paid'. It seems to me, therefore, that no question of a reduction of capital would arise by reason of the company entering into transactions with persons not members of the company, as a result of which the company would have no rights in respect of its property other than bare *dominium*. However, the argument for the respondent is, as I understand it, that the articles of association in this case envisage the return to the members of an interest in immovable property of a value equivalent to the capital subscribed by such members. There is, of course, no question here of the repayment to shareholders of any moneys, but clearly a return of capital may be effected by a distribution of assets. ... Here, I have no information as to how many shares have been issued in the applicant company nor as to what extent such shares are paid up. Indeed it is only impliedly stated in the papers that the company is the owner of a building. ... If the position is that the share capital initially provided for in the articles has been raised, and has not been utilized in the acquisition by the company of the building referred to in the articles, and such share capital exists in the form of moneys or other assets and it was not contemplated that these moneys or other assets were in any sense, to be returned or paid over to the shareholders, then no question of a reduction of capital could arise. I assume, however, that what is contemplated is that the share blocks referred to in . . . the amended articles will be issued to the person or persons who have provided the funds required to erect the company's building known as 'Rosslare', and that the moneys or assets to be provided as the consideration for the issue of share blocks have been used by the company to acquire land on which the building stands, and to erect such building. The second applicant and one Ronald Walker, described as an accountant, each subscribed in the memorandum for one share, and it appears from the minutes of the extra-ordinary general meeting held on 27 April 1971, at which it was resolved that the articles of association be amended, that the sole shareholders are still the second applicant and Walker. As I have already mentioned, I have no information as to the factual position, but it seems quite likely that the funds by means of which the first applicant acquired the land and erected the building known as 'Rosslare' were obtained by means of loans from the second applicant, and that it is proposed that all the remaining unissued shares will be allotted to the second applicant in consideration for a complete, or partial, extinction of the company's liability to the second applicant in respect of such loans. The second applicant would then presumably dispose of share blocks at a price sufficient to make him a profit on his investment in the company. Would the issue of the remainder of the shares in these circumstances to the second applicant constitute a return of capital to him? If it does not, then the Registrar cannot, so it seems to me, decline to register the amended articles by reason of this objection. In other words, if the facts may reasonably be such that the implementation of arts 4 and 6 is possible without an unauthorized reduction of capital being involved, then the articles themselves are not objectionable or contrary to the terms of underlying assumptions of the Companies Act. The fact that such articles *might* be used in such a way as to involve an unauthorized reduction of capital would not, in my view, constitute a valid objection to registration. I return, therefore, to the question of whether or not the issue of shares to the second applicant, in the circumstances I have described above, would constitute an unauthorized reduction of capital. If the judgment in *Jenkins's* case (*supra cit*) is correct and, assuming what Holmes JA called 'the absence of pitfalls of dissimilarity' in another country's statute (*Rishworth* v *Secretary for Inland Revenue* 1964 (4) SA 493 (AD) at 500E), then it would indeed involve a reduction of capital. The authorized share capital would, of course, remain unchanged, but this is not relevant since a reduction of share capital in terms of the Act does not necessarily embrace a reduction of *authorized* share capital, see *Ex parte Associated Lead Manufacturers (Pty) Ltd* [*85*, p 152 above]. What I am here concerned with is the *issued* share capital of the company, cf Cilliers en Benade *Maatskappyereg* 233n6, or what is described in Gower *Modern Company Law* 3 ed 104 as 'a rigid yardstick fixing the minimum value of the net assets which must be raised initially and then, so far as possible, retained in the business', and at 122, as 'a fund of credit'. Much reliance was placed in *Jenkins's* case upon the decision of the House of Lords in *Trevor* v *Whitworth* (1887) 12 App Cas 409, and, indeed, what was decided in that case, namely that a company has no power to purchase its own shares, is a clearly recognized principle in our law. . . . Clearly, a return of capital may take place not only by the return of money, but by what Lord Radcliffe termed 'money's worth' in the *Westburn Sugar Refineries* case [*89* below]. Here, of course, the ownership of the immovable property will remain vested in the company, but the amended articles clearly contemplate that it will receive no income, other than the levy payable in terms. . . . of the amended articles. It is, I think, also relevant to mention at this stage that the amended articles require each holder of a share block to lend to the company, free of interest, an amount to be specified in an annexure to the articles, which is to be used to discharge loans owing to 'unsecured loan creditors (vendors)' and repayment of capital and/or interest on a mortgage bond passed over the company's immovable property . . . The terms of these articles seem to indicate that a further fact must be added to the presumptive picture which I have sought to infer as a probable or, at least, possible one, and that is that there is a mortgage bond over the company's property.

On the basis of the facts envisaged in this judgment the company has acquired land and the building known as Rosslare, not by means of share capital, but by means of loans. In these circumstances I doubt whether it is correct to speak of the company's immovable property as constituting its capital. It is, of course, 'capital' in the sense that it is a fixed asset of the company, but the 'capital' with which I am here concerned is the issued share capital of the company. On the facts envisaged, the position immediately before the allotment of the unissued shares to the second applicant would be that the issued share capital was R2 and the company would be the owner of (mortgaged) immovable property not 'burdened' with shareholders' rights of occupation. The company would also owe a substantial sum to the second applicant on loan account. Upon allotment of the unissued shares to the second applicant, the company would still be the owner of (mortgaged) immovable property now 'burdened' with the second applicant's rights as a shareholder, but the loan account would have been extinguished. Assuming in favour of the respondent, that the immovable property of the company could be regarded as the share capital (or its equivalent) of the company, it by no means follows that the value of that capital or its equivalent has been diminished. Disregarding the fact that there is a mortgage bond in existence, the amount of the loan account might be such that:

(*a*)   if the company were to lease portions of its premises in the ordinary way to outsiders at current market rental the nett return to the company might be entirely consumed in interest payable in respect of the loan account; or

(*b*)   if the company sold its property the nett proceeds of the sale might well be entirely consumed in discharging the company's liability on the loan account.

In other words, the result of giving effect to the arrangements envisaged in the amended articles might well be that the *value* of the capital remained unchanged. . . . In any event with due respect to the court in *Jenkins's* case, I have some doubts as to the correctness of the decision.

Prima facie, there is something to be said for the arguments advanced by the Solicitor-General as *amicus curiae*.

Quite apart from these considerations, I have difficulty with the notion that a reduction of capital is constituted by the grant to shareholders of rights in the company's property which merely has the effect of extinguishing the profit-making capacity of that property but does not at the same time return the property itself to shareholders. After all, it is clear that losses of fixed assets, e g by a fall in value of immovable property, need not be made good before treating a revenue profit as available for dividend, cf *Bolton* v *Natal Land & Colonisation Co* [1892] 2 Ch 124 [*345* below] Cf Also the remarks of Lindley LJ in *Lee* v *Neuchatel Asphalte Co* (1889) 41 ChD 1 at 24 [*344* below].

I have, accordingly, come to the conclusion that the respondent's objection is not well-founded. . . .

NOTES

Rosslare is critically discussed by R C Beuthin 1972 *Annual Survey* 230 and (1972) 89 *SALJ* 428.

Associated Lead Manufacturers was approved by Trengove J in *Ex parte Republic Real Estate Corporation* 1972 (1) SA 98 (W).

Any scheme which amounts to the distribution by a company of part of its subscribed capital amongst its shareholders is a reduction of capital, see e g *Australian Oil Exploration Ltd* v *Lachberg* (1959) 32 *Australian Oil Exploration Ltd* v *Lachberg* (1959) 32 *Australian LJR* 301, where A company, finding itself in financial difficulties, sold its shares in B company to C company at undervalue in consideration of an undertaking by C company to allow shareholders in A company to subscribe for its shares.

In *Lawrie* v *Symington* (1969) SLT 221, it was held that a replacement of preference shares by loan stock involves the repayment of capital to shareholders in terms of s 67(2) of the UK Act 1948.

Where a company does not possess power in its articles to reduce or increase capital, a resolution to do so is ineffective: *The Oregon Mortgage Company Ltd* 1910 SC 964; *Metropolitan Cemetery Co Ltd* 1934 SC 65.

The special resolution altering the articles and the special resolution of reduction can be passed at the same meeting, s 201.

[87] Bellerby v Rowland and Marwood's Steamship Company Ltd

[1902] 2 Ch 14

COLLINS MR: . . . The forfeiture of shares is distinctly recognized by the Companies Act, and by the articles contained in the schedule, which, in the absence of other provisions, regulate the management of a limited liability company. It does not involve any payment by the company, and it presumably exonerates from future liability those who have shown themselves unable to contribute what is due from them to the capital of the company. Surrender no doubt stands on a different footing. But it also does not involve any payment out of the funds of the company. If the surrender were made in consideration of any such payment it would be neither more nor less than a sale, and open to the same objections. If it were accepted in a case when the company were in a position to forfeit the shares, the transaction would seem to be perfectly valid. There may be other cases in which a surrender would be legitimate. . . .

NOTES

On the surrender of old shares for new, see also *Teasdale's Case* (1873) 9 Ch App 54; *Eichbaum* v *City of Chicago Grain Elevators Limited* [1891] 3 Ch 459; *Rowell* v *John Rowell & Sons* [1912] 2 Ch 609.

[88] *Ex Parte* **Vlakfontein Gold Mining Co Ltd**
1970 (2) SA 180 (T)

GALGUT J: The duties of a court which is asked to confirm a reduction of capital are:

(*a*) to ensure that the relevant formalities and provisions of the Companies Act have been duly complied with; . . .

(*b*) to consider whether the proposed reduction is fair and equitable as between the shareholders and particularly as between different classes of shareholders; . . .

(*c*) to safeguard the interests of existing creditors;

(*d*) to safeguard the interests of the general public, that is to say, persons who may in the future have dealings with the company or may be minded to invest in its securities, or who may in some manner become creditors in the future; . . .

. . . The Act has imposed on the court the task of deciding whether a reduction should be confirmed. If the confirmation is to be a mere formality it seems the task could have been left in the hands of the Registrar of Companies.

[For a discussion of *Vlakfontein*, see B O'Rourke (1970) 87 *SALJ* 161, who welcomes the decision as a 'reassertion of discretionary power'. In *Vlakfontein*, Galgut J was reluctant to confirm a reduction by future repayments. 'I do not think that a court ought lightly to confirm a reduction of capital which in the main is purely dependent on the future activities and profit-making ability of a company' (at 185A). The 1973 Act deals with this method of reduction in s 84(4) and (5).]

[89] *Ex parte* **Westburn Sugar Refineries Ltd**
[1951] AC 625, [1951] 1 All ER 881, 1951 SC (HL) 57

The main questions in this case were (1) whether in a reduction of capital it was competent for a company to pay off capital by transferring to the shareholders assets the value of which might be in excess of the amount by which the capital was reduced; (2) whether the fact that the reduction might have an ulterior motive, eg to escape the consequences of possible nationalization by transferring valuable assets to shareholders, was a reason for the court to withhold its sanction. The House of Lords reversed the decision of the Scottish Court of Session which had refused to confirm the reduction.

LORD REID: . . . In this case the statutory conditions have been satisfied. The question is whether the court should confirm the reduction of capital proposed. The only unusual features of this case are that the appellants propose to pay off part of their share capital not with money but by transferring to the shareholders shares of another company, and that the value of the shares proposed to be so transferred greatly exceeds the amount by which the appellants' share capital is to be reduced. But there is nothing novel in paying off share capital other-wise than with money; it has long been recognized that this is not incompetent.

The real questions in this case are whether it is competent in a reduc-tion of capital to pay off share capital by transferring assets whose value clearly exceeds the amount by which the share capital of the company is reduced; and if this is competent, whether it is proper in this case to allow it to be done. As regards competency 'the statute has not prescribed the manner in which the reduction is to be carried out, nor has it prohibited any method of effecting that object' (per Lord Herschell LC in *British and American Trustee & Finance Corporation Ltd* v *Couper* [1894] AC 399 at 405). And in the same case Lord Watson said (at 410): 'I do not find a single expression in the Act tending to indicate that the discretion of the court to grant or refuse such an application does not extend to every possible mode of reducing capital.'

The terms of the Act are as wide today as they were then. At first sight it may seem strange that the appellants' proposal should be compe-tent; but once it has been recognized that paying off capital can be done otherwise than by payment of money, there cannot be any requirement of exact correspondence between the amount of capital paid off and the value of the assets used to pay it off, because in many cases it is impossible to make any exact valuation of such assets. So the most that could be required would be an approximate correspondence; but I can see no reason why it must be held that the statute has imposed any such vague or difficult limitation. . . .

. . . Are the circumstances of this case such that the court ought to confirm the appellants' proposal?

. . . In the first place the interests of creditors must be safeguarded; but here that has been done. Secondly the interests of shareholders may have to be considered; but in this case there has been no opposition by any shareholders at any time and it is difficult to see how there could be any prejudice to any single shareholders. And thirdly there is the public interest to consider. . . . Lord Carmont [in the Court of Session] took the view that there is or may be an ulterior object behind the present petition, namely to avoid in part the consequences of possible future legislation. The fact that the petition may have such an ulterior object may be a good reason for making quite certain that the existing law is complied with in every respect, but it cannot in my judgment be by itself a ground for dismissing the petition. The petition must be judged by the law as it exists today.

LORD RADCLIFFE: Two reasons are advanced by Lord Carmont for his view. One is that on general grounds of public policy the court ought not to aid a company threatened with nationalization to 'eviscerate' itself by parting with valuable assets. My Lords, I do not think that the contingency of nationalization has any relevance to the public policy that courts of justice should support. If the reduction is objectionable on other grounds, it will not become the more acceptable because it may have been proposed in view of a pending measure of nationalization; conversely, the threat of nationalization cannot render improper what is otherwise unobjectionable.

[90] *In re* **London and New York Investment Corporation**
[1895] 2 Ch 860

A company which had founders' shares, preference shares and ordinary shares, had suffered a considerable loss of capital. Under the constitution of the company, in the event of liquidation, losses of capital were to fall first on founders' shares. The preference shares were preferred both as to capital and dividend. The court confirmed a scheme of reduction which involved the total elimination of the founders' shares and threw the remainder of the loss upon the ordinary shares.

STIRLING J: . . . Where there are different classes of shares the loss on a reduction ought to fall on those who would have to bear it if there were a winding-up. . . .

[Similarly, *In re Floating Dock Company of St Thomas Ltd* [1895] 1 Ch 691.]

[91] **British and American Trustee and Finance Corporation Limited (and Reduced)** *v* **Couper**
[1894] AC 399 (HL)

A company which had carried on business in England and the United States, determined to discontinue its American business. It was decided that the American investments should be made over to the American shareholders, their shares being cancelled, and that the English shareholders should take the English assets, receiving an agreed sum by way of adjustment. A special resolution was accordingly passed providing that the capital should be reduced by paying off the shares held by the American shareholders. All the creditors of the company either were paid or assented to the arrangement, but confirmation of the reduction was opposed by one shareholder. The House of Lords, overruling the decision of the Court of Appeal, confirmed the reduction.

LORD HERSCHELL LC: . . . There can be no doubt that any scheme which does not provide for uniform treatment of shareholders whose rights are similar, would be most narrowly scrutinized by the court, and that no such scheme ought to be confirmed unless the court be satisfied that it will not work unjustly or inequitably. But this is quite a different thing from saying that the court has no power to sanction it. . . .

LORD MACNAGHTEN: My Lords, I agree. . . . The Companies Act, 1867, declares that any company limited by shares may by special resolution so far modify the conditions contained in its memorandum, if authorized so to do by its regulations as originally framed or as altered by special resolution, as to reduce its capital. The power is general. The exercise of the power is fenced round by safeguards which are calculated to protect the interests of creditors, the interests of shareholders, and the interests of the public. Creditors are protected by express provisions. Their consent must be procured or their claims must be satisfied. The public, the shareholders, and every class of shareholders individually and collectively, are protected by the necessary publicity of the proceedings and by the discretion which is entrusted to the court. Until confirmed by the court the proposed reduction is not to take effect, though all the creditors have been satisfied. When it is confirmed the memorandum is to be altered in the prescribed manner, and the company as it were makes a new departure. With these safeguards, which certainly are not inconsiderable, the Act apparently leaves the company to determine the extent, the mode, and the incidence of the reduction, and the application or disposition of any capital moneys which the proposed reduction may set free. . . .

. . . There are authorities in which it seems to be laid down that a proposed reduction of capital cannot be confirmed if it involves a purchase by the company of its own shares, and for that reason alone. That of itself, however, cannot be a sufficient objection. The shares are not to be purchased out of the company's capital, but out of moneys withdrawn from the capital and set free by the reduction. A company cannot employ any part of the capital with which it is registered, so long as it forms part of its capital, in the purchase of its own shares. But if it proposes to reduce its capital in accordance with the statutory provisions which empower it to do so, there is no reason why it should not employ the fund set free by the reduction in the purchase of shares which it is intended to extinguish. . . . The fact that a thing is prohibited if it is done in the wrong way, and at a time when the circumstances of the case do not justify it, is no reason for holding the thing prohibited it if is to be done in the right way and when it is justified by circumstances.

[Counsel for the respondent] did not press this point as constituting in itself a sufficient answer to the application. The reduction he said was not objectionable simply because it involved a purchase by the company of its own shares, but because a purchase by a company limited by shares of some of its own shares must involve dealing with shareholders, members of one and the same class, in different ways. You cannot, he said, reduce or extinguish some of a class of shares without equally reducing or extinguishing all the others of the same class. That was the objection which in the opinion of the Court of Appeal would have been fatal to the application of the Denver Hotel Company [*In re Denver Hotel Co* [1893] 1 Ch 495] if the court had regarded the transaction as really a purchase of shares. The words of [the section] 'cannot in our opinion', says Lindley LJ, 'be considered so as to enable a company to prefer one shareholder to another of the same class as himself by buying up his shares'. With all deference I venture to think that mode of stating the proposition is really begging the question. It assumes that the person whose shares are to be purchased is getting a preference—an undue advantage for himself at the expense of his fellow shareholders. But why should that assumption be made? The person whose shares are bought gets money or money's worth. The persons on whose behalf the company buys have their own shares improved by the value of the shares extinguished. If the parties to the transaction come to the conclusion that the bargain is a fair one, why should the court say that there is a preference on the one side or on the other? If there is nothing unfair or inequitable in the transaction, I cannot see that there is any objection to allowing a company limited by shares to extinguish some of its shares without dealing in the same manner with all other shares of the same class. There may be no real inequality in the treatment of a class of shareholders although they are not all paid in the same coin or in coins of the same denomination. . . .

NOTES

That the courts are fully at large in deciding whether a reduction of capital should or should not be confirmed, was reaffirmed in *Ex parte Vlakfontein Gold Mining Co Ltd,* *88* above. See also *In re William Jones & Sons Ltd* [1969] 1 WLR 146, [1969] 1 All ER 913.

See further *Bannatyne* v *Direct Spanish Telegraph Company* (1886) 34 ChD 287; *In re Gatling Gun Ltd* (1890) 43 ChD 628 (court has power to sanction a special resolution for the reduction of only some of the shares of a company); *In re James Colmer Ltd* [1897] 1 Ch 524, esp at 527, per Romer J: 'I think that in a proper case the court has power to confirm a resolution for reduction of capital, notwithstanding the voting powers may thereby be affected'; *In re Mackenzie and Company Ltd* [1916] 2 Ch 450; *Ex parte Greys Clothing and Associated Industries Ltd* 1948 (3) SA 376 (W) (reduction confirmed where it became necessary because certain preference shares had been surrendered by holders for conversion into ordinary shares). In *In re Nixon's Navigation Co* [1897] 1 Ch 872 the court confirmed a scheme of reduction under which a portion of the capital of the company was to be returned to the shareholders, although a part of the capital so returned was to be immediately borrowed again by the company from shareholders on debentures. That there can be no objections on principle against this procedure was also held in *Ex parte Vlakfontein Gold Mining Co Ltd, 88* above.

In *Ex parte Mackay Bros Ltd (and Reduced)* 1934 WLD 44 the court confirmed a reduction which took the form of cancelling certain of the issued and fully paid-up shares, and issuing to those shareholders in lieu thereof acknowledgements of debt for less than the nominal amount of the shares, bearing interest and repayable over a term of years. In *In re Durban North Estates Ltd* 1947 (4) SA 568 (N) the court sanctioned a reduction whereby a certain amount was repaid to shareholders in cash while unsecured debentures were issued to them in respect of the balance. See also *Ex parte Dunell Ebden & Co* 1933 EDL 228 and *Ex parte South African Clothing Industries Ltd (and Reduced)* 1939 WLD 270.

The court has power to confirm a reduction of capital effected by the purchase by a company of its own shares: *Ex parte Reserve Investment Co Ltd* 1916 WLD 52. See also *In re Denver Hotel Co* [1893] 1 Ch 495; *Ex parte Rattham and Son (Pty) Ltd* 1959 (2) SA 741 (SR).

A return to members of paid-up capital may be effected by dividing among the members part of the company's assets either in money or in kind, e g by giving them shares in another company: *Ex parte Union Construction Company (Pty) Ltd (and Reduced)* 1937 WLD 98; *Ex parte Hume Steel South Africa (Pty) Ltd (and Reduced)* 1937 WLD 102; *Ex parte National Industrial Credit Corporation Ltd* 1950 (2) SA 10 (W).

There is no rule that where the articles provide that, in the case of a winding-up, losses are to be borne by the members in proportion to the capital paid up on their shares, the same principle must be applied in the case of any reduction of capital as between shares in the same class with different amounts paid up: *In re Credit Assurance and Guarantee Corporation Ltd* [1902] 2 Ch 601.

In the case of *In re Development Company of Central and West Africa* [1902] 1 Ch 547 the court rejected a scheme which involved the issue to each deferred shareholder of 100 £1 ordinary shares in exchange for each £1 deferred share on the ground that it involved the issue of £70 000 nominal capital in exchange for £700 nominal capital without any consideration to the company.

In *Ex parte African Russian Oil Products (Pty) Ltd (and Reduced)* 1934 WLD 75 the court refused to sanction a reduction which, prima facie, appeared to be part of a scheme which would constitute a fraud on the minority of shareholders in another company which held shares in the applicant company. In *Ex parte Seafoods Successors Ltd* 1957 (3) SA 73 (N) the court refused to approve a reduction before a loan which the company had made to its holding company in contravention of s 86*bis*(1) [now s 37] had been repaid.

A reduction can be given retrospective effect: *Amalgamated Packaging Industries Ltd* 1963 (1) SA 335 (SR).

Shares may be repaid at a premium: *Re Trocadero Building and Investment Company* (1960) 33 Australian LJR 446; *Re Rank Radio & Television Ltd* Supplement 22 vol 6 *Justice of the Peace and Local Government Review* 30 November 1963 (confirming a reduction under which the holders of ordinary 5s shares received a premium of 30s per share). See also *Inland Revenue Commissioners* v *Universal Grinding Wheel Co Ltd* [1955] AC 807 at 820, [1955] 2 All ER 29 (HL) at 34; *Re Saltdean Estate Co Ltd* [1968] 3 All ER 829.

If a reduction of capital is not objectionable on any other ground, the courts are not concerned with the fact that it has an ulterior motive, for example, the avoidance of certain taxes: *Ex parte Westburn Sugar Refineries Ltd* [1951] AC 625, [1951] 1 All ER 881 (HL), 89 above; *David Bell Ltd* 1954 SC 33; *In re African Film Products Ltd* 1959 (4) SA 76 (W).

The minute of reduction must set out the complete picture, for the benefit of creditors, shareholders and future investors: *Ex parte Rhodesian Pulp and Paper Industries* 1959 (2) SA 735 (SR), where the reduction was followed by an increase of capital, effected by the creation and issue of new shares.

The provisional liquidator of a company may apply to court for approval of a scheme of reduction forming part of a compromise: *Ex parte Provisional Liquidator Hugo Franco (Pty) Ltd* 1958 (4) SA 397 (W).

The court can sanction a reduction where the company has already ceased to exist and is being wound up: *In re African Films Production, Ltd (in voluntary liquidation)* 1959 (4) SA 76 (W).

Where a reduction of capital is to be effected by return of capital paid up on part of a class of shares only, and not all the members of that class have consented, the preferable practice is to proceed by way of a scheme of arrangement rather than by a reduction: *Re Robert Stephens Holdings Ltd* [1968] 1 All ER 195 (Ch).

A reduction of capital is not infrequently combined with an increase or reorganization of capital: e g *Ex parte Allen Wack and Sheppard Ltd (and Reduced)* 1936 WLD 25; *Ex parte Rhodesian Pulp and Paper Industries Ltd* 1959 (2) SA 735 (SR). In *Ex parte Carrig Diamonds Ltd* 1966 (1) SA 572 (W), where the proposed reduction of capital was combined with a subdivision, consolidation, and increase of shares in one set of special resolutions, the court confined itself to the confirmation of the reduction, without pronouncing upon the validity of the ordinary resolutions relating to the disposal of the shares after the reorganization. (For a critical review of *Ex parte Carrig Diamonds Ltd* see 1966 *Annual Survey* 255–8.)

On preference shareholders and the reduction of capital, see p 177 below.

7   *Shares, Debentures and Bonds*

I GENERAL

A TEXT

A 'share' means a share in the share capital of a company: *92*. It includes stock, and in relation to a prospectus includes debentures and any rights or interests in a company or in or to shares or debentures, s 1 s v 'share'. A share is movable property transferable in the manner provided by the Companies Act and the articles of the company, s 91. Shares may be converted into stock and vice versa, s 100.

Shares may be created with or without a par value (see S W L de Villiers 'Some Comments on No Par Value Shares in terms of the Draft Companies Bill' (1972) 5 *CILSA* 348; Karl Pretorius 'Aandele sonder Pari-waarde in Oëskou' (1974) 3 *Responsa Meridiana* 63). Capital consisting of par value shares may be converted into stated capital consisting of no-par value shares and vice versa, s 75(1)(*f*) and (*g*).

A public company can create share warrants to bearer (s 101), a private company cannot as it must restrict the right to transfer its shares, s 20(1)(*a*). Unlike nominative shares, bearer shares are negotiable instruments.

For the purpose of the provisions dealing with share transfers, shares and debentures which are listed on a stock exchange are included under the term 'securities', s 134(*c*). (On listing of shares, see p 59 above.)

Where shares and, more particularly, shares not listed on a stock exchange have to be valued a large number of factors have to be taken into consideration, including the value of the company's assets, its goodwill, its dividend yield, its present and prospective profitability, and the possibility of capital appreciation: *93*.

As long as the 1926 Act was in force it was usual to make in the articles of association provision for calls on not fully paid-up shares

and for the forfeiture of shares on default in the payment of calls. The
articles also used to give the company a lien over the shares of a member
for his liability to the company. As shares may no longer be issued or
allotted unless they are fully paid-up (s 92(1)), these issues cannot
arise with regard to shares issued or allotted under the 1973 Act.

B CASES

[92] Borland's Trustee v Steel Brothers & Company Ltd
[1901] 1 Ch 279

FARWELL J: . . . A share is the interest of a shareholder in the company measured by a sum of money, for the purpose of liability in the
first place, and of interest in the second, but also consisting of a series
of mutual covenants entered into by all the shareholders *inter se*. . . .
The contract contained in the articles of association is one of the original
incidents of the share. A share is not a sum of money settled in the way
suggested, but is an interest measured by a sum of money and made up
of various rights contained in the contract, including the right to a sum
of money of a more or less amount. . . .

[Approved by Innes CJ in *Liquidators, Union Share Agency* v *Hatton*
1927 AD 240 at 250–1. See also Lord Russell of Killowen in *Commissioners
of Inland Revenue* v *Crossman* [1937] AC 26 at 66, [1936] 1 All ER 762
(HL) at 787: 'A share in a limited company . . . is the interest of a person
in the company, that interest being composed of rights and obligations
which are defined by the Companies Act and by the memorandum and
articles of association of the company. . . .']

[93] Dean v Prince
[1954] Ch 409, [1954] 1 All ER 749

The articles of association of a private company provided that if a
member died, his shares should be purchased by the surviving directors
at a price to be certified by an auditor as a fair value. A director who
held a controlling interest in the company died. The company's auditor
made his valuation of the shares on the basis that the company was to
be wound up at once. He was of the bona fide belief that the shares
had no value on any other basis, having regard to the losses made by
the company. Nor did he make any allowance for the fact that the shares
in question carried control. In an action by the deceased director's
wife, who was his executrix, the court of first instance held that the
valuation was invalid and not binding, because the auditor had proceeded on the wrong basis in making his valuation. The Court of Appeal
reversed the decision.

DENNING LJ: The task of the auditor here was to act as an expert
and not as an arbitrator, and, as an expert, he was to certify what, in
his opinion, was the fair value of the shares. The draftsman of [the
articles] obviously was aware that there is a special virtue in an expert's
valuation. The reason is that it is so much a matter of opinion that it is
very difficult to say it was wrong. But difficult as it is, nevertheless, if

the courts are satisfied that the valuation was made under a mistake, they will hold it not to be binding on the parties. . . .

In this case the judge has upset the valuation on the ground that the auditor failed to take into account some factors and proceeded on wrong principles. I will take the points in order.

1. *The right to control the company.* The judge said that the auditor should have taken into account the fact that the one hundred and forty shares were a majority holding and would give a purchaser the right to control the company. I do not think that the auditor was bound to take that factor into account. Test it this way. Suppose it had been Mr Prince [another director] who had died, leaving only thirty shares. Those thirty shares, being a minority holding, would fetch nothing in the open market. But does that mean that the other directors would be entitled to take the shares for nothing? Surely not. No matter which director it was who happened to die, his widow should be entitled to the same price per share, irrespective of whether her husband's holding was large or small. It seems to me that the fair thing to do would be to take the whole two hundred shares of the company and see what they were worth, and then pay the widow a sum appropriate to her husband's holding. At any rate, if the auditor was of opinion that that was a fair method, no one can say that he was wrong. The right way to see what the whole two hundred shares were worth, would be to see what the business itself was worth, and that is what the auditor proceeded to do.

2. *Valuation of the business 'as a going concern'.* The judge seems to have thought that the auditor should have valued the business as a going concern. I do not think the auditor was bound to do any such thing. The business was a losing concern which had no goodwill, and it is fairly obvious that, as soon as Mrs Dean had sold the one hundred and forty shares to the other two directors — as she was bound to do — she would in all probability call in the moneys owing to herself and to her husband amounting to over £2 000. The judge said that she was not likely to press for the moneys because that would be 'killing the goose that laid the eggs', but he was wrong about this, because as soon as she sold the shares, she would have got rid of the goose and there was no reason why she should not press for the moneys. She was an executrix and the company's position was none too good. It had only £1 200 in the bank to meet a demand for £2 200. In these circumstances, the auditor was of opinion that there was a strong probability of the company having to be wound up, and he rejected the going-concern basis. For myself, I should have thought he was clearly right, but, at any rate, no one can say that his opinion was wrong.

3. *Valuation of the assets of the business.* Once the going-concern basis is rejected, the only possible way of valuing the business is to find out the value of the tangible assets. The judge thought that the assets should have been valued as a whole *in situ.* It was quite likely, he said, that 'someone could have been found who would make a bid for the whole thing, lock, stock and barrel'. But the judge seems to have forgotten that no one would buy the assets *in situ* in this way unless he could also buy the premises, and that the company had no saleable interest in the premises. In respect of part of the premises the company had only a

monthly tenancy. In respect of the rest, the company had only a contract for the purchase of the premises on paying £200 a year for twenty-five years. It had no right to assign this contract, and its interest was liable to be forfeited if it went into liquidation, either compulsory or voluntary; and the probability was, of course, that, if it sold all the assets, it would go into liquidation, and hence lose the premises. The company could, therefore, only sell the assets without the premises. That is how the auditor valued them and no one can say that he was wrong in so doing.

4. *Valuation on a 'break-up' basis*. The auditor instructed the valuer to value the plant and machinery at the break-up value as loose chattels on a sale by auction. The judge thought that was a wrong basis because it was equivalent to a forced sale. I would have agreed with the judge if the business had been a profitable concern. The value of the tangible assets would then have been somewhere in the region of £4 000 or £5 000, being either the balance sheet figure of £4 070 or Mr Pressley's figure of £4 835. But the business was not a profitable concern. It was a losing concern, and it is a well-known fact that a losing concern cannot realize the book value of its assets. There is an element to be taken into account which is sometimes spoken of as 'negative goodwill'. It comes about in this way. If a business is making a loss, that shows that its assets, regarded as an entity, are not a good investment. A purchaser will decline, therefore, to buy on that basis. He will only buy on a piece-meal basis, according to what the various assets, taken individually, are worth, and it is obvious that on a sale of assets piecemeal, the vendor will suffer heavy losses as compared with the book figures. The auditor was, therefore, quite justified in asking the valuer to value the assets as loose chattels sold at an auction. At any rate, if he honestly formed that opinion, no one can say he was wrong.

5. *The special purchaser*. The judge thought that some one could have been found to buy the one hundred and forty shares who would use his majority holding to turn out the two directors, and reorganize the factory and put in his own business. In other words, that the shares would have a special attraction for some person (namely, the next-door neighbour) who wanted to put his own business into these premises. I am prepared to concede that the shares might realize an enhanced value on that account, but I do not think it would be a fair price to ask the directors to pay. They were buying these shares—under a com-pulsory sale and purchase—on the assumption that they would continue in the business as working directors. It would be unfair to make them pay a price based on the assumption that they would be turned out. If the auditor never took that possibility into account, he cannot be blamed, for he was only asked to certify the fair value of the shares. The only fair value would be to take a hypothetical purchaser who was prepared to carry on the business if it was worth while to do so, or other-wise to put it into liquidation. At any rate, if that was the auditor's opinion, no one can say he was wrong. . . .

NOTES

On the valuation of shares, see further *Commissioners of Inland Revenue* v *Crossman* [1936] AC 26, [1936] 1 All ER 762 (HL); *Short* v *Treasury Commissioners* [1948] AC 534. [1948] 2 All ER 509 (HL); *Crabtree* v *Hinchcliffe* [1972] AC 707, [1971] 3 All ER 967 (HL),

Where shares are listed on a stock exchange the stock exchange price is generally taken as their true value: *383, 385* below.

In *Jones* v *Jones* [1971] 1 WLR 840, [1971] 2 All ER 676 (Ch), noted (1971) *JBL* 220, it was held that where shares in a private company have to be valued 'on an assets basis', 'as between a willing vendor and a willing purchaser of a business being carried on as a going concern', a valuation based on 'break-up' values is based on an erroneous principle.

Where shares in a private company have to be valued on the hypothesis that they are being sold in the open market, the value of the shares must be assessed on the basis that the preconditions for the transfer of the shares have been fulfilled and that the owner is free to sell them in the open market, but that the price which a purchaser would be prepared to pay for them would be affected by the fact that the shares are subject to restrictions on transfer. The fact that there are plans to remove the restrictions and make a public issue should only be taken into account if it was generally known: *Lynall* v *IRC* [1971] 3 All ER 914 (HL).

A buyer of shares at a price to be fixed by the company's auditors is entitled to refuse to pay the price so fixed if it is manifestly unjust and unfair, and bears no relationship to the real value of the shares: *Dublin* v *Diner* 1964 (1) SA 799 (N). See also *Estate Milne* v *Donohoe Investments (Pty) Ltd* 1967 (2) SA 359 (AD).

On the liability of an accountant for making negligently an erroneous valuation, see *Arenson* v *Arenson*, *368* below.

II CLASSES OF SHARES; MORE PARTICULARLY, PREFERENCE SHARES; VOTING RIGHTS

A TEXT

Except where the constitution of a company otherwise provides, all shares rank equally: *94*. The memorandum or (the more usual practice) the articles of association may authorize the creation of different classes of shares.

There are three main classes of shares: ordinary shares, preference shares and deferred shares. (As to the meaning of 'ordinary preferred' and 'preferred ordinary' shares, see *In re Powell-Cotton's Resettlement* [1957] Ch 159, [1957] 1 All ER 404.) A company, if so authorized by its articles, may by special resolution convert any of its shares, whether issued or not, into shares of another class, s 75(1)(i).

A person holding ordinary shares in a company is law's 'normal' or 'typical' shareholder. He is entitled to a dividend if and when declared. Preference shareholders are almost invariably entitled to a preferential dividend. They may or may not be preferred as to capital on a winding-up. Unless the company's constitution otherwise provides, preference shares do not participate in the profits of the company over and above the fixed dividend: *95, 96*; also *105* below. Like dividends generally (p 558 below), the preference dividend may not be paid out of capital and becomes payable only if and when declared: *97, 98*; also *108* below. In a winding-up arrear dividends on preference shares are not payable unless previously declared and then only if surplus assets are available: *99*; also *103* below.

Unless otherwise provided preference shares enjoy no preference as to capital in a winding-up or on a reduction of capital: *100*; also *95*. If the shares are preferred as to capital they are repaid first but do not (unless the constitution otherwise provides) participate in surplus assets: *101–105*.

If so authorized by its articles, a company may issue redeemable preference shares. Such shares may only be redeemed out of the profits of the company which would otherwise have been available for dividend or out of the proceeds of a fresh issue of shares made for the purposes of redemption, notice of redemption to be given to the Registrar, s 98. Such a redemption does not amount to a reduction of capital, s 98(3). Nor does it amount to an increase of capital for the purposes of s 75(3) if a company redeems redeemable preference shares out of a fresh issue of shares, s 98(2). (See Scaevola 1976 *SA Chartered Accountant* 62.)

A company may convert preference shares into redeemable preference shares, see s 99.

Deferred shares, also called vendors', promoters', founders', or management shares, as the case may be, receive no dividend until the holders of preference shares have received their preferential dividend and the holders of ordinary shares have received a specified minimum dividend.

In a public company all shares carry equal voting rights, ss 193, 195(1) (but see 195(4)): *106, 209* below.

The articles may provide that preference shares shall not carry the right to vote, except (a) during any period during which the preference dividend or any part of it remains in arrear and unpaid, or (b) in regard to any proposed resolution which directly affects the rights attached to such shares or the interests of preference shareholders, including a resolution for the winding up of the company or for the reduction of its capital, s 194(1)(a): *107, 108*.

The voting rights of a member of a private company are determined by its articles, s 195(2). In the absence of other provision every member has a right to vote in respect of each share held by him, s 193.

B CASES

[94] **Birch v Cropper**
(1889) 14 App Cas 525

The capital of a company consisted of ordinary shares, partly paid up, and preference shares, fully paid up. The company was voluntarily wound up. After the discharge of debts and liabilities and the repayment to the ordinary and preference shareholders of the capital paid on their shares, surplus assets remained. The court held that they ought to be divided among all the shareholders, not in proportion to the amounts paid on the shares, but in proportion to the shares held by them.

LORD MACNAGHTEN: Every person who becomes a member of a company limited by shares of equal amount becomes entitled to a proportionate part in the capital of the company, and, unless it be otherwise provided by the regulations of the company, entitled, as a necessary consequence, to the same proportionate part in all the property of the company, including its uncalled capital. He is liable in respect of all moneys unpaid on his shares to pay up every call that is duly made upon him. But he does not by such payment acquire any further or other interest in the capital of the company. His share in the company is just what it was before. His liability to the company is diminished by the amount paid. His contribution is merged in the common fund. And that is all. . . .

The ordinary shareholders say that the preference shareholders are entitled to a return of their capital, with 5 per cent interest up to the day of payment, and to nothing more. That is treating them as if they were debenture-holders, liable to be paid off at a moment's notice. Then they say that at the utmost the preference shareholders are only entitled to the capital value of a perpetual annuity of 5 per cent upon the amounts paid up by them. That is treating them as if they were holders of irredeemable debentures. But they are not debenture-holders at all. For some reason or other the company invited them to come in as shareholders, and they must be treated as having all the rights of shareholders, except so far as they renounced those rights on their admission to the company. There was an express bargain made as to their rights in respect of profits arising from the business of the company. But there was no bargain—no provision of any sort—affecting their rights as shareholders in the capital of the company.

Then the preference shareholders say to the ordinary shareholders, 'We have paid up the whole of the amount due on our shares; you have paid but a fraction of yours. The prosperity of a company results from its paid-up capital; distribution must be in proportion to contribution. The surplus assets must be divided in proportion to the amounts paid up on the shares.' That seems to me to be ignoring altogether the elementary principles applicable to joint-stock companies of this description. I think it rather leads to confusion to speak of the assets which are the subject of this application as 'surplus assets' as if they were an accretion or addition to the capital of the company capable of being distinguished from it and open to different considerations. They are part and parcel of the property of the company—part and parcel of the joint stock or common fund—which at the date of the winding-up represented the capital of the company. It is through their shares in the capital, and through their shares alone, that members of a company limited by shares become entitled to participate in the property of the company. The shares in this company were all of the same amount. Every contributory who held a preference share at the date of the winding-up must have taken that share and must have held it on the terms of paying up all calls duly made upon him in respect thereof. In paying up his share in full he has done no more than he contracted to do; why should he have more than he bargained for? Every contributory who was the holder of an ordinary share at the date of the winding-up took his share and held it on similar terms. He has done all he contracted to do; why should he have less than his bargain? When the preference shareholders and the ordinary shareholders are once placed on exactly the same footing in regard to the amounts paid up upon their shares, what is there to alter rights which were the subject of express contract? . . .

[95] Will v United Lankat Plantations Company Ltd
[1912] 2 Ch 571

A claim by holders of 10 per cent preference shares that they were entitled to dividends equally with ordinary shareholders after provision for a 10 per cent cumulative dividend on the preference shares was rejected by the Court of Appeal and the House of Lords.

FARWELL LJ: . . . the fallacy of the ingenious argument of [counsel for the respondent, a preference shareholder] is this. They treat shares as though they were born into the world, all equal; and as if preference was a kind of subsequent attachment to them; but the whole of the attributes of a preference share are limited and defined on its birth. It has a preference, and such a preference as is given to it by resolution. . . .

[Affirmed by the House of Lords [1914] AC 11.]

Cf *Steel Company of Canada* v *Ramsay* [1931] AC 270.

[96] *In re* National Telephone Company
[1914] 1 Ch 755

SARGANT J: . . . it appears to me that the weight of authority is in favour of the view that either with regard to dividend or with regard to the rights in a winding-up, the express gift or attachment of preferential rights to preference shares, on their creation, is, prima facie, a definition of the whole of their rights in that respect, and negatives any further or other right to which, but for the specified rights, they would be entitled.

[97] Buenos Ayres Great Southern Railway Company Ltd v Preston
[1947] Ch 384, [1947] 1 All ER 729

After incurring heavy losses on revenue account for several years, a company made profits in one year sufficient to pay the full dividends on preference shares. The directors, however, considered that it would be unwise to pay such dividends and decided to transfer the profits to reserve. The court held that they had power to do so and that the preference shareholders were not entitled to claim their dividends.

ROMER J: Having regard to [the] articles, it is clear that the dividends on the ordinary capital were payable only out of the net profits of the company in the sense that the powers of the company or the board to carry profits to reserve overrode the rights of the shareholders to dividend. The procedure would be that the board would consider the profits of the company on the one hand and its requirements as to maintenance and so on on the other. Having decided the amount of profit, if any, which was available, the directors would make the necessary recommendation to the company and the company would consider the matter. . . .

. . . In other words, the dividend would be payable, and payable only, out of profits available for dividend in the sense attributed to that phrase in the modern cases. . . .

... The preference shareholders were not given a contractual right to be paid a preference dividend out of the balance on profit and loss account in each year but only out of the profits which are available for dividend. ...

NOTES

Preference shares which participate in the profits of the company over and above the preferential dividend are called 'participating preference shares'. See *Re Saltdean Estate Ltd, 103* below, also *re Catalinas Warehouses and Mole Co Ltd* [1947] 1 All ER 51, where the preference shareholders were given a preferential dividend of 4 per cent, the ordinary shareholders a dividend of 4 per cent, and the balance of the profits was to be applied in paying a dividend to both classes of shareholders treated as one class.

[98] Webb *v* Earle
(1875) LR 20 Eq 556

The directors in accordance with the articles and with the consent of a general meeting, issued 10 per cent preference shares. It was held that if the profits of one year could not meet the dividend in full, the deficiency could be paid out of subsequent profits.

JESSEL MR: I am of opinion that the defendants are right. The words are very simple. The resolution authorized the capital of the company to be 'increased by the issue of 25 000 new shares of £10 each, such shares being preference shares, with such amount of preferential dividend, and with or without a power of redemption on terms to be arranged, with or without the option within a specified time of turning the preference shares into ordinary stock, and with or without such other rights and privileges, or with such restrictions, and to be issued at such price and on such terms and conditions as the directors of the said company may deem expedient'. Consequently these shares must be part of the capital entitled to preferential dividend, whatever that may mean.

Then the directors exercise the power by a contract by letter. The preferential capital authorized is £250 000, carrying dividend at £10 per cent per annum, payable half-yearly, and entitled to a pro rata participation in surplus dividends after £10 per cent has been paid on the ordinary share capital of £650 000. ...

When you look at the resolution, articles, and letter together, it clearly means this, that the dividend on the preference shares is to be paid out of the dividend declared, if there is one—in other words, that the right is restricted to this, that it is to be paid out of what is declared so far as it will go, and that the preference shareholders cannot get any more, and that they cannot get it when there is no dividend declared. They are to have it if there is anything to pay; if there is nothing to pay they are to go without until there is something to pay; but it does not mean that if there is not enough to pay one half-year they are not to have it the next half-year, or the third or fourth or fifth half-year. ...

It really comes to nothing more than that. The preference shareholders are to have a dividend of £10 per cent per annum, but it is to be paid as on preference capital, that is, so far as the profits shall extend; there is nothing to prevent them going to the profits of a subsequent period when they are sufficient to make it up. ...

NOTES

See, further, *Staples v Eastman Photographic Materials Co* [1896] 2 Ch 303 and *Godfrey Phillips Ltd v Investment Trust Corporation Ltd* [1953] *Ch* 449,]1953] 1 *All* ER 7; also *In re Mackenzie & Co Limited* [1916] 2 Ch 450.

[99] Re W Foster & Son Ltd
[1942] 1 All ER 314

BENNETT J: This company was incorporated in 1892 with a nominal capital of £30 000 divided into 3 000 shares of £10 each. Of those 3 000 shares, 1 000 were preference and the remaining 2 000 were ordinary shares. The preference shares are wholly paid up; the ordinary shares have been paid up to the extent of £7 per share. The company is now a private company, and its financial year ends on 31 August in each year. On 31 August 1940 it paid its preference dividend and no subsequent dividend has been declared; on that date the profit available for dividend was £1 899, and out of this it paid the dividend at the rate of 10 per cent on the preference shares and a dividend of 5 per cent on the ordinary shares, and carried forward £522 4s 9d. The company made profits in the period which followed after 31 August 1940, and on 21 July 1941 it passed a resolution by which it went into liquidation, the liquidation commencing on that date. The assets of the company have realized enough to repay to the holders of the preference shares the whole of their paid-up capital and to repay to the holders of the ordinary shares the whole of their paid-up capital and to leave a substantial surplus.

The first question asked by the summons is:

Whether any payment by way of dividend on shares or interest on capital ought to be made to the holders of the preference shares in respect of any period since 31 August 1940, and if so whether the dividend or interest on or in respect of such preference shares ought to be paid down to the commencement of the winding-up of the company or down to the date of repayment of the capital on such preference shares or down to some other and what date and at what rate the same ought to be paid. . . .

. . . The real question, in my opinion, is whether, as a matter of principle, the court can, in dealing with surplus assets after the company has gone into liquidation, regard any part of the surplus assets as being profits and so available for distribution amongst the shareholders in accordance with the rights under the company's articles of association, or whether once the company has gone into liquidation, everything that the company has, after it has satisfied its debts, is to be regarded as surplus assets and to be distributed among the members without regard to the particular provisions in the articles dealing with the payment of dividends which, prima facie, apply only while the company is a going concern. . . .

. . . Prima facie, when a winding-up has commenced, a dividend is no longer payable. Prima facie, a dividend is a payment made to the shareholder whilst the company is a going concern, and when, as is the case with this company, there is a provision in the articles of association which enables the directors to declare a dividend, and which gives the shareholders no right to a dividend unless the directors declare it, the shareholders have no right as against the company to be paid a dividend. . . .

. . . In the present case, having regard to the fact that the liquidation began on 21 July 1941, although the company had earned profits from the end of its last financial year, that is to say, from 31 August 1940, the preference shareholders had no right to anything out of the surplus assets in respect of the preferential dividend which the memorandum confers. . . .

NOTES

Everything, of course, turns on the relevant provisions of the company's constitution, e g *In re W J Hall & Co Ltd* [1909] 1 Ch 521; *In re Espuela Land and Cattle Co* [1909] 2 Ch 187; *In re New Chinese Antimony Co Ltd* [1916] 2 Ch 115; *In re Springbok Agricultural Estates Ltd* [1920] 1 Ch 563; *In re Roberts and Cooper Ltd* [1929] 2 Ch 383; *In re Dominion Tar and Chemical Co Ltd* [1929] 2 Ch 387; *In re Walter Symons Ltd* [1934] Ch 308; *In re Wood, Skinner & Co Ltd* [1944] Ch 323; *In re F de Jong & Co Ltd* [1946] Ch 211, [1946] 1 All ER 556; *In re E W Savory Ltd* [1951] 2 All ER 1036; *In re Wharfedale Brewery Co Ltd* [1952] Ch 913, [1952] 2 All ER 635.

The conclusion to be drawn from these cases is that with the slightest encouragement from the articles the courts will conclude that the arrear dividends of preference shareholders have to be paid out of surplus assets with priority over the claims of ordinary shareholders even if no declaration of dividends has been made prior to the winding-up. But see also *Re William Bedford Ltd* [1967] VR 490, noted (1968) 41 *Australian LJ* 438. Whether the surplus assets represent accumulated profits which might have been distributed by way of dividend, does not matter: *In re New Chinese Antimony Company Limited (supra)*; *Dimbula Valley (Ceylon) Tea Co Ltd v Laurie* [1961] 1 Ch 353, But cf *In re Bridgwater Navigation Company* [1891] 2 Ch 317.

[100] *In re* Quebrada Railway, Land and Copper Company
(1889) 40 ChD 363

NORTH J: I should have been prepared to sanction the proposed reduction of capital if I had felt myself at liberty to do so. But I do not. It seems to me that the proposal that the whole burden of the loss which has been incurred shall be thrown upon the ordinary shareholders is not fair as between the two classes of shareholders. The preference shareholders have a preference as regards dividend, but they have no preference as regards capital. Prima facie, having regard to the memorandum and articles of association, all the shares ought to be reduced *pari passu*, that is, rateably, and that is not what it is proposed to do. The resolution, therefore, produces an inequality among shareholders who ought to share the loss equally. . . .

[101] Scottish Insurance Corporation Ltd *v* Wilsons & Clyde Coal Co Ltd
[1949] AC 462, [1949] 1 All ER 1068 (HL)

A coal-mining company had been nationalized and its assets transferred to the National Coal Board. It was the intention of the company ultimately to go into voluntary liquidation. In the meantime, it proposed to reduce its capital by returning their capital to the holders of preference shares, which would be extinguished thereby. Article 141 of the company's articles of association provided that the company might convert any undivided profits into capital and distribute it among the ordinary shareholders. Articles 159 and 160 stated that in the event of a winding-up the preference stock ranked before the ordinary stock. The preference shareholders objected to the scheme on the ground that it deprived them of the opportunity of sharing in a distribution of surplus assets on the liquidation of the company. They contended that the reduction was unfair and unequitable and ought not to be confirmed by the court. The Scottish Court of Session (Lord Cooper dissenting) and the House of Lords (Lord Morton of Henryton dissenting) rejected this contention, and confirmed the reduction.

VISCOUNT MAUGHAM: My Lords . . . my conclusion is that taking these articles together it is reasonably clear that subject to the payment to the preference shareholders of their capital and their preferential dividends if any not yet paid . . . the whole of the reserve funds and other assets of the company, including the proceeds of sale of the capital assets, are appropriated to the ordinary shareholders and in that sense belongs to them to the exclusion of the preference shareholders. . . .

. . . In my view it is a sound prima facie rule that profits which have been appropriated, subject to possible application for the benefit of the company, to the ordinary shareholders to the exclusion of the preference shareholders must, in the absence of some other consideration, remain the property of the former on a winding up. . . .

LORD SIMONDS: . . . In the formal case which they have presented to the House of the element of unfairness on which the appellants insist is that the reduction deprives them of their right to participate in the surplus assets of the company on liquidation and leaves the ordinary stockholders in sole possession of those assets. But in their argument both in the Court of Session and before your Lordships they have further relied on the fact that they have been deprived of a favourable 7 per cent investment which they cannot hope to replace and might have expected to continue to enjoy. They further contend that the deprivation of these rights, which would in any case have been an unmerited hardship, is rendered the more unfair because it is likely to be followed at an early date by liquidation of the company or, as it is less accurately expressed, because it is itself only a step in the liquidation of the company.

The first plea makes an assumption, viz that the articles give the preference stockholders the right in a winding up to share in surplus assets, which I for the moment accept but will later examine. Making that assumption, I yet see no validity in the plea. The company has at a stroke been deprived of the enterprise and undertaking which it has built up over many years: it is irrelevant for this purpose that the stroke is delivered by an Act of Parliament which at the same time provides some compensation. Nor can it affect the rights of the parties that the only reason why there is money available for repayment of capital is that the company has no longer an undertaking to carry on. . . . Whether a man lends money to a company at 7 per cent or subscribes for its shares carrying a cumulative preferential dividend at that rate, I do not think that he can complain of unfairness if the company, being in a position lawfully to do so, proposes to pay him off. . . .

It will be seen, my Lords, that, even making an assumption favourable to the appellants, I reject their first plea. But it is perhaps necessary, in case there should be a division of opinion which would make this a decisive issue, that I should shortly examine the assumption. . . .

It is clear from the authorities, and would be clear without them, that, subject to any relevant provision of the general law, the rights *inter se* of preference and ordinary shareholders must depend on the terms of the instrument which contains the bargain that they have made with the company and each other. . . . Reading the relevant articles, as a whole, I come to the conclusion that arts 159 and 160 are exhaustive of the rights of the preference stockholders in a winding up. The whole tenor of the articles, as I have already pointed out, is to leave the ordinary stockholders masters of the situation. If there are 'surplus assets' it is because the ordinary stockholders have contrived that it should be so . . .

[102] *Re* **Chatterley-Whitfield Collieries Ltd**
[1948] 2 All ER 593

The capital of a colliery company was £400 000, divided into 20 000 six per cent preference shares of £10 each and 20 000 ordinary shares of £10 each. Under the Coal Industry Nationalization Act 1946, the company's colliery undertaking was nationalized. The company decided to embark upon certain other activities and to reduce its capital which was now in excess of the wants of the company.

A special resolution, as empowered by the articles of association, was passed to reduce its capital to £200 000 by returning to the preference shareholders the whole capital paid up on their shares. Certain preference shareholders objected. The Court of Appeal (Evershed LJ dissenting) confirmed the reduction.

LORD GREENE MR: . . . It is a clearly recognized principle that the court, in confirming a reduction by the payment off of capital surplus to a company's needs, will allow, or rather require, that the reduction shall be effected in the first instance by payment off of capital which is entitled to priority in a winding-up. Apart from special cases where by agreement between classes the incidence of reduction is arranged in a different manner, this is and has for years been the normal and recognized practice of the courts, accepted by the courts and by business men as the fair and equitable method of carrying out a reduction by payment off of surplus capital. I know of no case where this method has, apart from agreement, been departed from. Every person who acquires shares in a company has only himself to blame if he does not know this, and I have no doubt that it is well recognized by business men. . . .

In the argument before us there seemed to me at times to be involved some idea that preference shareholders, so far from being entitled to be paid off first, ought to be regarded as being entitled *not* to be paid off first, ie that a company having once issued preference shares, is bound either to keep them for ever, irrespective of the fact that it has surplus capital sufficient to pay them off, or at any rate is only entitled to reduce its capital by spreading the reduction rateably over its preference and its ordinary capital, with the result that the company will always be left with a certain amount of preference capital. The theory at the bottom of this idea appears to be that a preference shareholder subscribes his capital on the basis that he is to receive a preferential dividend of an agreed amount and that it is unfair to him to oust him from the company and thus deprive him of his contractual expectations of dividend. Apart from the fact that no such principle has ever been recognized by the court, it is, in my opinion, unsound for the reason that it ignores the facts (1) that the risk of a reduction of capital taking place is as much an element in the bargain as the right to a preferential dividend, and (2) that the well-known practice of the courts involves what (as I have endeavoured to point out) is really in accordance with sound business practice and, moreover, is based on the recognized analogy of priorities as to capital in a winding-up, viz that, at any rate where preference shares are not entitled to participate in surplus assets, they are to be paid off first on a reduction, and references to the reasonable expectations of preference shareholders which are intended to suggest that there is something inequitable in this form of treatment, have, in my judgment, no support either in practice or on principle, and are unsound.

ASQUITH LJ: . . . It is not in dispute that an unwanted surplus exists, and it is not in dispute that the proposed method of reducing capital is perfectly consistent with the preference shareholders' contractual rights. The sole residual question is whether the scheme is 'fair'. . . .

What, then, is the criterion of fairness? One test surely is whether the scheme is consistent with the reasonable expectations of a share-holder of the class in question, in the sense that it involves no more than the realization of a risk which he knows he is assuming when he acquires shares of that class. To be paid off in full is just such a risk as the pur-chaser of a preference share carrying a high rate of interest knows he is incurring. He must be taken to know of s 55 of the Companies Act [ie the United Kingdom Act of 1929, corresponding to s 44 of the South African Act of 1926, s 82 of the 1973 Act]. He must be taken, in my view, to know more, namely, that a prudent company will cut the millstone of onerous prior charges or senior stocks from its neck as soon as money becomes cheaper or the company finds itself in possession of a surplus of cash not needed to carry on its business. This risk is the price the preference shareholder pays for solid advantages, namely, for what is in the present case a high, as well as a well-secured, rate of fixed dividend, and a first charge on the assets in a liquidation. . . .

[Decision of the Court of Appeal affirmed in the House of Lords in *Prudential Assurance Company Ltd* v *Chatterley-Whitfield Collieries Ltd* [1949] AC 512, [1949] 1 All ER 1094].

[103] *Re* Saltdean Estate Co Ltd
[1968] 1 WLR 1844, [1968] 3 All ER 829 (Ch)

BUCKLEY J: This is a petition for the confirmation by the court of a reduction of the capital of the company, Saltdean Estate Co Ltd. The company was incorporated in 1926 with an authorized share capital of

£1 000 divided into one thousand shares all of one class, but, in consequence of an increase of capital in 1932, the authorized capital was
reorganized and is now £12 500 divided into twenty thousand preferred
shares of 10s each and fifty thousand ordinary shares of 1s each. All the
shares of each class have been issued and are fully paid up. The company
has resolved by special resolution to reduce its capital to £2 500, divided
into fifty thousand ordinary shares of 1s each, by repaying the full amount
of the capital paid-up on the preferred shares with a premium of 5s a
share. It is this reduction which the court is asked to confirm.

The rights of participating in profits and assets of the company which
were attached to the two classes of shares on the creation of the preferred
shares in 1932, are now to be found in art 21 and art 24 of the company's
articles of association, in the following terms.

'21. ... the net profits of the company which the directors shall
determine, to distribute by way of dividend in any year shall be
applied, First, in payment of a dividend at the rate of 10 per cent per
annum on the amounts paid up or credited as paid-up on the preferred
shares for the time being issued, Secondly, in payment among the
holders of the ordinary shares for the time being issued of a sum
equivalent to the total sum paid by way of dividend to the holders of
the preferred shares, and Thirdly, the balance of profits shall be divided
as to 50 per cent among the holders of the preferred shares and 50
per cent among the holders of the ordinary shares for the time being
issued.

'24. If the company shall be wound-up there shall first be paid to
the holders of the preferred shares rateably the amounts paid up or
credited as paid up thereon. The surplus assets (if any) shall be applied
in repayment of the capital paid up or credited as paid up on the
ordinary shares at the commencement of the winding-up; and the
excess (if any) shall be distributed among the members holding
ordinary shares in proportion to the number of ordinary shares held
by them respectively at the commencement of the winding-up.'

Every share carries one vote on a poll at a general meeting. . . . Under
art 8 of the company's articles of association, any right belonging to
any class of shares may be affected, modified, dealt with or abrogated
in any manner with the sanction of an extra-ordinary resolution of a
class meeting of the holders of that class of shares. No class meeting has
been convened to consider the proposed reduction of the company's
capital, but the owner of all, or virtually all, the ordinary shares
approves it.

The company's business has been very profitable. In the seven years
ended 30 September 1966, the amounts distributed by way of dividend
amongst the preferred shareholders in each year have respectively
amounted to 200 per cent, 275 per cent, 125 per cent, 150 per cent,
50 per cent, 100 per cent, and 100 per cent (gross) on the amount paid
up on the preferred shares. For the period from 1 October 1966 to
31 March 1968, £10 000 (gross) has been or is proposed to be distributed
in dividend amongst the holders of preferred shares—that is, a dividend
at the rate of 100 per cent. At 31 March 1968, a sum of £324 924 stood

to the credit of the company's revenue reserve representing undistributed profits. If this last amount were to be distributed by way of dividend, one half, or approximately £162 500, would go to the preferred shareholders, representing 1625 per cent on their paid-up capital. Compared with these figures, the 15s per 10s share which it is proposed that the holders of preferred shares shall receive on the reduction of the company's capital naturally seems disappointing to them. The question I have to consider is whether this proposal is unfair.

The evidence satisfies me that the sum of £15 000 proposed to be paid to or on account of the preferred shareholders on the reduction of the company's capital is not needed by the company. So far as it represents a return of paid-up capital, that capital is in excess of the company's needs.

It has long been recognized that at least in normal circumstances, where a company's capital is to be reduced by repaying paid-up share capital, in the absence of agreement or the sanction of a class meeting to the contrary, that class of capital should first be repaid which would be returned first in a winding-up of the company. . . .

In the present case the preferred shareholders are entitled to prior repayment of capital in a winding-up and, consequently, if the company has more paid-up capital than it needs and wishes to repay some part of it, the first class of capital to be repaid should prima facie be the preferred shares.

A company called High Trees Investment Trust Ltd, however, which holds eighty preferred shares of the company, opposes the petition, contending that, in the circumstances of this particular case, the proposed reduction will operate unfairly to the preferred shareholders.

First, it is said that the proposed cancellation of the preferred shares will constitute an abrogation of all the rights attached to those shares which cannot validly be effected without an extraordinary resolution of a class meeting of preferred shareholders under art 8 of the company's articles. In my judgment, that article has no application to a cancellation of shares on a reduction of capital which is in accord with the rights attached to the shares of the company. Unless this reduction can be shown to be unfair to the preferred shareholders on other grounds, it is in accordance with the right and liability to prior repayment of capital attached to their shares. The liability to prior repayment on a reduction of capital, corresponding to their right to prior return of capital in a winding-up, is a liability of a kind of which Lord Greene . . . said that anyone has only himself to blame if he does not know it. It is part of the bargain between the shareholders and forms an integral part of the definition or delimitation of the bundle of rights which make up a preferred share. Giving effect to it does not involve the variation or abrogation of any right attached to such a share. Nor, in my judgment, has s 72 of the Companies Act 1948, on which the preferred shareholders place some reliance, any application to this case. That section relates to variation of rights attached to shares, not to cancellation of shares.

The preferred shareholders' main ground of complaint about the proposed reduction is that, as they contend, it is discriminatory. It will deprive the preferred shareholders of any opportunity of participating in the enjoyment not only of the future fruits of the company's prosperity but also of those which have already been garnered. It is said that the preferred shares of the company are not like preference shares with a limited interest in the profits of the company: as a class they carry a right to at least an equal share with the class of ordinary shares in the distributed profits. As regards participation in profits, they are, it is said, what are called 'equity' shares. This is true so far as it goes, but it should be noted that the profits which, under art 21, the preferred shareholders are entitled to share equally with the ordinary shareholders, are only those which the directors decide shall be distributed. Moreover, the preferred shareholders' only right under art 24 in a winding-up is a preferential right to repayment of paid-up capital.

Counsel for the preferred shareholders has contended that, on the true construction of the company's articles, the undistributed trading profits of the company are appropriated to the preferred and ordinary share-holders and belong to the two classes of shareholders in equal shares as undrawn profits. . . . He further submits, in connexion with this con-struction, that 'surplus assets' in art 24 means capital assets in excess of what is required to repay capital paid up on the preferred shares and does not include any undistributed trading profits. . . .

In art 21, read alone, it seems to me to be reasonably clear that the 'balance of profits' there referred to is what is left of the fund of profits mentioned earlier in the same article—that is, the net profits which the directors determine to distribute in dividend in any year—after making the payments first and secondly directed to be made out of it. If this is so, this article says nothing about any profits which are left undistributed. On this view, undrawn profits would remain part of the general fund of unappropriated assets of the company.

Is there anything in art 24 inconsistent with this view? I think not. The word 'assets' here means prima facie any property of the company available for distribution in a winding-up, including any such property out of which paid-up capital could properly be repaid. For this purpose it is not normally necessary to distinguish between assets representing contributed capital and assets representing undrawn profits. . . . The natural meaning of art 24, in my judgment, is that all the property of the company available for distribution in a winding-up and remaining after repaying all paid-up capital, belongs to the ordinary shareholders. Article 21 and art 24, so construed, are mutually consistent. This is, in my judgment, their clear and undoubted meaning.

The only real alternative to construing the expression 'balance of profits' in art 21 in the way I have indicated is to read the word 'profits' here as extending to all profits of the company of any kind. There seems to be no reason to confine it to trading profits. It would, therefore, include profits on capital account. But if these profits were all to be treated as appropriated to and belonging to the shareholders by virtue of art 21 in such a way that their ownership would be unaffected by a winding-up, there could never be any 'excess' to be distributed amongst the ordinary shareholders under art 24.

I therefore reach the conclusion that, on the true interpretation of the company's articles, if the company were now to be liquidated, all the undistributed profits would belong to the ordinary shareholders.' The preferred shareholders, opposing the petition, say that notwithstanding this and notwithstanding that in a winding-up the first capital to be repaid would be that paid-up on the preferred shares, the proposed reduction of capital is unfair to the preferred shareholders and should not be confirmed by the court. They say, as seems to be the case, that there is no present prospect of the company being wound up; that it can be regarded as certain that there will continue to be large distributions of profits in which, if the preferred shares were still to exist, the holders of them would participate equally with the ordinary shareholders; and that it is unfair that this right should be bought out at the price of no more than 15s for a 10s share. . . . The fact is that every holder of preferred shares of the company has always been at risk that his hope of participating in undrawn or future profits of the company might be frustrated at any time by a liquidation of the company or a reduction of its capital properly resolved on by a sufficient majority of his fellow members. This vulnerability is and has always been a characteristic of the preferred shares. Now that the event has occurred, none of the preferred shareholders can, in my judgment, assert that the resulting state of affairs is unfair to him.

For these reasons the opposition to this petition fails. I will confirm the reduction of the company's capital. . . .

[104] Levin *v* Felt and Tweeds Ltd
1951 (2) SA 401 (AD)

A company passed a special resolution authorizing the reduction of capital by the repayment to all preference shareholders of their capital from an amount which it was sought to borrow by the raising of a mortgage over all its assets. The scheme also involved the payment to the preference shareholders of all arrear dividends on their shares.

The appellant and several other ordinary shareholders opposed the confirmation of the reduction by the court on the ground that the scheme was devised solely in the interests of the preference shareholders. They also contended, *inter alia*, that the fact that the directors who proposed the resolution were shareholders in a company which held such preference shares should have been disclosed. Their opposition was unsuccessful.

CENTLIVRES CJ: . . . In the case I am now considering, the proposed reduction of capital does not involve any alteration of rights as between the different classes of shareholders or as between any other persons. In view of the fact that the preference shareholders are, in terms of the special resolution of 29 July 1946, entitled on a liquidation or winding-up in priority to the ordinary shareholders to repayment of their capital and arrears of dividend, whether declared or not, there is, in my opinion, nothing unfair or inequitable in a scheme, such as the one now before the court, whereby on a reduction of capital the preference shareholders only are repaid the capital which they have invested in the company as well as the arrear dividends on their shares. In *Re Chatterley-Whitfield Collieries Ltd* [1948] 2 All ER 593 [*102* above] at 596 Lord Greene MR said:

'It is a clearly recognized principle that the court, in confirming a reduction by the payment off of capital surplus to a company's needs, will allow, or rather require, that the reduction shall be effected in the first instance by payment off of capital which is entitled to priority in a winding-up.'

I can see no reason why the same principle should not be applied to arrear dividends in respect of which preference shareholders have priority rights in a winding-up. It therefore seems to me that in the present case the ordinary shareholders, of which the appellant is one, have no ground for complaining that there is any interference with their rights. Their rights are not being interfered with. [It was] contended that the rights of the ordinary shareholders were being altered, because when they invested money in the company, they relied on the fact that the capital of the company was as it then was and that any reduction of capital affects their rights. The answer to this contention is that when the ordinary shareholders invested their money in the company they must be taken to have known that under the Companies Act the court may confirm a reduction of capital voted for by three-fourths of the shareholders and that on such a reduction of capital the preference shareholders are entitled to be paid out first. . . .

[As to the question of non-disclosure, the learned Chief Justice said, after referring to a number of English decisions:]

These cases seem to lay down that, when the passing of a resolution results in a direct pecuniary benefit to directors, the shareholders should, before being asked to vote on the proposed resolutions, be told what that pecuniary benefit is. I have not found any case where it has been held that, in circumstances similar to those of the present case, the directors should have disclosed the fact that they were substantial shareholders in a company which was the holder of preference shares in another company when it was proposed to reduce the capital of that other company by returning to the preference shareholders the amount they had paid on their shares. When such a reduction of capital takes place the preference shareholders are entitled, as I have pointed out, to be repaid their capital and the mere fact that it has not been disclosed that the directors who propose the necessary resolution are shareholders in a company which holds such preference shares does not, in my opinion, vitiate the passing of the resolution. It cannot be said that the real object of the passing of the resolution in this case was to benefit the directors concerned: the object was to obtain better financial facilities for the respondent company. . . .

[105] *Ex parte* **Betty:** *In re* **First Mutual Investment Trust Ltd**
(In Liq)
1974 (1) SA 127 (W)

GALGUT J: The applicant is the liquidator of the First Mutual Investment Trust Ltd (In Liq.). All the assets of the company have been realized. It appears that after payment of all liabilities, the cost of winding-up and the repayment of the capital of the preference and ordinary shares there will be a surplus of R54 000.

The applicant asks for an order declaring whether, on a true construction of the articles of association of the company, the above surplus ought to be distributed on the basis that the holders of the preference shares are entitled to participate with the holders of the ordinary shares rateably in proportion to the nominal amount of the shares held by them respectively or upon the footing that the holders of the preference shares have no right to participate in such distribution. . . .

The company was registered on 2 July 1928 and initially had a capital of £10 000 divided into 10 000 shares of £1 each. In terms of art 47 of Table A which forms part of the company's articles of association, the company was empowered to increase its share capital.

On 27 October 1943, a special resolution was passed and subsequently registered in the company's office whereby the nominal capital of the company was increased from £10 000 to £60 000 divided into 60 000 ordinary shares of ten shillings each, and 60 000 preference shares of ten shillings each. An extract from the said resolution reads as follows:

'That the additional capital of £50 000 be issued in terms of the aforegoing resolution and divided into two classes of shares, namely:

(i) 5½ per cent cumulative preference shares which will be entitled to a cumulative preferential dividend calculated at the rate of 5½ per cent per annum on the capital paid up or credited as paid up thereon with the further right to receive out of any additional profits which the directors may from time to time determine to divide amongst shareholders after provision has been made for payment of a dividend of 8 per cent on ordinary shares and a bonus (non-cumulative) not exceeding in any one year a total bonus of 1½ per cent on the nominal value of the shares with the additional right in the event of the winding-up of the company of priority over the ordinary shares to a return of capital and payment of any arrears of preferential dividend whether declared or not up to the date of the commencement of the winding-up and that such preference shares carry the same rights and privileges as to voting or otherwise as the ordinary shares in the company. (All the underlining is my own).

(ii) Ordinary shares which shall rank *pari passu* with and bear and carry the same rights and privileges as the existing ordinary shares in the company.' . . .

My attention has been drawn to the fact that when this resolution defining the rights of preference shareholders was passed in October 1943 the prevailing judicial opinion was that, unless the articles of association provided otherwise, the preference shareholders were entitled to share in the surplus assets with the ordinary shareholders. . . .

. . . This approach however was changed in 1949 in the House of Lords decision of *Scottish Insurance Corp Ltd* v *Wilsons & Clyde Coal Co Ltd* [1949] AC 462 [*101* above], which specifically disapproved of the decision in *Metcalfe's* case. See also *Re Isle of Thanet Electricity Supply Co Ltd* [1950] 1 Ch at 176.

In the latter case the article in question stated that . . .

'The preference shares shall confer the right in winding-up of the company of repayment of capital together with arrears (if any) and whether earned or not of the preferential dividend to the date of the commencement of the winding-up in priority to the ordinary shares . . . .'

It was held (see p 172) that the language of this article on the rights of preference shareholders on winding up was exhaustive. The decision in the *Scottish Insurance* case, *supra*, was therefore followed. . . . There is no direct authority in South Africa on the point in issue. There can be no doubt that prior to 1949 judicial opinion was that in the absence of anything to the contrary in the articles preference shareholders had a right in winding up to participate in surplus assets. Since the *Scottish Insurance* case (*supra*) the thinking has changed.

I have always understood the position to be, that, in the absence of some indication to the contrary, such profits as remain after the payment of dividends to the preferent shareholders are available for ordinary shareholders; therefore, if in a winding-up there are surplus assets which result from profits, such surplus assets should, again in the absence of some indication to the contrary, be available to the ordinary shareholders. This view accords with the decision in the *Scottish Insurance* case (*supra*). However, the view which I have formed as to the meaning to be given to the article in question purely as a matter of interpretation and without having regard to the judicial pronouncements referred to renders it unnecessary to discuss the question of what weight, if any, should now be attached to the state of the law in 1943.

As I read the article the preferent shareholders are given the

'cumulative preferential dividend of $5\frac{1}{2}$ per cent with a further right to receive a bonus of $1\frac{1}{2}$ per cent out of additional profits remaining after ordinary shareholders had been awarded a dividend of 8 per cent; in the event of a winding up, the preferent shareholders are given priority over the ordinary shareholder to a return of capital and arrear dividends'.

However, there then follow the words underlined by me. These words give the preference shares the same rights and privileges as ordinary shareholders as to voting rights and otherwise. It will be noted that the article in question is one sentence. The words may well refer to the rights which shareholders are to have only in winding up or generally in all circumstances, ie before and in winding up. The first part of the sentence sets out the rights the preferent shareholder has as to dividends and also as to a bonus. The second part of the sentence deals with the priorities in winding up. It seems probable that the underlined words were meant to refer to the rights and privileges of the shareholders winding up. If this is so then the words 'or otherwise' refer to rights and privileges other than voting rights. Such other rights can only refer to the right to share in surplus assets. Even if the underlined words refer also to the rights and privileges prior to winding up it seems to me that the words 'or otherwise' can only refer to the right to share profits over and above those declared by way of dividends and the bonus referred to. I am further of the view that the first part of the sentence shows that it was not intended to limit the preferent shareholder to his cumulative payment dividend of $5\frac{1}{2}$ per cent. He is entitled to a bonus of $1\frac{1}{2}$ per cent after the ordinary shareholder has received a dividend of 8 per cent. This being so it seems to me that the article undertakes that after the preferent shareholders have received their dividends and the bonus and the ordinary shareholders have received 8 per cent, the remaining profits, if any, and hence surplus assets, if any, should be apportioned between preferent shareholders and ordinary shareholders. This view would also give weight to my interpretation of the words 'or otherwise'.

It follows from what has been said above that I am of the view that the contention advanced on behalf of the preferent shareholders must be upheld.

NOTES

See also *In re The Isle of Thanet Electricity Supply Company Ltd* [1950] 1 Ch 161, [1949] 2 All ER 1060, where Wynn-Parry J said: '. . . In my judgment the effect of the authorities as now in force is to establish . . . two principles . . . : first, that, in construing an article which deals with rights to share in profits, that is, dividend rights, and rights to share in the company's property in a liquidation, the same principle is applicable; and, second, that that principle is that, where the article sets out the rights attached to a class of shares to participate in profits while the company is a going concern or to share in the property of the company in liquidation, prima facie, the rights so set out are in each case exhaustive. . . .'

For a case in which under the company's constitution preference shareholders were entitled to participate rateably with ordinary shareholders in surplus assets, see *Dimbula Valley (Ceylon) Tea Co Ltd* v *Laurie* [1961] 1 All ER 769 (Ch) (*357* below). It was held there that in the circumstances capitalization of a reserve fund resulting from a revaluation of unrealized fixed assets for the benefit of ordinary shareholders did not encroach upon the rights of the preference shareholders to participate in 'surplus assets', but had to be equated to payment of a dividend. See, also, Murray A Pickering 'The Problem of the Preference Share' (1963) 26 *MLR* 499.

In *In re Old Silkstone Collieries Ltd* [1954] Ch 169, [1954] 1 All ER 68 the court refused to sanction a scheme of reduction by the repayment of the preference stocks at par, on the ground that it was not fair and equitable to the preference shareholders; similarly, in *In the Matter of Vacola Manufacturing Co Ltd* [1966] VR (Supreme Court of Victoria, Australia) 97, noted (1966) 40 *Australian LJ* 55, the court refused to sanction a reduction, despite the fact that it was in strict accordance with the rights of the preference shareholders, on the ground that it was unfair to them, because the amount in excess of the wants of the company was to be returned in its entirety to the ordinary shareholders.

A scheme of reduction under which preference shares were repaid and cancelled was held not to amount to an abrogation of the rights of the preference shareholders in *Re Saltdean Estate Co Ltd, 103* above. See also *Re William Jones & Sons* [1969] 1 WLR 146, [1969] 1 All ER 913, where a scheme of reduction under which preference shares were repaid and cancelled was confirmed although the preference shareholders were entitled to be repaid in full and then, after repayment in full of the ordinary shares, to share rateably with ordinary shares in any surplus up to a fixed amount.

In *Anglo-Transvaal Collieries Ltd* v *SA Mutual Life Assurance Society* 1976 (4) SA 655 (T), preference shareholders were in terms of the memorandum entitled to receive a fixed preferential dividend but not to participate in profits, and to rank in a winding-up in priority to ordinary shareholders. There was a general provision that otherwise all shares were to rank *pari passu*. Applying the principle in *Ex parte Betty, 105* above, the court held that the preference shareholders were entitled to participate on an equal basis with ordinary shareholders in an offer of unsecured convertible notes.

[106] Hopkinson v Bloemfontein District Creamery
1966 (1) SA 159 (O)

SMUTS AJ: This is the return day of a rule issued by this court calling on all interested parties to show cause why the existing art 69 of the articles of association of Bloemfontein Creamery Limited should not be declared to be void and of no effect. . . .

Confirmation of the rule is opposed by 13 of the members of the respondent company. It appears from the papers that the respondent, a public company, was registered with limited liability under the laws of the Orange River Colony on 19 October 1909. It has a nominal share capital of R200 000 divided into 100 000 ordinary shares of R2 each and an issued share capital of R163 632, consisting of 81 816 ordinary shares of R2 each.

Article 69 of the articles of association, to which the applicant objects as being invalid, reads as follows:

'Every member shall have one vote, and one vote only, whether on a show of hands or on a poll.'

The question of the validity of art 69 of the respondent company depends on whether it is in conflict with the provisions of s 62*quat*. This application is, therefore, mainly concerned with the correct interpretation of s 62*quat* [now ss 193, 195]. . . .

Whether in the present case one seeks to ascertain the true intention of the legislature by applying the test of the ordinary grammatical meaning of the words used or whether the matter is approached by considering the words in the context in which they are used . . . the result, in my view, is the same.

Applying the ordinary meaning of the words used as the test to determine the intention of the legislature, I turn firstly to the wording of ss (2) which is that:

'Every member shall have a right to vote in respect of each share held by him.'

I agree . . . that this does not mean that a shareholder is entitled to one vote for each share held by him. Apart from the fact that the subsection does not state that each share is to carry one vote, it appears clearly from the proviso to ss (3) that it is contemplated by the legislature that articles of association may make provision that, above a stated number of shares, voting rights will not increase in direct proportion to the number of shares held, but in some defined lower proportion. In such a case, votes above the stated number will not confer one vote per share but will carry individually a lower voting power. What the legislature had in mind, when ss (2) was introduced, was evidently to ensure that no voteless shares be issued. [Counsel for the applicant] also did not contend that each share must necessarily confer one vote. He contended, however, that ss (2) and (3), when read together, indicate that the legislature intended that the financial stake that a shareholder has in a company should be recognized in the form of conferring on a member who has invested a larger amount of money in a company than his co-member, a greater voting power than that held by such co-member. [Counsel for the respondent] disputed this contention and relied on the proviso to ss (3) wherein it is stated that

'. . . the articles of association of a company may make provision applying equally to all members that the votes to which any member is entitled shall be limited to a stated number'.

He contended that this right of limitation justifies a provision that all members shall have only one vote on a poll, no matter what their respective shareholding may be. If he is correct the application must fail.

Subsection (3) commences by providing that:

'The proportion of the total votes in a company which each member shall have in respect of the shares held by him shall be the proportion which the nominal value of such shares bears to the nominal value of all the issued capital of the company.'

As stated in *Henochsberg on the Companies Act* 2 ed 143, the effect of this provision is that each member must, in the case of public companies, be given voting rights proportionate to the par value of the shares held by him, so that, if there are 50 cent shares and R2 shares, holders of the former would have one vote and holders of the latter four votes in respect of each share. It is clear from the words I have quoted that, but for the proviso following on these words, the voting power of members *inter se* would be determined by the nominal value of each member's shareholding, since voting power would depend on the proportion which the nominal value of each member's shareholding bears to the nominal value of the issued capital. Members would accordingly exercise voting power in accordance with the extent of their investment in a company's shares. . . .

[It is stated in the second part of the proviso] that it is permissible to restrict voting power by means of a provision, which is to apply equally to all members, that, above a stated number, the votes to which a member will be entitled shall not increase in direct proportion to the number of shares held, but in some defined lower proportion. This provision, however, still recognizes that the member with the greater shareholding is entitled to more votes than his co-member who holds less shares. . . . If it is permissible to limit each member to one vote on a poll, it will mean that what I regard as the dominent portion of s 62*quat*(3) may be completely defeated by a provision that no member shall have more than one vote. If such a result were contemplated, I find it strange that the trouble was taken to state the scheme contained in the first portion of ss (3). The use of the plural, 'votes', in the phrase 'that the votes to which any member is entitled', is also an indication that the legislature contemplated and intended that a person in respect of whom limitation of votes could be prescribed should in any event have more than one vote. Reading the section as a whole it appears to me that the legislature, after deciding on the scheme stated in what I have called the dominant portion of ss (3), realized the possibility of one or more persons being able to buy a very large number of shares and thus to obtain an excess of voting power. It was then made possible to limit this power by appropriate provisions in the articles of association while at the same time still recognizing that effect was to be given to the fact that a greater investment had in fact been made by one member than another. This intention is clearly expressed in the second part of the proviso. . . . Restriction of voting power is clearly allowed but not complete equation of all members irrespective of the value of their shareholding. . . .

I conclude that art 69 is invalid as being in conflict with s 62*quat*(3), read with ss (1) and (2), in so far as it limits members to one vote only on a poll being taken, irrespective of the value of each respective shareholding in the company.

[Smuts AJ also held that art 69 was valid in so far as it dealt with voting on a show of hands.]

[For a critical review of *Hopkinson*, see 1966 *Annual Survey* 258–60.]

[107] *In re* Holders Investment Trust Ltd
[1971] 1 WLR 583, [1971] 2 All ER 289

MEGARRY J: Unopposed petitions by a company for the confirmation of a reduction of capital are a commonplace of the Companies' Court; but an opposed petition such as the one I have before me is a comparative rarity. The company, Holders Investment Trust Ltd (which I shall call 'the company') was incorporated in 1933 and has an authorized capital of £2 275 000. What is in issue before me is a reduction of capital which is to be effected by cancelling 1 250 000 5 per cent cumulative redeemable preference shares of one pound each, redeemable at par on 31 July 1971, and allotting to the holders the same nominal amount of 6 per cent unsecured loan stock 1985/90. The preference shares are all issued and fully paid up, and confer the right on a winding up to repayment of capital and arrears of dividend in priority to any other class of shares, but no further right to participate in the profits or assets.

The remaining share capital consists of £834 600 stock and 1 800 000 'A' non-voting ordinary shares of two shillings each, which have been issued and are fully paid up. In addition, there are 104 000 ordinary shares of two shillings each which have not been issued. The proposed reduction has been duly authorized by a special resolution of the company; and a separate class meeting of the preference shareholders also passed an extraordinary resolution approving the reduction. At that meeting, however, the trustees of the Lionel Barber Voluntary Settlement, who hold 95 000 of the preference shares, voted against the resolution; I shall call them the 'opposing trustees'. The trustees of another settlement, who hold 30 000 of the preference shares, were not in agreement as to how they should vote, and so did not vote. The resolution was carried by the requisite majority because nearly 90 per cent of the preference shares are vested in the trustees of three trusts set up by Mr William Hill, and they voted in favour of the resolution. These trustees (whom I shall call 'the supporting trustees') also hold some 52 per cent of the ordinary stock and shares. . . .

Put briefly [Mr D's] opposition to the confirmation of the reduction is twofold. First, he contends that the extraordinary resolution of the preference shareholders was not valid and effectual because the supporting trustees did not exercise their votes in the way that they ought to have done, namely, in the interests of the preference shareholders as a whole. Instead, being owners of much ordinary stock and many shares as well, they voted in such a way as to benefit the totality of the stocks and shares that they held. Secondly, [Counsel for the opposing trustees] contends that even if the extraordinary resolution was valid, the terms on which the reduction of capital is to be effected are not fair, in particular in that the increase in the rate of interest from 5 per cent to 6 per cent is not an adequate recompense for having the right of repayment or redemption postponed from 31 July 1971 until at earliest 31 October 1985, and at latest some unspecified date in 1990. I may say at the outset that it is common ground that the proposed reduction is not in accordance with the class rights of the preference shareholders.

The statutory guidance given to the court in such cases is meagre. On the facts of this case, s 66(1) of the Companies Act 1948 gives an admitted power to effect a reduction of capital, 'subject to confirmation by the court'; and s 67(1) authorizes the company to 'apply to the court for an order confirming the reduction'. By s 68(1), the court 'may make an order confirming the reduction on such terms and conditions as it thinks fit'. It is accepted that the result is that the court exercises a discretionary jurisdiction which provides a safeguard for minorities.

[Counsel for the supporting trustees] put before me four propositions based on the authorities. Discarding what does not apply in this case, and putting the matter shortly, I think that three relevant propositions emerge. First, a reduction of capital which is not in accordance with the class rights is nevertheless regular if it is effectually sanctioned in accordance with the regulations of the company. Second, there is an effectual sanction to the modification of class rights if those holding a sufficient majority of the shares of that class vote in favour of the modification in the bona fide belief that they are acting in the interests of the general body of members of that class. Third, the burden of proof depends on whether or not there is any such sanction. If there is, the court will confirm the reduction unless the opposition proves that it is unfair; if there is not, the court will confirm the reduction only if it is proved to be fair. . . . Whatever may be said about the precise formulation of the propositions, their substance was, I think, common ground between the parties. Accordingly, I must first consider the validity of the class resolution.

In the *British America* case [1927] AC 369 Viscount Haldane, in speaking for a strong Board of the Judicial Committee, referred, at 371, to

'a general principle, which is applicable to all authorities conferred on majorities of classes enabling them to bind minorities; namely, that the power given must be exercised for the purpose of benefiting the class as a whole, and not merely individual members only . . .',

and see also at 373. The matter may, I think, be put in the way in which Scrutton LJ put it in the *Shuttleworth* case [1927] 2 KB 9, where the question was the benefit of the company rather than of a particular class of members. Adapting his language at p 23, I have to see whether the majority was honestly endeavouring to decide and act for the benefit of the class as a whole, rather than with a view to the interests of some of the class and against that of others. . . .

I pause here to point the obvious. Without guidance from those skilled in these matters, many members of a class may fail to realize what they should bear in mind when deciding how to vote at a class meeting. The beneficial owner of shares may well concentrate on his own personal interests: even though he regards the proposal per se as one to be rejected, collateral matters affecting other interests of his may lead him to vote in favour of the resolution. Trustees, too, are under a fiduciary duty to do the best they properly can for their beneficiaries. A proposal which, in isolation, is contrary to the interests of those owning the shares affected may nevertheless be beneficial to the beneficiaries by reason of the improved prospects that the proposal will confer on other shares in the company which the trustees hold on the same trusts: and that, in essence, is what is in issue here. As I have mentioned, of the £1 250 000 preference shares in question, almost 90 per cent are vested in the supporting trustees, who also own some 52 per cent of the ordinary stock and shares.

[After referring to an exchange of letters in which the solicitors of the 'supporting trustees' sought the advice of a firm of stockbrokers, His Lordship continued:]

That exchange of letters seems to me to make it perfectly clear that the advice sought, the advice given, and the advice acted upon, was all on the basis of what was for the benefit of the trusts as a whole, having regard to their large holdings of the equity capital. From the point of view of equity, and disregarding company law, this is a perfectly proper basis: but that is not the question before me. I have to determine whether the supporting trustees voted for the reduction in the bona fide belief that they were acting in the interests of the general body of members of that class. From first to last I can see no evidence that the trustees ever applied their minds to what under company law was the right question, or that they ever had the bona fide belief that is requisite for an effectual sanction of the reduction. Accordingly, in my judgment there has been no effectual sanction for the modification of class rights. It may be observed that I have said nothing as to the burden of proof on the issue whether the sanction to the modification of class rights has been validly given, and I propose to continue to say nothing. However that burden lies, in my judgment there was no effectual sanction. The result is therefore that on the issue of fairness the burden of proof devolves on those supporting the reduction to prove that it is fair. Unless this burden is discharged, confirmation of the reduction will be refused.

[108] Utopia Vakansie-Oorde Bpk v Du Plessis
1974 (3) SA 148 (AD)

Section 62*quat* (4) of the 1926 Act [now s 194] provided, in the Afrikaans version, as follows:

„Die statute van 'n maatskappy mag bepaal dat die reg om te stem opgeskort word —

(a) ten opsigte van voorkeuraandele op sodanige voorwaardes as wat bepaal mag word, maar onderworpe daaraan dat die reg om te stem ten volle uitgeoefen kan word —

(i) gedurende dié tydperk wanneer die voorkeurdiwidend of 'n
deel daarvan agterstallig en onbetaald bly en dié tydperk
loop vanaf 'n dag wat nie meer dan ses maande of so 'n
korter tyd dan ses maande wat die statute mag bepaal, na
die betaaldatum van die diwidende is nie; en

(ii) ten opsigte van 'n voorgestelde besluit wat regstreeks 'n reg
verbonde aan dié aandele of die belange van die houers
daarvan raak, insluitende 'n besluit dat die maatskappy
gelikwideer word;

(b) ten opsigte van aandele waarop 'n opvordering of ander bedrag
aan die maatskappy verskuldig en betaalbaar is, gedurende die
tydperk wanneer die opvordering of ander som of 'n deel daarvan
onbetaald bly."

In *Utopia Vakansie-Oorde* the following questions arose:

(1) Is the preferential dividend in arrears and unpaid ('agterstallig
en onbetaald') when no dividend has been declared, or only when a
dividend has been declared but not paid?

(2) When can a proposed resolution be said to affect 'the interests'
('die belange') of the preference shareholders?

TROLLIP JA: 1. Die doel van die sub-artikel [(4)(a)(i)] is klaarblyklik
om te verseker dat in spesifieke gevalle die stemreg aan voorkeuraandeelhouers toegeken moet word. Die bogenoemde beweerde betekenis daarvan
skep onmiddellik twee voor-die-hand-liggende moeilikhede. Eerstens,
volgens dié uitleg, sou dit al te maklik vir direkteure of gewone aandeelhouers wees om dié stemreg te verydel deur voorkeurdiwidende nie te
verklaar nie. Tweedens, gewoonlik verklaar maatskappye nie sulke
dividende as hulle nie die bedrag daarvan kan of wil betaal nie; derhalwe sou die sub-artikel, aldus uitgelê, op weinige gevalle van toepassing
wees: so weinig dat die bestaan van enige besondere behoefte daarvoor
sterk bevraagteken kan word. Uit die staanspoor blyk dit meer waarskynlik te wees dat die bedoeling van die sub-artikel is om die gewone
gevalle te betrek, nl, waar die voorkeurdiwidende nie verklaar word nie,
asook waar dit verklaar word maar nie betaal word nie.

2. Weliswaar is die gewone of primêre, maar ietwat enge, betekenis
van ,,agterstallig" verskuldig, betaalbaar, en onbetaald. By uitstek sal
dit 'n voorkeurdiwidend behels wat verklaar is maar onbetaald bly.
Maar die woord het ook 'n wyere of sekondêre betekenis, naamlik as
iets wat agterweë (,,behindhand") bly, dws, iets wat op of voor 'n
sekere tydstip moes of sou gedoen gewees het, maar nie gedoen is nie.
Kyk, bv, *Woordeboek van die Afrikaanse Taal* sv ,,agterstallig", vierde sin;
Oxford English Dictionary, en veral die *Imperial and Standard Dictionaries*
sv ,,arrear" en ,,in arrear", asook *Van der Merwe* v *Reynolds* 1972 (3) SA
740 (AA) op 746D-H. In die lg sin, indien die verklaring van 'n voorkeurdiwidend nie op die beoogde tydstip geskied het nie, kan dit, myns
insiens, heeltemal tereg gesê word dat die voorkeurdividend agterstallig
(in arrear) is. . . .

3. Die wyere betekenis van ,,agterstallig" sal natuurlik ook die enge of
primêre sin daarvan dek. Die vraag is, derhalwe, word die woord in sy
enge of wyere betekenis in die sub-artikel gebesig? Indien die lg, sal

dit ook 'n verklaarde maar onbetaalde voorkeurdividend insluit. Daar is na my mening twee aanduidings in die sub-artikel self dat die wyere betekenis bedoel is. As slegs die enge sin beoog is, sou, eerstens, die uitdrukking ,,verskuldig en betaalbaar'', in plek van ,,agterstallig'', gebruik gewees het—vgl sub-art (4)(*b*) waar dié frase gebesig word om die enge begrip uit te druk ivm onbetaalde opvorderings en ander bedrae wat op aandele verskuldig is; en sou, tweedens, dit onnodig gewees het om ,,en onbetaald'' aan ,,agterstallig'' in sub-art (4)(*a*)(i) te koppel, want ,,agterstallig'' in die enge sin beteken op sigself verskuldig, betaalbaar, en onbetaald. Trouens, die koppeling van ,,en onbetaald'' dien o a om die begrip van 'n onverklaarde en onbetaalde dividend volkome uit te druk.

4. Weliswaar is dit . . . ietwat onvanpas of selfs teenstrydig om van 'n ,,agterstallige dividend (arrears of dividend)'' te praat alvorens die betrokke bedrag as dividend verklaar is. Maar hoe tegnies verkeerd die uitdrukking ook al mag wees, word dit in gewone handels- asook regstaal goedgekeur as 'n kort, handige uitdrukking om 'n onverklaarde voorkeurdividend te beskrywe. . . .

Om my mening oor die juiste uitleg van art 62*quat*(4)(*a*)(i) op te som, vir sover dit die onderhawige saak betref: die bevoegdheid van die houers van die kumulatiewe voorkeuraandele om te stem kan ten volle uitgeoefen word gedurende die tydperk daarin gemeld as die voorkeurdividend daarop òf nie verklaar word nie òf verklaar word maar onbetaald bly.

Om terug te keer tot die feite van hierdie saak: geen dividend op die voorkeuraandele is verklaar of betaal op of sedert 9 Januarie 1972 nie, dws 'n maand na die tweede jaarlikse algemene vergadering van die maatskappy. Na my mening is dit, kragtens die sub-artikel, agterstallig en bly dit onbetaald. Derhalwe is respondent, solank dit agterstallig en onbetaald bly, geregtig om by algemene vergaderings van die maatskappy te stem. Regter Viljoen het tereg tot daardie slotsom geraak.

* * *

[As to the question when a proposed resolution can be said to affect directly the 'interests' ('belange') of preference shareholders, Trollip JA said:]

,,Belange (interests)'' is 'n woord van breë betekenis. In die samehang van art 62*quat*(4)(*a*)(ii) beteken dit iets anders as ,,regte'', want dit is daarmee saamgekoppel. ,,'n Reg verbonde aan dié aandele'' bedoel die spesifieke regte wat volgens die betrokke bepalings aan die aandele kleef. Gewoonlik sal hierdie regte van 'n vermoëns- of geldelike aard wees, want normaalweg sou voorkeuraandele in 'n winsgewende maatskappy nie om sentimentele, altruïstiese, of liefdadige redes geneem of verkry word nie, maar om geld daarin te belê en, tot 'n mate, 'n deel in sy onderneming te verkry. ,,Die belange van die houers daarvan'' is die belange of voordele wat uit daardie regte voortvloei, meesal a g v die genot of gebruik daarvan. Derhalwe sal die betekenis van ,,belange'', ondanks die gewone breë betekenis daarvan, gewoonlik ook beperk moet word tot belange of voordele van 'n vermoëns- of geldelike aard. (Gerieflikheidshalwe word hulle hierna die geldelike belange en voordele genoem.) Dit is derhalwe ook vanselfsprekend dat „die belange" wat geraak moet word, nie die gewone belange van die maatskappy en sy aandeelhouers in die algemeen is nie, maar die besondere geldelike belange en voordele van die voorkeuraandeelhouers as 'n groep. Dit verklaar waarom die spesifieke geval van die likwidasie van 'n maatskappy [and now, also of the reduction of capital, s 194(1)(*b*)] uitdruklik in die subparagraaf behandel word, anders sou voorkeuraandeelhouers in dié belangrike geval nie 'n stemreg hê nie. Die woord „raak (affect)" het ook normaalweg 'n breë begrip. Miskien moet dit hier beperkend uitgelê word (vgl *White* v *Bristol Aeroplane Co Ltd* (*supra*) op 44A–E, en *Re John Smith's Tadcaster Brewery Co Ltd* [1953] 1 All ER 518 (CA) op 522A). Maar dit is nie nodig om oor die presiese betekenis daarvan hier te beslis nie. Dit is voldoende om te sê, eerstens, dat „die belange" ten minste in 'n besigheidsin geraak moet word („affected as a matter of business" — vgl lord Greene MR in *Greenhalgh* v *Arderne Cinemas Ltd* [1946] 1 All ER 512 (CA) op 518A; en ook Gower *Modern Company Law* 3e uitg, 512–13) en, tweedens, dat „raak" die begrippe van „verander", „verswak", en „benadeel" insluit. Ek beklemtoon dat die betrokke voorgestelde besluite „die belange" van die voorkeuraandeelhouers *regstreeks* moet verander, verswak of benadeel, soos oorsaak en gevolg, want „regstreeks" kwalifiseer „raak" en nie „belange" nie. Dit is nie voldoende dat voorkeuraandeelhouers 'n regstreekse belang besit wat indirek geraak sal word nie; hulle belang, al is dit direk, sal nogtans regstreeks geraak moet word om aan die vereistes van die sub-paragraaf te voldoen, alhoewel die direktheid daarvan natuurlik 'n relevante oorweging sal wees. . . .

. . . Trouens die gebruik van die uitdrukking, „'n besluit wat regstreeks die belange raak", in plaas van, bv, „'n besluit wat die belange mag raak", is opvallend en dui aan dat die bepaling, as geheel gelees en uitgelê, 'n noue eerder as 'n wye betekenis moet hê. Die Wetgewer se bedoeling was blykbaar dat, indien die voorkeurdiwidende opbetaald is, die voorkeuraandeelhouers se reg om in die bestuur van die maatskappy in te meng, streng beperk moet word.

Om my uitleg van art 62*quat*(4)(*a*)(ii) vir die doeleindes van die onderhawige saak op te som: voorkeuraandeelhouers het die reg om te stem ten opsigte van enige voorgestelde besluit indien dit die besondere geldelike belange of voordele voortvloeiend uit die regte verbonde aan die aandele en behorende aan die houers daarvan as 'n groep, regstreeks en in 'n besigheidsin verander, verswak, benadeel, of andersins raak.

III VARIATION OF CLASS RIGHTS

A TEXT

Where the rights of a class of shareholders are set out in the memorandum they are unalterable except (*a*) where the memorandum itself provides for their alteration, s 56(5), or (*b*) in connection with a compromise or arrangement under s 311, p 632 below. Where they are contained in the articles they may be varied by special resolution, s 62: *109.* (See also above, pp 92–3.) On variation of class rights and oppression, see *Rights and Issues Investment Trusts Ltd* v *Stylo Shoes Ltd* [1965] Ch 250, [1964] 3 All ER 628.

Usually, the memorandum or articles of association provide that the rights attached to a class of share may only be varied if a specified proportion of the holders of the issued shares of that class consents or a resolution sanctioning the variation is passed at a separate meeting of the holders of those shares. (Table A art 7, Table B art 9.) If the rights attached to any class of shares are so varied, the holder of a share of that class may, if he considers himself unfairly treated, apply to court for a remedy under s 252 on the ground of oppressive or unfairly prejudicial conduct, s 102.

An issue of new shares or of a new class of shares or a subdivision of shares does not constitute a variation of the rights of existing shareholders merely because it changes the balance of voting power: *110.*

B CASES

[109] Campbell *v* Rofe
[1933] AC 91 (PC)

LORD THANKERTON: . . . The law may be summarized as follows: While the memorandum must state the amount of capital, divided into shares of a certain fixed amount, provision as to the character of the shares and rights to be attached to them is more properly made by the articles of association, which may be altered from time to time by special resolution of the company. If equality of the shareholders is expressly provided in the memorandum, that cannot be modified by the articles of association. If nothing is said in the memorandum, the articles of association may provide for the issue of the authorized capital in the form of preference shares; if the articles do not so provide, or do provide for equality *inter socios*, the power to issue preference shares may be obtained by alteration of the articles. If the memorandum prescribes the classes of shares into which the capital is to be divided and the rights to be attached to such shares respectively, the company has no power to alter that provision by special resolution. . . .

NOTES

'The term "class . . ." must be confined to those persons whose rights are not so dissimilar as to make it impossible for them to consult together with a view to their common interest': per Bowen LJ *Sovereign Life Assurance Co* v *Dodd* [1892] 2 QB 573 at 583 (*374* below).

[110] White *v* Bristol Aeroplane Company Ltd
[1953] Ch 65, [1953] 1 All ER 40

The company had an issued share capital of £3 900 000, consisting of £600 000 preference stock of £1 each and £3 300 000 ordinary stock. It proposed increasing its share capital by way of capitalization of undistributed profits by (*a*) 660 000 new preference shares of £1 each ranking *pari passu* with the existing preference stock, and (*b*) 2 640 000 ordinary shares of 10*s* each ranking *pari passu* with the existing ordinary stock.

Article 62 gave the company in general meeting power to issue the aforementioned new shares. Article 68 stated:

'all or any of the rights or privileges attached to any class of shares forming part of the capital for the time being of the company may be affected, modified, varied, dealt with, or abrogated in any manner with the sanction of an extraordinary resolution passed at a separate meeting of the members of that class. . . .'

Article 83 provided:

'. . . preference shares or preference stock shall not confer on the holders thereof the right in respect thereof to receive notice of or to attend or vote at a general meeting unless the meeting is convened [*inter alia*] . . . to consider a resolution directly affecting their rights or privileges as a separate class.'

The plaintiff, a holder of preference stock, on behalf of himself and the other preference stockholders, applied for an interdict to restrain the company from proceeding with the scheme without the sanction of an extraordinary resolution passed at a separate meeting of the preference shareholders.

The court of first instance granted the order prayed for, but on appeal the judgment was reversed.

SIR RAYMOND EVERSHED MR: . . . The question shortly is: will the effect of this proposed distribution, if carried out, be to 'affect' the rights of the preference stockholders?

It is necessary, first, to note . . . that what must be 'affected' are the rights of the preference stockholders. The question then is—and, indeed, I have already posed it—are the rights which I have already summarized 'affected' by what is proposed? It is said in answer—and I think rightly said—No, they are not; they remain exactly as they were before; each one of the manifestations of the preference stockholders' privileges may be repeated without any change whatever after, as before, the proposed distribution. It is no doubt true that the enjoyment of, and the capacity to make effective, those rights is in a measure affected; for as I have already indicated, the existing preference stockholders will be in a less advantageous position on such occasions as entitled them to register their votes, whether at general meetings of the company or at separate meetings of their own class. But there is to my mind a distinction, and a sensible distinction, between an affecting of the rights and an affecting of the enjoyment of the rights, or of the stockholders' capacity to turn them to account. . . .

. . . I have no doubt . . . that . . . what is here suggested will 'affect' the preference stockholders 'as a matter of business'; but we are concerned with the question whether the rights of the preference stockholders are 'affected', not as a matter of business, but according to the articles, that is, according to their meaning construed under the rules of construction and as a matter of law. . . .

ROMER LJ: The rights attached to a class of shares within the meaning of such an article as this, are those attached by the resolutions creating such shares or by the articles of association of the company as amended from time to time by any relevant resolution; and accordingly, regard must be had to such resolutions and to the constitution of the company for the purpose of finding out what the rights of the preference stockholders are.

The rights attaching to the preference stockholders are those which are conferred by arts 62 and 83; and the only relevant article for present purpose is art 83. Under that article it is provided . . . that on a poll every member present in person or by proxy shall have one vote for every share held by him, or in the case of the preference stock, one vote for every £1 of preference stock held by him. It is suggested that, as a result of the proposed increase of capital, that right of the preference stockholders will in some way be 'affected'; but I cannot see that it will be affected in any way whatever. The position then will be precisely the same as now—namely, that the holder of preference stock will have on a poll one vote for every £1 of preference stock held by him. It is quite true that the block vote, if one may so describe the total voting power of the class, will, or may, have less force behind it, because it will *pro tanto* be watered down by reason of the increased total voting power of the members of the company; but no particular weight is attached to the vote, by the constitution of the company, as distinct from the right to exercise the vote, and certainly no right is conferred on the preference stockholders to preserve anything in the nature of an equilibrium between their class and the ordinary stockholders or any other class. . . .

NOTES

The principle in *White* v *Bristol Aeroplanes* was applied, *inter alia*, in *In re John Smith's Tadcaster Brewery Co Ltd* [1953] Ch 308, [1953] 1 All ER 518. But see also *In re Old Silkstone Collieries Ltd* [1954] Ch 169, [1954] 1 All ER 68. See further *In re Schweppes Ltd* [1914] 1 Ch 322; *Greenhalgh* v *Arderne Cinemas Ltd* [1946] 1 All ER 512; *Levin* v *Felt and Tweeds Ltd* 1951 (2) SA 401 (AD); *Rights & Issues Investment Trusts Ltd* v *Stylo Shoes Ltd* [1965] Ch 250, [1964] 3 All ER 628.

A rateable reduction on all shares, including preference shares, though it will result in diminishing the actual preferential dividend, is not an alteration of the rights of the preference shareholders so as to require their sanction as a variation of their rights: *In re Mackenzie & Co Ltd* [1916] 2 Ch 450.

A cancellation of shares is not the same as a variation of the rights attached to the shares: *Re Saltdean Estate Co Ltd: 103* above.

IV SHARE REGISTERS AND THEIR RECTIFICATION, SHARE CERTIFICATES, AND VARIOUS OTHER LISTS, REPORTS AND ENTRIES RELATING TO SHARES

A TEXT

Every company is required to keep a register of members, ss 105–115. This register is open to inspection by members, s 113. The register is prima facie evidence that a person on the register is a member of the company, s 109. Section 115 provides for the rectification of the register where the name of a person is wrongfully entered in or omitted from the register: *111, 112*.

Every company limited by shares is obliged to keep a register of allotment of shares, s 93, and to issue share certificates, s 96. See also s 140. (As to the numbering of shares, see s 95.) A share certificate is prima facie evidence of the title of the member mentioned therein to the shares, s 94, and creates two estoppels: an estoppel as to title: *113, 114*; and an estoppel as to payment: *115*.

Schedule 3 para 8 makes provision for the disclosure in the prospectus of details regarding different classes of shares. Paragraph 10 requires disclosure of the number of shares issued or to be issued otherwise than for cash. Details regarding shares and their allotment must be specified both in the annual return of a company, s 173(1)(*h*), and the directors' report, s 299, read with Schedule 4 para 5.

B CASES

[111] Orr NO *v* Hill
1929 TPD 865

TINDALL AJP: It might be contended that the word 'rectification' in the section [now s 115] means putting right something which, at the present time, is wrong on the register. . . . But, in my opinion, we should not place that narrow construction on the word. I think the word 'rectification' covers an alteration of the register so as to make it reflect the state of affairs which the applicant is entitled to claim that it ought to reflect.

[112] Verrin Trust & Finance Corporation (Pty) Ltd *v* Zeeland House (Pty) Ltd
1973 (4) SA 1 (C)

In an application in terms of s 32 of the 1926 Act for the rectification of the first respondent's share register by restoring the applicant company's name to it, on the ground that it had been removed therefrom without sufficient cause, the applicant alleged that the transfer out of the applicant's name had been effected by means of false or forged share certificates. No order was made on the application.

CORBETT J: At the hearing of the matter Mr A on behalf of the applicant explained that the application was simply one, in terms of s 32 of the Companies Act, for the restoration to the share register of the company of a name (viz Verrin) that was once there but had been removed therefrom without sufficient cause. The basis of the application was (*a*) that the share certificates belonging to Verrin and reflecting Verrin as being the holder of 999 of the 1 000 issued shares in the company were never presented to the company—nor were any properly completed transfer forms so presented—when the transfer of the shares to Penwarden on 10 March 1967 was registered by the company by means of an appropriate entry in the share register; and (*b*) that although Graaff's Investment and Southern Life now appear in the share register as the holders of the 1 000 issued shares (ie the 999 shares transferred to Penwarden and the one share held by Prouse, as nominee of Verrin), the transfer thereof to them was effected by means of false or forged share certificates. Mr A emphasized that Verrin was not seeking any order for the delivery to it of the disputed shares or as to true ownership in the shares or as to the rights and obligations, *inter se*, of Verrin and the present shareholders: Verrin was merely claiming as against the company that the latter correct its share register as a prelude, so to speak, to any litigation that might subsequently ensue in regard to title to the shares or for damages or other relief arising out of the transactions in question. Counsel contended that when a shareholder's name is removed from the register under a forged transfer or by virtue of a forged certificate, he is entitled to have it restored to the register, irrespective of questions of title to the shares in question, and he likened such an application for rectification of the register to a spoliation application. . . . The true nature of an application under s 32 was considered by Stratford JA in the case of *Jeffery* v *Pollak and Freemantle* 1938 AD 1 at 18–19. In his judgment the learned judge of appeal stated that essentially such an application is concerned with title to be on the register and not with the ownership of the shares in issue. Consequently —

'. . . there is no onus on the person previously on the register to prove his ownership and secondly the court is not necessarily concerned with ownership at all, for, as is admitted, the right to be on the register may be independent of ownership'.

A court hearing such an application may, therefore, quite properly confine itself to the minor and direct dispute as to whether the register should be rectified or not and leave it to the parties thereafter to debate the question of ownership in a trial action. On the other hand, in terms of ss (3), the court is empowered to investigate all questions in dispute between the parties and would, accordingly, be entitled to determine the issue as to ownership, if so advised. . . .

The jurisdiction which the court exercises under s 32 is a discretionary one and an applicant under the section is not entitled to an order *ex debito justitiae*. . . .

Even assuming, as I have done, that Verrin has established, prima facie, that its name was originally removed from the company's share register without sufficient cause, it seems to me that this case raises questions of very considerable difficulty and complexity both in regard to Verrin's title to be restored to the register and in regard to title to the shares themselves.

In so far as the difficulty and complexity in this matter relates to the question of title to the shares (as distinct from title to be on the register), I consider that, upon the peculiar circumstances of this case, this is a relevant factor in exercising a discretion against the grant of an order on motion. Although, as was pointed out in *Jeffrey* v *Pollak and Freemantle* (*supra*), title to be on the register and title to the disputed shares are distinct issues and a court confronted with an application under s 32 is entitled to confine itself to the former issue and leave the latter, and other related issues, to be debated in a separate trial action, I do not read this case as deciding that in all instances the court is obliged to follow this course or that in deciding how to exercise its discretion the court cannot have regard to the issue as to title. Indeed there appear to be a number of decisions indicating that, in England at any rate, a contrary view is taken.

As I have indicated, the issue as to title is a matter of considerable difficulty and complexity and not one that is amenable to decision on motion. Title to shares and title to be on the register are very closely interrelated in this case and in truth the real dispute between the parties relates to the proprietorship of the shares and, through them, of Zeeland House. Moreover, it seems to me that a separation of these issues, . . . could be productive of inequity and substantial practical inconvenience. . . .

To put the whole position very shortly, I have come to the conclusion that, having regard to all circumstances, this is a case where the enquiry as to title to be restored to the register should not be divorced from the general and more fundamental enquiry as to title to the shares themselves; and that, for the reasons stated, these enquiries cannot, and should not, be undertaken summarily by means of an application under s 32.

NOTES

The judgment in *Orr NO* v *Hill* deals with the circumstances under which rectification should be made retrospective. See further *In re Contributories Rosemount GM Syndicate* 1905 TH 169 at 185, per Bristowe J: 'Under the Act membership depends on registration. The power to rectify the register . . . therefore, enables the court when settling the list of contributories to place on the register, and thereby constitute members, persons who at the date of the winding-up were not actually members, but had bound themselves to become such. By this process there are swept into the net (as is manifestly right) not only members, but also persons who ought to be members, but for want of compliance with a formal requirement are not so. . . .' In *In re Sussex Brick Company* [1904] 1 Ch 598 it was held that the power given to the court of rectifying the register of members is exercisable whether a company is in liquidation or not, and that it is not, in the case of liquidation, limited to rectification for the purpose of settling the list of contributors. Per Vaughan Williams LJ: '. . . when it is right that an order for rectification should be made — whether the order be for rectification by taking a name off the register or by putting a name on — the court may make an order, not only that the right name shall be put on or taken off, as the case may be, but that the register shall be treated as if the name had been on or off at the time it ought in fact to have been on or off. . . .'

That the court's power to rectify the register is discretionary was affirmed by the Rhodesion Appellate Division in *Bondi* v *Wood NO* 1976 (3) SA 680 (RAD), where rectification was refused because the applicants, who were also the directors of the company, were themselves at least partially responsible for the wrong entry in the register regarding their own shares.

Where a person contracted to take fully-paid shares in a company and shares were issued to him at a discount, with the risk of personal liability (see below, *138*), he may be entitled to repudiate the contract, but rectification is not the right remedy: *Burstein* v *Mindel* 1959 (2) SA 56 (SR). Unilateral removal of a member's name from the register may amount to an act of spoliation: *Rooibokoord Sitrus (Edms)* v *Louw's Creek Sitrus Koöperatiewe Maatskappy (Edms) Bpk* 1964 (3) SA 601 (T).

See further *Waja* v *Orr, Orr NO and Dowjee Co Ltd* 1929 TPD 865; *Nurick* v *Bron Syndicate (Prop) Ltd* 1936 OPD 76; *Jeffery* v *Pollak and Freemantle* 1938 AD 1; *Estate Boyce* v *The East Rand Greyhound Racing Association (Pty) Ltd* 1939 WLD 332; *Ex parte East Rand Wine & Spirit Co (Pty) Ltd* 1941 (2) PH E15 (W); *In re Globe Cinema (Pty)*

Ltd 1946 EDL 82; *Neviol Lights (SA) (Pty) Ltd* v *White* 1949 (1) SA 988 (W); *In re MI Trust (Pty) Ltd* v *Morny's Motor Supplies (Pty) Ltd* 1952 (3) SA 262 (W); *Peer* v *Greenhouse (Pty) Ltd* 1952 (4) SA 614 (N); *Thole* v *Trans-Drakensberg Bank Ltd* 1967 (2) SA 214 (D); *Davis* v *Buffelsfontein Gold Mining Co Ltd* 1967 (4) SA 631 (W); *Ex parte Keir & Cawden (South Africa) Ltd* 1968 (2) SA 207 (T).

[113] *In re* **Bahia and San Francisco Railway Company**
(1868) LR 3 QB 584

A company, on the strength of a forged transfer, registered S and G as holders of five shares, owned by T, giving them certificates stating that they were the registered holders of the five shares. X purchased the five shares in good faith and was registered as their holder. When it was discovered that the transfer to S and G was a forgery, the company was ordered to restore T's name to the register. In an action by X against the company it was held that X was entitled to recover from the company damages for the loss of the shares.

CockBURN CJ: I am of opinion that our judgment must be for the claimants. . . . The company are bound to keep a register of shareholders, and have power to issue certificates certifying that each individual shareholder named therein is a registered shareholder of the particular shares specified. This power of granting certificates is to give the shareholders the opportunity of more easily dealing with their shares in the market, and to afford facilities to them of selling their shares by at once showing a marketable title, and the effect of this facility is to make the shares of greater value. The power of giving certificates is, therefore, for the benefit of the company in general; and it is a declaration by the company to all the world that the person in whose name the certificate is made out, and to whom it is given, is a shareholder in the company, and it is given by the company with the intention that it shall be so used by the person to whom it is given, and acted upon in the sale and transfer of shares. It is stated in this case that the claimants acted bona fide, and did all that is required of purchasers of shares; they paid the value of the shares in money on having a transfer of the shares executed to them, and on the production of the certificates which were handed to them. It turned out that the transferors had in fact no shares, and that the company ought not to have registered them as shareholders or given them certificates, the transfer to them being a forgery. That brings the case within the principle . . . that, if you make a representation with the intention that it shall be acted upon by another, and he does so, you are estopped from denying the truth of what you represent to be the fact.

The only remaining question is, what is the redress to which the claimants are entitled? In whatever form of action they might shape their claim, and there can be no doubt that an action is maintainable, the measure of damages would be the same. They are entitled to be placed in the same position as if the shares, which they purchased owing to the company's representation, had in fact been good shares, and had been transferred to them, and the company had refused to put them on the register, and the measure of damages would be the market price of the shares at that time. . . .

[114] **Ruben & another** *v* **Great Fingall Consolidated**
[1906] AC 439

Rowe, the secretary of the defendant company, applied to the plaintiffs for a loan of £20 000. He stated that he required the money to enable him to purchase shares in the defendant company. The plaintiffs arranged with a bank to advance the money to Rowe against a transfer of the shares into plaintiffs' names. Rowe forged a transfer in the name of one Storey as transferor. The transfer was duly executed by the bank and the plaintiffs delivered it to Rowe in exchange for a share certificate. The share certificate purported to state that the bank was the registered owners of 5 000 shares; it purported to be signed by two directors, the seal of the company was affixed to it and it was countersigned by Rowe himself as secretary. In fact the signatures of the two directors were forged by Rowe and the company's seal was affixed by him fraudulently. The bank advanced Rowe £20 000 on the account of the plaintiffs. When the fraud was discovered the plaintiffs were obliged to repay this sum to the bank. The plaintiffs then sued the company for damages. The court held that the company was not estopped by the forged certificate from disputing the claim of the plaintiffs.

LORD MACNAGHTEN: Ruben and Ladenburg are the victims of a wicked fraud. No fault has been found with their conduct. But their claim against the respondent company is, I think, simply absurd.

The thing put forward as the foundation of their claim is a piece of paper which purports to be a certificate of shares in the company. This paper is false and fraudulent from beginning to end. The representation of the company's seal which appears upon it, though made by the impression of the real seal of the company, is counterfeit, and no better than a forgery. The signatures of the two directors which purport to authenticate the sealing are forgeries pure and simple. Every statement in the document is a lie. The only thing real about it is the signature of the secretary of the company, who was the sole author and perpetrator of the fraud. No one would suggest that this fraudulent certificate could of itself give rise to any right or bind or affect the company in any way. It is not the company's deed and there is nothing to prevent the company from saying so.

Then how can the company be bound or affected by it? The directors have never said or done anything to represent or lead to the belief that this thing was the company's deed. Without such a representation there can be no estoppel.

The fact that this fraudulent certificate was concocted in the company's office and was uttered and sent forth by its author from the place of its origin cannot give it an efficacy which it does not intrinsically possess. The secretary of the company, who is a mere servant, may be the proper hand to deliver out certificates which the company issues in due course, but he can have no authority to guarantee the genuineness or validity of a document which is not the deed of the company. . . .

NOTES

As to the effect of a share certificate, see also *Moosa v Lalloo* 1957 (4) SA 207 (N), 216–17. The principle in *In re Bahia and San Francisco Railway Co* (1868) LR 3 QB 584 (113) was followed, *inter alia*, in England in *Hart v Frontino and Bolivia South American Gold Mining Co Ltd* (1870) LR 5 Exch 111; *In re Ottos Kopje Diamond Mines Ltd* [1893] 1 Ch 618; *Balkis Consolidated Co Ltd v Tomkinson* [1893] AC 396; *Dixon v Kennaway & Co* [1900] 1 Ch 833.

[115] **Burkinshaw v Nicolls**
(1878) 3 App Cas 1004

LORD CAIRNS LC: . . . My Lords . . . it would paralyse the whole of the dealings with shares in public companies if, a share being dealt with in the ordinary course of business, dealt with in the market with the representation upon it, by the company, that the whole amount of the share was paid, the person who so took it was to be obliged to disregard the assertion of the company, and, before he could obtain a title, must go and satisfy himself that the assertion was true, and that the money had been actually paid. In the first place, as a matter of business, we know that the affairs of mankind could not be conducted if that were necessary; but in the next place, even if such a person were minded to make the investigation, he would be absolutely without the means of making it—it would be impossible for him to obtain accurate information as to whether this state of things was true or not. . . .

NOTES

See further *Bloomenthal v Ford* [1897] AC 156; *In re Contributories Rosemount GM Syndicate* 1905 TH 169, esp at 204–6; *Reynolds Vehicle and Harness Factory Ltd in liquidation v Zietsman* (1907) 3 Buch AC 74; *In re Coasters Ltd* [1911] 1 Ch 86. Even an original allottee may be able as against the company to rely on a certificate that the shares were fully paid up; *Parbury's case* [1896] 1 Ch 100; *Albatross Fishing Corporation (Pty) Ltd v Ramsay* 1968 (2) SA 217 (C).

V DEBENTURES AND BONDS

A TEXT

A company, if so authorized by its memorandum or by its articles, may create and issue debentures, s 116. 'Debenture' includes debenture stock, s 1 s v 'Debenture'. A debenture is a formal acknowledgment of debt by a company: *116*. It may be secured or unsecured, s 116. No debenture, debenture certificate or prospectus relating to debentures may be issued by a company unless the term 'debenture' or such other term denoting a debenture used therein is qualified by the word 'secured' or 'insecured', as the case may be, s 125. The debenture or debenture certificate must be signed by one director and an officer duly authorized thereto by the directors and must state the conditions of the debenture. Most debentures are notarially executed, but this is not essential. If a debenture is notarially executed it may be registered in a deeds registry as if it were a notarial bond. The power to raise money by debentures includes the power to secure an existing debt in this way: *Liquidators Union and Rhodesia Wholesale Ltd* v *Official Manager of the Company* (1923) 44 NLR 358.

As to issue, allotment, prospectus and transfer debentures are, generally speaking, subject to the same rules as shares (see the definition of 'share' in s 1, and the definition of 'security' in s 134). Unlike shares, however, debentures may be issued at a discount: *117*.

Debenture holders are creditors, not members of the company. Interest on debentures is payable even if the company has earned no profits.

Debentures become redeemable at the time specified or upon the commencement of the winding-up of the company, whichever is the earlier. The company is not entitled to redeem debentures before the fixed date: *Knightsbridge Estates Trust Ltd* v *Byrne* [1940] AC 613. Redeemed debentures may be reissued, s 124.

Debentures may be secured by the binding of movable or immovable property, s 117. The binding of movable property may be effected by a deed of pledge and the delivery of the movable property concerned, by a notarial bond or surety bond, or by the cession of incorporeal rights, present or future, s 117(1). The binding of immovable property may be effected by a mortgage bond or surety bond, s 117(3). A wholly owned subsidiary has power to mortgage any of its property as collateral security for the issue of debentures by its holding company, s 117(4). Mortgage bonds and notarial bonds must be registered in the deeds registry, s 118.

Pledges, notarial bonds and mortgage bonds may be constituted in favour of one or more debenture holders or of a trustee for the debenture holders, s 117(1). A director or officer of the company cannot be appointed as a trustee for the debenture holders, s 122. Subject to exceptions a trustee for the debenture holders cannot be exempted from or indemnified against liability for breach of trust where he fails to show the degree of care and negligence required from him as a trustee, s 123.

A notarial bond over movables confers upon the holders a 'floating charge' over the movable property of the company, but does not prevent the company from disposing of movables prior to winding-up in the ordinary course of business: *118*. On a winding-up the holders have a preferential right in the 'free residue': Insolvency Act 24 of 1936 s 102.

A mortgage bond over immovable property confers upon the secured debenture holders a specific charge over the mortgaged property in question which cannot be defeated by any subsequent alienation, hypothecation or attachment.

Debentures issued at different dates rank in preference concurrently with one another as from the date when the pledge was constituted or the bond registered, s 120.

Every holder of a debenture secured by a pledge or a bond executed in favour of a trustee for debenture holders generally may, unless the deed of pledge, bond or trust deed otherwise provides, enforce his rights under the debenture as soon as it has been issued to him in the same manner as if he himself were the pledgee or holder of the bond, s 121(1).

Unsecured debentures do not confer any preferential rights upon the holders, who rank on the winding-up of the company as con-current creditors.

Like shares, debentures are normally transferred by a security transfer form and registration of the transfer in the register (in this case, the debenture holders' register) of the company. Since nominative debentures are not negotiable instruments, all defences available against the transferor can be set up against the transferee unless the company by its conduct has estopped itself from doing so: *In re Natal Investment Co: Financial Corporation's Claim* (1868) 3 Ch App 355; *Higgs* v *Northern Assam Tea Company Ltd* (1869) LR 4 Exch 387; *Christie* v *Taunton, Delmard, Lane & Co* [1893] 2 Ch 175. Bearer debentures are negotiable instruments, *119*, but it would seem that the 1973 Act does not permit the issue of bearer debentures, see e g ss 126(4), 127, 128.

Companies are obliged to keep registers of debenture-holders, s 128, and pledges and bonds, s 127.

B CASES

[116] Coetzee *v* Rand Sporting Club
1918 WLD 74

WARD J: . . . I am not aware that the word 'debenture' has been defined precisely. Bowen LJ says in *English and Scottish Mercantile Investment Company* v *Brunton* [1892] 2 QB 700 at 712:'It seems that there are three usual forms of debenture. . . . The first is a simple acknowledgment, under seal, of the debt; the second an instrument acknowledging the debt, and charging the property of the company with repayment; and the third an instrument acknowledging the debt, and charging the property with repayment and further restricting the company from giving any prior charge.' It does not follow that there may not be other forms, but it 'is not necessary to go into that. I think the word imports an acknowledgment of debt. It is derived from *debentur*. Stroud says it seems to have originated from *debentur mihi* with which various forms of acknowledgment commenced. . . .

NOTES

See further *Lemon* v *Austin Friars Investment Trust Ltd* [1926] Ch 1; *Edmonds* v *Blaina Furnaces Co* (1887) 36 ChD 215; *English and Scottish Mercantile Investment Co* v *Brunton* [1892] 2 QB 700, esp at 712. Debentures of a company are not stock or shares in the company (*Sellar* v *Charles Bright & Co Ltd* [1904] 2 KB 446), but where the phrase 'stocks and shares' is used in a will, it may be the intention of the testator that debentures are to be included, e g *In re Purnchard's Will Trusts* [1948] Ch 312, [1948] 1 All ER 790.

[117] Campbell's case
(1876) 4 ChD 470

Directors issued debentures at $7\frac{1}{2}$ per cent discount. Some of the debentures were taken by Mr Campbell, a director. The court held that Mr Campbell was not liable to the company for the difference between $92\frac{1}{2}$ per cent and par.

BACON V-C: This case, in one point of view, is of importance, because it has been argued as if it fell within the principle which the courts of equity have always adhered to, not to permit an agent, or director, or any person in a fiduciary character, and having power and influence in the concern, to make a profit by his dealings with the concern.

But the fact that any profit was made I find to be wholly wanting in this case. There was no profit. The directors publish a prospectus, in which they say, 'We are going to issue bonds at par'. It is all very well to say so, but when they come to issue these bonds, people will not take them at par. What are they to do? They find they cannot place them at par, and they sell them on the best terms they can, and, except in the two particular cases mentioned, they issue all these debentures on the same terms as those on which the debentures taken by Mr Campbell were issued. What is there unlawful in that? What is there to prevent the directors buying on the same terms as other people? ... The directors did that which it was lawful for them to do—they issued debentures at a certain discount. Mr Campbell took them as other people took them, and paid his money for them. He derived no sort of profit from them; the advantage, if any, was all on the side of the company. . . .

NOTES

An irregularity in the issue of the debentures cannot be set up by the company against even the original debenture holder if he has a right to presume *omnia rite acta*, and if the debenture is transferable, the irregularity and, *a fortiori*, any equitable defence against the original holder cannot be asserted by the company against a bona fide transferee for value: *Webb* v *Herne Bay Commissioners* (1870) LR 5 QB 642; *In re Romford Canal Co* (1883) 24 ChD 85.

The rule that debentures may be issued at a discount does not apply where the debenture holders are given the immediate right to exchange the debentures at par for fully paid shares, as this would provide a means by which the rule that shares may not be issued at a discount could be circumvented: *Mosely* v *Koffyfontein Mines Ltd* [1904] 2 Ch 108.

[118] London and Westminster Bank v Receivers Grand Junction Railways
(1904) 21 SC 404

DE VILLIERS CJ: . . . The debentures now in question do not describe any of the property of the company beyond stating that 'the whole property and assets of the company subject only to the reservation in the next clause are hereby pledged and given as a first charge in security for the due payment of this bond and all debentures issued under it'. The reservation in the next clause is as follows: 'The company reserves power and right to deal with any property and assets, provided the proceeds of such shall be placed to credit of capital and not to that of revenue account.' I have already, in the *African Banking Corporation* case (1903) 20 SC 599, indicated my views in regard to these provisions, and I will here only add that the debenture holders, in my opinion, acquire no greater rights under the bond than are enjoyed by the holder of a duly registered general bond. There are no earmarked assets, movable or immovable, upon which the charge can operate, and the only preference which the debenture holders can claim in the winding-up of the company is that they shall be paid before any of the unsecured creditors can share in the distribution of its assets as they existed at the date of the order for winding-up. By a series of cessions, some of which almost have the appearance of juggles, the construction of the railways passed out of the hands of the company to a partnership, having the same title as the company, and from the partnership to the Thames Ironworks and Shipbuilding Company, and then again from the last-named company to the defendant, Hills. On 20 July 1898, Hills and the firm of John Walker and Sons agreed with the company to pay all its debts, including the debentures theretofore issued by it. At that time £170 000 worth had been issued. . . . It is now contended that by reason of the partnership having taken over the liabilities of the company, the preference which would have been awarded to the debenture holders as against the company should be extended to the assets of the partnership. No fresh bond was passed by the partnership, and I fail to see how the bond passed by the company can in any way create a preference against assets belonging to another *persona* and not specially pledged or mortgaged to the debenture holders before they became the property of the partnership. The bond, as I have said, operates as a general bond, and can only affect the assets of the *persona* which passed the bond, and that is the company. . . .

NOTES

See further *Wallace v Evershed* [1899] 1 Ch 891; *In re Benjamin Cope & Sons Ltd* [1914] 1 Ch 800; *In re Automatic Bottle Makers* [1926] Ch 412.

In *In re H H Vivian & Co Ltd* [1900] 2 Ch 654 a company, in terms of its objects clause, carried on three distinct businesses supplemental to one another. The court held that debenture holders with a floating charge could not restrain the company from selling one of these businesses.

A mere promise to pass a general bond does not confer any preferent right upon the creditor: *Loewenthal v Syferfontein Gold and Coal Estates Ltd* 1904 TH 316.

Where three companies issued joint debentures charging their several undertakings and assets for all the debentures, it was held that the charges were valid to the extent to which the moneys advanced had come into the hands of each company: *In re Johnston Foreign Patents Co Ltd* [1904] 2 Ch 234.

[119] African Banking Corporation *v* Official Liquidator Grand Junction Railways Ltd

(1907) 24 SC 296

DE VILLIERS CJ: . . . The debentures now in question entitle the bearer or registered holder to receive, at its due date, the amount thereof and interest due thereon. They were issued under the provisions of Act 43 of 1895, s 6 of which entitles the holder of a debenture covered by a bond, as those in question were, to enforce his rights under the debenture, and dispenses with the necessity of giving notice to the debtor of the cession of any debenture as would be required in the case of an ordinary cession of debt in order to protect the cessionary against the payment of the debt by the debtor to the original creditor. The company is bound to pay the amount when due to the holder, and as against him the company could not plead in compensation a debt due by a former holder, or claim the benefit of a payment made to such former holder. Of course, if the company had issued the debentures without authority, it would not be bound to pay; but if, while acting within the powers conferred on it by its memorandum of association, it had been overreached by those who induced it to issue the debentures in favour of the original holders, a subsequent bona fide holder is entitled to claim the amount due on the face of the debenture. Having regard to commercial practice in England . . . to the terms of the Act under which the debentures were issued, to the reasons for the judgment given in *Van Blommestein* v *Holliday* (1904) 21 SC 11, and to the commercial practice in this Colony, so far as I am entitled to take judicial cognizance of it, I am of opinion that the debentures may be regarded as negotiable instruments. . . .

NOTES

It would appear that bearer debentures are no longer permitted, see p 207 above.

8   *Members*

I Membership in General

A TEXT

'On the registration of the memorandum and articles the corporate body comes into existence, and is composed of the subscribers of the memorandum and of all other persons who may from time to time become members', Bowen LJ in *Nicol's* case (1885) 29 ChD 421 at 444.

A person becomes a member of a company—

(a) by subscribing to the memorandum of association; or
(b) by allotment of shares (see p 236, below); or
(c) by transfer of shares (see p 251, below).

A subscriber of the memorandum becomes a member as soon as the company is incorporated, *120*, any other person who agrees to become a member (more particularly, an allottee or transferee) when his name is entered on the register of shareholders, s 103. A company cannot become a member of itself by purchasing its own shares, p 145 above. On the other hand, unless these 'common powers' are expressly excluded, a company can acquire shares in another company, form and have an interest in another company, amalgamate with another company, take part in the management or control of the business of another company, and enter into partnership with another company or person, s 34 and Schedule 2(a), (k), (l) and (m). However, a subsidiary company cannot become a member of its holding company, s 39 (see above, p 52).

On insolvency of a member his shares vest in his trustee: Insolvency Act 24 of 1936 s 20(1)(a) (cf *In re W Key & Son Ltd* [1902] 1 Ch 467). On the death of a member his shares fall into his estate: *Lombard* v *Suid-Afrikaanse Vroue-Federasie* 1968 (3) SA 473 (AD). See also s 397(1)(*b*) and Table A arts 15 and 16, Table B arts 16 and 17. (On an invalid *pactum successorium* relating to a member's rights in an interest fund in a co-operative society, see *Borman en De Vos NNO* v *Potgieters-russe Tabakkorporasie Bpk* 1976 (3) SA 488 (AD).)

A member of a company has an interest in the company entitling him, subject to the constitution, to (*a*) a share in the profits of the company; (*b*) attendance and vote at meetings of the company; (*c*) a share in the surplus assets (if any) when the company is wound up.

Once shares are fully paid up—and no company may any longer allot or issue shares unless they are fully paid up, s 92(1)—a member is free of liability. See *Edmonton Country Club Ltd* v *Case* (1974) 44 DLR (3d) 554 (SC), where it was held that a corporation, whatever its powers, has no power to impose on its members an annual assessment for the purpose of providing operating revenue, since such a power would be incompatible with the concept of limited liability. '[These resolutions] are *ultra vires* because they offend the basic jural principle which has given limited liability companies their vitality, that a share-holder who has paid for his shares is thereafter free of pecuniary obligation in respect of those shares', per Dickson J at 562. An exception applies where a public company has been carrying on business for more than six months with fewer than seven members, the statutory minimum, s 66.

Holding shares in and being a member of a company is not the same thing. A person may hold shares as beneficial 'owner' through a nominee or trustee; or, having acquired shares by transfer, may not trouble about having himself registered as a member. The right to be on the register is independent of the ownership of the shares: *Davis* v *Buffelsfontein Gold Mining Co Ltd* 1967 (4) SA 631 (W). The company is concerned only with the person who is registered as a member and is not bound to see to the execution of any trust in respect of shares, s 104: *121, 122*. On the distinction between the registered holder of shares and the person who is beneficially entitled to them, see also *Brodie* v *Secretary for Inland Revenue* 1974 (4) SA 702 (AD), esp at 712ff. The beneficial owner of shares that have been stolen is entitled to recover the shares or share certificates from the possessor: *154* below.

Members may, and often do, lend money to their company, but a condition in the articles for compulsory loans by members to their company is of no force or effect, s 59(2). (As to the position before the commencement of the 1973 Act, see *Rosslare (Pty) Ltd* v *Registrar of Companies* 1972 (2) SA 524 (D), *86* above). A company may lend money to its members provided,

(1) that loans to its directors are, subject to narrowly circumscribed exceptions, prohibited (p 384 below); and

(2) that a company may not provide financial assistance for the purchase or subscription of its own shares or shares of its holding company, p 214 below.

B CASES

[120] *In re* **London and Provincial Consolidated Coal Company**
(1877) 5 ChD 525

The memorandum of association of a company was signed on its formation by nine people. Thereafter at a meeting of the directors it was resolved that no shares be allotted to three of the subscribers and their deposit moneys were returned to them.

The court held that the directors had no power to remit the shares.

MALINS V-C: . . . the decisions have been uniform that wherever any person signed a memorandum of association, he must be put on the list of contributories, although no shares may have been allotted to him.

. . . If I were to accede to this application on the part of these three gentlemen, it seems to me to follow that the persons who sign the memorandum of association, seven in number, as provided by the Act, have only — as of course they may very well do — to call a meeting, and at that meeting to resolve that they shall be released from their shares and the liability attaching to them, or all but one, or all but two, and the consequences would be that although those persons who sign a memorandum of association must of course be contributories, as expressly stated by the Act of Parliament, they may at any time escape their liability, and say by resolution among themselves that everyone who signed the memorandum, except one or except two, as the case may be, shall be freed. . . .

NOTES

Cf *Evans's* case (1867) 2 Ch App 427; *Migotti's* case (1867) LR 4 Eq 238; *Forbes and Judd's* case (1870) 5 Ch App 270; *Mackley's* case (1875) 1 ChD 247; *Moosa* v *Lalloo* 1957 (4) SA 207 (N) at 210.

[121] **Société Générale de Paris** *v* **Tramways Union Company Ltd**
(1884) 14 QBD 424

LINDLEY LJ: . . . If a shareholder in a company governed by the Companies Act . . . does not transfer his shares, but agrees to transfer them or to hold them upon trust for another, either absolutely or by way of security, there can be no doubt as to the validity of the agreement, nor as to the effect of it as between the parties to it. As between them the agreement or trust can be enforced; but as regards the company the shareholder on the register remains shareholder still. He is the person to exercise the rights of a shareholder, for example, to vote as such, to receive dividends as such, and to transfer the shares. On the other hand, he, and he alone, is liable for calls and to be put on the list of contributories if the company is wound up. The person having the beneficial interest in the shares has, as against the company, no right to them. . . .

[122] **Musselwhite** *v* **C H Musselwhite & Son Ltd**
[1962] 1 Ch 964, [1962] 1 All ER 201

The plaintiffs had sold their shares in a private company to X, payment of the purchase price to be made in instalments over five years.

Executed transfers and the share certificates were deposited with the company's solicitors, who were to hold them in trust until payment was made in full, the plaintiffs remaining on the register in the meantime. The company sent notice of a general meeting to X, but not to the plaintiffs. The court held that the meeting was invalid, since the plaintiffs, as the registered members, had not received notice of it.

RUSSELL J: In my judgment, so far as voting powers are concerned, an unpaid vendor remaining on the register is not to be regarded as in a weaker position, so far as the exercise of voting powers is concerned, than a mortgagee. . . . In the one case the mortgagee is deliberately put on the register to safeguard his money lent: in the other case the vendor is deliberately left on the register until all is paid to safeguard his purchase—money due.

In my judgment, an unpaid vendor remaining on the register after the contract of sale retains vis-á-vis the purchaser the prima facie right to vote in respect of those shares.

[It was also held in *Musselwhite* that, prima facie, the purchaser in such a case has no right to say how the shares should be voted.]

NOTES

In *Sammel* v *President Brand GM Co Ltd* 1969 (3) SA 629 (AD) Trollip JA defined a nominee as follows (at 666D): ' "Nominee" . . . is not defined in Act. The ordinary meaning is a person who is nominated or appointed; in the context it therefore means a person nominated or appointed by the transferee company to hold the shares in his name on its behalf, that is, he is simply an agent of the transferee company for that purpose. . . . The policy of the law is that a company shall concern itself only with the registered holder and not the owner or beneficial owner of the shares.' The question whether a person who holds as a trustee is a nominee was left open (667A). See further *Simpson* v *Molson's Bank* [1895] AC 270; *Liquidators Karroo and Eastern Board of Executors* v *Cronje* 1926 CPD 370; *Dowjee Company Ltd* v *Waja* 1929 TPD 66. As to the legal relationship between trustees under a trust deed and the beneficiaries under the trusts, see *Kirby* v *Wilkins* [1929] 2 Ch 444; *Butt* v *Kelson* [1952] Ch 197, [1952] 1 All ER 167, and *Re Whichelow* [1954] 1 WLR 5, [1953] 2 All ER 1558, also *Pender* v *Lushington* (176 below).

II COMPANY PROVIDING ASSISTANCE FOR THE PURCHASE OF ITS OWN SHARES

A TEXT

No company may give, whether directly or indirectly, and whether by means of a loan, guarantee, the provision of security or otherwise, any financial assistance for the purpose of or in connection with a purchase or subscription made or to be made by any person of or for any shares of the company, or where the company is a subsidiary company, of its holding company, s 38: *123–129B*. The responsible directors are personally liable to the company for breach of trust: *128*, *129B*. Among the exceptions to the rule is the lending of money in the ordinary course of its business by a company whose main business is the lending of money, s 38(2)(*a*): *129*.

B CASES

[123] **Gradwell (Pty) Ltd** *v* **Rostra Printers Ltd**
1959 (4) SA 419 (AD)

SCHREINER JA: In the early part of 1956 the appellant company acted as agent in the negotiation of a contract between the two respondents, whereby the first respondent sold to the second respondent (*a*) all the issued shares of a company called Printing House Limited, and (*b*) the loan indebtedness of the latter to the first respondent. I shall call the appellant company Gradwell, the first respondent Rostra, the second respondent Crowden and Printing House Limited, the company. In terms of the contract Gradwell was entitled to commission from Rostra and was to be paid £1 000 out of the purchase price by Crowden. Gradwell received that sum but was to hold it in trust until the contract was carried out. After the contract had been entered into Crowden claimed that it was invalid and cited Gradwell and Rostra as respondents in an application before the Witwatersrand Local Division for an order declaring the contract to be of no force and effect and directing Gradwell to repay the £1 000. Rostra did not oppose the proceedings but Gradwell did. . . .

Crowden claims that the contract was invalid because it infringed s 86*bis*(2) of the Companies Act (Act 46 of 1926, now s 38). The first portion of the subsection reads —

'No company shall give, whether directly or indirectly, and whether by means of a loan, guarantee, the provision of security or otherwise, any financial assistance for the purpose of or in connection with a purchase or subscription made or to be made by any person of or for any shares in the company or in any company to which it is a subsidiary. . . .'

There follow three provisos which exclude from the subsection's prohibition the lending of money in the ordinary course of its business by a company which ordinarily lends money, and the provision or loan of money by a company for the acquisition of its shares by its employees.

Subsection (3) subjects a company that contravenes the section to a fine not exceeding £100.

The terms of the contract appear from an offer contained in a letter, dated 12 March 1956, from Crowden to Rostra, the offer being accepted by Rostra in a letter dated 23 March 1956. Crowden begins the letter of 12 March 1956 by offering to purchase from Rostra the total issued share capital of the company and Rostra's claim against the company upon the terms that follow. For present purposes the important terms are these —

'1. You warrant and/or undertake that as at the effective date, as hereinafter defined: — . . .

(*d*) Save for . . . taxes the company's only liabilities and obligations will be: —

(i) A first mortgage bond in favour of the United Building Society; and

(ii) the loan account owing to yourselves and which will be acquired by us on the acceptance of this offer.

'2. The purchase consideration payable by us to you for the said shares and the said loan account is the sum of £42 500 less the amount owing at the effective date under the aforesaid mortgage bond in favour of the United Building Society, and the said purchase price shall be payable:

(a) As to the sum of £1 000 in cash on the acceptance of this offer, which amount shall be paid to Messrs B T Gradwell (Pty) Ltd, who shall hold the same in trust pending the transfer of the shares and the loan account to us and the completion of the other formalities . . .

(b) for the balance of the purchase price a banker's or an approved building society guarantee shall be furnished to you. . . .

'3. Immediately after delivery to you . . . of the guarantee . . . you shall deliver to us: — . . .

(b) All books and records of the company. . . .

(d) Share certificates in respect of the total issued share capital in the company. . . .

(e) A cession in our favour of the loan account owing by the company to yourselves. . . .

'8. The agreement constituted by this offer, if accepted, shall be subject to our being able to arrange a first mortgage bond over the property of the company for an amount of £30 000 bearing interest at 7% per annum, and otherwise upon the terms and conditions usually applicable to a building society bond.

'If the said bond is arranged you shall be obliged to procure that the company passes all necessary resolutions and signs all documents necessary to effect cancellation of the existing bond in favour of the United Building Society and the simultaneous registration of the said new bond, and the proceeds of the said bond shall be utilised as follows: —

(a) liquidation of the existing bond in favour of the United Building Society;

(b) payment to you on account of the purchase price of the shares and the loan account, the subject of this offer, and the simultaneous reduction of your loan account against the company.

In that event the balance of the purchase price payable by us to you in terms of para 2(b) shall be reduced by the amount paid to you out of the proceeds of the said bond.

'9. It is hereby recorded that this offer is made through the agency of Messrs B T Gradwell (Pty) Ltd and you shall be liable for payment of the commission in respect of the transaction.'

From the balance sheet it appears that substantially the sole asset of the company was a piece of land in Johannesburg with buildings thereon, shown at cost, namely £66 178. The liabilities consisted substantially of (a) £10 255, owed on bond to the United Building Society, and (b) £40 258, owed on loan account to Rostra. The issued shares were

£20 000 of £1 each. At the balance sheet value of the property there would be a surplus of assets over liabilities to an amount of £15 665, which would give the shares a value of some 15*s* each, but if the purchase price of £42 500 were taken to represent the value of the property there would be an £8 005 excess of liabilities over assets and the shares would be worthless. In terms of clause 2 Crowden would have to provide £42 500 less £10 255. This balance of £32 245 would have to be paid as to £1 000 on acceptance of the offer and as to £31 245 by a guarantee furnished within 45 days thereafter. But if the machinery provided in clause 8 came into operation the £30 000 provided by the new bond would pay off the United Building Society bond of £10 255 and £19 745 of the loan account, leaving £20 513 still due by the company to Rostra. The purchase price payable by Crowden would at the same time be reduced by £19 745 from £32 245 to £12 500.

In broad outline the case for Gradwell was that clause 8 does not provide for the giving by the company of financial assistance either to Rostra or to Crowden, since it amounts to no more than provision for the payment by the company of the whole of its debt to the United Building Society and of part of its debt to Rostra. The effect of the transaction contemplated by the clause is not, so it was argued, the provision by the company of the means to purchase the shares plus a loan account of £40 258, but the adjustment of the company's affairs so as to reduce its loan account to £20 513, thus making what was to be purchased of less worth. No doubt this would help Crowden to effect its apparent purpose of acquiring control over the property by buying the shares and eliminating the indebtedness due to the United Building Society and Rostra, since it could now do so by paying £12 500 instead of £32 245. But this was because what it was buying was the smaller and therefore cheaper article, not because it was being assisted to buy the larger, more expensive, one. Making the smaller one available, though achieved by the financial process of paying off part of the loan account, was not the giving of financial assistance by the company.

For Crowden emphasis was laid on what was said to be the apparent intention of the legislature to prohibit and penalize and therefore invalidate a wide range of transactions. Attention was drawn to 'whether directly or indirectly' in the subsection and to the words 'or otherwise', which it was contended should not be limited by the preceding enumeration. The words 'made or to be made', it may be observed, seem to cover assistance provided even after the purchase or subscription. Although it was conceded that generally payment of a debt owed by the company would not be described as the giving of financial assistance to the payee or any other person, it would be properly so described where the payment was made not in the ordinary course of the company's business and to advance its interests but as part of a scheme designed solely to facilitate by financial means the purchase of shares in the company. It was argued that a provision of finance under such a scheme is invalid even though it incidentally discharges a debt owed by the company. In relation to the terms of the contract counsel for Crowden relied strongly on the obligation to provide £42 500 under clause 2. There was only one purchase price payable in respect of the shares and the loan account taken together, and any financing of the payment of that purchase price in whole or in part must, it was argued, assist in paying for the shares. And the operations envisaged by clause 8 would enable the purchase price to be furnished in part by using the property of the company as security.

For Gradwell it was argued that the words 'or otherwise' should be construed *ejusdem generis* with loan, guarantee and the provision of security. For Crowden it was contended that the words 'or otherwise' must be given their full, independent operation. I do not think, however, that in this case it matters whether the words 'or otherwise' are given a restricted meaning or not. Loan, guarantee and the provision of security are certainly ways in which a company could provide financial assistance in the purchase of its shares. It could lend money to the purchaser or guarantee or secure his borrowings from someone else. But the method employed can hardly determine what is the giving of financial assistance within the meaning of the subsection. Loan, guarantee and the provision of security may, I apprehend, be used also for other purposes than the giving of financial assistance. It would consequently not advance the reasoning to enquire whether the method used was similar to loan, guarantee or the provision of security instead of asking directly whether the giving of financial assistance covers the payment of a debt that is due and payable. In the present case the company was itself to borrow the money and its property was to be used to secure the loan. Thereby it would incur a liability but it would receive a corresponding amount of money. The question whether it was to give financial assistance would depend not on how it obtained the money—by loan, secured or not, by realizing assets or otherwise—but on what it was to do with the money when available.

We were pressed by counsel for Crowden with the importance of the purpose of the whole transaction. The purpose of Crowden and Rostra was inevitably that of the company, the actions of which were entirely controllable by Rostra. The purpose must be taken to have been to help Crowden to buy and Rostra to sell the company's shares. But this does not carry Crowden to success. Unless what was to be done would amount to giving of financial assistance within the meaning of the subsection the purpose and the connection would not be important.

Having money available the company could part with it in various ways that would enable the recipient to purchase the company's shares with the money. It could for instance buy an asset, not required for the purposes of its business, in order to provide the seller of the asset with money with which to buy the shares. It was contended on behalf of Crowden that this would be giving financial assistance. If the purchase of the asset were effected at a price known to be inflated, this would no doubt be the giving of financial assistance. It would indeed be equivalent to a gift and would clearly involve a reduction of the company's capital. It was one of the illustrations given by Lord Greene in *In re VGM Holdings Ltd* [1942] Ch 235 at 240. It is, I think, significant that the Master of the Rolls did not mention the case of the purchase of an asset at a fair price with the object of enabling the seller of the asset to buy the shares. But whatever may be the position in such a case the paying off of an existing debt seems to be decidedly more difficult to bring within the notion of giving financial assistance. The payer's assets and liabilities are put into a different form but the balance is unchanged. And the same applies to the financial position of the payee. Here the company would have no more and no less after the completion of the transaction than before. And the same would apply to Rostra. The company would owe more to its mortgagee and correspondingly less to Rostra. The price to be paid by Crowden would be less by the difference in the value of the assets to be acquired. Its financial position would be unchanged—only its investment would be smaller. Where there is an anticipation of the date when a debt becomes due and payable the position may possibly be different, but where the debt is presently due and payable and the debtor can have no answer to the creditor's demand for payment, it would be straining the language to hold that by paying his debt the debtor gives the creditor financial assistance.

The appeal is allowed and the judgment of the Witwatersrand Local Division dismissing the application is restored.

[*Gradwell* was criticized by I B Murray in (1960) *77 SALJ* 17, and defended by P Friedlander ibid 246. I B Murray replied ibid 381.]

[124] **Karnovsky v Hyams**
1961 (2) SA 368 (W)

CLAASSEN J: This is a matter in which the excipients contend that the respondent's declaration against them is bad in law and discloses no cause of action.

The action arises out of a contract whereby the respondent (plaintiff in the action) purchased from the defendants all the issued shares, which are fully paid up, in a property owning company. This company owes the sellers of the shares a sum of £49 600. It was stipulated in the deed of sale that in order to secure the payment of this debt by the company to the sellers, the company was bound to pass a first mortgage bond over its fixed property in favour of the sellers of the shares. Clause 2 of the agreement of sale reads as follows:

'The parties record that the amount owing by the Company to the sellers is the sum of forty-nine thousand six hundred pounds (£49 600). In order to secure the payment by the Company to the sellers of the said sum of forty-nine thousand six hundred pounds (£49 600), the Company shall pass in favour of the sellers a first mortgage bond over the property hereinafter described. The said sum shall bear interest at the rate of six per centum (6%) per annum, reckoned from the 1st day of March 1960, and payable quarterly in arrear. The capital sum shall be repaid on the 31st day of December 1963.'

There is nowhere in the agreement or the declaration any suggestion that the debt was not due and payable, and there was no suggestion to the contrary during the course of the arguments.

The plaintiff [alleged] that in the bona fide and reasonable belief that the agreement was valid and binding he had paid a portion of the purchase price of the shares. He claimed an order declaring that the agreement was void, and further claimed repayment of that portion of the purchase price which he had paid.

The basis of the plaintiff's attack on the agreement of sale is s 86*bis*(2) of the Companies Act which provides that —

> 'No company shall give, whether directly or indirectly, and whether by means of a loan, guarantee, the provision of security or otherwise, any financial assistance for the purpose of or in connection with a purchase made or to be made by any person of any shares in the company or in any company to which it is subsidiary . . .'.

A breach of this subsection is made an offence and renders the company liable to a fine not exceeding £100, according to s 86*bis*(3).

This subsection of the Act is difficult to construe and all the implications thereof are far from clear. It is undoubtedly one of the objects of s 86*bis*(2) of the Companies Act to protect a company from being prejudiced financially, defrauded or from having its capital diminished by decreasing the surplus of assets over liabilities. Such an inference, in my view, is in harmony with the South African case of *Gradwell (Pty) Ltd* v *Rostra Printers Ltd & another* 1959 (4) SA 419 (AD) [*123* above]. It is also worth while to bear in mind the origin of the prohibition in English legislation from which the relevant section was originally taken over. In the case of *In re VGM Holdings Limited* [1942] ChD 235 Lord Greene MR said at 239:

> 'Those whose memories enable them to recall what had been happening after the last war for several years will remember that a very common form of transaction in connection with companies was one by which persons—call them financiers, speculators, or what you will—finding a company with a substantial cash balance or easily realizable assets such as war loans, bought up the whole or the greater part of the shares of the company for cash and so arranged matters that the purchase money which they then became bound to provide was advanced to them by the company whose shares they were acquiring, either out of its cash balance or by realization of its liquid investments. That type of transaction was a common one, and it gave rise to great dissatisfaction and, in some cases, great scandals. I think that it is not illegitimate to bear in mind that notorious practice in considering the ambit of the section . . .'.

It is clear, I think, that it was an object of the legislation to prohibit immoral transactions which had the effect of illegally enriching one or more persons at the expense of a company. It is well known that a company may not buy its own shares for such a transaction would have the effect of reducing its capital without the approval of the court contrary to the provisions of the Companies Act. It seems to me that it is probable that one type of transaction which it was intended to prohibit was the transaction in connection with the purchase of shares which directly or indirectly had the effect of reducing the capital of the company. If a transaction is real and not fictitious, and in the ordinary course of sound business methods, the court would, in my view, be slow to condemn such a transaction on the basis of s 86*bis*(2), unless the court, when in possession of the full facts, could say that on a balance of probabilities the transaction if carried out would constitute a criminal offence. . . .

There are three parties concerned in the present transaction: the purchaser, the sellers and the company. It is relevant to the enquiry to answer the question whether either the purchaser or the sellers have been financially assisted in the transaction and whether the company has been financially prejudiced.

The defendant filed an exception alleging that the plaintiff's declaration was bad in law and disclosed no cause of action. Mr R submitted that the provision for the passing of the bond did not in the circumstances disclosed in the declaration and the agreement attached thereto fall within the prohibition of s 86*bis*(2). This submission seems to me to be correct. I cannot say in what way financial aid is rendered to anyone for the purpose of or in connection with the purchase of the shares in the company. The persons who are selling the shares were in control of the company; they now sell their shares and there is a provision in the deed of sale that all the present directors should resign and an undertaking is given that the purchaser and/or his nominees will be appointed as directors. This means that the sellers of the shares are stepping completely out of the company and are giving up any control they may have had through the board of directors. While they still had control they may have been satisfied to leave the debts owing to them by the company unsecured but when they step out completely and the control passes into other hands, it seems to me that, while not demanding payment, they are acting normally and in business-like manner in stipulating that their loan accounts be secured by mortgage bond over the fixed assets of the company. In doing that there is nothing immoral or contrary to sound business methods.

Mr N argued that these sellers of the shares get a benefit which they did not have before: whereas before they were unsecured creditors, they now become secured creditors; their personal right has now become a real right. That is no doubt true. He then submitted that they will therefore be financially assisted. But does the company not get a *quid pro quo*? Instead of having to pay the amount of the loan accounts at once the company gets an extension of time until 31 December 1963, and has to pay interest at the legal rate of 6 per cent per annum. If the debt were paid by the company then in terms of the authorities that would not amount to giving financial aid to the sellers of the shares. If something less were done, namely a bond registered over immovable assets of the company, it cannot be said, in my opinion, that financial assistance is being given to the sellers of the shares. But even if one were to assume that the loan was in any event only payable during 1963 or later, as to which there is no suggestion anywhere, it is on a balance of probabilities unlikely that the sellers of the shares would have given up all control of the company without some safeguard. That safeguard is rendered in the form of a mortgage bond; as they had given up their safeguard of personal control for the safeguard of a mortgage bond I cannot say that the sellers or the purchaser have thereby been assisted financially. There has been no suggestion in the documents before the court, or even during the arguments, that the purchaser has in any way been assisted financially.

Nor can it, in my opinion, be said that the company will be prejudiced financially. True, those fixed assets will now become bonded, but there is nothing unfair in that in view of the time given to pay off the loan accounts and in view of the control which the sellers have given up. . . . Therefore it does not seem to me that clause 5 of the declaration read with clause 2 of the agreement of sale are on a balance of probabilities capable of a conclusion that the agreement constitutes a breach of s 86*bis*(2) of the Act, and that the company will on a balance of probabilities be liable to conviction and a fine in accordance with s 86*bis*(3).

[125] Albert *v* Papenfus
1964 (2) SA 713 (E)

Windsor Hotel (Pty) Ltd which owned the Windsor Hotel in East London, was a 'one-man' company. Of its issued share capital of 7 000 shares of £1 each, the plaintiff held 6 998 shares, his wife one share, and the defendant one share. The defendant expressed the desire to purchase or lease the hotel, and the plaintiff stated that he and his wife were prepared to hand over at any time provided they received a total, secure income of R600 per month for their shares. After some negotiations it was agreed that the plaintiff and his wife were to receive a permanent income of R600 per month, to be calculated on a secured amount of R90 000 at 8 per cent per annum.

The way this was put into effect was as follows: 'The company opened a 'goodwill' account of R90 000 in favour of the plaintiff and secured it by a mortgage bond. The defendant entered into a deed of suretyship for the company's debt to the plaintiff, and in return the shares of the plaintiff and his wife were transferred to the defendant. Some time later, the company, having gone into liquidation, defaulted on the bond and the plaintiff sued the defendant under the deed of suretyship.

The court held that the transaction amounted to a contravention of s 86*bis*(2), and that both the bond and the suretyship were invalid.

MUNNIK J: It is common cause and trite law that if the main obligation is unenforceable as being tainted with illegality, the guarantor's obligation is equally unenforceable. . . .

The defendant's contention as I have already stated is that there never was any amount owing by the company to the plaintiff in respect of goodwill, but that the true transaction was one in terms of which the purchase price was R90 000 for which liability was assumed by the company and secured by a mortgage bond over the company's immovable property, with the defendant as surety.

If . . . this is the true position then it admits of no doubt that the company in the words of s 86*bis*(2) gave 'financial assistance' in connection with the purchase of the shares. . . .

It seems to me that the plaintiff's denial proceeds from his failure to appreciate that his *de facto* control of the company through his possession of 6 998 out of 7 000 shares did not make him the owner of the hotel business, but that the hotel business belonged to the company as a distinct and separate *persona*.

It follows therefore that whatever goodwill attached to the hotel belonged to the company. The plaintiff admits that the company's liability to the plaintiff for R90 000 did not appear on the books prior to the signing of the deed of sale. I find it difficult to understand how it could have. It seems to me inescapable that unless the plaintiff had a legally enforceable claim against the company for R90 000 it cannot be said that a liability for this amount existed. I am of the opinion that on the admitted facts not only is it improbable that such a claim existed but it is legally impossible for it to have existed.

One assumes that the ordinary commercial practice prevails in the hotel industry as well as the other fields of business activity. A successful hotel manager is one who runs the hotel in such a way that its profits are satisfactory to the owners. People come to the hotel because he is running it. The value of his services in this connection no doubt bears a relationship to the quantum of his salary. In that way he is rewarded for his diligence, but whatever he does must enure to the benefit of his employer and therefore the concept of his building up a personal saleable goodwill is to me incomprehensible. The matter may be tested very simply. Could he sell that asset to a third party? The answer is that he could not. He could by virtue of his reputation place a premium on his services in a similar capacity. In other words his goodwill would possibly enable him to command a higher salary elsewhere.

Even if I am wrong in my view that the plaintiff could not sell his goodwill to the company the transaction to my mind is still hit by s 86*bis*(2). I say this because it is clear on the papers that the question of the plaintiff's alleged goodwill only arose after the sale had been concluded.

A careful reading of the deed of sale together with the extracts from the plaintiff's affidavit and his attorney's letters as set out above lead one inexorably to the conclusion . . . that the plaintiff first fixed a price based upon the income he wanted and thereafter ways and means of securing payment of this income were devised and it was then that the device of opening a goodwill account to create a previously non-existent liability to justify the passing of the bond over the company's assets was arrived at.

For the company to have opened a goodwill account and credited the plaintiff with R90 000 in respect thereof amounted to the assumption by the company without a *quid pro quo* of a previously non-existent liability and the company therefore became the poorer by R90 000.

Whatever view one takes of the matter, that is whether the plaintiff's alleged goodwill was saleable or not, I am satisfied on the papers before me that the defendant has discharged the onus of proving on a balance of probability a contravention of s 86*bis*(2).

I turn now to [the] alternative contention, viz that the bond or suretyship is not invalidated by the contravention of s 86*bis*(2).

For this proposition [counsel for the plaintiff] relies upon the judgment of Roxburgh J in *Victory Battery Co Ltd* v *Curry's Ltd* [p 235 below], which . . . paraphrased, stated that the section was only contravened if the financial assistance was valid; if therefore the financial assistance was not valid the section was not contravened; therefore proof of contravention of the section necessarily means that the financial assistance (whatever form it took) was valid and consequently whatever flows therefrom is equally valid.

This reasoning seems to me to be in direct conflict with . . . numerous decisions in our law. . . .

To hold otherwise would mean that the whole object of s 86bis(2) could in practice be defeated by anyone willing to pay at most a penalty of R1 000—which in many cases may constitute an attractive and profitable commercial proposition.

It follows from what I have said that the defendant has succeeded in her defence to the extent necessary for resisting the plaintiff's claim and provisional sentence is accordingly refused.

[126] Bay Loan Investment (Pty) Ltd v Bay View (Pty) Ltd
1972 (2) SA 313 (C)

In this case it was held that the securing of the loan indebtedness by a company to the person surrendering control of that company by reason of the sale by him of his shares in the company does not constitute the rendering of financial assistance by the company as contemplated by s 86bis(2) of Act 46 of 1926 (now s 38).

VAN WINSEN J: It appears from the papers filed with the Court that Messrs Tollman, Shapiro and the Estate Late Solomon Tollman in April 1968 sold their total shareholding in defendant company to Corlett Drive West Rand (Pty) Ltd. At the time of the sale the sellers and one other were loan creditors of defendant company, and it was a term of the contract that a second mortgage bond be passed by defendant company in favour of the existing loan account creditors or their nominee to secure the defendant company's indebtedness to them. The bond sued upon is the bond passed in terms of this contract and it recites that it is in respect of money lent and advanced but does not say that the money was advanced by the plaintiff company, and it can be taken as admitted that it was intended to secure money owing by defendant company to the loan creditors above referred to.

[Dealing first with the effect of s 54 of the Deeds Registries Act 47 of 1937 which provides that no mortgage bond shall be passed in favour of a person as agent or nominee of a principal, Van Winsen J arrived at the conclusion that a bond passed in contravention of this section is not a nullity. He then addressed himself to the question whether the transaction was void as a contravention of what is now s 38.]

There is authority in our case law to support the proposition that should a company contract in breach of the terms of s 86bis(2) the contract is void and security given by the company in terms of such a contract is also null and void. . . .

The question is therefore whether the present transaction is in breach of the provisions of s 86bis(2). . . .

It was argued that the financial assistance afforded lay in the fact that the purchasers of the shares undertook to procure that defendant company would pass a second bond in favour of the existing loan account creditors to secure the balance of the loan accounts and interest thereon at 8½ per cent. In pursuance of this undertaking defendant company passed the bond presently being sued upon. It is to be noted that the company was merely securing an existing loan indebtedness. It does not appear from the papers that by agreeing to pay 8½ per cent interest on the unpaid balance of the loans the company was undertaking to do more than it was in any event obliged to do. The company was accordingly in no worse position as a result of the undertaking to pay what it was in any event obliged to pay. As I understand the decision in *Gradwell (Pty) Ltd* v *Rostra Printers Ltd* 1959 (4) SA 419 (AD), *123* above, it was there laid down that where, as a result of the transaction in issue the balance of the company's liabilities remain unchanged, eg where it undertakes to pay off an existing debt and it has accordingly not been impoverished, it cannot be said to have rendered financial assistance in the purchase of its shares in contravention of s 86*bis*(2). This decision appears to have been so understood in *Miller* v *Muller* (1965 (4) SA 458 (C)) at 466; *Lindner & another* v *Vogtmannsberger & another* 1965 (4) SA 108 (O) at 112; *Karnovsky & others* v *Hyams* 1961 (2) SA 368 (W), *124* above. Cf too *Albert* v *Papenfus* (*125* above) at 718, and *Curtis' Furnishing Stores Ltd* v *Freedman* [1966] 2 All ER 955.

It might be argued that the company is worse off in that what in all probability were unsecured loans have now been secured under a mortgage bond, and that the giving of this mortgage bond was a material factor in promoting the conclusion of the contract of the purchase of the shares by Corlett Drive. I assume the latter is in fact the case, since no doubt the sellers of the shares, no longer in control of defendant's company, would want to be secured in some other way in regard to the payment to them of their loans to the company before acceding to the agreement of purchase and sale of their shares in the company. The question, however, still is whether the giving of security amounts to affording 'financial assistance' within the meaning of s 86*bis*(2). On the facts presently before me I think the answer to this is in the negative. In any event, the section does not appear to me to be intended to counter what would be a perfectly normal business transaction, and one dictated by prudent business considerations. I am in respectful agreement with the views of Claassen J as expressed in *Karnovsky & others* v *Hyams* (*supra*), namely, that the securing of the loan indebtedness by the company to the person surrendering control of that company by reason of the sale by him of his shares in that company does not constitute the rendering of financial assistance by the company as contemplated by s 86*bis*(2). Accordingly the second defence to defendant's claim for provisional sentence also fails.

[127] Manufacturers Development Co v Diesel & Auto Engineering Co
1975 (2) SA 776 (W)

In terms of an agreement Speedy Engineering (Pty) Ltd purchased the shares of a group of companies from their holders. In order to provide Speedy Engineering with funds the companies sold their plant and equipment to the applicant and received them back from him under 'lease-back' agreements. Moneys from the proceeds of these sales were used to assist Speedy Engineering in the purchase of the shares. The main question before the court was whether the sale of the property to the applicant was void as a contravention of s 38.

NICHOLAS J: The applicant relied for the indebtedness of the respective respondents on certain lease-back agreements concluded between the respective respondents and the applicant. Respondents allege that during the early part of January 1974, a company, Speedy Engineering (Pty) Ltd, which is the respondent in matter No 12, desired to acquire the shares in certain other of the respondent companies for a total of R855 000. Speedy Engineering did not, however, have at its disposal sufficient money to pay the purchase price and an arrangement was accordingly made, in terms of which the companies, the shares in which were being purchased, would sell their assets to the applicant for an aggregate of R396 660, and the applicant would then 'lease back' the assets to the companies concerned. The sum of R396 660, it is then alleged, was used by the seller companies for the purpose of providing financial assistance to Speedy in the purchase of the shares in those companies. If those allegations are well-founded, then it is plain that the companies concerned provided financial assistance to Speedy in contravention of s 38 of the Companies Act 61 of 1973. The respondents allege that, because the applicant knew of the way in which the purchase price was going to be applied by the companies concerned, the 'lease-back agreements' were invalid and of no force or effect.

I asked for legal argument from [Counsel for the respondents] in support of this submission. He stated that he has been unable to find any case decided under s 38 of the present Companies Act, or s 86*bis* of the previous Companies Act, which supported his submission. [He] relied on cases of illegality of contract generally. In none of those cases, however, was it held that the mere fact that a purchaser of property knew that the proceeds of a sale were going to be applied by the seller in contravention of a statutory provision, rendered the sale invalid, or rendered invalid an agreement in terms of which the assets sold were leased back by the purchaser to the seller.

[128] **Wallersteiner *v* Moir** (*1*)
[1974] 3 All ER 217 (CA)

LORD DENNING MR: Section 54(1) of the Companies Act 1948 says:
'... it shall not be lawful for a company to give ... any financial assistance ... in connection with a purchase ... made or to be made by any person of or for any shares in the company, or ... in its holding company. ...'

That section was first introduced in the Companies Act 1929. It was enacted so as to deal with a mischief which was described by Lord Greene MR in *Re VGM Holdings Ltd* [[1942] Ch 235, 239, [1942] 1 All ER 224, 225]:

'Those whose memories enable them to recall what had been happening for several years after the last war will remember that a very common form of transaction in connection with companies was one by which persons—call them financiers, speculators, or what you will—finding a company with a substantial cash balance or easily realizable assets, such as war loan, bought up the whole, or the greater part, of the shares of the company for cash, and so arranged matters that the purchase money which they then became bound to provide was advanced to them by the company whose shares they were acquiring, either out of its cash balance or by realization of its liquid investments. That type of transaction was a common one, and it gave rise to great dissatisfaction and in some cases, great scandals.'

Lord Greene MR spoke those words in the year 1942. Since that time financiers have used more sophisticated methods. You have only to look at such cases as *Steen* v *Law* [*129* below] and *Selangor United Rubber Estates Ltd* v *Cradock* (*No* 3) [p 235 below] to see the devices which they use. Circular cheques come in very handy. So do puppet companies. The transactions are extremely complicated, but the end result is clear. You look to the company's money and see what has become of it. You look to the company's shares and see into whose hands they have got. You will then soon see if the company's money has been used to finance the purchase. The present case is an excellent example. In March 1962 Hartley Baird Ltd was a public company. Ten million of its shares, worth £500 000, were held by Camp Bird Ltd. Camp Bird had charged them to the Pearl Assurance Co Ltd to secure a loan of £125 000. It would have cost an honest buyer £625 000 to get them for his own benefit, free of the charge.

By September 1972 Dr Wallersteiner (in the name of his creature, the Rothschild Trust) had acquired all those shares for his own benefit and free of any charge. But he had not paid a penny for them. He had done it by two means: (1) by loans which Hartley Baird made to him (in the name of his company, IFT of Nassau); (2) by commissions which he said he had earned in the name of the Liechtenstein company. Those loans to IFT were for £284 981 11s 4d and £50 000. They were repayable by IFT by instalments over the succeeding years. One or two instalments were paid, but none thereafter. IFT has no assets. So the sums have been lost to Hartley Baird.

It is clear that those loans by Hartley Baird to IFT greatly assisted the acquisition of the shares by Rothschild Trust; and that Dr Wallersteiner was the moving spirit behind it. In those circumstances to my mind Dr Wallersteiner was guilty of misfeasance, apart altogether from s 54 of the Companies Act 1948. It was a misfeasance of the same quality as that which took place in *Re VGM Holdings Ltd* [[1942] Ch 235, [1942] 1 All ER 224]. But it was also a plain breach of s 54. What is the remedy for such breach? By s 54(2) the company and every officer who is in default is liable to a fine not exceeding £100. That is a trifling sanction. In *Essex Aero Ltd* v *Cross* [17 November 1961, unreported] Harman LJ said: '. . . the section was not enacted for the company's protection but for that of its creditors . . . the company cannot enforce it.' I do not agree. I think the section was passed so as to protect the company from having its assets misused. If it is broken, there is a civil remedy by way of an action for damages. Every director who is a party to a breach of s 54 is guilty of a misfeasance and breach of trust; and is liable to recoup to the company any loss occasioned to it by the default. That is shown by *Steen* v *Law* [*129* below] and *Selangor* v *Cradock* (*No 3*) [p 235 below]: see also Halsbury's *Laws of England* [4 ed, vol 7 para 208 pp 117, 118]. In those cases defaulters were held liable for the loss. So should Dr Wallersteiner be held liable here.

The loss on the 'circular cheque' transaction was £215 334 lost by Hartley Baird, and £19 440 lost by Baldwins. In each case with interest. The loss on the '£50 000 transaction' was £50 000. It was in form repaid by IFT to Hartley Baird on 31st January 1964 but immediately relent to IFT on the same terms. Hartley Baird have undoubtedly lost the £50 000 owing to the misfeasance of Dr Wallersteiner. They are not to be defeated by the paper device of a repayment and relending.

[*Wallerstein* v *Moir* (*No 1*) is noted by J H Farrar & N V Lowe (1975) 38 *MLR* 455. In *Wallerstein* v *Moir* (*No 2*) [1975] 1 All ER 849 (CA) the court dealt with the assessment of damages and costs.]

[129] Steen *v* Law
[1964] AC 287, [1963] 3 All ER 770 (PC)

For taxation reasons, IVM, a proprietary company, of which the two appellants were the only directors and which had one other shareholder, decided to become the wholly owned subsidiary of a public company, AMH. The three holders of IVM shares sold them to AMH for £200 000. IVM lent AMH £200 000, which AMH used to pay the IVM shareholders for their shares.

This clearly amounted to financial assistance. The question was whether the lending of money was part of, and effected in the ordinary course of the business of IVM so as to bring it within the exception of s 148(1) of the Companies Act 1936 of New South Wales, corresponding to s 54 of the English Companies Act 1948 and s 38 of our Act.

VISCOUNT RADCLIFFE: 'The lending of money', to be part of the ordinary business of a company, must be what may be called a lending of money in general, in the sense, for example, that money-lending is part of the ordinary business of a registered money-lender or a bank. Such lenders are not obliged to accept their borrowers; but it is characteristic of their business that, if they do lend, the money made available is at the borrower's free disposition and is not, except in special circumstances, confined to special uses or restricted to particular and defined purposes. Unless the lending of money as part of the ordinary business of a company is understood in this sense, the absurd result would be reached that any lending operations of which it made a practice, however restricted their purpose or remote from general money-lending, would qualify the company to ignore the prohibition of the section and finance purchases of its shares, provided that it could describe such advances as made in the ordinary course of its business. Thus a company which, for instance, lent money from time to time to trade suppliers or purchasers could claim that the lending of money was part of its ordinary business and that it was accordingly one of the companies intended to be protected by s 148(1)(a), if it chose to make loans in connexion with the purchase of its shares. Yet it is not possible to suppose that the section could have been intended to provide any exemption or relief for such cases, for there could be no good reason for allowing a company to use previous lendings for quite different purposes as the justification for share purchase loans, which the legislation is in general intended to forbid.

This interpretation is supported by the fact that in the proviso the 'ordinary business of a company' is associated with 'lending . . . of money in the ordinary course of its business'. The latter words are not intended, their lordships think, to be synonymous with the 'ordinary course of business' itself, and seem to refer more particularly to advances of a scale and for a purpose similar to those regularly made by the company in carrying out its business. Such a construction accords naturally with the idea of general money-lending, provided that the advances do not amount to a departure from the usual order of business: but it is, on the other hand, virtually impossible to see how loans, big or small, deliberately made by a company for the direct purpose of financing a purchase of its shares could ever be described as made in the ordinary course of its business.

Now the only lending of money in which IVM can be said to have taken a part since it set up its business was the inter-company transfers of funds which were made to enable the merchandising companies to fulfil their obligations and support the guarantee fund and the drawings of company moneys on loan account by the three members of the Steen family. Neither type of operation was effected on commercial terms or at interest. In their lordships' opinion such operations did not render the lending of money part of the ordinary business of IVM within the meaning of proviso (a) to s 148(1), and it follows that the advance of the £200 000 was not a loan that was protected from the ban imposed by the section.

[*Steen* v *Law* is also authority for the proposition that the directors who were responsible for the contravention of the section are personally liable to indemnify the company for its loss even where they were ignorant of the law.]

[129A] Lomcord Agencies (Pty) Ltd v Amalgamated Construction Co (Pty) Ltd
1976 (3) SA 86 (D & CLD)

Commercial Properties (Pty) Ltd entered into a prospecting contract with the trustees of Magnet Quarries (Pty) Ltd, a company then still in the course of formation. The prospector was given the right to purchase the property for R200 000 'which amount will be satisfied by the prospector raising a loan account in its books of account in favour of the owner in that amount'. The prospective shareholders of Magnet Quarries entered into an agreement with the plaintiff under which the plaintiff was given the right to purchase the entire share capital of Magnet Quarries together with the loan account of R200 000 due to Commercial Properties (Pty) Ltd for R509 000 — R200 000 for the loan account, and R309 000

for the shares. The total amount of R509 000 was to be secured (i) by
the registration of a first mortgage bond of R200 000 over the property
of Magnet Quarries and (ii) by the pledging of all shares to a firm
of attorneys.

The question before the court was whether this agreement amounted
to the giving of financial assistance by Magnet Quarries for the purchase
of its own shares.

HEFER J: . . . what is to be decided is whether the factors thus pleaded
by the defendant amount to the rendering of financial assistance by
Magnet Quarries within the meaning of that expression in s 38(1).

I have no doubt that it does not. The effect of the scheme, as pleaded by
the defendant himself, is simply that the plaintiff will acquire the loan
account, an unsecured debt owing by the company to Commercial
Properties, which he will cede to the grantors (sellers), and the company's
land will be mortgaged to secure the claim. Instead of owing the R200 000
to Commercial Properties, it will owe it to the grantors as cessionaries *in
securitatem debiti*. The company will thus be no poorer after the implementation of the scheme: it will be left with exactly the same assets
and liabilities. Concededly its land will now be mortgaged, but that does
not change the situation. Unlike cases such as *Karroo Auctions (Pty) Ltd* v
Hersman, 1951 (2) SA 33 (E), and *Saambou Nasionale Bouvereniging* v
Ligatex (Pty) Ltd; Ex parte Stuart: In re Saambou Nasionale Bouvereniging v
Ligatex (Pty) Ltd 1976 (1) SA 868 (E) (where the companies concerned
assumed additional liability by passing bonds over their properties in
connection with the sale of their shares) the company in the present
case will mortgage its property as security for its own existing debt and
thus it will assume no additional liability at all. (Cf *Gradwell (Pty) Ltd*
v *Rosta Printers Ltd & another* 1959 (4) SA 419 (AD); *Karnovsky & others*
v *Hyams* 1961 (2) SA 368 (W); Cilliers & Benade *Company Law
(Practitioner's Edition)* 273–4.

Mr M tried to counter this by arguing that the company will indeed
assume additional liability. In developing his argument, he referred to the
fact that the loan account would be ceded to the grantors merely *in
securitatem debiti*, and that the plaintiff will thus retain at least the right to
have it re-ceded to him upon satisfaction of his debt to the grantors (*Lief
NO* v *Dettmann* 1964 (2) SA 252 (AD) at 271). This entails (so the
argument ran) that the company would be liable in terms of the bond
and, even after discharging that liability, the loan account is to be re-ceded
to the plaintiff, leaving the company still indebted to the plaintiff for
the full R200 000.

This argument is quite obviously fallacious. It implies a complete
disregard of the truism, firstly, that a mortgage is 'only accessory to an
obligation' . . . and, secondly, that by redeeming the mortgage the mort-
gagor discharges the obligation in respect of which it was passed. As I
have indicated earlier, the defendant in its plea has completely correlated
the bond with the loan account, and it follows that, should the company
redeem the bond, the loan account (in security of which the bond is to
be passed) will obviously be discharged *ipso jure*.

To my mind, the scheme for which the agreement between the plaintiff and the prospective shareholders in Magnet Quarries provides, accordingly does not amount to the rendering of financial assistance within the meaning of s 38(1), on the construction of the agreement pleaded by the defendant.

[129B] Jacobson *v* Liquidator of M Bulkin & Co Ltd
1976 (3) SA 781 (T)

M Bulkin Co Ltd had four directors, B, J, L and O. In 1969 J, L and O sold their shares to B. In order to assist B in acquiring their shares the company agreed to lend and advance to J, L and O R50 000 each less the amount standing to their respective credits in the loan account of the company—a total of R37 780,86, reducing the advances to them to a total of R112 219,14. Their shares were then transferred to B who took over their indebtedness to the company. In 1972 the company was placed under liquidation. The liquidator sued B, J, L and O for payment of R112 219,14. J and L excepted to the claim as disclosing no cause of action. Their exception was dismissed.

LE GRANGE J: [Counsel for the defendants] conceded, for the purposes of his argument, that the effect of the agreement and the transactions which implemented it was such that a loan was made by the company to the first defendant, Bulkin, to assist him in acquiring the shares of the other shareholders in the company. But, Mr K submitted, not all assistance by a company afforded to a purchaser of shares in that company is hit by the prohibition . . . in s 86*bis*(2) What the section prohibits, he submitted, is financial assistance which effects a diminution of a company's capital assets. Financial assistance which is afforded 'in the ordinary course of sound business' and which has not such an effect is not prohibited by the section. Mr K submitted that in a series of decisions in our Courts it has, in effect, been laid down that the one and only test whether financial assistance afforded to a buyer of shares by the company is hit by the section is the test of what might be called 'impoverishment'.

Mr K pointed out that the plaintiff made no allegations in his particulars of claim which, if proved, could enable a Court to find that impoverishment of the company had resulted from the agreement and its implementation; there were no allegations from which the inference could be drawn that the agreement had not been concluded 'in the ordinary course of sound business'. Upon implementation of the agreement, he submitted, the company's books of record would have shown that no change in its financial position had been effected. Instead of R112 219,14 in the bank or the indebtedness of the retiring shareholders in that sum, the books would have shown a debt in that amount owing by Bulkin. Just as in the *Gradwell* case, he submitted, there would have been a change in the company's assets and liabilities but the balance between them would not have been disturbed. . . .

It was further submitted on behalf of the excipients that the summons could not sustain a cause of action because no allegation was made that the plaintiff was unable to recover the R112 219,14 from Bulkin on some legal ground other than one founded on the loan agreement. Although the agreement was illegal and, consequently, unenforceable, the plaintiff had not pleaded that he was unable, in law, to recover any amount equal to Bulkin's indebtedness from Bulkin. He referred to a large number of decisions including *Jajbhay* v *Cassim* 1939 AD 537, and submitted that equitable principles of our law afford the plaintiff a right of action against Bulkin. Failure by the plaintiff to allege that he had instituted an action against Bulkin based on one or other of those equitable principles and had failed to recover thereon, or that no such cause of action was available to the plaintiff, he submitted, rendered the plaintiff's pleading excipiable: the plaintiff sought to recover an alleged loss of a sum of money, the proximate cause of which loss could not *ex facie* the pleading be said to have been the alleged breach of duty by the directors.

Mr S, who appeared for the plaintiff, submitted that the contention that the South African Courts have adopted impoverishment as the sole test in deciding whether a transaction is hit by s 86*bis*(2) is based on misreading of those decisions to which Mr K referred. He drew attention to the most recent exposition of the corresponding provisions of s 54 of the English Companies Act by Lord Denning MR in *Wallersteiner* v *Moir* (1974) 3 All ER 217 (CA) at 238. In that case Lord Denning, after pointing out that financiers have since the last war used very sophisticated methods of circumventing s 54 of the English Act, said:

'You have only to look at such cases as *Steen* v *Law* 1964 AC 287 and *Selangor United Rubber Estates* v *Cradock* (1968) 1 WLR 1555 to see the devices which they use. Circular cheques come in very handy. So do puppet companies. The transactions are extremely complicated, but the end result is clear. You look to the company's money and see what has become of it. You look to the company's shares and see into whose hands they have got. You will then soon see if the company's money has been used to finance the purchase.'

It [was] obvious, Mr S submitted, that by way of agreement and the book-entries pleaded, the company transferred R140 000, to which it was entitled, to the retiring shareholders. By means of the same agreement and entries in the books of record of the company the shares of the retiring shareholders got into the hands of Bulkin. Such a transaction was clearly one in contravention of s 86*bis*(2) of the Companies Act (cf *S* v *Hepker & another* 1973 (1) SA 472 (W) at 478G) without any resort to an enquiry whether the transaction had resulted in the impoverishment of the company. The loan of the money to Bulkin which enabled him to purchase the shares was void and unenforceable. It would be futile to institute an action against him based on the illegal agreement. One remedy only was available to the liquidator of the company and that was to sue the directors who had devised and executed the scheme to put the money of the company into the pockets of the retiring shareholders and the shares of the latter into the hands of Bulkin. Their conduct caused the loss of R112 219,14 to the company. . . .

Section 86*bis*(2) [s 38] was certainly drawn in the widest and most general of terms. The language used makes it clear that the question whether the section has been contravened does not depend on the manner in which assistance is given (see the *Gradwell* case, *supra*, at 425B). The prohibition is not confined to financial assistance to the purchaser; it is directed

'to financial assistance to whomsoever given, provided that it be for the purpose of a purchase of shares or in connection with a purchase of shares'.

(See *E H Dey (Pty) Ltd (in Liquidation)* v *Dey* 1966 VR 464 at 469–470.) The words in which the prohibition is couched do not in any way refer to the financial position of the company. Since the decision in the *Gradwell* case, *supra*, however, it appears that it is generally accepted that the Courts, in deciding whether there has been a contravention of the section, will have regard to the question whether the transaction adversely affected the financial position of the company. (See, e g *Miller* v *Muller* [1965 (4) SA 458 (C)] at 466A; *Bay Loan Investment (Pty) Ltd* v *Bay View (Pty) Ltd* [*126* above] at 317A, and cases there cited.) Business transactions are often complicated and the Courts appear to exhibit great reluctance to stigmatise as 'financial assistance' transactions which are perfectly normal business transactions dictated by prudent business considerations. (See *Bay Loan Investment (Pty) Ltd* v *Bay View (Pty) Ltd*, *supra*, at 317D–G.) A close examination of a complicated transaction, which on the face of it appears to afford 'financial assistance', might reveal that the transaction is an honest transaction which advances, or at least serves, the interests of the company. In such a case it could be said that a mere change in the company's financial structure would not necessarily have the effect of giving 'financial assistance'; the change effected might make the *merx* more marketable, that is all. Examples of such transactions . . . are the paying off of an existing debt at a time when the debt was due and payable (the *Gradwell* case, *supra*) and the securing by mortgage of an existing loan indebtedness (*Bay Loan Investment's* case, *supra*). Such transactions in the view of the Courts left the company's overall financial position unchanged and therefore the transactions did not effect an impoverishment of the company. But, it appears to me, though the Court may often derive considerable assistance from a consideration of such a nature it cannot be called the true or sole criterion in an enquiry as to whether there has been a contravention of the section. (See article by R C Beuthin (1973) 90 *SALJ* 211 and Ian B Murray (1960) 77 *SALJ* 381 at 382.)

If the 'impoverishment test' is applied in respect of the transactions in question then it appears to me that there has been an impoverishment of the company. In terms of the agreement the company, upon a sale of its assets, in effect exchanged the major portion of the cash proceeds thereof for a claim against Bulkin. By doing so the company deprived itself of money which it could have utilized in its business and exposed its asset, on the face of the transaction, to an unwarranted risk. In the *Gradwell* case, *supra*, the company undertook to make arrangements to pay off an existing debt, then due and payable; in the instant case the company lent money to the retiring shareholders (or caused a book entry to that effect to be made) for the sole purpose of creating an indebtedness which could be taken over by Bulkin. . . . Could it be said that such a transaction was in the normal course of the company's business; that it was 'dictated by prudent business considerations'? I think not.

But if I have understood Mr K's argument he did not seek to apply the 'impoverishment test' as I have applied it. Mr K, it appears to me, applied the so-called test in a manner which makes the operation of the prohibition dependent upon the financial position of the borrower of the money at the time when the loan is made or at the time when repayment of the loan is desired. If his submission is correct then a company which lends money to a person to enable him to purchase shares in that company does not contravene the section if the debtor is a millionaire or if he furnishes ample security for the loan but does so if the borrower is a man of straw. The proposition that the legality of the loan depends on the eventual ability of the debtor to repay the loan does not merit consideration. . . .

I now turn to the argument that the plaintiff's pleading is excipiable because it does not allege that the money is irrecoverable from Bulkin in an action founded on some cause of action other than the loan agreement. Mr K conceded that the authorities cited by Mr S show that no action can be maintained on an agreement concluded in contravention of s 86*bis*(2) because it is void and unenforceable (the decision of the Full Court in *Crowden Products (Pty) Ltd* v *Gradwell (Pty) Ltd, supra,* settled any doubt which there might, possibly, have been in this Division). . . .

The question which was debated is not without difficulty but at the conclusion of argument on the point I considered that Mr K had failed to spell out a cause of action against Bulkin which the plaintiff could have utilised with success. . . .

There is nothing which Bulkin received from the company which he could be compelled to restore to the company. A claim for payment of R112 219,14 against B founded in the doctrine of enrichment would have been one for the enforcement of an illegality as much as a claim based upon the contract of loan.

In none of the English and Australian authorities cited by Mr S and the other decisions of the English Courts which I read, which deal with the remedy available to a company where the company has given financial assistance in contravention of the provisions of the applicable statute, has it been suggested that a company could recover the amount expended by it from the borrower of the company's funds by founding an action on the equitable principles to which Mr K referred. In the *Dressy Frocks* case, *supra,* at 395, Street CJ pointed out that a company in such circumstances

'is not left without a remedy, inasmuch as the directors participating in this illegal transaction may themselves be required to make good to the company the loss which it would otherwise sustain. . . .'

In the *Wallersteiner* case, [*128*], at 239 (by Lord Denning MR) and at 255 (by Scarman LJ) it was held that s 54 of the Companies Act 1948 was enacted not only for the protection of creditors but also to protect company funds; the remedy for loss occasioned by a contravention of the section was said to be one by way of action for damages against the defaulting directors. There are no decisions of our Courts precisely in point but it appears to me that an application of the principles of our law produces a similar result.

[The learned judge proceeded to say that even if the views which he had expressed as to the recoverability of the R112 219,44 from B were wrong, the exception failed on another ground.] ... The company parted with R112 219,14 in exchange for an unenforceable claim against B. *Prima facie* that sum represents the company's loss, which was directly caused by the breach of duty on the part of the directors. The question whether the amount claimed, or any part thereof, could be recovered from B in a suit based on some other cause of action is not germane to the issue whether the pleading on which the plaintiff has based the action of his choice is excipiable.

NOTES

R C Beuthin 1973 *Annual Survey* 234–5 considers that the real problem in *Bay Loan Investments* was one of severance. See also *Karroo Auctions (Pty) Ltd v Hersman* 1951 (2) SA 33 (E) where the court drew a distinction between an executory and an executed contract (doubtful whether this case can still be regarded as good law); *R v Herholdt* 1957 (3) SA 236 (AD) where the company gave indirect assistance to a purchaser of its shares by interposing an intermediary; *Lindner v Vogtmannsberger* 1965 (4) SA 108 (O): 'section only contravened if, upon scrutiny of the transaction as a whole, it appears that financial assistance has been given to the purchaser of the shares . . .' (per De Villiers J at 112); and *Miller v Muller* 1965 (4) SA 458 (C) where Corbett J said (at 466): 'In deciding whether financial assistance has been given the courts have enquired as to whether the company has been impoverished as a result of the transaction. . . .'

In *Saambou Nasionale Bouvereniging: Ex parte Stuart v Ligatex (Pty) Ltd* 1976 (1) SA 868 (C) there were two separate transactions: a loan agreement under which the defendant company incurred a liability of R85 000 to the plaintiff, and in return received the full R85 000; and a second agreement by which the directors of the company, in contravention of s 86*bis*(2) (now s 38) utilized the funds so acquired to finance the purchase of their shares in the company. The court held, on the facts, that the loan contract was entirely separate from the illegal agreement and could therefore be enforced.

This should be compared with *Goss v E C Goss & Co (Pty) Ltd* 1970 (1) SA 602 (D), where the court held that the two transactions in question were not severable.

See further *Crispette & Candy Co Ltd v Michaelis NO* 1948 (1) SA 404 (W); *Pires v American Fruit Market (Pty) Ltd* 1952 (2) SA 337 (T); *Harrison v Harrison* 1952 (3) SA 417 (N); *Straiton v Cleanwell Dryers (Pvt) Ltd* 1960 (1) SA 355 (SR); *London Ranch (in liquidation) v Hyreb Estate* 1963 (2) SA 570 (E) at 573–4; *Secretary for Inland Revenue v Smant* 1973 (1) 754 (AD), a tax case, discussed by E B Broomberg (1973) 90 *SALJ* 127; and *S v Hepker* 1973 (1) SA 472 (W) at 478–80 (discussed by R C Beuthin (1973) 90 *SALJ* 211 and 1973 *Annual Survey* 256–8.

In England there has been a turn-about. In *Victor Battery Co Ltd v Curry's Ltd* [1946] Ch 242, [1946] 1 All ER 519 the court decided that where a company gives by means of a security, which in that case was a debenture, financial assistance for the purchase of its own shares, the security is valid and enforceable.

In *Selangor United Rubber Estates Ltd v Cradock (No 3)* [1968] 1 WLR 1555, [1968] 2 All ER 1073 (Ch) Ungoed Thomas J took a different view. He held that a transaction in contravention of s 54 (s 38 of our Act) is not only a criminal offence but, in accordance with principle, void. This was followed in *Heald v O'Connor* [1971] 1 WLR 497, [1971] 1 All ER 1105, where the court held that a debenture given by a company as security for moneys lent to enable a person to purchase shares in the company, in contravention of s 54, was illegal and void, and that it made no difference in this respect whether the giving of the security was *ultra vires* the company or not.

Curtis's Furnishing Stores Ltd v Freedman [1966] 2 All ER 955 confirms that the test is whether or no the company has become poorer as a result of the transaction. Thus, if a company, in order to allow a sale of its shares to go through, releases a debt owing to it by the seller without receiving adequate consideration, the transaction is hit by the prohibition.

Curtis's case also supports the proposition that directors who act in contravention of the provision render themselves personally liable. Cross J said (at 960): 'If a director who is about to retire and sell his shares makes a bargain with his intended successors and the purchasers of his shares that when they are in control of the company they will procure it to make a present to him out of its assets and this is done, the recipient is in my judgment as guilty of misfeasance as the directors who actually procure the company to make the gift.'

The loans to the trustees in *Hogg* v *Cramphorn Ltd, 227* below, were not hit by the prohibition, because they fell within the exception of s 54(1)(*b*) (s 38(2)(*b*) of our Act).

In Australia it is settled law now that transactions in contravention of the provision corresponding to s 54 of the English Act are invalid, see Reginald Barrett (1974) 48 *SALJ* 6.

In Canada, the position is the same. Thus, in *Murray and Murray* v *C W Boon & Co Ltd* [1974] 2 WWR 620 (Alta), where the company had granted a chattel mortgage of its assets to secure the purchase price of its shares, the court held that the transaction was *ultra vires* and the chattel mortgage invalid.

It does not, apparently, amount to a contravention of s 54 if the buyer of a company's shares uses a dividend declared by the company to repay moneys borrowed by him to pay for the shares, *Re Wellington Publishing Co Ltd* [1973] 1 NZLR 133, noted by Francis Dawson (1974) 90 *LQR* 452. See also *Weinberg on Take-overs and Mergers* 3 ed (1971) para 1807.

On giving financial assistance in connection with a 'take-over' bid, see J H Farrar in *New Law Journal* (1967), 565, 593, and R C Beuthin (1968) 85 *SALJ* 194.

III ALLOTMENT OF SHARES

A TEXT

Allotment is the appropriation of shares to a person by the company. The practice used to be to leave the allotment of shares entirely to the board of directors, but s 221 now provides that notwithstanding anything contained in its memorandum or articles, the directors of a company shall not have the power to allot or issue shares without the prior approval of the company in general meeting. This approval may take either the form of a general authority to the directors to allot or issue shares in their discretion or of a specific authority in respect of any particular allotment or issue, s 221(2). In the former case, the general rule applies that directors must exercise discretionary powers entrusted to them in the best interests of the company, p 388 below.

Section 222 imposes important restrictions on the allotment of shares to a director or his nominee, or to a body controlled by a director or his nominee.

The contract of allotment is concluded by offer and acceptance. Where the application for shares is made by post the contract becomes binding when the notice of allotment is posted to the applicant, unless he has agreed to dispense with notice: *130–133*. The allottee becomes a member of the company when his name is entered on the register, s 103: *134*. As to register and return of allotments, s 93. Failure to keep a register or make a return of allotments does not affect their validity:

Moosa v *Lalloo* 1957 (4) SA 207 (N) at 220. As to the correction of an incorrect return of allotment, see *Ex parte Northern Transvaal (Messina) Copper Exploration Ltd* 1938 WLD 258. See also *Ex parte Keir & Cawder (South Africa) Ltd* 1968 (2) SA 207 (T), where the company had made a return of allotment, without regard to s 70*dec* [now s 222]. The court under s 32 [now s 115] approved the cancellation of the original form and the lodging of a new correct form.

At common law an application for shares may be withdrawn prior to allotment: *135*. The allottee can repudiate the contract if he was induced by misrepresentation to subscribe for his shares: *136*.

A company issuing a prospectus may not proceed to allotment until the minimum subscription has been received, ss 165, 167. Application forms for shares offered to the public must have the prospectus attached to them, ss 166, 167.

No company may allot shares offered to the public unless the application for the shares is received before the expiration of a period of four months after the registration of the prospectus, s 164. Where a prospectus is issued generally (see above p 108) no allotment may be made until the third day after the day on which the prospectus is first issued ('opening of the subscription lists') or such later time (if any) as may be specified in the prospectus, s 168. An application for shares which is made in pursuance of an offer made generally is not revocable before the expiration of the third day after the opening of the subscription lists, or the giving of a public notice before the third day under s 160 having the effect of excluding or limiting the liability of the person giving such notice, s 168(4). Where the prospectus states that application has been made or will be made for the shares offered thereon to be dealt in on a stock exchange, any allotment of shares is conditional on a listing being granted, s 169.

An irregular allotment may be validated by the court, s 97.

Subject to exceptions, shares may not be issued at a discount, ss 80, 81: *137, 138*. Shares having no par value of a class already issued may not be issued at a price lower than an amount arrived at by dividing that part of the stated share capital contributed by already issued shares of that class unless the issue price is authorized by a special resolution, s 82(1); but see also (4).

Shares may be issued at a premium. A sum equal to the aggregate amount of the premiums must be transferred to the 'share premium account', which may only be reduced in accordance with the provisions applicable to the reduction of capital, s 76(1): *139*. This applies also in respect of share premium funds accumulated before the 1973 Act came into force, s 76(4) and (5). The share premium account may, however, be applied by the company in paying up unissued shares to be issued to members as fully paid capitalization shares, or in providing for the premium payable on redemption of any redeemable preference shares or of any debentures of the company, or in writing off the expenses or commission or discount referred to in s 76(3). A company is under no duty to issue shares at the best price, as long as there is no breach of the fiduciary duties of the directors or fraud on the minority: *140.*

Capitalization or bonus shares may only be issued (*a*) in respect of a commission authorized by the Act; (*b*) by way of capitalization of profits; (*c*) out of a capital redemption reserve fund, s 98(4); or (*d*) out of a share premium account, s 76(3) (cf *In re Eddystone Marine Insurance Co* [1893] 3 Ch 9; *Swan Brewery Company Ltd* v *R* [1914] AC 231 (PC)). For taxation purposes the application of profits towards bonus shares may be equivalent to the distribution of a dividend: *CIR* v *Legal and General Assurance Society Ltd* 1963 (3) SA 876 (AD).

Shares may not be allotted unless the issue price has been paid in full, either in cash or for a consideration other than cash: *141, 142.* Where shares are allotted otherwise than for cash, the contracts must be lodged with the Registrar, s 93(2), (3)(*b*) (see also Schedule 3 para 11).

A company may not give financial assistance to a subscriber for its own shares (see pp 214 above).

Where an issue is underwritten, the requirements of s 153 must be complied with. (As to underwriting commission, see s 80 and Schedule 3 paras 14 and 15.) And where shares are to be traded in on a stock exchange application for a listing must be made to the stock exchange concerned. Modern company practice favours selling shares through a bank or issuing house, private placings and, where the company has already been in business for some time, 'rights issues' (on 'rights offers', 'letters of allocation', and prospectus, see pp 108–9 above).

B CASES

[130] Nicol's case: Tufnell & Ponsonby's case
(1885) 29 ChD 421

CHITTY J: There is no difference, as has been often pointed out, between a contract to take shares and any other contract. What is termed 'allotment' is generally neither more nor less than the acceptance of the company of the offer to take shares. To take the common case, the offer is to take a certain number of shares, or such a less number of shares as may be allotted. That offer is accepted by the allotment either of the total number mentioned in the offer or a less number, to be taken by the person who made the offer. This constitutes a binding contract to take that number according to the offer and acceptance. To my mind there is no magic whatever in the term 'allotment' as used in these circumstances. It is said that the allotment is an appropriation of a specific number of shares. It is an appropriation, not of specific shares, but of a certain number of shares. It does not, however, make the person who has thus agreed to take the shares a member from that moment; all that it does is simply this—it constitutes a binding contract under which the company is bound to make a complete allotment of the specified number of shares, and under which the person who has made the offer and is now bound by the acceptance is bound to take that particular number of shares.

[131] Household Fire Insurance Company *v* Grant
(1879) 4 Ex D 216

THESIGER LJ: In this case the defendant made an application for shares in the plaintiff's company under circumstances from which we must imply that he authorized the company, in the event of their allotting to him the shares applied for, to send the notice of allotment by post. The company did allot him the shares, and duly addressed to him and posted a letter containing the notice of allotment, but upon the finding of the jury it must be taken that the letter never reached its destination. In this state of circumstances, Lopes J has decided that the defendant is liable as a shareholder. . . . I am of the opinion that he did so rightly. . . .

. . . Now, whatever in abstract discussion may be said as to the legal notion of its being necessary, in order to the effecting of a valid and binding contract, that the minds of the parties should be brought together at one and the same moment, that notion is practically the foundation of English law upon the subject of the formation of contracts. Unless, therefore, a contract constituted by correspondence is absolutely concluded at the moment that the continuing offer is accepted by the person to whom the offer is addressed, it is difficult to see how the two minds are ever to be brought together at one and the same moment. . . . But on the other hand it is a principle of law, as well established as the legal notion to which I have referred, that the minds of the two parties must be brought together by mutual communication. An acceptance, which only remains in the breast of the acceptor without being actually and by legal implication communicated to the offerer, is no binding acceptance. How then are these elements of law to be harmonized in the case of contracts formed by correspondence through the post? I see no better mode than that of treating the post office as the agent of both parties. . . . But if the post office be such common agent, then it seems to me to follow that, as soon as the letter of acceptance is delivered to the post office, the contract is made as complete and final and absolutely binding as if the acceptor had put his letter into the hands of a messenger sent by the offerer himself as his agent to deliver the offer and receive the acceptance. . . .

. . . How then can a casualty in the post, whether resulting in delay, which in commercial transactions is often as bad as no delivery, or in non-delivery, unbind the parties or unmake the contract? To me it appears that in practice a contract complete upon the acceptance of an offer being posted, but liable to be put an end to by an accident in the post, would be more mischievous than a contract only binding upon the parties to it upon the acceptance actually reaching the offerer, and I can see no principle of law from which such an anomalous contract can be deduced. . . .

[Baggallay LJ arrived at the same result, but Bramwell LJ dissented.]

[132] McKenzie *v* Farmers' Co-operative Meat Industries Ltd
1922 AD 16

MAASDORP JA: . . . Now if we consider the circumstances surrounding the transaction in question, we find that the letter of application for shares was in the following terms: 'I hereby apply for 100 shares of one pound each in the above company, payable 2*s* on application, 2*s* on allotment and the balance as may be requested, for which I enclose cheque. I agree to accept the above number of shares or any lesser number that may be allotted to me and to abide by the articles of association which I authorize you to sign on my behalf.'

Here we have the expressed intention on the part of the defendant that the company should on receipt of his application forthwith proceed to allot shares to him and that their secretary should sign the articles on his behalf. This is wholly inconsistent with an intention that the contract should not be binding on the defendant until he received notice of acceptance. It was laid down in the case of *Nel* v *The King*, decided by this court in May 1921, that although it is a general rule that it is necessary that the communication of an acceptance should be made to the offeror in order to effect a contract, it is clear that it is competent for the latter to dispense with such a notification, either expressly or impliedly, and to notify the manner in which the acceptance may be manifested.

In the present case the defendant dispensed with the communication of acceptance as an essential to the conclusion of the contract by requesting the plaintiff to allot the shares to him upon receiving the application. By such allotment the plaintiff manifested his acceptance of the application, and he did so in the manner indicated by the defendant. . . .

[133] Pretorius *v* Natal South Sea Investment Trust
1965 (3) SA 410 (W)

VIEYRA J: The respondent is a public company incorporated . . . on 2 June 1961. The object of the company was to erect blocks of flats on an area of ground in the holiday resort known as Margate on the Natal south coast and to give shareholders rights of occupation to specified flats, so far as legally possible, on the same basis as if they held the *dominium* thereof. The capital is R1 325 divided into 1 250 management shares of 10c each and 1 200 shares of R1 each. Included in the latter are groups of nine shares, each group entitling the holder to exercise rights of occupation to a particular flat. The first directors and the only ones ever to have been appointed are one Eliasov and one Mueller.

As a result of Eliasov's activities, several persons in Rhodesia, including the applicants, were induced to take steps to acquire shares in the respondent company so as to become entitled to flats in the proposed building. In respect of each flat the following documents had to be signed:

(*a*) an offer to purchase the shares addressed to the respondent, irrevocable for a period of fifteen days;

(*b*) an undertaking to observe various conditions in respect of the occupancy of the flat;

(*c*) an authorization to let the flat and apply rentals in reduction of the applicant's indebtedness, as also a mandate to furnish the flat for a sum of R600, payable on call;

(*d*) a statement in lieu of prospectus.

The applicants executed these documents about the end of May 1962, and a cheque for £4 820 was handed over to Eliasov, made up of four deposits of £905 on each of the flats and £300 in respect of furniture for each one. A promissory note, payable in May 1963, for £10 500, was handed over for the balance. In June 1962 copies of all documents were returned to the applicants, the offer to purchase the shares showing a purported acceptance by the respondent signed by Mueller, as director. By this time building operations on the site in question had already been commenced by South Coast Builders and Contractors (Pty) Ltd, which was subsequently responsible for placing the company under judicial management. These operations continued until December 1962 when they ceased prior to completion because of defaults by the respondent.

Despite the purported acceptance of the offer to purchase shares, no formal allotment of shares was made until 19 August 1963 when at a meeting of directors appropriate resolutions were passed to that end. The fact of the passing of these resolutions was at no time communicated to the applicants. On 1 October 1963, the respondent was placed under a final order of judicial management.

Turning now to the first submission made on behalf of the applicants, the argument runs as follows. The offer to purchase shares was at no time accepted by the respondent. The purported acceptance in June 1962 was of no avail because the acceptance was by one director only, and there is no resolution of the board of two directors appointing one of them as manager or managing director or delegating powers to one of them in terms of the relevant regulations of the articles of the respondent company. The allotment eventually made was out of time, the offer having by then lapsed, nor did that purport to be a ratification of the purported acceptance by Mueller. Finally even if the allotment was timeously made and constituted an acceptance it was at no time communicated to the offerors.

Eliasov . . . says that Mueller was at all material times duly authorized to accept the offer to take shares on behalf of the company. . . . Mueller supports this allegation. Neither Mueller nor Eliasov states when and in what form the authority contended for was granted. The articles of the company require decisions to be taken at meetings of the board, save that a resolution in writing signed by both directors shall be as effective as if passed at a meeting. There is no minute of any meeting clothing Mueller with the authority he claims, nor is there any signed resolution to the same effect. Accordingly the purported acceptance is of no avail.

Regarding the allotment, as stated by Baggallay LJ in *Re Scottish Petroleum* (1883) 23 ChD 413 (CA) at 430:

'To constitute a binding contract to take shares in a company where such contract is based upon application and allotment it is necessary that there should be an application by the intending shareholders, an allotment by the directors of the company of the shares applied for, and a communication by the directors to the applicant of the fact of such allotment having been made.'

See also *Ex parte The Master* 1913 TPD 38 at 41. Accordingly, quite apart from the question as to whether the offer had lapsed because of the effluxion of a reasonable time, the failure in this case to communicate the fact of allotment to the applicants is fatal to a reliance on such allotment being an acceptance of the offer.

But despite the correctness of these submissions there is still room in the circumstances of the present matter for the view that the manifestation of mutual assent required for a valid agreement . . . has occurred by conduct of the parties. It is to be noted that between the time that the applicants signed the offers to take shares and the date when they for the first time raised the point that no contract had been entered into there is a lapse of some fifteen months. During that period the money paid on account of the purchase price of the shares as also in respect of the furniture for the flats had been received by the respondent and had not been returned. The promissory note had also been received and presented for payment. This conduct by itself might well be construed as consistent only with an intention on the part of the directors to accept the offers, for it appears to be unequivocal: It would be difficult to explain the failure to return the money and promissory note on any other basis. This manifestation was not hidden from the applicants. They were fully aware thereof and yet made no demur nor asked for a return of their money.

[The application of the applicants for the removal of their names from the register of shareholders by way of rectification under s 32 was accordingly refused.]

NOTES

See further *Moosa v Lalloo* 1957 (4) SA 207 (N) at 219, per Caney J: 'An allotment, by which shares are acquired from a company, is a contract. Although a share is created and comes into existence upon its original issue by the company, and not before issue (with the consequence that he who subscribes for it does not purchase it from the company), the right to it springs from offer and acceptance. No ceremonious ritual, nor any magic formula, is required for the process of allotting the share. It may be effected by way of offer on the part of the company to the allottee, accepted by him, or, as is more usual, by way of offer (an application for shares) by him, accepted on behalf of the company; a contract of allotment may be effected in any manner in which a contract may be concluded, even by implication from conduct. . . .' When a company has dealt with the authorized number of shares, its powers of allotment and issue are exhausted, and any shares issued beyond that number are a nullity: *Moosa v Lalloo (supra)* at 224.

Application and allotment must agree in terms: 'There can be no proper allotment until either the special terms contained in the application have been accepted by the directors, or until the allotment on terms different from those in the application has been accepted by the applicant': per Solomon JA in *Whittle v Henley NO* 1924 AD 138 at 148. Thus, where an application is made subject to a condition there is no contract unless the condition is accepted—see *Ex parte the Master: In re Niagara Ltd (in liquidation)* 1913 TPD 38. Unless the allotment is made within a reasonable time, the applicant is not bound to accept the shares.

In *Raubenheimer v Palmer* 1934 WLD 170 an unrehabilitated insolvent had entered into a contract to take shares. Without deciding whether the contract was initially valid, the court held that he was a member of the company since, on the facts, both he and the company had confirmed the allotment after his rehabilitation.

An irregular or *ultra vires* allotment is void, or at least voidable. See *Ex parte Gunn NO: In re Contributories of Krog Engineering (Pty) Ltd (in liquidation)* 1965 (3) SA 231 (O), where it was held that in the event of the allotment being *ultra vires*, the allottee escapes liability for calls. In *Thole v Trans-Drakensberg Bank Ltd* 1967 (2) SA 214 (N) the articles limited the shares any member might hold to 5 000. Shares in excess of that number were issued to the plaintiff. The court ordered rectification of the register. (Cf *In re Homer District Consolidated Gold Mines* (1888) 39 ChD 546; *In re Portuguese Consolidated Copper Mines* (1889) 42 ChD 160.) Where only the procedure followed is irregular, the defect can be cured by subsequent ratification by the board of directors; see *Meaker v Boere Saamwerk Bpk* 1930 EDL 127. An allotment improperly made by the directors is capable of ratification by the shareholders: *Bamford v Bamford* [1968] 2 All ER 655, noted by K W Wedderburn (1968) 31 *MLR* 688.

An agreement to take shares must be distinguished from an agreement to place shares: *Gorrissen's* case (1873) 8 Ch App 507.

On the principle that where an offer is made through the post, a contract comes into being as soon as the acceptance is posted, see *Cape Explosives Works Ltd v South African Oil and Fat Industries Ltd* 1921 CPD 244; *Kerguelen Sealing and Whaling Co Ltd v CIR* 1939 AD 487.

The company must prove that notice of allotment has been posted to the applicant. *Adamanta Diamond Mining Company Ltd v Smythe* (1883) 1 HCG 406.

See further *Betz v Worcester Exploration and Gold Mining Co* (1888) 6 SC 79; *Rissik v Liquidators of the Olifant's Vlei Gold Mining Co Ltd* (1894) 1 Off Rep 255; *Botha v Myburgh, Krone en Kie Bpk (in liquidation)* 1923 CPD 482; *Union Rhodesia Wholesale Ltd v Becker* 1926 EDL 314; *SA Tungsten Mines Ltd (in liquidation) v Van Zyl* 1928 CPD 122; also, *Fern Gold Mining Co v Tobias* (1890) 3 SAR 134.

[134] **Doornkop Sugar Estates Ltd *v* Maxwell**
1926 WLD 127

FEETHAM J: . . . It is the entry on the register which makes a person who has agreed to take shares a member of a company.

An allotment is only made complete by the entry upon the register of the name of the person to whom the company has agreed to make the allotment. . . .

NOTES

Though entry upon the share register is required to make the allottee a member of the company, the contract of allotment is complete as soon as the offer to take shares has been accepted and the allottee has the rights inherent in his shares: *Moosa v Lallo* 1957 (4) SA 207 (N) at 221, 222.

[135] *In re* **London and Northern Bank:** *Ex parte* **Jones**
[1900] 1 Ch 220

COZENS-HARDY J: It is settled law that an offer is to be deemed accepted when the letter of acceptance is posted. . . . The withdrawal, in order to be effectual, must be before the offer is clinched by the posting of the letter of acceptance. The question I have to decide is this—was the letter of allotment posted before the letter withdrawing the offer was received by the company?

NOTES

See further *International Diamond Mining Co, De Beer's Mine (Ltd) v Webster* (1882) 2 EDC 131; *Fern Gold Mining Co v Tobias* (1890) 3 SAR 134; *African Finance and Investments Ltd v Van der Spuy* 1920 CPD 596.

[136] Adamanta Diamond Mining Company *v* Wege
(1883) 2 HCG 172

LAURENCE J: I concur in the Judge-President's expression of regret that in this case it is impossible for the court, on the facts proved, to relieve the defendant from the liabilities arising out of his contract with the plaintiff company. There can be little doubt, I think, from the facts disclosed in this and in another case in which the same company brought a similar action, that the late Mr Richter, who was at once a vendor, promoter, director and secretary, did make certain representations as to the prospects of the company which influenced many persons, including the present defendant, in applying for shares, and that those representations—whether owing to the failure of subscribers to pay their calls and thus supply the necessary working capital, or for other reasons—have up to the present time remained unfulfilled. It is also possible that Mr Wege, living as he did in the country and only occasionally visiting Kimberley, regarded these shares as a genuine investment, and did not apply for them merely for speculative purposes. . . .

. . . For the defence to succeed, the defendant must show firstly that misrepresentations of such a nature as to render voidable a contract induced thereby were made by the plaintiff company, or its authorized representative; secondly, that in point of fact he was induced by those misrepresentations to enter into the contract; thirdly, that there has been no subsequent *laches* or acquiescence on his part disentitling him to relief. Now the defendant has not satisfied me on any of these points. . . . The statements made by Richter no doubt depicted the prospects of the company, as is usual in such cases, in a sort of hue of *couleur de rose*; but I cannot say that any positive misrepresentation has been proved. . . .

NOTES

See also *Thesse* v *Woodstock Sweets Co Ltd* 1915 CPD 594; *Pathescope (Union) of South Africa Ltd* v *Mallinick* 1927 AD 292; *Meskin* v *Anglo-American Corporation of SA Ltd* 1968 (4) SA 793 (W).

The fact that a shareholder made a mistake as to the effect of the allotment—he thought mistakenly that there would be no liability in regard to the shares—does not justify repudiation: *Estate Boyce* v *East Rand Greyhound Racing Association (Pty) Ltd* 1939 WLD 332. Nor is repudiation justified on the ground that a share certificate shows the nominal capital incorrectly: *Agricultural Co-operative Union Ltd* v *Chadwick* (1922) 43 NLR 135: 'The most that could be claimed . . . is a certificate correctly reflecting the capital of the company': per Dove Wilson JP (at 136). But see also *Burstein* v *Mindel* 1959 (2) SA 56 (SR).

In *Tiger-Eye Investments (Pty) Ltd* v *Riverview Diamond Fields (Pty) Ltd* 1971 (1) SA 351 (C) the court found that the second appellant had allotted shares to the first appellant in fraud of the respondent's prior rights to the shares. It confirmed the decision of the trial court setting aside the allotment to the first appellant and directed the second appellant to reallot the shares to the respondent.

[137] Ooregum Gold Mining Company of India Ltd *v* Roper
[1892] AC 125

A company which was in want of money and whose original shares stood at a discount issued preference shares of £1 each with 15*s* credited as paid, leaving a liability of 5*s* per share. The House of Lords held that the issue was beyond the company's powers.

LORD MACNAGHTEN: My Lords, your Lordships are called upon to determine whether it is or is not competent for a company limited by shares to issue shares at a discount so as to relieve persons taking shares so issued from liability to pay up their amount in full. It was suggested that different considerations might apply to shares in the capital with which a company is originally registered and shares in additional capital created afterwards. But it seems to me to be perfectly clear that, for the present purpose, no distinction can be drawn between one portion of the capital of a company limited by shares and another.

The question turns upon the construction of the Companies Act 1862. The provisions of the Act are, I think, plain enough if one bears in mind the condition of things which existed before the principle of limited liability was introduced in 1855. Before that time there was no way known to the law by which persons trading in partnership could restrict their liability. They were liable to the uttermost farthing. At last the legislature intervened and authorized persons who proposed to trade in partnership to form themselves into a registered company with a declared capital and shares of a fixed amount, and then limited the liability of the partners as members of the company to the amount unpaid upon their shares.

But all this legislation proceeds on the footing of recognizing and maintaining the liability of the individual members to the company until the prescribed limit is reached. The memorandum of association of a company limited by shares must contain 'the amount of capital with which the company proposes to be registered divided into shares of a certain fixed amount'. It must also contain 'a declaration that the liability of the members is limited'. Neither the liability nor the limitation is defined in the memorandum itself. And so the declaration carries you back to the earlier part of the section, where you are told what is meant by 'a company limited by shares'. It is a company 'formed on the principle of having the liability of its members limited to the amount unpaid upon their shares'. That must mean that the liability of a member continues so long as anything remains unpaid upon his shares. Nothing but payment and payment in full can put an end to the liability. . . .

To sum the matter up, I cannot, I think, do better than adopt the language Mr Buckley has used in speaking of the Limited Liability Acts. 'The dominant and cardinal principle of these Acts', he says, 'is that the investor shall purchase immunity from liability beyond a certain limit, on the terms that there shall be and remain a liability up to that limit.' Whether this liability is one of 'the conditions of the memorandum', within the meaning of that expression in the Act of 1862, as Lord Selborne seems to have thought (*Dent's* case (1873) 8 Ch App 768), or a condition attached by the Act to a company limited by shares and of the essence of such a company, though it may not be found contained within the four corners of the memorandum, is a matter of little or no importance. In either view of the case it is plain that the condition is one which cannot be dispensed with by anything in the articles of association, or by any resolution of the company, or by any contract between the company and outsiders who have been invited to become members of the company and who do come in on the faith of such a contract. . . .

[138] Welton v Saffery
[1897] AC 299

A company issued shares at a discount, being authorized by its articles to do so. The company was wound up in due course and it was found possible to pay the debts and the costs of liquidation out of its assets. The House of Lords held (Lord Herschell dissenting) that the holders of the shares issued at a discount were liable to pay the amounts unpaid on their shares for the adjustment of the rights of contributories *inter se*.

LORD HALSBURY LC: My Lords, in respect of the liability to pay up the shares so far as it is necessary to satisfy creditors and the cost of winding-up, I believe no doubt exists in the minds of any of your Lordships. Since the *Ooregum* case [*137*, above], in this House it would be impossible to contend that that question is not covered by authority. But it is said that, where the only object in making a call is to settle the rights of the shareholders *inter se*, the law laid down in the *Ooregum* case does not conclude the question.

My Lords, I am unable to accede to that view. I think the legislature, in permitting the existence of a company limited by shares and with limited liability, created a machinery which makes it impossible by any expedient, either by company or shareholder, to act otherwise than in pursuance of the provisions of the statute. Whether for the purpose of settling the rights *inter se*, or for the purpose of satisfying creditors, it appears to me that the statute enforces upon company and shareholder alike conformity to the rule laid down, that a share for a fixed amount shall make the person agreeing to take that share liable for that amount. . . .

NOTES

In *Liquidator Seta Diamonds Ltd* v *Knox* 1915 WLD 109 the company issued in exchange for 20 000 shares of 5s each 20 000 new shares of £1 each without any payment by the shareholders. It was held that those who, with knowledge of the facts, took new for old shares, were liable on winding-up for the unpaid balance of 15s per share. See further *In re Weymouth and Channel Islands Steam Packet Co* [1891] 1 Ch 66; *Hirsche* v *Sims* [1894] AC 654 (directors answerable to company for allotting shares at a discount); *Hilder* v *Dexter* [1902] AC 474 (*140* below); *In re Development Company of Central and West Africa* [1902] 1 Ch 547; *In re White Star Line Ltd* [1938] Ch 458, [1938] 1 All ER 607; *In re Derham and Allen Ltd* [1946] Ch 31.

Debentures may be issued at a discount, but the issue of debentures at a discount may not be used as an indirect means of issuing shares at a discount: *Mosely* v *Koffyfontein Mines Ltd* [1904] 2 Ch 108.

If a man agrees to accept shares at a discount he cannot subsequently obtain removal of his name from the share register even if he was not aware of the legal consequences. But if he agrees to accept fully paid shares and shares are issued to him at a discount, he may repudiate the contract: *Burstein* v *Mindel* 1959 (2) SA 56 (SR).

[139] Henry Head & Company Ltd v Ropner Holdings Ltd
[1952] Ch 124, [1951] 2 All ER 994

HARMAN J: The defendant company is what is popularly known as a holding company and was incorporated at the end of 1948, having as its first and paramount object the acquisition for amalgamation purposes of two shipping companies formerly carried on separately under the same management. The amalgamation was of the simplest kind. The shareholders in the two companies were willing to sell their shares in the two companies in exchange for shares in the holding company. At that point there arose the question of the rate of capitalization. Sometimes this figure is a merely nominal figure; at other times it is designed to reflect the true value of the assets being acquired. In the present case a valuation of the assets of the two companies was procured from a firm of accountants. No doubt those calculations were based on information given by persons having a knowledge of shipping, a know-ledge which accountants would not have, and they merely valued the physical assets of the two companies, leaving out questions of profit-earning capacity, goodwill and so forth. They then apparently arrived at a value of the assets of each of the constituent companies and advised that the one having slightly larger assets than the other should issue by way of capital profit dividend a sufficient sum to its shareholders to reduce the value of the assets to an equality with the other company.

At that point it was possible to advise, and the advice was given, that a pound-for-pound capitalization—that is to say, a pound of the new company's shares for a pound's worth, nominal, of the constituent company's shares—was a fair method of performing the amalgamation. Accordingly, there was issued in the aggregate to the shareholders in the two companies the entire authorized capital of the holding company, which was £1 759 606. That did not, however, do anything more than represent the aggregate of the nominal value of the shares of the con-stituent companies. The real value of the shares was, if the valuation was right, approximately £5 000 000 in excess of that sum. The issuing company has therefore acquired for its shares assets worth between six and seven millions, if that valuation be, as I think I must suppose it to be for these purposes, a true reflection of the value of the assets acquired at the time of their acquisition. When the balance sheet of the holding company appears for the year ended 31 March 1949, one finds on the left-hand side the issued capital set out, and below that, under the words Capital Reserve, Share Premium Account (less formation expenses), rather over £5 000 000. On the other side is stated the value of the shares in the subsidiary companies as valued in the way I have mentioned, and they are valued at rather under £7 000 000. When the consolidated balance sheet is looked at, a rather more express statement is found, namely: share premium account, being the excess of the value of the net assets of subsidiary companies at the date of acquisition over the book value of the investments (less formation expenses); and that is what this £5 000 000 figure is.

The directors have been advised that they are bound to show their accounts in that way, and, not only they, but the plaintiffs, who are large shareholders, regard that as a very undesirable thing, because it fixes an unfortunate kind of rigidity on the structure of the company, having regard to the fact that an account kept under that name, namely, the share premium account, can only have anything paid out of it by means of a transaction analogous to a reduction of capital. It is, in effect, as if the company had originally been capitalized at approximately £7 000 000 instead of £1 750 000.

The question which I have to determine is whether the defendants were obliged to keep their account in that way. That depends purely on s 56 of the Companies Act 1948 [corresponding to s 76 of our Act]. . . . [Under that section] the share premium account can be distributed in the same restricted way and with the same leave of the court as if paid-up share capital was being returned to the shareholders.

Counsel for the plaintiff company asks who would suppose that a common type of transaction of the sort now under consideration was the issue of shares at a premium and says that nobody in the city or in the commercial world would dream of so describing it. It is with a sense of shock at first that one hears that this transaction was the issue of shares at a premium. Everybody, I suppose, who hears those words thinks of a company which, being in a strong trading position, wants further capital and puts forward its shares for the subscription of the public at such a price as the market in those shares justifies, whatever it may be, 30s a £1 share, £5 a £1 share, or any price obtainable; and the 10s or £4 above the nominal value of a share which it acquires as a result of the transaction is no doubt a premium. That is what is ordinarily meant by the issue of shares at a premium. The first words of ss (1) are: 'Where a company issues shares at a premium.' If the words had stopped there, one might have said that the subsection merely refers to cash transactions of that sort, but it goes on to say 'whether for cash or otherwise'.

What 'otherwise' can there be? It must be a consideration other than cash, namely, goods or assets of some physical sort. Continuing, the subsection contains the words 'a sum equal to the aggregate amount or value of the premiums on those shares shall be transferred to an account, to be called "the share premium account" '. Apparently, if the shares are issued for a consideration other than cash and the value of the assets acquired is more than the nominal value of the shares issued, you have issued shares at a premium; and I think that counsel for the plaintiff company was constrained to admit that, in the ordinary case, that was so. This subsection at least has that much result; but he says that the line must be drawn somewhere. It cannot apply, he says, where the issuing company has no assets at all other than the assets which it will acquire as the price of the issue of shares. 'Premium' (he argues) means something resulting from the excess value of its already existing assets over the nominal value of its shares. I am much attracted by that. I have every desire to reduce the effect of this section to what I cannot help thinking would be more reasonable limits, but I do not see my way to limiting it in that way. It is not stated to be a section which only applies after the company has been in existence a year, or after the company has acquired assets, or when the company is a going concern, or which does not apply on the occasion of a holding company buying shares on an amalgamation. Whether that is an oversight on the part of the legislature, or whether it was intended to produce the effect it seems to have produced, it is not for me to speculate. All I can say is that this transaction seems to me to come within the words of the section, and I do not see my way to holding as a matter of construction that it is outside it. If that is so, the inevitable result is that the action must fail.

NOTES

See also *In re Duff's Settlements* [1951] Ch 923, [1951] 2 All ER 534. Utilization of the share premium account for writing off a portion of the consideration paid by the company in acquiring shares in its subsidiaries does not fall within any of the exceptions in s 86*quat*(2) (now s 76): *Ex parte National Packaging Co Ltd* 1965 (1) SA 542 (W).

[140] Hilder *v* Dexter
[1902] AC 474

In order to raise capital, a company offered shares at par to the appellant and certain other persons, with an option to take further shares at par within a certain time. The appellant subscribed for shares. The market price having risen to a premium, he desired to exercise his option to take further shares. The House of Lords, reversing the decision of the Court of Appeal, decided that this was not a forbidden application of shares or capital money directly or indirectly in payment of commission, discount or allowance within the meaning of s 8(2) of the Companies Act 1900 (UK) (corresponding to s 80 of the 1973 Act).

LORD DAVEY: It [s 8(2)] is in the following terms:

'(2) Save as aforesaid no company shall apply any of its shares or capital money either directly or indirectly in payment of any commission, discount, or allowance to any person in consideration of his subscribing or agreeing to subscribe, whether absolutely or conditionally, for any shares of the company. . . .'

. . . The first words to be construed are, 'apply any of its shares or capital money'. I think that those words naturally mean apply its capital, either in the form of shares before issue, when they may be described as potential capital, or in the form of money derived from the issue of its shares. 'In payment of any commission, discount, or allowance': I think this means payment by the company. The words 'discount or allowance' seem to mean the same thing, namely, a rebate on what would justly be due from the subscriber on his shares. The advantage which the appellant will derive from the exercise of his option is certainly not a 'discount or allowance', because he will have to pay 20*s* in the pound for every share. Nor is it, in my opinion, a commission paid by the company, for the company will not part with any portion of its capital which is received by it intact, or indeed with any moneys belonging to it. But the words relied on are, 'either directly or indirectly', and the argument seems to be that the company, by engaging to allot shares at par to the shareholder at a future date, is applying or using its shares in such a manner as to give him a possible benefit at the expense of the company in this sense, that it forgoes the chance of issuing them at a premium. With regard to the latter point, it may or may not be at the expense of the company. I am not aware of any law which obliges a company to issue its shares above par because they are saleable at a premium in the market. It depends on the circumstances of each case whether it will be prudent or even possible to do so, and it is a question for the directors to decide. But the point which, in my opinion, is alone material for the present purpose is that the benefit to the shareholder from being able to sell his shares at a premium is not obtained by him at the expense of the company's capital. . . .

NOTES

Cf *Lowry* v *Consolidated African Selection Trust Ltd* [1940] AC 648. On modern 'share incentive' schemes, see D S Ribbens 1976 *SA Chartered Accountant* 88, 127.

[141] *In re* Wragg Ltd
[1897] 1 Ch 796

LINDLEY LJ: . . . I understand the law to be as follows. The liability of a shareholder to pay the company the amount of his shares is a statutory liability. . . . [These] debts, like other debts, can be discharged in more ways than one—eg by payment, set-off, accord and satisfaction, and release—and, subject to the qualifications introduced by the doctrine of *ultra vires*, or, in other words, the limited capacity of statutory corporations, any mode of discharging [the] debt is as available to a shareholder as to any other . . . debtor. It is, however, obviously beyond the power of a limited company to release a shareholder from his obligation without payment in money or money's worth. It cannot give fully paid-up shares for nothing and preclude itself from requiring payment of them in money or money's worth. . . .

. . . That shares cannot be issued at a discount was finally settled in the case of the *Ooregum Gold Mining Co of India* v *Roper* [1892] AC 125. . . . It has, however, never yet been decided that a limited company cannot buy property or pay for services at any price it thinks proper, and pay for them in fully paid-up shares. Provided a limited company does so honestly and not colourably, and provided that it has not been so imposed upon as to be entitled to be relieved from its bargain, it appears to be settled . . . [that] agreements by limited companies to pay for property or services in paid-up shares are valid and binding on the companies and their creditors. . . .

. . . It is not law that persons cannot sell property to a limited company for fully paid-up shares and make a profit by the transaction. We must not allow ourselves to be misled by talking of value. The value paid to the company is measured by the price at which the company agrees to buy what it thinks it worth its while to acquire. Whilst the transaction is unimpeached, this is the only value to be considered. . . .

[142] *In re* White Star Line Ltd
[1938] Ch 458, [1938] 1 All ER 607

CLAUSON LJ: . . . The reported authorities establish . . . that a payment is an effective payment in money's worth if the consideration given by way of payment is something which is bona fide regarded by the parties to the payment as fairly representing the sum which the payment is to discharge . . . but that if the consideration given by way of payment is a mere blind or clearly colourable or illusory . . . the so-called payment is ineffectual for the purpose. The question whether the consideration is colourable is one of fact in each case.

NOTES

See further *Moosa v Lalloo* 1957 (4) SA 207 (N) at 220, per Caney J: 'The fact that payment is deferred or is to be made by instalments or by reference to calls does not detract from the allotment being one for cash. The contrast is between shares to be paid for by money and those to be paid for otherwise than by money, for example, by property, goods, services, or a business. . . .'

In *Motor Fuels Corporation (in liquidation)* v *Linder Bros* (1927) 48 NLR 279 a creditor of the company for rent accepted shares in satisfaction of his claim. The court held that his liability on the shares was extinguished, approving of the principle laid down by James LJ in *Spargo's* case (1873) 8 Ch App 407, that any bona fide transaction between a company and a shareholder which, if the company brought an action against him for calls, could support a plea of payment, is payment in cash.

In *Pellat's* case (1867) 2 Ch App 527 it was held that it was not competent for a company to contract that the calls in respect of what remains to be paid up on shares should not be paid in money, but should be set off against goods to be supplied to the company by the shareholders.

In *National House Property Investment Co Ltd* v *Watson* 1908 SC 888 it was held that it is *ultra vires* for directors to agree that an allottee whose firm was to be appointed to a certain office in the company, should be at liberty to pay up the balance due upon his shares by fees to be earned by his firm.

A promise by a shareholder to discharge at some future date a debt due by the company to a third party is not equivalent to payment in cash, nor is the giving of a promissory note, but, of course, as soon as payment is actually made by him, the shareholder is discharged: *Simon v Master of the Supreme Court* 1912 TPD 459; *In re Biltong Asbestos Co Ltd* 1925 CPD 356.

Semble, where there is an agreement that certain shares are to be allotted as fully paid up, the fact that this agreement has not been lodged with the Registrar as prescribed does not render the allottees liable to pay for the shares. Cf *Reynolds Vehicle and Harness Factory Ltd (in liquidation)* v *Zietsma* (1907) 3 Buch AC 74, and *In re Standard Engineering Works Ltd* 1922 CPD 573.

In England it has been held that a contract for the allotment of shares can be specifically enforced: *Northern Counties Securities Ltd* v *Jackson & Steeple Ltd* [1974] 1 WLR 1133, [1974] 2 All ER 625 (Ch).

See further *Poole, Jackson and Whyte's* case (1878) 9 ChD 322; *Kent's* case (1888) 39 ChD 259; *In re Jones, Lloyd & Co Ltd* (1889) 41 ChD 159; *In re Eddystone Marine Insurance Co* [1893] 3 Ch 9; *In re Macdonald, Sons & Co* [1894] 1 Ch 89; *Chapman's* case [1895] 1 Ch 771; *Larocque v Beauchemin* [1897] AC 358; *Markham and Darter's* case [1899] 1 Ch 414; *In re Innes & Co Ltd* [1903] 2 Ch 254; *Mosely v Koffyfontein Mines Ltd* [1904] 2 Ch 108; *In re Contributories Rosemount Gold Mining Syndicate* 1905 TH 169; *Famatina Development Corporation Ltd* v *Bury* [1910] AC 439; *Gardner v Iredale* [1912] 1 Ch 700; *Hong Kong and China Gas Co Ltd* v *Glen* [1914] 1 Ch 527; *In re Contat's Collieries* (1898) 15 SC 12, followed in *Ex parte Van Buuren Medicine Co Ltd* 1914 CPD 179; *Middelburg Prospecting Syndicate Ltd (in liquidation)* v *Goodwin* 1906 TS 899; *Ex parte St John's Land and Colliery Syndicate Ltd* (1910) 27 SC 144; *Ex parte Mutual House and Land Association Ltd (in liquidation)* 1912 CPD 904; *African Woodworks Co Ltd (in liquidation)* v *Warden* 1923 CPD 535.

IV TRANSFER OF SHARES

A TEXT

Unless otherwise provided, shares in a public company are freely transferable, s 91: *143*. The articles may place restrictions on the transfer of shares and must do so in the case of a private company, s 20(1)(*a*) (see Table B art 11): *144–146*. Where a company is under investigation under s 254 or 255 the Minister of Economic Affairs may impose restrictions on the transfer of shares, s 256. The transfer of a share of a company being wound up without the consent of the liquidator is void, s 341(1).

In most cases the transfer of shares is effected in pursuance of a contract of sale: *147*. The transfer is a contract by which the transferor makes over his rights as a shareholder to the transferee: *148*.

The formalities of transfer are regulated by ss 133ff and the company's articles of association (see Table A arts 10ff, Table B arts 12ff). Special rules apply to the transfer of 'securities'—listed shares and debentures (s 134 s v 'security'). Securities are transferred by a securities transfer form, which is usually completed by the transferor with the transferee's name left in blank and handed over to the transferee together with the share certificates, s 135(1)(*a*). Alternatively, a securities transfer form and a broker's transfer form may be completed, s 135(1)(*b*). Neither form need be attested. Section 136 deals with certification by a company that a security has been lodged with it for transfer, and the effect of such certification. Persons lodging instruments of transfer in respect of a security are deemed to warrant that the instruments are genuine and have to indemnify the company if they are not, s 138.

A forged transfer is a nullity: *Barton* v *North Staffordshire Railway Company* (1888) 38 ChD 458; *Davis* v *Buffelsfontein Gold Mining Co Ltd* 1967 (4) SA 631 (W).

As soon as the transferee's name is substituted in the company's share register for that of the transferor, the former becomes, the latter ceases to be, a member. If a company refuses to register the transferee, it must notify him as provided in s 137. As between the transferor and the transferee ownership of the shares passes independent of registration: *149, 150*.

Shares may be sold '*cum*' or '*ex*' dividend. If nothing is said the buyer is only entitled to dividends declared or bonus shares issued after the date of the sale: *151*.

Share certificates are not negotiable instruments, but where a person entrusts scrip with a blank transfer to another, e g as a pledge or for the purpose of safe-keeping, he may be estopped from claiming the shares from a third party who has acquired them bona fide and for value from that other person: *152, 153*.

The usual way of pledging shares is by handing the pledgee the scrip, together with a transfer form signed in blank by the pledgor: *154*.

When a stockbroker purchases shares on behalf of a client, the scrip does not become the property of the client until it is allocated or delivered to him: *155*. Delivery of scrip from stockbroker to stockbroker in stock exchange transactions nowadays takes place by a computerised clearing house scheme, under which the net balance in each security owed to and by each broking firm by and to other broking firms is settled. Thus broker A who bought shares in a particular security from broker B will not necessarily get the scrip which broker B sold him but may get scrip sold by broker C or D. And if the sales of a particular share by his clients exceeded purchases by his clients A may get no shares at all.

All the indications are (it is already happening overseas) that before long the delivery of scrip in stock exchange transactions will be entirely replaced by computerised book entries.

A stockbroker who holds clients' shares may not pledge those shares at all if they are fully paid but must keep them separate and identified as his clients' property. The only exception is the case where a broker has made a loan to his client who has delivered his scrip to the broker as security for the loan. If the shares are not fully paid for, the broker may pledge them only for the amount still owing by the client on those shares and then only with the written consent of the client on a form specially provided for such purpose: *S* v *McPherson* 1972 (2) SA 348 (EC), *155* below, at 357E. If the client does not pay the stockbroker the purchase price in cash the stockbroker is obliged to sell the securities for the account of the purchaser, as provided in s 13 of the Stock Exchanges Control Act 7 of 1947: *156*. On repudiation of the purchase of securities where the stockbroker fails to deliver, see s 13B of the Stock Exchanges Control Act 7 of 1947.

Regulations promulgated under s 27 of the Stock Exchanges Control Act prescribe the accounting records to be kept by stockbrokers, R1817, *Reg Gaz* 2379, GG 5309 of 8 October 1976.

The publication of particulars regarding shares to be bought or sold by a person other than a stock exchange are prohibited, p 109 above.

B CASES

[143] Weston's case
(1868) 4 Ch App 20

PAGE WOOD LJ: . . . The very object of all parties who enter into these companies is to have shares which are not like shares in ordinary partnerships, but which are transferable; and all the articles are framed on the supposition that they are so transferable. Indeed, it has always been a subject of discussion whether the establishment of joint stock companies were or were not politic, for that very reason that the partners can immediately get rid of all their liabilities. I was therefore greatly surprised at the argument which had been addressed to us today, namely that unless there is something in the articles which makes the shares transferable, they are not transferable at all, except by a resolution of a general meeting. I apprehend the shares are transferable by virtue of the statute, and that the province of the articles is to point out the mode in which they shall be transferred, and the limitations (if any) to which a shareholder shall be subjected before he can transfer. . . .

It would be a very serious thing for the shareholders in one of these companies to be told that their shares, the whole value of which consists in their being marketable and passing freely from hand to hand, are to be subject to a clause or restriction which they do not find in the articles. . . .

[144] *In re* **Smith and Fawcett Ltd**
[1942] Ch 304, [1942] 1 All ER 542

LORD GREENE MR: . . . The principles to be applied in cases where the articles of a company confer a discretion on directors with regard to the acceptance of transfers of shares are, for the present purposes, free from doubt. They must exercise their discretion bona fide in what they consider—not what a court may consider—is in the interests of the company, and not for any collateral purpose. . . .

There is nothing, in my opinion, in principle or in authority to make it impossible to draft such a wide and comprehensive power to directors to refuse to transfer as to enable them to take into account any matter which they conceive to be in the interests of the company, and thereby to admit or not to admit a particular person and to allow or not to allow a particular transfer for reasons not personal to the transferee but bearing on the general interests of the company as a whole—such matters, for instance, as whether by their passing a particular transfer the transferee would obtain too great a weight in the councils of the company or might even perhaps obtain control. The question, therefore, simply is whether on the true construction of the particular article the directors are limited by anything except their bona fide view as to the interests of the company. In the present case the article is drafted in the widest possible terms, and I decline to write into the clear language any limitation other than a limitation, which is implicit by law, that a fiduciary power of this kind must be exercised bona fide in the interests of the company. Subject to that qualification, an article in this form appears to me to give the directors what it says, namely an absolute and uncontrolled discretion. . . .

[145] **Richter NO** *v* **Riverside Estates (Pty) Ltd**
1946 OPD 209

DE BEER J: . . . I would . . . add a few remarks on the interpretation and application of the following provision in the articles of association: 'The director or directors may, at any time, in their absolute and uncontrolled discretion and without assigning any reason therefor, decline to register any proposed transfer of a share or shares in the company.' The provision is couched in very wide terms even should the ambiguous, if not sinister, phrase 'uncontrolled discretion' be ignored. It appears to be subject to this one limitation only, namely, that the directors bona fide considered and decided against the proposed transfer. As they need not assign any reason for their decision, it would be difficult, if not impossible, for an applicant ever to succeed in establishing that such decision was not bona fide where no such reasons are given. . . .

It does, however, appear that if the directors do specify the reasons which prompted their action, the court is entitled to examine them though it will be loath to interfere . . . unless it is shown that the directors acted on a wrong principle . . . or that they acted unreasonably, mala fide or arbitrarily. In purporting to give their reasons for the refusal to register the proposed transfer, the directors advanced an argument which is unsound; but it is specifically stated that this unsound reason is only one of the reasons which influenced them. I do not, therefore, think the court is entitled to embark on a speculative investigation in an attempt to discover, if possible, whether any valid reasons may, or may not, in fact, exist justifying the decision of the directors. It appears from the minutes that the question was 'discussed at length' before arriving at the decision to decline the proposed transfer and if, thereafter, one of the reasons given by them is found to be untenable, I fail to see how the court, from this fact, could infer that they acted on a wrong principle or arbitrarily or mala fide. . . .

[146] Lyle & Scott Ltd & Scott's Trustees *v* British Investment Trust Ltd
[1959] AC 763, [1959] 2 All ER 661 (HL)

A company's articles provided that every shareholder 'desirous' of transferring his shares was to inform the secretary, and that other shareholders were to have the rights to purchase the shares at a price to be fixed by the auditor of the company. It was held that a shareholder could not evade this obligation by an agreement under which he sold the shares to a third party, binding himself to put the purchaser as fully in control of the company as he could without registering transfers of the shares.

VISCOUNT SIMONDS: . . . The question is not whether what has been done is a breach of the first part of the article but whether it demonstrates with sufficient clearness that Scott's trustees are persons desirous of transferring their ordinary shares. It appears to me that there is no room for doubt that that is just what they are. . . . For, since it is the admitted fact that they entered into the agreement for sale of their shares and have received and retain the price, it follows that, whether or not they have yet done all that they ought as vendors to do, they hold the shares as trustees for the purchaser. They are bound to do everything that in them lies to perfect the title of the purchaser. They cannot compel the company to register him as the holder of the shares, but everything else they must do, and it is straining credulity too far to suppose that everything else would not already have been done, if it had not been hoped to gain some tactical advantage by delay. In my opinion, it is not open to a shareholder, who has agreed to do a certain thing and is bound to do it, to deny that he is desirous of doing it.

Against this view it was urged that they were not desirous of transferring their shares within the meaning of the article because they had not a general desire but a particular desire to transfer only to Mr Fraser at a certain price. This makes nonsense of the article, the purpose of which would be wholly defeated if it did not apply to a desire to transfer to a particular person, who might be the person whom the company particularly wished to exclude. Then it was contended that they were not desirous of transferring their shares, because their task had been done and their desire satisfied. I think, my Lords, that this ingenious and almost humorous plea ignores that they have elsewhere pleaded and vigorously relied on the fact that the transfer has not been completed.

If, then, Scott's trustees are, as I hold they are, shareholders desirous of transferring their ordinary shares, what follows?

I have already indicated that a shareholder who has agreed to sell his shares and has received the price is to be deemed to be desirous of transferring them. At once, therefore, the machinery of the article is put in motion and he must inform the secretary of the number that he desires to sell, which is *ex hypothesi* the number he has agreed to sell. The price is then fixed in the manner prescribed by the article and so the matter proceeds. . . . I have already indicated that his desire must be deemed to continue so long as he adheres to his contract of sale. . . .

NOTES

See further *In re Gresham Life Assurance Society* (1872) 8 Ch App 446; *In re Bede Steam Shipping Co Ltd* [1917] 1 Ch 123; *Adam v Central India Estates Ltd* 1922 WLD 135; *Waja v Orr, Orr NO and Dowjee Co Ltd* 1929 TPD 865 at 875–6; *Berry and Stewart v Tottenham Hotspur Football and Athletic Co Ltd* [1935] Ch 718; *Hunter v Hunter* [1936] AC 222; *Charles Forte Investments Ltd v Amanda* [1964] 1 Ch 240, [1963] 2 All ER 940; *Rayfield v Hands* (52 above); also *Karsen v Hansen* 1944 (2) PH E8 (C); *Sachs v Gillibrand* 1959 (2) SA 233 (W); *Konyn v Viedge Bros Ltd* 1961 (2) SA 816 (E) (court 'cannot give effect to a proved intention which the draftsman failed to reflect in the language he employed': per O'Hagan J at 825); *Mendonides v Mendonides* 1962 (2) SA 190 (W); *SA Vroue Federasie v Thackeray NO* 1967 (2) SA 468 (T).

There is no effective transfer of shares if the restrictions on transfer imposed by the articles are not observed: *Lombard v Suid-Afrikaanse Vroue-Federasie* 1968 (3) SA 473 (AD). A transfer may be set aside if the approval of the directorate was obtained by fraudulent misrepresentations: *Payne's case* (1869) LR 9 Eq 223; see also *In re Discoverers' Finance Corporation Ltd* [1910] 1 Ch 312.

In *Robinson v Chartered Bank* (1865) LR 1 Eq 32 the court considered, but did not decide, the question whether it was a reasonable ground of objection that the proposed transferee was the nominee of a rival bank with which the shares were deposited as a security.

Where the articles give the directors a discretion to refuse to register a transfer by a shareholder if he is indebted to the company, the time at which it is to be determined whether he is indebted or not is when the transfer is sent in to the company for registration, and not when it comes before a board meeting: *In re Cawley & Co* (1889) 42 ChD 209.

In *In re Hackney Pavilion Ltd* [1924] 1 Ch 276 the executrix of a deceased member, under the articles, had the right to be registered as a member, subject to the directors' absolute discretionary right to decline such registration. At a board meeting of the two directors, one proposed and one opposed the transfer. It was held that the right to decline transfer was not exercised and that, consequently, the executrix was entitled to be registered as a new member. This was followed by the House of Lords in *Moodie v W & J Shepherd (Bookbinders) Ltd* [1949] 2 All ER 1044. On the effect of undue delay in bringing transfers before the board of directors, see *Re Swaledale Cleaners Ltd* [1968] 1 All ER 1132, [1968] 1 WLR 1710.

Unless clearly otherwise stated, restrictions on the transfer of shares in the articles apply only to transfers to non-members: *Greenhalgh v Mallard* [1943] 2 All ER 234; *Greenacre v Falkirk Iron Co Ltd* 1953 (4) SA 289 (N). In the last-mentioned case it was further held that under the article in question a corporation which was a member of the company was entitled to transfer its shares to trustees. In *Estate Milne v Donohoe Investments (Pty) Ltd* 1967 (2) SA 359 (AD), the restrictions of the transfer on shares applied even between members.

The fact that a member knows that the company is about to be wound up voluntarily does not take away his power to transfer his shares: *In re Taurine Co* (1883) 25 ChD 118. On the other hand, it was held in *Chappel's case* (1871) 6 Ch App 902 that there can be no transfer of shares after the company has ceased to be a going concern, having transferred its business to another corporation.

Harris v Joyce & McGregor (Pty) Ltd 1970 (1) SA 665 (C) dealt with the construction of a clause in a will providing for the transfer of shares of a deceased member to his or her widow or widower or other relations.

Where the articles of a private company provided that on the death of a member his shares were to be offered to 'the other members' and there were only two members, one of whom died, it was held that his shares had to be offered to the sole surviving member, the plural including the singular: *Jarvis Motors (Harrow) Ltd* v *Carabott* [1964] 3 All ER 89, [1964] 1 WLR 1101. On sale of shares by an executor, see *Lombard* v *Suid-Afrikaanse Vroue-Federasie* 1968 (3) SA 473 (AD).

The fact that the company's auditor to whom the valuation at which the shares are to be offered to other shareholders is entrusted by the articles, is himself a shareholder, does not preclude him from doing the valuing provided he exercises an honest judgment: *Estate Milne* v *Donohoe Investments (Pty) Ltd* 1967 (2) SA 359 (AD).

[147] Stewart *v* Ryall
(1887) 5 SC 146

DE VILLIERS CJ: . . . Where no fixed time for delivery has been stipulated for, the scrip must be delivered within a reasonable time. Where the contract fixes the time, the delivery must be made at the time thus fixed. It is not to the purpose, to say that in the present case the defendant sustained no damage through the delay, seeing that the shares did not fall in value during the interval. It is the nature of the thing sold which we must, among other matters, consider in determining whether or not the time agreed upon for its delivery is an essential part of the contract. Shares of all kinds, and more especially shares in gold-mining companies, are in their nature of such a fluctuating value that neither the vendor nor the purchaser can be presumed to have regarded the time agreed upon for the delivery as an unimportant ingredient in the contract. If the vendor sues for the price it lies upon him, as pointed out by Voet (19.1.23), to prove that he has performed everything which was stipulated to be performed on his part. If the delivery of the shares on a fixed day was an essential ingredient of the contract, it is not sufficient to prove that the plaintiff was willing and ready to deliver them six days after. The defendant, although not damnified by the delay, is freed from the obligation which he would have incurred if the plaintiff had performed his part of the contract. . . .

[148] Jeffrey *v* Pollak and Freemantle
1938 AD 1

In October 1933 the applicant (Mr Jeffrey) instructed his broker (Mr Hunt) to purchase 65 shares in the S Company for him. The broker purchased a parcel of 120 shares, notified the applicant that he had bought the 65 shares for him, and was paid the price thereof by the applicant. The applicant signed a transfer form as transferee and requested the broker to have the shares registered in his (the applicant's) name. Instead of doing so, the broker sold the whole parcel of 120 shares. In January 1934 the broker purchased a further 100 shares in the same company, transferred them to himself, and on the same day transferred 65 to the applicant. The broker did not use the transfer form signed by the applicant, but a new form upon which he signed the applicant's name as transferee. The applicant's name was placed on the register of members. The share certificate was sent to the broker who was instructed by the applicant to keep it for him. In October 1935 the broker sold the shares to the respondent and 'transferred' them to him by means of the forging of the applicant's name on a transfer form. Shortly afterwards, the broker went insolvent. The respondent having been placed on the register of members of S Company by virtue of the forged transfer form, the applicant applied for an order rectifying the register of members of S Company by restoring his name to the register. The Witwatersrand Local Division granted the application, but on appeal the Transvaal Provincial Division reversed the decision. On appeal the order of the Witwatersrand Local Division was restored, the Appellate Division holding that the applicant was the owner of the shares.

STRATFORD JA: There seems to me to have been, both in counsel's argument and in his illustrations, a failure to appreciate that we have here to deal with the cession of a right of action (a right *in personam*) and not with the transferring of the ownership in a chattel. The four requisites for transferring ownership mentioned by counsel are necessary to effect transfer of *dominium* in a thing (right *in rem*) but in general all that is necessary to transfer a right of action is a contract of cession. I have said 'in general' because in some cases cession of a right against another cannot be effected without the obligator's consent, or only by the observance of certain formalities. Also, if there is a document which evidences the title to the right it must be delivered to the cessionary (*Smith* v *Farrelly's Trustees* 1904 TS 949)—but not because this is the equivalent to delivery of possession of a chattel, but because the delivery of the document is a requisite formality of cession in such cases. There can be no delivery of a *jus in personam*. Such a right passes on cession effected with such formalities as the case may require. 'A share is a *jus in personam*, the ownership of which passes by cession in due form' (per Innes CJ in *Liquidators, Union Share Agency* v *Hatton* 1927 AD 240 at 251).

. . . The appellant's instruction to Hunt was to acquire 65 shares in the company of no particular identifiable numbers. The numbered identification was of no consequence to him whatsoever and never is, or can be, of any concern in the mind of any buyer of shares. Consequently when Hunt had these 65 shares registered in his name in January these were the very things to which the mandate related and which he desired to acquire. I should say here that the requirements mentioned in the case of *Farrelly's Trustees* is supplied by Hunt's receipt from the company of the certificate for the 65 shares. Hunt undoubtedly must be taken in law to have received this certificate on behalf of his client the appellant. Thereafter he retained the custody of the certificate by the permission and on behalf of the appellant. When, therefore, the appellant became aware of the registration in his name and accepted dividends in respect of the shares he manifested the necessary *animus acquirendi* in respect of them. . . .

NOTES

Letters of renunciation of bonus shares in favour of a nominee and of acceptance by that nominee do not, normally, amount to a 'transfer' of shares: *In re Pool Shipping Co Ltd* [1920] 1 Ch 251.

In *Goodchild* v *Wellborne* [1941] 2 All ER 449 it was held that where it was the intention of the parties to the transfer to carry on an illegal business through the company, the contract was unenforceable.

As to the rule that the scrip must be delivered within a reasonable time, see also *Goldschmidt* v *Adler* (1884) 3 SC 117; *Stewart* v *Sichel* (1886) 4 SC 435; *Joel* v *Dolman* (1888) 6 SC 137; *Green* v *Andrews* (1889) 10 NLR 18; *Wolff* v *Pickering* (1895) 12 SC 429.

In *Globe Electrical Transvaal* v *Brunhuber* 1970 (3) SA 99 (E) an option to purchase shares was held to be invalid because there were factors which rendered the price uncertain and unascertainable.

In *Dublin* v *Diner* 1964 (1) SA 799 (D) shares were sold at the valuation to be placed thereon by the company's auditors. The court held that if the price fixed was so grossly excessive as to bear no relationship at all to the value of the shares and was manifestly an unjust and unfair price, the purchaser was justified in refusing to pay it. The question whether the purchaser could elect whether to repudiate the sale or to carry it out at a fair price, was left open.

In *Hare* v *Nicoll* [1966] 2 QB 130, [1966] 1 All ER 285 (CA) it was held that where there is an option to repurchase shares the time fixed for payment is of the essence.

The seller is entitled to the purchase price in full against delivery of the shares: *Smith and Warren* v *Harris* (1888) 5 HCG 193.

As to the requirements of offer and acceptance, see further *Biet* v *Trubshawe* (1887) 8 NLR 65 and *Castines* v *O'Flagherty Brothers* (1887) 8 NLR 115.

A voting agreement does not run with the shares so as to bind the transferee: *Greenhalgh* v *Mallard* [1943] 2 All ER 234 (*175* below).

On the enforcement of an agreement to transfer shares, *De Kock* v *Davidson* 1971 (1) SA 428 (T).

As to the question when a deed of sale of the share capital of a company is a liquid document, see *Onay* v *Schmulian* 1971 (1) SA 626 (W).

If a prospective seller of shares hands the auditor's report without comment to the prospective buyer his action is capable of the construction that he represents to the buyer that the auditor's report is correct and can be relied upon: *Prima Toy Holdings (Pty) Ltd* v *Rosenberg* 1974 (2) SA 477 (C).

[149] Farrar's Estate *v* Commissioner for Inland Revenue
1926 TPD 501

STRATFORD J: It is well-established law that the passing of the property in shares is effected independently of and prior to registration.

[150] Moosa *v* Lalloo
1956 (2) SA 237 (N)

The plaintiff sued the defendants for the price of the shares in a private company which he had sold to them. He tendered the shares, together with duly completed transfer forms. The defendants pleaded that under the articles of the company in question no share could be transferred to a person who was not already a member of the company without the previous approval of the directors, and that the directors had not approved of the transfer from the plaintiff to the defendants, who were not members of the company. The court held that the plea did not disclose a good defence.

CANEY J: . . . [Counsel for] the excipient contended that the obligation of the seller of shares, in relation to the delivery of them, is to tender the share certificates together with a transfer form, or transfer forms, duly executed, so that the transferee may use them for the purpose of obtaining transfer of the shares; it is then for the buyer of the shares to lodge them with the company for the purpose of obtaining registration of transfer of them. The seller, [he] contended, does not warrant to the buyer that the company will register transfer in his favour.

[As against this, it was] contended that the seller of shares must do everything in his power to give transfer.

The legal situation in England appears to be summarized in a passage in the 16th edition of Palmer *Company Precedents* Part I at 503, as follows:

> 'An agreement for the sale of a share does not bind the seller to procure the registration of the transfer. His duty is performed when he hands over to the transferee a duly executed transfer. But until registration of the transfer the transferor is a trustee of the shares for the transferee. If the buyer wishes to protect himself he must buy with "registration guaranteed".'

That, in my judgment, is also our law. In *McGregor's Trustees* v *Silberbauer* (1891) 9 SC 36 at 38 De Villiers CJ put a transfer of shares on the same basis as a cession of action, in contrast to transfer of immovable property by registration. In *Randfontein Estates Ltd* v *The Master* 1909 TS 978 at 981, 982 Innes CJ said shares

> 'are simply rights of action—*jura in personam*—entitling their owner to a certain interest in the company, its assets and dividends. As between those in whose names they are registered in the books of the company, and any other person with whom the registered holders deal, they may be freely assigned, even though the original registration remains unaltered. And that is the ordinary way in which such shares are dealt with; they pass from hand to hand, and form the subject of many transactions without the original registration in the books of the company being disturbed. It is true that the company cannot be forced to register the transfer of shares until any claim which it has against the registered holder is satisfied. But that does not affect the right of the holder to freely transfer his interest in them, without registration. If a registered holder sells shares, endorses them in blank, and delivers the scrip to the purchaser, and then becomes insolvent, it is clear that those shares do not form part of his insolvent estate, and his trustee cannot claim them. . . . And that shows the difference between property of this nature and landed property. In regard to the latter the court cannot go behind the register; in regard to the former it can—and that is a vital distinction.'

In *Jeffrey* v *Pollak and Freemantle* 1938 AD 1 at 24 the principle of *McGregor's Trustees* v *Silberbauer* (*supra*) was approved, in the following terms:

> 'The principle enunciated in *Silberbauer's* case (and I think generally accepted as good law) is that a cession of shares is complete as between the parties when the cedent has done all in his power to divest himself of his right of action and to put the transferee in a position to demand recognition by the obligor (the company)'.

Again, on the same page,

> 'In that case McGregor as registered owner of the shares had executed a transfer as transferor—there was nothing that he could do or be called upon to do, and the cessionary was furnished with every requisite to complete his claim against the company.'

It is immaterial that the shares are those of a private company, or that they are not dealt in on the stock exchange. . . . It may be that if the articles prohibit a sale of shares of a private company save amongst members (as distinct from requiring the directors' approval to register a transfer) the situation would be different: but that is not . . . this case.

NOTES

See further *Nation's* case (1866) LR 3 Eq 77; *In re Overend, Gurney & Co: Walker's* case (1866) LR 2 Eq 554; *Hayes Bros v Jameson* (1886) 7 NLR 30; *McGregor's Trustees v Silberbauer* (1891) 9 SC 36; *Moore v North Western Bank* [1891] 2 Ch 599; *Spencer v Ashworth, Partington & Co* [1925] 1 KB 589; *Moosa v Lalloo* 1957 (4) SA 207 (N).

As Professor R C Beuthin states (1967 *Annual Survey* 227): 'It will always be a matter of construction of the particular articles in question as to whether they place restrictions only on the right to compel registration by the company of an instrument of transfer, or whether they in fact place restrictions, for example, on a member's right to conclude any juristic act which might oblige him to cede his *jura in personam*. There is even no reason why the articles should not place restrictions on the very right of cession itself. All these would have somewhat differing results.'

A purchaser of shares at a valuation by the company's auditors is not obliged to pay the price fixed by them if it is manifestly unjust and unfair, bearing no relationship to the true value of the shares: *Dublin v Diner* 1964 (1) SA 799 (N), p 259 above.

A company can be compelled by action to register a valid and absolute transfer: *R v Lambourn Valley Rail Co* (1888) 22 QBD 463. The directors cannot refuse to pass a transfer merely because it omits some, in the circumstances, immaterial particulars: *In re Letheby & Christopher Ltd* [1904] 1 Ch 815. The transferor is under an implied obligation not to prevent or delay the registration of the transferee: *Hooper v Herts* [1906] 1 Ch 549.

Where the directors, acting under powers conferred on them by the articles, refuse to register a transferee, the transferor holds the shares henceforth as trustee for the transferee and must account to him for dividends, bonus shares and other benefits received. Conversely, the transferee must indemnify the transferor against future calls: *Kellock v Enthoven* (1874) LR 9 QBD 241; *Levi v Ayers* (1878) 3 App Cas 824; *Hardoon v Belilios* [1901] AC 118; *Stevenson v Wilson* 1907 SC 445.

In *Fyfe's* case (1869) 4 Ch App 768, where it was due to delays on the part of the company that the transferee was not registered as a shareholder at the time of the winding-up order, the court ordered that the transferee be placed on the list of contributories instead of the transferor. See also *Hill's* case (1867) 4 Ch App 769n and *In re National Bank of Wales: Taylor, Phillips* and *Rickard's* cases [1897] 1 Ch 298.

In *Longman v Bath Electric Tramways Ltd* [1905] 1 Ch 646 a share certificate, together with the transfer, was lodged with the company. The company by mistake returned the share certificate to the transferor who fraudulently used it to obtain an advance from an innocent party. The court held that the company owed no duty of safe custody to the public at large and was therefore not liable to the third party for the loss caused to him by the fraud of the transferor.

On transfer of shares by an executor in a deceased estate, see *Lombard v Suid-Afrikaanse Vroue-Federasie* 1968 (3) SA 473 (AD).

[151] Logan v Beit
(1890) 7 SC 197

DE VILLIERS CJ: The phrase 'cum rights' must prima facie be taken to refer to rights accruing at or after the date of the sale, and not to bonus shares which had been distributed among the shareholders three weeks before the date of the sale. . . . By our law error or mistake on the part of one of the parties to a contract will, under certain circumstances, entitle him to restitution, but it must be *justus error*, that is to say, a mistake which is reasonable and justifiable. In the present case there may be some doubt as to the meaning of the term 'rights' but, whatever the meaning may be, the plaintiff was not reasonably justified in supposing that rights which shareholders had already acquired in the way of bonus shares were intended to be sold under the phrase 'cum rights'. If the additional shares had been intended to be sold they would have been added to the number of shares mentioned in the broker's note, and a proportionate reduction would have been made in the price per share. If the plaintiff did not know that the shares had already been distributed he could, upon inquiry, have ascertained the fact; at all events the defendant was not responsible for the plaintiff's ignorance. Under these circumstances there appears to me not to have been such *justus error* on the plaintiff's part as to entitle him to relief. . . .

NOTES

See also *In re Wimbush* [1940] Ch 92, [1940] 1 All ER 229, where it was held that the purchaser is entitled to any dividend declared after the sale. 'The purchaser had bought the tree and with it the fruits that are ripening on the tree' (per Morton J). In South African law it is a general principle that on conclusion of a contract of sale, the risk and the right to fruits pass to the seller, unless otherwise stipulated.

[152] United South African Association Ltd *v* Cohn
1904 TS 733

The plaintiff company entrusted scrip indorsed in blank to one of its clerks. The clerk stole some of the certificates and sold them to the defendant who purchased them in good faith. The court held that the plaintiff company was estopped from disputing the defendant's title.

INNES CJ: . . . If scrip certificates indorsed in blank by a transferor were negotiable instruments the inquiry would present little difficulty. No matter what taint of illegality might be connected with the manner in which Maxwell obtained the documents, the defendant would be entitled to retain them, just as much as if he had purchased a cheque duly in order, or a bank-note. But I do not think that these certificates can be called negotiable in the legal sense of the word. They entitle the holder to claim registration as a shareholder in the syndicate; but until that is effected the prior registered owner is regarded by the syndicate as the absolute owner. The real owner can exercise no rights in respect of his interest except the right of registering or disposing of it. He cannot vote at meetings or draw dividends, and the syndicate is not bound to transfer the shares to him if it holds any lien over them. The articles of association leave no doubt on these points, and the effect is to prevent the characteristics of negotiability from attaching to the certificates. . . . The question still remains whether the company, having indorsed the certificates in blank, and placed them under the control and custody of its clerk, can demand them back from a holder who purchased them from the clerk in good faith.

No doubt the general rule of law is that a man cannot be held to have parted with the ownership of property taken from him fraudulently and against his will, and that a thief cannot convey good title to stolen property even to an innocent purchaser for value. But scrip certificates indorsed in blank do not stand in the same position as ordinary property.

The evidence shows that, by the rules of the Stock Exchange and by admitted custom, such certificates pass freely from hand to hand, are considered as the property of the person to whom they are delivered, and are accepted as sufficient in all transactions in which the delivery of shares constitutes a necessary element. Indeed, one of the rules of the Exchange provides that scrip certificates shall not be deemed good delivery unless indorsed in blank by the registered holder. Without such indorsement the certificates cannot be dealt in; with it, they are freely saleable, and their delivery is universally accepted without question as the performance of the contract. . . .

. . . If we endeavour to extract the principle which lies at the root of the decisions to which I have referred, it will be found to be this: The original owner was estopped because he did two things—first, by indorsing the scrip in blank, he represented to all who saw it that it was scrip intended to pass from hand to hand, and to which the holder for the time being could give a good title; and second, by entrusting it to the custody and control of a third person, he placed that person in a position to hand the scrip over, ostensibly as its owner, to innocent purchasers or others who advanced money on it. This governing consideration was not that the person entrusted with the scrip had the possession of it, in a juridical sense, but that he had the actual physical custody and control. And, if that be so, it is impossible to draw any logical distinction between the case where the custodian is a broker and the case where he is a banker, a clerk or a private person. Brokers are not the only people who sell shares. One of the witnesses for the plaintiff hazarded the assertion that it was not practicable for an auditor to check the signatures of directors on the scrip which he counted, because he would have to know the signature of everyone in Johannesburg. In other words, all men in Johannesburg were potential directors. That was, of course, a gross exaggeration; but if he had said that a large proportion of the population were either actual or potential shareholders, and therefore possible vendors of shares, he might have been much nearer the truth. At any rate there must be a large number of men who are not brokers, but who from time to time do sell shares; and the same rule should apply in the case of blank indorsed scrip entrusted to the custody of private persons as would apply if it had been deposited with a broker. Nor ought the fact that the custodian is in the employ of the real owner to make any difference, so far as the applicability of the doctrine of estoppel is concerned, provided only that the actual custody and control of the scrip be parted with by the owner and given to the servant. . . .

It is not necessary to say what the position of an owner of blank indorsed scrip would be if the documents were abstracted, say, by picking his pocket, or rifling his safe, or if by similar means they were taken from an agent to whom he had entrusted them. Under such circumstances an innocent purchaser of the stolen scrip might have difficulty in resisting the claims of the original owner. That question need not be decided, because it is not the one the court is called upon to settle. The custody and control of the scrip in the present instance was not retained by the true owner, but was handed over entirely to one of his clerks. When the scrip was deposited in the safe of the Rand Safe Deposit Company, the only key of which was handed over to Maxwell, it was as much under his individual and personal control as if he had been allowed to take it home and lock it up in his private bureau. And that being so, the company must be regarded as having placed it in his hands. . . .

[153] Oakland Nominees (Pty) Ltd v Gelria Mining & Investment Co (Pty) Ltd
1976 (1) SA 441 (AD)

The plaintiff, a mining and investment company, was the beneficial owner of certain shares which were registered in the name of its broker's nominee company. The secretary of the nominee company, who had authority to sign transfer forms on its behalf, stole the shares (share certificates) and sold them to the defendant, who purchased them in good faith and for value. The stockbroker went insolvent and the plaintiff sued the defendant for the shares. The defendant pleaded estoppel. His defence failed.

HOLMES JA: In the Witwatersrand Local Division the present respondent successfully sued the appellant for an order declaring it to be the lawful owner of 2 000 shares in Gledhow Sugar Co Ltd, which shares were registered in the name of the appellant; and for an order declaring the appellant to be obliged to deliver the relevant certificate and the transfer forms. . . .

Although both sides dealt with the case on the footing that the plaintiff's claim was vindicatory, what was claimed was basically a declaration that the shares were vested in Gelria. Although 'ownership' may, juristically, not be accurate in relation to the rights of the person in whom the shares vest, for convenience the descriptive labels of 'owner' and 'ownership' will be retained in this judgment.

The action arose out of the collapse of a firm of stockbrokers known as Louis Witkin, Farber and Co. I shall for convenience refer to the firm as Witkin. The background to the case may be summarized as follows —

(i)   The respondent (to whom I shall refer as Gelria, or the plaintiff, as contextual clarity may require) deals in shares. It had for many years been a client of Witkin and had done all of its share dealings through that firm.

(ii) It is a practice among brokers of the Johannesburg Stock Exchange (JSE) to have a nominee company. The practice is accepted as proper by the JSE. Shares acquired by a broker's client, or by the broker himself, are often transferred into the name of such a company, which then holds the shares as nominee for the client or broker, as the case may be. This practice has certain advantages. For example, shares which have been sold can be transferred on behalf of the client by the broker, acting through the nominee company, and rights can be taken up. This is particularly useful in the case of clients who are not readily available.

(iii) Barnfri Nominees (Pty) Ltd was a nominee company controlled by Witkin. I shall refer to it as Barnfri. . . .

(iv) At all material times one Poplak was employed by Witkin in a senior, managerial capacity. He was also the secretary of Barnfri from 1960 until the date of his death. In 1956 the directors of Barnfri passed a resolution, which remained in force, in terms of which 'transfer deeds and other instruments be signed by one director, or, alternatively, by the secretary . . .'. Such deeds and instruments so signed were to be binding on the company. Hence Poplak was empowered to sign all transfer forms on behalf of Barnfri.

(v) In March 1972 certificates in respect of 2 200 shares in the Gledhow Sugar Co Ltd (Gledhow) were delivered to Witkin, being purchases made by it for Gelria on the JSE.

(vi) Gelria knew that Barnfri was a nominee company controlled by Witkin. In accordance with Gelria's instructions, Witkin caused the above-mentioned certificates in respect of Gledhow shares to be sent to the offices of the transfer secretaries of Gledhow for the registration of transfer of the shares into the name of Barnfri. Accordingly, these 2 200 shares were duly registered in the name of Barnfri under a share certificate No 25256, and the said share certificate was delivered by the transfer secretaries to Witkin in April 1972. Entries were made in Witkin's scrip register and safe custody ledger, recording that the said share certificate No 25256, for 2 200 shares in Gledhow registered in the name of Barnfri, was being held by Witkin in safe custody for Gelria.

(vii) On or about 29 December 1972, on the JSE, Poplak caused Witkin to sell to the partnership known as R S Mennie, stockbrokers and members of the JSE, 2 000 shares in Gledhow for the sum of R7 800. The partnership of R S Mennie later became incorporated as a company. (I shall refer to the partnership and the company as Mennie.) It was marked a 'No offset' transaction. As will appear later, this expression ordinarily means that the identical shares sold will be delivered.

(viii) On 2 January 1973 Poplak stole the said share certificate No 25256 from the safe custody of Witkin and caused it, together with securities transfer form No 10131, to be submitted to C G Smith & Co Ltd (Smith), the transfer secretaries of Gledhow; and also caused Smith, on 4 January 1973, to make the necessary certified deed endorsement, covering 2 000 shares, on the said securities transfer form. This securities transfer form, when submitted to Smith, contained in Part A thereof the details required by the Securities Transfer Act 69 of 1965. It contained the rubber stamp of the selling broker, ie Witkin's stamp. Each broker has such a rubber stamp, approved by the JSE to be used for this purpose. It also contained in Part A the rubber stamp of Barnfri, as transferor, above the handwritten signature of Poplak, as secretary for Barnfri. Part B of the securities transfer form was blank. This portion is usually left blank to be completed by a transferee. (It is plain that the old share certified No 25256 was cancelled and was replaced by two certified securities transfer forms, one being No 10131 for 2 000 shares, and the other being for 200 shares.)

(ix) In all respects this securities transfer form was in the form set out in the First Schedule to the Securities Transfer Act 69 of 1965, as amended, read with Government Notice 703 in *Government Gazette* 2375 dated 2 May 1969.

(x) Section 2 of the Act provides that a security may be transferred by means of a securities transfer form which is defined as the form set out in the First Schedule to the Act.

(xi) Section 3(1)(*a*) of the Act is to the effect that if the transfer secretary of a company

'endorses on any instrument of transfer referred to in section 2 and executed by or on behalf of the transferor, that the certificate relating to the security in question has been lodged with the company, the company shall, for the purposes of this section, be deemed to have certified that instrument'.

(xii) Section 3(3) of the Act reads —

'(3) . . . the delivery to any person of any instrument of transfer certified in terms of sub-sec (1) shall confer on that person the same rights as that person would have acquired before the commencement of this Act upon delivery to him of a certificate for the securities in question and an instrument of transfer signed by the transferor in blank.'

The foregoing statutory provisions were in force then: they have since been included in the Companies Act 1973 [ss 133ff] . . .

(xiii) On 9 January 1973, in performance of the sale referred to in (vii) *supra*, Poplak caused Witkin to deliver to Mennie the securities transfer form No 10131, completed and certified. The delivery was effected through the clearing house of the JSE. Mennie duly paid (also through the clearing house) the sum of R7 800 in settlement of the purchase price.

(xiv) On 17 January 1973 Poplak committed suicide. On 18 January 1973 the estate of Witkin was provisionally sequestrated and the order was made final on 30 January 1973. Thereafter Gelria's attorneys wrote to Mennie's attorneys advising the latter that Gelria was bringing a 'vindicatory' action in respect of the 2 000 Gledhow shares.

(xv) Correspondence followed and it was arranged that the 2 000 shares could be transferred from Barnfri into the name of Oakland Nominees (Pty) Ltd (the appellant) which is a nominee company controlled and owned by Mennie. Registration took place on or about 27 March 1973. Certificate No 25794 was issued. It was agreed that such registration of transfer of the shares would not be used as a defence. In other words, the action was to be decided as if the shares were held by Mennie or, put another way, as if the appellant were put into the shoes of Mennie. . . .

South African law of estoppel in regard to ownership

Our law jealously protects the right of ownership and the correlative right of the owner in regard to his property, unless, of course, the possessor has some enforceable right against the owner. Consistent with this, it has been authoritatively laid down by this court that an owner is estopped from asserting his rights to his property only —

(a) where the person who acquired his property did so because, by the *culpa* of the owner, he was misled into the belief that the person, from whom he acquired it, was the owner or was entitled to dispose of it; or

(b) (possibly) where, despite the absence of *culpa*, the owner is precluded from asserting his rights by compelling considerations of fairness within. the broad concept of the *exceptio doli*. . . .

As to the formulation in (b), *supra*, the occasion has not yet arisen for its further development by this court. Certainly it does not arise in the present appeal, having regard to the pleadings, the evidence, and the arguments in this court.

As to (a), *supra*, it may be stated that the owner will be frustrated by estoppel upon proof of the following requirements —

(i) There must be a representation by the owner, by conduct or otherwise, that the person who disposed of his property was the owner of it or was entitled to dispose of it. . . .

(ii) The representation must have been made negligently in the circumstances.

(iii) The representation must have been relied upon by the person raising the estoppel.

(iv) Such person's reliance upon the representation must be the cause of his acting to his detriment. . . .

. . . [C]ompany share certificates with blank transfer forms are not, in law, negotiable instruments. There is therefore no basis, in law, for regarding them as being excepted from the principle stated above; although their transferability, as distinct from negotiability, may, depending on the circumstances, be relevant in considering the question of negligent representation, *supra*.

It is therefore necessary to examine the facts of the present case, in the light of the evidence, in order to ascertain whether the defendant established the four requirements of a plea of estoppel. . . .

[After dealing with the facts His Lordship continued:]

One is now in a position to deal with the question, posed earlier herein, whether the first requirement of the plea of estoppel was established, namely, whether Gelria, by conduct, represented to Mennie that Barnfri, as a nominee company, had authority to dispose of the Gledhow shares in question.

In the light of all of the evidence, the trial court answered this in the negative. Barnfri's name, as reflected in share certificate No 25256, and, more relevantly, in the certified securities transfer form No 10131, was Barnfri Nominees (Pty) Ltd. It was therefore apparent to anyone confronted therewith that this was a nominee company, subject to instructions from the beneficial owner. As the learned judge put it —

'The registration in the name of a nominee company merely indicates that the nominee is holding for and on behalf of the beneficial holder. All members of the JSE would know this, and Mennie certainly has not suggested that it did not know. There was therefore no representation *to Mennie* or any other member of the JSE that Barnfri had the beneficial owner's authority to sell.'

I agree with the foregoing. In the result, it cannot be said that Gelria's conduct fell within the following criterion formulated by Trollip J (as he then was) in *Electrolux (Pty) Ltd* v *Khota & another* 1961 (4) SA 244 (W) at 247:

'To give rise to the representation of *dominium* or *jus disponendi*, the owner's conduct must be not only the entrusting of possession to the possessor but also the entrusting of it with the *indicia* of the *dominium* or *jus disponendi*. Such *indicia* may be the documents of title and/or of authority to dispose of the articles, as, for example, the share certificate with a blank transfer form annexed. . . .'

It is true that it would be recognized that Barnfri had power to transfer the shares. But power does not mean authority—the *jus disponendi*. To acquire this *jus* Barnfri would have to refer to its principal, Gelria or someone duly acting on its behalf.

This is not a case where an owner of shares has left them with his broker together with share transfer forms signed in blank, which ordinarily constitutes a representation by him that he intended the shares to be transferred. No such representation was made by the plaintiff in the present case. The plaintiff did not put the shares in transferable form, nor did it proclaim that it was its intention to have the shares transferred. When Mennie (or his scrip clerk) received the certified securities transfer form No 10131 in the name of *Barnfri Nominees*, the representation was that they were held by a nominee who was subject to instructions. This is not a case of a representation that the person holding the shares was authorized to transfer them *without reference to the owner*, as appears to be the case in some of the old cases cited in argument. . . .

To sum up on this issue, the representation averred in the plea was not established.

Was Gelria negligent in its conduct? The trial judge answered this in the negative, saying —

'Ebels [the sole director and sole beneficial shareholder of Gelria] had dealt with Witkin and Poplak for very many years. He instructed that Gelria's shares should be registered in the name of Barnfri. In so doing he followed an accepted practice of many years standing. He knew that it was a nominee company which "held" the shares as it were as a trustee. The shares were to be kept in the safe custody of Witkin until he instructed they should be sold. He knew that Witkin, its employees and Poplak, had access to the shares, He knew that someone would sign the transfer documents as and when the shares were to be transferred. It has been suggested that he should have realized that by so registering and leaving the shares he was taking a risk, namely that Witkin or Poplak or someone in Witkin's employ could get possession of the shares and dispose of them. In *Grosvenor Motors (Potchefstroom) Ltd* v *Douglas* 1956 (3) SA 420 (AD) at 428 Steyn JA says:

> "Misplaced confidence in one person is not synonymous with negligence towards another. The existence of negligence must depend on the facts of each case. . . ."

The facts in the present case do not in my view prove that Ebels was negligent. His conduct was that of a normal man of affairs. He had every reason to trust Witkin and Poplak. He could not reasonably foresee that either of them would steal his shares.

He accepted that his shares were being held as it were in trust pending his instructions.'

I agree with the foregoing. I would add that it was not suggested to Mr Ebels in cross-examination that the plaintiff should have anticipated that Poplak might act dishonestly, or that the plaintiff had conducted its affairs negligently in having the shares registered in Barnfri's name and in leaving them with Witkin in safe custody. To sum up on this issue, it was not established that the plaintiff was negligent as pleaded.

Did Mennie, in paying for the shares, rely on the fact that the beneficial owner had registered them in the name of a nominee and left them with his broker for safe-keeping? And was this the cause of Mennie's acting to its detriment? . . .

The trial judge's appraisal of the evidence was as follows—

> 'The registration in the name of the nominee company was not the real reason why Mennie paid for shares and so altered its position for the worse. Poplak caused Witkin to sell the shares. Thereafter he, Poplak, fraudulently appended Barnfri's signature and imprinted Witkin's "approved" rubber stamp. The evidence shows that it was the presence of the rubber stamp that firstly caused the transfer secretary "Smith" to certify the securities transfer form and what is more important, caused Mennie to accept that the Barnfri signature was a proper and authorized signature and to accept delivery of the temporary document of title (ie the certified securities transfer form . . .) and to make the payment of R7 800. This means that even if Gelria was negligent and even if the registration in the name of Barnfri was calculated to mislead others, the evidence shows that the real and direct cause which led Mennie to accept delivery of the shares and to make payment was Witkin's rubber stamp placed on the document by Poplak and not the representation by Gelria.'

I am in general agreement with the foregoing. It would be wrong to say that the requirement is that the representation which is relied upon must be the cause of the defendant's *loss*. Such a formulation would emasculate the defence of estoppel, for the cause of the defendant's loss is nearly always the villainy of the intermediary. In estoppel by negligent representation we are concerned with the effect of the representation on the state of mind of the defendant, ie that his reliance on it was the cause of his *having entered into the transaction* (in the present case, by Mennie's acceptance of the delivered share certificate). This state of mind precedes his loss. Hence the requirement is that the representation and his reliance on it must be the cause of his *having acted as he did*—to his detriment.

To sum up on this issue, Mr Mennie did not give any evidence. There is no direct testimony in proof of the averments in the plea that, 'by reason of the plaintiff's said negligent representation', Mennie accepted the securities transfer form and paid the purchase price of the shares; and that he would not have so acted had it not been for the plaintiff's said representation. Nor was there any such evidence from Mennie's scrip clerk (Miss McKinnon) whose duty it was to scrutinize the scrip delivered in respect of this transaction. There was no evidence that either Mennie or Miss McKinnon had been misled by any representation by Gelria, or by the fact that the shares were registered in the name of Barnfri Nominees (Pty) Ltd. On the contrary, Miss McKinnon accepted the share certificate and passed it for payment because of the broker's stamp thereon; and she indicated that it was a matter of indifference to her who might have signed it. Finally, in view of her evidence, it cannot be said that there was proof, by inference, of the aforementioned averments in the plea.

In these circumstances it cannot be said either that Mennie or Miss McKinnon relied on any representation by Gelria or, if they did, that such reliance was the cause of their acting as they did to Mennie's detriment.

To sum up with regard to the plea of estoppel, not one of the four requisites of that defence was established.

NOTES

Another vindicatory action in respect of shares in which the defence of estoppel failed was *Standard Bank* v *Stama (Pty) Ltd* 1975 (1) SA 730 (AD).

See further *Smith and Rause* v *Philips* (1893) Hertzog 50; *Tripp* v *Henderson* (1894) 15 NLR 182; *African Mining and Financial Association Ltd* v *Oppenheimer* (1897) 4 Off Rep 314; *African Mining and Financial Association* v *De Catelin and Muller NO* (1897) 4 Off Rep 344; *Van Blommestein* v *Holliday* (1904) 21 SC 11; *Longman* v *Bath Electric Tramways Ltd* [1905] 1 Ch 646; *Fry* v *Smellie* [1912] 3 KB 282; *Sprinz* v *Rayton Diamonds Ltd* 1926 WLD 23; *West* v *Pollak and Freemantle* 1936 WLD 37; confirmed on appeal, 1937 TPD 64; *West* v *De Villiers* 1938 CPD 96.

Estoppel does not operate where the third party acted on the faith of a forged transfer (*Jeffery* v *Pollak and Freemantle* 1938 AD 1; *Davis* v *Buffelsfontein Gold Mining Co Ltd* 1967 (4) SA 631 (W)) or where the shares alone are handed over without a transfer (*Rees* v *Jackson and Blyth* (1894) 1 Off Rep 285).

Where a party to whom shares are pledged by a transfer in blank and the handing over of the scrip, pledges them to someone else, the latter is not protected if he knows of the rights of the true owner: *Sykes* v *Venning & Creighton and the Standard Bank* (1889) 10 NLR 89. See also *In re Tahiti Cotton Co: Ex parte Sargent* (1874) LR 17 Eq 273. But cf *France* v *Clark* (1884) 26 ChD 257.

[154] *In re* Tahiti Cotton Company: *Ex parte* Sargent
(1874) LR 17 Eq 273

JESSEL MR: . . . Mr Fry borrows what I will call for shortness' sake £450 of a Mr Cannon, a sharebroker. He deposits with him as security the transfers of certain shares not quite filled up, that is, there was no date to them, and there was no name of the transferee; they were what are commonly called blank transfers. The deposits were made on two different occasions as a security. He hands to him also certificates of shares. I have no doubt that without express words Mr Cannon was authorized, and was intended to be authorized by Mr Fry, if necessary, to fill up the blanks, and get the shares registered. The object and meaning of the whole transaction was, that if the money was not paid, Mr Cannon should do this. . . .

NOTES

Handing over of shares under an oral agreement that they are to be pledged is sufficient in our law to constitute a valid pledge: *Bernstein v Mankowitz's Assignees* 1933 CPD 466.

See further *Hanau and Wicke v Standard Bank* (1891) 4 SAR 130 and *Smith v Farrelly's Trustee* 1904 TS 949, per Smith J: '. . . For a valid pledge of an incorporeal right the law requires the right to be ceded by the pledgor, and to be vested in the pledgee to hold as security for a debt. As a general rule no particular form of words need be used to effect a cession, and it may be effected either verbally or by a written instrument. . . . Where . . . the evidence of the right is contained in the written instrument which records it, then the right cannot be completely ceded unless the instrument is delivered to the cessionary. . . .' (The last statement needs qualification now—see e g *Labuschagne v Denny* 1963 (3) SA 538 (AD).)

A creditor who sends the share certificates pledged to him together with the completed transfer forms to the company concerned to have them registered in his name does not thereby lose his lien over the share certificates: *De Wet NO v Die Bank van die OVS Bpk* 1968 (2) SA 73 (O).

On the nature and effect of a pledge of shares, see also *Oertel NO v Brink* 1972 (3) SA 669 (W), further M L Benade (1964) 27 *THR-HR* 279.

[155] S *v* McPherson
1972 (2) SA 348 (EC)

In this criminal trial the accused, a stockbroker, was charged, *inter alia*, with 50 counts of theft. On 24 of these counts the accused pleaded guilty. His plea of not guilty on another 19 counts was accepted by the State. This left 7 counts on which the State and the defence joined issue. Basically, it was alleged that the accused had received share certificates which were either the property of his clients or the property of some other persons, and that, in breach of his legal duties towards such clients or other persons, the accused used such scrip for his own purposes, namely by pledging it as security for loans extended to him by banking or other institutions.

ADDLESON J: The seven counts now in issue are . . . all cases where the accused was instructed to buy shares on behalf of clients and ordered the shares in question from Max Pollak and Freemantle and received shares from Max Pollak and Freemantle of the same sort as those ordered for his clients. It is moreover common cause that on each of these seven counts he pledged the shares he thus received with the institutions alleged, as security for loans advanced to him by such institutions, and that, after uplifting them at the later date set out in column 6 of annexure A, he then caused them to be registered in the name of the client and/or delivered them to the client.

The sole enquiry in regard to these seven counts is therefore whether the accused had the right to use, that is to pledge, these shares as he did. This in turn involves the question whether the clients had any right in such shares at the time the accused pledged them. It was common cause between the defence and the State that, if at the time of such pledging and until the shares were uplifted from pledge the clients in question had no ownership or other essential legal interest in the shares, the accused could not by pledging them, have committed theft as against such clients, or fraud as against the financial institutions concerned in that, as far as fraud is concerned, he would not then have falsely been representing that he had the right to pledge such shares.

However, before we deal with the facts and the legal position relating to the clients' ownership or other legal interest in such shares, it is necessary to refer to certain statutory provisions on which emphasis was placed by the State, both in the indictment and in argument, and by certain witnesses who were tendered by the State as experts on the law and custom relating to a stockbroker's rights and obligations vis-à-vis a client for whom he has bought shares.

It was common cause, as set out in para 1(c) of the indictment, that at all material times the conduct of the accused's stockbroking business was subject to the provisions of the Stock Exchanges Control Act 7 of 1947, the regulations made by the Minister of Finance under that Act, the Rules of the Johannesburg Stock Exchange and the regulations made under those Rules by the committee of the Johannesburg Stock Exchange and the customs and usages of the Johannesburg Stock Exchange.

The principal statutory provisions on which the State relied were rules 163 and 163*bis* of the Rules of the Johannesburg Stock Exchange. There are analogous provisions in s 20 of the Stock Exchanges Control Act and in sub-rule (T)(ii) of the regulations made under that Act, but it is not necessary to refer to them in this judgment, nor for present purposes is it necessary to set out the terms of rule 163 but I shall quote briefly the relevant passages from rule 163*bis* as far as it concerns these counts. Rule 163*bis* provides as follows:

'(i) (a) Subject to the provisions of para (b) of this sub-rule and of sub-rule (4) hereof, (aa) the aggregate of the amount of money a member may borrow against the security of a client's stocks or shares and the amount of money a member may borrow by other use of such client's stocks or shares, shall not exceed the amount owing to the member by the client against such stocks or shares. (bb) Such member shall not re-pledge or use more of a client's stocks or shares than are necessary for this purpose.

(b) . . .

(ii) Stocks or shares belonging to a client against which the client owes money to a member and which are not re-pledged or used in terms of sub-rules (i) and (iv), shall be so segregated and distinguished that they can at all times be identified as the client's property. Under no circumstances may use be made of such stocks or shares except as provided for in sub-rules (i) and (iv) hereof. . . .

(iv) Notwithstanding the provisions of sub-rule (i) hereof, stocks or shares referred to therein which have been pledged in terms of a pledge form referred to in sub-rule (v) may in isolated cases only be used by a member for such purposes as the client owning them may by means of a special agreement in writing agree to, provided that an agreement between a member and his client shall not for the purposes of this sub-rule be deemed to be a special agreement if such agreement: (*a*) does not stipulate the number of shares or nominal value of stocks which may be used by the member and the company by which such stocks or shares have been issued; (*b*) is required by a member as a condition precedent to transacting business on behalf of a client.

(v) With effect from 1st January, 1963 no member may re-pledge or use his client's stocks or shares for borrowing purposes unless they have been pledged to him in terms of such pledge form as may from time to time be prescribed by the committee.'

The effect of these statutory provisions is that a stockbroker who holds clients' shares may not pledge those shares at all if they are fully paid but must keep them separate and identified as his clients' property. The only exception is the case where a broker has made a loan to his client who has delivered his scrip to the broker as security for the loan. None of these exceptions apply to the counts now under consideration. If the shares are not fully paid for, the broker may pledge them only for the amount still owing by the client on those shares and then only with the written consent of the client on a form specially provided for such purpose.

The above provisions of rules 163 and 163*bis* were made much of by the State in its evidence, of the expert witnesses and in argument, and were, we think, accepted without dispute by the defence. We feel, however, that Mr O was correct in his contention that the provisions of these Rules have no direct application to the seven counts with which we are now concerned. The accused is not charged with a contravention of the Act, the Rules or the regulations, nor is he at present facing charges, either civil, criminal or disciplinary, that he acted in breach of the customs and usages of stockbroking or of the Johannesburg Stock Exchange. He is charged with the common law crimes of theft, alternatively fraud, and his breach of the regulations or of stockbroking practice can only be relevant if such breach brings his actions within the type of criminal conduct which constitutes theft or fraud. In the present case, having regard to the issue between the State and the defence, he can only be convicted of theft if the clients in question had ownership or some 'special property or interest' in the shares at the time of the pledging. See Hunt *South African Criminal Law and Procedure* vol 2 pp 590 to 602, to which work we shall hereafter in this judgment refer to as Hunt vol 2. For the same reason the accused can only be convicted of fraud if, at the time he pledged the shares, he did not have the right to represent that he was entitled to pledge them because the ownership or some other special property or interest vested in the client. See Hunt vol 2 above at pp 714 and following pages. If there was no such ownership or special property or interest in the client at the time of such pledging, the fact that the accused breached rules 163 and 163*bis* (if indeed he could breach them when the client had no ownership or other special interest in the shares) or that he breached any other statutory enactment or acted contrary to his other legal duties as a stockbroker, cannot suffice to bring home a charge of theft or fraud against him.

It appears that the question whether the client had acquired ownership or any other relevant interest in the shares at the time of the pledging, depends on whether or not the shares in question had been allocated to the client at such time. . . .

[The learned judge then set out the evidence of certain employees of the accused and proceeded:]

There is ample evidence that it is for the broker to decide which shares received by him shall be allocated to clients who have ordered such shares and in what order he shall allocate them. It is clear, for example, that if clients X, Y and Z had instructed the accused to purchase 100 De Beers deferred shares for each of them, and on a particular day the broker received 200 De Beers deferred from Johannesburg, it was in his discretion to decide not to allocate any of those shares to X but to allocate them to Y and Z, even if X had ordered those shares before Y and Z. Various reasons might motivate his decision, such as the fact that Z was a very good client or that X was a bad payer or that it was inconvenient to 'split' a parcel of shares which had arrived from Johannesburg. Leaving aside his obligation eventually to deliver shares to a client of the type and at the price which the client had ordered, the broker is under no obligation to earmark a particular share certificate received by him from the market to a client who has ordered the number and type of shares which the certificate represents. . . .

[The learned judge then dealt with the evidence and proceeded:]

It seems clear from this evidence that whatever may be the position in regard to a possible failure by a broker to fulfil his other duties to his client, the scrip does not become the property of the client until it is allocated to him; and that allocation consists in the physical act of clearly identifying the scrip in the name of the client by pinning-up, that is by attaching a docket to the scrip, stating the name of the client and describing the shares in question and by keeping the scrip apart from other scrip.

[The learned judge found, on the facts, that this had not been done by the accused with the scrip in issue, and that, in consequence, a charge of theft at common law could not succeed. Nor did he accept the contention of the State that even if allocation has not taken place, the client had a 'special property or interest in the shares' which was capable of being stolen:]

. . . [T]he fallacy lies in the suggestion not supported by legal principle that a broker who receives for a client, scrip which he has not yet allocated, is a trustee in respect of such scrip. If, by using such a term, the expert witnesses for the State meant that the broker has contractual and statutory duties towards his client in regard to such scrip, we would agree. But we cannot find that a broker is a trustee in relation to such scrip in the sense that the client has any legal interest in, or right to, unallocated scrip, which right would be capable of being stolen at common law.

[156] McKay v Stein
1951 (3) SA 1 (AD)

Centlivres CJ: This is an appeal from an order made by the Witwatersrand Local Division upholding an exception to a declaration on the ground that the declaration disclosed no cause of action.

The declaration alleged that the plaintiff was a duly licensed stock and sharebroker and that, acting on the instructions of the defendant, he purchased on his behalf on 6 June 1949 five hundred shares in the Union Free State Mining & Finance Co Ltd for £1 012 10s, which he (the plaintiff) duly paid. The declaration proceeded as follows:

'7. Immediately after plaintiff purchased the shares as aforesaid defendant wrongfully and unlawfully repudiated the said contract between him and plaintiff and refused to pay the said purchase price or any of the said disbursements. Thereafter defendant wrongfully and unlawfully failed to comply with his obligations under s 13(1) of Act 7 of 1947, and plaintiff, on 28 June 1949, acting in pursuance of s 13(5) of the said Act, sold the said shares on the Union Stock Exchange for the account of defendant for the sum of £291 5s.

8. Plaintiff says that the market price at which the said shares could have been sold on the Union Stock Exchange on 21 June 1949, being the date forthwith after the expiration of the period of 14 days after the purchase of the said shares, was 13s 4½d per share.

10. In the premises there is a balance of account in favour of plaintiff of £740 6s 5d, being the sum of £1 026 19s 3d (ie the abovementioned sum of £1 012 10s, plus stamp, tax and brokerage charges) less £286 12s 10d (ie the aforementioned sum of £291 5s less stamp, tax and brokerage charges).

11. From the said sum of £740 6s 5d plaintiff deducts the sum of £43 2s 6d, being the difference between the market price of the said shares on 21 June 1949 and on 28 June 1949, leaving a balance due and payable by defendant to plaintiff of £697 3s 11d . . .'

Plaintiff accordingly claimed the sum of £697 3s 11d interest *a tempore morae* and costs of suit.

Section 13 of the Stock Exchanges Control Act 7 of 1947 is, in so far as it is relevant to this case, as follows:

'(1) If any stockbroker buys any stocks or shares on behalf of any person, that person shall, not later than fourteen days after the purchase —

(a) pay to the stockbroker the amount payable by him in respect of the stocks or shares; or

(b) deposit with the stockbroker such stocks or shares as (either alone or together with any stocks or shares so bought which may be held by the stockbroker in respect of the amount owing to him by the purchaser in pursuance of the purchase) may be necessary to provide the minimum cover in respect of the said amount. . . .

(5) If any person has not complied with the provisions of subsection (1) . . . at least seven days before the expiration of the relevant period

referred to therein, the stockbroker concerned shall forthwith give him written notice of his obligation to act in terms of this subsection, and if such person fails to comply with the said provisions, such stock-broker shall—

(*a*) in the case of a non-compliance with the provisions of subsection (1) . . . sell for the account of that person, so much of the stocks or shares held by him in terms of the said provisions, as may be necessary to reduce the debt in question to an amount in respect of which any such stocks or shares not sold by the stockbroker, provide the minimum cover.

(7) The provisions of this section shall not be interpreted as rendering ineffective any contractual obligation to make any payment or to deposit, deliver or cede any stocks or shares before the expiry of the relative period referred to in subsection (1). . . .'

The declaration to which exception was taken was an amended declaration. The plaintiff had previously filed a declaration in which he had claimed from the defendant the sum of £740 6*s* 5*d* which is mentioned in para 10 of his amended declaration. Defendant excepted to the original declaration on the ground that it disclosed no cause of action. Millin J upheld the exception for the following reasons (see *McKay* v *Stein* 1950 (4) SA 692 (W) at 700):

'As the declaration stands, the sale by the plaintiff on which he bases his claim to a balance in his favour appears to have been made at a time outside the time fixed by the statute. It may be that there were special circumstances which made a sale on 28 June a sale "forthwith" within the meaning of the statute; but the plaintiff has not pleaded these circumstances, and therefore it is impossible to say from the declaration that he acted within the terms of the statute.
  It follows that no cause of action is disclosed for a claim by the plaintiff to recover a balance in his favour.' . . .

Counsel for the plaintiff accepted the position that the broker's obligation was to sell 'forthwith' and both counsel for the plaintiff and counsel for the defendant agreed that 'forthwith' meant 'as soon as is reasonably possible'. It is clear from the amended declaration that it is based on the position that plaintiff was, in the circumstances stated, under an obligation to sell forthwith.
In his reasons for judgment Ramsbottom J, who heard the argument on the exception to the amended declaration said:

'The argument put forward by Mr P on behalf of the defendant (the excipient) was as follows: At common law, a stockbroker whose client has repudiated a sale made on his behalf has one of two remedies; he may either refuse to accept the repudiation and hold the client to his contract, claiming reimbursement and remuneration, or he may accept the repudiation as a breach of the contract of agency and claim damages. In the latter event, damages are assessed as at the date of the acceptance of the repudiation or within a reasonable time from that date. Act 7 of 1947 has effected a change. A stockbroker who has bought shares and whose client has repudiated may still hold the client to the contract and claim reimbursement, tendering delivery, as in *Samons* v *Freedman* 1950 (1) SA 156 (W), and he can still accept the repudiation and claim damages. But the Act obliges him, if he has not accepted the repudiation but has kept the contract alive, and if he has not received payment or cover, to sell the shares "forthwith" after the lapse of 14 days from the date of purchase. If he carries out his statutory duty and sells on the prescribed date, he is given a remedy against the client—a new remedy which did not exist at common law. The sale is "for the account of" the client and is regarded as having been effected on the client's instructions. The stockbroker can then claim the difference between what he paid for the shares on the client's behalf, plus other disbursements and brokerage, less what the shares realized when sold, and also his disbursements and brokerage in connection with the sale. But, so Mr P argued, this statutory remedy is contingent upon the performance of the statutory duty; the stockbroker cannot sell at some later date, and then claim from his client as if he had carried out his statutory obligation; the statute does not fix a date for the assessment of damages for breach, but gives a new remedy to a stockbroker who has refused to accept his client's repudiation and who has kept the contract alive.

I do not think that there is any answer to Mr P's argument. It is common cause that the declaration means that the plaintiff refused to accept the defendant's repudiation; it was so interpreted by Millin J, and this exception has been argued on that basis. Consequently this is not a claim for damages; if it were, damages would have to be claimed as at the date of the acceptance of the repudiation— and the repudiation has not been accepted. It is clear that the plaintiff is claiming the statutory remedy. But the statute gives a remedy upon the performance of a statutory duty, and the stockbroker cannot, in my opinion, while claiming to keep the contract alive, sell the shares at some date which he selects, and claim from his client what he would have been able to claim if he had performed his statutory obligation.'

If the judgment in the court *a quo* is correct it seems to follow that:

(1)	the plaintiff has lost any remedy he might have had against the defendant, as he has sold the shares and can no longer tender them to the defendant and claim reimbursement and

(2)	he has rendered himself liable to be prosecuted under s 25(1)(*b*)(ii) and liable to a fine not exceeding £500 or to imprisonment for a period not exceeding one year or to both such fine and imprisonment.

If on a proper construction of the Act these dire consequences result, a court of law cannot come to the relief of the plaintiff.

It was contended by Mr P on behalf of the defendant that the plaintiff would, if the judgment of the trial court was correct, not be without a remedy as he could still sue the defendant for damages based on the difference between the contract price and the market price of the shares on 7 June, the day on which the defendant repudiated the contract. This contention would no doubt be sound, if the plaintiff had accepted the defendant's repudiation but the inference to be drawn from the declaration is that there was no such acceptance. The plaintiff was not bound to accept the repudiation by the defendant: he was fully entitled—and there is nothing in the Act to deprive him of this right—to hold the shares up to 20 June for delivery to the defendant against payment of the cost of the shares plus brokerage charges and stamp duty and tax. Under s 13(5) of the Act, however, the defendant having failed on or before 20 June to carry out the obligation imposed on him by ss (1) of that section, the plaintiff was bound to sell all the shares for the account of the defendant. I say all the shares, because the minimum cover which had to be provided by the defendant under that subsection was 50 per cent of the amount they would realize at the buyers' price last quoted in the lists issued under the authority of a stock exchange in the Union before the date on which the cover is provided. See the definition of 'minimum cover' in s 1 of the Act. As the shares had fallen in value after their date of purchase, half of the contract price would not have been realized if they had been sold on 21 June at the price quoted in the stock exchange list.

I shall assume, as was decided in *Samons* v *Freedman* (*supra*), that if the plaintiff had commenced legal proceedings against the defendant before 20 June and claimed payment from defendant against delivery of the shares, plaintiff would not have been compelled by s 13(5) of the Act to sell the shares forthwith after 20 June. In the present case, however, the plaintiff did not adopt that course and I may add that, even although the plaintiff did not accept the defendant's repudiation on 7 June of the contract, he was under no obligation to institute proceedings for payment on or before 20 June. But not having so instituted such proceedings, he could not retain the shares after 20 June for the purpose of delivering them to the defendant against payment, for under s 13(5) he was bound to sell the shares forthwith for the account of the defendant. . . . Does the failure of the plaintiff to sell the shares on 21 June result in his having forfeited any claim he might have had against the defendant? There is nothing in the Act which expressly decrees such a forfeiture nor can such a forfeiture in my opinion be inferred by necessary implication from the words used by the legislature. Moreover a deprivation of rights is not lightly to be inferred. . . . It does not seem to me to be likely that the legislature in enacting s 13(5) intended that if a broker through inadvertence, sickness or any other cause failed to sell forthwith shares bought by him on behalf of a client, he should lose all right of recourse against his client. Such a conclusion is not necessary in order to carry out the object of the legislature. As to what the object of the legislature was, I agree with the views of Millin J, which he stated in *McKay* v *Stein* (*supra*) at 697:

> 'As to the manifest object of the legislator in enacting s 13, it cannot be doubted that this was to discourage the giving of credit to people who desire to speculate in stocks and shares without having the means to pay for shares bought on their behalf or to provide shares which may have been sold on their behalf. The evident intention is that where principals do not, within 14 days, comply with their statutory obligations, the broker, by selling, or buying, as the case may be, is to close the account in so far as minimum cover is not available.

Thus, where shares have been bought on the principal's behalf, and they fall in value, after the sale, and neither money nor minimum cover is provided by the principal, it is necessary, in order to close the account, to sell all the shares bought on the principal's behalf. On any other view, the broker would be left with the shares in his possession for which the principal has neither paid nor given security, and the result would be the giving of credit in circumstances in which the legislators have been at pains to prohibit the giving of credit.'

There is no danger of defeating the object of the legislature if it is held in the present case that the plaintiff has not lost his right of recourse against the defendant. That object is sufficiently safeguarded by the fact that the plaintiff has rendered himself liable to be prosecuted under s 25(1)(*b*)(ii) for a contravention of s 13(5). . . .

For these reasons it seems to me that the plaintiff's declaration does disclose a cause of action. The appeal is allowed with costs and the order made by the Witwatersrand Local Division is set aside . . .

NOTES

Since *McKay* v *Stein* s 13 of the Stock Exchanges Control Act has been amended in important respects, but it is generally accepted that there has been no change in regard to the effect of a failure on the stockbroker's part to sell the shares of his defaulting client as provided in the section, see *Amm* v *Mia* 1974 (4) SA 138 (T) at 143B, C, where Myburgh J followed *McKay's* case. But see also *Dalrymple, Frank & Co* v *Schochat* 1972 (2) SA 15 (W), where Snyman J, after referring to the statement of Millin J in *McKay* v *Stein* 1950 (4) SA 692 (W) at 697, quoted with approval by Centlivres CJ in *McKay's* case, said (at 17A):

'I must accept therefore that the provision in s 13(5) was made, not for the benefit of particular individuals, but as a matter of public policy to curb speculation. Consequently a broker and his client have no right to waive it.'

He concluded (at 18F, G):

'The effect of s 13(5) is to render ineffective or unenforceable any contract, compromise or novation in conflict with s 13(5). The section provides that the broker shall "sell for the account" of the client. In other words it may be said that the legislature constitutes the broker the "statutory agent" of his former common law principal. By so doing it renders unenforceable the rights which had accrued to him at common law. It follows that his client, if sued under such a contract, has a good defence to the action. The only remedy available to such a broker is a claim for the difference (if any) between the price at which he bought the shares for his client and the price obtaining on the date on which it was his statutory duty to "sell out" against his client.'

Special rules apply to 'bear sales', ie sales of listed securities of which the seller is at the time of the sale neither the owner nor entitled to become the owner, Stock Exchanges Control Act 7 of 1947 s 1 s v 'bear sale'.

On a stockbroker's liability, see Philip J Hoblin Jr 'A Stockbroker's Implied Liability to its Customer for Violation of a Rule of a Registered Stock Exchange' (1970) 39 *Fordham LR* 253.

V 'RIGGING THE MARKET'

A TEXT

'Rigging the market' is a statutory offence under s 21A of the Stock Exchanges Control Act 7 of 1947, which provides that 'No person shall by means of any statement, promise or forecast which he knows to be misleading induce any other person to buy or sell listed securities, or directly or indirectly, whether within or outside a stock exchange, by means of the creation of fictitious transactions or the spreading of false reports, attempt to stimulate activities or influence the prices of securities on a licensed stock exchange'. It has long been a crime at common law: *157, 158*.

B CASES

[157] R *v* De Berenger
King's Bench (1814) 3 M & S 67, 105 ER 536

'De Berenger and seven others were tried at the London sittings . . . before Lord Ellenborough CJ upon an indictment for a conspiracy [and convicted].

The indictment set forth by way of general inducement, that at the time of committing the several offences, etc, there was and for a long time before, to wit, two years and upwards, had been an open and public war between our lord the King and his allies, and the then ruler of France, to wit, Napoleon Bonaparte, and the people of France; and the third count stated that the defendants on February 19 in the 54th year of the King unlawfully contriving, etc, by false reports, rumours, arts, and contrivances, to induce the subjects of the King to believe that a peace would soon be made between the King and his subjects, and the people of France, and thereby to occasion without any just or true cause a great increase and rise of the public Government funds and Government securities of this kingdom, and to injure and aggrieve the subjects of the King, who should on February 21 purchase and buy any part or parts, and share or shares of and in the said public Government funds, etc, then and there to wit on February 21 unlawfully, etc, did conspire, etc, to make and propagate and cause to be made and propagated, unto and among divers subjects, etc, in the country of Kent, etc, and also unto and among divers subjects, etc, at London, and places adjacent thereto, divers false reports and rumours that the said N Bonaparte was killed, and that a peace would soon be made between the King and his subjects, and the people of France, and that the defendants would by such false reports and rumours, as far as in them lay, occasion an increase and rise in the prices of the public Government funds and other Government securities, with a wicked intention thereby to injure and aggrieve all the subjects of the King who should, on February 21, purchase or buy any part or parts, share or shares of and in the said public Government funds, and other Government securities, etc' . . .

LORD ELLENBOROUGH CJ: I am perfectly clear that there is not any ground for the motion in arrest of judgment. A public mischief is stated as the object of this conspiracy; the conspiracy is by false rumours to raise the price of the public funds and securities; and the crime lies in the act of conspiracy and combination to effect that purpose, and would have been complete although it had not been pursued to its consequences, or the parties had not been able to carry it into effect. The purpose itself is mischievous, it strikes at the price of a vendible commodity in the market and if it gives it a fictitious price, by means of false rumours, it is a fraud levelled against all the public, for it is against all such as may possibly have any thing to do with the funds on that particular day. It seems to me also not to be necessary to specify the persons, who became purchasers of stock, as the persons to be affected by the conspiracy, for the defendants could not, except by a spirit of prophecy, divine who would be the purchasers on a subsequent day. The excuse is, that it was impossible they should have known, and if it were possible, the multitude would be an excuse in point of law. But the statement is wholly unnecessary, the conspiracy being complete independently of any persons being purchasers. I have no doubt it must be so considered in law according to the cases. . . .

[158] S v Marks
1965 (3) SA 834 (W)

HILL J: In count 8, the accused is charged with the crime of *falsitas*, it being alleged

'In that whereas at all relevant times the accused was in fact and in terms of s 381 (10) of Act 56 of 1955 a person who controlled or governed three companies known respectively as Annyspruit Coal Development and Exploration Co Ltd, Western Main Reefs Ltd and Unicorn Investments Ltd, or was a member of a body or group of persons which did so; . . .

'And whereas at all relevant times the accused was a member of the Johannesburg Stock Exchange:

'Now therefore during the period 1 April 1958 to 20 February 1959, and at or near Johannesburg, in the district of Johannesburg, the said accused did wrongfully, unlawfully, falsely and with intent thereby to defraud give out and pretend to the public at large and to the members of the Johannesburg Stock Exchange and their employees that:

(1) there was a bona fide and active market in the shares of the following companies: Unicorn Investments Ltd, Western Main Reefs Ltd and Annyspruit Coal Development and Exploration Co Ltd;

(2) there was a large and genuine demand by the public for the said shares;

(3) the said shares were increasing in price and value as a result of a genuine and large demand by the public for, and an active market in these shares;

(4) the said shares were worth the market price or more than the market price;

(5) the market prices were not a true and fair reflection of the value of the said shares;

(6) there was demand for the said shares on the Stock Exchange, London:

'And did by means of the said false pretences and to their loss and prejudice (actual and potential) influence and induce:

(a) the members of the public and the members of the Johannesburg Stock Exchange and their employees to buy, sell and deal in the said shares at the market prices thereof;

(b) the members of the Johannesburg Stock Exchange and their employees to enter into carrying deals and time bargains in these shares according to the market prices thereof:

'Whereas in truth and in fact the accused, when he gave out and pretended, well knew that:

(1) there was not a bona fide and active market in the said shares;

(2) there was not a large and genuine demand by the public for the said shares;

(3) the said shares were not increasing in price and value as a result of a genuine and large demand by the public for, and an active market in these shares;

(4) the said shares were not worth the market price or more than the market price;

(5) the market prices were not a true and fair reflection of the value of the said shares;

(6) there was no demand for the said shares on the Stock Exchange, London.

'And thus the said accused is guilty of *falsitas*.'

What is alleged in the count is a form of fraud commonly known as 'rigging the market' and the charge is confined to the shares of the three public companies in which the accused was interested, namely, Unicorn Investments Ltd, Western Main Reefs Ltd and Annysspruit Coal Development and Exploration Co Ltd.

The case of *The King* v *De Berenger & others* [*157* above] appears to be the first case of a market rig detected in England. . . .

In South Africa the question of what constitutes rigging was considered by De Waal JP on a motion to quash an indictment in the case of *R* v *McLachlan and Bernstein* 1929 WLD 149. At p 156 the learned Judge-President expressed the view that three essential elements are required to constitute the crime of 'rigging the market':

'(1) the rigger must hold a parcel of shares (generally a large parcel) which he wishes to off-load on the ignorant public, and which he cannot otherwise off-load than by a fraudulent market manipulation — by the artificial creation of a fictitious market, (2) the shares must be intrinsically valueless or practically valueless, or, at any rate, intrinsically far below the level at which the rigger intends and hopes to off-load and (3) as a result of a successful "rig", the unsuspecting public must be left in possession of the worthless scrip, at which moment of time the rigger withdraws his support by ceasing to operate, as an inevitable result whereof the shares recede to their original value, that is to the value at which they stood before the "rig" commenced.'

As pointed out by the Hon E R Roper in his treatise *Stock Exchange Law in South Africa* at 82, with reference to *R* v *McLachlan and Bernstein*, it is not a necessary element of rigging that shares should be valueless or that members of the public should be left with worthless scrip on their hands and in support of his view the learned author refers to *R* v *De Berenger* (*supra*), where the securities affected were British Government stocks.

The learned Judge-President, however, did make the qualification, in the passage above quoted, that the shares must at least be far below the 'value' at which the rigger hopes to off-load and that as a result of the operation shares recede to the 'value' at which they stood before the commencement of the rig.

I do not think that by saying that it is essential that the rigger must hold a parcel of shares which he wishes to off-load upon the public, the learned Judge-President meant that a parcel of shares is a necessary prerequisite for the perpetration of a rig. It is only at the time when the rigger wishes to benefit by the result of his rigging operations that he must have a parcel of shares to off-load upon the buying public at a profit. The rigger may manipulate market dealings by placing buying and selling orders without becoming the holder of any shares but with the view to acquiring, at some stage during the operation, a quantity of shares for off-loading at a later stage when the prices have risen to the desired level. Or the rigger may have the right to a call or an option to buy shares which he would exercise when a profit could be made as a result of his manipulations. It may even happen that a person or persons who have control of a company would procure an increase of the capital of the company with the motive of acquiring the additional shares at a particular price and selling them at a profit. Reference has been made earlier in this judgment to the increase of the capital of Unicorn Investments Ltd on 28 November 1958 from 50 000 shares to 64 000 shares at 10*s* each. The additional 14 000 shares were issued at 10*s* each to the accused, I Isakow and their respective wives. No cash was paid to the company but the amounts payable to the company were simply transferred to loan accounts. . . .

. . .

The State set out to prove that the accused rigged the market in the shares of the three companies by various devices such as the introduction of assets into the companies at 'blown up' prices to create a false impression that the companies owned valuable assets; the acquisition by the accused of large quantities of shares in the companies to enable him to control the market; causing a large turnover in the shares by buying and selling his own shares either personally or through agents in order to create the false impression that there was a genuine demand by the public for the shares and an active market in the shares; causing a constant upward trend in the prices by buying at increased prices and selling at a loss.

[The court convicted the accused of the crime of 'rigging the market'.]

NOTES

Under s 21B of the Stock Exchanges Control Act 7 of 1947 no person may publish or issue to the public or circulate any written comment which relates to the trading results of any company or which may influence the value of the securities of any company unless such comment is accompanied by the name of the person or persons who compiled it or disclosure of the source from which it was obtained. If any information is disclosed by a company to registered holders of listed securities which may influence the price of such securities it must be made available at the same time for immediate publication to the president of the stock exchange concerned and the press, s 9C(3) of the Act. Various 'manipulative' practices are specifically prohibited by the Rules of the Stock Exchanges. On the liability of a company for negligently misleading press releases, see (1973) 122 *U of Pen LR* 162.

9 *The Company in General Meeting*

I MEETINGS

A TEXT

The general meeting is the organ through which the members of a company act: *159, 160*. There are two kinds of general meetings: annual general meetings and other general meetings.

Every company must hold annual general meetings. Its first meeting must be held within eighteen months after its incorporation, subsequent meetings not more than six months after the end of every ensuing financial year and within not more than fifteen months after the last preceding annual general meeting, s 179(1); see also (3) and (4). At each annual general meeting the annual financial statements of the company, consisting of a balance sheet, an income statement, a directors' report and an auditor's report must be laid before the meeting, as provided in ss 286ff.

General meetings other than the annual general meeting may, subject to the provisions of the articles, be held from time to time. Usually, the articles give the directors power to convene general meetings, see Schedule 1 Table A art 34, Table B art 33. The directors are obliged to call a general meeting on the requisition of 100 members of the company or of members holding not less than one-twentieth of the voting capital of the company, s 181: *161, 162*.

A number of provisions take care of special situations. A general meeting may be called by two or more members of the company holding not less than one-tenth of the issued share capital or, in the case of a company not having a share capital, by not less than 5 per cent in number of the members, s 180. The Registrar may call or direct the calling of a meeting, on the application of a member or his legal representative if all the directors have become incapacitated or have ceased to be directors, s 182. The court, on its own initiative or on the application of the Registrar, a director, or a member, has power to order a general meeting to be called whenever it is for any reason impracticable to call a meeting in the manner in which meetings are ordinarily called or to conduct it in the ordinary fashion, or for any other good reason, s 183: *163.*

Unless the articles otherwise provide, notice of meeting must be served on members in the manner prescribed in Table A (art 35) or B (art 34) as the case may be, s 187. The length of notice is twenty-one days for the annual general meeting and a meeting for the passing of a special resolution, and fourteen days for any other general meeting, s 186. The articles may prescribe longer but not shorter periods of notice, s 186(1), but a majority of members holding not less than 95 per cent of all the total voting rights may agree to have a meeting called on shorter notice, s 186(2).

Failure to give notice as required to all registered shareholders renders the meeting and any resolutions passed at it invalid, provided (1) that notice need only be given to shareholders within reasonable reach, *Majola Investments (Pty) Ltd* v *Uitzigt Properties (Pty) Ltd* 1961 (4) SA 705 (T), and (2) that any defect in giving notice can be cured by the consent of all the members of the company: *164.*

The annual general meeting deals with all matters prescribed by the Act, including the sanctioning of a dividend, the consideration of the annual financial statements, the election of the directors and the appointment of an auditor, as well as with any other business laid before it. All business laid before any other general meeting is considered special business, Table A art 36 and Table B art 35. If any special business is to be transacted at a meeting the nature of such business must be clearly stated in the notice: *165–167.*

B CASES

[159] Mayor etc of Merchants of the Staple of England v Governor and Company of Bank of England
(1887) 21 QBD 160

WILLS J: . . . The acts of a corporation are those of the major part of the corporators, corporately assembled. By 'corporately assembled' it is meant that the meeting shall be one held upon notice which gives every corporator the opportunity of being present. . . .

[160] Boschoek Proprietary Company Ltd v Fuke
[1906] 1 Ch 148

An irregularity in the constitution of the board of directors does not invalidate resolutions of a general meeting convened by them.

SWINFEN EADY J: . . . This meeting was called by the only persons acting as directors, and the persons who for upwards of three months had been acting as the board; the resolution for calling it was passed at a board meeting; notice of it was duly sent to every shareholder, and one of the objects of the meeting was to confirm the acts theretofore done by persons purporting to act as directors. Under these circumstances, I must consider any informality in convening the meeting as a mere irregularity, and not sufficient to invalidate any resolution passed at it. . . .

NOTES

In *Taylor v Machavie Claims Syndicate Ltd* 1912 WLD 187, A and B (with C as an alternate to B) were the sole directors of a company under whose articles the directors were given powers to convene a meeting of shareholders whenever they thought fit. A convened a meeting without consulting B or C, but B and C by their conduct subsequently ratified A's action. The court held that the meeting was validly held.

A meeting is not properly convened if it is summoned by the secretary of the company without the authority of the board of directors: *In re Haycraft Gold Reduction and Mining Co* [1900] 2 Ch 230. But see also *D Frenkel Ltd v Liquidators Susman Jacobs & Co Ltd* 1918–23 GWL 182, where it was held that in accordance with the presumption *omnia rite esse acta* it must be assumed, until the contrary is proved, that the secretary of a company when convening a meeting, does so on the authority of the directors.

If all shareholders of a company consent to a transaction, it is not necessary that they should hold a meeting in one place or room to express that consent simultaneously: *Parker and Cooper Ltd v Reading* [1926] Ch 975, p 288 below.

The directors can be restrained from fixing a particular date for a meeting for the purpose of preventing certain shareholders from exercising their voting powers: *Cannon v Trask* (1875) LR 20 Eq 669.

In the absence of express authority, the directors of a company have no power to postpone a properly convened general meeting: *Smith v Paringa Mines Ltd* [1906] 2 Ch 193.

[161] **MacDougall *v* Gardiner**
(1875) 10 Ch App 606

JAMES LJ: If a general meeting is wanted for any purpose, then the directors, if they think it for the interests of the company, have power to call a general meeting; but I do not think that the court has any jurisdiction to compel the directors to call the meeting, when they may honestly think it not for the interests of the company to do so. Then if the directors do not call the meeting, it is left to the shareholders to call it, with these restrictions, that before the company can be called together, and before they can be put to any such inconvenience, one-fifth [now 100 members or members holding one-twentieth of the voting capital, s 181] of the shareholders must give in a requisition to the directors, and if one-fifth do not join in it, then there is no power to call the meeting.

Now, what power have we to say that a general meeting is to be called, if the directors do not think it right, and if one-fifth of the shareholders will not sign a requisition for the purpose? We have no authority, and there is, as it appears to me, no reason why we could interfere to do that which the shareholders have a right to do for themselves. . . .

[162] **Ball *v* Metal Industries Ltd**
1957 SC 315

Shareholders requisitioned an extraordinary general meeting for the appointment of three new directors. Subsequently, the chairman of the company gave notice of intention to move at the meeting a resolution for the removal from office of one of the existing directors. The court interdicted the company from proceeding with this resolution.

LORD HILL WATSON: The removal of a director from the board is a matter of very considerable importance. I think it would be quite wrong that a matter of this nature should be brought by a shareholder before an extraordinary general meeting of the company, convened pursuant to s 132 [corresponding to s 181 of our Act], when the matter is not covered by the terms of the requisition, and when the directors have not convened the meeting . . . for that particular purpose.

NOTES

In *Lurie v Sacks* 1972 (2) SA 396 (O) a clause in the articles provided that a person becoming entitled to shares by transmission on the death of a member 'shall, until transfer has been effected, be entitled to the same dividends and other advantages to which he would be entitled if he were the registered holder of the share'. The court held that this clause did not authorize the person concerned to requisition and convene a meeting. The word 'advantages' had to be restricted 'to matters germane to the concept of dividends, such as rights issues' (at 399 B, C, per Hofmeyr J). On requisitioned meetings, see further *Isle of Wight Railway Co v Tahourdin* (1883) 25 ChD 320; *In re State of Wyoming Syndicate* [1901] 2 Ch 431; *Brayshaw v Cameron* 1903 TH 496; *Fruit and Vegetable Growers' Association Ltd v Kekewich* [1912] 2 Ch 52.

[163] Allen *v* Wisbeach Court (Pty) Ltd
1974 (2) SA 59 (C)

Application was made to the court under s 62(2) of the 1926 Act (which corresponds broadly to s 183 of the present Act but differs from it in important respects) to order a general meeting to be called of a private company which had neither members nor directors, all its members being deceased.

BAKER J: Section 62(2) contemplates the calling of a meeting of a company by the court, *inter alia*, of its own motion. The court is empowered to order a meeting to be called, held and conducted in such manner as the court thinks fit, but . . . in this particular case it is not possible to call such a meeting, because there are no members left alive. It seems to me clear that s 62(2) contemplates that at least one member must be in existence. The concluding sentence of s 62(2) provides that:

'The said directions may include a direction that one member present in person or by proxy shall be deemed to constitute a meeting.'

This, prima facie, means that the meeting of the company contemplated by the subsection must be a meeting of members of the company. As all members and directors are now dead, there is nobody who can attend any such meeting, and it would be a *brutum fulmen* for the court to order one to be held.

NOTES

Being more widely worded than s 62(2) was, s 183 empowers the court to order a meeting to be called even where not a single director or member of the company is left. In *Rothschild v Radiola (Pty) Ltd* 1964 (4) SA 133 (W) it was held that the court will act under the section only where the equities require that it should come to the assistance of the person or persons who are at a disadvantage because of the deadlock. See further *Otto v Klipvlei Diamond Areas (Pty) Ltd* 1958 (2) SA 437 (T) and *Yende v Orlando Coal Distributors* 1961 (3) SA 314 (W).

[164] *In re* Bailey, Hay & Co Ltd
[1971] 1 WLR 1357, [1971] 3 All ER 693

Notices concerning an extraordinary general meeting to pass resolutions for the voluntary winding up of the company and the appointment of a liquidator were issued one day short of the required period. The court held that the defect in the notices was cured by the unanimous agreement of the corporators.

BRIGHTMAN J : It is established law that a company is bound in a matter, *intra vires* the company, by the unanimous agreement of all its corporators. I refer to *In re Express Engineering Works Ltd* [1920] 1 Ch 466 and *Parker and Cooper Ltd* v *Reading* [1926] Ch 975. I quote two brief passages from the latter case. At p 982 Astbury J says: '. . . where a transaction is *intra vires* the company and honest the sanction of all the members of the company, however expressed, is sufficient to validate it . . .'. At p 983: '. . . the company was bound in a matter *intra vires* by the unanimous agreement of its members.'

I consider that on the particular facts of this case all the corporators ought to be treated as having assented on 9 December 1965 to the company being wound up on that day. In my judgment, the case falls within the principle of the decisions in the two cases I have mentioned. Admittedly three of the five corporators did not vote in favour of the resolution, but they undoubtedly suffered it to be passed with knowledge of their power to stop it. The true quality of the acts of such corporators on 9 December is not to be judged exclusively by reference to what they did or did not do on that day, but is also to be judged in the light of what they did and did not do thereafter.

What these corporators did and did not do after 9 December 1965 down to 10 December 1969, when they swore their affidavits disclosing this defence, points, in my view, to one conclusion only. The conclusion is that they outwardly accepted the resolution to wind up as decisively as if they had positively voted in favour of it. If corporators attend a meeting without protest, stand by without protest while their fellow-members purport to pass a resolution, permit all persons concerned to act for years on the basis that that resolution was duly passed and rule their own conduct on the basis that the resolution is an established fact, I think it is idle for them to contend that they did not assent to the purported resolution.

In the circumstances I have set out I see no injustice in treating them as having agreed to the liquidation. . . .

Secondly, the fertilizer company is, in my view, barred by laches from now disputing that the company is in liquidation. The fertilizer company is setting up a positive case against the liquidator, a case which inevitably involves a claim that the liquidator has no status whatever and is wrongly in possession of the company's assets. In my judgment, the equitable doctrine of laches is applicable to that situation just as if the fertilizer company were seeking a remedy against the liquidator.

NOTES

See also *Ex parte Smith & Co Ltd* (1929) 50 NLR 49; *Gundelfinger* v *African Textile Manufacturers Ltd* 1939 AD 314; *Silver Garbus & Co (Pty) Ltd* v *Teichert* 1954 (2) SA 98 (N).

[165] Tiessen *v* Henderson
[1899] 1 Ch 861

KEKEWICH J: ... The question is ... whether each shareholder as and when he received the notice of the meeting, in which I include the circular of the same date, had fair warning of what was to be submitted to the meeting. A shareholder may properly and prudently leave matters in which he takes no personal interest to the decision of the majority. But in that case he is content to be bound by the vote of the majority; because he knows the matter about which the majority are to vote at the meeting. If he does not know that, he has not a fair chance of determining in his own interest whether he ought to attend the meeting, make further inquiries, or leave others to determine the matter for him. ...

[166] Lace *v* Modderfontein Gold Mining Company
(1894) 1 Off Rep 275

AMESHOFF J: ... Clause 56 of the articles of association provides that the notices calling a general meeting shall set forth the general nature of the business. The notice in question mentioned as the subject-matter to be discussed at the meeting, and eventually to be adopted, with or without amendment, a certain proposal for the reconstruction of the company which had been made to the directors. The notice further set out the terms of that proposal. At the general meeting, however, a second offer was made, in somewhat different terms from those of which notice had been given. That proposal was accepted, and it is now challenged. I am of opinion that the general meeting had no right to deal with this second proposal. I cannot agree with the interpretation put upon the notice, which is, that the question to be dealt with was reconstruction in general under any conditions whatever. This surely cannot be brought within the general terms of 'with or without amendments'. ...

[167] Kaye *v* Croydon Tramways Company
[1898] 1 Ch 358

A provisional agreement was made between two companies for the sale of the undertaking of the one to the other. Under the agreement the buying company agreed to pay, in addition to the sum payable to the selling company, a substantial sum to the directors of the selling company as compensation for loss of office. The notice convening the meeting of shareholders to consider the agreement described it as an agreement for the sale of the undertaking, without mentioning the provision for the payment of compensation to the directors. *Held*, that the notice did not fairly disclose the purpose for which the meeting was convened.

LINDLEY MR: ... Now comes the question—to my mind a difficult question—whether, in ordinary fairness of language, one can say that this notice does, to use the words of the Companies Clauses Act, 'specify

the purpose for which the meeting is called'. On behalf of the company
it is argued that it does—that the purpose is to confirm the agreement.
That, no doubt, is true by the card, but, in my opinion, this notice
has been most artfully framed to mislead the shareholders. It is a tricky
notice, and it is to my mind playing with words to tell shareholders that
they are convened for the purpose of considering a contract for the
sale of their undertaking, and to conceal from them that a large portion
of the purchase-money is not to be paid to the vendors who sell that
undertaking. I am perfectly alive to the danger of putting into notices,
especially notices by advertisement, more than the Act of Parliament
requires, and I agree that all that the Act of Parliament requires is that
the purpose shall be stated. But it must be stated fairly: it must not be
stated so as to mislead; and one of the main purposes of this agreement,
so far as the directors care about it, is that they shall get a large sum of
money without disclosing the fact to their shareholders. I do not think
that this notice discloses the purpose for which the meeting is convened.
It is not a notice disclosing that purpose fairly, and in a sense not to mislead those to whom it is addressed. It follows that, although in my judgment this contract is one which the companies can lawfully enter into,
it is a contract which the selling company has not yet adopted—that is
to say, the resolution which was passed under this notice is not one which
is binding upon absent or dissenting shareholders. . . .

NOTES

See also *Henderson* v *Bank of Australasia* (1890) 45 ChD 330, per Chitty J: 'The notice
which specifies . . . the objects of the meeting is to be a fair notice, intelligible to the
minds of ordinary men, the class of men who are shareholders in the company, and to
whom it is addressed.'

On sufficiency of notice, see further *In re Bridgport Old Brewery Co* (1867) 2 Ch App
191; *Imperial Bank of China, India and Japan* v *Bank of Hindustan, China and Japan* (1868)
LR 6 Eq 91; *Grant* v *United Kingdom Switchback Railways Co* (1888) 40 ChD 135; *Betts
& Co Ltd* v *Macnaghten* [1910] 1 Ch 430; *Smith* v *Hofmeyr* 1911 WLD 222, esp at 228;
Baillie v *Oriental Telephone and Electric Co Ltd* [1915] 1 Ch 503; *Pacific Coast Coal Mines
Ltd* v *Arbuthnot* [1917] AC 607; *Choppington Collieries Ltd* v *Johnson* [1944] 1 All ER 762;
Ex parte Carrig Diamonds Ltd 1966 (1) SA 572 (W); *Merion Court Durban Ltd* v *Kidwell*
1976 (4) SA 584 (N).

In *Dolly Varden Mines Ltd* v *Sunshine Exploration Ltd* (1967) 64 DLR (2d) 283 (British
Columbia Supreme Court) the directors of a company decided to submit an agreement
with another party to a general meeting of the company, at which it was discussed and
approved. The notice of the general meeting did not mention the agreement, as it ought
to have done. The court held that the other party had no *locus standi* to object to the
validity of the contract on the ground that insufficient notice was given by the company
to its members. Cf *In re Miller's Dale and Ashwood Dale Lime Co* (1885) 31 ChD 211.

In *In re Wemmer Gold Mining Co* (1890) 6 HCG 6 the constitution of the company
provided that a notice calling an extraordinary meeting of shareholders should specify
the day, place and hour of meeting. An extraordinary meeting was called by notice to
be held immediately after the ordinary meeting convened for a certain day. The court
held (*a*) that this amounted to proper notice; and (*b*) that the fact that the ordinary
meeting had fallen through did not affect the legality of the extraordinary meeting.

In the absence of provision to the contrary in the articles, preference shareholders with
no voting rights have no right to be summoned to general meetings: *In re Mackenzie &
Co Ltd* [1916] 2 Ch 450.

The notice convening the statutory meeting must state the fact that it is the statutory
meeting: *Gardner* v *Iredale* [1912] 1 Ch 700.

Expenses incurred by the directors in informing the shareholders by circular of their
policy and reasons for it and in sending out proxy papers are properly payable out of

the funds of the company: *Peel* v *London and North Western Railway Co* [1907] 1 Ch 5 (*183*, below).

Business not completed at a lawfully adjourned meeting may be completed at the adjourned meeting though the notice calling the adjourned meeting does not state the purpose again for which it was convened: *Scadding* v *Lorant* (1851) 3 HL Cas 418, 10 ER 164.

On notices in general, see further *Torbock* v *Lord Westbury* [1902] 2 Ch 871; *Ex parte Eastern Districts Sporting Club Ltd* 1927 WLD 131.

In calculating the period of notice, twenty-one days (or fourteen days) means twenty-one (or fourteen) clear days, exclusive of the day of service and of the day on which the meeting is to be held: s 4 of the Interpretation Act 33 of 1957. See also *Transvaal Consolidated Land and Exploration Co Ltd* v *Registrar of Companies* 1910 TPD 1247; *In re Hector Whaling Ltd* [1936] Ch 208; *Neil M'Leod & Sons Limited* 1967 SC 16.

See further *African Organic Fertilizers and Associated Industries Ltd* v *Premier Fertilizers Ltd* 1948 (3) SA 233 (N).

II Procedure at Meetings; Resolutions

A TEXT

Unless the articles of association otherwise provide, any meeting of the company may elect any member to be the chairman, s 191. As a rule the articles of association provide that the chairman of the board of directors shall preside at general meetings, and that if the company has no chairman or if the chairman does not turn up in time or is unwilling to act, the members present may elect one of their number as chairman, Table A art 40, Table B art 39. The chairman conducts the meeting. Every member has a right to attend, speak, vote and propose amendments: *168–170*. A corporation may authorize any person to act as its representative at a meeting of a company of which it is a member, s 188.

Unless the articles provide for a greater number of members to constitute a quorum, the quorum for general meetings is, in the case of a public company, three members entitled to vote personally present, or if a member is a body corporate, represented; in the case of a private company having two or more members, two members entitled to vote, present in person or by proxy or, if a member is a body corporate, represented; and in the case of a wholly-owned subsidiary (p 52 above), the representative of the holding company, s 190. Where a private company has only one member, such member present in person or by proxy, constitutes the meeting, s 184. Otherwise, it is presumably still the rule that one person cannot constitute a meeting: *171*.

There are resolutions pure and simple, and special resolutions. Ordinary resolutions are passed by a simple majority of the members present and entitled to vote. They take effect as from the date on which they are passed, s 203(2). The chairman has no casting vote, in addition to his ordinary vote, unless the articles give him one (see Table A art 43,

Table B art 44). Special resolutions require 21 clear days' notice, specifying the intention to propose the resolution as a special resolution, the terms and effect of the resolution and the reasons for it, s 199(1) (and see *165–167* above). With the consent of a majority in number of the members having the right to attend and vote and holding in the aggregate not less than 95 per cent of the total votes of all such members, a resolution may be proposed and passed as a special resolution at a meeting of which less than 21 clear days' notice has been given, s 199(1) and (3).

At the meeting at which the special resolution is to be passed members holding in the aggregate not less than one-fourth of the total votes of all the members entitled to attend and vote at the meeting must be present in person or by proxy, and, on a show of hands, not less than three-fourths of the members present in person or by proxy, or where a poll has been demanded, not less than three-fourths of the total votes to which they are entitled, must vote in favour of the resolution, s 199(1). If less than one-fourth of the total votes of all the members entitled to attend and vote are present or represented at the meeting, the meeting stands adjourned, and at the adjourned meeting the resolution is passed if not less than three-fourths of the members present in person or by proxy vote for it even if less than one-fourth of the total votes are represented, s 199(2).

A special resolution must be lodged with the Registrar for registration, s 200. Until registered, it does not take effect, s 203(1). It would seem that registration does not operate with retrospective effect (see P E J Brooks (1972) 35 *THRHR* 170).

In certain cases special notice of a resolution (ordinary or special) is required, see e g ss 220(1), 279(1). In this case notice of the intention to move the resolution must be given to the company not less than 28 days before the meeting, and the company must give its members notice of the resolution at the same time and in the same manner as it gives notice of the meeting or, if that is not practicable, by advertisement in a newspaper not less than 21 days before the meeting, as laid down in s 186(3).

On the requisition of a certain number of members, resolutions which the requisitionists intend to move at a forthcoming meeting must be circulated by the company, at the expense of the requisitionists, to all members before the meeting, s 185.

No share may be without voting rights (on voting rights, see p 172 above). In casting their votes shareholders are not required to consider any interests but their own: *172, 173*. It follows that in contradistinction to directors (p 459 below) they can bind themselves by voting agreements: *174, 175*. On the voting of shares held in trust: *176*.

Voting takes place on a show of hands or by poll, ss 197, 198. On a show of hands every member present in person has one vote, irrespective of the number of shares he holds or represents, s 197(1): *177*. On a poll any member present or his proxy is entitled to exercise all his voting rights, s 197(2): *178*. The right to demand a poll on any question other than the election of the chairman of the meeting or the adjournment of the meeting cannot be excluded by the articles, s 198(1)(*a*), nor can it be rendered ineffective beyond the limits set out in s 198(1)(*b*). On the effect of a declaration by the chairman that a special resolution has been carried, see s 199(4). The articles usually provide that unless a poll is demanded a declaration by the chairman that a resolution has or has not been carried and an entry to that effect in the minute book of the company shall be conclusive evidence of that fact, Table A art 42, Table B art 42: *179*.

Section 189 entrenches the right to appoint proxies, who may or may not be members of the company. A proxy has the right to attend and speak. He may vote on a poll but not on a show of hands, s 189(1). A member of a private company may not appoint more than one proxy for the same meeting, s 189(1). At meetings of private companies having two or more members, proxies of members may be counted in the quorum, s 190. Every notice calling a meeting of a company having a share capital and every proxy form issued at the company's expense must contain a statement that a member entitled to attend and vote at the meeting is entitled to appoint a proxy and that a proxy need not be a member of the company, s 189(2). (In *Babic* v *Milinkovic* (1971) 22 DLR (3d) 732 (BC) the Supreme Court of British Columbia held that failure of a corporation to comply with the corresponding provision in the British Columbia Companies Act RSBC 1960 c 67, rendered all resolutions taken at the meeting irrevocable nullities.) As to the instrument of proxy, see s 189(3), (5) and (6), and Table A arts 50–52 and Table B arts 51–53: *180–183, 183A*. The period prescribed in the articles for lodging proxies prior to a meeting may not exceed 48 hours, s 189(3).

Adjournment of a meeting takes place by the chairman with the consent of the meeting: *184*. On compulsory adjournment, see s 192.

Minutes of proceedings must be kept as prescribed in s 204. They create a rebuttable prescription that the meeting to which they relate has been duly held and convened, and the proceedings thereat have been duly had, s 205: *185, 186*. Members are entitled to inspect the minutes and to be furnished with copies of them, s 206 (cf *Gans* v *SPCA* 1962 (4) SA 543 (W)).

No report purporting to be a report of the proceedings at a meeting of the company may be circulated or advertised at the expense of the company unless it contains a fair summary of all material questions and comments relevant to any matter before the meeting which have been asked or made by members taking part in the proceedings, s 207.

B CASES

[168] Cohen and Ehrlich *v* Witwatersrand Gold Mining Company

(1895) 2 Off Rep 277

KOTZE CJ: . . . The company proposed to increase its capital, and with that object a special general meeting of shareholders was called, by a notice published in the newspapers, to consider an offer for the increase of the capital of the company. The particulars of that offer were set out in the notice, but the names of those who had made the offer were not mentioned. It was proposed to increase the share capital of the company from 250 000 to 300 000 shares of £1 each. Of the 50 000 new shares, 30 000 were to be issued at 52s 6d each to shareholders in the existing capital, in proportion to the registered shares held by them. The guarantors undertook to take up at 52s 6d each all shares not so taken up by present shareholders within the period of option. The guarantors were to get 7 500 of the new shares at 52s 6d each, with an option on the balance of 12 500 shares for a period of twelve months. It appears that certain shareholders in England considered the published offer to be too low. It is also said that one Struben had made a higher offer, although nothing to that effect appears on the record. At the meeting the chairman informed the meeting that Barnato Brothers and the Anglo-French Company were the guarantors and that they had increased their offer from 52s 6d to 56s per share, and he then laid the amended offer before the meeting for consideration. Cohen, a shareholder, expressed his opinion that there was no necessity to increase the capital, but, if such increase of capital was necessary, he would be prepared to take up 30 000 shares at 60s each, and the remaining 20 000 at the same price. The chairman ruled that the offer made by Cohen was out of order, as it was a new offer. He thereupon laid the second offer of Barnato Brothers and the Anglo-French Company, which he called an amended offer, before the meeting for consideration. This offer was accepted by the majority of shareholders. Now for what reasons did the chairman pass over Cohen's offer? Barnato's proposal had no preference over that of Cohen. Both proposals were made in the same form, but Cohen's offer was higher than that of Barnato Brothers and the Anglo-French Company. The fact that the last-mentioned were the guarantors of the published offer can make no difference, as they were not mentioned in the notice to shareholders, but were announced only at the meeting. . . . The chairman clearly erred in giving preference to the offer of Barnato Brothers and the Anglo-French Company. By doing so he exceeded his powers. If the increased offer of Barnato Brothers and the Anglo-French Company could be put to the meeting, then likewise the proposal of Cohen could with equal right have been put to the meeting. Neither offer was published in the notice. It is the duty of the court to protect the interests of the minority against the majority when necessary. . . .

[The order granted by the court of first instance, interdicting the company from carrying out the resolution, was accordingly confirmed.]

[169] Wall v London and Northern Assets Corporation
[1898] 2 Ch 469

LINDLEY MR: . . . Mr Cozens-Hardy raised various points of irregularity, which I shall dispose of very shortly, because I think they mostly are not points with which this court has anything to do. The only new one is the point about the closure. It appears that there was a discussion about this matter at a meeting of shareholders of the Assets Company, and, after having heard the views—I do not say of all those who opposed, but of one or two of them—the meeting came to the conclusion that they had heard enough, and did not want to hear any more, and thereupon the chairman declared the discussion closed. That is said to be a matter calling for the interference of this court. I do not think so. I think it would be a very bad precedent that we should interfere in such a case. I am aware of the importance of the observations made by Lord Eldon in *Const* v *Harris* (1824) T & R 496 at 525, in which he said, 'I call that the act of all' (he was speaking of the meeting of large companies), 'which is the act of the majority, provided all are consulted, and the majority are acting bona fide, meeting, not for the purpose of negativing, what any one may have to offer, but for the purpose of negativing, what, when they are met together, they may, after due consideration, think proper to negative: For a majority of partners to say, We do not care what one partner may say, we, being the majority, will do what we please, is, I apprehend, what this court will not allow.' I think that principle is as important, and, perhaps, more important, to bear in mind now than it was sixty or seventy years ago; but Lord Eldon does not mean that a minority who are bent on obstructing business and resolved on talking for ever should not be put down. He means that the majority are not to be tyrannical. After hearing what is to be said, they may say, 'We have heard enough. We are not bound to listen till everybody is tired of talking and has sat down. . . .'

[170] Carruth v Imperial Chemical Industries Ltd
[1937] AC 707, [1937] 2 All ER 422

The capital of the respondent company consisted of preferred, ordinary and deferred shares. The company applied for an order confirming a reduction of its capital, affecting the holders of ordinary and deferred shares. Under the constitution of the company, the reduction had to be approved by separate class meetings of the holders of these shares as well as by a special resolution of the company in general meeting.

A circular notice containing the scheme of reduction was sent to the shareholders together with (1) a notice of an ordinary general meeting of the company to be held at a certain place on 1 May 1935 at 10.30 am, and three other notices of other meetings to be held at the same place on the same day, namely (2) a notice of an extraordinary general meeting of the company for the purpose of passing, among other resolutions, a resolution for reduction of the capital; (3) a notice of a separate meeting of the ordinary shareholders; (4) a notice of a separate meeting of deferred shareholders; the three last-mentioned meetings to be held respectively at 10.45 am, 11 am, and 11.15 am or as soon thereafter as the meeting immediately preceding should be concluded, with the object of passing as an extraordinary resolution a resolution consenting to the reduction and reorganization of the company's capital.

At the meeting 1 600 shareholders were present of whom 565 were holders of deferred shares. The notice convening the extraordinary general meeting was taken as read. The chairman stated that the extraordinary general meeting would be followed by a meeting of the ordinary shareholders, and then by a meeting of deferred shareholders; and he proposed to make one speech and to take the vote at the two meetings to follow without any further speeches. He then held the three meetings in succession, all the shareholders remaining, and took polls at each meeting. In the result the resolutions were carried with the requisite majorities. The court was divided as to the regularity of the proceedings, but confirmed the scheme of reduction.

LORD BLANESBURGH: ... My Lords, had the order of procedure foreshadowed in the notices convening the meetings been in any true sense realized, no objection technical or substantial would have now been competent. The form of notice seemed to presuppose that there had to be three specific meetings—the first an extraordinary general meeting consisting of all shareholders in the company—preference, ordinary and deferred—at which the scheme in all its details, as affecting the company generally, would be submitted for approval by special resolution; the second, a meeting of the ordinary shareholders only at which the scheme as affecting their particular class interests would be submitted to them separately for approval by extraordinary resolution; and the third, a corresponding meeting of deferred shareholders only, similarly convened to approve of the scheme as specially affecting their class interests in the sense already discussed. These meetings were convened for 10.45 am, 11 am and 11.15 am, or so soon thereafter as the immediately preceding meeting should be concluded. But on the day itself no attempt was made to separate the shareholders alone entitled to be present at either class meeting from the whole body of shareholders summoned for, entitled to be present at, and to take part in, the general meeting. These did so assemble·at the appointed hour of 10.45 am to the number of about 1 600, and after the show of hands on the resolutions and a poll demanded in writing by the chairman to be taken immediately, they were informed that their voting papers on the poll would be collected at the doors after the close of the final, the deferred shareholders', meeting. In other words, all present were invited to remain seated as they were until the business of the last of the meetings, which only a fraction of the assembly was entitled to attend, had concluded. ...

... The proceedings at each separate meeting (if such it can be called, with the whole general body of shareholders remaining in their places) consisted in the chairman reading the extraordinary resolution, then calling for a show of hands, and thereupon, whether the result was for or against the resolution, demanding a poll to be taken at once. And that was all.

Now, my Lords, in the above circumstances I ask myself when did either separate class meeting commence? The business of each meeting certainly commenced with the chairman's speech to the general meeting. He said so. But if the class meetings then commenced they did so before the time for which either was convened, probably two hours before. It must also on that view be taken that there were one general and two separate meetings proceeding simultaneously under one chairman. If, however, the separate meeting, say of the deferred shareholders, did not commence until after the proceedings of the ordinary shareholders' meeting had concluded—and this is the view of the company—then it was a meeting at which nothing in fact took place and nothing was intended or arranged to take place except that the resolution should be read, a show of hands asked for, with neither explanation given nor discussion invited, and then a poll demanded to be taken at once. The separate meeting on this hypothesis consisted in a resolution read, a show of hands asked for, and a poll demanded. Is this the position to which a deferred shareholder attending that meeting at the appointed time, and not earlier, may properly be relegated? That must be the contention. But when it is remembered that all this took place in the presence of the great bulk of the shareholders of all classes originally assembled, it seems to be impossible to hold that any meeting on that day was a separate class meeting in any sense of those words not wholly inappropriate. A far more accurate description of the relevant proceedings of the day regarded objectively would be that they consisted of one general meeting and two separate polls. Let it be agreed that the result of each of the two separate polls was accurate in every particular; still it is a separate meeting and not a separate poll that is required by this company's memorandum of association. And there is a wealth of meaning in the distinction.

But nevertheless it is, doubtless, because of the accuracy of the result of the polls—the final deliverance—that the procedure adopted is in its result sought to be justified. And it is at this very point, as it seems to me, that one material defect in the procedure is disclosed. For if I must condescend upon the question, what essential condition of a separate meeting was on this occasion broken, I would say that one such breach consisted in this, that the meeting was so held that there could not be a reliable show of hands—an essential preliminary basis for all subsequent procedure including the demand for and the taking of the poll. It is true that the chairman at the deferred meeting said that only deferred shareholders were to hold up their hands. No one, however, can say, the chairman perhaps, least of all, whether all of the shareholders present not being deferred shareholders were obedient to his command. . . . A show of hands is the constitutional method of declaring the will of a meeting. It stands as the resolution of the meeting, unless the declaration of the chairman that the proposed resolution is thereby carried or lost is subsequently displaced by the result of a poll thereafter duly demanded and taken. But from the very nature of the case there can, I suggest, be no valid demand for a poll unless there has been a valid show of hand. And that there was a valid show of hands at this so-called separate meeting it is impossible to affirm. . . .

... The opportunity afforded to the class of discussing their own affairs undisturbed by opposing or conflicting interests is the modest protection against possible oppression offered by a class meeting. How weak that protection often is, owing to conflicting interests within the class itself, is only too well known and is illustrated perhaps in this case. But the protection is worth preserving *faute de mieux*. ...

LORD RUSSELL OF KILLOWEN: ... The question which has given me the chief anxiety in this case is the question whether a separate meeting of the deferred shareholders, within the meaning of those words, was held. ...

... There are many matters relating to the conduct of a meeting which lie entirely in the hands of those persons who are present and constitute the meeting. Thus it rests with the meeting to decide whether notices, resolutions, minutes, accounts, and such like shall be read to the meeting or be taken as read; whether representatives of the Press, or any other persons not qualified to be summoned to the meeting, shall be permitted to be present, or if present shall be permitted to remain; whether and when discussion shall be terminated and a vote taken; whether the meeting shall be adjourned. In all these matters, and they are only instances, the meeting decides, and if necessary a vote must be taken to ascertain the wishes of the majority. If no objection is taken by any constituent of the meeting, the meeting must be taken to be assenting to the course adopted. It is not a case, as was suggested in argument, of those present at a meeting waiving rights of those who have elected not to attend; it is a case of those who have elected to attend regulating the conduct of the meeting, a question in which those who have chosen to stay away have no voice. I am, however, far from assenting to the view that all that is necessary to constitute a valid resolution by a separate class of shareholders, or a valid separate meeting of a class of shareholders, is that a separate vote of the class be taken in such circumstances as to ensure that all members of the class shall have an opportunity of voting, and that no one who is not a member of the class shall vote. Prima facie a separate meeting of a class should be a meeting attended only by members of the class, in order that the discussion of the matters which the meeting has to consider may be carried on unhampered by the presence of others who are not interested to view those matters from the same angle as that of the class; and if the presence of outsiders was retained in spite of the ascertained wish of the constituents of the meeting for their exclusion, it would not, I think, be possible to say that a separate meeting of the class had been duly held. In the present case, however, the deferred shareholders present, with knowledge that many were in the room who held no deferred shares, and that it was proposed that no further discussion should take place, but that a vote on the resolution should be taken, raised no objection, or at all events no audible objection, of any kind. In those circumstances they must be taken to have assented to the meeting being so conducted, and the resolution was accordingly a valid extraordinary resolution passed at a meeting of the deferred shareholders. ...

*Met groot genoeë stuur die Uitgewers
hierdie boek aan u vir 'n bespreking
daarvan in u blad.*

*Hulle sal dit op prys stel as u aan
hulle twee afskrifte stuur van enige
sodanige resensie wat in u blad mag
verskyn — een afskrif vir die
skrywer en die ander vir hulself.*

PRYS

JUTA & KIE., BEPERK

KAAPSTAD · WYNBERG · JOHANNESBURG

NOTES

If a shareholder present at a meeting protests neither against its legality nor against the appointment of the chairman, he cannot subsequently do so if the irregularities are such as could have been put right at the meeting: *Marting v Van Oordt, Russel & Co (Pty) Ltd* 1939 CPD 106.

In the absence of mala fides on the part of the conveners, proceedings are not invalidated if, owing to an unexpectedly large attendance, some persons who are entitled to be present at a meeting find that there is no accommodation for them. It is sufficient if provision is made for the accommodation of all who can reasonably be expected to come: *Bentote v Public Service Co-operative Stores Ltd* 1943 TPD 180.

[171] **Sharp *v* Dawes**
(1876) 2 QBD 26

MELLISH J: . . . In this case, no doubt, a meeting was duly summoned, but only one shareholder attended. It is clear that, according to the ordinary use of the English language, a meeting could no more be constituted by one person than a meeting could have been constituted if no shareholder at all had attended. No business could be done at such a meeting. . . .

NOTES

See also *Miller v Black and Black & Co Ltd* 1925 TPD 832; *Dowjee Co Ltd v Waja* 1929 TPD 66, esp at 77–8; *In re James Prain & Sons Ltd* 1947 SC 325: 'unless the word "meeting" bears a special meaning under the constitution of the company, a meeting cannot be composed of one individual, even if he holds proxies of other members'; and *Ingre v Maxwell* (1964) 44 DLR (2d) 765 (British Columbia Supreme Court): 'It is an untenable proposition that one member can hold a meeting.' Where, however, only one member of the company or a class of members is left, there may be a 'meeting' of one member only: *East v Bennett Brothers Ltd* [1911] 1 Ch 163; *Jarvis Motors (Harrow) Ltd v Carabatt* [1964] 3 All ER 89, [1964] 1 WLR 1101. On quorum at class meetings, see *Hemans v Hotchkiss Ordnance Co* [1899] 1 Ch 115. See also 375 below, and R Baxt 'Can a Single Shareholder Constitute a Meeting?' (1970) 44 *ALJ* 83.

Where the required quorum is 'three members personally present', it is satisfied if only two individuals are present, but one of them holds shares both as an individual and as a trustee on a trust: *Neil M'Leod & Sons Limited* 1967 SC 16. On the position that arises where only one shareholder is left or all the shareholders have died, see also, respectively, *Lombard v Suid-Afrikaanse Vroue-Federasie* 1968 (3) SA 473 (AD) and (1968) 41 *Australian LJ* 509.

In *Ex parte X Co* 1942 EDC 74 six out of nine shareholders resided outside South Africa and could not be communicated with. The court authorized the shareholders resident in South Africa to act as a quorum at a meeting to decide certain urgent matters. In *Ex parte Pollak* 1950 (4) SA 701 (W) one shareholder was authorized by the court to act as quorum.

If the articles state that 'no business shall be transacted at a general meeting unless a quorum is present when the meeting proceeds to business' it is sufficient if there is a quorum present at the beginning of the meeting: *In re Hartley Baird Ltd* [1955] Ch 143, [1954] 3 All ER 695. Failing provision to this effect in the articles it would seem (though the matter is controversial) that the quorum must be maintained throughout the meeting. In America, the prevailing view is that it is sufficient if the quorum is present at the commencement of the meeting.

In *In re Romford Canal Co* (1883) 24 ChD 85 a resolution to issue debentures was passed at a meeting at which an insufficient number of shareholders were present. The court held that the irregularity could not be set up against a bona fide transferee for value of the debentures. In *In re Miller's Dale and Ashwood Dale Lime Co* (1885) 31 ChD 211 it was held that a statutory defect in a resolution affects only the position of the company and its shareholders *inter se* and does not concern creditors. Cf *Dolly Varden Mines Ltd v Sunshine Exploration Ltd* (1967) 64 DLR (2d) 283, where it was decided that an outsider has no right to object that the meeting which approved a contract to which he is a party was called on insufficient notice.

In *M Harris Ltd* 1956 SC 207 the articles of a company provided that 'no business shall be transacted at any general meeting of the company . . . unless a quorum of members is present at the time when the meeting proceeds to business. Such quorum shall consist of two members of the company, of whom EB . . . shall be one. . . .' The court held that on the wording of this clause there could not be a quorum unless EB was present in person. Representation by a proxy or attorney was not sufficient.

[172] Northern Counties Securities Ltd *v* Jackson & Steeple Ltd
[1974] 1 WLR 1133, [1974] 2 All ER 625 (Ch)

The plaintiffs and the defendant company had entered into an agreement containing an option for the issue of certain shares to the plaintiffs, which option both parties treated as having been exercised. Brightman J made an order for the specific enforcement of this agreement, and the defendant company gave an undertaking to the court to use its best endeavours to obtain a stock exchange quotation for, and permission to deal in, the shares, in accordance with the option agreement. Under the Stock Exchange Rules, approval of the issue and allotment of the new class of shares by a general meeting of the company was a necessary prerequisite for the grant of a quotation for and permission to deal in the shares. The court held that under the order for specific performance, the directors of the defendant company were obliged to call an extraordinary general meeting, and place the matter fairly before the meeting, but that neither the shareholders nor the directors in their capacity as shareholders were obliged to exercise their votes in favour of the issue of the new shares.

WALTON J (at 1144): . . . what [Counsel for the company] submitted was that although it is perfectly true that the act of the members, in passing certain special types of resolutions, binds the company, their acts are not the acts of the company. There would, he submitted, be no real doubt about this were it not for the use of the curious expression 'the company in general meeting'—which, in a sense, drags in the name of the company unnecessarily. What that phrase really means, he submitted, is 'the members (or corporators) of the company assembled in a general meeting', and that if the phrase is written out in full in this manner it becomes quite clear that the decisions taken at such a meeting, and the resolutions passed thereat, are decisions taken by, and resolutions passed by, the members of the company, and not by the company itself. They are therefore in the position of strangers to the order and are not in contempt by their act in voting as they please, whatever its effect may be.

In my judgment, these submissions . . . are correct. I think that, in a nutshell, the distinction is this: when a director votes as a director for or against any particular resolution in a director's meeting, he is voting as a person under a fiduciary duty to the company for the proposition that the company should take a certain course of action. When a shareholder is voting for or against a particular resolution he is voting as a person owing no fiduciary duty to the company and who is exercising his own right of property, to vote as he thinks fit. The fact that the result of the voting at the meeting (or at a subsequent poll) will bind the company cannot affect the position that, in voting, he is voting simply in exercise of his own property rights.

Perhaps another (and simpler) way of putting the matter is that a director is an agent, who casts his vote to decide in what manner his principal shall act through the collective agency of the board of directors: a shareholder who casts his vote in general meeting is not casting it as an agent of the company in any shape or form. His act therefore, in voting as he pleases, cannot in any way be regarded as an act of the company.

NOTES

See also Lord Maugham in *Carruth* v *Imperial Chemical Industries Ltd* [1937] AC 707 (HL) at 765: '. . . the shareholder's vote is a right of property, and prima facie may be exercised by a shareholder as he thinks fit in his own interest.' On the right to vote of joint holders of shares, see R B (1972) 46 *ALJ* 90.

[173] Clemens *v* Clemens Bros Ltd & another
[1968] 2 All ER 268 (Ch)

The nominal capital of a family company was £2 000. It was divided into 200 preference shares and 1 800 ordinary shares of £1 each. The plaintiff held 100 preference shares and 800 ordinary shares, her aunt 100 preference shares and 1 000 ordinary shares. Under the company's articles (art 6), members of the company had a right of pre-emption if another member wished to transfer his shares. The aunt was a director of the company, the plaintiff was not. There were four other directors.

The directors proposed to increase the share capital from £2 000 to £3 650 by the creation of another 1 650 shares of £1 each. Each one of the four directors other than the aunt was to receive 200 of the new shares, the balance of 850 shares was to be placed in a trust fund to provide benefits for long-term employees.

At an extraordinary meeting of the company resolutions were passed to increase the capital, set up a trust fund, and provide for the allotments to the directors. The plaintiff sued her aunt (referred to in the judgment as Miss Clemens) for an order setting the three resolutions aside. The court granted the order.

FOSTER J: . . . For the plaintiff it was submitted that the proposed resolutions were oppressive, since they resulted in her losing her right to veto a special or extraordinary resolution and greatly watered down her existing right to purchase Miss Clemens's shares under art 6. For the defendants it was submitted that if two shareholders both honestly hold differing opinions, the view of the majority must prevail and that shareholders in general meeting are entitled to consider their own interests and vote in any way they honestly believe proper in the interests of the company.

There are many cases which have discussed a director's position. A director must not only act within his powers but must also exercise them bona fide in what he believes to be the interests of the company. The directors have a fiduciary duty, but is there any, or any similar, restraint on shareholders exercising their powers as members at general meetings?

Menier v *Hooper's Telegraph Works* [*310* below] is a very clear case, since it involved the majority shareholders expropriating the company's assets to the exclusion of the minority. In *North-West Transportation Co Ltd* v *Beatty* [*253* below] Sir Richard Baggallay said (at 593):

'The general principles applicable to cases of this kind are well established. Unless some provision to the contrary is to be found in the charter or other instrument by which the company is incorporated, the resolution of a majority of the shareholders, duly convened, upon any question with which the company is legally competent to deal, is binding upon the minority, and consequently upon the company, and every shareholder has a perfect right to vote upon any such question, although he may have a personal interest, in the subject-matter opposed to, or different from, the general or particular interests of the company. On the other hand, a director of a company is precluded from dealing, on behalf of the company, with himself, and from entering into engagements in which he has a personal interest conflicting, or which possibly may conflict, with the interests of those whom he is bound by fiduciary duty to protect; and this rule is as applicable to the case of one of several directors as to a managing or sole director. Any such dealing or engagement may, however, be affirmed or adopted by the company, provided such affirmance or adoption is not brought about by unfair or improper means, and is not illegal or fraudulent or oppressive towards those shareholders who oppose it.'

Here I find for the first time the word 'oppressive', but in that case the question in issue was whether a director could exercise his vote as a shareholder in general meeting to ratify a voidable contract to which he was party.

In *Allen* v *Gold Reefs of West Africa Ltd* [*53* above] Lindley MR said:

'The power thus conferred on companies to alter the regulations contained in their articles is limited only by the provisions contained in the statute and the conditions contained in the company's memorandum of association. Wide, however, as the language of s 50 [corresponding to s 10(2) of the English Companies Act 1948 and s 62 of our Act] is, the power conferred by it must, like all other powers, be exercised subject to those general principles of law and equity which are applicable to all powers conferred on majorities and enabling them to bind minorities. It must be exercised, not only in the manner required by law, but also bona fide for the benefit of the company as a whole, and it must not be exceeded. These conditions are always implied, and are seldom, if ever, expressed.'

In *Greenhalgh* v *Arderne Cinemas Ltd* [*315* below] Evershed MR said:

'Certain things, I think, can be safely stated as emerging from those authorities. In the first place, it is now plain that "bona fide for the benefit of the company as a whole" means not two things but one thing. It means that the shareholder must proceed on what, in his honest opinion, is for the benefit of the company as a whole. Secondly, the phrase, "the company as a whole", does not (at any rate in such a case as the present) mean the company as a commercial entity as distinct from the corporators. It means the corporators as a general body. That is to say, you may take the case of an individual hypothetical member and ask whether what is proposed is, in the honest opinion of those who voted in its favour, for that person's benefit.'

If that is right, the question in the instant case which must be posed is this: did Miss Clemens, when voting for the resolutions, honestly believe that those resolutions, when passed, would be for the benefit of the plaintiff? . . .

In *Ebrahimi* v *Westbourne Galleries Ltd* [*213* below] the House of Lords was dealing with . . . the 'just and equitable' ground for winding up a company. Lord Wilberforce said:

'The "just and equitable" provision does not . . . entitle one party to disregard the obligation he assumes by entering a company, nor the court to dispense him from it. It does, as equity always does, enable the court to subject the exercise of legal rights to equitable considerations; considerations that is, of a personal character arising between one individual and another, which may make it unjust, or inequitable, to insist on legal rights, or to exercise them in a particular way.'

I think that one thing which emerges from the cases to which I have referred is that in such a case as the present Miss Clemens is not entitled to exercise her majority vote in whatever way she pleases. The difficulty is in finding a principle, and obviously expressions such as 'bona fide for the benefit of the company as a whole', 'fraud on a minority' and 'oppressive' do not assist in formulating a principle.

I have come to the conclusion that it would be unwise to try to produce a principle, since the circumstances of each case are infinitely varied. It would not, I think assist to say more than that in my judgment Miss Clemens is not entitled as of right to exercise her votes as an ordinary shareholder in any way she pleases. To use the phrase of Lord Wilberforce, [[1973] AC at 379, [1972] 2 All ER at 500], that right is 'subject . . . to equitable considerations . . . which may make it unjust . . . to exercise [it] in a particular way'. Are there then any such considerations in this case? . . .

I do not doubt that Miss Clemens is in favour of the resolutions and knows and understands their purport and effect; nor do I doubt that she genuinely would like to see the other directors have shares in the company and to see a trust set up for long service employees. But I cannot escape the conclusion that the resolutions have been framed so as to put into the hands of Miss Clemens and her fellow directors complete control of the company and to deprive the plaintiff of her existing rights as a shareholder with more than 25 per cent of the votes and greatly reduce her rights under art 6. They are specifically and carefully designed to ensure not only that the plaintiff can never get control of the company but to deprive her of what has been called her negative control. Whether I say that these proposals are oppressive to the plaintiff or that no one could honestly believe they are for her benefit matters not. A court of equity will in my judgment regard these considerations as sufficient to prevent the consequences arising from Miss Clemens using her legal right to vote in the way that she has and it would be right for a court of equity to prevent such consequences taking effect.

[*Clemens* is noted by D D Prentice (1976) 92 *LQR* 502.]

[174] **Greenwell v Porter**
[1902] 1 Ch 530

As executors and trustees under a will, the defendants in this action held a large number of shares in a company called Robinson's Brewery Ltd. In 1898 they required money for the estate, and they agreed to sell a large block of shares to the plaintiff, Walpole Greenwell. The agreement provided, *inter alia*, that the defendants were to do all things within their power for obtaining the election, as directors of Robinson's Brewery Ltd, of one Aynsley Greenwell and one Trevor White, and to vote at all times for and not against the re-election of these two. Aynsley Greenwell and Trevor White were duly appointed directors of the company. The defendants were the other directors. In December 1901 Trevor White retired by rotation from office and was proposed for re-election. On a show of hands, there was a majority in favour of the motion but the defendants demanded a poll with the intention of opposing his re-election. The plaintiff thereupon sued the defendants for an injunction restraining them from voting against the re-election of Trevor White. The injunction was granted.

SWINFEN EADY J: . . . The plaintiff has brought this action to enforce the agreement so far as regards the provision as to voting. The agreement was entered into as part of a transaction under which the defendant executors sold to the plaintiff for a large price a considerable block of shares, and it appears from the evidence that it was at the time considered by all parties, and certainly by the executors, that it was to the interest of their testator's estate that the block of shares should be sold, that the terms were advantageous, and that at that time it was to the interest of the estate that the money should be obtained by a sale of shares in the way the transaction was carried into effect. The plaintiff stipulated as part of the transaction that he should have the benefit of the agreement.

Three of the defendant executors seek now to escape from performing the agreement. They say, in the first place, that the agreement was *ultra vires*—that as executors they had no power to, what they term, delegate their discretion as executors. At the present moment I am not satisfied that that point has any validity whatever. It will be observed that the sale of the shares retained by the executors is not tied up. . . . On the facts as they are at present before me, I am of opinion that the arrangement embodied in the agreement was for the benefit of the executors and their estate, and that it was not beyond the powers of the executors to enter into it.

The next point made was that, so far as regards shares held by any of the defendants in their individual capacity, because they were directors they could not enter into an agreement with regard to their voting in respect of these shares; and that, although an ordinary shareholder might do so, still, if the shareholder happened to be a director, that fact precluded him from entering into such an agreement. No authority was produced for such a proposition, and I do not consider it well founded. . . .

[175] Greenhalgh *v* Mallard
[1943] 2 All ER 234

On 28 March 1941, G agreed to subscribe for £11 000 worth of debentures in a private company, that sum being immediately needed by the company to pay a pressing debt. Certain shares were also to be allotted to G and to the three existing directors, and G was to be appointed a director. As G was a minority shareholder, and would not be able to control the company, a collateral agreement was entered into at the time between G and the three directors whereby the three agreed to vote with and support G when required by him so to do. In the circumstances then prevailing, the result would be to give G control of sufficient votes to enable him to carry an ordinary resolution. The intention and expectation of the parties was that this should be the position.

Later each of the three directors sold all his shares except 100 to other shareholders. G complained that he thereby lost his controlling position.

Held that there was no restrictive covenant affecting the shares in the hands of the purchasers.

LORD GREENE MR: . . . If the contract is such that it only imposes an obligation to vote in respect of whatever shares the contracting parties happen to have available, it follows that directly they sell their shares the contract is at an end — until possibly they acquire more shares. . . . Here the sale by these directors of their shares is not something which is out of their power under the contract; it is something which, under the contract, they are perfectly entitled to do. The obligation under the contract is an obligation which, in my opinion, endures so long, and so long only, as the contracting party has power to use his vote. Therefore, to sell the shares cannot be said to be a breach of the contract.

The argument that the restrictive covenant follows the shares in the hands of the purchasers is based on the same assumption as to the nature of the contract, because it necessarily assumes that the contract is one that has been entered into for, I suppose, some indefinite time, at any rate, for the lives of the parties. If the contract on its true construction ceases to operate when the shares are sold, then in the hands of the purchaser there can be no question of a continuing obligation which runs with the shares. The contract has come to an end. . . .

I think it is plain that the obligation is only to vote in respect of whatever shares the three directors might have or from time to time acquire. Any other construction would mean that never could any. of them sell one single share; there would have been an obligation to keep the shares, and, if the appellant had survived the three directors, or any of them, it would have passed to their legal personal representatives.

I cannot see how any other limit could be drawn. . . . I cannot bring myself to see that this document can be construed as imposing an absolute duty on the owner of the shares not to sell them. An obligation of that kind may have unforeseeable results. If it had been so intended, nothing would have been easier than to say so, but a mere undertaking by the shareholder to vote in a particular way, cannot by implication impose upon him a prohibition against the sale of his shares. . . .

[Luxmoore and Goddard LJJ concurred.]

NOTES

See also *Stewart* v *Schwab* 1956 (4) SA 791 (T) (*208* below); further, *North-West Transportation Company Ltd* v *Beatty* (1887) 12 App Cas 589 (PC) (*253* below); *Puddephatt* v *Leith* [1916] 1 Ch 200; *In re Coronation Syndicate Ltd* 1903 TH 254; *Unity Investment Co (Pty) Ltd* v *Johnson* 1932 CPD 275; *Marting* v *Van Oordt, Russel & Co (Pty) Ltd* 1939 CPD 106.

On the obligation of a shareholder bound by a voting agreement to ensure that his successors comply with it, see *Consolidated Crusher Holdings (Pty) Ltd* v *Plen* 1968 (1) PH A2 (T).

Voting trusts, common in America, do not seem to be used to any extent in England or South Africa.

[176] Pender *v* Lushington

(1877) 6 ChD 70 (see also *307* below)

JESSEL MR: . . . It is admitted that the votes tendered were the votes of persons on the register of shareholders, and it is admitted that they had been possessed of those shares for at least three months previously to the time of holding the general meeting, which is what is required by the 59th article. That being so, their votes were rejected on this ground: It was said that the persons who gave the votes were trustees for other persons. . . .

. . . The first observation which strikes one is that these are votes at general meetings. How are you to ascertain who is to vote? That is pointed out by the articles of association. First, who are to be summoned to attend the general meetings? You find by art 48 that notice is to be given to 'the members hereinafter mentioned'. What does the word 'members' mean in that article? . . . A member is a man who is on the register. . . .

. . . It comes, therefore, to this, that the register of shareholders, on which there can be no notice of a trust, furnishes the only means of ascertaining whether you have a lawful meeting or a lawful demand for a poll, or of enabling the scrutineers to strike out votes.

The result appears to me to be manifest, that the company has no right whatever to enter into the question of the beneficial ownership of the shares. Any such suggestion is quite inadmissible, and therefore it is clear that the chairman had no right to inquire who was the beneficial owner of the shares, and the votes in question ought to have been admitted as good votes independently of any inquiry as to whether the parties tendering them were or were not, and to what extent, trustees for other persons beneficially entitled to the shares. . . .

NOTES

On voting by joint holders of shares, see *Burns* v *Siemens Brothers Dynamo Works Ltd* [1919] 1 Ch 225; *Munro* v *Ekerold* 1949 (1) SA 584 (SWA) (cf Table A art 47, Table B art 48). On the insolvency of a member his shares vest in the trustee in his insolvent estate who may exercise the vote in respect of the shares (cf Table A art 19, Table B art 20).

As to the relationship between trustees and the beneficiaries under a trust in respect of shares see *Kirby* v *Wilkins* [1929] 2 Ch 444; *Butt* v *Kelson* [1952] 1 Ch 197, [1952] 1 All ER 167; *Re Whichelow* [1953] 2 All ER 1558; also p 212, above.

[177] *In re* **Horbury Bridge Coal, Iron and Waggon Company**
(1879) 11 ChD 109

The articles of a company provided that every member was to have one vote for every share held by him and that, unless a poll was demanded, a declaration by the chairman that a resolution had been carried and an entry to that effect in the book of proceedings of the company were to be sufficient evidence of the fact without proof of the number or proportion of the votes recorded in favour of or against such resolution.

At a meeting, at which five members of the company were present, an extraordinary resolution to wind up the company was passed. Kippax was proposed as liquidator and an amendment was moved that Masterman be appointed. Three members voted for Masterman, and two for Kippax, but the two members voting for Kippax held a greater number of shares than the three who voted for Masterman. No poll was demanded.

JESSEL MR: The facts are for this purpose beyond controversy. There were five persons present corporeally. . . .

Of the five persons present two only voted for Mr Kippax. Three voted against him. The two who voted for him held more shares in the company than the three who voted against him, and according to the law of this company there was a vote for every share. No poll was demanded, and consequently no poll was taken.

The neat point is, whether the chairman was right in deciding that Mr Kippax was duly elected because the two persons, including himself, who voted for Mr Kippax held more shares in the company than the three who were against him. I think he was not.

We will first of all consider what may be termed the common law of the country as to voting at meetings. It is undoubted . . . that, according to such common law, votes at all meetings are taken by show of hands. Of course it may not always be a satisfactory mode—persons attending in large numbers may be small shareholders, and persons attending in small numbers may be large shareholders, and therefore in companies provision is made for taking a poll, and when a poll is taken the votes are to be counted according to the number of shares, in some cases according to the number of shares absolutely, as in this company, viz a vote for every share, while in other companies there is another scale, and the number of votes increases, but not so rapidly as the number of shares, and there is a limit to the number of votes which a single shareholder can have.

Now, that being the common law mode of voting, is there anything in the Companies Act or in the articles of association which shews that any other mode is to be adopted; for in the absence of provision to the contrary the common law will prevail? So far from finding anything in the Act or the articles to the contrary, what little I do find on the subject confirms the view that the voting is to be taken by a show of hands.

[The court accordingly declared that Masterman, and not Kippax, had been elected as liquidator.]

NOTES

On a show of hands, a person who represents a corporation (s 188), even if he is a member of the company, has only one vote and is not entitled, in addition to his vote in his personal capacity, to cast a vote on behalf of the company he represents: *Vrede Gold Exploration Co Ltd* v *Lubner* 1973 (2) SA 331 (C).

[178] **Williams** *v* **Wilco Timbers (Pty) Ltd**
1950 (3) SA 105 (W)

The articles of association of a company provided, *inter alia*, that the office of a director should be vacated if not less than 90 per cent of the registered shareholders of the company requested him in writing to resign. The court had to decide whether 90 per cent had to be counted by persons or by votes.

ROPER J: . . . The ordinary method of ascertaining the wishes of the majority of members of a joint stock company is to count the number of votes cast for and against the particular proposal which is before the meeting, each share held representing one vote. . . . A majority in the number of votes cast is regarded as a majority of the members, even though the individual members casting them may be in a minority, counted by heads. This is well known to everybody who has any experience of the conduct of company business and must have been well known to the members of this particular company who passed the amended article. It is quite common in ordinary parlance to refer to a majority ascertained in this way, ie by votes, as a majority of the shareholders, even though it is not a majority of shareholders counted by heads. . . .

. . . Accordingly, when the phrase 'ninety per cent of the registered shareholders of the company' is used, I think it means ninety per cent ascertained in the same way as a 'majority' would be ascertained, namely according to votes. . . .

[179] *In re* **Caratal (New) Mines Ltd**
[1902] 2 Ch 498

BUCKLEY J: . . . I am asked to affirm the proposition that if the chairman makes a declaration, and in it actually gives the numbers of the votes for and against the resolutions which he is bound to recognize . . . and then declares that the result is that the required statutory majority has been obtained, although the numbers stated by him show that it has not been obtained, the declaration is conclusive. In my judgment that proposition cannot be supported. . . . It has been held that, if the chairman by his declaration affirms erroneously or without sufficiently ascertaining the facts but bona fide that a resolution has been carried, the court cannot go behind that declaration. Two cases establish that proposition, namely *In re Hadleigh Castle Gold Mines Ltd* [1900] 2 Ch 419, and *Arnot* v *United African Lands Ltd* [1901] 1 Ch 518. In the latter case there was confusion at the meeting, but the court came to the conclusion that the chairman had put the resolutions to the meeting properly and had declared them carried, and therefore declined to enter on an investigation as to what numbers voted for and against the resolutions. In the former case the meeting was a stormy one, and there was a considerable conflict of evidence as to what took place, and the court refused to entertain the question whether the resolution was carried by the requisite majority. But those decisions do not apply to a case where the chairman by his declaration finds the figures and erroneously in point of law holds that the resolution has been duly passed. . . .

NOTES

See also *Burstein* v *Yale* 1958 (1) SA 768 (W); further *MacDougall* v *Gardiner* (1875) 1 ChD 13; *Second Consolidated Trust Ltd* v *Ceylon Amalgamated Tea and Rubber Estates Ltd* [1943] 2 All ER 567.

Articles can validly provide that no objection shall be made to the validity of any vote except at the meeting or poll at which it is tendered: *Colonial Gold Reef Ltd* v *Free State Rand Ltd* [1914] 1 Ch 382; *Wall* v *Exchange Investment Corporation Ltd* [1926] Ch 143. See also *Marting* v *Van Oordt. Russel & Co (Pty) Ltd* 1942 CPD 106.

Where the articles provide that at general meetings, resolutions should be decided on a show of hands, the chairman cannot effectively declare a resolution carried, because there was no counter-motion, without calling for a show of hands: *In re The Citizens Theatre* 1946 SC 14.

A special resolution can be passed on a show of hands: *Etheridge* v *Central Uruguay Northern Extension Railway Co Ltd* [1913] 1 Ch 425.

On a show of hands the vote of each person present is counted as a single vote, even though he holds proxies: *Ernest* v *Loma Gold Mines Ltd* [1897] 1 Ch 1 (cf s 197(1)).

Unless otherwise provided in the articles the chairman can direct a poll to be taken then and there and is not bound to defer the poll to an adjourned meeting: *In re Chillington Iron Co* (1885) 29 ChD 159. (Cf *In re the Salisbury Gold Mining Co Ltd: Ex parte Hathorn* (1894) 15 NLR 232).

The representative of a company under s 188 comes to a meeting as the embodiment of his company, not as a proxy. It follows that he can vote not only on a poll but also on a show of hands. Otherwise if he comes as a proxy.

[180] Davey *v* Inyaminga Petroleum (1934) Ltd
1954 (3) SA 133 (W)

The articles of the respondent company provided as follows:

'Every instrument of proxy, whether for a specified meeting or otherwise shall, as nearly as circumstances will permit, be in the form or to the effect following:

Inyaminga Petroleum (1934) Limited

I
of
being a member of Inyaminga Petroleum (1934) Limited
and being entitled to
votes, hereby appoint
of
or, failing him,
of

as my proxy to vote for me and on my behalf at the
(ordinary or extraordinary, as the case may be)
general meeting of the Company to be held on the
day of
and at any adjournment thereof.
As witness my hand this   day of
1953
or in such other form as the directors shall from time to time approve.'

The proxy forms sent out to shareholders prior to the meeting and
lodged with them for the meeting substantially corresponded to this
form, except that the words: 'and entitled to . . . votes' were omitted.
At the meeting the chairman ruled that the proxies were invalid and
refused to admit them. The court held that the chairman had acted
correctly in rejecting the proxies, and that the fact that the forms had
been sent out to the shareholders by the secretaries of the company, did
not create an estoppel against the company, as the directors had not
approved the forms or authorized the secretaries to send them out.

MALAN J: The first contention on behalf of the applicants is that a
proxy need not be in precisely the same form as directed in the articles
but that compliance in substance therewith is sufficient and that in the
present case the failure to state the number of votes to which the shareholders granting the proxy are entitled is not a substantial departure
from the terms of the proxy required under the articles. It is said that
the number of shares to which the shareholders are entitled is readily
ascertainable by reference to the company's share-register and would
in any event be checked before a proxy is admitted for voting purposes.
I am of opinion that this contention cannot be sustained. The right of
a shareholder in a public company to appoint more than one proxy to
attend on the same occasion is recognized in s 61*quin* [now s 197(2)] of
the Companies Act. In addition ss (5) of that section provides that

> 'on a poll taken at a meeting of a company, a member entitled to
> more than one vote need not, if he votes, use all his votes or cast all
> votes he uses in the same way'.

It appears to me to be essential that the extent of the authority conferred upon the holder of the proxy should be disclosed therein. To
hold the contrary will lead to a most unsatisfactory result in that the
chairman or any other interested party will be obliged to accept the
verbal assurance of the holder of the proxy as to the number of votes
which he has been authorized to use. The insertion of the number of
votes which the holder is authorized to use is consequently most material
and not unimportant or formal. . . .
Moreover, a shareholder may hold shares as trustee or nominee of
other persons who may give him conflicting instructions. I am of opinion
that on both these grounds omission of the number of votes which may
be used by the proxy on a poll is a material defect and that without it
the proxy is incomplete, not in compliance with the requirements laid
down in the articles and thus invalid. . . .

[181] Shaw *v* Tati Concessions Ltd
[1913] 1 Ch 292

At a meeting a poll was demanded. The chairman directed the poll to be taken at a future date and closed the meeting. The court held that the adjournment of the poll was not an adjournment of the meeting, but a continuation of the original meeting, and that consequently no new proxies could be lodged.

SWINFEN EADY J: . . . The true legal position is this. There is an adjourned meeting, but the original meeting continues for the purpose of taking the poll until the poll is closed. Therefore proxies obtained and lodged later than forty-eight hours before the original meeting are not available. . . .

[See also *Jackson* v *Hamlyn* [1953] Ch 577, [1953] 1 All ER 887.]

[182] Cousins *v* International Brick Company Ltd
[1931] 2 Ch 90

LUXMOORE J: . . . Is there anything in the articles as between a shareholder and the company to preclude a shareholder who has given a proxy from attending a meeting or an adjourned meeting and voting in person, notwithstanding the fact that he has given a proxy? There is no authority touching the particular point, but on principle I do not think there is any ground in such a case for refusing the shareholder's vote and accepting that of the proxy. The proxy is merely the agent of the shareholder who appoints him. As between himself and the proxy he can determine the agency, and the agent is not entitled to vote if the agency is in fact determined. . . . A company finding votes cast in respect of the same shares is bound to consider which votes are to be accepted, and where the votes of a shareholder are cast by that shareholder himself in a manner justified by the articles, I think the company is, in the absence of any particular circumstances, bound to accept those votes, notwithstanding that a person who has been validly appointed as proxy in respect of the same shares has also purported to vote. The right of the shareholder to vote in person must, in my judgment, and in the absence of any special contract between himself and the company expressly precluding the right to vote in person where a proxy has been validly given, be paramount to the right of the proxy to vote in respect of the shares in question.

There is, in my judgment, no contract binding the shareholder vis-à-vis the company to exercise the option to vote either in person or by proxy at any time before the actual moment when the vote is to be given. . . .

LAWRENCE LJ: I agree. . . . The question is whether a shareholder by having appointed a proxy to vote for him at a particular meeting has precluded himself from voting personally at that meeting and whether, if he does vote personally, the chairman of the meeting is justified in rejecting his vote and accepting that of his proxy. . . . Every proxy is subject to an implied condition that it should only be used if the shareholder is unable or finds it inconvenient to attend the meeting.

The proxy is merely the agent of the shareholder, and as between himself and his principal is not entitled to act contrary to the instructions of the latter. . . . If the proxy insists on voting notwithstanding that the shareholder himself attends and votes and thus a double vote is given at the meeting in respect of the same shares, it is the duty of the chairman to reject the vote of the proxy as the personal vote is an unequivocal exercise on the part of the shareholder of his option to vote in person. . . .

[In *Ansett* v *Butler Air Transport (No 2)* (1958) 75 WN (NSW) 306, discussed by B J Herron in 'Proxy Voting at Company Meetings' (1958) 32 *Australian LJ* 249, the question was raised whether shareholders who, after having given proxies, attend the meeting personally and vote, render the proxies ineffectual so that the proxy holders cannot vote at a subsequent meeting at which the shareholders are not present. It is suggested that this depends upon whether the proxies were revoked or only temporarily suspended and that in doubt suspension must be presumed.]

[183] Peel *v* London and North Western Railway Company
[1907] 1 Ch 5

For some time there had been differences between the directors and a body of shareholders over the management's policy. Prior to certain general meetings the directors circularized the shareholders setting out the facts and appealing for support. With the circular was enclosed a stamped proxy paper containing the names of three of the directors as proxies, with a stamped envelope for return. The question before the court was whether the directors had acted legally in using the funds of the company in paying the expenses thus incurred.

BUCKLEY LJ: . . . A corporation in general can only act by its agents. It exists only in contemplation of law and not in physical fact. The only act which occurs to me at present that the corporation can personally do is to assemble in general meeting and pass a resolution. The convening of a general meeting, the use of such machinery as is necessary to express the view of the corporation in general meeting is, I think, as vital and important a corporate act as can be conceived. As a general principle it cannot be *ultra vires* to use the company's funds bona fide and reasonably for the purpose of obtaining the best expression of the voice of the corporators in general meeting.

The order which is under appeal affirms in substance two propositions. The first is that the directors ought not to seek to influence the votes of the shareholders; the second is one not so much of principle as of detail, namely that certain expenses, such as those of the stamps on proxy papers and for postage, are matters which ought not to be allowed. Let me say a word on each of these. As regards the first, is it proper that the directors should circulate amongst the shareholders in the company information for the purpose of guiding their judgment in questions of policy, and should endeavour to influence them in that matter by saying, 'Our views as your servants or managing partners are that the true policy is so and so, and we ask you to support us in it'? In my opinion it is not only within their power, but it is their manifest duty so to do. It is their duty, they knowing the proper working of the railway undertaking, if a question of policy of this sort is started, to say to the shareholders, 'In our view the policy which is suggested is wrong. We offer you our reasons for thinking so, and we ask you to support us by your vote in the interests of the undertaking in defeating the policy which is suggested.' . . .

. . . Secondly, as regards the question of detail, whether the proxy papers should be stamped and so on. . . . The true principle seems to me to be this: the company may legitimately do and may defray out of its assets the reasonable expense of doing all such acts as are reasonably necessary for calling the meeting and obtaining the best expression of the corporators' views on the questions to be brought before it. It may, or may not, be reasonable to pay for stamps upon proxies. I expect that it is necessary. There are many people who, if they received a proxy without a stamp, would not take the trouble to return it. If it is sent with the proxy stamped and the return postage stamp affixed, very likely it will come back.

. . . I wish to guard myself with one final observation. Those who are conversant with the affairs of joint stock companies are well aware that cases often arise in which the board in power are anxious to maintain themselves in power, to procure their own re-election, or to drive a policy not really in the interests of the corporation, but for some private purpose of their own, down the throats of the corporators at a general meeting, and in which they issue at the expense of the company circulars and proxy papers for the purpose of attaining that object. When a case of that kind comes before the court, I sincerely trust that the decision of this court in this case will not be cited as any authority for justifying the action of the directors. The point here decided is that directors bona fide acting in the interests of the corporation, and not to serve their own interests, are entitled and bound to inform and guide the corporators in matters affecting the corporate interests, and any expenses reasonably incurred in so doing may be borne out of the funds of the company. . . .

NOTES

At common law there is a right to demand a poll but not to appoint a proxy.

As to the rule that proxy forms must be in conformity with the articles, see also *Harben v Phillips* (1883) 23 ChD 14 (where articles prescribe attestation, unattested forms must be rejected). The proxy's authority depends upon the proxy: *In re Waxed Papers Ltd* [1937] 2 All ER 481; *Cameron v Getz* 1945 WLD 92.

'A mere misprint or some quite palpable mistake on the face of the document does not entitle the company to refuse to accept the proxy': *Oliver v Dagleish* [1963] 3 All ER 330 at 334, [1963] 1 WLR 1274 at 1278, per Buckley J. Nor is a proxy form which contains all the necessary information as to the date of the meeting invalid merely because it is undated: *Getz v Spaarwater Gold Mining Co Ltd* 1971 (2) SA 423 (W).

Where the proxy form provides for instructions on the part of the shareholder how to vote 'for' or 'against', are these instructions purely a matter between the shareholder and the proxy, which does not concern the company, or does it limit the proxy's powers so that the votes cast by him are not to be counted if he acts contrary to his instructions? This question was shortly discussed by Buckley J in *Oliver v Dagleish* but not decided. Certain is that a holder of proxies from different shareholders may cast some of the votes 'for' and others 'against', s 197(2).

On the proposition that reasonable expenditure incurred by the board in power in a 'proxy fight' in the interests of keeping the shareholders properly informed may be

charged to the company, see also *Wilson* v *London, Midland and Scottish Railway Co*
[1940] Ch 393, [1940] 2 All ER 92. On the question whether insurgents or, at least,
successful insurgents are entitled to a reimbursement of their expenses in the proxy
battle, see Dr Aaron Yoran, 'Restraints on Incumbent Directors in Intracorporate
Battle for Control'; (1973) 7 *U of Richmond LR* 431 at 455ff. On the position in
America, see L Loss *Securities Regulation* 859–66; also *Rosenfeld* v *Fairchild Engine and
Airplane Corp* 309 NY 168, 128 NE 2d 291 (1955); (1956) 56 *Columbia LR*. 633; *Levin*
v *Metro-Goldwyn-Mayer Inc* 264 F Supp 797 (SDNY 1967); Victor Brudney in (1966)
65 *Mich LR* 259 at 282–5; E R Aranow & H A Einhorn *Proxy Contests for Corporate
Control* 2 ed (1968).

The period prescribed in the articles for lodging proxies prior to a meeting may not
exceed 48 hours, s 189(3).

On a comparison of Anglo-American and South African proxy vote provisions, see
Robert D Levine (1969) 2 *CILSA* 363. 'Causation and Liability in Private Actions for
Proxy Violations' is the title of an article in (1970) 80 *Yale LJ* 107.

[183A]   ABC Limited

I...of..
being a member of ABC Limited hereby appoint
....of..or failing him
....of..or failing him
the Chairman of the meeting as my proxy to vote for me and on my behalf
at the general meeting of the Company to be held on the 10th day of
January, 1977 and at any adjournment thereof as follows:

	In favour of	Against	Abstention
Resolution No. 1 Special Resolution to increase the Company's authorized share capital			
Resolution No. 2 Special Resolution to reduce the Company's present share premium and place the amount so reduced to the credit of a 'special reserve'			
Resolution No. 3 Special Resolution to reduce the Company's share premium which will accrue as a result of the 'rights issue' and place the amount so reduced to the credit of a 'special reserve'			
Resolution No. 4 Special Resolution to change the name of the Company			
Resolution No. 5 Ordinary Resolution to place the new ordinary shares under the control of the directors			
Resolution No. 6 Ordinary Resolution to make application to the Supreme Court for the confirmation of the reduction of the Company's share premiums			

(Indicate instruction to proxy by way of a cross in space provided above.)
Unless otherwise instructed, my proxy may vote as he thinks fit.
Signed this..day of..
Signature..

Note

(i) A member entitled to attend and vote at the abovementioned meeting is entitled to appoint a proxy (who need not be a member of the Company) or more than one proxy (who also need not be members of the Company) to attend and speak and, on a poll, to vote in his stead.

(ii) Forms of proxy must be deposited at the office of the Transfer Secretaries, 59 Paradise Street, Johannesburg 2001, so as to be received not less than 48 hours before the time fixed for the meeting.

(iii) The authority of a person signing a proxy form under a power of attorney or on behalf of a company or pension fund must be attached to it unless that authority has already been recorded by the Company.

(iv) This proxy form must be signed by or on behalf of all joint shareholders. The vote/s of the senior of such joint holders who tender a vote (whether in person or by proxy) will be accepted to the exclusion of the vote/s of the other joint holder/s and for this purpose seniority will be determined by the order in which the names of the joint holders stand in the Company's register of members.

[184] National Dwellings Society v Sykes
[1894] 3 Ch 159

CHITTY J: . . . A question of some importance has been mooted in this case, with regard to the powers of the chairman over a meeting. Unquestionably it is the duty of the chairman, and his function, to preserve order, and to take care that the proceedings are conducted in a proper manner, and that the sense of the meeting is properly ascertained with regard to any question which is properly before the meeting. But, in my opinion, the power which has been contended for is not within the scope of the authority of the chairman, namely to stop the meeting at his own will and pleasure. The meeting is called for the particular purposes of the company. According to the constitution of the company, a certain officer has to preside. He presides with reference to the business which is there to be transacted. In my opinion, he cannot say, after that business has been opened, 'I will have no more to do with it; I declare the meeting dissolved, and I leave the chair'. . . . The meeting by itself . . . can resolve to go on with the business for which it has been convened, and appoint a chairman to conduct the business which the other chairman, forgetful of his duty or violating his duty, has tried to stop because the proceedings have taken a turn which he himself does not like. . . .

NOTES

If there are no objections to the adjournment of a meeting by the chairman, who leaves after having dissolved it, the remaining shareholders cannot thereafter elect another chairman and proceed with the business. Cf *R* v *Gaborian* (1809) 11 East 77, 103 ER 933.

[185] Kerr v John Mottram Ltd
[1940] Ch 657, [1940] 2 All ER 629

Clause 114 of the articles of association of defendant company provided as follows:

'The directors shall cause proper minutes to be made of all general meetings of the company and also of all appointments of officers and of the proceedings of all meetings of directors and committees and of the attendance thereat, and all business transacted at such meetings, and any such minute of any meeting, if purporting to be signed by the chairman of the next succeeding meeting, shall be conclusive evidence without any further proof of the facts therein stated.'

SIMONDS J: . . . This action raises a curious point upon which I am told, there is no previous decision. The plaintiff, Ewen Mackinnon Kerr, a shareholder in John Mottram Ltd, sues that company claiming specific performance of a contract for the sale to him by it of certain of its preference shares and ordinary shares, which it was in a position to sell by virtue of a lien given to it by arts 11 and 12 of the articles of association. For the purpose of establishing that contract he must lead evidence to show that it was in fact entered into without any qualification. Upon counsel for the plaintiff seeking to lead such evidence, objection was taken by counsel for the defendant company that he was not entitled to do so, inasmuch as that evidence was inconsistent with what was recorded in the minutes of a meeting of the company held on 7 February 1939. . . . Mr Jones, the secretary of the company, who was also a director, was called to prove that this was the minute book of the company, that the minutes relied on were those of the meeting in question, and that the signature was that of the chairman. That gave counsel for the plaintiff the opportunity of establishing, if he could, that the minutes were not a bona fide record of what took place and that they had been written up after the events, falsely and fraudulently, with a view to setting up a story which was not in accordance with the facts. I am quite satisfied, after hearing the evidence of Mr Jones, that the minutes are substantially correct and are a bona fide record of what took place on 7 February 1939. I am not saying that they are in every respect accurate; that I do not know, but of this I am satisfied, that they are not fraudulently written up. . . .

. . . Now, art 114 . . . represents the bargain between the shareholders as to what is to be, as between them, the value and effect of the minutes of the company as recorded in its minute book and signed by the chairman, and their bargain is that it is to 'be conclusive evidence without any further proof of the facts therein stated'. . . . That is to say, the minutes are to be regarded as evidence which is not to be displaced and is conclusive as between the parties who are bound by them. . . .

[186] Silver Garbus & Co (Pty) Ltd v Teichert
1954 (2) SA 98 (N)

HENOCHSBERG AJ: . . . Nel gave evidence to the effect that it was customary, in the case of small proprietary companies, for copies of so-called extracts from minutes to be sent to the company by solicitors or building societies, or others with whom they had transactions, for entry in the company's minute book, and that that entry was invariably made after the extract had been certified by an officer of the company. He also said that he never regarded such extracts as constituting a minute until the subject-matter of the extract had been confirmed by the directors at a subsequent meeting, and that, in the case of this company, no directors' meeting had been held since 17 November 1952.

Fortunately it is not necessary for me, in this case, to decide the propriety of the practice of certifying extracts from minutes when no meeting has in fact taken place, or before the resolutions contained in the extract have been passed, but I cannot say that it is a practice that meets with my approbation. . . .

NOTES

See further *R v Raisun and Pather* 1947 (2) SA 881 (W).

The entry of a resolution in a minute is not essential to the validity of the resolution, which may be proved *aliunde*: *In re Great Northern Salt and Chemical Works: Ex parte Kennedy* (1890) 44 ChD 472; *In re Fireproof Doors Ltd* [1916] 2 Ch 142. But note that special resolutions must be registered with the Registrar before they become effective: s 203.

A member is not entitled to see the minutes of a meeting or the transcript of the minutes before they are written up: *Gans v SPCA* 1962 (4) SA 543 (W).

III UNANIMOUS ASSENT AS SUBSTITUTE FOR A FORMAL RESOLUTION

A TEXT

In a number of cases English and South African courts have treated informal, unanimous assent of the shareholders as the equivalent of a formal resolution, passed at a properly convened meeting: *187, 188*; also *38* and *164* above and *190* below.

B CASES

[187] **Dublin *v* Diner**
1964 (1) SA 799 (D)

MILLER J: . . . I can find no justification for holding that the company would necessarily have to amend its articles of association in order to enable itself to sanction an irregular transaction concluded by directors or to authorize directors to do that which, without such sanction, they would not properly be able to do. In such circumstances, moreover, and particularly where there are only two shareholders, who are also the sole directors, it seems to me that the fact that there was no duly convened meeting of the shareholders for the purpose of sanctioning, or making, an allotment of shares, does not necessarily invalidate the transaction concluded pursuant to their agreement. In *Parker & Cooper Ltd v Reading* [1926] 1 Ch 975, to which Mr S, for the applicant, referred me, it was held that although the shareholders' assent to irregular transactions

concluded by the directors was not given at any actual meeting of shareholders, it was sufficient that 'every member of the company assented
to the purchase, and the company is bound in a matter *intra vires* by the
unanimous agreement of its members' (quoting the words of Lord Davey
in *Salomon* v *Salomon & Co* [1897] AC at 57). These decisions have recently
been applied by O'Hagan J in *Sugden* v *Beaconhurst Dairies (Pty) Ltd
& others* 1963 (2) SA 174 (E) at 180–1. There, too, the learned judge
had to deal with a case in which there were only two directors of a company, who were also its only shareholders. The issue in that case related
to the validity of a transaction falling within the ambit of s 70*dec*(2) of
the Act. O'Hagan J remarked:

> 'In my view, where the only two shareholders and directors express —
> whether at the same time or not — their joint approval of a transaction
> contemplated by s 70*dec*(2), their decision is as valid and effectual as
> if it had been taken at a general meeting convened with all the for-
> malities prescribed by the Act.'

(See also *Peter Buchanan Ltd and Macharg* v *McVey* [1955] AC 516 at
520–2.)

In the case now before me, although the 'minutes' are said to be
those of a meeting of shareholders, it is clear from all the surrounding
circumstances that in fact the only shareholders and directors of Ben-Oz
(Pty) Ltd agreed that 66 000 shares be allotted to the applicant. The
two shareholders in the company duly appended their signatures to
a document to manifest their approval of and agreement with the
'resolutions' contained therein, and although they may not have
specially designated their agreement to be in their capacity as directors,
it would be artificial in the extreme not to recognize their approval and
agreement in that capacity also. It seems to me, therefore, that whether
one views this as a case in which the company itself, through its only
shareholders, allotted shares to a director, or as a case in which the
allotment was made by the unaminous agreement of shareholders and
directors, the result is the same, and that result is that the transaction
is not impeachable by the company or any shareholder and gives rise
to an effective and valid allotment.

[188] *In re* Duomatic Ltd
[1969] 2 Ch 365, [1969] 1 All ER 161

For a period of approximately fifteen months, one Mr Elvins and one
Mr East were the only directors and the only ordinary shareholders
of the company. The articles of the company provided that the remuneration of directors should be determined from time to time by the company
in general meeting. No resolution was ever passed authorizing the directors
to receive any remuneration and neither of the directors had a contract
of service, but both according to their personal needs drew various sums,
totalling them up at the end of the year and entering them into the
accounts as 'directors' salaries'. After the company was being wound up,
the liquidator sought to recover from the two directors the sums paid
to them.

BUCKLEY J: It is common ground that none of the sums which I have mentioned were authorized by any resolution of the company in general meeting, nor were they authorized by any resolution of any formally constituted board meeting; but it is said on behalf of Mr Elvins that the payments were made with the full knowledge and consent of all the holders of voting shares in the company at the relevant times, and he contends that in those circumstances the absence of a formal resolution by the company in duly convened meeting of the company is irrelevant. . . .

In support of the first part of his argument Mr McC has relied on two authorities. The first was *In re Express Engineering Works Ltd* [1920] 1 Ch 466 where five persons formed a private company in which they were the sole shareholders, and they sold to it for £15 000, which was in fact, secured by debentures of the company, property which they had acquired for £7 000 a few days before. The contract for sale to the company and the issue of debentures was carried out at a meeting of the five individuals, who thereupon appointed themselves directors of the company. That meeting was described in the books of the company as a board meeting. The articles forbade any director to vote in respect of any contract or arrangement in which he might be interested; and in a winding up of the company the liquidator claimed that the issue of the debentures was invalid. In the court of appeal it was held, there being no suggestion of fraud, that the company was bound in a matter *intra vires* by the unanimous agreement of its members. Lord Sterndale MR in his judgment, at 469, referred to the earlier decision of the court of appeal in *In re George Newman & Co Ltd* [*239* p 414 below] and cited a passage from the judgment of Lindley LJ in that case, at 686, and went on himself to say that there were two differences between *Newman's* case and *Express Engineering Works*, first, the transaction in *Newman's* case was *ultra vires*, and, secondly, there never was a meeting of the corporators. Lord Sterndale MR in *In re Express Engineering Works Ltd* [1920] 1 Ch 466, 470 went on:

> 'In the present case these five persons were all the corporators of the company and they did all meet, and did all agree that these debentures should be issued. Therefore it seems that the case came within the meaning of what was said by Lord Davey in *Salomon v Salomon & Co Ltd* [1897] AC 22', and he quotes from Lord Davey. Lord Sterndale MR goes on: 'It is true that a different question was there under discussion, but I am of opinion that this case falls within what Lord Davey said. It was said here that the meeting was a directors' meeting, but it might well be considered a general meeting of the company, for although it was referred to in the minutes as a board meeting, yet if the five persons present had said, "We will now constitute this a general meeting", it would have been within their powers to do so, and it appears to me that that was in fact what they did.'

Warrington LJ said, at 470:

> 'It was competent to them'—that is, the five corporators of the company—'to waive all formalities as regards notice of meetings,

etc, and to resolve themselves into a meeting of shareholders and unanimously pass the resolution in question. Inasmuch as they could not in one capacity effectually do what was required but could do it in another, it is to be assumed that as business men they would act in the capacity in which they had power to act. In my judgment they must be held to have acted as shareholders and not as directors, and the transaction must be treated as good as if every formality had been carried out.'

Younger LJ said, at 471:

'I agree with the view that when all the shareholders of a company are present at a meeting that becomes a general meeting and there is no necessity for any further formality to be observed to make it so. In my opinion the true view is that if you have all the shareholders present, then all the requirements in connection with a meeting of the company are observed, and every competent resolution passed for which no further formality is required by statute becomes binding on the company.'

In that case there were no non-voting shares, but Mr McC contends that the presence of the non-voting shares in the present case does not matter. If he can establish that those who were entitled to attend and vote at general meetings of the company in fact agreed to all or any of these payments, then he says that that is tantamount to a resolution passed at a general meeting of the company, and that the agreement of those persons is binding on the company in the same way as a resolution of a general meeting is binding on the company.

In *Parker & Cooper Ltd* v *Reading* [1926] Ch 975, the second case relied upon by Mr McC, the directors of a company had created a debenture and proceedings were commenced to establish that the debenture and the resolution which authorized its issue and the appointment of a certain receiver under it were invalid. Astbury J referred to *In re Express Engineering Works Ltd* [1920] 1 Ch 466 and to *In re George Newman & Co Ltd* [1895] 1 Ch 674 and himself expressed this view [1926] Ch 975 at 984:

'Now the view I take of both these decisions is that where the transaction is *intra vires* and honest, and especially if it is for the benefit of the company, it cannot be upset if the assent of all the corporators is given to it. I do not think it matters in the least whether that assent is given at different times or simultaneously.'

Thus, the effect of his judgment was to carry the position a little further than it had been carried in *In re Express Engineering Works Ltd* [1920] 1 Ch 466, for Astbury J expressed the view that it was immaterial that the assent of the corporators was obtained at different times, and that it was not necessary that there should be a meeting of them all at which they gave their consent to the particular transaction sought to be upheld. In *Parker & Cooper Ltd* v *Reading* [1926] Ch 975, as in *In re Express Engineering Works Ltd* [1920] 1 Ch 466, no question arose about the position of any shareholders whose shares conferred no right of attending or voting at general meetings of the company.

The evidence in the present case, I think, establishes that Mr Elvins and Mr East both approved the accounts of the company for the year ended 30 April 1963, and, indeed, they signed a copy of those accounts; and the evidence is that that was done on an occasion when they met together with the auditor of the company. . . .

Mr W for the liquidator, has contended that where there has been no formal meeting of the company and reliance is placed upon the informal consent of the shareholders the cases indicate that it is necessary to establish that all shareholders have consented. He argues that as the preference shareholder is not shown to have consented in the present case, that requirement is not satisfied, and that the assent of those share-holders—that is to say, Mr Elvins and Mr East—who knew about these matters, and who did approve the figures relating to them in the accounts for the year ending 30 April 1963 is of no significance. It seems to me that if it had occurred to Mr Elvins and Mr East, at the time when they were considering the accounts, to take the formal step of constituting themselves a general meeting of the company and passing a formal resolution approving the payment of directors' salaries, that it would have made the position of the directors who received the remuneration, Mr Elvins and Mr Hanly, secure, and nobody could thereafter have disputed their right to retain their remuneration. The fact that they did not take that formal step but that they nevertheless did apply their minds to the question of whether the drawings by Mr Elvins and Mr Hanly should be approved as being on account of remuneration payable to them as directors, seems to lead to the conclusion that I ought to regard their consent as being tantamount to a resolution of a general meeting of the company. In other words, I proceed upon the basis that where it can be shown that all shareholders who have a right to attend and vote at a general meeting of the company assent to some matter which a general meeting of the company could carry into effect, that assent is as binding as a resolution in general meeting would be. The preference shareholder, having shares which conferred upon him no right to receive notice of or to attend and vote at a general meeting of the company, could be in no worse position if the matter were dealt with informally by agreement between all the shareholders having voting rights than he would be if the shareholders met together in a duly constituted general meeting.

Accordingly, the evidence that I have heard leads to the conclusion that the drawings by Mr Elvins and Mr Hanly during the accounting year ending 30 April 1963, which are covered by the item of directors' salaries £15 661 1s 8d in the profit and loss account cannot now be disturbed.

NOTES

See further *Advance Seed Co (Edms) Bpk* v *Marrok Plase (Edms) Bpk, 199* below, and *Avondson Trust (Pty) Ltd* v *Wouda* 1975 (2) SA 444 (T), where F S Steyn J said (at 447, 448):

'In *Sugden & others* v *Beaconhurst Dairies (Pty) Ltd & others* 1963 (2) SA 174 (E), O'Hagan J at 180 and 181, approved of the views quoted by him, which were expressed in *In re Express Engineering Works Ltd* [1920] 1 ChD 466, and in *Parker & Cooper Ltd* v *Reading* [1926] 1 ChD 975, and he concluded (at 181A):

"In my view, where the only two shareholders and directors express, whether at the same time or not—their joint approval of a transaction contemplated by s 70*dec*(2), their decision is as valid and effectual as if it had been taken at a general meeting convened with all the formalities prescribed by the Act."

The view that the decisions of a company can be taken without any vestige of formality was strikingly expressed by Mingswell Moore J in *Peter Buchanan Ltd and Macharg v McVey* [1955] AC 516 at the foot of 520:

"There was no formal meeting of the company to authorize the disposal of the property to the defendant, no resolution, however informal, to that effect. It is now settled law that neither meeting nor resolution is necessary. If all the corporators agree to a certain course then, however informal the manner of the agreement, it is an act of the company and binds the company. . . ." '

It would appear that an act which is *ultra vires* the company or which requires a special resolution cannot be authorized by the informal, unanimous consent of all the shareholders, *Quadrangle Investments* v *Witind, 38* above. In *L Taylor & Kie (Edms) Bpk* v *Grabe* 1976 (3) SA 75 (T) the court doubted whether participation in litigation could be authorized by such consent. See also R C Beuthin 'The Principle of Unanimous Assent' (1974) 91 *SALJ* 2. It does not necessarily follow that an act contrary to the articles which was committed in the past can never be validated by unanimous assent, see *Gohlke's* case, *190* below. Everything, it is suggested, must depend on the nature of the act.

10 *Directors*

I DEFINITION

A TEXT

Directors are the persons who direct and control the affairs of the company. A person who occupies the position of a director or alternate director is a 'director' for the purposes of the Act even if he is called by another name, s 1 sv 'director'. See also the Criminal Procedure Act 56 of 1955 s 381(10): *189*.

B CASES

[189] S *v* Marks
1965 (3) SA 834 (W) (See also *158*, above.)

HILL J: Before dealing with the question of the accused's criminal liability under the individual counts, I propose to deal with the allegation ... that at all relevant times the accused was, in fact and in terms of s 381(10) of Act 56 of 1955, a person who controlled or governed the three companies known respectively as Annysspruit Coal Development and Exploration Co Ltd, Western Main Reefs Ltd and Unicorn Investments Ltd.

In reply to a request for particulars as to the meaning of the phrase 'controlled or governed' the following information was supplied by the State:

'Apart from inferences to be drawn from the evidence demonstrating the accused's complete control of Annysspruit and Western Main Reefs he controlled or governed them by:

(*a*) being a director of companies which supplied their assets;

(*b*) financing them, paying their expenses and exercising control over their finances;

(*c*) being the majority shareholder thereof;

(*d*) controlling the share capital thereof;

(*e*) controlling the share market in and the market prices of their shares;

(f) dictating the policy and major transactions thereof and instructing the directors and secretaries thereof in the action to be taken;

(g) causing their directors, auditors and secretaries to act on his instructions . . .'

In ss (10) of s 381 of the Criminal Procedure Act, which deals with criminal proceedings against corporations, directors or servants of corporate bodies and members of associations, the word 'director' is defined as follows:

'In this section the word "director" in relation to a corporate body means any person who controls or governs that corporate body or who is a member of a body or group of persons which controls or governs that corporate body or where there is no such body or group, who is a member of that corporate body.'

In the Afrikaans text of the Criminal Procedure Act, which was signed by the Governor-General, s 381(10) reads as follows:

·(10) In hierdie artikel beteken die woord „direkteur" met betrekking tot 'n regspersoon iemand wat daardie regspersoon beheer of bestuur of wat lid is van 'n liggaam of groep persone wat daardie regspersoon beheer of bestuur of, waar daar nie so 'n liggaam of groep is nie, wat lid is van daardie regspersoon.'

In the *Afrikaanse Woordeboek* the following meanings to the word 'beheer' as a noun and as a verb are given:
'Beheer l.s.l. Bestuur en toesig, administrasie, kontrole. . . .'
The word 'bestuur' is described as follows:

's. 1. Beheer, leiding, reëling: Die bestuur oor iets hê. Geregtelike bestuur van 'n maatskappy (jur.). . . .'

One of the definitions of 'control' as a verb given in the *Oxford Dictionary* is

'to exercise restraint or direction upon the free action of; to hold sway over, exercise power or authority over; to dominate, command'.
Meanings given to the word 'govern' include:
'to rule or regulate the affairs of: to direct, guide or regulate in conduct or actions; to hold sway, prevail, have predominating or decisive influence.'

In the *Concise Oxford Dictionary* the word 'govern' is defined, *inter alia*, as

'regulate proceedings of (corporation, etc.); sway, rule, influence, regulate, determine, be the predominating influence'.

I am unable to agree with [the] contention that a reading of the dictionary references makes it clear that the words 'beheer' and 'bestuur' imply either complete control or, at least, effective control and that neither word suggests partial independent control in the sense of control of one or more company activities. In both the Afrikaans and English versions 'control' and 'govern' vary in meanings from merely guiding or influencing to commanding or ruling.

It seems to me that the connotation of the words 'control' and 'govern' as used in ss (10) of s 381 of the Act is wide enough to include the control of a company in any of its activities. If partial independent control is to be excluded, as suggested by counsel, the intended effect of the subsection would be rendered nugatory as the evil aimed at could then easily be avoided by leaving minor matters to the discretion of the appointed directors whilst the outsider exercises effective control over major matters of policy or business of the company.

In my opinion the accused more than merely usurped the function of a director of the three companies. He was tacitly accepted by the boards of directors of the companies as the person who in fact controlled or at least predominantly influenced the conduct of the affairs of the companies and I have no doubt that the control and governance of the companies as envisaged by the subsection was exercised by the accused.

NOTES

See also *R* v *Mall* 1959 (4) SA 607 (N) at 610–11, per Caney J: 'I consider . . . that there is no ground for limiting the clear language of ss (10) [of s 381 of the Criminal Procedure Act 1955] to those who are constitutionally and legally vested with the control and government of corporate bodies. The plain words are "any person who controls or governs . . . or who is a member of a body . . . which controls or governs . . .", that is to say, in fact "controls or governs". It is inconceivable that the legislature did not know and appreciate that corporate bodies, particularly companies, are sometimes controlled, wholly or partially, by persons who are not personally upon the board of directors but are represented there by a nominee; more particularly is a company which is subsidiary to another controlled by the directors of the latter, though they may not, or not all of them, be directors of the subsidiary. . . . An individual also may legally exercise control of a company by means of a nominee. . . . It is unlikely that the legislature did not intend to bring persons, exercising control from outside the company, possibly controlling the policy and controlling the acts of the company, within the net of criminal responsibility. The plain language of the subsection includes them and I see no ground for excluding them. Indeed, it is not beyond the bounds of possibility that a person should usurp the functions of a director; if that should happen I see no reason why he should not be treated as having brought himself within ss (10) and so taken upon himself the responsibilites placed on a director by the section.'

On directors generally, see S J Naudé *Die Regsposisie van die Maatskappydirekteure met besondere Verwysing na die Interne Maatskappyverband* (1970); G A Leveson *Company Directors. Law and Practice* (1970). On 'puppet' directors, see p 448 below.

II Appointment Qualifications and Disqualifications

A TEXT

Every public company must have at least two directors, every private company one, s 208(1); see Table A art 53 and Table B art 54. The articles may, and usually do, make provision for the appointment of alternate directors, Table A arts 57, 58, Table B arts 58, 59. Subject to the provisions of s 208(1), the number and method of appointment of directors is determined by the articles: *190*. If the articles do not otherwise provide, the first directors are appointed by the subscribers to the memorandum, s 209. Until directors are appointed every subscriber is deemed to be a director, s 208(2); see Table A art 53, Table B art 54 (cf *Ex parte Umtentweni Motels (Pty) Ltd* 1968 (1) SA 144 (N)). Where more than one director is to be elected at a meeting a separate resolution must be moved for each person to be appointed unless the meeting without dissent agrees to make the appointment by a single resolution, s 210: *191*. Subsequent directors are usually elected by the company in general meeting, Table A arts 66–69, Table B art 67. A third party may by vested with the right to appoint a director. Casual vacancies are usually filled by the directors, Table A art 72, Table B art 70.

Only a natural person may become a director, s 218(1)(*a*). Certain persons are disqualified from becoming or continuing as directors, ss 218(*b*)–(*d*), 219. (See also s 9 of the Financial Institutions (Investment of Funds) Act 56 of 1964, under which the court may declare a director convicted under the Act unfit to act as director of a financial institution.) The articles may apply further disqualifications, s 218(3) and Table A art 65 and Table art 66 (paras (*b*), (*d*) and (*e*) of these two articles are of special importance): *192, 193*. On incompatibility of offices, see *204, 205* below.

The articles may but need not prescribe the holding of a specified number of qualification shares, see Table A art 56, Table B art 57: *194–196*.

No person is capable of being appointed as a director before the issue of a certificate to commence business unless he has (*a*) signed and lodged with the Registrar his consent in writing to act as such; and (*b*) subscribed in the memorandum for the prescribed number of qualification shares, or signed and lodged with the Registrar a contract in writing to take from the company and pay for such shares, s 211 (1), (2), (4). Where a director is appointed after the issue of the certificate to commence business, his appointment does not take effect unless his written consent has been lodged with the Registrar and the company has been notified by the Registrar that the consent has been so lodged. On receipt of this notification his appointment becomes effective as from the date when it was made, s 211(3), (4). If qualification shares are required, he vacates his office if he does not obtain them within two months or such shorter period as the articles may prescribe, s 213. Bearer shares, for obvious reasons, do not count, s 213(1)(*b*). Apparently, unless the articles provide otherwise, a director cannot act before he acquires his qualification: *197*.

The acts of a director are valid notwithstanding any defect that is afterwards discovered in his appointment or qualification, s 214: *198, 199*.

Every company has to keep an up-to-date register of its directors and officers, containing the particulars set out in s 215, and to lodge a return reflecting these particulars with the Registrar, s 216(2), who maintains a central register of directors and officers, s 217. Persons appointed as directors or officers are obliged to provide the company with these particulars, s 216.

B CASES

[190] Gohlke and Schneider *v* Westies Minerale (Edms) Bpk
1970 (2) SA 685 (AD)

TROLLIP JA: In this appeal the only issue is whether the second appellant, to whom I shall refer by his surname, Wiehahn, was duly appointed a director of Sarusas Minerals (Pty) Ltd. . . . The latter is the second respondent and I shall call it, for brevity's sake, 'Sarusas'.

Sarusas was registered in South West Africa as a private company on 26 January 1965 primarily for the purpose of prospecting and mining for and dealing in precious and semi-precious stones, excluding diamonds. Its authorized share capital was R100 divided into 100 ordinary shares of R1 each. It can safely be inferred that the promoters were two persons, Gohlke and Schneider, and a company, Westies Minerale (Edms) Bpk, referred to herein as 'Westies', for soon after its incorporation, on 28 January 1965, they concluded a written agreement governing their respective rights and obligations in respect of Sarusas. In terms thereof they were to be the only shareholders, the shares being divided equally between Westies on the one hand and Gohlke and Schneider on the other hand. In return for its 50 shares Westies undertook to cede certain prospecting and mining rights to Sarusas, and in return for their 50 shares Gohlke and Schneider undertook to provide it with all the machinery and equipment needed for its operations. Clause 8 of the agreement, the critical provision on which this appeal turns, provides:

'Both Westies and Gohlke shall be entitled to appoint two directors each to the board of Sarusas. A fifth director shall be chosen by the two parties together and he shall act as chairman.'

('Gohlke', according to the agreement, meant both Gohlke and Schneider.)

It should be added here that Sarusas was itself a party to the agreement.

On the same day, 28 January 1965, in pursuance of that agreement, the two nominee subscribers to the memorandum of association of Sarusas appointed Gohlke, Schneider, and two other persons representing Westies, as directors. A directors' meeting was then held which vested the parties with their respective shareholdings and, as far as Sarusas was concerned, sanctioned the above agreement.

By the middle of 1967 Sarusas had apparently run into financial and other difficulties. Schneider and Gohlke then interested Wiehahn in its affairs; he was prepared to assist financially provided he was appointed a director. Consequently, on 24 July 1967, Schneider and Gohlke sent a letter signed by them to the secretary of Sarusas intimating that, in terms of clause 8 of the agreement, they 'nominated' Wiehahn to act as a director on the board of Sarusas, thereby replacing Gohlke, who tendered his resignation on the understanding that Wiehahn would take his place. This letter was considered at a meeting of the board on 27 July 1967, attended by Schneider, Gohlke, and Wiehahn, and by Westies's representatives and its attorneys. . . . The first three presumably maintained that by virtue of the letter Wiehahn had become a director, but that was resisted on behalf of Westies. Its objections were, firstly, that he was unacceptable as an individual, secondly, that Gohlke could not resign as a director without first having given one month's notice in writing to the board, as required by the articles, and, thirdly, that Wiehahn could not in any event become a director unless he was elected at a general meeting of members, as was also required by the articles. After discussion Wiehahn ultimately desisted from trying to participate in the meeting as a director and the meeting was adjourned.

On the following day, 28 July, Wiehahn discussed his appointment with Lombard and Schoeman again. It was common cause that the latter, on behalf of Westies, agreed to withdraw its objections to the 'appointment' of Wiehahn as a director. That was confirmed by them on the same day by telegram and letter to Wiehahn, and on 8 August by letters to Gohlke, Schneider, and the secretary of Sarusas. . . .

There is no doubt that thereafter Wiehahn believed that he had been duly appointed a director of Sarusas for he busied himself with its affairs and expended substantial sums of money on its behalf. Unfortunately, differences then arose between him and Westies about the conduct of its affairs, which subsequently culminated in an attitude by Westies that he had never been appointed a director. These proceedings were therefore launched in the court a quo in which Gohlke, Schneider, and Wiehahn claimed a declaratory order against Westies and Sarusas that he had been duly appointed a director. They were opposed by Westies on behalf of itself and Sarusas. Badenhorst JP dismissed the application. . . .

The appellants contended (a) that, according to the true interpretation of clause 8 of the agreement, the exercise of Gohlke's and Schneider's rights by the letter of 24 July 1967 per se resulted in the appointment of Wiehahn as a director of Sarusas; alternatively, (b) that, according to the facts, he was at some stage thereafter appointed a director by the unanimous agreement of all the shareholders.

As to (a), the respondents maintained that 'appoint' in clause 8 meant 'nominate for appointment in accordance with the provisions of the articles of association',

that Westies had merely withdrawn its objection to Gohlke's and Schneider's nominating Wiehahn for appointment as a director, that in terms of the articles only a general meeting of members could appoint Wiehahn, and that that had never happened (which was indeed true). The court a quo upheld that argument.

According to the Oxford English Dictionary the meaning of 'appoint' in the sense relevant here is 'to determine authoritatively, prescribe, decree, ordain', and, specifically in regard to an office, 'to ordain or nominate a person to an office . . . (or) to be an official'. In that context 'nominate', I think, means 'to appoint (a person) by name to hold some office or discharge some duty' rather than 'to propose, or formally enter, (one) as a proper person or candidate for election', which is also given as another meaning of 'nominate' in that dictionary. The *Standard Dictionary*, too, defines 'appoint' as 'to designate, fix upon, or select as being the person or subject for some position, object, or the like: as, to appoint to postmaster'. Thus, in my view, the ordinary meaning of 'appoint a director' is not merely to nominate or propose a person for appointment as a director but to effect his appointment as such.

Did the parties to the agreement use 'appoint' in that sense, its ordinary sense, in clause 8? I think that they did. They were to be the sole members of Sarusas, who, as such, would ordinarily be entitled to appoint its directors. And, indeed, in clause 8 they agreed who would be appointed, namely, those persons chosen by them. Having so agreed, they could hardly have intended that it should still be necessary for them formally to meet in general meeting to approve of and effect the appointment of anyone chosen by them as director. On the contrary, I think that clause 8 was expressly designed to constitute such an approval in advance and to render unnecessary the usual formalities of appointing directors. After all, Sarusas was itself made a party to the agreement with the object, *inter alia*, of being bound by any such appointment. Moreover, the parties must have contemplated that Gohlke and Schneider might exercise their rights under the clause by designating themselves as directors. It would not have been intended that before they became directors they and Westies would have to meet again in a formal general meeting to solemnly vote themselves on to the board. The above conclusion gives full force and effect to the phrase in clause 8, 'entitled to appoint'. If, on the other hand, that phrase meant nothing more than 'entitled to nominate for appointment', as contended for, it would virtually add nothing to the existing rights of the parties, for as members they already had the right anyway. Moreover, in that case one would also have expected a complementary provision in the agreement obliging the one party to vote for or approve of the nominees of the other party at the general meeting, for otherwise clause 8 would not have achieved the parties' manifest object of securing equal representation on the board. The absence of such a provision is dead against the construction contended for. . . .

In my view, therefore, clause 8 meant that a party's nominee would become a director of Sarusas on his merely nominating him as such.

Two English cases were referred to by the court *a quo* and in the argument before us. In *British Murac Syndicate Ltd* v *Alperton Rubber Co Ltd* [1915] 2 ChD 186 an agreement between the plaintiff syndicate and the defendant company provided that, so long as the former held at least 5 000 shares in the defendant, it should have 'the right of nominating two directors' on the board of the defendant. That entitlement was also incorporated in the defendant's articles. A dispute arose about the directors nominated by the plaintiff. One of the defendant's contentions was that in order to complete the appointment of the two directors something further had to be done beyond their mere nomination by the plaintiff. That was rejected by Sargant J, who said at 192:

'According to the true reading of the article I think that when the syndicate formally nominated the persons whom it selected those persons became directors then and there. It was suggested that some form of co-option on the part of the other directors was necessary. I do not think so, but in any case that step would be a mere formality, and the right of the plaintiff syndicate to choose the two directors seems to me to be perfectly clear.'

That decision accords with my conclusion. Indeed, the present is an *a fortiori* case, for clause 8 uses the word 'appoint'. The court *a quo* distinguished it on the ground that there the agreement had been incorporated in the company's articles. But, as will appear presently when I deal with s 16 of the SWA Companies Ordinance 19 of 1928, that merely rendered the agreement binding, not only on the company and the plaintiff, but also on all the other members of the company as if they too had signed it. And that is actually the very position in the present case by virtue of the parties' agreement, which per se rendered clause 8 binding on Sarusas and all its members. Hence there is no real distinction between the two cases in that respect.

The other case, *Plantations Trust Ltd* v *Bila (Sumatra) Rubber Lands Ltd* (1916) 85 LJ 801 (Ch) is clearly distinguishable, for there the agreement between the parties was that

> 'the defendant company would appoint two persons to be nominated by the plaintiff company, to be directors of the defendant company';

that is, a right to nominate was given to the plaintiff and an obligation to appoint those nominated was imposed on the defendant (see p 801). That is not the position here under clause 8.

[Counsel for the respondents] further contended that, if that was the true construction of clause 8, it was contrary to and sought to amend Sarusas' articles, which, according to ss 15, 16, and 65 of the Ordinance, rendered the clause ineffective, or at any rate unenforceable against Sarusas, since it had not been incorporated in the articles. More specifically the contention was that according to the articles only a general meeting of members could appoint directors, whereas clause 8, so construed, vested the right in each of the two parties to the agreement to appoint two directors without the holding of a general meeting.

Section 16 of the Ordinance, much relied upon by the court *a quo*, reads as follows:

> 'The memorandum and articles shall, when registered, bind the company and the members thereof to the same extent as if they respectively had been signed by each member, to observe all the provisions of the memorandum and of the articles, subject to the provisions of this Ordinance.'

In substance it is the same as the corresponding section in our Act and in the successive English Companies Acts. We are not concerned here with the memorandum for which the Ordinance elsewhere makes special provision. As to the articles, it will be immediately apparent that the section does not render them absolutely binding on the company and its members as though they were statutory enactments, which the court *a quo* seems to have assumed. The company and its members

are bound only to the same extent *as if* the articles had been signed
by each member, that is, as if they had contracted in terms of the articles.
The articles, therefore, merely have the same force as a contract between
the company and each and every member as such to observe their
provisions (see *Hickman* v *Kent or Romney Marsh Sheepbreeders' Association*
[1915] 1 ChD 881, the *locus classicus* on the point [*51* above], and
De Villiers v *Jacobsdal Saltworks* (*Michaelis and De Villiers*) (*Pty*) *Ltd*
1959 (3) SA 873 (O) [*202* below] at 876–7). Now that contract is not
made immutable or indefeasible by the Ordinance in any respect relevant
here. Consequently, I can see no reason why, as with any other contract,
it cannot be departed from by a bona fide agreement concluded between
the company and all its members to do something *intra vires* of the company's memorandum but in a manner contrary to the articles, and why
that agreement should not bind them, at least for as long as they remain
the only members. Of course, for it to bind new members and affect
outsiders, the agreement would probably have to be incorporated into
the articles by a special resolution which would have to be registered
(see s 15(1) [now s 62], which provides for the alteration of articles by a
special resolution, and s 65(1) [now ss 200, 203], which says that a special
resolution is not effective until it has been registered by the Registrar).
That situation does not arise and need not be considered here. Consequently, even if clause 8 is contrary to the articles, I think that it is
nevertheless binding on all the parties to it.

In any event, I do not think that the agreement does conflict with
the articles. . . .

The articles . . . only empower a general meeting to appoint directors
to fill vacancies caused by retirement or removal of directors, a situation
which did not arise in the present case. I agree, however, with Mr C
that the members must have inherent or implied general power to
appoint directors to fill other vacancies caused, for example, by resignation, death, incapacity, or disqualification. Usually, as a matter of
practice, they would exercise that power by ordinary resolution at a
general meeting. But the articles neither require that nor prohibit the
power from being exercised by their unanimous assent achieved otherwise than at such a meeting. After all, the holding of a general meeting
is only the formal machinery for securing the assent of members or the
required majority of them, and, if the assent of all the members is otherwise obtained, why should that not be just as effective? Thus in the case
of *Salomon* v *Salomon and Co Ltd* [1897] AC 22 one of the questions that
arose was whether the agreement whereby the company purchased the
vendor's business was valid, since there had been no independent board
of directors to render the company bound. No general meeting of members
of the company had been held to approve the agreement, but according
to the evidence they all knew of its terms and accepted them. At 57
Lord Davey said:

> 'I think it an inevitable inference from the circumstances of the
> case that every member of the company assented to the purchase, and
> the company is bound in a matter *intra vires* by the unanimous agree-
> ment of its members.'

The Privy Council case *Ho Tung* v *Man On Insurance Co Ltd* [1902] AC 232 is another example of the application of what, for convenience, I can term the principle of unanimous assent. . . .

Because the principle, as applied in those cases, is a sound one, giving effect to the substance rather than the mere form of the members' assent, I think that we should accept it as being settled law. Consequently, the assent of all the members and Sarusas, as evinced by the agreement of 28 January 1965, rendered clause 8 binding on all of them just as if they had approved it by ordinary resolution in general meeting.

[An order was accordingly made declaring that Wiehahn was duly appointed as a director of Sarusas in the place of Gohlke. For a critical discussion of the case, see R C Beuthin 1970 *Annual Survey* 276–9 and (1970) 87 *SALJ* 395. On the effect of the unanimous but informal consent of all the shareholders, see p 317 above.]

NOTES

See also *Flegg* v *McCarthy & Flegg* 1942 CPD 109 where a third director was appointed although the articles provided only for the appointment of two directors. 'The fact . . . that Eric Flegg's appointment as a director was technically or strictly not regular under the articles of association cannot in my opinion invalidate his appointment from time to time or render acts bona fide done by him as such in relation to the affairs of the company invalid, particularly when it is borne in mind that the only two persons interested in the matter, viz the other two directors, not only acquiesced in his appointment, but actually made it originally and subsequently confirmed it and for several years thereafter reappointed him . . .', per Jones J at 114. The court made an order directing the two original shareholders to vote in favour of a special resolution by which the articles were to be amended by making provision for the appointment of a third director. In *De Kock* v *Davidson* 1971 (1) SA 428 (T) the applicant was appointed as a director in terms of a compromise.

A company is bound by an agreement that certain directors are to be nominated by a third party: *British Murac Syndicate Ltd* v *Alperton Rubber Co Ltd* [1915] 2 Ch 186.

On *de facto* directors, see also *L Suzman (Rand) Ltd* v *Yamoyani* (2) *402 below*.

On the filling of casual vacancies see *Munster* v *Cammell Co* (1882) 21 ChD 183 and *Isle of Wight Railway Co* v *Tahourdin* (1883) 25 ChD 320. In the latter case it was held that where all the directors are removed, the shareholders in general meeting can fill vacancies on the board. In *Munster* v *Cammell Co* (*supra*) the articles provided that the directors might fill up any casual vacancy on the board. A casual vacancy occurred. Before it was filled by the board a general meeting was held but it did not fill the vacancy. The court held that under these circumstances the powers of the board to fill the vacancy remained. In *Gorfil* v *Marendaz* 1965 (1) SA 686 (T) the sole surviving director was held to be empowered to fill a casual vacancy. See also *Macson Development Co Ltd* v *Gordon* (1959) 19 DLR (2d) 465.

Where under the articles the power of appointing additional directors is given to the directors it is a question of construction of the articles (*a*) whether this power is to be exercised by all or by a majority (*Perrott and Perrott Ltd* v *Stephenson* [1934] Ch 171); and (*b*) whether the inherent powers of the company in general meeting to appoint directors is excluded (*Worcester Corsetry Ltd* v *Witting* [1936] Ch 640). Where the directors are unable to exercise the power conferred upon them by the articles of appointing additional directors, the company in general meeting can make the appointment: *Barron* v *Potter* [1914] 1 Ch 895, *271 below*.

In *Aitchison* v *Dench* 1964 (2) SA 515 (T) it was held that where the general meeting had never formally decided how many directors they would appoint, this could be done impliedly by electing a particular number within the limits laid down by the articles.

[191] Schachat *v* Trans-Africa Credit & Savings Bank Ltd
1963 (4) SA 523 (C)

BANKS J: On 15 March 1962, the annual general meeting of first respondent was held at its head office. . . . At that annual general meeting seven directors were elected including third respondent. During the course of the following month a number of directors resigned. It was subsequently ascertained that one had never accepted nomination and two others became disqualified, and the number of directors was reduced below the number fixed by the articles of association as the quorum.

Pursuant to the instructions of the Registrar of Banks an extraordinary general meeting was held in Cape Town on 4 September 1962. Applicant attended the meeting in his personal capacity as the holder of 50 shares, and as proxy for 34 shareholders. Applicant worked in co-operation with a group in East London representing approximately 105 shareholders and in addition collaborated with other individual shareholders, representing in all 185 shareholders. Applicant nominated four persons (including himself) for election to the board of directors of first respondent.

The shareholders from East London had prior to the meeting nominated seven persons for election to the board.

The third respondent nominated himself and fourth, fifth, sixth and seventh respondents. In addition there was one further nomination.

At the meeting the following were present:

  48 members present in person;
  20 authorized representatives of member companies;
335 members represented by proxies; and
  54 members represented under special powers of attorney lodged prior to the annual general meeting.

The chairman (third respondent) intimated that the meeting should decide on the number of directors to be elected and a motion that the number of directors be fixed at five was carried both on a show of hands and at a poll. . . .

The meeting then proceeded with the election of directors. The chairman explained the procedure to be followed. He stated that as the Act required separate resolutions on each director nominated, separate ballot papers had been prepared reflecting the name of each director. The number of votes to which each member was entitled had been left blank on the slips and members were requested to insert this number. The attention of members was drawn to the fact that each ballot paper provided for a vote 'for' and 'against' the nominated director. The chairman stated that the ballot papers had been prepared in this manner in case members decided to vote on a 'for' or 'against' basis, but that in view of the decision to elect five directors, it would only be necessary for members to vote for each of the five directors they selected and no votes need be cast 'against'. Applicant . . . objected to this procedure.

The result of the poll was that the third, fourth, fifth, sixth and seventh respondents were elected.

Section 69*bis*(2) of the Companies Act 46 of 1926 as amended reads as follows:

'69*bis*. (1) At a general meeting of a company a motion for the appointment of two or more persons as directors of the company by a single resolution shall not be made, unless a resolution that it shall be so made has first been agreed to by the meeting without any vote being given against it.

(2) Where motions for the appointment by separate resolutions of more than the number of directors to be elected, have been made and not withdrawn, all the resolutions shall be voted upon separately, and thereafter the result of the voting shall be determined in accordance with the number of votes cast in favour of each resolution.

(3) A resolution moved in contravention of this section shall be void. . . .'

In regard to the construction of s 69*bis* [s 210 is the corresponding section in the 1973 Act], it should be noted that s 69*bis* was inserted in the Act by s 43 of Act 46 of 1952. The corresponding section in the English Act is s 183, but in the English Act there is no provision similar to ss (2) of s 69*bis*. Section 183 of the English Act has always been regarded as sufficient to prevent the submission of a 'ticket' of directors to the voters. It would, in my view, have been unnecessary to add s 69*bis*(2) unless some additional object was sought to be achieved. In my view the object was to lay down a specific voting procedure.

At the meeting in question there were motions for the appointment by separate resolutions of more than the number of directors to be elected. In these circumstances the Act requires that each motion be voted upon separately. . . . [T]he fact that motions are voted on simultaneously does not mean that they are not voted on separately. . . . But, on the other hand, when the section enacts that a motion must be voted upon, it, in my view, means that it must be voted upon in the usual manner and it is carried or defeated according to whether there was a majority 'for' or 'against'. If motions are carried in respect of more candidates than there are vacancies, the result is to be determined 'in accordance with the number of votes cast in favour of each resolution'. The articles made provisions as to the procedure to be followed if all the places of the retiring directors are not filled.

According to the minutes of the meeting, which respondent accepts as correct, the chairman ruled that members need only vote for the five candidates they selected and that they need not vote 'against', presumably, other candidates. Each motion was, as a consequence, not voted upon and there was a failure to comply with the provisions of ss (2) of s 69*bis* of the Act.

NOTES

Schachat was followed in *Aitchison v Dench* 1964 (2) SA 515 (T), where Hiemstra J said (at 517): 'The words "all the resolutions shall be voted upon separately" to my mind mean that a candidate must be voted on as if his candidacy is a motion for his appointment. As with ordinary motions, votes for and against are to be called for. If he attracts a plurality of "against" votes, the motion for his appointment is defeated, and, if the opposite is the case, the motion is carried. This could cause a position where more candidates are approved of than there are candidacies. Only then the number of votes in favour of each candidate is taken into account and those with the highest number of favourable votes will fill the available vacancies. The method could conceivably also cause a position where all the candidates are rejected, but normally the articles will take care of a situation where the company is without a board.'

Our Companies Act does not make provision for cumulative voting. In cumulative voting each shareholder has the right to cast as many votes as are attached to his shares multiplied by the number of directors to be appointed, and he may cast all his votes in favour of one candidate or distribute them among the candidates in whatever way he desires. By concentrating all their votes on one candidate, a group of minority shareholders can elect a representative against the wishes of the majority group, thus ensuring that they do not remain unrepresented on the board.

[192] *In re* **The Bodega Company Ltd**
[1904] 1 Ch 276

Wolseley was a director of the company. On 24 December 1900 he became secretly concerned in a contract with the company but did not disclose his interest to the board; the transaction came to an end in June 1901. At general meetings of the company held on 8 July 1901 and in July 1902, Wolseley in the usual way retired from office and was re-elected a director. In February 1903 the board first discovered Wolseley's secret interest in the contract of December 1900. He then ceased to act as a director.

Held, that in terms of the articles Wolseley automatically vacated his office on 24 December 1900, but that his disqualification only continued so long as the contract continued, and that his re-elections in July 1901 and July 1902 were valid. It was accordingly decided that the company was entitled to recover from him the director's fees for the period 24 December 1900 to 8 July 1901.

FARWELL J: ... The company's articles contain, amongst others, this provision: 'The office of a director shall be vacated ... if he is concerned in or participate in the profits of any contract with the company not disclosed to and authorized by the board.' ... The question is this: Does the director, who is himself concerned in a contract not disclosed, thereupon ... *ipso facto,* ie automatically, vacate his office, or does anything further remain to be done? In my opinion it is quite plain on the words of the article that he *ipso facto,* or automatically, vacates his office on the act being done: there is no distinction between this and the other events mentioned in the article, eg bankruptcy, and in none of them is there any *locus poenitentiae* for him, or any means by which the directors can condone the offence or the act which causes the vacation. The office is vacated automatically, and if his co-directors wish him still to act, he has to be re-elected in the usual way; or the casual vacancy has to be filled up under the article to that effect. The directors have nothing whatever to do with the vacation of the office by an event over which they have no control, and with which they have nothing to do except to satisfy themselves that the fact has happened, if the fact be put in issue. ...

... Now the vacation of his office by the contract of 24 December 1900, which I will assume for the moment, was a vacation of his then office as a director ... did not in my opinion disqualify him from thereafter being elected as a director. I do not understand the article to mean that, if a man be concerned in a contract not disclosed, and he thereby vacates his office, he cannot be elected in a subsequent year. To my mind it is not a continuing disqualification unless the work to be done under the contract is a continuing work. If the work to be done under the contract ought to be reviewed by the director concerned in the contract, and the discretion which the company are entitled to expect from that director is still to be exercised after the next election, then, and then only, the re-election would be avoided by the continuing contract. But when, as here, it is a contract made once and for all for a particular purchase, and the matter comes to an end in the current year, then, I think, it only applies to the particular holding of the directorship for the current year. I am, therefore, of opinion that he vacated his office on entering into the contract, and that that vacation lasted until 8 July 1901 when he was re-elected. . . .

[See also *Nel* v *De Necker* 1948 (1) SA 884 (W).]

[193] *Ex parte* **Schreuder**
1964 (3) SA 84 (O)

ERASMUS R : Die aansoekdoener vra magtiging ingevolge art 68*bis*(1)(*c*) van die Maatskappywet 46 van 1926 [now s 218(1)(*d*)] om 'n direkteur te wees van 'n privaat maatskappy wat hy en sy eggenote van voorneme is om te stig en waarin hulle die enigste aandeelhouers en direkteure sal wees.

Die applikant word in sy aansoek beskryf as ,,'n eiendoms-, finansiële- en algemene agent en sakeman'' van Bloemfontein met ,,'n florerende praktyk'' en dit word gemeld dat ,,sekere persone en instansies . . . baie vertroue in'' sy ,,sakeondervinding en besigheidsvernuf'' het. Voorts word beweer dat hy redelik goed bekend met die bepalings van die Maatskappywet 46 van 1926 asook die hantering en behartiging van die sake en transaksies van privaat maatskappye is. Hy is begerig om op te tree as 'n direkteur van maatskappye veral omdat daar vir hom met 'n groot inkomste voordeel in sal wees met die oog op besparing van inkomstebelasting, hereregte en boedelbelasting. Sy aansoek is vergesel van agt beëdigde verklarings, vyf waarvan afkomstig van boere is, twee van prokureurs en één van 'n rekenmeester, almal waarvan in sy guns getuig.

In 1937 het die Rondgaande Hof op De Aar hom skuldig bevind op 'n aanklag van bedrog teenoor Barclay's Bank waarby 'n bedrag van £650 betrokke was en een van vervalsing van 'n tjek. Hy was gevonnis tot een jaar gevangenisstraf met dwangarbeid waarvan ses maande opgeskort was. Aan die begin van 1939 was hy ontslaan. Daarna het hy hom weer op spekulasie en 'n eiendomsagentbesigheid in Bloemfontein toegelê. Ongeveer 1948 het hy sy besigheid in 'n maatskappy omskep en strydig met art 68*bis*(1)(*c*) as direkteur opgetree. Dit het hy gedoen ten opsigte van sewe maatskappye. In 1951 het die Prokureur-generaal die aangeleentheid laat ondersoek. Die applikant was gearresteer, vervolg, skuldig bevind en met R150 beboet. Hy het as direkteur van al sy maatskappye bedank. Die publiek se vertroue in die applikant se maatskappye was geskok en die uiteinde was dat almal gelikwideer en die applikant se persoonlike boedel gesekwestreer was. Hierna is hy op 44 aanklagtes van diefstal en onder die Insolvensiewet vervolg. 'n Streekhof het hom aan vier klagtes van diefstal en vier oortredings onder die Insolvensiewet skuldig bevind en tot drie jaar gevangenisstraf veroordeel. Hy het in hoër beroep teen die skuldigbevindings na hierdie afdeling en later, op die skuldigbevindings wat nie deur die afdeling tersyde gestel is nie na die appelhof gegaan met die uiteindelike resultaat dat slegs een skuldigbevinding aan 'n oortreding van die Insolvensiewet bekragtig is. Sy vonnis is gewysig tot een van nege maande gevangenisstraf.

Artikel 68*bis*(1)(*c*) gee aan die hof 'n diskresie om 'n persoon as 'n direkteur van 'n maatskappy toe te laat wat enige tydstip skuldig bevind is aan diefstal, bedrog, vervalsing en sekere andere misdade waarvan gevangenisstraf sonder 'n keuse van 'n boete, of 'n boete hoër as vyftig rand opgelê is. Daar is egter nie 'n aanduiding in die artikel op watter gronde hierdie diskresie behoort uitgeoefen te word nie, maar in *Ex parte Erleigh* 1950 (2) PH E 14 (W), het Roper R bevind dat 'n hof sy diskresie ten gunste van 'n applikant alleen in buitengewone omstandighede behoort uit te oefen. Uiteraard die mags- en vertrouensposisie wat 'n direkteur van 'n maatskappy beklee, vereenselwig ek my eerbiediglik met hierdie beskouing. In *Ex parte Harrod* 1954 (4) SA 28 (SR) het Quénet R, soos hy toe was, net soos Roper R eerlikheid, die belange van die maatskappy sowel as die openbare belange in gedagte gehad toe hy die ooreenkomstige artikel, dws art 144 in die Rhodesiese Maatskappywet 47 van 1951 oorweeg het. Op bl 30 sê hy:

> „I infer that the Legislature intended to ensure that the management of a company's affairs and the shaping of its destiny would be in honest hands. . . . Prima facie, then, persons, seeking appointment should be honest and trustworthy."

Hy vervolg:

> „The section, taken as a whole, seeks to protect the shareholders to whom the directors owe a fiduciary duty. Had it been intended, however, that the protection should end there the right to grant relief would have been given to the shareholders and not to the court. The protection extends beyond the private interests of the shareholders and reaches to the public whose welfare may be injured by dishonest trading."

Watter persoon, liggaam of instansie se belange ook al op die spel is, blyk dit, myns insiens, onmiskenbaar dat die wetgewer uiteraard die posisie van 'n direkteur van maatskappye, die besondere misdade in die sub-artikel genoem, die vonnis van gevangenisstraf sonder 'n boete en die lae minimum-boete bokant R50, bedoel het dat die howe 'n aansoekdoener aan 'n streng toets van eerlikheid moet onderwerp en alle ander faktore word vir doeleindes van art 68*bis*(1)(*c*) daardeur oorskadu. Enige inligting wat bygevolg aan 'n hof verskaf word oor 'n applikant se betroubaarheid dra noodwendig meer gewig as sy bekwaamheid, besigheidsvernuf en kennis van maatskappye. Ten einde 'n applikant se eerlikheid te toets sal daar o a gelet word op die geaardheid en omvang van die misdaad wat hom gediskwalifiseer het; die omstandighede waaronder dit gepleeg is; die applikant se gedrag daarna oor 'n tydperk wat langer is na mate die ernstigheid van die oortreding, enige verdere misdaad waarby oneerlikheid betrokke kan wees en tot· hoe 'n mate ander' persone en instansies wat hom ken of waarmee hy te doen het, bereid is om hom te vertrou.

In die onderhawige geval was die twee oortredings wat hom in 1937 gediskwalifiseer het mi van 'n ernstige geaardheid en ofskoon dit beweer word dat hy redelik vertroud met die Maatskappywet is, gaan hy voort en tree op as 'n direkteur van sewe maatskappye. Nêrens beweer die applikant dat hy nie geweet het dat hy dit nie mag doen nie ofskoon hy 'n prokureur geraadpleeg het. Hierop is hy skuldig bevind. Die feit dat die applikant self beweer dat die publiek se vertroue in sewe van sy maatskappye ,,geskok'' was omdat hy nie geregtig was om as direkteur op te tree nie, het mi die indruk van sy valse voordoening verskerp en versprei.

[Application rejected. Confirmed by the full bench in 1965 (2) SA 174 (O).]

NOTES

See further *Ex parte Schreuder* 1974 (2) SA 358 (O), where Steyn J said (at 361H, 362A, B): 'Na my mening regverdig die hele opset van die Maatskappywet, soos uitgelê deur die aangehaalde gewysdes, die stel van hoë eise van eerlikheid en betroubaarheid aan 'n applikant wat ingevolge art 68*bis*(1)(*c*) magtiging aanvra, en was verwysing na buitengewone omstandighede' slegs 'n beklemtoning daarvan. Verder, alhoewel 'n Hof oorweging sal skenk aan die waarskynlikheid van 'n herhaling van een van die diskwalifiserende misdade, sou die Hof selfs oneerlike gedrag wat waarskynlik nooit daardie stadium sal bereik nie, ook oorweeg. Ek is verder van mening dat alhoewel eerlikheid en betroubaarheid die belangrikste oorweging is, dit slegs een van die faktore is. By 'n uitoefening van 'n diskresie van hierdie aard, is ek van mening dat dit nie wenslik is om al hierdie moontlike faktore te probeer weergee of die afsonderlike gewig daarvan te bepaal nie, aangesien in elke geval op sy eie feite beslis moet word of die applikant voldoen aan die hoë eise van die Maatskappywet, en of hy geregtig is op die aangevraagde toeskietlikheid.' Again, in *Ex parte R* 1966 (1) SA 87 (SR) Young J remarked: 'I accept that the object of the section is that the management of companies should not be in the hands of unscrupulous or disreputablemen; and, moreover, it seems that a conviction within the terms of s 144(1)(*d*) is to be regarded as some evidence that a person is within those categories; but in determining the issue the facts must be regarded as a whole, and no limited formula can necessarily be decisive. Exceptional circumstances may sometimes play an important part. Similarly, the possible consequences to shareholders and the public generally must be kept in view; but in the end the question must be whether in all the circumstances the applicant has satisfied the court that he has rehabilitated himself in the sense that he is worthy of trust in carrying out the functions which he is seeking permission to undertake. The exercise of judicial discretion is a far-roving enquiry in the fields of law and morality; but ultimately it boils down to the exercise of what has been called judicial common sense.'

The court may grant a person who is disqualified authority to be appointed as a director of a particular company or particular companies, or general power to become a director of any company at any time: *Ex parte Osband* 1944 WLD 176; *Ex parte K* 1971 (4) SA 289 (D). On applications by unrehabilitated insolvents, see *Ex parte Jacobson* 1944 OPD 112; *Ex parte Dworsky* 1970 (2) SA 293 (T); by convicted criminals, *Ex parte Taitz* 1946 TPD 211; *Ex parte Leal* 1962 (4) SA (O); *Ex parte Boland* 1967 (3) SA 655 (R). *R v Bradley* [1961] 1 WLR 398, [1961] 1 All ER 669 decided that a disqualification should be imposed as from the date of the conviction, and not as from a future date. In *Ex parte Hemphill* 1967 (2) PH E8 (N), it was held that no dispensation can be granted from s 68*bis*(3) (now s 218) which makes it an offence for any person who is disqualified from being a director to take part in the management of a company.

Section 68(3) of the 1926 Act made it an offence for a disqualified person to take part in, directly or indirectly, or be concerned in the management of a company. Section 218(2) of the new Act casts the net more widely. It punishes a disqualified person 'who purports to act as a director or directly or indirectly takes part in or is concerned in the management of any company'. It would therefore seem that the problem in S v *Nixon* 1971 (4) SA 495 (N) could no longer arise.

[194] Bainbridge *v* Smith
(1889) 41 ChD 462

The articles required a director 'to hold so and so many shares in his own right'.

LINDLEY LJ: The words in question have acquired . . . a conventional meaning which I for one am not prepared at present to disturb. I think that conventional meaning is this, that a person 'holding shares in his own right' means holding in his own right as distinguished from holding in the right of somebody else. I do not think the test is beneficial interest, the test is being on or not being on the register as a member, ie with power to vote, and with those rights which are incidental to full membership. It means that a person shall hold shares in such a way that the company can safely deal with him in respect of his shares whatever his interest may be in the shares. . . .

[On the same point see above pp 213–14; also *Pulbrook* v *Richmond Consolidated Mining Co* (1878) 9 ChD 610; *Howard* v *Sadler* [1893] 1 QB 1; *Sutton* v *English and Colonial Produce Co* [1902] 2 Ch 502, esp at 506, per Buckley J; *Boschoek Proprietary Co Ltd* v *Fuke* [1906] 1 Ch 148 (person registered as liquidator of a company holding shares does not hold these shares 'in his own right').]

[195] Balmoral Diamond Syndicate Ltd (in liquidation) *v* Liddle, Smith, Leeb, Harger and Schuller
1907 TH 89

A director who has received his qualification shares as a gift from the promoters is qualified, but must account to the company for the value of the shares.

MASON J: . . . The liability of a director to refund the value of qualification shares so received [ie from promoters] . . . rests upon general principles of law, as applicable in South Africa as they are in England and this liability is enforced however the transaction may be disguised. . . .

. . . Nor does it make any difference whether a director has received these qualification shares before or after allotment, as long as there is any question open between the company and the donor of the shares as to which the director might be called upon to act in the interests of the company; and this rule is applicable even if the contract under which the promoter obtains the shares is one that has already been signed on behalf of the company, or one under which the company has no discretion whether to accept the property or not. . . .

[On the same point see *Carling, Hespeler and Walsh's* cases (1875) 1 ChD 115; *Hay's* case (1875) 10 Ch App 593; *In re Englefield Colliery*

Co (1878) 8 ChD 388; *Mitcalfe's* case (1879) 13 ChD 169; *In re Carriage Co-operative Supply Association* (1884) 27 ChD 322; *Ex parte The Master: In re the Niagara Ltd (in liquidation)* 1912 TPD 896; *In re London and South Western Canal Ltd* [1911] 1 Ch 346.]

[196] *In re* Dover Coalfield Extension Ltd
[1908] 1 Ch 65

The Dover Company, in order to qualify one of its directors to become a director of the Kent Company, transferred to him the necessary qualification shares in the Kent Company in trust. The court held that he was not obliged to account to the Dover Company for the remuneration received by him as a director of the Kent Company.

COZENS-HARDY MR: I must say this is a very plain case. Certain shares in the Kent Company were held by the Dover Company. These shares were put with prefect propriety in the names of the respondent Cousins and another gentleman. That was communicated to the Dover Company in general meeting in plain language, and, even apart from that, it seems to me to be a perfectly proper transaction; and, indeed, there was no suggestion of any impropriety in it. In that state of things, of course, these gentlemen could not claim the dividends arising from the shares standing in their names; but they became by virtue of that circumstance in the position of being eligible to act as directors of the Kent Company, and they were entitled to remuneration for the services so rendered, not from the Dover Company, but from the Kent Company. The money was received, not by virtue of the shares held by the Dover Company, but by virtue of a separate contract with the Kent Company; and to hold that the mere fact that a director of a company holds his qualification shares as trustee for another company renders him accountable to the second company for the director's fees which he earns would, in my opinion, be going further than either authority or principle justifies the court in going. . . .

[196A] Dowjee Co Ltd *v* Waja
1929 TPD 66

SOLOMON J: [It was contended] that Orr was not qualified to act as a director because his shares were registered in his name as trustee in Dowjee's insolvent estate. Now the articles fix the qualification of a director as the holding of at least one share, and according to Mr D's contention Orr should have been registered as the holder of a share in his own name, in order to be a shareholder of the defendant company. Section 27 of the Companies Act of 1926 provides that no notice of any trust shall be entered on the register. In the registration of Orr notice of a trust was entered on the register of the defendant company. But I think the consequence of entering the trust on the register was not, as Mr D argues, to nullify the registration of the trustee as a shareholder. The section merely operates to relieve the company from any obligation to take notice of the trust, and not to relieve the trustee of all the obligations of a shareholder. The notice of the trust in the register is, therefore, to be taken *pro non scripto*, and Orr stands in the books as the shareholder. . . .

[But see also *Simpson* v *Molson's Bank* [1895] AC 270 (PC), esp at 279.]

[197] Carbonic Gas Company Ltd v Ziman
1938 TPD 102

Murray J: . . . If the articles provide that the holding of a certain number of shares is a qualification for election as a director, that share-holding must exist at the time of election, otherwise the appointment is defective and absolutely void; it cannot be rendered valid even by the subsequent acquisition of the prescribed qualification. If the articles, however, merely provide that the specified shareholding is a qualification for holding the office of director, such qualification may be obtained within two months (or such shorter period as the articles fix) but if at the end of such two months or shorter period the qualification has not been obtained, there is an automatic vacation of directorship, with a resultant incapacity for reappointment until qualified as required. But although given a certain time to qualify, it does not follow that the appointed director is entitled to act prior to acquiring qualification. Specific provision to this effect should appear in the articles; in the absence thereof, it would seem from statements in certain cases (*Brown's* case (1873) 9 Ch App 102 at 109; *Miller's* case (1876) 3 ChD 661 at 665; *In re Portuguese Consolidated Copper Mines Ltd* [1891] 3 Ch 28 at 35) — though it is not clear to me that such statements were necessary for the decision in each case — that the director must acquire his qualification before he acts as director. . . .

NOTES

In view of the wording of s 213(1)(a) the proposition that a director cannot act before he has acquired his qualification is open to doubt.

Unless otherwise stated in the articles, it is not sufficient that the director has the right to be registered as the holder of the requisite number of shares — he must actually be so registered: *Spencer* v *Kennedy* [1926] Ch 125. Registration as joint holder of the shares is sufficient: *Dunster's* case [1894] 3 Ch 473 (director held qualified where his firm held the shares); *Grundy* v *Briggs* [1910] 1 Ch 444.

Where the articles provide that no person shall be eligible as a director unless he holds a certain number of shares, the election of a person not holding such shares is void: *Mockford* v *Gordon and Abe Gordon (Pty) Ltd* 1949 (3) SA 1173 (W). The provision does not apply to directors appointed by the articles: *Dent's* case, *Forbes's* case (1873) 8 Ch App 768. See also *Meyer* v *Meyer, Sons & Co Ltd* 1926 CPD 109.

On the appointment to a casual vacancy of the very person who had vacated office because he had failed to acquire the requisite qualification, see *Greenacre* v *Falkirk Iron Co Ltd* 1953 (4) SA 289 (N).

In *Craven-Ellis* v *Canons Ltd* [1936] 2 KB 403, the plaintiff was appointed managing director of a company by an agreement which also provided for his remuneration. Neither the plaintiff nor his fellow directors obtained the requisite qualification shares. It was held that the agreement was void because it was made by directors lacking authority but that the plaintiff was entitled to recover remuneration for the work done by him on a *quantum meruit* basis.

A director does not automatically cease to hold office when the share qualification is raised: *Molineaux* v *London, Birmingham and Manchester Insurance Co* [1902] 2 KB 589. In *Lord Claud Hamilton's* case (1873) 8 Ch App 548, it was held that a resolution to the effect that the 'future qualification of a director shall be 100 shares' meant that the qualification of future directors should be 100 shares. In *Holmes* v *Keyes* [1958] 2 All ER 129, an election of directors had taken place on 23 December, and the result of the poll had been declared on 24 December. The court held that the two-month period for the acquisition of the qualification shares had to be counted from the 24th, the election meeting to be treated as continuing until the result of the poll was obtained. The election was therefore in order.

On tacit agreement to take the qualification shares from the company, see *Harward's* case (1871) LR 13 Eq 30; *Brown's* case (1873) 9 Ch App 102; *Miller's* case (1876) 3 ChD 661; *In re Wheal Buller Consols* (1888) 38 ChD 42; *In re Portuguese Consolidated Copper Mines Ltd* [1891] 3 Ch 28; *Isaacs's* case [1892] 2 Ch 158; *In re Printing, Telegraph and Construction Co of the Agence Havas* [1894] 2 ChD 392; *In re Hercynia Copper Co* [1894] 2 ChD 403; *Salton* v *New Beeston Cycle Co* [1899] 1 Ch 775; *Molineaux* v *London, Birmingham and Manchester Insurance Co Ltd* [1902] 2 KB 589.

As to the question whether an individual shareholder may sue to have an unqualified director restrained from acting, see *Meyer* v *Meyer, Sons & Co Ltd* 1926 CPD 109.

[198] Dawson *v* African Consolidated Land and Trading Company
[1898] 1 Ch 6

Clause 114 of the articles of the company provided that:

'All acts done at any meeting of the directors or of a committee of directors, or by any person acting as a director, shall, notwithstanding that it shall be afterwards discovered that there was some defect in the appointment of such directors or persons acting as aforesaid, or that they or any of them were disqualified, be as valid as if every such person had been duly appointed and was qualified to be a director.'

CHITTY LJ: I desire to say one word as to the 114th article. It is not framed so as to render valid a resolution passed by any persons who without a shadow of title assume to act as directors of a company. The case put by [counsel] that if three or four strangers went into the board-room and passed a resolution the clause would, according to the contention of the appellants, support their acts and make them valid, is disposed of by the mere reading of the clause. The clause is addressed, as is shown by the words 'some defect in the appointment of such directors or persons acting as aforesaid, or that they or any of them were disqualified', to cases of defective appointment or disqualification. . . .

[199] Marrock Plase (Pty) Ltd *v* Advance Seed Co (Pty) Ltd
1975 (3) SA 403 (AD)

This was an action against a company on a surety bond. The first defence, and the only one germane to the point under discussion, was that the resolution of the company authorizing the suretyship and bond was invalid in that Mr and Mrs De Lange who had passed the resolution, were not directors of the company. The question was whether s 69 (now s 214) applied.

TROLLIP JA: On 28 June 1971 appellant (herein called 'the Company') passed a second mortgage bond, as a surety bond, over its farm properties in favour of respondent (plaintiff). In terms of the bond the Company bound itself as surety and co-principal debtor for the indebtedness of one De Lange in the sum of R112 500 owed by him to plaintiff for seed potatoes. The Company allegedly authorized the suretyship and bond by a resolution passed by De Lange and his wife at a meeting of directors of the Company held on 5 March 1971. The certified extract of the minutes describes the De Langes as being present as 'the only share-holders and directors' of the Company. De Lange failed to pay the balance of his indebtedness, R40 500. So plaintiff sued the Company in the Northern Cape Division for payment of that amount, an order declaring the properties executable, and other ancillary relief.

The Company raised two defences —

1. The De Langes were not directors of the Company on 5 March 1971 and they therefore had no authority to bind it by the surety-ship and bond.
2. The suretyship and bond were *ultra vires* the Company and there-fore null and void.

The court *a quo* (Basson AJ) rejected both defences and gave judgment for the plaintiff as prayed. Hence the appeal by the Company.

To appreciate the true inwardness of the first defence, it is necessary to expand on the origin and career of the Company. It was registered as a private company on 7 August 1967 under the previous Companies Act 46 of 1926. (Incidentally, although that Act was repealed by the new Companies Act 61 of 1973, it was common cause that its provisions continued to govern the present dispute. It will be referred to as 'the Act'.) The nominal share capital of the Company was R100, divided into 100 shares of R1 each. The two signatories to the memorandum of association each subscribed for one share. They were clearly mere nominees and had no interest in the Company, which was formed for the De Langes as a family concern. Soon after the registration of the Com-pany, on 15 August 1967, the two subscribers, obviously acting in concert and in accordance with the instructions they received as nominees, signed transfer forms for their shares in blank, which must then have been handed to the De Langes.

On 23 August 1967 the De Langes purported to hold a meeting of 'shareholders'. Mrs De Lange attended as a shareholder; De Lange attended as the father and natural guardian of their two minor sons. According to arts 26 and 59 of the Company's articles he was entitled, vis-à-vis the Company, to represent them as shareholders. The minutes of the meeting say that it was resolved:

(*a*) That the De Langes be appointed directors. (The holding of shares is not required to qualify a person for appointment as a director — see art 68.)
(*b*) That the transfer of the subscribers' shares to Mrs De Lange and their sons be accepted.
(*c*) That additional shares be issued to Mrs De Lange (40) and their sons (30 each).
(*d*) That Mrs De Lange be appointed secretary and public officer of the Company.

(e) That the Company acquire certain farm properties for R36 000, of which R4 000 was immediately payable and the balance secured by first mortgage bond. (These properties were transferred to the Company on 6 June 1969 and were mortgaged by the surety bond as a second mortgage, as mentioned above.)

It is not clear whether, at the time of this meeting, the subscribers' transfer forms had been completed by Mrs De Lange and on behalf of her sons. But there is no doubt that they were then not shareholders or members of the Company, since their names had not been entered on the register of members, as is required by s 24(2) [now s 103(2)]. Indeed, their names were not so registered until 8 April 1969. In the meantime, however, the De Langes apparently acted as directors.

. . . [O]n 28 October 1971, the Company was taken over by certain two Oliviers. Mrs De Lange and her sons transferred all their shares to them. The De Langes resigned as directors and were replaced by the Oliviers. Hence, the latter controlled the Company when the plaintiff sued it in September 1972 in the present proceedings.

I now turn to consider the first defence raised by the Company, namely, that the De Langes were not directors on 5 March 1971 and so had no authority to bind it by the suretyship and bond.

The subscribers to the memorandum became members of the Company on its registration (s 24(1), now s 103(1)). Despite signing transfer forms for their shares, they remained the holders of the shares and members of the Company until the transferees' names were recorded in the members' register (art 20). They were also deemed to be the directors of the Company until other directors were appointed (s 66*ter*(2), now s 208). According to art 65 the first directors had to be appointed at the first meeting of shareholders. Now the subscribers, being initially the only shareholders, did not at any time appoint the De Langes as directors. All they did was to sign the transfer forms in blank. But the prospective transferees, Mrs De Lange and her sons, did not become shareholders and members of the Company, until their names had been entered on the members' register (s 24(2)). Until that happened the subscribers remained the holders and members (art 20). That had not happened by the time the meetings of 'shareholders' were held on 23 August 1967 and 8 April 1969. Hence, the De Langes could not vote at those meetings as or for shareholders (as the case may be). Their appointment as directors at the former meeting and its confirmation at the latter one were therefore defective. Nor was such defect cured merely by Mrs De Lange and her sons becoming members immediately after the latter meeting. Hence, when the resolution was passed by the De Langes on 5 March 1971 binding the Company to the suretyship and bond, they had not been properly appointed directors. . . .

[The applicability of s 69] to the instant situation was contested on one ground only: according to Mr L the section postulated, as a prerequisite to its application, that an actual (albeit defective) appointment must have been made, whereas here, in effect, no appointment of the De Langes as directors was ever made. *Morris* v *Kanssen & others* [1946] AC 459, and *Gorfil & another* v *Marendaz & others* 1965 (1) SA 686 (T), which followed it, were relied on. In *Morris's* case the relevant facts were, very briefly, that C and K were directors of a company, and S acted as one. As no general meeting was held in 1941, in terms of the articles they all ceased to be directors by the end of 1941. However, on 30 March 1942 C and S purported to hold a directors' meeting at which M was appointed a director and he and C and S were allotted shares. K and others disputed the validity of those acts, since C and S had by then ceased to be directors. M invoked the corresponding section in the English Companies Act (which is in identical terms to our s 69) and also the equivalent article in that company's articles of association. It was held that those provisions were inapplicable because, as at 30 March 1942, the appointment of C and S had ceased and there was thus no appointment that could then be said to be defective. Lord Simonds, delivering the unanimous opinion of the House of Lords, said at 471:

'There is, as it appears to me, a vital distinction between (a) an appointment in which there is a defect or, in other words, a defective appointment, and (b) no appointment at all. In the first case, it is implied that some act is done which purports to be an appointment but is by reasons of some defect inadequate for the purpose; in the second case, there is no defect; there is no act at all.'

And at 472, after referring to certain English cases, he said that the language used therein clearly indicated that—

'in the opinion of those learned Judges the section and article alike deal with slips or irregularities in appointments, not with a total absence of appointment'.

Gorfil's case (*supra*) was also decided on the basis that no appointment at all of the two directors concerned was made, so that, on the authority of *Morris's* case, s 69 was inapplicable.

Mr L argued that those cases were decisive here for these reasons: according to the articles only members of the Company can vote at a general meeting and appoint the first directors of the Company; only the subscribers could therefore have appointed the De Langes as directors at the meetings of 23 August 1967 and 8 April 1969; the purported action by the De Langes at those meetings in appointing themselves as directors was as devoid of all legal effect as if two complete strangers to the Company had held a meeting and appointed themselves as directors; here there was no slip or irregularity in their appointment, but, in effect, no appointment had been made at all: and consequently s 69

'cannot be utilized for the purpose of ignoring or overriding the substantive provisions relating to such appointment'

(Lord Simonds in *Morris's* case (*supra*) at 472).

That argument, ably advanced, cannot prevail for the following reasons. I entertain some doubt about whether *Morris's* case does not place an unduly restrictive interpretation on the section in question. It seems to confine its operation to cases in which a formal appointment has been made which turns out to be defective. But, as the section was enacted primarily for the protection of innocent persons who in good faith deal with the directors believing they have been properly appointed, I have some difficulty in understanding why 'appointment' in the section cannot be construed to include a *de facto* appointment too. If it is so construed, it would include the case where a person, without any formal appointment, acts as a director, or after the expiry of his term of office, continues to act as a director, with the acquiescence of the other directors or the shareholders. And if the lack of any formal appointment in such cases is due to bona fide inadvertence, is that not, *par excellence*, one of the very kind of defects comprehended by the section? I would have thought so. That *Morris's* and the other English cases have caused some difficulty in this regard appears from the observation of Gower *Modern Company Law* 3 ed 165:

'This distinction, drawn in these cases, between a defective appointment and no appointment at all, is a fine one, and it is far from clear what is regarded as a mere defect for this purpose.'

However, I need not give further voice here to my reservations about *Morris's* and *Gorfil's* cases. . . .

The *ratio decidendi* in each of them was that there had been no appointment whatsoever of the directors concerned. Here the De Langes were formally appointed directors at the meetings of 23 August 1967 and 8 April 1969. It is true that Mrs De Lange and her sons were then not yet members of the Company. But the De Langes held the transfer forms signed in blank. They and their children were the only persons interested in the Company. And although art 21 prohibits the transfer of any shares to anyone who is not already a shareholder unless the then existing directors approve of the transfer in writing, the subscribers, being the deemed directors (s 66*ter*(2)), by concertedly signing the transfer forms in blank and handing them to the De Langes, must be regarded as having duly approved in writing the transfer of the shares to Mrs De Lange and her sons. Hence, all that was required to regularize their membership was the formality of completing the transfer forms and entering their names on the members' register. Small lay or family companies of this kind, it is notorious, often fail to comply with the necessary formalities or technicalities of company law. And the triviality of the omission here is illustrated by this: if, on 8 April 1969, the auditor, then having the completed transfer forms for the two subscribers' shares before him, had entered the names of Mrs De Lange and her sons on the members' register as the transferees of those shares just before, instead of just after the meeting, the appointment of the De Langes as directors would have been effective. The present case, therefore, differs entirely from the one . . . of the two officious strangers coming from outside the Company and usurping office as directors. Here, I think, it was a true instance of a bona fide, inadvertent slip or irregularity rendering an actual appointment defective. So, in my view, s 69 does validate the resolution of 5 March 1971 binding the Company to the suretyship and bond.

NOTES

See further *Liquidators of the Republican and Colonial Loan Agency and Trust Co* v *The Natal Bank* (1894) 1 Off Rep 375 (a company may be bound by the *de facto* actions of a person who has for certain reasons become disqualified from being a director); *John Morley Building Co* v *Barras* [1891] 2 Ch 386; *British Asbestos Co Ltd* v *Boyd* [1903] 2 Ch 439; *Boschoek Proprietary Co Ltd* v *Fuke* [1906] 1 Ch 148; *Africa's Amalgamated Theatres Ltd* v *Naylor* 1912 WLD 107; *Dey* v *Goldfields Building Finance and Trust Corporation Ltd* 1927 WLD 180; *Gorfil* v *Marendaz* 1965 (1) SA 686 (T). In *Dowjee Co Ltd* v *Waja* 1929 TPD 66 and *Trek Tyres Ltd* v *Beukes* 1957 (3) SA 306 (W) it was held that only completed acts fall under s 69. See further *Ex parte Umtentwini Motels (Pty) Ltd* 1968 (1) SA 144 (D) at 150. On the question whether a third party who has bona fide dealt with a director whose appointment is invalid because the requirements of s 211 have not been complied with, is protected under s 214, see M J Oosthuizen, (1976) *Tydskrif vir die Suid-Afrikaanse Reg* 241.

Directors who bona fide acted as such without being qualified may be granted relief by the court under s 217 (now s 248): *In re Barry & Staines Linoleum Ltd* [1934] Ch 227; *In re Gilt Edge Safety Glass Ltd* [1940] Ch 495, [1940] 2 All ER 237.

On the question in what circumstances ss 423, 425 (ss 184, 185 of the old Act) apply to a *de facto* director or manager, see *R* v *Mall* 1959 (4) SA 607 (N) and *L Suzman (Rand) Ltd* v *Yamoyani* (2) 1972 (1) SA 109 (W), *402* below. In *Mall's* case Caney J held that for the purposes of s 185 a *de facto* director is one who has been elected or appointed as a director and in whose election or appointment some defect or irregularity exists, but not a person who in fact exercises the functions and enjoys the powers of a director without any colour of authority, whether he usurps those functions or is permitted by the directors to assume them.

III TERMS OF APPOINTMENT

A TEXT

The terms on which a director holds office may be found in the articles or in a service contract outside the articles (the latter will usually be the case with a full-time director). A contract outside the articles may embody the provisions of the articles: *200–202*; also *210*.

Though a director is not a servant of the company, the same person may be a director and, in a different capacity, or for special purposes, a servant: *203*. In this event, dismissal as an employee does not necessarily put an end to his directorship, pp 364–5 below. However, unless the articles otherwise provide, a person may not hold two offices in the company at the same time, e g those of director and secretary: *204, 205*.

On directors' remuneration more particularly, see p 383 below.

B CASES

[200] *In re* **New British Iron Company**
[1898] 1 Ch 324

Articles of association of a company provided that the remuneration of the board of directors 'shall be an annual sum of £1 000 . . .'.

WRIGHT J: . . . Article 62 fixes the remuneration of the directors at the annual sum of £1 000. That article is not in itself a contract between the company and the directors; it is only part of the contract constituted by the articles of association between the members of the company *inter se*. But where on the footing of that article the directors are employed by the company and accept office the terms of article 62 are embodied in and form part of the contract between the company and the directors. Under the article as thus embodied the directors obtain a contractual right to an annual sum of £1 000 as remuneration. . . .

[201] Ross & Company v Coleman
1920 AD 408

Under the articles of association of defendant company the plaintiff and four other persons were appointed directors and were entitled at their option to hold office for five years. The articles further provided that the directors should receive a salary of £480 per annum and that one-half of any surplus remaining on the working of any one year after payment of a dividend at the rate of 8 per cent should be payable to the directors who should divide it amongst themselves in such manner as the majority of them might decide. There was an article to the effect that 'no articles herein contained or hereafter made shall at any time, or upon any pretext, be rescinded, altered or added to, except by special resolution'.

In January 1919 a special resolution was passed deleting the clauses of the articles referring to the payment of directors and substituting a provision that the remuneration of directors should from time to time be settled by the company at its annual general meeting. The plaintiff resigned his directorate on the ground that the defendant company had broken its contract with him and sued for damages.

INNES CJ: . . . Articles of association are, in themselves, merely an agreement between the shareholders *inter se* —that agreement being, generally speaking, subject to amendment at the will of a specified majority, expressed in the prescribed manner. But when a shareholder is appointed to, and accepts the office of director, the intention both on his part and on the part of the company must be that his position— his rights and his obligations—shall be regulated by the articles. They are incorporated by implication into the contract. They regulate the terms on which the director undertakes to serve, and the benefits to which he becomes entitled. . . . [Plaintiff's counsel] admitted that, broadly speaking, any article could be altered, save where the alteration amounted to a breach of contract—in other words that no amendment of the articles could justify such a breach. That is no doubt so; but in the words of Lord Macnaghten (*British Equitable Assurance Co Ltd* v *Baily* [1906] AC 35 at 36) 'the simple question is, what was the contract'. The machinery for alteration was there, operative to the knowledge of the parties in respect of the entire matter of directors' remuneration. Was there anything in their agreement which prohibited any change during the plaintiff's period of service? Express prohibition there was none, and I can see no sufficient ground for implying a prohibition. When an article has been duly amended, the future operation of that article upon existing rights cannot be excluded unless the intention of the contracting parties to preserve such rights intact is beyond doubt. Here the plaintiff was given the option of remaining a director for five years (clause 75); during that period he could not be removed by special resolution (clause 84); nor was he under any obligation to retire (clause

86). But I find nothing in the articles which shows that during his period of service he was to enjoy fixity of remuneration. A director is entitled to such benefits as the articles may specify; the articles are subject to amendment; and any agreement as between the company and the director, that those benefits shall remain undiminished under all circumstances, must very clearly appear, if it is to be given effect to. The general rule, as pointed out by Lindley MR (*Allen* v *Gold Reefs of West Africa Ltd* [1900] 1 Ch 656, *53* above), is that existing rights founded or dependent upon alterable articles are limited as to their duration by the duration of the articles which confer them. I can see nothing in this case which takes it out of that principle. And in my opinion, it was competent for the shareholders . . . to alter, as the circumstances of the company might require, the remuneration assigned to the directors (including the original directors). It follows that the claim for damages founded on diminution of remuneration after the date of alteration was rightly disallowed. . . .

SOLOMON JA: . . . The plaintiff had no express agreement with the company: his contract is one which arises from the fact that he accepted office as a director, and that necessarily implies that the contractual relations of the parties are to be gathered from the articles of association as a whole. One of these articles specially provides that they may be altered by special resolution. As regards the plaintiff's remuneration, therefore, it was a term of the contract that the shareholders might at any time alter the regulations by which this was determined. The undertaking of the defendant company, in fact, was to pay the plaintiff the remuneration set forth in arts 97 and 98 subject to the right of the shareholders at any time to alter these articles and so change his remuneration. . . .

[202] De Villiers *v* Jacobsdal Saltworks (Michaelis and De Villiers (Pty) Ltd)
1959 (3) SA 873 (O)

In terms of the original articles of association of the defendant company the plaintiff was a director for life. As a result of an alteration of the articles he was made subject to election like all other directors. He claimed ·damages, contending that the substitution of the new articles for the old and the ensuing termination of his appointment as a director amounted to a breach of contract.

BOTHA JP: It is clear that while in terms of s 16 of the Companies Act 46 of 1926 a company's articles of association

'bind the company and the members thereof to the same extent as if they . . . had been signed by each member, to observe all the provisions . . . of the articles, subject to the provisions of this Act',

no right merely purporting to be given by an article to a person, whether a member or not, in a capacity other than that of a member, as, for instance, as solicitor or director, can be enforced against the company. A person may, however, enter into a contract with a company in the terms of one or more of the company's articles the terms of which may then by reason of the resulting contractual relationship between the company and such person be enforced by the latter against the company. But such a contract is a contract made upon the terms of an alterable article the alteration of which by the company in terms of its statutory powers (see s 15 [now s 62] of the Companies Act) can afford no valid ground for complaint by either of the contracting parties.

A company cannot be precluded or enjoined from altering its articles or from acting under the provisions of the articles as altered, but where a company causes loss or damage to another by acting under the articles as altered, an action for damages will lie against the company, but only if the act of the company under the articles as altered is inconsistent with the provisions of a then existing agreement entered into or arrangement made by the company prior to the alteration of its articles.

While a contract of employment between plaintiff and defendant company in the terms of art 42 may properly have been constituted by plaintiff's alleged appointment as director 'subject to the terms and conditions' contained in the said article, it could only have been a contract of employment upon the terms of an alterable article, the mere alteration of which by the company in terms of its statutory powers can afford the plaintiff no valid ground for complaint unless the termination of his appointment as director under the altered articles was inconsistent with a previous agreement or arrangement in terms of which his appointment as director for life was unconditional and not subject to the company's statutory power to alter its articles.

In *Southern Foundries Ltd and Federated Foundries Ltd* v *Shirlaw* (p 95, above) Viscount Maugham observed at 452 that:

'The right to alter its articles being inherent, if it is desired by a contract to give an employee or a third person a right of action if there should be an alteration of the articles which causes damage to him, I think it is very desirable to express such a term in clear language. Such a prohibition cannot be implied without very strong reasons.'

No such contract or arrangement is alleged by plaintiff in his declaration in the instant case. The only agreement alleged by him is the contract of employment which came about in consequence of his appointment as a director 'subject to the terms and conditions' contained in the defendant company's articles of association. The alteration from time to time of the articles by the company being an implied condition of such a contract, it is not capable of a construction inconsistent therewith, and the plaintiff cannot therefore, in the absence of an expressed allegation of a prior arrangement with the company whereby he was to be excluded from the operation of any subsequent alteration of the articles, found a valid claim upon the mere alteration of the articles.

NOTES

See further *Shindler* v *Northern Raincoats* [1960] 2 All ER 239 (*211* below); also *Shuttleworth* v *Cox Brothers & Co (Maidenhead) Ltd* [1927] 2 KB 9; *In re T N Farrer Ltd* [1937] Ch 352, [1937] 2 All ER 505; *Read* v *Astoria Garage (Streatham) Ltd* [1952] Ch 637, [1952] 1 All ER 922; *Nourse* v *The Farmers' Co-operative Co Ltd* (1905) 19 EDC 291; *Beyers* v *Grundling* 1967 (2) SA 131 (W) at 139; also R C Beuthin 'Appointment of Directors and Legal Effect of Articles' (1970) 87 *SALJ* 276.

[203] Lee *v* Lee's Air Farming Ltd
[1961] AC 12, [1960] 3 All ER 420 (HL)

The appellant's husband, who had founded Lee's Air Farming Ltd was the controlling shareholder and governing director of the company. He was also employed as its chief pilot. While piloting an aircraft of the company in the course of its business he was killed. The question was whether he was a worker of the company for purposes of workmen's compensation.

LORD MORRIS OF BORTH-Y-GEST: The court of appeal recognized that a director of a company may properly enter into a service agreement with his company, but they considered that, in the present case, inasmuch as the deceased was the governing director in whom was vested the full government and control of the company he could not also be a servant of the company. . . .

The substantial question which arises is, as their Lordships think, whether the deceased was a 'worker' within the meaning of the Workers' Compensation Act 1922 and its amendments. Was he a person who had entered into or worked under a contract of service with an employer? The court of appeal thought that his special position as governing director precluded him from being a servant of the company. On this view it is difficult to know what his status and position was when he was performing the arduous and skilful duties of piloting an aeroplane which belonged to the company and when he was carrying out the operation of top-dressing farm lands from the air. He was paid wages for so doing. The company kept a wages book in which these were recorded. The work that was being done was being done at the request of farmers whose contractual rights and obligations were with the company alone. It cannot be suggested that when engaged in the activities above referred to the deceased was discharging his duties as governing director. Their Lordships find it impossible to resist the conclusion that the active aerial operations were performed because the deceased was in some contractual relationship with the company. That relationship came about because the deceased as one legal person was willing to work for and to make a contract with the company which was another legal entity. A contractual relationship could only exist on the basis that there was consensus between two contracting parties. It was never suggested (nor in their Lordships' view could it reasonably have been suggested) that the company was a sham or a mere simulacrum. It is well established that the mere fact that someone is a director of a company is no impediment to his entering into a contract to serve the company. If, then, it be accepted that the respondent company was a legal entity their Lordships see no reason to challenge the validity of any contractual obligations which were created between the company and the deceased.

Nor in their Lordships' view were any contractual obligations invalidated by the circumstance that the deceased was sole governing director in whom was vested the full government and control of the company. Always assuming that the company was not a sham then the capacity of the company to make a contract with the deceased could not be impugned merely because the deceased was the agent of the company in its negotiation. The deceased might have made a firm contract to serve the company for a fixed period of years. If within such period he had retired from the office of governing director and other directors had been appointed his contract would not have been affected. The circumstance that in his capacity as a shareholder he could control the course of events would not in itself affect the validity of his contractual relationship with the company. When, therefore, it is said that one of his first acts was to appoint himself the 'only pilot of the company', it must be recognized that the appointment was made by the company, and that it was none the less a valid appointment because it was the deceased himself who acted as the agent of the company in arranging it. In their Lordships' view it is a logical consequence of the decision in *Salomon's* case that one person may function in dual capacities. There is no reason, therefore, to deny the possibility of a contractual relationship being created as between the deceased and the company. If this stage is reached then their Lordships see no reason why the range of possible contractual relationships should not include a contract for services, and if the deceased as agent for the company could negotiate a contract for services as between the company and himself there is no reason why a contract of service could not also be negotiated. It is said that therein lies the difficulty, because it is said that the deceased could not both be under the duty of giving orders and also be under the duty of obeying them. But this approach does not give effect to the circumstance that it would be the company and not the deceased that would be giving the orders. Control would remain with the company whoever might be the agent of the company to exercise it. The fact that so long as the deceased continued to be governing director, with amplitude of powers, it would be for him to act as the agent of the company to give the orders does not alter the fact that the company and the deceased were two separate and distinct legal persons. If the deceased had a contract of service with the company then the company had a right of control. The manner of its exercise would not affect or diminish the right to its exercise. But the existence of a right to control cannot be denied if once the reality of the legal existence of the company is recognized. Just as the company and the deceased were separate legal entities so as to permit of contractual relations being established between them, so also were they separate legal entities so as to enable the company to give an order to the deceased.

NOTES

See also *Boulting* v *Association of Cinematograph Television and Allied Technicians* [1963] 2 QB 606, [1963] 1 All ER 716. In that case, Lord Denning MR said (at 624): 'I am quite aware that a senior member of the staff (who is not a director) may properly be considered to be a "person employed". But I do not think that the chairman or directors or managing directors of a company can properly be considered "persons employed" within the meaning of the [Trade Disputes Act 1906].' Upjohn LJ said (at 634): 'True it is as directors they [the Boulting brothers] are not employees, but it cannot, I think, be doubted that a managing director may for many purposes be properly regarded as an employee.'

For the proposition that a director may also be, in a different capacity, a servant of the company, see further *Normandy* v *Ind, Coope & Co Ltd* [1908] 1 Ch 84; *In re Beeton & Co Ltd* [1913] 2 Ch 279; *French Hairdressing Saloons Ltd* v *National Employers Mutual General Insurance Association Ltd* 1931 AD 60; *R* v *Berman* 1932 CPD 133; *Kerr* v *Walker* 1933 SC 458; *Moresby White* v *Rangeland Ltd* 1952 (4) SA 285 (SR).

A director may be at the same time a manager. On the distinction between the post of director and that of manager, see *R v Mall* 1959 (4) SA 607 (N) and *L Suzman (Rand) Ltd v Yamoyani* (2) 402 below. In the former case Caney J said (at 622, 623):

'There is . . . a material difference between the situation of a director and that of a manager. Directors are required by statute; they are essential to a company, and their functions and duties are defined by law. They are appointed by the shareholders and are vested with the management and control of the company. They represent the company, and there is a degree of permanence attaching to their position. They act as a body, save so far as powers are lawfully delegated. . . . To regard as a director a person with no appointment, a person meddling in the company's affairs, runs counter to the whole idea of company law.

A manager, on the other hand, is an employee of the company and his services are engaged by the directors; he is not legally essential to the company, his contract may be of a formal nature or otherwise; his position may be inferred from conduct, and he may continue in employment for a long time or a short time. His position is not defined by law, indeed he may be a general manager, manager of a department, office manager or whatsoever. It is always a question of fact what he is and what his functions are. . . .'

[204] Robinson *v* Randfontein Central Gold Mining Company Ltd

1917 WLD 78

BRISTOWE J: . . . I come now to the question of incompatibility of office. There is no doubt in England an ancient common-law rule that the acceptance by a public or corporate official of an office inconsistent with one which he already holds involves the vacation of the first office. . . .

. . . The rule is not a substantive rule of law, but depends on an implied act on the part of the person who accepts the second office, or an implied contract between him and the appointor. . . .

. . . Having regard to these authorities it must I think be admitted that without the authorization of the articles no power to appoint a director to another office of profit under the company resides with the board; for the powers of the board are defined by the articles and everything not permitted by the articles is beyond their authority. But it was not disputed that such a power may be given. . . .

[205] Dey *v* Goldfields Building Finance and Trust Corporation Ltd

1927 WLD 180

The secretary of a company had been appointed as a director.

Held, where a person is appointed to an office incompatible with the one held by him, the usual result is that the first office is held to be vacated. However, this result only follows because the law implies an act of resignation on his part of the first office. If there is proof that he was to continue in his first office, this implication is rebutted and he is then ineligible for the second post.

GREENBERG J: . . . In the present case I have first to consider whether the two offices, ie that of secretary and director, are incompatible, and it appears to me that they are. The director is one of a body which stands in the position of master, and the secretary stands in the position of servant. . . .

. . . I do not think there is any room for an implied surrender, where there is actual proof of the intention to the contrary. [It was] contended that the implication was an irrebuttable presumption, but I am not disposed to agree with that contention. The point can be put in another way, that the directors only have power to appoint persons to offices which are compatible with each other, and they have no power to appoint a person who continues to hold an office incompatible with the new office. . . . The result is that in my opinion the appointment of Mr Silcock as director is bad and must be set aside. . . .

NOTES

See also *Iron Ship Coating Co* v *Blunt* (1868) LR 3 CP 484 and *Astley* v *New Tivoli Ltd* [1899] 1 Ch 151.

The correctness of *Dey* v *Goldfields* has been doubted: see 1961 *Chartered Secretary* 111; 1961 *Commercial Law Reporter* 200. Certain it is that the articles of association may, and usually do, authorize dual appointments.

IV REMOVAL, RESIGNATION, RETIREMENT

A TEXT

The period of office of directors is as fixed by the articles of association, which may provide for rotation: *206* (see Table A arts 66, 67. A system of rotation is a stock exchange requirement for listed companies: p 59 above.)

A director automatically ceases to hold office—

(*a*) if he fails to obtain his qualification shares in time, s 213(1);

(*b*) if he becomes disqualified from holding office in terms of the provisions of s 218 or 219, or of the articles of the company, (see Table A art 65, Table B art 66; also *In re Bodega, 192* above);

(*c*) when the company is being wound up.

Subject to the terms of his contract, a director may at any time resign from office: *207*. (See Table A art 65(*c*), Table B art 66(*c*).)

A company may by ordinary resolution remove a director before the expiration of his period of office, notwithstanding anything in its articles or in any agreement between it and him, s 220: *208, 209*. (As to the giving of special notice and representations by the director concerned see ss (2) and (3).) Such removal does not deprive the director of any right he may have to claim damages, s 220(7): *210–212*.

Where in a quasi-partnership company the removal of a director takes place contrary to an agreement between the shareholders or is otherwise inequitable, the director may be entitled to a winding-up order on the 'just and equitable' ground (s 344(*h*)) or to relief under s 252: *213*; see also *208* below.

B CASES

[206] Grundt *v* Great Boulder Proprietary Gold Mines Ltd
[1948] Ch 145, [1948] 1 All ER 21

The articles of the company provided:

'If at any general meeting at which an election of directors ought to take place the place of any director retiring by rotation is not filled up, he shall, if willing, continue in office until the next ordinary meeting in the next year, and so on from year to year until his place is filled up, unless it shall be determined at any such meeting on due notice to reduce the number of directors in office.'

At the annual general meeting in July 1947 G retired by rotation but a resolution for his re-election was lost on a show of hands. There was no resolution to reduce the number of directors in office.

It was held that G continued in office in terms of the company's article.

LORD GREENE MR: . . . 'Absurdity' I cannot help thinking, like public policy, is a very unruly horse, because there may very well be considerations which would be well understood by the persons concerned to work the particular document in question, which do not readily present themselves to the mind of a judge. . . . The article is contemplating that the number of directors in office in the previous year is temporarily going to be reduced by retirement by rotation. If that vacancy is not filled, the company will be minus a director. The number of directors to run the company's affairs which have been found necessary or desirable in the previous year, will in the next year, be reduced by one. It seems to me quite a reasonable view to take that in those circumstances the company may do one of two things: it may either restore the number of directors by filling the vacancy—which it can do either by re-electing the retiring director or by electing somebody in his place—or it can decide that the previous number of directors was unnecessarily large, and resolve to reduce accordingly the number of directors in office. Unless the company signifies its intention to do one or other of those two things, I can well understand it being thought that a director, who, after all, has been tried in office for two or three years or whatever it may be, should continue in office rather than that the number of directors which had previously been found necessary to run the company should be reduced. It seems to me that is a perfectly sensible business attitude for people to take in the running of a company. . . .

NOTES

See further *In re Consolidated Nickel Mines Ltd* [1914] 1 Ch 883; *Mills v Durban Roodepoort Mining Syndicate Ltd* 1925 WLD 108; *Eyre v Milton Proprietary Ltd* [1936] Ch 244; *In re David Moseley & Sons Ltd* [1939] Ch 719, [1939] 2 All ER 791; *Parsons v Langemann* 1948 (4) SA 258 (C).

[207] Glossop *v* Glossop
[1907] 2 Ch 370

NEVILLE J: . . . I have no doubt that a director is entitled to relinquish his office at any time he pleases by proper notice to the company, and that his resignation depends upon his notice and is not dependent upon any acceptance by the company, because I do not think they are in a position to refuse acceptance. Consequently, it appears to me that a director, once having given in the proper quarter notice of his resignation of his office, is not entitled to withdraw that notice, but, if it is withdrawn it must be by the consent of the company properly exercised by their managers, who are the directors of the company. But, of course, that is always dependent upon any contract between the parties, and that has to be ascertained from the articles of association.

NOTES

On the same point see *Mills v Durban Roodepoort Mining Syndicate Ltd* 1925 WLD 108; *Latchford Premier Cinema Ltd v Ennion* [1931] 2 Ch 409; also *Matthews v Garment Workers Union (Natal)* 1955 (4) SA 42 (N). Resignation takes effect when it is tendered, not when it is accepted: *Rosebank Television & Appliance Co (Pty) Ltd v Orbit Sales Corporation (Pty) Ltd* 1969 (1) SA 300 (T): '. . . there are cases which decide that the tender of a resignation is a unilateral act: it does not require to be accepted or concurred in by the party receiving it, nor is the latter entitled to refuse to accept it, or to decline to act on it', per Nicholas J at 302.

[208] Stewart *v* Schwab
1956 (4) SA 791 (T)

DE WET J: . . . The applicant alleges that the third respondent company known as Westonaria Foundry (Pty) Ltd was formed and registered in July 1947 by himself and the first and second respondents for the purpose of conducting a foundry business. He alleges that in February 1948 a written agreement was entered into which was signed only by himself and the first respondent, but it is alleged that the second respondent agreed to the terms of this agreement, which is stated to be an agreement of 'partnership'.

The material terms of this agreement are that the sole shareholders of the company shall be the applicant and the first and second respondents, who shall hold respectively 875, 875 and 3 050 shares of a nominal value of £1; that the applicant and the first and second respondents shall be the directors of the company and be entitled to draw a minimum amount of £30 per month each; that notwithstanding the disparity in shareholding each director shall have 'equal power'; that the partnership shall continue for an indefinite time subject to the right of each partner to withdraw on three months' notice, whereupon the remaining partners shall have the right to purchase his shareholding in the company, and the partner withdrawing would be paid out in a specified manner. It is provided that the applicant and the first respondent shall devote their whole time and attention to the conduct of the company's business. . . .

. . . At a directors' meeting on 13 June 1956 without any previous warning to the applicant, a resolution was passed dismissing him from the service of the company, and a further resolution was passed that a special meeting should be convened for the purpose of removing the applicant as a director, in terms of s 69*ter* of the Companies Act 46 of 1926 [now s 220].

Application is now brought for an interdict restraining the first and second respondents from voting at a meeting of shareholders in support of the resolution removing the applicant from his office as a director of the company pending an action for a permanent interdict.

The first question is whether the first and second respondents have impliedly bound themselves by contract not to vote in favour of the contemplated resolution. It seems to me that the three parties have agreed that their relationship *inter se* would be that of three partners.

If in fact there had been a partnership the relationship could only have been brought to an end by dissolution of the partnership, and it seems to follow that it must have been contemplated that their relationship would continue until the company was dissolved. . . .

. . . The second question which arises is whether an agreement by shareholders in regard to the exercise of their votes is a valid agreement. Two English decisions in favour of the validity of such an agreement were cited, namely *Greenwell* v *Porter* [1902] 1 Ch 530, and *Puddephat* v *Leith* [1916] 1 Ch 200. The correctness of these decisions has not been questioned. . . .

. . . Thirdly, the question arises whether the shareholders are entitled to vote to remove a director from office in breach of an agreement with him by virtue of the provisions of s 69*ter* of the Companies Act. . . . Section 69*ter*(1) reads:

'A company may by ordinary resolution remove a director before the expiration of his period of office, notwithstanding anything in its articles or in any agreement between it and him.'

Subsection (6) preserves to a director so removed the right in a proper case to claim compensation for damages.

It seems to me that the words 'notwithstanding anything in its articles or in any agreement between it and him' give a clue to the intended scope of ss (1). In the absence of clear words to that effect it seems to me that this section should not be interpreted so as to authorize a breach of an agreement between shareholders and a director because in terms the provision only authorizes the disregard of the company's articles and of agreements between the company and director. . . . [Interdict granted.]

NOTES

The question whether *Stewart* v *Schwab* was correctly decided was raised but not decided in *Desai* v *Greyridge Investments (Pty) Ltd* 1974 (1) SA 509 (AD). Cf *Ebrahimi* v *Westbourne Galleries, 213* below, and *Bentley-Stevens* v *Jones,* p 371 below.

[209] Swerdlow *v* Cohen 1977 (1) SA 178 (W)

Article 42 of a private company's memorandum provided, inter alia, that questions arising at any meeting of members were to be decided by majority but that as long as the applicant and the first and second respondents were members no resolution was to be of force and effect unless all of them were in favour of the resolution. At a general meeting a resolution was passed, against the applicant's opposition, removing the applicant from office as a director. The applicant prayed for a declaration that the resolution was invalid. The court dismissed his application, holding that he had been validly removed in terms of s 220(1)(*a*).

BOTHA J: Counsel for the applicant argued that the special voting powers conferred upon the three named shareholders in art 42(3) precluded the application of s 220(1)(*a*) in this case. In support of his argument he relied strongly upon the persuasive authority of . . . *Bushell* v *Faith* [1970] AC 1099. . . . [A]rt 9 of the company in that case provided as follows: 'In the event of a resolution being proposed at any general meeting of the company for the removal from office of any director, any shares held by that director shall on a poll in respect of such resolution carry the right to three votes per share. . . .'

The sisters, being dissatisfied with the conduct of their brother as a director of the company, requisitioned a general meeting of the company, at which a resolution was proposed to remove him from his office. On a poll, the sisters voted for the resolution and the brother against. One of the sisters applied in the court of first instance for a declaration that the brother had been removed from his office, relying upon the provisions of s 184(1) of the English Companies Act, 1948 which is . . . the exact counterpart of our s 220(1)(a). For the sister it was contended that art 9 was overridden by s 184(1) and, therefore, void, with the result that the resolution must be taken to have been passed by 200 votes to 100. For the brother it was contended that art 9 was valid and applicable, with the result that the resolution must be taken to have been defeated by 300 votes to 200. The learned judge of first instance upheld the sister's contention. In an appeal by the brother, the court of appeal unanimously upheld the appeal. . . . A further appeal by the sister was dismissed in the House of Lords by a majority of four to one.

The *ratio* of the majority judgments (in particular, those of Lord Upjohn and Lord Donovan) seems to me to be fairly, if briefly, reflected in the headnote of the report, as follows:

'. . . that art 9 was valid and applicable, despite the provisions of s 184(1), since Parliament was only seeking to make an ordinary resolution sufficient to remove a director and had not sought to fetter a company's right to issue a share with such rights or restrictions as it thought fit and these need not be of general application but could be attached to special circumstances and particular types of resolution. Accordingly the resolution had been defeated.'. . .

[After referring to the passage in Cilliers and Benade, 2nd ed, p 190n6, in which the learned authors submit that *Bushell* v *Faith* should not be followed in South Africa, since South African company law, unlike English company law, is based on the principle of equality of voting rights, Botha J continued:]

It seems to me that the learned authors are confusing the position in a public company with that of a private company. It is true, of course, that our law does not recognize the 'unfettered' right of a company, either public or private, to issue shares with *any* rights or restrictions as it may think fit, or to allocate voting rights in *any* way it pleases. But what are the fetters on a company in this regard, in our law? In the case of a public company, by virtue of the provisions of s 195(1) . . . there is no room for allocating weighted or loaded voting rights to certain shares or classes of shares. . . . But in a private company, subject only to the prohibition against non-voting shares contained in s 193(1), there is no principle of equality of voting rights, the company can allocate voting rights as it pleases, and there is no difference in general principle between the English law and our law in relation to a situation such as occured in *Bushell* v *Faith*. . . . In *Bushell* v *Faith* . . . art 9 . . . was directed specifically and exclusively at a proposed resolution for the removal from office of any director. Art 42(3) in the present case is not thus restricted; it is of general application. Thus, it may be said that, if the validity of art 9 in the face of s 184(1) had been correctly upheld, the operation of art 42(3) in the present case should *a fortiori* be held not to have infringed s 220(1)(*a*). For this reason I think that it is unavoidable that I should express my own view on the correctness or otherwise of the actual decision in *Bushell* v *Faith*. . . .

The reasoning in *Bushell* v *Faith* comes to this, that in counting the votes cast on a proposed resolution for the removal of a director, to see whether a bare majority has been achieved, the operation of an article conferring more votes per share on a certain share or class of shares than in respect of others, is not excluded by s 184. . . . In my view, however, the restrictive interpretation of the words 'notwithstanding anything in its articles' in the aforegoing reasoning cannot be extended beyond the limits of articles providing for the general pattern of voting rights. . . . Clearly, the expression 'notwithstanding anything in its articles' in s 184, as in s 220, was directed at any provision purporting to require more than a bare majority of votes for the removal of a director. . . . I am reverting to art 9 in *Bushell* v *Faith* and my respectful concurrence with the minority judgment of Lord Morris. Art 9 was a 'device' the 'unconcealed' effect of which was 'to make a director irremovable'; it purported to make the voting power of a director threatened with removal greater than it actually was and its object was thus to circumvent and to thwart the provisions of s 184. . . . Lest I be misunderstood, I would add that even an article purporting to deal with voting rights only may in some circumstances fall foul of ss 184 and 220. . . . [T]he words 'notwithstanding anything in its articles' are of wide import and I can perceive of no reason why they should be restricted to articles dealing specifically and in terms with resolutions for the removal of a director. . . . Thus, if the articles of a company provided that a majority of three-quarters of the votes would be required for all resolutions in general, such a provision would be inoperative in the particular case of a proposed resolution for the removal of a director; in respect of such a resolution, a bare majority of votes will be sufficient to carry the resolution, notwithstanding the provision of the articles. The position will be the same where the articles require all resolutions generally to be passed unanimously. . . . To hold otherwise would be to run counter to the evident intention of the legislature that directors should be removable by a bare majority of votes, irrespective of *anything* in the articles.

NOTES

On *Bushell* v *Faith*, referred to in *Swerdlow*, see R C Beuthin (1969) 86 *SALJ* 489, and Dr Aaron Yoran (1973) 7 *U of Richmond* LR 431, at 475. Dr Yoran suggests that s 184 of the English Act should be amended so as to 'invalidate circumventing devices . . .'.

[210] Shuttleworth *v* Cox Brothers & Co (Maidenhead)
[1927] KB 9 (CA)

The articles of association of a company provided that the plaintiff and four others should be the first directors of the company, and that they should be permanent directors but that a director should become disqualified on the happening of one of six specified events. Subsequently a special resolution was passed altering art 22 by adding a seventh event disqualifying a director—a request in writing by all his co-directors that he should resign. A request to this effect was made to the plaintiff. He sued the company for damages.

SCRUTTON LJ: . . . In my opinion Avory J was right in holding that there was no evidence on which a reasonable jury could find that the directors acted otherwise than in good faith. In my view the plaintiff's failure to account for 22 items continuing up to and after the writ, all of which were ultimately admitted, was a very serious default in the management of the company; the directors considered this alteration of the articles under careful advice, with no precipitation, and with a genuine desire to remedy the evil, which was forced upon them, of having a man, whom they could admittedly have dismissed with notice from the post of manager, still sitting with them as a director in spite of his laxity in the management of the business entrusted to him; and I can see no evidence to justify the jury in finding that their determination was taken maliciously, or with any desire to spite the plaintiff, or from any motive but that of doing what they thought best in the interest of the company. If there was no evidence of lack of good faith, the other finding of the jury makes an end of this appeal. That finding is that the alteration of the article was for the benefit of the company. That would apparently conclude this case but for one point which Mr Porter raised—namely, that art 22 in its original form constituted a contract between the company and the plaintiff, that he should be a permanent director for life, except in the events specified in that article, a contract which could not be varied without the consent of both parties; and that the plaintiff never consented to the article in its altered form. That argument would be sound if he could show a contract outside the articles; for then an alteration of the articles would not affect the contract. A good example of that principle is *Nelson* v *James Nelson & Sons* [[1914] 2 KB 770]. There the articles of association of a company empowered the directors to appoint a managing director and to revoke his appointment. They appointed by a separate document in writing a managing director for a specified term. During the term they tried to use the articles to revoke the appointment. The court held that the contract being outside the articles could not be altered without the consent of both parties. But if a contract is contained in the articles it must be, as the articles themselves are, subject to alteration in accordance with the power given by s 13 of the Companies (Consolidation) Act 1908. Consequently the plaintiff's contract, if any, is not a contract constituting him a permanent director unconditionally, but is a contract constituting him a permanent director subject to the power of terminating his appointment in accordance with the articles or any modification of the articles sanctioned by the Companies Act. So far, therefore, the appeal fails.

Then Mr Porter advanced an argument based on an expression of Petersen J in *Dafen Tinplate Co* v *Llanelly Steel Co* [[1920] 2 Ch 124]. He contended that the question is not what the shareholders think, but what the court thinks is for the benefit of the company—I suppose he would treat the verdict of the jury in the same way—that the court must be satisfied that the alteration of the articles is genuinely for the benefit of the company, and that in this case the court on the materials before it ought to be of opinion that this alteration was not genuinely for the benefit of the company and ought therefore to reject the honest opinion of the shareholders and the equally honest opinion of the jury and declare that the alteration is invalid. To adopt that view would be to make the court the manager of the affairs of innumerable companies instead of the shareholders themselves. I think it is a mistaken view, based on a misunderstanding of an expression used by Lindley MR in *Allen's* case [*53* above] and by Lord Sterndale MR in *Sidebottom's* case [[1920] 1 Ch 154]. Speaking of the power of altering articles, Lindley MR said: 'It must be exercised, not only in the manner required by law, but also bona fide for the benefit of the company as a whole.' . . . The important words are 'exercised bona fide for the benefit of the company'. I do not read those words as importing two conditions, (1) that the alteration must be found to be bona fide, and (2) that, whether bona fide or not, it must be in the opinion of the court for the benefit of the company. I read them as meaning that the shareholders must act honestly having regard to and endeavouring to act for the benefit of the company. . . . So with regard to the passage, relied on . . . from the judgment in the *Dafen Tinplate Co's* case, I can only say, if Petersen J means that, whatever the honest decision of the shareholders may be, it is the opinion of the court, and not that of the shareholders, which is to prevail, I disagree with that interpretation of the words of Lindley MR in *Allen's* case. If the learned judge merely means that the court will interfere where the decision of the shareholders, though honest, is such that no reasonable men could have come to it upon proper materials, I do not object to that explanation, and I should be prepared to act accordingly; but as reported I think the test laid down by the learned judge is erroneous for the reasons I have given. I think the appeal fails and must be dismissed.

[211] Shindler *v* Northern Raincoat Co Ltd
[1960] 1 WLR 1038, [1960] 2 All ER 239

The plaintiff had carried on business as a retailer in raincoats through the defendant company from 1946 until April 1958. In 1958 a public company purchased the £2 000 share capital of the defendant company from the plaintiff and his wife for £25 000. A service agreement was entered into between the plaintiff and the defendant company under which the latter undertook to employ the plaintiff as managing director for ten years, at a fixed salary of £3 000 per annum and a commission of 10 per cent on its net profits in excess of £15 000 before tax. In terms of this agreement the business of the defendant company was carried on by the plaintiff from April until August 1958. Thereafter, a third company acquired the shares of the defendant company. In accordance with the directions of its new controllers the defendant company, at an extraordinary general meeting, passed resolutions removing the plaintiff from office and terminating his service contract forthwith. In this it relied on a clause in its articles providing that the appointment of a managing director was to be subject to determination by the company in general meeting.

An action by the plaintiff for damages for wrongful dismissal was successful.

DIPLOCK J: Since on 21 November 1958, the plaintiff was removed from office as a director and thus *ipso facto* ceased to be managing director and his tenure of office was determined by the defendant company in general meeting, it was contended on behalf of the defendant company that, as a matter of law, he was not wrongfully dismissed. In support of that contention, counsel for the defendant company relied on a number of cases, of which the most important are *Bluett* v *Stutchbury's Ltd* (1908) 24 TLR 469 and the decision of Harman J in *Read* v *Astoria Garage (Streatham) Ltd* [1952] 1 All ER 922.

The argument for the defendant company on this matter derives some support from the cases referred to and from another case, *Nelson* v *James Nelson & Sons Ltd* [1914] 2 KB 770. The argument is put thus—where a company's articles of association include art 68, the directors have no power to appoint a managing director on terms which purport to exclude the company's right to terminate his appointment *ipso facto* on either his ceasing to be a director or if the company shall by resolution in general meeting resolve that his tenure of office as managing director be determined. That argument can be put in alternative ways, either that the agreement for a fixed term which does not incorporate the right of the company set out in art 68 is *ultra vires,* or else that the agreement for a fixed period of employment must be subject to the implied term that it is determinable in either of the circumstances set out at the end of art 68.

It seems to me that this point is concluded against the defendant company by the decision of the House of Lords in *Southern Foundries (1926) Ltd* v *Shirlaw* [1940] AC 701, [1940] 2 All ER 445. That case was somewhat complicated and gave rise to a division of opinion in the House of Lords. Two of their Lordships (Viscount Maugham and Lord Romer) who were most familiar with the Chancery side came to one conclusion and three of their Lordships (Lord Atkin, Lord Wright and Lord Porter) who were perhaps more familiar with the common law side, came to another. There are some references in subsequent cases in the Chancery Division which suggest that it is difficult to ascertain what *Southern Foundries (1926) Ltd* v *Shirlaw* determined. It does, however, seem to me that all five of their Lordships . . . were agreed on one principle of law which is vital to the defendant company's contention in the present case. That principle of law is that laid down in *Stirling* v *Maitland* (1864) 5 B & S at 852, 122 ER at 1047, where Cockburn CJ said:

'. . . if a party enters into an arrangement which can only take effect by the continuance of a certain existing state of circumstances, there is an implied engagement on his part that he shall do nothing of his own motion to put an end to that state of circumstances, under which alone the arrangement can be operative.'

Applying that respectable principle to the present case, there is an implied engagement on the part of the defendant company that it will do nothing of its own motion to put an end to the state of circumstances which enables the plaintiff to continue as managing director. That is to say, there is an implied undertaking that it will not revoke his appointment as a director, and will not resolve that his tenure of office be determined.

It is necessary to say a word about the circumstances of the *Southern Foundries* case. Mr Shirlaw, the plaintiff in that case, had a ten-year contract as managing director of Southern Foundries Ltd. At the time when he was appointed, the articles of the company were not in the form of art 68 of Table A of the Companies Act 1929. The relevant articles were these:

> '90. The directors may from time to time appoint any one or more of their body to be managing director or managing directors for such period and upon such terms as they think fit. . . .
>
> '91. A managing director shall not while he continues to hold that office be subject to retirement by rotation, and he shall not be taken into account in determining the rotation of retirement of directors, but he shall, subject to the provisions of any contract between him and the company, be subject to the same provisions as to resignation and removal as the other directors of the company, and if he ceases to hold the office of director he shall *ipso facto* and immediately cease to be a managing director.'

Then art 105 is important:

> 'The company may by extraordinary resolution remove any ordinary director before the expiration of his period of office, and may, if thought fit, by ordinary resolution appoint another director in his stead. . . .'

Thus there was in the articles in force at the time when the managing director's agreement was entered into, an article which enabled the company by extraordinary resolution to determine his appointment by removing him as a director. Subsequently, the articles were changed and an article was inserted which gave another company, Federated Foundries Ltd, a stranger to the contract of employment, power at any time, by an instrument in writing, to remove from office any director of Southern Foundries Ltd. The matter which gave rise to a dissension of opinion in the House of Lords was whether, when Federated Foundries Ltd exercised that power by removing Mr Shirlaw, this constituted wrongful dismissal of Mr Shirlaw. The majority of the House held that the fact that it was done by a third party, who was given power to do so under the new article, did not prevent this being wrongful dismissal although it was done by a stranger to the contract and might not, therefore, be said to come directly within the principle in *Stirling* v *Maitland*. The minority took the view that it could not be brought within the principle in *Stirling* v *Maitland* because the articles were altered in good faith and the act was an act of a third party. They would have held that because of this there was no breach of contract. All of their Lordships made quite plain their view, that if the company itself had exercised the power under the original articles by removing the plaintiff as director by extraordinary resolution, that would have been a breach of the implied term laid down in *Stirling* v *Maitland* and would have given rise to the right for damages.

[212] Nourse v Farmers' Co-operative Company Ltd
(1905) 19 EDC 291

KOTZE JP: . . . Reliance has been placed, on behalf of the plaintiffs, on the last clause of the agreement between them and the company. It has been contended that in no event, short of fraud or criminal conduct, could the company dismiss the plaintiffs as managing directors without first giving them six months' written notice to that effect. With this contention I do not agree. The wording of the clause is certainly somewhat involved, but its meaning seems plain enough. It provides that in the event of continued absence (unless caused by illness), habitual drunkenness, insanity or failure to fulfil the terms of the agreement, the managing directors can be dismissed on six months' written notice. Now this clause was introduced wholly for the benefit of the plaintiffs and must as against them be strictly construed. But, apart from that, there are many acts short of fraud or criminal conduct which would not be embraced in any of the causes of dismissal included in this clause and would yet justify the dismissal of a managing director. For instance, disobedience of the resolutions of the board of directors, breach of trust on the part of the managing directors, or the doing of anything that may tend or is calculated to prejudice or injure the business or the employer, never mind how attentive and assiduous the servant may otherwise be in the affairs of the business. This is so even although no actual prejudice or damage has resulted or been sustained. . . .

NOTES

Although s 220 now makes it possible to remove a director before the expiration of his period of office notwithstanding anything in the articles or his contract, the aforementioned cases are still relevant to the question of damages.

Whether the procedure prescribed in s 220 must be followed if a director is to be summarily dismissed is a question which does not appear to have cropped up so far. Having regard to the spirit of the section, which aims at ensuring that the director should have the opportunity of putting his case before the general meeting, the answer is, presumably, yes. Generally, see further *Walker* v *Kenns Ltd* [1937] 1 All ER 566; *James* v *Thomas H Kent & Co Ltd* [1951] 1 KB 551, [1950] 2 All ER 1099; also *Bold* v *Brough, Nicholson & Hall Ltd* [1964] 1 WLR 201, [1963] 3 All ER 849 where the damages awarded to the wrongfully dismissed director covered: (1) loss of salary and commission; (2) diminution in pension and loss of life insurance cover under the defendant company's staff pension and assurance scheme; (3) the amount of premiums payable under the defendant company's discretionary pension and life assurance scheme which, the company had undertaken to pay on behalf of the plaintiff.

In *Yetton* v *Eastwoods Froy Ltd* [1966] 3 All ER 353, an action for damages for dismissal, the court held that refusal of the plaintiff, who had been dismissed as managing director, to accept reappointment at the existing salary as assistant managing director was, in view of the reduction in status, not unreasonable.

On the duty arising from a condition in a contract of sale of shares not to vote for the removal of a director, see *Adams* v *North* 1933 CPD 100.

In *Bersel Manufacturing Co* v *Berry* [1968] 2 All ER 552 (HL) husband and wife were permanent life directors of a private company and had power to terminate the directorship of any of the ordinary directors by notice in writing. The wife having died, it was held that this power was now exercisable by the husband alone.

On removal of directors, see also D Botha 'Some Aspects Concerning the Removal of Directors' 1973 *De Rebus Procuratoriis* 465.

Where a director serves the company in the dual capacity of a director and an employee, his dismissal as a servant does not necessarily put an end to his directorship;

the company may still have to go through the procedure of s 220 to remove him from office as a director. Nor does his removal as a director necessarily put an end to his contract of employment as a servant, *203* above.

[213] Ebrahimi *v* Westbourne Galleries Ltd
[1973] AC 360 (HL), [1972] 2 All ER 492

LORD WILBERFORCE: My Lords, the issue in this appeal is whether the respondent company Westbourne Galleries Ltd should be wound up by the court on the petition of the appellant who is one of the three shareholders, the personal respondents being the other two. The company is a private company which carries on business as dealers in Persian and other carpets. It was formed in 1958 to take over a business founded by the second respondent (Mr Nazar). It is a fact of cardinal importance that since about 1945 the business had been carried on by the appellant and Mr Nazar as partners, equally sharing the management and the profits. When the company was formed, the signatories to its memorandum were the appellant and Mr Nazar and they were appointed its first directors. Of its issued share capital, 500 shares of £1 each were issued to each subscriber and it was found by the learned judge, after the point had been contested by Mr Nazar, that Mr Ebrahimi paid up his shares out of his own money. Soon after the company's formation the third respondent (Mr George Nazar) was made a director, and each of the two original shareholders transferred to him 100 shares, so that at all material times Mr Ebrahimi held 400 shares, Mr Nazar 400 and Mr George Nazar 200. The Nazars, father and son, thus had a majority of the votes in general meeting. Until the dispute all three gentlemen remained directors. The company made good profits, all of which were distributed as directors' remuneration. No dividends have ever been paid, before or after the petition was presented.

On 12 August 1969 an ordinary resolution was passed by the company in general meeting, by the votes of Mr Nazar and Mr George Nazar, removing Mr Ebrahimi from the office of director, a resolution which was effective in law by virtue of s 184 of the Companies Act 1948 and art 96 of Part I of Table A. Shortly afterwards the appellant presented his petition to the court.

This petition was based in the first place upon s 210 of the Companies Act 1948, [s 111*bis* of the 1926 Act and s 252 of the 1973 Act], the relief sought under this section being an order that Mr Nazar and his son be ordered to purchase the appellant's shares in the company. In the alternative it sought an order for the winding-up of the company. The petition contained allegations of oppression and misconduct against Mr Nazar which were fully explored at the hearing before Plowman J [1970] 1 WLR 1378. The learned judge found that some were unfounded and others unproved and that such complaint as was made out did not amount to such a course of oppressive conduct as to justify an order under s 210. However, he made an order for the winding up of the company under the 'just and equitable' provision. . . . The appellant did not appeal against the rejection of his case under s 210 and this House is not concerned with it. The company and the individual respondents appealed against the order for winding up and this was set aside by the court of appeal. The appellant now seeks to have it restored.

My Lords, the petition was brought under s 222(f) of the Companies Act 1948, [s 344(h) of our Act] which enables a winding-up order to be made if 'the court is of the opinion that it is just and equitable that the company should be wound up'. This power has existed in our company law in unaltered form since the first major Act, the Companies Act 1862. Indeed, it antedates that statute since it existed in the Joint Stock Companies Winding up Act 1848. For some 50 years . . . the words 'just and equitable' were interpreted so as only to include matters *ejusdem generis* as the preceding clauses of the section, but there is now ample authority for discarding this limitation. There are two other restrictive interpretations which I mention to reject. First, there has been a tendency to create categories or headings under which cases must be brought if the clause is to apply. This is wrong. Illustrations may be used, but general words should remain general and not be reduced to the sum of particular instances. Secondly, it has been suggested, and urged upon us, that (assuming the petitioner is a shareholder and not a creditor) the words must be confined to such circumstances as affect him in his capacity as shareholder. I see no warrant for this either. No doubt, in order to present a petition, he must qualify as a shareholder, but I see no reason for preventing him from relying upon any circumstances of justice or equity which affect him in his relations with the company, or, in a case such as the present, with the other shareholders.

One other signpost is significant. The same words 'just and equitable' appear in the Partnership Act 1892 s 25 as a ground for dissolution of a partnership and no doubt the considerations which they reflect formed part of the common law of partnership before its codification. The importance of this is to provide a bridge between cases under s 222(f) of the Act of 1948 and the principles of equity developed in relation to partnerships.

The winding-up order was made following a doctrine which has developed in the courts since the beginning of this century. As presented by the appellant, and in substance accepted by the learned judge, this was that in a case such as this the members of the company are in substance partners, or quasi-partners, and that a winding-up may be ordered if such facts are shown as could justify a dissolution of partnership between them. The common use of the words 'just and equitable' in the company and partnership law supports this approach. Your Lordships were invited by the respondents' counsel to restate the principle on which this provision ought to be used; it has not previously been considered by this House. The main line of his submission was to suggest that too great a use of the partnership analogy had been made; that a limited company, however small, essentially differs from a partnership; that in the case of a company, the rights of its members are governed by the articles of association which have contractual force; that the court has no power or at least ought not to dispense parties from observing their contracts; that, in particular, when one member has been excluded from the directorate, or management, under powers expressly conferred by the Companies Act and the articles, an order for winding up whether on the partnership analogy or under the just and equitable provision, should not be made. Alternatively, it was argued that before the making of such an order could be considered the petitioner must show and prove that the exclusion was not made bona fide in the interests of the company.

My Lords, I must first make some examination of the authorities in order to see how far they support the respondents' propositions and, if they do not, how far they rest upon a principle of which this House should disapprove. . . .

The real starting point is the Scottish decision in *Symington* v *Symington's Quarries Ltd* (1905) 8 F 121. There had been a partnership business carried on by two brothers who decided to transfer it to a private limited company. Each brother was to hold half the shares except for a small holding for a third brother to hold balance for voting. A resolution was passed in general meeting by the votes of one brother together with other members having nominal interests that he should be sole director. The other two brothers petitioned for a winding-up under the just and equitable provision and the court so ordered. The reasons for so doing, given by some of their Lordships of the First Division, are expressed in terms of lost substratum or deadlock—words clearly used in a general rather than a technical sense. The judgment of Lord M'Laren, which has proved to be the most influential as regards later cases, puts the ground more generally. He points out, at 130, that the company was not formed by appeal to the public: it was a domestic company, the only real partners being the three brothers:

'In such a case it is quite obvious that all the reasons that apply to the dissolution of private companies, on the grounds of incompatibility between the views or methods of the partners, would be applicable in terms to the division amongst the shareholders of this company. . . .'

In England, the leading authority is the Court of Appeal's decision in *In Re Yenidjee Tobacco Ltd* [*21*] above.

[After dealing with that case and one or two other cases, his Lordship continued:]

There are three recent cases which I should mention since they have figured in the judgments below. *In re Lundie Brothers Ltd* [1965] 1 WLR 1051 was, like the present, a decision of Plowman J. This was a case where the petitioner, one of three shareholders and directors, was excluded from participation in the management and from directors' remuneration. Plowman J, applying partnership principles, made a winding-up order under the just and equitable clause. If that decision was right it assists the present appellant. The court of appeal in the present case disagreed with it and overruled it, in so far as it related to a winding-up. The respondent argues that this was the first case where exclusion of a working director, valid under the articles, had been treated as a ground for winding up under the just and equitable clause and that as such it was an unjustifiable innovation.

In re Expanded Plugs Ltd [1966] 1 WLR 514 was, on the other hand, approved by the court of appeal in the present case. The case itself is a paradigm of obscure forensic tactics and, as such, of merely curious interest; its only importance lies in the statement, contained in the judgment, at 523, that since the relevant decisions were carried out within the framework of the articles the petitioner must show that they were not carried out bona fide in the interests of the company. I shall return, in so far as it limits the scope of the just and equitable provision, to this principle but I should say at once that I disagree with it.

In *In re K/9 Meat Supplies (Guildford) Ltd* [1966] 1 WLR 1112 there was a company of three shareholder/directors one of whom became bankrupt; the petitioner was his trustee in bankruptcy. It was contended that the company was a quasi-partnership and that since s 33 of the Partnership Act 1890 provides for dissolution on the bankruptcy of one of the partners a winding-up order on this ground should be made. Pennycuick J rejected this argument on the ground that, since the 'partnership' had been transformed into a company and since the articles gave no automatic right to a winding-up on bankruptcy, bankruptcy of one member was not a ground for winding up of itself. He then proceeded to consider whether the just and equitable provision should be applied. In my opinion, this procedure was correct and I need not express an opinion whether, on the facts, it was right to refuse an order.

Finally I should refer to the Scottish case of *Lewis v Haas* 1970 SLT (Notes) 67 where the two main shareholder/directors each held 49 per cent of the shares, the remaining 2 per cent being held by a solicitor. Lord Fraser, in the Outer House, while accepting the principle that exclusion from management might be a ground for ordering a winding-up, did not find the facts sufficient to support the use of the just and equitable clause.

This series of cases (and there are others: *In re Davis & Collett Ltd* [1935] Ch 693; *Baird v Lees* 1924 SC 83; *Elder v Elder & Watson* 1952 SC 49; *In re Swaldale Cleaners Ltd* [1968] 1 WLR 1710; *In re Fildes Bros Ltd* [1970] 1 WLR 592; *In re Leadenhall General Hardware Stores Ltd* [(1971) 115 SJ 202]) amounts to a considerable body of authority in favour of the use of the just and equitable provision in a wide variety of situations, including those of expulsion from office. The principle has found acceptance in a number of Commonwealth jurisdictions.

In *In re Straw Products Pty Ltd* [1942] VLR 222 Mann CJ said, at 223:

'All that Hinds has done in the past in exercise of his control has been within his legal powers. The question is whether he has used those powers in such a way as to make it just and equitable that Robertson should be allowed by the court to retire from the partnership. The analogy of a partnership seems to me to clarify discussion.'

In *In re Wondoflex Textiles Pty Ltd* [1951] VLR 458 was a case where again the company was held to resemble a partnership. The petitioner, owner of a quarter share, was removed from office as director by the governing director exercising powers under the articles. Thus the issue, and the argument, closely resembled those in the present case. The judgment of Smith J contains the following passage, at 467:

'It is also true, I think, that, generally speaking, a petition for winding up, based upon the partnership analogy, cannot succeed if what is complained of is merely a valid exercise of powers conferred in terms by the articles. . . . To hold otherwise would enable a member to be relieved from the consequences of a bargain knowingly entered into by him. . . . But this, I think is subject to an important qualification.

Acts which, in law, are a valid exercise of powers conferred by the articles may nevertheless be entirely outside what can fairly be regarded as having been in the contemplation of the parties when they became members of the company; and in such cases the fact that what has been done is not in excess of power will not necessarily be an answer to a claim for winding up. Indeed, it may be said that one purpose of [the just and equitable provision] is to enable the court to relieve a party from his bargain in such cases.'

My Lords, in my opinion these authorities represent a sound and rational development of the law which should be endorsed. The foundation of it all lies in the words 'just and equitable' and, if there is any respect in which some of the cases may be open to criticism, it is that the courts may sometimes have been too timorous in giving them full force. The words are a recognition of the fact that a limited company is more than a mere judicial entity, with a personality in law of its own: that there is room in company law for recognition of the fact that behind it, or amongst it, there are individuals, with rights, expectations and obligations *inter se* which are not necessarily submerged in the company structure. That structure is defined by the Companies Act and by the articles of association by which shareholders agree to be bound. In most companies and in most contexts, this definition is sufficient and exhaustive, equally so whether the company is large or small. The 'just and equitable' provision does not, as the respondents suggest, entitle one party to disregard the obligation he assumes by entering a company, nor the court to dispense him from it. It does, as equity always does, enable the court to subject the exercise of legal rights to equitable considerations; considerations, that is, of a personal character arising between one individual and another, which may make it unjust, or inequitable, to insist on legal rights, or to exercise them in a particular way.

It would be impossible, and wholly undesirable, to define the circumstances in which these considerations may arise. Certainly the fact that a company is a small one, or a private company, is not enough. There are very many of these where the association is a purely commercial one, of which it can safely be said that the basis of association is adequately and exhaustively laid down in the articles. The superimposition of equitable considerations requires something more, which typically may include one, or probably more, of the following elements: (i) an association formed or continued on the basis of a personal relationship, involving mutual confidence; this element will often be found where a pre-existing partnership has been converted into a limited company; (ii) an agreement, or understanding, that all, or some (for there may be 'sleeping' members), of the shareholders shall participate in the conduct of the business; (iii) restriction upon the transfer of the members' interest in the company—so that if confidence is lost, or one member is removed from management, he cannot take out his stake and go elsewhere.

It is these, and analogous, factors which may bring into play the just and equitable clause, and they do so directly, through the force of the words themselves. To refer, as so many of the cases do, to 'quasi-partnerships' or 'in substance partnerships' may be convenient but may also be confusing. It may be convenient because it is the law of partnership which has developed the conceptions of probity, good faith and mutual confidence, and the remedies where these are absent, which become relevant once such factors as I have mentioned are found to exist: the words 'just and equitable' sum these up in the law of partnership itself. And in many, but not necessarily all, cases there has been a pre-existing partnership the obligations of which it is reasonable to suppose continue to underlie the new company structure. But the expressions may be confusing if they obscure, or deny, the fact that the parties (possibly former partners) are now co-members in a company, who have accepted, in law, new obligations. A company, however small, however domestic, is a company not a partnership or even a quasi-partnership and it is through the just and equitable clause that obligations, common to partnership relations, may come in.

My Lords, this is an expulsion case, and I must briefly justify the application in such cases of the just and equitable clause. The question is, as always, whether it is equitable to allow one (or two) to make use of his legal rights to the prejudice of his associate(s). The law of companies recognizes the right, in many ways, to remove a director from the board. Section 184 of the Companies Act 1948 confers this right upon the company in general meeting whatever the articles may say. Some articles may prescribe other methods: for example, a governing director may have the power to remove (compare *In re Wondoflex Textiles Pty Ltd* [1951] VLR 458). And quite apart from removal powers, there are normally provisions for retirement of directors by rotation so that their re-election can be opposed and defeated by a majority, or even by a casting vote. In all these ways a particular director-member may find himself no longer a director, through removal, or non-re-election: this situation he must normally accept, unless he undertakes the burden of proving fraud or mala fides. The just and equitable provision nevertheless comes to his assistance if he can point to, and prove, some special underlying obligation of his fellow member(s) in good faith, or confidence, that so long as the business continues he shall be entitled to management participation, an obligation so basic that, if broken, the conclusion must be that the association must be dissolved. And the principles on which he may do so are those worked out by the courts in partnership cases where there has been exclusion from management ... even where under the partnership agreement there is a power of expulsion. ...

I come to the facts of this case. It is apparent enough that a potential basis for a winding-up order under the just and equitable clause existed. The appellant after a long association in partnership, during which he had an equal share in the management, joined in the formation of the company. The inference must be indisputable that he, and Mr Nazar, did so on the basis that the character of the association would, as a matter of personal relation and good faith, remain the same. He was removed from his directorship under a power valid in law. Did he establish a case which, if he had remained in a partnership with a term providing for expulsion, would have justified an order for dissolution? This was the essential question for the judge. Plowman J dealt with the issue in a brief paragraph in which he said [1970] 1 WLR 1378, 1389:

... while no doubt the petitioner was lawfully removed, in the sense that he ceased in law to be a director, it does not follow that in removing him the respondents did not do him a wrong. In my judgment, they did do him a wrong, in the sense that it was an abuse of power and a breach of the good faith which partners owe to each other to exclude one of them from all participation in the business upon which they have embarked on the basis that all should participate in its management. The main justification put forward for removing him was that he was perpetually complaining, but the faults were not all on one side and, in my judgment, this is not sufficient justification. For these reasons, in my judgment, the petitioner, therefore, has made out a case for a winding-up order.'

Reading this in the context of the judgment as a whole, which had dealt with the specific complaints of one side against the other, I take it as a finding that the respondents were not entitled, in justice and equity, to make use of their legal powers of expulsion and that, in accordance with the principles of such cases as *Blisset* v *Daniel* 10 Hare 493, the only just and equitable course was to dissolve the association. To my mind, two factors strongly support this. First, Mr Nazar made it perfectly clear that he did not regard Mr Ebrahimi as a partner, but did regard him as an employee. But there was no possible doubt as to Mr Ebrahimi's status throughout, so that Mr Nazar's refusal to recognize it amounted, in effect, to a repudiation of the relationship. Secondly, Mr Ebrahimi, through ceasing to be a director, lost his right to share in the profits through directors' remuneration, retaining only the chance of receiving dividends as a minority shareholder. . . .

I must deal with one final point which was much relied on by the court of appeal. It was said that the removal was, according to the evidence of Mr Nazar, bona fide in the interests of the company; that Mr Ebrahimi had not shown the contrary: that he ought to do so or to demonstrate that no reasonable man could think that his removal was in the company's interest. This formula 'bona fide in the interests of the company' is one that is relevant in certain contexts of company law and I do not doubt that in many cases decisions have to be left to majorities or directors to take which the courts must assume had this basis. It may, on the other hand, become little more than an alibi for a refusal to consider the merits of the case, and in a situation such as this it seems to have little meaning other than 'in the interests of the majority'. Mr Nazar may well have persuaded himself, quite genuinely, that the company would be better off without Mr Ebrahimi, but if Mr Ebrahimi disputed this, or thought the same with reference to Mr Nazar, who prevails is simply the majority view. To confine the application of the just and equitable clause to proved cases of mala fides would be to negative the generality of the words. It is because I do not accept this that I feel myself obliged to differ from the court of appeal.

NOTES

Applying *Ebrahimi*, the Court of Chancery held in *Bentley-Stevens* v *Jones* [1974] 2 All ER 653 (Ch) that, assuming that the dismissed director was a quasi-partner, the company had still the statutory right to remove him from office, and refused his application for an interlocutory injunction. His only remedy was to apply for a winding-up order. But see *Stewart* v *Schwab* 208 above.

Rights and Duties of Directors

I THE LEGAL STATUS OF DIRECTORS

A TEXT

A company is a diarchy. Its organs are the general meeting of share-holders and the board of directors, analogues of parliament and executive government in a democratically ruled republic. For some purposes directors are agents, for others trustees of the company, but neither is fully descriptive of their status: *214, 215*. As a board they are the 'controlling mind' of the company (Chapter 12).

Directors are not the servants of either the shareholders or the company, though they may work for the company in the dual capacity of director and servant (p 347 above). Within the area of management entrusted to them by the articles they are not subject to directions of the shareholders in general meeting: *216, 217*. Nevertheless, it is the company in general meeting which is the supreme organ of the company. The directors are subject to the general meeting in that it is the shareholders in general meeting who 'hire and fire' them. Major changes in the structure of the company, such as alterations of the articles, increases and reductions of capital, the issue and allot-ment of shares, compromises, amalgamations and reconstructions, require the assent of the shareholders, in most instances by special resolution. In all companies which adopt the standard set of articles, the exercise of their powers by the directors is subject to such regulations as the company in general meeting may lay down, Table A art 59, Table B art 60 (see M S Blackman (1975) 92 *SALJ* 286). Irregular or improper acts of the director, provided they are not illegal, *ultra vires* the company, or in fraud of the minority, may be ratified by a general meeting or by the unanimous consent of all the shareholders: *218–220.* The company in general meeting can exercise all powers which are not delegated to the directors (G D Goldberg (1970) 33 *MLR* 133), and, if there are no directors or the directors are incapacitated or otherwise unable to act, the shareholders in general meeting may act in their stead: *221.*

B CASES

[214] Ferguson *v* Wilson
Court of Appeal in Chancery (1866) LR 2 Ch App 77

The plaintiff sought specific performance of a resolution of the board of directors of a company under which he alleged that he was entitled to have a certain number of shares allotted to him. In the alternative, he sought damages from the directors for their failure to allot shares to him. On the latter claim:

CAIRNS LJ: . . . What is the position of directors of a public company? They are merely agents of a company. The company itself cannot act in its own person, for it has no person; it can only act through directors, and the case is, as regards those directors, merely the ordinary case of principal and agent. Wherever an agent is liable those directors would be liable; where the liability would attach to the principal, and the principal only, the liability is the liability of the company. This being a contract alleged to be made by the company, I own that I have not been able to see how it can be maintained that an agent can be brought into this court, or into any other court, upon a proceeding which simply alleges that his principal has violated a contract that he has entered into. In that state of things, not the agent, but the principal, would be the person liable.

[215] Selangor United Rubber Estates Ltd *v* Cradock
Chancery Division [1968] 1 WLR 1555, [1968] 2 All ER 1073
(see also p 235 above)

UNGOED THOMAS J: . . . The first question of law that arises is how far directors are trustees of their companies' funds. . . .

On occasion directors have been said to be trustees and on occasion not to be trustees. Like so many interminable arguments in philosophy, economics and everyday life, its resolution depends largely upon definition of terms, in this case of 'trustees' and then on the ambit of its proper application to directors.

Directors are clearly not trustees identically with trustees of a will or marriage settlement. In particular, so far as at present relevant, they have business to conduct and business functions to perform in a business manner, which are not normally at any rate associated with trustees of a will or marriage settlement. All their duties, powers and functions *qua* directors are fiduciary for and on behalf of the company. So property in their hands or under their control is theirs for the company, ie for the company's purposes in accordance with their duties, powers and functions. However much the company's purposes and the directors' duties, powers and functions may differ from the purposes of a strict settlement and the duties, powers and functions of its trustees, the directors and such trustees have this indisputably in common—that the property in their hands or under their control must be applied for the specified purposes of the company or the settlement; and to apply it otherwise is to misapply it in breach of the obligation to apply it to those purposes for the company or the settlement beneficiaries. So, even though the scope and operation of such obligation differs in the case of directors and strict settlement trustees, the nature of the obligation with regard to property in their hands or under their control is identical, namely, to apply it to specified purposes for others beneficially. This is to hold it on trust for the company or the settlement beneficiaries as the case may be. That is what holding it on trust means. That is why a misapplication of it is equally in each case a breach of trust. This is just not treating as a breach of trust something which is not a breach of trust. No ground has been suggested for treating it as a breach of trust except that it is a breach of trust. . . .

In *Re City Equitable Fire Insurance Co Ltd, 234* below, Romer J said: 'It has sometimes been said that directors are trustees. If this means no more than that directors in the performance of their duties stand in a fiduciary relationship to the company, the statement is true enough. But if the statement is meant to be an indication by way of analogy of what those duties are, it appears to me to be wholly misleading. I can see but little resemblance between the duties of a director and the duties of a trustee of a will or of a marriage settlement. It is indeed impossible to describe the duty of directors in general terms, whether by way of analogy or otherwise. The position of a director of a company carrying on a small retail business is very different from that of a director of a railway company.' . . .

In *Russell* v *Wakefield Waterworks Co* [(1875) LR 20 Eq 474] Sir George Jessel MR in a passage explaining that the appropriate person to apply to the court for repayment of misapplied funds of a company was not the shareholders, but the company, said: 'The answer was, that where the owner of the trust fund is an incorporated company, the corporation is the only party to sue; the stranger has nothing whatever to do with the individual corporators; and although in a sense it is their property, because individual corporators make up the corporation, yet in law it is not their property, but the property of the corporation, and therefore the right person to sue is the corporation, who is the *cestui que trust* or equitable owner of the fund. That I take to be the general rule of this court. In this court the money of the company is a trust fund, because it is applicable only to the special purposes of the company in the hands of the agents of the company, and it is in that sense a trust fund applicable by them to those special purposes; and a person taking it from them with notice that it is being applied to other purposes cannot in this court say that he is not a constructive trustee.'

In *Re Lands Allotment Co* [[1894] 1 Ch 616] Lindley LJ said: 'Although directors are not properly speaking trustees, yet they have always been considered and treated as trustees of money which comes to their hands or which is actually under their control; and ever since joint stock companies were invented directors have been held liable to make good moneys which they have misapplied upon the same footing as if they were trustees. . . .'

In *Re Forest of Dean Coal Mining Co* [(1878) 10 ChD 450] Sir George Jessel MR, in dealing with the responsibility of directors in respect of debts due to a company, said: 'Traders have a discretion as to whether they shall sue their customers, a discretion which is not vested in the trustees of a debt under a settlement.' He added: 'Again, directors are called trustees. They are no doubt trustees of assets which have come into their hands, or which are under their control, but they are not trustees of a debt due to the company. . . . A director is the managing partner of the concern, and although a debt is due to the concern I do not think it is right to call him a trustee of that debt which remains unpaid, though his liability in respect of it may in certain cases and in some respects be analogous to the liability of a trustee. So much for the question of unpaid debts.'

So, in my view, in general as in this case, a credit in a company's bank account which the directors are authorized to operate are moneys of the company under the control of those directors and are held by them on trust for the company in accordance with its purposes. . . .

[For comments on *Selangor*, see M R Chesterman & A S Grabiner (1969) 32 *MLR* 328.]

[216] Automatic Self-Cleansing Filter Syndicate Company Ltd *v* Cuninghame
[1906] 2 Ch 34

By the articles of association of a company the general management and control of the company were vested in the directors, subject to such regulations as might be made by extraordinary resolution (three-quarter majority). At a general meeting of the company a resolution was passed by a simple majority of the shareholders for the sale of the company's assets on certain terms, directing the directors to carry the sale into effect. The directors were of the opinion that a sale on those terms was not for the benefit of the company and declined to carry the sale into effect. *Held*, that they could not be compelled to do so.

Cozens-Hardy LJ: . . . If you once get clear of the view that directors are mere agents of the company, I cannot see anything in principle to justify the contention that the directors are bound to comply with the votes of the resolutions of a simple majority at an ordinary meeting of the shareholders. I do not think it true to say that the directors are agents. I think it more nearly true to say that they are in the position of managing partners appointed to fill that post by a mutual arrangement between all the shareholders. . . .

[217] John Shaw & Sons (Salford) Ltd *v* Shaw
[1935] 2 KB 113

GREER LJ: ... A company is an entity distinct alike from its shareholders and its directors. Some of its powers may, according to its articles, be exercised by directors, certain other powers may be reserved for the shareholders in general meeting. If powers of management are vested in the directors, they and they alone can exercise these powers. The only way in which the general body of the shareholders can control the exercise of the powers vested by the articles in the directors is by altering their articles, or, if opportunity arises under the articles, by refusing to re-elect the directors of whose actions they disapprove. They cannot themselves usurp the powers which by the articles are vested in the directors any more than the directors can usurp the powers vested by the articles in the general body of shareholders. ...

NOTES

See further *Gramophone and Typewriter Ltd* v *Stanley* [1908] 2 KB 89; *Marshall's Valve Gear Co Ltd* v *Manning, Wardle & Co Ltd* [1909] 1 Ch 267; *Salmon* v *Quin & Axtens Ltd* [1909] AC 442; *Scott* v *Scott* [1943] 1 All ER 582; *Wessels & Smith* v *Vanugo Construction (Pty) Ltd* 1964 (1) SA 635 (O) at 637; also *Cape United Sick Fund Society* v *Forrest* 1956 (4) SA 519 (AD); K A Aickin (1967) 5 *Melbourne University LR* 448; K W Wedderburn (1968) 31 *MLR* at 690; Colin Jack Cohen 'The Distribution of Powers in a Company' (1973) 90 *SALJ* 262.

[218] Grant *v* United Kingdom Switchback Railways Company
(1888) 40 ChD 135

COTTON LJ: ... The ratifying a particular contract which had been entered into by the directors without authority, and so making it an act of the company, is quite a different thing from altering the articles. To give the directors power to do things in future which the articles did not authorize them to do, would be an alteration of the articles, but it is no alteration of the articles to ratify a contract which has been made without authority. ...

[219] *In re* Express Engineering Works Ltd
[1920] 1 Ch 466

Five persons formed a private company in which they were the sole shareholders and directors. They sold to the company for £15 000 in debentures property which they had acquired prior to the incorporation of the company for £7 000. The contract of sale and the issue of the debentures were approved at a meeting of the five stated to be a board meeting. The articles of the company provided that no director should vote in respect of any contract in which he might be interested.

It was held that as there was no suggestion of fraud and the matter was *intra vires*, the company was bound by the unanimous agreement of its members.

WARRINGTON LJ: It happened that these five directors were the only shareholders of the company, and it is admitted that the five, acting together as shareholders, could have issued these debentures. As directors they could not but as shareholders acting together they could have made the agreement in question. It was competent to them to waive all formalities as regards notice of meetings etc and to resolve themselves into a meeting of shareholders and unanimously pass the resolution in question. Inasmuch as they could not in one capacity effectually do what was required but could do it in another, it is to be assumed that as business men they would act in the capacity in which they had power to act. In my judgment they must be held to have acted as shareholders and not as directors, and the transaction must be treated as good as if every formality had been carried out. . . .

[220] **Bamford v Bamford**
[1970] Ch 212, [1969] 1 All ER 969 (CA)

HARMAN LJ: This appeal from Plowman J is concerned with a popular modern subject—the subject of take-overs. The company in question, Bamfords Ltd, is a public company, making agricultural implements somewhere in the Midlands, incorporated in 1916, having under its present articles (dating from 1958, so in quite a modern form) a capital of £1 000 000, all now in shares of similar rights with a nominal value of 4s, and 500 000 of them remaining unissued. From 1966 onwards, another member of the Bamford family (this being largely a family company) kept on making proposals to amalgamate his business (which was that of making earth-moving machinery and whom I shall call 'Excavators') with that of Bamfords. He did not receive a very hearty welcome. In 1967 he started to make bids for taking over his cousins' company. The division roughly was that three directors, the defendants Vincent, Richard and John, were of one school of thought: another one, the plaintiff Rupert, was I think on the other side of the line; and the other party one needs to mention is the defendant Frederick H Burgess Ltd who were a private company who acted I think as distributors of Bamfords' agricultural machinery on a large scale and who the defendants' side thought it would be a good thing to engage in the Bamford business in order to promote its sales and so forth and, incidentally, to make a take-over by Excavators more difficult. The proposal on one side was for Excavators to buy everybody out—anyway enough to obtain control—and the three Bamford defendants proposed instead to get Burgesses into the company by issuing the unissued shares to that company or to Mr Burgess, its managing director, and thus obtain his sympathy and help.

The ball opens with a resolution of the board of Bamfords, made on 20 November 1967, to allot the 500 000 unallotted shares to Burgesses at par. On the next day a writ was issued to prevent that being done, that being issued on behalf of Rupert and another Bamford—Anthony. Just before that allotment, the defendant directors had issued a circular to the shareholders, of whom there were a good many in number outside the family on both sides of the dispute. The first writ was issued on 21 November and its purpose was to have it declared that the allotment was bad because it was made for an improper motive, namely, as a

move in the take-over war and not in the best interests of Bamfords. As
a counter to that the defendant directors gave notice of a general meeting
for 15 December 1967 at which they proposed to ask the general meeting
to approve of what they had done, and they sent out a circular about
that. There was another writ, on 1 December, attempting to stop that
meeting and to have it declared that anyhow any resolution passed at
it was a nullity. The meeting nevertheless was held on 15 December
and there a resolution was passed. The resolution which was passed was
in these terms:

> 'That this general meeting of [Bamfords] hereby ratifies and approves
> the allotment to [Burgesses] on 20 November 1967 of 500 000 shares
> of 4s 0d each in the capital of the company at a price of 4s 0d per share
> paid in full on allotment.'

That having been passed, the action proceeded with interlocutory motions
on each side and various moves and counter-moves; and it was eventually
suggested, on the part of the defendants, that this was a suitable case
for a preliminary point to be taken. The point was that, the general
meeting of 15 December having passed the resolution ratifying what the
directors had done, it did not matter if the allotment when it was made
was an allotment made for a purpose beyond the powers of the directors
because it was not made within the trust purposes of their power. It
was eventually decided to set the matter down and an order was made;
and the preliminary point of law was argued on 4 April 1968.

The preliminary point was in these terms:

> 'On the assumption (which is made solely for the purposes of the
> hearing of this preliminary point of law) that the allotment by the
> board of [Bamfords] of 500 000 shares at par to [Burgesses] on
> 20 November 1967 was not made bona fide in the interests of [Bam-
> fords], because it was a tactical move in a battle for control of [Bam-
> fords], having as its primary purpose to make it more difficult for
> [Excavators] to obtain such control.
>
> 'Whether as a matter of law and on the true construction of the
> memorandum and articles of association of [Bamfords] such allotment
> was capable of being effectively ratified and/or approved by an ordinary
> resolution of a general meeting of [Bamfords].'

The learned judge decided that point of law in this way:

> 'Declare that as a matter of law and on the true construction of the
> memorandum and articles of association of [Bamfords] such allotment
> was capable of being effectively ratified and approved or approved
> by an ordinary resolution of a general meeting of [Bamfords].'

If that is right, that is an end of the action, as has been recognized by the
fact that the order goes on to order both actions to be consolidated and
to stand dismissed. Now there is an appeal to this court.

The notice of appeal gives as its grounds these:

> '(i) That on the true construction of the articles of association of
> [Bamfords] the power to allot the shares purported to be allotted to

[Burgesses] on 20 November 1967 was vested in the directors of
[Bamfords] and in them alone and that the company in general meeting
had no residual power to make or ratify or approve an allotment of
the said shares. (ii) That an allotment not made bona fide in the
interests of [Bamfords] is void and thus incapable of ratification or
approval.'

Now to me from the very start that sounded odd, and I shall be forgiven
if, after all the eloquence which we have had in this case, I am expressing
the view which I have held throughout—that this is a tolerably plain
case. It is trite law, I had thought, that if directors do acts, as they do
every day, especially in private companies, which, perhaps because there
is no quorum, or because their appointment was defective, or because
sometimes there are no directors properly appointed at all, or because
they are actuated by improper motives, they go on doing for years,
carrying on the business of the company in the way in which, if properly
constituted, they should carry it on, and then they find that everything
has been, so to speak, wrongly done because it was not done by a proper
board, such directors can, by making a full and frank disclosure and
calling together the general body of the shareholders, obtain absolution
and forgiveness of their sins; and provided the acts are not *ultra vires*
the company as a whole everything will go on as if it had been done all
right from the beginning. I cannot believe that is not a common-place
of company law. It is done every day. Of course, if the majority of the
general meeting will not forgive and approve, then the directors must
pay for it.

It will be remembered that in . . . *Regal (Hastings) Ltd* v *Gulliver,*
[*243* below] decided in the House of Lords, Lord Russell of Killowen
in the course of his speech made a very significant observation about
this. In that case certain directors had acquired some shares by reason
of the fact that they were directors of a certain company. They afterwards sold those shares at a profit. It was held that they must account
for the profit because it had been obtained as a result of their directorships and therefore was in the nature of trust property of the company.
Lord Russell said this:

'The suggestion that the directors were applying simply as members
of the public is a travesty of the facts. They could, had they wished,
have protected themselves by a resolution (either antecedent or subsequent) of the Regal shareholders in general meeting. In default of
such approval, the liability to account must remain.'

So that Lord Russell considers it obvious that they could, either by getting
a previous approval or a subsequent ratification, retain the profit, which
otherwise they must disgorge.

So it seems to me here that these directors, on the assumptions which
we have to make, made this allotment in breach of their duty—mala
fide, as it is said. They made it with an eye primarily on the exigencies
of the take-over war and not with a single eye to the benefit of the company, and therefore it is a bad allotment; but it *is* an allotment. There
is no doubt that the directors had power to allot these shares. There is

no doubt that they did allot them. There is no doubt that the allottees are on the register and are for all purposes members of the company. The only question is whether the allotment, having been made, as one must assume, in bad faith, is voidable and can be avoided at the instance of the company—at their instance only and of no one else, because the wrong, if wrong it be, is a wrong done to the company. If that be right, the company, which had the right to recall the allotment, has also the right to approve of it and forgive it; and I see no difficulty at all in supposing that the ratification by the decision of 15 December in the general meeting of the company was a perfectly good 'whitewash' of that which up to that time was a voidable transaction; and that is the end of the matter. Unfortunately, so it seems to me, the matter has been bedevilled by the course that the case has taken. The learned judge delivered a very long and elaborate judgment in which he went through the whole line of cases to show that the general meeting of the company by ordinary resolution cannot override or usurp the authority of the directors where the conduct of the business is entrusted to them. I see no quarrel with any of those cases and I do not see that anybody can say there is any question about it. I will only mention one of them because it has an observation or so which may be useful. It is *North-West Transportation Co Ltd* v *Beatty* [*253* below], a Privy Council case. The decision of the board was delivered by Sir Richard Baggallay. The point, as stated in the headnote, was that a voidable contract, fair in its terms and within the powers of the company, had been entered into by its directors with one of their number as sole vendor. It was, therefore, of course, voidable; but it was said, and said quite properly, that the general meeting could set that right. Sir Richard Baggallay said this:

'The general principles applicable to cases of this kind are well established. Unless some provision to the contrary is to be found in the charter or other instrument by which the company is incorporated, the resolution of a majority of the shareholders, duly convened, upon any question with which the company is legally competent to deal, is binding upon the minority, and consequently upon the company, and every shareholder has a perfect right to vote upon any such question, although he may have a personal interest in the subject-matter opposed to, or different from, the general or particular interests of the company. On the other hand, a director of a company is precluded from dealing, on behalf of the company, with himself, and from entering into engagements in which he has a personal interest conflicting, or which possibly may conflict, with the interests of those whom he is bound by fiduciary duty to protect; and this rule is as applicable to the case of one of several directors as to a managing or sole director. Any such dealing or engagement may, however, be affirmed or adopted by the company, provided such affirmance or adoption is not brought about by unfair or improper means, and is not illegal or fraudulent or oppressive towards those shareholders who oppose it.'

So that Sir Richard Baggallay had no doubt that a voidable transaction of that sort could be set right by the company in general meeting if the matter was properly explained to the shareholders.

The learned judge, having gone through these cases at great length, came to the conclusion that though it was true that the general meeting could not override the directors it could affirm that which they had done; but he arrived at this result by what to my mind is a curiously unapt process. He said that the right to allot shares if not delegated to anybody else is in the company in general meeting: in this case by art 12 that power has been delegated to the directors: but in the present instance the directors, having regard to their equivocal position, cannot exercise the power: it therefore remains to the company and the company can do what it has done, and it has what is termed in the notice of appeal a 'residual' power. That might be all very well if the company in general meeting had ever made an allotment. It never did anything of the sort. It merely ratified that which the directors had already done and prevented its being undone. Therefore it seems to me that to talk of 'residual' power is entirely beside the mark, with all respect to those who think otherwise.

[The decision of the court below was confirmed on the ground that the improper allotment by the directors had been validated by ratification of the company in general meeting.]

NOTES

See also *Dublin* v *Diner* 1964 (1) SA 799 (D) at 801, 802, and *Avondson Trust (Pty) Ltd* v *Wouda* 1975 (2) SA 444 (T). In *Houldsworth* v *Evans* (1868) LR 3 HL 263 it was held that where the shareholders know that the directors have exceeded their powers but allow things to remain unimpeached for years, they must be taken to have retrospectively sanctioned what has been done.

Other cases are: *Phosphate of Lime Co Ltd* v *Green* (1871) LR 7 CP 43; *Irvine* v *Union Bank of Australia* (1877) 2 App Cas 366; *Browne* v *La Trinidad* (1887) 37 ChD 1; *In re Portuguese Consolidated Copper Mines Ltd* (1890) 45 ChD 16; *Hugo and Haines* v *Transvalia Co* (1892) 4 SAR 278; *Sparks & Young* v *John Hoatson* (1906) 27 NLR 634; *In re Parker and Cooper Ltd* v *Reading* [1926] Ch 975; *Silver Garbus & Co (Pty) Ltd* v *Teichert* 1954 (2) SA 98 (N) at 102; *Burstein* v *Yale* 1958 (1) SA 768 (W) at 771; *Marshall Industrials Ltd* v *Khan* 1959 (4) SA 684 (N); *Sugden* v *Beaconhurst Dairies* 1963 (2) SA 174 (E); *Dublin* v *Diner* 1964 (1) SA 799 (N). I B Murray, in (1953) 70 *SALJ* 424–5, casts doubt on the proposition that any irregularity can be cured by consent of all the shareholders, citing *EBM Co Ltd* v *Dominion Bank* [1937] 3 All ER 555 (PC) at 566, and the remarks of Scott LJ in *Re Cleadon Trust* [1938] 4 All ER 518 (CA) at 533 in support of his criticism. See further *Gründling* v *Beyers* 1967 (2) SA 131 (W) and *In re Olympus Consolidated Mines Ltd* 1958 (2) SA 381 (SR) at 384.

[221] Alexander Ward and Co Ltd *v* Samyang Navigation Co Ltd
[1975] 2 All ER 424 (HL)

The main question in this case was whether an action instituted on behalf of a company which at the relevant time had no directors by two individuals acting without the authority of the company could be ratified by the liquidator after the company had gone into liquidation.

LORD HAILSHAM OF ST MARYLEBONE: My Lords, I would dismiss this appeal. These proceedings originated on 5 November 1970 when the pursuers (now respondents to this appeal) issued a summons which constituted at the same time warrants for the laying-on of arrestments *ad fundandam jurisdictionem* and on the dependence. The conclusion of the summons was for the payment of a sum of money a little in excess of £160 000.

The original pursuers (the respondent company) are a limited company registered in Hong Kong. The appellants (defenders in the proceedings) are a limited company registered in Korea. Nothing, apart from the arrestment *ad fundandam jurisdictionem* which was executed on a ship owned by the appellants and lying in a Scottish shipyard, would have given the Scottish courts jurisdiction to try the issues between the parties. The actual arrestments were recalled by interlocutor of 5 December 1970, the appellants having consigned the sum of £165 000 by way of caution pursuant to an interlocutor of the Lord Ordinary of the previous day.

In due course the appellants lodged defences including a plea-in-law in the following terms: '4. The pursuers not being the company have no title to sue.' . . .

The facts, as they must be assumed from the pleadings and the preliminary proof, are that, at the time of the issue of the summons and the warrants for the arrestments, the proceedings had not been properly constituted, having been initiated on the instructions of two individuals named Ward and Irons, who acted without authority from the respondent company. At the time of the issue of the proceedings and, until it went into liquidation, the company had no directors, and had held no general meetings at least since 1967. . . .

In the course of his cogent and erudite argument before your Lordships' House, counsel for the appellants rested his case on two principal contentions: (1) that the arrestment *ad fundandam jurisdictionem* is not available to the liquidator since both arrestments had been laid by Ward and Irons without authority from the company and this arrestment is available only to him who has used it; (2) that the liquidator could not ratify either the laying-up of the arrestments or the raising of the action as at that time the respondent company was not competent to perform these acts by any agent let alone the two persons who in fact had performed them. I will deal with the second contention first since, as will be seen, this is the real point in the case and, on the view I take, the decision on the first flows from the decision on the second.

I begin by pointing out, not as a pure piece of pedantry, but as bearing on my opinion on both parts of the case, that the ratification relied on is not that of the liquidator, but that of the company acting by the liquidator. The proceedings were *ab initio* in the name of the company. By the time he was sisted and adopted the proceedings, the liquidator was authorized to act for the company. It is not simply an exercise in semantics to point out that if there was a ratification of the acts of Ward and Irons, it was a ratification by the company acting through the liquidator and not by the liquidator acting on his own behalf. The question for consideration is whether the company could ratify through the liquidator and not whether the liquidator could ratify for the benefit of the company.

Clearly, if and in so far as the company could ratify the acts of Ward and Irons, the company has done so by adopting the proceedings and, on the general principle governing the law of ratification '*Omnibus ratihabitio retrotrahitur et mandato priori aequiparatur*', the ratification dates back to the acts ratified, and so to the time when the arrestments were laid, and the summons issued. Appellants' counsel relied, however, basically on the contention that none of these acts can be ratified by the company as, he urged, the second of the three conditions laid down by Wright J in *Firth* v *Staines* [[1897] 2 QB 70 at 75] viz that 'at the time the act was done the agent must have had a competent principal' had not been fulfilled, because the respondent company had neither appointed directors nor held a general meeting and so was incapable of instructing solicitors or other agents to do the acts alleged to have been ratified. Thus, it was contended, the company was not a competent principal within the meaning of the requirement.

With respect, however, this argument is a *non sequitur* which would only become cogent if one adopted a false and question-begging meaning to the word 'competent'. In my opinion at the relevant time the company was fully competent either to lay arrestments or to raise proceedings in the Scottish courts. The company could have done so either by appointing directors or as I think by authorizing proceedings in general meeting which, in the absence of an effective board, has a residual authority to use the company's powers. It had not taken, and did not take, the steps necessary to give authority to perform the necessary actions. But it was competent to have done so, and in my view it was therefore a competent principal within the meaning of the second of Wright J's three conditions.

[His Lordship then proceeded to deal with the second point, relating to the peculiarly Scottish procedure known as *arrestment ad fundandam jurisdictionem*.]

II RIGHTS

A TEXT

A director has a right to the exercise of his office: *222*. By virtue of their office directors are entitled to inspect and take extracts from the company's books: *223*.

A director .has no right to remuneration unless such right is given to him by the articles or by his service contract (see above p 347). As a rule the articles leave it to the company in general meeting to fix directors' fees: *224* (cf Table A arts 54, 55; Table B arts 55, 56). Tax-free payments are prohibited, s 225.

A director is entitled to compensation for expenses bona fide incurred on behalf of the company, but in the absence of specific authority in the articles or a resolution of the company, he is not entitled to travelling expenses to directors' meetings: *225* (cf Table A art 55, Table B art 56).

No company may make any payment or grant any benefit or advantage to a director or past director of the company or of its controlled or controlling company or of any company controlled by its controlling company by way of compensation for loss of office, in connection with his retirement, or in connection with a reconstruction or amalgamation under s 313 or a take-over scheme under s 314, unless full particulars have been disclosed to the members of the company and the payment, benefit or advantage has been approved by special resolution, s 227. (See S W L de Villiers (1972) 5 *CILSA* 340; R C Beuthin 1973 *De Rebus Procuratoriis* 465.) In connection with a take-over scheme a director or past director may not be paid more for his shares than other shareholders, s 227(3).

No company may make a loan to one of its directors or managers or to the director or manager of its holding company or a company which is a subsidiary of its holding company, or to a company or body corporate which is controlled by one or more of the directors or managers of the company or of its holding company or of any company which is a subsidiary of its holding company, or provide any security to any person in connection with an obligation of such director, manager or company, s 226(1). (See also ss (1)(A). For exceptions, see ss (2) and (3).)

When shares or debentures are issued in connection with a share option plan directors may not be treated more favourably than other members or debenture-holders, ss 222, 223.

The annual financial statements of a company must disclose the aggregate amount of the directors' emoluments; the aggregate amount of directors' and past directors' pensions; and the aggregate amount of compensation paid to directors in respect of loss of office, s 297. The statements must also show any loans made to directors, ss 295, 296.

In England it has been held that in estimating the money value of a benefit received by a director otherwise than in cash the sum actually spent on it by the company, of which he received the benefit, is the decisive figure, not 'a notional sum which he could or would or might have spent' if he had had to purchase the benefit himself: *Rendell* v *Went (Inspector of Taxes)* [1964] 2 All ER 464 at 468, [1964] 1 WLR 650 at 660, per Viscount Radcliffe.

B CASES

(a) Right to Exercise of Office

[222] Pulbrook v Richmond Consolidated Mining Company
(1878) 9 ChD 610

JESSEL MR: ... The first question is, whether a director who is improperly and without cause excluded by his brother directors from the board from which they claim the right to exclude him, is entitled to an order restraining his brother directors from so excluding him.

In this case a man is necessarily a shareholder in order to be a director, and as a director he is entitled to fees and remuneration for his services, and it might be a question whether he would be entitled to the fees if he did not attend meetings of the board. He has been excluded. Now, it appears to me that this is an individual wrong, or a wrong that has been done to an individual. It is a deprivation of his legal rights for which the directors are personally and individually liable. He has a right by the constitution of the company to take a part in its management, to be present, and to vote at the meetings of the board of directors. He has a perfect right to know what is going on at these meetings. It may affect his individual interest as a shareholder as well as his liability as a director, because it has been sometimes held that even a director who does not attend board meetings is bound to know what is done in his absence.

Besides that, he is in the position of a shareholder, of a managing partner in the affairs of the company, and he has a right to remain managing partner, and to receive remuneration for his services. It appears to me that for the injury or wrong done to him by preventing him from attending board meetings by force, he has a right to sue. He has what is commonly called a right of action, and those decisions which say that, where a wrong is done to the company by the exclusion of a director from board meetings, the company may sue and must sue for that wrong, do not apply to the case of wrong done simply to an individual. There may be cases where, by preventing a director from exercising his functions, in addition to its being a wrong done to the individual, a wrong is also done to the company, and there the company have a right to complain. But in a case of an individual wrong, another shareholder cannot on behalf of himself and others, not being the individuals to whom the wrong is done, maintain an action for that wrong. That being so, in my opinion, the plaintiff in this case has a right of action. . . .

NOTES

Approved in *Robinson v Imroth* 1917 WLD 159. See also *Nel v De Necker* 1948 (1) SA 884 (W), further *Joubert v Van Aardt* 1923 OPD 238.

In *Hayes v Bristol Plant Hire Ltd* [1957] 1 All ER 685, [1957] 1 WLR 499 it was held that the fact that the articles do not require a director to hold a share qualification and do not give him a right to specified remuneration, does not preclude him from suing for relief if he is unlawfully excluded from the board.

[223] Wes-Transvaalse Boeresake (Edms) Bpk *v* Pieterse
1955 (2) SA 464 (T)

RAMSBOTTOM J: . . . The law is reasonably clear. A director has the right to inspect books and documents in accordance with the provisions of s 90(2) [now s 284(3)] of the Companies Act, which provides:

'The books and accounts shall be kept at the registered office of the company or at such other place as the directors think fit and shall at all times be open to inspection by directors.'

A director has the right to have the assistance of an accountant to make that inspection effectual. But the latter right is not unqualified —the company has the right, if good cause exists, to object to the accountant or other professional assistant, and it has the right to demand an undertaking that the accountant will not disclose information gained in the course of the inspection. . . .

... I think that if a director claims the right to inspect the books of a company assisted by an accountant, the company must be entitled to ask for a reasonable time to consider whether or not it has good grounds to object to the accountant produced, and to consider whether or not to impose a condition of non-disclosure of information, and to have a directors' meeting for that purpose if necessary. ...

NOTES

See also *Möller v Spence* (1885) 4 SC 46; *Lochoff v Jewish Daily Press Ltd* 1942 WLD 255. The proper custodian of the books of a company is its secretary: *Randfontein Township Syndicate's Directors v De Kock* 1910 WLD 30. See also *Strand Rink and Recreation Co Ltd v Jones* 1913 CPD 519.

(b) Remuneration and Other Benefits

[224] *Re* Richmond Gate Property Co Ltd
[1965] 1 WLR 335, [1964] 3 All ER 936

The applicant was joint managing director of the respondent. Under art 9 of the company's articles, article 108 of Table A of the English Companies Act applied, which is in these terms:

'A managing director shall receive such remuneration (whether by way of salary, commission or participation in profits, or partly in one way and partly in another) as the directors may determine.'

After a short life the company went into a members' voluntary liquidation. No remuneration for the directors had been determined. The applicant lodged proof for £400 as remuneration due to him as managing director either under contract or under a *quantum meruit*. The liquidator's rejection of the claim was upheld by the court.

PLOWMAN J: The effect of art 9 of the articles, coupled with art 108 in Table A, coupled with the fact that the applicant was a member of the company, in my judgment is that a contract exists between himself and the company for payment to him of remuneration as managing director, and that remuneration depends on art 108 of Table A and is to be such amount 'as the directors may determine'; in other words, the managing director is at the mercy of the board, he gets what they determine to pay him, and, if they do not determine to pay him anything, he does not get anything. That is his contract with the company, and those are the terms on which he accepts office. Since there is an express contract with the company in regard to the payment of remuneration, it seems to me that any question of *quantum meruit* is automatically excluded.

NOTES

See also *Phillips v Base Metals Exploration Syndicate Ltd (in liquidation)* 1911 TPD 403, per Wessels J: ... 'There is no implication in law that a person who acts as the director or managing director of a company is entitled to any payment for any services he renders on behalf of the company ...'; further *Brown v Nanco (Pty) Ltd, 328A* below.

In *Blythe v Phoenix Foundry Ltd, Wilson & Muir* 1922 WLD 87 it was held that directors cannot pass a valid resolution to increase their own remuneration unless all shares in the company are held by them. See also *In re George Newman & Company* [1895] 1 Ch

674, *239* below; *Normandy v Ind, Coope & Co Ltd* [1908] 1 Ch 84; *In re the Coliseum (Barrow) Ltd* [1930] 2 Ch 44. A director may not vote at a board meeting at which his own remuneration is being considered: *Gundelfinger v African Textile Manufacturers Ltd* 1939 AD 314; *Trek Tyres Ltd v Beukes* 1957 (3) SA 306 (W). In *In re Duomatic Ltd* [1969] 2 Ch 365, [1969] 1 All ER 161 (Ch), *188* above, the only two shareholders–directors, without constituting themselves a general meeting or passing a formal resolution, had tacitly approved the drawings by them as being on account of directors' remuneration. The court held that their assent was as binding as a resolution in general meeting.

While the directors *qua* directors cannot determine their own remuneration, the shareholders in general meeting may fix a global sum as directors' fees and leave it to the directors to decide how to distribute it among themselves.

Whether a director who has served part of a year only is entitled to a proportionate amount of the director's fees depends upon the wording of the articles or his contract, as the case may be: *Inman v Ackroyd & Best Ltd* [1901] 1 QB 613; *McConnell's Claim* [1901] 1 Ch 728; *Moriarty v Regent's Garage and Engineering Co Ltd* [1921] 2 KB 766.

In *Caridad Copper Mining Co v Swallow* [1902] KB 44, the articles provided that each of the directors should receive out of the funds of the company as a remuneration for his services a certain sum per annum to be paid at such times as the directors might determine. The court held that it was a condition precedent to the right of a director to sue for remuneration in respect of a year's service that the directors should have determined a time for payment.

Even where there is no provision for remuneration, the company can vote fees to its directors, but such fees are in the nature of a gratuity, and the directors cannot claim for them in competition with ordinary creditors. See *Hutton v West Cork Railway Co* (1883) 23 ChD 654; *Liquidators of Grand Hotel and Theatre Co v Haarburger* 1907 ORC 25. Where the remuneration is fixed by or under the articles or by contract, on the other hand, the directors can claim their remuneration like ordinary creditors.

Directors' fees may be paid by way of a percentage on the profits of the company. In *Edwards v Saunton Hotel Co Ltd* [1943] 1 All ER 176 a director was entitled to a fixed salary plus a commission of 20 per cent on the 'profits available for distribution'. The court held that the profits were to be ascertained apart from the liability to pay commission and that proper provision had to be made for depreciation, but that the company was not entitled to deduct income tax before arriving at the profits for the purpose of calculating the director's commission. Everything must naturally depend upon the instrument in question: see *In re Peruvian Guano Co* [1894] 3 Ch 690; *Johnston v Chestergate Hat Manufacturing Co Ltd* [1915] 2 Ch 338, and *LC Ltd v G B Ollivant & Co Ltd* [1944] 1 All ER 510.

In *Frames v Bultfontein Mining Co* [1891] 1 Ch 140 the directors were entitled to a percentage of the net profits of the company. The company went into voluntary liquidation and made a large profit on the sale of its undertakings and assets. The court held that the directors were not entitled to a share in this profit.

Under Table A art 55 and Table B art 56 a director may be paid extra remuneration for extra services.

A notice concerning an extraordinary meeting of shareholders to ratify remuneration illegally paid in the past to directors must make fair and full disclosure of the facts: *Baillie v Oriental Telephone and Electric Co Ltd* [1915] 1 Ch 503.

Where the agreement providing for remuneration is invalid, remuneration may become payable on a *quantum meruit*: *Craven-Ellis v Canons Ltd* [1936] 2 KB 403, [1936] 2 All ER 1066.

In the absence of a stipulation to the contrary, persons who are nominated by a company as directors of another company are not obliged to account to the company by which they were nominated for the directors' remuneration received by them: *In re Dover Coalfield Extension Ltd* [1908] 1 Ch 65 (*196*, above). On the other hand, as a general rule a person who obtains appointment as a director as a result of a discretion vested in him as a trustee of shares is liable to account to the trust estate for the remuneration received by him as a director: *In re Macadam* [1946] Ch 73, [1945] 2 All ER 664. The position is otherwise where the trustee receives remuneration from the company independently of any use by him of the trust holding: *In re Gee* [1948] Ch 284, [1948] 1 All ER 498, followed in *Re Northcote's Will Trusts* [1949] 1 All ER 442. See also *Re Llewellin's Will Trusts* [1949] 1 All ER 487.

On the legal position of trustees and beneficiaries who are appointed as directors on the strength of the shares which they hold in trust, see further *Butt* v *Kelson* [1952] Ch 197, [1952] 1 All ER 167; *Re Whichelow* [1953] 2 All ER 1558.

As to interruption of prescription in respect of an amount due to a director by confirmation of the accounts of the company meeting, see *Markham* v *South African Financial and Industrial Co Ltd* 1962 (3) SA 669 (AD); also *In re The Coliseum (Barrow) Ltd* [1930] 2 Ch 44; *In re Transplanters (Holding Company) Ltd* [1958] 2 All ER 711; and *Consolidated Agencies Ltd* v *Bertram Ltd* [1965] AC 470, [1964] 3 All ER 282. Generally speaking a director, because of his fiduciary position, cannot on behalf of the company acknowledge his own claim. See below p 436.

On the release of a director from a debt owed by him to his company, see *Curtis's Furnishing Stores Ltd (in liquidation)* v *Freedman* [1966] 2 All ER 955, [1966] 1 WLR 1219.

[225] Young v Naval, Military, and Civil Service Co-operative Society of South Africa Ltd
[1905] 1 KB 687

FARWELL J: . . . A paid agent is bound to discharge all the duties incidental to his agency for the payment agreed on, and cannot make extra charges for work properly within the scope of his employment as agent. . . . I ask myself, then, if remuneration to a director for his services does or does not include his travelling expenses to and from the board room, and I am of opinion that it does. It is the chief part of the ordinary business of a director to attend board meetings. Directors as a rule do not reside at the registered office of the company, where board meetings are usually held. The director lives where he pleases and suits his own convenience. He is paid a fixed sum for attending and advising with his co-directors. His expense in getting there is included in his salary, because it is necessarily incidental to the duty undertaken by him that he should be in that particular place. He has undertaken for a fixed sum to do work at particular meetings of himself and others. He cannot perform his obligations without attending, and such attendance, being necessary for, is paid by the remuneration for, such work. . . .

[It was accordingly held that in the absence of express provision in the articles, directors who are remunerated for their services are not entitled to travelling expenses incurred in attending board meetings. Payment may, however, be authorized by the company in general meeting.]

NOTES

See further *Standard Bank* v *Liquidators of Cobb & Co* (1876) 5 Buch 186.

In England art 76 of Table A now enables a company to pay directors their expenses in attending directors' meetings. There is no corresponding provision in our model articles. But cf Table A art 55 and Table B art 56.

On the question whether expenditure on proxies may be charged to the company, see *183* and pp 313–14.

On directors' remuneration generally, see also 383 above.

III DUTIES

A TEXT

The paramount duty of directors, individually and collectively, is to exercise their powers in the best interests of the company: *226–230.*

They must conduct its affairs honestly, with due care and skill: *231–234*. If they authorize the use of the company's funds for the purchase of its own shares, or pay dividends out of capital, they can be held liable in damages: *235*; see also *Cohen NO v Segal, 84* above. The same holds true if they act *ultra vires*, or beyond their powers as directors, or (rather obviously) if they despoil the company by fraud or theft: *236, 237*.

They must not allow themselves to be placed in a situation where their personal interests and the interests of their company conflict or may possibly conflict: *238*. They must not make presents to themselves out of the company's funds: *239*. They are accountable to the company for any profits they may make in the performance of their duties and may not, without the approval of the company in general meeting, appropriate to themselves assets, advantages and opportunities which belong properly to the company: *240–246*. And even the approval of the company in general meeting cannot authorize them to benefit themselves at the expense of the minority: *247*.

Unless the articles authorize it, a director may not, without the informed consent of a general meeting of shareholders, contract with his company: *248, 249*. If a director is materially interested in a contract or proposed contract to be entered into by the company, or becomes interested in it after the company has entered into it, he must make full disclosure to the board of directors, as provided in ss 234ff: *250*. A register of interests of directors in contracts has to be kept, and is open to inspection by members, s 240. The standard set of articles provides that a director shall vacate his office if he fails to declare his interest in a contract as required by law, Table A art 65(*e*), Table B art 66(*e*).

Unless the articles otherwise provide, a director may not vote at a directors' meeting on a contract in which he is interested, but there is nothing to preclude him from voting on it at a general meeting in his capacity as a shareholders: *251–253*.

Unless he has assumed office under a service contract which restrains competition, a director of company A is not, it would seem, precluded from accepting a directorship in company B, even if the two companies are in competition, but if he does he must keep confidential information which he acquires as director of company A from company B, and vice versa, and must, generally, take care not to subordinate the interests of one of the companies to those of the other: *254, 255*. Sections 215 and 216 which compel every director and officer of a company to disclose to the company all directorships held in other companies, and which oblige the company to enter this information in its register of directors and officers whence it eventually makes its way into the central register kept by the Registrar, ensures that every shareholder can find out at any time what other directorships the directors of his company hold.

At common law a director could freely deal in the shares of his company, provided that he did not fraudulently withhold from the other party material information of which he stood possessed: *256, 257*; but cf *258*. The Companies Act imposes important restrictions on 'insider trading'. First, directors may not deal in options in respect of listed shares or debentures of their company or its controlled or controlling company or a company controlled by its controlling company, s 224. Secondly, a director may not effect a 'bear sale' of a security of his company, i e (in the main) a sale where prior to the completion of the transaction by delivery, the director repurchases the security, s 13A of the Stock Exchanges Control Act 7 of 1947. Thirdly, it is an offence for a director, past director, officer or other person who has inside information which, if it became publicly known, would materially affect the price of the company's securities, to deal in these securities to his advantage before the information is publicly announced, s 233 (and see s 229 s v 'officer', 'past director', and 'person'). Fourthly, every public company has to keep a register of the material interests of its directors, past directors, officers and 'persons' in the shares and debentures of the company. 'Interest' includes an option, s 229 s v 'interest'. (Thus, *S* v *Newman* 1973 (3) SA 968 (T), where it was held that under s 70*nov*(11) of the old Act a director was not obliged to notify the company of an option to acquire shares before he had exercised it, would go the other way today.)

The Act imposes diverse statutory duties on directors. Most are enforced by criminal sanctions, but there may be civil liability as well. Some sections expressly provide for civil liability in one shape or other, e g ss 50(3), 160, 181(5), 222(2)(*a*), 227(2). Others, such as s 284 which requires a company to keep proper records, are silent on the point, but personal liability for default follows from the principles governing breach of statutory duty: *259*.

The duties of 'puppet', alternate or nominee directors are in no way less onerous than those of other directors. Thus a puppet director cannot escape liability for negligence, breach of duty or breach of trust by laying the blame on the person who (perhaps without being formally a director himself) put him into office and pulled the strings: *260*. Conversely, the puppeteer cannot escape liability by relying on the fact that he was not, formally, a director: *261* (and see s 1 s v 'director').

It is not possible, in the articles of association or by contract, to exempt directors from personal liability for negligence, default, breach of duty or breach of trust, s 247. However, the court may relieve a director who has acted honestly and reasonably from liability, s 248. (Section 248 extends to *ultra vires* acts: *In re Claridge's Patent Asphalte Company, Ltd* [1921] 1 Ch 543. On the question whether the company may take out an indemnity insurance for its directors, see Joseph Bishop Jnr (1968) 77 *Yale LJ* 1078. See further John Birds

'The Permissible Scope of Articles excluding the Duties of Company Directors' (1976) 39 *MLR* 394.)

On personal liability of directors on a winding-up of the company, ss 423, 424; see also ss 425, 426; on their criminal liability for offences committed by the company, p 498 below.

B CASES

(a) General

[226] **Treasure Trove Diamonds Ltd v Hyman**
1928 AD 464

The capital of Treasure Trove Diamonds Ltd was £235 000 divided into 940 000 shares of five shillings each. On 14 April 1928 the board of directors decided to increase the capital to £285 000 by the creation of 2 000 000 deferred shares of 6d each, these shares to rank equally with the ordinary shares as to voting power, share for share, and to issue these shares to an investment corporation at par. The shareholders were informed of this decision by circular, but no mention was made in the circular of the fact that the deferred shares were to rank equally with the ordinary shares as to voting rights. The petitioner was a shareholder.

CURLEWIS JA: . . . The petitioner's complaint is that in the circular no information was given of this special voting right . . . that the effect of the special voting rights was to give to the holders of the two million 'deferred shares' the entire management and control of the Treasure Trove Company for the £50 000 subscribed by them, and that such control and management was taken from the subscribers of £235 000 to the capital of the Treasure Trove Company, that the shareholders of the latter company were not advised by the directors of their intention to create the said 'deferred shares', and that the shareholders had no opportunity of expressing their view as to whether such 'deferred shares' with the special rights to dividend and voting should be created and whether they should be given an opportunity of subscribing for the same, and that he verily believes that if the shareholders had been consulted they would not have consented thereto unless they had been given an opportunity of subscribing for the whole of such 'deferred shares'. . . .

. . . Where wide powers are conferred on directors by the articles of association of a company in respect of the issue of shares, as in the present case, those powers are primarily given to them for the purpose of enabling them to raise capital for the purposes of the company, and the directors as occupying a fiduciary position towards the company must exercise those powers bona fide solely for the benefit of the company as a whole, and not for an ulterior object. . . .

. . . On the facts disclosed on the affidavits and documents before us, in the absence of a full and satisfying explanation on the part of the directors I have come to the conclusion that prima facie they establish that the directors of the Treasure Trove Company did not act bona fide and solely in the interest of that company when they entered into the agreement with the Investment Corporation whereby the two million deferred shares were issued to that corporation for the sum of £50 000 and that the paramount object was not so much the obtaining of the fresh capital of £50 000 but to enable the Investment Corporation to obtain control of the Treasure Trove Company, and that therefore the court below was justified in granting the provisional interdict pending action.

This interdict is only provisional in its nature, and it may be that at the trial when evidence is heard, the directors may satisfy the court that they acted entirely bona fide, and that what now looks on the face of it a transaction with an ulterior motive and not for the benefit of the company, was quite genuine. . . .

[226A] Mills v Mills
High Court of Australia (1938) 60 CLR 150

N was managing director of a company, and also a large ordinary shareholder. Relations between N and A, his nephew, who was a director and a holder of a large number of preference shares, had become strained.

N, prior to the events in question, had had a controlling vote in the company, by reason of his own shares, the votes of a relative who as a matter of habit voted with him, and the votes attaching to certain shares held by N on family trusts. N was forced to resign from these trusts and his control of ·the company was thus threatened. The directors (A dissenting) under powers conferred by the articles resolved that certain accumulated profits be capitalized, and distributed to ordinary shareholders in the form of bonus shares. One effect of this arrangement was to ensure N's continued control of the company. A challenged the validity of the directors' resolution on the grounds that it had not been passed bona fide in the interests of the company as a whole. The validity of the resolution was upheld.

LATHAM CJ: . . . It is urged that the rule laid down by the cases is that directors must act always and solely in the interests of the company and never in their own interests. It is clear that, if it is established that the directors did not act bona fide in the interests of the company, the court in a properly constituted action will set aside their resolution. Thus, if directors issue shares only for the purpose of conserving their own power, the resolution creating the shares will be set aside or an injunction will be granted to prevent the holding of a proposed meeting. . . . But before the exercise of a discretionary power by directors will be interfered with by the court it must be proved by the complaining party that they have acted from an improper motive or arbitrarily and capriciously. . . .

It must . . . be recognized that as a general rule, though not invariably, directors have an interest as shareholders in the company of which they are directors. Most sets of articles of association actually require the directors to have such an interest, and it is generally desired by shareholders that directors should have a substantial interest in the company so that their interests may be identified with those of the shareholders of the company. Ordinarily, therefore, in promoting the interests of the company, a director will also promote his own interests. I do not read the general phrases which are to be found in the authorities with reference to the obligations of directors to act solely in the interests of the company as meaning that they are prohibited from acting in any matter where their own interests are affected by what they do in their capacity as directors. Very many actions of directors who are shareholders, perhaps all of them, have a direct or indirect relation to their own interests. It would be ignoring realities and creating impossibilities in the administration of companies to require that directors should not advert to or consider in any way the effect of a particular decision upon their own interests as shareholders. A rule which laid down such a principle would paralyse the management of companies in many directions. Accordingly, the judicial observations which suggest that directors should consider only the interests of the company and never their own interests should not be pressed to a limit which would create a quite impossible position.

Directors are required to act not only in matters which affect the relations of the company to persons who are not members of the company but also in relation to matters which affect the rights of shareholders *inter se*. Where there are preference and ordinary shares a particular decision may be of such a character that it must necessarily affect adversely the interests of one class of shareholders and benefit the interests of another class. In such a case it is difficult to apply the test of acting in the interests of the company. The question which arises is sometimes not a question of the interests of the company at all, but a question of what is fair as between different classes of shareholders. Where such a case arises some other test than that of 'the interests of the company' must be applied, and the test must be applied with knowledge of the fact already mentioned that the law permits directors, and by virtue of provisions in articles of association often requires them, to hold shares, ordinary or preference, as the case may be. A director who holds one or both classes of such shares is not, in my opinion, required by the law to live in an unreal region of detached altruism and to act in a vague mood of ideal abstraction from obvious facts which must be present to the mind of any honest and intelligent man when he exercises his powers as a director. It would be setting up an impossible standard to hold that, if an action of a director were affected in any degree by the fact that he was a preference or ordinary shareholder, his action was invalid and should be set aside.

[227] **Hogg *v* Cramphorn Ltd**
[1967] Ch 254, [1966] 3 All ER 420

The company had a capital of 96 000 £1 preference shares and 40 000 £1 ordinary shares. 90 293 preference shares and 35 888 ordinary shares were issued. Article 10 of the company's articles of association provided that its shares were to be under the control of the directors, who might allot or otherwise dispose of them to such persons, on such terms and conditions, and at such times as they might think fit. Article 75 laid down that on a poll every member was to have one vote for every share (preference, ordinary or deferred) held by him.

The directors learnt that a take-over bid was to be made to shareholders. In the bona fide belief that the acquisition of control by the prospective take-over bidder would not be in the best interests of the company or its staff, the directors decided to forestall his move. They attached ten votes each to the 5 707 unissued preference shares and allotted them to a trust, controlled by the chairman of the board of directors, a partner in the company's auditors and an employee of the company. In order to enable the trustees to pay for the shares, they provided them with an interest-free loan out of the company's reserve fund. Subsequently they advanced another £28 293 by way of an interest-free loan to the trustees, to enable them to buy further preference shares. These transactions were challenged by the plaintiff, an associate of the prospective take-over bidder, who was the registered holder of fifty ordinary shares in the company.

The court held that on a proper interpretation of the company's articles of association, it was incompetent for the directors to attach special voting rights to the 5 707 preference shares.

BUCKLEY J: It does not, however, in my opinion follow from this that the plaintiff is entitled on this ground to have the allotment of the 5 707 shares set aside. It may well be that the trustees whose application was conditional on the shares carrying ten votes each on a poll could do so, but I think that they must be entitled to waive noncompliance with this condition and to elect, if they choose, to retain these shares without special voting rights attached. The matter rests, in my judgment, between the trustees and the company. The plaintiff, in my opinion, whether suing on his own behalf or in a representative capacity, is not competent to procure this allotment to be set aside.

I now turn to what has been the main matter of debate in this case, which is whether the allotment of the 5 707 shares was an improper use by the directors of their discretionary and fiduciary power under article 10, to decide to whom these unissued shares should be allotted.

It is common ground that the scheme of which this allotment formed part was formulated to meet the threat, as the directors regarded it, of Mr Baxter's offer. The trust deed would not have come into existence, nor would the 5 707 shares have been issued as they were, but for Mr Baxter's bid and the threat that it constituted to the established management of the company. It is also common ground that the directors were not actuated by any unworthy motives of personal advantage, but acted as they did in an honest belief that they were doing what was for the good of the company. . . . I am satisfied that Mr Baxter's offer, when it became known to the company's staff, had an unsettling effect on them. I am also satisfied that the directors and the trustees of the trust deed genuinely considered that to give the staff through the trustees a sizeable, though indirect, voice in the affairs of the company would benefit both the staff and the company. I am sure that Col Cramphorn and also probably his fellow directors firmly believed that to keep the management of the company's affairs in the hands of the existing board would be more advantageous to the shareholders, the company's staff and its customers than if it were committed to a board selected by

Mr Baxter. The steps which the board took were intended not only to ensure that, if Mr Baxter succeeded in obtaining a shareholding which, as matters stood, would have been a controlling shareholding, he should not secure control of the company but, also, and perhaps primarily, to discourage Mr Baxter from proceeding with his bid at all.

Counsel for the defendants has submitted that a trading company and its board of directors are fully entitled to take an interest in who becomes a member of the company and to arrange or influence matters in such a way that a particular person shall not become a member. In the present case, he says that the board was entitled to try to kill Mr Baxter's bid, if in doing so they acted in good faith, having regard to what they believed to be the interests of the company, and if the means they employed were lawful. The establishment of an employee's trust, was, he says, *intra vires* the company and *intra vires* the board under the general delegation of powers to them, and the loan made by the company to the trustees did not in any way conflict with s 54 of the Companies Act 1948 [s 38 of our Act]. Counsel for the plaintiff does not dispute the right and power of the company or of the board on a company's behalf to establish in proper circumstances a trust of shares in the company for the benefit of employees, and concedes that the scheme adopted by the board involved no contravention of s 54. Counsel for the defendants says that this scheme was one which conferred a genuine benefit on the employees, in that it conferred on their trustees an influential voice on the counsels of the company, as well as providing some perhaps rather modest financial benefit for employees. There is no doubt that the staff thoroughly appreciated and approved the board's action in establishing the trust. Counsel for the defendants says that the scheme was rightly regarded by the board as being in the interests of the shareholders both on the ground that it tended to cement the loyalty of the staff and on the ground that it would be likely to prevent the displacement of an experienced management by an inexperienced one. On these grounds he contends that the establishment of the trust fund, the issue of the 5 707 shares with special voting rights and the making of the interest-free loans to the trustees were justified as reasonably incidental to the favourable conduct of the company's business, and so *intra vires* not only the company, but also the board.

Accepting, as I do, that the board acted in good faith and that they believed that the establishment of a trust would benefit the company and that avoidance of the acquisition of control by Mr Baxter would also benefit the company, I must still remember that an essential element of the scheme, and indeed its primary purpose, was to ensure control of the company by the directors and those whom they could confidently regard as their supporters. Was such a manipulation of the voting position a legitimate act on the part of the directors? Somewhat similar questions have been considered in the well-known cases of *Punt* v *Symons & Co Ltd* [1903] 2 Ch 506 and *Piercy* v *S Mills & Co Ltd* [1920] 1 Ch 77. In *Punt* v *Symons* directors had issued shares with the object of creating a sufficient majority to enable them to pass a special resolution depriving other shareholders of special rights conferred on them by the company's articles. In *Piercy* v *Mills* directors had issued shares

with the object of creating a sufficient majority to enable them to resist
the election of three additional directors, whose appointment would
have put the two existing directors in a minority on the board. In each
case the directors were held to have acted improperly. In the earlier
case, Byrne J said (at 515–16):

'A power of the kind exercised by the directors in this case is one
which must be exercised for the benefit of the company: primarily
it is given them for the purpose of enabling them to raise capital
when required for the purposes of the company. There may be
occasions when the directors may fairly and properly issue shares in
the case of a company constituted like the present for other reasons.
For instance, it would not be at all an unreasonable thing to create
a sufficient number of shareholders to enable statutory powers to be
exercised; but when I find a limited issue of shares to persons who
are obviously meant and intended to secure the necessary statutory
majority in a particular interest, I do not think that is a fair and bona
fide exercise of the power.'

In the later case, Peterson J . . . said (at 84–5):

'The basis of the decisions in these two cases I have referred to is
that directors are not entitled to use their powers of issuing shares
merely for the purpose of maintaining their control or the control
of themselves and their friends over the affairs of the company, or
merely for the purpose of defeating the wishes of the existing majority
of shareholders. That is, however, exactly what has happened in the
present case. With the merits of the dispute as between the directors
and the plaintiff I have no concern whatever. The plaintiff and his
friends held a majority of the shares of the company, and they were
entitled, so long as that majority remained, to have their views prevail
in accordance with the regulations of the company; and it was not,
in my opinion, open to the directors, for the purpose of converting a
minority in voting power into a voting majority, and solely for the
purpose of defeating the wishes of the existing majority, to issue the
shares which are in dispute in the present action.'

With those observations I respectfully agree.

It is not, in my judgment, open to the directors to say, 'We genuinely
believe that what we seek to prevent the majority from doing will harm
the company and, therefore our act in arming ourselves or our party
with sufficient shares to outvote the majority is a conscientious exercise
of our powers under the articles, which should not be interfered with.'
Such a belief, even if well-founded, would be irrelevant. . . . These
considerations lead me to the conclusion that the issue of the 5 707
shares with the special voting rights which the directors purported to
attach to them could not be justified by the view that the directors
genuinely believed that it would benefit the company if they could
command a majority of the votes in general meetings. . . . The power to
issue the shares was a fiduciary power and if, as I think, it was exercised
for an improper motive, the issue of these shares is liable to be set aside.

Counsel for the defendants, however, contends that the present case
is distinguishable from those which I have cited in an important respect.

In both *Punt* v *Symons* and *Piercy* v *Mills*, the majority and minority were already arrayed for battle on a specific issue when the latter attempted to create reinforcements by issuing additional shares. If the question whether that issue should be allowed to stand had been referred to a general meeting at which the newly issued shares were excluded from voting, the resulting answer would in each case have been a negative one. Such a meeting would have served no useful purpose. In the present case, on the other hand, no battle had been joined when the 5 707 shares were issued; the directors were merely fearful that Mr Baxter would acquire control and that in any ensuing battle they would find themselves outnumbered. In the event, as I have said, Mr Baxter's offer lapsed. One cannot say what the result would have been if the directors had sought the approval of a general meeting before making the issue, and it is very possible that if the issue of the shares were now submitted to the company for approval it would be approved.

Counsel for the plaintiff says, no doubt rightly, that the company in general meeting could not by ordinary resolution control the directors in the exercise of the powers under art 10. He goes on to say, I think with less justification, that what they could not ordain a majority could not ratify. There is, however, a great difference between controlling the directors' exercise of a power vested in them and approving a proposed exercise by the directors of such a power, especially where the proposed exercise of the power is of a kind which might be assailed if it had not the manifest approval of the majority. Had the majority of the company in general meeting approved the issue of the 5 707 shares before it was made, even with the purported special voting rights attached (assuming that such rights could have been so attached conformably with the articles), I do not think that any member could have complained of the issue being made; for in these circumstances, the criticism that the directors were, by the issue of the shares, attempting to deprive the majority of their constitutional rights would have ceased to have any force. It follows, in my opinion, that a majority in a general meeting of the company at which no votes were cast in respect of the 5 707 shares could ratify the issue of those shares. Before setting the allotment and issue of the 5 707 shares aside, therefore, I propose to allow the company an opportunity to decide in general meeting whether it approves or disapproves of the issue of these shares to the trustees. Counsel for the defendants will undertake, on behalf of the trustees, not to vote at such a meeting in respect of the 5 707 shares.

The execution of the trust deed and the allotment of the 5 707 shares were, as I have said, integral parts of one scheme, of which the degree of control assured to the directors through the trustees by the creation of the 5 707 votes purported to be attached to these shares was the principal objective. The execution of the deed, is accordingly, in my judgment, tainted with the same vice, if it be a vice, as the issue of the shares. If the issue of the shares is to be set aside, so, I think must the deed: if the issue of the shares is to stand, so may the deed.

. . . [T]he loan of £28 293 to the trustees was tainted with the same vice as the rest of the scheme, that is to say, it was an integral part of a scheme for securing for the directors the support of a controlling body

of votes. The loan was not made with the single-minded purpose, or even
with the primary purpose, of benefiting the company otherwise than by
securing that control for the directors or facilitating their securing that
control. Accordingly, although I do not question that the loan was made
with honourable intentions, the making of it was not, in my judgment,
a conscientious exercise by the directors of their powers to make loans
of the company's funds for the purposes of the company's business or
purposes reasonably incidental thereto. The loan was, consequently, in
my judgment, *ultra vires* the directors and invalid unless sanctioned or
ratified by the company in general meeting. . . . In these circumstances I
propose to stand the action over for a specified period to enable the
directors, if so advised, to convene a general meeting to consider such
resolutions as may be submitted to it. . . . Counsel for the defendants will
undertake that at any such meeting the trustees will not vote in respect
of the 5 707 shares, but I do not think that there is any need for me to
disfranchise any other shares from voting at the meeting.

[The general meeting was held and ratified each and every action
of the directors.]

[For comments on *Hogg* v *Cramphorn* see L S Sealy [1967] *Camb LJ* 33;
688; R C Beuthin (1967) 84 *SALJ* 349; Ross W Parsons (1967) 5 *Melbourne University LR* 448; J K Walsh (1967) 8 *U West Aust L Rev* 85.]

[228] Harlowe's Nominees Pty Ltd *v* Woodside (Lakes Entrance) Oil Company No Liability
(1968) 42 *ALJR* 123 (Austr HC)

The plaintiff, a substantial shareholder in the defendant company,
had been making extensive purchases of shares in the latter through
the exchange. The directors of the defendant company made an allotment of shares to another company, the effect of which, the plaintiff
alleged, was to prevent it acquiring the degree of voting power it had
expected to obtain. The plaintiff contended that the defendant company
had no need of additional capital and that the issue of shares had been
made for a collateral purpose.

THE COURT: At the threshold of the argument for Harlowe on the
appeal was a submission of law which was put in the form of a corollary
upon the undoubted general proposition that a power vested in directors
to issue new shares is a fiduciary power which the directors are not entitled
to exercise otherwise than bona fide for the benefit of the company as a
whole. The suggested corollary is that an exercise of the power cannot
be maintained as having been bona fide in the interests of the company
unless the company had at the time of the exercise an immediate need
of the capital to be paid up on the new shares. In many a case this may
be true as a proposition of fact; but in our opinion it is not true as a
general proposition of law. To lay down narrow lines within which the
concept of a company's interests must necessarily fall would be a serious
mistake.

The principle is that although primarily the power is given to enable capital to be raised when required for the purposes of the company, there may be occasions when the directors may fairly and properly issue shares for other reasons, so long as those reasons relate to a purpose of benefiting the company as a whole, as distinguished from a purpose, for example, of maintaining control of the company in the hands of the directors themselves or their friends. An inquiry as to whether additional capital was presently required is often most relevant to the ultimate question upon which the validity or invalidity of the issue depends; but that ultimate question must always be whether in truth the issue was made honestly in the interests of the company. Directors in whom are vested the right and the duty of deciding where the company's interests lie and how they are to be served may be concerned with a wide range of practical considerations, and their judgment, if exercised in good faith and not for irrelevant purposes, is not open to review in the courts. Thus in the present case it is not a matter for judicial concern, if it be the fact, that the allotment to Burmah would frustrate the ambitions of someone who was buying up shares as opportunity offered with a view to obtaining increased influence in the control of the company, or even that the directors realized that the allotment would have that result and found it agreeable to their personal wishes. But if, in making the allotment, the directors had an actual purpose of thereby creating an advantage for themselves otherwise than as members of the general body of shareholders, as for instance by buttressing their directorships against an apprehended attack from such as Harlowe, the allotment would plainly be voidable as an abuse of the fiduciary power, unless Burmah had no notice of the facts. The decisive fact now, however, is that the judge's findings were against the negative proposition which Harlowe set itself to establish, and it seems to us impossible in all the circumstances of the case for a court of appeal to hold that the proposition was made out. The findings to which we refer are reflected in several passages in his Honour's reasons, but one quotation will suffice. Speaking of Donaldson, Hughes-Jones and Humphris, his Honour said: 'I am sufficiently convinced of their credibility to hold that they at least did not make a placement with Burmah to thwart or prevent any possible influence or control of any shareholder of the Woodside company. I also hold that although I believe the directors' opinion of the needs of the company was imprecise, probably intuitive and maybe erroneous, yet each one of them addressed his mind to the relevant problem and exercised the power to issue shares, bona fide, in order to raise money for the company's future requirements which they believe would exist. I am of the view that this was generally [? genuinely] held by each of them and their desire was to give financial stability to the company in its future programme.'

[229] Howard Smith Ltd v Ampol Petroleum Ltd
[1974] AC 821, [1974] 2 WLR 689, [1974] 1 All ER 1126 (PC)

The plaintiff company (Ampol), together with a related company, controlled 54,9 per cent of the issued shares of R W Miller (Holdings) Ltd. Ampol had submitted a bid to Miller for the remaining shares

but this had been rejected as too low by the board. A rival take-over bid
by Howard Smith Ltd, at a slightly higher price, was then rejected by
Ampol. To overcome Ampol's opposition, the board of Miller allotted
unissued shares to Smith, providing needed capital but placing Ampol
in a minority position and making likely the acceptance of the Smith
bid by all shareholders other than Ampol. Ampol sought, successfully,
to invalidate the allotment.

LORD WILBERFORCE: The directors, in deciding to issue shares, forming
part of Millers' unissued capital, to Howard Smith, acted under clause 8
of the company's articles of association. This provides, subject to certain
qualifications which have not been invoked, that the shares shall be under
the control of the directors, who may allot or otherwise dispose of the
same to such persons on such terms and conditions and either at a
premium or otherwise and at such time as the directors may think fit.
Thus, and this is not disputed, the issue was clearly *intra vires* the directors.
But *intra vires* though the issue may have been, the directors' power
under this article is a fiduciary power: and it remains the case that an
exercise of such a power though formally valid, may be attacked on the
ground that it was not exercised for the purpose for which it was granted.
It is at this point that the contentions of the parties diverge. The extreme
argument on one side is that, for validity, what is required is bona fide
exercise of the power in the interests of the company: that once it is
found that the directors were not motivated by self-interest—ie by a
desire to retain their control of the company or their positions on the
board—the matter is concluded in their favour and that the court will
not enquire into the validity of their reasons for making the issue. All
decided cases, it was submitted, where an exercise of such a power as
this has been found invalid, are cases where directors are found to have
acted through self interest of this kind.

On the other side, the main argument is that the purpose for which the
power is conferred is to enable capital to be raised for the company, and
that once it is found that the issue was not made for that purpose,
invalidity follows.

It is fair to say that under the pressure of argument intermediate positions were taken by both sides, but in the main the arguments followed
the polarization which has been stated.

In their Lordships' opinion neither of the extreme positions can be
maintained. It can be accepted, as one would only expect, that the
majority of cases in which issues of shares are challenged in the courts
are cases in which the vitiating element is the self-interest of the directors,
or at least the purpose of the directors to preserve their own control of
the management. . . .

Further it is correct to say that where the self-interest of the directors
is involved, they will not be permitted to assert that their action was
bona fide thought to be, or was, in the interest of the company; pleas to
this effect have invariably been rejected—just as trustees who buy
trust property are not permitted to assert that they paid a good price.

But it does not follow from this, as Howard Smith asserts, that the
absence of any element of self interest is enough to make an issue valid.

Self-interest is only one, though no doubt the commonest, instance of improper motive; and, before one can say that a fiduciary power has been exercised for the purpose for which it was conferred, a wider investigation may have to be made. . . .

On the other hand, taking Ampol's contention, it is, in their Lordships' opinion, too narrow an approach to say that the only valid purpose for which shares may be issued is to raise capital for the company. The discretion is not in terms limited in this way: the law should not impose such a limitation on directors' powers. To define in advance exact limits beyond which directors must not pass is, in their Lordships' view, impossible. This clearly cannot be done by enumeration, since the variety of situations facing directors of different types of company in different situations cannot be anticipated. No more, in their Lordships' view, can this be done by the use of a phrase—such as 'bona fide in the interest of the company as a whole', or 'for some corporate purpose'. Such phrases, if they do anything more than restate the general principle applicable to fiduciary powers, at best serve, negatively, to exclude from the area of validity cases where the directors are acting sectionally, or partially: ie improperly favouring one section of the shareholders against another. . . .

In their Lordships' opinion it is necessary to start with a consideration of the power whose exercise is in question, in this case a power to issue shares. Having ascertained, on a fair view, the nature of this power, and having defined as can best be done in the light of modern conditions the, or some, limits within which it may be exercised, it is then necessary for the court, if a particular exercise of it is challenged, to examine the substantial purpose for which it was exercised, and to reach a conclusion whether that purpose was proper or not. In doing so it will necessarily give credit to the bona fide opinion of the directors, if such is found to exist, and will respect their judgment as to matters of management; having done this, the ultimate conclusion has to be as to the side of a fairly broad line on which the case falls. . . .

Their Lordships were referred to the recent judgment of Berger J in the Supreme Court of British Columbia in *Teck Corporation Ltd* v *Millar* [(1973) 33 DLR (3d) 288 (BC)]. This was concerned with the affairs of Afton Mines Ltd in which Teck Corporation Ltd, a resource conglomerate, had acquired a majority shareholding. Teck was indicating an intention to replace the board of directors of Afton with its own nominees with a view to causing Afton to enter into an agreement (called an 'ultimate deal') with itself for the exploitation by Teck of valuable mineral rights owned by Afton. Before this could be done, and in order to prevent it, the directors of Afton concluded an exploitation agreement with another company 'Canex'. One of its provisions, as is apparently common in this type of agreement in Canada, provided for the issue to Canex of a large number of shares in Afton, thus displacing Teck's majority.

Berger J found that—

'. . . their [sc the directors'] object was to obtain the best agreement they could while . . . still in control. Their purpose [was] in that sense to defeat Teck. But, not to defeat Teck's attempt to obtain

control, rather it was to foreclose Teck's opportunity of obtaining for
itself the ultimate deal. That was . . . no improper purpose.'

His decision upholding the agreement with Canex on this basis appears
to be in line with the English and Australian authorities to which reference
has been made.

By contract to the cases of *Harlowe* and *Teck*, the present case, on the
evidence, does not, on the findings of the trial judge, involve any considerations of management, within the proper sphere of the directors.
The purpose found by the judge is simply and solely to dilute the majority
voting power held by Ampol and Bulkships so as to enable a then
minority of shareholders to sell their shares more advantageously. So
far as authority goes, an issue of shares purely for the purpose of creating
voting power has repeatedly been condemned. . . . In the leading Australian case of *Mills* v *Mills* [(1938) 60 CLP 150] it was accepted in the
High Court that if the purpose of issuing shares was solely to alter the
voting power the issue would be invalid. . . . The constitution of a
limited company normally provides for directors, with powers of management, and shareholders, with defined voting powers having power to
appoint the directors, and to take, in general meeting, by majority vote,
decisions on matters not reserved for management. Just as it is established
that directors, within their management powers, may take decisions
against the wishes of the majority of shareholders, and indeed that the
majority of shareholders cannot control them in the exercise of these
powers while they remain in office . . . so it must be unconstitutional for
directors to use their fiduciary powers over the shares in the company
purely for the purpose of destroying an existing majority, or creating a
new majority which did not previously exist. To do so is to interfere
with that element of the company's constitution which is separate from
and set against their powers. If there is added, moreover, to this immediate purpose, an ulterior purpose to enable an offer for shares to proceed
which the existing majority was in a position to block, the departure
from the legitimate use of the fiduciary power becomes not less, but all
the greater. The right to dispose of shares at a given price is essentially
an individual right to be exercised on individual decision and on which
majority, in the absence of oppression or similar impropriety, is entitled
to prevail. Directors are of course entitled to offer advice, and bound to
supply information, relevant to the making of such a decision, but to
use their fiduciary power solely for the purpose of shifting the power to
decide to whom and at what price shares are to be sold cannot be related
to any purpose for which the power over the share capital was conferred
on them. That this is the position in law was in effect recognized by the
majority directors themselves when they attempted to justify the issue
as made primarily in order to obtain much needed capital for the company. And once this primary purpose was rejected as it was by Street J,
there is nothing legitimate left as a basis for their action, except honest
behaviour. That is not, in itself, enough.

Their Lordships therefore agree entirely with the conclusion of Street J
that the power to issue and allot shares was improperly exercised by the
issue of shares to Howard Smith.

[230] S v Hepker
1973 (1) SA 472 (W)

This was a criminal case in which the accused were charged, *inter alia*, with fraud.

HIEMSTRA J: At this point I wish to make some general remarks. The proposition of law underlying all these charges is that directors are not allowed knowingly to bind their companies to transactions which are unprofitable to the company and are intended to serve the directors' own ends. That is so even when they hold all the shares and even when all the members of the board agree with full knowledge of the facts. The basis of this proposition is that the company is a person in law and that the directors stand in a fiduciary relationship towards it. This position is not artificial; it is very real because the company's fate always affects others besides the directors. There are creditors who may suffer and there are staff members who may lose their employment.

To have investigated and finally disposed of a commercial fraud of this magnitude took years and probably cost several hundreds of thousands of rands in unproductive expenditure. It has taken up tens of thousands of man-hours of highly skilled people. Frauds like these are difficult to detect and to prove in a court of law, and detection usually takes place only when the company has collapsed. The business methods which have come to light here are bad for the economy of the country and bad for the commercial image of the country.

The courts have the duty to uphold standards of business morality and I want to dispel any idea that companies which are wholly owned by directors can be managed as if the directors are the only persons who count.

The concept of creditors having recourse only against a company as such, leaving shareholders immune beyond their shareholdings, was a legal invention of surpassing significance for the industrial expansion of the world. But it has placed great responsibility upon directors. Because of its limited liability, directors have a duty to manage the company strictly on a basis of fairness to all those who deal with it and who have no means of knowing its internal affairs. The courts will not be tolerant to deviations from this indispensable commercial guideline. This includes persons who are not formally appointed to the board but nevertheless take part in management, and also those who allow themselves to be used as dummies on a board by acting under the command of others.

NOTES

On the same point, see further *Ashburton Oil No Liability v Alpha Minerals No Liability* (1971) 45 *ALJR* 162 (Austr HC) and *Teck Corporation v Millar* (1973) 33 *DLR* (3d) 288 (BCSC), referred to by Lord Wilberforce in his judgment in *Smith v Ampol.*

For comments on *Howard Smith v Ampol*, see J R Birds (1974) 37 *MLR* 580; J H Farrar (1974) 33 *CLJ* 221; R B (1974) 48 *ALJ* 319.

In *Alexander v Automatic Telephone Co* [1900] 2 Ch 56 directors who required shareholders to make payments on application and allotment of shares but who without the consent of the other shareholders excluded themselves from such a liability in respect of their own shares were held liable to the company for the contributions they should have made. In view of the provisions of s 222 this situation can no longer arise.

For a general discussion of minority shareholders' rights arising out of improper share issues, see C J H Thomson 'Share Issues and the Rule in *Foss* v *Harbottle*' (1975) 49 *ALJ* 134, and N C A Franzi (1976) *Melbourne LR* 392.

Directors are 'trustees' in the exercise of their power to call meetings, to issue and allot shares, or to approve or reject share transfers. See e g *Pergamon Press Ltd* v *Maxwell* [1970] 2 All ER 809 (Ch) where the court refused to order the directors to call a meeting, holding that their power to call a meeting was a fiduciary power to be exercised in good faith in the interests of the company as a whole, with which a court of law should not lightly interfere.

As it happens, the leading cases on the principle that directors are under a duty to act in the best interests of their company have to do with the issue and allotment of shares. This particular issue is likely to play a diminishing role in South Africa in future. Section 221 ordains that 'notwithstanding anything contained in its memorandum or articles, the director of a company shall not have the power to allot or issue shares of the company without the prior approval of the company in general meeting'. In terms of s 221(2) the approval may be in the form of a general authority to the directors to allot or issue any shares in their discretion, or of a specific authority in respect of any particular allotment or issue of shares. Where the approval has taken the form of a specific authority, the question whether the directors have acted in the best interests of the company can no longer arise. It can still arise, however, where the approval has taken the form of a general authority to the directors to allot or issue shares in their discretion. Moreover, in as far as they deal with the general issue what it means that directors must act in the best interests of the company, cases *226–229* remain relevant.

Where an action of the directors has received the approval, general or specific, of a general meeting, a dissatisfied minority shareholder may be able to obtain relief under s 252 (see below, p 511).

(b) The Duty of Care and Skill

[231] Marquis of Bute's case
[1892] 2 Ch 100

STIRLING J: . . . Neglect or omission to attend meetings is not, in my opinion, the same thing as neglect or omission of a duty which ought to be performed at those meetings. If, indeed, he [the defendant director] had had knowledge or notice either that no meetings of trustees or managers were being held, or that a duty which ought to be discharged at those meetings was not being performed, it might be right to hold that he was guilty of neglect or omission of the duty. That, however, is not this case. . . .

[232] Dovey v Cory
[1901] AC 477 (affirming the decision in *In re National Bank of Wales* [1899] 2 Ch 629, see p 408 below)

EARL OF HALSBURY LC: . . . The charge of neglect appears to rest on the assertion that Mr Cory, like the other directors, did not attend to any details of business not brought before them by the general manager or the chairman, and the argument raises a serious question as to the responsibility of all persons holding positions like that of directors, how far they are called upon to distrust and be on their guard against the possibility of fraud being committed by their subordinates of every degree. It is obvious if there is such a duty it must render anything like an intelligent devolution of labour impossible. Was Mr Cory to turn himself into an auditor, a managing director, a chairman, and find out whether auditors, managing directors, and chairmen were all alike deceiving him? That the letters of the auditors were kept from him is clear. That he was assured that provision had been made for bad debts, and that he believed such assurances, is involved in the admission that he was guilty of no moral fraud; so that it comes to this, that he ought to have discovered a network of conspiracy and fraud by which he was surrounded, and found out that his own brother and the managing director (who have since been made criminally responsible for frauds connected with their respective offices) were inducing him to make representations as to the prospects of the concern and the dividends properly payable which have turned out to be improper and false. I cannot think that it can be expected of a director that he should be watching either the inferior officers of the bank or verifying the calculations of the auditors himself. The business of life could not go on if people could not trust those who are put into a position of trust for the express purpose of attending to details of management. . . .

[233] *In re* **Brazilian Rubber Plantations and Estates Ltd**
[1911] 1 Ch 425

NEVILLE J: . . . I have to consider what is the extent of the duty and obligation of directors towards their company. It has been laid down that so long as they act honestly they cannot be made responsible in damages unless guilty of gross negligence. There is admittedly a want of precision in this statement of a director's liability. In truth, one cannot say whether a man has been guilty of negligence, gross or otherwise, unless one can determine what is the extent of the duty which he is alleged to have neglected. A director's duty has been laid down as requiring him to act with such care as is reasonably to be expected from him, having regard to his knowledge and experience. He is, I think, not bound to bring any special qualifications to his office. He may undertake the management of a rubber company in complete ignorance of everything connected with rubber, without incurring responsibility for the mistakes which may result from such ignorance; while if he is acquainted with the rubber business he must give the company the advantage of his knowledge when transacting the company's business. He is not, I think, bound to take any definite part in the conduct of the company's business, but so far as he does undertake it he must use reasonable care in its despatch.

Such reasonable care must, I think, be measured by the care an ordinary man might be expected to take in the same circumstances on his own behalf. He is clearly, I think, not responsible for damages occasioned by errors of judgment. . . .

[234] *In re* **City Equitable Fire Insurance Company Ltd**
[1925] Ch 407*

An investigation of a company's affairs in the course of winding-up disclosed a shortage in the funds of over £1 200 000. This shortage was due mainly to the deliberate fraud of the managing director, Bevan, for

---

* In so far as it concerns the duties of auditors, this case is dealt with elsewhere (*366* below).

which he was convicted and sentenced. The liquidator sought to make the other directors, all of whom had acted honestly throughout, liable for negligence.

In dealing with the duties of directors, the learned judge in the court *a quo* made the following remarks:

ROMER J: . . . It has sometimes been said that directors are trustees. If this means no more than that directors in the performance of their duties stand in a fiduciary relationship to the company, the statement is true enough. But if the statement is meant to be an indication by way of analogy of what those duties are, it appears to me to be wholly misleading. I can see but little resemblance between the duties of a director and the duties of a trustee of a will or of a marriage settlement. It is indeed impossible to describe the duty of directors in general terms, whether by way of analogy or otherwise. The position of a director of a company carrying on a small retail business is very different from that of a director of a railway company. The duties of a bank director may differ widely from those of an insurance director, and the duties of a director of one insurance company may differ from those of a director of another. In one company, for instance, matters may normally be attended to by the manager or other members of the staff that in another company are attended to by the directors themselves. The larger the business carried on by the company the more numerous, and the more important, the matters that must of necessity be left to the managers, the accountants and the rest of the staff. The manner in which the work of the company is to be distributed between the board of directors and the staff is in truth a business matter to be decided on business lines. . . .

. . . There are . . . one or two . . . general propositions that seem to be warranted by the reported cases: (1) A director need not exhibit in the performance of his duties a greater degree of skill than may reasonably be expected from a person of his knowledge and experience. A director of a life insurance company, for instance, does not guarantee that he has the skill of an actuary or of a physician. In the words of Lindley MR: 'If directors act within their powers, if they act with such care as is reasonably to be expected from them, having regard to their knowledge and experience, and if they act honestly for the benefit of the company they represent they discharge both their equitable as well as their legal duty to the company': see *Lagunas Nitrate Co* v *Lagunas Syndicate* [1899] 2 Ch 392 at 435. It is perhaps only another way of stating the same proposition to say that directors are not liable for mere errors of judgment. (2) A director is not bound to give continuous attention to the affairs of his company. His duties are of an intermittent nature to be performed at periodical board meetings, and at meetings of any committee of the board upon which he happens to be placed. He is not, however, bound to attend all such meetings, though he ought to attend whenever, in the circumstances, he is reasonably able to do so. (3) In respect of all duties that, having regard to the exigencies of business, and the articles of association, may properly be left to some other official, a director is, in the absence of grounds for suspicion, justified in trusting that official to perform such duties honestly. . . .

. . . A director who signs a cheque that appears to be drawn for a legitimate purpose is not responsible for seeing that the money is in fact required for that purpose or that it is subsequently applied for that purpose, assuming, of course, that the cheque comes before him for signature in the regular way having regard to the usual practice of the company. If this were not so, the business of a large company could not be carried on. In the case of an insurance company, for instance, the cheques to be signed at the board meeting would often include cheques in payment of insurance claims. If a claim appears to have been examined into and passed by the manager or other proper official for the purpose, a director who signs the necessary cheque in payment of the claim (the cheque being brought before him in the customary way) cannot be expected to investigate the whole matter over again, for the purpose of satisfying himself that the claim is well founded. A director must of necessity trust to the officials of the company to perform properly and honestly the duties allocated to those officials. In many large companies—it was so in the case of the City Equitable —it is the duty of the manager to pay the salaries and wages of the staff. For that purpose cheques are drawn by the directors in his favour, the exact amounts required being calculated by him. So long as there is nothing suspicious about the amount, the directors are justified in trusting him to calculate it correctly, and to use the proceeds of the cheque for the purpose for which it was drawn. . . .

. . . Before any director actually signs, or at any rate parts with a cheque signed by him, he should satisfy himself that a resolution has been passed by the board, or committee of the board, as the case may be, authorizing the signature of the cheque. In the case where a cheque has to be signed between meetings, he must, of course, obtain the confirmation of the board subsequently to his signature. . . .

. . . It is the duty of each director to see that the company's moneys are from time to time in a proper state of investment, except in so far as the company's articles of association may justify him in delegating that duty to others. . . . If the shareholders had desired to leave hundreds of thousands of pounds of the company's money under the sole control of Bevan, they would have done so. But the shareholders had preferred to have associated with Bevan a board of six or seven other directors, and it was not for these other directors to leave Bevan to discharge one of the most important of the duties that had been entrusted by the shareholders to the board as a whole, however reasonable and however safe it might have seemed to the directors to do so. Still less would it be permissible to leave the control of the company's temporary investments to the general manager. It is not any part of the function of a manager of an insurance company to decide upon the method of investment of the company's cash resources. His advice and assistance will no doubt be sought. But the responsibility for the ultimate decision as to investment must rest with the directors or, when the articles permit, with a committee of the directors. . . .

. . . The list of investments which, in my opinion, the directors should have obtained in connection with and for the purposes of the balance sheet in each year would have been a list that showed in detail all the investments that were lumped together in the balance sheet under general headings, in order that the directors might form some idea for themselves as to whether the total sum brought in as the value of the investments under each general heading was justified for the purpose of the balance sheet and of the dividend that they were recommending. . . .

. . . Having regard to the high reputation that Bevan possessed in the City of London and elsewhere it is not difficult to understand how the respondent directors allowed themselves to be satisfied with the assurances given by him fortified by the certificate of the auditors. As it turned out, the respondent directors were being tricked and defrauded by Bevan and so were the auditors themselves, and neither these directors nor the auditors received from the officials of the company the protection and assistance that they were entitled to expect. For the moment, however, I am only concerned with the respondent directors, and, though I feel considerable sympathy with them in being surrounded by officials whom events have shown to be unreliable, and in being led by a chairman whom events have shown to be a daring and unprincipled scoundrel, I also feel bound to express my opinion that in the particular matter that I am now considering they did less than the law required of them. When presenting their annual report and balance sheet to their shareholders, and when recommending the declaration of a dividend, directors ought not to be satisfied as to the value of their company's assets merely by the assurances of their chairman, even as distinguished and honourable as Bevan appeared at the time to be, nor with the expression of the belief of an auditor as competent and trustworthy as Mr Lepine was and still is. As I have already stated, a list of the company's assets should have been prepared, and this was never done. . . .

. . . But it is not the duty of a director of such a company as the City Equitable to see in person to the safe custody of securities. That is one of the matters which the directors must almost of necessity leave to some official who is at the office daily, such as the manager, accountant or secretary.

NOTES

See also *In re National Bank of Wales Ltd* [1899] 2 Ch 629 at 672 per Lindley MR: '. . . it is plain that directors are not liable for all the mistakes they make, although, if they had taken more care, they might have avoided them. . . . Their negligence must be, not the omission to take all possible care; it must be much more blameable than that; it must be in a sense culpable or gross.'

That reliance on an apparently trustworthy person may be a good defence is expressly recognized by s 284(4) in connection with the keeping of proper accounting records.

See further *Grey v Lewis* (1869) LR 8 Eq 526 (*ultra vires* acts and breach of trust); *In re New Mashonaland Exploration Co* [1892] 3 Ch 577 (directors cannot be held liable for breach of trust unless it can be shown that they did not bona fide exercise their judgment and discretion in what they considered to be the best interests of the company); *Trustees of the Orange River Lead and Asbestos Co v King* (1892) 6 HCG 260; *In re Sharpe* [1892] 1 Ch 154; *Hirsche v Sims* [1894] AC 654 (directors held personally liable for allotting shares at a discount); *In re Kingston Cotton Mill Co (No 2)* [1896] 1 Ch 331; *Lagunas Nitrate Co v Lagunas Syndicate* [1899] 2 Ch 392 (negligence); *Préfontaine v Grenier* [1907] AC 101 (negligence).

The fact that the directors took legal advice will not necessarily protect them from liability. See (1961) 70 *Yale LJ* 987–8, dealing with the standard of care required from directors; also *Boyce NO v Bloem* 1960 (3) SA 855 (T).

On contribution between directors, see *Ashhurst* v *Mason* (1875) LR 20 Eq 225; *Ramskill* v *Edwards* (1885) 31 ChD 100.

On the liability of outside directors for misleading corporate statements under the American Securities Regulations, see *Lanza* v *Drexel & Co* 479 F 2d 1277, noted (1954) 59 *Cornell LR* 728.

As a rule the misconduct of directors is not a ground upon which the court will consider it just and equitable to wind up a company, unless the misconduct has produced insolvency: *In re Anglo-Greek Steamship Co* (1866) LR 2 Eq 1.

Where a company is being wound up or placed under judicial management, and it appears to the court that any business of the company has been carried on with intent to defraud creditors of the company or creditors of any other person or for any fraudulent purpose, the court may declare that any of the company's directors, whether past or present, shall be personally liable without limitation for all or any of the debts or other liabilities of the company, s 424. See also *S v Jousof* 1965 (3) SA 259 (T), where a director was convicted under ss 134(1) and 135(3) of the Insolvency Act 24 of 1936, read with s 185 [now s 425] of the Act, in that he, in managing a company, had failed to keep proper records and had contracted debts without reasonable expectations that the company would be able to discharge them. On sections 424, 425, see below p 719.

[235] Flitcroft's case

(1882) 21 ChD 519

JESSEL MR: ... The facts are these. The directors had for several years been in the habit of laying before the meetings of shareholders reports and balance sheets which were substantially untrue, inasmuch as they included among the assets as good debts a number of debts which they knew to be bad. They thus made it appear that the business had produced profits when in fact it had produced none. The meetings acting on these reports declared dividends which the directors paid. ... A limited company by its memorandum of association declares that its capital is to be applied for the purposes of the business. It cannot reduce its capital except in the manner and with the safeguards provided by statute, and ... it clearly is against the intention of the legislature that any portion of the capital should be returned to the shareholders without the statutory conditions being complied with. A limited company cannot in any other way make a return of capital, the sanction of a general meeting can give no validity to such a proceeding, and even the sanction of every shareholder cannot bring within the powers of the company an act which is not within its powers. If, therefore, the shareholders had all been present at the meetings, and had all known the facts, and had all concurred in declaring the dividends, the payment of the dividends would not be effectually sanctioned. One reason is this — there is a statement that the capital shall be applied for the purposes of the business, and on the faith of that statement, which is sometimes said to be an implied contract with creditors, people dealing with the company give it credit. The creditor has no debtor but that impalpable thing the corporation which has no property except the assets of the business. The creditor, therefore, I may say, gives credit to that capital, gives credit to the company on the faith of the representation that the capital shall be applied only for the purposes of the business, and he has therefore a right to say that the corporation shall keep its capital and not return it to the shareholders, though it may be a right which he cannot enforce otherwise than by a winding-up order. It follows then that if directors who are quasi trustees for the company improperly pay away the assets to the shareholders, they are liable to replace them. It is no answer to say that the shareholders could not compel them to do so. I am of opinion that the company could in its corporate capacity compel them to do so, even if there were no winding-up. . . .

[Directors held jointly and severally liable. See also *Cohen* v *Segal NO*, *84* above, and *333* below.]

[236] R v Milne and Erleigh (7)
1951 (1) SA 791 (AD)
See *32*, pp 57, 58 above.

[237] S v De Jager
1965 (2) SA 616 (AD)

HOLMES JA: I turn now to the appeal by the first appellant (De Jager) in respect of his conviction on count 1.

It alleged the theft of several sums of money by De Jager from FGG over the period January 1961 to June 1962. The trial court held that De Jager was a director of FGG; that, in conspiracy with a co-director, Shaban, he caused payments totalling R22 665 to be paid out of FGG's funds; that such payments were unauthorized and were for his own purposes and not for the benefit of FGG, and constituted theft. The payments and their nature were admitted, but the defence was that there was no theft because De Jager was entitled to a credit of R25 000 in his loan account against which he was entitled to draw, and this exceeded the R22 665 which he had caused to be paid out. In this regard De Jager said in evidence that on 5 June 1961 Shaban sold to FGG his shares in National Castor Industries Ltd for R50 000, and that, by way of payment, it was agreed that the loan account of each of them in FGG was to be credited with R25 000. The trial court did not believe De Jager and found that no such sale ever took place. The correctness of that finding is the first issue in the appeal.

According to the minute book of FGG, De Jager, Shaban, and one Shapero were the directors until 3 June 1961 when they resigned and Strydom and Webb became the new directors. They were the puppets of De Jager and Shaban respectively. To support his evidence of the sale, De Jager relied on a document, exh 261, which was found by the police among the papers of FGG. It purports to reflect the minutes of an extraordinary general meeting of FGG held on 5 June 1961 under the chairmanship of Strydom. It records, *inter alia*, the passing of a resolution to buy from De Jager and Shaban their shares in National Castor Industries Ltd for £25 000.

The trial court regarded this document as a sham. It was not in the minute book. And the court held that Strydom, a humble Railways pensioner who was De Jager's 'stooge', did not preside at any meeting on 5 June 1961 or vote for the 'resolution' referred to in the document.

Now it seems clear, on the evidence, that the ostensible resignation of De Jager and Shaban as directors and the appointment of the puppet directors on 3 June 1961 was a sham, and, *de jure*, can be disregarded. Indeed, this was common cause in argument in this court. De Jager and Shaban continued to control the company and occupied the position of directors and fell within the definition of 'director' in s 229 [now s 1] of the Companies Act. . . .

[The next . . .] submission was that in any event there was in law no theft from FGG because the beneficial shareholders were Shaban and De Jager, who must be taken to have agreed to the abstractions; and therefore in effect the company was a consenting party. Reliance was placed on the decision in *R v Jona* 1961 (2) SA 301 (W). In that case the sole beneficial shareholder and director of a private company had abstracted various amounts for his own purposes and was charged on 20 counts of theft from the company. The trial court acquitted him of theft. One of the reasons was that, on all the evidence, there was a reasonable possibility that the accused bona fide believed that he had the right to take the moneys in the circumstances, especially as he was the sole beneficial shareholder and director. I can find no fault with that reasoning. Another ground for the acquittal was that in law there could be no theft because the owner (the company) acting through the sole beneficial shareholder and director (the accused), consented to the abstractions. . . . The learned judge said:

> 'Now in this case all the shareholders in Continental—all the shareholders being Dr Jona himself—all the directors (all the directors being Dr Jona himself) knew perfectly well that the money was being taken, consented to the money being taken. And the company, as such, in this case, as represented by the whole of its directorate and by the whole of its shareholders, agreed to Dr Jona taking money out of the company. In my view it can never be said in a case such as that that there is theft.'

In the present case FGG was a public company which, according to the evidence, was formed with the object of acquiring shares in and taking an interest in the spheres of banking, insurance, and general finance, with a view to being established as a deposit-receiving institution. It was given permission to operate as such by the Registrar of Banks. De Jager was a director. He abstracted company funds (not in the nature of salary) for his own purposes, not for the benefit of the company.

. . . It is argued that it cannot be theft because the company consented inasmuch as the beneficial shareholders, De Jager and Shaban, must have been agreeable to the payments.

In my view [this] contention cannot succeed. It involves the proposition that De Jager, in his capacity as shareholder, could be a party to the company's agreeing to be despoiled by him in his capacity as director. It also in effect gives a general right to the company to distribute its assets to shareholders. This offends against certain principles of company law basic to the concept of limited liability as introduced by Parliament —at any rate in regard to companies limited by shares, as this one was, namely:

(*a*) The company is a separate legal *persona*, owning the assets.
(*b*) The directors manage the affairs of the company in a fiduciary capacity to it.

(*c*) The shareholders' general right of participation in the assets of the company is deferred until winding-up, and then only subject to the claims of creditors.

Neither shareholders nor directors nor the company itself can violate the foregoing, whatever the memorandum or articles may say.

The appellant's contention is an attempt to have it both ways. On the one hand he would retain the advantage of limited liability as a shareholder. On the other hand he would seek to absolve himself from the fiduciary duty which a director owes to the company, helping himself to its assets via its supposed consent to which he was a party.

To allow this would be to avoid basic legal consequences of incorporation as a company. To combine in substance the common-law advantages of individual ownership with the statutory benefits of limited liability without regard to fiduciary duties as director—this would not be company law at all.

For these reasons I hold that De Jager cannot be heard to say that the fact that he and Shaban were sole beneficial shareholders enabled him as director to use company funds for his own purposes.

As to whether De Jager had a bona fide belief that he could do this, in *Rex* v *Milne and Erleigh* [*236*, above] Centlivres CJ said:

'Indeed it is difficult to imagine that any person of ordinary intelligence would believe that he had a power to despoil a company in relation to which he stood in a fiduciary capacity.'

... In my view the trial court correctly found the first appellant (De Jager) guilty of the theft of R22 665 on count 1, and the appeal against the conviction fails.

RUMPFF JA (dissenting): Fraud may be committed on creditors or on shareholders or on the company by directors, or directors may steal from the company or the majority of shareholders may commit fraud on the minority but I am not aware of any provision whereunder the shareholders of a company commit theft when the company (through a resolution of the shareholders) disposes of its assets in a manner which is not *ultra vires* the memorandum. There is also, in my view, no duty on the shareholders when they meet as shareholders to act in the interests of the company. They can decide what they like—within the objects of the memorandum—and when they decide, the company has decided.

NOTES

R v *Milne and Erleigh 32* above was followed in *R* v *Herholdt* 1957 (3) SA 236 (AD), where the appeal court reaffirmed that directors commit theft if they make out of the company's coffers payments to themselves which they are not authorized to make and which they do not bona fide believe themselves authorized to make. That they look upon these payments as loans which they intend to repay is no defence. In the course of his judgment, Fagan JA said: 'A director's goodwill towards the company of which he is a director is part of the duty which he owes the company by virtue of his being a director. If grateful shareholders vote him a bonus or an increase in salary, or any other form of remuneration or token of their appreciation, well and good; but he cannot use his power as a director, nor can his co-directors use theirs, to give him, out of the company's coffers, underhand benefits to which he is not lawfully entitled in order to retain his goodwill or to reward him for it, any more than a clerk may take money out of the till, or be given it by a fellow-clerk, as an inducement or a reward for serving the firm well' (at 260). See also *George Newman & Co 239* below.

Again, in *S v Berliner* 1966 (4) SA 535 (W) Boshoff J remarked (at 537): 'Where . . . a person takes another's money without authority to do so and intending to consume it, he commits theft, even if he intends to return other money, if it is proved that he did not, when he took it, believe that he had the right to take it or that the owner, had he been consulted, would have consented to its taking. Where the consent that the taker might have relied on is that of an agent of the owner, it must be such as the agent, acting honestly in the interests of his principal and within knowledge of the facts, might have been expected to give.'

See also *EBM Co Ltd v Dominion Bank* [1937] 3 All ER 555 (PC), where a company, acting through its directors, and not by its shareholders in general meeting, had purported to apply its property for the benefit of those directors: also *Curtis's Furnishing Stores Ltd v Freedman* [1966] 2 All ER 955, [1966] 1 WLR 1219.

In the Canadian case of *R v Smith* (1962) 36 DLR (2d) 613 (Ontario Ct of Appeal), where directors of a company had used company funds to purchase shares which they had pledged with a bank to secure an overdraft, it was held that the fact that the accused honestly intended to redeem the shares and pay back the company, and that they actually did so, was no defence.

On theft by directors, see also R C Beuthin (1965) 82 *SALJ* 479.

A director (or other person) may make a misrepresentation to a company even if he makes it through a board of directors all of whom are aware of its falsity. While the knowledge of the directors is in ordinary circumstances the knowledge of the company, this is not so 'if the knowledge of the director is the knowledge of a director who is himself *particeps criminis*, that is, if the knowledge of an infringement of the right of the company is only brought home to the man who himself was the artificer of such infringement', per Viscount Dunedin in *J C Houghton & Co v Nothard, Lowe & Wills* [1928] AC 1 at 14, quoted with approval by Hoexter AJ in *R v Kritzinger* 1971 (2) SA 57 (AD) at 59, 60.

On fraud (civil or criminal) by director on company, see further *S v Isaacs* 1968 (2) SA 187 (N); *Woomack v Commercial Vehicles Spares (Pvt) Ltd* 1968 (3) SA 419 (R); *S v Ressel* 1968 (4) SA 224 (AD); also *Reg v Sinclair* [1968] 3 All ER 241, [1968] 1 WLR 1246 (misuse of company's funds).

On the liability of a director for wrongful acts committed by his fellow directors, see *Land Credit Company of Ireland v Lord Fermoy* (1870) 5 Ch App 763 (director not liable for fraud committed by other directors without his knowledge); *Cargill v Bower* (1878) 10 ChD 502 (director not liable for fraud committed by other directors unless he either expressly authorized or tacitly permitted its commission); *Barlow v The Friend PP Co Ltd* 1909 ORC 110.

(c) Fiduciary Duties

[238] S *v* Heller
1971 (2) SA 29 (AD)

HOLMES JA: The meaning and effect of that legal principle is, we think, really this: the agent's authority and hence his duty is to act *solely* for the benefit of his principal. For if he were allowed to act for the principal's and also his own or another's benefit, situations could easily arise in which his duty to his principal might conflict with his interest to serve himself or the other person; and it is the policy of the law, in sustaining the fiduciary relationship between the parties, to avoid and not to encourage or facilitate such situations. Hence, unless otherwise agreed, the agent is not authorized so to act. . . . That his principal is not prejudiced by his so acting is irrelevant; the position simply is that the agent's act falls outside the ambit of what his principal bargained for. *Story on Agency* 9 ed sums up that position lucidly in s 210 by saying:

'This rule (that agents cannot bind their principals where they have an adverse interest in themselves) is founded upon the plain and obvious consideration, that the principal bargains, in the employment, for the exercise of the disinterested skill, diligence, and zeal of the agent, for *his own exclusive benefit*. It is a confidence necessarily reposed in the agent, that he will act with a *sole regard* to the interests of his principal, as far as he lawfully may; and, even if impartiality could possibly be presumed on the part of an agent, where his own interests were concerned, that is not what the principal bargains for. . . .'

(Our italics.)

On the other hand, the fact that the agent or a third person also derives a benefit from the agent's act does not necessarily mean that this act is unauthorized, for apart from cases where that is actually within the parties' agreement, it might be merely an inevitable or incidental consequence of the agent's duly performing his mandate with the sole intention of benefiting his principal. To take a simple but apposite example: that a managing director of a company also derives an advantage as a shareholder thereof from a transaction which he duly carries out on its behalf and for its benefit obviously would not render his act unauthorized.

[239] *In re* George Newman & Co
[1895] 1 Ch 674

Mr Newman was the chairman of a private company in which he and his family held substantially all the shares. On behalf of the company he purchased the right to a building agreement to be obtained from a third party. The party objected to the company as a tenant and proposed to substitute Mr Newman. Mr Newman thereupon sold the benefit of the agreement to the company at an advance of £10 000, £3 000 of which he applied for his own use. A further £3 500 was spent by him out of the assets of the company upon his private house. The payments were made out of money borrowed by the company for the purposes of the business. All these transactions were sanctioned by resolutions of the directors and informally approved by the shareholders.

The company went into liquidation and the official receiver and liquidator claimed from Mr Newman a refund of the sums of £3 000 and £3 500. The action succeeded.

LINDLEY J: . . . The presents made by the directors to Mr Newman, their chairman, were made out of money borrowed by the company for the purposes of its business; and this money the directors had no right to apply in making presents to one of themselves. The transaction was a breach of trust by the whole of them; and even if all the shareholders could have sanctioned it, they never did so in such a way as to bind the company. It is true that this company was a small one and what is called a private company; but its corporate capacity cannot be ignored. Those who form such companies obtain great advantages, but accompanied by some disadvantages. A registered company cannot do anything which all its members think expedient, and which, apart from the law relating to incorporated companies, they might lawfully do. An incorporated company's assets are its property and not the property of the shareholders for the time being; and, if the directors misapply those assets by applying them to purposes for which they cannot be lawfully applied by the company itself, the company can make them liable for such misapplication as soon as any one properly sets the company in motion. All this is familiar law and must be borne in mind in deciding the present case. Mr George Newman and his co-directors evidently ignored their legal position entirely. They regarded Mr George Newman as the company, and it never seems to have occurred to them that he and his brothers could not do as they liked with what they regarded as their own property, or rather as his, for he and his children held the bulk of the shares. . . . Directors have no right to be paid for their services, and cannot pay themselves or each other, or make presents to themselves out of the company's assets, unless authorized so to do by the instrument which regulates the company or by the shareholders at a properly convened meeting. The shareholders, at a meeting duly convened for the purpose, can, if they think proper, remunerate directors for their trouble or make presents to them for their services out of assets properly divisible among the shareholders themselves. Further, if the company is a going concern, the majority can bind the minority in such a matter as this. But to make presents out of profits is one thing and to make them out of capital or out of money borrowed by the company is a very different matter. Such money cannot be lawfully divided among the shareholders themselves, nor can it be given away by them for nothing to their directors so as to bind the company in its corporate capacity. . . .

NOTES

See also *Brown v Nanco (Pty) Ltd* 1976 (3) SA 832 (W).

[240] Parker *v* McKenna
(1874) 10 Ch App 96

A company having passed resolutions to increase its capital by the issue of new shares, the directors entered into an agreement with a certain Mr Stock for him to take at a premium all the shares not taken up by the existing shareholders. When Mr Stock proved unable to take all the shares which he was supposed to take under this agreement, the directors took over from him considerable numbers of shares at the agreed price and afterwards disposed of them at a profit. It was held that they were liable to account to the company for these profits.

LORD CAIRNS LC: . . . Now, the rule of this court, as I understand it, as to agents, is not a technical or arbitrary rule. It is a rule founded upon the highest and truest principles of morality. No man can in this court, acting as an agent, be allowed to put himself into a position in which his interest and his duty will be in conflict. If Stock had bought these shares and paid for them, and become the absolute owner of them, the directors were as free as any person in the market to go to Stock and to become the purchasers from him of those shares. The agency in that case would have been over, and there would have been no longer any conflict between interest and duty. Here the agency had not terminated. The court will not inquire, and is not in a position to ascertain, whether the bank has lost or not lost by the acts of the directors. All that the court has to do is to examine whether a profit has been made by an agent, without the knowledge of his principal, in the course and execution of his agency. . . .

[241] Boston Deep Sea Fishing and Ice Company v Ansell
(1888) 39 ChD 339

The defendant was the managing director of the plaintiff company. He contracted on behalf of the company for the construction of certain fishing-smacks, and, unknown to the company, took a commission from the shipbuilders. The defendant was also a shareholder in an ice company and a fish-carrying company which paid, in addition to the ordinary dividends, bonuses to shareholders who were owners of fishing-smacks and employed the companies. The defendant employed these companies for the plaintiff's smacks but received the bonuses for himself.

Held: (a) that the receipt of a commission from the shipbuilding company was a good ground for the dismissal of the defendant from office; and (b) that he had to account to the plaintiff company for the bonuses received from the ice and carrying companies.

Bowen LJ: . . . I will, first of all, deal with what is the cardinal matter of the whole case; whether the plaintiffs were justified or not in dismissing their managing director as they did. This is an age, I may say, when a large portion of the commercial world makes its livelihood by earning, and by earning honestly, agency commission on sales or other transactions, but it is also a time when a large portion of those who move within the ambit of the commercial world, earn, I am afraid, commission dishonestly by taking commissions not merely from their masters, but from the other parties with whom their master is negotiating, and with whom they are dealing on behalf of their master, and taking such commissions without the knowledge of their master or principal. There never, therefore, was a time in the history of our law when it was more essential that courts of justice should draw with precision and firmness the line of demarcation which prevails between commissions which may be honestly received and kept, and commissions taken behind the master's back, and in fraud of the master. . . .

. . . There can be no question that an agent employed by a principal or master to do business with another, who, unknown to that principal or master, takes from that other person a profit arising out of the business which he is employed to transact, is doing a wrongful act inconsistent with his duty towards his master, and the continuance of confidence between them. He does the wrongful act whether such profit be given to him in return for services which he actually performs for the third party, or whether it be given to him for his supposed influence, or whether it be given to him on any other ground at all; if it is a profit which arises out of the transaction, it belongs to his master, and the agent or servant has no right to take it, or keep it, or bargain for it, or to receive it without bargain, unless his master knows it. . .

[242] **Robinson *v* Randfontein Estates Gold Mining Company Ltd**
1921 AD 168

By the beginning of the century large mineral interests in the farms Randfontein, Uitvalfontein and Waterval were held by a number of associated companies, all members of the Robinson group, of which the Randfontein Estates Gold Mining Company Ltd, the plaintiff, was the principal or parent company. The defendant was the chairman of the board of directors of the plaintiff company.

The plaintiff company's interest in the farm Waterval took the form of a lease of the mineral rights. The defendant, as director of the plaintiff company, would have preferred to purchase the farm for the company, but he could not come to terms with its owner.

Later the defendant, through an agent, bought an undivided half-share of Waterval for £60 000 and sold it soon after for £275 000 to the Waterval Trust Company, a concern formed by the plaintiff company for the purpose of acquiring and holding, for a brief space, the farm Waterval. All its shares were held by the plaintiff company and the price of £275 000 was paid to the defendant by draft drawn on the plaintiff company. The court held that the plaintiff company was entitled to claim from the defendant the profit of £215 000 made by him on this transaction.

INNES CJ: . . . Where one man stands to another in a position of confidence involving a duty to protect the interests of that other, he is not allowed to make a secret profit at the other's expense or place himself in a position where his interests conflict with his duty. The principle underlies an extensive field of legal relationship. A guardian to his ward, a solicitor to his client, an agent to his principal afford examples of persons occupying such a position. As was pointed out in *The Aberdeen Railway Company* v *Blaikie Bros* (1854) 2 Eq Rep 1281 (HL), *248* below, the doctrine is to be found in the civil law (*Digest* 18.1.34.7), and must of necessity form part of every civilized system of jurisprudence. It prevents an agent from properly entering into any transaction which would cause his interests and his duty to clash. If employed to buy, he cannot sell his own property; if employed to sell, he cannot buy his own property; nor can he make any profit from his agency save the agreed remuneration; all such profit belongs not to him, but to his principal. There is only one way by which such transaction can be validated, and that is by the free consent of the principal following upon a full disclosure by the agent. In such a case the special relationship *quoad* that transaction falls away and the parties deal at arm's length with one another. The general doctrine is clear enough; but the remedies available to a principal who discovers that he has purchased his agent's own property depend upon considerations of some nicety. Obviously he is not bound by the contract unless he chooses; he may elect therefore either to repudiate or confirm it. But, if he wishes it to stand and also claims the resulting profit, he must show that such profit arises from transactions completely covered by the prohibitive operation of the relationship. . . . Now the question of the remedies available against a director who, without due disclosure, disposes of his own property to his company has been dealt with in a number of comparatively recent English decisions. . . . It is clear from these decisions that, in every such inquiry, regard must be had to the relationship in which the director stood to the company when he acquired the property. The test is, not what honour would dictate, but what the law will allow. And that depends upon his duty to the company at the date of acquisition. If he was under no obligation at that time to acquire the property for the company, instead of for himself, then his non-disclosure would entitle it to repudiate the sale and restore the original position because, as already explained, the transaction could not bind the company without its free consent. It could affirm the contract, but only by an acquiescence in its terms. The acquisition being untainted by any breach of duty, the company's only claim to the subject-matter would be based on the contract. It could not seek to retain the property at a price reduced by a deduction of the director's profit. For that would amount to a new contract between the parties. When, however, the director's default extends further than non-disclosure, when a breach of duty attended the original acquisition, then the company may, if it chooses, retain the property purchased and also demand a refund of the profits. . . . The test is expressed, for the most part, in terms peculiar to the English law; but the principle which underlies it is not foreign to our own. For it rests upon the broad doctrine that a man, who stands in a position of trust towards another, cannot, in matters affected by that position, advance his own interests (eg by making a profit) at that other's expense. An examination of what is involved in the remedy explains its principle. The director, in the case assumed, intends to acquire the property for himself alone; he has no idea of acquiring the equitable ownership for the company. No such *animus* enters into the transaction. His sole object is to secure the *dominium* in order to resell to the company at a profit. But the law refuses to give effect to that intention; it treats the acquisition as one made in the interests of the company. That can only be because it was a duty of the director to acquire the property for the company, if he acquired it at all. Its acquisition for himself would, under the circumstances, be a breach of faith which the courts will not allow him to set up. . . . But even if the relationship between the defendant and the company could not be fitly described as one of agent and principal, I should still hold that it was fiduciary. I had occasion in *Hull* v *Turf Mines Ltd* 1906 TS 68 to remark upon the anomalous and undesirable positions which arise in the working of the group system. It is a system much in vogue in the Transvaal, and it exists in the present instance under the new regime as it did under the old. It involves the management and direction of the policy and affairs of the various companies by some controlling authority through nominee directors. Whether the control is exercised by a man who is himself a director or by someone outside makes little difference in principle. In either case the system is peculiarly liable to abuse. Unless the board is moulded to the will of the controlling authority the system cannot work. An independent set of directors would be fatal. Hence the temptation to deprive the nominees of all discretion until, as in the present case, they are completely under the thumb of the controlling authority and it is practically impossible for them to exercise an independent judgment. There may be something to be said for that position from the point of view of administrative efficiency. But it carries its own danger. Power thus obtained involves a corresponding responsibility. A man, who procures the election of a board of directors under circumstances which make it impossible for them to exercise an independent judgment, must, in my opinion, observe the utmost good faith in his dealings with the company, which he has, of set purpose, deprived of independent advice. The duty to do so arises from the circumstances which he has chosen to bring about. And it is wholly inconsistent with the obligations of good faith that the defendant should have made for himself these profits by the method which the evidence discloses. That being so, he ought not to be allowed to retain them — whether he can accurately be described as an agent of the company when he acquired the property or not. . . .

[See also *Robinson* v *Randfontein Estates Gold Mining Co Ltd* 1923 AD 155.]

[243] **Regal (Hastings) Ltd** *v* **Gulliver**
[1942] 1 All ER 378

Regal (Hastings) Ltd owned a cinema. The directors decided to acquire two other cinemas with a view to the sale of the undertaking of the company as a going concern. For this purpose they formed a subsidiary company ('Amalgamated') with a capital of £5 000 in £1 shares. The owner of the two cinemas offered them a lease but required a personal guarantee of the rent by the directors unless the paid-up capital of the subsidiary company was £5 000. As the directors wished to avoid giving the guarantee, Regal (Hastings) subscribed for 2 000 shares in the subsidiary at par and the remaining 3 000 shares were taken at par by the directors and their friends, Regal (Hastings) being unable to take more than 2 000 shares. Ultimately the sale of the three cinemas was carried through by the sale of all the shares in the company and the subsidiary. The shares in 'Amalgamated' which had been taken by the directors were sold by them at a profit of £2 16s 1d per share. Regal successfully sued them for this profit.

LORD RUSSELL OF KILLOWEN: We have to consider the question of the respondents' liability on the footing that, in taking up these shares in Amalgamated, they acted with bona fides, intending to act in the interest of Regal.

Nevertheless, they may be liable to account for the profits which they have made, if, while standing in a fiduciary relationship to Regal, they have by reason and in course of that fiduciary relationship made a profit. . . .

The rule of equity which insists on those, who by use of a fiduciary position make a profit, being liable to account for that profit, in no way depends on fraud, or absence of bona fides; or upon such questions or considerations as whether the profit would or should otherwise have gone to the plaintiff, or whether the profiteer was under a duty to obtain the source of the profit for the plaintiff, or whether he took a risk or acted as he did for the benefit of the plaintiff, or whether the plaintiff has in fact been damaged or benefited by his action. The liability arises from the mere fact of a profit having, in the stated circumstances, been made. The profiteer, however honest and well-intentioned, cannot escape the risk of being called upon to account.

... My Lords, I have no hesitation in coming to the conclusion, upon the facts of this case, that these shares, when acquired by the directors, were acquired by reason and only by reason of the fact that they were directors of Regal, and in the course of their execution of that office. ...

... The directors standing in a fiduciary relationship to Regal in regard to the exercise of their powers as directors, and having obtained these shares by reason and only by reason of the fact that they were directors of Regal and in the course of the execution of that office, are accountable for the profits which they have made out of them. The equitable rule laid down in *Keech* v *Sandford* (1726) Sel Cas Ch 61, and *Ex parte James* (1803) 8 Ves 337, and similar authorities applies to them in full force. It was contended that these cases were distinguishable by reason of the fact that it was impossible for Regal to get the shares owing to lack of funds, and that the directors in taking the shares were really acting as members of the public. I cannot accept this argument. ... The suggestion that the directors were applying simply as members of the public is a travesty of the facts. They could, had they wished, have protected themselves by a resolution (either antecedent or subsequent) of the Regal shareholders in general meeting. ...

LORD MACMILLAN: The sole ground on which it was sought to render [the defendants] accountable was that, being directors of the plaintiff company and therefore in a fiduciary relationship to it, they entered in the course of their management into a transaction in which they utilized the position and knowledge possessed by them in virtue of their office as directors, and that the transaction resulted in a profit to themselves.

The issue thus becomes one of fact. The plaintiff company has to establish two things: (i) that what the directors did was so related to the affairs of the company that it can properly be said to have been done in the course of their management and in utilization of their opportunities and special knowledge as directors; and (ii) that what they did resulted in a profit to themselves.

LORD PORTER: The legal proposition may, I think, be broadly stated by saying that one occupying a position of trust must not make a profit which he can acquire only by use of his fiduciary position, or, if he does, he must account for the profit so made.

Directors, no doubt, are not trustees, but they occupy a fiduciary position towards the company whose board they form. Their liability in this respect does not depend upon breach of duty but upon the proposition that a director must not make a profit out of property acquired by reason of his relationship to the company of which he is director. It matters not that he could not have acquired the property for the company itself—the profit which he makes is the company's, even though the property by means of which he made it was not and could not have been acquired on its behalf. . . .

[It will be realized that in 'disgorging their profits' the former directors in fact had to pay them over to the purchasers of the cinemas who were by now in control of the company. In the result the purchasers achieved a reduction of the purchase price by the profit made by the former directors on the sale of their shares in the subsidiary company to them. The chairman of the directors, who did not take the shares beneficially, was held not liable to repay the profits made by those who took the shares from him, as the latter were not in a fiduciary relationship to the company.]

[244] **Peso Silver Mines Ltd (NPL)** *v* **Cropper**
(1966) 58 DLR (2d) 1 (Supreme Court of Canada)

Peso Silver Mines was incorporated as a private company in March 1961 and converted into a public company later that year. In April 1961 the defendant was appointed as its managing director. Early in 1962 a certain Dr A, consulting geologist for Peso, told the Peso directors, including the defendant, that several claims held by one Dickson, a prospector, could be acquired by Peso. All the claims were in the near vicinity of the claims held by Peso. Peso's board of directors decided that it was inadvisable for Peso to acquire the claims, mainly because its financial resources at the time were somewhat strained. Subsequently, the defendant, Dr A, and two other directors of Peso, purchased the claims from D at the price at which they had been offered to Peso, and caused a new private company, Cross Bow Mines Ltd, to be formed to take them over. A public company, Mayo Silver Mines Ltd, was then incorporated to develop the claims held by Cross Bow Mines Ltd.

The control of Peso changed, and the new directors fell out with the defendant, who was dismissed. Peso now sued the defendant to account to the company for the shares held by him in Cross Bow Mines Ltd and Mayo Silver Mines Ltd. The action was dismissed by the court of first instance. This was affirmed, on appeal, by the British Columbia Court of Appeal (Norris JA dissenting), and, on further appeal, by the Supreme Court of Canada.

CARTWRIGHT J (who delivered the judgment of the Supreme Court of Canada, after quoting extensively from *Regal (Hastings)* (*243*, above), said:

On the facts of the case at bar I find it impossible to say that the respondent obtained the interests he holds in Cross Bow and Mayo by reason of the fact that he was a director of the appellant and in the course of the execution of that office.

When Dickson, at Dr A's suggestion, offered his claims to the appellant it was the duty of the respondent as director to take part in the decision of the board as to whether that offer should be accepted or rejected.

At that point he stood in a fiduciary relationship to the appellant. There are affirmative findings of fact that he and his co-directors acted in good faith, solely in the interests of the appellant and with sound business reasons in rejecting the offer. There is no suggestion in the evidence that the offer to the appellant was accompanied by any confidential information unavailable to any prospective purchaser or that the respondent as director had access to any such information by reason of his office. When, later, Dr A approached the appellant it was not in his capacity as a director of the appellant, but as an individual member of the public whom Dr A was seeking to interest as a co-adventurer.

The judgments in the *Regal* case in the court of appeal are not reported but counsel were good enough to furnish us with copies. In the course of his reasons Lord Greene MR said:

'To say that the company was entitled to claim the benefit of those shares would involve this proposition: Where a board of directors considers an investment which is offered to their company and bona fide comes to the conclusion that it is not an investment which their company ought to make, any director, after that resolution is come to and bona fide come to, who chooses to put up the money for that investment himself must be treated as having done it on behalf of the company, so that the company can claim any profit that results to him from it. That is a proposition for which no particle of authority was cited; and goes, as it seems to me, far beyond anything that has ever been suggested as to the duty of directors, agents, or persons in a position of that kind.'

In the House of Lords, Lord Russell of Killowen concluded his reasons, at 391, with the following paragraph:

'One final observation I desire to make. In his judgment Lord Greene MR stated that a decision adverse to the directors in the present case involved the proposition that, if directors bona fide decide not to invest their company's funds in some proposed investment, a director who thereafter embarks his own money therein is accountable for any profits which he may derive therefrom. As to this, I can only say that to my mind the facts of this hypothetical case bear but little resemblance to the story with which we have had to deal. . . .'

If the members of the House of Lords in *Regal* had been of the view that in the hypothetical case stated by Lord Greene the director would have been liable to account to the company, the elaborate examination of the facts contained in the speech of Lord Russell of Killowen would have been unnecessary.

The facts of the case at bar appear to me in all material respects identical with those in the hypothetical case stated by Lord Greene and I share the view which he expressed that in such circumstances the director is under no liability. I agree with the conclusion of the learned trial judge and of the majority in the court of appeal that the action fails.

[Norris JA in his dissenting judgment in *Peso Silver Mines* in the lower court ((1966) 56 DLR (2d) 117) said: 'It is clear from . . . the evidence, that at the time of the acquisition of the claims the respondent [and his fellow director] in substance acknowledged and were aware that:

(1) the information as to the claims came to them in the course of and in the execution of their duties as directors;

(2) in that sense the information was "confidential";

(3) they owned a duty to the shareholders to "protect" their interests in respect of the potential value of the claims;

(4) whatever action was taken with regard to the claims must be taken on behalf of the Peso shareholders;

(5) they were consequently trustees for the shareholders;

(6) they had a duty to account to the shareholders in respect of the claims.

'I propose now to deal shortly with a number of points argued by counsel for the respondent:

(1) That there was no secret profit.

Lord Wright in the *Regal* case deals with this matter as follows ([1942] 1 All ER) at 392: "The rule in such cases is compendiously expressed to be that an agent must account for net profits secretly (that is, without the knowledge of his principal) acquired by him in the course of his agency. . . ."

'There is no doubt that the profit here was acquired without the knowledge and assent of the shareholders.

(2) That the information was not "confidential".

The evidence shows that the information was acquired by the respondent in the course of the execution of his duties as managing director. . . .

(3) That the learned trial judge was correct in his statement as follows:

". . . I find as a fact that the defendant was not only able to acquire the property without . . . making . . . use of confidential information he acquired in the course of the exercise of his office as a director . . . but that there was no evidence to suggest that D made his offer only to the plaintiff's directors or that he made his offer to them first."

'In my opinion the onus was on the respondent to show that the transaction was one into which he could properly enter.

'In my opinion the appellant has satisfied the burden of proof on it and the respondent has failed to meet the onus on him.

'Whether or not "it was . . . fortuitous" that the appellant's geologist referred the claims to the company was, in this case, quite irrelevant. The information was disclosed to the appellant's directors by its geologist and thus became confidential . . .

(4) . . . [dealing with the credibility of the witnesses].

(5) Some argument was presented to the effect that because of the complexity of modern business, modern practice and the modern way of life, the strict rule laid down in the *Regal* and other cases should not be applied.

'With the greatest respect, it seems to me that the complexities of modern business are a very good reason why the rule should be enforced strictly in order that such complexities may not be used as a smoke screen or shield behind which fraud might be perpetrated. The argument is purely and simply an irrelevant argument of expediency as to what the law should be, not what it is. It might as well be said that such an argument if given effect to would open the door to fraud, and weaken the confidence which ordinary people should have in dealing with corporate bodies. In order that people may be assured of their protection against improper acts of trustees it is necessary that their activities be circumscribed within rigid limits. No great hardship is imposed on directors by the enforcement of the rule, as a very simple course is available to them which they may follow. As Lord Russell of Killowen said in the *Regal* case at 389:

"[*The directors*] *could, had they wished, have protected themselves by a resolution (either antecedent or subsequent) of the Regal shareholders in general meeting. In default of such approval, the liability to account must remain.*"]

[245] Industrial Development Consultants Ltd *v* Cooley
[1972] 1 WLR 443, [1972] 2 All ER 162

The defendant, an architect, had been managing director of the plaintiff company, which offered comprehensive construction services, such as engineering, architecture and project management services. Following his appointment, the defendant had sought to obtain design and supervision contracts for the plaintiff company from the Eastern Gas Board in connection with four depots the latter planned to build. The Eastern Gas Board indicated to the defendant that they were not prepared to do business with the plaintiff company but that they were prepared to engage the defendant personally. Thereupon, the defendant resigned his appointment with the plaintiff company, on the pretext of ill-health, and accepted the work from the Eastern Gas Board. The defendant was held liable to account to the plaintiff company for all benefits accruing under the contract with the Eastern Gas Board.

ROSKILL J: [The plaintiffs] . . . say that his [the defendant's] duty required him to obtain that business for and only for the plaintiffs. Put in another way, the plaintiffs say he allowed his duty and his interests to conflict. His duty, they say, required him to seek and obtain this work for the plaintiffs while his financial interests required him, or led him to believe that it was in his interest, to obtain that selfsame work for his own benefit. They say that he set about a deliberate policy of obtaining that contract for himself when his duty required him to obtain it for the plaintiffs and, as a result, he became in gross breach of what the plaintiffs claim to have been his fiduciary duty to them, thus rendering himself accountable to them for the profits resulting from that breach of fiduciary duty which the plaintiffs claim at all material times he was under.

The defendant by way of defence says that that claim for an account is unfounded. Counsel for the defendant has argued that at no time was there any fiduciary duty or any breach of such duty of which the defendant was guilty. He says with force that if there is any remedy that remedy lies in damages; it is not a remedy enforceable by way of relief in the nature of an account. As regards any possible claim for damages, counsel says that the plaintiffs have not suffered any damage because they would never themselves have got the work which the defendant got for himself. It is further contended there was no breach of any duty, fiduciary or otherwise, when the defendant obtained this highly valuable work for himself.

The first matter that has to be considered is whether or not the defendant was in a fiduciary relationship with his principals, the plaintiffs. Counsel for the defendant argued that he was not because he received this information which was communicated to him privately. With respect, I think that argument is wrong. The defendant had one capacity and one capacity only in which he was carrying on business at that time. That capacity was as managing director of the plaintiffs. Information which came to him while he was managing director and which was of concern to the plaintiffs and was relevant for the plaintiffs to know, was information which it was his duty to pass on to the plaintiffs because between himself and the plaintiffs a fiduciary relationship existed.

Therefore, I feel impelled to the conclusion that when the defendant embarked on this course of conduct of getting information on 13 June, using that information and preparing those documents over the weekend of 14/15 June and sending them off on 17 June, he was guilty of putting himself into the position in which his duty to his employers, the plaintiffs, and his own private interests conflicted and conflicted grievously. There being the fiduciary relationship I have described it seems to me plain that it was his duty once he got the information to pass it to his employers and not to guard it for his own personal purposes and profit. He put himself into the position when his duty and his interests conflicted.

Does accountability arise? It is said: 'Well, even if there were that conflict of duty and interest, none the less, this was a contract with a third party in which the plaintiffs never could have had any interest because they would have never got it.' That argument has been forcefully put before me by counsel for the defendant.

The remarkable position then arises that if one applies the equitable doctrine on which the plaintiffs rely to oblige the defendant to account, they will receive a benefit which on Mr Smettom's evidence at least it is unlikely they would have got for themselves had the defendant complied with his duty to them. On the other hand, if the defendant is not required to account he will have made a large profit as a result of having deliberately put himself into a position in which his duty to the plaintiffs who were employing him and his personal interests conflicted. I leave out of account the fact that he dishonestly tricked Mr Hicks into releasing him on 16 June although counsel for the plaintiffs urged that that was another reason why equity must compel him to disgorge his profit. It is said that the plaintiffs' only remedy is to sue for damages either for breach of contract or maybe for fraudulent misrepresentation. Counsel for the plaintiffs has been at pains to disclaim any intention to claim damages for breach of contract save on one basis only and he has disclaimed specifically any claim for damages for fraudulent misrepresentation. Therefore, if the plaintiffs succeed they will get a profit which they probably would not have got for themselves had the defendant fulfilled his duty. If the defendant is allowed to keep that profit he will have got something which he was able to get solely by reason of his breach of fiduciary duty to the plaintiffs.

When one looks at the way the cases have gone over the centuries it is plain that the question whether or not the benefit would have been obtained but for the breach of trust has always been treated as irrelevant.

In one sense the benefit in this case did not arise because of the defendant's directorship; indeed, the defendant would not have got this work had he remained a director. However, one must . . . look at the passages in the speeches in *Regal*, having regard to the facts of that case to which those passages and those statements were directed. I think counsel for the plaintiffs was right when he said that it is the basic principle which matters. It is an overriding principle of equity that a man must not be allowed to put himself in a position in which his fiduciary duty and his interests conflict. The variety of cases where that can happen is infinite. The fact there has not previously been a case precisely of this nature with precisely similar facts before the courts is of no import. The facts of this case are, I think, exceptional and I hope unusual. They seem to me plainly to come with this principle.

[For comments on *Cooley*, see D D Prentice (1972) 50 *Can BR* 623; H Rajak (1972) 35 *MLR* 655; J G Collier (1972) 30 *Camb LJ* 222; A Yoran (1973) 89 *LQR* 187].

[246] Canadian Aero Service Ltd *v* O'Malley
(1974) 40 DLR (3d) 371 (SCC)

The plaintiff company offered mapping and geophysical exploration services, mainly to governments, either governments requiring the services directly or governments sponsoring these services for other governments as part of foreign aid programmes. The two defendants had been directors of the plaintiff company and had been involved in carrying out preparatory work for the plaintiff in connection with a project in Guyana. The Canadian government later invited the plaintiff company and others to submit tenders for this project. At this time, the defendants resigned their offices with the plaintiff company, and formed their own surveying company, which sought, and was awarded, the contract. The defendants were held liable to the plaintiff company for loss of the contract.

LASKIN J: I do not think it matters whether O'Malley and Zarzycki were properly appointed as directors of Canaero or whether they did or did not act as directors. What is not in doubt is that they acted respectively as president and executive vice-president of Canaero for about two years prior to their resignations. To paraphrase the findings of the trial judge in this respect, they acted in those positions and their remuneration and responsibilities verified their status as senior officers of Canaero. They were 'top management' and not mere employees whose duty to their employer, unless enlarged by contract, consisted only of respect for trade secrets and for confidentiality of customer lists. Theirs was a larger, more exacting duty which, unless modified by statute or by contract (and there is nothing of this sort here), was similar to that owed to a corporate employer by its directors. I adopt what is said on this point by Gower *Principles of Modern Company Law* 3 ed (1969) at 518 as follows:

'... these duties, except in so far as they depend on statutory provisions expressly limited to directors, are not so restricted but apply equally to any officials of the company who are authorized to act on its behalf, and in particular to those acting in a managerial capacity.'

It follows that O'Malley and Zarzycki stood in a fiduciary relationship to Canaero, which in its generality betokens loyalty, good faith and avoidance of a conflict of duty and self-interest. Descending from the generality, the fiduciary relationship goes at least this far: a director or a senior officer like O'Malley or Zarzycki is precluded from obtaining for himself, either secretly or without the approval of the company (which would have to be properly manifested upon full disclosure of the facts), any property or business advantage either belonging to the company or for which it has been negotiating; and especially is this so where the director or officer is a participant in the negotiations on behalf of the company.

An examination of the case law in this court and in the courts of other like jurisdictions on the fiduciary duties of directors and senior officers shows the pervasiveness of a strict ethic in this area of the law. In my opinion, this ethic disqualifies a director or senior officer from usurping for himself or diverting to another person or company with whom or with which he is associated a maturing business opportunity which his company is actively pursuing; he is also precluded from so acting even after his resignation where the resignation may fairly be said to have been prompted or influenced by a wish to acquire for himself the opportunity sought by the company, or where it was his position with the company rather than a fresh initiative that led him to the opportunity which he later acquired.

[After citing from *Regal (Hastings) Ltd* v *Gulliver* [*243* above], Laskin J continued:]

I need not pause to consider whether on the facts in *Regal (Hastings) Ltd* v *Gulliver* the equitable principle was over-zealously applied; see for example Gower op cit at 535–7. What I would observe is that the principle, or, indeed, principles, as stated, grew out of older cases concerned with fiduciaries other than directors or managing officers of a modern corporation, and I do not therefore regard them as providing a rigid measure whose literal terms must be met in assessing succeeding cases. In my opinion, neither the conflict test, referred to by Viscount Sankey, nor the test of accountability for profits acquired by reason only of being directors and in the course of execution of the office, reflected in the passage quoted from Lord Russell of Killowen, should be considered as the exclusive touchstones of liability. In this, as in other branches of the law, new fact situations may require a reformulation of existing principle to maintain its vigour in the new setting.

The reaping of a profit by a person at a company's expense while a director thereof is, of course, an adequate ground upon which to hold the director accountable. Yet there may be situations where a profit must be disgorged, although not gained at the expense of the company, on the ground that a director must not be allowed to use his position as such to make a profit even if it was not open to the company, as for example, by reason of legal disability, to participate in the transaction. An analogous situation, albeit not involving a director, existed for all practical purposes in the case of *Boardman et al* v *Phipps* [[1967] AC 46], which also supports the view that liability to account does not depend on proof of an actual conflict of duty and self-interest. Another, quite recent, illustration of a liability to account where the company itself had failed to obtain a business contract and hence could not be regarded as having been deprived of a business opportunity is *Industrial Development Consultants Ltd* v *Cooley* a judgment of a court of first instance [*245* above].

What these decisions indicate is an updating of the equitable principle whose roots lie in the general standards that I have already mentioned, namely, loyalty, good faith and avoidance of a conflict of duty and self-interest. Strict application against directors and senior management officials is simply recognition of the degree of control which their positions give them in corporate operations, a control which rises above day accountability to owning shareholders and which comes under some scrutiny only at annual general or at special meetings. It is a necessary supplement, in the public interest, of statutory regulation and account-ability which themselves are, at one and the same time, an acknowledg-ment of the importance of the corporation in the life of the community and of the need to compel obedience by it and by its promoters, directors and managers to norms of exemplary behaviour.

Counsel for O'Malley and Zarzycki relied upon the judgment of this court in *Peso Silver Mines Ltd* (*NPL*) v *Cropper* [*244* above], as representing affirmation of what was said in *Regal* (*Hastings*) *Ltd* v *Gulliver* respecting the circumscription of liability to circumstances where the directors or senior officers had obtained the challenged benefit by reason only of the fact that they held those positions and in the course of execution of those offices. In urging this, he did not deny that leaving to capitalize on their positions would not necessarily immunize them, but he submitted that in the present case there was no special knowledge or information obtained from Canaero during their service with that company upon which O'Malley and Zarzycki had relied in reaching for the Guyana project on behalf of Terra.

There is a considerable gulf between the *Peso* case and the present one on the facts as found in each and on the issues that they respectively raise. In *Peso*, there was a finding of good faith in the rejection by its directors of an offer of mining claims because of its strained finances. The subsequent acquisition of those claims by the managing director and his associates, albeit without seeking shareholder approval, was held to be proper because the company's interest in them ceased. What is before this court is not a situation where various opportunities were offered to a company which was open to all of them, but rather a case where it had devoted itself to originating and bringing to fruition a particular business deal which was ultimately captured by former senior officers who had been in charge of the matter for the company. Since Canaero had been invited to make a proposal on the Guyana project, there is no basis for contending that it could not, in any event, have obtained the contract or that there was any unwillingness to deal with it.

It is a mistake, in my opinion, to seek to encase the principle stated and applied in *Peso*, by adoption from *Regal (Hastings) Ltd* v *Gulliver*, in the strait-jacket of special knowledge acquired while acting as directors or senior officers, let alone limiting it to benefits acquired by reason of and during the holding of those offices. As in other cases in this developing branch of the law, the particular facts may determine the shape of the principle of decision without setting fixed limits to it. So it is in the present case. Accepting the facts found by the trial judge, I find no obstructing considerations to the conclusion that O'Malley and Zarzycki continued, after their resignations, to be under a fiduciary duty to respect Canaero's priority, as against them and their instrument Terra, in seeking to capture the contract for the Guyana project. They entered the lists in the heat of the maturation of the project, known to them to be under active government consideration when they resigned from Canaero and when they proposed to bid on behalf of Terra.

In holding that on the facts found by the trial judge, there was a breach of fiduciary duty by O'Malley and Zarzycki which survived their resignations I am not to be taken as laying down any rule of liability to be read as if it were a statute. The general standards of loyalty, good faith and avoidance of a conflict of duty and self-interest to which the conduct of a director or senior officer must conform, must be tested in each case by many factors which it would be reckless to attempt to enumerate exhaustively. Among them are the factor of position or office held, the nature of the corporate opportunity, its ripeness, its specificness and the director's or managerial officer's relation to it, the amount of knowledge possessed, the circumstances in which it was obtained and whether it was special or, indeed, even private, the factor of time in the continuation of fiduciary duty where the alleged breach occurs after termination of the relationship with the company, and the circumstances under which the relationship was terminated, that is whether by retirement or resignation or discharge.

There remains the question of the appropriate relief against O'Malley and Zarzycki, and against Terra through which they acted in breach of fiduciary duty. In fixing the damages at $125 000, the trial judge based himself on a claim for damages related only to the loss of the contract for the Guyana project, this being the extent of Canaero's claim as he understood it. No claim for a different amount or for relief on a different basis, as, for example, to hold Terra as constructive trustee for Canaero in respect of the execution of the Guyana contract, was made in this court. Counsel for the respondents, although conceding that there was evidence of Terra's likely profit from the Guyana contract, emphasized the trial judge's finding that Canaero could not have obtained the contract itself in view of its association with Spartan Air Services Limited in the submission of a proposal. It was his submission that there was no evidence that that proposal would have been accepted if Terra's had been rejected and, in any event, there was no evidence of Canaero's likely share of the profit.

Liability of O'Malley and Zarzycki for breach of fiduciary duty does not depend upon proof by Canaero that, but for their intervention, it would have obtained the Guyana contract; nor is it a condition of recovery of damages that Canaero establish what its profit would have been or what it has lost by failing to realize the corporate opportunity in question. It is entitled to compel the faithless fiduciaries to answer for their default according to their gain. Whether the damages awarded here be viewed as an accounting of profits or, what amounts to the same thing, as based on unjust enrichment, I would not interfere with the quantum.

[247] Cook v Deeks
[1916] 1 AC 554

The stock of the Toronto Construction Co, a company carrying on the business of railway construction contractors, was held in equal shares by one Cook, one G S Deeks, one G M Deeks and one T R Hinds, who also constituted the board of directors. The company carried out several large construction contracts for the Canadian Pacific Railway Co. When Messrs Deeks and Mr Hinds learned that a new contract was coming up, they obtained this contract in their own names, to the exclusion of the company, and formed a new company, the Dominion Construction Co to carry out the work. At a general meeting of shareholders of the Toronto Construction Co resolutions were passed owing to the voting power of G S Deeks, G M Deeks and T R Hinds, approving the sale of part of the plant of the Toronto Construction Co to the Dominion Construction Co, and a declaration was made that the Toronto Construction Co had no interest in the new contract with the Canadian Pacific Railway Co.

In an action by Mr Cook against Messrs Deeks and Mr Hinds, the Privy Council held that the benefit of the contract belonged properly to the Toronto Construction Co and that the directors could not validly use their voting power as shareholders to vest it in themselves.

LORD BUCKMASTER LC: . . . The management of Messrs Deeks and Hinds of the affairs of the construction company was eminently satisfactory; but so far as railway construction was concerned the whole of their reputation for the efficient conduct of their business had been gained by them while acting as directors of the Toronto Construction Co. In 1911, and probably at an earlier date, the three defendants had settled that they would no longer continue business relationships with the plaintiff. It is unnecessary to seek the cause of the quarrel, or to determine whether they had good reason for the opinion that they had formed. There was nothing to compel them to work with or for the plaintiff, and it is impossible to see that they were bound to continue their relationship with him by any legal or moral consideration. They were, however, involved with him in different reciprocal duties, by reason of their relationship in connection with the Toronto Construction Co, and if they desired freedom to act, without regard to the restrictions that those relationships imposed, it was necessary that they should terminate their position as directors and shareholders in the company and place it in dissolution. This they could easily have accomplished owing to the fact that they held three-fourths of the share capital. It is suggested that they might also have resolved at a general meeting of the company that the company should no longer continue the work.

This would have been all but equivalent to a resolution of voluntary liquidation; but even this step was not taken. While still retaining their position as directors, while still actually acting as managers of the company, and with their duties to the company of which the plaintiff was a shareholder entirely unchanged, they proceeded to negotiate with Mr Leonard for the new Shore Line contract, in reality on their own behalf, but in exactly the same manner as they had always acted for the company, and doubtless with their claims enforced by the expeditious manner in which they, while acting for the company, had caused the last contract to be carried through. . . .

Two questions of law arise. . . . The first is whether, apart altogether from the subsequent resolutions, the company would have been at liberty to claim from the three defendants the benefit of the contract which they had obtained from the Canadian Pacific Railway Co; and the second, which only arises if the first be answered in the affirmative, whether in such event the majority of the shareholders of the company constituted by the three defendants could ratify and approve of what was done and thereby release all claim against the directors. . . .

It is quite right to point out the importance of avoiding the establishment of rules as to directors' duties which would impose upon them burdens so heavy and responsibilities so great that men of good position would hesitate to accept the office. But, on the other hand, men who assume the complete control of a company's business must remember that they are not at liberty to sacrifice the interests which they are bound to protect, and, while ostensibly acting for the company, divert in their own favour business which should properly belong to the company they represent.

Their Lordships think that, in the circumstances, the defendants T R Hinds and G S and G M Deeks were guilty of a distinct breach of duty in the course they took to secure the contract, and that they cannot retain the benefit of such contract for themselves, but must be regarded as holding it on behalf of the company.

There remains the more difficult consideration of whether this position can be made regular by resolutions of the company controlled by the votes of these three defendants. . . .

If, as their Lordships find on the facts, the contract in question was entered into under such circumstances that the directors could not retain the benefit of it for themselves, then it belonged in equity to the company and ought to have been dealt with as an asset of the company. Even supposing it be not *ultra vires* of a company to make a present to its directors, it appears quite certain that directors holding a majority of votes would not be permitted to make a present to themselves. This would be to allow a majority to oppress the minority. . . . In the same way, if directors have acquired for themselves property or rights which they must be regarded as holding on behalf of the company, a resolution that the rights of the company should be disregarded in the matter would amount to forfeiting the interest and property of the minority of shareholders in favour of the majority, and that by the votes of those who are interested in securing the property for themselves. Such use of voting power has never been sanctioned by the courts. . . .

NOTES

For comments on *Peso Silver Mines, 244* above, see D D Prentice (1967) 30 *MLR* 450; H R H (1968) 85 *SALJ* 71; (1968) 3 *New Zealand Universities LR* 77; for comments on *O'Malley*, D D Prentice (1974) 37 *MLR* 464; S W Beck (1975) 53 *Can BR* 771.

As Aaron Yoran (1973) 89 *LQR* 188 points out, the modern approach to the question whether there has been an improper usurpation of a corporate opportunity by a director is not to ask whether the information had its source with the company or was the property or in the line of business of the company, but whether on the facts the director acted unfairly towards the company in taking advantage of the opportunity. The Canadian case of *Abbey Glen Property Corporation* v *Stumborg* [1976] 2 WWR 1 (Alta) adopts this approach. See also *Hawrelak* v *City of Edmonton* [1976] 1 SCR 387. *O'Malley, 246* above, supports Gower's view (3 ed 518) that the fiduciary standard applicable to directors applies also to executive officers in managerial or quasi-managerial positions.

In *Phipps* v *Boardman* [1967] 2 AC 46 solicitors for a trust which held shares in a company negotiated the acquisition by themselves of a personal controlling interest in the company. In the course of negotiations for the purchase of the shares, the solicitors (defendants in this action) made use of information which they had obtained by reason of their representation of the shareholding of the trust. The 'take-over bid' by the defendants proved very successful both for them and the trust, substantial capital distributions being made to shareholders well in excess of the amounts paid for the shares. A beneficiary under the trust sought to recover from the defendants the proportion of the profit made by them on their transactions attributable to the plaintiff's share in the trust fund. The House of Lords (by a majority of three to two) held that the defendants were accountable, subject to a liberal allowance for their skill and work in producing the profit. The decision in *Regal (Hastings) Ltd* v *Gulliver, 243* above, was applied.

Lord Guest said (at 117) '. . . Applying these principles to the present case I have no hesitation in coming to the conclusion that the appellants hold the Lester and Harris shares as constructive trustees and are bound to account to the respondent. It is irrelevant that the trustees themselves could not have profited by the transaction. It is also irrelevant that the appellants were not in competition with the trustees in relation to the shares. . . . In the present case the knowledge and information obtained by Boardman was obtained in the course of the fiduciary position in which he had placed himself. The only defence available to a person in such a fiduciary position is that he made the profits with the knowledge and assent of the trustees. It is not contended that the trustees had such knowledge or gave such consent.'

Lord Upjohn (dissenting) said (at 123, 124): '. . . Rules of equity have to be applied to such a great diversity of circumstances that they can be stated only in the most general terms and applied with particular attention to the exact circumstances of each case. The relevant rule for the decision of this case is the fundamental rule of equity that a person in a fiduciary capacity must not make a profit out of his trust which is part of the wider rule that a trustee must not place himself in a position where his duty and his interest may conflict. . . . The phrase "possibly may conflict" requires consideration. In my view it means that the reasonable man looking at the relevant facts and circumstances of the particular case would think that there was a real sensible possibility of conflict; not that you could imagine some situations arising which might, in some conceivable possibility in events not contemplated as real sensible possibilities by any reasonable person, result in a conflict.'

See also *S* v *Berliner* 1966 (4) SA 535 (W) at 536, per Boshoff J: 'It is the duty of all agents, including directors of companies, to conduct the affairs of their principals in the interests of the principals and not for their own benefit. If an act is done which falls within the terms of an express power but is done by the agent for his own benefit and not for the benefit of his principal, it is an unauthorized act.'

In *Magnus Diamond Mining Syndicate* v *Macdonald and Hawthorne* 1909 ORC 65 the defendants, while directors and managers of a company, acquired information as to the value of certain diamondiferous property. They thereupon purchased the property in competition with the company without disclosing their intention to the company. The court decided that the defendants were obliged to transfer the property to the company and to account to it for profits already received.

In *Cranleigh Precision Engineering Ltd* v *Bryant* [1964] 3 All ER 289, [1965] 1 WLR 1293 the defendant had acquired valuable technical information as the plaintiff's managing director and subsequently sought to turn this information to his own advantage and that of a company formed by him. The court granted an interdict restraining both the defendant and his company from committing a breach of his duty of confidence. See also *Measures Bros Ltd v Measures* [1910] 1 Ch 336.

The same fiduciary standards which apply to directors, apply also to officers of the company, in particular senior executives; see Gower 3 ed 518; *O'Malley's* case, *246* above, at 381.

Generally a director, *qua* director, is not liable to account for profits made on pre-incorporation contracts, but he may be liable to account for such profits *qua* promoter: see 97 above; further *Albion Steel and Wire Co v Martin* (1875) 1 ChD 580; *Ex parte The Master (In re Ferreira Produce Co Ltd in liquidation)* 1912 TPD 1104.

On liability for gifts received from promoters, see *Madrid Bank v Pelly* (1869) *LR* 7 Eq 442; *Nant-Y-Glo and Blaina Ironworks Co v Grave* (1878) 12 ChD 738; *Eden v Ridsdales Railway Lamp and Lighting Co Ltd* (1889) 23 QBD 368.

Where an agent enters into a contract in the name of his principal but in his own interests, the principal cannot repudiate the contract as against the third party if the latter acted bona fide: *Hambro v Burnard* [1904] 2 KB 10.

With the consent of a general meeting a director may keep profits made by him in the exercise of his office provided there is no fraud on the minority.

See further *General Exchange Bank v Horner* (1870) LR 9 Eq 480; *In re Imperial Land Company of Marseilles* (1877) 4 ChD 566; *Phosphate Sewage Co v Hartmont* (1887) 5 ChD 394; *In re Cape Breton Co* (1885) 29 ChD 795, affirmed *sub nom Cavendish Bentinck v Fenn* (1887) 12 App Cas 652; *In re Oxford Benefit Building and Investment Society* (1886) 35 ChD 502; *Ladywell Mining Co v Brookes* (1887) 35 ChD 400; *Mayor of Salford v Lever* [1891] 1 ChD 168; *In re Washington Diamond Mining Co* [1893] 3 Ch 95; *Grant v Gold Exploration and Development Syndicate Ltd* [1900] 1 QB 233; *Shaw v Holland* [1900] 2 Ch 305; *Costa Rica Railway Co Ltd v Farwood* [1901] 1 Ch 746; *In re Lady Forrest (Murchison) Gold Mine Ltd* [1901] 1 Ch 582; *Bath v Standard Land Co Ltd* [1911] 1 Ch 618; *R v Alexander* 1936 AD 445; *Refco v Amicor Investments* 1964 (3) SA 184 (FC); also *Bell Houses Ltd v City Wall Properties Ltd* [1966] 2 QB 656, [1966] 2 All ER 674 (CA) and *Lindgren v L & P Estates Co Ltd* [1968] Ch 572, [1968] 1 All ER 917.

On the fiduciary duties of directors, see M S Blackman *The Fiduciary Doctrine and its Application to Directors of Companies* (1970) (Ph D Thesis, U of Cape Town); further, Ross W Parsons 'The Director's Duty of Good Faith' (1967) 5 *Melbourne Univ LR* 395; L S Sealy 'The Director as Trustee' (1967) *CLJ* 83; Sir Douglas Menzies 'Company Directors' (1959) 33 *ALJ* 156; 'Corporate Opportunity' (1961) 74 *Harv LR* 765; Gareth Jones 'Unjust Enrichment and the Fiduciary's Duty of Loyalty' (1968) 84 *LQR* 472; Allen B Afterman 'Directors' Duties in Joint-Venture and Parent–Subsidiary Companies' (1968) 42 *ALJ* 168.

On the question whether controlling shareholders owe a fiduciary duty (which may overlap with their fiduciary duty as directors) to other shareholders, see p 510 below.

(d) Contracts between a Director and his Company

[248] Aberdeen Rail Co *v* Blaikie Bros
House of Lords (1854) 1 Macq 461, 2 Eq Rep 1281

The defendant company entered into a contract to purchase a quantity of chairs from the plaintiff partnership. At the time that the contract was concluded, a director of the company was a member of the partnership. The court held that the company was entitled to avoid the contract.

LORD CRANWORTH LC: . . . This, therefore, brings us to the general question, whether a director of a railway company is or is not precluded from dealing on behalf of the company with himself or with a firm in which he is a partner. The directors are a body to whom is delegated the duty of managing the general affairs of the company. A corporate body can only act by agents, and it is, of course, the duty of those agents so to act as best to promote the interests of the corporation whose affairs they are conducting. Such an agent has duties to discharge of a fiduciary character towards his principal, and it is a rule of universal application that no one having such duties to discharge shall be allowed to enter into engagements in which he has or can have a personal interest conflicting or which possibly may conflict with the interests of those whom he is bound to protect. So strictly is this principle adhered to that no question is allowed to be raised as to the fairness or unfairness of a contract so entered into. It obviously is, or may be, impossible to demonstrate how far in any particular case the terms of such a contract have been the best for the *cestui que trust* which it was impossible to obtain. It may sometimes happen that the terms on which a trustee has dealt or attempted to deal with the estate or interests of those for whom he is a trustee have been as good as could have been obtained from any other person; they may even at the time have been better. But still so inflexible is the rule that no inquiry on that subject is permitted.

The English authorities on the subject are numerous and uniform. . . .

It is true that the questions have generally arisen on agreements for purchases or leases of land, and not, as here, on a contract of a mercantile character. But this can make no difference in principle. The inability to contract depends not on the subject-matter of the agreement, but on the fiduciary character of the contracting party, and I cannot entertain a doubt of its being applicable to the case of a party who is acting as manager of a mercantile or trading business for the benefit of others no less than to that of an agent or trustee employed in selling land.

Was, then, Mr Blaikie so acting in the case now before us? If he was, did he, while so acting, contract, on behalf of those for whom he was acting, with himself? Both these questions must obviously be answered in the affirmative. Mr Blaikie was not only a director, but, if that was necessary, the chairman of the directors. In that character it was his bounden duty to make the best bargains he could for the benefit of the company. While he filled that character, viz on 6 February 1846, he entered into a contract on behalf of the company with his own firm for the purchase of a large quantity of chairs at a certain stipulated price. His duty to the company imposed on him the obligation of obtaining these iron chairs at the lowest possible price. His personal interest would lead him in an entirely opposite direction—would induce him to fix the price as high as possible. This is the very evil against which the rule in question is directed; and I see nothing whatever to prevent its application here. I observe that Lord Fullerton seemed to doubt whether the rule would apply where the party whose act or contract is called in question, is only one of a body of directors, not a sole trustee or manager. But, with all deference, this appears to me to make no difference. It was Mr Blaikie's duty to give to his co-directors, and through them to the company, the full benefit of all the knowledge and skill which he could bring to bear on the subject. He was bound to assist them in getting the articles contracted for at the cheapest possible rate. As far as related to the advice he should give them, he put his interest in conflict with his duty, and whether he was the sole director, or only one of many can make no difference in principle. The same observation applies to the fact, that he was not the sole person trading with the company. He was one of the firm of Blaikie Brothers with whom the contract was made, and so was interested in driving as hard a bargain with the company as he could induce them to make. . . .

[249] Imperial Mercantile Credit Association *v* Coleman
(1871) 6 Ch App 558

LORD HATHERLEY LC: . . . No director of a company can, in the absence of any stipulation to the contrary, be allowed to be a partaker in any benefit whatever from any contract which requires the sanction of a board of which he is a member. . . . The company have a right to the services of their directors, whom they remunerate by considerable payments; they have a right to their entire services, they have a right to the voice of every director, and to the advice of every director in giving his opinion upon matters which are brought before the board for consideration. . . .

. . . However, the question then remains, whether the company cannot stipulate that this is a benefit of which they do not desire to avail themselves, and if they are competent so as to stipulate, whether they may not think that in large financial matters of this description it is better to have directors who may advance the interests of the company by their connection, and by the part which they themselves take in large money dealings, than to have persons who would have no share in such transactions as those in which the company is concerned.

It is not for me to say which was the wiser or better course of the two, nor do I think that this court professes to lay down rules for the guidance of men who are adult, and can manage and deal with their own interests. It would be a violent assumption if anything of that kind were attempted. It must be left to such persons to form their own contracts and engagements, and this court has only to sit here and construe them, and also to lay down certain general rules for the protection of persons who may not have been aware of what the consequences would be of entrusting their property to the management of others where nothing is expressed as to the implied arrangement. In this case it does appear to me that there was a distinct contemplation of directors being interested in the concerns of the company, and acting and voting when the matter came before the board of directors, and that the shareholders took such precautions as they thought necessary. . . .

[The decision was reversed by the House of Lords (1873) LR 6 HL 189, but not so as to affect the validity of the passages cited.]

NOTES

As to the rule that, unless otherwise provided in the articles, a director cannot contract with his company unless a general meeting, after full disclosure, approves of the contract, see further *In re Republic of Bolivia Exploration Syndicate Ltd* [1914] 1 Ch 139; *Transvaal Lands Co v New Belgium (Transvaal) Land and Development Co* [1914] 2 Ch 488; *EBM Co Ltd v Dominion Bank* [1937] 3 All ER 555 (PC); *Gundelfinger v African Textile Manufacturers Ltd* 1939 AD 314. But see also *Hely-Hutchinson v Brayhead Ltd* [1968] 1 QB at 570, [1967] 2 All ER at 27–8, where Roskill J denied that there was a rule of the common law that a director could not validly contract with his company. His judgment was affirmed by the court of appeal (see p 488 below).

Release of a director from a debt owed by him to his company may amount to a wrongful act: *Curtis's Furnishing Stores Ltd (in liquidation)* v *Freedman* [1966] 2 All ER 955, [1966] 1 WLR 1219.

In *Re Transplanters Ltd* [1958] 2 All ER 711, [1958] 1 WLR 822 it was held that for the purpose of interruption of prescription in respect of a loan made to a director the balance sheets of the company did not constitute an acknowledgment of the debt because they were signed by the director himself (as required by the Act) and in view of his fiduciary position it was not competent for him to acknowledge on behalf of the company a debt owed to himself. The approval of the balance sheets by the auditors did not help, for they were not agents for the purpose of giving such acknowledgments. See also above p 388.

On the winding-up of a company directors rank equally with other creditors for advances bona fide made by them to the company: *Standard Bank* v *Liquidators of Cobb & Co* 1876 Buch 186.

Generally, on contracts between a director and his company, S J Naudé 'Kontraksluiting tussen Direkteur en Maatskappy' (1970) 30 *THRHR* 142.

[250] S v Heller
1964 (1) SA 524 (W)

Trollip J: According to the common law, s 70*quin*(1) of the Companies Act, and the articles of the companies concerned . . . a director must disclose the nature of his interest in any transaction with the company. That certainly includes revealing his identity in the transaction as vendor or otherwise. Must he also disclose the fact and extent of his profit?

According to the common law, material facts relating to the nature of his interest must ordinarily be disclosed, ie those

'which if disclosed, would influence the mind of a reasonable person in determining whether to enter into the proposed contract or transaction at all, or deciding upon the terms of such contract or transaction, having regard to its class and character'.

(Spencer Bower *Actionable Non-disclosure* p 16 para 30.) Consequently, where the transaction is one of selling things to the company it would normally be the duty of the director to disclose the exact extent of the profit which he will make as a result of the transaction, as that would be a material fact in the above sense, especially if the actual value of the property was not readily or easily determinable.

That principle undoubtedly applies where the director is liable in common law to account to the company for his profit on the transaction, because then the fact and extent of that profit are most material facts which have to be disclosed.

The articles of each of the companies concerned, however, enable a director to contract with the company and provide that he is not

'liable to account to the company for any profit . . . realized by any such contract or arrangement by reason only of such director holding that office or the fiduciary relation thereby established but it is declared that the nature of his interest must be disclosed by him . . .'.

That article does not lessen but entrenches the director's duty to disclose the fact and extent of his profit for which, at common law, he would be liable to account to the company because, being material facts, they would be included in 'the nature of his interest'. . . .

It is relevant to emphasize here that it is clear from the *Robinson* case that a director is only liable to account for his profit on a resale of his property to the company if, when he originally acquired it, he was already the company's director or agent and under a fiduciary duty to acquire it for the company and not for himself. If he was not a director when he acquired it and he acquired it for himself he would generally not be liable to account for his resulting profit even if his intention at the time was to become a director and to resell to the company, because at that stage he would not have been under any legal obligation to the company and would therefore be 'at liberty to carry out or abandon (the plan) at his own will'.

So much then is clear, and can be accepted as being within the knowledge of experienced directors like the accused. The uncertainty, however, exists where a director is not liable at common law to account for his profit. Is there then any duty on him to disclose it? It may be that non-liability to account means that the fact and extent of his profit are not material and therefore need not be disclosed; but in some circumstances those facts may possibly still be material and therefore have to be disclosed because, although the profit is not recoverable, the fact and extent thereof might still be factors that would be weighed by a reasonable person in determining whether to enter into the transaction upon the terms proposed or at all.

Section 70*quin*(1) of the Companies Act further complicates the matter by requiring a director to disclose not only 'the nature' but also 'the extent' of his interest. Section 199 of the English Act . . . requires a disclosure of only 'the nature' of the interest and not its extent.

It is possible that by deliberately adding 'and extent' in s 70*quin* our legislature intended, at any rate in regard to selling transactions in which a director is interested, to compel a disclosure of the fact and extent of his profit. As against that there is subsection (5) of the section in which a general notice that a director is a member of a specified company or firm, and is to be regarded as interested in any contract made with it, shall be deemed to be a sufficient declaration of the interest in terms of s 70*quin*(1). A similar provision occurs in the articles of the companies. That suggests that 'the nature and extent of his interest' in subsection (1) or 'the nature of his interest' in the articles is to have a limited connotation, and that in a selling transaction all the director need declare is, for example, that he is the vendor or part-vendor (that would be 'the nature' of his interest) and that he owns the whole or a specified part of the *merx*, as the case may be (that would be 'the extent' of his interest). I need express no views on any of those obscure and doubtful aspects. I have referred to them to show the uncertainty of the present position and the difficulty that a director must find himself in in deciding whether or not it is necessary for him to declare the fact and extent of his profit in any particular transaction when that profit is not recoverable by the company. On the other hand it is necessary to emphasize that if the director knows that by his not declaring the fact and extent of his profit his co-directors or the company itself will infer that he is not making any profit, and that they will regard that as material then, irrespective of the articles or the Companies Act, he would be obliged to disclose that information.

NOTES

In view of the wording of s 234 which requires a director '*who is in any way, whether directly or indirectly, materially interested* in a contract . . . which has been or is to be entered into be the company or who becomes so interested in any such contract after it has been entered into' to declare '*his full interest and full particulars thereof*', the doubts which arose as to how far this obligation extends in *S* v *Heller* and the older English cases, such as *Liquidators of Imperial Mercantile Credit Association* v *Coleman* (1873) LR 6 HL 189, are not likely to trouble the courts any more.

One of the questions in *Hely-Hutchinson* v *Brayhead Ltd* (p 488 below) was whether the failure of a director to disclose his interests in a contract, as required by the Act, apart from rendering him liable to criminal penalties, renders the contract unenforceable. Lord Denning MR said (at 585): 'It seems to me that when a director fails to disclose his interest, the effect is the same as non-disclosure in contracts *uberrimae fidei*, or non-disclosure by a promoter who sells to the company property in which he is interested. . . . Non-disclosure does not render the contract void or a nullity. It renders the contract voidable at the instance of the company and makes the director accountable for any secret profit which he has made.'

This accords with our law, as stated in *Robinson* v *Randfontein Estates*, 242 above.

On the question what 'being interested in' means, cf *Stellenbosch Farmers' Winery* v *Distillers Corporation* 1962 (1) SA 458 (AD).

[251] *In re* Greymouth Point Elizabeth Railway and Coal Co Ltd
[1904] 1 Ch 32

The material articles of the company provided, *inter alia*, as follows:

'104. Subject to the provisions of article 106, any director may enter into a contract with the company, or be interested in any operation or business undertaken or assisted by the company. . . .'

'106. No director·shall vote on any matters relating to the contract, operation, business, or office, with, in, or to which he shall be con-nected, interested, or appointed; and, if he does so vote, his vote shall not be counted.'

'116. The directors may meet together for the despatch of business . . . and determine the quorum necessary for the transaction of business: until otherwise determined, two directors shall be a quorum.'

In 1894 the company created a series of £90 000 first mortgage deben-tures secured by a trust deed, and allotted and issued debentures to the aggregate amount of £88 800, leaving a balance of £1 200 unissued.

During 1897 the company was in financial difficulties, and advances amounting to £2 069 were made to the company by John and Joseph McDonald, two of the directors. At a board meeting held on 10 December 1897 it was resolved that debentures to the value of £1 200 should be sealed and issued to John and Joseph McDonald in consideration of and part security for their said advances and a small further advance then made. The only directors present at this meeting were the two McDonalds and another director.

In October 1900 the usual debenture-holder's action was commenced against the company, and a receiver and manager was appointed. In May 1901 judgment was obtained, and certain accounts and inquiries were directed. It then transpired that no debentures had been issued to the two McDonalds under the resolution of 10 December 1897 and a summons was taken out by John McDonald and the executors of Joseph McDonald (who had died in 1900), claiming a declaration that they were entitled to rank as first mortgage debenture-holders of £1 200 *pari passu* with the other debenture-holders of £88 800. It did not appear whether the two McDonalds had or had not voted on the resolution of 10 December 1897; but there was evidence that all parties had acted in good faith, and that the McDonalds had not pressed for the issue to themselves of the debentures for £1 200 because they thought that the resolution was a sufficient security for them.

FARWELL J: I think that the meaning of art 116 is that the two directors to form the quorum for the despatch of business must be two directors who are capable of voting on the business before the board; otherwise it is idle. In the present case there were three directors present, and I take it that they voted for giving debenture security to two of themselves in consideration of a large sum of money then owing to the two directors, and a small sum of money then advanced or to be advanced. The giving of the security was a matter on which two of the directors could not vote under art 106; and, moreover, if there had been otherwise a quorum, I think the other directors would have been justified in asking them to retire while the question of giving them security was discussed, because they were interested against the company. Certainly it is a case in which the company is entitled to have the benefit of all the protection it can get from the independent directors. On the construction of the articles I think . . . that the two directors were not capable of voting on the question, and, therefore, there was no quorum, and no valid contract for the issue of debentures to the two McDonalds.

[252] *In re* North Eastern Insurance Company Ltd
[1919] 1 Ch 198

The articles provided that no director should be disqualified from contracting with the company but that no director should vote on such a contract; further that the directors themselves should determine the quorum for the transaction of business, three being the quorum unless otherwise determined. Y, D, C and L were directors. At a meeting of the board, it was resolved by D, C and L, Y not participating in the resolution, that a debenture for £350-odd be issued to Y to secure the repayment of certain loans made by him to the company; and similarly resolved by Y, C and L, D not participating, that a debenture be issued to D for a like purpose.

P O LAWRENCE J: . . . The question is whether the resolutions so passed are valid resolutions. In my judgment they are not. The real point is whether the issue of the debentures ought to be regarded as part of one entire transaction in which both directors were jointly interested. I think it ought to be so regarded. If either of the resolutions in question had not been passed . . . the transaction agreed upon would not have been carried out. In my judgment, therefore, Y was interested in the issue of the debenture to D and D was interested in the issue of the debenture to Y. . . .

[253] North-West Transportation Company Ltd *v* Beatty
(1887) 12 App Cas 589 (PC)

SIR RICHARD BAGGALLAY: . . . Unless some provision to the contrary is to be found in the charter or other instrument by which the company is incorporated, the resolution of a majority of the shareholders, duly convened, upon any question with which the company is legally competent to deal, is binding upon the minority, and consequently upon the company, and every shareholder has a perfect right to vote upon any such question, although he may have a personal interest in the subject-matter opposed to, or different from, the general or particular interests of the company.

The only unfairness or impropriety which, consistently with the admitted and established facts, could be suggested, arises out of the fact that the defendant J H Beatty possessed a voting power as a shareholder which enabled him, and those who thought with him, to adopt the by-law, and thereby either to ratify and adopt a voidable contract, into which he, as a director, and his co-directors had entered or to make a similar contract, which latter seems to have been what was intended to be done by the resolution passed on 7 February.

But the constitution of the company enabled the defendant, J H Beatty, to acquire this voting power; there was no limit upon the number of shares which a shareholder might hold, and for every share so held he was entitled to a vote; the charter itself recognized the defendant as a holder of 200 shares, one-third of the aggregate number; he had a perfect right to acquire further shares, and to exercise his voting power in such a manner as to secure the election of directors whose views upon policy agreed with his own, and to support those views at any shareholders' meetings. . . . To reject the votes of the defendant upon the question of the adoption of the by-law would be to give effect to the views of the minority and to disregard those of the majority. . . .

NOTES

See also *Northern Counties Securities Ltd* v *Johnson & Steeple Ltd, 173* above.

A director may vote at a board meeting when his appointment as a managing director is being considered, provided no salary or remuneration is attached to the appointment. If his appointment is to be made at a salary he may not vote and is not counted in the quorum: *Foster* v *Foster* [1916] 1 Ch 532; *Trek Tyres Ltd* v *Beukes* 1957 (3) SA 306 (W). In *Foster* it was held that the appointment by directors of one of their number as chairman or managing director, without a service contract or additional remuneration, does not amount to a contract on which that director cannot vote, but is merely a delegation of their powers.

An alternate director is a director in his own capacity and is not prevented from voting on a matter in which the director to whom he is an alternate is interested.

In *Mendonides* v *Mendonides* 1962 (2) SA 190 (N) the articles required for the transfer of shares by a member to a non-member the previous approval in writing of the directors. The company had three shareholders, all of them directors. Two of them intended to transfer their shares to a non-member. They called a directors' meeting, at which a resolution to approve of the transfers was carried with their votes against the votes of the third shareholder-director. The latter thereupon applied to court for an interdict restraining his fellow directors from proceeding with the transfers. The company's articles of association provided that:

'A director shall not be disqualified by his office from entering into contracts, arrangements, or dealings with the company, nor shall any contract, arrangement, or dealing with the company be voided, nor shall a director be liable to account to the company for any profit arising out of any contract, arrangement, or dealing with the company by reason of such director being a party to or interested in or deriving profit from any such contract, arrangement, or dealing, and being at the same time a director of the company, provided that such director, unless the whole of his interest is apparent on the face of the contract, discloses to the board with sufficient particularity at or before the time when such contract, arrangement, or dealing is determined upon his interest therein or if his interest be subsequently acquired, provided that he on the first occasion possible discloses to the board the fact that he has acquired such interest. But no director shall vote as a director in regard to any contract, arrangement, or dealing in which he is interested or upon any matter arising thereout, and if he shall so vote his vote shall not be counted, nor shall he be reckoned for the purpose of constituting a quorum of directors.'

The applicant contended, *inter alia*, that the transfers were invalid because in terms of this provision his fellow directors were precluded from voting on the transfers of their own shares. The court held that as the business before the directors in approving the share transfers was not any contract, arrangement or dealing of the company or involving it as a party, it was not affected by the article.

See also *English and Devenish* v *Liquidators of the New Rietfontein Deep Level Gold Mining Co* (1895) 2 Off Rep 249; *Burland* v *Earle* [1902] Ac 83; *In re Express Engineering Works Ltd* [1920] 1 Ch 466; *Blythe* v *The Phoenix Foundry Ltd* 1922 WLD 87; *Victors Ltd (in liquidation)* v *Lingard* [1927] 1 Ch 323; *In re Cleadon Trust Ltd* [1939] Ch 286, [1938] 4 All ER 518; *Levin* v *Felt & Tweeds Ltd* 1951 (2) SA 401 (AD) (*000 above*).

(e) Directorships in Competing Companies

[254] London and Mashonaland Exploration Company Ltd v New Mashonaland Exploration Company Ltd

[1891] WN 165

Motion on behalf of the plaintiff company to restrain the defendant company from publishing any announcement that Lord Mayo was one of its directors, and to restrain Lord Mayo from authorizing or permitting any such publication, and from acting as director of the defendant company.

The above-named companies were incorporated for the same object, and were rival companies. The plaintiff company was registered in March 1891 and in the following month a resolution was passed at a meeting of the directors appointing Lord Mayo a director and chairman. The plaintiff company alleged that Lord Mayo accepted the appointment and approved of a prospectus privately circulated wherein his name appeared as director and chairman, and that numerous applications for shares had been received upon the faith of such prospectus. In July the prospectus of the defendant company was circulated with the name of Lord Mayo at the head of its list of directors. It was admitted that Lord Mayo had never acted as a director, nor attended any board meeting of the plaintiff company, and that he had never agreed, either expressly or by the articles of association, not to become a director of any similar company.

CHITTY J said, even assuming that Lord Mayo had been duly elected chairman and director of the plaintiff company, there was nothing in the articles which required him to give any part of his time, much less the whole of his time, to the business of the company, or which prohibited him from acting as a director of another company; neither was there any contract express or implied to give his personal services to the plaintiff company and to no other company. No case had been made out that Lord Mayo was about to disclose to the defendant company any information that he had obtained confidentially in his character of chairman: the analogy sought to be drawn by the plaintiff company's counsel between the present case and partnerships was incomplete: no sufficient damage had been shown, and no case had been made for an injunction: the application was wholly unprecedented, and must be dismissed with costs.

[255] Scottish Co-operative Wholesale Society Ltd *v* Meyer
[1959] AC 324; [1958] 3 All ER 66, 1958 SC (HL) 40

In 1946 the Scottish Co-operative Wholesale Society formed a subsidiary company to enable it to participate in the manufacture of rayon materials and to get licences to manufacture rayon cloth, the manufacture of which was controlled until 1952. The society appointed three nominee directors to the board of its subsidiary. After the removal of the controls, the society adopted the policy of transferring the business of the subsidiary to itself, thus bringing the activities of the subsidiary to a virtual standstill. An application against the society by the independent shareholders of the subsidiary on the ground of oppression under s 210 of the Companies Act 1948 succeeded (*319* below, where a fuller statement will be found). One of the questions raised in argument related to the duties of the nominee directors.

LORD DENNING: . . . What, then, is the position of the nominee directors here? Under the articles of association of the textile company the co-operative society was entitled to nominate three out of the five directors, and it did so. It nominated three of its own directors and they held office, as the articles said, 'as nominees' of the co-operative society. These three were therefore at one and the same time directors of the co-operative society—being three out of twelve of that company—and also directors of the textile company—three out of five there. So long as the interests of all concerned were in harmony, there was no difficulty. The nominee directors could do their duty by both companies without embarrassment. But, so soon as the interests of the two companies were in conflict, the nominee directors were placed in an impossible position. Thus, when the realignment of shareholding was under discussion, the duty of the three directors to the textile company was to get the best possible price for any new issue of its shares . . . whereas their duty to the co-operative society was to obtain the new shares at the lowest possible price—at par, if they could. Again, when the co-operative society determined to set up its own rayon department, competing with the business of the textile company, the duty of the three directors to the textile company was to do their best to promote its business and to act with complete good faith towards it; and in consequence not to disclose their knowledge of its affairs to a competitor, and not even to work for a competitor, when to do so might operate to the disadvantage of the textile company (see *Hivac Ltd* v *Park Royal Scientific Instruments Ltd* [[1946] Ch 169]), whereas they were under the selfsame duties to the co-operative society. It is plain that, in the circumstances, these three gentlemen could not do their duty by both companies, and they did not do so. They put their duty to the co-operative society above their duty to the textile company in this sense, at least, that they did nothing to defend the interests of the textile company against the conduct of the co-operative society. They probably thought that 'as nominees' of the co-operative society their first duty was to the co-operative society. In this they were wrong. By subordinating the interests of the textile company to those of the co-operative society, they conducted the affairs of the textile company in a manner oppressive to the other shareholders.

It is said that these three directors were at most only guilty of inaction—of doing nothing to protect the textile company. But the affairs of a company can, in my opinion, be conducted oppressively by the directors doing nothing to defend its interests when they ought to do something—just as they can conduct its affairs oppressively by doing something injurious to its interests when they ought not to do it.

The question was asked: What could these directors have done? They could, I suggest, at least on behalf of the textile company, have protested against the conduct of the co-operative society. They could have protested against the setting up of a competing business. But then it was said: What good would that have done? Any protest by them would be sure to have been unavailing, seeing that they were in a minority on the board of the co-operative society. The answer is that no one knows whether it would have done any good. They never did protest. And it does not come well from their mouths to say it would have done no good, when they never put it to the test. . . .

Your Lordships were referred to *Bell* v *Lever Brothers Ltd* [[1932] AC 161 at 195], where Lord Blanesburgh said that a director of one company was at liberty to become a director also of a rival company. That may have been so at that time. But it is at the risk now of an application under s 210 [s 252 of our Act] if he subordinates the interests of the one company to those of the other.

NOTES

See also *Premier Medical & Industrial Equipment (Pty) Ltd* v *Winkler* 1971 (3) SA 866 (W), where it was held that a managing director may not compete with his company and may not make use of confidential information which came into his possession, even after the termination of his employment. On the other hand, in the absence of a restraint of trade clause he may after the termination of his employment set up in competition with his old company.

For a full statement on the subject see S J Naudé 'Toestemming deur 'n Maatskappy tot Mededinging deur 'n Direkteur' (1972) 89 *SALJ* 217.

(f) 'Insider Trading'

[256] Gilbert's Case
(1870) LR 5 Ch App 559

The directors of a company agreed to make a call in order to prevent the transfer of numerous shares which was threatened by some shareholders. However, the declaration of the call was postponed for several days so that one of the directors could transfer some of his shares to his clerk and thus avoid liability on them. The board approved and registered the transfer. The registration was held void, and the transferor placed on the list of contributories.

GIFFARD LJ: ... I quite agree ... that because a man is a director he is not necessarily a trustee of the shares he holds for the general body of shareholders; and in a vast variety of circumstances he is just as free to deal with his shares—except perhaps his qualification, which he cannot deal with without giving up his directorship—as any other person.
But [that does] not cover this case. ...

[257] Percival *v* Wright
[1902] 2 Ch 421

Certain shareholders wrote to the secretary of the company asking if he knew anyone disposed to purchase shares. Negotiations took place and eventually the chairman of the company and two other directors purchased the shares of the plaintiffs at £12 10*s* per share. The plaintiffs subsequently discovered that, prior to and during their own negotiations for sale, the chairman and the board had been approached by a third party with a view to the purchase of the entire undertaking of the company at prices which represented considerably over £12 10*s* per share. In the event the negotiations with the take-over bidder proved abortive.
The plaintiffs asked to have the sale of their shares to the chairman and the other two directors set aside on the ground that the defendants as directors ought to have disclosed the negotiations with the take-over bidder when treating for the purchase of the plaintiff's shares. Their action was dismissed with costs.

SWINFEN EADY J: ... Directors must dispose of their company's shares on the best terms obtainable, and must not allot them to themselves or their friends at a lower price in order to obtain a personal benefit. They must act bona fide for the interests of the company.
The plaintiffs' contention in the present case goes far beyond this. It is urged that the directors hold a fiduciary position as trustees for the individual shareholders, and that, where negotiations for sale of the undertaking are on foot, they are in the position of trustees for sale. The plaintiffs admitted that this fiduciary position did not stand in the way of any dealing between a director and a shareholder before the question of sale of the undertaking had arisen, but contended that as soon as that question arose the position was altered. No authority

was cited for that proposition, and I am unable to adopt the view that any line should be drawn at that point. It is contended that a shareholder knows that the directors are managing the business of the company in the ordinary course of management, and impliedly releases them from any obligation to disclose any information so acquired. That is to say, a director purchasing shares need not disclose a large casual profit, the discovery of a new vein, or the prospect of a good dividend in the immediate future, and similarly a director selling shares need not disclose losses, these being merely incidents in the ordinary course of management. But it is urged that, as soon as negotiations for the sale of the undertaking are on foot, the position is altered. Why? The true rule is that a shareholder is fixed with knowledge of all the directors' powers, and has no more reason to assume that they are not negotiating a sale of the undertaking than to assume that they are not exercising any other power. . . . The contrary view would place directors in a most invidious position, as they could not buy or sell shares without disclosing negotiations, a premature disclosure of which might well be against the best interests of the company. . . .

. . . There is no question of unfair dealing in this case. The directors did not approach the shareholders with the view of obtaining their shares. The shareholders approached the directors, and named the price at which they were desirous of selling. . . .

[258] **Diamond v Oreamuno**
(1969) 248 NE 2d 910
(NY Court of Appeals)

Directors of a company, MAI, knowing that because of an increase in expenses, profits had fallen drastically, sold their shares on the market at $28 a share, before the information was made public. Subsequently, the shares dropped to $11. By virtue of their common law fiduciary duties, they were held liable to the company for the difference, although the company was not the party who had suffered the loss.

FULD CJ: It is well established, as a general proposition, that a person who acquires special knowledge or information by virtue of a confidential or fiduciary relationship with another is not free to exploit that knowledge or information for his own personal benefit but must account to his principal for any profits derived therefrom. This, in turn, is merely a corollary of the broader principle, inherent in the nature of the fiduciary relationship, that prohibits a trustee or agent from extracting secret profits from his position of trust.

In support of their claim that the complaint fails to state a cause of action, the defendants take the position that, although it is admittedly wrong for an officer or director to use his position to obtain trading profits for himself in the stock of his corporation, the action ascribed to them did not injure or damage MAI in any way. Accordingly, the defendants continue, the corporation should not be permitted to recover the proceeds. They acknowledge that, by virtue of the exclusive access which officers and directors have to inside information, they possess an unfair advantage over other shareholders and, particularly, the persons who had purchased the stock from them but, they contend, the corporation itself was unaffected and, for that reason, a derivative action is an inappropriate remedy.

It is true that the complaint before us does not contain any allegation of damages to the corporation but this has never been considered to be an essential requirement for a cause of action founded on a breach of fiduciary duty. This is because the function of such an action, unlike an ordinary tort or contract case, is not merely to compensate the plaintiff for wrongs committed by the defendant but, as this court declared many years ago, 'to prevent them, by removing from agents and trustees all inducement to attempt dealing for their own benefit in matters which they have undertaken for others, or to which their agency or trust relates'.

Just as a trustee has no right to retain for himself the profits yielded by property placed in his possession but must account to his beneficiaries, a corporate fiduciary, who is entrusted with potentially valuable information, may not appropriate that asset for his own use even though, in so doing, he causes no injury to the corporation. The primary concern, in a case such as this, is not to determine whether the corporation has been damaged but to decide, as between the corporation and the defendants, who has a higher claim to the proceeds derived from the exploitation of the information. In our opinion, there can be no justification for permitting officers and directors, such as the defendants, to retain for themselves profits which, it is alleged, they derived solely from exploiting information gained by virtue of their inside position as corporate officials.

In addition, it is pertinent to observe that, despite the lack of any specific allegation of damage, it may well be inferred that the defendants' actions might have caused some harm to the enterprise. Although the corporation may have little concern with the day-to-day transactions in its shares, it has a great interest in maintaining a reputation of integrity, an image of probity, for its management and in insuring the continued public acceptance and marketability of its stock. When officers and directors abuse their position in order to gain personal profits, the effect may be to cast a cloud on the corporation's name, injure stockholder relations and undermine public regard for the corporation's securities.

[*Diamond* v *Oreamuno*, discussed, *inter alia*, in (1970) 83 *Harv LR* 1421 and (1969) 37 *Fordham LR* 477, was followed in *Schein* v *Chasen* 478 F (2d) 817, noted in (1973) 87 *Harv LR* 675.]

NOTES

It will be noticed that s 233 of the 1973 Act makes 'insider trading' a statutory offence but says nothing about civil liability. There are, however, always the common-law rules about fraud to fall back on. A director who with inside knowledge of impending disaster to his company would sell his shares to another shareholder or even an outsider without telling him about it, might well be liable to the buyer in damages for fraudulent concealment. Cf *Pretorius* v *Natal South Sea Investment Trust* 1965 (3) SA 410 (N) at 418. But see also *Meskin NO* v *Anglo-American Corporation of SA Ltd* 1968 (4) SA 793 (W).

Percival v *Wright* above was distinguised in *Allen* v *Hyatt* (1914) 30 TLR 444 where directors who had purchased shares from shareholders by representing (falsely) that the shares were needed to effect an amalgamation with another company were held liable to account to the shareholders for profits made on the transactions on the ground that they were acting as agents for the shareholders.

The Jenkins Committee recommended special statutory civil liability rules to apply to corporate insiders who trade securities on the basis of inside information not generally available to the public (para 89 Cmnd 1749, 1962).

In America, too, the majority view used to be that a director trading as an individual in respect of his own shares owes no duty to shareholders to disclose to them facts likely to affect the future value of the shares that are known to the directors, but not to the shareholders. 'A director of a corporation may freely purchase its stock, and occupies no relationship of trust to an individual stockholder which prohibits his using whatever advantage his position may afford him through knowledge of its business and condition superior to that of the stockholder with whom he deals': *Du Pont* v *Du Pont* 242 Fed 98 (1917) at 136. Today the prevailing opinion, in the evolution of which *Strong* v *Repide* 213 US 419, 53 LED 853 (1909), seems to have been seminal, is that a director renders himself guilty of fraud if he purchases the holdings of a minority shareholder without disclosing to him 'special circumstances', such as 'an assumed sale, merger or other factor condition enhancing the value of the stock, known by the officer or officers, not known by the stockholder, and not to be ascertained by an inspection of the books' (*Buckley* v *Buckley* 230 Mich 504, 202 NW 955 (1925)). See Loss *Securities Regulation* (1961) 1445–8.

As regards listed securities there are various statutory safeguards against 'insider trading'. Section 16(*a*) of the Securities Exchange Act 1934 prescribes disclosure. Section 16(*b*) seeks to discourage 'short-swing' speculation by insiders with advance information by rendering them liable to account to the company for any profit realized from any purchase and sale, or any sale and purchase, within a period of less than six months. (For details see L Loss *Securities Regulation* (1961) 1037ff; also (1962) 30 *Chicago LR* 121 and (1969) *Rev Int de Droit Comparé* 743.

Under the Federal Securities Exchange Act of 1934 and Rule 10*b*–5 promulgated thereunder by the SEC it is unlawful for any person by means of interstate commerce or of the mail or of the facilities of a stock exchange to use manipulative or deceptive devices in connection with the purchase or sale of any securities. The courts have held that the purpose of this provision is, *inter alia*, to secure fair dealings in securities markets by providing full disclosure of inside information: *SEC* v *Texas Gulf Sulphur Co* 401 F 2d 833 (1968); *Reynolds* v *Texas Gulf Sulphur Co* 309F Supp 548 (1970); *SEC* v *Texas Gulf Sulphur Co* 312 F Supp 77 (1970); *Shapiro* v *Merrill, Lynch* 495 F 2d 228 (1974).

A useful series of articles on the US Federal Securities Laws will be found in (1975) 32 *Washington and Lee Law Review* 571ff; see also Bernard J Davies 'Canadian and American Attitudes on Insider Trading' (1975) 25 *U of Toronto LJ* 215.

For a discussion of the English cases, see G K Morse 'Insider Trading' (1973) *JBL* 118. For comparisons between US law and English law on insider trading, see Louis Loss 'Fiduciary Concept as Applied to Trading by Corporate Insiders in the United States' (1970) 33 *MLR* 34; E J Wright 'Insider Trading in Corporate Securities – Can We Learn from America?' (1971) 4 *NZUL Rev* 209. See also A Yoran *Insider Trading in Israel and England* (1972).

(g) Statutory Duties

[259] R v Milne and Erleigh (5)
1950 (4) SA 604 (W)

LUCAS AJ: . . . Where a managing director is in charge . . . of the affairs of the company . . . a duty is thrown upon him to see that the books are properly kept and that the entries in them, in respect of substantial matters, are correct.

Illustrations were used in argument as to the difficulty of the managing director being responsible for every sixpence that was spent, and it is clear that the legislature recognized that there must be some limit to the responsibility of directors or officials of companies in respect of books, because, although requiring full statements of the business affairs of the company, an exception was made in respect of retail trade, and it is

quite clear that it would be absurd to expect the manager of a departmental store to have a record of every pound of sugar that was sold or
for every pair of bootlaces. But the policy of the Companies Act appears
to me to require that somebody must be responsible for the proper
keeping of the books of a company, and it is sufficient for my judgment
for me to restrict the liability to see that proper entries are made in
matters which would normally be expected to fall within the ken of a
man in the position of E. . . .

(h) 'Puppet' Directors

[260] Selangor United Rubber Estates Ltd v Cradock (No 3)
[1968] 1 WLR 1555, [1968] 2 All ER 289

This was an action for damages against various defendants on the
ground that they had provided, in contravention of s 54 of the English
Companies Act 1948 (s 38 of ours) financial assistance to one Mr Cradock
for the purchase of the company's own shares (p 235 above). Among the
defendants were one Mr Barlow-Lawson and one Mr Jacob who as the
'puppets' of Mr Cradock (who himself was not a member of the board
of directors of the plaintiff company) had effected the transfer of the
company's funds to him. They were held liable.

UNGOED THOMAS J: . . . The allegation against Barlow-Lawson and
Jacob is that they procured that the £232 500 of the plaintiff's money
should be misapplied for the purpose of financing stock in the plaintiff
by Cradock, in bad faith and in breach of their duties as directors and as
part of an arrangement between them, Cradock, Contanglo, District
[Bank Ltd] and Woodstock [Trust Ltd] or some of such defendants to
which the others were privy. They both deny that they were aware that
the plaintiff's money was to be used for such a purpose.

Barlow-Lawson had a small engineering business and had before
the war been an estate agent. . . . He gave the impression of being somewhat flamboyant and happy-go-lucky. . . .

He said that he regarded going on the board of the plaintiff as a
'splendid opportunity' to be a director of a public company. . . .

He authorized the transfer of the plaintiff's moneys on deposit to
Woodstock at 8 per cent without security and without any inquiry about
Woodstock. He said: 'I was quite happy to do what I was told to do by
the virtual owner of the company', and added 'because I obviously
would have thought that he would not have invested the company's
money in something where it would be lost.' Later, he added: 'He said
it was all right, yes, and I naturally took his word, not only was he a
respectable sort of bloke, in my opinion, quite wealthy but also the
owner of the company.'. . . He admitted that he was 'simply . . . the
hands and eyes of Mr Cradock'. . . .

Jacob was an employee of Cradock and his companies. He was engaged
in managing properties and was paid by those companies £2 500 a year
less PAYE, plus the use of a car and expenses. . . . Jacob said that he
was told by Cradock that he was going to be a director of the plaintiff

and that his money and that of the plaintiff were to be transferred to Woodstock and that he realized that that would involve a resolution of the directors, including himself. He said that he voted for the resolution and the removal of the plaintiff's account from National [Bank Ltd] to District [Bank Ltd] because Cradock wanted that. He made no inquiries about the resolutions and never considered the interests of other shareholders than Cradock, but did what Cradock, the majority shareholder, asked him to do. He said that, if Cradock acted honestly, the arrangement was honest, if dishonest it was dishonest, but that there seemed nothing wrong with it, within his knowledge at the time. . . .

It seems to me, however, that both Barlow-Lawson and Jacob were nominated as directors of the plaintiff to do exactly as they were told by Cradock, and that that is in fact what they did. They exercised no discretion or volition of their own and they behaved in utter disregard of their duties as directors to the general body of stockholders or creditors or anyone but Cradock. They put themselves in his hands, not as their agent or adviser, but as their controller. They were puppets which had no movement apart from the strings and those strings were manipulated by Cradock. They were voices without any mind but that of Cradock; and with that mind they are fixed in accordance with the view which I have already expressed on the law. They doubtless hoped for the best but risked the worst; and that worst has befallen them. . . .

[The court refused to relieve the defendants from liability under s 448 (s 248 of our Act) because, even assuming that their participation in the breach of s 54 had not been dishonest 'to dispose of large sums, constituting virtually the whole of the plaintiff company's assets, without any regard whatsoever for minority shareholders, and without consideration, but blindly at the behest of the majority shareholders who nominated them to the board is not to act reasonably'.]

[261] S *v* Shaban
1965 (4) SA 646 (W)

The accused was charged with fraud, arising from his conduct as a director of companies. Broadly stated, the charges related to an alleged misuse of the funds of an insurance company of which he was a director. One of his defences was that at the relevant time he had resigned from his directorship and that one Strydom and one Webb were the directors. The court found, on the facts, that Strydom and Webb were his 'puppets' or 'stooges' who signed everything that was put before them 'without the foggiest notion of what they were doing'. The defence failed.

HIEMSTRA J: I want to destroy any idea that puppets can be lawfully employed in our company system. By that I mean persons placed on boards who pretend to have taken part in resolutions of which they know nothing. The Companies Act knows directors and through practice the concept of nominees has arisen, but they are still lawfully elected directors whose functions as such are not a hollow pretence. Our law does not know the complete puppet who pretends to take part in the management of a company whilst having no idea what it is to which he puts his signature. It is utterly foreign to the basic concepts of our law and the courts will punish it as fraud. The more is this so when an entire board consists of puppets manipulated from outside by persons who are ostensibly unconnected with the company. . . .

The pretence in which the accused took part was that he and De Jager were no longer directors and had no part whatever in directing or controlling the affairs of the company and that they had been replaced by Strydom and Webb. The accused was without a doubt a party to this façade.

He is found guilty.

NOTES

See also *Wallerstein v Moir (1), 23* above, and *S v Hepker, 230* above.

Directors in Action

I DIRECTORS AS THE CONTROLLING MIND OF THE COMPANY

A TEXT

Within the framework of the company's constitution, the board of directors is the 'controlling mind' of the company. It directs its affairs and represents it in its dealings with third parties: *262–265*. (Cf Table A arts 59, 60. As to the formalities of contracts, see ss 69, 70. On contracts of sale of land, more especially, see p 470 below.)

Statutory restrictions on the powers of directors are imposed by ss 221, 222 with regard to the issue and allotment of shares; and by s 228 with regard to the sale of the whole or substantially the whole of the undertaking of the company or the whole or the greater part of the assets of the company: *266, 267*.

B CASES

[262] **Small v Smith**
(1884) 10 App Cas 119

The question was whether a bond granted by the directors of a building society was binding on the society.

LORD WATSON: . . . It appears to me that the true test to apply in such a case is not to consider whether the act might have been competently performed by an individual, or by directors who were not fettered by regulations, or articles, or a memorandum of association. The real test is to consider whether the act is authorized by the statutory rules of the society, which perform a twofold function; in the first place, they define the power of the directors, and in the second place, they ensure that all who deal with the directors shall have notice of the precise limits of their authority. We cannot assume that the directors have power to do everything which may be usually done by unfettered directors, or by individuals. We must consider whether the rules confer, either expressly or by any fair implication, authority upon the directors to grant a bond . . . binding upon the society. . . .

[263] Lennard's Carrying Company Ltd v Asiatic Petroleum Company Ltd
[1915] AC 705

A ship and her cargo were lost owing to unseaworthiness. The owners of the ship were a limited company. The managers of that company were another limited company, whose managing director, a Mr Lennard, managed the ship on behalf of the owners. He knew, or ought to have known, of the ship's unseaworthiness, but took no steps to prevent the ship from putting to sea.

The purchasers of the cargo and endorsees of the bills of lading sued the owners of the ship for their loss. Under s 502 of the British Merchant Shipping Act, then in force, the owner of a sea-going ship was not liable to make good 'any loss or damage happening without his fault'. The owners of the ship sought to bring themselves within this exemption, claiming that they were not liable for Mr Lennard's fault. The trial judge found for the plaintiffs and this was confirmed on appeal by the court of appeal, and on further appeal by the House of Lords.

VISCOUNT HALDANE: Now, my Lords, did what happened take place without the actual fault or privity of the owners of the ship who were the appellants? My Lords, a corporation is an abstraction. It has no mind of its own any more than it has a body of its own; its active and directing will must consequently be sought in the person of somebody who for some purposes may be called an agent, but who is really the directing mind and will of the corporation, the very ego and centre of the personality of the corporation. That person may be under the direction of the shareholders in general meeting; that person may be the board of directors itself, or it may be, and in some companies it is so, that that person has an authority co-ordinate with the board of directors given to him under the articles of association, and is appointed by the general meeting of the company, and can only be removed by the general meeting of the company. My Lords, whatever is not known about Mr Lennard's position, this is known for certain, Mr Lennard took the active part in the management of this ship on behalf of the owners, and Mr Lennard, as I have said, was registered as the person designated for this purpose in the ship's register. Mr Lennard therefore was the natural person to come on behalf of the owners and give full evidence not only about the events of which I have spoken, and which related to the seaworthiness of the ship, but about his own position and as to whether or not he was the life and soul of the company. For if Mr Lennard was the directing mind of the company, then his action must, unless a corporation is not to be liable at all, have been an action which was the action of the company itself within the meaning of s 502.

[See also *The Lady Gwendolen* [1965] P 294, [1965] 2 All ER 283 (CA) and L H Leigh (1965) 28 *Mod LR* 584.]

[264] H L Bolton & Company v T J Graham & Sons
[1957] 1 QB 159, [1956] 3 All ER 624 (CA)

Under the English Landlord and Tenant Act 1954 the plaintiffs, tenants of certain business premises, were entitled to a renewal of their tenancy unless the landlords intended to occupy these premises them-selves for the purposes of their business. The question was whether the defendant company had effectively formed this intention. The directors of a group of cement companies, to which the defendant company belonged, had decided to build a new warehouse and office block on certain land owned by the defendant company. The directors of the defendant company caused notice to vacate to be given to the tenants, but there had been no formal meeting of their board and no formal resolution to occupy the land for the purposes of their business. The plaintiffs claimed that under these circumstances the defendant company as the landlords of the premises in question had not formed the intention to occupy the premises itself and that, in consequence, the plaintiffs were entitled to a new tenancy.

The Court decided in favour of the defendant company.

DENNING LJ: . . . Counsel for the tenants urges that the landlords have not shown the necessary intention. He says there must at least be a board meeting. In view of the recent decision of this court in *Austin Reed Ltd* v *Royal Assurance Company Ltd* (so far unreported) he has to concede that the decision of the board need not formally be recorded in a minute, but he says that, even though it is not formally recorded, there must be a board meeting by which there is a collective decision, and it is not sufficient that individual directors should individually be of one mind. . . .

The judge [of first instance] has found that the landlord company, through their managers, intend to occupy the premises for their own purposes. [Counsel for the tenants] contests this finding and he has referred us to cases decided in the last century, but I must say that the law on this matter and the approach to it have developed very considerably since then. A company may in many ways be likened to a human body. They have a brain and a nerve centre which controls what they do. They also have hands which hold the tools and act in accordance with directions from the centre. Some of the people in the company are mere servants and agents who are nothing more than hands to do the work and cannot be said to represent the mind or will. Others are directors and managers who represent the directing mind and will of the company, and control what they do. The state of mind of these managers is the state of mind of the company and is treated by the law as such. So you will find that in cases where the law requires personal fault as a condition of liability in tort, the fault of the manager will be the personal fault of the company. . . . So also in the criminal law, in cases where the law requires a guilty mind as a condition of a criminal offence, the guilty mind of the directors or the managers will render the company themselves guilty. . . .

. . . So here the intention of the landlord company can be derived from the intention of their officers and agents. Whether their intention is the company's intention depends on the nature of the matter under consideration, the relative position of the officer or agent and the other relevant facts and circumstances of the case. Approaching the matter in that way, although there was no board meeting, nevertheless, having regard to the standing of these directors in control of the business of the company, having regard to the other facts and circumstances which we know, whereby plans had been prepared and much work done, it seems to me that the judge was entitled to infer that the intention of the landlord company was to occupy the holding for their own purposes. . . .

[265] CIR *v* Richmond Estates (Pty) Ltd
1956 (1) SA 602 (AD)

One of the questions was whether the respondent company held certain properties as an investment or as stock-in-trade. The special court found on the facts that at the end of 1948 the company had decided not to sell its properties but to retain them as an investment.

CENTLIVRES CJ: Counsel for the Commissioner attacked the . . . finding of fact . . . on the ground, if I understand him correctly, that, as there was no formal resolution by the respondent showing a change of intention and policy, there was no evidence on which the Special Court for Income Tax Appeals could arrive at that finding and for this contention he relied on the following statement of Benjamin J in *Wilson* v *Commissioner for Inland Revenue* 1926 CPD 63 at 70:

'The company being an artificial entity, its intentions must be determined from its formal acts.'

In *Wilson's* case the bulk of the shares were held by a deceased estate and there were two other shareholders who held a substantial number of shares. I shall assume that in the case of such a company the only method of arriving at the intention of the company is that stated by Benjamin J. In the present case we have what is commonly called a one-man company, the one man being Caplan, who was its sole director as well as its managing director. In these circumstances the absence of formal resolutions is not surprising. A company is an artificial person with no body to kick and no soul to damn and the only way of ascertaining its intention is to find out what its directors acting as such intended. Their formal acts in the form of resolutions constitute evidence as to the intentions of the company of which they are directors but where a company has only one director, who is also the managing director and the sole beneficial owner of all its shares, I can see no reason in principle why it should be incompetent for him to give evidence as to what was the intention of the company at any given time. In such a case it is, perhaps, not going too far to say that his mind is also the mind of the company.

NOTES

See also F S Steyn J in *Avondson Trust (Pty) Ltd* v *Wouda* 1975 (2) SA 444 (T): '. . . in a legal person where the normal pressures of motivation, interest and action cannot be unravelled as in a natural person, the manifest intent of its officials and directors, its resolutions and subsequent actions should be jointly considered to ascertain whether the company did indeed accept a benefit [conferred upon it by others] or not . . .' (at 447H). 'With a single director . . . and sole substantial shareholder, a decision of the company cannot be distinguished from the frame of mind and interest of that sole director and shareholder' (at 448D).

The doctrine that the directors are the 'controlling mind' of the company is known as the 'organic theory'. On the identification of a company with its managing director for the purposes of a 'reasonable precautions' clause in an insurance policy, see *Aetna Ins Co v Dormer Estates (Pty) Ltd* 1965 (4) SA 656 (N), which should be compared with *Aviation Ins Co Ltd v Burton Construction Ltd* 1976 (4) SA 769 (AD), where a breach of the Aviation Regulations by a pilot of the insured company was held not to amount to a breach of the warranty clause by the company.

Normally, the knowledge of directors is the knowledge of the company, but a director cannot be taken to have disclosed his own fraud to the company: *In re European Bank* (1870) 5 Ch App 358; *J C Houghton & Co v Nothard, Lowe and Wills Ltd* [1928] 1 AC 1, esp at 14. (But cf *Randbank Bpk v Santam Versekerings Maatskappy Bpk* 1965 (4) SA 363 (AD).) Where the same person is a director of two companies, the one company has not necessarily knowledge of everything that is within his knowledge as a director of the other company: *In re Marseilles Extension Railway Co* (1871) 7 Ch App 161; *In re Hampshire Land Co* [1896] 2 Ch 743; *Kwei Tek Chao v British Traders and Shippers Ltd* [1954] 2 QB 459 *sub nom Chao v British Traders and Shippers Ltd* [1954] 1 All ER 779. Cf *In re Fenwick, Stobart & Co Ltd* [1902] 1 Ch 507 (where a man acts as secretary of two companies, a fact which comes to his knowledge as secretary of one company is not notice to him as secretary of the other company unless it is his duty to the first company to communicate his knowledge to the second company). Again, knowledge acquired by a director independently in his personal capacity cannot be necessarily imputed to his company: *In re David Payne & Co Ltd* [1904] 2 Ch 608, esp at 618–19. See further *John Henshall Ltd v Harvey* [1965] 2 QB 233, [1965] 1 All ER 725. In *R v Kritzinger* 1971 (2) SA 57 (AD) (first reported in 1953 (2) PH H109 (AD)), it was held that a person can perpetrate a fraud upon a company by making a misrepresentation to its board of directors even if all the members of the board (including the malefactor himself) are aware of its falsity. See also *S v Heller* 1971 (2) SA 29 (AD), *238* above.

Admissions by directors are not necessarily binding on the company: *Simmons NO v Gilbert Hamer & Co Ltd* 1963 (1) SA 897 (N) at 918–22. As regards an admission of guilt, see *R v Fruit Growers (Pvt) Ltd* 1966 (2) SA 180 (RAD).

In *Connock's (SA) Motor Co Ltd v Sentraal Westelike Ko-operatiewe Maatskappy Bpk* 1964 (2) SA 47 (T), estoppel was raised as a defence to the company's claim. Trollip J said (at 53): '. . . where the representor is a company the knowledge of the relevant facts that is required is its actual or imputed, and not merely constructive knowledge. . . . That would, therefore, include the knowledge of any of its agents or servants possessed or acquired by him in the course of his employment under such circumstances and being of such a nature that it was his duty to communicate it to the proper authority in the company . . . unless that agent or servant is perpetrating a fraud on the company in relation to the matters of which he so possesses or acquires knowledge. . . .'

On constructive notice to a company, see also *African Films Ltd v Bijou Theatres Ltd* 1925 OPD 31.

On company's signature see *Firwood Sweet Manufacturers (Pty) Ltd v Ager Motors* 1959 (2) PH A 28 (N) (company's name plus director's signature); *Jones v John Barr & Co (Pty) Ltd* 1967 (3) SA 292 (W) (signature by rubber stamp); *Meyer v Roberts* 1971 (1) SA 328 (O) (company bound by a cheque signed on its behalf by a director irrespective of whether the director signed above or below the dotted line, as long as it is clear that he signed on behalf of the company). See also p 497 below.

On powers of directors, see further *Smith v Paringa Mines Ltd* [1906] 2 Ch 193 (directors, in the absence of express authority in the articles, have no power to postpone a general meeting of the company properly convened); *Peel v London and North Western Railway Co* [1907] 1 Ch 5 (*183*). Where the constitution of the company vests the control of litigation in the directors, the question may arise whether the shareholders have parallel, or at least residual powers of litigation. See *Alexander Ward & Co Ltd v Samyang Navigation Ltd*, *221* above, and *Re Argentum Reductions (UK) Ltd* [1975] 1 WLR 186, [1975] 1 All ER 608, noted by K W W (1976) 39 *MLR* 327.

Actions on behalf of the company must be instituted by the directors (*John Shaw & Sons (Salford) Ltd v Shaw* [1935] 2 KB 113; *Kempff v Visse* 1958 (1) PH F 6 (T)), but in court a company must be represented by counsel—not by its managing director even if he be sole shareholder: *Frinton and Walton Urban District Council v Walton and District Sand and Mineral Co Ltd* [1938] 1 All ER 649; *Tritonia Ltd v Equity and Law Life Assurance Society* [1943] AC 584, [1943] 2 All ER 401; *Yates Investments (Pty) Ltd v CIR* 1956 (1) SA 364 (AD); *Ramsey v Fuchs Garage (Pty) Ltd* 1959 (3) SA 949 (C). In an application by a company proper proof must be adduced that the application was authorized by the company: *Mall (Cape) (Pty) Ltd* v *Merino Ko-operasie Bpk* 1957 (2) SA 347 (C); *Griffiths & Inglis (Pty) Ltd* v *Southern Cape Blasters (Pty) Ltd* 1972 (4) SA 249 (C). The general meeting of shareholders decides whether an action is to be instituted against the directors of the company: *Pender* v *Lushington* (1877) 6 ChD 70.

Where the articles of a company give the directors borrowing powers without stating that these powers are to be exclusive, the company itself retains its general power to borrow, which it may exercise through properly authorized agents: *Mercantile Bank of India Ltd* v *Chartered Bank of India, Australia and China, and Strauss & Co* [1937] 1 All ER 231.

The single director of a private company can effectively sign his own authorization, *African Peach Growers Bpk* v *Bouwer* 1973 (4) SA 654 (T).

[266] Lindner *v* National Bakery (Pty) Ltd
1961 (1) SA 372 (O)

The applicant had purchased the assets of a company in liquidation and sold them to the second respondent as trustee of a new company to be formed. The deed of sale provided, *inter alia*, that should the second respondent dispose of the shares of the new company or should the assets of that company be sold, the applicant should be given the first option to acquire these shares or assets.

The new company (first respondent) was duly incorporated. It took delivery of the assets in question and made certain payments to the applicant. The applicant then learnt that it had sold its business to one J without notifying the applicant.

Alleging that the sale to J was in breach of the agreement with him, the applicant applied for an order interdicting the two respondents from proceeding with the sale to J, without giving him an opportunity of exercising his option. The respondents contended, first, that the pre-emption clause in favour of the applicant required for its valid adoption by the respondent company a resolution of its shareholders in general meeting in terms of s 70*dec*(2) [now s 228], and that, as no such resolution had been passed, the clause was not binding on the respondents; secondly, that even if the clause had been approved in general meeting, it would not be binding on the respondent company. The terms of s 70*dec*(2) were such as to put it beyond the power of any company to grant a right of pre-emption in respect of its undertaking or the whole or the greater part of its assets. The clause was therefore incapable of being ratified, adopted or confirmed.

SMUTS AJ: Although it may be so that until such time as a resolution authorizing a sale of the assets of first respondent is passed, applicant will not, due to the provisions of s 70*dec*(2), be able to enforce a sale to him by first respondent, I do not think that [the pre-emption clause] is devoid of any effect at all.

Normally a right of pre-emption, as it is usually framed, enables the grantee thereof to enforce a sale to him on the same terms offered to the grantor by a prospective purchaser once the grantor has decided to sell to such purchaser, on the terms offered. . . .

The grantee, once he becomes aware that the grantor has agreed to sell to a third party, may, if he pleases, compel the grantor to submit to him the offer which he, the grantor, has received from the third party so as to enable him, the grantee, to accept such offer. The grantee need, however, not go that far and can simply interdict the grantor from transferring ownership until such time as the grantor submits to him the terms of the offer he has received.

Reverting now to the provisions of [the agreement] the pre-emption clause provides that should the assets of the company to be formed be sold applicant is to be given the 'first option' to acquire such assets on the same terms and conditions as are bona fide offered to the company by any purchaser.

The offer which the first respondent undertakes to submit to the applicant for his acceptance must obviously be a valid offer, that is to say, an offer of such a nature that if accepted it will constitute a valid agreement of sale between the parties. If it is necessary that such an offer should be sanctioned by a resolution of shareholders in general meeting it will be the duty of first respondent to seek to obtain such a resolution from its shareholders. If it is unable to obtain such a resolution first respondent can of course not be compelled to submit an offer to applicant for his acceptance. But that does not mean that first respondent can then sell its assets as it pleases. The undertaking to submit a valid offer to applicant on the same terms as those offered to a third party to whom first respondent is prepared to sell carries with it, as a necessary implication, the duty and obligation not to sell to a third party until such time as a valid offer has first been made to applicant.

As far as I am aware there is nothing to prevent a company through its directors from entering into such an undertaking. Such an undertaking does not contravene the provisions of s 70*dec*(2), as it is not a disposal of any assets. It merely prohibits the company from disposing of its assets pending the fulfilment of a condition, namely, that the company makes a valid offer of sale to applicant which is not accepted by him within 30 days.

The fact that the directors may not be able to persuade the shareholders to consent to the offer being made to applicant does not appear to me to affect the validity of the undertaking or its binding effect on first respondent. If the shareholders refuse to consent the result is simply that the company cannot dispose of its assets; it does not lead to an invalid disposal and therefore s 70*dec*(2) is not contravened. . . .

[The pre-emption clause] would therefore not require for its valid adoption by the company a resolution of shareholders in terms of s 70*dec*(2). The company could validly adopt it by the resolution of its directors. . . .

[*Lindner* v *National Bakery (Pty) Ltd* is noted in (1961) 78 *SALJ* 135.]

[267] Sugden v Beaconhurst Dairies (Pty) Ltd
1963 (2) SA 174 (E)

Action for the implementation of four agreements for the sale of land by the defendant company. The agreements related to four portions of the farm 'Bleakhouse'.

O'HAGAN J: The case made out by the applicants is a simple one for the performance of contracts of sale on the face of them valid and enforceable.

... It is said [by the defendant company] that the requirements of s 70*dec*(2) of the Companies Act were not complied with when the various contracts of sale were concluded. ... According to a schedule ... the company owned fixed assets valued at R208 183,30, and of these the whole farm 'Bleakhouse' was shown at a value of R110 000 — more than half of the total. For the company it was argued that the directors' decision to sell this property, followed by four separate sales to the three applicants, constituted a disposal of the 'greater part of the assets of the company', and that inasmuch as the directors' action had not received the approval of the company in general meeting, the sales were void.

At the times relevant to this matter ... there were only two shareholders in and directors of the company. They were A M L Crawford and J R Crawford. ...

... In February 1962 a mandate to sell the whole farm was given to the auctioneer by A M L Crawford on behalf of the company. The auction took place on 28 April. On the same day, according to a company minute, a meeting of directors resolved to authorize the auctioneer to accept Sugden's increased offer of R30 000; and this authority was recorded in writing by A M L Crawford on behalf of the company on the conditions of sale which Sugden had signed. The auctioneer then signed an acceptance of the offer. Another minute reveals that on 14 May a directors' meeting resolved that the auctioneer be authorized to accept on the company's behalf the two offers made by the third applicant for portions 2 and 3 of the farm. On the same day the auctioneer signed the conditions of sale accepting the two offers.

On 18 July another meeting of directors was held. Both A M L Crawford and J R Crawford were present. It was resolved that the auctioneer be authorized to accept on the company's behalf the second applicant's offer for portion 4 of the farm; and it was resolved further that the resolutions taken on 28 April and 14 May be confirmed.

In my opinion it is to be inferred from all the evidence that the decision to dispose of 'Bleakhouse', and the implementation of that decision, was founded upon the joint consent and approval of both of the company's two shareholders and directors. ... It is true that s 70*dec*(2) prescribes the formality of a general meeting for the approval of a resolution to which the subsection relates; but inasmuch as the subsection was designed for the benefit of shareholders why should the shareholders not be able to waive compliance with the formalities that are ordinarily attendant upon the convening of a general meeting? In my view, where the only two shareholders and directors express — whether at the same time or not — their joint approval of a transaction contemplated by s 70*dec*(2), their decision is as valid and effectual as if it had been taken at a general meeting convened with all the formalities prescribed by the Act.

In the result I hold that the sales to the three applicants are not invalid through want of compliance with the requirements of s 70*dec*(2).

NOTES

The approval by the general meeting can be supplied retrospectively: *In re Olympus Consolidated Mines Ltd* 1958 (2) SA 381 (SR).

On s 70*dec*(2) of the old Act, which has now been replaced by s 228, see K van Dijkhorst *Huldigingsbundel Daniel Pont* (1970) 372; Basil Wunsh (1971) 88 *SALJ* 351. On s 228 of the 1973 Act, see D S Ribbens (1976) 36 *THRHR* 162.

II The Board of Directors—The Managing Director

A TEXT

When it is stated in the articles that the business of the company shall be managed by 'the directors' (Table A art 59, Table B art 60), 'the directors' means the board of directors. The powers of the company vest in the directors as a collective, a board, and not as individuals.

Directors act at board meetings, of which proper notice must be given to all directors, and at which a quorum must be present: *268–272*. (See Table A arts 75–82, Table B arts 73–82.) On minute books and attendance registers, see ss 242–246. With the consent of all the directors, a formal board meeting may be dispensed with: *273*. The articles may provide that a resolution signed by the directors shall be as valid as if passed at a meeting, see ss 236 and 242(2), and Table B art 76.

Unlike shareholders, directors cannot fetter their discretion by voting agreements: *274, 275*.

The articles may give the board of directors power to delegate all or some of its powers to a committee of one or more of its members (cf Table A art 80, Table B art 79), or to appoint a managing director (cf Table A arts 61, 62, Table B arts 62, 63): *276–279*.

The board of directors (or, inasmuch as the company's powers have been delegated to them, the executive committee or managing director) may authorize the chairman of the board, a director, a secretary, a manager, or some other servant of the company or an outsider to act as an agent of the company, either generally or in certain matters: *280*.

A contract which is outside the powers of the directors because it is *ultra vires* the company is nevertheless binding on the company, s 36 (see p 78 above). A contract which is outside the powers of the directors because they lack the necessary authority is not binding on the company but may be validated by the company in general meeting or by the assent of all the shareholders. The same holds true of any irregularity in their proceedings.

B CASES

[268] D'Arcy *v* The Tamar, Kit Hill and Callington Railway Co
(1867) LR 2 Exch 158

Two directors declared their approval to the raising of a bond in a letter to the secretary, the third one gave the secretary his oral consent when he met him in the street. The court held that the bond was invalid.

PIGOTT B: . . . No doubt this is the deed of the company if it is the deed of the directors properly done; the question is, whether it is so done. The special Act . . . makes 'the quorum of *a meeting* of directors' three, and the general act speaks also of meetings of directors. Three directors have given their assent to the issuing of this bond, but were they a meeting? Clearly they were not; but, on the contrary, the secretary casually picked up three members of the body of directors, and obtained their assents separately. The seal has been affixed without the authority of a meeting of directors, and the bond is therefore invalid.

[*D'Arcy* v *The Tamar Railway Co* was referred to with approval by Rumpff CJ in *S* v *Naudé* 1975 (1) SA 681 (AD) at 700–1.]

[269] Bottomley's case
(1880) 16 ChD 681

The articles provided that the business of the company be conducted by a specified number of directors. It was held that a call made or forfeiture of shares declared by less than this number was invalid.

JESSEL MR: . . . The shareholders have entrusted the management of their business to a certain number of persons, not to any other number. They say, in effect, 'there shall not be less than five, nor more than seven, who shall manage our business; less than five shall not be the managers'. If, in an ordinary case, persons appointed seven people to be their attorneys, and said, 'they shall conduct the business not being less than five', would anybody say that if the attorneys were below five they could conduct the business? Is there any distinction between that case and this? Or take the case of a man going away and leaving his business to three clerks, and giving them power to act for him, and to draw bills, not less than two to act together—could any one of them draw bills? I do not see the distinction on principle. The contract of this partnership, or quasi-partnership, is that the business shall be managed by not less than a certain number of persons: what right has a court of justice to say that it shall be managed by a less number, without the shareholders being consulted? . . .

[270] *In re* Homer District Consolidated Gold Mines
(1888) 39 ChD 546

A company, which had five directors, invited applications for 106 000 preference shares. At a meeting of all the directors it was resolved not to allot any shares until application for 14 000 shares had been received. The company received applications for only 3 000 shares. Thereupon two directors (two being the quorum) held a meeting and resolved to cancel the previous resolution and allot at once the shares applied for. The meeting was held at two o'clock, a few hours' notice having been given to two of the directors who did not attend. The fifth director was abroad and no notice was sent to him.

Held, that the allotment was void.

NORTH J: . . . It seems to me that what was done was as irregular as possible. Without wishing to suggest any fraud on the part of the two directors present, the conclusion I come to as to their acts is that they did think it desirable that the shares should be allotted as soon as possible. They knew that Witt and Simpson had opposed the allotment of shares till a larger number were applied for. They proposed to do what they may have thought they could do; they thought they could get rid of the opposition of their co-directors, and pass a resolution that would bind the company.

With regard to the notice of the meeting, it was such as had never before been given in the history of the company. The shortest notice that had ever been given before was a notice for the next day. The notice was sent out in a most irregular way. What is more, it was expressed in such a way (I cannot help thinking intentionally so expressed) as not to give Witt and Simpson notice of what was to be done. On that notice at two o'clock, the two directors present knowing that one of the other two summoned could not be present till three, and not knowing whether the other could come, proceeded at once to rescind a resolution passed by the board two weeks before. In my opinion that was about as irregular as anything could be. No doubt a bare quorum is capable to act and bind the company at a meeting duly convened, with proper notice given to the other directors, at which therefore all the other directors may, if they please, be present; but, these two directors met, having abstained from telling the others what they intended to do, and proceeded to pass these resolutions in the full belief, and, I think, knowledge, that if the others had had notice and been able to be there they would have objected; and further than that, with notice as to one that he would be there at three, they proceeded to pass their resolution at two. They ought certainly to have waited. I do not say that would have been enough. I come to the conclusion that what was done on that occasion was not the act of the board of directors, and did not bind the company, and had not the effect of getting rid of the resolutions previously passed by the board. . . .

[271] **Barron v Potter**
[1914] 1 Ch 895

The British Seagumite Company Ltd, a private company, was incorporated in January 1912. According to art 21 of the articles of association the number of directors was to be not less than two or more than ten. Article 26 stated that the quorum of directors was to be two, unless otherwise fixed by the directors.

Early in 1914 there were two directors only, W J Potter, the chairman and managing director, and Canon Barron. The conduct of the company's business was at a standstill as Canon Barron refused to attend any board meeting with Mr Potter.

On 21 February Mr Potter sent to Canon Barron a notice requesting him to attend a board meeting at the company's office on 24 February. This notice, however, was not received by Canon Barron until a later date.

Canon Barron happened to arrive by train at Paddington Station on 23 February and was met on the platform by Mr Potter who, according to his evidence, seeing Canon Barron alight from the train, walked by his side along the platform and said to him, 'I want to see you, please'. Canon Barron replied, 'I have nothing to say to you'. Mr Potter then said, 'I formally propose that we add the Reverend Charles Herbert, Mr William George Walter Barnard, and Mr John Tolehurst Musgrave as additional directors to the board of the British Seagumite Company Limited. Do you agree or object?' Canon Barron replied, 'I object and I object to say anything to you at all'. Mr Potter then said, 'In my capacity as chairman I give my casting vote in their favour and declare them duly elected'. He continued to walk with Canon Barron a few steps and then said, 'That is all I want to say. I thank you. Good day.'

WARRINGTON J: . . . In my opinion . . . there was no directors' meeting at all for the reason that Canon Barron to the knowledge of Mr Potter insisted all along that he would not attend any directors' meeting with Mr Potter or discuss the affairs of the company with him, and it is not enough that one of two directors should say, 'This is a directors' meeting' while the other says it is not. Of course if directors are willing to hold a meeting they may do so under any circumstances, but one of them cannot be made to attend the board or to convert a casual meeting into a board meeting, and in the present case I do not see how the meeting in question can be treated as a board meeting. . . . There was therefore no board meeting at which Canon Barron was present. Mr Potter was alone present, so that there was no quorum, and I must hold that the three additional directors named by him were not validly appointed. . . .

[272] African Organic Fertilizers and Associated Industries Ltd v Premier Fertilizers Ltd
1948 (3) SA 233 (N)

BROOME J: . . . I . . . accept the principles that notice of a directors' meeting must be given to every director who is within reach, and that the question whether a director is within reach depends upon the circumstances, including the nature of the business to be transacted. If the business to be transacted were contentious, the degree of inaccessibility would have to be very great. If, on the other hand, the business were not contentious but required immediate attention, the degree of inaccessibility would be very much less, particularly where the absent director knew and approved of the formal business to be transacted. . . .

NOTES

See also *Majola Investments (Pty) Ltd* v *Uitzigt Properties (Pty) Ltd* 1961 (4) SA 705 (T) where it was held, *inter alia*, that if the articles do not provide otherwise, directors may meet on oral notice. On notice of directors' meetings, see further *Browne* v *La Trinidad* (1887) 37 ChD 1; *La Compagnie de Mayville* v *Whitley* [1896] 1 Ch 788; *Young* v *Ladies' Imperial Club* [1920] 2 KB 523.

The articles may permit the directors to appoint a quorum of one: *In re Fireproof Doors Ltd* [1916] 2 Ch 142; *Sugden* v *Beaconhurst Dairies (Pty) Ltd* 1963 (2) SA 174 (E) at 182. Where the articles do not prescribe a quorum, the number of directors who usually act will constitute a quorum: *Lyster's* case (1867) LR 4 Eq 233.

In *Blythe* v *The Phoenix Foundry Ltd* 1922 WLD 87 the articles provided that the number of directors should be not less than two or more than five, and that three directors should constitute a quorum. The court held that when only two directors were left to act, these two constituted a quorum. Similarly, in *Gorfil v Marendaz* 1965 (1) SA 686 (T), where the quorum was two, and the directors had the right under the articles to fill casual vacancies, it was held that if as a result of death or resignation only one director was left, he had the power to fill a casual vacancy. The court stressed that he had to act at a meeting, even though it had to be a meeting of himself alone. 'The general way in which directors act is at a meeting, but for there to be a meeting, even of one, there must be some formality to show that that is intended' (per Clayden J at 690).

In *Wagenaar v Krugersdorp Stone Crushers (Pty) Ltd* 1954 (3) SA 452 (W) the articles prescribed (*a*) that the board of directors had to be unanimous; and (*b*) that no director should vote on a matter in which he was interested. It was held that where a director is interested, the rule of unanimity is satisfied by the unanimous assent of the other directors.

If six out of seven directors meet in a different capacity and for a different purpose they are not the board: *Barber's* case (1877) 5 ChD 963.

A resolution taken at an irregular meeting is invalid: *In re Sly, Spink & Co* [1911] 2 Ch 430; *Wessels & Smith v Vanugo Construction (Pty) Ltd* 1964 (1) SA 635 (O).

However, while the assent of directors must ordinarily be expressed formally in a resolution duly minuted, the courts have tended to accept an informal assent in certain circumstances as effective, especially in small private companies or where the irregularity is one which can be easily remedied and is certain to be remedied, see e g *Bentley-Stevens v Jones* [1974] 2 All ER 653 (Ch); also *Collie's Claim, 273* below.

Urgent proceedings involving a director may exceptionally be instituted by the other directors without calling a directors' meeting first: *Ex parte Aloe Engineering Industries (Pty) Ltd* 1965 (2) SA 151 (W).

In several cases, e g *Silver Garbus & Co (Pty) Ltd v Teichert* 1954 (2) SA 98 (N), the court expressed its disapproval of the practice of certifying extracts from minutes when in fact no directors' meeting has been held (*186* above). On the keeping of minutes, see further *Hearts of Oak Assurance Co Ltd v James Flower & Sons* [1936] Ch 76.

[273] Collie's claim
(1871) LR 12 Eq 246

The quorum of directors prescribed by the articles was three. A letter containing an agreement with another party was signed by two directors in the office of the company and handed to the other party who forwarded it to the third director in the country. The latter returned it to the other party, signed by himself and a fourth director.

Held, that the agreement, though informal according to the internal regulations of the company, was binding on the company.

BACON V-C: . . . It is said that the formal authority to enter into the agreement was wanting, for that article providing that the acts of directors shall be binding means that they shall act in their 'combined wisdom'; and that nothing shall be valid that is not done by three of them together.

Now, first of all, there is no such thing said in the articles. I quite agree that the 'combined wisdom' is required in this sense, that they must all be of one mind. But I do not know that it is necessary they shall all meet in one place. I can conceive a great many circumstances which I do not say happened in this case, but which may happen in any case, where the actual presence of the three directors cannot be procured, but where their combination can be most effectually secured by correspondence, by transmission of messages, or by other means which may be resorted to. If you are satisfied that the persons whose concurrence is necessary to give validity to the act did so concur, with full knowledge of all that they were doing, in my opinion the terms of the law are fully satisfied, and it is not necessary that whatever is done by directors should be done under some roof, in some place, where they are all three assembled. . . .

[274] Coronation Syndicate Ltd v Lilienfeld and the New Fortuna Company Ltd
1903 TS 489

SOLOMON J: . . . No doubt there are certain cases in which a court would make an order upon directors to convene a meeting of shareholders. Where, for instance, there are statutory provisions requiring directors to call meetings at certain times, and the directors in disregard of their duties refuse to obey these provisions, a court of justice might be invoked for the purpose of compelling the directors to do their duty. Or where the articles of association provide that upon requisition of shareholders the directors shall call a meeting, and the directors refuse to respond to such a requisition. . . . But the present case is a very different one. Here the directors of a company have bound themselves by contract with a third person, who is not even a shareholder, to call a general meeting and to submit and support certain proposals for increasing the capital of the company.

It appears to me that there is a very great difference in principle between the case of a shareholder binding himself by such a contract and the directors of the company undertaking such an obligation. The shareholder is dealing with his own property, and is entitled to consider merely his own interests, without regard to the interests of the other shareholders. But the directors are in a fiduciary position, and it is their duty to do what they consider will best serve the interests of the shareholders. If, therefore, they have bound themselves by contract to do a certain thing, and thereafter have bona fide come to the conclusion that it is not in the interests of the shareholders, that they should carry out their undertaking, I do not think that the court would be justified in interfering with their discretion and compelling them to do what they honestly believe would be detrimental to the interests of the shareholders. . . .

[275] Ringuet v Bergeron
[1960] SCR 672 (Supreme Court of Canada)

Shareholders had entered into an agreement to acquire control of a company. Each party undertook (1) to vote for each other's election to the board of directors; (2) to ensure the election of the defendant R as president, of the defendant P as vice-president and general manager, and of the plaintiff B as secretary-treasurer and assistant general manager; (3) to vote unanimously at all meetings. The agreement further provided that on a breach by it of one of the parties his shares were to be transferred to the others.

The plaintiff B was subsequently excluded from the management. He sued for breach of contract. The sole defence was that the contract was contrary to public order in that it imposed restrictions on the freedom of decision of directors. The trial court accepted this defence and dismissed the action. The court of appeal reversed the decision and a further appeal to the Supreme Court of Canada was dismissed by a majority of three to two.

JUDSON J [for the majority]: Did the parties of this agreement tie their hands in their capacity as directors of the company so as to contravene the requirements of the Quebec Companies Act, which provides that 'the affairs of the company shall be managed by a board of not less than three directors'? I agree with the reasons of the learned Chief Justice that this agreement does not contravene this or any other section. . . . It is no more than an agreement among shareholders owning or proposing to own the majority of the issued shares of a company to unite upon a course of policy or action and upon the officers whom they will elect. There is nothing illegal or contrary to public order in an agreement for achieving these purposes. Shareholders have the right to combine their interests and voting powers to secure such control of a company and to ensure that the company will be managed by certain persons in a certain manner. This is a well-known, normal and legal contract and one which is frequently encountered in current practice and it makes no difference whether the objects sought are to be achieved by means of an agreement such as this or a voting trust. Such an arrangement is not prohibited either by law, by good morals or public order.

It is important to distinguish the present action, which is between contracting parties to an agreement for the voting of shares, from one brought by a minority shareholder demanding a certain standard of conduct from directors and majority shareholders. Nothing that can arise from this litigation . . . can touch on that problem.

NOTES

See also *Northern Counties Securities Ltd* v *Jackson & Steeple Ltd*, *173* above, further *Boulting* v *Association of Cinematograph, Television and Allied Technicians* [1963] 2 QB 606, [1963] 1 All ER 716, where Lord Denning MR stated (at 626–7) that it was unlawful for a director to bind himself to act in accordance with the instructions of another person or body. It followed, *inter alia*, that a nominee director may not bind himself to act in accordance with the directors or interests of his patron or to subordinate the interests of the company to the interests of his patron (cf p 390 above). But see also *Stewart* v *Schwab*, *208* above.

[276] *In re* **Newspaper Proprietary Syndicate Ltd**
[1900] 2 Ch 349

COZENS-HARDY J: A managing director is only an ordinary director entrusted with some special powers. . . .

[277] **Nelson** *v* **James Nelson & Sons Ltd**
[1914] 2 KB 770

SWINFEN EADY LJ: Unless there is a power given to the directors by the articles to appoint a managing director it is not competent for them to make such an appointment. . . . The articles may give a power to the directors to appoint one of their members to be managing director, but no power to revoke or cancel the appointment. The company may keep that power in its own hands to be exercised in general meeting.

[278] Moresby White v Rangeland Ltd
1952 (4) SA 285 (SR)

TREDGOLD CJ: ... The term 'managing director' has become virtually a term of art in company law and is applied to a director who is vested by the board of directors with all or a substantial part of its general powers of the control of the affairs of the company. He is the direct and immediate representative of the board, fully recognized as such for certain legal purposes. Acts within his ostensible authority bind the company in its dealings with other parties. A fully accredited managing director, acting in that capacity, acts as the company itself, just as the board so acts, and he could not properly be described as the servant of the company. But it does not follow that every director to whom is delegated any part of the management of the company thereby becomes a managing director. His relation to the company cannot be determined by the description applied to him. It falls to be decided in the light of the actual terms of the agreement between the company and himself. ...

[279] H Holdsworth & Co (Wakefield) Ltd v Caddies
[1955] 1 WLR 352, 1955 SC 27, [1955] 1 All ER 725 (HL)

The plaintiff (respondent) in this action was formerly managing director of the British Textile Company and the beneficial owner of all its shares. In November 1947 the defendant (appellant) company purchased from him the whole share capital of the British Textile Company. In terms of the agreement the defendant company was bound to procure that the plaintiff be appointed to the board of the defendant company and be appointed managing director of the British Textile Company, and this was duly done. In April 1949 a second agreement was entered into by which the plaintiff was appointed managing director of the defendant company for a period of five years. At that time the appellant company controlled, apart from the British Textile Company, two other subsidiaries. In May 1950 the board of directors of the defendant company resolved that the plaintiff should confine his attentions to the British Textile Company only. The plaintiff regarded this decision by which he was ordered to devote his full time to a subsidiary of the defendant company as a breach of the second agreement between himself and the defendant company and sued the company for damages. He succeeded in the lower court but on appeal the decision was reversed.

VISCOUNT KILMUIR LC: ... The most important clause in the second agreement is clause 1, and I therefore set it out in full:

'[The respondent] shall be and he is hereby appointed a managing director of the [appellant] company and as such managing director he shall perform the duties and exercise the powers in relation to the business of the company and the businesses (howsoever carried on) of its existing subsidiary companies at the date hereof which may from time to time be assigned to or vested in him by the board of directors of the company. . . .'

. . . If one then asks what are the duties which he shall perform and what are the powers he shall exercise, the answer, from the words of the clause, is the powers and duties which may from time to time be assigned to, or vested in, him by the board of directors. If one then asks how shall he perform and exercise them, the answer is in relation to the business of the appellant company and the businesses (howsoever carried on) of its existing subsidiary companies at the date of the contract. . . .

. . . I cannot find either in the statute or in the cases in which the matter has been considered anything to prevent a board of directors appointing a managing director and limiting his duties according to their own wishes. . . .

EARL JOWITT: . . . I think that, on the true construction of clause 1 of the agreement of 1949, the respondent was to perform such duties and exercise such powers in relation to the business of the appellant company, and to perform such duties and exercise such powers in relation to the business of the Textile Company and the other subsidiaries, as might from time to time be vested in him by the appellant company's board. In directing the respondent on 10 May 1950 to confine his attention to the Textile Company, the board of the appellant company were, in my opinion, merely exercising the right given to them by the agreement.

The Lord President [who delivered judgment in the court below] took a different view, because he considered that the appointment of managing director was

> 'a well-recognized title in company administration, carrying responsibilities of a familiar nature and involving sundry obligations and liabilities under the Companies Act. The [respondent] was not appointed to perform such duties, if any, as the board might assign to him.'

The Lord President, having formed this view, no doubt considered that the resolution which called on the respondent to devote his whole time to the affairs of the Textile Company prevented him from carrying out those responsibilities, obligations and liabilities which, on this view, he had the right to perform for the appellant company, by virtue of his office as their managing director. My Lords, with the greatest respect for the Lord President, I do not think that the respondent, by the mere fact that he was appointed managing director of the appellant company, had any responsibilities, obligations or liabilities which would prevent the appellant company ordering him to devote his full time to a subsidiary, and I am of the opinion that the appellant company had, by clause 1 of the agreement, expressly preserved their right to call on the respondent to devote his time to the affairs of the Textile Company if they judged this course desirable. . . .

NOTES

The maxim *delegatus delegare non potest* does not apply to directors, whose powers are original, not delegated. (See K A Aicken in (1967) 5 *Melbourne University LR* 448 at

459.) However, since their powers are delimitated by the constitution of their company they cannot, unless otherwise provided by the articles, delegate discretionary powers entrusted to them, such as the power of allotment of shares. See *Howard's* case (1866) 1 Ch App 561; *Cartmell's* case (1874) 9 Ch App 691; *Foster* v *Foster* [1916] 1 Ch 532; *Gründling* v *Beyers* 1967 (2) SA 131 (W) at 150. They can, however, delegate ministerial functions of a routine character: see (1961) 47 *Virginia LR* 278.

A managing director with all the powers of the board, who is authorized to appoint another to act for him, has power to appoint another person to bring a petition in court: *Shell Company of SA Ltd* v *Vivier Motors (Pty) Ltd* 1959 (3) SA 971 (W).

As to the authority of a managing director to apply for the sequestration of the estate of a debtor of the company, see *Trek Tyres Ltd* v *Beukes* 1957 (3) SA 306 (W).

It depends on the constitution of the company whether a managing director can (1) sign promissory notes alone on behalf of the company: *Insurance Trust and Investment (Pty) Ltd* v *Mudaliar* 1943 NPD 45; (2) bind the company by his admissions: *Simmons NO* v *Gilbert Hamer & Co Ltd* 1963 (1) SA 897 (N).

On the distinction between a managing director and a manager, see *Kuter* v *South African Pharmacy Board* 1954 (2) SA 423 (T): 'Where in any case the line comes between a person who is a managing director and a person who is a manager cannot, I think, be defined at large': per Clayden J. See also F J Willett, 'Conflict between Modern Managerial Practice and Company Law' (1967) 5 *Melbourne University LR* 481.

On the ostensible authority of a managing director, see *SA Securities Ltd* v *Nicholas*, 289 below.

[280] Dickson *v* Acrow Engineers (Pty) Ltd

1954 (2) SA 63 (W)

ROPER J: . . . This is an action for recovery of the sum of £1 192 alleged to be due from the defendant company, by way of commission, to the plaintiff who had been a director and the executive, or working, director of the company from the end of 1946 until March 1950.

The declaration alleges that in December 1947 by agreement between himself and one W A de Vigier, acting on behalf of the company, he became entitled, in addition to his salary and director's fees, to a commission of 5 per cent on the net profits of the company after deducting or allowing for the dividend payable on the preference shares. Plaintiff alleges that the sum claimed is commission due . . . for the period 1 July 1947 to 10 March 1950. Alternatively, the plaintiff claims the sum of £1 000, alleging that on 20 March 1950 it was agreed between him and De Vigier that the defendant would pay him £1 000 in full settlement of his claim for commission. . . .

At the conclusion of the evidence counsel for the plaintiff intimated that he would not press the main claim; therefore, the only claim which I am concerned with is that for £1 000.

The defendant company is registered under the company laws of South Africa, and is an offshoot of an English company named Acrow (Engineers) Limited which was established in or about 1936 by W A de Vigier in order to manufacture and sell certain types of implements and materials used in the building trade. . . . The South African company, which is the defendant in this case, was floated in December 1946 with a share capital of £60 000. At all material times the majority of shares has been held either by De Vigier himself or by the London company, in which he holds the controlling interest. . . .

. . De Vigier compiled for the attention of the plaintiff a document described as 'Outline of policy to be pursued in the Union of South Africa'. . . . This document was handed to the plaintiff when he came out to South Africa in 1946 in order to establish the company. The company was incorporated in December 1946, De Vigier, the plaintiff, and Barnes were appointed as directors, and the plaintiff was appointed working director at a salary of £1 500 per annum. . . .

. . . I find [on the facts] that De Vigier did offer £1 000 to the plaintiff in settlement of his claim for commission, and that the plaintiff accepted it. . . .

The question now is, whether the company is bound by De Vigier's promise. [Counsel for the plaintiff] sought to bring the case within the rule of *Royal British Bank* v *Turquand* [p 471 below] . . . that persons dealing with a company are not expected to inquire into the regularity of internal proceedings of the company but are entitled to assume that they are regular. . . . I do not consider, however, that this case can be decided on that line of decisions. In my view the question is whether De Vigier had implied authority to bind the company. It is clear that such authority can be inferred from a course of dealing inside the company itself. . . .

. . . It is important in the present case to observe that the South African company was formed specifically in order to sell Acrow products in South Africa. It was financed almost entirely by funds provided either by De Vigier personally or by the London company in which he held the controlling interest. . . . Furthermore, De Vigier was in a position to exercise absolute control over the policy and operations of the company. . . . Under the articles De Vigier, as holder of the majority of issued shares, was entitled not merely to appoint directors and dismiss them, whether appointed by himself or not, but to give them such powers and authority as he might deem fit. The directors were, therefore, in the hollow of De Vigier's hand. If a director opposed his wishes he could be dismissed by him instantly. Any opinion held by directors could therefore be voiced as opinion and might be discussed with De Vigier, but it was impossible for any director to enforce his views to the point of disagreement without risking the loss of his directorship. It is true that the article contains a proviso that these powers are without prejudice to the power of the company in general meeting to appoint and remove directors, managing directors and managers. But as De Vigier was the majority shareholder he would have as much power at a general meeting as at a directors' meeting, and the power to oppose his wishes as to the appointment or dismissal of a managing director was therefore non-existent. I feel, therefore, that the board of directors in South Africa, excepting De Vigier himself, was a 'puppet board'. . . .

[The facts] are sufficient to satisfy me that by the course of dealing followed inside the company and acquiesced in by the other directors, there was constituted an implied mandate to De Vigier to manage and control the affairs of the company.

In my view, therefore, the company is bound by De Vigier's promise, and it is ordered to pay plaintiff's claim of £1 000 with costs. . . .

NOTES

Authority to act may be granted to a director informally by his fellow directors (*Marshall Industrials Ltd* v *Khan* 1959 (4) SA 684 (D)) or may be implied from a course of dealing in the company (*Majola Investments (Pty) Ltd* v *Uitzigt Properties (Pty) Ltd* 1961(4) SA 705 (T)). See also *Pretorius* v *Natal South Sea Investment Trust* 1965 (3) SA 410 (W).

Where under the constitution of the company some act has to be done, or some document signed, by 'at least two directors or their nominees', it is not sufficient if the act is done or document signed by one person only, who is both a director in his own right and the nominee of another director: *Equitee Nominees Limited* v *Tucker* (1967) 41 *Australian LJR* 80.

The secretary of a company may be its authorized agent: *Beer* v *London and Paris Hotel Company* (1875) 20 Eq Cas 412.

In *Gin* v *John Fitchat & Sons Ltd* 1924 OPD 54, it was held that without a resolution of the directors authorizing him to do so, a general manager cannot represent the company in transactions which do not form part of its ordinary business.

The requirement that an agent for the purchase or sale of land must be authorized by his principal in writing (Formalities of Contracts of Sale of Land Act 71 of 1969 s 1) does not apply to a person expressly or impliedly authorized by a company to act on its behalf, s 69(1)(*a*) (formerly s 72(1)(*a*)): *African Peach Growers (Edms) Bpk* v *Bouwer* 1973 (4) SA 654 (T). Cf *Suid-Afrikaanse Sentrale Koöperatiewe Graanmaatskappy Bpk* v *Thanasaris* 1953 (2) SA 314 (W). See further B R Bamford (1963) 80 *SALJ* at 82, and p 143 above.

13   *Outsider Protection*

I OSTENSIBLE AUTHORITY AND THE RULE IN ROYAL BRITISH BANK v TURQUAND

A TEXT

While the rule is that a contract or other transaction entered into by directors acting outside their authority is not binding on the company, the company is bound if the lack of authority on the part of the directors is due to the fact that the company was without capacity or power to perform the act (in other words, that it was *ultra vires* the company), s 36, see above p 78. Where the act was *intra vires* the company but beyond the powers of the directors, the company is bound if the third party was in good faith and the contract or other transaction fell within the ostensible authority of the director, manager, secretary or other officer of the company who entered into it or is covered by the rule in *Royal British Bank* v *Turquand* (also known as the 'Indoor Management Rule'): *England: 281–287; South Africa: 288–292.*

In England the practical importance of the rule in *Royal British Bank* v *Turquand* has been greatly reduced. Third parties who have dealt with the company in actual good faith (the doctrine of constructive notice has been abrogated for this purpose) will prefer to rely on s 9(1) of the European Communities Act which provides that in favour of a person dealing with a company in good faith the power of directors shall be deemed to be free of any limitation in the company's constitution, see above p 80. *Royal British Bank* v *Turquand* will continue to apply with regard to managers and other officers unless the courts decide to give the term 'directors' in s 9(1) an extensive interpretation (see D D Prentice (1973) 89 *LQR* 518). The first Directive of the EEC (*33* above), on which s 9 is based, speaks of limitations on the authority of 'organs' of the company, not of directors.

In South Africa where s 36 protects third parties against lack of authority on the part of the directors only where it is the result of lack of capacity or power on the part of the company, the doctrine of ostensible authority and the rule in *Royal British Bank* v *Turquand* (which to a large extent overlap) will continue to flourish, unless the Standing Committee on Company Law Reform decides to bring s 36 into conformity with either s 9(1) of the European Communities Act or the First EEC Directive.

Reference has been made earlier to s 214, a statutory rule providing that 'the acts of a director or manager shall be valid notwithstanding any defect that may afterwards be discovered in his appointment or qualification' (see above, p 326).

B CASES

[281] Royal British Bank v Turquand

(1856) 6 E & B 327, 119 ER 886

The Royal British Bank sued Turquand as the official manager of the Coalbrook Steam, Coal, and Swansea and London Railway Company, on a bond, signed by two directors, whereby the Coalbrook Steam, Coal, and Swansea and London Railway Company acknowledged itself to be bound to the Royal British Bank in an amount of £2 000. Under the constitution of the Coalbrook Company, the directors might borrow on bond such sums as should, from time to time, by a general resolution of the company, be authorized to be borrowed, and the defendant pleaded that there had been no such resolution.

JERVIS CJ: . . . We may now take for granted that the dealings with these companies are not like dealings with other partnerships, and that the parties dealing with them are bound to read the statute and the deed of settlement. But they are not bound to do more. And the party here, on reading the deed of settlement, would find not a prohibition from borrowing, but a permission to do so on certain conditions. Finding that the authority might be made complete by a resolution, he would have a right to infer the fact of a resolution authorizing that which on the face of the document appeared to be legitimately done.

[282] Mahony v East Holyford Mining Company

(1875) LR 7 HL 869

A mining company was founded by W and certain of his friends and relations. The memorandum and articles were registered and subscriptions were obtained from applicants for shares. These moneys were paid into the bank which had been described in the prospectus as the company's bank. A communication was sent to the bank by a person who described himself as the company's secretary, to the effect that in accordance with a resolution passed that day, the bank was to pay out cheques signed by 'either two of the following three directors' (who were named, and whose signatures were attached), and countersigned by himself. The bank thereafter honoured cheques so signed. When the funds of the company were almost exhausted, the company was ordered to be wound up. It was then discovered that no meeting of shareholders had been held, and no appointment of directors and secretary made, but that W and his friends and relations had held themselves out to be directors and secretary and had appropriated the subscription moneys.

It was held that the liquidator could not recover the amount of the cheques from the bank which it had paid in good faith.

KELLY CB: . . . If the shareholders and members of the company permitted Wadge, McNally, and Hoare to act as directors, to have possession of the office of the company, and of the books of the company, to transact, as directors, all such business as required to be transacted, such shareholders knowing, as from the articles of association they must have known, that from the moment the company was incorporated, directors could be appointed at once by the first seven members, or a majority of them; and that there was business which required the immediate action of directors, and such shareholders yet taking no steps themselves to appoint any directors *de jure* to transact that business — the jury might and should find that the shareholders permitted these persons to be *de facto* in possession of the office of directors; and that if they did so they were bound, at least as to innocent third persons, by the acts of those directors *de facto*, just as if they had been regularly appointed by the majority of the seven. . . .

LORD HATHERLEY: A banker dealing with a company must be taken to be acquainted with the manner in which, under the articles of association, the moneys of the company may be drawn out of his bank for the purposes of the company. . . .

. . . And the bankers must also be taken to have had knowledge, from the articles, of the duties of the directors, and the mode in which the directors were to be appointed. But, after that, when there are persons conducting the affairs of the company in a manner which appears to be perfectly consonant with the articles of association, then those so dealing with them, externally, are not to be affected by any irregularities which may take place in the internal management of the company. They are entitled to presume that that of which only they can have knowledge, namely the external acts, are rightly done, when those external acts purport to be performed in the mode in which they ought to be performed. For instance, when a cheque is signed by three directors, they are entitled to assume that those directors are persons properly appointed for the purpose of performing that function, and have properly performed the function for which they have been appointed. Of course, the case is open to any observation arising from gross negligence or fraud. . . .

[283] **Biggerstaff v Rowatt's Wharf Ltd**
[1896] 2 Ch 93

LINDLEY LJ: . . . What must persons look to when they deal with directors? They must see whether according to the constitution of the company the directors could have the powers which they are purporting to exercise. Here the articles enabled the directors to give to the managing director all the powers of the directors except as to drawing, accepting, or indorsing bills of exchange and promissory notes. The persons dealing with him must look to the articles, and see that the managing director might have power to do what he purports to do, and that is enough for a person dealing with him bona fide. . . .

[284] Houghton & Co v Nothard, Lowe and Wills Ltd

[1927] 1 KB 246 (CA), affirmed by the House of Lords [1928] AC 1

A director of the defendant company, without the authority of the board, entered on behalf of the company into an agreement with the plaintiffs. The plaintiffs sought to hold the company liable (a) under the rule in *Royal British Bank* v *Turquand*; (b) on estoppel on the ground that the agreement was known to the company through two of its directors. The court of appeal and the House of Lords decided that the plaintiffs could not succeed under either (a) or (b).

In the court of appeal, the following remarks were made on the rule in *Royal British Bank* v *Turquand*:

SARGANT LJ: . . . In this case it is quite clear that neither Mr Maurice Lowe, as a director, not Mr Prescott, as the secretary of the defendant company, had any authority to make any such contract on behalf of the company as that alleged. . . . The management of the business of the company was in the usual course and under the express provisions of art 71 of Table A, in the hands of the directors, that is of the board of directors; and there had been no delegation to Mr Maurice Lowe or to the secretary of the power of the board to enter into a contract of this character. . . .

. . . Next as to the power to delegate which is contained in the articles of association. In a case like this where that power of delegation had not been exercised, and where admittedly Mr Dart and the plaintiff firm had no knowledge of the existence of that power and did not rely on it, I cannot for myself see how they can subsequently make use of this unknown power so as to validate the transaction. They could rely on the fact of delegation, had it been a fact, whether known to them or not. They might rely on their knowledge of the power of delegation, had they known of it, as part of the circumstances entitling them to infer that there had been a delegation and to act on that inference, though it were in fact a mistaken one. But it is quite another thing to say that the plaintiffs are entitled now to rely on the supposed exercise of a power which was never in fact exercised and of the existence of which they were in ignorance at the date when they contracted. No case was cited to us in which a binding obligation has been constructed out of so curious a combination; and I cannot see any principle on which an obligation could be so constructed.

But even if Mr Dart, and through him the plaintiffs, had been aware of the power of delegation in the articles of the defendant company, this would not in my judgment have entitled him or them to assume that this power had been exercised in favour of a director, secretary or other officer of the company so as to validate the contract now in question. The learned judge, indeed, has said that this follows from a well-recognized line of cases . . . and holds that the plaintiffs were entitled to assume that anything necessary to delegate any of the functions of the board to one director or two directors had been done as a matter of internal management. But, in my opinion, this is to carry the doctrine of presumed power far beyond anything that has hitherto been decided, and to place limited companies, without any sufficient reason for so doing, at the mercy of any servant or agent who should purport to contract on their behalf. On this view, not only a director of a limited company with articles founded on Table A, but a secretary or any subordinate officer might be treated by a third party acting in good faith as capable of binding the company by any sort of contract, however exceptional, on the ground that a power of making such a contract might conceivably have been entrusted to him. . . .

. . . I know of no case in which an ordinary director, acting without authority in fact, has been held capable of binding a company by a contract with a third party, merely on the ground that that third party assumed that the director had been given authority by the board to make the contract. . . .

[285] British Thomson-Houston Co Ltd *v* Federated European Bank Ltd

[1932] 2 KB 176

A guarantee given to the plaintiffs was signed on behalf of the defendant bank by one of its directors. The same director had written to the plaintiffs during the negotiations for the giving of the guarantee, signing the letter 'for and on behalf' of the company, as 'Chairman'.

Under the articles of association of the defendant bank the directors had power to delegate their powers to one of their number, but they had not done so in respect of guarantees, which had to be signed by two directors. In an action on the guarantee, the bank denied liability on the ground that the guarantee had not been signed by two directors.

Scrutton LJ: . . . We find that [the articles] confer upon the directors two powers: (1) to delegate to one or more of their number any of the powers of the board of directors, and (2) to decide who shall sign contracts and other documents on the company's behalf. Then *Royal British Bank* v *Turquand* [*281*, above] and *Mahony* v *East Holyford Mining Co* [*282*, above] decide that if the articles of association give a power, persons dealing with the company, though they are deemed to have notice of the extent of the power, are not bound to inquire into what is called the 'indoor management' of the company to see whether the power has been properly and regularly exercised with all the prescribed formalities, and if they find an officer of the company openly exercising an authority which the directors have power to confer upon him, they are relieved from the duty of further inquiry and are entitled to assume that the power has been regularly and duly conferred.

A difficulty in the way of the plaintiffs is raised by the judgment of Sargant LJ in *Houghton & Co* v *Nothard, Lowe & Wills Ltd* [*284* above], where one director of a company purported to pledge certain future profits of the company by a contract which was said to be beyond his powers. It was a question whether his act was or was not within the powers conferred by one of the company's articles of association. Sargant LJ held, and Atkin LJ agreed with him, that, assuming that the articles enabled the directors to delegate to the particular director power to perform the act, it was not enough for the pledgees to rely upon their constructive knowledge of the effect of the articles where the power of delegation had not in fact been exercised and where the pledgees had no actual knowledge that the power existed, and did not rely on its existence. This case was considered in *Kreditbank Cassel* v *Schenkers Ltd* [1927] 1 KB 827 (CA) where, besides the decision in *Houghton's* case, there were other good reasons disentitling the plaintiffs from recovering; first, they were seeking a remedy against the drawers of a bill whose names had been forged; secondly, the person who was vouched as having authority to sign the names of the drawers was one whose position must have raised doubts whether such authority would ever have been reposed in him. All three members of the court held that the facts of the case ought certainly to have put the plaintiffs upon inquiry before they discounted the bill; they also held that as the drawers' names were forged they were not liable upon the bill; and thirdly, they held themselves bound to follow the decision in *Houghton's* case. But Atkin LJ held that in certain circumstances the inquiry, whether directors have in fact nominated one of their number to do the act relied on, need not be made — namely, where directors have power to nominate one of their number to do acts on their behalf, and a director is found acting in a matter in which normally a director would have power to act for his company. In that case, in the view of Atkin LJ, a person dealing with the company would not be obliged to inquire whether the director had been formally invested with authority to do the act. Assuming that to be correct, in the present case we have a director acting in matters which are normally entrusted to directors. The learned judge held that the chairman of a board of directors, a title which N Pal is permitted to assume, was a person acting normally in the affairs of the defendant company. In my opinion he came to the right conclusion. The plaintiffs were entitled to assume that N Pal was duly authorized to act for the company.

[286] Freeman & Lockyer v Buckhurst Park Properties (Mangal) Ltd
[1964] 2 QB 480, [1964] 1 All ER 630

Kapoor, a property developer, and one Hoon formed a private company which purchased Buckhurst Park Estate. The board of directors consisted of Kapoor, Hoon, a nominee of Kapoor's, and a nominee of Hoon's. The articles of the company contained power to appoint a managing director, but none was appointed. Kapoor, though never appointed as such, acted as managing director. He instructed the plaintiffs, a firm of architects, to do certain work for the company, which they did. The court held that the company was liable for their fees.

DIPLOCK LJ: The county court judge made the following findings of fact: (1) that the plaintiffs intended to contract with Kapoor as agent for the company, and not on his own account; (2) that the board of the company intended that Kapoor should do what he could to obtain the best possible price for the estate; (3) that Kapoor, although never appointed as managing director, had throughout been acting as such in employing agents and taking other steps to find a purchaser; (4) that Kapoor was so acting was well known to the board. . . .

The county court judge did not hold (although he might have done) that actual authority had been conferred upon Kapoor by the board to employ agents. He proceeded on the basis of apparent authority, that is, that the defendant company had so acted as to be estopped from denying Kapoor's authority. This rendered it unnecessary for the judge to inquire whether actual authority to employ agents had been conferred upon Kapoor by the board to whom the management of the company's business was confided by the articles of association.

It is necessary at the outset to distinguish between an 'actual' authority of an agent on the one hand, and an 'apparent' or 'ostensible' authority on the other. Actual authority and apparent authority are quite independent of one another. Generally they co-exist and coincide, but either may exist without the other and their respective scopes may be different.

An 'actual' authority is a legal relationship between principal and agent created by a consensual agreement to which they alone are parties. Its scope is to be ascertained by applying ordinary principles of construction of contracts, including any proper implications from the express words used, the usages of the trade, or the course of business between the parties. To this agreement the contractor is a stranger; he may be totally ignorant of the existence of any authority on the part of the agent. Nevertheless, if the agent does enter into a contract pursuant to the 'actual' authority, it does create contractual rights and liabilities between the principal and the contractor.

An 'apparent' or 'ostensible' authority, on the other hand, is a legal relationship between the principal and the contractor created by a representation, made by the principal to the contractor, intended to be and in fact acted upon by the contractor, that the agent has authority to enter on behalf of the principal into a contract of a kind within the scope of the 'apparent' authority, so as to render the principal liable to perform any obligations imposed upon him by such contract. To the relationship so created the agent is a stranger. He need not be (although he generally is) aware of the existence of the representation but he must not purport to make the agreement as principal himself. The representation, when acted upon by the contractor by entering into a contract with the agent, operates as an estoppel, preventing the principal from asserting that he is not bound by the contract. It is irrelevant whether the agent had actual authority to enter into the contract.

In ordinary business dealings the contractor at the time of entering into the contract can in the nature of things hardly ever rely on the 'actual' authority of the agent. His information as to the authority must be derived either from the principal or from the agent or from both, for they alone know what the agent's actual authority is. All that the contractor can know is what they tell him, which may or may not be true. In the ultimate analysis he relies either upon the representation of the principal, that is apparent authority, or upon the representation of the agent, that is, warranty of authority.

The representation which creates 'apparent' authority may take a variety of forms of which the commonest is representation by conduct, that is, by permitting the agent to act in some way in the conduct of the principal's business with other persons. By so doing the principal represents to anyone who becomes aware that the agent is so acting that the agent has authority to enter on behalf of the principal into contracts with other persons of the kind which an agent so acting in the conduct of his principal's business has usually 'actual' authority to enter into.

In applying the law as I have endeavoured to summarize it to the case where the principal is not a natural person, but a fictitious person, namely, a corporation, two further factors arising from the legal characteristics of a corporation have to be borne in mind. The first is that the capacity of a corporation is limited by its constitution, that is, in the case of a company incorporated under the Companies Act, by its memorandum and articles of association; the second is that a corporation cannot do any act, and that includes making a representation, except through its agent.

[The learned judge then dealt with the effect of the *ultra vires* doctrine on the authority of an agent of the company. In view of the provisions of s 36 of our Act and s 9 of the UK European Communities Act this part of the judgment is no longer relevant either in South Africa or (unless the other contracting party was in actual bad faith) in the UK (see pp 80–1 above). Diplock LJ continued:]

The second characteristic of a corporation, namely, that unlike a natural person it can only make a representation through an agent, has the consequence that in order to create an estoppel between the corporation and the contractor, the representation as to the authority of the agent which creates his 'apparent' authority must be made by some person or persons who have 'actual' authority from the corporation to make the representation. Such 'actual' authority may be conferred by the constitution of the corporation itself, as, for example, in the case of a company, upon the board of directors, or it may be conferred by those who under its constitution have the powers of management upon some other person to whom the constitution permits them to delegate authority to make representations of this kind. It follows that where the agent upon whose 'apparent' authority the contractor relies has no 'actual' authority from the corporation to enter into a particular kind of contract with the contractor on behalf of the corporation, the contractor cannot rely upon the agent's own representation as to his actual authority. He can rely only upon a representation by a person or persons who have actual authority to manage or conduct that part of the business of the corporation to which the contract relates.

The commonest form of representation by a principal creating an 'apparent' authority of an agent is by conduct, namely, by permitting the agent to act in the management or conduct of the principal's business. Thus, if in the case of a company the board of directors who have 'actual' authority under the memorandum and articles of association to manage the company's business permit the agent to act in the management or conduct of the company's business, they thereby represent to all persons dealing with such agent that he has authority to enter on behalf of the corporation into contracts of a kind which an agent authorized to do acts of the kind which he is in fact permitted to do usually enters into in the ordinary course of such business. The making of such a representation is itself an act of management of the company's business. Prima facie it falls within the 'actual' authority of the board of directors.

If the foregoing analysis of the relevant law is correct, it can be summarized by stating four conditions which must be fulfilled to entitle a contractor to enforce against a company a contract entered into on behalf of the company by an agent who had no actual authority to do so. It must be shown:

(1) that a representation that the agent had authority to enter on behalf of the company into a contract of the kind sought to be enforced was made to the contractor;

(2) that such representation was made by a person or persons who had 'actual' authority to manage the business of the company either generally or in respect of those matters to which the contract relates;

(3) that he (the contractor) was induced by such representation to enter into the contract, that is, that he in fact relied upon it; and

(4) [no longer relevant] that under its memorandum or articles of association the company was not deprived of the capacity either to enter into a contract of the kind sought to be enforced or to delegate authority to enter into a contract of that kind to the agent.

The confusion which, I venture to think, has sometimes crept into the cases is in my view due to a failure to distinguish between these four separate conditions, and in particular to keep steadfastly in mind (*a*) that the only 'actual' authority which is relevant is that of the persons making the representation relied upon, and (*b*) that the memorandum and articles of association of the company are always relevant (whether they are in fact known to the contractor or not) to the questions (i) whether condition (2) is fulfilled, and (ii) whether condition (4) is fulfilled, and (but only if they are in fact known to the contractor) may be relevant (iii) as part of the representation on which the contractor relied.

In each of the relevant cases the representation relied upon as creating the 'apparent' authority of the agent was by conduct in permitting the agent to act in the management and conduct of part of the business of the company. Except in *Mahony* v *East Holyford Mining Co Ltd* [*282 above*] it was the conduct of the board of directors in so permitting the agent to act that was relied upon. As they had, in each case, by the articles of association of the company full 'actual' authority to manage its business, they had 'actual' authority to make representations in connection with the management of its business, including representations as to who were agents authorized to enter into contracts on the company's behalf. The agent himself had no 'actual' authority to enter into the contract because the formalities prescribed by the articles for conferring it upon him had not been complied with. In *British Thomson-Houston Co* v *Federated European Bank Ltd* [*285* above] where a guarantee was executed by a single director, it was contended that a provision in the articles, requiring a guarantee to be executed by two directors, deprived the company of capacity to delegate to a single director authority to execute a guarantee on behalf of the company, that is, that condition (4) above was not fulfilled; but it was held that other provisions in the articles empowered the board to delegate the power of executing guarantees to one of their number, and this defence accordingly failed. In *Mahony's* case no board of directors or secretary had in fact been appointed, and it was the conduct of those who, under the constitution of the company, were entitled to appoint them which was relied upon as a representation that certain persons were directors and secretary. Since they had 'actual' authority to appoint these officers, they had 'actual' authority to make representations as to who the officers were. In both these cases the constitution of the company, whether it had been seen by the contractor or not, was relevant in order to determine whether the persons whose representations by conduct were relied upon as creating the 'apparent' authority of the agent had 'actual' authority to make the representations on behalf of the company.

The cases where the contractor's claim failed, namely, *Houghton & Co* v *Nothard, Lowe & Wills* [*284* above], *Kreditbank Cassel GmbH* v *Schenkers Ltd* [[1927] 1 KB 827 (CA)] and the *Rama Corporation* case [[1952] 2 QB 147, [1952] 1 All ER 554], were all cases where the contract sought to be enforced was not one which a person occupying the position in relation to the company's business which the contractor knew that the agent occupied would normally be authorized to enter into on behalf of the company. The conduct of the board of directors in permitting the agent to occupy that position, upon which the contractor relied, thus did not of itself amount to a representation that the agent had authority to enter into the contract sought to be enforced, that is, condition (1) was not fulfilled. The contractor, however, in each of these three cases sought to rely upon a provision of the articles giving to the board power to delegate wide authority to the agent as entitling him to treat the conduct of the board as a representation that the agent had had delegated to him wider powers than those usually exercised by persons occupying the position in relation to the company's business which the agent was in fact permitted by the board to occupy. Since this would involve proving that the representation on which he in fact relied as inducing him to enter into the contract comprised the articles of association of the company as well as the conduct of the board, it would be necessary for him to establish first that he knew the contents of the articles (that is, that condition (3) was fulfilled in respect of any representation contained in the articles) and secondly that the conduct of the board in the light of that knowledge would be understood by a reasonable man as a representation that the agent had authority to enter into the contract sought to be enforced, that is that condition (1) was fulfilled.

In the present case the findings of fact by the county court judge are sufficient to satisfy the four conditions, and thus to establish that Kapoor had 'apparent' authority to enter into contracts on behalf of the company for their services in connection with the sale of the company's property, including the obtaining of development permission with respect to its use. . . .

I think the judgment was right, and would dismiss the appeal.

[287] **Panorama Developments (Guildford) Ltd *v* Fidelis Furnishing Fabrics Ltd**
[1971] 2 QB 711, [1971] 3 All ER 16 (CA), [1971] 3 WLR 440

By letters written on the defendant company's notepaper the secretary of the company had fraudulently ordered from the plaintiffs, a car hire company, 'self-drive' cars on various dates, falsely stating that they were wanted by the company for business purposes. In fact the defendant company knew nothing about the transactions. Both the trial court and the court of appeal held that the defendant company was liable to the plaintiffs for the amount of the hire.

LORD DENNING MR: [Counsel for the company] says that the company is not bound by the letters which were signed by Mr Bayne as 'Company Secretary'. He says that, on the authorities, a company secretary fulfils a very humble role; and that he has no authority to make any contracts or representations on behalf of the company. He refers to *Barnett, Hoares & Co v South London Tramways Co* [(1887) 18 QBD 815 at 817] where Lord Esher MR said:

'A secretary is a mere servant; his position is that he is to do what he is told, and no person can assume that he has any authority to represent anything at all. . . .'

Those words were approved by Lord Macnaghten in *George Whitechurch Ltd v Cavanagh* [[1902] AC 117 at 124]. They are supported by the decision in *Ruben v Great Fingall Consolidated* [[1906] AC 439]; they are referred to in some of the textbooks as authoritative. But times have changed. A company secretary is a much more important person nowadays than he was in 1887. He is an officer of the company with extensive duties and responsibilities. This appears not only in the modern Companies Acts, but also by the role which he plays in the day-to-day business of companies. He is no longer a mere clerk. He regularly makes representations on behalf of the company and enters into contracts on its behalf which come within the day-to-day running of the company's business. So much so that he may be regarded as held out as having authority to do such things on behalf of the company. He is certainly entitled to sign contracts connected with the administrative side of a company's affairs, such as employing staff, and ordering cars, and so forth. All such matters now come within the ostensible authority of a company's secretary. Accordingly I agree with the judge that Mr R L Bayne, as company secretary, had ostensible authority to enter into contracts for the hire of these cars and, therefore, the company must pay for them. Mr Bayne was a fraud. But it was the company which put him in the position in which he, as company secretary, was able to commit the frauds. So the defendants are liable. I would dismiss the appeal, accordingly.

[288] **Paddon and Brock Ltd** *v* **Nathan**

1906 TS 158

SMITH J: This was an action tried before the Second Civil Magistrate of Johannesburg, in which the plaintiff was the holder of a promissory note, and the defendants were the indorsers. The note, which was for £360, was made on 14 October 1905 and was due at the expiration of two months. It was made by G W Paddon to the order of Stonestreet who indorsed it to the Bank of Africa. The note also purported to bear the indorsement of the defendant company, of the plaintiff, and of one Rosenberg. Several defences were raised to the claim in the magistrate's court. . . . The only one which is really material is the last one, which was that the note was made for the private purposes of G W Paddon, and that the indorsement by the defendant company, by him, was unauthorized.

The facts are very short, and practically there is no dispute about them. G W Paddon, the maker of the note, was, at the time when the note was made, the managing director of the defendant company. He was desirous of raising money for his own purposes; he went to the plaintiff with the note now sued upon, and asked him to lend him money. The plaintiff had had a prior transaction with G W Paddon of a similar nature, which had not been entirely satisfactory, because G W Paddon's cheque had been dishonoured, and on this occasion the plaintiff says he refused to lend Paddon the money unless he obtained the indorsement of the defendant company as further security for the loan. Thereupon in the plaintiff's presence, G W Paddon indorsed the note with the name of the defendant company. The plaintiff asked him whether he was authorized to sign, to which Paddon replied: 'You must be a fool to ask that, because I am the boss of the whole concern.' . . .

. . . It is admitted that the note was made by Paddon for his own private purposes, and that the defendant company has had no benefit whatever from it. It also seems to me to be clear that the plaintiff must have known that the note was made for Paddon's private purposes. It was apparent on the face of the note itself. . . .

. . . Had the plaintiff any ground for believing Paddon was authorized by the company? In answer to that, it is said that the inquiry he made of Paddon was sufficient, and the cases of *Mahony* v *The Liquidator of the East Holyford Mining Company* [*282* above], *Biggerstaff* v *Rowatt's Wharf Ltd* [*283* above], and the *Royal British Bank* v *Turquand* [*281* above] were relied upon. Those cases only show that where the directors of a company do an act which under the articles of association they might or could have power to do, persons dealing with them are not bound to investigate the private concerns of the company and to ascertain whether a condition precedent which may exist to the due exercise of that power has in fact been performed. . . .

. . . It was the duty of the plaintiff in this matter to look to the articles and ascertain whether the managing director had the power, and was authorized to indorse the note. If he had done so, he would have seen that the only authority which the managing director had was to indorse the note for the purposes of the company. It is clear, as I have already pointed out, that the plaintiff knew that this note was not for the purposes of the company. . . .

[The company was, accordingly held not liable. See also *Harcourt* v *Eastman NO* 1953 (2) SA 424 (N) at 428, per Holmes J: 'Even if M as a director had authority to sign guarantees on behalf of the company, he was not acting within the scope of his authority in using the company's credit for his private debts.' Further *In re David Payne and Company Ltd* [1904] 2 Ch 608.]

[289] SA Securities Ltd *v* Nicholas
1911 TPD 450

WESSELS J: . . . All that it is necessary that a person dealing with a managing director should do is refer to those outside documents of the company, and to see from them whether the managing director might or might not have such powers as he alleges that he has. If it is found that the managing director might have such powers, then a person is entitled to deal with him on the footing that he possesses them. . . .

. . . It seems to me that the mere fact of appointing a man as managing director gives him prima facie certain powers. It was held by Blackburn J in *Gibson* v *Barton* (1875) LR 10 QB 329, that 'The manager would be, in ordinary talk, a person who has the management of the whole affairs of the company; not an agent who is to do a particular thing, or a servant who is to obey orders, but a person intrusted with power to transact the whole of the affairs of the company'. Prima facie that is what is meant when a person is appointed managing director of a company; he is appointed manager for the board of directors, and is held out as having the power of exercising in his own person all powers of management which the board might themselves exercise. A person dealing with an official of a company, such as a managing director, has not access to the minutes of the company or the board, or to any documents relating to the internal management of the company; he has only access to the articles of association. And, unless the articles contain something restricting the powers of the directors as regards the appointment of a managing director, a person dealing with the managing director is entitled to assume that he has all the powers which his position as managing director would ostensibly give him. . . .

[290] Insurance Trust and Investments (Pty) Ltd *v* Mudaliar
1943 NPD 45

BROOME J: . . . As there was no resolution of the directors authorizing Black alone to sign promissory notes for the company it would appear to follow that Black had no actual authority to sign the promissory note sued on in the present case, and that the only remaining question is whether the company is nevertheless liable on the ground of estoppel. . . .

. . . The circumstances in which such an estoppel will arise are too numerous to set out, and in any case they are not propositions of law but merely examples of the application to various sets of facts of a single legal principle. If the matter is looked at in this light, all difficulty in regard to the plaintiff's knowledge or want of knowledge of the contents of the articles disappears. It is for the plaintiff to plead and prove the estoppel he relies on. If he relies on the contents of the articles as constituting a representation, he must prove that he knew the contents. But he may rely on quite a different representation, for instance, that the company held out a particular officer as having authority. In every case he must, of course, prove, not only the representation, but that he acted upon it to his prejudice. . . .

. . . It is common cause that Black alone had no actual authority to sign promissory notes for the appellant company, for the directors had by resolution given authority to two directors to do so. Is the appellant company estopped from denying Black's authority? The replication alleges an estoppel based upon a representation by the appellant company that Black had authority. I have already set out the respondent's own account of the transaction which we are entitled to accept. What does it show? That the loan was asked for by Black and not by the appellant company. That the transaction took place in the respondent's house which he used as an office, and not in the offices of the appellant company. That the money was paid to Black and not to the appellant company, and was paid in cash at Black's special request. That the promissory note and receipt were typed out then and there by Black and signed by him. Where in all this is there any evidence of a representation made by the appellant company? Respondent dealt with Black and Black alone. Whatever representations were made were made by him. If they had been made by Black in the company's office while apparently transacting the company's business the case might be stronger, but even then the whole transaction was so unusual that it would be difficult to fix responsibility for them upon the company. It is immaterial that Black 'runs the company' or that he was managing director, if in fact he was. The company is a different entity, and it can only be estopped upon a representation which it has itself made. A representation by an officer, however important he may be, made in the course of negotiating a personal transaction of his own cannot be regarded as a representation made by the company. . . .

[291] The Mine Workers' Union *v* Prinsloo
1948 (3) SA 381 (AD)

GREENBERG JA: . . . In regard to the question whether the presumption that the necessary acts of internal management have been performed depends on the third party's knowledge of the constitution, the present case is wholly covered by *Turquand's* case and does not depend on the later extension or development of the rule, evidenced by *Mahony's* case [*282* above] and the large number of cases which have since been decided in regard to the question of the due appointment or authority of a director or directors who have entered into a particular contract. It was in a case of this latter class (*Houghton & Co* v *Nothard, Lowe & Wills Ltd* [*284* above]) that Sargant LJ said that a third party could not rely on the supposed exercise of a power which was never in fact exercised and of the existence of which he was in ignorance at the time of the contract. It appears to me that this statement cannot be regarded as authoritative in view of what was said about it in the later cases of *Kreditbank Cassel GmbH* v *Schenkers Ltd* [[1927] 1 KB 827 (CA)] and *British Thomson-Houston Co Ltd* v *Federated European Bank Ltd* [*285* above].

I do not think that the validity of a transaction such as the one in question in *Turquand's* case is to be decided on a subjective basis, depending on whether the other party does or does not know of the constitution or whether — as would follow if the basis were subjective — even though he knew of the constitution, he did or did not apply his mind to the question whether the internal acts of management had been performed. It seems to me that the true position is that the necessary acts of internal management are presumed to have been performed and not that a particular person is entitled to assume that they have. . . . I have already said that this presumption does not arise when the other contracting party knows that the acts have not been performed. . . .

[292] Wolpert v Uitzigt Properties (Pty) Ltd
1961 (2) SA 257 (W)

Action for provisional sentence on four promissory notes for £1 500 each. Each of the promissory notes bore the rubber stamp of the defendant company, and below that the signature 'T McAlpine', one of its directors, followed by the word 'director'. The company denied liability on the ground that the notes had not been signed by all its directors, as required by its articles.

CLAASSEN J: In the present case the board of directors of the first defendant were by art 47(*h*) given the power:

'To determine who shall be entitled to sign on the Company's behalf bills, notes, receipts, acceptances, endorsements, cheques, releases, contracts and documents.'

It is therefore clear that a single director or any other person, even the office boy, could have been given authority to sign a promissory note on behalf of the company. Would a third party dealing with a single director be justified, without enquiry, in assuming that such a single director would have authority to bind the company? And would the company in fact be bound where, as in a case like the present, it has not been proved on a balance of probabilities that such authority has been given?

I fail to see on what principle anyone with either express or constructive knowledge of an article such as 47(*h*) can assume that if he deals with anyone who purports to act on behalf of a company that particular person is a person who has been authorized under the article in question. After all, all he is entitled to assume is that someone has been appointed, but how can he assume that a specific person or persons have been appointed?

In such a case where A purports to act for the company I cannot conceive of any principle which can debar a company from denying that A has been appointed. Why should a company in this respect be different from an ordinary human being? Everyone knows that any person may appoint an agent to act for him. But that does not stop the principal denying that he has appointed a particular agent who purports to act for him. . . . If a company's official is acting within the usual authority of that type of agent the company is normally bound and the articles are only relevant if they make it clear that he had no actual authority. If any further formal act of internal management is required this can be assumed to have taken place by reason of the *Turquand* rule. If the act is outside the usual scope of authority mere knowledge that actual authority might have been conferred on the official is not sufficient to estop the company and the consequences of *omnia praesumuntur rite ac solemniter esse acta* do not help the third party. He must inquire further and either ensure that the official has actual authority or elicit some further facts which estop the company from denying it. And these further facts would, probably, have estopped the company (unless the articles made it clear that the official could not have had actual authority) even if they had been elicited without any actual exploration of the articles, which therefore continued to be irrelevant.

Two question arise:

(*a*) When does one deal with or contract with a company?

(*b*) Who are the apparent agents of a company?

In my opinion a party deals with or contracts with a company when he does so through the following apparent agencies of the company:

(1) The board of directors. . . .

The board is ordinarily the organ of a company vested with plenary authority on matters *intra vires* the company. There is therefore no difficulty in applying the *Turquand* rule in cases where the board has contracted.

(2) (*a*) The managing director. See *Biggerstaff* v *Rowatt's Wharf Ltd* [*283* above] concerning which case it was said in *Houghton & Co* v *Northard, Lowe and Wills* [*284* above]: 'But there the agent whose authority was relied on had been acting to the knowledge of the company as a managing director, and the act done was one within the ordinary ambit of the powers of a managing director in the transaction of the company's affairs. It is I think clear that the transaction there would not have been supported had it not been in this ordinary course, or had the agent been acting merely as one of the ordinary directors of the company.' In the case of *SA Securities* v *Nicholas* 1911 TPD 450 the head-note says:

'Unless the articles of association of a company restrict the powers which the directors may delegate to a managing director, anyone dealing bona fide with the managing director is entitled to assume that he has all the power which his position as such ostensibly would give him.'

(*b*) The chairman of the board of directors, where the circumstances are such that it can be assumed that he was in a position equivalent to that of a managing director. There seems to be no reason why a chairman should not be treated as an ordinary director. And a party dealing with such a director without actual authority from the board or the managing director usually does so at his peril.

(3) Any person or persons such as an ordinary director, a branch manager, a secretary, a committee of directors or a combination of a director and secretary, who have express or implied authority. Such implied authority can be inferred, when the official acting on behalf of the company purports to exercise an authority which that type of official usually has even though the official is exceeding his actual authority . . . but the company would not be bound:

 (i) If the person or persons so acting acted beyond their usual authority. If they did, the third party may still be protected under (4) below.
 (ii) If the party knew that the official was acting beyond his actual authority.
(iii) If the circumstances are such as to put him on inquiry.
(iv) If the registered documents of the company make it clear that the official concerned has no actual authority.

Under this heading it would, in my opinion, be irrelevant whether the third party knew the contents of the registered documents of the company or not.

(4) Those mentioned under (3) in circumstances where they have had ostensible authority. That is to say, they had no actual authority which such officials usually have, but the company is estopped from denying such authority. Such estoppel operates where

 (i) the company (not the official acting for the company) has represented the official as having authority,
 (ii) the party relied on such representation, and
(iii) he altered his position by reason of such reliance.

Under this heading the third party cannot rely on the registered documents of the company . . . in his favour, unless he knew about them and relied on them.

In all the above cases (1) to (4) the *Turquand* rule can be applied so that if any one of the enumerated agents had contracted with the third party, but there was still an act of internal organization not completed in order to complete the necessary authority, the company would be bound.

It is also necessary to draw attention to the fact that the position of an ordinary director may vary from company to company. In some companies, particularly in large public companies, he usually only attends board meetings, and only takes part in the decisions of the board, but he takes no part in the internal running of the affairs of the company. In other companies again, and that is often true of private companies, the ordinary director besides attending board meetings, also takes an active part in the day-to-day running of the affairs of the company. If that is the case, he may also have some managerial functions and then his implied or ostensible authority would be wider than in the case of a director who merely attends board meetings.

Looking back to what I have written it seems to me quite clear that the agencies mentioned under (1) and (2) above, are merely instances of agencies having express or implied authority; because if the third party is dealing with the board of directors as a whole or a managing director he will usually be safe, since it is usual to confer the widest powers of management on those organs, but if he deals with a single director he will not normally be protected, because a single director usually has no authority to bind the company.

Coming now to the facts of the present case, it is clear that McAlpine was an ordinary director. It was not contended that he had ostensible authority. On my findings he did not have express authority. So all that is left, is to inquire whether on the facts implied authority can be inferred.

The mere fact that McAlpine used the company's rubber stamp does not in the circumstances lead to an inference that he had implied authority. No course of dealing has been set out in the papers. The only person who could inform the court as to how it came about that he used the stamp of the company was McAlpine, and he has remained silent on the point. In terms of s 90 of the Bills of Exchange Proclamation it is express or implied authority which entitles a person to use a company's stamp. It cannot be argued that because he used it, therefore he must have had express or implied authority. If he had authority then he could have bound the company without using the stamp by merely printing in the name of the company and signing as a director.

I therefore come to the conclusion that McAlpine did not have implied authority tó bind the company nor was it contended that he did have such authority. Provisional sentence must therefore be refused.

NOTES

On the difference between actual and ostensible authority, see also *Hely-Hutchinson* v *Brayhead Ltd* [1968] 1 QB 549, where Lord Denning MR said (at 583): 'I need not consider at length the law on the authority of an agent, actual, apparent or ostensible. That has been done in the judgments of this court in the case of *Freeman & Lockyer (a firm)* v *Buckhurst Park Properties (Mangal) Ltd* [286 above]. It is there shown that actual authority may be express or implied. It is express when it is given by express words, such as when a board of directors pass a resolution which authorizes two of their number to sign cheques. It is implied when it is inferred from the conduct of the parties and the circumstances of the case, such as when the board of directors appoint one of their number to be managing director. They thereby impliedly authorize him to do all such things as fall within the usual scope of that office. Actual authority, express or implied, is binding as between the company and the agent, and also as between the company and others whether they are within the company or outside it.

'Ostensible or apparent authority is the authority of an agent as it appears to others. It often coincides with actual authority. Thus, when the board appoint one of their number to be managing director, they invest him not only with implied authority, but also with ostensible authority to do all such things as fall within the usual scope of that office. Other people who see him acting as managing director are entitled to assume that he has the usual authority of a managing director. But sometimes ostensible authority exceeds actual authority. For instance, when the board appoint the managing director, they may expressly limit his authority by saying he is not to order goods worth more than £500 without the sanction of the board. In that case his actual authority is subject to the £500 limitation, but his ostensible authority includes all the usual authority of a managing director. The company is bound by his ostensible authority in his dealings with those who do not know of the limitation. He may himself do the "holding-out". Thus, if he orders goods worth £1 000 and signs himself "Managing Director for and on behalf of the company", the company is bound to the other party who does not know of the £500 limitation. . . . Even if the other party happens himself to be a director of the company, nevertheless the company may be bound by the ostensible authority. Suppose the managing director orders £1 000 worth of goods from a new director who has just joined the company and does not know of the £500 limitation, not having studied the minute book, the company may yet be bound.' Lord Pearson said (at 493): 'The difference and the relationship between actual authority and ostensible authority were explained by Diplock LJ in *Freeman & Lockyer v Buckhurst Park Properties (Mangal) Ltd*. There is, however, an awkward question arising in such cases how the representation which creates the ostensible authority is made by the principal to the outside contractor. I agree entirely with what Diplock LJ said that such representation has to be made by a person or persons having actual authority to manage the business. Be it supposed for convenience that such persons are the board of directors. Now there is not usually any direct communication in such cases between the board of directors and the outside contractor. The actual communication is made immediately and directly, whether it be express or implied, by the agent to the outside contractor. It is, therefore, necessary in order to make a case of ostensible authority to show in some way that such communication which is made directly by the agent is made ultimately by the responsible parties, the board of directors. That may be shown by inference from the conduct of the board of directors in the particular case by, for instance, placing the agent in a position where he can hold himself out as their agent and acquiescing in his activities, so that it can be said that they have in effect caused the representation to be made. They are responsible for it and, in the contemplation of law, they are to be taken to have made the representation to the outside contractor.

'For the present purpose it is important to note that actual authority and ostensible authority are not mutually exclusive, and indeed, as Diplock LJ pointed out, they generally co-exist and coincide.'

On ostensible authority in our law, see *Claude Neon Lights (SA) Ltd v Daniel* 1976 (4) SA 403 (AD).

As to the authority of a company secretary, see also *Re Maidstone Buildings Provisions Ltd* [1971] 1 WLR 1085, [1971] 3 All ER 363 (Ch), where it was held that the secretary of the company was not, *qua* secretary, a party to the carrying on of the business of the company within the meaning of s 332(1) of the English Companies Act (s 424(1) of ours). 'So far as the position of a secretary as such is concerned, it is established beyond all question that a secretary, while merely performing the duties appropriate to the office of secretary, is not concerned in the management of the company. Equally I think he is not concerned in carrying on the business of the company. On the other hand, it is equally well established, indeed it is obvious, that a person who holds the office of secretary may in some other capacity be concerned in the management of the company's business', per Pennycuick J at 368. But see *Panorama Developments, 287* above.

On the powers of a secretary, see further *65* above and K E Lindgren 'Development of the Power of the Modern Company Secretary to Bind his Company' (1972) 46 *ALJ* 385.

A manager can bind the company in transactions which form part of his everyday business.

A commercial traveller has no ostensible authority to act on behalf of his company, nor is his knowledge imputed to the company: *S v Schwartz* 1972 (2) SA 295 (C) at 299.

In *Mahomed v Ravat Bombay House (Pty) Ltd* 1958 (4) SA 704 (T), where promissory notes had been signed by one director only, and not by two, as required by the articles, the court, applying the rule in *Royal British Bank v Turquand*, held the company liable. Cf *Wolpert v Uitzigt Properties (Pty) Ltd* (*292* above), where on practically identical facts the court arrived at the opposite result. *Mahomed's* case was criticized by G A Mulligan in (1960) 77 *SALJ* 332.

In *Sugden v Beaconhurst Dairies (Pty) Ltd* 1963 (2) SA 174 (E) O'Hagan J, applying the rule in *Royal British Bank v Turquand*, held (at 182) that 'where directors are empowered to fix a quorum for the transaction of their business, an outside person is entitled to assume that a resolution certified by a director and secretary of the company has been passed by a quorum duly fixed in terms of the articles'.

As a rule a director himself cannot rely on the rule in *Turquand's* case. As Lord Simonds put it in *Morris v Kanssen* [1946] AC 459, [1946] 1 All ER 586: 'It is a rule designed for the protection of those who are entitled to assume, just because they cannot know, that the person with whom they deal has the authority which he claims. . . .

'What then is the position of the director or acting director who claims to hold the company to a transaction which the company has not, though it might have, authorized? Your Lordships have not in this case to consider what the result might be if such a director had not himself purported to act on behalf of the company in the unauthorized transaction. For here Morris was himself purporting to act on behalf of the company in a transaction in which he had no authority. Can he then say that he was entitled to assume that all was in order? My Lords, the old question comes into my mind, *"Quis custodiet ipsos custodes?"* It is the duty of directors, and equally of those who purport to act as directors, to look after the affairs of the company, to see that it acts within its powers and that its transactions are regular and orderly. To admit in their favour a presumption that that is rightly done which they have themselves wrongly done is to encourage ignorance and condone dereliction from duty. It may be that in some cases . . . a director is not blameworthy in his unauthorized act. It may be that in such a case some other remedy is open to him, either against the company or against those by whose fraud he was led into this situation, but I cannot admit that there is open to him the remedy of invoking this rule and giving validity to an otherwise invalid transaction. His duty as a director is to know; his interest, when he invokes the rule, is to disclaim knowledge. Such a conflict can be resolved in only one way . . .' (at 475–6, 592–3).

But see also *Hely-Hutchinson* v *Brayhead Ltd* [1968] 1 QB 549 (CA), where it was held that a director who contracts with his company as an outsider may be able to rely on the rule in *Royal British Bank*. (See R S Nock in (1967) 30 *MLR* at 708.)

In dealing with the managing director of a company a third person is entitled to assume that he has all the powers a managing director normally has, in as far as they are not curtailed by the articles: *SA Securities Ltd* v *Nicholas* 1911 TPD 450 (*289* above); *Moresby White* v *Rangeland Ltd* 1952 (4) SA 285 (SR) (*278* above). In America the president of a corporation is presumed to have all the powers which by usage or necessity are incidental to his office, being part of the usual course of the corporation's business.

That forgeries do not fall within the rule was also held in *Uxbridge Permanent Benefit Building Society* v *Pickard* [1939] 2 KB 248, [1939] 2 All ER 344. Nor does the rule in *Royal British Bank* v *Turquand* apply where the facts are such that the third party is put upon inquiry. See *A L Underwood Ltd* v *Bank of Liverpool* [1924] 1 KB 775, where it was held that the bank at which a director of a company keeps his private account is put on inquiry if he pays cheques made out to the company into his private account, and *B Liggett (Liverpool) Ltd* v *Barclays Bank Ltd* [1928] 1 KB 48, where the bank, contrary to its instructions, paid out cheques signed by one director only; also *Paddon & Brock Ltd* v *Nathan* 1906 TS 158 (*288* above); *Jones* v *John Barr & Co (Pty) Ltd* 1967 (3) SA 292 (W). In *Burstein* v *Yale* 1958 (1) SA 768 (W) it was held that a company is not bound by a contract with a third party where the third party knew that no resolution authorizing the contract was passed by the board of directors.

In *Service Motor Supplies Ltd* v *Hyper Investments Ltd* 1961 (4) SA 842 (AD) the articles provided that no resolution of the directors should be binding unless passed unanimously by the three directors of the company. One of the directors had negotiated with the respondent to hire its premises, the company had moved in and made alterations, and a lease had been signed by one of the directors. It was held that although there was no resolution of the appellant company to which all three directors had consented the appellant company was estopped from denying that the director who had signed the lease had authority to do so.

Mine Workers' Union v *J J Prinsloo* 1948 (3) SA 831 (AD) makes it clear that the rule in *Royal British Bank* v *Turquand* is not limited in its application to companies but applies to corporations generally. On its application to local authorities, see *Potchefstroomse Stadsraad* v *Kotze* 1960 (3) SA 616 (AD), discussed by E Kahn in 1960 *Annual Survey* 29–32, on its application to a trade union, *Grundling* v *Beyers* 1967 (2) SA 131 (W).

On *Royal British Bank* v *Turquand* in South Africa, see further *Acutt* v *Seta Prospecting and Developing Co Ltd* 1907 TS 799; *Welgedacht Exploration Co Ltd* v *Transvaal and Delagoa Bay Investment Co Ltd* 1909 TH 90; *Estate of Hoskings* v *Colonial Mutual Life Assurance Society Ltd* 1913 WLD 116; *SAIF Co-operative Society* v *Webber* 1922 TPD 49; *Legg & Co* v *Premier Tobacco Co* 1926 AD 132; *Treasure Trove Diamonds Ltd* v *Hyman* 1928 AD 464 (*226* above); *Roodepoort Settlement Committee* v *Retief* 1951 (1) SA 73 (O); *Silver Garbus & Co (Pty) Ltd* v *Teichert* 1954 (2) SA 98 (N); *Dickson* v *Acrow Engineers (Pty) Ltd*, *280* above; *Amalgamated Union of Building Trade Workers of SA* v *South African Operative Masons' Society* 1957 (1) SA 440 (AD); *National and Overseas Distributors Corporation (Pty) Ltd* v *Potato Board* 1958 (2) SA 473 (AD); *Christian Coloured Vigilance Council* v *Groenewald* 1961 (1) PH E 3 (C); *Goode, Durrant & Murray Ltd* v *Hewitt & Cornell* 1961 (4) SA 286 (N); *Leites* v *Contemporary Refrigeration (Pty) Ltd*

1968 (1) SA 58 (AD); G A Mulligan (1960) 77 *SALJ* 332–7.
On *Royal British Bank* v *Turquand*, and related questions, see further A Stiebel (1933) 49 *LQR* 350; J L Montrose (1934) 50 *LQR* 224; (1957) 55 *Michigan LR* 447 at 449; (1957) 57 *Columbia LR* 868; M L Benade (1962) 25 *THRHR* 195; M J Trebilcock (1966) 2 *Adelaide LR* 310; R S Nock (1967) 30 *MLR* 705.

II PERSONAL LIABILITY OF DIRECTORS

A TEXT

As a rule, a director is not personally liable to a third party on a contract into which he has entered in the name of his company: *293*. There are, however, several exceptional cases in which he may be personally liable:

(1) on the ground of breach of warranty of authority, where he has acted beyond his powers and this was not, actually or constructively, known to the other party: *294, 295*;

(2) where he has acted fraudulently as against the other party: *296*;

(3) where he wrongfully procured a breach of contract by the company or deliberately committed an act disabling the company from carrying out its duties under a contract: *Torquay Hotel Ltd* v *Cousins* [1969] 2 Ch 106 at 138, *Einhorn* v *Westmount Investments Ltd* (1969) 6 DLR (3d) 71 (*Torquay Hotel* v *Cousins* is discussed by K W Wedderburn (1970) 33 *MLR* 309);

(4) where he negligently inflicted damage on the other party: *297*;

(5) where he has bound himself personally for the liability of the company, e g as a surety or as maker or endorser of a bill: *298, 299*;

(6) where he has signed an order or negotiable instrument on behalf of the company without using its name as prescribed by the Act, s 50(3): *Abro* v *Softex Mattress*, *36* above.

(7) if he has formed the company for the purpose of doing a wrongful act or, being in control, directed that a wrongful thing be done: *Rainham Chemical Works Ltd* v *Belvedere Fish Guano Co* [1921] 2 AC 465 (HL) at 476, and *P S Johnson & Associates Ltd* v *Bucko Enterprises Ltd* [1975] 1 NZLR 311.

B CASES

[293] **Ferguson v Wilson**
(1866) 2 Ch App 77

CAIRNS LJ: . . . What is the position of directors of a public company? They are merely agents of a company. The company itself cannot act in its own person, for it has no person; it can only act through directors, and the case is, as regards those directors, merely the ordinary case of principal and agent. Wherever an agent is liable those directors would be liable; where the liability would attach to the principal, and the principal only, the liability is the liability of the company. This being a contract alleged to be made by the company, I own that I have not been able to see how it can be maintained that an agent can be brought into this court, or into any other court, upon a proceeding which simply alleges that his principal has violated a contract that he has entered into. In that state of things, not the agent, but the principal, would be the person liable. . . .

NOTES

See also *Anderson & Co* v *Reynolds and Tillard* (1884) 4 EDC 215; *Major* v *Business Corners (Pty) Ltd* 1940 WLD 84; *Phear and Quinton* v *Rodwell* 1949 (3) SA 1183 (SR).

[294] West London Commercial Bank Ltd *v* Kitson
(1884) 13 QBD 360

Directors held personally liable on bills which they accepted on behalf of the company without authority to do so.

BRETT MR: This is one of the simplest kinds of a common-law action. The defendants allow a bill to be drawn which they accept under these circumstances. They were directors of a company — a tramway company — which was formed under two private Acts of Parliament, the terms of which no one knew or was bound to know but they themselves, and they knew that by those Acts of Parliament they had no authority to accept bills for the company. . . . The acceptance was in this form: 'Accepted for and on behalf of the B and I Company, GK, FSP, directors; BW, Secretary.' The meaning of that is plain. It is that we accept as directors for and on behalf of the company, so that any one who should take the bill would assume that the company had power to accept it, and that the defendants, as directors, were authorized by the company to accept it. That is what this acceptance meant, and it was given in order that the bill might be discounted. By whom was the bill to be discounted? Surely not by the person who knew that the company had no power to accept, and that the defendants had no authority to do so for the company. The acceptance was meant to represent that the company had such power, and that the defendants had such authority. . . . That was a statement of fact to the persons who should discount the bill, and made so that they should suppose that there was such power and authority to accept the bill. It was made that it should be acted on, and it was acted on by the persons who it was intended should act on it. It was a false representation made by the defendants with the knowledge that it was false, and therefore the persons to whom it was made have a cause of action for such false representation. . . .

[295] Firbank's Executors *v* Humphreys
(1886) 18 QBD 54

LINDLEY LJ: . . . The position of affairs on 26 July 1882 may be thus shortly stated. The company was indebted to its contractor for work done, and could not pay those sums in cash, nor could it pay in cash for the work remaining to be done. Under these circumstances, and with a view to induce the contractor to abstain from pressing for cash, and also to induce him to continue the works, the company agreed to give him £18 400 debenture stock and security for the balance due under the original contract for making the line. Pursuant to this agreement the directors of the company gave him certificates for £18 400 debenture stock, and thereupon the contractor forbore to press the company for cash, and he proceeded to finish the line. The company was afterwards wound up, and it was then discovered that when the above agreement was made and the certificates were given the company had already issued the whole of the debenture stock which the company could then lawfully issue; whence it follows that the company could not then legally issue more, and that the certificates given by the directors for the £18 400 debenture stock were valueless. It further appears that the company cannot pay its unsecured creditors anything; but its debenture stock is and always was worth 20s in the pound. Under these circumstances the contractor claims to make the directors personally responsible for the value which the £18 400 debenture stock purported to be given him would have had if it had been validly issued. The learned judge who tried the case has decided in favour of the contractor, and has assessed the damages at £18 400, and the contractor is content with this sum. Whether the contractor is entitled to recover this amount from the directors depends upon two questions, viz: (1) Whether the directors are to be treated as having impliedly warranted that they, as agents of the company, had authority to issue £18 400 debenture stock? (2) What is the measure of damages for which they are liable if they are to be so treated?

The first question must, in my opinion, be answered in the contractor's favour. He could not know whether the company had or had not already issued the full amount of debenture stock which it was authorized to issue. He was justified in assuming that the directors had power to do what they did; and by giving him the debenture stock certificates they in truth represented to him that they had such power. . . . The fact that the directors were themselves deceived and did not know or suspect that they had not the power to do what they did is immaterial in cases of this description. Speaking generally, an action for damages will not lie against a person who honestly makes a misrepresentation which misleads another. But to this general rule there is at least one well-established exception, viz where an agent assumes an authority which he does not possess, and induces another to deal with him upon the faith that he has the authority which he assumes. The present case is within this exception, and the directors are liable to the contractor for the misrepresentation they made to him.

The next question is as to the amount of damages to which the contractor is entitled. The directors cannot be treated as having warranted the solvency of the company, and if genuine debenture stock of the company had been worthless, the measure of damages would have been nil, but in this case the company's debenture stock is and always has been worth twenty shillings in the pound. Consequently the value of £18 400 genuine debenture stock is the measure of the contractor's loss. . . .

NOTES

Although the decision in *Firbank* would now go the other way, in the UK under s 9 of the European Communities Act, in South Africa under s 36 of the 1973 Act, the case is still valuable as an illustration of the principle of warranty of authority as applied to company executives.

See also *Weeks* v *Propert* (1873) LR 8 CP 427; *Chapleo* v *Brunswick Permanent Benefit Building Society* (1881) 6 QBD 696; *Looker* v *Wrigley* (1882) 9 QBD 397; *Elkington & Co* v *Hurter* [1892] 2 Ch 452. In practice an action against the directors on the ground of breach of authority will but rarely lie, for, as a rule, a person who deals with a director of a company can discover the extent of his authority from a perusal of the company's constitution and is, therefore, deemed to have had knowledge of it.

[296]　Orkin Bros Ltd *v* Bell
1921 TPD 92

Directors of a company, which was in financial difficulties, purchased large quantities of goods on credit without believing that they would be paid for and with reckless indifference as to whether they could be paid for or not. The company shortly afterwards was placed in liquidation. The court decided that the directors were personally liable, jointly and severally, for the purchase price.

MASON J: ... There seems to me an implied representation when the directors or officers of limited companies order goods from a merchant that they believe the company will probably be able to pay, and, if they know that there is no likelihood of payment and no means of payment, they commit ... a fraud.

NOTES

See further *Brenes & Co* v *Downie* 1914 SC 97; *Armstrong* v *Strain* [1952] 1 KB 232, [1952] 1 All ER 139; *Ruto Flour Mills (Pty) Ltd* v *Moriates* 1957 (3) SA 113 (T); *Huworth's Properties (Pty) Ltd* v *Poynton* 1962 (4) SA 117 (D). Mere lack of judgment is not sufficient.

In *Briess* v *Woolley* [1954] AC 333, [1954] 1 All ER 909 it was held that if a director commits a fraud while acting as an agent on behalf of the shareholders to negotiate the sale of their shares, the shareholders are vicariously liable in damages to the third party even if they themselves were innocent of fraud.

Where a company is being wound up or has been placed under judicial management, and it appears to the court that any business of the company has been carried on with intent to defraud creditors of the company or creditors of any other person or for any fraudulent purpose, the court may declare that any of the company's directors, whether past or present, shall be personally liable, without limitation, for all or any of the debts or other liabilities of the company, s 424. The director must have knowingly been a party to the fraud: see *Hardie* v *Hanson* (1960) 33 *Australian LJR* 455, and pp 723–5 below.

[297]　Fairline Shipping Corporation *v* Adamson
[1974] 2 WLR 824, [1974] 2 All ER 967

The plaintiffs agreed with a company (Game and Meat Ltd), of which the defendant was managing director, to store perishable goods in a refrigerated store owned by the defendant. A letter was later sent to the plaintiffs on behalf of the defendant confirming the arrangement. An invoice for the first month's storage charges was also sent in the defendant's name. Because of failure to maintain a check on the temperature in the store-room, the goods were damaged. The company went into liquidation and the plaintiff sued the defendant personally alleging breach of contract, breach of duty by a bailee, and negligence.

KERR J: The real answer to the submission made on behalf of the defendant is in my judgment that the question of his liability in negligence to the plaintiffs is not necessarily excluded as a matter of law on the ground that there was no contract with him and that he is also not to be regarded as a bailee with a right to the legal possession of the goods. Depending on the facts, he may none the less owe a duty of care to the plaintiffs and be liable in negligence for breach of that duty. The fact that he was a director of Game & Meat and that the company was the contracting party does not necessarily exclude his personal liability. The legal position in this connection can be conveniently illustrated by reference to two cases, but such examples could easily be multiplied. In *Adler* v *Dickson* [1955] 1 QB 158 the plaintiff's contract with the defendant's employers, although excluding all liability for negligence, nevertheless did not preclude her from recovering damages in negligence from the defendant, a servant of the company with which she had contracted, because he owed her a personal duty of care apart from his contractual obligations to his employers, and because he was held to be in breach of that duty. That was a case of personal injury, but I do not see why a case of damage to the plaintiff's property must be regarded differently in law. Take the facts of *Morris* v *C W Martin & Sons Ltd* [1966] 1 QB 716. In that case the plaintiff's fur coat was stolen by a servant of the defendants, who were subcontractors and subbailees of the coat without any contractual or other nexus existing between the plaintiff and the defendants. The plaintiff recovered damages against the defendants for the loss of her coat because they were held responsible for the act of their servant. It is, however, clear that if she had chosen to sue the servant personally in the tort of conversion she would equally have succeeded, indeed with less difficulty. But would the position on this basis have been any different if instead of stealing the coat the servant had negligently caused or allowed it to be ruined in the process of cleaning it? If he had carelessly plunged it into a vat of green dye or left it in cleaning fluid for so long that it became destroyed by some foreseeable chemical action, could he not have been made liable in negligence as well as his employers? I do not see why it should follow as a matter of law that in such cases an action could only be maintained against his employers. A duty of care by somebody else's servant to the owner of goods, and a breach of that duty by a particular servant, may of course be much more difficult to establish than a wrongful conversion of the goods by such a servant. But this depends on the facts. Generally speaking, if an employer is liable to a plaintiff in tort on the basis of the doctrine *respondeat superior*, the servant can also be held personally liable, though in practice it is of course usually much more convenient and worth while to sue his employers. If this is the law as regards servants it cannot logically be more favourable to company directors.

It follows that in my view the crucial question in the present case is whether or not, on the facts, the defendant owed a duty of care to the plaintiffs in respect of their goods which were stored in his cold store, and, if so, whether he was in breach of that duty. In my view, both limbs of this question are to be answered in the affirmative on the special facts of this case which I have already reviewed. Game & Meat would only perform its duties in relation to these goods through its human servants and agents. At the relevant time the only persons through whom these duties could be performed were the directors. The only one of these who concerned himself with these goods in any way after their delivery was the defendant. The letter of 23 March dictated by him or on his behalf, in my view, reflected the true position, in that he regarded himself, and not Game & Meat, as concerned with the storage of these goods. On the facts of this case the defendant in my view assumed and owed a duty of care to the plaintiffs in respect of the storage of their goods in his premises and was in breach of that duty with the result that the plaintiff's goods were damaged. I therefore give judgment for the plaintiffs against the defendant in the agreed amount of £3 143,78.

[298] Steenkamp *v* Webster
1955 (1) SA 524 (AD)

A company had purchased a certain right from the plaintiff. The deed of sale was signed by the defendant (M D C Steenkamp) and one Van Staden, the sole directors of the company, as follows:

'M D C Steenkamp,
M P van Staden,
vir Hennenman Sand (Pty) Ltd'.

Clause 3 of the deed of sale provided as follows:

'3. Mnr M D C Steenkamp in sy private hoedanigheid verbind homself hiermee as borg en mede-prinsipale skuldenaar teenoor die verkoper vir die betaling van die gemelde koopsom soos in klousule 1 uiteengesit.'

Sued on this undertaking, the defendant (Steenkamp) denied that he signed the agreement as surety and co-principal debtor and pleaded that he signed it only in a representative capacity as a director of the company.

GREENBERG JA: ... The document on which the respondent based his claim no doubt sets out two agreements, one under which the company purchases from the respondent the assets mentioned and the other under which the appellant binds himself as surety for, and co-principal debtor with, the company for payment of the purchase price. But there is nothing to warrant the view that the respondent would have been prepared to enter into the agreement which provided for delivery against payment of only one-third of the price, without the security of the appellant's undertaking and the additional fact that the two agreements were jointly discussed and incorporated in one document is in conflict with that view, which I think must be rejected. On this basis the question for decision is whether the appellant must be held to have bound himself under clause 3. The principle on which it is to be ascertained whether he has so bound himself appears from the passage cited by the learned Chief Justice from *Williston on Contracts*, viz: that what is decisive is not whether the appellant assented but whether what he has done justified the respondent in concluding that he had assented. The respondent had signed the document which incorporated both agreements and it seems clear that he did not intend by that signature to agree to the sale and delivery without the appellant's assent to clause 3.

Nor was it contended on the appellant's behalf, and rightly so in my opinion, that the respondent's signature to the contract was an offer and that the appellant's was a counter-offer. Clause 3 unambiguously stipulates that he is to be a surety and co-principal debtor and, more especially as he was not making a counter-offer, the obvious way to signify his non-assent to the clause would have been either not to sign the document at all or to delete clause 3 or perhaps to record on the document that he did not agree to the clause. In the absence of such an indication it appears to me that he must be taken to have assented to all the contents of the document. . . .

NOTES

A director who adds his signature to the company's stamp or signature on a bill, cheque or promissory note, without adding 'pp' (*per procurationem*) or some other letters or words to make it clear that he is signing in a representative capacity, is likely to find that, in addition to binding the company, he has rendered himself personally liable. See e g *Associated Engineers Co Ltd* v *Goldblatt* 1938 WLD 139; *Francois* v *Blackie & Co Ltd* 1955 (2) SA 55 (N); *Hein* v *Hofmeyr* 1958 (1) SA 29 (W); *Jones* v *John Barr & Co (Pty) Ltd* 1967 (3) SA 292 (W); further I B Murray (1958) 75 *SALJ* 189; 1961 *Annual Survey* 272; Harry Silverberg, 'Personal Liability of Directors on Bills of Exchange' (1967) *Journal of Business Law* 116. But see *299*, below.

[299] Dickinson *v* SA General Electric Co (Pty) Ltd
1973 (2) SA 620 (AD)

Two cheques drawn in favour of the plaintiff were signed as follows:

Boiler Plant and Services (Pty) Ltd
Helen Dickinson
349445

Helen Dickinson was a director of Boiler Plant and Services (Pty) Ltd. The name of the company and the account number were imprinted on the cheques by the bank. The plaintiff sought to hold the defendant personally liable as drawer of the cheque.

Without deciding the issue the court clearly felt that the cheques were the company's cheques, and not the cheques of the defendant.

JANSEN JA: In view of what will be said in regard to the other points, it is unnecessary to decide whether *ex facie* the cheques the appellant is clearly a drawer or not, or whether there is at least some ambiguity. It is, therefore, desirable to leave aside the controversies raging around the so-called composite signature of a company (cf (1958) *SALJ* 189; (1961) *SALJ* 293; Cowen *Law of Negotiable Instruments* 4 ed 148 et seq). The whole question may well require reconsideration in view of recent banking practice. Although he considered himself bound by the decisions, the learned judge *a quo* [Nicholas J] in granting leave to appeal, directed attention to the following:

'It is common knowledge that the cheque forms supplied to' their customers by banks which have adopted computerization, have printed on them a name and a number. The name is that of the bank's customer in which the banking account is conducted; it is not, of course, a signature. The number is that by which the account is identified in the bank's records. Where, at any rate, a single signature is affixed to such a cheque, it may well be argued that, in the light of the circumstances to which I have just referred, that signature is intended to be and is to be interpreted as being the signature of the customer whose account it is. That may be so even where, as in the present case, the name of the customer as printed on the cheque is that of a company ('Boiler Plant and Services (Pty) Ltd') and the signature is the unqualified signature of a natural person ('Helen Dickinson').

Prima facie when a person has signed a cheque form such as the present he intends to write, and will be understood as writing, the signature of the customer of the bank whose name is printed on the cheque. If he intended to sign in his own person he would presumably strike out the printed name and number which appears on the cheque.'

In conjunction with this the argument is raised that s 24(1) of Act 34 of 1964 does not necessarily imply the converse, viz that unless eg a drawer adds words to his signature indicating that he signs for or on behalf of a principal, or in a representative capacity, he is personally liable. But on these matters, as has been indicated, it is not necessary to express any final opinion.

II CRIMINAL LIABILITY OF DIRECTORS

A TEXT

For the purpose of criminal liability, any act performed by a director or servant of the company in the exercise of his powers or the performance of his duties is deemed to be an act of the company. The director or servant of a company is personally liable to punishment for a criminal offence committed by the company unless he can prove that he had no part in the commission of the offence: s 381 of the Criminal Procedure Act 56 of 1955: *300–304.*

[300] Criminal Procedure Act
56 of 1955 s 381:

(1) For the purpose of imposing upon a corporate body criminal liability for any offence, whether under any law or at common law—

(*a*) any act performed, with or without a particular intent, by or on instructions or with permission, express or implied, given by a director or servant of that corporate body; and

(*b*) the omission, with or without a particular intent, of any act which ought to have been but was not performed by or on instructions given by a director or servant of that corporate body,

in the exercise of his powers or in the performance of his duties as such director or servant, or in furthering or endeavouring to further the interests of that corporate body, shall be deemed to have been performed (and with the same intent, if any) by that corporate body or, as the case may be, to have been an omission (and with the same intent, if any) on the part of that corporate body.

(2) In any prosecution against a corporate body, a director or servant of that corporate body shall be cited, as representative of that corporate body, as the offender, and there-

upon the person so cited may, as such representative, be dealt with as if he were the person accused of having committed the offence in question: Provided that—

(a) if the said person pleads guilty, the plea shall not be valid unless the corporate body authorized him to plead guilty;

(b) if at any stage of the proceedings the said person ceases to be a director or servant of that corporate body or absconds or is unable to attend, the court or magistrate concerned may, at the request of the prosecutor, from time to time substitute for the said person, any other person who is a director or servant of the said corporate body at the time of the said substitution, and thereupon the proceedings shall continue as if no substitution had taken place;

(c) if the said person, as representing the corporate body, is committed for trial, he shall not be committed to prison but shall be released on his own recognizance to stand his trial;

(d) if the said person, as representing the corporate body, is convicted, the court convicting him shall not impose upon him in his representative capacity any punishment, whether direct or as an alternative, other than a fine, even if the relevant law makes no provision for the imposition of a fine, in respect of the offence in question, and such fine shall be payable by the corporate body and may be recovered by attachment and sale of any property of the corporate body in terms of section *three hundred and thirty-seven*;

(e) the citation of a director or servant of a corporate body as aforesaid, to represent that corporate body in any prosecution instituted against it, shall not exempt that director or servant from prosecution for that offence in terms of subsection (5).

(3) In any criminal proceedings against a corporate body, any record which was made or kept by a director, servant or agent of the corporate body within the scope of his activities as such director, servant or agent, or any document which was at any time in the custody or under the control of any such director, servant or agent within the scope of his activities as such director, servant or agent, shall be admissible in evidence against the accused.

(4) For the purposes of subsection (3) any record made or kept by a director, servant or agent of a corporate body or any document which was at any time in his custody or control shall be presumed to have been made or kept by him or to have been in his custody or control within the scope of his activities as such director, servant or agent, unless the contrary is proved.

(5) When an offence has been committed, whether by the performance of any act or by the failure to perform any act, for which any corporate body is or was liable to prosecution, any person who was, at the time of the commission of the offence, a director or servant of the corporate body, shall be deemed to be guilty of the said offence, unless it is proved that he did not take part in the commission of the offence, and that he could not have prevented it, and shall be liable to prosecution therefor, either jointly with the corporate body or apart therefrom, and shall on conviction be personally liable to punishment therefor.

(6) In any proceedings against a director or servant of a corporate body, in respect of an offence—

(a) any evidence which would be or was admissible against that corporate body in a prosecution for that offence, shall be admissible against the accused;

(b) whether or not such corporate body is or was liable to prosecution for the said offence, any document, memorandum, book or record which was drawn up, entered up or kept in the ordinary course of that corporate body's business, or which was at any time in the custody or under the control of any director, servant or agent of such corporate body, in his capacity as director, servant or agent, shall be *prima facie* evidence of its contents and admissible in evidence against the accused, unless and until he is able to prove that at all material times he had no knowledge of the said document, memorandum, book or record, in so far as its contents are relevant to the offence charged, and was in no way party to the drawing up of such document or memorandum or making of any relevant entries in such book or record.

(7), (8) and (9) [Deal with offences committed by a member of an association other than a corporate body.]

(10) In this section the word 'director' in relation to a corporate body means any person who controls or governs that corporate body or who is a member of a body or group of persons which controls or governs that corporate body or where there is no such body or group, who is a member of that corporate body.

(11) The provisions of this section shall be additional to and not in substitution for any other law which provides for a prosecution against corporate bodies or their directors or servants or against associations of persons or their members.

B CASES

[301] R v Van Heerden
1946 AD 168

DAVIS AJA: ... The first appellant (Universal Services (Pty) Ltd), which I shall call the company, sells coloured portraits and pictures and the frames therefor; the second appellant, W J van Heerden, is one of its two directors, and the third appellant, J L van Heerden, was at all material times its secretary. The fraud alleged in the charge, in so far as the convictions of the appellants were confirmed, and so far as is material to this appeal, was that they had falsely represented to certain four persons that certain frames which they sold were made of expensive imported American wood, whereas they well knew that they were not. The frames were sold by the company through the agency of the second appellant: they were locally made of South Africa pine or poplar. . . .
. . . Subsection (1) [of s 384 of Act 31 of 1917*], leaving out the portion dealing with omissions, is as follows:

'For the purpose of imposing upon a corporate body criminal liability for any offence, whether under any statute or statutory regulation or by-law or at common law—

(*a*) any act performed, with or without a particular intent, by or on instructions or with permission, express or implied, given by a director or servant of that corporate body . . . in the exercise of his powers or in the performance of his duties as such director or servant, or in furthering or in endeavouring to further the interests of that corporate body, shall be deemed to have been performed (and with the same intent, if any) by that corporate body. . . .'

It was contended that the second appellant, in making these misrepresentations, acted as an agent, and did not act either in his capacity as director or as a servant and that, consequently, the company does not fall under the provisions of this subsection. That he was not a servant, but an agent . . . I am prepared to assume. It was contended that he was acting solely as agent for his own benefit to earn his commission and in no way as director, and it was pointed out that there is no mention of agents in ss (1). . . . But the fact remains that he was a director, and it is indeed difficult to imagine a case where a company, employing one of its directors as its agent, would not be criminally responsible under this subsection for his unlawful acts if such acts were done as agent and

---

* Cf s 381(1) of Act 56 of 1955 (see above), which has replaced it, but is substantially in identical terms.

related to the affairs of the company. What the second appellant did here, as agent, he 'did with the permission, express or implied, given by' himself in his capacity as director. Moreover, even if I take it that in making the representations, he was not acting 'in the exercise of his powers or in the performance of his duties as director', there is still the remaining portion of the subsection. It was the company which was selling the frames: the second appellant admitted that the frames were a source of income to the company, that everything done to get orders or make delivery was in the interests of the company, and that it was his duty to sell as many frames as he could. In these circumstances, what he did was done, not only for himself, but also 'in furthering or endeavouring to further the interests of the corporate body', that is, of the company. . . .

[Appeal dismissed.]

NOTES

See further *R* v *Philips Dairy (Pty) Ltd* 1955 (4) SA 120 (T).

[302] **Herold NO v Johannesburg City Council**
1947 (2) SA 1257 (AD)

HATHORN AJA: . . . Section 384 of Act 31 of 1917 provides, in ss (2) [cf ss (2) of s 381 of Act 56 of 1955 which has replaced it, but is substantially in identical terms], that in any criminal proceedings against a corporate body, a director or servant shall be cited as representative of the corporate body and it goes on to enact in proviso (*d*) that upon conviction the court may not impose any punishment except a fine, and the fine shall be payable by the corporate body. Then ss (5) provides that when an offence has been committed for which any corporate body is or was liable for prosecution, a director or servant shall be deemed to be guilty of the offence, unless it is proved that he did not take part in the commission of the offence and that he could not have prevented it and the subsection proceeds to make him personally liable to conviction and punishment.

It is clear that when criminal proceedings are instituted under ss (2) the director or servant should be cited as representative of the corporate body, and it is equally clear that, if it is sought to charge a director or servant under ss (5), he should be cited as an individual, and the fact that he is a director or servant should be alleged in the body of the charge as one of the essential facts to be proved, and it would be an advantage if ss (5) were mentioned in order to show that he is being prosecuted under the provisions of that subsection. If charges take this form, the prosecutor, the accused and the court can have no doubt whatever about the identity of the accused. . . .

[303] **S v Louterwater Landgoed (Edms) Bpk**
1972 (2) SA 809 (C)

The first appellant, a private company, the second appellant, the company's sole director, and the third appellant, an employee of the company, were convicted, *inter alia*, of a contravention of s 21(1)(*c*)(ii) of the Forest Act 72 of 1968 in that they wrongfully lit a fire which spread and caused loss. The evidence showed that the third appellant had lit the fire and that it had spread through his negligence. The second appellant had had no knowledge of the fire.

BAKER AJ: Die vraag wat dus beantwoord moet word is wat is die aanspreeklikheid van die maatskappy en die daadwerklike beheerder daarvan vir 'n vuur wat aangesteek is deur 'n werknemer (dienaar of agent) van die maatskappy agerend binne die bestek van sy hoedanigheid as sulks en ingevolge algemene instruksies om so 'n vuur aan te steek, welke vuur as gevolg van die nalatigheid van bedoelde dienaar versprei het en skade veroorsaak het, op 'n datum wat nie deur die direkteur bepaal is nie en onder omstandighede aan die direkteur onbekend, waar hy hoegenaamd geen stappe kon gedoen het om die brand te reël of te verbied of die verspreiding daarvan te beheer nie. Die onwetenheid van die direkteur is ook die onwetenheid van die maatskappy.

Artikel 381 van die Strafproseswet, insoverre dit op die aanspreeklikheid van eerste appellant betrekking het, lui soos volg:

„(1) Ten einde 'n regspersoon strafregterlike aanspreeklikheid op te lê weens 'n misdryf, hetsy wetteregterlike of gemeenregtelik, word—

(*a*) enige daad wat deur of in opdrag of met uitdruklike of stilswyende toestemming van 'n direkteur of dienaar van daardie regspersoon, met of sonder 'n besondere opset, verrig word; en

(*b*) die versuim, met of sonder 'n besondere opset, om 'n daad te verrig wat verrig moes geword het maar nie verrig is nie, deur of in opdrag van 'n direkteur of dienaar van daardie regspersoon, by die uitoefening van sy bevoegdhede of die uitvoering van sy pligte as so 'n direkteur of dienaar, of ter bevordering of gepoogde bevordering van die belange van daardie regspersoon, geag 'n daad met dieselfde opset, as daar opset by is, deur daardie regspersoon verrig te gewees het of, na gelang van die geval, 'n versuim en met dieselfde opset, as daar opset by is, aan die kant van daardie regspersoon te gewees het.''

Tweede appellant is 'n direkteur binne die betekenis van hierdie subartikel (sien subart (10) en *R* v *Mall & others* 1959 (4) SA 607 (N), en derde appellant 'n dienaar (vgl *R* v *van Zyl* 1960 (1) SA 371 (SWA) te bl 372D). Tweede appellant het die aansteek van die tweede vuur in algemene terme gemagtig, maar hierdie „daad'' is nie, na my mening, die „daad'' wat in para (*a*) van bostaande subartikel beoog word nie: die „daad'' wat daarin beoog word is 'n misdryf, en die aansteek van 'n vuur per se is nie, in terme van art 21(1)(*c*) van Wet 72 van 1968, 'n misdryf nie. Dit is die nalatigheid van die aansteker, sy dienaar of sy agent wat tot verspreiding lei wat die maatskappy strafregtelike verantwoordelikheid op die hals haal. As eerste appellant dus vir die optrede van tweede appellant aanspreeklik gehou moet word, moet dit onder para (*b*) geskied, en moet dit bewys word dat tweede appellant „versuim" het om iets te doen en dat dié versuim strafbaar was. Al versuim wat tweede appellant ten laste gelê kan word is die versuim om díe vuur te beheer of te keer sodat verspreiding en die daaropvolgende skade nie sou plaasgevind het nie. Ek het reeds gesê dat tweede appellant niks van die vuur geweet het nie. Hy kon dit dus nie keer nie. Sy „versuim" is dus geen versuim nie, en sy optrede of gebrek aan optrede kan geen strafregtelike aanspreeklikheid op die eerste appellant oplê nie.

Wat betref derde appellant is dit 'n ander saak. Hy as dienaar het versuim om die vuur te beheer en dit het gelei tot die verwoesting van die berg. Sy versuim lei regstreeks tot die aanspreeklikheid van eerste appellant en eerste appellant is derhalwe skuldig, ingevolge art 381(1) van die Strafproseswet, van 'n oortreding van art 21(1)(*c*)(ii) van Wet 72 van 1968.

[304] S *v* Klopper
1975 (4) SA 773 (AD)

Kotzé AJA: Die appellant, as beskuldigde nr 1, is in die Witwatersrandse Plaaslike Afdeling skuldig bevind op een uit 16 aanklagtes waarop hy tereggestaan het, nl aanklag 15. Hy is gevonnis tot gevangenisstraf wat op sekere voorwaardes opgeskort is.

Aanklag 15 het betrekking op 'n sirkulêre, bewysstuk 107 by die verhoor, waarin aansoek aangevra word deur 'n maatskappy, Gainmore Mutual Bpk (hierna Gainmore genoem) vir die aankoop van vyf miljoen aandele van 50 sent elk van die maatskappy se onuitgereikte gemagtigde aandelekapitaal. Die aanklag lê die appellant, ter alle saaklike tye 'n direkteur van Gainmore soos bedoel in art 381 van die Strafproseswet 56 van 1955, ten laste dat hy wederregtelik en onwettiglik, persoonlik of uit hoofde van art 381(5), die misdaad van poging tot bedrog gepleeg het deur aan ongenoemde lede en aandeelhouers van Gainmore sekere valse voorstellings deur middel van die gemelde sirkulêre te doen, ten einde hulle te beweeg om tot hulle verlies en nadeel, aandele in Gainmore op te neem en hulle aldus te bedrieg.

Die skuldigbevinding het voortgevloei uit 'n bevinding dat die appellant hom nie van die bewyslas gekwyt het nie deur aan te dui dat hy die pleeg van die misdaad nie kon verhoed het nie soos vereis word deur subart (5) van art 381 van die Strafproseswet.

Pasvermelde bevinding het tot gevolg gehad dat, op versoek van die appellant, 'n regsvraag luidens art 366 van die Strafproseswet 56 van 1955 vir oorweging deur hierdie Hof, voorbehou is. Die Verhoorregter het die regsvraag as volg geformuleer:

> „Het die Hof korrek beoordeel dat beskuldigde nr 1 se geestestoestand, subjektief gesproke, nl, dat hy nie bewus was van die wanvoorstelling wat vervat is in bewysstuk 107 nie en wat veroorsaak is deur sy nalate om dit met redelike agsaamheid te lees, nie 'n uitweg vir hom bied uit sy middellike aanspreeklikheid onder art 381(5) van die Strafkode nie?"

Subartikel (5) van art 381 bepaal:

„Wanneer 'n misdryf gepleeg is hetsy deur die verrigting van 'n daad of deur die versuim om 'n daad te verrig, waarvoor 'n regspersoon vervolg kan word of kon geword het, word enigiemand wat ten tyde van die pleeg van die misdryf 'n direkteur of dienaar van die regspersoon was, geag aan bedoelde misdryf skuldig te wees tensy dit bewys word dat hy nie aan die pleeg van die misdryf deelgeneem het en dit nie kon verhoed het nie, en kan hy saam met die regspersoon of afsonderlik weens daardie misdryf aangekla word, en by skuldigbevinding persoonlik daarvoor gestraf word."

Die Verhoorregter het aan subart (5) 'n breë vertolking verleen en beslis dat die uitdrukking „nie kon verhoed . . . nie," nalatigheid deur 'n direkteur nie uitsluit nie. Hy het gedeeltelik op gesag van die uitspraak in *S* v *Salama Taxis (Pty) Ltd & others* 1964 (1) SA 371 (K), beslis dat dit die oogmerk van die Wetgewer, met die bepaling, is om te verseker dat 'n direkteur van 'n regspersoon op sy hoede geplaas word en dat, waar hy die moontlikheid van 'n oortreding deur 'n regspersoon kan voorsien, hy verplig is om daarteen te waak. Versaak hy hierdie plig op nalatige wyse word hy persoonlik deur aanspreeklikheid getref.

In hierdie hof het die Staat, benewens te steun op die uitspraak in die hof *a quo*, aangevoer dat die tweede voorbehoudsbepaling in subart (5) so vertolk behoort te word dat dit daarop neerkom dat die getuienis, objektief beskou, op 'n oorwig van waarskynlikhede aandui dat die beskuldigde redelike maatreëls getref het om die pleeg van die tenlastegelegde misdaad te verhoed. So nie, verplaas hy nie die bewyslas nie. Of anders gestel: dat die beskuldigde onder 'n verpligting staan om toe te sien dat misdrywe nie gepleeg word waarvoor die regspersoon vervolg kan word nie, en dat hy redelike stappe moet neem om uit te vind of sodanige misdrywe gepleeg word of op hande is. As gesag vir hierdie standpunt word hoofsaaklik gesteun op die minderheidsuitspraak van Schreiner AR, in *R* v *Limbada & another* 1958 (2) SA 481 (AA) op 484–5; *R* v *Van den Berg* 1955 (2) SA 338 (AA) op 341; *R* v *Kekane & others* 1955 (4) SA 378 (T) op 383–4, *S* v *Salama Taxis (Pty) Ltd (supra); S* v *Poole* 1975 (1) SA 924 (N).

Mnr *Cillié* het op versoek van die hof namens die appellant verskyn. Ons spreek aan hom ons dank uit vir sy bystand. Sy standpunt is dat 'n subjektiewe toets toegepas word: Indien dit op die feite blyk dat die beskuldigde die pleeg van die misdaad nie kon verhoed nie, weens sy eerlike onbewustheid dat die misdaad gepleeg word, kwyt hy hom van die bewyslas in weerwil van sy onagsaamheid.

Die passasie in die uitspraak van Schreiner AR in die saak van *Limbada* het betrekking op subart (7) van art 381, wat in die tersaaklike deel enersluidend met subart (5) is, en lees as volg:

„But when an accused person is charged under s 381(7) of Act 56 of 1955 or its predecessor, although in form he is charged with what may fairly be called the main offence, the substance of the matter may well be, I think, that he is being charged with a statutory offence under the subsection, read with the main offence. The reason why I think that this may be the more acceptable view is that the accused is not merely saddled with the burden of proving that he did not take part in the commission of the offence, but he must also prove 'that he could not have prevented it'. A partner who proves that he was not a *socius criminis* in the main offence, is nevertheless convicted if he cannot prove the second requirement. It seems somewhat artificial to say that he is guilty of the main offence although it is established that he was not a party to it. If this should be the correct view the subsection would be one of the essentials of the crime with which the accused is really charged and would have to be alleged."

Die meerderheidsuitspraak, geskryf deur Steyn AR (soos hy toe was), gaan van die standpunt uit dat die subartikel nie 'n nuwe misdryf skep nie, maar die beskuldigde slegs aan 'n bewyslas onderwerp:

> „What it does is to deem an accused, in the circumstances described therein, to be guilty of an offence committed by another. . . . In the circumstances so described it casts an onus of proof upon the accused and in effect directs the court to find him guilty if he does not discharge that *onus*. It is essentially, therefore, an evidential provision (cf *R v Milne and Erleigh* (7) 1951 (1) SA 791 (AD) at 831), and does not bring into existence a distinct though mutable offence, having as one of its essentials the commission of some other offence. In each case in which its provisions are invoked, the accused would, if found guilty, have to be convicted of such other offence and not of a contravention of this sub-section. That does not mean that the matters required to be proved before reliance can be placed upon it, need not be averred in the indictment or charge. If the prosecution rests its case upon the subsection, the accused is, I think, entitled to be informed of that fact, just as much as he is entitled to other details necessary to acqaint him with the nature of the case he has to meet. But that goes to part-ticularity rather than to the substance of the offence."

(Op bl 486.)

Op die oog af is die twee uitsprake teenstrydig. Dit is, na my mening, onnodig om te oorweeg of dit inderdaad so is. Indien in ag geneem word dat dit in *Limbada* se saak gegaan het oor die inhoud van die akte van beskuldiging, is beide benaderings versoenbaar met die uitleg dat, benewens 'n bewyslasverskuiwing in die eerste deel van die voorbehouds-bepaling, die tweede deel daarvan 'n vorm van strafpligtigheid oplê in die sin dat die oortreding van die dader aangesien word as dié van die lid van die vereniging (onder subart (7)) of van die direkteur of dienaar (onder subart (5)) tensy op 'n oorwig van waarskynlikhede bewys word dat die lid, direkteur of dienaar die pleeg van die misdryf nie kon verhoed nie. So beskou, verleen die sub-artikels nie steun aan die Staatsbetoog dat slegs 'n objektiewe uitleg sin aan die tweede voorbehoudsbepaling verleen nie—selfs 'n subjektiewe vertolking vestig strafpligtigheid waar dit nie onder die geneme reg bestaan nie.

In die *Van den Berg*-saak het die Verhoorhof beskuldigdes nrs 1 en 2 skuldig bevind op 'n aanklag van brandstigting. Laasgenoemde het die brand gestig terwyl eersgenoemde, sy vennoot, skuldig bevind is ingevolge die bepalings van subart (7) van art 348 van Wet 31 van 1917—die voorganger van subart (7) van art 381 van die huidige Strafproseswet. Op appèl het Greenberg AR op 341 gesê:

„In the passages I have cited it is twice conceded that the first appellant may have been unaware of the act of the second appellant in causing the fire, and if he was so unaware, then he has proved, in terms of the subsection, that he did not take part in the commission of the offence and could not have prevented it; it may be that ignorance caused through deliberately abstaining from making enquiries may not avail a member of an association but this position does not arise here."

In die onderhawige geval is daar geen sprake van 'n opsetlike versuim om navrae te doen nie. Die appellant se gebrek aan kennis het uit nalatigheid ontstaan. Sover die aangehaalde uittreksel gaan, is dit eerder strydig met die Staatsbetoog as ondersteunend daarvan.

Die *Kekane*-saak is beslis op grond van 'n bevinding op bl 384 dat

„there is no evidence at all to show that any of the eight other accused could not have prevented the third accused from breaking the rules of the club and thus committing the offences with which they were all charged".

In die *Salama Taxis*-saak, wat ten grondslag van die beslissing in *Poole* se saak lê, was 'n huurmotor-maatskappy gemagtig om slegs nie-Blanke passasiers te vervoer. 'n Werknemer van die maatskappy (derde appellant) het die magtiging oortree deur Blanke passasiers te vervoer. 'n Direkteur van die maatskappy (tweede appellant), wat as gevolg hiervan voor 'n landdros tereg gestaan het op 'n oortreding van Wet 39 van 1939, is skuldig bevind ingevolge die bepalings van subart (5). Op appèl het Corbett R (soos hy toe was), bevind dat die bewyslas nie gekwyt word bloot deur getuienis uit die mond van die direkteur dat hy die pleeg van die misdryf nie kon verhoed nie. Die geleerde regter het bygevoeg op 376:

„It seems to me for a person in his position merely to tell the court that he could not have prevented the commission of the offence is not sufficient to discharge the onus placed upon him by s 381(5) of the code. I think in those circumstances he should have given evidence of objective facts designed to enable the the court to come to a conclusion as to whether or not he could have prevented the commission of the offence. Thus he could have told the court whether appellant No 3 had been informed about the condition contained in the certificate, as to whether the need to observe this condition had been impressed upon the third appellant or any other servant of the company; and possibly also as to what steps had been taken by appellant No 2 to check whether such conditions were being observed by the servants of the company. Had he done so and had this evidence been accepted by the magistrate, he would no doubt have succeeded in discharging this onus. But, in my view, a mere statement that he could not have prevented it is not sufficient, even in the absence of cross-examination, to discharge the onus."

Hierbo het ek die mening uitgespreek dat *Limbada* se saak nie strydig is met 'n subjektiewe vertolking nie. Met uitsondering van die *Salama Taxis*-

en *Poole*-sake, bevat die uitsprake waarop die Staat steun geen duidelike rigsnoer dat 'n objektiewe uitleg toegepas behoort te word nie. Na my mening behoort subart (5), wat—soos reeds aangedui—'n vorm van strafpligtigheid oplê, op die mins verswarende wyse uitgelê te word. Ten einde 'n objektiewe vertolking te regverdig, behoort 'n kwalifikasie, soos bv „redelikerwyse" of „sonder nalatigheid" voor die woorde „kon verhoed het nie" ingelees te word. Sonder so 'n kwalifikasie in te voeg— waarvoor ek in 'n strafbepaling, soos hierdie, geen regverdiging kan sien nie—is dit onmoontlik om te beslis dat die Wetgewer 'n objektiewe uitleg wou voorskryf. Dit geld veral in 'n geval soos die onderhawige waar die aanklag poging tot bedrog is—'n misdryf wat op opset berus. 'n Bevestigende antwoord op die voorbehoude regsvraag, sou inhou dat strafaanspreeklikheid op grond van *culpa* opgelê kan word tov 'n misdryf waarvan opset 'n essensiële element is. Dit is moeilik om te aanvaar. My mening soos hierbo vermeld lei tot 'n konklusie wat, oa, harmonieer met ondervermelde beslissings:

(a) *R* v *Milne and Erleigh* (7) 1951 (1) SA 791 (AA). Die Verhoofhof het Erleigh skuldig bevind op 'n aanklag van diefstal van 80 000 aandele. Milne is, uit hoofde van subart (7) van art 384 van Wet 31 van 1917, skuldig bevind as Erleigh se vennoot. Centlivres HR verklaar, sonder motivering, op bl 831:

> „The only material on which it could be argued that this burden was discharged was the fact that Milne paid for the 40 000 shares he received by a cheque drawn in favour of ETC. Had this fact been related to credible evidence by him to the effect that *he was not aware* (ek kursiveer) that Erleigh was taking the shares from NUG he might well have succeeded in discharging the burden. But in the absence of such evidence the name of the payee is equivocal; the cheque might have been so drawn as a safety measure."

(b) *R* v *Kapelus* 1944 TPD 70, 'n saak waar, onder sub-art (5) van art 384 van Wet 31 van 1917, beslis is dat 'n direkteur wat die werknemer in sy pligte voorgelig het en nie by die oortreding teenwoordig was nie, die bewyslas gekwyt het.

(c) *R* v *SA Butcheries* (*Pty*) *Ltd* 1952 (2) PH H113 (C) waar met betrekking tot art 384 van Wet 31 van 1917 verklaar word:

> „The words in the Act must be given a reasonable meaning and in each case the particular circumstances must be looked at."

(d) *R* v *Couvaras* 1946 OPD 392. Ten aansien van art 384 van Wet 31 van 1917 sê Van Den Heever R (soos hy toe was), op 397:

> „Die misdryf was die uitreiking van vervalste dokumente. Klaarblyklik had die appellant daaraan geen aandeel nie, want hy het eers daarvan bewus geword in Desember. Hoe hy dit kon verhinder gaan my verstand te bowe, want selfs die Gode kan gedane sake nie ongedaan maak nie. Reeds uit die voorbehoudsbepaling blyk duidelik dat die Wetgewer deur die woorde ‚en het niet heeft kunnen verhinderin' te besig, nie kon beoog het om in die verenigingslewe elke lid in die algemeen sy broeder se

hoeder te maak nie. Wat die Wetgewer bedoel het kom op dieselfde neer as die aanspreeklikheid van die Romeinse *dominus
conscius;* dit stel voorop dat die persoon, wat aangespreek word,
bewus was van die voornemens van sy medelid en dat hy by magte
was om dit te verhinder. Versuim om die medelid later te verklap
staan teenoor die begrip wildvreemd. Meer nog: ek kan my nie
voorstel dat die Wetgewer bedoel het om elke vennoot tot onbe-
soldigde speurder teenoor sy compagnons aan te stel nie; dit sou
direk indruis teenoor die begrip vennootskap. Hy moes nie *in
abstracto* kon verhinder nie, maar *in concreto,* met inagneming van
die bedryfsorganisasies. Dit so synde kon appellant nie regtens
op hierdie aanklag skuldigbevind word nie."

Uit wat voorafgaan kom ek, met respek, tot die gevolgtrekking dat die
sake van *Salama Taxis* en *Poole,* waar die geleerde Regters se aandag nie
gevestig is op die sake *Couveras* en *Milne and Erleigh* nie en gevolglik nie
die voordeel daarvan geniet het nie, verkeerd beslis is.

Ek kom, uit hoofde van die oorwegings hierbo vermeld, tot die slotsom
dat die antwoord op die regsvraag „Nee" is. Bygevolg word die skuldigbevinding en vonnis ter syde gestel.

NOTES

See also *S* v *Hepker* 1973 (1) SA 472 (W). In *Biba Ltd* v *Stratford Investments Ltd* [1972]
3 WLR 902, a director was found liable in contempt for the breach of an undertaking
by his company, embodied in an order of court, not to infringe a certain trademark,
the property of the plaintiffs.

Whether the company is charged through its officer or the officer is charged in his
personal capacity is a matter of interpretation of the summons or indictment: *R* v *Beelen*
1940 TPD 215. A director can be charged in his personal as well as his representative
capacity, but 'in the absence of any further allegations in the summons the citing of a
director or servant of the company is an indication that it is the company and not the
individual that is charged' (per Fischer JP in *R* v *Hammersma* 1941 OPD 39 at 41).
See further *R* v *Levin* 1944 EDL 247; *R* v *Kalak (Pty) Ltd* 1948 (1) SA 1063 (T).

A company is not criminally liable for the acts of an employee if the act was not done
in furthering or endeavouring to further the interests of the company: *R* v *Barney's
Super Service Station* 1956 (4) SA 107 (T).

On the whole subject, see further *R* v *Oudtshoorn Munic* (1908) 25 SC 257; *R* v
Hewertson 1937 CPD 5; *R* v *Kalell (Pty) Ltd* 1939 TPD 224; *Durban Baking Co Ltd*
v *R* 1945 NPD 136; *R* v *Raisun and Pather* 1947 (2) SA 881 (W); *R* v *De Lange* 1949
(3) SA 1088 (T); *R* v *Murray and Stewart (Pty) Ltd* 1950 (1) SA 194 (C); *R* v *Dracoulis*
1951 (3) SA 752 (C); *R* v *Richardson NO* 1951 (4) SA 284 (T); *R* v *Darwin Supply
Stores (Pvt) Ltd* 1957 (2) SA 519 (SR); *Symington NO* v *Die Meester* 1960 (4) SA 70 (O);
also *Nyasaland Transport Co Ltd* v *R* 1962 R & N 721; *John Henshall (Quarries) Ltd*
v *Harvey* [1965] 2 QB 233 [1965] 1 All ER 725.

Special rules apply under s 425 to offences under the Insolvency Act 24 of 1936,
see e g *S* v *Jousof* 1965 (3) SA 259 (T), where a director was convicted under ss 134(1)
and 135(3) of that Act, read with s 185 (now s 425) of the Companies Act, in that he, in
managing a company, had failed to keep proper records and had contracted debts
without reasonable expectation that the company would be able to discharge them.

According to *R* v *City Silk Emporium (Pty) Ltd and Meer,* 1950 (1) SA 825 (GW);
R v *RSI (Pty) Ltd* 1959 (1) SA 414 (E), and *R* v *Smith* 1960 (4) SA 364 (O), a company
cannot be charged with an offence under s 132(c) or (d), 134(1), 135(1) or 135(3)(a) of
the Insolvency Act, since the statutory provisions make it clear that these offences can
only be committed by a natural person.

On criminal liability of a company, especially for offences under the Insolvency Act,
see T B Barlow in (1946) 63 *SALJ* 520, and Michael Imber in (1960) 77 *SALJ* 237.

The latter criticizes *R v City Silk Emporium (supra)* on the ground that it overlooked ss (11) of s 381 of Act 56 of 1955. On English law, see L H Leigh *The Criminal Liability of Corporations In English Law* (1969).

On the definition of a director in ss (10) of s 381 of the Criminal Procedure Act, see *189* above.

Majority Rule and Minority

Protection

I Introductory

Company law is based on the premise that within the framework of the Companies Act companies are self-governing republics in which the majority should be allowed to govern unhindered by outside interference. From this follow two basic rules: the 'Non-Intervention' Rule (II below) and the 'Proper Plaintiff' Rule (III below). Both are subject to common-law and statutory exceptions.

II The 'Non-Intervention' Rule and the Exceptions to it

A TEXT

Except when a deadlock in the management of a company renders intervention by the courts imperative, the courts will not interfere with the domestic management of companies acting within the law and their constitution: *305, 306*. Acts of the company, resolutions regularly passed at directors' meetings or general meetings of the company, will not be set aside by the courts at the behest of dissatisfied minority shareholders even where they can show that their interests have been detrimentally affected by them. Unlike directors who must always place their duty to the company first shareholders owe no fiduciary duties to the company or their fellow-shareholders and may, within limits, vote their shares as they please: *307*. Nor are there any restrictions on the way in which they can dispose of their shares. At common law there exists no rule restraining controlling shareholders from cashing in on their privileged position by selling their shares at a premium: *308*; but cf *309*. In practice, this freedom has been greatly curtailed by s 314(2)(*a*), which lays down that no takeover offer shall be made unless it is made in the same terms to all the shareholders of the shares or of a particular class of shares of the offeree company, and, as far as listed shares are concerned, by the stock exchange rules relating to take-over bids p 656 below).

The principle of non-intervention is subject to exceptions if the majority acts illegally, *ultra vires*, or in fraud of the minority: *310–315.*

So far the common law. It is supplemented by statutory provisions of which s 252 is the most important one. (On inspections and investigations, IV below.)

Section 252 provides, in substance, that any member of a company who considers that any particular act or omission of a company is unfairly prejudicial, unjust or inequitable, or that the affairs of the company are being conducted in a manner unfairly prejudicial, unjust or inequitable to him or to some part of the members, may apply to court for relief, s 252(1): *316.* Where the act complained of relates to an alteration of the memorandum of the company under ss 55 or 56, a reduction of capital under s 83 (p 150 above), a variation of class rights under s 102, or the conversion of a private company into a public company or vice versa under s 22, application must be made within six weeks after the passing of the relevant special resolution, s 252(2). If the court finds the complaint justified, it may make whatever order it thinks fit, including an order for the purchase of the shares of any member or members of the company by other members of the company. Thus, the court may order the company to buy the disgruntled shareholder out or order the controlling shareholders to sell their shares to the company.

To justify the intervention of the court, it is not sufficient that the act complained of is prejudicial to the dissenting shareholder; it must be unfairly prejudicial, unjust or inequitable. In determining whether it is, the courts will no doubt take the common-law rules on acts in fraud of a minority as well as the case law on minority oppression under s 111*bis* of the 1926 Act (*317–322*) into account. However, s 252 of the present Act goes very much further than either the common law rule or s 111*bis* of the old Act. It is difficult to envisage that an act which amounts to a fraud on the minority or is oppressive could be anything other than unfairly prejudicial, unjust or inequitable. On the other hand, an action may be unfairly prejudicial, unjust or inequitable although it amounts neither to a fraud on the minority nor to oppression within the meaning of s 111*bis* of the 1926 Act.

B CASES

[305] Yende *v* Orlando Coal Distributors
1961 (3) SA 314 (W)

DOWLING J: In general, the policy of the courts has been not to interfere in the internal domestic affairs of a company, where the company ought to be able to adjust its affairs itself by appropriate resolutions of a majority of the shareholders.

[306] Featherstone v Cooke

(1873) LR 16 Eq 298

Trade Auxiliary Company v Vickers

(1873) LR 16 Eq 303

MALINS V-C: ... With regard to private partnerships, nothing is of more frequent occurrence than the quarrels of partners. If partners quarrel, oust each other from the management, or so conduct themselves that the partnership cannot go on with advantage, it is every day's practice for the court to interfere by injunction, and appoint a receiver if necessary. With regard to public companies, I apprehend the same principle is applicable. If a state of things exists in which the governing body are so divided that they cannot act together, and there is the same kind of feeling between the members as there is frequently in the case of private partnerships, it is clearly within the rule of this court to interfere, and it will do so. I have referred already to the case of the *Trade Auxiliary Company*, where there being quarrels between the directors ... one set being in possession of the office shut the doors against the others, and those who were excluded employed Irish labourers to ram the door down, and when they got in tried to exclude the others. ...

... The court will not interfere with the internal affairs of joint stock companies unless they are in a condition in which there is no properly constituted governing body, or there are such dissensions in the governing body that it is impossible to carry on the business with advantage to the parties interested. In such a case the court will interfere, but only for a limited time, and to as small an extent as possible. ...

NOTES

See also e g *Miller* v *Miller* 1963 (2) SA 199 (SR); *Moosa NO* v *Mavjee Bhawan (Pty) Ltd* 1967 (3) SA 131 (T).

[307] Pender v Lushington

(1877) 6 ChD 70 (See also *176* above)

JESSEL MR: ... A man may be actuated in giving his vote by interests entirely adverse to the interests of the company as a whole. He may think it more for his particular interest that a certain course may be taken which may be in the opinion of others very adverse to the interests of the company as a whole, but he cannot be restrained from giving his vote in what way he pleases because he is influenced by that motive. There is ... no obligation on a shareholder of a company to give his vote merely with a view to what other persons may consider the interests of the company at large. He has a right, if he thinks fit, to give his vote from motives or promptings of what he considers his own individual interests.

This being so, the arguments which have been addressed to me as to whether or not the object for which the votes were given would bring about the ruin of the company, or whether or not the motive was an improper one which induced these gentlemen to give their votes, or whether or not their conduct shows a want of appreciation of the principles on which this company was founded, appear to me to be wholly irrelevant. . . .

NOTES

Thus, a shareholder, and a director in his capacity as a shareholder, may vote in a general meeting in his own interest on a contract between the company and himself: *North-West Transportation Company* v *Beattie* (1887) 12 App Cas 589 (*253* above); *Gundelfinger* v *African Textile Mfrs Ltd* 1939 AD 314; *Northern Counties Securities Ltd* v *Jackson & Steeple Ltd*, *173* above. See also Earl Sneed (1960) 58 *Mich LR* 961, (1965) 49 *Minnesota LR* 745. But see also *Clemens* v *Clemens Bros*, *173* above.

[308] United Trust (Pty) Ltd v SA Milling Company
1959 (2) SA 426 (W)

KUPER J: This application for an interdict pending the decision of an action concerns the shareholders of the fourth respondent, Jno W Quinn & Co (Pty) Ltd. . . . In order to understand the present dispute it is necessary to trace the history of the holdings of the shares in Quinn by the interested parties. Quinn has carried on a bakery and confectionery business on a considerable scale for many years. It was registered on 14 March 1918 with a capital of £25 000 divided into 25 000 shares of £1 each, all of which were held by the first applicant, United Trust (Pty) Ltd. . . . On 9 January 1936 United entered into an agreement with the second respondent Posner, in terms of which United sold 12 500 shares in Quinn to Posner. Clause 8 of the agreement provided that

'the parties hereto acknowledge that they have a common interest in the Quinn Company and the Premier Company and they agree to work together in all ways for the furtherance of the interests of the companies and to vote for and support all motions and proposals which are calculated to benefit the Companies, submitted to any meeting of directors or shareholders.'

Notwithstanding the provisions of clause 8, the effect of the sale was to create two groups of interested persons in the affairs of Quinn. On the same date United and Posner jointly sold 2 500 shares in Quinn to one Fisher, who was then employed by Quinn and was one of its directors. Clause 7 of the agreement of sale provided that

'The purchaser hereby agrees and undertakes that the votes to which he is entitled as a shareholder in Jno W Quinn & Co Ltd, by virtue of the purchase hereby concluded and also by virtue of any further shares in the Company, acquired or held by him at any time hereafter, shall always be cast as to one half in such manner as the United Trust Ltd shall require, and as to the remaining one half in such manner as the said Maurice Posner or his successors shall require.'

On 14 December 1939 United and Posner jointly undertook that Quinn would allot 5 000 shares to one MacFarlane—the present secretary of Quinn—and MacFarlane agreed that the votes to which he would

be entitled would be controlled in the same manner as the votes of
Fisher. Similarly on 12 July 1943 United and Posner jointly sold 3 926
shares to the third applicant, Jaffee, on the same condition. From time
to time between 1936 and ... 1958, the issued and paid-up share capital
was increased, and on the latter date it was £100 000 divided into
100 000 shares of £1 each. The additional shares to which Posner
became entitled as well as portion of the shares he already held were,
with the consent of all the interested parties, taken up by members of
Posner's family and by a trust company created by Posner. . . . United
took up its additional shares, and Jaffee (who has a substantial interest
in United) was permitted to part with some of his shares to a trust
company created by him.

On 13 November 1958 Fisher, MacFarlane, Jaffee and his trust
company held between them 26 373 shares, all governed by the restriction of voting control to which I have referred. Of the balance, United
held 36 813 shares and Posner and the members of his family and his
trust company held between them 36 814 shares. Consequently the
Posner group held the majority control by one vote. . . .

On the 14th day of November 1958 the Posner group and Fisher
and MacFarlane sold all their shares in Quinn to the first respondent
(hereinafter referred to as SA Milling) and on the same day in circumstances described hereafter, all the shares so sold were transferred to
SA Milling. . . .

[Counsel for the applicant] argued that a decision of the majority
shareholders can be impeached if it was not passed bona fide for the
benefit of the company as a whole. He referred to the case of *Greenhalgh* v *Arderne Cinemas Ltd* [1951] ChD 286 (*175* above), in support of
that contention. The court of appeal decided that the phrase 'for the
benefit of the company as a whole' means that a shareholder must proceed upon what in his honest opinion is for the benefit of the company
as a whole, namely for the benefit of the corporators as a general body.
It was competent, in the view of the court, to impeach a special resolution if its effect is to discriminate between the majority shareholders
and the minority shareholders so as to give the former an advantage
of which the latter are deprived. . . .

. . . But in none of [the cases decided in England] nor in any decided
in our courts was a decision of majority shareholders, taken outside a
meeting of the company, to dispose of their own shares impeached on
the ground of the duty of the majority to vote for the benefit of the
company as a whole. It was suggested that the principle should be
extended, and reference was made to the following passage in *Modern
Company Law* (2 ed) by Professor L C B Gower at 524:

> 'Can they (majority shareholders acting as such and not as directors)
> then sell their controlling block for a larger price than that which
> the other shareholders can obtain? In England it has always been
> assumed that they can. In the United States, however, a number of
> courts have held that they must account to the other shareholders
> on the ground that they are selling control of corporate property.
> There is, in theory, no reason why the English courts should not adopt

the same view; it would be easy to treat this case as an example of appropriation of the company's property as exemplified in *Menier* v *Hooper's Telegraph Works* (1874) 9 Ch App 350, and *Cook* v *Deeks* [1916] 1 AC 554. And, clearly, there are sound grounds for so doing, for the only reason why they get a larger price is because their shares enable the holders to appoint the board, and thereby to gain control of assets which belong not to themselves but to the company as a whole.'

I do not agree with this statement. The action of the majority can only be impeached if they receive a larger price at the expense of other shareholders. If the majority sell their control to a third party the minority is in exactly the same position as it was before the sale except that the control is to be exercised by B instead of A. Of course the position is different if the action of the majority is fraudulent, in the sense in which that word is used in regard to oppression of the minority, but in the absence of that essential the majority must be entitled, without hindrance, to sell their shares as a block at the best price they can obtain for those shares.

[309] Jones v Ahmanson & Co
(1969) 81 Cal Rptr 592, 460 P 2d 464
(SC of California)

The plaintiff was a member of a minority group of shareholders in a savings and loan association. The defendants had formerly owned the remaining shares. Most of the association's earnings had been retained since incorporation, resulting in a high book value for the shares; in addition, management had also provided the investing public with little information about the association and, as a result, there was no active public market in the association's shares. In 1959, following increased investor interest in savings and loan companies, the defendants, who were officers of the associations, in their personal capacities, formed a holding company (United) and exchanged each of their association shares for 250 shares of United. No similar offer of exchange was made to minority shareholders. A subsequent offer made was on much less favourable terms. Following a split of United's shares and a public offering, the market price of United's shares rose dramatically. There continued to be no active public market in the association's shares. The plaintiff brought a class action on behalf of herself and other minority shareholders for personal relief alleging a breach of fiduciary duty by the association's controlling shareholders. The court held that a cause of action was established.

TRAYNOR CJ: We are faced at the outset with defendants' contention that if a cause of action is stated, it is derivative in nature since any injury suffered is common to all minority stockholders of the association. Therefore, defendants urge, plaintiff may not sue in an individual capacity or on behalf of a class made up of stockholders excluded from the United Financial exchange. . . .

It is clear from the stipulated facts and plaintiff's allegations that she does not seek to recover on behalf of the corporation for injury done to the corporation by defendants. Although she does allege that the value of her stock has been diminished by defendants' actions, she does not contend that the diminished value reflects an injury to the corporation and resultant depreciation in the value of the stock. Thus the gravamen of her cause of action is injury to herself and the other minority stockholders. . . .

Defendants take the position that as shareholders they owe no fiduciary obligation to other shareholders, absent reliance on inside information, use of corporate assets, or fraud. This view has long been repudiated in California. The courts of appeal have often recognized that majority shareholders, either singly or acting in concert to accomplish a joint purpose, have a fiduciary responsibility to the minority and to the corporation to use their ability to control the corporation in a fair, just, and equitable manner. Majority shareholders may not use their power to control corporate activities to benefit themselves alone or in a manner detrimental to the minority. Any use to which they put the corporation or their power to control the corporation must benefit all shareholders proportionately and must not conflict with the proper conduct of the corporation's business. . . .

Defendants assert, however, that in the use of their own shares they owed no fiduciary duty to the minority stockholders of the association. They maintain that they made full disclosure of the circumstances surrounding the formation of United Financial, that the creation of United Financial and its share offers in no way affected the control of the association, that plaintiff's proportionate interest in the association was not affected, that the association was not harmed, and that the market for association stock was not affected. Therefore, they conclude, they have breached no fiduciary duty to plaintiff and the other minority stockholders. . . .

The increasingly complex transactions of the business and financial communities demonstrate the inadequacy of the traditional theories of fiduciary obligation as tests of majority shareholder responsibility to the minority. These theories have failed to afford adequate protection to minority shareholders and particularly to those in closely held corporations whose disadvantageous and often precarious position renders them particularly vulnerable to the vagaries of the majority. Although courts have recognized the potential for abuse or unfair advantage when a controlling shareholder sells his shares at a premium over investment value (*Perlman* v *Feldmann* 219 F 2d 173, 50 ALR 2d 1134 [premium paid for control over allocation of production in time of shortage]; *Gerdes* v *Reynolds Sup* 28 NYS 2d 622 [sale of control to looters or incompetents]; *Porter* v *Healy* 244 Pa 427, 91 A 428; *Brown* v *Halbert* 271 ACA 307, 76 Cal Rptr 781 [sale of only controlling shareholder's shares to purchaser offering to buy assets of corporation or all shares]) or in a controlling shareholder's use of control to avoid equitable distribution of corporate assets (*Zahn* v *Transamerica Corporation* (3 Cir 1946) 162 F 2d 36, 172 ALR 495 [use of control to cause subsidiary to redeem stock prior to liquidation and distribution of assets]), no comprehensive rule has emerged in other jurisdictions. Nor have most commentators approached the problem from a perspective other than that of the advantage gained in the sale of control. Some have suggested that the price paid for control shares over their investment value be treated as an asset belonging to the corporation itself (Berle & Means *The Modern Corporation and Private Property* (1932) 243), or as an asset that should be shared proportionately with all shareholders through a general offer (Jennings 'Trading in Corporate Control' (1956) 44 *Cal LR* 1 39), and another contends that the sale of control at a premium is always evil (Bayne 'The Sale-of-Control Premium: the Intrinsic Illegitimacy' (1969) 47 *Tex LR* 215).

The additional potential for injury to minority shareholders from majority dealings in its control power apart from sale has not gone unrecognized, however. The ramifications of defendants' actions here are not unlike those described by Professor Gower as occurring when control of one corporation is acquired by another through purchase of less than all of the shares of the latter: 'The [acquired] company's existence is not affected, nor need its constitution be altered; all that occurs is that its shareholders change. From the legal viewpoint this methodological distinction is formidable, but commercially the two things may be almost identical. If . . . a controlling interest is acquired, the [acquired] company . . . will become a subsidiary of the acquiring company . . . and cease, in fact though not in law, to be an independent entity.

'This may produce the situation in which a small number of dissentient members are left as a minority in a company intended to be operated as a member of a group. As such, their position is likely to be unhappy, for the parent company will wish to operate the subsidiary for the benefit of the group as a whole and not necessarily for the benefit of that particular subsidiary.' (Gower *The Principles of Modern Company Law* 2 ed (1957) 561.) Professor Eisenberg notes that as the purchasing corporation's proportionate interest in the acquired corporation approaches 100 per cent the market for the latter's stock disappears, a problem that is aggravated if the acquiring corporation for its own business purposes reduces or eliminates dividends (Eisenberg 'The Legal Role of Shareholders and Management in Modern Corporate Decision-making' (1969) 57 *Cal LR* 1132). . . .

. . . The case before us, in which no sale or transfer of actual control is directly involved, demonstrates that the injury anticipated by these authors can be inflicted with impunity under the traditional rules and supports our conclusion that the comprehensive rule of good faith and inherent fairness to the minority in any transaction where control of the corporation is material properly governs controlling shareholders in this state.

If, after trial of the cause, plaintiff has established facts in conformity with the allegations of the complaint and stipulation, then upon tender of her association stock to defendants she will be entitled to receive at her election either the appraised value of her shares on the date of the exchange, 14 May 1959, with interest at 7 per cent a year from the date of this action or a sum equivalent to the fair market value of a 'derived block' of United Financial stock on the date of this action with interest thereon from that date, and the sum of $927,50 (the return of capital paid to the original United Financial shareholders) with interest thereon from the date United Financial first made such payments to its original shareholders, for each share tendered. The appraised or fair market value shall be reduced, however, by the amount by which dividends paid on association shares during the period from 14 May 1959 to the present exceeds the dividends paid on a corresponding block of United Financial shares during the same period.

[For comments on *Jones* v *Ahmanson* see (1970) 83 *Harv LR* 1904, (1970) 70 *Columb LR* 1079.]

NOTES

In America the prevailing view now is that controlling shareholders who sell their shares to outsiders at a premium are liable to account for it to their fellow-shareholders, (1) if they sold control to persons they had reason to believe would 'loot' the company and who did so loot it; (2) if the premium was obtained for an asset or opportunity which rightfully belonged to the company. In *Donahue* v *Rodd Electrotype* 328 NE 2d 502 (1975), noted (1975) 89 *Harv LR* 423, the court held that where a controlling shareholder in a 'close' corporation sells his own shares to the company, he is under a duty to cause the corporation to offer to purchase a proportionate number of shares from the minority, and it has been suggested that whenever a controlling shareholder assumes a dominant role in the management of the company, selecting and directing the directors, he becomes liable to all the fiduciary duties of a director: (1961) 74 *Harv LR* at 770.

In *Western Mines Limited* v *Shield Development Company Limited* [1976] 2 WWR 300 (BC), a Canadian case, it was proposed to call a general meeting of shareholders to increase the number of directors from 12 to 29 and to elect directors to fill the vacancies thereby created. The purpose of the exercise was to put men acceptable to the controlling shareholders into office. The articles contained a complete code for fixing the number and election of directors and for any increases in their number between annual general meetings. The court decided that the inherent power of shareholders to appoint directors did not exist in this case, and that, even if it existed, it could not be used for the purpose of gaining control. Approving G D Goldberg's statement in (1970) 33 *MLR* 177 at 183 that 'under Table A the shareholders in general meetings are able to exercise all the powers of the company which are not either specially delegated to the directors (which category includes the day-to-day control of the business) or required by the Act or the articles to be done by some special procedure; provided always that such exercise does not constitute a fraud on the minority'. Anderson J said (at 307):

'I agree with the learned author, except that I think he should have added that the shareholders cannot exercise their inherent powers for an improper purpose. The purpose of increasing the number of directors or of filling vacancies in the board of directors is to serve the needs of the company, namely, to have a more effective and efficient board. In my opinion, the shareholders like the directors, must use their powers to achieve the objects for which their powers were given. The power to enlarge the board of directors (if it exists) must be used for legitimate purposes and not as an indirect means of gaining control of the board of directors'.

Professor Gower *Modern Company Law* 3 ed 578 expresses the view that in the UK sale of control at a premium is unlikely to lead to civil liability, a view that draws some support from *Re Grierson, Oldhams & Adams Ltd* (*383* below).

Generally, see K W Wedderburn [1957] *CLJ* 194, [1958] *CLJ* 93; (1967) 30 *MLR* 77, (1968) 31 *MLR* 688; B H McPherson (1960) 77 *SALJ* 297; (1963) 36 *ALJ* 404; Robert N Leavell (1961) 35 *Tulane LR* 331; George D Hornstein (1967) *JBL* 282; Stanley M Beck *Studies in Canadian Company Law* (1967) 545; (1974) 52 *Can BR* 159; N A Bastin (1968) *JBL* 320; A Barak (1971) 20 *ICLQ* 22; H H Mason (1972) 46 *ALJ* 67; also with special reference to American law, Alfred Hill (1957) 70 *Harv LR* 986; Adolf A Berle (1958) 58 *Col LR* 1212; Edward J Grenier (1962) 19 *Washington & Lee LR* 165; A J Boyle (1964) 13 *ICLQ* 185; William D Andrews (1964) 78 *Harv LR* 505; George B Javaras (1965) 32 *Chicago LR* 420; Anonymous (1964) 31 *Chicago LR* 725; A J Boyle (1969) *JBL* 120; D J Dykstra (1967) 116 *U Pa LR* 74. As to what constitutes a 'controlling interest' see *Mendes* v *Commissioner of Probate Duties* (1967/8) 41 *ALJR* 108 (High Court of Australia).

[310] Menier *v* Hooper's Telegraph Works
(1874) 9 Ch App 350

JAMES LJ: . . . The minority of the shareholders say in effect that the majority has divided the assets of the company, more or less, between themselves, to the exclusion of the minority. I think it would be a shocking thing if that could be done, because if so the majority might divide the whole assets of the company, and pass a resolution that everything must be given to them, and that the minority should have nothing to do with it. Assuming the case to be as alleged by the bill, then the majority have put something into their pockets at the expense of the minority. If so, it appears to me that the minority have a right to have their share of the benefits ascertained for them in the best way in which the court can do it, and given to them.

[311] Hoole *v* Great Western Railway Company
(1867) 3 Ch App 262

LORD CAIRNS LJ: . . . If the arrangement which has been proposed is legal, is *intra vires*, the company, through their general meetings, have power to carry it into effect; if, on the other hand, it is *ultra vires*, if it is illegal, any member of the company may dissent from it, and has a right to appeal to this court to be protected against its effects. . . .

[312] Bishop *v* Nannucci Ltd
(1908) 25 SC 464

The company adopted by special resolution new articles limiting the rights of shareholders. A minority objected.

HOPLEY J: Now, it is clear that these [new] articles relate entirely to the internal administration of the company, and that they are not *ultra vires* as being opposed to or beyond the scope of the operations of the company, as set forth in the memorandum of association. As regards their bona fides it is significant that they were drawn up by the company's attorney, and it is given in Nannucci's evidence, and not contradicted, that they were considered to be in the interests of the company as a whole—their object being to confine the membership to a limited class, and to keep the processes used by the company secret. . . . There is, therefore, nothing in the articles objected to which is apparently *ultra vires* or mala fide, or even unusual. But it was contended that they could not be forced upon an unwilling minority in derogation of their existing rights which had accrued under the earlier and freer constitution of the company. Without saying that these articles are incapable of being worked and utilized in an illegal or oppressive way, such, for instance, as fixing a wholly unfair value on the shares and calling it a 'fair value' or attempting to deprive members entirely of their right to approach the courts of the land for the redress of genuine grievances, it does not appear to me that in the present action any point of that kind arises for consideration. . . . If members really have such grievances, I have no doubt they could be redressed; but the articles being in themselves unobjectionable, it is impossible to hold that members of the company in general meeting were not empowered to adopt them as though they had originally been the articles of the company. Members who join a joint stock company, regulated by the Companies Act, know that their articles of association are capable of, and subject to, such alterations as the majority of the shareholders may choose to adopt. They need not join a company, but, once in it, they must abide by the covenants *inter se* imposed on the members by the majority, and companies in which nearly all the shares are in one hand, or in a few hands, are no exception to the rule.

[313] Sidebottom *v* Kershaw, Leese and Company Ltd
[1920] 1 Ch 154

The defendant company, a private trading company, passed a resolution to alter its articles of association by providing that the directors (who held the majority of the shares) should have power to require shareholders who carried on business in competition with the company to transfer their shares, at their fair value, to the directors. The plaintiff, who held a minority of the shares and carried on a competing business, brought action for a declaration that the resolution was invalid.

WARRINGTON LJ: Now it is quite plain that an article providing for the compulsory sale by a member of the company of his shares is good if it is contained in the original articles; that is to say that it is a regulation of the company within the meaning of the statute. If that be so, and if such an article could be a regulation of the company within the meaning of the statute, then it is equally plain that it is one of the things which may be introduced by an alteration effected by special resolution. . . . That leaves as the only question to be decided whether the power itself was exercised bona fide for the benefit of the company. In the present case the object of the article was to enable this private trading company to get rid as a shareholder of any member who was either carrying on a business in direct opposition or who was a director of any company carrying on a business in direct competition. . . . Now, looking at it from the point of view of the ordinary business man engaged in trade, might he not quite well take the view that it would not be to the advantage of this private company—which is, after all, in many respects like a private firm, although not so in law—or rather that it would be to the disadvantage of this private company that one of its members should be carrying on a business in direct competition, or be a director of a company carrying on business in direct competition? That membership of the company gives some opportunities, possibly, according to the constitution of this body, not very great opportunities, of getting behind the scenes and knowing what the company is doing, there can be no doubt, and it might be greatly to the disadvantage of the company that knowledge so acquired should be exercised by a competitor. Therefore it is desirable that, if there was reason to suppose that it would be exercised, they should have power to remove that competitor from his advantageous position of shareholder. If that be so, and there being in this case no suggestion of fraud, it seems to me that the only inference one can draw is that the company were, in passing this special resolution, acting bona fide for the benefit of the company at large. It may be that a particular course may be to the disadvantage of some individual shareholder; but, notwithstanding that, it might still be for the benefit of the company at large that that course should be pursued. But it is then said that this step was taken with the special object of ridding the company of a particular shareholder, whose name is given in the affidavits, who was known to be a competitor, and that for that reason the resolution was not passed bona fide. I am entirely unable to follow that. I have no doubt that the fact that there was this competitor, and probably the knowledge that he was doing harm to the company, awoke the directors to the disadvantage in which they were placed by having such a man as one of their shareholders; but that is a very different thing from saying that they passed this resolution with the mala fide and dishonest intention of getting rid of a shareholder whom they did not wish to remain in the company.

[314] Dafen Tinplate Company Ltd *v* Llanelly Steel Company (1907) Ltd

[1920] 2 Ch 124

By altering its articles the company empowered the majority of shareholders to compel any member to sell his shares at a price to be fixed from time to time by the directors to a person (whether a member or not) determined by the directors. The court held that the company could not confer such power on the majority.

PETERSON J: . . . Having regard to the decision in *Sidebottom's* case [1920] 1 Ch 154 [*313*], it appears that a resolution altering the articles in such a way as to enable the shareholders to compel a shareholder who is actively interested in a competing firm to transfer his shares would be valid on the ground that it was an alteration which was bona fide for the benefit of the company. But in this case the resolution which was passed went much further than the protection of the company from action by shareholders which could be properly considered to be detrimental to its interests. The resolution as passed enables the majority of the shareholders to compel any member to transfer his shares, although there may be no complaint of any kind against his conduct and it cannot be suggested that he has done, or contemplates doing, anything to the detriment of the company. It is an unrestricted power which authorizes the majority, if they think proper, or if they consider it in their own interests to require the transfer of his shares by any shareholder other than the Briton Ferry Company. It is true that the directors may offer the shares to any person, whether a member of the company or not; but having regard to the way in which the board is constituted, no one can doubt that if the majority desired to acquire the shares, the directors would offer the shares to the remaining shareholders. As drawn, the resolution authorizes the majority at their will and without any reason, other than the desire to get into their hands the whole of the shares in the company, to expropriate the shares of the minority. . . .

... In my view it cannot be said that a power on the part of the majority to expropriate any shareholder they may think proper at their will and pleasure is for the benefit of the company as a whole. To say that such an unrestricted and unlimited power of expropriation is for the benefit of the company appears to me to be confusing the interests of· the majority with the benefit of the company as a whole. In my opinion the power which, in this case, has been conferred upon the majority of the shareholders by the alteration of the articles of association in this case is too wide and is not such a power as can be assumed by the majority. . . .

[The new article was accordingly declared to be invalid.

Peterson J stated (at 140) that the question was not whether the shareholders bona fide believed that the alteration was for the benefit of the company, but whether the court considered that it was in fact for its benefit. This statement was disapproved in *Shuttleworth* v *Cox Brothers & Company (Maidenhead) Ltd 210* above.]

[315] Greenhalgh *v* Arderne Cinemas Ltd
[1951] Ch 286, [1950] 2 All ER 1120

The articles of a private company provided *inter alia* that no shares were to be transferred to a person not a member of the company so long as a member of the company was willing to purchase them at a fair value. In order to allow certain majority shareholders to sell their shares to an outsider, a special resolution was passed altering the articles so as to permit a member to transfer his shares to non-members with the sanction of the company in general meeting, without first offering them to the other members. The plaintiff attacked the validity of the special resolution on the ground that the interests of the minority of the shareholders had been sacrificed to those of the majority. The court held that the special resolution could not be impeached.

EVERSHED MR: . . . This is a special resolution, and, on authority, [counsel] says, the validity of a special resolution depends upon the fact that those who passed it did so in good faith and for the benefit of the company as a whole. . . . I think it is now plain that 'bona fide for the benefit of the company as a whole' means not two things but one thing. It means that the shareholder must proceed upon what, in his honest opinion, is for the benefit of the company as a whole. The second thing is that the phrase 'the company as a whole' does not (at any rate in such a case as the present) mean the company as a commercial entity, distinct from the corporators: it means the corporators as a general body. That is to say, the case may be taken of an individual hypothetical member and it may be asked whether what is proposed is, in the honest opinion of those who voted in its favour, for that person's benefit.

I think that the matter can, in practice, be more accurately and precisely stated by looking at the converse and by saying that a special resolution of this kind would be liable to be impeached if the effect of it were to discriminate between the majority shareholders and the minority shareholders, so as to give to the former an advantage of which the latter were deprived. . . .

... This resolution provides that anybody who wants at any time to sell his shares can now go direct to an outsider, provided that there is an ordinary resolution of the company approving the proposed transferee. Accordingly, if it is one of the majority who is selling, he will get the necessary resolution. This change in the articles, so to speak, franks the shares for holders of majority interests but makes it more difficult for a minority shareholder, because the majority will probably look with disfavour upon his choice. But, after all, this is merely a relaxation of the very stringent restrictions on transfer in the existing article, and it is to be borne in mind that the directors, as the articles stood, could always refuse to register a transfer. A minority shareholder, therefore, who produced an outsider was always liable to be met by the directors (who presumably act according to the majority view) saying, 'We are sorry, but we will not have this man in'. . . . I think that this case is very far removed from the type of case in which what is proposed, as in the *Dafen* case, is to give a majority the right to expropriate a minority shareholder, whether he wanted to sell or not, merely on the ground that the majority shareholders wanted the minority man's shares.

NOTES

As to the setting aside of shareholders' resolutions on the ground that they are *ultra vires* or illegal or in fraud of the minority, see further *Cook* v *Deeks, 247* above; also *Bloxam* v *Metropolitan Railway Co* (1868) 3 Ch App 337; *Flitcroft's* case *235* above; *Wood* v *Odessa Waterworks Co* (1889) 42 ChD 636; *Cohen and Ehrlich* v *Witwatersrand Gold Mining Co* (1895) 2 Off Rep 277 (*168* above); *English and Devenish* v *Liquidators of the New Rietfontein Deep Level Gold Mining Co* (1895) 2 Off Rep 249, esp at 255; *Allen* v *Gold Reefs of West Africa Ltd* [1900] 1 Ch 656; *Borland's Trustee* v *Steel Brothers & Co Ltd* [1901] 1 Ch 279; *British Equitable Assurance Co Ltd* v *Baily* [1906] AC 35; *In re Consolidated South Rand Mines Deep* [1909] 1 Ch 491; *Ex parte Oregon Mortgage Co Ltd* 1910 SC 964 (a resolution by a company to reduce its capital is ineffective if it has no power to do so under its articles); *Dominion Cotton Mills Company Ltd* v *Amgot* [1912] AC 546 (PC); *Brown* v *British Abrasive Wheel Co* [1919] 1 Ch 290; *Ex parte African Russian Oil Products (Pty) Ltd* 1934 WLD 75; *Levin* v *Felt & Tweeds Ltd* 1951 (2) SA 401 (AD); *Sorenson* v *Executive Committee Tramway & Omnibus Workers Union (Cape)* 1974 (2) SA 454 (C). Further *Sammel* v *President Brand GM Co, 384* below.

See also *Gundelfinger* v *African Textile Manufacturers Ltd* 1939 AD 314, where Stratford CJ said (at 325): '. . . if what is resolved, either at a board meeting or at a general meeting, is within the powers of either, and effects something in the interests of the company as a whole, there is no improper use of a majority's voting power.'

The fact that a shareholder present at a meeting votes for a resolution does not preclude him from attacking its validity subsequently on the ground that it was not authorized by the constitution of the company: *Ex parte Oregon Mortgage Co Ltd* 1910 SC 964; *Hawson* v *LHC Corporation of SA Ltd* 1949 (3) SA 592 (C).

Cramphorn's case (*227* above) shows that there can be cases where the wrongful act is open to ratification, but where nevertheless the minority can sue as long as it is not ratified.

In America, where a company may repurchase its own shares, there have been several cases in recent years on the extent to which this may be done in order to fight off a control bid by a raider: see e g Carlos L Israels (1964) 64 *Columbia LR* 1446 esp at 1452-7, and Victor Brudney (1966) 65 *Mich LR* 259, esp at 263-82.

On interim relief, see *Ex parte Aloe Engineering Industries Ltd* 1965 (2) SA 151 (W).

Ordinary creditors and debenture holders have no *locus standi* to object to resolutions of the company: *Mills* v *Northern Railway of Buenos Ayres Co* (1870) 5 Ch App 621; *Lawrence* v *West Somerset Mineral Railway Co* [1918] 2 Ch 250.

On the whole subject see B H McPherson in (1960) 77 *SALJ* 297.

[316] Porteus *v* Kelly
1975 (1) SA 219 (W)

Application for an interdict restraining the respondent from holding a meeting and taking a certain resolution.

NICHOLAS J: The general rule is that the court has no jurisdiction to and will not interfere with the internal management of companies acting within their powers unless a fraud has been perpetrated upon the minority. . . . Counsel for the applicant put forward two bases on which, it was submitted, the court could and should interfere in the present case: the one was that the case fell within s 252 of the Companies Act 61 of 1973; and the other was that the passing of the proposed resolution would constitute a fraud on the applicant.

[After quoting from s 252, Nicholas J continued:]

Counsel referred to authority (*Bader & another* v *Weston & another* 1967 (1) SA 134 (C) at 147–8, which was decided under the corresponding s 111*bis* of the previous Companies Act 46 of 1926) to the effect that the court has a wide and unfettered discretion as to what order it should make and that it is not restricted to orders in regard to the matters specifically mentioned in s 252(3) or matters *ejusdem generis* therewith. The first question to be considered, however, is whether at this stage the applicant has *locus standi* under ss (1) to apply for an order under the section, and whether the court has jurisdiction under ss (3) to grant an order. In the present case it is said that the 'complaint' (which is necessary in an application under the section) is a complaint that an 'act . . . is unfairly prejudicial, unjust or inequitable'; and that the act complained of is the passing of the resolution, alternatively the calling of the meeting at which such resolution will be proposed. But something to be done in the future is not yet an 'act', which is something done or performed; and, although the calling of a meeting is an 'act', such calling cannot in itself be 'unfairly prejudicial, unjust or inequitable' to the applicant. Counsel for the applicant argued that there was no reason in principle why, if the court could interfere after the resolution was passed, it could not interfere to prevent it being passed. It may well be that in this, as in other cases, prevention of an act would be better than curing it after it has been committed, but the answer is that the section does not provide therefor. This may be a *casus omissus*. But

'The court cannot speculate upon whether Parliament might have overlooked something or might have done something if it had not overlooked something and in any event it cannot supplement the Act by providing for a *casus omissus*.'

(*Walker* v *Carlton Hotels* (*SA*) *Ltd* 1946 AD 321 at 330, per Watermeyer CJ).

In my opinion, therefore, the case does not fall within s 252.

In regard to the second contention advanced on behalf of the applicant, the well-established rule is that

'shareholders may vote at a meeting of a company in favour of their own interests provided that it is in an ordinary legitimate manner on a matter within the scope of the company's powers'.

But a majority cannot of course oppressively and fraudulently use their votes to defraud a minority. . . .

If in the present case, the proposed resolution should be passed, it will be passed not by the first four respondents but by the requisite majority, which could be constituted by the remaining fifteen shareholders. It is nowhere alleged that those shareholders are party to any fraud or oppression—indeed, it is stated in the applicant's founding affidavit that

'the said shareholders have not been joined because they have not been parties to the events detailed'

in the papers filed on behalf of the applicant. That being so, there is no basis on which the court would be entitled to interfere on the ground of alleged fraud at this stage.

[317] Irvin and Johnson Ltd *v* Oelofse Fisheries Ltd
1954 (1) SA 231 (E)

REYNOLDS J: . . . At page 335 of Pyemont *Company Law of South Africa* (6 ed) it is stated that the petitioner to comply with s 111*bis* must allege and prove three things, meaning all of them:

(*a*) That the company's affairs are being conducted in a manner oppressive to some part of the members, including himself.

(*b*) That the facts would justify the making of a winding-up order, on the ground that it is just and equitable that the company be wound up.

(*c*) That to wind up the company would unfairly prejudice that part of the members.

While, however, agreeing that these three essentials should be shown, it seems to me that there is a fourth essential. It must be shown that the order that the court can make—if it does make it—can remedy the complaints in such a manner that the company can then continue to function properly and will in all probability not perish. This seems to be so from the wording of ss (2) of s 111*bis* that the court makes its order 'with a view to bringing to an end the matters complained of' for it would be futile to grant an order which would leave the company so to perish. . . .

NOTES

It will be seen that requirements (*b*) and (*c*) have been dropped in s 252, and that (*a*) has been greatly expanded. The cases that follow must be read in the light of these changes.

[318] Elder *v* Elder & Watson
1952 SC 49

LORD PRESIDENT (Cooper): . . . The introduction into s 210 [corresponding to s 111*bis* of our old Act] of condition (iii) refers us back to the pre-1947 practice under the 'just and equitable' clause, and is a salutary reminder of the fact that the new remedy is not lightly to be accorded. Under the former practice winding-up has been ordered in many types of case which involved no true element of oppression to shareholders, eg where the substratum of the company had vanished, and such cases will doubtless continue to arise. On the other hand the justice and equity which led to the grant of a winding-up order have often been found in conduct reasonably capable of being described as 'oppressive' to some part of the company's members, the oppression being usually exerted by a person with predominating voting power which was employed for his own advantage to the detriment of a helpless minority. The decisions indicate that conduct which is technically legal and correct may nevertheless be such as to justify the application of the 'just and equitable' jurisdiction, and, conversely, that conduct involving illegality and contravention of the Act may not suffice to warrant the remedy of winding-up, especially where alternative remedies are available. Where the 'just and equitable' jurisdiction has been applied in cases of this type, the circumstances have always, I think, been such as to warrant the inference that there has been, at least, an unfair abuse of powers and an impairment of confidence in the probity with which the company's affairs are being conducted, as distinguished from mere resentment on the part of a minority at being outvoted on some issue of domestic policy. . . . The essence of the matter seems to be that the conduct complained of should at the lowest involve a visible departure from the standards of fair dealing, and a violation of the conditions of fair play on which every shareholder who entrusts his money to a company is entitled to rely.

[319] Meyer v Scottish Co-operative Wholesale Society
1954 SC 381 [See also 255 above.]

In an action under s 210 of the Companies Act 1948 (UK) (which corresponds substantially to s 111*bis* of the South African 1926 Act), two independent shareholders in a not wholly owned subsidiary company applied to court for an order on the holding corporation (a wholesale co-operative society) in its capacity as shareholder in the subsidiary company, to purchase their shares in the subsidiary company. The burden of their complaints was that the holding company, in which they did not hold any shares, had deliberately used its controlling powers to bring about a decline in the business of the subsidiary company, and, having no further use for that company, intended to bring its activities to a virtual standstill.

The holding corporation pleaded that on the facts alleged no relevant case was disclosed for the invocation of s 210, and that, accordingly, the application should be dismissed forthwith. It argued *inter alia* that what the petitioners were complaining about was the action of the society in the conduct of its own affairs, and not the action of an oppressive majority in conducting the affairs of the subsidiary company.

Another point taken by the parent corporation was that, in terms of s 210, the oppression must affect 'some part' of the members, and that, therefore, the section could not be invoked in any case where all the members, as distinguished from a part, were affected.

The court refused to dismiss the petition without proof of the facts.

LORD PRESIDENT (Cooper): It is . . . desirable to point out (*a*) that a person invoking s 210 must make it appear that the oppression of which he complains has arisen in the conduct of the affairs *of the company in question*, and not in the independent conduct of the affairs of some other company, firm or individual; (*b*) that the section contemplates a complaint that the affairs of the company in question *are* being conducted in a manner oppressive to the complainer (and perhaps others), and that the court's intervention must be aimed at 'bringing to an end the matters complained of'; and (*c*) that the manifest purpose of the section is to provide, as an alternative to the normal remedy of liquidation under the 'just and equitable' clause, a different remedy under which the company, instead of being wound up, may continue to operate as a going concern freed from the taint of oppression in the administration of its affairs. The circumstances which may arise in cases of this type are so infinitely various that I wish to guard myself against suggesting that all or any of the above requirements are rigidly and inevitably indispensable, especially as it may often be no easy matter to determine in an individual case how far each is satisfied. . . .

. . . It is said, first that what the petitioners are complaining about is the action of the society in its conduct of its own affairs, and not the action of an oppressive majority in conducting the company's affairs. In the peculiar circumstances of this case I cannot at this stage sustain this objection. The company was a subsidiary, differing only in form from a branch of the society, and controlled by the society by nominee directors who did not even hold qualification shares. . . . In my view, the section warrants the court in looking at the business realities of a situation and does not confine them to a narrow legalistic view. The truth is that, whenever a subsidiary is formed as in this case with an independent minority of shareholders, the parent company must, if it is engaged in the same class of business, accept as a result of having formed such a subsidiary an obligation so to conduct what are in a sense its own affairs as to deal fairly with its subsidiary. Until the facts are ascertained, I am unable to hold that this objection is valid.

It is said, next, that assuming there was 'oppression' in the sense already defined, that oppression is at an end and nothing that the court can now do will 'bring to an end the matters complained of'. But what is here complained of is a course of conduct which began years ago and which was still being pursued months after this petition was presented, with the object and effect of depressing the value of the shares. The petitioners are still shareholders in a live concern and no action has even yet been taken to put the company into liquidation and so to complete the transformation of a subsidiary into a branch. The Dean of Faculty was, I feel, justified in describing the petitioners as in effect the victims of a continuing wrong, the damaging consequences of which still persist and are capable of being rectified. At least I am not meantime prepared to negative this proposition.

There are three further criticisms to be met. The respondents maintained that since November 1953 the petitioners could, in terms of the formation agreement, have compelled the society to buy them out at a price fixed by the auditor. No doubt they could; but by November 1953 a large part of the mischief had already been done through devaluation of the shares, and it would be small consolation to the petitioners to be bought out at the assumedly low figure which would be fixed so late in the day. Doubtless the petitioners could have terminated their contract long ago on giving reasonable notice, but this would have entailed the sacrifice of positions to which they evidently attached value and for which they were being remunerated at substantial salaries. It does not appear to me that the petitioners can be denied resort to s 210, assuming that they are entitled to invoke the section, merely because they did not incur a serious sacrifice at some earlier date, in order to obtain contractual terms the nature of which they could not accurately foresee.

Secondly, the respondents argued that s 210 was excluded because it was conceded that it was just and equitable that the company should be wound up. This appears to me to involve a fallacy. It is a condition precedent to the application of s 210 that the court should be of opinion that, questions of unfair prejudice apart, the facts would justify the making of a winding-up order on 'just and equitable' grounds; and this is all that I think that the concession means. It does not mean that the company has been wound up, or must inevitably be wound up. . . .

. . . Finally, a point is taken with regard to the statutory requirement that the oppression must affect 'some part of the members', the suggestion being that s 210 is not available in any case where all the members, as distinguished from a part, are in the same boat. In other words, it is maintained that the section has no operation where Samson destroys himself as well as the Philistines in a single catastrophe the point being that in this case the society hold 4 000 of the shares the value of which they are said to have deliberately depressed. I have come to think that this is to give too narrow a meaning to this remedial provision, and to place on the words 'some part' an emphasis which they were not intended to bear. The most dangerous type of 'oppressor' is the person who, having other fish to fry, can afford deliberately to curtail or even destroy the business of a company in which he holds perhaps the majority of the shares, and, if the section bears the meaning suggested by the respondents, it will fail of effect in a class of case to which its spirit is plainly applicable. It is not essential for the application of s 210 that the oppressor should have made a profit as a result of his oppression, and I see no sufficient reason for inferring as a requirement that he must not *qua* shareholder have made a loss or the same loss pro rata as the complainer. The section is not concerned with the results to the oppressor but with the results to those who complain of the oppression. When the section inquires whether the affairs of the company are being conducted in a manner oppressive to some part of the members including the complainer, that question can still be answered in the affirmative even if, *qua* member of the company, the oppressor has suffered the same or even a greater prejudice. . . .

[An appeal by the Society was dismissed *sub nom Scottish Co-operative Wholesale Society Ltd* v *Meyer* [1959] AC 324, [1958] 3 All ER 66 (HL), [1958] SC (HL) 40.]

LORD KEITH OF AVONHOLM said: 'My Lords, if the society could be regarded as an organization independent of the company and in competition with it, no legal objection could be taken to the actions and policy of the society. . . . But that is not the position. In law, the society and the company were, it is true, separate legal entities. But they were in the relation of parent and subsidiary companies, the company being formed to run a business for the society which the society could not at the outset have done for itself unless it could have persuaded the respondents to become servants of the society. This the respondents were not prepared to do. The company, through the knowledge, the experience, the connexions, the business ability and the energies of the respondents, had built up a valuable goodwill in which the society shared and which there is no reason to think would not have been maintained, if not increased, with the co-operation of the society. The company was in substance, though not in law, a partnership consisting of the society and the respondents. Whatever may be the other different legal consequences following on one or other of these forms of combination one result, in my opinion, followed in the present case from the method adopted, which is common to partnership, that there should be the utmost good faith between the constituent members. In partnership the position is clear. As stated in *Lindley on Partnership* (11 ed) 401:

> "A partner cannot, without the consent of his co-partners, lawfully carry on for his own benefit, either openly or secretly, any business in rivalry with the firm to which he belongs."

It may not be possible for the legal remedies that would follow in the case of a partnership to follow here, but the principle has, I think, valuable application to the circumstances of this case.

'In these circumstances, I have no doubt the conduct of the society was oppressive.'

[In the result an order was made compelling the society to buy the petitioners out at £3 15s per share, this being the value which the shares would have had at the commencement of the proceedings had it not been for the effect of the oppressive conduct of the society.]

[320] Aspek Pipe Co (Pty) Ltd *v* Mauerberger
1968 (1) SA 517 (C)

TEBBUTT AJ: . . . It is quite clear, in my view, that an applicant for relief under this section [111*bis*] must show that the affairs of the company are being conducted in a manner oppressive to him as a member, or to some part of the members of the company as members of that company. In other words the conduct complained of must be oppressive to the petitioner *qua* shareholder and member . . . and not to him in some other capacity such as a director or servant or employee or agent of the company (ibid).

It is also clear that it is in respect of the conduct of the 'affairs of the company' that such conduct must be oppressive . . . and that it must be established that those responsible for conducting the affairs of the company have embarked upon a course of conduct which is oppressive to those who do not possess controlling powers. . . .

I am . . . in respectful agreement with what was said by Cillié J in

Livanos v *Swartzberg & others* 1962 (4) SA 395 (W) at 397 that for relief under the section it is unnecessary for an applicant to establish tyrannical abuse of power. He would be entitled to relief, in my view, if he establishes that the majority shareholders are using their greater voting power unfairly in order to prejudice him or are acting in a manner which does not enable him to enjoy a fair participation in the affairs of the company. . . . It is essential not to confuse the rights which the majority shareholders undoubtedly have to manage the affairs of a company and to determine its policy with lack of probity and unfair dealing in the affairs of the company. Anyone who becomes a minority shareholder in a company does so with the obvious knowledge that where his point of view conflicts with that of the majority, the latter's will is likely to prevail. He invests his money in a company on that premise and cannot be heard to complain if the affairs of the company are not conducted as he desires. He is, however, entitled to complain if the majority voting power is being abused or unfairly used to his prejudice as a shareholder. . . . As stated by Van den Heever AJP (as he then was) in *Richter NO* v *Riverside Estates (Pty) Ltd* 1946 OPD 209 at 227:

> 'It is trite law that privileged shareholders or directors of a company may not use their powers oppressively and in an unconscionable manner. That does not mean, on the other hand, that a person may become a shareholder on express terms of inequality and invoke a form of equitable relief in order radically to amend the legal relations between himself and the company.' . . .

It remains to add but three further comments on the section before I consider the facts of this case in the light of what I feel the legal approach should be. In the first place, the words 'affairs of the company *are being conducted*' (my italics) imply a continuing state of affairs. . . . Secondly, it is not necessary that, in doing what they did, the majority had any expectation of personal profit or pecuniary advantage in mind. The oppressors may have as their ultimate object the downfall of the company, which may bring with it financial loss to themselves, but may be conducting the affairs of the company with that object in mind in order to prejudice the minority. Again the oppression may consist in a wilful disregard of the minority shareholders' rights. . . . Thirdly, the motive underlying the conduct will generally not be relevant to the inquiry. The result rather than the motive is the material thing and it is not the motive for the conduct but the conduct itself to which the court must look and the effect which it has on other members of the company.

[*Aspek Pipe* v *Mauerberger* is discussed by N L Chadwick (1968) *Rhod LJ* 126.]

[321] **Hart v Pinetown Drive-in Cinema (Pty) Ltd**
1972 (1) SA 464 (D)

This was an application for the winding up of a company under s 111(g) of the 1926 Act on the ground that it was just and equitable that the company should be wound up.

MILLER J: ... It appears from the profit and loss account for the year ending 30 June 1970 that the net revenue derived by the respondent from the sale of tickets for cinema performances was (I give round figures only) R63 000. After deduction of the cost of advertising and other incidental expenses the gross profit was R59 000. The net result, however, was a loss of R4 000. It appears from the account that the cost of carrying on the business amounted to R31 000 of which R15 000 was for salaries. Administrative costs amounted to R6 000 and 'management fees' to R22 500. ... The respondent also derived income from its catering department which is run in conjunction with the exhibiting of films. The net profit from catering and advertisements amounted to some R20 000. In consequence, after deducting therefrom the losses sustained on the cinema business proper, the net profit of the company was R16 000. The company's undistributed profit as at the date of the account stood at R40 000. The balance sheet of the company reveals that it owns substantial assets which considerably exceed its liabilities.

Although this application is brought under the provisions of s 111(*g*) and not under s 111*bis*, what the applicant principally contends for is that the affairs of the respondent are being conducted by the majority shareholder in a manner oppressive to the applicant as a minority shareholder. It is for an applicant who relies upon that ground to place before the court facts which, if true, would warrant a conclusion that he justifiably lacks confidence in the conduct and management of the company's affairs and hence that it would be just and equitable that the company should be wound up. ... For that lack of confidence to be justifiable, the conduct complained of must be unfair, or, as Lord Simonds has expressed it, must be 'burdensome, harsh and wrongful' to a member or members of the company (*Scottish Co-operative Wholesale Society Ltd* v *Meyer* [1958] 3 All ER 66 (HL) at 71; and see *Marshall* v *Marshall (Pty) Ltd & others* 1954 (3) SA 571 (N) at 580). A minority shareholder may, because he is in the minority, feel a sense of grievance or be in a state of permanent frustration through his inability to persuade the majority to his point of view, but he would not merely on that account be able to justify lack of confidence in the management of the company. The conduct complained of must 'lack that degree of probity' which a member is entitled to expect in the conduct of the company's affairs. (See *Re Jermyn Street Turkish Baths Ltd* [1971] 3 All ER 184 (CA) at 199.)

Paragraphs 7 and 9 of the petition contain the essence of the applicant's complaint. Reading those paragraphs together, it is fair to accept that the applicant alleges (i) that the affairs of the company are conducted without regard for his interests as a minority shareholder and to his prejudice; (ii) that one of the reasons of the majority shareholder for so conducting the company's affairs is that it desires to compel the applicant to sell his shares for much less than their value; (iii) that the affidavit of Mr M and the company accounts show that the 'management fee' paid by the respondent is not a genuine fee at all, for it bears no relationship whatsoever to the services (if any) rendered by the majority shareholder. It is the third of these allegations that contains the sting of the complaint. The first two allegations are more in the nature of expressions of belief or opinion than positive statements of fact. A bald statement that the management has no regard for the applicant's interests would not be of much avail without facts from which the court could for itself assess the justice or otherwise of such a charge. Nor would the applicant's contention regarding the reasons which prompt the management to act as it does suffice in the absence of facts from which it could be deduced on the balance of probabilities that those were indeed the reasons. The facts upon which the applicant relies in support of the allegations reflected in (i) and (ii) above, are those reflected in (iii), namely, the figures revealed by the company's accounts and Mr M's report of what happened at the annual general meeting. . . .

. . . In the final resort, the applicant's case must depend upon the allegation that the accounts reveal that the management fee is not genuine in that it bears no relationship whatever to the services rendered or the work performed. If that allegation were substantiated by the accounts or by any other evidence, there might be a great deal to be said for the view that there was a lack of probity in the conduct of the company's affairs and that those managing such affairs were using the power which their majority holding gave them, not in the interests of the company and through it of the shareholders, but for other purposes; and that they were not only unmindful of the applicant's interests but were in truth acting unfairly and wrongfully, in a manner oppressive to him as a minority shareholder.

The accounts do not, in my view, enable the court to draw any inference, with the requisite degree of conviction (that is, on a sufficiently strong balance of probabilities) that the management fee of R22 500 is bogus and bears no relationship to the work done. There is, in the petition and its annexures, no evidence whatever of the nature of the services actually rendered by those for whom the fee is said to be a payment or reward, nor is there evidence of the work involved in conducting the affairs of the company. It is one thing to say that R22 500 is a very substantial sum to be paid in respect of management fees in a company such as the respondent appears to be but an entirely different thing to say that it is so large a sum that it can bear no real relationship to the services rendered. The latter allegation could rarely, if ever, be shown to be justified without evidence of the duration and nature of the services rendered or the degree of complexity of management and direction of the company. Nor does the account given by Mr M of what was done and said at the company meeting resolve the difficulty in the applicant's way. Accepting, as I must, for present purposes, that the chairman of the company admitted that the bulk of the profit was appropriated for fees and other charges, there is no evidence that such appropriation was or was admitted to be unlawful or in any way untoward. It is necessary to bear in mind, too, that even if the fee were to be regarded as unduly generous, that would not of itself mean that those accepting such a fee were necessarily acting oppressively. As Buckley LJ observed in *Re Jermyn Street Turkish Baths Ltd* (*supra*) at 199:

'Oppression must, we think, import that the oppressed are being constrained to submit to something which is unfair to them as the result of some overbearing act or attitude on the part of the oppressor. If a director of a company were to draw remuneration to which he was not legally entitled or in excess of the remuneration to which he was legally entitled, this might no doubt found misfeasance proceedings or proceedings for some other kind of relief, but it would not, in our judgment, of itself amount to oppression. Nor would the fact that the director was a majority shareholder in the company make any difference, unless he had used his majority voting powers to retain the remuneration or to stifle proceedings by the company or other shareholders in relation to it.'

It is recognized that relief of the kind now sought might be granted without evidence of oppressive conduct if there has been destruction of or irreparable damage to the proper relationship between the members of a domestic company who stand towards one another in substantially the same way as partners do. That is the second of the principles referred to by Trollip J (as he then was) in *Moosa's* case [1967 (3) SA 131 (T) at 137]; ie the principle derived from the decision in *Re Yenidje Tobacco Co* [*21* above]. But this is not the case sought to be made by the applicant, who claims that he is being prejudiced by the oppressive manner in which the majority shareholder conducts the affairs of the company.

NOTES

In *Benjamin* v *Elysium Investments (Pty) Ltd* 1960 (3) SA 467 (E) (noted by B H McPherson in (1961) 24 *MLR* 368), it was held that an application under s 111*bis* of the 1926 Act could be brought by a member who shared voting control equally with another. This was approved in *Livanos* v *Swartzberg* 1962 (4) SA 395 (W). In *Re Bellador Silk Ltd* [1965] 1 All ER 667, an application under s 210 of the English Act was refused because (*a*) the true purpose of the petitioner was to bring pressure to bear to achieve a purpose alien to s 210, viz repayment of a loan owed by the company to the petitioner's group of companies; and (*b*) there was no prospect of a dividend on winding-up. See, however, N A Bastin (1968) *JBL* 320, suggesting that (*b*) should not concern the court.

Re H R Harmer Ltd [1959] 1 WLR 62, [1958] 3 All ER 689 (noted by K W Wedderburn in (1959) *Cambridge LJ* 37) was the case of a dictatorial father, in his late eighties, who as managing director and chairman of the board of a family firm did not permit his sons, who were minority shareholders and directors, any effective say in the running of the company. The court made an order demoting him to the position of an expert adviser, at a fixed salary. The fact that the sons had obtained their shares from their father as gifts was considered to be irrelevant.

In *Breetveldt* v *Van Zyl* 1972 (1) SA 304 (T) Margo J held that in an application under s 111*bis* the petitioner ought to specify the nature of the relief sought. It remains to be seen whether the same rule will be applied to an application under s 252 of the present Act.

Other cases of importance were *Taylor* v *Welkom Theatres (Pty) Ltd* 1954 (3) SA 339 (O); *Marshall* v *Marshall (Pty) Ltd* 1954 (3) SA 571 (N); *Marsh* v *Odendaalrus Cold Storage Ltd* 1963 (2) SA 263 (W); *Moosa NO* v *Mavjee Bhawan (Pty) Ltd* 1967 (3) SA 131 (T); *Woomack* v *Commercial Vehicles Spares (Pvt) Ltd* 1968 (3) SA 419 (R).

Of recent English cases, see *Re Five-Minute Wash Service Ltd* [1966] 1 WLR 745, [1966] 1 All ER 242; *Re Jermyn Street Turkish Baths Ltd* [1971] 1 WLR 1042, [1971] 3 All ER 184 (CA). On minority protection under s 210 of the English Act (s 111*bis* of the 1926 South African Act), see also D D Prentice (1972) *Current Legal Problems* 124 and, commenting on *Re Tivoli Freeholds Ltd* [1972] VR 445, (1973) 89 *LQR* 338.

III THE 'PROPER PLAINTIFF' RULE (FOSS V HARBOTTLE) AND THE
EXCEPTIONS TO IT

A TEXT

If a wrong has been committed against a company the proper person
to sue is the company, as the injured party, and not an individual
shareholder: *Foss* v *Harbottle*, *322*. This does not preclude an individual
shareholder from suing a third party who has infringed his personal
rights: *323*.

Like the 'non-intervention' rule, the rule in *Foss* v *Harbottle* is
subject to exceptions. Individual shareholders may take action in respect
of a wrong done to a company by its directors, officers or controllers
if the act was

(*a*) illegal or *ultra vires* the company; or
(*b*) in fraud of the company, and the wrongdoers are in control,
and will not allow action to be brought.

The action (known in America as a 'derivative stockholders' action)
must be brought by the shareholders in a representative capacity, on
behalf of themselves and all the other shareholders, except the real
defendants, and the company must be joined as co-defendant. No action
may be brought in respect of an internal irregularity which could be
put right by an ordinary resolution of the company in general meeting:
324–328.

Again, the common-law remedy is supplemented by a statutory
remedy. Where a company has suffered damages or loss or has been
deprived of any benefit as a result of any wrong, breach of trust or
breach of faith committed by any director or officer of that company
or by any past director or officer while he was in office, and the company has not instituted proceedings for the recovery of such damages,
loss or benefit, any member of the company may initiate proceedings
on behalf of the company against the alleged wrongdoer: *328A*.
Before doing so he must serve written notice on the company calling
upon it to institute such proceedings within one month from the date of
service of the notice, as prescribed in s 266(2). If the company fails
to institute action and the member applies to court, the court, if
satisfied that there is a prima facie case, may appoint a provisional
curator ad litem and direct him to conduct an investigation and report
to the court on the return day of the provisional order, s 266 (3). On
the return day the court may either discharge the provisional order
or confirm the appointment of the *curator ad litem* for the company
and issue directions as to the institution of the proceedings, s 266(4).
The fact that the company has in general meeting ratified or condoned
the alleged wrong breach of trust or breach of faith, or passes a resolution ratifying or condoning it, is no bar either to the provisional

proceedings or the making of a final order, s 266(1) and (4). As to the powers of the curator see s 267.

There is nothing in the Act to say that the representative (or derivative) shareholders' action of the common law is to be abolished, but it is likely that in practice it will be largely replaced by proceedings under s 266. The old cases remain useful because (*a*) they are necessary for the understanding of the English and American case law; (*b*) they provide some guidance as to the kind of situation in which an application under s 266 is likely to succeed; (*c*) there might be occasionally a shareholder who prefers to bring the common-law action because he wishes to retain the conduct of the proceedings in his own hands.

On s 266, see M S Blackman 'Majority Rule and the Statutory Derivative Action' (1976) 36 *THRHR* 27.

B CASES

[322] Foss *v* Harbottle

(1843) 2 Hare 461, 67 ER 189

WIGRAM V-C: . . . The Victoria Park Company is an incorporated body, and the conduct with which the defendants are charged in this suit is an injury not to the plaintiffs exclusively; it is an injury to the whole corporation by individuals whom the corporation entrusted with powers to be exercised only for the good of the corporation. And from the case of *Attorney-General* v *Wilson* (1840) Ct & Ph 1, it may be stated as undoubted law that a bill or information by a corporation will lie to be relieved in respect of injuries which the corporation has suffered at the hands of persons standing in the situation of the directors upon this record. This bill, however, differs from that in *Attorney-General* v *Wilson* in this that, instead of the corporation being formally represented as plaintiffs, the bill in this case is brought by two individual corporators, professedly on behalf of themselves and all the other members of the corporation, except those who committed the injuries complained of — the plaintiffs assuming to themselves the right and power in that manner to sue on behalf of and represent the corporation itself.

It was not, nor could it successfully be, argued that it was a matter of course for any individual members of a corporation thus to assume to themselves the right of suing in the name of the corporators. In law the corporation and the aggregate members of the corporation are not the same thing for purposes like this; and the only question can be whether the facts alleged in this case justify a departure from the rule which, prima facie, would require that the corporation should sue in its own name and in its corporate character, or in the name of someone whom the law has appointed to be its representative. . . .

. . . It would be too much to hold that a society of private persons associated together in undertakings, which, though certainly beneficial to the public, are nevertheless matters of private property, are to be deprived of their civil rights *inter se* because, in order to make their common objects more attainable, the Crown or the legislature may have conferred upon them the benefit of a corporate character. If a case should arise of injury to a corporation by some of its members, for which no adequate remedy remained, except that of a suit by individual corporators in their private characters, and asking in such character the protection of those rights to which in their corporate character they were entitled, I cannot but think that the principle so forcibly laid down by Lord Cottenham in *Wallworth* v *Holt* (1841) 4 My & Cr 619 at 635 (see also 17 Ves 320, per Lord Eldon), and other cases would apply, and the claims of justice would be found superior to any difficulties arising out of technical rules respecting the mode in which corporations are required to sue.

But, on the other hand, it must not be without reasons of a very urgent character that established rules of law and practice are to be departed from, rules which, though in a sense technical, are founded on general principles of justice and convenience. . . .

. . . It is only necessary to refer to the clauses of the Act to show that, whilst the supreme governing body, the proprietors at a special general meeting assembled, retain the power of exercising the functions conferred upon them by the Act of incorporation, it cannot be competent to individual corporators to sue in the manner proposed by the plaintiffs. . . .

[323] Edwards *v* Halliwell
[1950] 2 All ER 1064

The constitution of a trade union provided that contributions were not to be altered until a ballot vote of the members had been taken and a two-thirds majority obtained. A delegate meeting of the union, without taking any ballot, passed a resolution increasing the contributions of members. The plaintiffs, two members of the union, sued two members of the executive committee of the union and the union itself for a declaration that the resolution was invalid. The action succeeded.

JENKINS LJ: . . . The rule in *Foss* v *Harbottle*, as I understand it, comes to no more than this. First, the proper plaintiff in an action in respect of a wrong alleged to be done to a company or association of persons is prima facie the company or the association of persons itself. Secondly, where the alleged wrong is a transaction which might be made binding on the company or association and on all its members by a simple majority of the members, no individual member of the company is allowed to maintain an action in respect of that matter for the simple reason that, if a mere majority of the members of the company or association is in favour of what has been done, then *cadit quaestio*. No wrong had been done to the company or association and there is nothing in respect of which anyone can sue. If, on the other hand, a simple majority of members of the company or association is against what has been done, then there is no valid reason why the company or association itself should not sue. In my judgment, it is implicit in the rule that the matter relied on as constituting the cause of action should be a cause of action properly belonging to the general body of corporators or members of the company or association as opposed to a cause of action which some individual member can assert in his own right.

The cases falling within the general ambit of the rule are subject to certain exceptions. It has been noted in the course of argument that in cases where the act complained of is wholly *ultra vires* the company or association the rule has no application because there is no question of the transaction being confirmed by any majority. It has been further pointed out that where what has been done amounts to what is generally called in these cases a fraud on the minority and the wrongdoers are themselves in control of the company, the rule is relaxed in favour of the aggrieved minority who are allowed to bring what is known as a minority shareholders' action on behalf of themselves and all others. The reason for this is that, if they were denied that right, their grievance could never reach the court because the wrongdoers themselves, being in control, would not allow the company to sue. Those exceptions are not directly in point in this case, but they show, especially the last one, that the rule is not an inflexible rule and it will be relaxed where necessary in the interests of justice.

There is a further exception which seems to me to touch this case directly . . . noted by Romer J in *Cotter* v *National Union of Seamen* [1929] 2 Ch 58. He pointed out that the rule did not prevent an individual member from suing if the matter in respect of which he was suing was one which could validly be done or sanctioned, not by a simple majority of the members of the company or association, but only by some special majority, as, for instance, in the case of a limited company under the Companies Act, a special resolution duly passed as such. As Romer J pointed out, the reason for that exception is clear, because otherwise, if the rule were applied in its full rigour, a company which, by its directors, had broken its own regulations by doing something without a special resolution which could only be done validly by a special resolution could assert that it alone was the proper plaintiff in any consequent action and the effect would be to allow a company acting in breach of its articles to do *de facto* by ordinary resolution that which according to its own regulations could only be done by special resolution. That exception exactly fits the present case inasmuch as here the act complained of is something which could only have been validly done, not by a simple majority, but by a two-thirds majority obtained on a ballot vote. In my judgment, therefore, the reliance on the rule in *Foss* v *Harbottle* in the present case may be regarded as misconceived on that ground alone.

I would go further. In my judgment, this is a case of a kind which is not even within the general ambit of the rule. It is not a case where what is complained of is a wrong done to the union, a matter in respect of which the cause of action would primarily and properly belong to the union. It is a case in which certain members of a trade union complain that the union, acting through the delegate meeting and the executive council in breach of the rules by which the union, and every member of the union are bound, has invaded the individual rights of the complainant members, who are entitled to maintain themselves in full membership with all the rights and privileges appertaining to that status so long as they pay contributions in accordance with the tables of contributions as they stood before the purported alterations of 1943, unless and until the scale of contributions is validly altered by the prescribed majority obtained on a ballot vote. Those rights, these members claim, have been invaded. The gist of the case is that the personal and individual rights of membership of each of them have been invaded by a purported, but invalid, alteration of the tables of contributions. In those circumstances, it seems to me the rule in *Foss* v *Harbottle* has no application at all, for the individual members who are suing sue, not in the right of the union, but in their own right to protect from invasion their own individual rights as members. . . .

NOTES

See also *Pender* v *Lushington* (1877) 6 ChD 70, where it was held that a shareholder whose vote had been improperly rejected by the chairman at a general meeting of the company had a right to sue the directors in his own name, and *Petersen* v *Amalgamated Union of Building Trade Workers of SA* 1973 (2) SA 140 (E), where two expelled members of a trade union sued for reinstatement; further *Goldex Mines Ltd* v *Revill* (1974) 54 DLR (3d) 672 (Ont CA), noted by B V Slutsky (1976) 39 *MLR* 331, where it was held that a contravention of the proxy rules provides a basis for a personal (as distinguished from a derivative) action by injured shareholders.

[324] Hichens *v* Congreve
(1828) 4 Russ 562, 38 ER 917

THE LORD CHANCELLOR (Lyndhurst): Upon the face of the bill I cannot help considering the transactions stated in it to be fraudulent. Sir William Congreve entered into a negotiation with Flattery for the purchase of the property in question at the price of £10 000 for a joint stock company of which he was to be a member and director. After the treaty was begun, the two Clarkes associated themselves with Sir William Congreve in the scheme; and the negotiation with Flattery went on. The object was, the purchase of the Arigna mines, in order that they might be conveyed to a company by whom they were to be worked; and the company was to consist, not of Congreve and the Clarkes alone, but of a considerable body of shareholders.

It appears that, in the course of these negotiations, Congreve and the Clarkes became desirous of making a profit out of the original transaction for the purchase of Flattery's interest in the mines. The first plan, which occurred to them, was, that a conveyance for the sum of £10 000 should be made to persons nominated by them, who were afterwards to convey to the company for £25 000. If such a transaction had taken place, and the particulars had been concealed from the company, it could not have been sustained; for, considering the situation in which Congreve and the Clarkes stood with reference to the company, it would have been incumbent on them to have communicated the real price at which the mines had been purchased of Flattery. This objection seems to have occurred to them; and, accordingly, another shape was given to the proceedings. The plan now adopted was this—that a conveyance should be executed directly from Flattery to trustees for the company; and although Flattery had agreed to convey the property for £10 000, that in this conveyance it should be stated that the purchase-money was £25 000, in order that the difference might be put into the pockets of Sir William Congreve and the two Clarkes, and some other individuals whom they might choose to nominate. Such a transaction is so incorrect, that it is quite impossible that any court of justice could permit it to stand: and if, after the conveyance had been so made, reciting that the price paid to Flattery was £25 000, a company of shareholders was formed, who acted upon that representation, they could, in justice, be chargeable only with the money actually paid to Flattery; and if a larger sum was taken out of their funds, they would be entitled to call on the individuals, into whose hands it came, to refund it. In substance, therefore, the plaintiffs are entitled to relief.

The only other question is, whether, in point of form, there is any objection to this bill? . . .

Here is a fund in which all the shareholders are interested; £15 000 has been improperly taken out of it: a fraud has been committed on them all. Is it necessary that all should come into a court of justice, for the purpose of joining in a suit with a view to obtain redress? . . .

It is said that there is nothing on the face of the bill which shows that the shareholders are so numerous, that they could not all be joined as parties without inconvenience. I think it does appear sufficiently, that, if all were joined, the number of complainants would be inconveniently great; first, because the shares are six thousand in number, and, secondly, because it appears by the act of parliament that there were then upwards of two hundred shareholders. It is clear, therefore, that justice would be unattainable, if all the shareholders were required to be parties to the suit.

It is said, each shareholder might file a bill to recover his proportion of the money. Such a course would produce enormous inconvenience. Are two hundred bills to be filed, in order to do justice in this matter? If justice can be done in one suit, the court will sustain such a proceeding; for to require all the shareholders to be parties, or to leave each shareholder to file a separate bill to redress his own wrong, would, in substance, be a denial of justice.

In the present case, it appears to me that justice may be done in one suit. All the shareholders stand in the same situation; the property has been taken out of their common fund; they are entitled to have that property brought back again for the benefit of the concern. When all parties stand in the same situation, and have one common right, and one common interest, in what respect can it be inconvenient that two, or three, or more, should sue in their own names for the benefit of all?

[325] Atwool *v* Merryweather
(1867) 5 Eq 464 n

A company was formed for the acquisition of a mine from one Merryweather. The purchase price was £7 000, of which £4 000 was to be paid in cash and £3 000 in shares of the company. The capital was fixed at £30 000, divided into 6 000 shares of £5 each, but only 2 000 shares were taken, on which £3 940 was received. This money was paid to Merryweather, and 600 shares were registered in his name as paid up, in part payment of the £7 000. The company had six directors, including Merryweather and one Whitworth.

Subsequently it was discovered that the mine was worthless. Inquiries showed that Merryweather had applied to Whitworth for assistance in disposing of the mine and that Merryweather had intended to sell it for £4 000. Merryweather and Whitworth then decided upon the scheme to form a company and sell the mine to it for £7 000, of which Merryweather was to get £4 000, while the remaining £3 000 was to be paid to Whitworth for his assistance. This agreement was concealed from the other incorporators and directors who believed that £7 000 was bona fide to be paid as the purchase price of the mine.

In the earlier action of *East Pant Du United Lead Mining Company Ltd* v *Merryweather* (1864) 2 Hem & M 254, certain shareholders sued Merryweather in the name of the company to relieve the company from liability on the contract with him, and to recover the moneys already paid to him. The action was disapproved by a majority of the shareholders, including Merryweather and Whitworth, who moved that the action be struck off as unauthorized by the company. The court, in this earlier action, held that it had no alternative but to order accordingly. Although it was true that it was the object of the action to set aside a fraudulent acquisition of shares by a member whose votes in respect of those shares made it impossible to obtain a majority in favour of an action against him, the fact remained that there was no authority for bringing the action in the name of the company.

Subsequently, action was brought by a shareholder, on behalf of himself and all the other shareholders except the defendants to the action, against Merryweather, Whitworth, and the company, for the purpose of setting aside the contract for the purchase of the mine and compelling repayment from Merryweather and Whitworth of the sum of £3 940 or such portions as had been received by them, and a return of the 600 shares allotted to Merryweather. This action succeeded.

PAGE WOOD V-C: . . . I think that, upon principle, a contract of this kind cannot stand, and that there is not such a defect in the constitution of the suit as would be fatal according to the authority of *Foss* v *Harbottle* [*322* above]. . . .

Looking at the facts as they come out, I am clearly of opinion that this arrangement, by which Merryweather was to have £4 000 and Whitworth £3 000, was concealed from everybody, and that Merryweather assisted in that concealment by allowing his name to appear as the sole vendor, and taking the purchase-money.

Upon such a transaction the court will hold that the whole contract is a complete fraud. I do not in the least say that where persons with their eyes open know that the agent who secures them the bargain is going to take money for it, that would not be all right enough. If the company knew this gentleman was to have this amount as promotion-money, well and good. . . . But here it is a simple fraud, and nothing else. Merryweather, knowing Whitworth's position with regard to the company, and that as an honest man Whitworth was bound to tell the company what price he bought the mines for, agreed that the mine should be sold to the company for £7 000, and that the real price, £4 000, should not be disclosed to the company.

With regard to the frame of the suit, a question of some nicety arises how far such relief can be given at the instance of a shareholder on behalf of himself and other shareholders on the ground that the transaction might be confirmed by the whole body if they thought fit, and that the case would fall within *Foss* v *Harbottle*, according to which the suit must be by the whole company. On the previous occasion, when it was desired to take proceedings to set aside this transaction, a gentleman took upon himself to file a bill in the name of the company. A motion was made to take that bill off the file, as the person filing the bill was not the solicitor of the company, and was not authorized to file the bill, and I ordered the bill to be taken off the file. There was a majority against setting aside this transaction. The number of votes for rescinding the transaction was 324, and 344 the other way. But Merryweather, in respect of the shares obtained by this sale, which I have held cannot stand, had 78 votes, and Whitworth 28, making altogether 106 out of 344. If I were to hold that no bill could be filed by shareholders to get rid of the transaction on the ground of the doctrine of *Foss* v *Harbottle*, it would be simply impossible to set aside a fraud committed by a director under such circumstances, as the director obtaining so many shares by fraud would always be able to outvote everybody else. . . .

[326] MacDougall v Gardiner
(1875) 1 ChD 13

JAMES LJ: . . . I think it is of the utmost importance in all these companies that the rule which is well known in this court as the rule in *Mozley* v *Alston* (1847) 1 Ph 790, and *Lord* v *Copper Miners' Company* (1848) 2 Ph 740, and *Foss* v *Harbottle* [*322*, p. 535 above], should be always adhered to; that is to say, that nothing connected with internal disputes between the shareholders is to be made the subject of a bill by some one shareholder on behalf of himself and others, unless there be something illegal, oppressive, or fraudulent — unless there is something *ultra vires* on the part of the company *qua* company, or on the part of the majority of the company, so that they are not fit persons to determine it; but that every litigation must be in the name of the company, if the company really desires it. Because there may be a great many wrongs committed in a company — there may be claims against directors, there may be claims against officers, there may be claims against debtors; there may be a variety of things which a company may well be entitled to complain of, but which, as a matter of good sense, they do not think it right to make the subject of litigation; and it is the company, as a company, which has to determine whether it will make anything that is wrong to the company a subject-matter of litigation, or whether it will take steps itself to prevent the wrong from being done. . . .

MELLISH LJ: . . . Looking to the nature of these companies, looking at the way in which their articles are formed, and that they are not all lawyers who attend these meetings, nothing can be more likely than that there should be something more or less irregular done by them—some directors may have been irregularly appointed, some directors as irregularly turned out, or something or other may have been done which ought not to have been done according to the proper construction of the articles. Now, if that gives a right to every member of the company to file a bill to have the question decided, then if there happens to be one cantankerous member, or one member who loves litigation, everything of this kind will be litigated; whereas, if the bill must be filed in the name of the company, then, unless there is a majority who really wish for litigation, the litigation will not go on.

In my opinion, if the thing complained of is a thing which in substance the majority of the company are entitled to do, or if something has been done irregularly which the majority of the company are entitled to do regularly, or if something has been done illegally which the majority of the company are entitled to do legally, there can be no use in having a litigation about it, the ultimate end of which is only that a meeting has to be called, and then ultimately the majority gets its wishes. Is it not better that the rule should be adhered to that if it is a thing which the majority are the masters of, the majority in substance shall be entitled to have their will followed? . . . Of course, if the majority are abusing their powers, and are depriving the minority of their rights, that is an entirely different thing, and there the minority are entitled to come before this court to maintain their rights. . . .

[327] **Burland v Earle**
[1902] AC 83 (PC)

LORD DAVEY: It is an elementary principle of the law relating to joint stock companies that the court will not interfere with the internal management of companies acting within their powers, and in fact has no jurisdiction to do so. Again, it is clear law that in order to redress a wrong done to the company or to recover moneys or damages alleged to be due to the company, the action should prima facie be brought by the company itself. These cardinal principles are laid down in the well-known cases of *Foss v Harbottle, 322*, and *Mozley v Alston* (1847) 1 Ph 790 and in numerous later cases which it is unnecessary to cite. But an exception is made to the second rule, where the persons against whom the relief is sought themselves hold and control the majority of the shares in the company, and will not permit an action to be brought in the name of the company. In that case the courts allow the shareholders complaining to bring an action in their own names. This, however, is mere matter of procedure in order to give a remedy for a wrong which would otherwise escape redress, and it is obvious that in such an action the plaintiffs cannot have a larger right to relief than the company itself would have if it were plaintiff, and cannot complain of acts which are valid if done with the approval of the majority of the shareholders, or are capable of being confirmed by the majority. The cases in which the minority can maintain such an action are, therefore, confined to those in which the acts complained of are of a fraudulent character or beyond the powers of the company. A familiar example is where the majority are endeavouring directly or indirectly to appropriate to themselves money, property, or advantages which belong to the company, or in which the other shareholders are entitled to participate. . . . It should be added that no mere informality or irregularity which can be remedied by the majority will entitle the minority to sue, if the act when done regularly would be within the powers of the company and the intention of the majority of the shareholders is clear. . . .

[See also *334* , below, dealing with a different aspect of the case.]

[328] **Pavlides v Jensen**
[1956] Ch 565, [1956] 2 All ER 518

DANCKWERTS J: . . . The defendants are Tunnel Asbestos Cement Company Ltd and three directors of that company. The action purports to be a minority shareholder's action, on behalf of the plaintiff and all other shareholders in the company except the three defendant directors. The capital of the company consists of 600 000 ordinary shares of 10*s* each and 600 000 deferred shares of 1*s* each. . . . The plaintiff is the holder of 1 980 deferred shares in the capital of the company, which have, therefore, a nominal value of £99. He has held these shares since 1936. The deferred shareholders have, after the payment of a dividend of 5 per cent to the ordinary shareholders, an equal interest with the ordinary shareholders in the profits of the company; but by article 74 of the company's articles the holders of the deferred shares are not entitled to receive notices of or to attend or vote in person or by proxy at any general meeting of the company. Five hundred and seventy-eight thousand of the ordinary shares and the greater part of the deferred shares are held by another company, called Tunnel Portland Cement Company Ltd of which the defendant directors are also directors.

The complaint of the plaintiff relates to a sale of an asbestos mine in Cyprus, which was acquired by the defendant company (according to the statement of claim) in 1936 for about £142 000 and was resold in 1947 for about £182 000 to Cyprus Asbestos Mines Ltd in which the company holds 25 per cent of the issued capital. This sale was carried through by the defendant directors, and was not submitted to the approval of the defendant company in general meeting. The plaintiff alleges that the conduct of the defendant directors in effecting the sale was grossly negligent, because it was at an undervalue, the true value of the mine (according to the plaintiff's allegations) having been 'somewhere in the neighbourhood of £1 000 000'. If the allegations be true, this was, of course, a wrong to the defendant company for which the defendant company but no one else would be entitled to bring an action. The plaintiff claims that he is entitled to the assistance of the court in the manner of this action because (1) he is unable to requisition or attend a general meeting of the company under the terms of its articles and (2) the alleged delinquent directors are in a position to control the defendant company and so prevent the company taking any action against them. . . .

. . . It is contended on behalf of the defendants that the matters in respect of which the plaintiff complains, and in particular the question whether proceedings should be taken against the directors, is a matter of internal management of the company, with which, on the principle stated in *Foss* v *Harbottle*, the court normally will not interfere. It is contended further on behalf of the defendants that the present case—based on negligence of directors—is not within the few recognized exceptions to the above-mentioned rule, namely cases of *ultra vires*, illegality, or fraud (including fraudulent oppression of a minority by the majority of the shareholders). Further, it is said, the case is not a case where the control of the voting power is in the hands of the directors of the company whose actions are impugned; for they are not the shareholders; the shares are held by another company of which the defendant directors merely happen also to be among the directors.

For the plaintiff, it is contended that the above-mentioned exceptions are not exhaustive, and the court will grant relief wherever justice requires on any ground, and particularly where an otherwise helpless minority shareholder is in need of assistance by the court. As regards control, it is contended that, except for an immaterial period, the defendant directors, being a majority of the directors of Tunnel Portland Cement Company Ltd (the holders of the vast bulk of the shares of the company), were in a position to stifle any attempt to institute proceedings in the name of the company against them. . . .

[After quoting from a passage in *Buckley on the Companies Acts*, in which the author deals with the exceptions to the rule in *Foss* v *Harbottle*, Danckwerts J continued as follows:]

. . . The phrases in the passage which I have quoted most favourable to the plaintiff in the present case are the reference to 'a wrong done to the corporation', as well as cases of fraud and *ultra vires*, and the statement that the general rules stated are not inflexible and any case in which the claims of justice require that an action in which the company is not plaintiff should be entertained may be made an exception. It would appear that these are based on statements by Sir George Jessel MR in *Russell* v *Wakefield Waterworks Company* (1875) LR 20 Eq 474. In that case Sir George Jessel said (ibid at 480) of the rule in *Foss* v *Harbottle*:

'. . . that is not a universal rule; that is, it is a rule subject to exceptions, and the exceptions depend very much on the necessity of the case; that is, the necessity for the court doing justice.'

Later, Sir George Jessel said (LR 20 Eq at 482) (after referring to *Atwool* v *Merryweather*):

'As I have said before, the rule is a general one, but it does not apply to a case where the interests of justice require the rule to be dispensed with. . . .'

. . . The wide expressions used in *Buckley on the Companies Acts* and by Sir George Jessel in the above-mentioned case are not supported by the statement of the law by Lord Davey in the Privy Council case of *Burland* v *Earle*.

[After quoting from the passage by Lord Davey quoted on p 542 above, Danckwerts J continued:]

These observations, indeed, indicate how the principles involved may easily be misstated. Lord Davey refers to an action by share-holders (instead of the company) being allowed 'in order to give a remedy for a wrong which would otherwise escape redress'. But he points out that this is purely a matter of procedure and he expressly confines the cases in which such proceedings can be brought to those in which the acts complained of are of a fraudulent character (in which he includes appropriation by a majority in fraud of the minority of the shareholders) or beyond the powers of the company. Where the act com-plained of is within the powers of the company and the intention of the majority of the shareholders, in other cases than these exceptions the action is not maintainable. Lord Davey adds ([1902] AC at 94) that:

'Unless otherwise provided by the regulations of the company, a shareholder is not debarred from voting or using his voting power to carry a resolution by the circumstance of his having a particular interest in the subject-matter of the vote.'

On the facts of the present case, the sale of the company's mine was not beyond the powers of the company, and it is not alleged to be *ultra vires*. There is no allegation of fraud on the part of the directors or appropriation of assets of the company by the majority shareholders in fraud of the minority. It was open to the company, on the resolution of a majority of the shareholders, to sell the mine at a price decided by the company in that manner, and it was open to the company by a vote of the majority to decide that, if the directors by their negligence or error of judgment had sold the company's mine at an undervalue, proceedings should not be taken by the company against the directors. Applying, therefore, the principles as stated by Lord Davey, it is impossible to see how the present action can be maintained. . . .

[*Pavlides* v *Jensen* was critically noted by Professor L C B Gower in (1956) 19 *MLR* 538. (See also (1957) 74 *SALJ* 443.) It should be noted that under s 228 of our Act, directors can no longer dispose of the whole or the greater part of the assets of the company without the approval of a general meeting.]

[328A] **Brown *v* Nanco (Pty) Ltd**
1976 (3) SA 832 (W)

Some shareholders applied under s 266 for the appointment of a pro-visional curator *ad litem* to investigate a claim which the respondent company was alleged to have against four of its directors.

ELOFF J: The claim in question is said to have arisen from the payment to four of the respondent's directors of remuneration which they were not, in terms of its articles, empowered to make. The applicants have *locus standi* to bring this application as shareholders of the company. They hold 19,75 per cent of the issued share capital.

The relevant clauses in the articles of the respondent company provide as follows:

'66. The remuneration of the directors shall from time to time be determined by the company in general meeting.

87. A director may hold any other office or position of profit in the company, other than that of auditor, in conjunction with his directorship, and may be appointed thereto upon such terms as to remuneration, tenure of office and otherwise as may be arranged by the directors.' . . .

It appears to be common cause that pursuant to art 66, the company fixed the remuneration of the directors in respect of the years ended 28 February 1973 and 28 February 1974 in particular amounts, and that they, ie the directors, in addition authorized the payment to four of them of certain further amounts which in the accounts were styled 'management commissions'. The latter payments are explained by . . . the accountant of the respondent company. He says:

'The duties which devolve upon the directors who are, or were, in receipt of what I have called a "management commission" are arduous, manifold and responsible.'

He then describes those duties, and goes on to say that when he was consulted by the respondent company, he advised it as to the proper remuneration payable to the directors. His advice was to this effect: A low initial salary for the persons concerned was to be the starting point, since it was uncertain what the future business prospects were. (The low initial salary, I infer from the papers, was that which was approved of by the company in general meeting.) Subsequent remuneration would depend upon the results achieved so as to assess the contribution made by the persons concerned more accurately, as also the respondent's ability to afford an adequate remuneration at a later stage. . . .

The issue raised necessitates a determination of the meaning and effect of art 87, which I quoted earlier herein, and which seems to me to be the only clause which could possibly have justified the payments under discussion. That clause has of course to be read in the light of the background of the common law, which is that a director of a company has no right to any remuneration of any sort at all unless such right is given him by the articles of the company, or by his contract (*In re George Newman & Co* [1895] 1 ChD 674 at 686, quoted with approval in, *inter alia, Phillips* v *Base Metal Exploration Syndicate Ltd (in Liquidation)* 1911 TPD 403 at 406).

The approach in the present case should then be that, unless there was a proper appointment of the persons concerned in terms of art 87 to hold positions of profit in the company in conjunction with their directorships upon such terms as to remuneration, tenure of office, or otherwise, as may be arranged, they could not validly have been paid the remuneration under consideration.

I think it is a fair reading of the affidavit of [the accountant] that the four directors were not appointed to offices of profit, but performed duties so burdensome that it was considered that the remuneration fixed by the company in general meeting was not adequate, and they should receive extra remuneration, the amount of which was fixed in the light of the profits earned by the company.

Article 87 seems to me to require that there should at least be an appointment to a specific post with a prior formulation of rights and obligations in a manner sufficiently clear and definite to found a contract. I do not think that anything of that sort was done in the present case.

In any event I do not consider that I need, for present purposes, be convinced that the payment of the amounts under discussion was unauthorized. The section under which this application was brought does not require that at this stage. . . .

What ss (3) seems to contemplate is that once the court considers that there is a prima facie cause of action it should enjoin the *curator ad litem* to investigate the matter further. The investigation has to be directed to whether it will really be worth while taking action. His investigation may prompt him to conclude that, while there may be prima facie grounds for the proceedings, the case is not of sufficient strength to justify the litigation desired by the applicants. Or his investigation may lead him to the conclusion that there is not even a prima facie cause of action. What is clear is that the court need not at this stage of the proceedings be satisfied that there is a probability of success.

In my opinion the requirements of ss (3)(*b*) have been complied with. As for ss (3)(*c*), I do not think that much further need be done by way of investigation into the facts. The directors of the company seem to have placed all the relevant factual data before the court, and the curator's investigation will probably be limited to the question of the inferences which can properly be drawn from those facts. But I do think that such an investigation is justified.

In my opinion a case for relief has been made out.

NOTES

On the historical development of the rule in *Foss v Harbottle* see especially A J Boyle in (1965) 28 *MLR* 317.

One of the reasons for the rule in *Foss v Harbottle* is the undesirability of a multiplicity of actions for the same wrong: *326* above, also *Goodall v Hoogendoorn Ltd* 1926 AD 11 at 16. Another is the futility of allowing an action to be brought to redress a wrong which would cease to be a wrong if ratified by the majority in general meeting. A third reason is given by Richard R Lee (1957) 35 *North Carolina Law Review* 279–84: 'The real objection to permitting a shareholder to recover directly for his proportionate share of the damage inflicted upon the corporation of which he is a member is not that the injury was done to the corporate entity rather than to him, but that the result of such recovery is a return of corporation assets to shareholders without first satisfying corporate creditors.'

In America illegal political contributions and bribes paid to foreign government officials have been held to be recoverable by shareholders from directors and managers with a derivative stockholders' action.

The action cannot be brought by a creditor: *Lawrence v West Somerset Mineral Railway Co* [1918] 2 Ch 250.

Where the wrongful act has caused no loss to the company no action will be permitted: *Heyting v Dupont* [1964] 2 All ER 843, [1964] 1 WLR 843. (See also the judgment of the trial court in [1963] 3 All ER 97, where the rule in *Foss v Harbottle* was regarded as one relating to jurisdiction. For a full discussion of *Heyting v Dupont*, see Anthony Boyle (1964) 27 *MLR* 479, 603; K W Wedderburn (1964) *CLJ* 39.)

Even where the irregular action of the executive could be confirmed by a general meeting, individual members are able to maintain the action if it is, as a practical proposition, impossible to go through the necessary procedure in time. '*Foss v Harbottle* should not be applied if the result may be to deprive the majority of an opportunity of carrying out their will. In other words, if the constitutional machinery of the body cannot operate in time to be of practical effect, the court, in my view, should entertain

the suit of a member or members not supported by the association', per Goulding J
in *Hodgson v NALGO* [1972] 1 All ER 15 at 24. (See D D Prentice (1972) 55 *MLR* 318.)

The rule in *Foss v Harbottle* has been adopted in South Africa: *Cohen v Directors of
Rand Collieries Ltd* 1906 TS 197; *Robinson v Imroth* 1917 WLD 159; *Meyer v Meyer
Sons & Co Ltd* 1926 CPD 109 (in exceptional cases an individual shareholder can sue
to have a director who is not duly qualified restrained from acting); *Eales v Turner*
1928 WLD 173; *Moti v Moti and Hassim Moti Ltd* 1934 TPD 428; *Garment Workers'
Union v Smith* 1936 CPD 249; *Cooper v Garrett* 1945 WLD 137; *Mockford v Gordon
and Abe Gordon (Pty) Ltd* 1949 (3) SA 1173 (W); and *Vrede Gold Exploration Ltd v Lubner*
1973 (2) 331 (C), where it was held that if the directors have no 'direct and substantial
interest' in the proceedings, it is not necessary to join them. But see also *Thomas Ltd
v May* 1952 (3) SA 750 (SR), where it was held that though the company is the only
proper plaintiff to sue for damages the company has suffered, a minority shareholder is
entitled to sue the controlling shareholder for damages arising out of his negligent
conduct in the administration of the affairs of the company, provided he limits his claim
to his own personal loss, resulting from the company's shares having become valueless.

On the applicability of *Foss v Harbottle* to a registered trade union, see *Gründling v
Beyers* 1967 (2) SA 131 (W) at 139.

Shareholders can have the directors restrained from committing illegal or *ultra vires*
acts: see e g *Davison v Gillies* (*343* below).

The representative minority shareholders' action at common law is limited to cases
where the directors or officers have acted illegally, *ultra vires* or fraudulently (see p 534
above). Whether there is a further exception to *Foss v Harbottle*, viz 'where the interests
of justice require that the rule be disregarded' (Gower 3 ed 585) is doubtful, *328*. Proceedings under s 266 may be instituted whenever a company has suffered damages
or loss as a result of '*any* wrong, breach of trust or breach of faith' committed by a
director or officer or past director or officer. This clearly includes damages or loss
suffered as a result of a negligent act. Nor is ratification or condonation of the wrong
a bar to proceedings under s 266.

IV Inspections and Investigations, and Other Statutory Safe-guards

A TEXT

The Minister of Economic Affairs may appoint one or more
inspectors to investigate the affairs of a company and report thereon,

(a) if 100 members or members holding not less than one-twentieth
of the shares issued apply for such investigation, s 257(1);

(b) if it appears to the Minister that there are circumstances suggesting
fraud, illegality, oppression or any other form of misconduct, be
it in connection with the formation or the management of the
company, or that its members have not been given all the information with respect to its affairs which they might reasonably
expect, s 258(2).

The Minister must appoint one or more inspectors if (i) the company
by special resolution, or (ii) the court by order, declares that the
affairs of the company ought to be so investigated, s 258(1): *329, 330*.

As to the powers of an inspector appointed to investigate the affairs
of a company to investigate into the affairs of related (controlled or
controlling) companies, see s 259. Section 260 deals with the production
of documents and evidence on investigation (but see s 264).

After the report of the inspector has been submitted to the Minister as prescribed by s 261, the Minister, if he decides to proceed, may (*a*) apply to court for the winding-up of the company or for an order under s 252; or (*b*) bring in the name of the company an action for damages in respect of any fraud, delict or other misconduct in connection with the promotion or formation of the company or the management of its affairs, or for the recovery of any property of the company which has been misapplied or wrongly retained, s 262: *330*. A copy of the report of the inspector is admissible in any legal proceedings as evidence of his opinion, s 265. As to the expenses of the investigation, see s 263.

Special provision is made for an investigation into membership, the ownership of shares, and the control of a company, ss 254, 255 (see also s 253). If it appears to the Minister that owing to the unwillingness of the persons concerned to co-operate there is difficulty in finding out the relevant facts about any shares, he may by notice 'freeze' the shares as regards transfers, voting right, rights issues and payments, as detailed in s 256.

While ss 252, 266, and 253–265 constitute major statutory safeguards for shareholders who consider that the directors or shareholders of the company are abusing their powers, other provisions which directly or indirectly provide some measure of protection are scattered throughout the Companies Act. The rules as to special resolutions are one example; s 272 which empowers the Minister to appoint a joint auditor to the auditor of the company if 100 members or members holding one-twentieth of the issued share capital so demand, another.

B CASES

[329] **Breetveldt *v* Van Zyl**
1972 (1) SA 304 (T)

Among the remedies applied for in this case was an order for the investigation into the affairs of several companies under s 95*bis* of the 1926 Act (s 258(1) of the present Act).

MARGO J: There remains for consideration the applicants' claim for an order, under s 95*bis*(1)(*a*)(ii) of the Companies Act, declaring that the affairs of the companies ought to be investigated by an inspector appointed by the Minister of Economic Affairs.

Section 95*bis*(1) reads as follows:

'Without prejudice to his powers under section 95, the Minister

(*a*) shall appoint one or more inspectors to investigate the affairs of a company and to report thereon in such manner as he may direct if—

(i) the company by special resolution; or
(ii) the Court by order,
declares that its affairs ought to be investigated by an inspector appointed by the Minister; and

(*b*) may do so if it appears to the Minister that there are circumstances suggesting —

   (i) that its business is being conducted with intent to defraud its creditors or the creditors of any other person or otherwise for a fraudulent or unlawful purpose or in a manner oppressive of any part of its members or that it was formed for any fraudulent or unlawful purpose; or

   (ii) that persons concerned with its formation or the management of its affairs have in connection therewith been guilty of fraud, delict or other misconduct towards it or towards its members; or

   (iii) that its members have not been given all information with respect to its affairs which they might reasonably expect.' . . .

As far as I am aware, there is no reported case in our courts in which an application for relief under s 95*bis*(1)(*a*)(ii) has succeeded. See *Irvin and Johnson Ltd* v *Gelcer & Co (Pty) Ltd* 1958 (2) SA 59 (C); *Buckingham & others* v *Combined Holdings and Industries Ltd* 1961 (1) SA 326 (E); *Yende* v *Orlando Coal Distributors (Pty) Ltd & others* 1961 (3) SA 314 (W); *Candice Investments* v *Harmony Gold Mining Co Ltd* 1961 (4) SA 123 (W); *Nafte* v *Allied Minerals Ltd* 1966 (3) SA 94 (W).

It is desirable to refer briefly to the principles emerging from these cases. In the *St Martin Preserving Co Ltd* case [[1965] 1 QB 603] Phillimore J at 613C held that the words 'affairs of the company' in s 165 of the English Act include the company's goodwill, its profits or losses, its contracts and assets, including its shareholding in and ability to control the affairs of a subsidiary, and of a sub-subsidiary; and Winn J at 618G held that the phrase 'affairs of the company' comprises all its business affairs, interests or transactions, all its investment or other property interests, all its profits and losses or balance of profits or losses, and its goodwill. Lord Parker CJ concurred in both these judgments. With respect, I would think that the same interpretations ought to be applied to the term 'the affairs of a company' in s 95*bis*(1)(*a*) of our Act, save that I would go further and include such matters as the internal management and administration of the company.

In the *Gelcer* case (*supra*) Herbstein J, dealing with the requirement in s 95*bis*(1)(*a*) that the Minister must appoint one or more inspectors if the court by order declares that the company's affairs ought to be investigated, examined the meaning of the words 'ought to be investigated'. The learned judge concluded, at 62C–F, that the word 'ought' conveys the idea that the court should function if it deems it right or advisable to order an investigation and not only if some prima facie case is made out; and that the power of the court would appear to be wider than that of the Minister, for it is not confined to the circumstances set out in paras (i), (ii) and (iii) of s 95*bis*(1)(*b*). The court can thus make the required declaration if, on a consideration of all the facts placed before it, it deems it advisable or desirable that the affairs of the company should be investigated. Herbstein J, at 62G, having quoted from Professor Gower's *Modern Company Law* (the first edition of the work cited above) p 515, in which the learned author said that the most likely

ground of action 'is that there is a suspicion of some grave impropriety
. . .', said:

'If the court is entitled to act on "a suspicion of some grave impropriety", it should be satisfied that the suspicion is well-founded and
that it has a solid and substantial basis. A mere feeling that something
might be wrong should not be, and in my opinion is not, enough.'

The reasons for a refusal of a declaration under s 95*bis* in *Gelcer's*
case (see p 64) were that no case of fraud or impropriety had been made
out, that there was not even a suspicion of fraud, and that no case had
been made out justifying interference by the court in what was essentially
a domestic quarrel between two groups of shareholders.

In *Buckingham's* case (*supra*) O'Hagan J, with whom Van der Riet J
concurred, referring to the legal conclusions of Herbstein J in *Gelcer's*
case, said, at 332H:

'I think it is inherent in the reasoning of the learned judge that the
factors enumerated in sub-paras (1) (ii) and (iii) of s 95*bis*(1)(*b*), which
may prompt the Minister to order an investigation, are criteria to
which the court might properly and usefully have regard in determining whether it should come to the aid of an applicant for relief.'

At 333A O'Hagan J said:

'It seems to me . . . that for the purpose of s 95*bis* the court is concerned only with issues of substance, not minor irregularities which
might occur from time to time in any commercial organization. If
the substantial complaints appear to be well-founded, lesser grievances
may tip the balance in favour of the applicants' case, but if the chief
elements in the applicants' contentions do not in any way warrant
the order which is sought, little else calls for consideration.'

The reasons for refusing relief under s 95*bis* in *Buckingham's* case
(see pp 333–4), were that the main complaints had been known to the
directors and shareholders for several years, and had been investigated
and inquired into in the past; that a complaint in regard to the payment
of certain dividends had long since been redressed; that a complaint
of fraud and theft by a former secretary, some five years previously,
had been investigated by the police; that in regard to the remaining
complaints, in which oppression was alleged, the court was being asked
to enquire into events which directors and shareholders had left buried
for many years; that various subsequent incidents did not amount to
oppression, that the matter had been investigated by the police, and that
a request to the Minister for the appointment of an inspector had been
considered and refused.

In *Yende's* case (*supra*) Dowling J, at 316B–D, said that, in general,
the policy of the courts has not been to interfere in the internal domestic
affairs of a company, where the company ought to be able to adjust its
affairs itself by appropriate resolutions of a majority of the shareholders.
On the papers in that case there appeared to be nothing to prevent the
applicant from requisitioning a general meeting of the company to
redress his complaint.

In *Nafte* v *Allied Minerals Ltd* (*supra*) the application was such as to require the court itself to embark upon an extensive enquiry into the affairs of the company, in which many facts were in dispute. De Wet JP at 95A said:

'I have difficulty in believing that the legislature, in enacting the provision in question, envisaged a procedure of this nature. It seems to me that the provision in question should only be invoked when undisputed facts can be placed before the court pointing to the desirability of an inquiry by an inspector. However, the procedure has been sanctioned in previous cases, eg in *Buckingham & others* v *Combined Industries* 1961 (1) SA 326 (E), where the court was faced with a similar inquiry on an unnecessarily bulky record. In *Irvin and Johnson* v *Gelcer & Co (Pty) Ltd* 1958 (2) SA 59 (C) at 63 the opinion is expressed that the court could act on a suspicion of some grave impropriety provided it is satisfied that the suspicion is well-founded and has a solid and substantial basis, and this opinion is approved in the *Buckingham* case (*supra*). On the other hand, in my opinion, the court should only act if it is satisfied that some object is likely to be achieved, eg where in terms of s 95*sext*, the inquiry may lead to the winding-up of the company on the petition of the Minister or when the Minister may take steps for recovery of damages or property by the company.'

At 95E the learned Judge-President said:

'The further suggestion that an inquiry should be ordered merely to satisfy disgruntled shareholders that there is no legitimate cause for complaint is a suggestion which I cannot entertain. Further, when the evidence before the court merely points to a suspicion that a director or shareholder has been guilty of criminal conduct not clearly related to the affairs of the company, this appears to me to be a matter for police investigation and not for an investigation by an inspector appointed by the Minister.'

I am in respectful agreement with each of the legal propositions cited above from the judgments in *Gelcer's* case, *Buckingham's* case, *Yende's* case and *Nafte's* case (all *supra*). In my view there is no conflict between the approach in *Nafte's* case and that in the two earlier cases of *Gelcer* (*supra*) and *Buckingham* (*supra*). In particular, the proposition in *Nafte's* case, that s 95*bis*(1)(ii) should be invoked only when undisputed facts can be placed before the court, means no more than this, that the grounds which make it advisable or desirable that the affairs of the company should be investigated should be undisputed or clearly established. Obviously if those grounds are disputed, the court cannot be expected, for the purposes of deciding an application under s 95*bis*(1)(*a*)(ii), to enter upon an extensive investigation of its own into the affairs of the company. But that does not mean that the existence of any material dispute rules out an order under the section. Indeed, one can readily envisage circumstances in which the existence of a dispute between the board of directors and the shareholders would by itself establish the very ground upon which an investigation becomes desirable.

Turning now to the facts of the present case, I think that the first and second applicants have only themselves to blame for much of their troubles. Their neglect in the handling of their own interests, and their readiness to leave matters entirely in the hands of the first respondent, a young man in his early twenties with no particular training or experience, attract the comment *vigilantibus non dormientibus subvenit lex.* However, notwithstanding this indifference and neglect on their part, and notwithstanding the enthusiastic praise in the affidavit of the companies' auditor, . . . for the excellence of the first respondent's administration, it is evident from the papers that there are circumstances which make it desirable that there should be an investigation.

For obvious reasons, any expression of opinion on those circumstances should be avoided at this stage. I therefore restrict myself to stating the following conclusions:

(*a*) There have been transfers of shares in the companies which appear to require more explanation than has been offered by the first respondent.

(*b*) There appears to have been an attempt by the first respondent, without the requisite authority, to transfer a controlling interest in certain, if not all, of the companies to himself. He says that in fact these transfers were not put into effect, but the fact that they were attempted at one stage is disturbing.

(*c*) The moneys admittedly advanced by the second applicant for the development of the companies appear to have been regarded by the first respondent as personal loans to himself. On either basis the moneys were to be used for the companies, and it is desirable to investigate how such moneys were in fact applied.

(*d*) There appears to have been a withdrawal by the first respondent of moneys standing to the credit of the companies in circumstances which merit further examination. It is true that the second respondent says that he withdrew these moneys on the advice of the auditor, but at the time the companies were short of funds, and it is by no means clear that this transaction was authorized.

(*e*) The evidence suggests extravagance in the leasing of premises and in the monthly running expenses of the companies.

(*f*) At least one of the companies has had a default judgment taken against it for a substantial sum of money.

(*g*) The first respondent's reaction to requests for information on behalf of the second applicant have been such that an important shareholder has not been given all the information with respect to the affairs of the companies which he might reasonably expect. Cf s 95*bis*(1)(*b*)(iii) of the Companies Act. Indeed, the first respondent's admitted response to the requests by the second applicant's attorneys raises a prima facie inference that information is being deliberately withheld.

(*h*) Though the applicant's evidence on the alleged statements by the first respondent, that the patents had been disposed of for R2 000 is in part self-contradictory, and though the first respondent denies these statements, there is prima facie evidence that statements by the first respondent to the Press, in regard to the development and disposal of the patent rights, to the extent that the making of such statements is not disputed, do not tally in material respects with the actual position in the companies. Regard being had to all the circumstances, this too is a disturbing feature.

(i) The management and administration of the companies appears to have been in the hands of the first respondent throughout, and he has been responsible for the events referred to above.

In my view, these several conclusions, as I have stated them, are reasonably clearly established on the papers and are within the several principles discussed above.

As to whether any object is likely to be achieved by an investigation, it is reasonable to suppose that the facts to be elicited will enable these various matters to be cleared up. It may be that the prima facie unsatisfactory features to which I have referred can be fully explained, and that no further action will be required. Or it may be shown that there has been mismanagement, and that a desirable solution is one or other of the remedial steps permitted by the Act. These are matters which cannot be prejudged.

I am accordingly of the opinion that an investigation should be ordered of the affairs of the third, fourth, fifth and sixth respondents. . . .

[330] Maxwell v Department of Trade
[1974] 2 WLR 338, [1974] 2 All ER 122 (CA)

Inspectors had been appointed under s 165 (ss 257, 258 of our Act) to investigate the affairs of a public company. The inspectors prepared an interim report which was published by the Department of Trade and which was highly critical of the plaintiff (the chairman and chief executive of the company). The plaintiff brought an action against the inspectors and the Department claiming a declaration that the inspectors had acted in breach of the rules of natural justice in that, having formulated their tentative criticisms of him, they had failed to give him an opportunity of answering those criticisms before signing their report, and further that they had failed to put to the plaintiff all relevant statements made by other witnesses, or in documents, which were prejudicial to him so as to give him an opportunity of answering them. Relief was denied.

LAWTON LJ: For many decades now the British public have become accustomed to reading about inquiries started by the government of the day or a Minister. Sometimes the inquiries are held, as was the one in this case, under powers given by a statute; others are held because a Minister wants to find out something. The subject-matter of inquiry may range from questions touching the integrity of Ministers (the Lynskey Inquiry), and national security (the Vassall Inquiry), to questions whether a youth was assaulted by two police officers (the Thurso Inquiry). Some inquiries are held in public and a few take on some of the characteristics of a state trial; others are held in private. Whenever inquiries are held the British public expects them to be conducted fairly; and on many occasions in the past 60 years the courts have said that they must be conducted fairly.

From time to time during that period lawyers and judges have tried to define what constitutes fairness. Like defining an elephant, it is not easy to do, although fairness in practice has the elephantine quality of being easy to recognize. As a result of these efforts a word in common usage has acquired the trappings of legalism: 'acting fairly' has become 'acting in accordance with the rules of natural justice', and on occasion has been dressed up with Latin tags. This phrase in my opinion serves no useful purpose and in recent years it has encouraged lawyers to try to put those who hold inquiries into legal straitjackets.

For the purposes of my judgment I intend to ask myself this simple question: did the inspector act fairly towards the plaintiff?

This question cannot be answered without knowledge of what the inspector's were inquiring into. They had been appointed by the Department of Trade and Industry to investigate the affairs of International Learning Systems Corporation Ltd and Pergamon Press Ltd and to report thereon (see s 165(*a*) of the Companies Act 1948). The department made the appointment not because there were circumstances suggesting that the businesses of these companies were being conducted dishonestly or that those connected with their management had been guilty of fraud (see s 165(*b*)(i) and (ii)), but because it had been suggested by the Takeover Panel that Pergamon Press Ltd's shareholders might not have been given all the information with respect to its affairs which they might reasonably have expected (see s 165(*b*)(iii)).

In their terms of reference the inspectors were specifically instructed to report on this matter of information. It followed that they had to find out first what information had been given and then to express their opinion whether enough had been given. What was to be done if they were of the opinion that not enough information had been given, or the affairs of the two companies were in disorder, was not for them to decide. The inspectors were not instructed to investigate any charge against the plaintiff or any other officer of these companies; their duty was to find out what had happened, and to report their opinion. This was a very different task from that which is sometimes imposed on those holding inquiries when they are asked to decide whether allegations of specific misconduct have been made out. . . . That which fairness calls for in one kind of inquiry may not be called for in another. Those conducting an inquiry are in the best position to decide what fairness calls for.

In all these cases there are, in my judgment, two facets of fairness: what is done and how it is done. Doing what is right may still result in unfairness if it is done in the wrong way.

As to what was done, once it became apparent to the inspectors that the plaintiff might be open to criticism in their report, on many occasions they put to him the substance of what other witnesses had said about him which could, if they accepted the evidence, be the basis for criticism. On a few occasions they did not, and by the standards of perfection it might have been better if they had. In putting the substance of what had been said by other witnesses the inspectors were, no doubt, trying to do what those holding inquiries had been enjoined to do by Lord Loreborn LC in *Board of Education* v *Rice* [1911] AC 179, 182, namely to give any one in the plaintiff's position a fair opportunity for correcting or contradicting any relevant statement prejudicial to his view.

What they did not do was to give the plaintiff an opportunity of correcting or contradicting the opinions which they were minded to report to the department as to what evidence they thought credible and what inferences they should draw from such evidence. The plaintiff submits they should have done so, and that their omission constituted unfairness. I do not agree. The plaintiff's submission was founded on some observations made by Sachs LJ during the hearing of what was the first of a series of proceedings which have been started by the plaintiff in respect of this inquiry: see *Re Pergamon Press Ltd* [1971] Ch 388, 405. The learned Lord Justice was there commenting on what the court, of which he was a member, had been told the inspectors had promised to do. The inspectors had said more than what had been reported and that which had not been reported altered the sense. Further, endorsing with his approval what the inspectors were reported to have said was not necessary for the purpose of deciding the appeal. The researches of counsel have not produced any other case which has suggested that at the end of an inquiry those likely to be criticized in a report should be given an opportunity of refuting the tentative conclusions of whoever is making it. Those who conduct inquiries have to base their decisions, findings, conclusions or opinions (whichever is the appropriate word to describe what they have a duty to do) on the evidence. In my judgment they are no more bound to tell a witness likely to be criticized in their report what they have in mind to say about him than has a judge sitting alone who has to decide which of two conflicting witnesses is telling the truth. The judge must ensure that the witness whose credibility is suspected has a fair opportunity of correcting or contradicting the substance of what other witnesses have said or are expected to say which is in conflict with his testimony. Inspectors should do the same but I can see no reason why they should do any more.

There was little criticism of the way the inspectors had done what they did. It was submitted, however, that when putting to the plaintiff for his comments the substance of what witnesses had said they did not make plain what was the sting of their questions, with the result that the plaintiff was deprived of an opportunity of refuting any injurious criticism which was founded on his answers. An example was said to be provided by conclusion (c) in para 319 of the inspectors' report which was to the effect that the plaintiff knew that an offer document contained a false statement. In order to deal with this kind of criticism it is necessary to consider how the inquiry was conducted. Both the inspectors were distinguished professional men. The plaintiff is clearly intelligent and quick witted; he has had an exceptionally wide experience of life and when the inquiry started he was a member of Parliament. He did not have to have spelt out to him the relevance and point of every question he was asked. The inspectors must have appreciated this. It is manifest from the transcript that they treated him throughout with courtesy and patience. . . .

I should say in conclusion that I am doubtful whether, even if I had found on the merits in favour of the plaintiff, I would have adjudged that he was entitled to a declaration that the inquiry had been conducted unfairly or that specified criticisms had been made unfairly. That was the only relief he asked for from this court. Below he had asked for an injunction against the department to restrain further publication of the report, but this he could not get because the department represents the Crown. He had also asked for a declaration that the report was null and void; but before this court, without abandoning this, his counsel did not ask for such a declaration. For my part I cannot see how any such declaration could ever be made in respect of a report made to the Minister under s 165. The courts cannot declare null and void events which have happened. What they can do is to declare that the making of a report shall have no legal consequences. . . . The report in this case itself neither produced, nor could directly produce, any legal consequences. On receiving it the Minister had to decide what action to take; and even if the inquiry had been conducted unfairly the report might have contained information which the Minister would be under a duty to consider for the purpose of performing his statutory duty to safeguard the interests of shareholders. The fact is that a declaration to the effect that the inquiry had been conducted unfairly or that specified criticisms had been made unfairly would produce no practical result. The Minister would not be stopped from initiating proceedings if he thought that the facts justified such a course. It was submitted that such a declaration would protect the plaintiff's reputation. It might; but the protection would only be temporary if the Minister initiated proceedings; and in any proceedings the fact that the inquiry had been conducted unfairly would be irrelevant. In my judgment a man who has been unfairly criticized in a report made under s 165 is in the same position as one who had been unfairly criticized in a speech made in Parliament. He has suffered 'damnum' but not 'injuria'. Cases may occur (although they are unlikely to do so as long as the Minister appoints competent and experienced professional men as inspectors) in which the inspectors had behaved so unfairly that the public interest requires a court to say so. In my judgment, even if there had been unfairness in the conduct of this inquiry, which there was not, this is not such a case.

NOTES

See also the case of *Re Allied Produce Co Ltd* [1967] 1 WLR 1469, where Buckley J emphasized the distinction between a contested and uncontested application for a winding-up order in relation to the weight to be attached to an inspector's report; further *Re Travel & Holiday Clubs Ltd* [1967] 1 WLR 711, [1967] 2 All ER 606, and *Re SBA Properties Ltd* [1967] 1 WLR 799, [1967] 2 All ER 615.

In the Australian case of *Testro Bros (Pty) Ltd* v *Tait* (1963) 109 CLR 353, (1963–4) 37 *ALJR* 100, it was held that an inspector in charge of an investigation of a company's affairs is not obliged to give the company an opportunity of placing its side of the case before him, before he makes his report to the Minister.

On the admissibility of evidence given before an inspector, see *R* v *Harris* [1970] 3 All ER 746 and *Karak Rubber Co Ltd* v *Burden* [1971] 3 All ER 1118.

See also R D Fraser 'Administrative Powers of Investigation into Companies' (1971) 34 *MLR* 260 and Gerard Nash (1965) 38 *ALJ* 111 and (1967) 8 *University of West Aust LR* 143.

Dividends and Profits

I Dividends

A TEXT

A dividend is a share in the profits of a company. The manner in which profits are to be divided is determined by the constitution of the company. As a rule the articles provide that dividends are declared by the company in general meeting but that no dividend may exceed the amount recommended by the directors (see Table A art 84, Table B art 83) and that the directors may pay interim dividends (see Table A art 85, Table B art 84): *331*.

Usually the articles prescribe that no dividend may be paid otherwise than out of profits (see Table A art 86, Table B art 85), but, irrespective of what the constitution of the company says, dividends may not be paid out of capital: *332, 333*; also *Flitcroft's* case, *235* above, and *Cohen NO v Segal, 84* above. A company which issues shares in order to raise money for the construction of works, buildings or a plant, which cannot be made profitable for a lengthened period, may pay interest out of capital, subject to the requirements of s 79 being satisfied.

A company is not obliged to distribute all its profits by way of dividend but may place part or all of them to reserve (see Table A art 87, Table B art 86): *334, 335*. Instead of paying a dividend out of them, profits may be applied in paying up unissued shares to be issued to members as capitalization or bonus shares: *336–338*.

Unless payment in some other way is authorized by the articles dividends must be paid in cash: *339*. The fact that the company has not sufficient ready cash available does not prevent it from declaring a dividend—it may borrow the necessary moneys (but see also *346*, below).

A dividend becomes due if and when declared: *340*. In the winding up of a company a contributory is not entitled to set off against his liability to the company any amount due to him by the company in respect of dividends, s 397(2)(b).

As to the rights of preference shareholders, see above, p 171.

If shares are sold, a dividend declared after the date of the sale belongs to the buyer, unless the sale is 'ex dividend' (see above, p 252).

B CASES

[331] Nicholson v Rhodesia Trading Company
[1897] 1 Ch 434

The articles of a company provided that the final dividend was to be sanctioned at the annual general meeting and accounts up to a date within three months of that meeting were to be submitted.

NORTH J: . . . In my opinion, on the construction of those articles, a dividend is to be sanctioned only at the annual ordinary general meeting of the company to be held in July or August, when the accounts up to a period within three months of the meeting and other full information have to be submitted to the shareholders; and they are to have the opportunity, among other things, of fully considering the expenditure and the income of the company. If the directors could obtain the sanction of a dividend in the way proposed, without submitting the accounts required by the articles, by calling an extraordinary meeting, it would be giving the go-by to the provisions made for the protection of the shareholders. I am of opinion, therefore, that a dividend cannot be sanctioned at an extraordinary meeting; and that, even if it could be sanctioned, it would be necessary to follow the requirements of the articles, and lay before the company the matters required to be so laid down before them by the articles. In the present case they cannot do this, because the accounts are brought down only to August last, which is much more than three months ago. . . .

[332] Rance's case
(1870) 6 Ch App 104

MELLISH LJ: . . . In my opinion . . . a declaration of bonus without any profit or loss account having been made out is a mala fide proceeding on the part of the directors. . . . I quite agree that if directors or a proper actuary had made out a profit and loss account the court ought to assume, very strongly indeed, that it was a correct account, and ought not without very strong reasons showing that it was done mala fide, to set it aside, or declare a dividend made upon it improper. But, if directors choose to declare a bonus or a dividend without making out any account at all, and if shareholders choose to vote that dividend or bonus, knowing that they have got no account before them, knowing that the directors do not even profess to have made a profit out of which that bonus or dividend can be declared, I cannot help thinking that under those circumstances it lies on the parties who contend that such bonus or dividend was properly declared, to show that it was made out of profits. . . .

[333] Moxham *v* Grant
[1900] 1 QB 88

Directors illegally distributed part of the capital of a company among its shareholders who received their shares knowing that they were paid out of capital. After the company was being wound up the court ordered the directors to replace the money. It was held that the directors were entitled to an indemnity from the shareholders.

COLLINS LJ: . . . When the circumstances of this case are considered, it cannot be disputed that the liquidator could have enforced his claim to recover the capital improperly distributed against the individual shareholders to the extent of the amounts that they had received. He could also enforce against the directors his claim in respect of the whole sum. That is what he has done; and we, therefore, start with these facts. The directors who distributed the money were liable, and the persons to whom it was distributed were also liable, and the former were compelled to pay the whole amount distributed. Moreover, that payment has operated in relief of the shareholders. On those facts—namely, a payment under compulsion by one of a sum of money for which another was liable, and in relief of that other—there is an implication of law that the payer has a right to be recouped by the person relieved. . . .

NOTES

Moxham v *Grant* appears to be the only case in England where the director's right of recourse against shareholders was affirmed. The prevailing American view appears to be that shareholders who bona fide received an improperly paid dividend are not liable to repay it. In South Africa, the matter would be dealt with, presumably, in accordance with the principles governing unjust enrichment.

The memorandum or the articles can prohibit the payment of dividends out of unrealized profits or out of non-trading profits. See e g *Quadrangle Investments (Pty) Ltd* v *Witind Holdings Ltd, 34* above, where the memorandum provided that profits resulting from the sale of investments should not be treated as revenue available for the payment of dividends.

On payment of dividends out of capital see further *Turquand* v *Marshall* (1869) 4 Ch App 376; *Holmes* v *Newcastle-upon-Tyne Freehold Abattoir Co* (1875) 1 ChD 682; *In re National Funds Assurance Co* (1878) 10 ChD 118; *In re Alexandra Palace Co* (1882) 21 ChD 149; *In re Denham & Co* (1883) 25 ChD 752; *Leeds Estate Building and Investment Co* v *Shepherd* (1887) 36 ChD 787; *In re Sharpe* [1892] 1 ChD 154; *Dovey* v *Cory* [1901] AC 477 (*341* below); *Towers* v *African Tug Co* [1904] 1 Ch 558.

The constitution of a company cannot validly provide that the capital contributed by one class of shareholders shall be applied, if necessary, so as to make good a preferential dividend to be paid to another class of shareholders: *Guinness* v *Land Corporation of Ireland* (*83* above). A third party can validly undertake to make up the profits of a company to a certain amount or to guarantee a minimum dividend: *In re South Llanharran Colliery Co* (1879) 12 ChD 503. See also *In re Menell et Cie Ltd* [1915] 1 Ch 759; *In re Walters' Deed of Guarantee* [1933] Ch 321.

There is no onus on the directors to prove that dividends were in fact paid out of profits: *In re City Equitable Fire Insurance Co Ltd* [1925] Ch 407 at 477.

Any shareholder can sue to have payment of a dividend out of capital restrained.

[334] **Burland *v* Earle**
[1902] AC 83 (PC)

LORD DAVEY: ... Their Lordships are not aware of any principle which compels a joint stock company, while a going concern, to divide the whole of its profits amongst its shareholders. Whether the whole or any part should be divided, or what portion should be divided and what portion retained, are entirely questions of internal management which the shareholders must decide for themselves, and the court has no jurisdiction to control or review their decision, or to say what is a 'fair' or 'reasonable' sum to retain undivided, or what reserve fund may be 'properly' required. And it makes no difference whether the undivided balance is retained to the credit of profit and loss account, or carried to the credit of a rest or reserve fund, or appropriated to any other use of the company. These are questions for the shareholders to decide subject to any restrictions or directions contained in the articles of association or by-laws of the company.

If the company may form a reserve or retain a balance of undivided profits, it must, it would seem, have power to invest the moneys so retained. [Counsel] for the respondents contended that the company, in the absence of express power to invest, could employ the money only in its own business. This contention has no support either in principle or in authority. . . .

. . . If it appeared that under the guise of investing undivided profits or the reserve fund the directors were, in fact, embarking the moneys of the company in speculative transactions, or otherwise abusing the powers vested in them for the management of the company's business, different considerations would of course arise. . . .

[335] **Dodge *v* Ford Motor Company**
(1919) 204 Mich 459, 170 NW 668

Action to compel the defendant company to declare a dividend. The trial court made an order in terms of the prayer. The Ford Motor Co appealed.

OSTANDER J: The rule which will govern courts in deciding these questions is not in dispute. . . . This court, in *Hunter* v *Roberts, Throp & Co* 83 Mich 63, 71; 47 NW 131, 134, recognized [it] in the following language:

> 'It is a well-recognized principle of law that the directors of a corporation, and they alone, have the power to declare a dividend of the earnings of the corporation, and to determine its amount. Courts of equity will not interfere in the management of the directors unless it is clearly made to appear that they are guilty of fraud or misappropriation of the corporate funds, or refuse to declare a dividend when the corporation has a surplus of net profits which it can, without detriment to its business, divide among its stockholders, and when a refusal to do so would amount to such an abuse of discretion as would constitute a fraud, or breach of that good faith which they are bound to exercise towards the stockholders.'

When plaintiffs made their complaint and demand for further dividends, the Ford Motor Company had concluded its most prosperous year of business. The demand for its cars at the price of the preceding year continued. It could make and could market in the year beginning 1 August 1916 more than 500 000 cars. Sales of parts and repairs would necessarily increase. The cost of materials was likely to advance, and perhaps the price of labour; but it reasonably might have expected a profit for the year of upwards of $60 000 000. It had assets of more than $132 000 000, a surplus of almost $112 000 000, and its cash on hand and municipal bonds were nearly $54 000 000. Its total liabilities, including capital stock, was a little over $20 000 000. It had declared no special dividend during the business year except the October 1915 dividend. It had been the practice, under similar circumstances, to declare larger dividends. Considering only these facts, a refusal to declare and pay further dividends appears to be not an exercise of discretion on the part of the directors, but an arbitrary refusal to do what the circumstances required to be done. These facts and others call upon the directors to justify their action, or failure or refusal to act. In justification, the defendants have offered testimony tending to prove, and which does prove, the following facts: It had been the policy of the corporation for a considerable time to annually reduce the selling price of cars, while keeping up, or improving, their quality. As early as in June 1915 a general plan for the expansion of the productive capacity of the concern by a practical duplication of its plant had been talked over by the executive officers and directors and agreed upon.... The erection of a smelter was considered, and engineering and other data in connection therewith secured. In consequence, it was determined not to reduce the selling price of cars for the year beginning 1 August 1915 but to maintain the price and to accumulate a large surplus to pay for the proposed expansion of plant and equipment, and perhaps to build a plant for smelting ore. It is hoped, by Mr Ford, that eventually 1 000 000 cars will be annually produced. The contemplated changes will permit the increased output.

The plan, as affecting the profits of the business for the year beginning 1 August 1916 and thereafter, calls for a reduction in the selling price of the cars. It is true that this price might be at any time increased, but the plan called for the reduction in price of $80 a car. The capacity of the plant, without the additions thereto voted to be made (without a part of them at least), would produce more than 600 000 cars annually. This number, and more, could have been sold for $440 instead of $360, a difference in the return for capital, labour, and materials employed of at least $48 000 000. In short, the plan does not call for and is not intended to produce immediately a more profitable business, but a less profitable one; not only less profitable than formerly, but less profitable than it is admitted it might be made. The apparent immediate effect will be to diminish the value of shares and the returns to shareholders.

It is the contention of plaintiffs that the apparent effect of the plan is intended to be the continued and continuing effect of it, and that it is deliberately proposed ... to continue the corporation henceforth as a semi-eleemosynary institution and not as a business institution. In support of this contention, they point to the attitude and to the expressions of Mr Henry Ford.

Mr Henry Ford is the dominant force in the business of the Ford Motor Company. No plan of operations could be adopted unless he consented, and no board of directors can be elected whom he does not favour. . . .

> 'My ambition', said Mr Ford, 'is to employ still more men, to spread the benefits of this industrial system to the greatest possible number, to help them build up their lives and their homes. To do this we are putting the greatest share of our profits back into the business.'

The record, and especially the testimony of Mr Ford, convinces that he has to some extent the attitude towards shareholders of one who has dispensed and distributed to them large gains and that they should be content to take what he chooses to give. His testimony creates the impression, also, that he thinks the Ford Motor Company has made too much money, has had too large profits, and that, although large profits might be still earned, a sharing of them with the public, by reducing the price of the output of the company, ought to be undertaken. We have no doubt that certain sentiments, philanthropic and altruistic, creditable to Mr Ford, had large influence in determining the policy to be pursued by the Ford Motor Company—the policy which has been herein referred to.

There is committed to the discretion of directors, a discretion to be exercised in good faith, the infinite details of business, including the wages which shall be paid to employees, the number of hours they shall work, the conditions under which labour shall be carried on, and the price for which products shall be offered to the public.

It is said by appellants that the motives of the board members are not material and will not be inquired into by the court so long as their acts are within their lawful powers. As we have pointed out, and the proposition does not require argument to sustain it, it is not within the lawful powers of a board of directors to shape and conduct the affairs of a corporation for the merely incidental benefit of shareholders and for the primary purpose of benefiting others, and no one will contend that, if the avowed purpose of the defendant directors was to sacrifice the interests of shareholders, it would not be the duty of the courts to interfere.

Defendants say, and it is true, that a considerable cash balance must be at all times carried by such a concern. But, as has been stated, there was a large daily, weekly, monthly, receipt of cash. The output was practically continuous and was continuously, and within a few days, turned into cash. Moreover, the contemplated expenditures were not to be immediately made. . . . So that, without going further, it would appear that, accepting and approving the plan of the directors, it was their duty to distribute on or near 1 August 1916 a very large sum of money to stockholders.

In reaching this conclusion, we do not ignore, but recognize, the validity of the proposition that plaintiffs have from the beginning profited by, if they have not lately, officially, participated in, the general policy of expansion pursued by this corporation. We do not lose sight of the fact that it had been, upon an occasion, agreeable to the plaintiffs to increase the capital stock to $100 000 000 by a stock dividend of $98 000 000. These things go only to answer other contentions now made by plaintiffs, and do not and cannot operate to estop them to demand proper dividends upon the stock they own. It is obvious that an annual dividend of 60 per cent upon $2 000 000 or $1 200 000 is the equivalent of a very small dividend upon $100 000 000 or more.

The decree of the court below fixing and determining the specific amount to be distributed to stockholders is affirmed.

NOTES

Dodge v *Ford Motor Company*, decided in 1919, has remained an isolated case. In small private companies it happens occasionally that the majority shareholders use a combination of high salaries for the directors (themselves) and low (or no) dividends to squeeze inconvenient minority shareholders out. The remedy is an application under s 252, but the onus on the complainant is a heavy one, see *321* above.

[336] Commissioners of Inland Revenue v Blott
[1921] 2 AC 171

Held (Lord Dunedin and Lord Sumner dissenting) that for tax purposes bonus shares constituted capital, and not income.

VISCOUNT HALDANE: . . . I think that it is, as matter of principle, within the power of an ordinary joint stock company with articles such as those in the case before us to determine conclusively against the whole world whether it will withhold profits it has accumulated from distribution to its shareholders as income, and as an alternative not distribute them at all, but apply them in paying up the capital sums which shareholders electing to take up unissued shares would otherwise have to contribute. If this is done the money so applied is capital and never becomes profits in the hands of the shareholder at all. What the latter gets is no doubt a valuable thing. But it is a thing in the nature of an extra share certificate in the company. His new shares do not give him an immediate right to a larger amount of the existing assets. These remain where they were. The new shares simply confer a title to a larger proportion of the surplus assets, if and when a·general distribution takes place as in a winding-up. In these assets the undistributed profits now allocated to capital will be included, profits which will be used by the company for its business but henceforth as part of its issued share capital. . . .

[337] Pool v The Guardian Investment Trust Company Ltd
[1922] 1 KB 347

Where a dividend is paid, partly in cash and partly in shares in another company, the whole dividend constitutes income, and must be distinguished from a division of profits by the issue of bonus shares.

SANKEY J: . . . As Pitney J points out in giving the judgment of the Supreme Court of the United States [*Eisner* v *Macomber* (1920) 252 US

189 at 206], the fundamental relation of capital to income has been much discussed by economists, the former being likened to the tree or the land, the latter to the fruit or the crop; the former depicted as a reservoir supplied from springs, the latter as the outlet stream to be measured by its flow during a period of time. He cites on the subsequent page various definitions, one of which was that income may be defined as the gain derived from capital, from labour, or from both combined, and points out that the essential matter is that income is not a gain accruing to capital but a gain derived from capital.

Applying the metaphor of a reservoir to *Blott's* case [1921] 2 AC 171, the facts found therein may be stated as follows: From the reservoir of capital certain proceeds were allowed to flow down the outlet stream, but these proceeds were not allowed to reach the shareholder. The company enlarged the area of the reservoir and put back the proceeds into the enlarged reservoir; in other words, the proceeds in that case never became the profit or gain or income of the shareholder, but were put back into the capital of the company and the unissued shares issued to the shareholder in respect thereof.

In the present case just the opposite has happened. The proceeds have been allowed to flow down the outlet stream, but they have not been put back into capital. They have been allowed to reach the shareholder in the form of a cash payment and a dividend in specie of the shares of another company, or, as Lord Halsbury put it in *Tennant* v *Smith* [1892] AC 150 at 156, there has been a distribution of money and of money's worth. I am far from saying that there can never be a distribution of capital to the shareholders of the company. There might certainly be such a distribution in the case of the voluntary winding-up of a company and the division of its capital assets among the shareholders, but in the present case I am entirely unable to say that there was any distribution of capital, as distinguished from profits or gains. . . .

[338] Hill v Permanent Trustee Company of New South Wales Ltd

[1930] AC 720 (PC)

A company carrying on pastoral farming in New South Wales sold substantially the whole of its lands, livestock and other assets in 1925, ceasing to carry on business. In 1926 a dividend was declared and paid as 'a distribution of capital assets in advance of the winding-up'. In 1927 a further dividend was paid out of the sale of the breeding stock. The Privy Council decided that the dividends constituted 'income' in the hands of the recipients.

LORD RUSSELL OF KILLOWEN: . . . A limited company not in liquidation can make no payment by way of return of capital to its shareholders except as a step in an authorized reduction of capital. Any other payment made by it by means of which it parts with moneys to its shareholders must and can only be made by way of dividing profits. Whether the payment is called 'dividend' or 'bonus', or any other name, it still must remain a payment on division of profits. . . .

... Other considerations arise when a limited company with power to increase its capital and possessing a fund of undivided profits, so deals with it that no part of it leaves the possession of the company, but the whole is applied in paying up new shares which are issued and allotted proportionately to the shareholders, who would have been entitled to receive the fund had it been, in fact, divided and paid away as dividend.

... The result of such a dealing is obviously wholly different from the result of paying away the profits to the shareholders. In the latter case the amount of cash distributed disappears on both sides of the company's balance sheet. It is lost to the company. The fund of undistributed profits which has been divided ceases to figure among the company's liabilities; the cash necessary to provide the dividend is raised and paid away, the company's assets being reduced by that amount. In the former case the assets of the company remain undiminished, but on the liabilities' side of the balance sheet (although the total remains unchanged) the item representing undivided profits disappears, its place being taken by a corresponding increase of liability in respect of issued share capital. In other words, moneys which had been capable of division by the company as profits among its shareholders have ceased for all time to be so divisible, and can never be paid to the shareholders except upon a reduction of capital or in a winding-up. . . .

NOTES

See further *Bouch* v *Sproule* (1887) 12 App Cas 385; *In re Bates* [1928] Ch 682.

[339] Wood *v* Odessa Waterworks Company
(1889) 42 ChD 636

STIRLING J: . . . The question . . . is whether it is within the power of a majority of the shareholders to insist against the will of a minority that the profits which have been actually earned shall be divided, not by the payment of cash, but by the issue of debenture-bonds of the company bearing interest at £5 per cent and repayable at par by an annual drawing extending over 30 years. . . . Now the rights of the shareholders in respect of a division of the profits of the company are governed by the provisions in the articles of association. . . . Those articles provide that the directors may, with the sanction of a general meeting, declare a dividend to be paid to the shareholders. Prima facie that means to be paid in cash. The debenture-bonds proposed to be issued are not payments in cash; they are merely agreements or promises to pay; and if the contention of the company prevails a shareholder will be compelled to accept in lieu of cash a debt of the company payable at some uncertain future period. In my opinion that contention ought not to prevail. . . .

... It was said that nothing could be more reasonable than that this company should be able to pay dividends in the manner proposed, or by the division in specie of assets of the company, eg fully paid-up shares in another company held by the defendant company. With those considerations, however, I have nothing to do. They might properly have been weighed by the framers of the articles of association. . . .

[340] Bond *v* Barrow Haematite Steel Company
[1902] 1 Ch 353

FARWELL J: . . . The necessity for the declaration of a dividend as a condition precedent to an action to recover is stated in general terms in *Lindley on Companies* 5 ed 437. . . . [T]he shareholder has no right to any payment until the corporate body has determined that the money can properly be paid away. . . .

NOTES

Where the directors declare an interim dividend without naming a time for payment, shareholders do not acquire an enforceable right to payment until a date for payment is set: *Potel* v *IRC* [1971] 2 All ER 504 (Ch).

'Neither the court nor the liquidator can assume the function of declaring a dividend after a company has gone into liquidation': per Simonds J in *In re Syston and Thurmaston Gas, Light and Coke Co Ltd* [1937] 2 All ER 322 at 324. See also *Inland Revenue Commissioners* v *Burrell* [1924] 2 KB 52.

See further *New Union Goldfields Ltd* v *CIR* 1950 (3) SA 392 (AD), esp at 402; *Boyd* v *CIR* 1951 (3) SA 525 (AD), esp at 534. But see also *Estate McGregor* v *De Beers Cons Mines* (1903) 20 SC 284.

On recovery of a loan lent to a company in trust for the specific purpose of enabling it to pay a declared dividend, where this purpose can no longer be carried out owing to the company's having gone into liquidation, see *Quistclose Investments Ltd* v *Rolls Razor Ltd* [1968] Ch 540, [1968] 1 All ER 613 (CA).

The right to a dividend is 'property' within the meaning of the Succession Act: *Estate Brownstein* v *CIR* 1957 (3) SA 512 (AD).

II PROFITS AVAILABLE FOR DIVIDEND

A TEXT

Profits are the earnings of the company less the expenses of making them (cf *Vulcan Motors and Engineering Company* v *Hampson* [1921] 3 KB 597). Subject to the proviso that dividends may not be paid out of capital (see above, p 558), it is left to the judgment of the business men in charge of the company to determine what profit is available for dividend: *341, 342*.

There is no rule that the paid-up capital of a company must be intact before a dividend can be paid out of the excess of revenue over expenses. It follows that losses of fixed capital need not be made good before treating a revenue profit as available for dividend. Losses of circulating capital in the current accounting period must be made good before a dividend may be paid, but trading losses in past accounting periods can normally be ignored: *343–352*.

Realized profits on the sale of fixed assets and other non-trading profits may be treated as profit available for dividend if there is an overall surplus of assets over liabilities: *353, 354*. Whether an unrealized increase in the value of fixed assets may be added to the revenue account is controversial, but if a bona fide revaluation of fixed assets, which were previously written down, shows an appreciation in their real value over their written-down value, sums written off in the past may be written back to revenue account: *355–357*.

The share premium account and the capital redemption reserve fund may not be treated as a profit available for dividend but may be applied in paying up unissued shares to be issued to members as fully-paid capitalization shares, ss 76(3), 98(4): *358*.

Substantial repairs or improvements which may be expected to last for some years may be charged to capital account or distributed as a charge on revenue account over a number of years.

Clause 14 of Schedule 4 to the Companies Act requires fixed assets to be distinguished from current assets. Clause 16 deals with the value to be placed on fixed assets, clause 25 with the value to be placed on current assets. On depreciation of fixed assets, see clauses 16(1)(*b*) and 141. Clause 36(*e*) lays down that profits or losses on the realization of non-trading, and fixed and other non-current capital assets, must be shown separately in the income statement. Furthermore, if not otherwise shown, the following must be stated by way of note in the profit and loss account: any material respects in which any items included in the income statement are affected by transactions not usually undertaken by the company or otherwise by circumstances of an exceptional or non-recurrent nature, by any change in the basis of accounting or by any change in the methods for the determination of the amounts of any assets, clause 43 (cf *Lord Kylsant's* case, p 116 above).

B CASES

[341] Dovey *v* Cory
[1901] AC 477

LORD MACNAGHTEN: . . . I do not think it desirable for any tribunal to do that which Parliament has abstained from doing—that is, to formulate precise rules for the guidance or embarrassment of business men in the conduct of business affairs. There never has been, and I think there never will be, much difficulty in dealing with any particular case on its own facts and circumstances; and, speaking for myself, I rather doubt the wisdom of attempting to do more. . . .

[342] Stringer's case [*In re* Mercantile Trading Company]
(1869) 4 Ch App 475

A company was formed in England during the American Civil War to run the blockade maintained by the Federal States and trade with the Confederacy. In 1864 a dividend was declared upon a balance sheet in which the ships engaged in running the blockade, cotton in the Confederate States, and a debt due from the Confederate Government, were estimated at their full nominal value. The victory of the Federal Government led to the failure of the company. A number of its ships had been lost. The cotton appropriated to it in the Confederate States had been destroyed or captured. The debt due from the Confederate

Government was worthless. On the winding-up of the company, the liquidator sought to obtain repayment by the managing director of the dividend received by him on the grounds that the balance sheet had been delusive and the dividend paid out of capital. The action failed.

SELWYN LJ: . . . If it is made to appear that for the purposes of fraud, or for any other improper motive, a company has declared and paid a wholly delusive and improper dividend, and has thereby in effect taken away from its creditors a portion of the capital which was available for the debts of those creditors, I entertain no doubt that the court would have full jurisdiction, and would exercise it by ordering the repayment of the money so improperly paid. But in the present case we have to consider whether this dividend was, in truth, a dividend declared under such circumstances. . . .

. . . I think that . . . the company was fully justified in putting a value on the ships and on the Confederate debt; and inasmuch as it is clear that, having regard to the extremely hazardous nature of the operations in which the ships were engaged, no insurance of them could be effected, the valuation of the ships became a matter of mere estimate; and inasmuch as with respect to the value of the obligation on the part of the Confederate Government, there could be no fixed principle on which it could be valued—for it depended upon the views which different persons might take, and we know well what different views were taken by very eminent persons with respect to the probable conclusion of that great struggle—I think the company was justified in doing that which, in truth, is done in almost every business, namely taking the facts as they actually stood, and forming an estimate of their assets as they actually existed, and then drawing a balance so as to ascertain the result in the shape of profit or of loss. . . .

. . . If we were to lay down as a rule that there must be actually cash in hand, or at the bankers of the company, to the full amount of the dividend declared, we should be laying down a rule which, in my judgment, would be inconsistent with what I understand and believe to be the custom of all companies of this description, and also inconsistent with mercantile usage, and we should be laying down a rule which would open the door to and encourage a very great amount of litigation, because there are very few dividends indeed which would not be open to more or less question if such a rule as that were laid down. I think that in the absence of any fraudulent intent as against the shareholders, or as against the creditors or the public, the court ought not to be astute in searching out minute errors in calculation, in an account honestly made out and openly declared. . . .

. . . The mode in which the matter was done was fair enough. The books were put into the hands of an accountant, calculations were made, and a certain conclusion was arrived at. True it is, no doubt, that these proceedings were full of risk; but although, on the one hand, there might be a great loss everyone knows that whenever there was a success the profits were something very enormous, and upon the balance sheets as taken from the books it did appear that there was a profit of £42 000, and it was proposed out of that to divide somewhere about £28 000, the profits, I agree, not being profits in hand. The fault that is found with that is, that the estimate was an erroneous estimate; that too sanguine a view was taken of the prospects of success; and that there ought to have been a very much less sum put upon the face of the balance sheet as assets than really was put there. But I do not think that anyone can say it was not at this date possible for honest persons carrying on this trade, entertaining the view which they did entertain as to their prospects, honestly to make out such a balance sheet as this, and honestly to believe that those were profits fairly divisible between them. As I have said before, this was not done in any under-hand manner; the whole thing was patent and open; it was known, or capable of being known, by every shareholder. . . .

[343] **Davison v Gillies**
(1879) 16 ChD 347n

The articles of association of a tramway company provided that no dividend should be declared except 'out of profits' and that the directors should, before recommending a dividend, set aside 'out of profits', subject to the sanction of the company, 'a reserve fund for maintenance, repairs, depreciation, and renewals'. The company declared a dividend, without having set aside a reserve fund adequate for the maintenance of the tramways which had become worn out. On an application by the shareholders, the court granted an order restraining the company from paying the dividend.

JESSEL MR: . . . The result . . . of the articles, as I read them, is that a dividend shall only be declared out of net profits.

. . . What are net profits? A tramway company lay down a new tramway. Of course the ordinary wear and tear of the rails and sleepers, and so on, causes a sum of money to be required from year to year in repairs. It may or may not be desirable to do the repairs all at once; but if at the end of the first year the line of tramway is still in so good a state of repair that it requires nothing to be laid out on it for repairs in that year, still, before you can ascertain the net profits, a sum of money ought to be set aside as representing the amount in which the wear and tear of the line has, I may say, so far depreciated it in value as that that sum will be required for the next year or next two years.

Take the case of a warehouse. Supposing a warehouse-keeper, having a new warehouse, should find at the end of the year that he had no occasion to expend money in repairs, but thought that, by reason of the usual wear and tear of the warehouse, it was a thousand pounds worse than it was at the beginning of the year, he would set aside £1 000 for a repair or renewal or depreciation fund before he estimated any profits; because, although the sum is not required to be paid in that year, still it is the sum of money which is lost, so to say, out of capital, and which must be replaced. I should think no commercial man would doubt, that this is the right course—that he must not calculate net profits until he has provided for all the ordinary repairs and wear and tear occasioned by his business. In many businesses there is a regular sum or proportion of some kind set aside for this purpose. Shipowners, I believe, generally reckon so much a year for depreciation of a ship as it gets older. Experience tells them how much they ought to set aside; and whether the ship is repaired in one year or another makes no difference in estimating the profits, because they know a certain sum must be set aside each year to meet the extra repairs of the ship as it becomes older. There are very many other businesses in which the same thing is done. That being so, it appears to me that you can have no net profits unless this sum has been set aside. . . .

Now, when I come to look at these articles, I think that is what is intended, and that that is the meaning of the reserve fund. What the company intended to do was this: inasmuch as they knew that maintenance, repairs, depreciation and renewals would be wanted, and inasmuch as they knew that according to the ordinary commercial rules they ought not to calculate the net profits until they had provided for this which was sure to happen, they said, 'We will set aside a sum of money which we will call a reserve fund for this purpose'. Although not expended during the year, it is a reserve fund set aside for expenditure in the following years, taken out of profits before a dividend is made. It appears to me, therefore, that these articles do recognize what seem to me sound commercial principles.

[See also *Dent* v *London Tramways Co* (1880) 16 ChD 344; *Edwards* v *Saunton Hotel Co Ltd* [1943] 1 All ER 176.]

[344] Lee *v* Neuchatel Asphalte Company
(1889) 41 ChD 1

LINDLEY LJ: . . . This company was formed in 1873 . . . for the purpose of working a concession, which may be called a lease, of some asphalt mines or mineral property in Switzerland. The original lease was afterwards extended, and the company may be treated as having been formed for the purpose of acquiring a lease which will run out in 1907. It is obvious with respect to such property, as with respect to various other properties of a like kind, mines and quarries and so on, every ton of stuff which you get out of that which you have bought with your capital may, from one point of view, be considered as embodying and containing a small portion of your capital, and that if you sell it and divide the proceeds you divide some portion of that which you have spent your capital in acquiring. It may be represented that that is a return of capital. All I can say is, if that is a return of capital it appears to me not to be such a return of capital as is prohibited by law. . . .

. . . There is nothing at all in the Act about how dividends are to be paid, nor how profits are to be reckoned; all that is left, and very judiciously and properly left, to the commercial world. It is not a subject for an Act of Parliament to say how accounts are to be kept; what is to be put into a capital account, what into an income account, is left to men of business. . . .

. . . This company having been formed for the purposes to which I have alluded, the articles contain clauses about distribution of profits. . . . [Clause 100] says: 'The directors may, before recommending any dividend on any of the shares, set aside out of the net profits of the company such sum as they think proper as a reserve fund to meet contingencies, or for equalizing dividends, or for repairing or maintaining the works connected with the business of the company or any part thereof, and the directors may invest the sum so set apart as a reserve fund . . . but they shall not be bound to form a fund or otherwise reserve moneys for the renewal or replacing of any lease, or of the company's interest in any property or concessions.'

First of all, let us see what that means. We are dealing with a lease for a limited number of years, which is a wasting property; and while it is wasting the capital spent in acquiring it is wasting. The article says in so many words that although in every year the capital may be wasted by working out the mine so that at the end there may be nothing left, yet this company is formed on the principle that it shall not be obliged to replace year by year that which is so wasted. [We are told] that is contrary to law. Let us see whether that is made out.

. . . I may safely say that the Companies Acts do not require the capital to be made up if lost. They contain no provision of the kind. There is not even any provision that if the capital is lost the company should be wound up, and I think this omission is quite reasonable. The capital may be lost and yet the company may be a very thriving concern. As I pointed out in the course of the argument, . . . suppose a company is formed to start a daily newspaper; supposing it sinks £250 000 before the receipts from sales and advertisements equal the current expenses, and supposing it then goes on, is it to be said that the company must come to a stop, or that it cannot divide profits until it has replaced its £250 000 which has been sunk in building up a property which if put up for sale would perhaps not yield £10 000? That is a business matter left to business men. If they think their prospects of success are considerable, so long as they pay their creditors, there is no reason why they should not go on and divide profits, so far as I can see, although every shilling of the capital may be lost. It may be a perfectly flourishing concern, and the contrary view I think is to be traced to this, that there is a sort of notion that the company is debtor to capital. In an accountant's point of view, it is quite right, in order to see how you stand, to put down company debtor to capital. But the company do not owe the capital. What it means is simply this: that if you want to find out how you stand, whether you have lost your money or not, you must bring your capital into account somehow or other. But supposing at the winding-up of the concern the capital is all gone, and the creditors are paid, and there is nothing to divide, who is the debtor? No one is debtor to any one. If there is any surplus to divide, then, and not before, is the company debtor to the shareholders for their aliquot portions of that surplus. But the notion that a company is debtor to capital, although it is a convenient notion, and does not deceive mercantile men, is apt to lead one astray. The company is not debtor to capital; the capital is not a debt of the company.

Having shown from the Acts (negatively, of course, because this is a negative proposition, and can only be proved by looking through the Acts) that the Acts do not require the capital to be made up if lost,

I cannot find anything in them which precludes payment of dividends so long as the assets are of less value than the original capital. . . .

. . . If a company is formed to acquire and work a property of a wasting nature, for example, a mine, a quarry, or a patent, the capital expended in acquiring the property may be regarded as sunk and gone, and if the company retains assets sufficient to pay its debts, it appears to me that there is nothing whatever in the Act to prevent any excess of money obtained by working the property over the cost of working it, from being divided amongst the shareholders, and this in my opinion is true, although some portion of the property itself is sold, and in some sense the capital is thereby diminished. If it is said that such a course involves payment of dividend out of capital, the answer is that the Act nowhere forbids such a payment as is here supposed. . . .

. . . You must not have fictitious accounts. If your earnings are less than your current expenses, you must not cook your accounts so as to make it appear that you are earning a profit, and you must not lay your hands on your capital to pay dividend. But it is, I think, a misapprehension to say that dividing the surplus after payment of expenses of the produce of your wasting property is a return of capital in any such sense as is forbidden by the Act   . .

. . . As regards the mode of keeping accounts, there is no law prescribing how they shall be kept. There is nothing in the Acts to show what is to go to capital account or what is to go to revenue account. We know perfectly well that business men very often differ in opinion about such things. It does not matter to the creditor out of what fund he gets paid, whether he gets paid out of capital or out of profit net or gross. All he cares about is that there is money to pay him with, and it is a mere matter of bookkeeping and internal arrangement out of what particular fund he shall be paid. Therefore you cannot say that the question of what ought to go into capital or revenue account is a matter that concerns the creditor. The Act does not say what expenses are to be charged to capital and what to revenue. Such matters are left to the shareholders. They may or may not have a sinking fund or a deterioration fund, and the articles of association may or may not contain regulations on those matters. If they do, the regulations must be observed; if they do not, the shareholders can do as they like, so long as they do not misapply their capital and cheat their creditors. In this case the articles say there need be no such fund, consequently the capital need not be replaced; nor, having regard to these articles, need any loss of capital by removal of bituminous earth appear in the profit and loss account. . . .

[*Lee* v *Neuchatel* represents the victory of the 'profits or earned surplus rule' over the 'capital maintenance' or 'balance sheet surplus rule', of the '*res* theory' over the '*quantum* theory'. The capital that must not be diminished by return to the shareholders in the form of dividend or otherwise is not defined in terms of the nominal, paid-up capital, but 'of the assets contributed by the shareholders in payment for their shares, or assets into which these original assets have been converted'. See R M Bryden in *Studies in Canadian Company Law* I (1967) 280–1.]

[345] **Bolton v Natal Land and Colonization Company**

[1892] 2 Ch 124

ROMER J: . . . This is an action which seeks to restrain the defendants from paying a certain dividend, which has not yet been paid, for the year 1885. It . . . is not concerned with any other dividends that have been paid by the company. Now, it appears that for the year 1885 there were profits earned sufficient to pay the proposed dividend; profits about which there could be no question that they were rightly brought in as sums available for dividend in this year. . . . But what is said is this. It is said that if you look at the balance sheet you will find that a certain value is put as against the properties of the company in South Africa; and this sum put in the balance sheet as the value of these properties is, they say, in excess of the true value, and the plaintiff produces some evidence . . . to show that in 1885 the true value of these properties was less than the value put in the balance sheet; and then it is said that on that ground they ought to treat as a loss to be put in the profit and loss account for this year the difference between the true value, as they say, of these properties and the value placed upon the properties in the balance sheet; and that, if that was done, then, instead of there being a profit for the year 1885 available for payment of dividend, there would be no profit at all.

It does not appear to me that the ground on which the plaintiff bases this claim is one on which the court can act, and say that the payment of this dividend ought to be stopped. I am not persuaded that the difference between the two values that I have referred to ought to be put against the profit and loss account in this year. The account as it stands certainly is not a fictitious account. Really all that the plaintiff's case amounts to is this: that if his evidence be correct, some portion of the capital of the company has been lost—that is to say, that the assets, if truly valued, do not make good the share capital of the company; but it does not appear to me that that in itself is a ground for impeaching the profit and loss account in this balance sheet of 1885. I think the case is covered by that of *Lee v Neuchatel Asphalte Company.* . . .

But, it is said, with a view of escaping from that case, that formerly this company had dealt with the increased values of these very properties as affording a ground for paying profits by placing part of the increased values of the properties over cost price to the credit of the profit and loss accounts. Now, on examination, I can only find two balance sheets in which that can be said to have been done at all—the balance sheet of 1873 and the balance sheet of 1882. What was done in the balance sheet of 1882 was this. Under peculiar circumstances the company appear to have debited to the profit and loss account the whole of the loss arising by reason of a certain debt of £72 326-odd having proved a bad debt; and they debited that loss undoubtedly in that year to the profit and loss account; but they only did that as part of a balance sheet in which on the opposite side in that profit and loss account they put as a set-off an increase in the value of the properties in Africa over the cost price. That does not afford in itself a ground for holding this company bound to always bring into the profit and loss account an increase or diminution of the value of these properties, nor enable the plaintiff to say that because an error has been committed, or a course adopted in 1882, the balance sheet for this year must be made out on the principle he has insisted upon, or enable the balance sheet of 1885 to be attacked by saying that the past erroneous system, if there had been a system, or what was done in 1882, should be now set right by altering the profit and loss account of this year. . . .

[346] Verner v General and Commercial Investment Trust
[1894] 2 Ch 239

The income of an investment company from its investments exceeded its expenses, but owing to a fall in the market price of some of its investments the value of its assets was considerably diminished. The court held that the company was not precluded from declaring a dividend.

LINDLEY LJ: . . . The broad question raised by this appeal is, whether a limited company which has lost part of its capital can lawfully declare or pay a dividend without first making good the capital which has been lost. I have no doubt it can—that is to say, there is no law which prevents it in all cases and under all circumstances. Such a proceeding may sometimes be very imprudent; but a proceeding may be perfectly legal and may yet be opposed to sound commercial principles. We, however, have only to consider the legality or illegality of what is complained of.

As was pointed out in *Lee* v *Neuchatel Asphalte Company*, there are certain provisions in the Companies Acts relating to the capital of limited companies; but no provisions whatever as to the payment of dividends or the division of profits. Each company is left to make its own regulations as to such payment or division. The statutes do not even expressly and in plain language prohibit a payment of dividend out of capital. But the provisions as to capital, when carefully studied, are wholly inconsistent with the return of capital to the shareholders, whether in the shape of dividends or otherwise, except, of course, on a winding-up and there can, in my opinion, be no doubt that even if a memorandum of association contained a provision for paying dividends out of capital such provision would be invalid. The fact is that the main condition of limited liability is that the capital of a limited company shall be applied for the purposes for which the company is formed, and that to return the capital to the shareholders either in the shape of dividend or otherwise is not such a purpose as the legislative contemplated.

But there is a vast difference between paying dividends out of capital and paying dividends out of other money belonging to the company, and which is not part of the capital mentioned in the company's memorandum of association. The capital of a company is intended for use in some trade or business, and is necessarily exposed to risk of loss. As explained in *Lee* v *Neuchatel Asphalte Company*, the capital even of a limited company is not a debt owing by it to its shareholders, and if the capital is lost, the company is under no legal obligation either to make it good, or, on that ground only, to wind up its affairs. If, therefore, the company has any assets which are not its capital within the meaning of the Companies Acts, there is no law which prohibits the division of such assets amongst the shareholders. Further, it was decided in that case, and, in my opinion, rightly decided, that a limited company formed to purchase and work a wasting property, such as a leasehold quarry, might lawfully declare and pay dividends out of the money produced by working such wasting property, without setting aside part of that money to keep the capital up to its original amount.

There is no law which prevents a company from sinking its capital in the purchase or production of a money-making property or undertaking, and in dividing the money annually yielded by it, without preserving the capital sunk so as to be able to reproduce it intact either before or after the winding-up of the company.

A company may be formed upon the principle that no dividends shall be declared unless the capital is kept undiminished, or a company may contract with its creditors to keep its capital or assets up to a given value. But in the absence of some special article or contract, there is no law to this effect; and, in my opinion, for very good reasons. It would, in my judgment, be most inexpedient to lay down a hard and fast rule which would prevent a flourishing company, either not in debt or well able to pay its debts, from paying dividends so long as its capital sunk in creating the business was not represented by assets which would, if sold, reproduce in money the capital sunk. Even a sinking fund to replace lost capital by degrees is not required by law.

It is obvious that dividends cannot be paid out of capital which is lost; they can only be paid out of money which exists and can be divided. Moreover, when it is said, and said truly, that dividends are not to be paid out of capital, the word 'capital' means the money subscribed pursuant to the memorandum of association, or what is represented by that money. Accretions to that capital may be realized and turned into money, which may be divided amongst the shareholders, as was decided in *Lubbock* v *British Bank of South America* (*353* below).

But, although there is nothing in the statutes requiring even a limited company to keep up its capital, and there is no prohibition against payment of dividends out of any other of the company's assets, it does not follow that dividends may be lawfully paid out of other assets regardless of the debts and liabilities of the company. A dividend presupposes a profit in some shape, and to divide as dividend the receipts, say for a year, without deducting the expenses incurred in that year in producing the receipts, would be as unjustifiable in point of law as it would be reckless and blameworthy in the eyes of business men. The same observation applies to payment of dividends out of borrowed money. Further, if the income of any year arises from a consumption in that year of what may be called circulating capital, the division of such income as dividend without replacing the capital consumed in producing it will be a payment of a dividend out of capital within the meaning of the prohibition which I have endeavoured to explain.

It has been already said that dividends presuppose profits of some sort, and this is unquestionably true. But the word 'profits' is by no means free from ambiguity. The law is much more accurately expressed by saying that dividends cannot be paid out of capital, than by saying that they can only be paid out of profits. The last expression leads to the inference that the capital must always be kept up and be represented by assets which, if sold, would produce it; and this is more than is required by law. Perhaps the shortest way of expressing the distinction which I am endeavouring to explain is to say that fixed capital may be sunk and lost, and yet that the excess of current receipts over current payments may be divided, but that floating or circulating capital must be kept up, as otherwise it will enter into and form part of such excess, in which case to divide such excess without deducting the capital which forms part of it will be contrary to law. . . .

[See also the following passages from the judgment of Stirling J in the court of first instance ([1894] 2 Ch 239 at 259): '. . . I think it is not made out that the payment of a dividend is beyond the power of the company. Whether it is prudent that a dividend should be paid is not for me to decide, but for the men of business of whom the company is constituted. I base my decision on the peculiar nature of the constitution of this particular company; and it is not to be assumed that I should have arrived at the same conclusion if I had been dealing with an ordinary trading company—if, for example, the object of the company had been to carry on the business of a stockholder, and the investments had been the ordinary stock-in-trade of that business.

'It follows from my view of the nature of the company that the shareholders would not be entitled to divide for the purpose of dividend any increase in the value of the investments however great. . . .']

[347] **Wilmer *v* McNamara & Company Ltd**
[1895] 2 Ch 245

STIRLING J: . . . It is necessary . . . to consider whether the depreciation in goodwill . . . is to be treated as loss of 'fixed' capital or of 'floating or circulating' capital. . . . Depreciation of goodwill seems to me to be loss of 'fixed' capital. It closely resembles the loss which a railway company might be said to sustain if it were found that a line which had been made, say ten years ago, at a certain cost, could now be made for a very much smaller amount, and consequently would not yield, if it were sold, the price expended in making it. . . .

[348] *In re* **National Bank of Wales Ltd**
[1899] 2 Ch 629

LINDLEY MR: . . . The liquidator has taken the view that the dividends declared and paid by the company, when Mr John Cory was a director, were all paid out of the capital of the company; and the evidence adduced is directed to prove that such was the case. But when this evidence is examined, it seems quite plain that the dividends were not in fact paid out of any part of the money forming the paid-up nominal capital of the company, but were paid notwithstanding the loss of such capital, and without making it good. What was done was this: the accounts were made up annually. Such losses incurred during the year as the directors recognized as losses were written off or provided for by carrying sums of money over to a reserve fund, and the balance of the receipts in each year over the outgoings in the same year, after making some allowance for bad debts and deductions for sums carried over to the reserve fund, were treated as the profits of that year, and were distributed as dividends. Losses written off in one year were not brought forward the next year, so as to diminish the profits of that year, but were simply ignored, a fresh start being made every year, and dividends being paid out of the excess of the annual receipts over the annual expenses. The effect of this was to throw all bad debts, written off and not provided for by an increase of the reserve fund, on to the capital; to diminish the paid-up capital year by year, and nevertheless to keep paying dividends out of the excess of the annual receipts over the current expenses. It is obvious that this method of procedure, if long continued, would ultimately exhaust the paid-up capital of the company, and the first disastrous year in which the current outgoings exceeded the current incomings would produce great embarrassment. Such a mode of dealing with the company's assets, however reprehensible, must nevertheless not be confounded with paying dividends out of the paid-up capital of the company. The paid-up capital of a limited company cannot be lawfully returned to the shareholders under the guise of dividends or otherwise. Even an article of association authorizing the payment of interest to shareholders on the amounts paid upon their shares cannot authorize a payment of such interest out of capital but paid-up capital which is lost can no more be applied in paying dividends than in paying debts. Its loss renders any subsequent application of it impossible. There was no such dealing with the paid-up capital of the company in this case as to amount to an illegal application for it. Further, it is not possible for the court to say that the law prohibits a limited company, even a limited banking company, from paying dividends unless its paid-up capital is intact. Suppose a heavy unexpected loss is sustained, which must be met if there are assets with which to meet it. Such an application of capital is a perfectly legitimate use of it. There is no law which in the case supposed prevents the payment of all future dividends until all the capital so expended is made good. Many honest and prudent men of business would replace a large loss of capital by degrees, and would reduce the dividends, but not stop them entirely, until the whole loss was made good. No law compels them to pay none at all. There are cases in which no honest competent man of business would think of charging particular debts or expenses to capital.

We are certainly not prepared to sanction the notion that all debts incurred in carrying on a business can be properly permanently charged to capital, and that the excess of receipts over other outgoings can be afterwards properly divided as profit as if there had been no previous loss. No honest competent man engaged in trade or commerce would carry on business on such a principle. But, excluding cases in which everyone can see that a particular debt or outlay cannot be reasonably charged to capital, it may be safely said that what losses can be properly charged to capital, and what to income, is a matter for business men to determine, and it is often a matter on which the opinions of honest and competent men will differ. There is no hard and fast legal rule on the subject.

There can, however, be no doubt that, if expenses or payments are obviously improperly charged to capital, and are so charged simply to swell the apparent profits, and to make it appear that dividends may properly be declared, dividends declared and paid under such circumstances cannot be treated as legitimately paid out of profits, and can no more be justified than if they were paid out of capital. . . .

. . . It is not denied that in this case the annual receipts did exceed the annual outgoings, and, the dividends having been paid out of the excess, the allegation that they were paid out of capital is not accurate. But, as already pointed out, it does not at all follow that the course adopted by the directors in declaring dividends year after year as they did was legally justifiable. It cannot be denied that the balance sheets and profit and loss accounts concealed the truth, as now known, from the shareholders, and were, as it now turns out, grievously misleading. The shareholders were never told that the paid-up capital was being constantly diminished by bad debts, as now appears to have been the case. . . .

[But cf Lord Davey in the appeal from the foregoing case, *sub nom Dovey v Cory* [1901] AC 477 at 493: '. . . I desire to express my dissent from some propositions of law which were laid down in the court of appeal, and upon which your Lordships thought it right to hear the respondent's counsel. The learned judges seem to have thought that a joint stock company, incorporated under the Companies Acts, may write off to capital losses incurred in previous years, and may in any subsequent year if the receipts for that year exceed the outgoings, pay dividends out of such excess without making up the capital account. If this proposition be well founded, it appears to me that a company whose capital is not represented by available assets need never trouble itself to reduce its capital . . . in order to enable itself to pay dividends out of current receipts. . . .']

[349] **Bond *v* Barrow Haematite Steel Company**
[1902] 1 Ch 353

Action by preference shareholders to obtain payment of their fixed cumulative preference dividend. They alleged that sufficient profits were available for the purpose. The defendant company proved that it had suffered a realized loss of capital exceeding £200 000, arising from the surrender of certain leasehold mines acquired by the company for supplying themselves with iron ore, the pulling down of certain blast furnaces and the sale of certain cottages used in connection therewith, as well as a loss by general depreciation of assets estimated at over £50 000. The company contended that there ought to be no distribution of profits until losses were made good.

The court decided in favour of the company, on the principle that, unless the articles provide otherwise, preference shareholders (like other shareholders) are not entitled to a dividend unless and until declared (*340*, above). It then addressed itself to the question whether, assuming the articles of the respondent company gave the preference shareholders a right to a dividend if the profits were available, the plaintiffs were right in their contention that the profits were available in this case.

FARWELL J: . . . It has been proved to my satisfaction that the company has sustained an actual ascertained and realized loss of capital to an amount exceeding £200 000, and has also lost capital by estimate and valuation to an amount exceeding £50 000. The various sums claimed by the plaintiffs as available to pay their dividends amount to about £240 000. If, therefore, these ascertained and estimated losses have to be made good before any dividend can properly be paid, there are obviously no funds out of which to pay dividends. The defendants allege and the plaintiffs deny that the company are bound to make good these losses before paying any dividend. The question is one of very considerable difficulty on the authorities, but the result of those authorities is, in my opinion, that there is no hard and fast rule by which the court can determine what is capital and what is profit. . . .

. . . It is, however, necessary to bear in mind that the two propositions — (1) that dividends must not be paid out of capital, and (2) that dividends may only be paid out of profits — are not identical, but diverse. The first is the requirement of the statutes, and cannot be dispensed with; the latter is in Table A or the articles of the particular company, and is one of the regulations of this company which has to be construed. A company which has a balance to the credit of its profit and loss account is not bound at once to apply that sum in making good an estimated deficiency in value of its capital assets. It may carry it to a suspense account or to reserve, and if the assets subsequently increase in value the amount neither has been nor will be part of the capital. If, therefore, a part of that balance is used in paying a dividend, that dividend is not paid out of capital, because the sum has never become capital, although it still remains a question whether it has been paid out of profits or not. It has been pointed out by Lindley LJ in *Lee* v *Neuchatel Asphalte Company* that there is nothing in the statutes requiring a company to keep up the value of its capital assets to the level of its nominal capital. The requirement is merely negative, that dividends shall not be paid out of capital, and the balance to the credit of profit and loss account does not automatically become part of the capital assets because the value of the actual capital assets has depreciated to an amount equal to or exceeding that balance.

The real question for determination, therefore, is whether there are profits available for distribution, and this is to be answered according to the circumstances of each particular case, the nature of the company, and the evidence of competent witnesses. There is no single definition of the word 'profits' which will fit all cases. . . . All the authorities, however, agree, I think, that circulating capital must be kept up.

Now, in the present case the £200 000 realized loss arises by the surrender of the leases of certain mines, by the pulling down of certain furnaces, and on the sale of certain cottages. The company is a smelting company on a very large scale, and for the convenience of its works and by way of economy they acquired the leases of the surrendered mines in order to supply themselves with their own ore instead of buying it as required. The ore was used exclusively for the purposes of the company's works. The mines were drowned out and the cost of pumping them out was prohibitive. The company, therefore, surrendered the leases, pulled down the blast furnaces, and sold the cottages therewith. . . . I think that the money invested in those items is properly regarded in this company as circulating capital. Suppose the company had bought enormous stocks of ore sufficient to last for ten years, it could hardly be said that the true value of so much of this as remained from time to time ought not to be brought into the balance sheet, and I can see no difference in principle for the purpose of the account between ore *in situ* and ore so bought in advance. The blast furnaces and cottages are mere accessories to the ore, and resemble a building for housing the stores bought in advance already mentioned.

There is more difficulty about the remaining £50 000. I think that the onus is on the plaintiffs to show that it is fixed capital, and that in a company of this nature such fixed capital may be sunk or lost. They have not done this, and the evidence, so far as it goes, is the other way. But this is not an actual loss, but depreciation by estimate, and the plaintiffs really relied on *Lee v Neuchatel Asphalte Company* as an authority for this proposition as a universal negative, namely 'that no company owning wasting property need ever create a depreciation fund'. In my opinion, that is not the true result of the decision. It must be remembered that in that case there had been no loss of assets. The company's assets were larger than at its formation, and the court decided nothing more than the particular proposition that some companies with wasting assets need have no depreciation fund. For instance, I cannot think that it would be right for the defendant company to purchase out of capital the last two or three years of a valuable patent, and distribute the whole of the receipts in respect thereof as profits without replacing the capital expended in the purchase. It is for the court to determine in each case on evidence whether the particular company ought, or ought not, to have such a fund. . . .

There is no doubt as to the opinion of the witnesses in this case, and, further, the opinion of the directors cannot be altogether disregarded. The courts have, no doubt, in many cases, overruled directors who proposed to pay dividends, but I am not aware of any case in which the court has compelled them to pay when they have expressed their opinion that the state of the accounts did not admit of any such payment. In a matter depending on evidence and expert opinion, it would be a very strong measure for the court to overrule the directors in such a manner.

[350] *In re* **Spanish Prospecting Company Ltd**
[1911] 1 Ch 92

Under a service agreement with the Spanish Prospecting Company, P and V were to receive a fixed salary per month, subject to the proviso that they should not be entitled to draw their salary 'except only out of profits (if any) arising from the business of the company which may from time to time be available for such purpose, but such salary shall nevertheless be cumulative, and accordingly any arrears thereof shall be payable out of any succeeding profits available as aforesaid'.

In the course of its business the Spanish Prospecting Company acquired certain shares and debentures in another company. When the Spanish Prospecting Company was subsequently voluntarily wound up, these shares and debentures were realized at a profit, and the question before the court was whether this was a profit arising from the business of the company for the purpose of the service agreement with P and V. The court of appeal, overruling the decision of the court of first instance, held that it was.

FLETCHER MOULTON LJ: . . . The word 'profits' has in my opinion a well-defined legal meaning, and this meaning coincides with the fundamental conception of profits in general parlance, although in mercantile phraseology the word may at times bear meanings indicated by the special context which deviate in some respects from this fundamental signification. 'Profits' implies a comparison between the state of a business at two specific dates usually separated by an interval of a year. The fundamental meaning is the amount of gain made by the business during the year. This can only be ascertained by a comparison of the assets of the business at the two dates.

For practical purposes these assets in calculating profits must be valued and not merely enumerated. An enumeration might be of little value. Even if the assets were identical at the two periods it would by no means follow that there had been neither gain nor loss, because the market value—the value in exchange—of these assets might have altered greatly in the meanwhile. A stock of fashionable goods is worth much more than the same stock when the fashion has changed. And to a less degree but no less certainly the same considerations must apply to buildings, plant, and other fixed assets used in the business, because one form of business risk against which business gains must protect the trader is the varying value of the fixed assets used in the business. A depreciation in value, whether from physical or commercial causes, which affects their realizable value is in truth a business loss.

We start therefore with this fundamental definition of profits, namely if the total assets of the business at the two dates be compared, the increase which they show at the later date as compared with the earlier date (due allowance of course being made for any capital introduced into or taken out of the business in the meanwhile) represents in strictness the profits of the business during the period in question.

But the periodical ascertainment of profits in a business is an operation of such practical importance as to be essential to the safe conduct of the business itself. To follow out the strict consequences of the legal conception in making out the accounts of the year would often be very difficult in practice. Hence the strict meaning of the word 'profits' is rarely observed in drawing up the accounts of firms or companies. These are domestic documents designed for the practical guidance of those interested, and so long as the principle on which they are drawn up is clear their value is diminished little if at all by certain departures from this strict definition which lessen greatly the difficulty of making them out. Hence certain assumptions have become so customary in drawing up balance sheets and profit and loss accounts that it may almost be said to require special circumstances to induce parties to depart from them. For instance, it is usual to exclude gains and losses arising from causes not directly connected with the business of the company, such, for instance, as a rise in the market value of land occupied by the company. The value assigned to trade buildings and plant is usually fixed according to an arbitrary rule by which they are originally taken at their actual cost and are assumed to have depreciated by a certain percentage each year, though it cannot be pretended that any such calculation necessarily gives their true value either in use or in exchange. These, however, are merely variations of practice by individuals. They rest on no settled principle. They mainly arise from the sound business view that it is better to underrate than to overrate your profits, since it is impossible for you to foresee all the risks to which a business may in future be exposed. For instance, there are many sound business men who would feel bound to take account of the depreciation in value of business premises (or in the value of plant specially designed for the production of a particular article) although they would not take account of appreciation in the same arising from like causes.

To render the ascertainment of the profits of a business of practical use it is evident that the assets, of whatever nature they may be, must be represented by their money value. But as a rule these assets exist in the shape of things or rights and not in the shape of money. The debts owed to the company may be good, bad, or doubtful. The figure inserted to represent stock-in-trade must be arrived at by a valuation of the actual articles. Property, of whatever nature it be, acquired in the course of the business has a value varying with the condition of the market. It will be seen, therefore, that in almost every item of the account a question of valuation must come in. In the case of a company like that with which we have to deal in the present case this process of valuation is often exceedingly difficult, because the property to be valued may be such that there are no market quotations and no contemporaneous sales or purchases to afford a guide to its value. It is not to be wondered at, therefore, that in many cases companies that are managed in a conservative manner avoid the difficulty thus presented and content themselves by referring to assets of a speculative type without attempting to affix any specific value to them. But this does not in any way prevent the necessity of regarding them as forming a part of the assets of the company which must be included in the calculation by which *de facto* profits are arrived at. Profits may exist in kind as well as in cash. For instance, if a business is, so far as assets and liabilities are concerned, in the same position that it was in the year before with the exception that it has contrived during the year to acquire some property, say mining rights, which it had not previously possessed, it follows that those mining rights represent the profits of the year, and this whether or not they are specifically valued in the annual accounts.

But though there is a wide field for variation of practice in these estimations of profit in the domestic documents of a firm or a company, this liberty ceases at once when the rights of third persons intervene. For instance, the revenue has a right to a certain percentage of the profits of a company by way of income tax. The actual profit and loss accounts of the company do not in any way bind the Crown in arriving at the tax to be paid. A company may wisely write off liberally under the head of depreciation, but they will be only allowed to deduct the sum representing actual depreciation for the purpose of calculating the profits for income tax. The same would be the case if a person had a right to receive a certain percentage of the profits made by the company. In the absence of certain stipulations to the contrary, 'profits' in cases where the rights of third parties come in mean actual profits, and they must be calculated as closely as possible in accordance with the fundamental conception or definition to which I have referred.

. . . The capital value of goodwill is an alternative to profits, not part of them. It is the price at which a person renounces his rights to future profits. Hence the goodwill of a business can never appear in the calculation of its profits. . . .

[351] Ammonia Soda Company v Chamberlain

[1918] 1 Ch 266 (CA, dismissing the appeal against the judgment of Peterson J, *356*, below)

SWINFEN EADY LJ: . . . The Companies Acts do not impose any obligation upon a limited company, nor does the law require, that it shall not distribute as dividend the clear net profit of its trading unless its paid-up capital is intact or until it has made good all losses incurred in previous years. . . .

. . . The distinction between 'fixed' capital and 'circulating' capital is not to be found in any of the Companies Acts; it appears to have first found its way into the Law Reports in *Lee* v *Neuchatel Asphalte Company*. . . . What is fixed capital? That which a company retains, in the shape of assets upon which the subscribed capital has been expended, and which assets either themselves produce income, independent of any further action by the company, or being retained by the company are made use of to produce income or gain profits. A trust company formed to acquire and hold stocks, shares, and securities, and from time to time to divide the dividends and income arising therefrom, is an instance of the former. A manufacturing company acquiring or erecting works with machinery and plant is an instance of the latter. In these cases the capital is fixed in the sense of being invested in assets intended to be retained by the company more or less permanently and used in producing an income. What is circulating capital? It is a portion of the subscribed capital of the company intended to be used by being temporarily parted with and circulated in business, in the form of money, goods or other assets, and which, or the proceeds of which, are intended to return to the company with an increment, and are intended to be used again and again, and to always return with some accretion. Thus the capital with which a trader buys goods circulates; he parts with it, and with the goods bought by it, intending to receive it back again with profit arising from the resale of goods. A banker lending money to a customer parts with his money, and thus circulates it, hoping and intending to receive it back with interest. He retains, more or less permanently, bank premises in which the money invested becomes fixed capital. It must not, however, be assumed that the division into which capital thus falls is permanent. The language is merely used to describe the purpose to which it is for the time being appropriated. This purpose may be changed as often as considered desirable, and as the constitution of the bank may allow. Thus bank premises may be sold, and conversely the money used as circulating capital may be expended in acquiring bank premises. The terms 'fixed' and 'circulating' are merely terms convenient for describing the purpose to which the capital is for the time being devoted when considering its position in respect to the profits available for dividend. Thus when circulating capital is expended in buying goods which are sold at a profit, or in buying raw materials from which goods are manufactured and sold at a profit, the amount so expended must be charged against, or deducted from, receipts before the amount of any profits can be arrived at. This is quite a truism, but it is necessary to bear it in mind when you are considering what part of current receipts are available for division as profit. . . .

WARRINGTON LJ: . . . In this case the plaintiff, the Ammonia Soda Company Ltd, claims to recover from two ex-directors the amount of certain dividends paid to preference shareholders, on the alleged ground that they were paid either (*a*) out of capital, or (*b*) at all events otherwise than out of profits, the articles of association providing that no dividend should be paid except out of profits of the company. It is unnecessary for me to restate the facts in detail; it is enough shortly to mention those which raise the question.

At the end of the year 1910 there stood to the debit of the profit and loss account the sum of £19 028 5s 4d, being the net loss on the trading of the company up to that time. By 31 July 1911 this loss had been reduced by subsequent profits to £12 970 18s 3d. During the period ending on the same date the total amount allowed for depreciation of buildings and machinery had been the sum of £13 702 15s 7d. The plaintiff company's land, if entered on the same footing as that previously adopted, namely at cost with certain additions, the nature of which it is unnecessary to specify, would have stood at £63 246 and some odd shillings. The directors, however, determined to enter it in the balance sheet for the period ending 31 July 1911 at £83 788, namely £20 542 more than the £63 246, and to carry the £20 542 to a reserve account. This they did, and to this reserve account they charged, amongst other sums, the £12 970 18s 3d standing to the debit of profit and loss. The result was to wipe off this debit. Subsequently considerable profits in trading were made, and out of these the dividends in question were paid.

In arriving at the amount of the profit for purposes of dividend there were deducted from the gross returns all money employed in earning them, including wages, cost of material, depreciation of buildings and machinery, and so forth. It is not suggested that any expense of this nature which ought to have been deducted was not deducted. That such proper deductions must be made is, I believe, all that Lindley LJ meant in the passages relating to circulating capital contained in his two judgments in *Verner's* case and in *In re National Bank of Wales*. As to the value of the land, the directors honestly believed that it was worth at least the extra £20 000 and I am quite satisfied that they had reasonable grounds for that belief. I am myself prepared to go further, and to say that the plaintiff company has failed to prove that the land was not of at least the value adopted by the directors.

There is ... one accepted restriction on the powers of companies incorporated under the Companies Acts, namely that they must not under the guise of dividends or in any other way return to their shareholders money subscribed for their shares unless it be with the sanction of the court under the appropriate statutory provisions.

It has been asserted in this case, not for the first time, that there is a further restriction—suggested to be a corollary of the rule I have just mentioned—which would make it illegal for a company to pay dividends out of the profits of a current year, unless it first makes good deficiencies in paid-up capital occasioned by losses in previous years; or, to put the contention in a broader form, no dividends can properly be paid out of profits so long as there are losses previously incurred and not made good. In my opinion this alleged restriction has no foundation in law. ...

I am, of course, far from saying that in all such cases dividends can properly be paid without making good the previous loss; the nature of the business and the amount of the loss may be such that no honest and reasonable man of business would think of paying dividends without providing for it. In such a case I apprehend the court would take the view that a payment which no honest and reasonable man of business would think it right to make could not properly be made by directors.

We have no such case here. Even without taking credit for the appreciation of the land I think the dividends paid were properly paid. ...

SCRUTTON LJ: ... In the first place, as to whether the dividends were paid out of capital—assuming all the facts in the plaintiff company's favour—£19 000 was lost in the years 1909–11. What was lost? It was not profits, because there were no profits to lose. It could be nothing else than capital that was lost, and when you have lost a thing you cannot use it for anything else, because you have lost it. You cannot pay dividends out of a thing which you have lost, because it is not there to pay dividends out of. Therefore I come to the conclusion which was come to in the three cases I have mentioned—that it is inaccurate to say that if in subsequent years you pay dividends, having lost capital in previous years, you are paying the dividends out of the capital that you lost in the previous years. It is only possible to support that suggestion by treating the profit when made in a subsequent year as in some way automatically turned into capital and as replacing the capital which has been lost, and by saying that what was made as profit has in some way automatically become capital and must be treated as capital. I can find no foundation for that in the statutes or in the decisions. ...

[352] **Wall v London and Provincial Trust Ltd**

[1920] 1 Ch 45, [1920] 2 Ch 582

The accounts of an investment company were kept on the basis that profit or loss on a change of investment was carried to capital account, while net receipts over expenditure were carried to revenue account. Dividends were paid out of revenue account without regard to depreciation in the market value of the company's investments. In 1900 the company issued debenture stock at par. In 1918, through a fall in the value of securities, the directors were able to redeem part of this debenture stock at a discount. The investments of the company had fallen approximately commensurately. It was held that the discount could not be carried to revenue account.

YOUNGER J (at the first hearing, for an interlocutory injunction, ie interim interdict): . . . It [is] . . . in my judgment . . . impossible to affirm that such a transaction as the present had resulted in a profit to the company unless it were at the same time established that there remained in the hands of the company in respect of it an asset equivalent in value to the profit alleged. If, for example, the whole £50 000 raised by this issue of debenture stock had been lost by the company the day after its receipt, the company, if the stockholders accepted £10 000 in respect of their claim for repayment, would not have made a profit of £40 000 on the transaction as the argument seems to affirm: the company would in fact have made a loss of £10 000. . . .

. . . It is true, as I have said, that in the case of such a company as we have here capital and revenue accounts are distinct accounts and you may operate upon a credit balance on the second account irrespective of loss on the first. But the accounts are distinct. There is a gulf set between them not spanned by any bridge. You must not carry any asset from one to the other. The price of being entitled to distribute as dividend a revenue balance regardless of a capital loss is that you may not supplement a deficiency of revenue by carrying to the credit of that account a gain on capital however realized. . . . This statement in respect of companies adopting the double account system is, I think, of universal application. In other words, the transfer from the one account to the other is inadmissible in the case of such companies even if after transfer made the real as distinct from the mere book-keeping equilibrium of the capital account is not thereby disturbed. *A fortiori* and for reasons far more cogent than any considerations of accountancy no such transfer can be made as it is here sought to make it regardless altogether of that equilibrium — regardless, in other words, of the true value of the remaining capital assets of the company.

The truth is that in accounts kept as this company is required to keep its accounts an appreciation in capital assets can never increase the dividend fund. If for the purpose of dividend a company like this desires to gain the benefit of an appreciation in capital values it must adopt the single account system and, as a consequence, value its entire assets for the purpose of every dividend distribution. That is not in accordance with the constitution of this company as it stands, and the present value of its assets offers no inducement to effect any immediate change in that direction. . . .

SARGANT J (at the trial): . . . Apart altogether from the special provisions of the defendant company's articles, I am clear that the directors could not dissociate the single item of gain now in question from the items of loss, and treat it as a profit susceptible of being divided as dividend. Before the transaction the capital of the company was represented by certain investments charged with debenture stock; and the value both of the investments and of the debenture stock had become seriously depreciated, with the result that the value of the equity of redemption was some 30 to 40 per cent less than the nominal amount of the issued capital of the company. Then an arrangement was made under which part of the debenture stock was paid off, at or somewhere above its depreciated value, out of some of the assets on which it was charged, some at least of these assets being realized for that purpose at their depreciated value. The net result is that the capital of the company is now represented by a less amount of investments, subject to a smaller charge of debenture stock, and that substantially the same proportion of the issued capital is still unrepresented by available assets.

This state of circumstances is one which might justify a petition for a reduction of capital, but it seems wholly inappropriate for rendering divisible as profit an item of gain representing a reduction in liability, which has been wiped out over and over again by previous or simultaneous losses in respect of the assets charged with the liability. Profit for this purpose is not constituted by one individual gain, but by a surplus of gains of all kinds over losses of all kinds during some definite period. . . .

NOTES

See further *In re Kingston Cotton Mill Co* (2) [1896] 1 Ch 331; *In re Crichton's Oil Co* [1901] 2 Ch 184, affirmed by the court of appeal [1902] 2 Ch 86; *Lawrence v West Somerset Mineral Railway Co* [1918] 2 Ch 250; and *Rosslare (Pty) Ltd v Registrar, 86* above (a fall in the value of fixed assets need not be made good before a revenue profit may be distributed as a dividend).

In a paper on 'Witwatersrand Gold Mines Considered as Companies Formed to Work Properties of a Wasting Nature', read at a meeting of the Chartered Accountants Students' Society of London on 27 April 1898, Mr Howard Pim FCA said, *inter alia*:

'We may . . . conclude that in the case of gold mining companies . . . the interests of shareholders are so large in proportion to those of creditors, and the latter can be so easily safeguarded in each individual case, that no objections sufficiently strong can be urged to prevent the distribution of the funds arising from the companies' working irrespective of their being capital or revenue, and, further, that there is no law to this effect. In support of this proposition, the following additional reasons can be put forward:

(a) We have a precedent for this course in the case of single-ship companies, where, to quote Mr Bogle . . . "the general practice is for the net earnings to be paid away as made, after deducting maintenance and some reserve for contingencies'.

(b) We are not considering the accounts of a complicated result of our civilization— such as a bank or a trading company, but of an example of the simplest and most primitive form of commercial enterprise. However magnificent the equipment, however delicate and elaborate the chemical and mechanical appliances used to separate the gold from the ores, viewed as a commercial undertaking these wasting propositions are on the same level as one single transaction of a fishmonger or greengrocer, who buys perishable goods, knowing that he runs the risk of their spoiling before he has succeeded in disposing of them all.

(*c*) There is also a more fundamental reason why return of capital should be allowed, which I will now mention in anticipation of a later argument. In the case of a continuing business, such as a bank or trading company, the capital is advanced for the purpose of carrying out an indefinite number of transactions extending over an indefinite period; in fact, *the assumption is that the business goes on for ever*, while in the case of a gold mine or other wasting business the capital is advanced for the purpose of carrying out *one* transaction—the exhaustion of the claims. . . .'

He said further: '. . . There is a distinction to be drawn between wasting and continuing businesses and nothing commercially unsound in returning to shareholders in the form of dividends the capital of companies formed to work a wasting asset, for in this case the capital is subscribed for the purpose of carrying out a single transaction— the exhaustion of the property—and granted proper precautions no one is prejudiced by the return. In the case of continuing businesses, among which are numbered all trading concerns, the conditions are different. There the capital is subscribed for the purpose of carrying out an indefinite number of transactions extending over an indefinite period; consequently the completion of one transaction only sets free the funds involved in order that they may be at once re-employed in further business of a similar nature. . . .' ·

[353] Lubbock *v* British Bank of South America
[1892] 2 Ch 198

A banking company with a paid-up capital of £500 000 sold part of its undertakings for £875 000. After providing for all its liabilities, it was left with a surplus of £205 000. The court held that the £205 000 could be treated as profit available for dividend.

CHITTY J: . . . The capital of the bank is intact, and the account shows it, and after providing for the capital, there remains a surplus which rightly goes to the profit and loss account. All that the company is required to do, by force of the Companies Act, is to keep its capital intact, and not to pay dividends out of its own capital; in other words, to keep that capital for its creditors, and any others who may be concerned therein. . . ,

. . . I have great difficulty in following the first portion of the argument for the plaintiff, because it was said that what was sold was part of the capital of the company, and that what came in over and above the £500 000 was an accretion to capital, therefore it must be kept intact as part of the capital. That has, with great respect to the counsel who put forward this argument, nothing to do with the matter. The sale being an authorized sale, it is immaterial what is the thing sold. I put during the argument a humble illustration. A man's business is to make boots and shoes. He has £10 000 which he takes into that business as his capital. He makes boots and shoes, and spends the whole of his £10 000 in doing it, and he sells and gets back from his customers a certain sum on the sale. He compares then, assuming he has sold all, what he has got back with his expenditure in producing the boots and shoes, and putting them on the market, and if he finds he has his £10 000 (I am treating it apart from any question of debts outstanding, supposing it is a good solid sale) then his capital is intact, and the rest, if there is a rest remaining in his hands, is profit. On the other hand, if he has only £9 000 his capital is not intact, and he has lost. It is exactly the same principle that has to be applied to a trading company under the Companies Act, and the capital that has to be regarded for the purpose of the Act of Parliament is the capital according to the Act and not the things, whether houses, goods, boots and shoes, or hats, or whatever it may be for the time being representing the capital, in the sense of being things in which the capital has been laid out. Where the company is formed to work a wasting property, such as a mine or a patent, different considerations may apply. . . .

The result, therefore, is to my mind plain, that on the facts of this case, £205 000 is profit. . . .

[354] Foster *v* New Trinidad Lake Asphalt Company Ltd
[1901] 1 Ch 208

In 1897 the defendant company purchased the property and assets of the old Trinidad Company, including promissory notes for 100 000 dollars given to the old Trinidad Company in 1894 by the New York and Bermudez Company. The defendant company did not consider these notes of any value and they did not appear as assets in its balance sheets. In 1900 the New York and Bermudez Company paid to the defendant company 127 355 dollars in payment of the notes and arrear interest. The directors of the defendant company looked on this payment as a windfall and proposed to treat it as a profit available for dividend.

BYRNE J: There is no doubt that the debt formed part of the assets originally purchased by the defendant company, and as such, part of its original capital assets, but it is argued that as the debt was not regarded or treated as an asset of value upon the purchase, and as it has not appeared in the former balance-sheet as part of the assets of the company, and as the only entry in relation to it in the books of the company is a journal entry carrying the notes to a profit-and-loss account, it ought to be regarded as a windfall in the nature of an unexpected profit, and as divisible accordingly amongst the shareholders. I cannot accept this view. Although the agreement for sale does not enumerate the debt or notes in question in the schedule which purports, according to its heading, to be a statement of assets and liabilities of the old Trinidad Asphalt Company, that schedule is . . . an enumeration of matters and things which the vendor warranted to be included in the property sold, or the equivalent in value thereof. Some of the items in the schedule may have been overvalued, some undervalued, and no doubt fluctuations in value of the assets have supervened, but the amount of this debt is a distinct item of the property purchased which has since been realized by payment. It appears to me that the amount in question is prima facie capital, and that I have no evidence which would justify me in saying that it has changed its character because it has turned out to be of greater value than expected.

. . . I think that I ought to grant an injunction until judgment or further order to restrain the defendants from distributing 100 000 dollars as dividend without reference to the other business or assets of the defendant company. I must not, however, be understood as determining that this sum or a portion of it may not properly be brought into profit and loss account or be taken into account in ascertaining the amount available for dividend. That appears to me to depend upon the result of the whole accounts for the year. It is clear, I think, that an appreciation in total value of capital assets, if duly realized by sale or getting in of some portion of the assets, may in a proper case be treated as available for purposes of dividend. . . . If I rightly appreciate the true effect of the decisions, the question of what is profit available for dividend depends upon the result of the whole accounts fairly taken for the year, capital, as well as profit and loss, and although dividends may be paid out of earned profits in proper cases, although there has been a depreciation of capital, I do not think that a realized accretion to the estimated value of one item of the capital assets can be deemed to be profit divisible amongst the shareholders without reference to the result of the whole accounts fairly taken. . . .

NOTES

In *Crompton v Reynolds and Gibson* [1952] 1 All ER 888, a partnership firm took over the assets and liabilities of another firm. These assets included a book debt which was acquired at a written-down figure, but which was later collected in full, a profit of £50 000 being thereby made by the partnership firm. The partnership carried on the business of cotton brokers. The court held that the £50 000 was not a trading profit liable to income tax as it did not accrue in the course of the partnership's trade, but an accretion of value analogous to the profit made by the sale of a fixed asset.

See further *Cross v Imperial Continental Gas Association* [1923] 2 Ch 553.

[355] Bishop *v* Smyrna and Cassaba Railway Company (No 2)
[1895] 2 Ch 596

An investment made by a company on capital account fell in value. The amount of depreciation was debited to revenue. Subsequently the company went into liquidation. By that time the investment had risen again in value and the liquidator in his accounts credited as 'appreciation' the amount which had previously been debited as depreciation. It was held that he was entitled to do so.

KEKEWICH J: . . . What we have now is not the mere increase in value of an item of investment, but the rehabilitation of the value of the investment. It is writing back what was before written off; and I cannot for myself see why, since the amount written off was treated as a deduction from profits in former accounts, the amount that is now written up should not be treated as profits in the same way. It seems to me to be not an accretion of principal, but a restitution of what was before taken away—taken away from profits, and therefore a restitution to profits. . . .

[356] Ammonia Soda Company *v* Chamberlain
[1918] 1 Ch 266[1]

PETERSON J: . . . The plaintiffs in substance allege that the debit to profit and loss account, amounting to £19 028, or, after deducting the profits up to 31 July 1911 and return income tax, £12 960 18s 3d,

[1] On appeal in *351* above.

ought to have been made good out of profits before there were any profits available for dividend. The greater part ($£3\ 722\ 15s\ 7d$) of this debit of $£19\ 028$ represented a depreciation of $2\frac{1}{2}$ per cent on buildings and $7\frac{1}{2}$ per cent on plant and machinery which had been written off as representing a diminution in value of these assets. The question is whether it is prohibited to utilize and increase in the value of the fixed assets for the purpose of wiping out this deficiency in the value of the capital assets. Sir Woodburn Kirby and Mr Gibson both expressed the view that it could not. Sir Woodburn's opinion was that it was contrary to all principles of commercial accountancy to write up the value of a fixed asset and apply the surplus so obtained to meet a deficit on trading, and Mr Gibson stated that such a course was absolutely wrong and 'illegal'. Sir Woodburn also accepted the proposition that it is a recognized and accepted principle of commercial accountancy that nothing should be taken into profit unless it is first realized. This, however, goes too far, for stock and book debts are habitually brought into profit and loss account before being realized, and probably Sir Woodburn intended to confine his statement to fixed assets. I am not satisfied that the proposition that it is contrary to all principles of commercial accountancy to utilize an increase in the value of a fixed asset for the purpose of getting rid of a debt which represents loss of paid-up capital is not too wide. It may be a precept of prudence and yet be far removed from the sphere of the categorical imperative. Assuming that a company ought to keep the value of its assets up to the amount of the liabilities and paid-up capital, or, in other words, to see that its paid-up capital is intact, why should it be absolutely precluded from stating the true value of its assets? If an agricultural company has land under which valuable coal measures are discovered, it is difficult to see why it should not be allowed to show in its balance sheet the increased value of its lands. If it is necessary or proper that a company shall maintain its assets at the amount of its paid-up capital and liabilities, there would not appear to be anything illegitimate in showing that the assets are equal to the paid-up capital and liabilities. Nor for this purpose can it matter that the increased value is due to the fixed assets. The paid-up capital is represented by both fixed and circulating capital, and it seems somewhat arbitrary that circulating capital may be shown at its true value while fixed capital must not. Take the case of a depreciation fund. The effect is that the value of the assets as shown in the account is diminished by the amount of the depreciation fund. If the assets in fact increase in value to the extent of the depreciation fund, there is no rule which prohibits a company from wiping out the depreciation fund from the liabilities side of the account. . . .

. . . It is one thing to treat an unrealized increase in value of a fixed asset as profit and to pay dividends out of it as profits; but it appears to me to be a different question whether in considering whether there is a deficiency in paid-up capital owing to past losses, which ought to be made good out of future profits, the real value of the assets can be ascertained with the object of discovering if in fact there is a deficiency in the paid-up capital. . . .

[357] **Dimbula Valley (Ceylon) Tea Co Ltd v Laurie**
[1961] Ch 353, [1961] 1 All ER 769

The capital of Dimbula Valley Tea Company consisted of ordinary and preference shares. Article 5 of the original articles of association provided: 'The ten thousand preference shares in the original capital shall confer on the holders the following rights: (*a*) The right to receive out of the profits of the company a cumulative preferential dividend at the rate of 6 per cent per annum on the amount for the time being paid up thereon. . . . (*b*) The right in the event of the company being wound up to be paid out of the surplus assets of the company the amount paid up in respect of such preference shares and all arrears (if any) of dividend thereon up to the date of the commencement of the winding-up in priority to the other shareholders, and to participate in any further surplus assets of the company after payment of the amount paid up in respect of the other shares rateably with the other shareholders in proportion to the amount paid up on the said preference shares and the other shares respectively.'

Subsequently, the company adopted a so-called capitalization article, providing that the company might at any time pass a resolution that 'any sum not required for the payment or provision of any fixed preferential dividend and (A) for the time being standing to the credit of any reserve fund or reserve account of the company, including premiums received on the issue of any shares or debentures of the company, or any sum arising from any operation creating an excess of assets on capital account, or (B) being undivided net profits in the hands of the company, be capitalized, and that such sum be appropriated as capital to and amongst the shareholders who would have been entitled thereto if the same had been distributed by way of dividend.'

One of the questions the court was called upon to decide was whether the company had acted legally in capitalizing a reserve resulting from a revaluation of the company's capital assets.

BUCKLEY J: I come now to the question of the effect of the capitalization article . . . in the company's new articles of association. The first submission of counsel for the preference shareholder with regard to this was that if this article in any respect varied, or purported to vary, the rights of the preference shareholders, it is to that extent not binding on them. This must be right, because the rights of the preference shareholders are by reference written into the memorandum of association and so are only capable of variation by a scheme of arrangement sanctioned by the court under the Companies Acts. . . . Accordingly the question raised by the originating summons in respect of art 140 involves first the consideration whether under the terms of that article amounts standing to the credit of all, or some, and if so which, of the accounts referred to in . . . the summons can be capitalized, and secondly the consideration whether the power to capitalize so construed conflicts with any right of the preference shareholders.

Counsel for the preference shareholder concedes that capitalization is authorized by the article under all of the heads mentioned in the question except reserves resulting from the revaluation of capital assets.

He relies, in this connexion, on *Westburn Sugar Refineries Ltd* v *Inland Revenue Comrs* [1960] Taxation Reports 105. In that case a revaluation in 1948 of the company's buildings, plant and machinery disclosed an excess of £155 910 over book values. This excess was carried to capital reserve. In the following year the company capitalized £152 250 of the amount on capital reserve. In 1950 the company, having carried out certain other transactions, reduced its capital by repaying part of its paid-up capital. This reduction was confirmed, the application for confirmation being carried as far as the House of Lords [*89* above]. In those proceedings the propriety of the 1949 capitalization was not in issue, but it does not seem to have struck anybody that there might have been anything wrong about it. Later the question whether the capitalization attracted profits tax as being a capitalization of a 'distributable sum' within the Finance Act 1951 s 31(5), came before the Court of Session. The Lord President, Lord Clyde, ... after holding that the capitalization having been of an increment in the value of fixed assets, the subject-matter could not have been utilized in making a distribution within the meaning of the section, went on to say, as a separate ground for his decision, that it would have been illegal for the company to have distributed the amount in question. After referring to a passage in *Palmer's Company Law* 20 ed (1959) 645, which for myself I read as saying that by law an unrealized profit resulting merely from revaluation of fixed assets can be treated as a profit for dividend purposes, but that this is not normally to be regarded as a wise commercial practice, but which the Lord President (Lord Clyde) seems to have interpreted otherwise, he said ([1960] Taxation Reports at 107):

> 'I am of opinion that these observations are sound, and that particularly in the case of an appreciation, which is neither realized nor immediately realizable, it would be illegal to distribute the surplus.'

Then Lord Sorn said (ibid at 109):

> 'In my view capital profits are not distributable until they are realized.'

Founding himself on these observations counsel for the preference shareholder contends that a reserve fund resulting from a revaluation of fixed assets cannot legitimately be distributed by way of dividend. Consequently, he says, it cannot legitimately be capitalized. It is to be observed that art 140 provides that the capitalized sum is to be

> '... appropriated as capital to and amongst the shareholders who would have been entitled thereto if the same had been distributed by way of dividend in the shares and proportions in which they would have been so entitled ...'.

These words are common form in articles of this kind, and I think that it is correct to say that a capitalization of this sort is in essence the declaration of a dividend combined with the application of that dividend on behalf of the shareholders entitled to participate in it in paying up shares to be allotted and issued to them in satisfaction of their rights of participation. ... As a general rule only that which could be distributed in dividends can be capitalized. Where the rights of various classes of shares to participate in profits differ from their rights of participating in a winding-up, any other view or arrangement would lead to anomalous results. The exception to this general rule is that a sum standing to the credit of a share premium account or of a capital redemption reserve fund may not be distributed, except as provided by the Companies Act 1948 s 56(1) or s 58(1), but may be capitalized under s 56(2) or s 58(5) [corresponding to ss 76 and 98 of our Act]. . . . A share premium account and a capital redemption reserve fund are, however, statutory creatures and these statutory provisions governing their distribution are of a special and artificial character. This exception from the general rule which I have formulated accordingly does not, in my judgment, in any way discredit the rule.

If, therefore, the Scottish court was right in holding that a reserve fund constituted as a result of a revaluation of unrealized fixed assets could not legally be distributed, it would seem to me to follow that it likewise could not legally be capitalized. It has, I think, long been the generally accepted view of the law in this country (though not established by judicial authority) that, if the surplus on capital account results from a valuation made in good faith by competent valuers and is not likely to be liable to short-term fluctuations, it may properly be capitalized. . . . Indeed, as I have pointed out, this was actually done by Westburn Sugar Refineries Ltd. For myself, I can see no reason why, if the valuation is not open to criticism, this should not be so, or even why, in any case in which the regulations of the company permit the distribution by way of dividend of profit on capital account, a surplus so ascertained should not be distributed in that manner. After all, every profit and loss account of a trading concern which opens and closes with a stock figure necessarily embodies an element of estimate. The difference between ascertaining trading profits by, amongst other things, estimating the value of the stock in hand at the beginning and end of the accounting period and ascertaining capital profits by comparing an estimated value of the assets with their book value appears to me to be a difference of degree but not of principle. Moreover, if a company has fluid assets available for payment of a dividend, I can see nothing wrong in its using those assets for payment of a dividend and at the same time as a matter of account treating that dividend as paid out of a capital surplus resulting from an appreciation in value of unrealized fixed assets. The proper balance of the company's balance sheet would not be disturbed by such a course of action. The company would be left with assets of sufficient value to meet the commitments shown on the liabilities side of its balance sheet, including paid-up share capital. . . .

For these reasons I reach the conclusion that, unless it conflicts with the rights of the preference shareholders, art 140 authorizes capitalization of a reserve resulting from the revaluation of capital assets.

As, for the same reasons, I have also reached the conclusion that the company could legitimately distribute a capital surplus of this nature by way of dividend, that is to say, exclusively amongst the ordinary shareholders at any time when the preference dividend has been paid in full, a capitalization exclusively for the benefit of the ordinary shares in similar circumstances could not, in my opinion, encroach on the rights of the preference shareholders.

NOTES

Buckley J's view that an unrealized increase in the value of fixed assets may be treated as a profit is supported by D G Rice in (1961) 24 *MLR* 525. See also L C B Gower *Modern Company Law* 3rd ed 118. But see also B J S Wimble in (1951) *SA Accountant* 446, and R R Pennington in (1962) *Accountancy* 304. Current accountancy practice seems to be that an unrealized increase in the value of a capital asset may only be treated as profit if (1) the articles do not prohibit it; (2) the increase is not due to short-term market fluctuations; and (3) on a bona fide revaluation of all fixed assets it is clear that the share capital of the company will remain intact after the distribution. Cf *Lubbock* v *British Bank* and *Foster* v *New Trinidad Lake* (*353, 354* above).

See further *Stapley* v *Read Brothers Ltd* [1924] 2 Ch 1, where it was held that, failing provision to the contrary in the articles, a company may write back to profit account so much of the depreciation written off goodwill as has proved to have been in excess of proper requirements.

[358] *In re* Duff's Settlements: National Provincial Bank Ltd *v* Gregson

[1951] Ch 923, [1951] 2 All ER 534

JENKINS LJ: . . . It is true that the section [s 56 of the English Companies Act 1948, s 76 of the South African Act 1973] does not in terms convert the share premium account into paid-up share capital, but merely makes the provisions of the Act relating to the reduction of share capital apply as if the share premium account was paid-up share capital. But the provisions thus made applicable are the essential provisions on which the distinction between share capital and divisible profit depends, and on which the implied prohibition against the distribution of paid-up share capital otherwise than in pursuance of a duly authorized reduction of capital is based. It is thus clear at all events that s 56 does take the share premium account out of the category of divisible profit and prevents it from being distributed by way of dividend. . . .

NOTES

Prior to the insertion of the section referred to in the respective Acts, a company could pay dividends out of assets representing share premiums: e g *Drown* v *Gaumont-British Picture Corporation Ltd* [1937] Ch 402, [1937] 2 All ER 609.

Where a company acquires the shares of another company, a dividend declared by the subsidiary out of pre-acquisition profits represents for the parent company capital, and not income, for it constitutes part of the asset for which the parent company paid out of capital. It follows that the parent company may not treat this dividend as profits available for dividend, Villiers & Benade 2 ed 285–6, A Weinberg *Take-overs and Amalgamations* 3 ed (1971) paras 1904–10.

Cases: 359–372

A TEXT

Every company is obliged to keep accounting records, s 284. Books and accounts are open to inspection by the directors, s 284(3) (and see Table A art 92, Table B art 91), but not by the shareholders (but see Table A art 93, Table B art 92). (On the meaning of 'books of account' see *Raubenheimer* v *Die Klein Karroo Landboukoöperasie Bpk* 1975 (1) SA 663 (C).)

In respect of every financial year (as determined in accordance with s 285) financial statements must be made out and laid before the annual general meeting, s 286(1). These statements must consist of a balance sheet, an income statement, a directors' report and an auditor's report, s 286. The statements must, in conformity with generally accepted accounting practice, fairly represent the state of affairs of the company as at the end of the financial year and the profit or loss of the company for that year, and must be in accordance with and include at least the matters prescribed by Schedule 4, including a statement of sources and application of funds (Schedule 4 cl 44), s 286(3): *359*. Among the items to be disclosed in the statements are loans given to, or securities provided for, directors or managers, legally or illegally, during the financial year, even if the loan has been repaid or the security cancelled, s 295, and loans made to or securities provided for a person before his appointment as a director or manager if the loan or security was still in existence at the time of his appointment, s 296. See also p 568 above and Schedule 4 cl 19. Holding companies have to present group financial statements, ss 288–91.

In addition to the annual financial statements, public companies have to send their members and debenture holders half-yearly interim reports, s 303, and provisional annual financial statements if the audited annual statements are not ready in time, s 304 (on private companies, see s 304(2), on exemptions and extensions of time, s 307).

Public companies have to send copies of their financial statements to the Registrar, ss 302(4), 306.

The annual financial statements must be approved and signed by the directors, as set out in s 298.

The directors' report must deal with the state of affairs, the business and the profit or loss of the company and, if it has subsidiaries, its subsidiaries, and must include at least the matters prescribed by Schedule 4.

Members and debenture holders of the company and judgment creditors of the company with *nulla bona* returns, are entitled to copies of the annual financial statements, s 309.

A side-effect of the insertion of a debt of the company in the financial statements of the company, if communicated by the company to the creditor, is that the running of extinctive prescription in terms of s 14 of the Prescription Act 68 of 1969 is interrupted: *360*.

The first auditor, who holds office until the conclusion of the first annual meeting, is appointed on incorporation of the company, s 269(1). Failing such appointment, the directors have to appoint him within 21 days after the date of incorporation, s 269(2). If they fail to do so, the Registrar may appoint the first auditor, s 269(4).

Every company must at each annual general meeting appoint an auditor or auditors to hold office until the next annual general meeting, s 270(1). Certain persons, including directors and officers of the company and persons not qualified to act as auditors under the Public Accountants' and Auditors' Act 51 of 1951, are disqualified for appointment, s 275.

In order to ensure that auditors enjoy some degree of independence, s 270(2) lays down that a retiring auditor shall be deemed to be reappointed at any annual general meeting without any resolution being passed unless (*a*) he is not qualified for reappointment; or (*b*) a resolution has been passed under s 278 by a majority of not less than three-fourths of the voting members present in person or by proxy not to reappoint him or to appoint someone else; or (*c*) he has given the company and the Registrar notice in writing of his unwillingness to be reappointed. On resignation, see s 280.

Where at an annual general meeting no auditor is appointed or reappointed, the directors must within 30 days appoint an auditor, failing which the Registrar may make the appointment, s 271(1).

On the application of 100 members or of members holding not less than one-twentieth of the issued share capital, the Minister may appoint an auditor to act jointly with any other auditor of the company, s 272.

The directors fill casual vacancies in the office of auditor, s 273.

The remuneration of auditors is determined by agreement with the company, s 283.

Section 281 gives the auditors a right of access to the accounting records, books and documents of the company, and its subsidiaries, and to such information and explanations as he thinks necessary for the performance of his duties. It also gives him the right to attend and be heard at general meetings. An auditor's working papers are his own property: *361*.

Auditors are employed by the company and not by management

and have an obligation to the shareholders to report illegal or improper activities by the management: *364*. No auditor may issue an unqualified certificate unless the requirements of s 26(1) and (1)*bis* of the Public Accountants' and Auditors' Act 51 of 1951 are satisfied. The auditor must report to the person in charge of the company any material irregularity which has caused or is likely to cause financial loss to the undertaking or to any of its members or creditors, s 26(3). If that irregularity is not dealt with to his satisfaction or rectified within 30 days after he has despatched his report, he must inform the Public Accountants' and Auditors' Board thereof, Public Accountants' and Auditors' Act, s 26(3). If the company has gone into liquidation without remedying the irregularity, he must also report the matter to the trustee or liquidator, ibid, s 26(3A).

For some purposes an auditor is an officer of the company, for others not: *362*. His duty is to examine the annual financial statements and various connected matters, as detailed in s 300, and to make a report to the members of the company to the effect that he has examined the statements and that in his opinion they fairly represent the financial position of the company and its subsidiaries (if any) and the result of its operations and the operations of its subsidiaries (if any), s 301(1): *363*. The words 'in conformity with generally accepted accounting practice' have presumably to be read into s 300(1), see p 597 above.

If the auditor finds himself unable to make such a report or to make it without qualification, he must so state, s 301(2).

An auditor is liable to the company for any loss caused to it by the negligent performance of his duties: *364–367*. Cf s 26(5) of the Public Accountants' and Auditors' Act, which provides that no action shall be instituted against an auditor or accountant in respect of any opinion expressed or statement made or statement, account or document certified by him in good faith in the ordinary course of his duties unless it is proved that he has acted maliciously or negligently. On liability of an accountant/auditor for a negligently false valuation of shares: *368*.

Auditors, like directors, cannot be exempted by contract from liability but may be relieved from liability by the court if they have acted honestly and reasonably, ss 247, 248.

That a third party with whom the auditor has no contractual nexus can hold the auditor liable in delict if he has suffered loss through reliance on a statement negligently made by the auditor would appear to be settled law by now, but the limits of this liability cannot be regarded as settled: *369–372*. Provision has been made for the establishment of a fund for the purpose of compensating any person for loss or damage suffered by him as a result of dishonesty or negligence of an accountant and auditor in the conduct of a public practice, s 21(1)(iA) of the Public Accountants' and Auditors' Act.

B CASES

[359] *Re* Press Caps Ltd
[1949] 1 Ch 434, [1949] 1 All ER 1013

A shareholder opposed a take-over bid on the ground that a freehold property, which constituted the major asset of the company, appeared on the balance sheet at a value of £29 349 (cost less depreciation), whereas its true value was in the neighbourhood of £90 000.

The court of first instance held that he was not bound under s 209(1) (corresponding to s 321(1) of our Act) to accept the offer.

VAISEY J said: 'If you find admitted so large a discrepancy as an undervaluation of the most important asset in the balance sheet of this company, an admitted undervaluation of no less than £60 000 I should have thought that threw a great deal of doubt on the appropriateness of the balance sheet as an estimate of value, and through that, therefore, it also threw doubt on the market price of the shares.'

The court of Appeal allowed the appeal. It considered that the Stock Exchange value of the shares had to be taken as the basis of the terms of transfer, and that the undervaluation of the property in the balance sheets was no indication that the price for the shares offered by the take-over bidder was unduly low.

WYNN-PARRY J: It is alleged that the balance sheet does not represent the true position. The learned judge seems to treat the balance sheet as containing a valuation of the freehold property. I do not so read it. The statement in the balance sheet does no more than accurately represent the state of the freehold property account in the books of the company. It is no more a valuation than the items: 'Patents and goodwill—at cost less accounts written off—as at July 1, 1946, £45 113.' The evidence on that item satisfies me that that asset was not, at the date of the balance sheet, worth anything like £45 000. The result, therefore, is that if one has to write up the one item, one must write down the other.

NOTES

Another case which illustrates that the truth as seen through the eyes of an accountant is not necessarily the same as the truth seen through the eyes of a layman, is *Re Grierson, Oldham & Adams Ltd, 383* below. See also *Prima Toy Holdings (Pty) Ltd* v *Rosenberg* 1974 (2) SA 477 (C) where Van Winsen AJP said (at 489):

'. . . It is argued that the auditor's report cannot be interpreted as conveying that the balance sheet and profit and loss account had been prepared in conformity with generally accepted accounting principles. One might suppose that it is notionally possible that a balance sheet and a profit and loss account prepared in violation of generally accepted accounting principles might nevertheless succeed in reflecting a true and fair view of the profits of a company. However, it seems justified to assume that accountancy principles in regard to the preparation of accounts are designed to produce accounts that give a fair reflection of profits of the company concerned and that it is for that reason that they are generally accepted by accountants. If an accountant certified that the accounts in question are prepared so as to afford a fair view of the profits of the company, it is not an unreasonable inference that he is saying that the preparation of such accounts was in accordance with generally accepted accounting principles.'

Different accounting methods may lead to different results but may be equally justifiable. In dealing with major construction contracts one firm may wait for 'substantial completion' before it enters its profit, while another firm may use the 'percentage of completion' method which involves booking profit proportionally to the progress of the work. Either method has its advocates among accountants.

In *Duple Motor Bodies Ltd* v *Inland Revenue Commissioners* [1961] 1 WLR 739, [1961] 2 All ER 167 a company carried on the business of building bodies for road vehicles to order. At the end of each accounting period they had a number of unfinished bodies on hand. The question before the court was, whether, in arriving at the value of work in progress for the purpose of computing the profits of the company for income tax purposes, the cost of direct materials and labour only should be taken into account ('direct-cost' method) or whether there should be added to the direct cost a proportion of indirect expenditure incurred, more particularly, overheads ('on-cost' method). It was common ground that there was no question of market value of work in progress as it could not be regarded as saleable in its unfinished state. The company had used for many years the 'direct-cost' method. The Inland Revenue Commissioners sought a declaration that the 'on-cost' method was the correct one. Without deciding which method was to the preferred, the court held that the facts and findings set out in the case did not justify the company to change from their established practice of using the 'direct-cost' method.

In the course of his judgment Lord Reid said ([1961] 1 WLR at 752, 753):

> 'There is one finding of the commissioners which rather puzzles me. "The accountancy profession as a whole is satisfied that either method will produce a true figure of profit for income tax purposes." This cannot mean that, taking a particular business in a single year, either method will produce a true figure; the methods will produce very different figures of profit and both cannot be true figures of profit for the same year. It may mean that, applied consistently over a period of years, both methods will for the whole period produce the same aggregate profit, and that appears to be approximately true. Or it may mean that one or other method will produce a true figure depending on the nature of the business and that seems to accord with the 'Recommendations' of the Institute. Normally a court attaches great weight to the view of the accountancy profession, though the court must always have the last word. But here the findings which I have summarized show that that assistance is not available on the issue which your Lordships have been invited to consider. The commissioners state that they were asked to decide between these methods as a broad matter of principle, and your Lordships were also invited to take that course. But I find that very difficult; if the accountancy profession cannot do that, I do not see how I can. The most I can do is to try to bring common sense to bear on the elements of the problem involved in this case on the assumption, which I am entitled to make, that common sense is the same for lawyers as for accountants.'

On the contradiction between the apparent meaning of the phrase 'true and fair view' and the meaning accountants have given it, see especially R Baxt 'True and Fair Accounts — A Legal Anachronism' (1970) 44 *ALJ* 541. In replacing the words 'every balance sheet shall give a true and fair view of the state of affairs of the company' in s 90*ter* of the 1926 Act with the words: 'The annual financial statements of a company shall, in *conformity with generally accepted accounting practice*, fairly present the state of affairs of the company . . .', s 286(3) of the 1973 Act replaces a myth with reality.

As regards the point in *Duple Motor Bodies*, it will be noted that any change in the basis of accounting must be stated, Schedule 4 cl 43(*b*).

How to conduct accounts in a time of inflation so as to 'fairly present the state of affairs' of a company is a question which is being widely debated. It has been suggested that 'current value' accounting should replace accounting based on historic costs.

[360] Markham *v* South African Finance and Industrial Co Ltd
1962 (3) SA 606 (AD)

The plaintiff claimed from the defendant company director's fees for the period from 1 July 1949 to 18 January 1958. The defendant submitted to judgment in respect of the three years preceding summons but pleaded prescription as regards the balance. The plaintiff's reply was that by inserting an item 'unsecured creditors' sundry—£11 961' in its accounts and balance sheets, for the years from 1950 to 1957, the defendant company had acknowledged its liability to him, thus interrupting the running of prescription in terms of s 6(1) of the Prescription Act 18 of 1943 (now s 14 of Act 68 of 1969). In the alternative, he relied for interruption of prescription on an item 'directors' fees—£1 250' in the 1957 accounts.

RUMPFF JA:

[After an examination of the authorities the learned judge arrived at the conclusion that in order to interrupt the running of prescription the acknowledgment of liability must be made by the debtor to the creditor or his agent. He continued:]

. . . The 1957 balance sheet contained the item 'directors fees—£1 250' for 1957, and also under the heading 'unsecured creditors', the item 'sundry—£11 961 4s 2d'. The report of the directors for 1957, which was signed by the secretary, contained the following paragraph:

'Provision of £1 250 has been made for directors' fees, in terms of the articles of association of the company, for the year ended 30 June 1957.'

The evidence before the court as to what happened at the annual general meeting on this issue is very brief. It is that the meeting, of which appellant was the chairman, by resolution adopted the balance sheet and the accounts for 1957. In regard to the item 'unsecured creditors, sundry— £11 961 4s 2d', there was no evidence before the trial court that the shareholders at the meeting, or the majority thereof, knew who these creditors were or what the amount was that was owed to each creditor, nor was there any evidence that at the meeting this particular item had been analysed.

On the evidence the appellant attended the meeting, to the knowledge of the other shareholders, as shareholder and director (and as chairman) and as creditor only in respect of the amount due to him in respect of directors' remuneration for the year ended 30 June 1957.

Although the confirmation of the accounts put before the meeting constituted an admission by the defendant of the contents of the accounts, the general admission of the amount of £11 961 4s 2d, owed to sundry creditors, cannot in my view, in the circumstances, be said to be an act done as between debtor and creditor so as to be an acknowledgment in terms of s 6(1) of the Prescription Act [now s 14 of the Prescription Act 68 of 1969] of any specific indebtedness to the plaintiff. The confirmation by defendant of the amount of £1 250, due to the directors in respect of the period ended 30 June 1957, stands on a different footing. To the knowledge of the shareholders who attended the meeting, the appellant was present as a director and as chairman, and therefore as a creditor for his share of the amount specifically admitted to be due to the directors. In these circumstances, the admission by defendant constituted, in my opinion, an act done as between the debtor and the creditor and therefore an acknowledgment of liability in terms of s 6(1) of the Prescription Act.

In the result, the appellant must fail on his main argument but he succeeds on his first alternative argument. The confirmation by the defendant of the amount of £1 250, as being a debt due to the directors, constituted an interruption of prescription in respect of £245, the appellant's share for the period 1 July 1956 to 28 December 1956, and this amount must be added to the amount awarded by the trial court.

[361] **Chantrey Martin v Martin**
[1953] 2 QB 286, [1953] 2 All ER 691

One of the questions in this case was whether in a law suit against a firm of auditors, the auditors can be compelled to produce (*a*) their working papers relating to the audit of a company's books; (*b*) correspondence conducted by them on behalf of the company with the Inland Revenue Department.

The court held that the working papers of auditors are their property and not that of their clients, and that they can, therefore, be ordered to produce them; but that correspondence conducted by them on behalf of a client with the Inland Revenue Department is the client's property and that consequently they cannot be ordered to produce it.

JENKINS LJ (giving the judgment of the court of appeal) : . . . We have no note of the judge's reasons for deciding that the remainder of the documents listed above should not be produced, but we were told by counsel that his decision was based on *Gibbon v Pease* [1905] 1 KB 810, where it was held that the plans prepared by an architect, employed by a building owner to carry out alterations to certain houses, were the property of the building owner. It would seem, therefore, that the judge took the view that the working papers, drafts, notes, calculations, and typed final accounts, brought into being by the plaintiffs in the course of, or as preliminaries to, the auditing of the client company's accounts, and the ascertainment of its tax liability, were by parity of reasoning the property of the client company, and accordingly that on the principle above stated the plaintiffs should not be compelled to produce them. . . .

. . . There are, however, other cases, to which we understand the judge was not referred, in which a different conclusion was reached in circumstances bearing a closer resemblance to those of the present case. In *Leicestershire County Council* v *Michael Faraday & Partners Ltd* [1941] 2 KB 205, [1941] 2 All ER 483 rating valuers were employed by a county council for five years to give advice and assistance in connection with the valuation of hereditaments in the council's area, and at the termination of the five years' agreement the council claimed to be entitled to all documents, books, maps and plans which had been prepared by or had come into the possession of the valuers in the course of, or for the purpose of, the performance of their duties. The court of appeal . . . rejected that claim, and held that the relationship between the county council and the valuers was that of client and professional man and not that of principal and agent; that the documents which the valuers had prepared in carrying out their expert work were their own property; and that, as the agreement did not contain any provision requiring the valuers to hand over the documents to the plaintiffs, they were not bound to hand them over.

In an earlier case, *London School Board* v *Northcroft* (reported in *Hudson on Building Contracts* 4 ed II 147) . . . a similar conclusion was reached by A L Smith J with respect to certain papers of calculations and memoranda prepared by quantity surveyors in the course of their employment by building owners on work which they had duly completed. Having regard to these two authorities we think that the proper conclusion in the present case is that (apart from correspondence with the Inland Revenue . . . to which we will return) all the documents listed above, other than the client company's ledgers, are the property of the plaintiffs. . . .

. . . It was, however, contended for the plaintiffs that even though these documents were their own property they should not be ordered to be produced, because they embodied information which was the subject of professional confidence as between the plaintiffs and the client company, and their production, and the consequent disclosure of their contents, would be a breach by the plaintiffs of their duty to the client company. Outside the area of legal professional privilege, which is not in question here, we do not think that this is a sufficient ground for refusing an order for production. . . .

. . . We think that (apart from the correspondence with the Inland Revenue) all the documents above listed (other than the ledgers) should be produced, but we think that the order should be made upon an undertaking by the defendant and the defendant's solicitors not to divulge their contents to any person otherwise than for the purposes of the present litigation, and not to use the information contained therein for any collateral purpose.

As to the correspondence with the Inland Revenue, this presumably comprises letters received from the Inland Revenue and copies of the letters written to the Inland Revenue. In conducting this correspondence the plaintiffs must, as it seems to us, have been acting as agents for the client company for the purpose of settling with the Inland Revenue the client company's tax liability. In *Leicestershire County Council* v *Michael Faraday & Partners* MacKinnon LJ distinguished that case from cases such as *Gibbon* v *Pease* in these words: '. . . but I think that those cases are radically different from the present case, as being concerned with the relative rights and duties of principal and agent. If an agent brings into existence certain documents while in the employment of his principal, they are the principal's documents and the principal can claim that the agent should hand them over.'

We are accordingly of opinion that these letters (both the copies of those sent and the originals of those received) should be considered as the property of the client company, with the result that on the principle above stated the plaintiffs should not be ordered to produce them. . . .

NOTES

In accordance with the principle that a person in possession of another's property who has incurred expenditure on that property with the consent of the owner, has a debtor-and-creditor lien over that property, an accountant who writes up books for a client has a lien on them for his fees: *Woodworth* v *Conroy* [1976] 2 WLR 338, [1976] 1 All ER 107 (CA). Not so, if his client furnishes him with a set of books, and the accountant prepares a statement for audit or income tax purposes upon the basis of the information contained therein. In this case, he has a lien on his statement, but not on the books: *Trustee of Walker* v *Jones, Cosnett & Ball* (1883) 2 SC 354 at 355. See also *Myra Foundation* v *Harvey* (1959) 76 ALR 2d 1313.

[362] **R** *v* **Shacter**
[1960] 2 Ch 252, [1960] 1 All ER 61

LORD PARKER CJ delivered the following judgment of the court: This appellant was convicted at Manchester Assizes together with one Shalam, who has not appealed, of publishing fraudulent statements and falsifying books of account contrary to s 83 and s 84 of the Larceny Act 1861, and also of frauds and defaults by officers of a company contrary to s 330(a) and s 331 of the Companies Act 1948, and of making a false entry contrary to s 328(1)(j). He now appeals by leave of the court.

The short facts so far as they are necessary for this appeal are that in 1950 one Maurice Shalam formed a private company to carry on a family business, and the appellant was appointed auditor. He was also appointed auditor of another company formed by Mr Shalam, the Wellington New Mills Company. He was appointed first on 22 June 1953 at an annual general meeting of the company, and his appointment was continued year by year after that. Apparently the companies, or one of them, got into financial difficulties and ultimately, with a view to obtaining an overdraft from a bank, certain figures were put before the bank including the stock position. These charges are made against the appellant in connexion with the putting forward of these figures to the bank.

The learned judge directed the jury in the course of his summing-up in these terms:

'There is no dispute Mr Maurice Shalam was director of the company and I direct you as a matter of law that if Mr Shacter was appointed auditor, and was exercising the office of auditor in 1953 — and that fact does not seem to be in dispute — then he would be an officer of the company.'

Accordingly, the first and main question which arises in this appeal is whether the appellant was at the material time an officer of the company. The argument for the appellant can be summarized as follows: An auditor, it is said, prima facie is not an officer. His duty is to safeguard the shareholders and not to help the directors, and he is not concerned with the day-to-day running or internal management of the company. It would be surprising, so runs the argument, to find him treated by the legislation as an officer, and great stress is laid on the definition clause in the Companies Act 1948 s 455(1) [corresponding to s 1 of our Act], where an officer is defined in these terms: '"officer", in relation to a body corporate, includes a director, manager or secretary'. Observe, it is said, that no reference is made to 'auditor'. That section, however, is a section of inclusive definition, and it is necessary to look more closely at the sections of the Act.

The first and perhaps most relevant section is s 159 [corresponding to s 270 of our Act]. Subsection (1) provides:

'Every company shall at each annual general meeting appoint an auditor or auditors to hold office from the conclusion of that, until the conclusion of the next, annual general meeting'.

In ss (5) and ss (6) of that section reference is again made to auditors appointed to hold office and to the office of auditor. Pausing there, it can well be asked to what office an auditor is being appointed unless it is an office in the company, and what officer he becomes unless it be an officer of the company?

Turning to s 161 [corresponding to s 275 of our Act], it is provided, so far as it is relevant, by ss (2):

'None of the following persons shall be qualified for appointment as auditor of a company — (*a*) an officer or servant of the company. . . . References in this subsection to an officer or servant shall be construed as not including references to an auditor.'

It follows from that, first, that an auditor becomes, or at any rate may become on his appointment, an officer of the company, otherwise the last sentence to which I have referred is unnecessary. Secondly, if he does become an officer of the company, it can only be by reason of being an auditor, for if he became an officer for any other reason he would under the subsection be disqualified. Further, in various sections of the Act, . . . reference is made to an auditor 'whether an officer of the company or not'. Those passages again show that an auditor may be an officer of the company, and this can, as I have already said, only be by reason of his appointment as auditor. Clearly, therefore, the Act contemplates that an auditor may at any rate be an officer by reason of his appointment under s 159.

The authorities concerned are all under the misfeasance section in earlier Acts dealing with civil liability, but they clearly show this, that an auditor appointed to fill an office is an officer, whereas an auditor appointed *ad hoc* for a limited purpose is not.

NOTES

Section 1 of our Act includes a secretary in the definition of 'officer', but excludes a secretary which is a body corporate.

Accountants, to whom Harman J in *Miles* v *Clarke* [1953] 1 All ER 779, [1953] 1 WLR 537, referred as 'the witch-doctors of the modern world', are for some purposes 'officers' of the company, but not for others, see e g *In re Western Counties Steam Bakeries and Milling Co* [1897] 1 Ch 617, and *Baker* v *McHardy* 1957 (4) SA 541 (N) (auditor not an officer, employee or servant for the purposes of the Liquor Act). Cf *Secretary for Inland Revenue* v *Somers Vine* 1968 (2) SA 138 (AD). In *Cornell and Millman NNO* v *Wolpert* 1976 (2) SA 563 (D) it was held that an auditor is not an officer of the company for the purposes of s 184 of the 1926 Act (s 424 of the 1973 Act).

In *Spackman* v *Evans* (1868) LR 3 HL 171 it was held (at 196) that auditors are not agents of the shareholders and that, in consequence, their knowledge of fraudulent acts of the directors cannot be imputed to the shareholders. Nor are auditors agents of the company for the purpose of making acknowledgments of debt: *Re Transplanters (Holding Company) Ltd* [1958] 2 All ER 711, [1958] 1 WLR 822.

[363] *In re* **Allen, Craig and Company (London) Ltd**
[1934] Ch 483

BENNETT J: . . . The auditors merely sent the reports and balance sheets to the secretary of the company, and they never got beyond the secretary. The directors never called a general meeting to consider these balance sheets and reports.

Mr Christie argued that, with respect to these two balance sheets, it was the duty of the auditors imposed by s 134(1) of the Companies Act of 1929 [ss 282, 301 of our Act] to make a report to the members. That is the plain wording of the section, and it is an admitted fact that the members of the company have never seen a report made by the auditors on those balance sheets.

The first thing to do is to interpret the section which lays down the duty of the auditors. The important words of the section are 'the members'. Does the statute impose on the auditors the duty of making their report to every member of the company? Now, if you give to the words their plain meaning it would seem that that obligation is imposed on them. But when you begin to reflect on the question it cannot, I think, have been the intention of the legislature to impose that duty on the auditors and it certainly has never been the practice, since the obligation has been imposed, for auditors themselves to send their report to every member of a company. . . .

. . . In my judgment the duty of the auditors, after having affixed their signatures to the report annexed to a balance sheet, is confined to forwarding that report to the secretary of the company, leaving the secretary of the company or the directors to perform the duties which the statute imposes of convening a general meeting to consider the report.

[364] *In re* **London and General Bank (No 2)**
[1895] 2 Ch 673

An auditor in a confidential report to the directors drew their attention to the insufficiency of the securities of the company. In his report to the shareholders he stated that the value of the assets was 'dependent on realization'. A dividend having been declared out of capital, the auditor was held liable.

LINDLEY LJ: . . . This is an appeal by Mr Theobald, one of the auditors of the above bank, which is being wound up, against an order made by Vaughan Williams J, under . . . the Companies (Winding-up) Act 1890. By this order Mr Theobald and the directors of the bank are declared jointly and severally liable to pay to the official receiver, as liquidator of the company, two sums of £5 946 12*s* and £8 486 11*s*, being respectively the amounts of dividends declared and paid by the bank for the years 1890 and 1891. The grounds on which this order was made on Mr Theobald are that these dividends were paid out of capital, and that such payment was made pursuant to resolutions of the shareholders based upon recommendations of the directors of the bank and upon balance sheets prepared and certified by Mr Theobald, and which did not truly represent the financial position of the company. . . .

... It is impossible to read s 7 of the Companies Act 1879 without being struck with the importance of the enactment that the auditors are to be appointed by the shareholders, and are to report to them directly, and not to or through the directors. The object of this enactment is obvious. It evidently is to secure to the shareholders independent and reliable information respecting the true financial position of the company at the time of the audit. . . . It is no part of an auditor's duty to give advice, either to directors or shareholders, as to what they ought to do. An auditor has nothing to do with the prudence or imprudence of making loans with or without security. It is nothing to him whether the business of a company is being conducted prudently or imprudently, profitably or unprofitably. It is nothing to him whether dividends are properly or improperly declared, provided he discharges his own duty to the share-holders. His business is to ascertain and state the true financial position of the company at the time of the audit, and his duty is confined to that. But then comes the question. How is he to ascertain that position? The answer is, by examining the books of the company. But he does not discharge his duty by doing this without inquiry and without taking any trouble to see that the books themselves show the company's true position. He must take reasonable care to ascertain that they do so. Unless he does this his audit would be worse than an idle farce. Assuming the books to be kept as to show the true position of a company, the auditor has to frame a balance sheet showing that position according to the books and to certify that the balance sheet presented is correct in that sense. But his first duty is to examine the books, not merely for the purpose of ascertaining what they do show, but also for the purpose of satisfying himself that they show the true financial position of the company. . . . An auditor, however, is not bound to do more than exercise reasonable care and skill in making inquiries and investigations. He is not an insurer; he does not guarantee that the books do correctly show the true position of the company's affairs; he does not even guarantee that his balance sheet is accurate according to the books of the company. If he did, he would be responsible for error on his part, even if he were himself deceived without any want of reasonable care on his part, say, by the fraudulent concealment of a book from him. His obligation is not so onerous as this. Such I take to be the duty of the auditor: he must be honest—ie he must not certify what he does not believe to be true, and he must take reasonable care and skill before he believes that what he certifies is true. What is reasonable care in any particular case must depend upon the circumstances of that case. Where there is nothing to excite suspicion very little inquiry will be reasonably sufficient, and in practice I believe business men select a few cases at haphazard, see that they are right, and assume that others like them are correct also. Where suspicion is aroused more care is obviously necessary; but, still, an auditor is not bound to exercise more than reasonable care and skill, even in a case of suspicion, and he is perfectly justified in acting on the opinion of an expert where special knowledge is required. . . . A person whose duty it is to convey information to others does not discharge that duty by simply giving them so much information as is calculated to induce them, or some of them, to ask for more. Information and means of information are by no means equivalent terms. Still, there may be circumstances under which information given in the shape of a printed document circulated amongst a large body of shareholders would, by its consequent publicity, be very injurious to their interests, and in such a case I am not prepared to say that an auditor would fail to discharge his duty if, instead of publishing his report in such a way as to insure publicity, he made a confidential report to the shareholders and invited their attention to it and told them where they could see it. . . .

. . . In this case I have no hesitation in saying that Mr Theobald did fail to discharge his duty to the shareholders in certifying and laying before them the balance sheet of February 1892, without any reference to the report which he laid before the directors and with no other warning than is conveyed by the words, 'The value of the assets as shown on the balance sheet is dependent upon realization'. . . .

[Lopes LJ concurred, and Rigby LJ gave a concurring judgment.]

[365] *In re* **Kingston Cotton Mill Company** (No 2)
[1896] 2 Ch 279

This was an action by the liquidators of a company against its auditors for payment of certain dividends improperly declared and paid out of the capital of the company on the faith of certain balance sheets signed by the auditors. In these balance sheets the manager of the company, a man of great ability and high repute, had deliberately overstated the value of the stock-in-trade, thus showing profits where in fact there were none. If the auditors had compared the different books and added to the stock-in-trade at the beginning of the year the amounts purchased during the year, and deducted the amounts sold, they would have seen that the statement of the stock-in-trade at the end of the year was so large as to call for explanation; but they did not do so. The court of appeal held that the auditors had not been negligent and were, therefore, not liable.

LOPES LJ: . . . It is the duty of an auditor to bring to bear on the work he has to perform that skill, care, and caution which a reasonably competent, careful, and cautious auditor would use. What is reasonable skill, care, and caution must depend on the particular circumstances of each case. An auditor is not bound to be a detective, or, as was said, to approach his work with suspicion or with a foregone conclusion that there is something wrong. He is a watch-dog, but not a bloodhound. He is justified in believing tried servants of the company in whom confidence is placed by the company. He is entitled to assume that they are honest, and to rely upon their representations, provided he takes reasonable care. If there is anything calculated to excite suspicion he should probe it to the bottom; but in the absence of anything of that kind he is only bound to be reasonably cautious and careful. . . .

It is not the duty of an auditor to take stock; he is not a stock expert; there are many matters in respect of which he must rely on the honesty and accuracy of others. He does not guarantee the discovery of all fraud. I think the auditors were justified in this case in relying on the honesty and accuracy of Jackson, and were not called upon to make further investigation.

. . . Auditors must not be made liable for not tracking out ingenious and carefully laid schemes of fraud when there is nothing to arouse their suspicion, and when those frauds are perpetrated by tried servants of the company and are undetected for years by the directors. So to hold would make the position of an auditor intolerable.

[366] *In re* City Equitable Fire Insurance Company Ltd
[1925] Ch 407

Dealing with the 'custom' of auditors to accept in the case of a 'responsible and reputable' bank a certificate of the bank as evidence that the securities exist —

ROMER J: . . . That it is the duty of a company's auditor in general to satisfy himself that the securities of the company in fact exist and are in safe custody cannot, I think be gainsaid. . . . An auditor may 'see' that the bank holds the securities in the sense that he satisfies himself of the fact. In the case of a responsible and reputable bank this . . . would seem to be the custom of auditors. But I think that it is a pity that there should be any such custom. It would be an invidious task for an auditor to decide as to any particular bank whether its certificate should be accepted in lieu of personal inspection. The custom, too, at once raises the question, much debated in the course of the evidence before me, whether the courtesy of accepting a certificate should be extended to an insurance company or a safe deposit company. Indeed, if once it be admitted that, in lieu of inspecting the securities personally, the auditor may rely upon the certificate of the person in whose custody the securities have properly been placed, the auditor would be justified in accepting the certificate of any official of the company who happened to be in charge of the safe in which the securities are placed, supposing such official to be a reputable and responsible person. At some time or another it will, I think, have to be considered seriously whether it is not the duty of an auditor to make a personal inspection, in all cases where it is practicable for him to do so, whatever may be the standing of the person or company in whose possession the securities happen to be. I do not, however, propose to investigate this question further upon the present occasion. For an auditor is not, in my judgment, ever justified in omitting to make personal inspection of securities that are in the custody of a person or company with whom it is not proper that they should be left, whenever such personal inspection is practicable. And whenever an auditor discovers that securities of the company are not in proper custody, it is his duty to require that the matter be put right at once, or, if his requirement be not complied with, to report the fact to the shareholders, and this whether he can or cannot make a personal inspection. . . .

[367] Tonkwane Sawmill Co Ltd *v* Filmalter
1975 (2) SA 453 (W)

BOSHOFF J: This is an action couched in delict for damages based on the alleged negligence of an auditor. The defendant was at all material times the auditor of the plaintiff and a company known as Tonkwane Estates Ltd. It is alleged that during the period May 1968 to March 1970 a sum of R2 179 was stolen from the plaintiff and a sum of R533,75 was stolen from Tonkwane Estates Ltd and that such losses occurred as a result of the negligence of the defendant who, failing to employ reasonable skill and care, adopted and accepted practices which allowed for defalcation to be undetected and did not at any time during the above period properly verify and audit the books of account of the companies and thereby determine that the sums of money drawn for and on behalf of both companies for the payment of wages exceeded the sums actually paid in respect of wages by each of the companies. . . .

In the nature of things, the obligations of an auditor depend to a very large extent on the nature of the contract between the auditor and the company which employs him and relevant legislation which may prescribe the duties of an auditor. In the instant case the plaintiff and Tonkwane Estates Ltd are companies which carry on business in Swaziland and are registered under the laws of Swaziland. No evidence was placed before the court as to the statutory duties of the defendant in respect of the companies and there is also no suggestion that the duties of the defendant were other than the ordinary duties of an auditor. In performing those duties he has to act with reasonable care and skill, that is to say, he must bring to bear on the work he has to perform that skill, care and caution which a reasonably competent, careful and cautious auditor would use; cf *Van Wyk* v *Lewis* 1924 AD 438 at 444. In the case of *Re London and General Bank Ltd, Ex parte Theobald (No 2)* [1895] 2 Ch 673 at 682–4 it was pointed out that an auditor is not an insurer and that in the discharge of his duty he is only bound to exercise a reasonable amount of care and skill and what in any particular case is a reasonable amount of care and skill depends on the circumstances of that case; that if there is nothing which ought to excite suspicion, less care may properly be considered reasonable than would be so considered if suspicion was or ought to have been aroused. In the case of *Re Kingston Cotton Mill Co (No 2)* [1896] 2 Ch 279 at 288 it was pointed out that an auditor is not bound to be a detective or to approach his work with suspicion or with a foregone conclusion that there is something wrong; he is a watchdog but not a bloodhound.

In the instant case it is common cause that in carrying out an audit, an auditor is entitled to conduct his audit by applying test checks. He is not necessarily obliged to check in detail all his clients' transactions or operations. The nature and extent of the tests which are to be applied must be decided by him in the light of all the circumstances and, in particular, on his assessment of the efficacy of a client's management and system of internal control and on whether his investigations reveal that the system is being effectively applied, and that management and management alone is responsible for the introduction and application of an effective internal control system. An audit is not a substitute for management control and no guarantee is given or to be implied that an audit will necessarily disclose fraudulent misappropriations. Responsibility for the financial control and accounts of an undertaking rests upon those who are entrusted by the proprietors with its direction and management.

It is for them to ensure that adequate records are maintained and that such accounts as may be required by statute or for other reasons, are prepared so as to give a true and fair view and such information as may be required by law or is considered desirable or useful as the particular circumstances may suggest. Management is responsible for safeguarding the assets of the undertaking and is not entitled to rely upon the auditor for protection against defects in its administration or control.

It is proper and necessary to add to all this the remarks of Lord Denning in *Fomento (Sterling Area) Ltd* v *Selsdon Fountain-Pen Co Ltd & others* [1958] 1 All ER 11 (HL) 23, namely, that an auditor is not to be confined to the mechanics of checking vouchers and making arithmetical computations. His vital task is to take care to see that errors are not made, be they errors of computation, or errors of omission or commission of downright untruths. To perform this task properly, he must come to it with an enquiring mind—not suspicious of dishonesty—but suspecting that someone may have made a mistake somewhere and that a check must be made to ensure that there has been none.

In my respectful view, this case must be considered in the light of these principles.

[The learned judge then analysed the evidence and concluded:]

In the circumstances it is difficult to come to the conclusion that the plaintiff has established a loss to the companies on a balance of probability, but even if I am wrong on this aspect of the case, the plaintiff still has to prove negligence on the part of the defendant. According to the defendant, he audited the books of the companies annually. He also did test-checks in December 1967, June 1968 and in April 1969, and found nothing irregular in the books of the companies. He has moved office three times since he ceased to be auditor of the companies, and is no longer in possession of his audit-programme. He was satisfied with the internal management of the companies and had no reason to suspect that the employees were not administering the financial affairs of the companies properly.

NOTES

'Auditors of a limited company are bound to know or make themselves acquainted with their duties under the articles of the company whose accounts they are appointed to audit, and under the Companies Acts for the time being in force . . .', per Astbury J in *Re Republic of Bolivia Exploration Syndicate Ltd* [1914] 1 Ch 139 at 171.

In *Dominion Freeholders Ltd* v *Aird* [1966] NSWR 293, noted (1966) 40 *ALJ* 237, the auditors, who in reliance upon a statement by the company's internal accountant, had certified an annual balance sheet and profit and loss account which did not give a true and fair view of the company's affairs, were held liable in damages to the company. Their claim for indemnification from the internal accountant failed, the court holding they could not delegate their statutory duty. The court added that there was no 'special relationship' between the auditors and the accountant so as to bring into operation the decision in *Hedley Byrne & Co Ltd* v *Heller 371* below. Both the accountant and the auditors owed their duties to the company, not to each other.

Unless a client elects to deal with an accountant individually, and not as a partner in his firm, his partners are liable for his professional negligence in conducting the affairs of the firm, *Kirkintilloch Equitable Society Ltd* v *Livingstone* 1971 SLT (Notes) 54.

In *Nelson Guarantee Corporation Ltd* v *Hodgson* [1958] NZLR 609 (noted (1959) *SA Accountant* 215) the annual audits of a company were behindhand because there was a delay in the preparation of the accounts. A new secretary embezzled moneys. The auditors were sued for damages by the company on the ground that this could not have happened if they had taken spots checks between audits. The court held that they were not liable. Their duty under the statutory audit was to report on the accounts when ready, not to make checks during the year.

The standard of care required of an accountant and auditor is not a static concept, and what was sufficient in 1900 or 1950 is not necessarily sufficient today. Failure to apply modern verification procedures may well amount to negligence, and it is generally accepted that it is now the duty of an auditor to check the stock by appropriate methods. See also *Thomas* v *Devonport Corporation* [1900] 1 QB 16; *Fomento (Sterling Area) Ltd* v *Selsdon Fountain-Pen Co Ltd* [1958] 1 WLR 45, [1958] 1 All ER 11 (HL); *In re Thomas Gerrard & Son Ltd* [1968] Ch 455, [1967] 2 All ER 525.

Generally on the standard of care expected of an auditor, R Baxt 'The Modern Company Auditor' (1970) 33 *MLR* 413.

[368] Arenson v Arenson
[1975] 3 WLR 815 (HL)

LORD SIMON OF GLAISDALE: My Lords, the question in this appeal is whether an accountant/auditor of a private company who on request values shares in the company in the knowledge that his valuation is to determine the price to be paid for the shares under a contract for their sale is liable to be sued if he makes his valuation negligently.

The first defendant, Archy Arenson (who has taken no part in the proceedings which have led to the instant appeal), was the controlling shareholder and chairman of a private company, A Arenson Ltd. He took his nephew, Ivor Arenson, the plaintiff in this action and the appellant before your Lordships, into the business, and Archy Arenson and his wife gave the appellant a parcel of shares in the company. By two documents ('the contract letters') dated 18 March 1964, and 1 October 1968 the appellant agreed with the first defendant (*inter alia*) as follows, the terms being common to both letters:

'5. In the event of my employment with the company terminating for whatsoever reason, I will offer to sell my shares to Mr Arenson' (the first defendant) 'and it is agreed that he will purchase them from me at the fair value. . . . 6. "Fair value" shall mean in relation to the shares in A Arenson Ltd, the value thereof as determined by the auditors for the time being of the company whose valuation acting as experts and not as arbitrators shall be final and binding on all parties.'

The respondents to this appeal, a firm of chartered accountants, were at all material times the auditors of the company. They are the second defendants in the action.

On 4 April 1970 the appellant's employment by the company ceased. It appears that the secretary of the company thereupon orally requested the respondents to value the appellant's shares. . . . The respondents replied to the company secretary by letter dated 13 May 1970, referring to the contract letters, and giving the 'fair value' of the shares as £4 916 13*s* 4*d*. On 11 June 1970 in reliance on that valuation, the plaintiff transferred his shares to the first defendant and received payment of £4 916 13*s* 4*d*.

A few months later the company 'went public', the transaction involving a report by the respondents. The appellant alleges that the transaction showed that the shares which he had sold were worth six times their value as assessed by the respondents. In consequence, on 19 August 1971 the appellant brought the action from which this appeal arises. Alleging that 'the said valuation was misconceived and erroneous in one or more fundamental respects and was made on a wrong basis or wrong bases', he in effect claimed from the first defendant the difference between what he had been paid for the shares and the sixfold sum which he asserts was their true value. Further or in the alternative, the appellant claimed damages from the respondents, alleging that they 'were negligent in making the said valuation'.

. . . [T]he respondents applied for an order . . . that the statement of claim should be struck out and the action dismissed as against them- selves (the respondents), on the ground that the statement of claim disclosed no reasonable cause of action against them. The matter was adjourned to Brightman J, who delivered a reserved judgment [1972] 1 WLR 1196. He held that a clear line of authority . . . established a principle whereby the appellant's claim against the respondents was misconceived and bound to fail. Brightman J stated the principle as follows, at 1205:

> '. . . where a person (though not an arbitrator) is in the position of an arbitrator, with a duty to hold the scales evenly between two other parties for the purposes of resolving by the exercise of his own judg- ment a matter that is not agreed between them, it is not expedient that the law should entertain an action against the opinion-giver alleging an error, whether negligent or not.'

I shall presume to call this 'Brightman J's formulation'. Although he did not use the term expressly, it is apparent that the judge considered the rule to be one of public policy.

The appellant appealed to the court of appeal. By reserved judgments delivered on 22 February 1973, they dismissed the appeal, Lord Denning MR dissenting [1973] Ch 346. The majority (Buckley LJ and Sir Seymour Karminski) relied on the same authorities as Brightman J. Buckley LJ summarized their effect in a passage which I presume to call 'Buckley LJ's formulation', at 370:

> '. . . these authorities establish in a manner binding upon us in this court that, where a third party undertakes the role of deciding as between two other parties a question, the determination of which requires the third party to hold the scales fairly between the opposing interests of the two parties, the third party is immune from an action for negligence in respect of anything done in that role.'

Later in his judgment, at 371, Buckley LJ reformulated the principle in such a way as to elucidate that by 'question' he meant 'matter in dispute or upon which other parties have opposed interests'. A clear distinction, in his opinion, was to be drawn between the position of a third party who is required to adjudicate in such a way and one to whom the parties delegate the function of ascertaining some matter of fact. Buckley LJ held the rule to be based on public policy (p 370), which, though not precluding a duty from arising, gives immunity from the consequences of its breach (pp 368–9). . . .

On 12 February 1974 your Lordships' House gave judgment in *Sutcliffe* v *Thackrah* [1974] AC 727. The plaintiff there had employed builders, who subsequently went into liquidation, to build a house for him, the contract being in the standard RIBA form. The defendants were appointed architects and quantity surveyors under the contract. The plaintiff brought an action in negligence against the defendants for (*inter alia*) over-certifying interim sums due from the plaintiff to the builders. The official referee found for the plaintiff and awarded him damages against the defendants. The court of appeal [1973] 1 WLR 888 reversed the decision on the ground that the defendants were acting in an arbitral capacity and were accordingly absolved from liability for negligence. Your Lordships' House restored the judgment of the official referee.

In consequence of the decision in *Sutcliffe* v *Thackrah*, the instant appellant applied to the court of appeal for leave to appeal immediately to your Lordships' House against their order of 9 July 1973 and, despite the respondents' opposition, the court of appeal on 22 July 1974 acceded to that application. . . .

Formally, the appeal to your Lordships is only against the costs order made by the court of appeal. But it has been rightly treated as raising the point of law which I posed at the outset of this speech — the legal issue falling to be decided on the basis that the facts set out in the statement of claim are correct.

. . . Counsel [for the respondents] founded his argument on four propositions: (1) judges and arbitrators enjoy immunity from suit in negligence in respect of their decisions; (2) such immunity is conferred by law on grounds of public policy, namely, the desirability of speedy and final settlement of disputes; (3) Lord Reid in *Sutcliffe* v *Thackrah* [1974] AC 727, 738 (Lord Hodson concurring) considered that 'many, probably most' of the decisions on which the court of appeal relied in that case, as in the instant one, could be justified on their facts, and only Lord Salmon specifically disapproved of any other than *Chambers* v *Goldthorpe* [1901] 1 KB 624; (4) the generic nature of the immunity recognized in those cases not specifically disapproved was marked by the long standing and reiterated use of the phrase 'quasi-arbitrator' . . . thereby according recognition that the role of the person concerned has some essential characteristic akin to that of an arbitrator. Counsel then went on to ask what this essential characteristic could be. Why should judges and arbitrators enjoy immunity from suit in negligence? Because, said counsel, they are in a particularly vulnerable situation; in the nature of things their decisions are liable to be displeasing to at least one of the parties affected thereby: as counsel put it, 'they are liable to be "shot at by both sides."' This, then, is the first essential characteristic which is shared by arbitrator and 'quasi-arbitrator', and the first prerequisite to constitute a person who is not an arbitrator under the Arbitration Act 1950 a 'quasi-arbitrator' so as to enjoy immunity from suit. The second such characteristic of an arbitrator, and prerequisite for immunity from suit, is that two or more parties have agreed to be bound by this decision on the question between them. The respondents satisfied both prerequisites; accordingly, they are 'quasi-arbitrators' and immune from suit in negligence in respect of their decision. So far as public policy is concerned no logical distinction can be drawn between the speedy and final settlement of disputes by an arbitrator and the obviation of disputes by a valuer in the position of the respondents: if public policy requires immunity in the one case, so it must also in the other.

Skilfully though this argument was deployed, I find it less than compelling. My main objections are that the journey starts at the wrong place and arrives at a wrong place. It starts with the immunity conferred on the arbitrator for reasons of public policy. But in my judgment this is a secondary and subordinate consideration of public policy. There is a primary and anterior consideration of public policy, which should be the starting point. This is that, where there is a duty to act with care with regard to another person and there is a breach of such duty causing damage to the other person, public policy in general demands that such damage should be made good to the party to whom the duty is owed by the person owing the duty. There may be a supervening and secondary public policy which demands, nevertheless, immunity from suit in the particular circumstances. . . . But that the former public policy is primary can be seen from the jealousy with which the law allows any derogàtion from it. Thus a barrister enjoys immunity, but only in respect of his forensic conduct (since his duty to the court may conflict with and transcend his duty to his client): *Rondel* v *Worsley* [1969] 1 AC 191. And a diplomatic envoy enjoys immunity, but only so long as he is in post (plus a reasonable time thereafter for him to wind up his official affairs). . . .

It is, in my view, wrong in principle to freewheel by analogy from the arbitrator's immunity, as if it were not exceptional, and as if the primary rule were not one of responsibility.

Not only does the argument start from the wrong place, it arrives at an impossible place. The respondents' contention would leave the instant case in absurd discrepancy with *Sutcliffe* v *Thackrah* [1974] AC 727 and throw the law into hopeless confusion.

. . . Lord Salmon [in *Sutcliffe* v *Thackrah* [1974] AC] said, at 759:

'. . . there are the most striking differences between the roles of the valuer and architect in the circumstances to which I have referred and the role of a judge or arbitrator. Judges and arbitrators have disputes submitted to them for decision.' . . .

There may well be other *indicia* that a valuer is acting in a judicial role, such as the reception of rival contentions or of evidence, or the giving of a reasoned judgment. But in my view the essential prerequisite for him to claim immunity as an arbitrator is that, by the time the matter is submitted to him for decision, there should be a formulated dispute between at least two parties which his decision is required to resolve. It is not enough that parties who may be affected by the decision have opposed interests—still less that the decision is on a matter which is not agreed between them.

The question which puzzled me as the argument developed was, what was the essential difference between the typical valuer, the auditor in the present case, and an arbitrator at common law or under the Arbitration Acts? It was conceded that an arbitrator is immune from suit, aside from fraud, but why? I find it impossible to put weight on such considerations as that in the case of an arbitrator (*a*) there is a dispute between parties, (*b*) he hears evidence, (*c*) he hears submissions from the parties, and that therefore he, unlike the valuer, is acting in a judicial capacity. As regards (*a*), I cannot see any juridical distinction between a dispute which has actually arisen and a situation where persons have opposed interests, if in either case an impartial person has had to be called in to make a decision which the interested parties will accept. As regards (*b*) and (*c*), these are certainly not necessary activities of an arbiter. Once the nature and the limits of the submission to him have been defined, it could well be that he would go down at his own convenience to a warehouse, inspect a sample of merchandise displayed to him by the foreman and return his opinion on its quality or value. I have come to be of opinion that it is a necessary conclusion to be drawn from *Sutcliffe* v *Thackrah* [1974] AC 727 and from the instant decision that an arbitrator at common law or under the Acts is indeed a person selected by the parties for his expertise, whether technical or intellectual, that he pledges skill in the exercise thereof and that if he is negligent in that exercise he will be liable in damages.

If this conclusion were to be established by law, I do not think the consequences would be dramatic or even noticeable. It would become a generally accepted term of a reference to arbitration—because the referee would insist on it—that he be given by the parties immunity from suit for negligence at the instance of either of them.

[In the result the House of Lords held that the respondents did not enjoy immunity and that, in consequence, the statement of claim disclosed a cause of action.]

[369] **Ultramares Corporation v Touche**
(1931) 255 NY 170, 174 NE 441, 74 ALR 1139

Cardozo Ch J: . . . The action is in tort for damages suffered through the misrepresentations of accountants, the first cause of action being for misrepresentations that were merely negligent, and the second for misrepresentations charged to have been fraudulent.

In January 1924 the defendants, a firm of public accountants, were employed by Fred Stern & Co Inc, to prepare and certify a balance sheet exhibiting the condition of its business as of 31 December 1923. They had been employed at the end of each of the three years preceding to render a like service. Fred Stern & Co Inc, which was in substance Stern himself, was engaged in the importation and sale of rubber. To finance its operations, it required extensive credit and borrowed large sums of money from banks and other lenders. All this was known to the defendants. The defendants knew also that in the usual course of business the balance sheet when certified would be exhibited by the Stern Company to banks, creditors, stockholders, purchasers, or sellers, according to the needs of the occasion, as the basis of financial dealings. Accordingly, when the balance sheet was made up, the defendants supplied the Stern Company with 32 copies certified with serial numbers as counterpart originals. Nothing was said as to the persons to whom these counterparts would be shown or the extent or number of the transactions in which they would be used. In particular there was no mention of the plaintiff, a corporation doing business chiefly as a factor, which till then had never made advances to the Stern Company, though it had sold merchandise in small amounts. The range of the transactions in which a certificate of audit might be expected to play a part was as indefinite and wide as the possibilities of the business that was mirrored in the summary.

By 26 February 1924 the audit was finished and the balance sheet made up. It stated assets in the sum of 2 550 671 dollars and liabilities other than capital and surplus in the sum of 1 479 956 dollars, thus showing a net worth of 1 070 715 dollars. Attached to the balance sheet was a certificate as follows:

'Touche, Niven & Co.,
Public Accountants,
Eighty Maiden Lane,
New York.
February 26, 1924.

Certificate of Auditors

We have examined the accounts of Fred Stern & Co Inc for the year ending December 31, 1923, and hereby certify that the annexed balance sheet is in accordance therewith and with the information and explanations given us. We further certify that, subject to provision for federal taxes on income, the said statement, in our opinion, presents a true and correct view of the financial conditions of Fred Stern & Co Inc as at December 31, 1923.

Touche, Niven & Co,
Public Accountants.'

Capital and surplus were intact if the balance sheet was accurate. In reality both had been wiped out, and the corporation was insolvent. The books had been falsified by those in charge of the business so as to set forth accounts receivable and other assets which turned out to be fictitious. . . .

. . . The plaintiff, a corporation engaged in business as a factor, was approached by Stern in March 1924 with a request for loans of money to finance the sales of rubber. Up to that time the dealings between the two houses were on a cash basis and trifling in amount. As a condition of any loans the plaintiff insisted that it receive a balance sheet certified by public accountants, and in response to that demand it was given one of the certificates signed by the defendants and then in Stern's possession. On the faith of that certificate the plaintiff made a loan which was followed by many others. . . . Nearly a year later, in December 1924, the house of cards collapsed. In that month, plaintiff made three loans to the Stern Company, one of 100 000 dollars, a second of 25 000 dollars, and a third of 40 000 dollars. For some of these loans no security was received. For some of the earlier loans the security was inadequate. On 2 January 1925 the Stern Company was declared a bankrupt. . . .

. . . The defendants owed to their employer a duty imposed by law to make their certificate without fraud, and a duty growing out of contract to make it with the care and caution proper to their calling. Fraud includes the pretence of knowledge when knowledge there is none. To creditors and investors to whom the employer exhibited the certificate, the defendants owed a duty to make it without fraud, since there was notice in the circumstances of its making that the employer did not intend to keep it to himself. . . . A different question develops when we ask whether they owed a duty to these to make it without negligence. If liability for negligence exists, a thoughtless slip or blunder, the failure to detect a theft or forgery beneath the cover of deceptive entries, may expose accountants to a liability in an indeterminate amount for an indeterminate time to an indeterminate class. The hazards of a business conducted on these terms are so extreme as to enkindle doubt whether a flaw may not exist in the implication of a duty that exposes to these consequences. . . .

. . . In the field of the law of torts a manufacturer who is negligent in the manufacture of a chattel in circumstances pointing to an unreasonable risk of serious bodily harm to those using it thereafter may be liable for negligence though privity is lacking between manufacturer and user. A force or instrument of harm having been launched with potentialities of danger manifest to the eye of prudence, the one who launches it is under a duty to keep it within bounds. Even so, the question is still open whether the potentialities of danger that will charge with liability are confined to harm to the person, or include injury to property. . . . In either view, however, what is released or set in motion is a physical force. We are now asked to say that a like liability attaches to the circulation of a thought or a release of the explosive power resident in words. . . .

We have said that the duty to refrain from negligent representation would become coincident or nearly so with the duty to refrain from fraud if this action could be maintained. A representation, even though knowingly false, does not constitute ground for an action of deceit unless made with intent to be communicated to the persons or class of persons who act upon it to their prejudice. Affirmance of this judgment would require us to hold that all or nearly all the persons so situated would suffer an impairment of an interest legally protected if the representation had been negligent. We speak of all 'or nearly all', for cases can be imagined where a casual response, made in circumstances insufficient to indicate that care should be expected, would permit recovery for fraud if wilfully deceitful. Cases of fraud between persons so circumstanced are, however, too infrequent and exceptional to make the radii greatly different if the fields of liability for negligence and deceit be figured as concentric circles. The like may be said of the possibility that the negligence of the injured party, contributing to the result, may avail to overcome the one remedy, though unavailing to defeat the other.

Neither of these possibilities is noted by the plaintiff in its answer to the suggestion that the two fields would be coincident. Its answer has been merely this, first, that the duty to speak with care does not arise unless the words are the culmination of a service, and, second, that it does not arise unless the service is rendered in the pursuit of an independent calling, characterized as public. As to the first of these suggestions, we have already had occasion to observe that given a relation making diligence a duty, speech as well as conduct must conform to that exacting standard. As to the second of the two suggestions, public accountants are public only in the sense that their services are offered to anyone who chooses to employ them. This is far from saying that those who do not employ them are in the same position as those who do.

Liability for negligence if adjudged in this case will extend to many callings other than an auditor's. Lawyers who certify their opinion as to the validity of municipal or corporate bonds, with knowledge that the opinion will be brought to the notice of the public, will become liable to the investors, if they have overlooked a statute or a decision, to the same extent as if the controversy were one between client and adviser. Title companies insuring titles to a tract of land, with knowledge that at an approaching auction the fact that they have insured will be stated to the bidders, will become liable to purchasers who may wish the benefit of a policy without payment of a premium. These illustrations may seem to be extreme, but they go little, if any, farther than we are invited to go now. Negligence, moreover, will have one standard when viewed in relation to the employer, and another, and at times, a stricter standard when viewed in relation to the public. Explanations that might seem plausible, omissions that might be reasonable, if the duty is confined to the employer, conducting a business that presumably at least is not a fraud upon his creditors, might wear another aspect if an independent duty to be suspicious even of one's principal is owing to the investors. . . .

. . . Our holding does not emancipate accountants from the consequences of fraud. It does not relieve them if their audit has been so negligent as to justify a finding that they had no genuine belief in its adequacy, for this again is fraud. It does no more than say that, if less than this is proved, if there has been neither reckless misstatement nor insincere profession of an opinion, but only honest blunder, the ensuing liability for negligence is one that is bounded by the contract, and is to be enforced between the parties by whom the contract has been made. We doubt whether the average business man receiving a certificate without paying for it, and receiving it merely as one among a multitude of possible investors, would look for anything more. . . .

[370] Candler v Crane, Christmas & Company
[1951] 2 KB 164, [1951] 1 All ER 426

The defendants, a firm of accountants and auditors, had prepared, by their clerk, a company's accounts and balance sheet which, to the knowledge of the clerk, were intended to be put before the plaintiff to induce him to invest money in the company. The accounts had been prepared negligently and did not give a true view of the state of the company's affairs. Relying on the accuracy of the accounts, the plaintiff subscribed the sum of £2 000 for shares in the company. He lost this money and sought to hold the defendants liable for the loss which he had sustained. It was admitted that the defendants had failed to use proper care and skill in the preparation and presentation of the accounts, but there was no fraud on their part.

The court of first instance dismissed the plaintiff's claim whose appeal to the court of appeal was dismissed, Denning LJ dissenting. The majority judges (Asquith and Cohen LJJ) held that in the absence of a contractual or fiduciary relationship between the parties, the auditors owned no duty to the plaintiff (as distinguished from the company employing them) to exercise care in preparing the accounts and giving their certificate.

Legal argument turned largely on the principles laid down in two English cases, *Le Lievre* v *Gould* [1893] 1 QB 491 and *Donoghue* v *Stevenson* [1932] AC 562.

In *Le Lievre* v *Gould* a surveyor had negligently given certificates certifying to the amount of work done by a builder in the erection of a home. A mortgagee had advanced money on the faith of these certificates and suffered loss for which he sought to hold the surveyor liable. There was no contract between the mortgagee and the surveyor. The court held that in the absence of a contractual relationship the surveyor owed the mortgagee no duty to be careful, and dismissed the action.

In *Donoghue* v *Stevenson* [1932] AC 562 a friend of the plaintiff had ordered for her in a café a bottle of ginger-beer manufactured by the defendant. The plaintiff alleged that after she had drunk part of the contents the decomposed remains of a snail had floated out of the bottle and that, as result, she had suffered shock and severe gastroenteritis. There was no contractual nexus between the plaintiff and the defendant, but the House of Lords held by a majority of three to two, that the manufacturer of an article of food, medicine, or the like, who sells it to a distributor in circumstances which prevent the distributor or consumer from discovering any defect, is under a legal duty to the ultimate purchaser or consumer to take reasonable care that the article is free from defects likely to cause injury to health.

DENNING LJ: . . . I come now to the great question in the case: Did the defendants owe a duty of care to the plaintiff? If the matter were free from authority, I should have said that they clearly did owe a duty of care to him. They were professional accountants who prepared and put before him these accounts, knowing that he was going to be guided by them in making an investment in the company. On the faith of those accounts he did make the investment, whereas, if the accounts had been carefully prepared, he would not have made the investment at all. The result is that he has lost his money. In the circumstances, had he not every right to rely on the accounts being prepared with proper care, and is he not entitled to redress from the defendants on whom he relied? I say he is.

. . . Before I consider the decision in *Le Lievre* v *Gould* I wish to say that, in my opinion, at the time it was decided current legal thought was infected by two cardinal errors. The first error was one which appears time and time again in nineteenth-century thought, namely that no one who is not a party to a contract can sue on it or on anything arising out of it. This error has had unfortunate consequences both in the law of contract and in the law of tort. . . . So far as tort is concerned, it led the lawyers of that day to suppose that, if one of the parties to a contract was negligent in carrying it out, no third person who was injured by that negligence could sue for damages on account of it. . . . This error lies at the root of the reasoning of Bowen LJ in *Le Lievre* v *Gould* [1893] 1 QB 491 at 502, when he said that the law of England

'. . . does not consider that what a man writes on paper is like a gun or other dangerous instrument . . .',

meaning thereby that, unless it was a thing which was dangerous in itself, no action lay. This error was exploded by the great case of *Donoghue* v *Stevenson* [1932] AC 562, which decided that the presence of a contract did not defeat an action for negligence by a third person, provided that the circumstances disclosed a duty by the contracting party to them. The second error was an error as to the effect of *Derry* v *Peek* [*69* above], an error which persisted for 35 years at least after the decision, namely that no action ever lies for a negligent statement even though it is intended to be acted on by the plaintiff and is, in fact, acted on by him to his loss. . . .

The first submission put forward by counsel for the defendants was that a duty to be careful in making statements arose only out of a contractual duty to the plaintiff or a fiduciary relationship to him. Apart from such cases no action, he said, had ever been allowed for negligent statements, and he urged that this want of authority was a reason against it being allowed now. This argument about the novelty of the action does not appeal to me. It has been put forward in all the great cases which have been milestones of progress in our law, and it has nearly always been rejected. If one reads *Ashby* v *White* (1703) 2 Ld Raym 938; *Pasley* v *Freeman* (1789) 3 Term Rep 51, and *Donoghue* v *Stevenson* one finds that in each of them the judges were divided in opinion. On the one side there were the timorous souls who were fearful of allowing a new cause of action. On the other side there were the bold spirits who were ready to allow it if justice so required. It was fortunate for the common law that the progressive view prevailed. . . .

The second submission of counsel for the defendants was that a duty to take care only arose where the result of a failure to take care will cause physical damage to persons or property. It was for this reason that he did not dispute two illustrations of negligent statements which I put in the course of the argument—the case of an analyst who negligently certifies to a manufacturer of food that a particular ingredient is harmless, whereas it is, in fact, poisonous, or the case of an inspector of lifts who negligently reports that a particular lift is safe, where it is, in fact, dangerous. The analyst and the lift inspector would, I should have thought, be liable to any person who was injured by consuming the food or using the lift, at any rate if there was no likelihood of intermediate inspection.

. . . Counsel said that that might well be so because the negligence there caused physical damage, but that the same would not apply to negligence which caused financial loss. . . . I cannot accept this as a valid distinction. I can understand that in some cases of financial loss there may not be a sufficiently proximate relationship to give rise to a duty of care, but if once the duty exists I cannot think that liability depends on the nature of the damage. . . .

. . . Let me now be constructive and suggest the circumstances in which I say that a duty to use care in making a statement does exist apart from a contract in that behalf. First, what persons are under such duty? My answer is those persons, such as accountants, surveyors, valuers and analysts, whose profession and occupation it is to examine books, accounts, and other things, and to make reports on which other people — other than their clients — rely in the ordinary course of business. Their duty is not merely a duty to use care in their reports. They have also a duty to use care in their work which results in their reports. Herein lies the difference between these professional men and other persons who have been held to be under no duty to use care in their statements, such as . . . trustees who answer inquiries about the trust funds. Those persons do not bring, and are not expected to bring, any professional knowledge or skill into the preparation of their statements. They can only be made responsible by the law affecting persons generally, such as contract, estoppel, innocent misrepresentation or fraud. It is, however, very different with persons who engage in a calling which requires special knowledge and skill. From very early times it has been held that they owe a duty of care to those who are closely and directly affected by their work apart altogether from any contract or undertaking in that behalf. . . . This reasoning has been treated as applicable not only to shoeing smiths, surgeons and barbers, who work with hammers, knives and scissors, but also to shipbrokers and clerks in the Custom House who work with figures and make entries in books

'. . . because their situation and employment necessarily imply a competent degree of knowledge in making such entries . . .'.

. . . The same reasoning has been applied to medical men who make reports on the sanity of others; see *Everett* v *Griffiths* [1920] 3 KB 163 at 182, 217. It is, I think, also applicable to professional accountants. They are not liable, of course, for casual remarks made in the course of conversation, nor for other statements made outside their work, or not made in their capacity as accountants, but they are, in my opinion, in proper cases, apart from any contract in the matter, under a duty to use reasonable care in the preparation of their accounts and in the making of their reports.

Secondly, to whom do these professional people owe this duty? I will take accountants, but the same reasoning applies to the others. They owe the duty, of course, to their employer or client, and also, I think, to any third person to whom they themselves show the accounts, or to whom they know their employer is going to show the accounts so as to induce him to invest money or take some other action on them. I do not think, however, the duty can be extended still further so as to include strangers of whom they have heard nothing and to whom their employer without their knowledge may choose to show their accounts. Once the accountants have handed their accounts to their employer, they are not, as a rule, responsible for what he does with them without their knowledge or consent. A good illustration is afforded by the decision in *Le Lievre* v *Gould* [1893] 1 QB 491 itself, which I certainly would not wish to call in question. The facts are somewhat differently stated in the various reports, but collecting them together they come to this: A surveyor there surveyed work for a building owner and handed certificates to him so that the owner could know the amounts which he had to pay the builder. The building owner then chose to show the certificates to his own mortgagees who advanced money on them instead of on the certificates of their own surveyor. The mortgagees then said that the owner's surveyor owed a duty of care to them. That was obviously untenable, because they should have had the work surveyed by their own surveyor. Indeed, they had actually stipulated for it. The relationship was, therefore, one in which the inspection of an intermediate person might reasonably be interposed, and was, consequently, too remote to raise a duty of care. . . . Excluding such cases as those, however, there are some cases—of which the present is one—where the accountants know all the time, even before they present their accounts, that their employer requires the accounts to show to a third person so as to induce him to act on them, and then they themselves, or their employers, present the accounts to him for the purpose. In such cases I am of opinion that the accountants owe a duty of care to the third person.

The test of proximity in these cases is: Did the accountants know that the accounts were required for submission to the plaintiff and use by him? . . .

. . . Thirdly, to what transactions does the duty of care extend? It extends, I think, only to those transactions for which the accountants knew their accounts were required. For instance, in the present case it extends to the original investment of £2 000 which the plaintiff made in reliance on the accounts, because the defendants knew that the accounts were required for his guidance in making that investment, but it does not extend to the subsequent £200 which he invested after he had been two months with the company. . . .

. . . It will be noticed that I have confined the duty to cases where the accountant prepares his accounts and makes his report for the guidance of the very person in the very transaction in question. That is sufficient for the decision of this case. I can well understand that it would be going too far to make an accountant liable to any person in the land who chooses to rely on the accounts in matters of business, for that would expose him, in the words of Cardozo CJ in *Ultramares Corporation* v *Touche* (1931) 174 NE 441 at 444, to

'. . . liability in an indeterminate amount for an indeterminate time to an indeterminate class'.

Whether he would be liable if he prepared his accounts for the guidance of a specific class of persons in a specific class of transactions, I do not say. I should have thought he might be, just as the analyst and lift inspector would be liable in the instances I have given earlier. . . .

. . . One final word. I think the law would fail to serve the best interests of the community if it should hold that accountants and auditors owe a duty to no one but their client. Its influence would be most marked in cases where the client is a company or firm controlled by one man. It would encourage accountants to accept the information which the one man gives them without verifying it, and to prepare and present accounts rather as a lawyer prepares and presents a case, putting the best appearance on the accounts they can without expressing their personal opinion of them. This is, to my way of thinking, an entirely wrong approach. There is a great difference between the lawyer and the accountant. The lawyer is never called on to express his personal belief in the truth of his client's case, whereas the accountant, who certifies the accounts of his client, is always called on to express his personal opinion whether the accounts exhibit a true and correct view of his client's affairs, and he is required to do this, not so much for the satisfaction of his own client, but more for the guidance of share-holders, investors, revenue authorities, and others who may have to rely on the accounts in serious matters of business. If we should decide this case in favour of the defendants, there will be no reason why accountants should ever verify the word of the one man in a one-man company because there will be no one to complain about it. The one man who gives them wrong information will not complain if they do not verify it. He wants their backing for the misleading information he gives them, and he can only get it if they accept his word without veri-fication. It is just what he wants so as to gain his own ends. And the persons who are misled cannot complain because the accountants owe no duty to them. If such be the law, I think it is to be regretted, for it means that the accountants' certificate, which should be a safeguard, becomes a snare for those who rely on it. I do not myself think that it is the law. In my opinion, accountants owe a duty of care not only to their own clients, but also to all those whom they know will rely on their accounts in the transactions for which those accounts are prepared. . . .

AsQUITH LJ: On two points I entirely agree with the judgment delivered by Denning LJ. I agree that the cause of action based on an alleged breach of duty occurring after the plaintiff became a shareholder cannot be made out if only because the damage relied on preceded the breach. I also agree, for the reasons he has given, that Fraser was clearly acting within the scope of his employment by the defendant firm in showing the draft accounts and giving certain other information to the plaintiff.

But I have the misfortune to differ from my brother on the more important point raised in this case. The point may be put in this way: assume that Fraser's negligent misrepresentations had been made by his employers, the partners in the defendant firm. Assume further, as the fact is, that there was no fraud and no contract or fiduciary relationship between them and the plaintiff. Would they, in those events, have been liable to the plaintiff in respect of damage incurred by him through acting on those negligent misrepresentations? The defendants say 'No'. They do not question that in the absence of fraud, contract and fiduciary relationship there are cases in which A may be under a legal obligation to B to use reasonable care for some purposes. Their proposition is that, under the conditions assumed in this case, the defendants were under no duty, sounding in tort, to the plaintiff to take care that their representations of fact should be true. They rely in support of this contention on *Le Lievre* v *Gould*, a decision binding on this court. I agree with the trial judge in considering that authority to be conclusive in their favour, unless it can be shown to have been overruled or to be distinguishable.

The plaintiff's case is that whatever may have been the position before *Donoghue* v *Stevenson* the rule applied by the majority of the House of Lords in that case necessarily involves the consequence that (even where fraud, contract and fiduciary relationship are absent) A will be liable to B for any negligent misrepresentations on which B acts to his detriment, provided always that there exists between A and B the necessary degree of so-called 'proximity'. It is argued for the plaintiff that there was sufficient proximity on the facts of this case. . . .

Singular consequences would follow if the principle laid down in the snail case were applied to negligent misrepresentation in every case in which the representee were proximate to the representor. The case has been instanced by Professor Winfield and referred to by my brother Denning of a marine hydrographer who carelessly omits to indicate on his map the existence of a reef. The captain of the *Queen Mary*, in reliance on the map and having no opportunity of checking it by reference to any other map, steers her on the unsuspected rocks, and she becomes a total loss. Is the unfortunate cartographer to be liable to her owners in negligence for some millions of pounds damages? If so, people will, in future, think twice before making maps. Cartography would become an ultra-hazardous occupation. Yet what line can be drawn between the map-maker and the defendants in the present case. If it be said that there is no proximity between the cartographer and those for whose use his map is designed, the reply surely is that there is just as much 'proximity' as there was between the manufacturer of the peccant ginger-beer bottle and its ultimate consumer.

In the present state of our law different rules still seem to apply to the negligent misstatement on the one hand and to the negligent circulation or repair of chattels on the other; and *Donoghue's* case does not seem to me to have abolished these differences. I am not concerned with defending the existing state of the law or contending that it is strictly logical—it clearly is not. I am merely recording what I think it is.

If this relegates me to the company of 'timorous souls', I must face that consequence with such fortitude as I can command.

[371] Hedley Byrne & Co Ltd *v* Heller & Partners Ltd
[1964] AC 465, [1963] 2 All ER 575 (HL)

In reliance on a favourable credit reference supplied by the defendant bank to his own bank the plaintiff extended credit to a customer of the defendant bank and lost heavily. Alleging that the defendant bank had acted negligently, he sued them for damages.

LORD MORRIS OF BORTH-Y-GEST: . . . My Lords, the important question of law which has concerned your lordships in this appeal is whether in the circumstances of the case there was a duty of care owed by the respondents, who I will call 'the bank', to the appellants, whom I will call 'Hedleys'. In order to recover the damages which they claim Hedleys must establish that the bank owed them a duty, that the bank failed to discharge such duty, and that as a consequence Hedleys suffered loss. . . .

My Lords, it seems to me that if A assumes a responsibility to B to tender him deliberate advice there could be a liability if the advice is negligently given. I say 'could be' because the ordinary courtesies and exchanges of life would become impossible if it were sought to attach legal obligation to every kindly and friendly act. But the principle of the matter would not appear to be in doubt. If A employs B (who might, for example, be a professional man such as an accountant or a solicitor or a doctor) for reward to give advice, and if the advice is negligently given, there could be a liability in B to pay damages. The fact that the advice is given in words would not, in my view, prevent liability from arising. Quite apart, however, from employment or contract there may be circumstances in which a duty to exercise care will arise if a service is voluntarily undertaken. A medical man may unexpectedly come across an unconscious man, who is a complete stranger to him, and who is in urgent need of skilled attention: if the medical man, following the fine traditions of his profession, proceeds to treat the unconscious man he must exercise reasonable skill and care in doing so. . . . I can see no difference of principle in the case of a banker. If someone who was not a customer of a bank made a formal approach to the bank with a definite request that the bank would give him deliberate advice as to certain financial matters of a nature with which the bank ordinarily dealt the bank would be under no obligation to accede to the request: if, however, they undertook, though gratuitously, to give deliberate advice (I exclude what I might call casual and perfunctory conversations) they would be under a duty to exercise reasonable care in giving it. They would be liable if they were negligent although, there being no consideration, no enforceable contractual relationship was created.

[After referring to several cases His Lordship continued:]

My Lords, these are but familiar and well-known illustrations, which could be multiplied, which show that irrespective of any contractual or fiduciary relationship and irrespective of any direct dealing, a duty may be owed by one person to another. It is said, however, that where careless (but not fraudulent) misstatements are in question there can be no liability in the maker of them unless there is either some contractual or fiduciary relationship with a person adversely affected by the making of them or unless through the making of them something is created or circulated or some situation is created which is dangerous to life, limb or property. In logic I can see no essential reason for distinguishing injury which is caused by a reliance on words from injury which is caused by a reliance on the safety of the staging to a ship, or by a reliance on the safety for use of the contents of a bottle of hair wash or a bottle of some consumable liquid. It seems to me, therefore, that if A claims that he has suffered injury or loss as a result of acting upon some misstatement made by B who is not in any contractual or fiduciary relationship with him the inquiry that is first raised is whether B owed any duty to A: if he did the further inquiry is raised as to the nature of the duty. There may be circumstances under which the only duty owed by B to A is the duty of being honest: there may be circumstances under which B owes to A the duty not only of being honest but also a duty of taking reasonable care. The issue in the present case is whether the bank owed any duty to Hedleys and if so what the duty was. . . .

Leaving aside cases where there is some contractual or fiduciary relationship there may be many situations in which one person voluntarily or gratuitously undertakes to do something for another person and becomes under a duty to exercise reasonable care. I have given illustrations. Apart from cases where there is some direct dealing, there may be cases where one person issues a document which should be the result of an exercise of the skill and judgment required by him in his calling and where he knows and intends that its accuracy will be relied on by another. . . .

My Lords, I consider that it follows and that it should now be regarded as settled that if someone possessed of a special skill undertakes, quite irrespective of contract, to apply that skill for the assistance of another person who relies on such skill, a duty of care will arise. The fact that the service is to be given by means of, or by the instrumentality of, words can make no difference. Furthermore if, in a sphere in which a person is so placed that others could reasonably rely on his judgment or his skill or on his ability to make careful inquiry, a person takes it on himself to give information or advice to, or allows his information or advice to be passed on to, another person who, as he knows or should know, will place reliance on it, then a duty of care will arise. . . .

LORD REID: A reasonable man, knowing that he was being trusted or that his skill and judgment were being relied on, would, I think, have three courses open to him. He could keep silent or decline to give the information or advice sought: or he could give an answer with a clear qualification that he accepted no responsibility for it or that it was given without that reflection or inquiry which a careful answer would require: or he could simply answer without any such qualification. If he chooses to adopt the last course he must, I think, be held to have accepted some responsibility for his answer being given carefully, or to have accepted a relationship with the inquirer which requires him to exercise such care as the circumstances require.

If that is right then it must follow that *Candler* v *Crane, Christmas & Co* [370, above] was wrongly decided. There the plaintiff wanted to see the accounts of a company before deciding to invest in it. The defendants were the company's accountants and they were told by the company to complete the company's accounts as soon as possible because they were to be shown to the plaintiff who was a potential investor in the company. At the company's request the defendants showed the completed accounts to the plaintiff, discussed them with him, and allowed him to take a copy. The accounts had been carelessly prepared and gave a wholly misleading picture. It was obvious to the defendants that the plaintiff was relying on their skill and judgment and on their having exercised that care which by contract they owed to the company, and I think that any reasonable man in the plaintiff's shoes would have relied on that. This seems to me to be a typical case of agreeing to assume a responsibility: they knew why the plaintiff wanted to see the accounts and why their employers, the company, wanted them to be shown to him, and agreed to show them to him without even a suggestion that he should not rely on them.

[In the result the bank was held not liable, because it had made it clear in advance that it was not assuming any duty of care, but as regards the principle, the Law Lords approved the dissenting judgment of Denning LJ.in *Candler* v *Crane, Christmas & Co.*]

[372] Lathern v Sher
1974 (4) SA 687 (W)

MARGO J: Since a fraudulent misrepresentation which is material, and which is intended to induce and does induce the representee to enter into a contract, gives the representee an action *ex delicto* for damages for the patrimonial loss caused thereby, there would appear to be no reason in principle why a negligent but non-fraudulent misrepresentation which is material, and which is intended to and does induce the representee to contract, should not create a similar right of action for damages *ex delicto*.

That there is no clear authority in our law for that proposition is not conclusive. In the history of Aquilian relief in modern times there have been progressive extensions to cover the demands of new situations. For example, in very recent times the Aquilian action has been applied to such delicts as unfair competition. . . .

. . . The extension of the Aquilian action to liability for negligent statements causing damage is itself a modern development, and has been achieved despite considerable controversy. *Cape of Good Hope Bank* v *Fischer* 4 SC 368, per De Villiers CJ at 376–7; *Perlman* v *Zoutendyk* 1934 CPD 151 per Watermeyer J at 161–2; *Fichardts Motors (Pty) Ltd* v *Nienaber* 1936 OPD 221, per Krause JP at 225; *Alliance Building Society* v *Deretitch* 1941 TPD 203 (where Barry J was on the whole opposed to this development); *Western Alarm System* v *Coini & Co* 1944 CPD 271, per Jones J at 276; *Herschel* v *Mrupe* 1954 (3) SA 464 (AD) in which, despite the varying opinions, all the judgments recognize liability in delict for negligent statements in certain circumstances; *Currie Motors (Pretoria) (Pty) Ltd* v *Motor Union Insurance Co Ltd* 1961 (3) SA 872 (T), per Bresler J at 876–7; *Hamman* v *Moolman* [1968 (4) SA 340 (AD)]; *Murray* v *McLean NO* 1970 (1) SA 133 (R), per Lewis J, as he then was, at 136A; *Bristow* v *Lycett* 1971 (4) SA 223 (RAD) per Beadle CJ at 238D.

NOTES

There have been several earlier cases in which the question of liability for negligent misrepresentations arose in South Africa. In *Perlman* v *Zoutendyk* 1934 CPD 151 the defendant, an auctioneer and sworn appraiser, had issued to the owner of certain land a certificate in which he valued the land at £4 500. In reliance on this certificate the plaintiff advanced the owner of the land £1 450 upon a mortgage of the property. The owner of the land became insolvent and the plaintiff lost the greater portion of the money advanced. The plaintiff sued the defendant for damages, alleging that at all material times the value of the land was not more than £390 and that the defendant had acted negligently in making his valuation. An exception that the declaration of the plaintiff disclosed no legal liability of the defendant was dismissed. The court held that in our law the circumstances which created a duty of care were considerably wider than in *Le Lievre* v *Gould*. Per Watermeyer J: 'In Roman-Dutch law the duty arises whenever the defendant whose act is complained of should reasonably have foreseen the probability of harm being caused by his act to another person, except, perhaps, in those cases in which the act complained of can be said to be justified or excused. . . .'

In *Herschel* v *Mrupe* 1954 (3) SA 464 (AD) the plaintiff's husband was killed in a collision between two motor vehicles, one of which was owned by the defendant. In reply to an inquiry by the attorney of the plaintiff, the defendant's attorneys innocently but incorrectly informed the plaintiff's attorney that the South British Insurance Company were the defendant's insurers. Acting on this information the plaintiff instituted action against the South British Insurance Company under the Motor Vehicle Insurance Act 1942 and as a result incurred wasted costs. The plaintiff then sued the defendant for the loss, alleging that the defendant had been negligent in supplying her with incorrect information. The Transvaal Provincial Division granted the defendant absolution from the instance and the appeal of the plaintiff to the Appellate Division was dismissed. Centlivres CJ, who dissented, considered that the case of *Perlman* v *Zoutendyk* had been correctly decided and that the defendant ought to be held liable, but the majority judges (Schreiner, Van den Heever, Hoexter and Fagan JJA), on varying grounds, held otherwise.

In *Currie Motors (Pretoria) (Pty) Ltd* v *Motor Union Insurance Co Ltd* 1961 (3) SA 872 (T) an insurer gave an insured person erroneous information about the renewal date of a car policy. As a result, the insured allowed the policy to lapse and the car was not insured when an accident occurred. The court held that if it could be shown that the insurer had acted negligently in supplying erroneous information, the insured was entitled to damages in delict.

As to liability for negligent statements in South African law see T W Price (1950) 67 *SALJ* 138, 257, (1951) 68 *SALJ* 78; R G McKerron (1963) 80 *SALJ* 483; P M A Hunt (1964) 81 *SALJ* 241, (1968) 85 *SALJ* 379.

In England there is still some uncertainty as to the circumstances in which liability will arise. See *Mutual Life and Citizens Assurance Co Ltd* v *Evatt* [1971] AC 793, [1971] 2 WLR 23 (PC), and *Esso Petroleum Company Ltd* v *Mardon* [1976] 2 All ER 5 (CA).

Lord Denning's statement in *Candler* v *Crane, Christmas & Co, 370* above, that accountants owe a duty of care to a third person to whom they themselves show the accounts, or to whom they know their employer is going to show the accounts so as to induce him to invest money or take some other action, but not to strangers of whom they have heard nothing and to whom their employer without their knowledge may choose to show the accounts, was applied in the New Zealand case of *Dimond Manufacturing Co Ltd* v *Hamilton* [1969] NZLR 609 and in the Canadian case of *Haig* v *Bamford* (1974) 6 WWR 236 (Sask CA).

In the New Zealand case the accountant, on whose alleged negligence the action was based, had no specific purchase or tender in contemplation at the time when he prepared the balance sheet, but he himself showed it to the plaintiff who later purchased the company, knowing that the plaintiff would rely upon it. 'Once he had done this I find the case indistinguishable from *Candler* v *Crane, Christmas & Co* in which the balance-sheet was prepared with a prospective purchaser in contemplation; for if the representation (as I have held) was constituted by the handing-over of the balance-sheet, or at least was not communicated to the representee till that time, it can hardly matter at what time the representee came into the contemplation of the representor, provided that it was before he did the final act, without which he would not have been liable at all' (per Turner J at 637). The firm of accountants, of which he was a member, was accordingly held liable. See also *Scott Group Ltd* v *McFarlane* [1975] 1 NZLR 582.

In the Canadian case of *Haig* v *Bamford* the plaintiff, in reliance on a financial statement prepared by the defendants in the ordinary course of their duties as accountants, invested some $29 000 in a company which subsequently collapsed, with the result that he lost his investment. When working on the company's accounts, the defendants did not discover that payments of $28 000 on two contracts recorded in the company's books as completed were in fact advance payments on contracts which had not yet been begun, and that the company, so far from having made a profit, as shown in its books, had suffered a substantial loss. When the defendants prepared the statement for the company, they knew that the company would use it to induce investors to put money into the company, but neither the defendants nor the company knew at that stage of the plaintiff as a prospective investor. The court of appeal, in a two-to-one decision, dismissed the action on the ground that the defendants were not under a duty of care to the plaintiff, who was not within their contemplation when they prepared their statement. To hold otherwise, would expose accountants, in the words of Cardozo CJ in *Ultramares Corporation* v *Touche, 369* above (quoted with approval by Lord Denning in *Candler* v *Crane, Christmas & Co, 370* above) to 'liability in an indeterminate account for an indeterminate time to an indeterminate class'.

In America, the privity doctrine is still predominant, but the authority of *Ultramares* v *Touche* has been weakened by cases such as *Fisher* v *Kletz* 266 F Supp 180 (1967), *Rusch Factors Inc* v *Levin* 284 F Supp 85 (1968) and *Shatterproof Glass* v *James* 466 SW 2d 873 (1971), 46 ALR 3d 968. In *Rusch Factors* and *Shatterproof Glass* the accountants were held liable to parties whose reliance was actually foreseen by them. In *Fisher* v *Kletz* the court held that accountants may have a common law duty to disclose to the investing and lending public the discovery of false and misleading statements in their already published financial statements.

There is unanimity on one point only: accountants cannot rely on the absence of a contractual tie with the plaintiff as a defence if they have acted dishonestly.

On *Hedley Byrne* and liability for negligent statements, see also A M Honoré (1964–65) 8 *Journal of the Society of Public Teachers of Law* 284; Arthur L Goodhart (1964) 74 *Yale LJ* 286; D G Hill (1962) 4 *Sydney LR* 75; D M Gordon (1964) 38 *Australian LJ* 39 and 79; Robert Stevens (1964) 27 *MLR* 121; D J Payne (1964) 6 *University of Western Australia LR* 467; R W Hodgin 'The Fortunes of Hedley Byrne' 1972 *JBL* 27; A F R 'The Aftermath of Hedley Byrne v Heller' 1973 *SLT* 109; R Baxt 'The Liability of Accountants and Auditors for Negligent Statements in Company Accounts' (1973) 36 *MLR* 42; C M Schmitthoff 1976 *JBL* 48. On the position in America see 'Accountants' Liabilities for False and Misleading Finance Statements' (1967) 67 *Col LR* 1437; Constantine N Katsoris 'Accountants' Third Party Liability—How Far Do We Go?' (1967) 36 *Fordham LR* 191.

On the liability of an accountant for non-disclosure of an error in the accounts which he discovers *after* he has audited and certified the accounts, see also (1968) 116 *University of Pennsylvania LR* 500.

17   *Compromises, Reconstructions and Take-overs*

I. COMPROMISES AND RECONSTRUCTIONS

A TEXT

If a compromise or arrangement is proposed between a company and its creditors or any class of them or between a company and its members or any class of them, the court may, on the application of the company or any creditor or member of the company or, in the case of a company being wound up, of the liquidator, or if the company is subject to a judicial management order, of the judicial manager, order a meeting of the creditors or class of creditors, or of the members or class of members to be summoned, s 311(1): *373–375*. An explanatory statement containing full information must be sent out with the notice summoning the meeting, s 312. If the compromise or arrangement is (1) approved by a majority in number representing three-fourths in value of the creditors or class of creditors, or a majority representing three-fourths of the votes exercisable by the members or class of members, present and voting either in person or by proxy at the meeting and (2) sanctioned by the court, it becomes binding on the creditors or the members concerned, and also on the company, or on the liquidators if the company is being wound up, or on the judicial manager if the company is subject to a judicial management order, s 311(2): *376–380*. The liability of a surety for the company is not affected, s 311(3), and see *Jeral Distributors* v *Rosen* 1975 (2) SA 149 (C). The court order does not become effective until a copy of it has been sent to the Registrar and registered by him, s 311(5).

If the compromise or arrangement involves a reconstruction of the company, ie a transfer of the undertaking to another company consisting substantially of the same members, or the amalgamation of two or more companies, the court may, either by the order sanctioning the compromise or by a subsequent order, make provision for the matters mentioned in paras (*a*) to (*f*) of ss (1) of s 313.

On the power of the liquidators in the voluntary winding-up of a company to accept shares for assets of the company, see s 390.

B CASES

[373] *Ex parte* **Payne Bros Ltd**
1945 NPD 8

SELKE J: . . . [The applicant] drew my attention . . . to the case of *In re Peach & Hatton Ltd* 1935 NPD 429. . . . In that case, Carlisle J expressed the view that section 103 [now s 311] applied only to a case where the company concerned was being administered as insolvent, or was liable to be so administered. I gather from his remarks that he was influenced to this view largely by the provision which was contained in ss (3) of the section as it then was, that: 'In this section the expression "company" means any company liable to be wound up under this Act.' The section at that time contained no definition or explanation of the word 'arrangement'. Since then, however, the section has been amended by s 64 of Act 23 of 1939, and in place of the former ss (3), has now been substituted a new subsection numbered (5), which, while retaining the provision that 'company' 'means any company liable to be wound up under this Act', also provides that:

'The expression "arrangement" includes a reorganization of the share capital of the company by the consolidation of shares of different classes or by the division of shares into shares of different classes or by both these methods.'

It seems to me, therefore, that whatever doubt may have existed formerly, this new definition or explanation of the word 'arrangement' shows beyond question that the application of the section is not now limited to companies which are insolvent or on the verge of insolvency. . . .

[374] **Sovereign Life Assurance Company** *v* **Dodd**
[1892] 2 QB 573

Here it was held that for the purposes of an arrangement between a life assurance company and its creditors insured persons whose policies have matured form a class of creditors distinct from those whose policies have not matured, and that separate meetings of these classes have to be held to make the arrangement binding upon their respective members.

BOWEN LJ . . . What is the proper construction of [the] statute? It makes the majority of the creditors or of a class of creditors bind the minority: it exercises a most formidable compulsion upon dissentient, or would-be dissentient, creditors; and it therefore requires to be construed with care, so as not to place in the hands of some of the creditors the means and opportunity of forcing dissentients to do that which it is unreasonable to require them to do, or of making a mere jest of the interests of the minority. If we are to construe the section as it is suggested on behalf of the plaintiffs it ought to be construed, we should be holding that a class of policy holders whose interests are uncertain may by a mere majority in value override the interests of those who have nothing to do with futurity, and whose rights have been already ascertained. It is obvious that those two sets of interests are inconsistent, and that those whose policies are still current are deeply interested in sacrificing the interests of those whose policies have matured. They are bound by no community of interest, and their claims are not capable of being ascertained by any common system of valuation. Are we, then, justified in so construing the Act of Parliament as to include these persons in one class? The word 'class' is vague, and to find out what is meant by it we must look at the scope of the section, which is a section enabling the court to order a meeting of a class of creditors to be called. It seems plain that we must give such a meaning to the term 'class' as will prevent the section being so worked as to result in confiscation and injustice, and that it must be confined to those persons whose rights are not so dissimilar as to make it impossible for them to consult together with a view to their common interest. . . .

[375] *Ex parte* **Massing & Ingham (Pty) Ltd**
1942 WLD 204

MILLIN J: . . . Section 103(1) of the Act with which I have to deal defines strictly what the court may do when any arrangement of this kind is proposed. All the court may do in a case like this is to order a meeting of the members of the company or class of member, as the case may be, to be summoned in the way the court directs. Then, under s 103(2), if the required majority is obtained at the meeting or meetings the arrangement shall, if sanctioned by the court, be binding. Thus, there is only one way in which the court may proceed before sanctioning a compromise or arrangement of this kind and that is by first ordering a meeting or meetings, as the case may be. In the case of a single person holding all the shares of a defined class a meeting may be dispensed with, ie his consent should be taken as equivalent to a meeting because one person cannot hold a meeting. In the case where it is possible to hold a meeting, that is to say, where there are two or more shareholders, a meeting must be held even if it appears from the evidence that they must all necessarily consent. . . .

NOTES

'It is elementary that if it is desired to distribute the assets of a company otherwise than strictly in accordance with the creditors' rights, the proper way to do it is by a scheme of arrangement under s 206. . . . Instead I am asked in effect to deprive the creditors of the protection afforded by s 206 and to sanction a conditional agreement of compromise under s 245', per Plowman J in *Re Trix Ltd* [1970] 1 WLR 1421 (Ch) at 1423, [1970] 3 All ER 397 at 398. (Section 206 corresponds to s 311, s 245 to s 386(4)(*b*), (*c*) and (*d*) of our Act.)

In *In re NFU Development Trust Ltd* [1972] 1 WLR 1548, [1973] 1 All ER 135 (Ch) it was held that a scheme whereby members' rights are totally surrendered without compensation is not a 'compromise' or 'arrangement' within the meaning of s 206, which implies some measure of accommodation on both sides.

For a scheme to be a scheme for the reconstruction of a company, 'substantially the business and the persons interested must be the same' per Buckley J in *In re South African*

Supply and Cold Storage Co Ltd [1904] 2 Ch 268 at 286, quoted with approval by Penny-cuick J in *Brooklands Selangor Holdings Ltd v Inland Revenue Commissioner* [1970] 1 WLR 429 at 445.

On the meaning of 'compromise' and 'arrangement', see further *Sneath v Valley Gold Ltd* [1893] 1 Ch 477; *Ex parte Cyrildene Heights (Pty) Ltd* 1966 (1) SA 307 (W); *Ex parte Bruyns* 1968 (1) SA 51 (W).

When a company transfers its business to a new company in consideration for shares, the consideration must be divided among different classes of members according to their rights and interests in the company: *Griffith v Paget* (1877) 5 ChD 894.

In re Gor Garage (Pty) Ltd 1963 (1) SA 375 (GW) it was held that a former director has no *locus standi* to apply.

In *Goode, Durrant & Murray (SA) Ltd v Stephenson NO (1)* 1961 (1) SA 655 (SR) Macdonald J put the principles which will guide the court in deciding whether to call a meeting thus (at 656): 'All that is necessary in my view is that this court should be satisfied on two points: firstly, that there is a proposal for a compromise or arrangement between the company and its creditors and, secondly, that there is a reasonable proba-bility that the requisite majority of creditors will accept the proposal.'

In *Ex parte Singh* 1950 (1) SA 471 (T) the court refused to call a meeting of creditors under s 103 because (*a*) one creditor whose claim exceeded one quarter of the total liabilities had stated that he was not prepared to accept the offer; (*b*) the offer contained various objectionable features; and (*c*) the court was not under the impression that it was a genuine offer.

While it is not the function of the court to say whether the compromise to be placed before the meeting is a good or a bad one, it will not authorize a meeting to be held if the offer is vague and the explanatory statement unsatisfactory: *Ex parte De Villiers* 1970 (2) SA 536 (C).

Substantial shareholders, who are concurrent creditors and yet whose interests differ widely from those of the other concurrent creditors, should meet separately from the other concurrent creditors: *Ex parte Borton* 1970 (1) SA 190 (E).

The court may give directions as to the manner in which the meeting is to be sum-moned and as to the proxy forms to be used: *Ex parte Judicial Managers CTC Bazaars (SA) Ltd* 1940 CPD 550, 1941 CPD 348. (About notices to creditors, see *Ex parte Beretta & Sons (Pvt) Ltd* 1963 (2) SA 146 (SR).)

A person appointed by the court to act as chairman of meetings under s 311 may not delegate his duties, and must comply strictly with the order of court under which he is appointed, and report to the court as directed: *Ex parte Simmons NO: In re Pola Invest-ments (Pty) Ltd* 1956 (4) SA 163 (T); *Ex parte Chenille Corporation of SA (Pty) Ltd* 1962 (4) SA 459 (T).

As to the voting rights of creditors with contingent claims, see *In re Unity Motors (Pty) Ltd* 1956 (4) SA 14 (W) (*377* below).

Meetings under s 311 are not subject to s 52 of the Insolvency Act. It follows, *inter alia*, that the vote of a creditor with a claim below R60 counts and that creditors may vote on claims ceded to them at any time before the meeting, *Ex parte MacRobert NO: In re Abor Trading Co Ltd (in liquidation)* 1956 (4) SA 588 (W).

A meeting may be dispensed with where the necessary meeting was held prior to the application to court, and the resolution was carried by the requisite majority of those present at the meeting, or where all the interested parties have agreed: *Ex parte Kinemas Ltd* 1933 WLD 75; *Ex parte Atkinson-Oates Motors Ltd* 1933 OPD 111; *Ex parte Handel House Ltd* 1940 GWL 52, (1940) 57 *SALJ* 390; *Ex parte Payne Bros Ltd* 1945 NPD 8; *Ex parte Jiffy Packing Co (Pty) Ltd* 1946 CPD 232; *Ex parte Hind Brothers & Company Ltd* 1947 (3) SA 373 (N); *Ex parte Schutex Industries (Pty) Ltd* 1950 (3) SA 714 (C). *Ex parte Hefferman's Supply Stores (Pty) Ltd* 1932 EDL 377 can no longer be regarded as good law.

On jurisdiction, see *Ex parte Pan-African Tanneries Ltd* 1950 (4) SA 321 (O); *In re Bobat: In re Kathorian Trading Co (Pty) Ltd* 1965 (2) SA 291 (N).

[376] *In re* **Bessemer Steel and Ordinance Company**
(1875) 1 ChD 251

MALINS V-C: . . . I think the agreement should be carried into effect. All the creditors of the company received notice of this meeting, and it must be presumed that those who did not attend left it to those who did to decide whether the agreement was advantageous or not, or they took so little interest in the matter that they did not think it worth their while to attend. At all events, I think that under the Act of Parliament only those creditors who were present at the meeting are to be attended to, and that three-fourths in value of those present are sufficient to sanction the contract. . . .

[This was followed in *Ex parte Liquidator Yum White Ltd* 1922 WLD 169, where the court held that it was not necessary that the creditors present at the meeting should constitute either a majority in number or three-fourths in value of the total creditors.]

[377] *In re* **Unity Motors (Pty) Ltd**
1956 (4) SA 14 (W)

KUPER J: . . . On 28 February 1956 this court granted leave to summon meetings of the preferent, secured and concurrent creditors of Unity Motors (Pty) Ltd . . . to consider an offer of compromise which the company wished to place before the creditors. The company was under provisional liquidation. K, who was the provisional liquidator of the company, was appointed the chairman of the meetings and he was obliged to report the results of the meetings to the court on 17 April 1956. . . .

The requisite meetings were duly held and the provisional liquidator in reporting the results to the court has also sought an order sanctioning the compromise in terms of s 103(2) of the Companies Act 46 of 1926 as amended. . . . For the purpose of this judgment I shall assume that there has been a compliance with the procedural requirements as set out in the order of court. . . .

. . . At the meetings the liquidator adopted the attitude that his sole duty was to act as chairman and therefore to report the results of the meetings to the court. He, therefore, accepted a certificate signed by the directors of the company setting out the creditors and their claims, he accepted the valuation of the assets of the company by the directors, he did not investigate the value and extent of the security held by the secured creditors and he did not investigate the books of the company. A number of disputes were raised at the meetings involving these questions and the liquidator did not determine any of the disputes but caused the creditors to vote on a number of alternative bases stating that the court would ultimately determine the correct basis. I understood from counsel that the liquidator was following the usual practice adopted by chairmen at meetings of this nature.

In my view the sooner this practice is altered the better the position will be for creditors of a company, and they are the persons whose interests are intended to be safeguarded by the provisions of s 103 and by the terms of the order of court. In most cases the offer of compromise is made by either the company or its directors and it is obviously in their interest to have the creditors accept as low an offer as possible. It is, therefore, completely wrong to compel creditors to approach such an offer on the basis of valuations made by the directors of the company without any investigation by the liquidator whose duty it is to represent the interests of the general body of creditors. The order of court required that a copy of the order should be sent 'to every creditor of the company whose claim is known to the provisional liquidator'. In my view this term required the provisional liquidator to examine the books of the company in order to ascertain who the creditors were, and in addition if he is aware of any creditor whose claim does not appear in the books he must send such a creditor notice. He does not comply with his duty merely by accepting the certificate of the directors setting out a list of creditors.

Furthermore, in my view, the liquidator should be required to state his view as to the business merits of the offer of compromise before the expenditure of the calling of meetings is incurred. In every case where the liquidator makes the original application for leave to summon meetings of creditors he expresses the view, based upon his investigation of the affairs of the company, that the acceptance of the proposed offer would prove to be to the benefit of creditors because on the final liquidation of the company the creditors would receive less than in terms of the offer. Where a director of the company makes the application either on his own behalf or on behalf of the company he should be required to obtain the view of the liquidator on the merits of the offer and this view should be placed before the court when the application is made. In this way the interests of creditors can be safe-guarded. In the instant case it seems to me that if the compromise was sanctioned the only persons who would receive a benefit, and a substantial benefit, would be the directors of the company at the expense of the creditors. . . .

. . . The three directors of the company had, it appears, personally guaranteed the accounts of several creditors of the company. At the meetings the directors stated that these guarantees were joint and several and the chairman accepted this statement without requiring the directors to exhibit the guarantees. The directors therefore claimed that each of them was a contingent creditor of the company to the full extent of each guarantee. If, therefore, they had guaranteed the claim of a creditor for the sum of £10 000 not only did the creditor vote in respect of his claim but each of the directors voted in respect of a contingent claim for £10 000 and consequently in respect of the one debt of the company for £10 000 votes for £40 000 were in fact cast. In this way the contingent claims of the directors amounted to £110 000. It was common cause that the requisite statutory majority was only obtained because the votes in regard to the £110 000 were cast in favour of accepting the compromise.

[It was] contended that the directors were contingent creditors and therefore entitled to cast their vote at meetings of creditors called pursuant to the provisions of s 103. The term creditor is not defined and [our attention was drawn] to the fact that in terms of s 113 [now 346(1)(*b*)] a contingent creditor is included in the term creditor as a person entitled to apply for a winding-up order. I do not think, however, that for the purpose of calculating the total liabilities of the company in terms of s 103 it is competent to add the claims of contingent creditors of the class here indicated. The total liabilities of the company are not increased because third parties have guaranteed the payment of debts of the company to creditors. The position is quite different where the company guaranteed the payment of a debt by a third person to his creditor, for in such a case if the company is called upon to discharge its guarantee its liabilities are increased by the amount it is called upon to pay. In the former case, furthermore, the contingent creditors could only become creditors after the company has been excussed. If the offer of compromise had been accepted by the statutory majority and sanctioned by the court, the result would be to prevent the contingent creditors from ever becoming creditors of the company, for the claim of the creditor against the company would be discharged.

But even if the directors were entitled to vote on their contingent claims, I do not think that the court would sanction the offer. In my view the directors used their vote in order to coerce the minority in order to protect their own interests at the expense of the ordinary trade creditors of the company. I have already referred to the fact that in the absence of vital information the arrangement was not such as a man of business would reasonably approve. The directors did not act bona fide in adopting this method of imposing their will on the other creditors of the company. . . .

[The application for the sanction of the compromise was accordingly refused.]

[378] Rosen *v* Bruyns NO
1973 (1) SA 815 (T)

CILLIÉ JP: This is an appeal against an order made on 12 April 1972 in this court by Claassen J sanctioning the acceptance of an offer of compromise made at a meeting of creditors of the Mammoth Construction and Drilling Co (Pty) Ltd which was under provisional liquidation, discharging that company from liquidation, revesting it with its assets and ordering an opposing creditor to pay the costs occasioned by his opposition.

The facts leading up to that order are the following: On 15 June 1971 the company was placed under provisional liquidation on the petition of a creditor, Hendrik Schalk Pienaar, and the respondent C A Bruyns was duly appointed provisional liquidator by the Master of the Supreme Court. A certain Isaac Nankin, who is a director of the company, submitted an offer of compromise with the creditors of the company to the respondent. It is not necessary to deal with all the particulars of the offer save to say that if accepted it would result in preferent and secured creditors being paid in full and concurrent creditors receiving a dividend of 5 cents in the rand, whereas on final liquidation, in the opinion of the respondent, there would be sufficient assets to cover the costs of the liquidation, but it is doubtful whether there would be

> 'any dividend that can approach the full payment of the preferent and secured creditors'.

That means that in the opinion of the respondent there would be no dividend for distribution among the concurrent creditors.

The provisional liquidator thereupon applied, in terms of s 103 of the Companies Act 46 of 1926 for an order for a meeting of creditors under his chairmanship to consider the offer of compromise. The application was opposed by Pienaar, but after hearing argument Trengove J ordered that meetings be held. . . .

The meetings were held and the respondent, as chairman, reported the result to the court as follows:

> 'Seven secured or preferent creditors, whose total claims amounted to R2 490 attended the said meeting by proxy and the offer of compromise was accepted by them unanimously; there were no objections in this regard and I beg leave to refer to annexure "E" annexed hereto being the minutes of the said meeting.
>
> On the same date at 2.15 pm the meeting of the concurrent creditors was held at the aforesaid address.
>
> The said meeting was attended by 25 creditors either in person or by proxy, whose claims totalled R143 314,77. Twenty-three of the aforesaid concurrent creditors with claims totalling R121 370,68 voted in favour of acceptance of the offer of compromise; two of the said concurrent creditors with claims totalling R21 944 voted against the acceptance of the offer of compromise.' . . .

The objecting creditor, now the appellant, alleges the following three irregularities concerning the meetings which were held:

(1) According to the list of registered letters sent to the creditors of the company two creditors were not given notice of the meeting.

(2) The publication of the notice convening the meeting was one day late.

(3) The notices convening the meeting were sent out two days late.

In these three respects the order of the court was not complied with and the respondent concedes that to be the case but argues that the court has power to condone these irregularities and should do so in this particular case. Notwithstanding some decisions to the contrary, I am respectfully of the opinion that the legal position is correctly set out by Trollip J in *Du Preez* v *Garber: In re Die Boerebank Bpk* 1963 (1) SA 806 (T). The learned judge says at 814—

> '. . . the court will not insist upon absolute or meticulous observance of all those terms and requirements, but will generally act on a substantial compliance therewith, if no prejudice or possible prejudice to anyone's legal interest has resulted from the non-observance of any of the prescribed formalities. The reason is that the object of those formalities is to ensure that the creditors and members are sufficiently informed of the compromise or arrangement, and are afforded a reasonable opportunity of considering and discussing it and of accepting or rejecting it. If that object has been attained through a substantial compliance with the prescribed formalities, and the statutory majority of creditors and members have agreed to the compromise or arrangement, it would then be sheer unnecessary formalism for the court to refuse to assume jurisdiction in the matter. . . .'

I think that in a case such as this where the irregularities are somewhat trifling, and it appears that prejudice is rather unlikely then, unless there is evidence before the court to show some possible prejudice to any creditor, the court would be entitled to assume that there was no prejudice. The court, therefore, in these circumstances condones the irregularities.

The second objection raised by the appellant was that the notice sent in terms of s 103*quat* of the Act and the proceedings at the different meetings were such that the creditors were not fully aware of the merits of the compromise when exercising their vote. . . .

Before the court relies on the creditors to be the best judges of whether the offer is advantageous to them and endorses their majority vote for its acceptance, it must be satisfied that they were sufficiently informed about the implications of the offer. . . . In this regard the court finds that the learned judge who sanctioned the acceptance, correctly considered that sufficient information was placed before the creditors to allow them to take a decision which the court should endorse.

That brings me to the third and difficult question of the separate classes of concurrent creditors which, it is alleged, should have met at different meetings to consider the offer. The appellant argued that all the concurrent creditors attended the same meeting

'whereas in fact by virtue of their different interests the concurrent creditors should have been divided into two, alternatively three, classes of creditors and meetings should have been held for each class of creditor'.

It was suggested that they should have been divided into —

(1)   those companies of which the offeror is a director;
(2)   the offeror and his wife;
(3)   other concurrent creditors.

There are a number of authoritative statements on what a 'class of creditors' means as used in s 103 of the Act. In laying down what has almost become a rule of practice, Solomon J, in *Ex parte Coleman: In re Argyle Dental Supplies Ltd (in liquidation)* 1933 WLD 177 at 190, relies for guidance on *Sovereign Life Assurance Co v Dodd* [*374* above]. There Bowen LJ dealt with the consideration of an arrangement between a company being wound up and creditors in terms of s 2 of the English Joint Stock Companies Arrangement Act of 1870, 'the prototype of s 103 of our Companies Act'. The learned judge said at 583:

'The word "class" is vague, and to find out what is meant by it we must look at the scope of the section, which is a section enabling the court to order a meeting of a class of creditors to be called. It seems plain that we must give such a meaning to the term "class" as will prevent the section being so worked as to result in confiscation and injustice, and that it must be confined to those persons whose rights are not so dissimilar as to make it impossible for them to consult together with a view to their common interest.'

In the Australian case of *Re Jax Marine (Pty) Ltd* (1967) 1 NS WR 145 Street J considered this statement in relation to s 181 of the Companies Act NSW 1961 and said at 149:

'If one finds a group of creditors whose claims against the company are of precisely similar legal character then, prima facie, they should be regarded as a class. It is similarity of rights that underlies the test enunciated by Bowen LJ. His Lordship's test is the guide for drawing the line at which rights become so dissimilar as to prevent them constituting a single class.'

In the argument advanced by the appellant such great stress was laid on the 'interest' of the creditor that sight was lost of the basis of the classification which is the dissimilarity of rights. With great respect it seemed to me that in some of the instances quoted here a similar excessive emphasis on interest could be perceived. Such an approach may lead to the constitution of meetings of creditors who hold similar views about the acceptance of the offer because of their common interest which may have little to do with their rights; this is undesirable because it is clearly envisaged that creditors with conflicting interests but similar rights should come together to discuss the acceptance of the offer of compromise. . . . If the determining factor for the classification is to be the interest of the creditor without sufficient regard to his rights it may well lead to a greater number of meetings than is necessary to arrive at the intention and wishes of the creditors. An indication that the legislature did not envisage a multiplicity of meetings appears from the fact that in s 103(2) no provision is made for the eventuality of different majority votes at different meetings of classes of creditors.

The common distinction between secured and unsecured creditors is clearly founded upon the dissimilarity of their rights. . . .

Using this criterion I have come to the conclusion that the rights of the companies with the offeror as a director, and of the offeror and his wife, and of the other concurrent creditors are not so dissimilar that the holders of these rights cannot consult together with a view to their common interest relating to the acceptance or refusal of the offer. Consequently this objection to the sanctioning of the compromise also fails.

[379] *Re* Hellenic & General Trust Ltd
[1975] 3 All ER 382 (Ch)

TEMPLEMAN J: This is an opposed application for the sanction by the court under s 206 of the Companies Act 1948 of an arrangement relating to the ordinary shares of the company, Hellenic & General Trust Ltd. [Sections 206 and 209 of the 1948 English Act correspond to ss 311 and 321 of ours.]

The company carries on business as an investment trust. The ordinary shares of the company are held as to 53,01 per cent by Merchandise & Investment Trust Ltd (known as 'MIT'). All the shares of MIT are held by Hambros Ltd and therefore MIT is a wholly owned subsidiary of Hambros. The objectors, National Bank of Greece SA, hold 13,95 per cent of the ordinary shares of the company proposed to be dealt with by the arrangement.

By the arrangement the ordinary shares of the company will be cancelled. New ordinary shares will be issued to Hambros and the company will thus become, like MIT, a wholly owned subsidiary of Hambros.

The former shareholders of the company will be paid by Hambros 48p per share for the loss of their former shares. The result is equivalent to a purchase by Hambros of the ordinary shares of the company at 48p per share.

Section 206 of the Companies Act 1948 provides, so far as material, that where an arrangement is proposed between a company and a class of its creditors or members the court may order a meeting of the class. Then, if a majority in number representing three-fourths in value of the class present and voting at the meeting agree to the arrangement, the arrangement shall, if sanctioned by the court, be binding on all the members of the class. Thus in the present case if there was a proper class meeting which agreed to the arrangement by the requisite majorities, and if this court sanctions the arrangement, then the objectors will lose their shares in the company and will receive 48p per share from Hambros instead. The objectors do not wish this to happen.

In the present case the court on the application of the company summoned a meeting of all the ordinary shareholders. A resolution agreeing to the arrangement was carried, some 91 per cent of the shareholders by value attending and voting. MIT, holding 53,01 per cent, voted in favour of the arrangement. The National Bank, holding 13,95 per cent of the ordinary shares, voted against the arrangement. The arrangement was approved by 86,61 per cent in number and 84,67 per cent in value of those who attended and voted. The votes of MIT were vital. If they had not attended and voted the requisite majority could not have been achieved against the opposition of the objectors, the National Bank of Greece. The National Bank now pursue their opposition to the arrangement in this court.

On their behalf counsel puts forward four objections. The first objection goes to jurisdiction, and the other three concern the discretion of the court in sanctioning an arrangement and the proper principles for the exercise of that discretion.

The first objection put forward is that the necessary agreement by the appropriate class of members has not been obtained. The shareholders who were summoned to the meeting consisted, it is submitted, of two classes. First there were the outside shareholders, that is to say the shareholders other than MIT; and secondly MIT, a subsidiary of Hambros. MIT was a separate class and should have been excluded from the meeting of outside shareholders. Although s 206 of the 1948 Act provides that the court may order meetings, it is the responsibility of the applicants to see that the class meetings are properly constituted, and if they fail then the necessary agreement is not obtained and the court has no jurisdiction to sanction the arrangement. Thus in *Re United Provident Assurance Co Ltd* [[1910] 2 Ch 477] the court held that holders of partly paid shares formed a different class from holders of fully paid shares.

The question therefore is whether MIT, a wholly owned subsidiary of Hambros, formed part of the same class as the other ordinary shareholders. What is an appropriate class must depend on the circumstances but some general principles are to be found in the authorities. In *Sovereign Life Assurance Co* v *Dodd* [*374* above] the court of appeal held that for the purposes of an arrangement affecting the policy-holders of an assurance company the holders of policies which had matured were creditors and were a different class from policy-holders whose policies had not matured. Lord Esher MR said (at 580):

'. . . they must be divided into different classes . . . because the creditors composing the different classes have different interests; and, therefore, if we find a different state of facts existing among different creditors which may differently affect their minds and their judgment, they must be divided into different classes.'

Bowen LJ said (at 583):

'It seems plain that we must give such a meaning to the term "class" as will prevent the section being so worked as to result in confiscation and injustice, and that it must be confined to those persons whose rights are not so dissimilar as to make it impossible for them to consult together with a view to their common interest.'

Vendors consulting together with a view to their common interest in an offer made by a purchaser would look askance at the presence among them of a wholly owned subsidiary of the purchaser.

In the present case on analysis Hambros are acquiring the outside shares for 48p. So far as the MIT shares are concerned it does not matter very much to Hambros whether they are acquired or not. If the shares are acquired a sum of money moves from parent to wholly owned subsidiary and shares move from the subsidiary to the parent. The overall financial position of the parent and the subsidiary remains the same. The shares and the money could remain or be moved to suit Hambros before or after the arrangement. From the point of MIT, provided MIT is solvent, the directors of MIT do not have to question whether the price is exactly right. Before and after the arrangement the directors of the parent company and the subsidiary could have been made the same persons with the same outlook and the same judgment. Counsel for the company submitted that since the parent and subsidiary were separate corporations with separate directors, and since MIT were ordinary shareholders in the company, it followed that MIT had the same interests as the other shareholders. The directors of MIT were under a duty to consider whether the arrangement was beneficial to the whole class of ordinary shareholders, and they were capable of forming an independent and unbiased judgment, irrespective of the interests of the parent company. This seems to me to be unreal. Hambros are purchasers making an offer. When the vendors meet to discuss and vote whether or not to accept the offer, it is incongruous that the loudest voice in theory and the most significant vote in practice should come from the wholly owned subsidiary of the purchaser. No one can be both a vendor and a purchaser and, in my judgment for the purpose of the class meetings in the present case, MIT were in the camp of the purchaser. Of course this does not mean that MIT should not have considered at a separate class meeting whether to accept the arrangement. But their consideration will be different from the considerations given to the matter by the other shareholders. Only MIT could say, within limits, that what was good for Hambros must be good for MIT. . . .

Accordingly I uphold the first objection, which is fatal to the arrangement. But in view of the careful arguments put forward by both sides I will consider the other objections which are raised by counsel for the bank and which are material if the class meeting in the present case, contrary to my view, was properly constituted.

The second objection is founded on the analysis of the arrangement as an offer by Hambros to acquire the ordinary shares for 48p. Section 209 of the 1948 Act provides safeguards for minority shareholders in the event of a takeover bid and in a proper case provides machinery for a small minority of shareholders to be obliged to accept a takeover against their wishes. Thus s 209 provides that where a scheme or contract involving the transfer of shares in a company to another company has been approved by the holders of not less than nine-tenths in value of the shares whose transfer is involved (other than shares already held at the date of the offer by, or by a nominee for, the transferee company or its subsidiary), the transferee company may give notice to any dissenting shareholder; and then, unless on an application made by the dissenting holder the court thinks fit to order otherwise, shall be entitled and bound to acquire those shares on the terms of the takeover bid. If the present arrangement had been carried out under s 209, MIT as a subsidiary of Hambros would have been expressly forbidden to join in any approval for the purposes of s 209, and in any event the National Bank could not have been obliged to sell because they hold ten per cent of the ordinary shares of the company.

The fact that an arrangement under s 206 produces a result which is the same as a takeover under s 209 is not necessarily fatal. It is not always so unfair as to preclude the court from exercising its discretion in favour of the scheme. Thus in *Re National Bank Ltd* [[1966] 1 WLR 819, [1966] 1 All ER 1006], where a similar objection was taken, Plowman J considered the argument that the scheme in that case ought to be treated as a s 209 case needing a 90 per cent majority. He said

'. . . I cannot accede to that proposition. In the first place, it seems to me to involve imposing a limitation or qualification either on the generality of the word "arrangement" in s 206 or else on the discretion of the court under that section. The legislature has not seen fit to impose any such limitation in terms and I see no reason for implying any. Moreover, the two sections, s 206 and s 209, involve quite different considerations and different approaches. Under s 206 an arrangement can only be sanctioned if the question of its fairness has first of all been submitted to the court. Under s 209, on the other hand, the matter may never come to the court at all. If it does come to the court then the onus is cast on the dissenting minority to demonstrate the unfairness of the scheme. There are, therefore, good reasons for requiring a smaller majority in favour of a scheme under s 206 than the majority which is required under s 209 if the minority is to be expropriated.'

Accepting that, the present proposals nevertheless seem to me to place the company in an inescapable dilemma. It cannot succeed under s 209 because of the express provisions of that section and the size of the shareholding of the objectors. It can only succeed under s 206 by using the votes of Hambros' subsidiary company, MIT, to secure the necessary majority. In these circumstances I agree with counsel for the National Bank that the court should not in the exercise of its discretion authorize the acquisition of the shares of the National Bank against the wishes of the bank. The company cannot succeed at all under s 209 and in my judgment they cannot fairly succeed under s 206.

The third alternative objection raised by counsel for the National Bank is that the arrangement is unfair to all the ordinary shareholders. I am satisfied that it is more than fair. The shares of the company are listed on the stock exchange and in common with other investment trust companies normally stand between 20 per cent and 25 per cent below the net asset value of the company's assets. Thus the offer price of 48p, if it represents the true net asset value of the shares, is 20 per cent to 25 per cent more than the shareholders can now obtain elsewhere. The assets of the company consist largely of cash and stock exchange investments, so that the ordinary shareholders, if they receive 48p instead of their existing shares, can follow the same outline of investment and will have roughly 48p to invest instead of a share worth on the stock exchange 36p. There has been independent advice provided to shareholders and I am quite satisfied that the offer is extremely fair.

Counsel for the company says that, that being so, I ought to ignore the earlier indications of unfairness, namely the effect of the s 209 machinery, and the exploitation of the s 206 machinery; and it may be that in some extraordinary case that would be true. But I cannot bring myself to believe that it would be right to exercise a discretion in favour of the company in the present case. It may be that there is some advantage in hanging on. At any rate the National Bank were entitled to say that they purchased more than 10 per cent, they could not be expropriated under s 209, and they object to expropriation, albeit it is said in the best interest of other shareholders, under s 206.

That leaves the final objection. Why, if the scheme is beneficial, is it not acceptable to the National Bank? In the first place they themselves seem to hold the opinion that there is some advantage in retaining their present shareholding. They voice some misgivings whether the company itself is not doing rather better out of the arrangement than appears to be the case. But substantially the objector's view is coloured by the fact that they will, as the evidence states, although I am not given details, become liable to a swingeing capital gains tax in Greece. Counsel for the company says the tax must be ignored because in considering their votes at a meeting under s 206 of the 1948 Act each shareholder must put himself in the impossible position of deciding what is in the best interests of the class. That appears from the judgment of Megarry J in *Re Holders Investment Trust Ltd* [[1971] 1 WLR 583, [1971] 2 All ER 289], and in particular the passage where Megarry J refers to a general principle that a power conferred on a majority of a class to bind minorities must be exercised for the purpose of benefiting the class as a whole and not merely individual members only. Similarly in *Re Grierson, Oldham & Adams Ltd* [*383* below], under s 209 of the 1948 Act it was held the test was one of fairness to the body of shareholders and not to individuals and the burden was on the applicants to prove unfairness and not merely that the scheme was open to criticism. Although under s 206 the onus is the other way round it is submitted that the test of fairness is exactly the same.

In a good many cases so it would be, but in the present case it seems to me that the individual loss which the National Bank will suffer from the scheme is one which should be borne in mind. When one adds together the three objections of counsel for the National Bank, first of all that it is really a scheme by Hambros to purchase the outside shareholding, secondly that under s 209 the scheme could not have been carried out against the wishes of the National Bank, and thirdly that it could not have been carried out under s 206 save with the votes of MIT, the wholly owned subsidiary of Hambros, it seems to me that it is unfair to deprive the National Bank of shares which they were entitled to assume were safe from compulsory purchase and which would have the effect of putting on to the National Bank a swingeing fiscal impost which, if the matter had proceeded under s 209, they could have avoided simply and quite properly by refusing to join in approving the scheme under that section.

Accordingly in the result, both as a matter of jurisdiction and as a matter of discretion, I am not prepared to make any order approving this scheme.

[*Hellenic Trust* is discussed by D D Prentice in (1976) 92 *LQR* 13.]

[380]　*Ex parte* **Venter & another NNO:** *In re* **Rapid Mining Supplies (Pty) Ltd (in Provisional Liquidation); African Gate and Fence Works Ltd Intervening**
1976 (3) SA 267 (O)

The co-provisional liquidators of a company in liquidation applied in terms of s 311 for an order sanctioning a compromise. Two creditors opposed, mainly on the ground that they had not been supplied with sufficient information. The application of the liquidators failed.

M T STEYN J: The purpose of the procedure laid down by s 311 of the Act is clear. In the words of Kotzé J in *Ex parte Borton NO* 1970 (1) SA 190 (E) at 191C–D, the section

> 'does not establish a rubber stamp procedure. It requires the summoning of meetings to consider and debate whether a proposed compromise is to be agreed to or not. The underlying intention of the section is to extend to creditors an opportunity of gathering
>> "an appreciation of the respective prospects under liquidation and the arrangement"
> —see the remarks of Trollip J in *Du Preez* v *Garber: In re Die Boerebank Bpk* 1963 (1) SA 806 (W) at 824G–H'.

Although Kotzé J was there referring to s 103 of the Companies Act of 1926, his words are to my mind equally apposite to s 311 of the present Act.

By virtue of s 339 the law relating to insolvency is applicable *mutatis mutandis* to companies in respect of any matter not specially provided for by the Companies Act. No provision is made in that Act regarding the order of preference in which creditors are to be paid and the provisions of the Insolvency Act therefore apply. In the offer of compromise preferent, secured and concurrent creditors are defined and basically given the same meaning as are ascribed to them in the Insolvency Law which will therefore be applicable *mutatis mutandis* to the implementation of the compromise if sanctioned.

The object of the Insolvency Act is to ensure a due distribution of assets among creditors in the order of their preference (per Innes JA in *Walker v Syfret NO* 1911 AD 141 at 166). *That* is to my mind also the object of the provisions of the Companies Act relating to winding-up and to compromise and arrrangements with creditors. The creditors of Rapid Mining must therefore be divided at least into the three above-mentioned classes for purposes of the payments offered in the offer of compromise and each of those classes must of necessity form an appreciation of their respective prospects under liquidation and the compromise as viewed from the position of their particular class.

To enable them to do so they must be properly informed as to all the relevant material facts including the effect of the offer of compromise and the consequences of the post-provisional liquidation administration of the company. What will be regarded as sufficient information in any particular case will depend upon the complexity of the facts and the kind of creditor to be enlightened. Thus, a relatively unsophisticated and modestly educated rural gentleman with little or no experience in matters of business and commerce, will require substantially more detailed information and explanatory comments thereon than an astute, well educated and experienced businessman. The more complicated the terms of an offer and/or the affairs of the company under consideration, the greater will the extent of the information and the explanatory comments necessarily have to be. . . .

. . . For that reason it is obligatory in terms of s 312(1) of the Act to send to creditors with every notice summoning a meeting a statement explaining the effect of the compromise or arrangement to be considered thereat. That statement must therefore be perfectly fair and contain all the information reasonably necessary for that purpose. . . .

Where there are different classes of creditors their interests will usually differ and may even clash, and the effect of a suggested compromise will usually also vary from class to class. The impact of such a compromise may, for example, be favourable or minimal as far as secured and/or preferent creditors are concerned, but may be very severe on concurrent creditors and may even be different as between creditors in the same class. That, to my mind, is the reason why s 311(2) of the Act contemplates separate meetings by the different classes of creditors and requires that an offer of compromise or an arrangement be agreed to separately by each class of creditors. Two classes of creditors, preferent and secured, are indirectly defined in the Insolvency Act, and by a process of elimination concurrent creditors are those who are unsecured and not entitled to any preference in the payment of their claim. That does not mean that such creditors must necessarily be regarded as being of one and the same class, or that a gathering together of all concurrent creditors in one meeting will be a sufficient separation of those creditors as a class for the purposes of s 311(2). The class to which a creditor belongs must be determined not only by the nature of his claim (ie preferent, secured or concurrent) but also by the rights or interests generated by that claim. In *Sovereign Life Assurance Co* v *Dodd* [1892] 2 QB 573, [1891–1894] All ER Reprint 246 (CA) Bowen LJ defines the term 'class', used in relation to a class of creditors, as follows on p 251H–I of the All ER Reprint:

> 'The word "class" used in the statute is vague, and to find out what it means we must look at the general scope of the section which enables the court to order a meeting of a "class of creditors" to be summoned. It seems to me that we must give such a meaning to the term "class" as will prevent the section being so worked as to produce confiscation and injustice, and that we must confine its meaning to those persons whose rights are not so dissimilar as to make it impossible for them to consult together with a view to their common interest.'

That definition was applied in South Africa by Solomon J in the matter of *Ex parte Coleman: In re Argyle Dental Supplies Ltd* (*in liq*) 1933 WLD 177 at 190 and has recently been reiterated in England. *Vide Re Hellenic & General Trust Ltd* [1975] 3 All ER 382 (Ch) at 385*f*. In the *Sovereign Life Assurance* case (*supra*) Lord Esher MR puts the criteria for differentiation of creditors into separate classes thus at 249 *in fin*—250B of the All ER Reprint:

> 'The Act provides that the persons to be summoned to the meeting, all of whom, it is to be observed, are creditors, are persons who can be divided into different classes, classes which the Act recognizes, though it does not define. The creditors, therefore, must be divided into different classes. What is the reason for prescribing such a course? It is because the creditors composing different classes have different interests, *and, therefore, if a different state of facts exists with respect to different creditors, which may affect their minds and judgments differently, they must be separated into different classes.*'

(My italics.)

Those remarks of Esher MR were also applied with approval in the *Hellenic and General Trust* case (*supra*) at 385*d–e*. In the interest of fairness and to ensure a useful and facile interchange of ideas, it is therefore, in my judgment, essential that only creditors with a sufficiently close identity of interests should be gathered together in one meeting; and that, to my mind, is what s 311(1) and (2) of the Act contemplates. . . .

There may, for example, be different classes of concurrent creditors, and, although such classes would in effect be merely sub-classes within the main class, they would have to be treated as separate classes and would have to meet separately. *Vide Ex parte Ruskin NO: In re Peace Distributors (Pty) Ltd* (*in liq*) 1959 (2) SA 747 (W) at 749E–G.

In the matter now under consideration the court decreed that the three main classes of creditors meet separately, and the order can be construed as requiring only one meeting for all concurrent creditors. Even if it should afterwards transpire that there were in fact different classes of concurrent creditors the gathering together of all such creditors in a single separate meeting would not necessarily invalidate such a meeting, but that fact may have a material influence on the exercise by the court of its discretion to grant or refuse an application to sanction the compromise or arrangement in respect of which such a single meeting was convened. . . . In my opinion, the responsibility for determining what creditors to summon to the different meetings as constituting separate classes rests ultimately with the applicant who applies for the holding of such meetings and thereafter for the sanctioning of a compromise agreed to by the requisite majorities at those meetings. If such meetings are incorrectly convened or constituted and different classes of creditors are improperly brought together in one meeting, the applicant runs the risk of having his application refused. . . . This is so even if no objection be raised that such a meeting is or was improperly constituted or no exception taken to the presence thereat of certain creditors as having interests competing in material respects with those of other creditors present thereat. The reason therefor is that the court must be satisfied that the provisions of the statute regarding creditors' meetings have been complied with, the aim of the statute being that a dissenting minority of creditors must not be unjustly overridden by a majority whose interests clash with those of such minority.

The over-all approach by the court to such an application was formulated as follows by Lindley LJ in the leading case of *In re Alabama, New Orleans, Texas and Pacific Junction Railway Co* [1891] 1 ChD 213 at 238–9:

'. . . but still, there is the statute, and what the court has to do is to see, first of all, that the provisions of that statute have been complied with; and, secondly, that the majority has been acting bona fide. The court also has to see that the minority is not being overridden by a majority having interests of its own clashing with those of the minority whom they seek to coerce. Further than that, the court has to look at the scheme and see whether it is one as to which persons acting honestly, and viewing the scheme laid before them in the interest of those whom they represent, take a view which can be reasonably taken by business men. The court must look at the scheme, and see whether the Act has been complied with, whether the majority are acting bona fide, and whether they are coercing the minority in order to promote interests adverse to those of the class whom they purport to represent; and then see whether the scheme is a reasonable one or whether there is any unreasonable objection to it, or such an objection to it as that any reasonable man might say that he could not approve of it.'. . .

In considering whether or not to sanction a compromise in terms of s 311(2) of the Act, it must however be borne in mind that a substantial compliance with the prescribed statutory formalities and requirements will be sufficient ground for granting the application. In the *Boerebank* case (*supra*) Trollip J, as he then was, explained this consideration as follows at 814C–H:

'The first duty of the court when asked to sanction a compromise or arrangement under s 103, which prima facie appears to have been agreed to by the requisite majorities of creditors or members, is to satisfy itself that the terms of its order for convening the meetings, and the statutory requirements of the Act, have been complied with, because upon that depends the jurisdiction of the court to confirm it and so bind all the creditors and members concerned. As in the present case the opposing creditors have strenuously contended that those formalities were not fully complied with in several respects, it is necessary, I think, to affirm at the outset that the court will not insist upon absolute or meticulous observance of all those terms and requirements, but will generally act on a substantial compliance therewith, if no prejudice or possible prejudice to anyone's legal interests has resulted from the non-observance of any of the prescribed formalities. The reason is that the object of those formalities is to ensure that the creditors and members are sufficiently informed of the compromise or arrangement, and are afforded a reasonable opportunity of considering and discussing it and of accepting or rejecting it. If that object has been attained through a substantial compliance with the prescribed formalities, and the statutory majority of creditors and members have agreed to the compromise or arrangement, it would then be sheer unnecessary formalism for the court to refuse to assume jurisdiction in the matter. Thus, in *Re Dynevor, Dyffryn and Neath Abbey Collieries Company* (1879) 11 ChD 605 it was held that where the necessary consents to an arrangement have in fact been given,

> "the court will not be astute to find technical defects in the proceedings".'

See also *Rosen* v *Bruyns NO* 1973 (1) SA 815 (T) at 818D–G: *Cohen NO* v *Nel & another* 1975 (3) SA 963 (W) at 969B–C.

Section 311(2) of the Act clearly requires a very substantial, almost an overwhelming, majority of each class of creditors in favour of a compromise as a prerequisite to it binding all creditors including expressly dissenting minorities in the various classes. Although the attainment of the required majorities is not an absolute prerequisite to the sanctioning of such compromise by the court, it is nevertheless clear that the court is bound to have regard to such majorities if attained and that an overwhelming majority in favour of the proposed compromise is very often quite rightly regarded as a strong indication that it is reasonable and beneficial to the interests of all classes of creditors. The fact of such an overwhelming majority is, however, not conclusive of the matter and does not invariably result in the compromise being sanctioned. The way in which the court should deal with the matter in the light of such a majority was explained thus by Lindley LJ in the *Chartered Bank* case [1893] 3 ChD 385 at 408–9:

> 'It is quite obvious from the language of the Act and from the mode in which it has been interpreted that the court does not simply register the resolution come to by the creditors. . . . If the creditors are acting on sufficient information and with time to consider what they are about and are acting honestly, they are, I apprehend, much better judges of what is to their commercial advantage than the court can be. I do not say it is conclusive, because there might be some blot in a scheme

which has passed unobserved and which might be pointed out later. But giving them the opportunity of observation, I repeat that I think they are much better judges of a commercial matter than any court, however constituted, can be. While, therefore, I protest that we are not to register their reasons, but to see that they have been properly convened and have been properly consulted, and have considered the matter from a proper point of view—that is, with a view to the interests of the class to which they belong, and which they are empowered to bind—the court ought to be slow to differ from them. It should do so unhesitatingly if there is anything wrong about it. But it ought not to do so, in my judgment, unless something is brought to the attention of the court to show that there has been some great oversight or miscarriage.'

Whilst agreeing with Lindley LJ as to the function of the court, Trollip J sounded a note of warning in the *Boerebank* case (*supra*) as to Lindley LJ's opinion regarding a court having to be slow to differ from the views of a majority of creditors, and said the following at 825G–H:

'Consequently, I think that before that approach is adopted, and the creditors' majority vote endorsed, the court must first be satisfied that they were sufficiently informed about the implications of the arrangement.'

I am in respectful agreement with what was said in the aforementioned cases regarding the functions of and approach by the court in matters of compromise or arrangements with creditors, but it is clear that the court has a very wide discretion in such matters and that what was said in those cases should be regarded merely as guides to, and not as fetters binding and limiting, the exercise of that discretion. In *Mahomed* v *Kazi's Agencies (Pty) Ltd & others* 1949 (1) SA 1162 (N) Broome J to my mind correctly summed up the position as follows on 1172:

'Many judges have endeavoured to lay down the principles which should govern a question under s 103 or the corresponding section of the English Acts, and in *In re Saratoga Investments (Pty) Ltd* 1941 NPD 117 at 142 Selke J has suggested that even if these general principles are correct there must still remain a residium of unfettered discretion in the court. I prefer to regard these so-called principles as no more than considerations which courts have found proper to be taken into account in particular cases, rather than as laying down the correct method of approach in all cases.'. . .

. . . [Counsel for the liquidators] contended that the facts were all clearly in favour of the compromise, even those facts which the creditors may have been unaware of, and that this was pre-eminently a matter for the application of the so-called 'Bwllfa principle' enunciated by Lord Macnaghten in the well-known case of *Bwllfa and Merthyr Dare Steam Collieries (1891) Ltd* v *Pontypridd Waterworks Co* [1903] AC 426 (HL) at 431 and recently approved of and applied by Megarry J in the case of *Re Goodwin* [1968] 3 All ER 12 at 15–16 and by Harcourt J in *S* v *National Board of Executors Ltd* 1971 (3) SA 817 (D) at 828A–G.

That principle may be formulated as follows: where facts are available they are to be preferred to prophecies. The underlying reason for the formulation and application of that principle is that it is not necessarily an exercise in impermissible hindsight to look at facts discovered or occurring subsequent to the act in issue and that it is sometimes, depending on the particular circumstances, the duty of the arbiter of fact, in the words of Lord Macnaghten, to

> 'avail himself of all information at hand at the time of making his award which may be laid before him. Why should he listen to conjecture on a matter which has become an accomplished fact? Why should he guess when he can calculate? With the light before him, why should he shut his eyes and grope in the dark?'

I agree that the 'Bwllfa principle' may apply to a request under s 311(2) for the sanctioning of a compromise agreed to by the creditors of a company. But can I in the matter now under consideration calculate instead of guessing? And do I have the light before me? I think not. How, for example, are preferent and secured creditors to be paid out of a fund that is clearly insufficient for that purpose? There is, *inter alia*, also uncertainty as to the present value of the remaining stock. . . .

Although a court should not be astute to find technical defects in the proceedings and should adopt a practical and fairly robust approach to applications for sanctioning-orders under s 311(2), and should rely on the 'Bwllfa principle' in appropriate cases, it should not, for the sake of practical convenience and a robustly swift adjudication, overlook or condone obvious defects which could result in prejudice to creditors, and should not sanction a compromise even if agreed to by an overwhelming majority of all the creditors if it is uncertain whether the compromise is capable of implementation according to its tenour.

I am therefore not prepared to sanction the compromise on the papers now before me.

NOTES

'Whilst I respectfully agree that a sanctioned compromise is not an order of court *ad factum praestandum* a contravention of which is punishable by committal for contempt, nevertheless the South African authorities to which I have referred establish that it is a contract which is binding on all the creditors, the members, the company, the receiver and the offeror, which derives its binding effect not from the actual consent of all the creditors, but by operation of law once the provisions of s 103 [now 311] have been complied with', per Franklin J in *Cohen NO v Nel* 1975 (3) SA 963 (W) at 968, 969. See also *Ex parte De Wet NO* 1971 (1) SA 256 (W).

'The general principles which guide a court in the exercise of its discretion in cases such as this are well known. . . . They are (i) whether the provisions of s 311 of the Act have been complied with in so far as concerns the holding of the meeting and the voting thereat; (ii) whether the statutory majority was acting bona fide, by which is meant no more than that they gave their votes strictly as creditors and were not acting, for example, for motives of sympathy or from some ulterior motive and (iii) whether the offer of compromise is of such a nature that a man of business would reasonably approve of it', per Kannemeyer J in *Borton NO v Dundas & Miller (Pty) Ltd* 1970 (3) SA 107 (E) at 108, 109. See also *Dundas & Miller (Pty) Ltd v Borton NO* 1971 (1) SA 106 (E), confirming the decision of Kannemeyer J.

The court will not sanction a scheme unless the offer is clear and unconditional and becomes final and binding on acceptance subject to the court's sanction: *Ex parte Standard Trading Co (Pty) Ltd* 1954 (4) SA 81 (W). In the same case the question was discussed, but not decided, whether an offer accepted by the creditors can be withdrawn prior to sanction by the court.

In *In re Saratoga Investments (Pty) Ltd* 1941 NPD 117 the court refused to sanction a compromise which differed from the proposal accepted at the meeting to the prejudice of one of the creditors. The court held that the position could not be met by treating that creditor who had assented to the compromise in its original form as though he had voted against it and become bound by the majority vote.

Where the provisions of the order of court have not been complied with, the scheme will not be sanctioned unless the court is satisfied that no interested party has been prejudiced: *Ex parte Meer: In re Indent Wholesalers v Meer's Retailers (Pty) Ltd* 1950 (3) SA 780 (N); *Ex parte Barton-Lister NO* 1951 (1) SA 208 (W); *Katz v Katzenellenbogen* 1955 (3) SA 188 (T); *Ex parte Simjee* 1956 (4) SA 733 (N); *Rosen v Bruyns NO 379* above. However, '... where there is an honest arrangement ... and everything is manifestly right, the court ought not to be astute to find out any little technical defect, if there is any, in the proceedings', per James LJ in *In re Dynevor, Dyffryn and Neath Abbey Collieries Co* (1879) 11 ChD 605.

In *Ex parte Milne NO: In re Khandaan Drive-In Cinema (Pty) Ltd* 1959 (1) SA 13 (N) the court condoned the failure of the judicial manager to hold separate meetings of preferred and concurrent creditors, as directed by the court; and in *Ex parte Chenille Corporation of SA (Pty) Ltd* 1962 (4) SA 459 (T) delegation of his duties by the chairman was condoned.

In *In re Fisher & Simmons Ltd* 1958 (3) SA 306 (W) an alteration of the company's memorandum so as to increase the rate of dividend on the company's preference shares was sanctioned by the court under s 103.

Where the ordinary shareholders have no interest in the assets because there is not sufficient for the claims of creditors and preference shareholders, a scheme of arrangement between the company and its creditors and preference shareholders can be sanctioned notwithstanding the dissent of the ordinary shareholders: *In re Tea Corporation Ltd* [1904] 1 Ch 12.

A reduction of capital may form part of an arrangement under s 311: *Ex parte Provisional Liquidator Hugo Franco (Pty) Ltd* 1958 (4) SA 397 (W).

'... if it appears that directors or others associated with the company have done any wrong to the company for which compensation could or might be recovered by the liquidator, or that an investigation in the winding-up proceedings might establish the validity of such clauses, then the court, in the interests of the public, and commercial morality, should weigh that, as one of the factors justifying the rejection of the compromise, against the other factors in favour of sanctioning it', per Trollip J in *Ex parte Chenille Corporation of SA (Pty) Ltd* 1962 (4) SA 459 (T) at 465.

On the need to place sufficient information before the court see also *Dundas & Miller v Borton NO* 1971 (1) SA 106 (E), *Rennie NO v Ruca Styles (Pty) Ltd* 1973 (4) SA 266 (C) and *Ex parte Cornelissen* 1976 (3) SA 286 (O) at 288.

In *Ex parte Wells NO* 1968 (4) SA 391 (W) an offer contained a clause that creditors had to lodge claims within 30 days, 'failing which they shall be deemed to have abandoned their claims'. The court held that this clause was offensive, but authorized a clause to the effect that all creditors who had notice of the submission of the offer and the meetings of creditors, who so failed to lodge their claims, were to be deemed to have abandoned them. See also *Ex parte Barnes NO* 1973 (2) SA 201 (W) and *Steel v Shanta Construction (Pty) Ltd* 1973 (2) SA 537 (T).

As to the principles guiding the courts in determining whether a compromise or arrangement should be sanctioned, further, *Urtel Bros v Western Province Co-operative Dairy Co Ltd* (1908) 18 CTR 863; *Ex parte A C Tayob & Co Ltd* 1930 TPD 758; *Ex parte Atkinson-Oates Motors Ltd* 1933 OPD 111; *Ex parte Coleman* 1933 WLD 177; *Ex parte Judicial Managers CTC Bazaars (SA) Ltd* 1941 CPD 458; *Mahomed v Kazi's Agencies (Pty) Ltd* 1949 (1) SA 1162 (N); *Ex parte Meer: In re Indent Wholesalers v Meer's Retailers (Pty) Ltd* 1950 (3) SA 780 (N); *Milne NO v Cook,* 1956 (3) SA 317 (N); *Ex parte Ruskin NO: In re Mimosa Mail Order House (Pty) Ltd* 1957 (4) SA 65 (W); *Ex parte Le Coultre: In re Morris Taxi Service* 1962 (2) SA 338 (N) (sanction refused because (1) it was not clear whether the majority had assented; (2) the offer was not in keeping with the realities of the situation). See further *Levin v Felt & Tweeds Ltd* 1951 (2) SA 401 (AD) at 410.

On the rule that a compromise sanctioned by the court does not become effective until a copy of it is registered (s 311(5)), see also *Ex parte De Wet* 1971 (1) SA 256 (W).

It was held in the same case that mere registration of the compromise does not discharge the company from liquidation.

At the sanctioning stage the judge has but a limited power to make modifications to the scheme. He may sanction it or refuse to sanction it, but he has no power to delete objectionable features and sanction it in part only: *Ex parte Union Whaling Co* 1973 (3) SA 550 (W). But see also *Penkin v Roeland Shoes (Pty) Ltd* 1972 (1) SA 513 (C), where Steyn J said (at 517): 'The court is not limited in its powers under s 103(2) to sanction or to refuse to sanction an arrangement or compromise. Circumstances can arise where a court would be entitled to vary the terms of such an agreement. Clearly, where all the parties consent to a variation of the terms of the compromise after its acceptance at the meeting but before sanction, the court would be authorized to vary the agreement accordingly. Similarly should the court deem it necessary for purposes of rendering the agreement efficacious to remove an ambiguity from its terms, without altering the meaning and effect of the arrangement it would, in my view, have the inherent power to do so. A variation of a compromise which gives it great efficacy without materially affecting its terms—so it seems to me—must be within the inherent power of the court when performing its statutory duties under the provisions of s 103(2).'

See also *Investments (Pty) Ltd v Crown Furniture Manufacturers (Pty) Ltd* 1963 (2) SA 271 (W) where it was held that implicit in the court's discretion under s 103 is the power to impose conditions for the more effective implementation of the scheme in the interests of members and/or creditors: *Ex parte Wells NO* 1963 (3) SA 257 (C) and *In re Chartered Bank of Australia* [1893] 3 Ch 540.

Once a scheme of arrangement has been sanctioned by the court, a variation cannot be effected by the mere acquiescence of the shareholders and creditors, but requires again the sanction of the court: *Srimati Premila Devi v Peoples Bank of Northern India Ltd* [1938] 4 All ER 337.

On the effect of an 'informal arrangement', see *Soffe Trust and Investment Co Ltd v Frontier Engineers Ltd* 1962 (3) SA 300 (SR).

Where after the meeting at which an offer was accepted by the requisite statutory majority a new offer is made, it will depend upon the circumstances whether the court will sanction the compromise or direct that another meeting be held to consider the new offer: *Ex parte Ruskin NO: In re Mimosa Mail Order House (Pty) Ltd* 1957 (4) SA 65 (W).

'A creditor cannot circumvent the effect of the compromise or seek to accelerate the payment of dividends by taking independent action to liquidate the company and so indirectly set at naught the order made by the court in pursuance of the terms of s 103 of the Act', per Diemont J in *Serein Investments (Pty) Ltd v Myb (Pty) Ltd* 1967 (4) SA 437 (C) at 439. See also *Ex parte Cyrildene Heights (Pty) Ltd* 1966 (1) SA 307 (W). For the effect of an order sanctioning a compromise after the company has been placed under judicial management, see *Ex parte Currie NO* 1966 (4) SA 546 (N).

A creditor who does not prove his claim in time may lose the right to participate in the distribution, *Steel v Shanta Construction (Pty) Ltd* 1973 (2) SA 537 (T).

The position of a receiver differs from that of a liquidator and has to be determined from the compromise, *Metal Box of SA Ltd v A S Dunstan (Pty) Ltd* 1974 (2) SA 208 (T).

In *South Africa Fabrics Ltd v Millman NO* 1972 (4) SA 592 (AD) an order placing a company under judicial management was discharged when an offer of compromise was sanctioned by the court under s 103(2) of the 1926 Act. The first respondent, who had been the judicial manager, was appointed the receiver. The compromise provided, *inter alia*, that he should have the same powers as he would have had as a liquidator and that creditors should prove their claims within 60 days. Leaving the question open of whether it was competent contractually to invest an individual with all the powers conferred by statute upon a liquidator, Ogilvie Thompson CJ said that it would, in his view, be contrary to the whole concept of the compromise to construe it as investing the receiver with the right, under ss 29 and 30 of the Insolvency Act, to set aside already completed transactions of the debtor company as voidable or undue preferences. On the other hand, the receiver was vested with plenary powers regarding the admission or rejection of claims, whence it followed that should he be of the opinion that any claim tendered to him for proof fell within the ambit of the provisions of s 26(2) of the Insolvency Act, rendered applicable by virtue of ss 181 and 182 of the Companies Act of 1926 (ss 339, 340 of the 1973 Act), he was bound to reject such claims.

See also *Lansdown NO v Baldwins Ltd* 1973 (3) SA 908 (W).

II TAKE–OVERS

A TEXT

A 'take-over scheme' is a scheme which involves the making of an offer by the offeror for acquiring shares of the offeree company which, together with any shares of that company already held by the offeror, will have the effect of (a) vesting the control of the offeree company directly or indirectly in the offeror or (b) the offeror acquiring all the shares or all the shares of a particular class of the offeree company. It does not include an offer made in the course of any individual negotiation with any shareholder for the acquisition of any such shares, s 314(1) sv 'take-over scheme'. A 'take-over offer' means an offer for the acquisition of shares under a take-over scheme, s 314(1) sv 'take-over offer'.

No take-over offer may be made unless it is made in the same terms to all the shareholders of the shares or of a particular class of shares of the offeree company, s 314(2)(a). (As to non-resident shareholders, see the proviso.) Annexed to the offer must be a take-over statement by the offeror which must contain at least the information set out in s 315, s 314(2)(b). Copies of the offer and the annexures to it must be lodged with the offeree company and the Registrar, s 314(2)(c) and (d). No take-over offer remains valid and capable of acceptance after the expiry of four months from the date of issue, and no take-over offer may be withdrawn within this period unless it is superseded by a fresh take-over offer by the offeror, or some other offeror makes a take-over offer, or the take-over offer is declared by the offeror to be unconditional, s 314(3). On an improved offer, see s 314(4).

Within two weeks after delivery to the offeree company by the offeror of a take-over offer, the directors of the offeree company must deliver a take-over statement to the offeror, copies of which the offeror must send to the shareholders of the offeree company and the Registrar, s 316. This statement must contain at least the information set out in s 317, including the number of shares of the offeree company held by the directors and the intention of each of the directors in relation to the take-over offer and his own shareholding; whether any of the directors of the offeree company is a director or shareholder of, or has any other interest in, the offeror or any company controlled by the offeror or by the controlling company of the offeror and if so, full disclosure of such interest; and particulars of any interest of any director of the offeree company in the take-over scheme and any payment, benefit or advantage or proposed payment, benefit or advantage from whatever source in connection with the take-over scheme. If the price to be paid to a director for his shares is in excess of the price offered to other holders of the shares, or he receives some other benefit or advantage not granted to other shareholders, such excess, benefit or advantage must be disclosed in the take-over statement, s 317(e) read with s 227(3).

With the consent in writing of all the shareholders of the offeree company the requirements of the Act in regard to take-over offers may be waived, s 319.

If a take-over offer under a scheme or contract involving the transfer of shares or any class of shares of a company to an offeror has within four months after the making of the offer in that behalf by the offeror been accepted by the holders of not less than nine-tenths of the shares or any class of shares whose transfer is involved (other than shares already held at the date on which the offer is issued by, or by a nominee for, the offeror or its subsidiary), the offeror may at any time within two months after such acceptance give notice to any shareholder who has not accepted the offer, that he or it desires to acquire his shares, and where such notice is given the offeror shall, unless on an application made by such shareholder within six weeks from the date on which the notice is given the court orders otherwise, be entitled and bound to acquire those shares on the terms on which under the scheme or contract the shares of the shareholders who have accepted the offer, are to be transferred to the offeror, s 321(1): *381–385*. Similar rules apply where in pursuance of any such scheme or contract, shares of an offeree company are transferred to a person or another company or its nominees, and those shares together with any other shares in the offeree company already held by the offeror comprise or include nine-tenths of the shares in the offeree company, s 321(3).

A different way of effecting a take-over is by means of an arrangement under s 311: *386*. (See S W L de Villiers 'Take-Overs under Sections 311 to 321 of the Companies Act 1973' (1973) 90 *SALJ* 350.)

In respect of companies listed or to be listed on a stock exchange, the provisions of the Act in regard to take-over bids are supplemented by the stock exchange rules. The guiding principle of the 'Requirements for Take-over Bids or Offers to Purchase . . .' of the Johannesburg Stock Exchange (April 1976) is that

'Directors whose shareholdings, together with those of their families and trusts, effectively control a company, or shareholders in that position who are represented on a board of a company, and who contemplate transferring control, should not, other than in special circumstances, do so unless the buyer undertakes to extend within a reasonable period of time a comparable offer to the holders of the remaining equity share capital whether such capital carries voting rights or not. In such special circumstances the Stock Exchange must be consulted in advance and its consent obtained.'

Another important rule bears on 'insider trading'. It provides that

'With a view to placing the shares beneficially owned by the Offeror Company and those person/s company/ies who have by agreement indicated their prior acceptance of the offer, on the same basis as those shareholders of the offeree company who accept the offer, the Directors of the offeror company shall ensure and submit a written undertaking, that during the period the offer remains open, neither it, nor its nominees or those associated with the offer or with the control of the offeror company, will sell directly or indirectly, or dispose of or alienate any of the shares in the offeree company which are beneficially owned by it or them.'

Exacting requirements are laid down regarding the information to be supplied in the circular from the offeror company to the shareholders of the offeree company and in the circular to be issued to the shareholders of the offeror company by its directors. Where the directors of the offeror company and the directors of the offeree company are identical or partly identical, and the directors of the offeree company recommend to their shareholders the acceptance of the offer and state that they intend to accept it in respect of their own shareholdings, a statement by the auditors of the offeree company is required that they consider the offer fair and reasonable.

B CASES

[381] *In re* **Evertite Locknuts (1938) Ltd**
[1945] Ch 220, [1945] 1 All ER 402

VAISEY J: . . . It will be observed that the section gives no indication of the ground on which the court could intervene and make an order preventing the transferee company from acquiring the shares of a dissenting shareholder. But, fortunately, the section [s 209 of the English Act, s 321 of ours] has already been considered by Maugham J in *In re Hoare & Co Ltd* (1934) 150 LT 374. The judge in that case considered the terms of the section in relation to the facts of the case then before him. I think that the decision is accurately summed up in the headnote, which says it was held:

'. . . that where not less than nine-tenths of the shareholders in the transferor company approve a scheme . . . prima facie the offer must be taken to be a fair one, and that the court will not "order otherwise". . .'

so as to prevent what is described, with more or less accuracy, as the expropriation of the dissenting shareholder's shares unless it is affirmatively established in the face of the apparent views of the large majority of the shareholders that the scheme is in point of fact unfair.

The judge in his judgment says,

'I think it is manifest that the reasons for inducing the court to "order otherwise" are reasons which must be supplied by the dissentients who take the step of making an application to the court, and that the onus is on them of giving a reason why their shares should not be acquired by the transferee company'.

After criticizing the use of the word 'expropriation' as being not altogether apt to the circumstances of that case, the judge goes on to say:

'Without expressing a final opinion on the matter, because there may be special circumstances in special cases, I am unable to see that I have any right to "order otherwise" in such a case as I have before me, unless it is affirmatively established that, notwithstanding the views of a very large majority of the shareholders, the scheme is unfair. . . .'

. . . In the present case, the dissenting shareholder who makes this application does so in respect of a holding of shares of the nominal value of £28; while the shareholders who, either originally or subsequently had become bound to transfer their shares, held shares of a nominal value of over £19 850, those being the figures relating, I think, only to the ordinary shares: the preference shareholders also affected by the proposal having agreed, I think, with practical unanimity to accept the offer.

The applicant does not say, and does not attempt to say, that the offer of 1s 3d for each 1s share which is made to him in common with the rest of the ordinary shareholders, is an unfair offer, an inadequate price. What he says is that at the time when the offer was made, and when he was called upon to consider whether or not he should accept it, he was without sufficient, or perhaps without any, information as to the relevant facts upon which he could have based his conclusion one way or the other. . . .

. . . The difficulty, I feel, is that, if once it is conceded that a scheme of this kind can be upset merely for the reason that a shareholder is not given all the information which he might require or might expect from the directors of the transferor company, there would be no limit to the inquiry which would have to be set on foot as to the extent to which his demands for disclosure ought to be conceded. It may be—I do not say that it is—possible that the present applicant has some grievance against the directors of the Evertite Locknuts (1938) Ltd. But I am quite satisfied in my own mind that I should be going much further than Maugham J was prepared to go in *In re Hoare & Co Ltd* if I said that it was not necessary for a dissentient shareholder, making an application under the Act, to establish unfairness, but that it would suffice if he merely said that he regarded himself, or was in fact, unprovided with all the materials upon which he could come to a just conclusion in regard to the acceptance or rejection of the offer. . . .

[382] *In re* **Bugle Press Ltd**
[1961] Ch 270, [1960] 3 All ER 791

The authorized and issued share capital of Bugle Press Ltd was 10 000 shares of £1 each fully paid. Nine thousand of these shares were held in equal moieties by J and S, who were the two directors of the company. The remaining 1 000 shares were held by the applicant. J and S formed a company, J and S (Holdings) Ltd, of which they held all the shares. J and S (Holdings) Ltd then offered to acquire the whole of the issued capital of Bugle Press Ltd at a price of £10 per share. The offer was based on a valuation by a firm of accountants. When the applicant refused to accept the offer, J and S as shareholders of 90 per cent of the shares in Bugle Press Ltd, approved the scheme, and J and S (Holdings) Ltd invoked the machinery of s 209 [corresponding to s 321 of our Act] for the acquisition of the applicant's one thousand shares at the price of £10 per share. The applicant thereupon applied for a declaration that J and S (Holdings) Ltd were not entitled to acquire the applicant's shares in Bugle Press Ltd.

The court of first instance granted the declaration prayed for and this was confirmed on appeal by the court of appeal.

HARMAN LJ: . . . In my judgment this is a barefaced attempt to evade that fundamental rule of company law which forbids the majority of shareholders, unless the articles so provide, to expropriate a minority. It would be all too simple if all you had to do was to form a £2 company and sell to it your shares and then force the outsider to comply. . . . The minority shareholder . . . having applied to the court under the section, had, like any other applicant, to prove his case, that is to say, to set up a case which the respondents had to answer. He did that, it seems to me, as it seemed to my Lord, quite simply by showing that the transferee company was nothing but a little hut built round his two co-shareholders, and that the so-called 'scheme' was made by themselves as directors of that company with themselves as shareholders and the whole thing, therefore, is seen to be a hollow sham. It was then for the transferee company to show that nevertheless there was some good reason why the scheme should be allowed to go on. The transferee company, whether because the two members did not wish to go into the witness-box and be cross-examined or for some other reason, did not file any evidence at all; they merely purported to rely on a copy of a valuation said to have been made on their behalf by a firm of chartered accountants. That valuation was not sworn to, nobody was able to cross-examine the authors of it and there is in my judgment no case in answer. The minority shareholder has nothing to knock down; he has only to shout and the walls of Jericho fall flat.

[*In re Bugle Press Ltd* was followed by the Supreme Court of Canada in *Esso Standard (Inter-America) Inc v J W Enterprises* [1963] SCR 144, (1963) 37 DLR 2d 598. The Standard Oil Company of New Jersey held all the shares of Esso Standard (Inter-America) Inc and 96 per cent of the shares of the International Petroleum Company Limited. Esso Standard made a take-over bid for the shares of the International Petroleum Company Limited, which was, naturally, accepted by Standard Oil. An application for the compulsory acquisition of the shares of certain minority shareholders under s 128 of the Canadian Companies Act (which corresponds to s 209 of the English Act and s 321 of ours) was rejected by the Court of Appeal for Ontario, and this was upheld by the Supreme Court of Canada. Judson J who delivered the judgment of the court, said (at 151):

'There is no distinction between *Bugle Press* and the present case either on fact or law. We have here 90 per cent ownership in Standard

Oil Company (New Jersey). The promoting force throughout is obviously that of Standard Oil and not its subsidiary. A transfer of shares from Standard Oil to Esso Standard is meaningless in these circumstances as affording any indication of a transaction which the court ought to approve as representing the wishes of 90 per cent of the shareholders. This 90 per cent is not independent. On this ground alone I would reject the appeal and hold that the section contemplates the acquisition of 90 per cent of the total issued shares of the class affected and that this 90 per cent must be independently held.']

[383] *Re* Grierson, Oldham & Adams Ltd
[1967] 1 All ER 192, [1967] 1 WLR 385

PLOWMAN J: Grierson, Oldham & Adams Ltd . . . was incorporated in the year 1894, and its business is that of shippers of wines and spirits. At all material times its issued share capital had consisted of 3 785 292 ordinary shares of 2s each and 100 500 preference shares of £1 each; and the preference shares were divided into two classes—50 000 5 per cent first cumulative preference and 50 500 7½ per cent second cumulative preference.

Mr Gurney-Champion holds 2 000 ordinary shares in the company. He bought those shares at various times during the first half of 1963, and in order to avoid a loss on his investment he needs to sell the shares for not less than 6s 7½d each. Mr Lightfoot also holds 2 000 ordinary shares in the company which he bought in 1959 at the price of 6s 9d, disregarding expenses. Those two holdings aggregate 4 000 ordinary shares, representing, in fact, something less than 0,1 per cent of the ordinary shareholding of the company.

The respondents to the summons, John Holt & Co (Liverpool) Ltd . . . are also in the wine and spirit business. . . .

In the autumn of 1965, Holts made an offer through Lazards for the whole of the issued share capital of the company; and that offer was announced to the Press on 15 September 1965, and on 27 September a circular was sent out in the usual way to all the company's shareholders. . . . Paragraph 1 is headed 'The Offer', and states as follows:

'On behalf of Holts we offer to acquire the whole of the issued share capital of Griersons, consisting of fifty thousand five per cent first cumulative preference shares of £1 each, 50 500 7½ per cent second cumulative preference shares of £1 each and 3 785 292 ordinary shares of 2s each, upon the following terms and conditions:

'A.   For each of the 5 per cent first cumulative
preference shares of £1, holders are offered   17s in cash,
                                                  free of all expenses

'For each of the 7½ per cent second cumulative preference shares of £1, holders are
offered   ..   ..   23s in cash,
                                                  free of all expenses

'For each of the ordinary shares of 2s,
holders are offered ..   ..   6s in cash
                                                  free of all expenses.'

The same paragraph goes on to state, among other things, that the offer is

'conditional upon irrevocable acceptances being received in accordance with the instructions set out below not later than 3 pm on 18 October 1965 . . . in respect of not less than ninety per cent . . . of the total nominal amount of the issued share capital of Griersons.'

In the next paragraph there is reference to Stock Exchange prices.

All I propose to refer to . . . is the fact that the middle market quotation for the ordinary shares on 14 September was 5*s* 9*d* and on 23 September it was also 5*s* 9*d* . . . So that from that circular it appears that ordinary shareholders were being offered 6*s* a share as against a middle market price of 5*s* 9*d*, that is to say, they were being offered 3*d* a share above the relevant Stock Exchange price.

Holts' offer was accepted by holders of more than 99 per cent of the shares in the company, but it was not accepted by the applicants. Accordingly on 28 January 1966 Holts served a notice on each of the applicants pursuant to s 209 [corresponding to s 321 of our Act] to the effect that it desired to acquire their shares and that unless they applied to the court on or before 28 February 1966, and the court otherwise ordered, Holts would be entitled and bound to acquire their shares on the terms of the offer; and the summons which is before me now was in fact issued on the last day, namely, 28 February 1966.

Now, the contentions which are put forward by the applicants in this case fall under two main heads. In the first place it is said that the price of 6*s* a share is unfair, taking into account the assets and future prospects of the company and the advantages which will accrue to Holts by the take-over; and secondly, it is said that it is unfair to the applicants that they should be compelled to sell their shares at a loss. Before considering those contentions in more detail, there are two or three general observations which I should make and which I think are justified by the authorities on this section to which I have been referred.

The first general observation is that the onus of proof here is fairly and squarely on the applicants, and, indeed, they accept that that is so. The onus of proof is on them to establish, if they can, that the offer was unfair. In *Re Hoare & Co Ltd* (1934) 150 LT 374 Maugham J had this to say:　　　·

'I have some hesitation in expressing my view as to when the court should think fit to order otherwise. I think, however, the view of the legislature is that where not less than nine-tenths of the shareholders in the transferor company approve the scheme or accept the offer, prima facie, at any rate, the offer must be taken to be a proper one, and in default of an application by the dissenting shareholders, which include those who do not assent, the shares of the dissentients may be acquired on the original terms by the transferee company. Accordingly, I think it is manifest that the reasons for inducing the court to "order otherwise" are reasons which must be supplied by the dissentients who take the step of making an application to the court, and that the onus is on them of giving a reason why their shares should not be acquired by the transferee company.' . . .

The second general observation which seems to me to be relevant is this: that, since this is not a case of a purchase of assets, but is a case of a purchase of shares, the market price on the Stock Exchange of those shares is cogent evidence of their true value; not conclusive evidence, of course, but cogent evidence. . . . In this case the applicants have set out to discharge a formidable onus, bearing in mind not only that the offer price was above the Stock Exchange price, but also that holders of over 99 per cent of the ordinary shares accepted it.

The third general observation which arises out of the arguments that have been put forward here concerns the question whether the test of the fairness of the offer is whether it is fair to the individual shareholder or whether it is fair to the body of shareholders as a whole. In my judgment, the test of fairness is whether the offer is fair to the offerees as a body and not whether it is fair to a particular shareholder in the peculiar circumstances of his own case.

. . . Now, after stating these general observations, let me refer in a little more detail to some of the points which have been put forward on the part of the applicants. They have complained that the market price was substantially higher than 6s a share for a number of years; and the evidence is that in 1959 the shares went as high as 7s 3d; in 1960, 7s 6d; 1961, 9s 9d; 1962, 8s 3d; 1963, 7s 7d; 1964, 7s 6d; 1965, 7s 3d: equally . . . in each of those years the lowest price for the shares was under 6s. However that may be, it seems to me that the real point is this—was 6s a fair price at the time when the offer was made, namely, in September 1965?

[Counsel for the applicants] says that September 1965 when the offer was made was a time when the shares were temporarily depressed; that the future prospects were good, and that the market price is not really a reliable guide in this case, particularly having regard to the fact that the accounts for the year ending 31 March 1965 which showed a substantial increase in profits were published simultaneously with the offer so that the market had no opportunity to adjust itself to the latest results. In answer to that, it has to be remembered that shareholders had three weeks in which to make up their minds whether to accept the offer or not; and it cannot be said that during that three weeks there was no time for the market to react, in which ever way it was likely to react in the particular circumstances of this case; nor can it be said that three weeks did not give the shareholders ample time in which to form their own view of the question whether 6s was a fair offer in the light of the accounts with which they were furnished at the same time. . . .

It is said that in the company's balance sheet the goodwill of the parent company is shown at a figure of £1 and that the freehold and leasehold properties have been valued either at 1959 values or at cost, part one way and part another; and it is said that those figures do not indicate the true value of either the goodwill or fixed assets. There seems to me to be a number of answers to that contention. First of all, as I have indicated earlier on, this is not a question of a purchase of assets, but a question of the purchase of shares. Secondly, the balance sheet does not purport to offer a current valuation of either the goodwill or of the fixed assets. It makes it perfectly plain what the basis is on which the properties are put in at those figures. Anybody looking at the balance sheet with ordinary intelligence would know that £1 is not being put forward as representing the value of the goodwill and that the figures in the balance sheet are not being put forward as the current value of the assets in question. There is also another point in relation to the matter that I am considering which counsel for the respondents pointed out, namely, that the balance sheet showed that the company had reserves totalling almost exactly the same amount as the amount of the issued ordinary share capital which would give each ordinary share a net book value of twice its value, that is to say, each 2*s* ordinary share would have a net book value of 4*s*, and counsel points out that the offer is 50 per cent in excess of that of 4*s* and 2*s* a share represents something like an additional £380 000 which Holts are paying for the ordinary shares. It seems to me that that is a matter which has to be balanced against any question of undervaluation.

Then, it is said that the price of 6*s* a share does not reflect the advantages accruing to Holts by their obtaining complete control of the company. Now, I agree with counsel that that might possibly be used as an argument to justify paying a shareholder with a controlling interest a larger price for the shares than the price paid to minority holders. In my judgment, however, it is not unfair to offer a minority shareholder the value of what he possesses, ie a minority shareholding.

. . . Counsel for the respondents says: 'on the figures the preference shareholders were dealt with proportionately better than the ordinary shareholders.' . . . [However] the question is not whether the preference shareholders were dealt with generously, but whether the ordinary shareholders were dealt with fairly; and whether the preference share-holders were dealt with over generously I do not know. . . . [T]he mere fact that they were dealt with generously or not generously at all, does not mean that the ordinary shareholders were not dealt with fairly. . . . It is possible to criticize, in cases like this, figures, offers and balance sheets and argue about matters of fairness and unfairness; but that is what makes the task of dissentients who come to the court under this section a very difficult task, one which, so far as reported cases go, they have never succeeded in discharging. They have not succeeded, except in *Re Bugle Press Ltd*, which is a different case that really lies outside the scheme of s 209; and, although I have sympathy for the applicants, who naturally did not want to face a loss on their investments, I have no doubt in the end that they have failed, like others before them, to discharge this heavy onus of proof, and, that being so, I am bound to dismiss this application.

[384] Sammel *v* President Brand Gold Mining Co Ltd
1969 (3) SA 629 (AD)

Free State Saaiplaas Gold Mining Co Ltd (Saaiplaas), incorporated in 1955, was insolvent. It had a large, assessed tax loss, and owed sub-stantial amounts to various loan creditors, who also held 56 per cent of the shares. In June 1965, a contract was concluded between Saaiplaas, the President Brand Gold Mining Co, and the loan creditors of Saaiplaas, in which it was agreed that the issued share capital of Saaiplaas was to be reduced from R25 438 800, divided into shares of R1 each, to R2 543 880, divided into shares of ten cents each, by writing off R22 894 920 as lost and not represented by assets. The reduced shares were to be consolidated into shares of R1 each and some seven and a half million new shares of R1 were to be created, which were to be issued at par to the loan creditors in settlement of their claims. President Brand undertook that thereafter it would offer to purchase the entire issued share capital of Saaiplaas at 60 cents per share. This offer was to be conditional on acceptance by the holders of not less than 90 per cent in value of the issued share capital.

Some 93 per cent of the shareholders of Saaiplaas accepted the offer. President Brand exercised its right under s 103*ter* (now s 321) to acquire compulsorily the balance. Some of the dissenting shareholders objected but did not succeed in persuading the court that the scheme was unfair.

TROLLIP JA: First, some general principles that are relevant. By becoming a shareholder in a company a person undertakes by his contract to be bound by the decisions of the prescribed majority of shareholders, if those decisions on the affairs of the company are arrived at in accordance with the law, even where they adversely affect his own rights as a shareholder (cf ss 16 and 24). That principle of the supremacy of the majority is essential to the proper functioning of companies. Thus, in *Levin* v *Felt & Tweeds Ltd* 1951 (2) SA 401 (AD) it was contended (p 411H) that the rights of the ordinary shareholders were being altered by the reconstruction of capital of the company, because, when they invested money in it, they relied on the fact that the capital of the company was as it then was, and that any reduction of capital therefore adversely affected their rights.

> 'The answer to this contention (said Centlivres CJ at 412A) is that when the ordinary shareholders invested their money in the company they must be taken to have known that under the Companies Act the court may confirm a reduction of capital voted for by three-fourths of the shareholders and that on such a reduction of capital the preference shareholders are entitled to be paid out first (ie before the ordinary shareholders).'

The same view was expressed by Evershed MR in answer to a similar contention in *Greenhalgh* v *Arderne Cinemas* [1951] Ch 286 (CA) at 292, which is quoted later in this judgment. Similarly in the present case, when the minority shareholders became members of Saaiplaas, they must be taken to have known that the prescribed majority of shareholders, if at any time it appeared to them to be necessary or desirable, could and might resolve that the company should take some action, even some unusual action as in the present case, which might adversely affect their rights as shareholders, but they undertook to be bound by any such decision if lawfully arrived at, and by the court's confirmation of it, if that were also required by law.

Now the resolutions approving the reconstruction plan for Saaiplaas were duly passed by the required majorities at a properly convened meeting of shareholders. Hence they were binding on the minority shareholders, unless they were contrary to the law. The only possible respect in which they could have offended against the law was if they perpetrated what is conveniently, although not quite accurately, described as a fraud on the minority shareholders. That is a limitation on the power of the majority which is not expressed in the Companies Act (except to the extent and for the purpose of s 111*bis* [now superseded by s 252], which is not relevant here), and is seldom, if ever, embodied in a company's articles of association; nevertheless, it is implied by the law. . . . It is true that it was neither alleged nor contended for the appellants that the resolutions constituted an actual fraud on the minority shareholders; but 'fraud' in that expression does not necessarily mean fraud in its technical sense; it is there used in its wider connotation of being any abuse or misuse of power by the majority of shareholders. It seems to me that at least part of the argument for the appellants amounted to maintaining the commission of a fraud on the minority of shareholders in that extended sense; in particular, the alleged circumvention or deprivation of the minority's rights could only be founded on that principle. It must therefore be considered.

The precise content and extent of the expression, 'fraud on the minority', has not yet been authoritatively and comprehensively defined, either here or in England, and such definition need not be now attempted. The expression is subjected to a critical and constructive analysis by Professor Gower in his *Modern Company Law* 2 ed 508–25. It suffices to say here that (1) merely because the whole or an effective part of the majority of shareholders are actuated in voting for a resolution at a general meeting by their own selfish interest, does not ordinarily constitute a fraud on the minority, for the rule is well established that a vote, being a proprietary right of shareholding, may be exercised by the shareholder in his own interests . . .; (2) that will not, however, entitle the majority to use their voting power to discriminate between themselves and the minority shareholders so as to give themselves an advantage at the expense of the minority . . .; and (3) generally, if a resolution is passed by the required majority bona fide for the benefit of the company as a whole, it can hardly be said to amount to a fraud on the minority shareholders. . . .

In regard to (3), two comments must be added. Firstly, according to *Greenhalgh's* case (*supra*) at 291, 'bona fide for the benefit of the company as a whole' does not mean (*a*) that the majority must have been bona fide, and (*b*) that the court must be objectively satisfied that the resolution was for the benefit of the company as a whole; it means, says Evershed MR,

'not two things but one thing. It means that the shareholder must proceed on what, in his honest opinion, is for the benefit of the company as a whole.'

I shall, however, assume, without deciding, in favour of the appellants that the expression does comprise the two elements (*a*) and (*b*). It is convenient to make that assumption in this case, for the resolutions in question had also to be confirmed by the court, which should and would have applied substantially the same objective test as in (*b*) above; and a similar objective test has to be applied under s 103*ter* in determining the fairness of the take-over scheme. Secondly, the Master of the Rolls also said

> '"the company as a whole" does not (at any rate in such a case as the present) mean the company as a commercial entity, distinct from the corporators; it means the corporators as a general body'.

He was there dealing, of course, with a solvent company. Where, as here, the shares of the company are fully paid up and it is insolvent, and the resolutions are intended to rescue it from insolvency, 'the company as a whole' must also include its creditors; indeed, their interests should be the paramount consideration in deciding what is for 'the benefit of the company as a whole'.

Good and instructive illustrations of the application of those principles are found in English law in the so-called 'expropriation' cases, that is, cases where the majority shareholders have sought by resolution to 'expropriate' the shares or rights of the minority shareholders; for example, *Brown* v *British Abrasive Wheel Co* [1919] 1 Ch 290 (Astbury J); *Dafen Tinplate Co Ltd* v *Llanelly Steel Co Ltd* [1920] 2 Ch 124 (Peterson J); *Sidebottom* v *Kershaw, Leese & Co Ltd* [1920] 1 Ch 154 (CA); *Shuttleworth* v *Cox Brothers & Co (Maidenhead) Ltd* [1927] 2 KB 9 (CA). In the first two cases it was held that the resolutions were impeachable as not having been passed bona fide for the benefit of the company as a whole but for the advantage of the majority at the expense of the minority shareholders, whereas in each of the last two cases the court of appeal arrived at a contrary conclusion. The facts in those latter two cases are worth quoting. In *Sidebottom's* case the majority shareholders (which included the directors) passed a special resolution altering the articles authorizing 'the expropriation' at full value and the transfer to nominees of the directors of the shares belonging to any shareholder who was competing with the company in business. In a suit at the instance of a minority shareholder, who was such a competitor, the court of appeal unanimously held that, whether or not the resolution was aimed at any particular shareholder, it was passed bona fide for the benefit of the company as a whole and was therefore valid. In *Shuttleworth's* case, the company's articles provided that plaintiff was to be a life director. The requisite majority of shareholders passed a special resolution altering the articles by adding that a director would be disqualified from office when all his co-directors requested him in writing to resign. Thereupon the plaintiff was duly called on to resign. The court of appeal unanimously held that, as the resolution was passed bona fide for the benefit of the company as a whole, it was valid. The principles applied in those last two cases accord fully with our law as expounded in *Gundelfinger's* case [1939 AD 314]: see *Fairham* v *Cape Town Mutual Aid Fund* 1949 (1) SA 919 (C) at 929–30.

Cases decided in a context of take-over bids are perhaps even more apposite and illustrative. In *Greenhalgh's* case (*supra*) an outside bidder offered to purchase the shares in a private company at 6*s* per share from any shareholder who was prepared to sell them. It is not clear whether the offer was made with a view to invoking the section, but that is not of importance to the point now under consideration. The articles, however, prohibited a sale to an outsider so long as any member was prepared to purchase the shares. The managing director, who held or controlled the majority of the shares, agreed to sell his shares to the bidder. He then proposed a special resolution altering the articles to enable any member, with the sanction of an ordinary resolution, to transfer his shares to any person named in the latter resolution so as to enable any member to take advantage of the offer. A general meeting passed the special resolution and an ordinary resolution sanctioning the transfer of some of the managing director's shares to the bidder. His remaining shares were to be transferred to the latter's nominees. The court of appeal unanimously held that the resolutions could not be impeached as they were passed bona fide for the benefit of the company as a whole and did not discriminate between majority and minority shareholders so as to give the former an advantage of which the latter were deprived. At 291 the Master of the Rolls said:

> 'If, as commonly happens, an outside person makes an offer to buy all the shares, prima facie, if the corporators think it a fair offer and vote in favour of the resolution, it is no ground for impeaching the resolution that they are considering their own position as individuals.'

It was also contended in that case that the resolutions deprived the minority shareholders of the right under the articles of buying the shares of the majority, if the latter wished to dispose of them. That contention was disposed of in substantially the same way as Centlivres CJ dealt with the similar argument in *Levin* v *Felt & Tweeds Ltd* quoted above. The Master of the Rolls said at 292:

> 'I think that the answer is that when a man comes into a company, he is not entitled to assume that the articles will always remain in a particular form; and that, so long as the proposed alteration does not unfairly discriminate in the way I have indicated, it is not an objection, provided the resolution is passed bona fide, that the right to tender for the majority holding of shares would be lost by the lifting of the restriction.'

In *Hogg* v *Cramphorn Ltd* [1967] Ch 254 (Buckley J) the directors of a company received an intimation of a proposed take-over bid for its shares, the object of which was to enable the bidder to obtain control of the company. The directors, who held and controlled a substantial number of shares but not the majority of them, thereupon devised and put into effect a scheme of issuing reserve shares to the trustees of a trust which they created for the benefit of the company's employees. With the expected support of the trustees as shareholders, the directors would command a majority of votes of shareholders. The object of the scheme was either to prevent the bidder from gaining control of the company through whatever shares he did acquire by his bid, or to discourage him altogether from proceeding with his bid. He, however, did proceed with making his bid formally to the shareholders, but he

made it conditional on its being accepted by the holders of 90 per cent
of the shares in value. That majority did not accept the offer and it
therefore lapsed. Nevertheless, the plaintiff, on behalf of himself and
other dissatisfied shareholders, because of the purpose of the scheme,
sued to have the issue of shares by the directors set aside. The court held
that, although the directors bona fide believed that the scheme was for
the benefit of the company as a whole, they could only issue new shares
to raise fresh capital, and it was therefore a breach of their fiduciary duty
as directors to have issued them for the abovementioned purpose, but
that could have been validly done by the majority of the shareholders
(excluding, of course, the trustees) at a general meeting (p 269). Such
a meeting was, with the leave of the court, called and ratified the issue
of shares [see 227 above].

The point to be underlined in the last two cases is that, in the former,
the object of the 'device' (to use the terminology of appellants' counsel
in the present case) was to facilitate the take-over bid by depriving those
shareholders, who did not want to accept the offer, of their pre-emptive
rights to the shares of those who wanted to accept it; and, in the latter,
the object was to frustrate the take-over bid in the above sense by the
dilution of existing voting rights through the creation of new voting
rights thereby ensuring a majority favourable to the directors. Both
'devices' were held to be valid if, as actually happened in the former
case, they were effected by the requisite majority of shareholders acting
bona fide for the benefit of the company as a whole and without unfairly
discriminating against any shareholders in the sense mentioned above.

As the reconstruction plan also involved a reduction of capital, indeed
it was an integral and vital element of it, the court's confirmation was
required—ss 44, 45 and 48. [On the position under the 1973 Act, see
p 150 above.] Section 48(1) endows a court with a discretion to confirm
or refuse confirmation. Before exercising that discretion in the present
case in favour of confirmation, the court had to be satisfied, even although
the application was unopposed, (a) that the resolutions were duly passed,
that is that they, inter alia, did not constitute a fraud on the minority
shareholders, for the validity of those resolutions is the foundation for
the proceedings (see ss 44 and 45), (b) that the rights of the creditors
were safeguarded or not prejudiced (cf ss 47 and 48 (1)), especially as
the company was insolvent, and (c) that the proposed reduction was fair
and equitable as between the majority and minority shareholders or the
creditor-shareholders and the others. See Levin's case (supra) 1951 (2)
SA 401 (AD) at 411E–G; Ex parte National Industrial Credit Corporation Ltd
1950 (2) SA 10 (W)—an unopposed application; British and American
Trustee and Finance Corporation v Couper [1894] AC 399, especially at 406,
per Lord Herschell LC:

> 'The interests of the dissenting minority of the shareholders . . . are
> properly safeguarded by this: that the decision of the majority can
> only prevail if it be confirmed by the court';

Carruth's case (supra) at 765, per Lord Maugham:

> '. . . the court, whether or not the petition is opposed, has a duty to
> consider whether the proposed reduction is a fair or unfair one';

Scottish Insurance Corporation Ltd v *Wilsons & Clyde Coal Company Ltd* [1949] AC 462 (HLSc), especially at 486, per Lord Simonds:

'. . . important though its (the court's) task is to see . . . that creditors are not prejudiced, it has the further duty of satisfying itself that the scheme is fair and equitable between the different classes of shareholders',

and at 499, per Lord Morton:

'It is this discretion, vested in the court, which properly safeguards the interests of a dissenting minority';

Ex parte Westburn Sugar Refineries Ltd [1951] AC 625 (HLSc), and unopposed application, especially at 629, per Lord Normand:

'But the powers of the shareholders (to reduce the capital) must be exercised so as to safeguard the rights of creditors, the just and equitable treatment of shareholders, and the interests of the investing public',

and at 632, per Lord Reid:

'What, then, is the duty of the court in considering a matter of this kind? In the first place the interests of creditors must be safeguarded. . . . Secondly, the interests of shareholders may have to be considered. . . . And thirdly there is the public interest to consider.'

Incidentally, in the last case it was held that, if the reduction is otherwise unobjectionable, the fact that it may have an ulterior motive (in that case, disposing of the assets of the company because it was threatened with nationalization) is no reason for not confirming the reduction. Similarly here, that a motive for the reduction was ultimately to ensure a successful take-over of the company's shares would not have been a reason for refusing confirmation, if the scheme was otherwise unobjectionable.

It is true that generally the court in such an application is only concerned with the actual reduction of capital. But here that was the vital and integral part of the wider reconstruction plan, which the court, in determining whether the reduction was fair and equitable or not, had therefore to consider as a whole (*Carruth's* case (*supra*) at 769, 770; *Ex parte Carrig Diamonds Ltd* 1966 (1) SA 572 (W) at 575D-G).

Now, after due disclosure to the shareholders of all the relevant and material facts relating to the reconstruction plan and take-over scheme, the resolutions for the reconstruction were duly passed by an overwhelming majority of shareholders at the general meeting of 23 July 1965. On 7 September the court, after a similar disclosure (in my view) in the petition and supporting documents . . . confirmed the reconstruction of capital; and, thereafter, the order of confirmation and the minute recording the reconstruction must have been registered by the Registrar of Companies. According to s 49(4) his certificate of such registration thereupon became

'conclusive evidence that all the requirements of this Act with respect to reduction of share capital have been complied with and that the share capital of the company is such as is stated in the minute'.

Dealing with the legal consequences of confirmation and registration of the order and minute, this court (per Stratford JA) in *Estate Walker* v *Estate Petersen* 1933 AD 23 at 30 said:

'Apart from the clear terms of the Act, we have in this approved minute an order of court of competent jurisdiction; that order could be set aside on appeal to a superior court, possibly also by a court of concurrent jurisdiction on some such ground as its procurement by fraud of one of the parties; but until so set aside it is as binding on the parties to it as any law of the land.' . . .

A few words should here be added about the contention that the plan circumvented or deprived the minority shareholders of their so-called rights under s 103*ter* to decline and defeat the take-over bid. I need only repeat that a shareholder's rights as such are not inviolate: they may be altered at any time in the manner and for the purposes canvassed above. For example, the proportion that his shares or the combined shares of the minority shareholders bears to the total issued shares, and therefore their relative voice in the company, can be diminished to below one-tenth either by the issue of new shares to others or in some other way. Section 103*ter* in no way affects that position; it does not prohibit such an alteration being made before or because of the prospective invocation of its provisions or at all; in particular, even if such an alteration were designedly done in order to facilitate or defeat the imminent invocation of its provisions, that would not vitiate it, provided that it was done, as it was in the present case, bona fide for the benefit of the transferor company as a whole and not merely to advantage the majority at the expense of the minority shareholders. (See the cases of *Sidebottom*, *Greenhalgh*, *Hogg* and *Westburn Sugar Refineries*, quoted above.)

Of course, if the majority of shareholders of a transferor company did force through a reorganization of its share capital, not bona fide for the benefit of the company as a whole, but solely to benefit themselves or the transferee company at the expense of the minority shareholders by thereby watering down their voting strength to below 10 per cent and thus enabling the transferee company to expropriate their shares under s 103*ter*, the position might well be entirely different. For then the action of the majority might possibly be mala fide or even fraudulent, which would be cognisable by the court in the exercise of its discretion. That would then approximate to the position in the *Bugle Press* and *Esso* cases presently to be discussed. But, for the reasons already given, that is clearly not the position in the present case.

Consequently both in law and in fact, I think that the court, in exercising its discretion under s 103*ter*, must act on the basis that the reconstruction plan was fair and equitable in all respects. . . .

I turn now to the other leg of the argument for the appellants: That the majority of nine-tenths in value, created by the reconstruction plan, was not an independent or disinterested majority, which s 103*ter* requires. More specifically the contention was that that majority, comprising the loan creditors, had, on 25 June 1965, bound themselves to President Brand to accept its offer for both their existing and new shares, so that, when the offer was made on 15 September, they were not the independent or disinterested shareholders that the section insists on. The English case of *In re Bugle Press Ltd* [1961] 1 Ch 270 (CA) and the Canadian case of *Re International Petroleum Co Ltd* 33 DLR (2d) 658 and 1963 SCR 144 (*sub nom Esso Standard (Inter-America) Inc*) were heavily relied upon.

As a matter purely of construction, our s 103*ter*, as originally enacted, did not require the nine-tenths majority in value to be independent of or disinterested in the transferee company before its provisions could be invoked. They could be so invoked simply

> 'if a scheme or contract . . . has . . . been approved by the holders of not less than nine-tenths in value of the shares affected'.

The view of the legislature then was that where shareholders holding not less than nine-tenths in value of the shares affected approved the scheme or accepted the offer, the offer must be taken to be a proper one, entitling the transferee company to use the provisions of the section; in any event, an inference could generally be drawn from such acceptances in the ordinary take-over case that the scheme was fair and reasonable to all the shareholders concerned. But obviously there could be special circumstances in a particular case which invalidated or weakened that inference or otherwise influenced the exercise of the court's discretion, as, for example, where there was some connection, interest, or dependence between the prescribed majority of the shareholders of the transferor company and the transferee company. The existence of such a circumstance, however, did not preclude the invocation of the section; it would merely have been relevant to the exercise of the court's discretion to order otherwise, and, in particular, to its assessment of the fairness of the scheme.

By s 86 of Act 46 of 1952 the section was amended to exclude shares held at the date of the offer by, or by a nominee for, the transferee company or its subsidiary from the reckoning of the nine-tenths majority in value. To the extent that such shareholders were therefore dependent on or interested in the transferee company, their approval of the offer was to be ignored in determining whether the nine-tenths in value had been attained and the section could be invoked. Otherwise the section was unaffected in its applicability and the above interpretation continued to apply.

I do not think that the *Bugle Press* and *Esso* cases [pp 658–60 above] decided anything different.

The *Bugle Press* case was decided on a section substantially the same as our s 103*ter*, as amended. It concerned three parties. They were the only shareholders in the Bugle Press Company, the transferor company. Two of them each held 4 500 shares and the third, the minority shareholder, 1 000 shares. Manifestly for the purpose of expropriating the latter's shares and acquiring them for themselves by means of the section, the two majority shareholders incorporated another company, the transferee company, in which they were the sole shareholders and directors. This transferee company thereupon, according to the plan, offered to purchase all the shares in the transferor company at £10 per share, based upon a valuation made by independent valuers. The majority shareholders, of course, accepted the offer, thereby constituting the nine-tenths in value required by the section. The minority share-holder refused the offer, and applied to court to 'order otherwise', which Buckley J did. His decision was confirmed on appeal. The association there between the majority shareholders and the transferee company was very close — the latter was for all practical purposes entirely equivalent to the former. Nevertheless, as the nine-tenths majority had been achieved, the court of appeal accepted that the case fell within the terms of the section (see p 286). Hence it said that the dissentient shareholder still had to satisfy the court that it ought to 'order otherwise', but that the above-mentioned circumstance was most relevant to the exercise of its discretion (p 286). Finally it held that, because the trans-feree company and the majority shareholders were virtually the same, and the latter were using the section for the ulterior purpose of expro-priating or evicting the minority shareholder, without its being shown that that was in the interests of the transferor company, the minority shareholder had discharged the onus of showing that, whether or not the price offered was fair, this was a special case with special circum-stances justifying the court's ordering otherwise.

The *Esso* case, decided by the Ontario and Canadian Courts of Appeal, was a similar case. A, the transferee company, was the wholly owned subsidiary of another company, C. C was the majority shareholder in the transferor company, B, holding about 96 per cent of its shares. C wanted to expropriate for itself the shares of the minority in B, so it caused A to make a take-over bid for all the shares in B, that is, the shares of itself and the minority shareholders. C, of course, accepted the offer itself, thereby creating the nine-tenths majority. Thereupon A sought to acquire the shares of the minority shareholders by invoking the section. For the same reasons as in the *Bugle Press* case, which was followed, the court ordered otherwise at the instance of some of the minority shareholders.

In each case it is clear that the majority shareholders could not have expropriated the shares of the minority for themselves by simply passing a resolution to that effect, for the resolution, not being bona fide for the benefit of the company as a whole but for the advantage of the majority at the expense of the minority, would have been a fraud on the minority, according to the cases discussed above. The take-over scheme was therefore merely a device to use the section to evade the law protect-ing the minority. As Harman LJ said in the *Bugle Press* case at 287,

'this is a barefaced attempt to evade the fundamental rule of company law which forbids the majority of shareholders, unless the articles so provide, to expropriate a minority'.

Not surprisingly, the court in each case refused to sanction that device, for what could not legally be done directly could not be allowed to be achieved indirectly. If, however, the proposed expropriation had been bona fide for the benefit of the company as a whole, the position would have been different. Both Lord Evershed MR and Harman LJ in effect pointed that out in the *Bugle Press* case at 287 and 288, and so did Laidlaw JA in his judgment in the *Esso* case (669–70 of 33 DLR (2d)), which was upheld on appeal. That also accords fully with the similar principle applicable to cases of the expropriation of minority rights by a resolution—see the authorities discussed above. . . .

The contention that, as a matter of construction, s 103*ter* requires for its applicability that the holders of the nine-tenths majority of countable shares must be independent of or disinterested in the transferee company is therefore rejected. If such a majority does accept a take-over offer made in pursuance of a scheme or contract the existence of any connection, interest or dependence between that majority and the transferee company is merely a factor to be taken into account by the court in exercising its discretion under the section, the weight to be given to it depending upon the circumstances of each case.

[*Sammel* v *President Brand* is noted by R C Beuthin (1970) 87 *SALJ* 276. See also *Sammel* v *President Brand Gold Mining Co Ltd* 1969 (3) SA 699 (W).]

[385] Mia *v* Anglo-Alpha Cement Ltd
1970 (2) SA 281 (W)

Cillié JP: On 12 July 1966 it was announced in the Press that Anglo-Alpha Cement Ltd, to which I shall refer as Anglo-Alpha or the respondent, wished to acquire the complete issued share capital of Union Lime Co Ltd, to which I shall refer as Union Lime. A circular dated 23 August 1966 was sent to all members of Union Lime containing the respondent's offer for this acquisition; in short it amounted to an exchange of shares in the proportion of two shares in Anglo-Alpha for every three shares held in Union Lime.

Apart from the exact terms of the exchange the 'particulars of the offer' in the circular contained, *inter alia*, the following: the offer would remain open until 13 September 1966 for acceptance by every member of Union Lime on that company's register or entitled to be placed thereon; acceptance would be irrevocable; the offer was made conditional upon its acceptance by the holders of 90 per cent in nominal value of the ordinary shares in Union Lime. It was stated specifically that s 103*ter* of the Companies Act 46 of 1926 as amended would apply to the offer and that, if the offer was accepted by as many shareholders as stipulated, the respondent would make use of the machinery set out in the section to acquire the shares of those holders who had not accepted the offer. . . .

On 16 September 1966 it was announced that shareholders holding 90,87 per cent of the issued share capital of Union Lime had accepted the offer.

The applicant is the registered and beneficial owner of 21 000 of Union Lime's 1 800 000 shares. He did not accept the offer. In a letter dated 7 October 1966 Anglo-Alpha gave him notice that, if he so wished, Anglo-Alpha would take over all his Union Lime shares in exchange for 14 000 shares in Anglo-Alpha. The applicant was not prepared to transfer his shares on that basis and he then received a final notice from Anglo-Alpha on 28 December 1966. This was to the effect that the holders of more than 96 per cent of the ordinary shares in Union Lime had by then accepted the offer; that Anglo-Alpha wanted to acquire his shares of that company by issuing 14 000 shares in the respondent company to him; that if he does not make application in terms of s 103*ter* of the

Act within the prescribed time Anglo-Alpha would be entitled and bound to acquire his Union Lime shares on the basis set out and that, if he does not agree to the exchange or makes no application, Anglo-Alpha would take such steps for the acquisition of his shares as it is entitled to do.

As a result of that notice the applicant brought the present application asking for an order that the respondent was not entitled to acquire his shares on the terms of the offer and directing the respondent to take them over at a cash price of R30 per share or at such other terms for cash as the court may think fit. . . .

Whether the court will 'think fit to order otherwise' as it is asked to do in this case, depends on the facts placed before it. Normally it will order otherwise if it comes to the conclusion that the offer which a shareholder may be compelled to accept is not a fair one. It has not been suggested that there are facts, other than those pointing to the fairness or unfairness of the offer, which should be considered in this case, before the court decides whether or not to order otherwise.

If the court does not make such an order or is not asked to make any order at all, the transferee company, that is Anglo-Alpha, will be entitled and bound to acquire the shares of the dissentient shareholder, that is the applicant, and on the terms contained in the offer accepted by the approving shareholders. Should the dissenting shareholder therefore not want his shares to be acquired by the transferee company on the basis of the offer, he must make application to the court 'to order otherwise', that means that the onus is on him to move and persuade the court to stop the process which would otherwise result in the acquisition of his shares by the transferee company as set out in the offer. In this case the applicant has the onus, therefore, of proving that the offer is unfair. Should he fail to do this the respondent will be entitled to acquire his Union Lime shares in exchange for its own shares as offered. No relevant reported South African cases on the interpretation of s 103*ter* was placed before the court, but the view set out above of where the burden of proof lies is in conformity with the well-known rule of our law, namely that

'if one person claims something from another in a court of law then he has to satisfy the Court that he is entitled to it'

(*Pillay* v *Krishna & another* 1946 AD 946 at 951).

In arriving at this view of the law the court was influenced by the decisions of the English Courts on the interpretation of similarly worded sections, s 209 of the English Companies Act of 1948, and s 155(1) of the English Companies Act of 1929.

In *Re Hoare & Co Ltd* (1934) 150 LT 374 (also reported at [1933] All ER 105) the court dealt with an offer by the transferee company to shareholders of the transferor company to acquire their shares partly for shares in the transferee company and partly for cash.

It may be relevant that the offer was accepted by shareholders representing 99,62 per cent of the total issued share capital of the transferor company. In his judgment Maugham J said the following:

'Accordingly, I think it is manifest that the reasons for inducing the court to "order otherwise" are reasons which must be supplied by the dissentients who take the step of making an application to the court, and that the onus is on them of giving a reason why their shares should not be acquired by the transferee company.'

And later:

'prima facie the court ought to regard the scheme as a fair one inasmuch as it seems to me impossible to suppose that the court, in the absence of very strong grounds, is to be entitled to set up its own view of the fairness of the scheme in opposition to so very large a majority of the shareholders who are concerned. Accordingly, without expressing a final opinion on the matter, because there may be special circumstances in special cases, I am unable to see that I have any right to order otherwise in such a case as I have before me, unless it is affirmatively established that, notwithstanding the view of a very large majority of shareholders, the scheme is unfair. There may be other grounds, but I see no other grounds available in the present case for the interference of the court.'

This dictum has been approved in a number of cases with one exception to which I shall refer later. At this stage I want to quote a passage from the judgment of Vaisey J in the case of *Re Sussex Brick Company Limited* [1960] 1 All ER 772. At 774 the learned judge says:

'I think that he (the applicant) is faced with the very difficult task of discharging the onus, which is undoubtedly a heavy one, of showing that he, being the only man in the regiment out of step, is the man whose views ought to prevail.'

To the same effect is the following passage of Plowman J in *Re Grierson, Oldham and Adams Ltd* [1967] 1 All ER 192 at 197:

'In this case the applicants have set out to discharge a formidable onus, bearing in mind not only that the offer price was above the Stock Exchange price, but also that holders of over 99 per cent of the ordinary shares accepted it.'

To say that an applicant has a heavy or formidable onus to discharge does not mean that the onus differs from the one which normally applies in civil cases, namely, proof on a balance of probabilities. The reference to the heavy onus is only an indication that, on the probability of the offer being a fair one, the scale is heavily loaded against the applicant by the fact that 90 per cent or more of the shareholders in value have accepted the offer.

Some English judges have stated what it is expected that an applicant should prove in these matters. For example, Vaisey J in *Re Sussex Brick Co Ltd* says at 292 and 293 of the report in [1961] 1 ChD 289:

'A scheme must be obviously unfair, patently unfair, unfair to the meanest intelligence.'

And

'It must be affirmatively established that, notwithstanding the view of the majority, the scheme is unfair, and that is a different thing from saying that it must be established that the scheme is not a very fair or not a fair one; a scheme has to be shown affirmatively, patently, obviously and convincingly to be unfair.'

Plowman J in *Re Grierson, Oldham and Adams Ltd* (*supra*) at 197 says:

'... the test of fairness is whether the offer is fair to the offerees as a body, and not whether it is fair to a particular shareholder in the particular circumstances of his own case.'

At 198 the learned judge says:

'... the fact that the applicants may be able to demonstrate that the scheme is open to criticism or is capable of improvement is not enough to discharge the onus of proof which lies on them'.

The applicant agreed that the onus would in ordinary circumstances be on him to prove the unfairness of the offer if he was to succeed. However, he relied on the statement of Maugham J in *Hoare's* case (*supra*) and contended that, because of 'special circumstances' which existed here, the onus rested upon the respondent to show that the offer was fair and reasonable, and, if he could not prove that the applicant would be entitled to judgment in his favour. . . .

. . . It is not necessary for me to go into details because I am of the opinion that the onus does not revert to the respondent because of special circumstances. It can merely be said that, in certain circumstances, the decision may go against the respondent if he leads no or insufficient evidence on fairness since the advantage he had obtained, through the overwhelming vote of the shareholders in favour of the offer, had diminished or disappeared as a result of particular circumstances. The so-called 'special circumstances' do not shift the onus because the overall onus to show that the offer is unfair still rests on the applicant; the circumstances merely affect the weight of the evidence and raise no rebuttable presumption of the unfairness of the offer nor do they mean that judgment will necessarily be in favour of the applicant if the respondent offers no evidence.

The first 'special circumstance' to which the applicant refers and which, so it was argued, was a reason why this was not an ordinary case, resulted from the relationship between Anglo-Transvaal Consolidated Investment Co Ltd (Anglo-vaal), Holderbank Financiere Glarus AG (Holderbank), the respondent and Union Lime. It was stated that Anglo-vaal and Holderbank together held more than 50 per cent of the issued shares in Union Lime and have *de facto* control of that company. Anglo-vaal, furthermore, is the parent company of a large group of companies including Union Lime and the respondent. An analysis is made of the specific shareholding in Union Lime and of the directors of the transferor and transferee companies, with allegations of a lack of independence and a conflict of duty and interest in the acceptance of the offer. In his petition the applicant summarizes his contention as follows:

'The special relationship between Union Lime, the respondent and the Anglo-vaal and Holderbank interests militates against a free determination of the actual value of Union Lime shares relative to a take-over by the respondent.'

This relationship may be a factor which could diminish the importance of the overwhelming vote in favour of the offer but it does not, by itself, show that the offer is unfair. From all the given facts it cannot be ascertained what the financial consequences of the relationship are nor how this relationship tends to enhance the value of Union Lime shares.

In considering whether the offer is a fair one it seems to me most important that sight should not be lost of the fact that the offer was not to purchase the shares for a cash amount but to exchange them for shares in the respondent company. It is therefore necessary to value the shares of the transferor and transferee companies on the same basis and compare the values when deciding on the fairness of the offer. Both shares in this case were freely sold on the Stock Exchange and it is, in my view, proper to compare the prices reached at the relevant times. Support for this view is to be found in a number of English cases. In *Re Press Caps Ltd* [1949] 1 All ER 1013 Wynn-Parry J says at 1018:

'. . . the final test of what is the value of a thing is what it will fetch if sold . . . if there exists a market, as, for instance, the Stock Exchange in the case of shares in respect of which there is a quotation or in respect of which there is permission to deal, there may be no need to sell, and *prima facie* the Stock Exchange markings can be taken as a satisfactory indication of the value of the shares in question.'

Similarly in the case of *Re Grierson, Oldham & Adams Ltd* (*supra*) Plowman J said at 197:

'. . . since this is not a case of a purchase of assets, but is a case of a purchase of shares, the market price on the Stock Exchange of those shares is cogent evidence of their true value; not conclusive evidence, of course, but cogent evidence.'

The middle market quotations of Union Lime shares during the six months preceding the public announcement of the offer ranged between 49 cents and 64 cents; the middle market quotation four days before the public announcement of the offer was 58 cents. At the beginning of August 1966, which is close to the date of the dispatch of the offer on the 23rd of that month, it rose to 71 cents. The middle market quotation of Anglo-Alpha on 8 July 1966 was 108 cents and this rose by 3 August to only 112 cents. Thus, immediately prior to the public announcement of the offer, the middle market value of three shares in Union Lime was 174 cents and the middle market of two Anglo-Alpha shares was 216 cents. On 3 August the middle market value of three Union Lime shares was 213 cents and the middle market value of two Anglo-Alpha shares was 224 cents.

The applicant's attack on this 'cogent evidence' of the comparative values of the two shares is the contention that the market price of Union Lime shares does not represent their true value; he claims that they are worth no less than R30 each. He acquired his shares between 1962 and 1966 and during that period their highest price on the Johannesburg Stock Exchange was below 100 cents per share. It is for the applicant to explain this substantial disparity. He arrives at his high figure, *inter alia*, by taking the net assets of Union Lime according to its balance sheet as at 30 June 1966, making no allowance for the provision for replacement which includes depreciation; he values the lime rights at R48 000 000 instead of the book value of R72 000; finally he adds R1 563 000 for

'goodwill in respect of potential profits earned since the date of the balance sheet'.

In this way he values the assets of Union Lime at R54 000 000, an amount which is divided by the number of shares (1 800 000) to give the value of each share as R30.

The respondent does not admit the correctness of these valuations or the methods of calculation employed in arriving at them, but says that it is impossible to decide on the fairness of the offer without comparing the values of the two shares and this can only be done properly if both shares are valued on the same basis. In this regard it means that, before any comparison can take place, the assets of and shares in Anglo-Alpha must be revalued employing the same methods as those used in the valuation of Union Lime's assets and shares. This the applicant has not done effectively or at all.

With this view of the respondent I agree and it is the main reason why I found that the applicant had not succeeded in discharging the onus of proving that the offer was not a fair one.

[386] *Ex Parte* Federale Nywerhede Bpk
1975 (1) SA 826 (W)

COETZEE J: Fed Nywerhede se aandelekapitaal bestaan uit gewone aandele van 50 sent elk en 5 persent kumulatiewe voorkeuraandele van R2 elk. Federale Volksbeleggings Bpk (,,FVB") en maatskappye deur hom beheer hou ongeveer 79 persent van die gewone uitgereikte aandele. Die voorkeuraandele verteenwoordig slegs ongeveer 5 persent van die totale uitgereikte aandelekapitaal. FVB het besluit dat Fed Nywerhede sy vol-filiaal moet word en van die buite-aandeelhouers moes dus ontslae geraak word. Die voorgestelde teenwaarde vir hulle aandele is FVB aandele (beide gewoon- en voorkeur-) in sekere proporsies wat nie ter sake is nie. Uit die stukke blyk dat tydens 'n direksievergadering van Fed Nywerhede op 17 Junie 1974, onder andere —

,,(1) die maatskappy kennis neem van die aanbod van Federale Volksbeleggings Bpk (FVB) om al die uitgereikte gewone aandele in die maatskappy wat nie reeds deur FVB regstreeks of onregstreeks gehou word nie, te verkry op die grondslag van (FVB aandele) vir elke 100 gewone aandele in die maatskappy;

(2) na aanleiding van hierdie aanbod die maatskappy 'n reëling-skema ingevolge art 311 van die Maatskappywet 1973 met sy gewone aandeelhouers aangaan om uitwerking te verleen aan die FVB aanbod".

Soortgelyke besluite is op dieselfde dag geneem ten opsigte van die voor-keuraandele. . . .

FVB se „aanbod", waarna ek hierbo verwys het, om al die uitgereikte aandele „te verkry", het 'n ander beslag gekry in die reëlingskema wat nou voor die Hof geplaas is. Hierdie reëlingskema heet een te wees „tussen Federale Nywerhede Bpk. en sy gewone aandeelhouers". FVB is glad nie 'n party daartoe nie en hy neem ook nie deel aan die huidige aansoek nie. Dit is 'n heel eenvoudige skema, die wese waarvan die kansellasie van die buite-aandele behels, „as teenprestasie" (kyk klousule 5(b)(iv)) waarvoor sekere FVB aandele in 'n besondere verhouding „deur FVB toegeken en uitgereik word . . ." aan hierdie buite-aandeelhouers. Dit word in die vooruitsig gestel dat wanneer die goedkeuring van die Hof aangevra word, die gebruiklike applikasie ook dan sal dien vir kapitaalvermindering om uitvoering te gee aan die skema. . . .

Ek het geen twyfel dat die voorstelle wat ek hierbo opgesom het op niks anders as 'n aandele oorname-aanbod (in die algemene sin) op gestelde voorwaardes neerkom nie, en die vraag ontstaan of daar nie gehoor gegee moet word aan die bepalings van art 314(2) van die Maatskappywet 1973 (waarna ek vervolgens sal verwys as die „huidige Wet"), waardeur die maak van 'n oorname-aanbod verbied word tensy daar aan sekere vereistes voldoen word nie. Dit is ook 'n vraag of 'n oorname-aanbod hoegenaamd afgehandel kan word by wyse van art 311 skema.

In *Maatskappyereg* 2e uitg van Cilliers en Benade, sê die skrywers die volgende op bl 323 en 324:

> „'n Oorname-aanbod word dikwels gedoen deur gebruik te maak van die reëlingskemaprosedure wat in art 311 voorgeskryf word wanneer die aanbieder voornemens is om al die uitgereikte aandele, of al die uitgereikte aandele van 'n bepaalde klas, te verkry. Die prosedure wat gevolg moet word om 'n reëling tussen 'n maatskappy en sy lede, of 'n klas van hulle, te bewerkstellig, is reeds volledig in § 2(2) van hierdie hoofstuk behandel. 'n Oorname word ingevolge art 311 deurgevoer deur dit in te klee in die vorm van 'n reorganisasie van die gemagtigde en uitgereikte aandelekapitaal of soms slegs die uitgereikte kapitaal van die maatskappy, waardeur die aanbieder in feite in die plek van die bestaande aandeelhouers te staan kom. Die reorganisasie word bewerkstellig dmv 'n reëlingskema tussen die maatskappy en die van sy aandeelhouers wie se aandele deur die aanbieder verkry staan te word. Die skema bepaal gewoonlik dat die uitgereikte aandelekapitaal wat nie alreeds deur of ten behoewe van die aanbieder besit word nie, dmv 'n kapitaal vermindering gekanselleer word; die opbrengs van die kansellasie, synde die bedrag op daardie aandele betaal, word tot krediet van 'n spesiale kapitaalreserwerekening geplaas; die aandelekapitaal van die maatskappy word onmiddellik daarna vermeerder, gewoonlik tot sy volle vorige bedrag, deur die skepping van nuwe aandele wat as ten volle betaald aan die aanbieder uitgereik word, aangesien die spesiale kapitaalreserwe vir die doel aangewend word; terselfdertyd betaal die aanbieder die ooreengekome teenprestasie aan die voormalige aandeelhouers van die doelwitmaatskappy. Ten gevolge van hierdie proses is die aanbieder die nuwe houer van al die uitgereikte aandele (of aandele van die bepaalde klas) in die doelwitmaatskappy."

In 'n voetnota op bl 324 word ten aansien van die laaste stelling in bogenoemde passasie, oa die volgende gesê:

„Die reëlingskemaprosedure bied talryke voordele bo die oorname-aanbodprosedure. Hulle is kortliks: (i) die kleiner meerderhede wat vir die goedkeuring van die skema vereis word; (ii) die tydsbesparing omdat die reëlingskemaprosedure vinniger is; (iii) besparing aan seëlregte; (iv) die sekerheid wat dit bied—die aanbieder sal nie aan 'n gedeeltelik voltooide oorname gebind word nie; (v) veel minder regulering en verantwoordelikheid vir die direkteure van die aanbieder (sien Weinberg *Take-Overs and Mergers* 63–5)."

Dit is doenlik om vlugtig na 'n brokkie voorgeskiedenis te verwys. Die Maatskappywet 46 van 1926 („die vorige Wet") het geen bepalings wat vergelykbaar is met arts 314 tot 320 van die huidige Wet bevat nie. In maatskappyregskringe is voorheen uiteenlopende opvattings daarop nagehou of 'n aandele oorname-aanbod hoegenaamd tuisgebring kon word onder art 103 van die vorige Wet. Daar was geen regspraak daaroor voor 1966 nie, toe *Re National Bank Ltd* [1966] 1 All ER 1006, gerapporteer is waarin Plowman J die volgende op bl 1012–13 sê:

„As regards counsel for the opposing shareholders' second objection, namely, that the scheme really ought to be treated as a s 209 case needing a 90 per cent majority, I cannot accede to that proposition. In the first place, it seems to me to involve imposing a limitation or qualification either on the generality of the word 'arrangement' in s 206 or else on the discretion of the court under that section. The legislature has not seen fit to impose any such limitation in terms and I see no reason for implying any. Moreover, the two sections, s 206 and s 209, involve quite different considerations and different approaches. Under s 206 an arrangement can only be sanctioned if the question of its fairness has first of all been submitted to the court. Under s 209, on the other hand, the matter may never come to court at all. If it does come to the Court then the onus is cast on the dissenting minority to demonstrate the unfairness of the scheme. There are, therefore, good reasons for requiring a smaller majority in favour of a scheme under s 206 than the majority which is required under s 209 if the minority is to be expropriated."

Dit was na aanleiding van hierdie uitspraak dat Weinberg in die eerste uitgawe van sy *Take-overs and Mergers* in 1968 (op bl 57–62) alreeds kategories kon aanvoer dat arts 206 en 209 van die Companies Act 1948 'n alternatiewe prosedure bied vir 'n „share-for-share exchange" in 'n „take-over bid". Dit is op dieselfde gesag wat *Cilliers en Benade, supra,* steun vir hul aangehaalde sienswyse. Daar is geen ander gewysdes op hierdie punt nie.

Dit is stellig so dat Plowman J se dicta hierbo aangehaal, *obiter* is. Daardie skema sou eerstens, die fisiese verdeling van die National Bank se besigheid ten gevolg gehad het wat, tweedens, uitreiking van aandele in die nuwe maatskappy, wat dus eintlik 'n afsplitsing van die ouer was, sou noodsaak. Dit kon dus kwalik aangemerk word as 'n „scheme or contract involving the *transfer* of shares" onder art 209 terwyl dit kon ressorteer as 'n tipiese „scheme of arrangement" onder art 206. 'n Ware „take-over bid" soos die finansiële gemeenskap hierdie uitdrukking gebruik, was dit nie. Nogtans meen ek, respekvol, was Plowman J se beslissing en sy motivering daarvoor prinsipieel gegrond en aanvaarbaar vir ons reg tydens die bewind van die vorige Wet. Daar is geen rede waarom 'n oornameaanbod nie by wyse van reëling onder art 103 vermag kon word nie, mits dit natuurlik inderdaad

> „'n skikking of reëling . . . *tussen 'n maatskappy* . . . *en sy lede*, of 'n klas van hulle . . ."

was. Indien, bv 'n reëlingskema wat voorgee 'n reëling te bevat *tussen* maatskappy A en sy aandeelhouers, slegs bepaal dat die aandeelhouers hulle A aandele aan maatskappy B verkoop of oormaak, kan dit myns insiens nie as 'n reëling *tussen* A en sy aandeelhouers beskou word nie. Inteendeel, dit is 'n reëling *tussen* B en die aandeelhouers van A wat laasgenoemde maatskappy min of niks mee uit te waai het, behalwe om in die gewone loop van sake mettertyd die oordrag van die aandele reël-matig te laat plaasvind nie. Vgl ook *Re NFU Development Trust Ltd* [1973] 1 All ER 135, waar Brightman J op bl 140F die volgende sê:

> „Section 206 is dealing with what is described as a 'compromise or arrangement . . . between a company and its creditors . . . or between the company and its members'. The word 'compromise' implies some element of accommodation on each side. It is not apt to describe total surrender. A claimant who abandons his claim is not compromising it. Similarly, I think that the word 'arrangement' in this section implies some element of give and take."

In die voorbeeld wat ek hierbo gegee het is daar aan die kant van maat-skappy A nòg „give" nòg „take" teenoor sy eie aandeelhouers. Onder-hewig dus aan bogenoemde voorbehoud, aanvaar ek dat die oorname-aanbod *in casu* as 'n reëling onder art 311 ingeklee kan word indien die posisie onder die huidige Wet nie verander het nie. Of dit wel so 'n reëling is, is 'n ander vraag waarop ek later sal terugkom.

Na die beslissing in *Re National Bank Ltd* het 'n belangrike ontwikkeling in Engeland plaasgevind toe daar in 1968 die „Panel on Take-Overs and Mergers" tot stand gekom het en *The City Code on Take-overs and Mergers* opgestel is. . . . Die bekende lojaliteit van die City aan sy finan-siële tradisies en aanvaarde gebruike het dit skynbaar onnodig gemaak om aan die *Code* statutêre krag deur inlywing daarvan by die Companies Act, te verleen. In die eerste „general principle" word dit bv gestel dat

> „persons engaged in such transactions should be aware that the spirit as well as the precise wording of these general principles and of the ensuing rules must be observed".

Die *Code* bevat 'n fyn uitgewerkte stel „general principles" en „rules" om oorname-aanbiedinge op 'n wyse wat billik teenoor belanghebbendes is, te laat vlot. Twee punte vermeld ek interessantheidshalwe *en passant*. Eerstens is dit, benewens genoteerde maatskappye, ook op ongenoteerde publieke maatskappye van toepassing, en tweedens,

,,offer includes, wherever appropriate, take-over and merger transactions howsoever effected''.

(My onderstreping.)

'n Betragting van arts 314–21 van die huidige Wet wat na 1968 opgestel is, oortuig mens dat daardeur gepoog word om etlike van die onder-
liggende beginsels van die *City Code* by ons maatskappyereg aan te pas
en in te lyf. Cilliers en Benade beskryf dit as volg op bl 314:

> ,,Die Wet skep vir die eerste keer 'n breë raamwerk van beginsels
> om die inhoud van en die prosedure vir die maak van 'n gewone
> oorname-aanbod te reël. Hierdie beginsels beoog om die belange van
> die aandeelhouer van die doelwitmaatskappy, wat hoofsaaklik
> verband hou met die prys of teenprestasie wat hy vir sy aandele
> aangebied word, te beskerm. 'n Billike prys, wat billike optrede ver-
> onderstel, is die doelwitaandeelhouer se belangrike beskerming teen
> benadeling. Ten einde hom in staat te stel om te besluit oor die billik-
> heid van die aangebode prys of teenprestasie, bestaan verdere
> beskermingsmaatreëls in die vorm van betroubare inligting mbt die
> waarde van sy aandele (en van enige ander aandele of sekuriteit wat
> betrokke is) en voldoende tyd om dit te oorweeg. Die direkteure van
> die doelwitmaatskappy is die mees gesaghebbende bron van inligting
> aangaande die waarde van die aandele en die meriete van die aanbod.
> Die aandeelhouer moet ook kan vertrou op die inligting vervat in die
> verklarings wat die aanbieder maak ivm die oorname-aanbod.''

Teen hierdie agtergrond gesien, beantwoord ek eers die volgende
vraag wat in hierdie aansoek ter sprake gekom het en geargumenteer is,
alvorens meer besonderlik na art 314(2) te verwys:

Is die reëlingskemaprosedure nog steeds beskikbaar vir die inkleding
van 'n oorname-aanbod, nou dat die Wetgewer in die huidige Wet hierdie breë raamwerk vir die maak daarvan ontwerp het, soos Cilliers en
Benade op cit beweer?

Ek meen dat, ten spyte van 'n mate van onsekerheid wat vloei uit die
bewoording van hierdie deel van die huidige Wet, die antwoord op hierdie
vraag tog bevestigend is, onderhewig aan dieselfde voorbehoud wat ek
hierbo beskryf het, nl dat dit werklik 'n reëling ,,*tussen die maatskappy* . . .
en sy aandeelhouers'' is. Artikel 311 is wesenlik 'n herverordening van art
103 van die vorige Wet wat vir baie dekades bestaan het. Alhoewel daar
nie 'n gerapporteerde Suid-Afrikaanse beslissing soos *Re National Bank*,
supra, op hierdie punt was nie, was die benadering van Plowman J
heeltemal versoenbaar met die algemene neiging van ons eie regspraak
oor die omvang en betekenis van art 103. Indien die Wetgewer dus
bedoel het om 'n verandering hieraan te weeg te bring, sou 'n mens iets
meer positiefs verwag het wat dit in daardie rigting dwing as slegs die
daarstelling van arts 314–321, wat moontlik beskou kan word as die
skepping van 'n uitgebreide metode van aandele-oorname wat nog steeds
'n alternatiewe een bly. Dit is natuurlik vreemd dat sulke weldeurdagte
bepalings, aan sommige waarvan selfs strafregtelike sanksies kleef, in
baie gevalle omseilbaar deur 'n art 311 reëlingskema mag blyk te wees.
Maar as so 'n resultaat strydig met die werklike bedoeling van die Wetgewer is, lê die remedie in laasgenoemde se eie hande.

Die volgende vraag betref die toepaslikheid van art 314(2).

Twee aspekte kom nou ter sprake: Is die verbod in sub-art (2) hoege-naamd op art 311 reëlingskemas van toepassing, en indien so, is die huidige een 'n oorname-aanbod binne die bedoeling van hierdie sub-artikel?

Mnr S, namens die applikant, het aanvanklik aangevoer dat die verbod onmoontlik kan slaan op reëlingskemas. Hy het betoog dat dit pertinent net betrekking het op die soort aanbod wat pas in die raamwerk van die verdere artikels tot en met art 321, nl een wat kan lei tot 'n oorname onder laasgenoemde artikel, omrede die woordbepaling in sub-art (1) alleen op daardie artikel slaan. Hierdie rede is myns insiens 'n misvatting wat so gou 'n skema of aanbod volgens die woordbepaling in sub-art (1) inderdaad 'n „oorname-aanbod" is, kom sub-art (2) in werking. Daar is niks in hierdie sub-artikel wat hierdie werking immers verder beperk tot slegs 'n „oorname-aanbod" wat vir doeleindes van uiteindelike aanwending van art 321 gedoen word nie. Hierdie benadering van mnr S postuleer dat sub-art (2) 'n aanhef het wat gelykluidend met die van sub-art. (1) is, min of meer soos volg:

> „Vir die doeleindes van hierdie artikel tot en met art 321, mag geen oorname-aanbod gemaak word nie tensy. . . ."

Dit is natuurlik nie so nie. Die uitdrukkings „oorname-aanbod" en „oornameskema" kom glad nie in die eerste deel van Hoofstuk XII voor nie sodat daar nie rede is om te dink dat die Wetgewer in art 314(2) 'n oorname-aanbod (soos nou gedefinieer) in gedagte het wat noodwendig iets verskillends is van wat moontlik binne die voorafgaande artikels ook kan val nie.

Daar kan egter 'n ander rede wees vir 'n engere vertolking van art 314(2) wat die uitdruklikheid daarvan afwater, nl die algemene raamwerk van hierdie hoofstuk in die huidige Wet waaruit daar moontlik 'n beperkende wetgewende bedoeling afgelei kan word. Hierdie benadering wat onge-twyfeld argumenteerbaar is kan moontlik gestuit word deur die eerste reël van wetsuitleg, nl dat die uitlegger nie buite die uitdruklike woorde van die Wet mag gaan nie. Aangesien afwykings van letterlike uitleg, onder-hewig aan 'n streng dissipline, in gepaste omstandighede nogtans moontlik is, kan hierdie 'n moeilike kwessie word om te beslis. Ek is glad nie oortuig dat hierdie benadering juis is nie maar gesien die uitsluitsel wat ek bereik het oor die vraag of die reëling *in casu* binne die trefwydte van „oorname-aanbod" val, selfs indien art 314(2) van toepassing is, is dit nie nodig om verder hierop in te gaan nie. Dit sou regsekerheid bevorder indien die Wetgewer sy bedoeling in hierdie verband duideliker maak. . . .

Vervolgens behandel ek nou die vraag of die reëlingskema *in casu* inder-waarheid as 'n reëling tussen die maatskappy en sy aandeelhouers beskou kan word. In hierdie verband is slegs die element van intrekking van aandele vir 'n teenwaarde ter sake. Die res van die skema is slegs onder-geskik en aanvullend. Alhoewel dit slegs vermag kan word deur 'n verdere spesiale aansoek om kapitaal te verminder, meen ek dat dit tog, prima facie (ek hoef op hierdie stadium nie finaal daaroor te beslis nie) as 'n „reëling" beskou kan word. Die intrekking van die aandele is iets wat beide die maatskappy en die aandeelhouers raak; in die geval van die maatskappy verander sy aandelekapitaalstruktuur en in geval van die aandeelhouers verval hul direkte seggenskap in die maatskappy. Dit kan dus 'n reëling *tussen* hulle wees omrede, wanneer die intrekking bewerkstellig word deur 'n spesiale besluit van 'n opvolgende ledevergadering en daaropvolgende Hofaansoek, 'n verpligting op Federale Nywerhede rus teenoor hierdie klas aandeelhouers om toe te sien dat die teenwaarde nl FVB aandele soos beskryf, aan hulle toegeken word. Dit is nie so uitgestippel in die skema nie, maar vir huidige doeleindes aanvaar ek dit as 'n redelike implikasie. As ek hier verkeerd oordeel en hierdie onderneming selfs nie stilswygend bestaan nie, bly daar geen kapstok oor om die gevolgtrekking dat dit 'n reëling is, aan op te hang nie want dan bly niks oor wat aangemerk kan word as 'n reëling *tussen* hulle nie. Slegs 'n onderneming om 'n ledevergadering ter vermindering van kapitaal te belê is nietsbeduidend indien afdwingbare regte oor en weer nie uit die totaliteit van die verrigtinge spruit nie. 'n Dictum van Brightman J (*NFU Development Trust*-saak op bl 140) is in hierdie verband insiggewend:

„Confiscation is not my idea of an arrangement. A member whose rights are expropriated without any compensating advantage is not, in my view, having his rights rearranged in any legitimate sense of that expression."

Dit is vanselfsprekend dat die woorde „compensating advantage" slegs slaan op 'n *afdwingbare* teenwaarde en nie op 'n blote verklaring dat 'n derde party voornemens is om sekere aandele uit te reik sonder dat enige regsverbondenheid teenoor die aandeelhouers geskep word nie.

Indien hierdie siening (*prima facie* altans) korrek is dat die skema wel 'n reëling is, is dit nogtans onbevredigend dat FVB nie 'n party daartoe is nie. As hy was, sou direkte verpligting op hom rus, voortvloeiend uit die goedgekeurde statutêre self, om aandele soos daarin uiteengesit uit te reik. Of dit, streng gesproke, moontlik is om FVB 'n party tot die reëling te maak (omrede die statutêre magtiging net bestaan ten opsigte van 'n reëling „tussen 'n maatskappy . . . en sy lede" wat, na goedkeuring, slegs die maatskappy en sy lede bind—kyk art 311(2)) hoef ek insgelyks my nie nou mee besig te hou nie. Vir geval egter daar moontlik twyfel ontstaan of FVB wel gebonde is teenoor Fed Nywerhede om aandele uit te reik op die terme wat in die skema beskryf word op tydstip van bekragtiging daarvan, het ek beveel dat die applikant 'n aanvaarbare kontrak tussen homself en FVB moet liasseer waarin FVB hom teenoor die aandeelhouers verbind om na goedkeuring van die skema, die aandele aan hul uit te reik, alvorens die Hofbevel deur die Griffier oorhandig word. Dit is in die tussentyd gedoen sedert ek die bevel gemaak het. . . .

NOTES

Where the time for acceptance under the original offer is extended, the notice of intention to acquire must still be made within the statutory period: *Musson* v *Howard Glasgow Associated Ltd* 1960 SC 371. The position is, of course, different where a new offer is made.

The 'take-over' company may fix a shorter period than the statutory four months for the acceptance of its offer: *In re Western Manufacturing* (*Reading*) *Ltd* [1956] Ch 436, [1955] 3 All ER 733. A circular sent to shareholders in connection with a merger or take-over is not a prospectus: *Government Stock and Other Securities Investment Co Ltd* v *Christopher* [1956] 1 WLR 237.

In *In re Castner-Kellner Alkali Company Ltd* [1930] 2 Ch 349 it was held that the fact that the 'take-over' company is offering to the dissentients shares wholly different from those offered to the assenting majority does not disqualify the company from availing itself of the opportunity to purchase the shares of the dissentients.

On acceptance of the take-over offer by each individual shareholder a binding contract of sale comes into existence between that shareholder and the company, conditional on the scheme going through: *Ridge Nominees Ltd* v *Inland Revenue Commissioners* [1962] 1 Ch 376 at 383.

In *Re Simco* [1971] 1 WLR 1455, [1971] 3 All ER 999 the company which was considering a take-over bid under s 209 had ordinary shares as well as convertible loan stock. If the holders of loan stock who had exercised their conversion rights but had not yet been allotted their shares were included, the requisite nine-tenths majority was there, but not if they were excluded. The court held that the holders of loan stock who by conversion had obtained an absolute right to an allotment of shares had to be counted in, but that stockholders who had not exercised their conversion rights were neither approving nor dissenting shareholders but creditors of the company.

In *Blue Metal Industries Ltd* v *Dilley* [1969] 3 WLR 357 (PC) the Privy Council decided that s 185 of the New South Wales Companies Act 1961, which substantially reproduces s 209 of the English Act, applies only to a scheme involving the transfer of shares in a single company to a single company, and not to one which involves the transfer of shares in a company to two other companies jointly. 'Acquisition of shares by two or more companies is not merely the plural of acquisition by one. It is a different kind of acquisition with different consequences. It would presuppose a different legislative policy', per Lord Morris of Borth-Y-Gest at 365.

On fighting the take-over bidder, see *Hogg* v *Cramphorn, 227* above; *Bamford* v *Bamford, 220* and Aaron Yoran 'Advance Defensive Tactics against Take-Over Bids' (1973) 21 *Am J Comp L* 53. On various take-over battles in South Africa, see S Nigel Mandy (1963) *SA Chartered Secretary* 287.

Take-overs fulfil a useful and economic function. The threat of a take-over bid exercises pressure on the incumbent directors to manage the company efficiently and treat their shareholders fairly, as regards dividends and otherwise. A successful take-over bid often (though not always) results in the replacement of a lazy, ineffectual or otherwise unsatisfactory management by an efficient one.

On take-overs see also L C B Gower 'Corporate Control: The Battle for the Berkeley' (1955) 68 *Harv LR* 1176 (discussing the *Savoy Hotel* case); Noyes Leech 'Transactions in Corporate Control' (1956) 10 *U of Pennsylvania LR* 725 (dealing especially with the position in America); K W Wedderburn (1960) 23 *MLR* 663; G Getz (1961) 78 *SALJ* 438; G W Penrose 'Some Aspects of the Take-over Bid' (1964) 9 *Juridical Review (NS)* 128; J H Farrar 'Finance of Take-over Bids' (1967) *New Law Journal* 565; J S McLennan 'Take-over Bids and the Court's Discretion' (1969) 86 *SALJ* 400; H Rajak 'Minority Rights and the Take-over Bid' (1970) 87 *SALJ* 12; B J Davies 'An Affair of the City: A Case Study in the Regulation of Take-overs and Mergers' (1973) 36 *MLR* 457; Francis Gurry 'Aspects of the Law of Contract in Relation to Take-over Offers' (1976) 50 *ALJ* 167. Leading English works on take-overs and mergers are M A Weinberg *Takeovers and Amalgamations* 3rd (1971) (a new edition was in the press at the time of writing) and P L Davies *The Regulation of Takeovers and Mergers,* 1976.

Winding-up and Judicial Management

I WINDING-UP

A company may be wound up by the court or voluntarily. A voluntary winding-up may be a creditor's or a member's winding-up, s 343.

(a) Grounds

A TEXT

The grounds on which a company may be wound up by the court are laid down in s 344. The most important ones, from a practical point of view, are:

1. The company commenced business before the Registrar certified that it was entitled to commence business, s 344(1)(b); but see s 347(3).

2. The company did not commence business within a year from its incorporation or suspended business for a whole year, s 344(1)(c): 387, 388.

3. Seventy-five per cent of the issued share capital of the company has been lost or has become useless for the company's business, s 344(1)(e).

4. The company is unable to pay its debts, s 344(1)(f), as specified in s 345: 389–391.

5. It appears to the court that it is 'just and equitable' that the company should be wound up, s 344(1)(h). Winding-up orders on this ground have been made in a variety of circumstances, ranging from 'failure of substratum' (40 and 41 above) to deadlock in the affairs of the company, from minority oppression to continued quarrels between incompatible fellow shareholders in a 'partnership' company: 392; further In re Yenidjee Tobacco Company Ltd, 21 above, In re Rhenosterkop

Copper Company, 40 above, *Re Baku Cons Oilfields Ltd*, 41 above, and (most importantly) *Ebrahimi* v *Westbourne Galleries Ltd*, 213 above.

Any of the parties mentioned in s 346 may apply for the winding-up of a company. It is within the discretion of the court whether to grant an order, s 347(1): *393*; also *387* and *390*. This is subject to the proviso that the court may not refuse an order on the ground only that the company has no assets or that its assets have been mortgaged to an amount equal to or in excess of its assets, s 347(1). Where the application is presented by members of the company and the court finds that the applicants are entitled to relief but that they are acting unreasonably in seeking to have the company wound up instead of pursuing some other remedy that is available to them (eg relief under s 252, p 511 above) it will refuse a winding-up order, s 347(2).

A company may be wound up voluntarily in the circumstances set out in s 349. In a members' voluntary winding-up the Master must be furnished with security for the payment of the debts of the company, unless he dispenses with such security on proof that the company has no debts, s 350. If the requirements of s 350 are not satisfied, the voluntary winding-up is a creditor's voluntary winding-up, s 351.

A company which is being wound up voluntarily remains a corporate body but from the commencement of the winding-up the powers of the directors cease unless their continuance is sanctioned, in a creditors' voluntary winding-up by the liquidator or the creditors, in a members' voluntary winding-up by the liquidator or the company in general meeting, s 353.

The court can intervene in a voluntary winding-up, ss 354(1), 388, and may convert a voluntary winding-up into a winding-up by the court, ss 346, 347.

B CASES

[387] Cluver & another v Robertson Portland Cement and Lime Co Ltd
1925 CPD 45

LOUWRENS J: The applicants are holders of 250 fully-paid-up shares. The company is perfectly solvent. It has assets of considerable value, and practically no debts. The applicants, therefore, have a sufficiently tangible interest to entitle them to apply for a winding-up order.

They apply for an order placing the company under liquidation in terms of s 135 ss (2) and (5) of Act 25 of 1892, wherein it is provided that a company may be wound up by the court under the following circumstances:

Subsection (2): Whenever the company does not commence its business within a year from its incorporation, or suspends its business for the space of a whole year. . . .

The court is not bound to order the winding-up of a company that has not commenced its business within a year from its incorporation. If, however, the fact that it has not commenced its business within a year is, in the circumstances of the case, a fair indication that the company has no intention of doing so within a reasonable time, then, I think, the court should exercise its discretion and order the winding-up. . . . But the court should not, at the instance of a shareholder, wind up a company merely on the ground of delay in commencing operations, if there is a reasonable prospect of its doing work in the near future, and if its objects have not been abandoned or become impossible. *Hull* v *Turf Mines Ltd* (1906 TS 68).

As to suspension of business for a year, the rule which has been followed in English cases in the interpretation of the section in the English Act corresponding to s 135(2) of our Act, is that the court will not order the winding-up of a company unless it is satisfied that there has been an intention on the part of the company to abandon its business or that it is unable to carry it on and, on the question of such intention, the court will have regard to the opinion and wishes of the majority of the shareholders. . . .

[After referring to the conflicting opinions of various experts as to the future prospects of the company Louwrens J continued:]

In view of the difference of opinion among the experts it is impossible for me, on motion, to hold that the company cannot reasonably be expected ever to become a paying one. Moreover, I agree with the opinion expressed by Lord Cairns in the case of *Diamond Fuel Co* (13 ChD 400), when he said, 'A winding-up petition is not to be used as a means of evoking a judicial opinion as to the probable success or non-success of the company as a commercial speculation.'

Nor should the court, unless a much stronger case is made out, interfere with the domestic forum which has been established for the management of the affairs of a company (*vide Langham Skating Rink Co* 5 ChD 669). As between shareholders, the court should not lightly interfere with the wishes of the majority, especially in the case of a company which is solvent, which was not created by fraud, and which the majority of shareholders consider will be able to carry on its business successfully. There are between 600 and 700 shareholders, and they hold between them 84 000 shares.

Holders of 36 000 shares have voted against winding-up, and only 29 shareholders, holding only 4 445 shares between them, have voted or asked for the winding-up. In about two months time there will be the next annual general meeting of the company, when the shareholders may again consider the matter, and if so desiring may avail themselves of the provisions of s 135(1) of the Act.

The applicants complain also of the conduct of some of the directors, and say that thousands of pounds have been spent by them in making fruitless journeys for the purpose of obtaining further capital, and in other ways, but, as was pointed out by Innes CJ in the case of *Hull* v *Turf Mines Ltd* (*supra*) at 75, the court will not wind up a solvent company merely for the purpose of inquiring into the conduct of the directors. Misconduct on the part of directors, and misapplication of funds may give ground for an action against the directors, but will not in themselves justify the winding-up of a solvent company capable of carrying on its business, especially against the wishes of the majority of the share-holders. . . .

I do not think a sufficiently strong case has been made out to induce me at this stage to order the winding-up of the company. . . .

[See also *Taylor* v *Macharie Claims Syndicate Ltd* 1912 WLD 197, where with the approval of all its shareholders the company did not commence business within one year. The court refused a winding-up order at the instance of a shareholder who without some convincing reason had changed his mind. This case and *Cluver's* case should be compared with *East Rand Deep Ltd* 1903 TS 616, where a winding-up order was made on the ground that a company had suspended its operations for more than a year.]

[388] Nakhooda *v* Northern Industries Ltd
1950 (1) SA 808 (N)

A company had been incorporated in 1946. Its objectives were to establish a modern mineral water factory and a large dry-cleaning business. By 1949 it had not done either, but its only activity had been money-lending. An application by a shareholder for the provisional winding-up of the company was granted.

SELKE J: There are . . . two main points which I must consider. . . . The first is whether the company, in terms of its memorandum of association, commenced business within the meaning of s 111(c) of the Companies Act. The . . . company's memorandum . . . discloses that the 'objects' of the company . . . are of the widest possible kind—so wide indeed, that after a moderately careful perusal of them all, I doubt whether almost anything lawful, done anywhere in the world, could legally be beyond the powers of this company. But, in my opinion, it does not follow that each sub-clause formulates a separate object of the company, as distinct from a mere power, even though the memorandum contains, as it does contain—a version of the so-called 'independent objects clause'.

I venture to think that if, in the course of the three and a half years of its existence, all that this company had done were to have borrowed or raised money in a manner authorized by this sub-clause, it would be fantastic to contend that it had 'commenced business' within the meaning of its memorandum of association.

The activities of the company in lending moneys . . . were said to fall under sub-paras (*p*) and (*q*). Sub-paragraph (*p*) reads:

'To invest and deal with the moneys of the company not immediately required in such manner as may from time to time be determined';

and (*q*) reads:

'To lend money to such persons or companies and on such terms as may seem expedient and in particular to customers and others having dealings with the company and to guarantee the performance of contracts by any such persons or companies.'

These clauses seem to me, as at present advised, to convey merely powers ancillary to the main objects of the company, and the exercise of them by the company in the circumstances of this case seems to me to represent no more the carrying on by it of its business or the pursuit of its objects than would the hire of an office for the secretary represent the carrying on by it of business under a sub-clause such as (*n*), which empowers the company to take on lease any buildings. For these reasons I think the petitioner is correct in his contention that the company has not 'commenced business'.

[389] **Mann *v* Goldstein**
[1968] 1 WLR 1091, [1968] 2 All ER 769 (Ch)

UNGOED-THOMAS J: To enable the companies court to make the winding-up order itself, not only must the petitioner have been shown to be entitled to present the petition, but also one of the grounds specified in s 222 of the Companies Act 1948 must be established: and the only such ground relied on in the petition and before me was that the company is unable to pay its debts. This requirement is additional to the precondition of presenting the petition, that the petitioner must be a creditor, and is not alternative to it. . . .

I come now to the allegation of lack of bona fides and to abuse of process. It seems to me that to pursue a substantial claim in accordance with the procedure provided and in the normal manner, though with personal hostility or even venom and from some ulterior motive, such as the hope of compromise or some indirect advantage, is not an abuse of the process of the court or acting mala fide but acting bona fide in accordance with the process. . . .

What then is the course for this court to take (i) when the creditor's debt is clearly established; (ii) when it is clearly established that there is no debt; and (iii) when the debt is disputed on substantial grounds?

(i) When the creditor's debt is clearly established it seems to me to follow that this court would not, in general at any rate, interfere even though the company would appear to be solvent, for the creditor would, as such, be entitled to present a petition and the debtor would have its own remedy in paying the undisputed debt which it should pay. . . .

(ii) When it is clearly established that there is no debt, it seems to me similarly to follow that there is no creditor, that the person claiming to be such has no locus standi and that his petition is bound to fail. Once that becomes clear, pursuit of the petition would be an abuse of process, and this court would restrain its presentation or advertisement. . . .

(iii) When the debt is disputed by the company on some substantial ground (and not just on some ground which is frivolous or without substance and which the court should, therefore, ignore) and the company is solvent, the court will restrain the prosecution of a petition to wind up the company. . . .

What, however, if the debt is disputed by the company on some substantial ground but it appears that the company is unable to pay its debts?

. . . [I]t is an abuse of the process of the court to prosecute a winding-up application otherwise than in accordance with the legitimate purpose of such a process. The legitimate purpose of such a process is to wind up a company on a ground specified in the Companies Act 1948, which, so far as material to this case, is the ground that it is unable to pay its debts. It is not its legitimate purpose to decide whether a petitioner claiming to be a creditor is a creditor, because s 224 makes it a prerequisite that he should be a creditor before he is even entitled to present a petition at all and before any consideration of the company's insolvency can become relevant. So, in my view, when a petitioning creditor's debt is disputed on such substantial ground this court should restrain the prosecution of the petition as an abuse of the process of the court even though it should appear to the court that the company is insolvent.

[390] **Rosenbach & Co (Pty) Ltd *v* Singh's Bazaars (Pty) Ltd**
1962 (4) SA 593 (D)

CANEY J: In Palmer *Company Precedents* 17 ed part II 26, it is said that 'under para (*d*) the court can wind up a company if it is commercially insolvent, that is, if it is unable to meet its current liabilities, including contingent and prospective liabilities as they come due'.

The proper approach in deciding the question whether a company should be wound up on this ground appears to me, in the light of what I have said, to be that, if it is established that a company is unable to pay its debts, in the sense of being unable to meet the current demands upon it, its day to day liabilities in the ordinary course of its business, it is in a state of commercial insolvency; that it is unable to pay its debts may be established by the means provided in para (*a*) or para (*b*) of s 112 [now s 345(i)(*a*) and (*b*)], or in any other way, by proper evidence. If the company is in fact solvent, in the sense of its assets exceeding its liabilities, this may or may not, depending upon the circumstances, lead to a refusal of a winding-up order; the circumstances particularly to be taken into consideration against the making of an order are such as show that there are liquid assets or readily realizable assets available out of which, or the proceeds of which, the company is in fact able to pay its debts. . . . Nevertheless, in exercising its powers the court will have regard to the fact that

> 'a creditor who cannot obtain payment of his debt is entitled as between himself and the company *ex debito justitiae* to an order if he brings his case within the Act. He is not bound to give time.'

Buckley, p 450.

This view is supported also by Palmer at 27:

> 'The fact that there is due to the petitioner a liquidated sum, that the debt is not disputed, and that the petitioner has demanded payment without success, affords cogent prima facie evidence of the company's inability to pay its debts, and is the evidence most commonly relied on.'

This appears to me to accord with sound business principles, for a concern which is not in financial difficulties ought to be able to pay its way from current revenue or readily available resources.

[391] **F & C Building Construction *v* Macsheil Investments**
1959 (3) SA 841 (D)

FANNIN J: This was the return day of a rule nisi issued out of this court calling upon the respondent (and all other interested persons) to show cause why it should not be wound up. . . . On the return day, the respondent did not appear to show cause, but Mr H appeared on behalf of Total Oil Products (Pty) Limited (whom I shall refer to as 'Total') to oppose the confirmation of the rule. Total is a creditor of the respondent company under four judgments totalling nearly £24 000, the first of them being for an amount of nearly £16 000 under a mortgage bond, which is a first charge over certain immovable property belonging to the respondent company. Total also has a registered notarial lease over all but a small portion of this immovable property, for a period of ten years from 1 April 1957, with a right of renewal for a further period of five years thereafter. This immovable property is the respondent company's only asset. It is common cause that the respondent is unable to pay its debts and is, in fact, insolvent. . . .

The petitioner is an unsecured creditor of the respondent company in an amount of £4 276, with interest and costs, under a judgment of this court, and has been unable to obtain payment. In the ordinary way, the petitioner would be granted a final winding-up order without any difficulty, but Total opposes on the ground that it would not be to the advantage or in the interests of creditors generally to grant a final winding-up order, and that the only result of a winding-up would be to reduce the amount which Total would receive on its secured claim. . . .

[Counsel] for the petitioner, did not seriously dispute the statements of fact made by Total. . . . [His] argument was *firstly* that his client was entitled, *ex debito justitiae*, and by virtue of s 117(1) of the Companies Act, to a final winding-up order, even if it appeared that the entire assets of the respondent company were likely to be consumed in paying preferent or secured claims. *Secondly*, he challenged the third of Total's propositions referred to above, and argued that the *concursus* of creditors would be entitled to direct the liquidator to repudiate, and have the property sold free of, the registered lease, leaving the lessee to prove a concurrent claim for damages. If this were so, he said, the property might well realize considerably more and so provide something for concurrent creditors. . . .

[His] first argument amounts, so it seems to me, to the proposition that a creditor who cannot get paid and who can show that the debtor company is unable, or is deemed under s 112 [now s 345] to be unable, to pay its debts, is entitled, as of right, to a winding-up order. Section 111 [now s 344] sets out the various grounds upon which a company *may* be wound up by the court, and it is plain in my view that it was never intended that whenever any of the grounds there set out are established the court must grant the order. Not only does the word 'may' ordinarily indicate a discretion, but a glance at the grounds set out will show that they could not all have been intended as founding an absolute right to a winding-up order. Furthermore, s 120(2) enjoins the court 'as to all matters relating to a winding-up' to have regard to the wishes of creditors or contributories as proved to it by any sufficient evidence. . . . The suggested rule that a creditor who cannot get paid his claim is entitled to an order *ex debito justitiae*, founded apparently on *Bowes* v *Hope Mutual Life Insurance Company* 11 HLC 389, applies in England only between the creditor and the company, see e g *Chapel House Colliery Co* (1883) 24 ChD 259, and not where there is a conflict between the creditors themselves. . . .

[Counsel for the petitioner] went on, however, to argue that s 117(1) of the Act [now s 347] applies to the present case, for, he said, the sole ground for Total's opposition is that the assets of the respondent company have been mortgaged to an amount equal to or in excess of those assets. That subsection specially provides that the court shall not refuse to make a winding-up order solely on that ground. I think, however, that [Counsel for the respondent] was right when he suggested that an important word in this part of the subsection is the word 'solely', and that if it can be shown that, in addition to the state of affairs referred to, there is no real possibility of any benefit to unsecured creditors, or to creditors generally, from a winding-up order, then s 117(1) does not preclude the refusal by the court of such an order. . . .

Total, the creditor which opposes a winding-up order, is a secured creditor for some £15 846, and an unsecured creditor for some £7 786. The petitioner is an unsecured creditor for some £4 726, and, being unable to recover its debt, claims to be entitled to have the respondent company wound up. The petitioner is entitled to such an order, despite the fact that the secured creditor will consume all the assets, as the probabilities indicate, unless it can be shown that there is no reasonable possibility that unsecured creditors will derive any benefit from the winding-up, and the onus is on the intervening creditor to show that. Assuming, for the purpose of deciding this aspect of the case, that the concurrent creditors will not be able to insist upon the property being sold free of the registered lease, I find that that onus has been discharged. . . .

[A winding-up order was accordingly refused.]

NOTES

That an application for liquidation should not be used to enforce a claim which is bona fide disputed, is settled law: *Badenhorst* v *Northern Construction Enterprises Ltd* 1956 (2) SA 346 (T); *In re LHF Wools Ltd* [1970] 1 Ch 27; *Meyer NO* v *Bree Holdings (Pty) Ltd* 1972 (3) SA 353 (T); *Walter McNaughtan (Pty) Ltd* v *Impala Caravans* 1976 (1) SA 189 (W). Where it is clear that the company is heavily indebted to the petitioner the fact that there is some dispute as to the precise amount of the debt is no answer to the petition: *Re Tweeds Garage Ltd* [1962] 1 All ER 121 (Ch).

To be a proper nulla bona return in terms of s 345(1)(*b*), the return must state that not sufficient assets, including immovable assets, to satisfy the debt were found: *Cornelissen NO* v *Welkom Tractors Auto (Pty) Ltd* 1971 (3) SA 114 (T).

That actual insolvency (excess of liabilities over assets) is not required but that commercial insolvency (inability to pay debts) is sufficient, was affirmed in *Ebrahim (Pty) Ltd* v *Pakistan Bus Services (Pty) Ltd* 1964 (4) SA 146 (N).

An application for a winding-up order by a creditor is not a proceeding for the recovery of a debt. It follows that s 11 of the Limitation and Disclosure of Finance Charges Act 73 of 1968 does not apply: *Prudential Shippers SA Ltd* v *Tempest Clothing Ltd* 1976 (2) SA 856 (W). But see also *Service Trade Supplies (Pty) Ltd* v *Cheviot Clothing Industries (Pty) Ltd* 1971 (1) SA 397 (W).

See further *In re Lympne Investments Ltd* [1972] WLR 523 (Ch); *In re Bryant Investment Co Ltd* [1974] WLR 826, [1974] 2 All ER 683 (Ch) (debt not yet due).

An applicant who has a valid claim for damages for breach of contract against a company is a 'contingent or prospective creditor' within the meaning of s 346(1)(*b*): *Gillis-Mason Construction Co (Pty) Ltd* v *Overvaal Trustees (Pty) Ltd* 1971 (1) SA 524 (T).

On inability to pay, see also *Phase Electric Co (Pty) Ltd* v *Zinman's Electrical Sales (Pty) Ltd* 1973 (3) SA 914 (W).

[392] **Moosa NO *v* Mavjee Bhawan (Pty) Ltd**
1967 (3) SA 131 (T)

TROLLIP J: The ground relied upon for a final winding-up order is that in para (*g*) of s 111 of the Companies Act, namely, that it is 'just and equitable' that the company should be wound up. That paragraph, unlike the preceding paragraphs of s 111, postulates not facts but only a broad conclusion of law, justice and equity, as a ground for winding up (see *Hull* v *Turf Mines Ltd* 1906 TS 68 at 75). In its terms and effect, therefore, s 111(*g*) confers upon the court a very wide discretionary power, the only limitation originally being that it had to be exercised judicially with due regard to the justice and equity of the competing interests of all concerned. (I say 'originally' because I am at present only dealing with the relevant sections of the Act as originally enacted; the effect on the court's discretionary power of the subsequent introduction into the Act of s 111*bis* and 117(2), through Act 46 of 1952, will be considered later.) Inevitably, in the course of time, the courts have evolved certain general principles which are useful as guides in particular cases for the exercise of that discretion. A most helpful collection and discussion of some of the leading decisions by the English, Australasian and Canadian courts (with some reference too to certain South African cases) appears in an article by B H McPherson, a lecturer in law at the University of Queensland, in (1964) 27 *Modern Law Review* 282, which [counsel] for the applicant made available to me.

Dealing with the winding-up at the instance of a member of a solvent company which is in the nature of a partnership—obviously the kind of company in question here—the author says at 303:

> 'There are in fact two principles which guide the court in exercising its discretion to wind up a domestic company of this kind: the first is that enunciated by Lord Shaw in *Loch* v *John Blackwood Ltd*: the second derives from *Re Yenidje Tobacco* [*21* above], where the majority of the court treated as the controlling consideration the absence of any hope of reconciliation and friendly co-operation between the members in the future. And these two principles are sufficiently distinct to make it possible for a member of a domestic company, who cannot bring his case within the first principle, nevertheless to succeed by basing it upon the second.'

As *Loch* v *John Blackwood* [1924] AC 783 and *Re Yenidje Tobacco Co* [1916] 2 Ch 426 (Court of Appeal) have both been followed here, each according to the appropriate circumstances, I think that the above thesis that the two principles are distinct and can be used conjointly or alternatively can be accepted as being a correct guide for our courts too. . . .

The principle enunciated by Lord Shaw in *Loch's* case at 788 is that it may be just and equitable for a company to be wound up where there is

'justifiable lack of confidence in the conduct and management of the company's affairs ... grounded on conduct of the directors, not in regard to their private life or affairs, but in regard to the company's business';

that lack of confidence is not justifiable if it springs merely from

'dissatisfaction at being outvoted on the business affairs or on what is called the domestic policy of the company',

but it is justifiable if in addition there is a lack of probity in the directors' conduct of those affairs. The other principle derived from the *Yenidje Tobacco Co* case, usually called the 'deadlock' principle, is founded on the analogy of partnership and is strictly confined to those small domestic companies in which, because of some arrangement, express, tacit or implied, there exists between the members in regard to the company's affairs a particular personal relationship of confidence and trust similar to that existing between partners in regard to the partnership business. Usually that relationship is such that it requires the members to act reasonably and honestly towards one another and with friendly co-operation in running the company's affairs. If by conduct which is either wrongful or not as contemplated by the arrangement, one or more of the members destroys that relationship, the other member or members are entitled to claim that it is just and equitable that the company should be wound up, in the same way as, if they were partners, they could claim dissolution of the partnership.

[His Lordship then considered the facts and continued:]

On those facts I think that second respondent's lack of probity in managing the company's borrowings and loans for his and his son's benefit from 1960 to 1964, and more especially his fraudulent conduct in regard to erf 197, the company's major asset, have justifiably ended the confidence of applicant and his wife in his management of the company's affairs, furnishing good cause for a winding-up order in terms of *Loch's* case (*supra*).

Secondly, I think that the principle in the *Yenidje Tobacco Company* case also applies, either additionally or alternatively. When second respondent originally assumed control of the company, by arrangement, explicit or implicit, a personal relationship of trust and confidence between all the members was created, in which it was contemplated that he would, vis-à-vis the others, manage the company reasonably, fairly and honestly and that, whenever necessary, for example at meetings, they would cordially co-operate in running the company's affairs. Although the proportion of their shareholdings altered in course of time, and Kalla succeeded to shares that some of them did not take up, that personal relationship continued to subsist.

However, the interminable litigation since 1953 and especially since 1963 between applicant and his wife and second respondent has engendered acute enmity and animosity between them in regard to the company's affairs. He admits that they are seriously at loggerheads. . . .

I have no doubt, too, that that hostility contributed materially to his misbehaviour at the meeting on 22 January 1965, which shows that it is now futile for them to meet together in general meetings. Moreover, they now seriously suspect his integrity in managing the company's affairs, which suspicions, even if the above findings on his lack of probity are pitched too high, are not without foundation. . . .

In other words, largely because of the second respondent's conduct, that fundamental personal relationship between him and the applicant's wife has been irreparably destroyed, thereby providing a good cause for winding-up. It is true she is a minority shareholder, but she is a substantial one, holding 10 per cent of the issued shares. The fact that she is only a minority shareholder does not, as has been previously pointed out, disentitle her from urging that cause, although regard must, of course, be paid to the views of the other shareholders before a final decision is made. . . .

I come to the conclusion, therefore, that on balance justice and equity are in favour of winding up the company.

[On the facts his Lordship held that the respondents had failed to show that the applicants acted unreasonably in seeking to have the company wound up instead of asking for relief under s 111*bis* (its greatly expanded equivalent in the 1973 Act is s 252) and confirmed the rule nisi for a final winding-up order.]

NOTES

See also *Heilig* v *The African Export and Import Co Ltd* 1928 WLD 44.

Examples of 'deadlock' cases are *Redler* v *Collier* 1923 CPD 458 and *Lawrence* v *Lawrich Motors* 1948 (2) SA 1029 (W), see p 44 above.

In *Ex parte Rhoprops Ltd* 1975 (3) SA 630 (R) the court refused to make a winding-up order on the 'just and equitable' ground because it considered that another remedy which did not involve the extinction of the company — rectification in that case — was open to the applicant.

In *Hart* v *Pinetown Drive-in-Cinema (Pty) Ltd* 1972 (1) SA 464 (D) the applicant's main complaint was that a large management fee which the company had paid to the majority shareholders bore no relationship whatever to the services rendered or the work performed. His application for the winding-up of the company on the 'just and equitable' ground failed. See *321*, p 530 above.

In *Re Chesterfield Catering Co Ltd* [1976] 3 All ER 294 (Ch) it was reaffirmed that a shareholder cannot apply for a compulsory winding-up unless he can show a 'sufficient' or 'tangible' interest. As a rule he has to show 'a prima facie probability that there will be assets available for distribution among the shareholders'. However, it is sufficient if he can show 'that he will, as a member of the company, achieve some advantage, or avoid or minimize some disadvantage, which would accrue to him by virtue of his membership of the company', per Oliver J at 299. A private advantage is not sufficient.

Re ABC Chewing Gum [1975] 1 All ER 1017 was a petition for a winding-up by a New York corporation which held one-third of the company's equity. The corporation came into the company on the basis that, though it would be a minority shareholder, it would have equal control with the majority shareholders. In order to achieve this position, the corporation and the majority shareholders had entered into an agreement, and the company had adopted a set of articles, which entitled the minority shareholders to appoint or remove a director, and which provided that decisions at board meetings were to be unanimous. The minority shareholders removed A, whom they had appointed as their director, from office and appointed B in his place. The majority shareholders, contrary to the terms of the shareholders' agreement, refused to recognize the substitution. Applying *Ebrahimi*, *213* above, the court held that the repudiation of the agreement by the majority shareholders constituted a ground which rendered a winding-up 'just and equitable'.

See also *In re Fildes Bros Ltd* [1970] 1 WLR 592 (Ch) and *In re Leadenhall General Hardware Stores Ltd* (1971) 115 SJ 202; further M R Chesterman 'The "Just and Equitable" Winding up of Small Private Companies' (1973) 36 *MLR* 129; M J Trebilcock 'A New Concern for the Minority Shareholder: *Ebrahimi* v *Westbourne Galleries Ltd*' (1973) 19 *McGill LJ* 106; B H McPherson 'Winding Up On The "Just and Equitable" Ground' (1964) 27 *MLR* 282.

Where there is prima facie evidence that the presentation of a petition for a winding-up order on the 'just and equitable ground' amounts to an abuse of the court process, an injunction restraining the petition may be granted, *Bryanston Finance* v *De Vries (No 2)* [1976] 2 WLR 41, [1976] 1 All ER 25 (CA).

[393] *In re* P & J Macrae Ltd
[1961] 1 WLR 229 (CA)

WILLMER LJ: The first ground of appeal put forward by the appellants in their notice of appeal is in the following terms: 'that in the circumstances of this case the judge was bound to dismiss the said petition having regard to the number and value of creditors opposing the same in the absence of evidence showing special circumstances why the wishes of such creditors should not be given effect to.'

In my judgment this ground of appeal will not bear examination. To say that the court is bound to dismiss the petition is to deprive the court of the discretion which Parliament has conferred by the clear terms of s 346(1) of the Act. If such were the case the court would be left, as I see it, with no judicial function to perform. The argument involves that in all cases the decision would have to be arrived at by a mere counting of heads. Had this been the intention, Parliament would surely have said so in plain terms, and the wording of s 346 must have been quite different. . . .

I have no doubt that where a majority of creditors do for good reason oppose a petition for the winding-up of a company, then, prima facie, they are entitled reasonably to expect that their wishes will prevail, in the absence of proof by the petitioning creditor of special circumstances rendering a winding-up order desirable in spite of their opposition. But I am certainly not prepared to accept the view that the bare fact of the opposing creditors being in a majority is of itself sufficient, still less conclusive. So to hold would be to leave the court with virtually no judicial function to perform, and to take away from it the discretion which the words of the Act plainly confer.

NOTES

Macrae was referred to with approval in *SAA Distributors (Pty) Ltd* v *Sport en Spe1 (Edms) Bpk* 1973 (3) SA 371 (C).

Though the wishes of the majority of creditors cannot fetter the court's discretion they will normally be followed, *Re ABC* [1961] 1 All ER 354. Thus the courts will normally refuse an application for the compulsory liquidation of a company which is in voluntary liquidation if it is opposed by a large majority of creditors, *In re Home Remedies Limited* [1943] 1 Ch 1; *Re B Karsberg* [1955] 3 All ER 854 (A).

Again the court will not readily order the winding-up of a company which has lost a great deal of its original capital if the majority of shareholders are determined to go on with the business and there is no fraud on the minority, *Fox* v *SA Protection Co* 1903 TH 412.

(b) *Effects*

A TEXT

When a winding-up order is made the company does not cease to exist, but its directors are *functus officio*: *394, 395*. But see also p 687.

In all windings-up, compulsory or voluntary, civil proceedings by or against the company are suspended until the appointment of a liquidator. Any attachment or execution put in force against the estate or assets of the company after the commencement of the winding-up is void, s 359(1). The court has a discretion to grant leave to continue an action suspended by the liquidation or allow execution to proceed, *Furstenberg* v *Smit* 1964 (3) SA 810 (O) and *CSAR* v *Geldenhuis Main Reef Gold Mining Co* (*in Liq*) 1908 TH 11. It also has power to grant leave to commence proceedings, *Furstenberg* v *Smit* (*supra*).

Concursus creditorum is established and there can be no set-off unless mutuality between the respective claims existed at the date of the winding-up order: *396*.

A winding-up is deemed to commence when the application for the winding-up is presented to the court, s 348. Section 348 does not mean that the launching of winding-up proceedings has the effect of granting the company a moratorium: *Prudential Shippers SA Ltd* v *Tempest Clothing Co Ltd* 1976 (4) SA 75 (W).

Share transfers effected after the commencement of a winding-up are void unless they are sanctioned by the liquidator, s 341(1). So is every disposition of its property (including rights of action) by a company being wound up which is unable to pay its debts unless the court otherwise orders, s 341(2). An application to the court to 'order otherwise' must be dealt with on its own facts, special regard being had to questions of good faith and honest intention on the part of the persons concerned, see *Re Steane's* (*Bournemouth*) *Ltd* [1950] 1 All ER 21 (Ch); *Re TW Construction Ltd* [1954] 1 All ER 744 (Ch); *Re Clifton Place Garage Ltd* [1970] 1 All ER 353 (CA).

In the winding-up of a company unable to pay its debts the provisions of the law relating to insolvency apply, *mutatis mutandis*, in respect of any matter not specially provided for by the Companies Act ss 339, 340 and 416: *397*. The provisions of the law relating to insolvency also apply in respect of voting, the manner of voting and voting by agents at creditors' meetings at any meeting called under s 351 or s 364, provided that in any winding-up by the court a director or former director of the company has no voting right in respect of the nomination of a liquidator on the ground of his loan account with the company or claims for arrear salary, travelling expenses or allowances due by the company or claims paid by the director or former director on behalf of the company, s 365(2)(*a*). The same applies to a person to whom such a right has been ceded, s 365(2)(*b*).

B CASES

[394] **Letsitele Stores (Pty) Ltd** *v* **Roets & others**
1958 (2) SA 224 (T)

The applicant company was the holder of a personal servitude. It was placed under liquidation but on a compromise being arrived at the liquidation was removed. The first question was whether as a result of the winding-up order the servitude had become extinguished, the second one whether, if it had become extinguished, the servitude revived when the company was revested with its assets.

WILLIAMSON J: In the first place it is clear that the servitude which was created was a personal servitude. It was therefore a servitude which would ordinarily lapse and become extinct upon the death of the grantee. . . .

The question was then argued as to whether the fact that this company was placed in liquidation and that thereafter the liquidation was discharged because of a compromise permits one to say that the servitude, if it lapsed originally, was then revived. . . . I do not find it necessary, however, to deal with the effect of the restoration of a company to its former status by the removal of a liquidation order; I have come to the conclusion, on a review of the authorities quoted, that in fact a liquidation of a company does not mean the 'death' of the company in the sense that the company no longer exists and has suffered 'civil death' and that such death is equivalent to the death of an individual which death if the individual was the holder of a personal servitude, would thereby extinguish such personal servitude. I think the effect of a liquidation is adequately and properly set out on p 343 of Pyemont's *Company Law of South Africa* 6 ed, where it is stated as follows:

'Immediately upon the winding-up order becoming operative the control of the company's affairs passes out of the hands of the directors and, upon the appointment of a liquidator, into those of a liquidator; but the company's corporate identity remains and its property remains vested in the corporation. The essential difference, however, is that the business is henceforth carried on not for the benefit of the members of the corporation but with a view only to its winding up and the distribution of its assets among the creditors in satisfaction of their debts and, when these are satisfied, for the division of any balance among contributories. The assets are therefore held upon a trust in which the creditors are interested, and they can apply to the court to have their rights enforced.'

That may be very different from the effect of a sequestration order in the case of an individual. Under a sequestration order the individual is divested of his assets and they become vested first in the Master and then in the trustee. That is not the effect of a liquidation order. The position under such an order seems to be correctly set out in the passage I have quoted above in view of the authorities to which I was referred.

In my view the liquidation of the applicant company did not in this case destroy the identity of the company. The company continued to exist; and if the company owned rights—for instance a right to a personal servitude such as trading rights over portion of a farm—those rights were not lost upon liquidation. What could be done with such a servitude by the liquidator is, of course, another matter because, being a personal right, it could not be transferred. It might be a worthless asset from the point of view of realization. But the mere fact of liquidation, in my view, did not destroy the existence of those rights. If such rights existed, they remained in force.

[395] Attorney-General *v* Blumenthal
1961 (4) SA 313 (T)

The question in this case was whether s 225*ter*(1) (now s 251) of the Act, which makes false statements by directors, other officers, and accountants an offence, covers a false statement made by a director after winding-up to the liquidator. The court answered it in the negative.

TROLLIP J: Section 225*ter* of the Companies Act was inserted by s 114 of the Companies Amendment Act 23 of 1939. Subsection (1) reads as follows:

> 'Every director, manager, secretary or other officer of a company or accountant or auditor of or employed by a company or any other person employed generally or engaged for some special work or service by the company who makes, circulates or publishes or concurs in making, circulating or publishing any certificate, written statement, report or account in relation to any property or affair of the company which is false in any material particular, shall, subject to the provision of subsection (2), be guilty of an offence and liable on conviction to a fine not exceeding five hundred pounds or imprisonment for a period not exceeding two years or to both such fine and imprisonment.'

It is clear that the offence is only committed if a person making the written statement was a 'director' at the time that he made it.

The crisp point that has been raised for our decision is whether, the company having been placed under compulsory winding-up on 13 January 1959, the accused was still a 'director' thereof in terms of and for the purposes of that subsection as at 8 January 1960 and 2 May 1960, when he made the written statements as alleged.

Section 229 [now s 1] says that a 'director' includes

> 'any person occupying the position of director or alternate director of a company, by whatever name he may be called'.

That merely broadens the ordinary meaning of 'director' to embrace a *de facto* director and it does not assist in solving the present problem. . . .

There is ample authority to support the correctness of Mr B's concession that on the granting of a compulsory winding-up order the powers of the directors of the company cease. Section 164(*c*) [now s 353(2)] of the Companies Act provides specifically that that is one of the consequences ensuing on a voluntary winding-up. There is no similar provision for companies under compulsory winding-up but that the same consequences also ensues in such cases is to be inferred from various sections of the Act, especially ss 124(2) and (3)(*b*), 128, 130, 139 and 142 [now ss 361, 368, 386, 391, 409]. . . .

I think that it follows too from the sections of the Companies Act referred to above that on winding-up the duties of the directors also cease. Special duties after winding-up may be imposed upon them expressly by the Act or other law but that is exceptional and does not affect the general principle.

It also seems to be accepted that, as either the cause or effect of the cessation of the powers and duties of the directors on liquidation (it is irrelevant for the present purposes which it is), the order for compulsory winding-up automatically terminates the directors' employment or operates to dismiss them. This happens whether the contract between the director and company is based merely on the articles of association or arises from a special agreement, the only difference being that in the former he may not, whilst in the latter case he might be entitled to damages for breach of contract. . . .

All the above show conclusively that on the granting of a compulsory winding-up order the powers, duties, remuneration, tenure of office, and any special contract of the director automatically cease. How complete the ouster of the directors from their position as such on compulsory liquidation is, is borne out by what Gower says in his *Modern Company Law* [3rd ed at 655]:

> 'Perhaps the most important rule of all is the basic principle of company liquidation, namely that on winding up the board of directors becomes *functus officio* and its powers are assumed by the liquidator. As we have seen, it is those in control who have the power to cause harm, ie generally the directors, or someone for whom they are nominees. Their removal is therefore almost invariably an essential preliminary to any remedial action, and this removal automatically occurs on liquidation.'

Now, if a director ceases on compulsory winding-up to be a director officially and functionally (as in my view he does) then I think he must also cease to be a director nominally, in fact for all purposes. . . . occasionally a statutory provision uses the expression 'director of the company' to mean or include a person who, although he has ceased to be a director, *was* a director at some relevant time in the past, as for example, when winding-up supervened. Whether the expression is used in that sense or not depends upon its context. If it is used in relation to a company that is under winding-up then in that context it would most probably be that it is being used in that special sense. And indeed, it is likely that it is the use of the expression in that sense in certain sections of chap IV [now c XIV] of the Companies Act in relation to winding-up that has given rise to this conception of a director continuing to be a kind of 'nominal' director after winding-up. The sections that I have in mind particularly are the following, all of which occur in chap IV and operate after a compulsory winding-up order has been granted: s 122 [now s 363] (verification of the statement of the company's affairs by persons 'who are at the time of the winding-up order the directors thereof'); s 148 [now s 362] (delivery up of the company's

property by any 'officer of the company' which includes a 'director' —
see s 229 [now s 1]); s 155 [now s 417] (private examination by the court
of 'any officer' of the company); s 156 (public examination of any person
who 'has been a director or officer'); ss 180*bis* and *ter* [now ss 415, 416]
(attendance and examination of 'the directors' at creditors meetings);
s 184 [now s 423] (damages against 'any past or present director');
s 185 (application of criminal provisions of Insolvency Law to any person
'who is or has been a director'); s 185*bis* [now s 424] (liability of 'the
directors, whether past or present', for fraudulent conduct of the company's business); s 186 [now s 426] (prosecution of 'any past or present'
director). . . .

In my view therefore on the granting of a winding-up order of a
company a director ceases to be a director, officially, functionally and
nominally, but the expression 'director of a company' in a statute might
in its context be used in a special sense to mean or include a person who
was a director at the time of the order.

The only remaining question is whether 'director' in the context
of s 225*ter*(1) was used in that special case. I do not think that it was.
It seems clear that in so far as an accountant, auditor or other person
is concerned the offence is only committed if he makes a written statement while he is employed by the company. By reason of such employment the section enjoins him to refrain from making any false statement
in relation to any property or affairs of the company while he is one of
its employees, and if he disobeys that injunction, it imposes a severe
penalty on him. . . .

Now a compulsory winding-up order operates to discharge an employee
of the company. . . . consequently s 225*ter* would not apply to a statement
made by an accountant, auditor or other person after the compulsory
winding up order had terminated his employment with the company.

I think that that gives the clue to the legislature's intention in regard
to a director, manager, secretary, or other officer of the company. It
was intended that he too only commits the offence and subjects himself to the more serious penalty if he makes the statement while his
particular relationship with the company that warrants the special
penalty under the section, still subsists.

According to what I have said above, that relationship is completely
terminated when a compulsory winding-up order is granted and I do
not think, therefore, that any statement made by a director etc thereafter
would be hit by s 225*ter*(1). . . .

[Mr Justice Trollip stressed that this does not mean that there are no
sanctions if a director makes false statements after winding-up. Where
the statement is made in writing, under oath, the penalties for perjury
apply, and in other cases s 249 (formerly s 225(1)) provides the necessary
sanction.]

NOTES

See also *R* v *Heyne* 1958 (1) SA 614 (W) (a company does not cease on liquidation)
and *Volkskas Bpk* v *Darrenwood Electrical (Pty) Ltd* 1973 (2) SA 386 (T) (since a director
becomes *functus officio* when a winding-up order is made he can no longer effectively
endorse cheques on behalf of the company).

[396] Thorne & another NNO *v* The Government
1973 (4) SA 42 (T)

Prior to its liquidation a company had entered into three building
contracts with the Government. One was for the erection of an hydro-
logical research station at Pienaars River, another for the construction
of a reservoir, pipelines and sewers at the new terminal building at Jan
Smuts Airport. The third one is not relevant for present purposes.

After the commencement of the winding-up the creditors resolved to
complete the Pienaars River project but to abandon the Jan Smuts
contract. In pursuance of this resolution the Pienaars River contract
was duly completed, and an amount of R44 611,76 became payable by
the Government to the applicants. As to the Jan Smuts contract, by
reason of the company's default the Government had to engage another
contractor to complete the works, in consequence of which the total cost
to the Government was increased by an amount in excess of R44 611,76.

MARGO J: The dispute between the parties is one in which the applicants contend that they are entitled to payment of the R44 611,76 under
the Pienaars River contract, and in which the Government contends that
it is entitled to retain that amount in part discharge of its claim to
damages under the Jan Smuts contract.

The applicants claim that their right to payment of the R44 611,76
arises from their administration of the company in liquidation. . . . The
Government, in asserting its claim to be entitled to retain the R44 611,76,
does not rely on any common-law principle of set-off. . . . [It] rests its
case entirely on the provisions of clause 18 of the Jan Smuts contract.
That clause contains a complex set of provisions. In so far as it is relevant
to the present inquiry, it provides that if the contractor should fail to
proceed with and complete the works as prescribed, the Government
may require the contractor to withdraw, and may then employ another
contractor; and that, if the cost of completing the contract should exceed
what is obtained from any guarantee, the Government may deduct such
excess

> 'from any sums due or to become due under this or any other contract
> heretofore or hereafter existing between the contractor . . . and the
> Government . . .'.

An identical clause 18 is contained in the Pienaars River contract,
but that clause could only have been invoked by the Government if
there had been a breach by the company of the Pienaars River contract.
I do not agree that clause 18 of the Jan Smuts contract effected any
variation of the Pienaars River contract. . . . The stipulation in clause 18
of the Jan Smuts contract was extrinsic to the Pienaars River contract,
and conferred on the Government a right to recoup itself from any
debts owing by it to the company under any previous or future contract.
But that did not affect the validity of the debt arising under the Pienaars
River contract. Since there was no breach of that contract, the right to
payment accrued as provided therein. Indeed, the Government admits
that it became indebted to the applicants under that contract. In effect,
clause 18 of the Jan Smuts contract provides nothing more than that the

Government may apply the moneys owing by it under that and any other debts to the payment of a debt owing to it by the company under the Jan Smuts contract.

Clause 18 of the Jan Smuts contract was therefore not imported into the Pienaars River contract. Thus, the obligations of the company under the Pienaars River contract (to which obligations the applicants became bound in electing to complete that contract) did not include any obligation to submit to a set-off or deduction by the Government of any payments becoming due by it under that contract. The company's agreement to such a set-off or deduction was made independently of the Pienaars River contract, and was not a burden or commitment assumed by the applicants in electing to complete that contract.

The question then is whether the Government is entitled to enforce the set-off arrangement in clause 18 of the Jan Smuts contract after the grant of the winding-up order and the consequent *concursus creditorum*.

In *Walker* v *Syfret NO* 1911 AD 141 at 160 Lord De Villiers CJ held that the effect of an order winding up a company is to establish a *concursus creditorum*, and nothing can thereafter be allowed to be done by any of the creditors to alter the rights of the other creditors. Innes JA at 166, after stating that a sequestration order crystallizes the insolvent's position, went on to say:

'the hand of the law is laid upon the estate, and at once the rights of the general body of creditors have to be taken into consideration. No transaction can thereafter be entered into with regard to estate matters by a single creditor to the prejudice of the general body. The claim of each creditor must be dealt with as it existed at the issue of the order.' . . .

In regard particularly to the question of set-off, the rule is that, once a *concursus creditorum* has been established, there can be no compensation unless mutuality between the respective claims existed at the date of the order. . . . The mutuality here required is that the reciprocal debts both existed and that both were liquidated and payable, before the *concursus creditorum* was established. . . . In the present case there was no such mutuality between the respective claims prior to the winding-up order. The applicants' claim to payment by the Government under the Pienaars River contract only accrued after the liquidation order; and the amount of the Government's claim to damages under the Jan Smuts contract was only ascertained after the liquidation order.

It cannot make any difference to the legal consequences of a *concursus creditorum* that the parties, in clause 18 of the Jan Smuts agreement, concluded a pre-liquidation agreement authorizing set-off. . . .

Contractual stipulations between the debtor and a creditor will not entitle the creditor to obtain a preference over other creditors in the *concursus* otherwise than in accordance with the order of preference laid down by law. . . .

Applying these considerations to the facts of the present case, I have come to the conclusion that, since there was no mutuality of debts prior to the winding-up order, the Government is not now entitled to effect a set-off, under clause 18 of the Jan Smuts contract or otherwise, between the respective debts which have arisen under the Pienaars River contract and the Jan Smuts contract. The Government is accordingly liable in full on the Pienaars River debt.

NOTES

A lien over goods of a company cannot be established after the commencement of winding-up: *Secretary for Customs and Excise* v *Millman NO* 1975 (3) SA 544 (AD).

On the effect of *concursus creditorum*, see also *Administrator, Natal* v *Magill, Grant & Nell (Pty) Ltd (in liq)* 1969 (1) SA 660 (AD).

[397] Galaxie Melodies (Pty) Ltd *v* Dally NO
1975 (4) SA 736 (AD)

BOTHA JA: In the Cape Provincial Division the plaintiff (respondent on appeal), in his capacity as liquidator of Suncraft (Pty) Ltd, provisionally liquidated on 27 December 1973, claimed an order declaring the sale of its book debts on 1 August 1973 to the defendant company (appellant on appeal) to be null and void in terms of s 34(1) of the Insolvency Act 24 of 1936, as read with s 181(1) [now s 340(1)] of the Companies Act 46 of 1926.

It is alleged in the particulars of claim that the book debts sold to the defendant on 1 August 1973 constituted the bulk of or, alternatively, all the assets of Suncraft (Pty) Ltd as at the aforesaid date, that the sale took place within a period of six months of Suncraft's liquidation, and that at no time did Suncraft publish a notice of its intention to alienate the said assets in the *Government Gazette* or in any newspaper circulating in the district in which Suncraft was carrying on business, as is required by s 34(1) of the Insolvency Act 1936, as read with s 181(1) of the Companies Act 1926. . . .

The simple question in this appeal is whether the words 'which . . . could, for any reason, be set aside . . .' in s 181(1) of the Companies Act should be restrictively construed as suggested by counsel for the defendant, viz as meaning

'which could for any reason be set aside by the court in terms of ss 26, 29, 30 or 31 of the Insolvency Act 1936',

or whether a wider signification, as contended for by counsel for the plaintiff, should be given to them. It is significant that the legislature did not in s 181(1) of the Companies Act qualify the words 'set aside' either by the words 'by the court' or by the words 'in terms of ss 26, 29, 30 or 31 of the Insolvency Act'. Indeed, by the use of the words 'for any reason', without any reference to the Insolvency Act or to the law relating to insolvent estates, the words 'set aside' seem to have been employed in a wide sense and not necessarily only in the sense used in ss 26, 29, 30 or 31 of the Insolvency Act. The question whether a disposition made by a company can, in terms of s 181(1) of the Companies Act, be set aside in the event of the company being wound up and unable to pay its debts, is, according to the language of that section, to be determined, not only by reference to the Insolvency Act, but also to any other law, including the common law (*Cornelissen NO* v *Universal Caravan Sales (Pty) Ltd* 1971 (3) SA 158 (AD) at 170) under which a disposition made by an individual can be set aside in the event of his insolvency. It is only when that question is determined in the affirmative that 'the provisions of the law relating to insolvent estates' are by s 181(1) made applicable, *mutatis mutandis*, to such a disposition made by a company.

The ordinary plain meaning of the words 'set aside' in s 181 ('opsygesit word' in the Afrikaans text) is to 'annul, quash, render void or nugatory': *Shorter Oxford Dictionary* p 1854.

An alienation referred to in s 34(1) of the Insolvency Act shall, in the circumstances therein set out, 'be void as against the trustee'. The alienation is not declared void in any absolute sense, but only as against the trustee. That means that it is within the discretion of the trustee whether to treat such an alienation as void or not. . . . If he waives his rights, the alienation remains standing. If he exercises his powers under the section and treats the alienation as void, he in effect avoids or annuls it, and, therefore, sets it aside in that sense. . . .

An order made by the court in declaring void an alienation made in conflict with the provisions of s 34(1), does not differ in substance from an order setting aside or declaring void a voidable disposition under ss 26, 29, 30 and 31 of the Act, as such an order is also an order 'declaratory of a right' (*Gunn & another NNO v Barclays Bank DCO* 1962 (3) SA 678 (AD) at 684). It is only in the effect of an order under s 34(1), and an order under ss 26, 29, 30 or 31, respectively, that there may be some difference, in that the effect of an order under s 34(1) is that the alienation in question is declared void *ab initio* (*Harrismith Board of Executors v Odendaal* [1923 AD 530], whereas the effect of an order under ss 26, 29, 30 or 31 is that the disposition in question is, subject to the provisions of ss 32(3) and 33, not invalidated *ab initio*, except perhaps as between the insolvent and the person to whom the disposition was made.

Section 34 of the Insolvency Act is clearly designed for the protection of the creditors of a trader who disposes of his business or assets. This appears particularly clearly from the provisions of ss (2) and (3) of that section. There can be no reason whatsoever why the legislature would have intended to deprive the creditors of a trading company in contrast to the creditors of an individual trader of the protection afforded by s 34, while affording them the protection provided for by ss 26, 29, 30 and 31 in the case of voidable dispositions. . . .

However, there is in my view a far more important consideration pointing away from a possible intention on the part of the legislature of depriving the creditors of a trading company of the protection of s 34. . . .

A trader facing insolvency may either recklessly or desperately in an endeavour to obtain cash money dispose of his assets at a price much below their true value. I know of no other legislative provisions mitigating the risk involved in such an eventuality to creditors of a trading company, and I cannot conceive of any reason why the legislature would have intended to deprive such creditors of the protection of s 34 in such circumstances.

NOTES

See also *Rousseau v Standard Bank* 1976 (4) SA 104 (C), where a payment made by the company within six months prior to its liquidation to its bank in reduction of an overdraft was set aside under s 29(1) of the Insolvency Act as a voidable preference.

On the applicability of ss 44 and 150 of the Insolvency Act, see respectively, *Ben Rossouw Motors* v *Druker NO* 1975 (1) SA 821 (W) and *Slabbert, Verster and Malherbe Bpk* v *Die Assistent Meester* 1977 (1) SA 107 (NC).

Section 182 of the 1926 Act (now s 339) renders s 156 of the Insolvency Act applicable. It follows that an injured workman employed by a construction company under winding up and unable to pay its debts can claim directly from the insurer of the company, *Woodley* v *Guardian Assurance Co of SA Ltd* 1976 (1) SA 758 (W).

(c) Liquidation

A TEXT

In any winding up a liquidator is appointed by the court, s 367. The general powers of a liquidator are defined in s 386. If a liquidator wishes to exercise any of the powers enumerated in ss (4), he must obtain, in a winding-up by the court, the authority of the creditors and members or contributors or, in the alternative, of the Master; in a creditors' voluntary winding-up, of the creditors; and in a members' voluntary winding-up, of the members, ss (3). The powers which fall into this category include the power to bring or defend an action; to compromise or admit a claim against the company; to enter into an arrangement; to submit a dispute to arbitration; to carry on or discontinue the business of the company; and to sell any movable or immovable property of the company.

The duties of a liquidator are set out in ss 391ff. In carrying out his duties the liquidator must have regard to the directions that are given to him by resolutions of creditors or members at general meetings, s 387(1). Failing directions or in the event of conflicting directions he may apply for directions to the Master and, in the last resort, to the court, s 387(2), (3) and (4). The court may also determine questions in a voluntary winding-up and, generally, exercise in a voluntary winding-up any of the powers which it might exercise if the company were being wound up by the court, s 388.

The word 'liquidator' as used in the Act includes a provisional liquidator, s 1 sv 'liquidator'. It follows that he has the same powers and duties as a final liquidator, but the Master may restrict his powers, s 386(6): *398*. Subject to the consent of the Master, the provisional liquidator may terminate any lease in terms of which the company is the lessee of movable or immovable property, s 386(2). In any winding-up meetings of creditors and members have to be held, as provided in ss 412–416. In a compulsory winding-up and a creditors' voluntary winding-up, the Master summons the first meeting of creditors and members, s 364, and claims have to be proved as in insolvency, s 366. Where the company is unable to pay its debts, directors and officers have to attend creditors' meetings, as provided in s 414 (see *Levin* v *Ensor NO* 1975 (2) SA 118 (D)) and may be examined as provided in s 415. In a compulsory winding-up the court may summon for examination any person known or suspected to have in his possession any property of the company, or believed to be indebted to the company, or any person whom the court deems capable of giving information concerning the trade, dealings, affairs or property of the company, s 417. (On examination by commissioners, see s 418.)

A director whose estate has been sequestrated after the winding-up of the company remains obliged to submit a statement of the company's affairs to the Master under s 363 (formerly s 122) and to attend the first and second meetings of creditors, under s 414 (formerly s 180*bis*(1)): *S* v *Cope* 1970 (3) SA 605(T).

An arrangement entered into between a company able to pay its debts and about to be or in the course of being wound up and its creditors is binding on the company if it is sanctioned by a special resolution of members and on its creditors if it is acceded to by three-fourths in number and value of such creditors, s 389(1). The arrangement is subject to review by the court on the application of a dissatisfied creditor or member, as set out in s 389.

Where a company is proposed to be or is being wound up voluntarily and the whole or part of its business or property is proposed to be transferred or sold to another company, the liquidator of the transferor company may, with the sanction of a special resolution of that company, accept in compensation for the transfer or sale, shares, policies or other like interests in the transferee company, for distribution among the members of the transferor company, or enter into any arrangement whereby the members of the transferor company participate in the profits of or receive any other benefit from the transferee company, s 390(1). This is subject to the proviso that in the case of a creditors' voluntary winding-up, the liquidator must also obtain the consent of three-fourths in number and value of the creditors present at a meeting called by him for that purpose, or the sanction of the court, s 390(1). A dissenting member of the transferor company may require the liquidators to purchase his interest or abstain from carrying the resolution into effect, s 390(3).

Arrangements in terms of ss 389 and 390 must not be confused with compromises or arrangements in terms of ss 311 and 313 (above p 632). Section 389 presupposes a company about to be or in the course of being wound up and able to pay its debts, while s 390 applies where a company is about to be or in the course of being wound up voluntarily.

After the liquidation and distribution account, which has been filed by the liquidator and lodged with the Master as provided in s 403, has been confirmed by the Master, the estate is distributed, s 409. A liquidator who has performed all his duties may apply to the Master for a certificate in completion of duties and the cancellation of the security given by him, s 385.

When a company has been completely wound up the Master transmits to the Registrar a certificate to that effect and the Registrar records the dissolution of the company and publishes notice thereof in the *Gazette*, s 419: *399*. Within two years of the dissolution, the court may declare the dissolution void, as provided in s 420.

B CASES

[398] *Ex parte* Klopper NO: *In Re* Sogervim SA (Pty) Ltd
1971 (3) SA 791 (T)

This was an application by a provisional liquidator for leave to sell the movable and immovable property of a company under compulsory winding-up. The application was refused.

BOSHOFF J: This brings me to the legal aspect—whether there was any justification at all for the applicant as a provisional liquidator to bring this application. This involves a consideration of the broad scheme of the Companies Act 46 of 1926, as amended, as far as a compulsory winding-up of a company is concerned.

On a winding-up order being made, all the property of the company is deemed to be in the custody or control of the Master until a liquidator or a provisional liquidator is appointed and is capable of acting as such. He is not capable of acting as such until he has given security to the satisfaction of the Master (s 124(3)(*b*) and (*c*) [now s 375]).

A liquidator is in a fiduciary position in relation to the company and the body of creditors. He is appointed by the Master for the purpose of conducting the proceedings in the winding-up (s 124(1) [now s 367]), and it is his duty to proceed forthwith to recover and reduce into possession all the assets and property of the company, movable and immovable, and to apply them so far as they extend in satisfaction of the costs of winding-up and the claims of the creditors, and to distribute the balance amongst those who are entitled thereto (ss 128 and 177 [now ss 391 and 342]). The creditors have a say in the appointment of a liquidator and he is consequently only appointed after the final winding-up order has been made and the Master has had the opportunity of summoning a meeting of creditors and a meeting of contributories for the purpose of determining the person whose name is to be submitted for appointment as liquidator. At the meeting of the creditors, claims will have to be proved in order to determine who are the creditors.

Although the meetings are to be held as soon as may be after the final winding-up order (s 180 [now s 412] and rule 25 of the winding-up rules), and the Master is to make the appointment of the liquidator as soon as possible after the meetings (rule 7(1)), it is inevitable that there must be some delay before the liquidator is appointed and capable of acting as such. By that time the Master should know something about the affairs of the company because the person or persons referred to in s 122(2) [now s 363] are required to submit a statement of the affairs of the company showing certain stated particulars and such other information as the Master may require, within fourteen days from the date of the winding-up order or within such extended time as the Master or the court may for special reason appoint (s 122(1), (2) and (3)).

. . . Every person who is required to submit such a statement must apply to the Master for instructions for the preparation of the statement and he must attend on the Master either before or after the statement has been submitted and give the Master all the information that he may require (rule 6(1) and (2)). The Master must transmit a duplicate of the statement to the liquidator on his appointment (s 122(1)). The liquidator in turn must as soon as practicable and, unless with the consent of the Master, not later than three months after the date of his appointment, submit to a general meeting of creditors and contributories a report, *inter alia*, as to the progress and prospects of the liquidation and as to any other matter which he may think fit or in regard to which he may desire the directions of the creditors or the contributories (s 129 [now s 402]).

Section 130 [now s 386] deals with the powers of liquidators and s 142 [now s 387] with the exercise of those powers. As will be seen from these sections, apart from certain administrative powers referred to in ss (1) of s 130, which the liquidator can exercise independently on his own initiative so as not to impose additional liability on the company, the liquidator must act on the authority of a resolution of creditors and contributories or under the directions of the Master or with the leave of the court. In terms of s 142(1) the liquidator must, in the administration of the assets of the company, subject to the provisions of the Act, have regard to any directions that may be given by the resolution of creditors or contributories at any general meeting. Where a matter has been submitted by the liquidator for the direction of creditors and contributories in general meeting, and no directions are given, or there is a difference, the liquidator may apply to the Master for directions; if the Master refuses to give directions, the liquidator may apply to the court for directions. He may also apply to court for directions in regard to any other particular matter arising under the winding-up (ss (2) and (3)). In this latter event, he must state in his petition the steps he has taken to ascertain the wishes of creditors and contributories and, if the matter had been submitted to a meeting of creditors or contributories, he must attach a copy of the minutes of the proceedings thereat to his petition (rule 36(2)).

A liquidator has power in terms of s 130(2)(*g*) to sell the movable and immovable property of the company by public auction or private contract with the authority mentioned in ss (4) of s 142, namely, a resolution of creditors and contributories or the directions of the Master.

When a provisional or final winding-up order is made the circumstances or the affairs of a company may be such that it is in the interest of the company and the general body of creditors that some other person than the Master should as soon as possible take all the property into his control and custody and attend to urgent matters for the preservation of the property and the beneficial winding-up of the company. To meet such a situation the Master has the power to appoint a provisional liquidator as soon as a provisional or final winding-up order is made and he then holds office until the appointment of a liquidator (s 124(2) [now s 368]). The Master, in appointing a provisional liquidator, may, under s 130(4) [now s 386(6)], restrict his powers. The extent to which his powers will be restricted will depend on the circumstances of each particular case. In the case of *Renwick & others* v *Transvaal Taxicab Co* 1910 TH 27 the learned judge stated that, because of the position of a provisional liquidator, he should be restricted in his powers. Indeed, a provisional liquidator should not be given power to do what may amount to a liquidation of a company prior to the statutory meetings of creditors and contributories being called and a final liquidator being appointed unless the circumstances really dictate such a course. In the case of *In re Lloyds Departmental Stores Ltd (in liquidation)* 1923 WLD 60 the creditors were in favour of the sale of the stock-in-trade which would have the effect of avoiding a monthly rental of £155 and result in a great saving to the creditors. The court was in the circumstances of that case prepared to give the provisional liquidator what it referred to as the unusual power to sell the stock-in-trade. It was also stated in that case that, where authority is sought by a provisional liquidator to sell practically all the stock-in-trade and assets of a company which has just been placed in liquidation, he should make out a very strong case indeed. . . .

In the instant case no exceptional circumstances exist for the granting of the powers asked by the applicant, and the application should therefore be refused.

NOTES

Ex parte Klopper NO: In re Sogervim SA (Pty) Ltd (398) was decided under the old Act but as a general statement of the process of liquidation it is still relevant. Under s 386(3) and (4) a liquidator as well as a provisional liquidator now requires the authority of creditors, members or the Master before he may sell movable or immovable property, but in the light of the pre-1973 Act case law it appears likely that at least in a compulsory winding-up or creditors' voluntary winding-up the Master will be inclined to restrict the powers of provisional liquidators under s 386(6) and that it will be only in exceptional circumstances that a provisional liquidator will be authorized by him to sell all the assets of the company, see *In re Texaphote (SA) Ltd (in liq)* 1927 WLD 130; *Ex parte Krumm NO: In re Tinsev (Pty) Ltd (in liq)* 1974 (2) SA 557 (D); and *Ex parte Paterson* 1974 (4) SA 281 (E). '. . . the liquidator in the winding-up of a company owes a duty both to that company and to the creditors. He owes a duty to the company to see that its assets are realized and its liabilities minimized to the best possible advantage of the company and he owes a duty to the creditors to see that they suffer the least loss and receive the most advantageous dividend', per Beadle ACJ in *Concorde Leasing Corporation (Rhodesia) Ltd* v *Pringlewood (NO)* 1975 (4) SA 231 (R) at 234, 235. He is not a trustee for the creditors or the shareholders but an agent of the company. If he performs a contract of the company or makes a new contract on its behalf there is no presumption that he does so in his personal capacity, *Stead Hazel & Co* v *Cooper* [1933] 1 KB 840. And in the absence of fraud, mala fides or personal misconduct an action for damages will not lie against him at the suit of either a creditor for a delay in paying his claim or of a shareholder for a delay in handing over to him his share in the surplus assets, *Knowles* v *Scott* [1891] 1 Ch 717.

He has power to continue a lease but is bound by a stipulation restricting or prohibiting the transfer of rights under the lease: *Durban City Council* v *Liquidator, Durban Icedromes*, 1965 (1) SA 600 (AD).

Where there are two liquidators they must act jointly: *Millman NO* v *Goosen* 1975 (3) SA 141 (O).

'[I]t is no excuse of a liquidator on whom responsible duties are imposed by statute to shelter himself behind the cloak of an ailing or dying principal. The liquidator is no figure-head nor is he a rubber-stamp. It [is] his duty to carry out his duties under the Act and, if he [is] unable to do so, to approach the Master with a proper explanation for his failure or inability to do so.

'It is the duty of every liquidator or trustee or executor to satisfy himself of the statutory and legal duties which such a responsible appointment entails, and to comply therewith to the best of his ability. If he is not able or prepared to do so, he should not accept such an appointment' (per Hart J in *Terrace Bay Holdings (Pty) Ltd* v *Strathmore Diamonds (Pty) Ltd* 1976 (3) SA 664 (SWA) at 667A and H.

Where a liquidator has elected, with the concurrence of the creditors and the Master, to abide by and continue with an executory contract into which the company has entered before liquidation, he is entitled to exact full performance by the other contracting party but in his turn has to perform in full the reciprocal duties imposed upon the company, *Ex parte Venter: In Re Rapid Mining Supplies (Pty) Ltd* 1976 (3) SA 267 (O).

[399] **Rapp and Maister Holdings** *v* **Ruflex Holdings**
1972 (3) SA 835 (T)

A company was voluntarily wound up by its members. After the surplus assets had been distributed among its members, the company was dissolved. A creditor of the company who was not paid a debt owing to him sought to recover from a shareholder his pro rata share in the excess which the shareholders received because the company had not discharged all the debts which it ought to have paid. The action failed.

GALGUT J: The defendant took exception to the summons as amplified by the particulars of claim on the ground that no cause of action was disclosed, in that defendant as a shareholder of Deimos could not be held liable for its debts.

Plaintiff sought to meet the exception by alleging that it could claim from defendant under a *condictio indebiti* in that defendant had been enriched at plaintiff's expense. The magistrate rejected the plaintiff's contentions and upheld the exception. The appeal is against that decision by the magistrate. . . .

It was urged that defendant has been enriched at the expense of plaintiff, and that, on this principle of our law, the plaintiff was entitled to recover by way of the *condictio indebiti*. Counsel pointed out that a creditor in a deceased estate who has not been paid is entitled to recover from the heir (or legatee) who had received more than he would have received if the creditor's claim had been paid. The *condictio indebiti* was available to such a creditor. . . .

He contended that by analogy and on principle the same remedy should be accorded to plaintiff. He submitted that the elements which were available to the unpaid creditor of a deceased estate, were for all practical purposes the same as those existing in the present case; that the two component elements of plaintiff's claim, were the element of indebtedness by the company (Deimos) to plaintiff and the further element that defendant had benefited at plaintiff's expense by reason of the distribution. Hence, so he argued, plaintiff could rely on the doctrine of unjust enrichment and the *condictio indebiti* was available to it. He quoted the following passage from the *South African Law of Obligations* by Lee and Honoré at para 688:

> 'When money, or other property which ought to have been transferred to the person, has been transferred to another, the rightful claimant may in some cases recover the property, or any benefit derived from it, from the person to whom it has been transferred.'

. . . He said money which ought to have been transferred to plaintiff had been transferred to defendant, and suggested that this was one of the cases in which the above dictum applied.

I cannot accept these submissions by counsel. Firstly, it is established under the common law that an action will lie at the instance of an unpaid creditor of a deceased person against an heir or legatee who has been paid more than he should have been paid out of the assets of the estate. Whether that action is described as a *condictio indebiti* or whether it is based upon the principle of unjust enrichment, does not matter. It is an action granted by the common law.

. . . There is no such common-law action available to an unpaid creditor of a company against a shareholder who has received more on dissolution of the company than he would have received, had the creditor been paid. Secondly it has been held that there is no general action for enrichment in our law. Before a plaintiff can succeed on a claim based on unjust enrichment he must show that his cause of action falls within the scope of one of the recognized actions for enrichment as our law. As plaintiff has no common law action to assist it and as the alleged enrichment does not arise from one of the recognized enrichment actions it must fail unless the Companies Act assists it. . . .

Counsel for respondent placed reliance on ss 138, 164(*e*) and 191 of the Act.

Section 138 [now s 408] provides that, when a liquidation account has lain for inspection as provided in the Act and when there has been no objection, or where objections have been lodged and dealt with, the Master shall confirm the account and his confirmation shall have the effect of a final sentence, save as against such persons as may be permitted by the court to reopen the account before any dividend has been paid thereunder.

Section 164(*e*) [which has no exact equivalent in the 1973 Act] reads:

'The following consequences shall ensue on the voluntary winding-up of a company —

(*e*) The liquidator may fix a time or times within which creditors of the company are to prove their claims or to be excluded from any distribution under any account lodged with the Master before those claims are proved . . .'.

Section 191 [now s 420] reads:

'(1) When a company has been dissolved, the court may, at any time within two years of the date of the dissolution, on an application by the liquidator of the company, or by any other person who appears to the court to be interested, make an order, upon such terms as the court thinks fit, declaring the dissolution to have been void, and thereupon such proceedings may be taken as might have been taken if the company had not been dissolved.'

Counsel for respondent urged that once an account had been confirmed the above provisions and s 138 in particular rendered the matter *res judicata*. He relied *inter alia* on dicta in *Gluckman* v *Jagger & Co* 1929 CPD 44 at 47 to 48; in *Appel* v *Estate Ginsberg* 1927 TPD 636 at 640; in *Callinicos* v *Burman* 1963 (1) SA 489 (AD) at 498. These cases were dealing with the sections in the Insolvency Act which in this regard have provisions similar to those in the Companies Act. They do indicate that, in the circumstances outlined in each of the cases, the confirmation of the liquidation account did have the effect of a final sentence. If it should come to pass that the facts in this matter ever come to be ventilated in a court of law it may well be that the present plaintiff could be met with a defence based on s 138 or s 164(*e*). . . . [T]here is nothing in the Companies Act which directly or indirectly assists the plaintiff or disturbs the common-law position as set out above.

II JUDICIAL MANAGEMENT

A TEXT

Judicial management is a half-way house between the life and death of a company. When by reason of mismanagement or for any other cause a company is unable or probably unable to meet its obligations but has not become or is prevented from becoming a successful concern and there is a reasonable probability that if it is placed under judicial management it will recover and become a successful concern, the court may, if it appears just and equitable, grant a judicial management order, ss 427, 428: *400, 401*.

The effect of a judicial management order is to place the company under the management, first of a provisional, and then of a final judicial manager, ss 429ff. The duties of a provisional and a final judicial manager are set out in ss 430 and 433. In important respects the rules governing winding-up apply, see e g ss 431(4) and 439, and as regards voidable and undue preferences and creditors meetings the rules are, generally, the same as on insolvency, ss 435(2), 436, 437.

If the judicial manager is at any time of the opinion that the continuation of the judicial management will not enable the company to become a successful concern, he must apply to the court for the cancellation of the judicial management order and the issue of an order for the winding-up of the company, s 433(*e*). If on the other hand on application by the judicial manager or any person having an interest in the company the court is satisfied that the purpose of the judicial management order has been fulfilled or that for any other reason it is undesirable that the order should remain in force the court may cancel the order and, if necessary, give directions for the resumption of the management of the company by its old officers or for the convening of a general meeting of members for the purpose of electing directors, s 440.

B CASES

[400] **Lief NO** *v* **Western Credit (Africa) (Pty) Ltd**
1966 (3) SA 344 (W)

SNYMAN J: A winding-up order, in its nature, is intended to bring about the dissolution of the company, whereas the purpose of a judicial management order is to save the company from dissolution. An important feature of a winding-up order is that upon such an order being granted there is a *concursus creditorum*. A judicial management order on the other hand usually provides for a moratorium in respect of the company's debt in the hope that it will lead ultimately to the payment of all creditors and the resumption by it of normal trading. Furthermore, it is true that for judicial management orders provision is made in the section for the order in which payments to creditors are to be effected, and that preference is given to older creditors over later ones. But this is the result of equitable considerations because of the granting of a moratorium. It is clear from all authority that it is not a form of *concursus creditorum* as in winding-up orders. A winding-up order is usually granted where a company is in fact insolvent, whereas a judicial management order is usually granted where a solvent company has run into financial difficulties because of mismanagement and because there is hope that with better management it will overcome its difficulties.

[401] Maynard *v* Office Appliances (SA) (Proprietary) Ltd
1927 WLD

BARRY J: In this matter the applicant asks the court to appoint a judicial manager in terms of s 195(2) of the Union Companies Act. It appears that the company is a private company registered on 25 March 1927, with a capital of £40 000, divided into 24 000 preferent or non-voting shares, and 16 000 deferred shares, entitling the holders to voting rights, and to surplus profits.

The applicant is the managing director and in charge of the business of the company at Cape Town. Cinamon and Tunley, two of the directors, who support the applicant in making the petition, are in charge at Durban and Johannesburg.

The respondent is the organiser and secretary of the company at Johannesburg engaged under a contract for $2\frac{1}{2}$ years at a salary of £1 800 a year. He also appears to be a director, but the validity of his appointment as such is challenged.

As the result of an investigation into the affairs of the company, which have been largely under the respondent's control (so it is said) it is alleged that the expenses of management have been excessive, and that the staff is too large and employees have been engaged at extravagant rates. In consequence the company has become financially embarrassed, and while quite solvent, cannot by reason of the heavy management costs meet its current liabilities. It is suggested that the company could have a successful career if the costs of management are reduced and the company is converted into a public one with an additional share capital. For this reason it is claimed that the company should be placed under judicial management in terms of the Act.

The applicant and the two directors Cinamon and Tunley hold the majority of the deferred shares in the company, and in addition the applicant is a creditor in the sum of £3 153, and a contingent creditor for a larger amount.

The respondent says that the cause of the company's financial embarrassment is not the heavy costs of management but the liabilities of Tunley and Company, which the company has assumed. He denies that he is responsible for the expenses of management, and says that this expenditure is in accordance with a scheme, of which the applicant and the two directors approve. Before, however, dealing with the facts in the present case, I think it is necessary to consider the provisions of s 195, and ascertain the circumstances in which the court will grant an order for the appointment of a judicial manager. . . .

Under ss (1) of s 195 [now s 427] in an application for the liquidation of a company, whenever it is just and equitable that the company should be wound up by reason of its mismanagement or its probable inability to meet its obligations or become a successful concern, or for some other cause the court may, if it is just and equitable to postpone the order for liquidation, grant a judicial management order instead of granting liquidation.

Subsection (2) provides that such an order can be granted on the application of a shareholder or creditor, if, by reason of mismanagement or any other cause, it is desirable to place the company under judicial management. . . .

It is a well-established principle that courts of law will not interfere with the internal management of companies, except in circumstances which are not present in this case. To quote the language of James LJ in *Macdougall* v *Gardiner* [*326*] at page 21: 'I think it is of the utmost importance to all these companies that the rule which is well known in this court as the rule in *Mozley* v *Alston* . . . and *Foss* v *Harbottle* should always be adhered to; that is to say, that nothing connected with internal disputes between the shareholders is to be made the subject of a bill by some one shareholder on behalf of himself and others, unless there be something illegal, oppressive, or fraudulent — unless there be something *ultra vires* on the part of the company *qua* company, or on the part of the majority of the company, so that they are not fit persons to determine it. . . .'

Applying these principles, if the facts show that there has been mismanagement in the conduct of the company's affairs, the court will not interfere on the application of a shareholder or an individual director. And the reason is that the directors can redress the mismanagement, or the shareholders can in the general meeting. If a director or shareholder is in a minority as regards the domestic policy of the company, a court will not assist him unless he can show something illegal on the part of the company or something oppressive or fraudulent on the part of the persons who control the company. It seems to me that ss (2) should be limited in its construction and that the same kind of mismanagement should be shown as is required in ss (1), although the application is not one for winding up the company. But, even if this is not the proper construction of ss (2), the court has a discretion and must consider whether, in the circumstances, it is desirable to place the company under judicial management.

Assuming that the affairs of the company are largely under the control of the respondent, as is alleged in para 5 of the petition, it is clear that the applicant and his co-directors can relieve him of such control, and themselves shape the domestic policy of the company's affairs. They can prevent a repetition of similar acts in the future. If the financial embarrassment of the company is due to the respondent's extravagant management, the applicant and his co-directors can themselves reduce the expenses of management, subject to existing obligations. If, as is alleged by the respondent, the costly management was authorized by the board of directors, the remedy lies in the hands of the board.

The steps proposed to remedy the financial embarrassment of the company are to reduce the costs of management, and to increase the capital of the company. It is suggested this object can be reached by appointing a judicial manager, but . . . this object can be attained by the directors themselves. Indeed the conversion of the company into a public one is one which the company alone can effect, and not the judicial manager. . . .

In the replying affidavit a number of creditors support the appointment of a judicial manager. There are also a number of American creditors, principals in agencies that the company holds: in terms of the company's contracts with these principals a right of cancellation is given in the event of the company's liquidation. The model clause is set out, and it is by no means clear that the appointment of a judicial manager may not similarly give rise to a right of cancellation. The views of the American creditors are not before the Court, and I have not their wishes before me, although it is stated that they have been advised of these proceedings.

In these circumstances, I do not think that the wishes of the largest South African creditors should be given undue weight.

I come to the conclusion, therefore, that the mismanagement in the present application is not such mismanagement as would entitle the court under the 'just and equitable rule' to appoint a judicial manager under s 195(2). And apart from the contruction I have placed under s 195(2), I do not think, in the circumstances, that, in the exercise of my discretion, it is desirable to appoint a judicial manager.

NOTES

See also *Ladybrand Hotel (Pty) Ltd v Segal* 1975 (2) SA 357 (O) where the court dealt in detail with the factors to be taken into consideration before a provisional order of judicial management is made final. Erasmus J stressed (at 359B) that '[a]n applicant basing his case for a judicial management order, which after all is a special concession and only granted in exceptional circumstances . . . on scanty information and generalisations does so at his own peril'. This applied especially when confirmation of the rule nisi was opposed, as it was in that case.

Considering that the reports submitted by the provisional judicial manager were incomplete and misleading, the learned judge concluded (at 363A–D):

'After consideration of the aspects mentioned in s 432(2) it does not appear to me that the applicant will, if placed under a final judicial management order, be enabled to become a successful concern and in view also of the first and third aspects of the application discussed in this judgment it is in my view not just and equitable that the rule be made final. The rule nisi is accordingly discharged.'

The respondents in the counter-application have asked that the applicant be placed under a winding-up order and that the costs of this application, including the respondents' costs of intervention in the applicant's application for a final judicial management order, form part of the costs of the winding-up of the applicant.

The onus is on the respondents to prove the counter-application, but generally it is accepted that, where a company is unable to pay its debts, an unpaid creditor has a right *ex debito justitiae* to have it placed in liquidation. See *Bahnemann* v *Fritzmore Exploration (Pty) Ltd* 1963 (2) SA 249 (T) at 250H.

In *Noordkaap Lewendehawe Ko-op Bpk* v *Schreuder*, 1974 (3) SA 102 (AD) the Appellate Division stressed that s 195 (now s 427) required ''n redelike waarskynlikheid' ('a reasonable probability') that the company, if placed under judicial management, would be enabled to pay its debts and become a successful concern.

Said Van Blerk JA (at 109H, 110A–C):

'Die hof *a quo* het nie alleen wat betref die vermeende nie-uitoefening van 'n diskresie fouteer nie, maar het ook die verkeerde benadering gevolg deur sy oordeel te baseer op 'n redelike moontlikheid instede van op 'n redelike waarskynlikheid. Artikel 195(1), reeds hierbo na verwys, skryf voor dat 'n Hof 'n geregtelike bestuursbevel kan verleen as dit van oordeel is dat daar 'n redelike waarskynlikheid bestaan dat die maatskappy in staat gestel sal word om aan sy verpligtinge·te voldoen.

Die verskil tussen die woorde ,,waarskynlikheid'' en ,,moontlikheid'' is wesenlik. In die regstaal word dit wat 'n moontlikheid is, beskou as minder seker as dit wat 'n waarskynlikheid is.

Die vermoedelike doel van die Wetgewer met die gebruik van die woord ,,waarskynlikheid'' kan aangeneem word, was om die regte van skuldeisers van 'n maatskappy wat nie betaling van hul eise kan kry nie omdat die maatskappy, soos in hierdie geval, kommersieel insolvent is, so min moontlik met 'n geregtelike bestuursbevel in te kort. Sodanige krediteure is op 'n aansoek wat wetlik in order is normaalweg geregtig op 'n likwidasiebevel. (Vgl Buckley *The Companies Acts* 13e uitg 450). As die woord ,,moontlikheid'' deur die Wetgewer gebruik was, kan dit vrywel ten gevolge hê dat die reg op 'n likwidasiebevel op die lange baan geskuif word. Dit kon nouliks die bedoeling van die Wetgewer gewees het.'

In *Guttman* v *Sunlands Township (Pty) Ltd* 1962 (2) SA 348(C) Herbstein J stated that the section does not require proof that the company will be able to function successfully in the future or that its debts will be settled within a reasonable time, but that the fact '[t]hat a creditor might be long delayed in the payment of his debts is a matter which, however, must be weighed by the court in deciding whether it would be just or equitable to postpone the liquidation' (at 352G).

In *General Leasing Corporation Ltd* v *Thorne NO* 1975 (4) SA 157 (C) it was held that the liabilities referred to in s 197B(1)(*bis*)(*a*) [now s 435(1)(*a*)] do not include one which arose by reason of the repudiation of a lease by the judicial manager.

Section 386(5) empowers the court to sanction the raising of money on the application of a liquidator or provisional liquidator, but not of a provisional judicial manager: *Ex parte Paterson NO: In re Goodearth Estates (Pty) Ltd* 1974 (4) SA 281 (E).

On the requirements of a judicial management order, see further *Bahnemann* v *Fritzmore Exploration (Pty) Ltd* 1963 (2) SA 249 (T); *Millman NO* v *Swartland Huis Meubeleerders (Edms) Bpk* 1972 (1) SA 741 (C).

On cancellation of an order for judicial management, see e g *Joubert NO* v *Consolidated Sand and Stone Supplies (Pty) Ltd* 1972 (3) SA 88 (C) and *Lapinsky NO* v *VJB Construction Mechanical and Electrical Engineers (Pty) Ltd* 1972 (2) SA 78 (O).

Part-payments made by a judicial manager to creditors of the company interrupt prescription: *S Cohen Ltd* v *Johnston & Johnston* 1970 (4) SA 332 (SWA).

The power given the court to stay proceedings against a company under judicial management (formerly s 196(1), now s 428(2)) extends to future as well as to pending proceedings: *Samuel Osborn (SA) Ltd* v *United Stone Crushing Co (Pty) Ltd (under judicial management)* 1938 WLD 229.

In *Rustomjee* v *Rustomjee (Pty) Ltd* 1960 (2) SA 753 (N) the court expressed doubt whether judicial management proceedings were really appropriate to a small private company.

III CORPORATE DELINQUENTS

When in the course of the winding-up or judicial management of a company, or otherwise it appears that any person who has taken part in the formation or promotion of the company, or any past or present director or any officer of the company has misapplied or retained or become liable or accountable for any money or property of the company or has been guilty of any breach of faith or trust in relation to the company the court, on the application of the Master or of the liquidator or of any creditor or member or contributory of the company may, after enquiry, order the delinquent promoter, director or officer to repay or restore the money or property or any part thereof, with or without interest, or to compensate the company in such manner as it deems just, s 423: *402, 403.*

Again, when it appears in a winding-up, judicial management or otherwise that business of the company was or is being carried on recklessly or fraudulently, the court may declare that any person who was knowingly a party to such conduct shall be personally liable, without any limitation of liability, for all or any of the debts or other liabilities of the company, s 424. On the application of the criminal sanctions of the Insolvency Act, see s 425.

Sections 414–18, 423 provide the chief tools for tracking down corporate wrongdoers.

B CASES

[402] L Suzman (Rand) Ltd v Yamoyani (2)
1972 (1) SA 109 (W)

MARGO J: This is an application by a creditor in a company known as Burke & Gannon (Pty) Ltd, now in liquidation, for an order under s 184 of the Companies Act 46 of 1926 [now s 423], directing an examination into the conduct of the respondent in relation to the affairs of the company.

Section 184(1) provides that:

'Where in the course of winding up a company it appears that any person who has taken part in the formation or promotion of the company, or any past or present director, manager or liquidator, or any officer of the company, has misapplied or retained or become liable or accountable for any money or property of the company, or has been guilty of any misfeasance or breach of trust in relation to the company, the court may on the application of the Master or the liquidator or of any creditor or contributory, examine into the conduct of the promoter, director, manager, liquidator or officer, and compel him to repay or restore the money or property or any part thereof, respectively with interest at such rate as the court thinks just, or to contribute such sum to the assets of the company by way of compensation in respect of the misapplication, retention, misfeasance or breach of trust as the court thinks just.' . . .

According to the papers the company conducted two retail businesses in shops close to the main railway station in Johannesburg. Prior to 8 September 1970, the sole beneficial shareholders of the company

were certain Christodoulakis and Roussos. On 8 September 1970, an
agreement was concluded whereby these persons sold the entire issued
shareholding in the company to a certain Milton Athanasellis (who is
referred to in the papers simply as Milton, an appellation which it is
convenient to adopt herein), and to Derek Brian Gavshon, the latter
acting as nominee for an undisclosed principal. It is common cause that
that principal was the respondent, who was to provide the greater part
of the moneys for the purchase price.

The agreement of sale provided that possession and occupation of
the assets of the company and of the stocks would be given by the sellers
to the purchasers on a date in September 1970, but the particular date
in September was left blank. It is not disputed that control of the assets
of the company and of the shops and the contents thereof was in fact
handed over to the respondent and Milton on 14 September 1970.

It is common cause that, at the end of every business day during the
next six weeks approximately, Milton brought almost all, if not all, of
the cash takings of the two businesses to the respondent. On each occasion
the respondent counted the cash and on the following day deposited it
in the bank account of Hillbrow Restaurant (Pty) Ltd, a company
controlled by the respondent. I assume that when the following day was
a Sunday, the banking of the money took place on the Monday. The
respondent himself admits that the total of the sums received by him
and banked in this way was R23 000 or R24 000. On 27 October 1970
the sellers of the shares cancelled the sale, and within a period of about
a week thereafter, that is on 3 November 1970, a provisional winding-up
order was granted against the company. That order was confirmed on
1 December 1970. . . .

The applicant's case is that the respondent, during the period of
approximately six weeks from 14 September 1970 was a *de facto* director
or manager. This is denied by the respondent, who contends that his
then interest as a shareholder-to-be, and his participation in the handling
of the money, did not make him either a director or a manager, *de facto*
or otherwise.

The first question to be determined is whether s 184 of the Companies Act includes among the persons subject to its provisions one who
has not been appointed a director or manager or officer of the company,
but who has acted *de facto* as such. . . .

In *R* v *Mall & others* 1959 (4) SA 607 (N) Caney J accepted that
s 185 applies to a *de facto* director.

I should here point out that s 185 provides that, in the circumstances
therein mentioned, the criminal provisions of the Insolvency Act shall
apply to

'any person who is or has been a director, manager, secretary, or other
officer of a company which is being or has been wound up'.

The difference between ss 184 and 185 is that s 185 is a substantive
provision, the purpose of which is to create offences, whereas s 184 is
an adjectival or procedural provision, which does not create any new
liability or new right. Section 184 merely provides a summary mode of
enforcing certain rights which might otherwise have been enforced by

the ordinary procedure of the court. . . .

. . . However, I agree that, if regard be had to the mischief aimed at in each section, then the considerations which the courts have applied in interpreting s 185 as covering *de facto* directors, managers and officers should be applied equally to the interpretation of s 184. . . .

The next step is to ascertain what is meant by *de facto* directors and *de facto* managers. It appears that there is a material difference between the situation of a *de facto* director and that of a *de facto* manager. As Caney J pointed out in *R v Mall (supra)* at 622–4, directors are required by statute. They are essential to a company, and their functions and duties are defined by law. They are appointed by the shareholders and are vested with the management and control of the company. They represent the company and there is a degree of permanence attaching to their position. They act as a body, save so far as powers are lawfully delegated. Their identity, the law intends, should be undoubted and easily discoverable from the company's records. Hence, said Caney J, to regard as a director a person with no appointment, a person meddling in the company's affairs, runs counter to the whole idea of company law.

These considerations led Caney J to hold, in regard to s 185, that a *de facto* director is one who has been elected or appointed as a director and in whose election or appointment some defect or irregularity exists, but not a person who in fact exercises the functions and enjoys the powers of a director without any colour of authority, whether he usurps those functions or is permitted by the directors to assume them. . . .

On the other hand, as Caney J went on to explain, a manager is an employee of the company and his services are engaged by the directors. He is not legally essential to the company, and his contract may be of a formal nature or otherwise. His position may be inferred from conduct, and he may continue in employment for a long or a short time. His position is not defined by law, and indeed he may be a general manager, manager of a department, office manager, or whatsoever. It is always a question of fact what he is and what his functions are, which may be easy or not easy of proof. *R v Kaloo* [1914 AD 17] at 20, and *R v Mall (supra)* at 623.

In the present case there is nothing to show that any step was taken to elect or appoint the respondent as a director of the company. The contention that he acted as a *de facto* director is therefore in conflict with what was laid down by Caney J in *R v Mall*. It should be mentioned that in that case Caney J's approach (at 622A) was that s 185 of the Companies Act is penal in nature and must be construed strictly. There is no such consideration in relation to s 184, and it may be that a person who has assumed and exercised the authority of a director, and has *de facto* functioned as a director vis-à-vis the company, would be subject to the provisions of s 184 even though no formal step had been taken to elect or appoint him. However, on the view I take of the undisputed facts, I find it unnecessary to decide this point.

On the meaning of the term 'manager' in s 184, Mr K, for the respondent, argued that what the legislature intended was a manager in the sense of a person entrusted with the management and control of the whole business of the company. . . . It seems to me that 'manager'

(Afrikaans 'bestuurder') is *ejusdem generis* with promoter, director, liquidator and officer, in the sense that each of these persons, by virtue of his position in the company, is vested or has been vested at some time, either alone or in association with others in the same position vis-à-vis the company, with the control and administration of the company's affairs and property, whether in whole or in part. That is the common basis of accountability under s 184(1). The persons made liable to account under these provisions are those who hold or have held one or other of the offices enumerated; the section does not extend to employees of the company in general.

However, I have difficulty in accepting that the concept of a manager in s 184(1) is limited to one who is or has been managing the affairs of the company as a whole. There is nothing in the section to that effect, and such an interpretation would impose an unwarranted restriction on an important part of these provisions. There is no reason why, if a company may have several promoters, directors, liquidators, or officers within the meaning of s 184(1), it may not also have several managers; and there is no reason why there should not be a division among such managers of the managerial control and administration of the company's affairs and property. That is a common situation in the management of large companies in this country, and it is a development which pre-dated the enactment of our Companies Act in 1926. As simple examples of such division of management one might refer to the manager of a company's administrative activities at its head office in Johannesburg, and the manager of its mines several hundred kilometres away; or to the production manager of a company, controlling all its factors, and its sales manager, in control of all distribution and receipts. In my view, all such managers would fall within the intended scope of s 184(1).

Whether or not a person is or was a manager, in the sense of exercising the requisite degree of managerial control and administration of the company's affairs or property, in whole or in part, is a matter which must depend on the facts of each case. . . .

I agree with Mr K, for the respondent, that before s 184(1) can be invoked against any person, the onus rests on the applicant to prove that such person was a promoter, or director, or manager, or liquidator or officer of the company within the meaning of the section.

Where there is a dispute on this aspect which cannot be resolved on the affidavits, it is a matter for the court to decide whether to refuse relief or to permit the issue to be resolved otherwise. In the exercise of its discretion, the court will no doubt have regard to the consideration that s 184(1) is a remedy designed to provide a swift and ready means of recovering company assets from or pursuing claims against persons in one or other of the categories listed in the section.

[In the result the application that the respondent be examined under s 184 (now s 423) of the Act was granted.]

[403] Lipschitz and Schwartz NNO *v* Markowitz
1976 (3) SA 772 (W)

COETZEE J: This matter . . . is one in which I dismissed the application and indicated that my reasons would be given later. These are the reasons.

The applicants are the liquidators of Landmark Construction (Pty) Ltd (in liquidation), to which I shall refer as 'Construction'. They rely on s 184 [now s 423] of the Companies Act 46 of 1926, in seeking an order that the respondent be examined to enable the court to compel him to contribute such sums to the assets of Construction as the court deems just. Directly or indirectly respondent controlled and managed a number of companies of which Construction was one. Others were, *inter alia*, Landmark Consolidated (Pty) Ltd, to which I shall refer as 'Consolidated', which was the sole beneficial shareholder of Construction and MS & J Investments (Pty) Ltd, to which I shall refer as 'MSJ'. These two companies figure prominently in the applicant's case. . . .

The facts relied on by the applicants to justify their seeking of the summary remedy under s 184 are concisely stated, and are fairly simple. The case made out is twofold:

Firstly, a debt of some R150 000, admittedly owing by Construction to Consolidated, was discharged by Consolidated at a time when the effect thereof was to prefer Consolidated above other creditors of Construction. . . .

Secondly, the shareholders of MSJ formed a syndicate which entered into a building contract with Construction in terms whereof the latter would be paid monthly instalments based on architects' certificates whereafter the respondent agreed, on behalf of Construction, also represented by himself, that the first R100 000 worth of work done by Construction would not be paid for by MSJ in terms of architects' certificates issued pursuant to the provisions of the standard lump sum contract, but would only be paid when the building work was completed by Construction. As a result of this arrangement work worth R111 300 carried out by Construction had not yet been paid for by the time that Construction was placed under liquidation. An action to recover this amount from MSJ has been instituted by the applicants and is pending. In respect of this matter the respondent's liability is alleged as follows in . . . the founding affidavit:

> 'We respectfully submit that the respondent was guilty of misfeasance or breach of trust in relation to Construction in regard to the contract with MS & J in that he utilised the creditors of Construction and thereby used Construction to finance the building work of MS and J, in which company he had a material interest via AGC Holdings. He did this at a time when Construction was in an illiquid position having regard to the fact that Kapmar and Ranpak were unable to effect payment of moneys due by them to Construction and Construction was compelled to borrow large sums of money from Consolidated to finance the building works of Kapmar and Ranpak and MS & J.'

[Counsel for the respondent] argued that it is settled that s 184 did not create any new causes of action but merely provided a summary remedy for the enforcement of existing causes of action recognized by law. . . . Once this is so, the problem can be approached by thinking away the liquidation and asking oneself the question whether Construction had any claim, on these facts, against the respondent. To this the answer is clearly in the negative. In both cases the emphasis falls purely on alleged prejudice of creditors and not on any invasion of Construction's own legal rights for which it might claim redress. In the first case a debt which is due and owing is repaid and, in the second case, an agreement is varied to postpone certain payments to the company, in both cases by the respondent acting for Construction when he was properly authorized to do so.

[After referring with approval to the statement of Nathan AJ in *Liquidators, Zululand Motor Co (Maritzburg) Ltd* v *Short* 1928 NPD 368 at 376, that

'There thus appears ample authority for the view that a person cannot be held liable under the misfeasance section of the Act unless he is already liable to pay a sum of money by some principle of ordinary law, or by virtue of a special clause of the Companies Act imposing upon him a particular liability,'

Coetzee J continued:]

There is no suggestion in the founding papers of any fraud which might have founded an action against the respondent.

[The application was accordingly dismissed.]

NOTES

An applicant with a substantial claim may apply for an order under s 423 even before he has proved his claim: see *L Suzman (Rand) Ltd* v *Yamoyami (1)* 1972 (1) SA 103 (W).

A claim for preliquidation work is not part of the administration costs, *Muller* v *Bryant & Flanagan (Pty) Ltd* 1976 (3) SA 210 (N).

In *Ensor NO* v *Syfret's Trust & Executor Co (Natal) Ltd* 1976 (3) SA 762 (D) it was held that ss 184(1) and 186*bis*(1) of the 1926 Act (now ss 423, 424) apply only to the persons mentioned therein, ie in s 423 to any person who has taken part in the formation or promotion of the company, or any past or present director or any officer of the company, and in s 424 to any person who was knowingly a party to the carrying on of the business.

Hefer J said (at 764G to 766C):

'One feature of s 184(1) which admits of no doubt is that it may only be invoked against the persons mentioned therein, ie against promoters, directors, managers, liquidators and officers of the company concerned (to whom I will in this judgment refer collectively as 'officers' in order to avoid constant repetition of the recital of the various offices): the court is clearly not entitled in terms of the section to examine into the conduct of or to make an order to repay or restore the company's money or property or to contribute to its assets, against anyone who is not an officer of the company concerned.

Then there is s 185*bis*(1) [now s 424(1)] which is, in turn, the basis of the second claim. This section reads as follows:

"If in the course of a winding-up or the judicial management of a company it appears that any business of the company has been carried on with intent to defraud creditors of the company or creditors of any other person or for any fraudulent purpose, the court, on the application of the Master or the liquidator or judicial manager or any creditor or contributory to the company, may if it thinks proper to do so, declare that any of the directors, whether past or present, of the company or other persons who were knowingly parties to the carrying on of the business in manner aforesaid, shall be personally responsible, without any limitation of liability, for all or any of the debts or other liabilities of the company as the court may direct."

Like s 184(1), s 185*bis*(1) is clearly of limited application regarding the persons against whom it may be invoked. The key words here are (apart from directors) "persons who were *knowingly parties* to the carrying on of the business in manner aforesaid".

What has to be decided, is whether either of these sections may be applied not only to the persons to whom they may be applied according to the express words used (officers of the company in the case of s 184(1), and persons who are knowingly parties to the fraud, in the case of s 185bis(1)), but also to persons who may be vicariously liable at common law for the conduct of such persons. And in deciding that question, I must obviously apply the rule that effect must be given to the words used in the statute under consideration: if they are clear, they must be applied according to their tenor; the court is not entitled in that case to depart from their ordinary meaning; it may only do so if there are compelling reasons to conclude that they do not express the true intention of the Legislature; in particular it is not the court's function to provide for a *casus omissus* on the part of the legislature or to accord an extended meaning to the words used unless it is justified by a consideration of the intention and object of the legislature. . . .

Bearing this in mind, I will deal firstly with s 184(1) and commence by referring to the fact that the legislature has made it applicable to officers of companies in plain and unequivocal language. It may be invoked in every case in which it appears in the course of a winding-up that an officer has been guilty of the kind of conduct described therein; it is that officer's conduct which may be examined, and it is against him that an order may be made to repay or restore the company's money or property or to contribute to its assets. No one else is even mentioned, and I do not think plainer language could have been employed to express the intention of limiting its operation to officers. . . .

Nor is there any reason for giving the words actually used, an extended meaning whereby persons other than officers may be brought within its ambit. On the contrary, all the indications are that the intention was to provide a remedy capable of limited use only. Thus it has been held that s 184(1) creates no new rights, but merely provides a special summary procedure for enforcing rights which may otherwise have been enforced by the ordinary procedure of the court (*Gunn NO v De Jager & others* 1968 (2) SA 625 (W) at 630; *L Suzman (Rand) Ltd v Yamoyani (2)* 1972 (1) SA 109 (W) at 112). But the right to employ this special remedy is not unlimited: it is not every type of right which the company has, which may be thus enforced (*Du Plessis v Gunn en andere* 1962 (4) SA 7 (O) at 11; *In Re Etic* [1928] ChD 861 at 871); it may only be employed in cases where an officer is guilty of the type of conduct described in the section, ie something in the nature of a breach of trust (*Du Plessis's* case at 12; *Re B Johnson & Co (Builders) Ltd* [1955] 2 All ER 775 (CA) at 781–2, and the cases cited there; *Selangor United Rubber Estates Ltd v Cradock & others* [1967] 2 All ER 1255 (ChD); and then only if the breach of trust was committed in relation to the company itself (*Goldberg NO v Turkstra* 1946 TPD 81). . . . It seems to me to be clear that the legislature intended a very special remedy which would be available in strictly circumscribed circumstances only, and to extend it to cover other cases, would be to offend against every principle of construction known to me.

The same reasoning applies generally to s 185bis(1). Again the legislature's intention has, to my mind, been expressed in the plainest language; the remedy provided here, is again a special one, aimed at those who participate in the fraudulent carrying on of a company's business (cf *Re Maidstone Buildings Provisions Ltd* [1971] 3 All ER 363 (ChD) at 368), and again I can conceive of no reason whatsoever for extending the words used to cover other persons as well. To my mind, neither s 184(1) nor s 185bis(1) may be invoked against persons not mentioned therein, and in particular not against persons who may be vicariously liable at common law for the conduct of persons against whom it may be invoked. It may be very reasonable and even desirable to extend their provisions to such cases, but the legislature has either overlooked them or advisedly not dealt with them, and it is not the function of the court to do what the legislature has, for some reason or other, failed to do.'

On interrogatories in terms of ss 180bis and 180ter of the 1926 Act (now ss 414 and 415) and attorneys costs incurred in connection therewith, see *Joel Melamed and Hurwitz v Simmons* 1976 (4) SA 189 (T).

At an examination by a commissioner under s 194(1) of the old Act (now s 418) creditors have a right to be represented: *Amod v Liquidators Greenhouse (Pty) Ltd* 1954 (4) SA 323 (N).

General Index

A

ACCOUNTS (*and see* FINANCIAL STATEMENTS, BALANCE SHEET, BOOKS)
  generally, 597ff
  compensation to directors for loss of office in, 384
  directors' remuneration must be stated in, 384
  group—*see* GROUP ACCOUNTS
  inspection of by directors, 383, 597
  loans to directors, particulars of, in, 384, 597
  members have no right to inspect, 597
  right of access of auditors to, 598

AGENCY, law of, applied to companies
  generally, 471ff, 488
  actual and ostensible authority, 470, 471ff, 488
  in relation to *ultra vires* acts, 78
    acts done in contravention of articles, 89, 470, 471, 489
    pre-incorporation contracts, 132, 142
  rule in *Royal British Bank* v *Turquand*, 471ff, 488–91

AGENT
  for non-existent principal, 132
  secretary may be authorized to act as, 470, 489
  warranty of authority, 491
  who may be, 470, 471, 488

ALLOCATION, letter of, 109

ALLOTMENT
  of debentures, 206
  of shares
    generally, 236ff
    as fully paid-up only, 144, 167
    how effected, 236, 242
    irregular, effect of, 236, 237, 242, 244
    meaning of, 236
    must be within reasonable time, 242
    notice of, sending of by post, 236
    power to make, 236
    register of, 236, 243
    return of, 236, 237
    statutory restrictions on, 144, 237, 238, 451
    to directors, 236, 384, 390
    unauthorized, 242
    when voidable, 108, 113, 237, 244
    ultra vires, 243

ALTERNATE DIRECTORS—*see* DIRECTORS, Alternate

AMALGAMATION, 211, 632

ANCILLARY OBJECTS, 68–9, 78

ANNUAL GENERAL MEETING—*see* MEETING

ANNUAL RETURN, 200

CAPITAL (*cont*)
  reduction of—*see* REDUCTION OF CAPITAL
  share, amount of must be stated in memorandum, 68, 144

CAPITAL REDEMPTION RESERVE FUND, 151
  issue of bonus shares out of, 238, 568
  not available for dividends, 568

CAPITALIZATION OF PROFITS
  by issue of bonus shares, 237, 238, 558, 568

CHAIRMAN
  casting vote by, 291
  declaration by, that resolution carried, 293, 309
  of general meeting, 291ff, 309
  of meeting held under s 311, 632, 635

CHARITABLE COMPANY—*see* ASSOCIATION NOT FOR PROFIT

CLASSES OF SHARES
  generally, 171ff
  disclosure in prospectus, 200
  variation of rights of, 69, 177, 188, 196–7, 199, 511

COMMENCEMENT OF BUSINESS
  generally, 129–30, 144, 686
  certificate, 129–30

COMPANIES ACT
  non-applicability of, 67
  history of company legislation, 7ff

COMPANY
  actions on behalf of, 455, 510, 534, 547
  benefactions by, 83–8
  cannot hold its own shares, 145, 149, 211
  capacity of, 78ff
  commencement of business of, 129–30, 144, 686
  constitution of, 68ff
  control of—*see* CONTROL
  criminal liability of, 498ff, 508
  definition of, 25
  deregistration of, 143
  dissolution of, 709
  distinct from members, 27ff
  distinguished from partnership, 45
  domicile of, 28, 34–40
  European, 66
  external, 50–1, 72, 107, 108
  history of, 1ff
  holding—*see* HOLDING AND SUBSIDIARY COMPANIES
  incorporation of—*see* INCORPORATION
  insolvency of, 686, 693, 698, 706 (*and see* INSOLVENT COMPANY)
  inspection of, 548–9
  investigation of ownership and control of, 549
  judicial management of, 714ff
  kinds of, 49–51
  knowledge of, 455
  legal nature of—*see* CORPORATE PERSONALITY
  multinational, 65ff
  nationality of, 28, 34–40
  organs of, 372ff, 451ff
  powers of—*see* POWERS OF COMPANY
  registration of, 68, 129
  representation of, at meetings, 291, 308, 309
    in court, 455

CREDITORS (*cont*)
    arrangement with company under s 389, 708
    contingent or prospective, 691, 693–4
    meetings of, on winding-up, 697, 698, 707–8, 714
        to consider compromise, 632, 634–5
        voting rights at, 632, 635
    rights of, on winding-up, 697, 698, 705, 706, 707–8, 711, 714
    when entitled to object to reduction of capital, 151

CRIMINAL LIABILITY—*see* OFFENCES

CURRENT ASSETS
    appreciation in value of, 567–8
    must be distinguished from fixed assets, 568, 584, 588

D

DEADLOCK
    intervention by court to avoid, 510–11, 686–7, 696

DEBENTURES (AND BONDS)
    generally, 205ff
    allotment of, 206
    bearer, 207, 210
    enforcement of, 206–7, 209
    includes debenture stock, 205
    interest on, 206
    issue of, 206
        at a discount, 206, 208, 246
        irregular, 208
        power to make, 205
        rules applicable to, 205–7, 384
        to directors, 384
    notarial, 205
    power to issue, 205
    ranking of, 206
    redemption of, 206
    register of debentures, pledges and bonds, 206–7
    rights of mortgagees, 207
    secured, 206–7
    transfer of, 207
    unsecured, 205, 207

DEFERRED SHARES, 171–2

DEREGISTRATION, 143

DIRECTOR(S)
    generally, 323ff
    actions against, 456
    actions on behalf of company instituted by, 455
    acts of, validity of, 326
    acts outside powers of, effect of, 78 (*and see* AGENCY)
    allotment of shares to, 236
    alternate, 323, 325, 390, 440
    appointment of, 325ff
        effect of defect in, 326, 332, 341–2, 347
        requirements for, 326
        terms of, 347
    appointment of auditors by, 459, 598
    appropriation of assets of company by, 389
    authority to act for company, 470, 471 (*and see* AGENCY)
    automatically ceasing to hold office, 354

INTEREST
 on debentures, 206
 payment of, out of capital, 558

INTERROGATORIES, 707–8, 725

INVESTIGATION
 of ownership and control of company, 549

J

JUDICIAL MANAGEMENT, 714ff, 717–18

JURISTIC PERSON — *see* CORPORATE PERSONALITY

L

LEGAL PERSONALITY — *see* CORPORATE PERSONALITY

LEGISLATION
 history of company legislation, 7ff

LIEN
 of accountant, over books, 604–5

LIQUIDATION (*and see* WINDING-UP), 707ff

LIQUIDATOR
 appointment of, 707
 duties, rights and powers of, 707ff, 711–12, 719, 724–5
 liability of, 711–12

M

MAIN OBJECT (*and see* AGENCY *and* ULTRA VIRES)
 generally, 68–9
 alteration of, 69
 determines capacity of company, 78
 includes ancillary objects and powers, 78

MANAGEMENT (*and see* CONTROL)
 generally, 451, 459
 interference with, by court, 510ff

MANAGER
 authority to act for company, 489
 distinguished from managing director, 468
 loans to, 384, 597
 who is, 353

MANAGING DIRECTOR — *see* DIRECTORS

MASTER (OF SUPREME COURT), 707–8, 711–12, 719

MEETING(S)
 generally, 284ff
 adjournment of, 291–3
 annual general
  appointment of auditor at, 598
  documents that must be tabled at, 284, 597
  notice required for, 285
  purpose of, 284
  when must be held, 284
 board
  agreement by directors *re* voting at, 459
  dispensing with, 459
  irregular, 459, 463
  minutes of — *see* MINUTES
  notice of, 459, 462
  quorum at, 459, 462–3

S

SCHEME OF ARRANGEMENT—*see* ARRANGEMENT, COMPROMISE

SECRET PROFIT—*see* DIRECTORS AND PROMOTERS

SECRETARY
  cannot be director, 347, 353, 354
  is an officer, 606
  is proper custodian of books, 386
  knowledge of, 455
  may be authorized to act as agent of the company, 470, 489

SECURITIES—*see* SHARES

SERVANTS
  of company, criminal liability of, 498ff, 508
    directors are not, 347, 352, 364–5

SHARE CAPITAL—*see* CAPITAL and SHARES

SHARE CERTIFICATE—*see* SHARES AND ESTOPPEL

SHAREHOLDERS—*see* MEMBERS

SHARES
  generally, 144ff, 167ff
  acquisition of, on take-over, 655–7
  allotment of—*see* ALLOTMENT
  'bear sales' of, 279, 390
  bearer, 167
  bonus, 237, 238, 558, 568
  cancellation of, 149, 151
  certificate, 200, 205, 252, 259, 261, 264, 270, 271
    estoppels relating to, 200, 252, 264, 270
  classes of, 171ff (*and see* CLASSES OF SHARES)
  consolidation of, 149
  conversion of, 149, 171
  dealing in own, by directors, 390
  deferred—*see* DEFERRED SHARES
  definition of, 167
  details of, in annual return and directors' report, 200
  financial assistance, cannot be given by company for purchase of its own shares,
    52, 145, 149, 212, 214ff
  founders', 172
  hawking of, 107ff
  include stock, 167
  issue of
    as fully paid-up only, 144, 167
    at a discount, 89, 145, 237, 246, 404
    at a premium, 237
    external company's shares, 107, 108
    to directors, 236, 384, 390
    to public, 108, 238
    new shares, 149, 237, 246, 404, 451
    unissued, not an increase of capital, 149
  listing of—*see* STOCK EXCHANGE
  management, 172
  no par value, 49, 68, 69, 144, 149, 167, 237
  of company, cannot be held by itself, 145, 149, 211
  offers to public, 107ff, 113
  passing of ownership in, 252
  payment for, 238, 251, 253, 259
  placing of, 107, 238
  pledge of, 252–3, 270–1